British Tax
Income Tax 2017–18

British Tax Guide: Income Tax 2017–18

Croner-i

HR • Tax • H&S • Audit & Accounting

Published by Croner-i Ltd
145 London Road
Kingston upon Thames KT2 6SR
United Kingdom
Telephone: +44 (0) 844 561 8166
E-mail: customer.services@croneri.co.uk
Website: croneri.co.uk

ISBN 978-1-78887-039-9

Previously published by Wolters Kluwer (UK) Ltd

British Library Cataloguing-in-Publication Data

A catalogue record for this book is available from the British Library.

Typeset by Innodata Inc., India.
Printed by Ovimex B.V. – The Netherlands

About the author

Warren Taylor CTA

Warren Taylor has advised individuals and companies on tax matters for over 30 years. Having been a senior employee and partner in a top ten practice for most of his career, he now runs his own consultancy business and has also acted as an examiner for the Chartered Institute of Taxation.

Preface

The *British Tax Guide: Income Tax 2017–18* is the twelfth edition of this work in its current format. Its aim is to provide clear, practical and accessible commentary on the tax issues likely to be of widespread interest to the vast majority of tax advisers in dealing with their clients' income tax affairs for 2017–18. To achieve that coverage, some less mainstream topics have been omitted or have been dealt with in summary form. The editor welcomes comments from readers on the scope and depth of the coverage.

The books in this series aim to provide clear, uncluttered, easy to read commentary on the main taxes rather than wholesale reproduction of source material. Useful cross references are included and are generally provided in separate footnotes rather than in the body of the text. In the CD and online versions of this work, those references are live links to relevant annotated legislation, cases, HMRC Manuals and other reference materials. The full references to Croner-i's main tax databases also make these books an ideal desktop companion to those services.

The worked examples have been fully updated to reflect the significant impact of the new basis of taxation of dividends and the introduction of both the savings investment allowance and dividend allowance. The two Finance Acts in 2017 saw further changes aimed at taking individuals with small or insignificant income sources out of the self-assessment system, for example trading allowance and rental income allowance. The changes to the taxation of non-domiciled individuals is likely to significantly diminish the tax planning opportunities for those individuals who are long-term residents in the UK.

Where appropriate significant changes effective from 6 April 2018 and later are referenced in this work.

The tax credits chapter was updated by Victoria Todd.

The *What's new* section lists the key developments over the past year.

Warren Taylor

November 2017

What's new in income tax?

There follows a series of summaries highlighting the main changes and developments relevant to income tax that have occurred since the last edition of *British Tax Guide: Income Tax*.

59-025	HMRC's power to issue a 'simple' assessment without the requirement to file a self-assessment tax return. (TMA 1970, s. 28H)
60-800	*Kaczmarczyk* [2017] TC 05744: Penalties for failure to file a tax return despite having no UK income.
60-800	*Richter* [2017] TC 05816: Imprisonment accepted as reasonable excuse for a late filing penalty.
61-000	*Pandey* [2017] TC 05706: Demonstration of 'reasonable excuse' in the application of penalties for an incorrect return.
61-000	Asset-based penalties for offshore income gains an asset movement.
61-000	Suspension of penalties for careless inaccuracies, new section and *Duncan* [2016] TC 05438.
62-000	*Singh* [2017] TC 05647: Importance of ensuring that an appeal is filed within the statutory time limits.
63-850	Serial tax avoiders: details of schemes covered.
66-000 to 66-900	Updating of the DOTAS regulations to reflect the HMRC guidance published September 2016 including the introduction of the 'financial products' hallmark.
69-300	New serial tax avoidance provisions from September 2016.
70-000	Reference to updated HMRC guidance to taxation of rental income: http://tinyurl.com/qfvf8ax.
70-300	Update list of rental income deduction that differ from normal trading income.
70-310	Rental allowance: tax free rental income up to £1,000.
70-320	Worked examples of the new restriction to mortgage interest costs deductions for residential property and the impact of carry forward of relief.
74-040	Reduction of the money purchase annual allowance from £10,000 to £4,000. (FA 2004, s. 227ZA)
74-410	Tax-free withdrawal from defined benefit pension schemes to fund pension and retirement advice.
76-300	*Abingdon Health Ltd* [2016] TC 05525: Loss of EIS relief as a result of failing to meet the 'preferential rights' restriction on qualifying shares.
79-000	Increased ISA limits from April 2017.
79-050	Lifetime ISA.

85-000	Extension of social investment tax relief to 5 April 2021. (ITA 2007, s. 257K)
92-220	Trading allowance: tax free trading income up to £1,000.
111-410	100% capital allowances on expenditure on electrical vehicle charging points. (CAA 2001, s. 45EA)
111-700	100% capital allowances on ultra-low emission vehicles extended to 31 March 2021.
112-600 to 112-615	Re-draft to reflect withdrawal of transitional rules for pre-2009 vehicles. Also proposed reduction in 'main rate' and ultra-low emission vehicles.
112-660	Reduction in thresholds for car lease tax relief restrictions with effect from April 2018.
112-600	From April 2018, cars will only be eligible for main rate capital allowances where CO_2 emission is below 110g/km.
130-270	Introduction of PAYE obligation for public sector organisations engaging intermediaries from April 2017. (ITEPA 2003, s. 61K)
131-660	*Tomlinson* [2017] TC 05943: Importance of the intention of both parties when establishing employment/self-employment status.
132-030	Order of priority on BIK charge where more than one individual may be taxable *Baylis* [2016] TC 05454.
132-080, 132-090, 140-405 and 141-300	Optional remuneration arrangements and 'salary sacrifice' post 5 April 2017.
132-050 and 132-395	Requirement to 'make good' private fuel cost by 6 July in the year following. (ITEPA 2003, s. 87)
133-510	Taxation of taxable benefit where assets made available to an employee. (ITEPA 2003, s. 205)
132-620 and 132-630	Updated van benefits and van fuel benefits rates from 5 April 2017.
132-810	Reduction in official rate of interest to 2.5% from 6 April 2017.
133-300 and 133-335	Trivial benefits exemption effective from 6 April 2016.
133-600	Impact of salary sacrifice rules on 'in-house' benefits.
142-100	New rules on the taxation of termination payments from 6 April 2018. (ITEPA 2003, s. 402A–402E)
143-370	Up to £500 worth of tax free provision of pension advice to employees. (ITEPA 2003, s. 308C)
147-010	Withdrawal of employee shareholder status provisions. (FA 2017, s. 12)

171-025	Deemed domicile provisions effective from 5 April 2017. (ITA 2007, s. 835BA)
190-220	Two-child limit introduced to the child element of CTC from 6 April 2017.
190-220	Family element of CTC limited to those who have responsibility for a child or qualifying young person born before 6 April 2017.
190-220	New CTC disability element created from 6 April 2017 – payable at two rates – disabled child rate and severely disabled child rate.
190-260	Changes to calculation of property income from 6 April 2017 to mitigate the impact of the residential landlord tax changes.
190-300	Changes to backdating rules for WTC and CTC to prevent dual entitlement to tax credits and Tax-Free Childcare and to preserve backdating for claimants who accidentally claim TFC.

Warren Taylor

Contents

Key data: income tax

Principles of income tax

Income tax rates

Note: See also ¶26-100 for rates applicable in Scotland from April 2016.

1-000 Structure of income tax rates: 2017–18

(ITA 2007, s. 9A, 10–15; FA 2016, s. 6)

Finance Act 2016 included legislation to separate the income tax rates that apply to savings (the savings rates), from those that apply to non-savings, non-dividends income (the main rates), with effect for the tax year 2017–18 (as the first tax year for which the Scottish Government can set Scottish rates of income tax (SI 2016/1161, reg. 3)) and subsequent tax years, in order to facilitate the devolution of income tax rates to Scotland (for Scottish taxpayers) and, in due course, to Wales (for Welsh taxpayers).

The savings and dividend rates are not being devolved and will apply across the UK whereas the main rates were devolved to Scotland from April 2017 (for Scottish taxpayers) and will be devolved, in due course, to Wales (for Welsh taxpayers).

Finance Act 2016 also created a default rate of income tax on non-savings, non-dividends income that will apply to, but is not limited to, trustees and non-residents.

The general effect of ITA 2007, s. 10–15 is outlined in the following table:

Type of taxpayer	Rates payable on savings income	Rates payable on most dividend income	Rates payable on other income
UK resident individual who is neither a Scottish taxpayer nor a Welsh taxpayer	Savings rates	Dividend rates	Main rates
Scottish taxpayer	Savings rates	Dividend rates	Scottish rates

Type of taxpayer	Rates payable on savings income	Rates payable on most dividend income	Rates payable on other income
Welsh taxpayer	Savings rates	Dividend rates	Main rates while ITA 2007, s. 11B is not in force; Welsh rates once in force
Non-UK resident individual	Savings rates	Dividend rates	Default rates
Non-individual, except some trustees subject to trust rate or dividend trust rate in certain circumstances	Default basic rate	Dividend ordinary rate	Default basic rate

Note

(1) The table does not address the effect of some exceptions referred to in ITA 2007, s. 10–15.

1-003 Income tax rates: 2017–18

(ITA 2007, s. 6–9; FA 2016, s. 6)

(Tax Reporter: ¶148-075ff.)

	Rate %	Taxable income band £	Tax on band £
Main rates(1)(2)			
Basic rate	20	1–33,500(3)	6,700
Higher rate	40	33,501–150,000	46,600
Additional rate	45	Over 150,000	
Default rates(4)			
Default basic rate	20	1–33,500(3)	6,700
Default higher rate	40	33,501–150,000	46,600
Default additional rate	45	Over 150,000	
Scottish rates			
Scottish basic rate	20	1–31,500	6,300
Scottish higher rate	40	31,501–150,000	47,400
Scottish additional rate	45	Over 150,000	

Other rates	Rate %	Taxable income
Savings rates		
Starting rate for savings[5]	0	£1–£5,000
Savings nil rate[6]	0	First £1,000 or £500
Savings basic rate	20	Savings income otherwise chargeable at basic rate or default basic rate
Savings higher rate	40	Savings income otherwise chargeable at higher rate or default higher rate
Savings additional rate	45	Savings income otherwise chargeable at additional rate or default additional rate
Dividend rates		
Dividend nil rate[7]	0	First £5,000
Dividend ordinary rate	7.5	Dividend income otherwise chargeable at basic rate or Scottish basic rate
Dividend upper rate	32.5	Dividend income otherwise chargeable at higher rate or Scottish higher rate
Dividend additional rate	38.1	Dividend income otherwise chargeable at additional rate or Scottish additional rate
Special rates for trustees' income[8]		
Trust rate	45	Trustees accumulated or discretionary income and other amounts under ITA 2007, Pt. 9, Ch. 3–6
Dividend trust rate	38.1	

Notes

(1) Income tax lock: F(No. 2)A 2015, s. 1 set a ceiling for the main rates of income tax at 20%, 40% and 45% respectively for tax years beginning on or after 18 November 2015 (Royal Assent) but before the date of the first parliamentary general election after that day.

(2) From 2017–18, the main rates are separated into the main rates, the savings rates and the default rates. From 6 April 2017, the main rates apply to non-savings, non-dividend income (income to which the main rates apply includes income from employment, property or pensions not subject to the Scottish rate of income tax). Prior to 6 April 2017, the main rates applied to all non-dividend income, including income from savings, employment, property or pensions.

(3) Autumn Statement 2016 confirmed the Government's commitment to raise the income tax personal allowance to £12,500 and the higher rate threshold to £50,000, by the end of this Parliament, on which figures the basic rate limit will increase to £37,500.

(4) Default rates apply from 6 April 2017 to non-savings and non-dividend income of any taxpayer that is not subject to either the main rates or the Scottish rates of income tax.

(5) The 'starting rate for savings' is available for savings income only. If an individual's taxable non-savings income (i.e. after deduction of their personal allowance) exceeds the starting rate, then the starting rate is not available and an individual's savings income is chargeable at the nil rate (to the extent available), the basic, higher or additional rate (as would otherwise apply).

(6) The savings allowance (the savings nil rate) is available to individuals with savings income. The savings allowance is £1,000 for basic rate taxpayers, £500 for higher rate taxpayers and nil for additional rate taxpayers. Savings income within the savings allowance is chargeable at the savings nil rate 0% (ITA 2007, s. 12A and 12B). The 'savings nil rate' is available in addition to the 'starting rate for savings' (where this is available) on savings income above the starting rate limit.

[7] The tax free dividend allowance operates as a 0% tax rate substituted for the dividend ordinary rate, dividend upper rate or dividend additional rate as would otherwise apply on the first £5,000 of an individual's dividend income (ITA 2007, s. 13A). From 2018-19, the dividend allowance will be reduced to £2,000 (F(No.2)A 2017, s. 8).

[8] The special trust rates do not apply to the first £1,000 slice of the 'trust rate income'. Instead, the normal income tax rates (currently the basic rate and dividend ordinary rate) apply as appropriate (ITA 2007, s. 491(1)–(3)).

1-004 Income tax rates: 2016–17

(ITA 2007, s. 6–15; FA 2015, s. 4; FA 2016, s. 1)

(Tax Reporter: ¶148-075ff.)

UK rates (England, Wales and Northern Ireland)

	Taxable income band £	Tax rate[1] %	Tax on band £
Basic rate	1–32,000	20	6,400
Higher rate	32,001–150,000	40	47,200
Additional rate	Over 150,000	45	
Starting rate for savings income	1–5,000	0	

Scottish rates

UK rate for England, Wales and Northern Ireland	Taxable income band £	UK rate paid in Scotland %	Scottish rate %	Total rate for Scottish taxpayers %
Basic rate 20%	1–32,000	10	10	20
Higher rate 40%	32,001–150,000	30	10	40
Additional rate 45%	Over £150,000	35	10	45

Savings, dividends and special trust rates

Starting rate for savings income[2]	0% up to starting rate limit
Rate on non-dividend savings income	0% on savings income charged at the savings nil rate[3] 20% up to basic rate limit 40% up to higher rate limit 45% thereafter
Dividend nil rate[5]	0% on first £5,000 dividends
Dividend ordinary rate	7.5%[5] up to basic rate limit

Dividend upper rate	32.5%[5] up to higher rate limit
Dividend additional rate	38.1%[5] above higher rate limit
Trust rate	45%[4]
Dividend trust rate	38.1%[4]

Notes

(1) Income tax lock: F(No. 2)A 2015, s. 1 set a ceiling for the main rates of income tax at 20%, 40% and 45% respectively for tax years beginning on or after 18 November 2015 (Royal Assent) but before the date of the first parliamentary general election after that day.

(2) The 'starting rate for savings' is available for savings income only. If an individual's taxable non-savings income (i.e. after deduction of their personal allowance) exceeds the starting rate limit, then the starting rate is not available and an individual's savings income is chargeable at the basic, higher or additional rate (as would otherwise apply). From 6 April 2016, a new savings allowance is available to individuals with savings income, 'the savings nil rate'.

(3) The savings allowance is £1,000 for basic rate taxpayers, £500 for higher rate taxpayers and nil for additional rate taxpayers. Savings income within the savings allowance is chargeable at the savings nil rate 0% (ITA 2007, s. 12A and 12B). The 'savings nil rate' is available in addition to the 'starting rate for savings' (where this is available) on savings income above the starting rate limit.

(4) The special trust rates do not apply to the first £1,000 slice of the 'trust rate income'. Instead, the normal income tax rates (currently the basic rate and dividend ordinary rate) apply as appropriate (ITA 2007, s. 491(1)–(3)).

(5) From April 2016, the dividend tax credit was abolished and replaced with a £5,000 tax-free dividend allowance. The allowance operates as a 0% tax rate substituted for the dividend ordinary rate, dividend upper rate or dividend additional rate as would otherwise apply on the first £5,000 of an individual's dividend income (ITA 2007, s. 13A).

1-005 Income tax rates: 2015–16

(ITA 2007, s. 6–15; FA 2014, s. 2)

(Tax Reporter: ¶148-075ff.)

2015–16

	Taxable income band £	Tax rate %	Tax on band £
Basic rate	1–31,785	20	6,357
Higher rate	31,786–150,000	40	47,286
Additional rate	Over 150,000	45	

Rate on non-dividend savings income	0% up to £5,000[1] 20% up to basic rate limit 40% up to higher rate limit 45% thereafter
Dividend ordinary rate (effective rate with tax credit)	10% up to basic rate limit 0%
Dividend upper rate (effective rate with tax credit)	32.5% up to higher rate limit 25%

Dividend additional rate (effective rate with tax credit)	37.5% above higher rate limit 30.6%
Trust rate	45%[2]
Dividend trust rate	37.5%[2]

Notes

[1] The starting rate is available for savings income only. If an individual's taxable non-savings income (i.e. after deduction of their personal allowance) exceeds the starting rate limit, then the starting rate is not be available.

[2] The special trust rates do not apply to the first £1,000 slice of the 'trust rate income'. Instead, the normal income tax rates (currently the basic rate and dividend ordinary rate) apply as appropriate (ITA 2007, s. 491(1)–(3)).

1-006 Income tax rates: 2014–15

(ITA 2007, s. 6–15; FA 2014, s. 1)

(Tax Reporter: ¶148-075ff.)

2014–15

	Taxable income band £	Tax rate %	Tax on band £
Basic rate	1–31,865	20	6,373
Higher rate	31,866–150,000	40	47,254
Additional rate	Over 150,000	45	

Rate on non-dividend savings income	10% up to £2,880[1] 20% up to basic rate limit 40% up to higher rate limit 45% thereafter
Dividend ordinary rate (effective rate with tax credit)	10% up to basic rate limit 0%
Dividend upper rate (effective rate with tax credit)	32.5% up to higher rate limit 25%
Dividend additional rate (effective rate with tax credit)	37.5% above higher rate limit 30.6%
Trust rate	45%[2]
Dividend trust rate	37.5%[2]

Notes

[1] A 10% starting rate applies to the first £2,880 of non-dividend savings income. The starting rate does not apply if non-savings income exceeds the personal allowance plus £2,880.

[2] The special trust rates do not apply to the first £1,000 slice of the 'trust rate income'. Instead, the normal income tax rates (currently the basic rate and dividend ordinary rate) apply as appropriate (ITA 2007, s. 491(1)–(3)).

1-008 Income tax rates: 2013–14

(ITA 2007, s. 6–15; FA 2013, s. 3)

(Tax Reporter: ¶148-075ff.)

2013–14

	Taxable income band £	Tax rate %	Tax on band £
Basic rate	1–32,010	20	6,402
Higher rate	32,011–150,000	40	47,196
Additional rate	Over 150,000	45	

Rate on non-dividend savings income	10% up to £2,790[(1)] 20% up to basic rate limit 40% up to higher rate limit 45% thereafter
Dividend ordinary rate (effective rate with tax credit)	10% up to basic rate limit 0%
Dividend upper rate (effective rate with tax credit)	32.5% up to higher rate limit 25%
Dividend additional rate (effective rate with tax credit)	37.5% above higher rate limit 30.6%
Trust rate	45%[(2)]
Dividend trust rate	37.5%[(2)]

Notes

(1) A 10% starting rate applies to the first £2,790 of non-dividend savings income. The starting rate does not apply if non-savings income exceeds the personal allowance plus £2,790.

(2) The special trust rates do not apply to the first £1,000 slice of the 'trust rate income'. Instead, the normal income tax rates (currently the basic rate and dividend ordinary rate) apply as appropriate (ITA 2007, s. 491(1)–(3)).

1-100 Personal allowances and reliefs

(ITA 2007, s. 35–46)

(Tax Reporter: ¶155-000ff.)

From 2016–17 onwards, there is one income tax personal allowance regardless of an individual's date of birth.

The Government has committed to raising the personal allowance to £12,500 by the end of its Parliamentary term (first announced at Summer Budget 2015, re-confirmed at Autumn Statement 2016).

For tax years up to 2012–13, higher (age-related) allowances were available for individuals attaining 'age 65–74' or age '75 and over' in the tax year. These allowances were frozen at 2012–13 rates and phased out between 2013–14 and 2015–16 as the basic personal allowance caught up with the frozen amounts of the former allowances.

Transferable tax allowances for married couples

(ITA 2007, Pt. 3, Ch. 3A)

(Tax Reporter: ¶156-725)

From the 2015–16 tax year, a spouse or civil partner who is not liable to income tax because their income is below their personal allowance or who is liable to income tax at the basic rate, dividend ordinary rate or the starting rate for savings has been able to elect to transfer a portion (set at 10%) of their personal allowance to their spouse or civil partner, with a corresponding reduction to the transferring spouse's personal allowance. Only a spouse or civil partner who is liable to income tax at the basic rate, dividend ordinary rate or the starting rate for savings can receive the transferred personal allowance. The transferred allowance is given effect as a reduction to the recipient's income tax liability at the basic rate of tax. Married couples or civil partners entitled to claim the married couple's allowance are not entitled to make a transfer.

Specific income allowances

From 6 April 2016, two 'allowances' were introduced for savings income and dividend income. Both 'allowances' operate as 0% rates of tax substituted for the rates that would otherwise apply. The savings allowance is available for up to £1,000 of a basic rate taxpayer's savings income and up to £500 of a higher rate taxpayer's savings income each year. The savings allowance is not available to additional rate taxpayers. The dividend allowance is available to all taxpayers on up to £5,000 of dividend income.

From 6 April 2017, two further £1,000 allowances each for property and trading income were introduced (amendments by Finance (No. 2) Bill 2017). The new allowances mean that individuals with property income below £1,000 or trading income below £1,000 do not need to declare or pay tax on that income. The trading income allowance also applies to certain miscellaneous income from providing assets or services. Those with income above the allowance may calculate their taxable profit either by deducting their expenses in the normal way or by electing for partial relief and simply deducting the relevant allowance from their gross income (instead of deducting expenses).

Type of relief[1]	2017–18 £	2016–17 £	2015–16 £	2014–15 £	2013–14 £
Personal allowance[2]					
All ages	11,500	11,000	—	—	—
– born after 5 April 1948	—	—	—	10,000	9,440
– born after 5 April 1938	—	—	10,600	—	—
– born after 5 April 1938 but before 6 April 1948	—	—	—	10,500	10,500
– born before 6 April 1938	—	—	10,660	10,660	10,660
Marriage allowance	1,150	1,100	1,060	—	—
Married couple's allowance[3]					
– born before 6 April 1935 and age 75 and over	8,445	8,355	8,355	8,165	7,915
– minimum amount of allowance	3,260	3,220	3,220	3,140	3,040
Maximum income before abatement of:					
– personal allowance[2]	100,000	100,000	100,000	100,000	100,000
– reliefs for older taxpayers	28,000	27,700	27,700	27,000	26,100
Abatement income ceiling					
Personal allowance (basic)	123,000	122,000	121,200	120,000	118,880
Single (age personal allowance)					
– born after 5 April 1938 but before 6 April 1948	—	—	—	28,000	28,220
– born before 6 April 1938	—	—	27,820	28,320	28,540
Married couple's allowance (only)	38,370	37,970	37,970	37,050	35,850
Married (age personal allowance and MCA)					
– relevant partner born after 5 April 1938 but before 6 April 1948	—	—	—	38,050	37,970
– relevant partner born before 6 April 1938	—	—	38,090	38,370	38,290

Type of relief[1]	2017–18 £	2016–17 £	2015–16 £	2014–15 £	2013–14 £
Blind person's allowance	2,320	2,290	2,290	2,230	2,160
Dividend allowance[4]	5,000	5,000	—	—	—
Personal savings allowance[5]					
Basic rate taxpayers	1,000	1,000	—	—	—
Higher rate taxpayers	500	500	—	—	—
Life assurance relief (policies issued before 14 March 1984)[6]	—	—	—[9]	12.5% of premiums	12.5% of premiums
'Rent-a-room' limit	7,500	7,500	4,250	4,250	4,250
Trading allowance[7]	1000	—	—	—	—
Property allowance[7]	1000	—	—	—	—

Notes

[2] From April 2010, the personal allowance is gradually withdrawn for income over £100,000 at a rate of £1 of allowance lost for every £2 over £100,000 until it is completely removed (ITA 2007, s. 35).

[3] The married couple's allowance is available only where at least one partner was born before 6 April 1935. Relief is given as a tax reduction at a rate of 10%.

[4] From 6 April 2016, a 0% rate of tax (the dividend nil rate) applies to the first £5,000 of dividend income received (ITA 2007, s. 13A). The dividend allowance will be reduced to £2,000 from April 2018-19 (F(No.2)A 2017, s. 8).

[5] From 6 April 2016, a 0% rate of tax applies to an individual's savings income (the savings nil rate or savings allowance). The savings nil rate applies to the first £1,000 of a basic rate taxpayer's savings income, or the first £500 of a higher rate taxpayer's savings income. The savings nil rate is not available to additional rate taxpayers (ITA 2007, s. 12A and 12B). The personal allowance, blind persons allowance, married couples allowance (MCA), income limit for MCA abatement (but not the £100,000 income limit for personal allowance abatement) are indexed by the annual percentage increase in CPI (RPI until 2014–15) for the year to September preceding the new tax year Amounts determined by the annual indexation order may be overridden by provision in a Finance Act. Existing legislation further provides that once the personal allowance has reached £12,500, it will be uprated in line with the national minimum wage (NMW) (and CPI based provisions would no longer apply). However, at Autumn Statement 2016, it was announced that once the personal allowance reaches £12,500, it will continue to be uprated in line with CPI rather than NMW.

[6] By relief at source. Abolished for payments becoming due and payable on or after 6 April 2015, and payments becoming due and payable before 6 April 2015 but actually paid on or after 6 July 2015 (FA 2012, s. 227 and Sch. 39, para. 23).

[7] Trading and property allowances introduced with effect from 6 April 2017. The allowances provide for full relief on trading and property income of up to each allowance of £1,000 (the trading allowance applies to miscellaneous income also). Individuals with gross income of up to the allowance do not have to declare or pay tax on this income. Where gross income is above the level of the allowance, individuals can either elect for partial relief and deduct the allowance from gross recepts instead of deducting actual expenses, or calculate profits applying normal rules. (ITTOIA 2005, Pt. 6A, as inserted by F(No.2)A 2017, Sch. 3)

1-110 High income child benefit charge

(ITEPA 2003, s. 681B–681H)

(Tax Reporter: ¶490-075)

The high income child benefit charge applies to individuals whose income exceeds £50,000 who are themselves, or whose partner is, in receipt of child benefit. The charge is levied on the partner with the highest income, irrespective of which partner claims the child benefit. The charge is calculated as the 'appropriate percentage' of child benefit payments received during the tax year which equates to 1% of the amount of child benefit received for every £100 of income over £50,000.

Adjusted Net Income	Appropriate percentage
£60,000 and over	100%
£50,001–£59,999	$\frac{ANI - L}{X}\%$
Up to £50,000	Nil

Where:

ANI = Adjusted Net Income
L = £50,000
X = £100

Adjusted Net Income is calculated as:

- net income (total income charged to income tax less income tax reliefs);
- less grossed up (at basic rate) gift aid donations;
- less gross pension contributions (before deduction of basic rate tax);
- add back any relief for payments to trade unions or police organisations (ITEPA 2003, s. 457 or 458) deducted in calculating net income.

Child benefit[1]	2017–18 £/week	2016–17 £/week	2015–16 £/week	2014–15 £/week	2013–14 £/week
Eldest qualifying child	20.70	20.70	20.70	20.50	20.30
Each other child	13.70	13.70	13.70	13.55	13.40

Note

(1) Individuals who elected not to continue to receive child benefit by 28 March 2013 were not liable for the charge for 2013–14. From 2014–15 onwards, individuals who opt out and whose payments stopped before the beginning of the tax year will not be liable for the charge and will otherwise be liable only for the period until payments stop.

1-120 Cap on income tax relief

(ITA 2007, s. 24A)

(Tax Reporter: ¶148-450)

From 6 April 2013, a limit applies to the amount of certain income tax reliefs that may be deducted from income under the Income Tax Act 2007, s. 24. The limit does not apply to charitable reliefs.

From	Amount of cap
6 April 2013[1]	greater of: – £50,000; or – 25% of adjusted total income

Note

[1] The limit applies for the tax year 2013–14 and subsequent tax years, and additionally, where loss relief is claimed for a tax year before 2013–14 in relation to losses made in 2013–14 or a later year. However, the limit does not apply in relation to property loss relief arising from a loss made in 2012–13 where the loss is claimed for relief against general income in the tax year 2013–14.

Limited reliefs	Legislation
Trade loss relief against general income (excluding relief for losses attributable to overlap relief and business premises renovation allowances (BPRA)) [and excluding deductions so far as made from profits of the trade or business to which the relief relates – see next table]	ITA 2007, s. 64
Early trade loss relief (first four years of trade, profession or vocation; excluding relief for losses attributable to overlap relief and BPRA) [and excluding deductions so far as made from profits of the trade or business to which the relief relates – see table below]	ITA 2007, s. 72
Post-cessation trade relief (qualifying payments or qualifying events within seven years of the permanent cessation of the trade) [and excluding deductions so far as made from profits of the trade or business to which the relief relates – see table below]	ITA 2007, s. 96
Property loss relief against general income (property business losses arising from capital allowances or agricultural expenses; excluding relief for losses attributable to BPRA) [and excluding deductions so far as made from profits of the trade or business to which the relief relates – see table below]	ITA 2007, s. 120

Limited reliefs	Legislation
Post-cessation property relief (qualifying payments or qualifying events within seven years of the permanent cessation of the UK property business) [and excluding deductions so far as made from profits of the trade or business to which the relief relates – see table below]	ITA 2007, s. 125
Employment loss relief against general income (certain circumstances where losses or liabilities arise from employment)	ITA 2007, s. 128
Former employees' deductions for liabilities (payment made by former employees for which they are entitled to claim a deduction from their general income in the year in which the payment is made)	ITEPA 2003, s. 555
Share loss relief on non-EIS/SEIS/SI shares (capital losses on the disposal, or deemed disposal, of certain qualifying shares)	ITA 2007, Pt. 4, Ch. 6
Losses on deeply discounted securities (losses on gilt strips and on listed securities held since at least 26 March 2003)	ITTOIA 2005, s. 446, 454[(4)]
Qualifying loan interest (interest paid on certain loans including loans to buy an interest in certain types of company or to invest in a partnership)	ITA 2007, Pt. 8, Ch. 1

Excluded reliefs	Legislation
Deductions attributable to business premises renovation allowances	CAA 2001, Pt. 3A
Deductions so far as made from profits of the trade or business to which the relief relates in respect of: • trade loss relief; • early trade loss relief; • post-cessation trade relief; • property loss relief; • post-cessation property relief.	ITA 2007, s. 64, 72, 96, 120 and 125
Deductions so far as attributable to a deduction for overlap relief profit in final tax year or on change of accounting date (allowed under ITTOIA 2005, s. 205 or 220) in respect of: • trade loss relief; • early trade loss relief.	ITA 2007, s. 64 and 72

Excluded reliefs	Legislation
Deductions for amounts of relief for share losses:	ITA 2007, Pt. 4, Ch. 6
• where the shares in question are qualifying shares to which EIS relief is attributable;	ITA 2007, s. 131(2)(a) ITA 2007, Pt. 5A
• where SEIS relief is attributable to the shares in question;	ITA 2007, Pt. 5B
• where SI tax relief is attributable to the shares in question.	

1-150 Gifts of assets

Nature of asset	Legislation	Effect of relief
Stock manufactured or sold by trader that is given to charity, etc. (Tax Reporter: ¶226-650)	CTA 2009, s. 105; ITTOIA 2005, s. 108	No amount is brought into account as trading receipt as result of the donation
Plant and machinery used by trader given to a charity, etc. (Tax Reporter: ¶238-235)	CAA 2001, s. 63	Disposal value is nil for capital allowances purposes
Stock manufactured or sold by trader that is given to a designated educational establishment and qualifies as plant or machinery in the donee's hands (Tax Reporter: ¶226-650)	CTA 2009, s. 105; ITTOIA 2005, s. 108	No amount is brought into account as a trading receipt as result of the donation
Plant or machinery used by trader that is given to a designated educational establishment and qualifies as plant and machinery in the donee's hands (Tax Reporter: ¶238-235)	CAA 2001, s. 63	Disposal value is nil for capital allowances purposes
Listed shares and securities and securities dealt with on a recognised stock exchange, units in unit trusts, etc. interests in land, that are given to a charity (Tax Reporter: ¶115-575; ¶716-640)	CTA 2010, s. 203; ITA 2007, s. 431	Full value of gift is deductible in calculating profits for IT or CT purposes

Nature of asset	Legislation	Effect of relief
Property settled by gift on a UK trust which has a charity as a beneficiary and the settlor retains an interest (Tax Reporter: ¶356-450)	ITTOIA 2005, s. 628	The trust income allocated to the settlor is reduced by an amount equal to the income paid to the charity in the year

1-200 Gifts to the nation

(FA 2012, Sch. 14)

For the tax year 2012–13 and subsequent tax years, a reduction in income tax and/or capital gains tax is available where an individual makes a gift of pre-eminent property to be held for the benefit of the public or the nation. The tax reduction is 30% of the value of the gift. A gift offer must be made and registered in accordance with the scheme and relief is available against the individual's liability for the year in which the gift offer is registered and/or any of the succeeding four tax years.

Pre-eminent property includes any picture, print, book, manuscript, work of art, scientific object or other thing that is pre-eminent for its national, scientific, historic or artistic interest, collections of such items and any object kept in a significant building where it is desirable that it remain associated with the building.

Administration

1-250 Submission dates for 2017–18 personal tax returns

(TMA 1970, s. 8)

(Tax Reporter: ¶180-125)

The *Taxes Management Act* 1970, s. 8 contains provisions concerning submission dates for returns issued on or after 6 April 2018 which relate to 2017–18, as follows:

- paper returns (whether or not HMRC are to calculate the tax liability) must be filed by 31 October 2018; and
- online returns must be filed by 31 January 2019.

There are the following exceptions:

Circumstances	Filing date[1]
Return issued after 31 July 2018 but before 31 October 2018	Three months from the date of issue (paper returns); 31 January 2019 (online returns)
Return issued after 31 October 2018	Three months from date of issue
Taxpayer wishes underpayment (below £3,000) to be coded out under PAYE in a subsequent year (paper returns)	31 October 2018
Taxpayer wishes underpayment (below £3,000) to be coded out under PAYE in a subsequent year (online returns)	30 December 2018

Note

[1] The time allowed for making a self-assessment when HMRC have served a notice to file a return is four years after the end of the tax year to which it relates (TMA 1970, s. 34A, as inserted by FA 2016, s. 168, with effect from 15 September 2016).

Withdrawing a notice to file a self-assessment return

(TMA 1970, s. 8B and 12AAA)

With effect in respect of returns for the tax year 2012–13 and subsequent tax years, HMRC will withdraw a notice to file a return, on request or otherwise, where they agree a self-assessment return is not required and cancel any late filing penalty already issued in respect of the outstanding return. A notice may only be withdrawn within the period of two years beginning with the end of the relevant year of assessment or period in respect of which the return is required or, in exceptional circumstances, such extended period as HMRC may agree.

Simple assessment

Simple assessment is a new HMRC assessment procedure which will remove the need for some customers to complete a tax return. From September 2017, HMRC will introduce simple assessments starting with two groups:

- *new state pensioners with income more than the personal tax allowance in the tax year 2016-17;*
- *PAYE customers, who have underpaid tax and who cannot have that tax collected through their tax code*

All existing state pensioners, who receive state pension over their personal allowance will be taken out of self-assessment for the tax year 2017-18, and will receive a simple assessment notification instead. (TMA 1970, s. 28H–28J and 59BA, as inserted by FA 2016, s. 167 and Sch. 23).

1-260 Digital reporting and record keeping (Making Tax Digital)

(TMA 1970, s. 12C and Sch. A1)

Finance (No. 2) Act 2017 provides powers to make regulations about digital record-keeping and reporting requirements for businesses within the charge to income tax. The measures will have effect from a day to be appointed by Treasury order. (TMA 1970, s. 12C and Sch. A1, as inserted by F(No.2)A 2017, s. 60).

Businesses (including self-employed and landlords) will be able to keep records of their income and expenditure digitally, and send summary updates quarterly to HMRC from their software (or app).

1-300 Payment dates 2017–18

(TMA 1970, s. 59A, 59B; SI 1996/1954)

(Tax Reporter: ¶182-725ff.)

Tax is paid on 31 January next following the year of assessment as a single sum covering capital gains tax(4) and income tax on all sources. Interim payments on account may be required. For 2017-18. the following due dates apply:

Type of assessment	Payment date
Self-assessment	
First interim payment[(1)]	31 January 2018
Second interim payment[(1)]	31 July 2018
Balancing payment	31 January 2019[(2)]
Simple assessment	31 January 2019[(3)]

Notes

(1) No interim payments are required if the tax paid in the preceding tax year was less than £1,000; or more than 80% of the tax due in the preceding year was collected at source. Otherwise, interim payments are calculated as 50% each of the net tax due for the preceding tax year (even if it is already clear that the actual liability for the year of assessment will exceed that for the preceding year). Where it is believed that the net tax due for the year of assessment will be less than the amount for the preceding year, a claim to reduce each payment on account accordingly can be made. Net tax is the excess of assessed tax over tax deducted at source (incl. tax credits on dividends before 6 April 2016). (TMA 1970, s. 59A).

(2) If a return is not issued until after 31 October 2018 and the taxpayer has notified chargeability by 5 October 2018, the due date for the final payment becomes three months from the issue of the return (TMA 1970, s. 59B).

(3) The due date for income tax and capital gains tax payable under a 'simple assessment' is three months after the day on which the simple assessment notice was given if given after 31 October following the year of assessment (TMA 1970, s. 59BA).

[4] Autumn Statement 2015 announced that from April 2019, a payment on account of any CGT due on the disposal of residential property will be required to be made within 30 days of the completion of the disposal. This will not affect gains on properties which are not liable for CGT due to private residence relief (PRR).

1-325 Direct recovery of debts

(F(No. 2)A 2015, s. 51 and Sch. 8)

HMRC have the power to recover debts due (including tax and tax credit debts) directly from the bank and building society accounts (including individual savings accounts) of debtors. This is also known as the direct recovery of debts (DRD). The power can only be used to recover debts of more than £1,000, and is subject to a number of statutory safeguards, including a 30-day right of objection and a limit of £5,000 as the minimum amount HMRC must always leave across a debtor's accounts above the amount that has been held.

1-350 Main penalty provisions 2017–18

Offence[4][5]	Penalty[1][2]		
Late return for 2010–11 and later years (FA 2009, Sch. 55; Tax Reporter: ¶181-500)			
Failure to submit by the filing date (by 31 October for paper return; by 31 January for online return)	£100		
Failure continues three months after the filing date by HMRC notice	£10 per day for a period up to 90 days beginning with the date specified in the notice (maximum £900)		
Failure still continues six months after the filing date)	The greater of £300 or 5% of the liability to tax shown by the return		
Failure still continues after 12 months	The greater of relevant percentage of liability shown by the return and £300		
	Relevant percentage		
	Category 1[3]	**Category 2**	**Category 3**
• withholding information deliberate and concealed	100%	150%	200%
• withholding information deliberate but not concealed	70%	105%	140%
• any other case	5%	5%	5%

<table>
<tr><th>Offence[4][5]</th><th colspan="3">Penalty[1][2]</th></tr>
<tr><td rowspan="23">Reductions for disclosure: maximum reduction weighted according to quality of disclosure determined as:
Disclosure of relevant information relating to domestic matter
• 30% for telling HMRC
• 40% for helping to quantify
• 30% for giving access to records
Discloses relevant information that relates to an offshore matter or offshore transfer
• telling HMRC
• helping to quantify
• giving access to records
• providing additional information</td><td colspan="3">**Tax years commencing on or after 6 April 2016**
Domestic matters</td></tr>
<tr><td>**Standard penalty**</td><td>**Prompted disclosure minimum**</td><td>**Unprompted disclosure minimum**</td></tr>
<tr><td>70%</td><td>35%</td><td>20%</td></tr>
<tr><td>100%</td><td>50%</td><td>30%</td></tr>
<tr><td colspan="3">**Offshore matters and offshore transfers**</td></tr>
<tr><td>**Standard penalty**</td><td>**Prompted disclosure minimum**</td><td>**Unprompted disclosure minimum**</td></tr>
<tr><td>70%</td><td>45%</td><td>30%</td></tr>
<tr><td>87.50%</td><td>53.75%</td><td>35%</td></tr>
<tr><td>100%</td><td>60%</td><td>40%</td></tr>
<tr><td>105%</td><td>62.50%</td><td>40%</td></tr>
<tr><td>125%</td><td>72.50%</td><td>50%</td></tr>
<tr><td>140%</td><td>80%</td><td>50%</td></tr>
<tr><td>150%</td><td>85%</td><td>55%</td></tr>
<tr><td>200%</td><td>110%</td><td>70%</td></tr>
<tr><td colspan="3">No reduction below £300</td></tr>
<tr><td colspan="3">**Tax years prior to 6 April 2016**</td></tr>
<tr><td>**Standard penalty**</td><td>**Prompted disclosure minimum**</td><td>**Unprompted disclosure minimum**</td></tr>
<tr><td>70%</td><td>35%</td><td>20%</td></tr>
<tr><td>105%</td><td>52.5%</td><td>30%</td></tr>
<tr><td>140%</td><td>70%</td><td>40%</td></tr>
<tr><td>100%</td><td>50%</td><td>30%</td></tr>
<tr><td>150%</td><td>75%</td><td>45%</td></tr>
<tr><td>200%</td><td>100%</td><td>60%</td></tr>
<tr><td rowspan="2">**Failure to notify chargeability**
For failures after 1 April 2010 (FA 2008, Sch. 41;
Tax Reporter: ¶181-350):</td><td colspan="3">**Percentage of potential lost revenue**</td></tr>
<tr><td>**Category 1[3]**</td><td>**Category 2**</td><td>**Category 3**</td></tr>
<tr><td>• failure deliberate and concealed</td><td>100%</td><td>150%</td><td>200%</td></tr>
<tr><td>• failure deliberate but not concealed</td><td>70%</td><td>105%</td><td>140%</td></tr>
<tr><td>• any other case</td><td>30%</td><td>45%</td><td>60%</td></tr>
</table>

<table>
<tr><th>Offence[4][5]</th><th>Penalty[1][2]</th></tr>
<tr>
<td>Reductions for disclosure: maximum reduction weighted according to quality of disclosure determined as:
Failures involving domestic matters and non-deliberate failures involving offshore matters
• 30% for telling HMRC
• 40% for helping to quantify
• 30% for giving access to records
Deliberate failures involving offshore matters and failures involving offshore transfers
• telling HMRC
• helping to quantify
• giving access to records
• providing additional information
[Note: The case A minimum applies if HMRC become aware of the failure less than 12 months after the time when the tax first becomes unpaid by reason of the failure, otherwise the case B minimum applies.]</td>
<td>
Tax years commencing on or after 6 April 2016
<table>
<tr><th colspan="5">Domestic matters</th></tr>
<tr><th>Standard penalty</th><th colspan="2">Prompted disclosure minimum</th><th colspan="2">Unprompted disclosure minimum</th></tr>
<tr><th></th><th>Case A</th><th>Case B</th><th>Case A</th><th>Case B</th></tr>
<tr><td>30%</td><td>10%</td><td>20%</td><td>0%</td><td>10%</td></tr>
<tr><td>70%</td><td colspan="2">35%</td><td colspan="2">20%</td></tr>
<tr><td>100%</td><td colspan="2">50%</td><td colspan="2">30%</td></tr>
</table>
<table>
<tr><th colspan="5">Offshore matters and offshore transfers</th></tr>
<tr><th>Standard penalty</th><th colspan="2">Prompted disclosure minimum</th><th colspan="2">Unprompted disclosure minimum</th></tr>
<tr><th></th><th>Case A</th><th>Case B</th><th>Case A</th><th>Case B</th></tr>
<tr><td>30%</td><td>10%</td><td>20%</td><td>0%</td><td>10%</td></tr>
<tr><td>37.5%</td><td>12.5%</td><td>25%</td><td>0%</td><td>12.5%</td></tr>
<tr><td>45%</td><td>15%</td><td>30%</td><td>0%</td><td>15%</td></tr>
<tr><td>60%</td><td>20%</td><td>40%</td><td>0%</td><td>20%</td></tr>
<tr><td>70%</td><td colspan="2">45%</td><td colspan="2">30%</td></tr>
<tr><td>87.5%</td><td colspan="2">53.75%</td><td colspan="2">35%</td></tr>
<tr><td>100%</td><td colspan="2">60%</td><td colspan="2">40%</td></tr>
<tr><td>105%</td><td colspan="2">62.5%</td><td colspan="2">40%</td></tr>
<tr><td>125%</td><td colspan="2">72.5%</td><td colspan="2">50%</td></tr>
<tr><td>140%</td><td colspan="2">80%</td><td colspan="2">50%</td></tr>
<tr><td>150%</td><td colspan="2">85%</td><td colspan="2">55%</td></tr>
<tr><td>200%</td><td colspan="2">110%</td><td colspan="2">70%</td></tr>
</table>
Tax years prior to 6 April 2016
<table>
<tr><th>Standard penalty</th><th colspan="2">Prompted disclosure minimum</th><th colspan="2">Unprompted disclosure minimum</th></tr>
<tr><th></th><th>Case A</th><th>Case B</th><th>Case A</th><th>Case B</th></tr>
<tr><td>30%</td><td>10%</td><td>20%</td><td>0%</td><td>10%</td></tr>
<tr><td>45%</td><td>15%</td><td>30%</td><td>0%</td><td>15%</td></tr>
<tr><td>60%</td><td>20%</td><td>40%</td><td>0%</td><td>20%</td></tr>
<tr><td>70%</td><td colspan="2">35%</td><td colspan="2">20%</td></tr>
<tr><td>105%</td><td colspan="2">52.5%</td><td colspan="2">30%</td></tr>
<tr><td>140%</td><td colspan="2">70%</td><td colspan="2">40%</td></tr>
<tr><td>100%</td><td colspan="2">50%</td><td colspan="2">30%</td></tr>
<tr><td>150%</td><td colspan="2">75%</td><td colspan="2">45%</td></tr>
<tr><td>200%</td><td colspan="2">100%</td><td colspan="2">60%</td></tr>
</table>
</td>
</tr>
<tr><td>Failure to keep and retain tax records (TMA 1970, s. 12B; Tax Reporter: ¶181-900)</td><td>Up to £3,000 per year of assessment</td></tr>
<tr><td>False statements to reduce interim payments (TMA 1970, s. 59A(6); Tax Reporter: ¶182-725)</td><td>Up to the difference between the amount correctly due and the amount paid</td></tr>
<tr><td>Failure to comply with an information notice (FA 2008, Sch. 36, para. 39 and 40; Tax Reporter: ¶186-550ff.)</td><td></td></tr>
<tr><td>• standard amount</td><td>£300</td></tr>
<tr><td>• continued failure</td><td>daily penalty of £60</td></tr>
<tr><td>Tax-related penalty where significant tax is at risk (FA 2008, Sch. 36, para. 50)</td><td>tax geared amount decided by Upper Tribunal</td></tr>
</table>

Offence[4][5]	Penalty[1][2]
Inaccurate information/documents in complying with an information notice (FA 2008, Sch. 36) Inaccuracy careless or deliberate	Up to £3,000 for each inaccuracy
Errors in returns Errors in returns for periods starting 1 April 2008 where return is filed on or after 1 April 2009 (FA 2007, Sch. 24; Tax Reporter: ¶184-850) • careless action • deliberate but not concealed action • deliberate and concealed action [Note: No penalty for inaccuracies that occur despite taking reasonable care.]	See table A below
Reductions for disclosure: maximum reduction weighted according to quality of disclosure determined as: *Domestic matters and careless inaccuracies involving offshore matters* • 30% for telling HMRC • 40% for helping to quantify • 30% for giving access to records *Deliberate inaccuracies involving offshore matters and inaccuracies involving offshore transfers* • telling HMRC • helping to quantify • allowing access to records • providing additional information	See tables B and C below

Table A – **Percentage of potential lost revenue**

Category 1[3]	**Category 2**	**Category 3**
30%	45%	60%
70%	105%	140%
100%	150%	200%

Tax years commencing on or after 6 April 2016

Table B – **Domestic matters**

Standard penalty	**Prompted disclosure minimum**	**Unprompted disclosure minimum**
30%	15%	0%
70%	35%	20%
100%	50%	30%

Table C – **Offshore matters and offshore transfers**

Standard penalty	**Prompted disclosure minimum**	**Unprompted disclosure minimum**
30%	15%	0%
37.5%	18.75%	0%
45%	22.5%	0%
60%	30%	0%
70%	45%	30%
87.5%	53.75%	35%
100%	60%	40%
105%	62.5%	40%
125%	72.5%	50%
140%	80%	50%
150%	85%	55%
200%	110%	70%

Offence[4][5]	**Penalty**[1][2]		
	Tax years prior to 6 April 2016 **Percentage of potential lost revenue**		
	Standard penalty	**Prompted disclosure minimum**	**Unprompted disclosure minimum**
	30%	15%	0%
	45%	22.5%	0%
	60%	30%	0%
	70%	35%	20%
	105%	52.5%	30%
	140%	70%	40%
	100%	50%	30%
	150%	75%	45%
	200%	100%	60%
Offshore asset moves (FA 2015, Sch. 21) Additional penalty for offshore asset moves from specified territory to non-specified territory on or after 26 March 2015 following an original deliberate failure penalty under: FA 2007, Sch. 24, para. 1; FA 2008, Sch. 41, para. 1; or FA 2009, Sch. 55, para. 6. See ¶1-370 for table of specified territories.	50% of original penalty		
General anti-abuse rule penalty (FA 2013, s. 212A and Sch. 43C) from 15 September 2016 Penalty where counteraction notice given under FA 2013, Sch. 43, para. 12, Sch. 43A, para. 8 or 9, or Sch. 43B, para. 8	60% of the value of the counteracted advantage		
Enabling offshore tax evasion or non-compliance (FA 2016, Sch. 20) from 1 January 2017 Penalty for engaging in offshore tax evasion or non-compliance where the tax at stake is income tax, capital gains tax or inheritance tax. Standard penalty: Where a penalty under FA 2015, Sch. 21, para. 1 arises:	The higher of: 100% of the potential lost revenue; or £3,000 The higher of: 50% of the potential lost revenue; or £3,000		

Offence[4][5]	Penalty[1][2]
Asset based penalty for offshore inaccuracies and failures (FA 2016, Sch. 22) for tax years commencing on or after 6 April 2016 Additional penalty where one or more standard offshore penalties and the offshore potential lost revenue in relation to a tax year exceeds £25,000. Standard offshore penalties means penalties under: FA 2007, Sch. 24, para. 1; FA 2008, Sch. 41, para. 1; or FA 2009, Sch. 55, para. 6 imposed involving offshore matters or offshore transfers and deliberate behaviour.	Lower of 10% of value of asset and offshore PLR x 10.
Reductions for: • disclosing to HMRC • providing a reasonable value • providing information or access to records to assist HMRC value the asset • special circumstances	Reduction factors Unprompted disclosure 50% Prompted disclosure 20%

Notes

[1] Interest is charged on penalties not paid when due. The due date is 30 days after the notice of determination of the penalty is issued.

[2] Defences of 'reasonable excuse' or 'special circumstances' may be available.

[3] FA 2015, s. 120 and Sch. 20 introduce a new category of penalty, category 0 from a date to be appointed. The new category of penalty will carry the lowest level of penalty equivalent to those currently in category 1 (i.e. 30%, 70% and 100%) and the penalty percentages for category 1 penalties will be increased to 37.5%, 87.5% and 125% respectively. New tables as follows:

Late return	**Relevant percentage**			
	Category 0	**Category 1**	**Category 2**	**Category 3**
• withholding information deliberate and concealed	100%	125%	150%	200%
• withholding information deliberate but not concealed	70%	87.5%	105%	140%
• any other case	5%	5%	5%	5%

Failure to notify chargeability	**Percentage of potential lost revenue**			
	Category 0	**Category 1**	**Category 2**	**Category 3**
• failure deliberate and concealed	100%	125%	150%	200%
• failure deliberate but not concealed	70%	87.5%	105%	140%
• any other case	30%	37.5%	45%	60%

Errors in returns	Percentage of potential lost revenue			
	Category 0	Category 1	Category 2	Category 3
• careless action	30%	37.50%	45%	60%
• deliberate but not concealed action	70.0%	87.50%	105%	140%
• deliberate and concealed action	100%	125%	150%	200%

(4) *Finance Act* 2016 contains the following changes:

- a new criminal offence that removes the need to prove intent for the most serious cases of failing to declare offshore income and gains (TMA 1970, s. 106B–106H, as inserted by FA 2016, s. 166, with effect from the tax year commencing on 6 April 2017 and subsequent tax years (SI 2017/970);
- increased public naming of tax evaders (FA 2009, s. 94, as amended by FA 2016, s. 164, with effect from 1 April 2017 (SI 2017/261)); and
- a new regime of warnings and escalating sanctions for those who persistently engage in tax avoidance schemes which HMRC defeats. Following the first defeat of a tax avoidance scheme, HMRC will place the taxpayer on a warning for five years. If the taxpayer uses any further schemes while under warning which HMRC defeats, the rate of penalty will be 20% for the first defeat, 40% for the second defeat and 60% for the third defeat. If HMRC defeat three tax avoidance schemes while the taxpayer is on warning, the taxpayer's details can be published. If three avoidance schemes which exploit reliefs are used while under warning and HMRC defeat them, the taxpayer will be denied further benefit of reliefs until the warning period expires. The regime comes into effect on 6 April 2017 (FA 2016, s. 159 and Sch. 18).

(5) Finance (No. 2) Act 2017 introduces a new penalty for any person who has enabled another person or business to use a tax avoidance arrangement that is later defeated by HMRC, with effect in relation to arrangements entered into on or after Royal Assent (F(No.2)A 2017, s. 65 and Sch. 16).

1-360 Offshore penalties – territory categories

The table below shows which territories are classified in 'category 1' and 'category 3' for the purposes of penalties for offshore non-compliance. Territories not listed here (other than the UK) are in 'category 2'. Penalties for domestic (UK) matters fall into category 1.

Territories are allocated into one of the categories depending upon the level of information exchange arrangements with the UK, with category 1 territories having the highest level of information sharing arrangements so penalties are the same as for penalties involving domestic matters, whereas territories in categories 2 and 3 have correspondingly poorer information exchange arrangements.

A new category of territory, category 0, is prospectively introduced by FA 2015, s. 120 and Sch. 20, with effect from a date to be appointed. The new category of penalty will apply to overseas territories making information exchange arrangements with the UK that meet the new Common Reporting Standard. It is envisaged that most or all territories currently in category 1 will, over time, make arrangements so as to fall within category 0 (FA 2015, Sch. 20).

Category 1	Category 3[(1)]
Anguilla	Albania
Aruba	Algeria
Australia	Andorra
Belgium	Bonaire, Sint Eustatius and Saba
Bulgaria	Brazil
Canada	Cameroon
Cayman Islands	Cape Verde
Cyprus	Colombia
Czech Republic	Congo, Republic of the
Denmark (not including Faroe Islands and Greenland which are in category 2)	Cook Islands
Estonia	Costa Rica
Finland	Curacao
France	Cuba
Germany	Democratic People's Republic of Korea
Greece	Dominican Republic
Guernsey (includes Alderney and Sark)	Ecuador
Hungary	El Salvador
Ireland	Gabon
Isle of Man	Guatemala
Italy	Honduras
Japan	Iran
Korea, South	Iraq
Latvia	Jamaica
Lithuania	Kyrgyzstan
Malta	Lebanon
Montserrat	Macau (China and Hong Kong are in category 2)
Netherlands (not including Bonaire, Sint Eustatius and Saba)	Marshall Islands
New Zealand (not including Tokelau)	Micronesia, Federated States of
Norway	Monaco
	Nauru

Category 1	Category 3[(1)]
Poland	Nicaragua
Portugal (includes Madeira and the Azores)	Niue
Romania	Palau
Slovakia	Panama
Slovenia	Paraguay
Spain (includes the Canary Islands and other overseas territories of Spain)	Peru
Sweden	Seychelles
Switzerland (from 24 July 2013)	Sint Maarten
United States of America (not including overseas territories and possessions of the United States of America which are in category 2)	Suriname
	Syria
	Tokelau
	Tonga
	Trinidad and Tobago
	United Arab Emiratess
	Uruguay

Note

(1) Before 24 July 2013, category 3 territories included additionally:
- Antigua and Barbuda;
- Armenia;
- Bahrain;
- Barbados;
- Belize;
- Dominica;
- Grenada;
- Mauritius;
- Saint Kitts and Nevis;
- Saint Lucia;
- Saint Vincent and the Grenadines;
- San Marino.

1-370 Offshore asset moves penalties: specified territories

(SI 2015/866)

Andorra	Anguilla	Antigua and Barbuda	Argentina
Aruba	Australia	Austria	The Bahamas
Bahrain[(1)]	Barbados	Belgium	Belize
Bermuda	Brazil	British Virgin Islands	Brunei Darussalam
Bulgaria	Canada	Cayman Islands	Chile

China	Cook Islands[(1)]	Colombia	Costa Rica
Croatia	Curaçao	Cyprus	Czech Republic
Denmark	Dominica	Estonia	Faroe Islands
Finland	France	Germany	Ghana[(1)]
Gibraltar	Greece	Greenland	Grenada
Guernsey	Hong Kong	Hungary	Iceland
India	Indonesia	Ireland	Isle of Man
Israel	Italy	Japan	Jersey
Korea (South)	Kuwait[(1)]	Latvia	Lebanon[(1)]
Liechtenstein	Lithuania	Luxembourg	Macau
Malaysia	Malta	Marshall Islands	Mauritius
Mexico	Monaco	Montserrat	Nauru[(1)]
Netherlands (including Bonaire, Sint Eustatius and Saba)	New Zealand (not including Tokelau)	Niue	Norway
Panama[(1)]	Poland	Portugal	Qatar
Romania	Russia	Saint Kitts and Nevis	Saint Lucia
Saint Vincent and the Grenadines	Samoa	San Marino	Saudi Arabia
Seychelles	Singapore	Sint Maarten	Slovak Republic
Slovenia	South Africa	Spain	Sweden
Switzerland	Trinidad and Tobago	Turkey	Turks and Caicos Islands
United Arab Emirates	Uruguay	Vanuatu[(1)]	

Note

(1) New entries added, and previous entries 'Albania' and 'United States of America (not including overseas territories and possessions)' omitted, by SI 2017/989, with effect from 3 November 2017.

1-400 Penalties for late payment of tax 2017–18

(FA 2009, Sch. 56)

(Tax Reporter: ¶182-875)

The current penalty regime for late payments under income tax self-assessment was introduced by FA 2009, Sch. 56 and applies from 6 April 2011 to payments for the tax year 2010–11 and later years.

Tax overdue	Penalty
30 days	5% of tax overdue
6 months	further 5% of tax overdue
12 months	further 5% of tax overdue

These penalties will be issued automatically and are in addition to the interest that will be charges on all outstanding amounts, including unpaid penalties, until payment is received.

Penalties apply to:

- final tax payments on self-assessments (this includes any amounts due as interim payments which remain unpaid);
- tax on inspector's amendments to a self-assessment made during or as a result of an audit; and
- discovery assessments.

1-450 Interest 2017–18

(FA 2009, s. 101–105 and Sch. 53 and 54)

(Tax Reporter: ¶182-925; ¶182-975)

The current regime for interest on overdue and overpaid tax was introduced by FA 2009, s. 101–105 and Sch. 53 and 54, with effect in relation to any self-assessment amount payable or repayable on or after 31 October 2011.

Late payment interest: is payable from the 'late payment interest start date':

Payment	Late payment interest start date
First interim payment[(1)]	31 January 2018
Second interim payment	31 July 2018
Final payment[(2)]	31 January 2019
Tax due on an amendment to a return	31 January 2019
Tax due on determination of appeal	31 January 2019

Notes

[(1)] Where the taxpayer has provided HMRC in good time with the information required to issue a statement of account ahead of the payment date of 31 January, but no statement is received before 1 January, interest on the tax to be paid will run from 30 days after the taxpayer is actually notified rather than from 31 January.

[(2)] Where notice to make a return is issued after 31 October following the end of the tax year, provided there has been no failure to notify chargeability under TMA 1970, s. 7, the date from which interest is payable becomes the last day in the period of three months beginning with the day notice to make a return was given.

Repayment interest: runs from the date of payment (deemed to be 31 January following the tax year in respect of tax deducted at source) to the date on which the order for the repayment is issued.

1-500 Rates of interest

(FA 2009, s. 101–102; SI 2011/2446)

(Tax Reporter: ¶182-925; ¶182-975)

The following table gives the rates of interest applicable in recent years.

From	Late payment %	Repayment %
23 August 2016	2.75	0.50
29 September 2009 to 22 August 2016	3.00	0.50

Notes

SI 2011/2446 sets the interest rates for the purposes of s. 101 and 102 at the Bank of England base rate plus 2.5% and minus 1% respectively. Changes in interest rates announced in Bank of England Monetary Policy Committee meetings take effect from the 13th working day following the meeting and apply in respect of interest running from before that date as well as interest running from on or after that date.

(1) Tax-related judgment debts: the Government will set the rate of interest which applies on taxation-related debts payable under a court judgment or order by HMRC to a rate equal to the Bank of England base rate plus 2%. The Government will also apply the late payment interest rate to taxation-related debts owed to HMRC under a court judgment or order. These changes will apply to new and pre-existing judgments and orders in respect of interest accruing on and after 8 July 2015 (F(No. 2)A 2015, s. 52).

1-600 Interest rates on certificates of tax deposit (CTD)

CTDs can be purchased to settle most tax liabilities, except PAYE, VAT and corporation tax falling due under Pay and File, or for subsequent encashment. (No CTDs are available for purchase for use against corporation tax liabilities since the start of the Pay and File regime.) A higher rate of interest is paid if the CTD is used in payment of tax. Interest is allowed/paid gross and is taxable.

Rates of interest vary according to the period for which the deposit is held. The rates in force at issue apply for one year; thereafter, the rate applicable is that on the most recent anniversary of the date of issue.

Details of how to purchase a CTD and use it in payment of tax can be found on the HMRC website at www.gov.uk/guidance/certificate-of-tax-deposit-scheme.

Rates applicable over recent years have been as follows:

Deposits on or after		Deposits under £100,000		Deposits of £100,000 or more									
				Deposits held for under 1 month		Deposits held for 1 to under 3 months		Deposits held for 3 to under 6 months		Deposits held for 6 to under 9 months		Deposits held for 9–12 months	
		Applied in payment of tax %	Cash value %	Applied in payment of tax %	Cash value %	Applied in payment of tax %	Cash value %	Applied in payment of tax %	Cash value %	Applied in payment of tax %	Cash value %	Applied in payment of tax %	Cash value %
7 May	1997	2.75	1.50	2.75	1.50	5.50	2.75	5.25	2.75	5.50	2.75	5.25	2.75
9 June	1997	3.00	1.50	3.00	1.50	5.50	2.75	5.50	2.75	5.50	2.75	5.50	2.75
11 July	1997	3.25	1.75	3.25	1.75	6.00	3.00	5.75	3.00	5.75	3.00	6.00	3.00
8 Aug.	1997	4.50	2.25	4.50	2.25	6.00	3.00	6.00	3.00	6.00	3.00	5.75	3.00
7 Nov.	1997	4.00	2.00	4.00	2.00	6.50	3.25	6.50	3.25	6.25	3.25	6.25	3.25
5 June	1998	4.00	2.00	4.00	2.00	6.50	3.25	6.25	3.25	6.25	3.25	6.00	3.00
9 Oct.	1998	3.75	2.00	3.75	2.00	6.25	3.25	5.75	3.00	5.50	2.75	5.25	2.75
6 Nov.	1998	3.25	1.75	3.25	1.75	5.75	3.00	5.25	2.75	5.00	2.50	4.75	2.50
11 Dec.	1998	3.00	1.50	3.00	1.50	5.25	2.75	4.75	2.50	4.50	2.25	4.25	2.25
8 Jan.	1999	2.50	1.25	2.50	1.25	5.00	2.50	4.50	2.25	4.00	2.00	4.00	2.00
5 Feb.	1999	1.75	1.00	1.75	1.00	4.50	2.25	4.00	2.00	3.75	2.00	3.75	2.00
9 Apr.	1999	1.75	1.00	1.75	1.00	4.25	2.25	4.00	2.00	3.75	2.00	3.75	2.00
11 June	1999	1.50	0.75	1.50	0.75	4.00	2.00	4.00	2.00	4.00	2.00	4.00	2.00
9 Sept.	1999	1.75	1.00	1.75	1.00	4.50	2.25	4.50	2.25	4.50	2.25	4.50	2.25
4 Nov.	1999	2.00	1.00	2.00	1.00	5.00	2.50	4.75	2.50	4.75	2.50	4.75	2.50
14 Jan.	2000	2.25	1.25	2.25	1.25	5.00	2.50	5.00	2.50	5.00	2.50	5.25	2.75
11 Feb.	2000	2.50	1.25	2.50	1.25	5.25	2.75	5.00	2.50	5.25	2.75	5.25	2.75
9 Feb.	2001	2.25	1.25	2.25	1.25	4.75	2.50	4.25	2.25	4.25	2.25	4.00	2.00
6 Apr.	2001	2.00	1.00	2.00	1.00	4.25	2.25	4.00	2.00	3.75	2.00	3.50	1.75
11 May	2001	2.00	1.00	2.00	1.00	4.00	2.00	4.00	2.00	3.75	2.00	3.75	2.00
3 Aug.	2001	1.50	0.75	1.50	0.75	4.00	2.00	3.75	2.00	3.75	2.00	3.75	2.00
19 Sept.	2001	1.25	0.75	1.25	0.75	3.50	1.75	3.25	1.75	3.25	1.75	3.00	1.50
5 Oct.	2001	1.00	0.50	1.00	0.50	3.25	1.75	3.00	1.50	3.00	1.50	3.00	1.50

Deposits on or after	Deposits under £100,000		Deposits of £100,000 or more									
			Deposits held for under 1 month		Deposits held for 1 to under 3 months		Deposits held for 3 to under six months		Deposits held for 6 to under 9 months		Deposits held for 9–12 months	
	Applied in payment of tax %	Cash value %	Applied in payment of tax %	Cash value %	Applied in payment of tax %	Cash value %	Applied in payment of tax %	Cash value %	Applied in payment of tax %	Cash value %	Applied in payment of tax %	Cash value %
9 Nov. 2001	0.50	0.25	0.50	0.25	2.75	1.50	2.50	1.25	2.25	1.25	2.25	1.25
7 Feb. 2003	0.25	Nil	0.25	Nil	2.75	1.25	2.25	1.00	2.25	1.00	2.00	1.00
11 July 2003	Nil	Nil	Nil	Nil	2.50	1.25	2.25	1.00	2.00	1.00	2.00	1.00
7 Nov. 2003	0.25	Nil	0.25	Nil	3.00	1.50	3.00	1.50	3.00	1.50	3.00	1.50
6 Feb. 2004	0.50	0.25	0.50	0.25	3.00	1.50	3.00	1.50	3.00	1.50	3.00	1.50
7 May 2004	0.75	0.25	0.75	0.25	3.25	1.50	3.25	1.50	3.25	1.50	3.25	1.50
11 June 2004	1.00	0.50	1.00	0.50	3.75	1.75	3.50	1.75	3.75	1.75	3.75	1.75
6 Aug. 2004	1.25	0.50	1.25	0.50	3.75	1.75	3.75	1.75	3.75	1.75	3.75	1.75
5 Aug. 2005	1.00	0.50	1.00	0.50	3.50	1.75	3.25	1.50	3.00	1.50	3.00	1.50
4 Aug. 2006	1.75	0.75	1.75	0.75	4.25	2.00	4.25	2.00	4.00	2.00	4.00	2.00
10 Nov. 2006	1.50	0.75	1.50	0.75	4.00	2.00	4.00	2.00	3.75	1.75	3.75	1.75
12 Jan. 2007	1.50	0.75	1.50	0.75	4.25	2.00	4.00	2.00	4.00	2.00	4.00	2.00
11 May 2007	2.00	1.00	2.00	1.00	4.75	2.25	4.50	2.25	4.50	2.25	4.50	2.25
6 July 2007	2.25	1.10	2.25	1.10	5.00	2.50	4.75	2.25	4.75	2.25	4.75	2.25
7 Dec. 2007	3.00	1.50	3.00	1.50	5.50	2.75	5.00	2.50	4.75	2.25	4.50	2.25
8 Feb. 2008	2.00	1.00	2.00	1.00	4.50	2.25	4.25	2.25	4.00	2.00	3.75	1.50
11 Apr. 2008	2.00	1.00	2.00	1.00	4.75	2.25	4.50	2.25	4.25	2.00	4.25	2.00
9 Oct. 2008	2.50	1.25	2.50	1.25	5.25	2.50	5.00	2.50	5.00	2.50	4.75	2.25
7 Nov. 2008	1.75	0.75	1.75	0.75	4.50	2.25	4.25	2.00	4.25	2.00	4.00	2.00
5 Dec. 2008	0.00	0.00	0.00	0.00	2.50	1.25	2.50	1.25	2.50	1.25	2.25	1.00
9 Jan. 2009	0.00	0.00	0.00	0.00	1.50	0.75	1.25	0.50	1.25	0.50	1.25	0.50
6 Feb. 2009	0.00	0.00	0.00	0.00	1.00	0.50	1.00	0.50	1.00	0.50	0.75	0.25
6 Mar. 2009	0.00	0.00	0.00	0.00	0.75	0.25	0.75	0.25	0.75	0.25	0.75	0.25

1-650 Remission of tax for official error

(ESC A19)

Arrears of income tax and capital gains tax may be given up if they result from HMRC's failure to make proper and timely use of information supplied by the taxpayer, or in certain circumstances by the taxpayer's employer or the Department for Work and Pensions.

The taxpayer must have reasonably believed that his or her affairs were in order. Tax will normally only be given up where there was a gap of 12 months or more between HMRC receiving the information that tax was due, and notifying the taxpayer of the arrears.

Taxation of business profits

2-000 Relief for fluctuating profits (farming and market gardening; creative artists): from 2016–17

(ITTOIA 2005, s. 221ff.)

(Tax Reporter: ¶272-300ff.; ¶268-300)

Two-year averaging

From 2016–17, marginal relief is removed and full two-year averaging relief is be availabe where the profits of one year are 75% or less of the profits of the other year (FA 2016, s. 25).

Five-year averaging

For 2016–17 and subsequent years, individuals are able to claim to average trading profits for income tax purposes over five consecutive tax years where the 'volatility' condition is met.

The volatility condition is that:

(a) one of the following is less than 75% of the other:
  (i) the average of the relevant profits of the first four tax years to which the claim relates;
  (ii) the relevant profits of the last of the tax years to which the claim relates; or

(b) the relevant profits of one or more (but not all) of the five tax years to which the claim relates are nil.

(ITTOIA 2005, s. 222A, as inserted by *Finance Act* 2016, with effect from the tax year 2016–17 (meaning that a five-year averaging claim with 2016–17 as the final year would involve averaging the profits of the years 2012–13 to 2016–17).)

2-005 Relief for fluctuating profits (farming and market gardening; creative artists): up to 2015–16

(ITTOIA 2005, s. 221ff.)

(Tax Reporter: ¶272-300ff.; ¶268-300)

Full averaging

Full averaging applied where profits of one of the tax years was less than 70% of profits for the other year or where profits of one (but not both) of the tax years was nil.

Marginal averaging

The amount of the adjustment to the profits of each relevant tax year, where lower profits are between 70% and 75% of higher profits, was computed as follows:

$$(D \times 3) - (P \times 0.75)$$

Where:

D is the difference between the relevant profits of the two years; and

P is the relevant profits of the tax year of which those profits are higher.

Marginal relief was removed by FA 2016, s. 25, with effect where the latest year is 2016–17 (and subsequent tax years).

2-010 Cash basis for small businesses

(ITTOIA 2005, Pt. 2, Ch. 3A)

(Tax Reporter: ¶206-481ff.)

From April 2013 eligible businesses may elect to calculate their profits on the cash basis instead of in accordance with generally accepted accountancy principles. The cash basis is optional but circumstances under which a business can leave the scheme are limited (businesses must continue to use the scheme until their circumstances change so that the cash basis is no longer suitable for them). Under the scheme, businesses calculate their taxable income by taking business income received in a year and deducting business expenses paid in a year. This means they do not need to adjust for debtors, creditors and stock, and generally do not have to distinguish between revenue and capital expenditure. Capital allowances remain available for expenditure on cars only. Businesses using the cash basis do not have to use the simplified flat rate expenses for their cars.

Eligible barristers are able to choose either to use the cash basis and simplified expenses or the accruals basis. The former cash basis for Barristers (also known as the alternative basis) under ITTOIA 2005, s. 160 (which was available in the seven years following their first holding themselves out for work) was repealed by Finance Act 2013 but barristers who were using the alternative basis for the tax year 2012-13 could continue to do so.

	Relevant max. Joining[(2)] £	Leaving Threshold[(2)] £
From 6 April 2017		
Standard	150,000	300,000
Recipients of universal credit[(1)]	300,000	
2016–17		
Standard	83,000	166,000
Recipients of universal credit[(1)]	166,000	
2015–16		
Standard	82,000	164,000
Recipients of universal credit[(1)]	164,000	
2014–15		
Standard	81,000	162,000
Recipients of universal credit[(1)]	162,000	
2013–14		
Standard	79,000	158,000
Recipients of universal credit[(1)]	158,000	

Notes

[(1)] Recipients of universal credit must use the cash basis for income assessment for UC purposes.

[(2)] Joining and leaving thresholds are prescribed by ITTOIA 2005, s. 31B (as amended by SI 2017/293, for tax the tax year 2017–18 and subsequent tax years).

Excluded businesses:

- companies;
- limited liability partnerships;
- partnerships with a non-individual partner during the basis period;
- lloyds underwriters;
- farming businesses with a herd basis election in effect for the tax year;

- farming and creative businesses with a profits averaging election in effect for the tax year;
- businesses that have claimed business premises renovation allowances within the previous seven years (ending immediately before the basis period);
- businesses that carry on a mineral extraction trade during the basis period for the tax year;
- businesses that still own an asset in respect of which research and development allowances have been claimed (at any time).

Simplified cash basis for unincorporated businesses

(F(No.2)A 2017, Sch. 2)

Finance (No. 2) Act 2017 introduces new rules relating to the calculation of the taxable profits of unincorporated businesses. This includes a simplified treatment of capital expenditure under the cash basis for trades, professions and vocations and the introduction of the cash basis for the calculation of taxable profits of property businesses. These changes will have effect for tax years from 2017-18 onwards, though for the 2017–18 tax year trading profits can be calculated using either the new rules or the existing rules.

2-020 Trade profits: deductions allowable at a fixed rate

(ITTOIA 2005, Pt. 2, Ch. 5A)

(Tax Reporter: ¶208-380)

From the tax year 2013–14, unincorporated businesses are entitled to use flat rates to calculate certain types of expenses rather than having to calculate actual amounts.

Expense	From 6 April 2013
Expenditure on vehicles	
Car or goods vehicle	
– first 10,000 miles	£0.45/mile
– above 10,000 miles	£0.25/mile
Motorcycle	£0.24/mile

Expense	From 6 April 2013
	Rate per Month £
Use of home for business[(1)(3)]	
25–50 hours per month	10.00
51–100 hours per month	18.00
101 hours or more per month	26.00
Or claim allowable portion of actual costs	
Premises used both as home and business premises[(2)(3)]	
Disallowance (for personal element of expenses)	
one occupant using premises as a home	350.00
two occupants using premises as a home	500.00
three or more occupants using premises as a home	650.00
Or identify allowable portion of actual costs	

Notes

[(1)] Deduction is given for each month or part of a month in relation to the number of hours spent wholly and exclusively on work done by the person in their home wholly and exclusively for the purposes of the trade (ITTOIA 2005, s. 94H).

[(2)] Available for premises which are mainly used for the purposes of carrying on the trade but also used by the person as a home. Instead of apportioning expenses between business and personal use, a deduction may be claimed for the full expense minus the relevant flat rate non-business use amount (ITTOIA 2005, s. 94I).

[(3)] *Finance Act* 2016 amends the simplified expenses regime, with effect for the tax year 2016–17 and subsequent tax years, to ensure that partnerships can fully access the provisions in respect of the use of a home and where business premises are also a home.

2-030 Limited liability partnerships: salaried members

(ITTOIA 2005, s. 863A–863G)

(Tax Reporter: ¶292-650)

From 6 April 2014, an individual member (M) of an LLP is treated as an employee for tax purposes (subject to PAYE and to tax on any benefits in kind) if all of the three conditions set out below are met. The rules apply only to LLPs formed under the *Limited Liability Partnership Act* 2000, not to general partnerships or limited partnerships that are formed under the Partnership Act 1890 and the Limited Partnership Act 1907, respectively.

Condition	Requirements for condition to be satisfied
Condition A: Disguised salary	Arrangements are in place under which: • M is to perform services for the LLP; and • it is reasonable to expect that at least 80% of the total amount payable by the LLP in respect of M's performance of those services will be 'disguised salary' (i.e. fixed, or variable but without reference to the overall amount of the profits or losses of the LLP; or not in practice affected by the overall profits or losses of the LLP).
Condition B: Significant influence	If the mutual rights and duties of the members and the LLP do not give M significant influence over the affairs of the partnership.
Condition C: Capital contribution	M's contribution to the LLP is less than 25% of the disguised salary which it is reasonable to expect will be payable in a relevant tax year in respect of M's performance of services for the partnership.

2-050 Car hire: leases starting from 6 April 2009

(ITTOIA 2005, s. 48ff.)

(Tax Reporter: ¶212-025)

Leased cars, where the lease begins from 6 April 2009 (for income tax purposes), suffer a 15% disallowance of relevant payments if CO_2 emissions exceed the limits set out below, otherwise no disallowance. This applies to all cars (not just those costing more than £12,000).

	CO_2 emissions
From 6 April 2013	Over 130g/km
6 April 2009 to 5 April 2013	Over 160g/km

2-060 Car hire: leases starting before 6 April 2009

(ITTOIA 2005, s. 48ff.)

(Tax Reporter: ¶212-050)

For leased cars where the lease began before 6 April 2009, the restricted deduction for hire charges of motor cars with a retail price greater than £12,000 is calculated as follows:

$$\text{Allowable amount} = \frac{£12{,}000 + ½\ (\text{retail price} - £12{,}000)}{\text{retail price}} \times \text{hire charge}$$

2-100 Time limits for elections and claims

(TMA 1970, s. 43(1))

(Tax Reporter: ¶191-635)

In the absence of any provision to the contrary, under self-assessment for the purposes of income tax, the normal rule is that claims are to be made within four years from the end of the tax year to which they relate.

Other specific income tax provisions are as below.

Provision	Time limit	Statutory reference
Averaging of profits of farmers or creative artists	first anniversary of the normal self-assessment filing date for the second tax year	ITTOIA 2005, s. 222
Stock transferred to a connected party on cessation of trade (or, from April 2009, profession or vocation) to be valued at higher of cost or sale price	first anniversary of the normal self-assessment filing date for the tax year of cessation	ITTOIA 2005, s. 178
Post-cessation expenses relieved against income and chargeable gains	first anniversary of the normal self-assessment filing date for the tax year	ITTOIA 2005, s. 257(4); ITA 2007, s. 96
Current and preceding year set-off of trading losses	first anniversary of the normal self-assessment filing date for the loss-making year	ITA 2007, s. 64

Provision	Time limit	Statutory reference
Three-year carry-back of trading losses in first four years of trade	first anniversary of the normal self-assessment filing date for the tax year in which the loss is made	ITA 2007, s. 72
Carry-forward of trading losses	normal rules apply (see above)	ITA 2007, s. 83ff.
Carry-back of terminal losses	normal rules apply (see above)	ITA 2007, s. 89

Taxation of investment income

3-000 Registered pension schemes

(FA 2004, Pt. 4, Ch. 1–7 and Sch. 28–36; SI 2014/1843)

From 6 April 2006, ('A' day) a revised set of rules applies to all forms of pension provision.

Age restrictions

Normal minimum pension age is 55 from 6 April 2010 (previously 50) except for retirement on ill-health grounds and some preserved lower retirement ages – see below.

From 2010–11 onwards, there is no minimum benefit age. Previously, benefits had to be taken by the age of 77 at the latest (age 75 before 22 June 2010).

Recent changes

- From 2017-18:
  - the Money Purchase Annual Allowance is reduced to £4,000 (F(No.2)A 2017, s. 7)
  - alignment of the UK tax treatment of payments out of "foreign pension schemes" with the UK's domestic tax regime and pension schemes used for those employed abroad; in particular:
  - funds in a registered pension scheme based outside the UK are subject to UK taxation consistent with the tax treatment of a UK based registered pension scheme;
  - tax the full foreign pension of UK residents, instead of 90%;
  - close specialist "section 615 schemes" to new pension saving if individuals wish to continue to be able to receive relief from tax in respect of annuity payments from those schemes; and
  - tax foreign pension lump sums paid to UK residents that are not already liable to UK tax.

(FA 2017, Sch. 3).

- introduce a new tax on transfers of pension savings to qualifying recognised overseas pension schemes (QROPS). The tax applies to transfers requested on or after 9 March 2017 (FA 2017, Sch. 4) (see ¶3-100);

- Finance Act 2016 legislated for a number of minor changes to the pensions tax rules to ensure that they operate as intended following the introduction of pension flexibility in April 2015, with effect from 15 September 2016, that:
  - remove the requirement that a serious ill-health lump sum can only be paid from an arrangement that has never been accessed;
  - replace the 45% tax charge on serious ill-health lump sums paid to individuals who have reached age 75 with tax at the individual's marginal rate;
  - enable dependants with drawdown or flexi-access drawdown pension who would currently have to use all of this fund before age 23 or pay tax charges of up to 70% on any lump sum payment, to continue to access their funds as they wish after their 23rd birthday;
  - remove the rule on paying a charity lump sum death benefit out of drawdown pension funds and flexi-access drawdown funds where the member dies under the age of 75 because the equivalent tax-free payment may be made as another type of lump sum death benefit;
  - enable money purchase pensions in payment to be paid as a trivial commutation lump sum;
  - enable the full amount of dependants benefits to be paid as authorised payments where there are insufficient funds in a cash balance arrangement when the member dies.

Tax relief on contributions

(ITEPA 2003, s. 308; FA 2004, Pt. 4, Ch. 4)

(Tax Reporter: ¶376-000ff.; ¶376-500ff.)

Type of contribution	Tax relief
Individual	the greater of £3,600 and the amount of the member's relevant UK earnings, subject to the annual allowance
Employer	No income tax for employee (not a taxable BIK) No NIC liability Tax deductible for employer[(1)]

Note

[(1)] Where contributions in a chargeable period exceed 210% of the contributions made in the immediately preceding chargeable period, relief for the excess of the current period contributions over 110% of the previous period's contributions (where that excess amounts to £500,000 or more) is to be spread forward into future chargeable periods. A fraction of the excess is to be treated as being paid in the current and subsequent periods (as below) with any remainder of the excess being relieved in the current period:

- excess £500,000 or more but less than £1m: one-half of excess allowed in current period and the next succeeding periods;
- excess £1m or more but less than £2m: one-third of excess allowed in the current period and the two following periods;
- excess £2m or more: one quarter of excess allowed in current period and the three following periods (FA 2004, s. 197).

3-050 Authorised payments limits

(ITEPA 2003, s. 636A; FA 2004, s. 164ff., Sch. 28 and 29)

(Tax Reporter: ¶378-000ff.)

Payments	Limits
Pension commencement	25% tax free lump sum (75% as pension income at marginal rate)
Capped drawdown	No new capped drawdowns from 6 April 2015 (previously, 150% on or after 27 March 2014 and 120% before)
Flexible drawdown[(1)]	No limit from 6 April 2015 (£12,000 minimum income requirement on or after 27 March 2014; previously £20,000)
Trivial commutation lump sum[(2)]	£30,000 on or after 27 March 2014 (previously £18,000)
Small pension pot[(2)]	£10,000; three lump sums on or after 27 March 2014 (previously £2,000; two lump sums)
Dependants' trivial commutation lump sum death benefit[(3)]	£30,000 from 6 April 2015 (previously, £18,000) all at dependant's marginal rate
Uncrystallised funds pension lump sum[(4)]	25% tax free 75% at marginal rate

Notes

(1) From 6 April 2015, there is no limit on how much can be taken from a flexi-access drawdown fund, but when benefits are first accessed from that fund, the money purchase annual allowance rules described in Pt. 4 are triggered in respect of that member.

(2) Apart from flexible drawdown, the only circumstances where an individual can normally take all of their pension pot as a single one-off payment is where their total pension savings in all funds are less than £30,000 (the trivial commutation limit for commutation periods beginning on or after 27 March 2014, previously, the limit was £18,000) or in certain circumstances where the value of a small pension pot is less than £10,000 (for payments made on or after 27 March 2014, previously the limit was £2,000). From 6 April 2015, a trivial commutation lump sum can be paid only in respect of a defined benefits arrangement. Those with relatively small amounts of money purchase savings will be able to take an UFPLS from this date, so there is no longer a need for trivial commutation lump sum rules for money purchase arrangements. To qualify for these payments, the individual must have reached normal minimum pension age (normally age 55) or satisfy the ill-health condition in FA 2004, Sch. 28, para. 1 (from 6 April 2015; previously, individuals had to have reached age 60). From 15 September 2016, a trivial commutation lump sum may be paid out of a money purchase scheme pension that is already in payment (FA 2004, Sch. 29, para. 7 and ITEPA 2003, s. 636B, as amended by FA 2016, s. 22 and Sch. 5).

(3) A trivial commutation lump sum death benefit can be paid to a dependant and, from 6 April 2015, to an individual in respect of any entitlement they had to receive any guaranteed pension payments of a lifetime annuity or scheme pension payable after the member's death. The whole lump sum will be taxable at the dependant's marginal rate.

[4] A new type of authorised lump sum payment (UFPLS) can be paid on or after 6 April 2015 directly from pension savings under a money purchase arrangement to certain individuals aged 55 or over. Individuals who meet the conditions to have an UFPLS can, therefore, if they wish, access as much of their money purchase pension savings as they want, without having first to designate the funds as available for drawdown. Where an UFPLS is paid, then this is flexible access and the money purchase annual allowance rules are triggered in respect of that member (FA 2004, s. 166(1) and Sch. 29, para. 4A).

3-075 Annual and lifetime allowances

(FA 2004, s. 214ff. and 227ff.)

(Tax Reporter: ¶386-000 and ¶384-000)

Since A-day, there have been no limits on the amount of pension savings an individual can have, but there are limits on the amount of tax relief that is available. These are the lifetime allowance and the annual allowance.

Year	Annual allowance limit(1)(2)(3)	Annual allowance income limit(4)	Money purchase annual allowance(5)	Lifetime allowance(6)(8)(9)(10)	Lifetime allowance charge(7)
2017–18	£40,000	£150,000	£4,000	£1m	25% as pension; 55% as lump sum
2016–17	£40,000	£150,000	£10,000	£1m	25% as pension; 55% as lump sum
2015–16(3) 9 July 2015 – 5 April 2016 ('post-alignment tax year')	£40,000	—	£10,000	£1.25m	25% as pension; 55% as lump sum
2015–16(3) 6 April 2015 – 8 July 2015 ('pre-alignment tax year')	£80,000	—			
2014–15	£40,000	—	—	£1.25m	25% as pension; 55% as lump sum
2013–14 and 2012–13	£50,000	—	—	£1.5m	25% as pension; 55% as lump sum
2011–12	£50,000	—	—	£1.80m	25% as pension; 55% as lump sum

Notes

Annual allowance

(1) An individual's annual allowance (AA) applies to all of that individual's pension arrangements for a year. It measures the 'pension input amount' for a tax year. That is the increase in the pension savings in that tax year (including contributions made by the individual and employer); and/or the increase in the value of the individual's pension rights (depending on the type of scheme, i.e. money purchase, defined benefit, etc.). If the 'pension input amount' for a year exceeds the AA for that year, the excess is subject to the charge. For future years the AA will be fixed by Treasury Order. Where for 2011–12 onwards, an annual allowance charge arises the annual allowance for that year may be increased by the unused annual allowance of the three immediately preceding years, except where the charge arises in 2015–16 or later and in a preceding year, the member or a dependant elected for flexible drawdown (in which case, no carry forward of unused annual allowance from that preceding year is possible) (FA 2004, s. 228A).

(2) An AA charge is the liability of the individual member of the scheme (or schemes where an individual is a member of more than one scheme), but provisions introduced from 6 April 2011 enable the member to transfer that liability onto the scheme administrator in certain circumstances (Tax Reporter: ¶386-010; FA 2004, s. 227–238). From 2011–12 onwards, the rate of tax to be charged on the excess is to be the 'appropriate rate'; that is, the rate or rates which would be charged on the excess if it was to be added to the individual's 'reduced net income' for the tax year concerned. That figure is the sum calculated at Step 3 of the prescribed method of calculating income tax liabilities. Any increase in the basic rate or higher rate bands due to pension contributions made under deduction of tax or gift aid payments is also taken into account for this purpose.

(3) From 6 April 2016, pension input periods are aligned with the tax year.

(4) From 6 April 2016, the existing £40,000 annual allowance is gradually reduced to £10,000 for those with incomes, including the amount of any pension savings, above £150,000. For each £2 of income above £150,000, an individual's annual allowance will reduce by £1 until the individual's income reaches £210,000 or over, when their annual allowance will be £10,000 (FA 2004, s. 228ZA and 228ZB).

(5) Where an individual has flexibly accessed their pension savings on or after 6 April 2015, an annual allowance will immediately apply to their future money purchase pension savings: the money purchase annual allowance rules. However, those individuals will retain an annual allowance for defined benefits pension savings, depending on the value of new money purchase pension savings. Unused annual allowance brought forward from earlier tax years will not be available to increase the money purchase annual allowance (FA 2004, s. 227ZA–227G).

Lifetime allowance

(6) An individual's lifetime allowance (LTA) is a measure of the total value of an individual's pension savings at the time that pension benefits begin to be taken. For future years the LTA will be fixed by Treasury Order.

(7) An LTA charge (55% on any excess over the LTA constituting a lump sum payment; and 25% on any excess over the LTA not used to pay a lump sum but to fund pension payments) is the joint and several liability of the individual and the pension scheme administrator (Tax Reporter: ¶384-050; FA 2004, s. 214–226).

(8) *Finance Act* 2013, Sch. 22 provided a transitional protection regime (fixed protection 2014) for individuals with UK tax relieved pension rights (or anticipated rights) of more than £1.25m who notified HMRC by 5 April 2014.

(9) *Finance Act* 2014 introduced a further transitional protection regime, individual protection 2014 (IP14) which entitled individuals with pension savings on 5 April 2014 of greater than £1.25m but who did not have primary protection to a lifetime allowance equal to the value of those savings, subject to an overall limit of £1.5m. SI 2014/1842 sets out relevant notice requirements.

(10) *Finance Act* 2016 reduced the lifetime allowance for pension contributions to £1m for the tax years 2016–17 and 2017–18. Finance Act 2016 also provides a requirement for the Treasury to make regulations before the start of tax year 2018–19 and each subsequent tax year, specifying the amount of the standard lifetime allowance for the year. The allowance will be increased by CPI (rounded up to the nearest £100) where the CPI for the year to the previous September is higher than it was 12 months earlier, otherwise, the allowance will remain the same as for the previous tax year (FA 2004, s. 218, as amended by FA 2016, s. 19). Transitional protection for pension rights already over £1m was introduced by way of two new transitional protections 'fixed protection 2016' and 'individual protection 2016', also from 6 April 2016 (FA 2016, Sch. 4).

3-100 Pension schemes: tax charges

Authorised payment charges

(FA 2004, s. 204–207)

(Tax Reporter: ¶383-000ff.)

Tax charges	Pre-6 April 2015	From 6 April 2015
Short service refund lump sum charge[1] (FA 2004, s. 205; Tax Reporter: ¶383-100)	20% up to £20,000; 50% on excess	20% up to £20,000; 50% on excess
Serious ill health lump sum charge[2] (FA 2004, s. 205A; Tax Reporter: ¶383-120)	55%	45% until 15 September 2016
Special lump sum death benefits charge[3] (FA 2004, s. 206; Tax Reporter: ¶383-150)	55%	45%
Authorised surplus payments charge (FA 2004, s. 207; Tax Reporter: ¶383-200)	35%	35%

Notes

[1] A tax charge arises where a registered pension scheme repays tax-relieved pension contributions to a member who has completed less than two years service ('short service refund lump sums'). The rate is 20% on the first £20,000 and 50% thereafter.

[2] There is no charge to income tax either on the individual or the scheme administrator on payment of a serious ill-health lump sum to a member who has not reached the age of 75 (unless the lifetime allowance is an issue). A serious ill-health lump sum paid to a member who has reached the age of 75 is taxed as pension income (at marginal rates) of the recipient member. However, before 16 September 2016, such payments were subject to the serious ill-health lump sum charge, which was an income tax charge on the scheme administrator at the rate of 45% (55% per cent where paid before 6 April 2015).

[3] Where a taxable lump sum death benefit listed below is paid on or after 6 April 2016 and directly from the pension scheme to an individual,

it is usually treated as the recipient's pension income and tax deducted under PAYE by way of the RTI process. The taxable lump sum death benefits this tax treatment relates to are:

- defined benefits lump sum death benefit
- uncrystallised funds lump sum death benefit
- pension protection lump sum death benefit
- annuity protection lump sum death benefit
- drawdown pension fund lump sum death benefit
- flexi-access drawdown fund lump sum death benefit.

But where the payment is to an individual who is receiving the payment in their capacity as:

- a trustee (but not a bare trustee)
- a personal representative
- a director of a company
- a partner in a firm, or
- a member of a limited liability partnership

the payment is not treated as their income for tax purposes and instead, the scheme administrator is liable to the special lump sum death benefits charge on the amount paid.

Other charges

(FA 2004, s. 208–213, 242)

(Tax Reporter: ¶383-500ff.; ¶388-500)

Charge	Rate
Unauthorised payments charge (FA 2004, s. 208; Tax Reporter: ¶383-550)	40%
Unauthorised payments surcharge[(1)] (FA 2004, s. 209; Tax Reporter: ¶383-600)	15%
Scheme sanction charge[(3)] (FA 2004, s. 239; Tax Reporter: ¶383-700)	40%
Deregistration charge[(4)] (FA 2004, s. 242; Tax reporter: ¶388-500)	40%
Overseas transfer charge (from 9 March 2017 on certain transfers to and from a QROPS)	25%

Notes

(1) A surcharge may be added to the unauthorised payment charge if a scheme pays out more than 25% of the scheme's fund in unauthorised payments.

(3) The scheme sanction charge is imposed at the rate of 40% of the aggregate of the 'scheme chargeable payments' (as defined by FA 2004, s. 241). The person liable to the scheme sanction charge is the scheme administrator. Where the scheme chargeable payment is also an unauthorised payment which has given rise to an unauthorised payments charge, the tax due under the scheme sanction charge is effectively reduced by the amount of tax actually paid (rather than charged) under the unauthorised payments charge.

(4) Where a registered scheme loses its registered status, a 'deregistration charge' of 40% of the aggregate value of the pension scheme's assets is levied on an payable by the scheme administrator.

(5) Finance Act 2017 introduces a 25% tax charge to pension transfers made to QROPS. Exceptions apply allowing transfers to be made tax free where people have a genuine need to transfer their pension, where:

- both the individual and the pension scheme are in countries within the European Economic Area (EEA);
- if outside the EEA, both the individual and the pension scheme are in the same country; or
- the QROPS is an occupational pension scheme provided by the individual's employer.

If the individual's circumstances change within five tax years of the transfer, the tax treatment of the transfer will be reconsidered. The changes will take effect for transfers requested on or after 9 March 2017. (FA 2004, s. 244A-244N, as inserted by Finance Act 2017, Sch. 4, Pt. 2).

3-150 Early retirement ages: retirement annuity contracts and personal pension schemes

From 6 April 2006

(FA 2004, Sch. 36, para. 23)

(Tax Reporter: ¶390-450)

Generally, if individuals take benefits from a registered pension scheme before age 55 they will be liable to a tax charge unless they are retiring due to ill-health. However, some individuals had unqualified rights on 5 April 2006 to take benefits before the normal minimum pension age. Where certain conditions are met these individuals may take their benefits earlier than age 55 without a tax charge. This is known as the individual's protected pension age. If an individual has a protected pension age, the tax rules provide that it replaces the prevailing normal minimum pension age for all purposes of the pensions tax legislation except for the lifetime allowance reduction that may apply where the protected pension age is less than 50 and benefits are taken before normal minimum pension age.

In order to exercise the right to a lower than normal pension age, the member must:

- be or have been in one of the occupations prescribed in the list at the *Registered Pension Schemes (Prescribed Schemes and Occupations) Regulations* 2005 (SI 2005/3451), Sch. 2, prior to 6 April 2006; and
- have had an 'unqualified right' to take a pension before the age of 50, prior to 6 April 2006 (an 'unqualified right' is when the individual needs no other party to consent to their request to take an early pension before it becomes binding upon the scheme or contract holder).

The list below will continue to apply to pension scheme members who are able to meet the conditions for a protected pension age lower than 50, as at 6 April 2006. All of the professions noted in the list below that have a retirement age of less than 50 are included in the list at SI 2005/3451, Sch. 2.

Profession or occupation		
Athletes (appearance and prize money)		
Badminton players		
Boxers		
Cricketers		
Cyclists		
Dancers		
Divers (saturation, deep sea and free swimming)		
Footballers		
Golfers (tournament earnings)		
Ice hockey players		
Jockeys – flat racing		
– national hunt		
Members of the reserve forces		
Models		
Motorcycle riders (motorcross or road racing)		
Motor racing drivers		
Rugby league players		

Profession or occupation		
Rugby union players		
Skiers (downhill)		
Snooker or billiards players		
Speedway riders		
Squash players		
Table tennis players		
Tennis players (including real tennis)		
Trapeze artistes		
Wrestlers		

3-175 Equalisation of and increase in pensionable ages for both men and women

For the purposes of social security legislation, an individual's pensionable age is determined by the following rules and tables. These gradually increase the pensionable age for women from the traditional age of 60 to bring it into line with that for men, while also increasing the ages for both sexes. Dates in the table below are grouped in one-month periods. A person born towards the end of one of these periods would have a slightly younger pension age than someone born at the beginning.

A man born before 6 December 1953 still attains pensionable age at age 65, while a woman born before 6 April 1950 attained pensionable age at age 60. The date the pensionable age is attained by individuals born after those dates is set out in the tables below. Table 1 relates to women born before 6 December 1953, while Table 2 relates to someone of either sex born on or after that date.

Under current law, the state pension age is due to increase to 68 between 2044 and 2046. However, the Government has announced plans to bring this timetable forward so that the state pension age will increase to 68 between 2037 and 2039. This change has yet to be enacted in legislation.

Table 1: Women

Date of birth (by month)	State pension age *y.m*	Pensionable age attained
06/04/50 to 05/05/50	60.1–60.0	06/05/2010
06/05/50 to 05/06/50	60.2–60.1	06/07/2010
06/06/50 to 05/07/50	60.3–60.2	06/09/2010
06/07/50 to 05/08/50	60.4–60.3	06/11/2010
06/08/50 to 05/09/50	60.5–60.4	06/01/2011

Date of birth (by month)	State pension age *y.m*	Pensionable age attained
06/09/50 to 05/10/50	60.6–60.5	06/03/2011
06/10/50 to 05/11/50	60.7–60.6	06/05/2011
06/11/50 to 05/12/50	60.8–60.7	06/07/2011
06/12/50 to 05/01/51	60.9–60.8	06/09/2011
06/01/51 to 05/02/51	60.10–60.9	06/11/2011
06/02/51 to 05/03/51	60.11–60.10	06/01/2012
06/03/51 to 05/04/51	61.0–60.11	06/03/2012
06/04/51 to 05/05/51	61.1–61.0	06/05/2012
06/05/51 to 05/06/51	61.2–61.1	06/07/2012
06/06/51 to 05/07/51	61.3–61.2	06/09/2012
06/07/51 to 05/08/51	61.4–61.3	06/11/2012
06/08/51 to 05/09/51	61.5–61.4	06/01/2013
06/09/51 to 05/10/51	61.6–61.5	06/03/2013
06/10/51 to 05/11/51	61.7–61.6	06/05/2013
06/11/51 to 05/12/51	61.8–61.7	06/07/2013
06/12/51 to 05/01/52	61.9–61.8	06/09/2013
06/01/52 to 05/02/52	61.10–61.9	06/11/2013
06/02/52 to 05/03/52	61.11–61.10	06/01/2014
06/03/52 to 05/04/52	62.0–61.11	06/03/2014
06/04/52 to 05/05/52	62.1–62.0	06/05/2014
06/05/52 to 05/06/52	62.2–62.1	06/07/2014
06/06/52 to 05/07/52	62.3–62.2	06/09/2014
06/07/52 to 05/08/52	62.4–62.3	06/11/2014
06/08/52 to 05/09/52	62.5–62.4	06/01/2015
06/09/52 to 05/10/52	62.6–62.5	06/03/2015
06/10/52 to 05/11/52	62.7–62.6	06/05/2015
06/11/52 to 05/12/52	62.8–62.7	06/07/2015
06/12/52 to 05/01/53	62.9–62.8	06/09/2015
06/01/53 to 05/02/53	62.10–62.9	06/11/2015
06/02/53 to 05/03/53	62.11–62.10	06/01/2016
06/03/53 to 05/04/53	63.0–62.11	06/03/2016
06/04/53 to 05/05/53	63.3–63.2	06/07/2016
06/05/53 to 05/06/53	63.6–63.5	06/11/2016
06/06/53 to 05/07/53	63.9–63.8	06/03/2017
06/07/53 to 05/08/53	64.0–63.11	06/07/2017
06/08/53 to 05/09/53	64.3–64.2	06/11/2017
06/09/53 to 05/10/53	64.6–64.5	06/03/2018
06/10/53 to 05/11/53	64.9–64.8	06/07/2018
06/11/53 to 05/12/53	65.0–64.11	06/11/2018

Table 2: Men and Women

Date of birth (by month)	State pension age[1] *y.m*	Pensionable age attained[1]
06/12/53 to 05/01/54	65.3–65.2	06/03/2019
06/01/54 to 05/02/54	65.4–65.3	06/05/2019
06/02/54 to 05/03/54	65.5–65.4	06/07/2019
06/03/54 to 05/04/54	65.6–65.5	06/09/2019
06/04/54 to 05/05/54	65.7–65.6	06/11/2019
06/05/54 to 05/06/54	65.8–65.7	06/01/2020
06/06/54 to 05/07/54	65.9–65.8	06/03/2020
06/07/54 to 05/08/54	65.10–65.9	06/05/2020
06/08/54 to 05/09/54	65.11–65.10	06/07/2020
06/09/54 to 05/10/54	66.0–65.11	06/09/2020
06/10/54 to 05/04/60	Age 66	[06/10/2020–05/04/2026]
06/04/60 to 05/05/60	Age 66 years and 1 month	[06/05/2026–05/06/2026]
06/05/60 to 05/06/60	Age 66 years and 2 months	[06/07/2026–05/08/2026]
06/06/60 to 05/07/60	Age 66 years and 3 months	[06/09/2026–05/10/2026]
06/07/60(2) to 05/08/60	Age 66 years and 4 months	[06/11/2026–05/12/2026]
06/08/60 to 05/09/60	Age 66 years and 5 months	[06/01/2027–05/02/2027]
06/09/60 to 05/10/60	Age 66 years and 6 months	[06/03/2027–05/04/2027]
06/10/60 to 05/11/60	Age 66 years and 7 months	[06/05/2027–05/06/2027]
06/11/60 to 05/12/60	Age 66 years and 8 months	[06/07/2027–05/08/2027]
06/12/60(3) to 05/01/61	Age 66 years and 9 months	[06/09/2027–05/10/2027]
06/01/61(4) to 05/02/61	Age 66 years and 10 months	[06/11/2027–05/12/2027]
06/02/61 to 05/03/61	Age 66 years and 11 months	[06/01/2028–05/02/2028]
06/03/61 to 06/04/77	Age 67	[06/03/2028–06/04/2044]
06/04/77 to 05/05/77	67.1–67.0	06/05/2044
06/05/77 to 05/06/77	67.2–67.1	06/07/2044
06/06/77 to 05/07/77	67.3–67.2	06/09/2044
06/07/77 to 05/08/77	67.4–67.3	06/11/2044
06/08/77 to 05/09/77	67.5–67.4	06/01/2045
06/09/77 to 05/10/77	67.6–67.5	06/03/2045
06/10/77 to 05/11/77	67.7–67.6	06/05/2045
06/11/77 to 05/12/77	67.8–67.7	06/07/2045
06/12/77 to 05/01/78	67.9–67.8	06/09/2045
06/01/78 to 05/02/78	67.10–67.9	06/11/2045
06/02/78 to 05/03/78	67.11–67.10	06/01/2046
06/03/78 to 05/04/78	68.00–67.11	06/03/2046
On or after 06/04/78	Age 68	[On or after 06/04/2046]

Notes

(1) Individuals born between 06/04/54 and 06/04/77 and those born on or after 06/04/78 attain state pension age at the age shown in column 2 (with figures in square brackets in column 3 being calculated date ranges). Otherwise, individuals attain state pension age at the date shown in column 3.

(2) A person born on 31 July 1960 is to be taken to attain the age of 66 years and four months at the commencement of 30 November 2026.

(3) A person born on 31 December 1960 is to be taken to attain the age of 66 years and nine months at the commencement of 30 September 2027.

(4) A person born on 31 January 1961 is to be taken to attain the age of 66 years and ten months at the commencement of 30 November 2027.

3-200 State retirement pensions

	Weekly rates			
	Full rate of state pension[1] £	Single person £	Married couple wife not a contributor £	Age addition (over 80) each £
From 6 April 2017	159.55	122.30	195.60	0.25
6/4/16 to 5/4/17	155.65	119.30	190.80	0.25
6/4/15 to 5/4/16	—	115.95	185.45	0.25
7/4/14 to 5/4/15	—	113.10	180.90	0.25
8/4/13 to 6/4/14	—	110.15	176.15	0.25
9/4/12 to 7/4/13	—	107.45	171.85	0.25
11/4/11 to 8/4/12	—	102.15	163.35	0.25

Note

(1) The *Pensions Act* 2014 introduced a new single tier pension from 6 April 2016. Individuals reaching pensionable age after that date are no longer entitled to the two-component state pension (the basic state pension and additional state pension based on amounts of National Insurance contributions (NICs) paid) but are instead entitled to a single-component flat-rate pension. Basic conditions of entitlement at the full rate include having attained pensionable age and having 35 or more 'qualifying years' of NICs (based on the individuals earnings factor reaching the qualifying amount for the tax year). Entitlement is subject to a minimum number of qualifying years (no more than ten) and pro-rated for individuals with fewer than 35 years. Transitional provisions apply for individuals who have paid, or are treated as having paid, NICs in respect of tax years before the introduction of the new state pension; for inheriting entitlement from a late spouse or civil partner who had made contributions prior to the introduction of the new state pension; for women who before 1977 elected to pay a reduced rate of NICs, and for sharing a pension with a former spouse or civil partner upon divorce.

3-300 Gilt-edged securities held by non-residents

(ITTOIA 2005, s. 713; ITA 2007, s. 893–897, 1024)

(Tax Reporter: ¶120-800)

Interest on all gilt-edged securities is payable gross. Interest may be paid net, if the holder wishes, by notice to the Registrar of Government Stock. Payment gross does not of itself imply that the interest is exempt from tax.

All gilt-edged securities are automatically given FOTRA status (Free Of Tax for Residents Abroad), thereby guaranteeing exemption from tax for holders not resident in the UK. Account holders receive interest on registered holdings of FOTRA securities without deduction of tax, unless they have asked for tax to be deducted.

3-350 Individual savings accounts (ISAs)

(ITTOIA 2005, s. 694–701; SI 1998/1870; SI 2004/1450)

(Tax Reporter: ¶315-000)

				2014–15[7]			
	2017–18	**2016–17[10]**	**2015–16**	**1 July 2014 – 5 April 2015**	**6 April 2014 – 30 June 2014**	**2013–14**	
	£	**£**	**£**	**£**	**£**	**£**	
'Adult' ISAs							
Maximum subscription limit	20,000	15,240	15,240	15,000	11,880	11,520	
Cash limit	—[4]	—[4]	—[4]	—[4]	5,940	5,760	
Junior ISAs/Child Trust Funds[5][6]							
Maximum subscription limit	4,128	4,080	4,080	4,000	3,840	3,720	
Lifetime ISA[11]							
Maximum subscription limit	4,000	—	—	—	—	—	
Government contribution	25%	—	—	—	—	—	
Help to buy ISA[9]							
Maximum savings per month	200	200	200	—	—	—	
Government contribution	25%	25%	25%	—	—	—	

Notes

[1] To open an ISA, an individual has to be aged 18 or over (or over the age of 16 for cash ISAs) and resident in the UK for tax purposes.

[2] All income and gains derived from investments within the account are tax free and withdrawals from the account will not attract any tax charge.

[3] From 6 April 2011, the ISA subscription limits have been increased in line with inflation. From 2012–13 onwards, the index used is the consumer prices index (CPI) (previously RPI).

[4] From 1 July 2014, the restriction that only 50% of the overall subscription limit may be invested in a cash ISA was removed. SI 1998/1870 was also amended to allow transfers to be made from a stocks and shares account to a cash account (SI 2014/1450).

[5] Children born between 1 September 2002 and 2 January 2011, living in the UK and in receipt of child benefit were eligible for a Child Trust Fund account. Child Trust Funds are now closed to new accounts but subscriptions can still be paid into existing accounts. Withdrawals are not permitted until the child has reached the age of 18, except in cases of terminal illness.

[6] Junior ISAs became available form 1 November 2011 to any child under 18, living in the UK, who is not eligible for a Child Trust Fund account. Withdrawals are not permitted until the child has reached the age of 18, except in cases of terminal illness.

[7] From 3 December 2014, if an ISA saver in a marriage or civil partnership dies, their spouse or civil partner will inherit their ISA tax advantages. From 6 April 2015, surviving spouses will be able to invest as much into their own ISA as their spouse used to have, on top of their usual allowance.

[8] From 6 April 2016, ISA savers can withdraw and replace money from their cash ISA without it counting towards their annual ISA subscription limit for that year (SI 1998/1870, as amended by SI 2016/16).

[9] From 1 December 2015, the 'Help to buy ISA' was launched for individuals saving for their first home. Individuals are able to save up to £200 per month with the Government topping up the account with £50 for every £200 saved (with a maximum of £3,000 for £12,000 savings). The accounts are only available for first time buyers and can be opened with an additional one off deposit of £1,000 (see *www.helptobuy.gov.uk/help-to-buy-isa/how-does-it-work/*).

[10] *Finance Act* 2016 introduces legislation to allow the ISA savings of a deceased person to continue to benefit from tax advantages during the administration of their estate (ITTOIA 2005, s. 694A, as inserted by FA 2016, s. 27).

[11] *The Lifetime ISA is available from 6 April 2017, can be opened by adults younger than 40 years old and allows adults to save up to £4,000 each year that they are younger than 50 years old and receive a government bonus of 25% (up to £1,000 a year), which can be withdrawn tax-free to buy a first home or when the individual turns 60.*

3-400 Enterprise investment scheme (EIS)

(ITA 2007, Pt. 5)

(Tax Reporter: ¶323-000ff.; ¶565-400ff.)

EIS relief is available for qualifying individuals who subscribe cash for the issue of qualifying shares issued by non-quoted trading companies (except those carrying on prohibited trades).

Qualifying EIS shares issued:[2][3]	Maximum individual investment[1]	Rate of IT relief on investment	Disposal of qualifying EIS shares	Carry back of EIS relief to previous tax year
On or after 6 April 2012 but before 6 April 2025	£1,000,000 per annum	30%	Capital gains not chargeable, losses allowable	Entire investment (subject to not exceeding £1,000,000 for the earlier year).
2011–12	£500,000 per annum	30%	Capital gains not chargeable, losses allowable	Entire investment (subject to not exceeding £500,000 for the earlier year).

Notes

[1] For an investment to qualify under EIS, the company must have raised no more than £5m (from 6 April 2012) under any or all risk capital schemes (VCT, EIS, SEIS and any other investment which is a State aid approved by the European Commission in accordance with the community guidelines on risk capital investments in SMEs), in the 12 months ending on the date of the relevant investment. From 18 November 2015, investments under the SITR will also count towards the company's annual maximum amount as will any 'relevant investments' the company's subsidiaries have received or used in the year and investments in any trade transferred from another company.

[2] EIS will cease to apply to new investments from 6 April 2025, unless the legislation is renewed. The date may be changed by Treasury Order and is set to be no later than ten years after the date of the European Commission's letter approving the EIS as compatible with state aids rules, following the formal notification of the scheme in June 2015 (ITA 2007, s. 157(1)(aa)).

[3] Finance (No. 2) Act 2017 amends the EIS and SEIS rules to allow companies that issue shares with rights to a future conversion into shares of another class in that company to qualify for relief, with effect for shares issued on or after 5 December 2016.

3-420 Seed enterprise investment scheme (SEIS)

(TCGA 1992, Sch. 5BB; ITA 2007, Pt. 5A)

(Tax Reporter: ¶319-000ff.; ¶568-500ff.)

SEIS relief is available to qualifying individuals who subscribe cash for the issue of qualifying shares in unquoted trading companies with fewer than 25 employees and assets of up to £200,000, carrying on or preparing to carry on new business.

Qualifying SEIS shares issued:[2]	Maximum individual investment[1]	Rate of IT relief on investment	Disposal of qualifying SEIS shares	Carry back of SEIS relief to previous year	Capital gains reinvestment limit[3]
2017–18 (from 2013–14)	£100,000 per annum	50%	Capital gains not chargeable, losses allowable	Entire investment (subject to not exceeding £100,000 for the earlier year)	50% of qualifying SEIS expenditure
2012–13	£100,000 per annum	50%	Capital gains not chargeable, losses allowable	N/A	100% of qualifying SEIS expenditure

Notes

(1) For an investment to qualify under SEIS, the company must have raised no more than £150,000 and must not have raised any capital under EIS or VCT.

(2) Finance (No. 2) Act 2017 amends the EIS and SEIS rules to allow companies that issue shares with rights to a future conversion into shares of another class in that company to qualify for relief, with effect for shares issued on or after 5 December 2016.

3-430 Social investment tax relief (SITR)

(TCGA 1992, s. 255A–255E, Sch. 8B; ITA 2007, Pt. 5B)

(Tax Reporter: ¶322-000ff.; ¶569-300ff.)

SITR is available to individual investors who invest in cash in new shares or new qualifying debt investments in qualifying social enterprises (an unquoted community interest company, community benefit society or charity with fewer than 250(6) full-time equivalent employees).

Relief is not available on any investment in respect of which the investor has obtained relief under the EIS, the SEIS or the CITRS.

Qualifying investment made[5]	Maximum individual investment[3]	Rate of IT on investment	Disposal of qualifying investment[1]	Carry back of SI relief to previous tax year
On or after 6 April 2015 and before 6 April 2019	£1m(4) per annum	30%	Capital gains not chargeable, losses allowable	From 2015–16, entire investment (subject to not exceeding £1m for the earlier year)
On or after 6 April 2014	£1m per annum	30%	Capital gains not chargeable, losses allowable(2)	—

Notes

(1) The exemption from capital gains applies where an investment on which income tax relief has been received (and not subsequently withdrawn) is disposed of after it has been held for at least three years. If no claim to income tax relief is made, the investment will not qualify for exemption from capital gains tax. Losses are eligible for relief in the normal way but the base cost is treated as reduced by the amount of the SI relief attributable to the asset.

(2) A capital gains tax deferral relief enables a capital gain arising from the disposal of any asset in the period from 6 April 2014 to 5 April 2019 to be deferred where the gain is reinvested (within the period one year before to three years after the gain arising) in shares or debt investments which also qualify for SITR income tax relief. It is not, however, necessary for the investor to have made a claim for SITR income tax relief.

(3) For an investment to qualify under SI, the social enterprise must (including its subsidiaries if a parent company) have no more than £15m in gross assets immediately before the investment and £16m immediately after the investment. Additionally, the social enterprise is restricted as to the amount of money it may raise under SITR, as determined by the formula:

$$\left(\frac{€200{,}000 - M}{RCG + RSI}\right) - T$$

Where: T is the total of any earlier SITR investments made in the previous three years;

M is the total of any other de minimis aid received in the previous three years by the social enterprise, or by a qualifying subsidiary;

RCG is the highest rate of capital gains tax in the previous three years; and

RSI is the highest rate of SITR income tax relief in the previous three years.

(4) At Autumn Statement 2014, it was announced that the annual investment limit would be increased to £5m per annum up to a total of £15m per organisation and relief to be extended to small scale community farms and horticultural activities, however, these changes have not yet been legislated. At Spring Budget 2017, it was confirmed that, as announced at Autumn Statement 2016, the amount of investment social enterprises aged up to seven years old can raise through SITR will increase to £1.5m, with effect for investments made on or after 6 April 2017. However, the current limit will continue to apply to older social enterprises.

(5) From 6 April 2016, all remaining energy generation activities are excluded from the venture capital schemes, as well as from the enlarged SITR (amendments by FA 2016, s. 28).

(6) Limit on number of full-time equivalent employees reduced to below 250 employees (previously 500 employees) with effect for investments made on or after 6 April 2017 (amendments by F(No.2)A 2017, Sch. 1). Finance (No. 2) Act 2017 also makes further amendments to the requirements for the SITR, with effect for investments made on or after 6 April 2017, including an increase in the amount of money newer social enterprises may raise from individual investors under the scheme.

3-450 Venture capital trusts (VCTs)

(TCGA 1992, s. 151A, 151B; ITTOIA 2005, s. 709; ITA 2007, Pt. 6)

(Tax Reporter: ¶326-000ff.)

A VCT is a specialised form of investment trust, which has been approved by the Board of HMRC. Certain tax advantages are obtained by individuals who subscribe for eligible shares issued by a qualifying VCT for the purposes of raising money.

Qualifying VCT Shares issued:(1)(2)(3)(4)(5)(6)(7)(8)(9)	Maximum individual investment	Rate of IT relief on investment	Dividends paid by VCT	Disposal of shares in VCT	Minimum holding period
On or after 6 April 2006 but before 6 April 2025	£200,000 per annum	30%	Exempt from IT in hands of investor	Exempt from CGT	5 years
2005–06 and 2004–05	£200,000 per annum	40%	Exempt from IT in hands of investor	Exempt from CGT	3 years
2000–01 to 2003–04	£100,000 per annum	20%	Exempt from IT in hands of investor	Exempt from CGT	3 years

Notes

(1) To obtain and retain HMRC's approval, a VCT must satisfy a number of detailed conditions. The main ones are as follows: it must be a non-close company whose shares are quoted on the stock exchange; its income must be wholly or mainly derived from investments in shares or securities; at least 70% (by value) of its total investments must comprise of 'qualifying holdings' (broadly, shares and securities in unquoted trading companies except those carrying on prohibited trades; no holding in any company (other than a VCT or a company that would qualify as a VCT but for the listing condition) can represent more than 15% of the value of the VCT's investments; the gross assets of the companies in which the VCT has invested may not exceed £15m immediately before the issue of shares to the VCT and £16m immediately afterwards.

(2) For an investment to qualify under VCT, the company must have raised no more than £5m (from 6 April 2012) through risk capital measures (VCT, EIS, SEIS or any other investment which is a State aid approved by the European Commission in accordance with the community guidelines on risk capital investments in SMEs). in the 12 months ending on the date of the relevant investment (ITA 2007, s. 292A). From 18 November 2015, investments under the SITR will also count towards the company's annual maximum amount as will any 'relevant investments' the company or group has received or used in the year and imported investments (in any trade transferred from another company).

(3) VCTs will no longer qualify for relief from 6 April 2025, unless the legislation is renewed. The date may be changed by Treasury Order and is set to be no later than ten years after the date of the European Commission's letter approving the VCT rules as compatible with state aids rules, following the formal notification of the scheme in June 2015.

(4) Finance (No. 2) Act 2017 amends the VCT rules to enable a new parent company, which has acquired an old company through a certain type of share for share exchange, to receive follow-on funding from a VCT on the basis of the old company's funding history, with effect for investments made, and relevant holdings issued, on or after 6 April 2017. Finance (No. 2) Act 2017 also provides a power for HM Treasury to make regulations on the exchange of non-qualifying investments held by a VCT for new shares or securities in the course of a share reorganisation or company reconstruction. This power has effect from Royal Assent.

Social venture capital trusts

Social venture capital trusts, a new scheme based on the existing VCT scheme, were announced at Autumn Statement 2014 and again at March Budget 2015. The scheme has yet to be legislated for.

3-465 Community investment tax relief

(ITA 2007, Pt. 7; CTA 2010, Pt. 7)

(Tax Reporter: ¶325-000ff.)

Tax relief is claimed on an annual basis at the rate of 5% of the 'invested amount' for the tax year (or accounting period for a corporate investor) in which the investment date falls and the four subsequent tax years (or accounting periods). If the investment is by way of a loan, the 'invested amount' is not necessarily the amount of the loan made available at the beginning of the five-year investment period. The tax relief cannot reduce the taxpayer's tax liability below zero for any single tax year (or accounting period).

3-500 Lease premiums

(ITTOIA 2005, s. 277; CTA 2009, s. 217)

(Tax Reporter: ¶300-110; ¶711-375)

Where a short-term lease (i.e. one not exceeding 50 years in duration) is granted, a proportion of any premium charged on the grant is assessable as property business profits. The amount of the premium to be treated as rental income, received at the time of the grant, is given by a formula:

$$P \times \frac{50 - Y}{50} = TP$$

Where:

- 'P' is total premium paid;
- 'Y' is duration of lease in complete years (ignoring the first year). Only whole years are counted, part years are ignored; and
- 'TP' is the amount of the premium taxed on the landlord as if it were rent.

Amount taken into account in calculating a chargeable gain will be the balance of the premium (TCGA 1992, s. 240 and Sch. 8, para. 5 and 7) for which the restriction of allowable expenditure is applicable:

Length of lease in complete years	Premium % chargeable as gain	Premium % chargeable as rent
Over 50	100	0
50	98	2
49	96	4
48	94	6
47	92	8
46	90	10
45	88	12
44	86	14
43	84	16
42	82	18
41	80	20
40	78	22
39	76	24
38	74	26
37	72	28
36	70	30
35	68	32
34	66	34
33	64	36
32	62	38
31	60	40
30	58	42
29	56	44
28	54	46
27	52	48
26	50	50
25	48	52
24	46	54
23	44	56
22	42	58
21	40	60
20	38	62
19	36	64
18	34	66
17	32	68
16	30	70
15	28	72
14	26	74
13	24	76
12	22	78
11	20	80
10	18	82
9	16	84
8	14	86
7	12	88
6	10	90
5	8	92
4	6	94
3	4	96
2	2	98
1 or less	0	100

The following arrangements relating to short leases may also cause amounts to be treated as rent paid to the landlord:

- the tenant carrying out work on the rented premises;
- the commutation of rent for some other type of payment;
- the payment of a lump sum from the surrender of a lease;
- the payment of a lump sum for the variation or waiver of a lease's terms; and
- the assignment of a lease which has been previously granted at undervalue.

Premiums paid by instalment

Where an amount of a premium is received by instalments any income tax or corporation tax due on the amount may be paid by instalments, at the taxpayer's request and by agreement with HMRC. The tax instalment period may not exceed eight years and must end on or before the time that the final instalment of the premium is due (ITTOIA 2005, s. 299 for income tax; and CTA 2009, s. 236(1)–(3) for corporation tax).

Relief for premiums paid

Where a tenant occupies land, under a short lease, for the purposes of a trade, profession or vocation and has paid a premium in respect of the lease; an amount of lease premium paid is allowed as a deduction in computing the business profits (ITTOIA 2005, s. 60 for income tax; and CTA 2009, s. 62 for corporation tax). The amount of the premium taxed as rent in the hands of the landlord (see above) is treated as if it were daily rent paid by the tenant over the course of the lease. The effective deduction for an accounting or basis period is therefore:

$$\frac{\text{TP}}{\text{Lease duration in days}} \times \text{No. of days in accounting or basis period} = \text{DRP}$$

Where:

- 'TP' is the amount of the premium taxed on the landlord as if it were rent; and
- 'DRP' is the amount of the deemed rent paid by the tenant.

Relief is also available, in respect of premiums paid, for the computation of property business profits where an intermediate landlord has paid a premium to the superior landlord for premises that are in turn sub-let to a tenant.

3-525 Restricted deductions for finance costs related to residential property

(ITTOIA 2005, s. 272A–272B, 274A–274B; ITA 2007, s. 399A–399B)

(Tax Reporter: ¶300-350)

Year	Restricted deduction[(1)]
2017–18	75%
2018–19	50%
2019–20	25%
2020–21	0%

Note

[(1)] In calculating for income tax purposes the profits of a property business, the deduction allowed for finance costs of a dwelling-related loan is restricted to the percentage shown of the amount that would be allowed apart from the restriction. A tax reduction for such costs is available instead and calculated by reference to the basic rate of income tax. The restriction and tax reduction will have effect for costs incurred on or after 6 April 2017.

3-550 Settlements on children

(ITTOIA 2005, s. 629(3))

(Tax Reporter: ¶356-300)

Income paid to or for the benefit of a minor child arising from capital provided by a parent is not treated as parents' income if it does not exceed £100 per tax year.

3-700 Time limits for elections and claims

(TMA 1970, s. 43)

In the absence of any provision to the contrary, for the purposes of income tax, the normal rule is that claims are to be made within four years from the end of the tax year to which they relate.

In certain cases, HMRC *may* permit an extension of the strict time limit in relation to certain elections and claims.

Provision	Time limit	Statutory reference
Averaging election for furnished holiday accommodation	12 months from 31 January following year to which claim applies	ITTOIA 2005, s. 326 (Tax Reporter: ¶303-170)
Set-off of property business loss against income of current or next year	12 months from 31 January following year of set-off	ITA 2007, s. 124 (Tax Reporter: ¶303-220)

Provision	Time limit	Statutory reference
Property business post-cessation relief	12 months from 31 January following year in which deduction to be made	ITA 2007, s. 125 (Tax Reporter: ¶303-230)
Set-off of loss on disposal of shares in unquoted trading company against income	12 months from 31 January following year in which loss arose	ITA 2007, s. 132 (Tax Reporter: ¶330-000ff.)
EIS, SEIS and SI relief	Five years from 31 January following tax year in which shares are issued (or previous tax year in relation to carry back claims)	ITA 2007, s. 202, 257EA and 257P (Tax Reporter: ¶323-120; ¶319-120)

Taxation of earnings

Company cars

4-000 Car benefits 2017–18

(ITEPA 2003, s. 139)

(Tax Reporter: ¶415-050ff.)

The benefit is calculated as a percentage of the list price of the car appropriate to the level of the car's CO_2 emissions. The 'appropriate percentage' depends upon whether the car was first registered on or after 1 January 1998 and whether it has a CO_2 emissions figure or is a diesel car. Relevant percentages are set out below.

For cars registered on or after 1 January 1998 (with CO_2 emissions figures)

CO_2 emissions[5]	2013–14 & 2012–13	2014–15	2015–16	2016–17	2017–18	2018–19[3]	2019–20[4]
50g/km or below	5%	5%	5%	7%	9%	13%	16%
51–75g/km			9%	11%	13%	16%	19%
Above 75g/km up to relevant threshold	10%	11%	13%	15%	17%	19%	22%

Equal to relevant threshold[(1)]	11%	12%	14%	16%	18%	20%	23%
Above relevant threshold: Increase per 5g/km[(1)]	1%	1%	1%	1%	1%	1%	1%
Up to maximum	35%	35%	37%	37%	37%	37%	37%
Diesel supplement[(2)]	3%	3%	3%	3%	3%	3%	3%

Notes

(1) Where CO_2 emissions are not a multiple of five, round down to the nearest multiple of five.

(2) All diesel cars are currently subject to a 3% addition (but subject to the absolute cap). The 3% diesel supplement was due to be abolished from 2016–17 (FA 2014, s. 24), however, FA 2016, s. 10 retains the diesel supplement in company car tax. Further provisions to remove the diesel supplement are expected to be made in a future Finance Bill, with effect from 6 April 2021.

(3) In 2018–19, the appropriate percentage of list price subject to tax will increase by two percentage points for cars emitting more than 75g/km CO2, to a maximum of 37%. In 2018–19, there will be a three percentage point differential between the 0–50 and 51–75g/km CO2 bands and between the 51–75 and 76–94g/km CO2 bands (FA 2015, s. 8).

(4) In 2019–20, the appropriate percentage of list price subject to tax will increase by three percentage points for cars emitting more than 75g/km CO2, to a maximum of 37%. There will be a three-percentage point differential between the 0–50 and 51–75g/km CO2 bands (FA 2016, s. 8).

(5) For 2020–21, lower bands will be introduced for the lowest emitting cars and the appropriate percentage for cars emitting greater than 90g/km CO2 will rise by one percentage point, see ¶4-002.

The relevant threshold is as follows:

Year	Relevant threshold
2017–18	95g/km
2013–14 to 2016–17	95g/km
2012–13	100g/km

Cars registered on or after 1 January 1998 without CO_2 emissions, or cars first registered before 1 January 1998

	2014–15 Registered		2015–16 Registered		2016–17	2017–18	2018–19[(2)]	2019–20[(2)]	2020–21[(3)]
	on or after 01/01/1998	before 01/01/1998	on or after 01/01/1998	before 01/01/1998					
Cylinder capacity of car with internal combustion engine in cubic centimetres									
• 1,400 or less	15%	15%	15%	15%	16%	18%	20%	23%	24%
• more than 1,400 but not more than 2,000	25%	22%	25%	22%	27%	29%	31%	34%	35%
• more than 2,000	35%	32%	37%	32%	37%	37%	37%	37%	37%

	2014–15 Registered		2015–16 Registered		2016–17	2017–18	2018–19[2]	2019–20[2]	2020–21[3]
	on or after 01/01/1998	before 01/01/1998	on or after 01/01/1998	before 01/01/1998					
Cars without an internal combustion engine									
• zero-emission cars registered on or after 1 January 1998	0%(1)	—	5%	—	7%	9%	13%	16%	2%
• any other case	35%	32%	37%	32%	37%	37%	37%	37%	37%
Diesel supplement[1]	3%	N/A	3%	N/A	3%	3%	3%	3%	

Notes

[1] All diesel cars registered on or after 1 January 1998 are currently subject to a 3% addition (but subject to the absolute cap). The 3% diesel supplement was due to be abolished from 2016–17 (FA 2014, s. 24), however, FA 2016, s. 10 retains the diesel supplement in company car tax. Further provisions to remove the diesel supplement are expected to be made in a future Finance Bill, with effect from 6 April 2021.

[2] Rates per FA 2015, s. 8 (amending ITEPA 2003, s. 140 and 142).

[3] Rates per FA 2016, s. 8 (amending ITEPA 2003, s. 140 and 142).

[4] Rates per Finance (No. 2) Act 2017, s. 2 (amending ITEPA 2003, s. 140 and 142).

4-002 Car benefits: table of percentages to 2019–20

Table of taxable percentages

(ITEPA 2003, s. 139)

(Tax Reporter: ¶415-720)

CO_2 emissions	Appropriate percentage						
	2013–14[1]	2014–15[1]	2015–16[1]	2016–17[1]	2017–18[1]	2018–19[1][2]	2019–20[1][3]
0	0	0	5	7	9	13	16
1–50	5	5					
51–75			9	11	13	16	19
76–94	10	11	13	15	17	19	22
95–99	11	12	14	16	18	20	23
100–104	12	13	15	17	19	21	24
105–109	13	14	16	18	20	22	25
110–114	14	15	17	19	21	23	26
115–119	15	16	18	20	22	24	27
120–124	16	17	19	21	23	25	28
125–129	17	18	20	22	24	26	29
130–134	18	19	21	23	25	27	30
135–139	19	20	22	24	26	28	31

CO_2 emissions	Appropriate percentage						
	2013–14[1]	2014–15[1]	2015–16[1]	2016–17[1]	2017–18[1]	2018–19[1][2]	2019–20[1][3]
140–144	20	21	23	25	27	29	32
145–149	21	22	24	26	28	30	33
150–154	22	23	25	27	29	31	34
155–159	23	24	26	28	30	32	35
160–164	24	25	27	29	31	33	36
165–169	25	26	28	30	32	34	37
170–174	26	27	29	31	33	35	
175–179	27	28	30	32	34	36	
180–184	28	29	31	33	35	37	
185–189	29	30	32	34	36		
190–194	30	31	33	35	37		
195–199	31	32	34	36			
200–204	32	33	35	37			
205–209	33	34	36				
210–214	34	35	37				
215–219	35						
220+							

Notes

[1] All diesel cars are subject to a 3% loading, but not to take the maximum figure above 37% (from 2015–16, previously, 35%). This addition was due to be abolished from 2016–17 (FA 2014, s. 24), however, FA 2016, s. 10 retains the diesel supplement in company car tax. Further provisions to remove the diesel supplement are expected to be made in a future Finance Bill, with effect from 6 April 2021.

[2] In 2018–19, the appropriate percentage of list price subject to tax will increase by two percentage points for cars emitting more than 75g/km CO2, to a maximum of 37%. In 2018–19, there will be a three percentage point differential between the 0–50 and 51–75g/km CO2 bands and between the 51–75 and 76–94g/km CO2 bands (FA 2015, s. 8).

[3] In 2019–20, the appropriate percentage of list price subject to tax will increase by three percentage points for cars emitting more than 75g/km CO2 to a maximum of 37%. There will be a three percentage point differential between the 0–50 and 51–75g/km CO2 bands (FA 2016, s. 8).

[4] Rates for 2020–21 as per Finance (No. 2) Act 2017, s. 2 are as follows:

2020–21						
CO_2 emissions	Electric range figure	Appropriate percentage	CO_2 emissions	Appropriate percentage	CO_2 emissions	Appropriate percentage
0		2	70–74	19	120–124	29
1–50 (split by zero emission miles)	130 or more	2	75–79	20	125–129	30
	70–129	5	80–84	21	130–134	31
	40–69	8	85–89	22	135–139	32
	30–39	12	90–94	23	140–144	33
	less than 30	14	95–99	24	145–149	34
51–54		15	100–104	25	150–154	35
55–59		16	105–109	26	155–159	36
60–64		17	110–114	27	160+	37
65–69		18	115–119	28		

4-015 Diesel cars: loading of appropriate percentage

(ITEPA 2003, s. 141)

(Tax Reporter: ¶415-740)

Most diesel cars have an appropriate percentage that is three points higher than an equivalent petrol car (but still subject to a 37% overall cap). See ¶4-000ff. for details of the petrol figures.

The 3% diesel supplement was due to be abolished from 6 April 2016 (FA 2014, s. 24), however, FA 2016, s. 10 retained the diesel supplement in company car tax. Further provisions to remove the diesel supplement are expected to be made in a future Finance Bill, with effect from 6 April 2021.

Fuel for company cars

4-140 Fuel benefit charges

(ITEPA 2003, s. 150)

(Tax Reporter: ¶416-000ff.)

The additional taxable benefit of free fuel provided for a company car is calculated using the same CO_2 percentages as are used for calculating the company car charge.

The fuel benefit is reduced to nil if the employee is required to make good the full cost of all fuel provided for private use, and does so.

A proportionate reduction is made where the company car is only available for part of the year, where car fuel ceases to be provided part-way through the year, or where the benefit of the company car is shared.

The CO_2 percentage figure is applied to a fixed amount in accordance with the following table:

Tax year	£
2017–18	22,600
2016–17	22,200
2015–16	22,100
2014–15	21,700
2013–14	21,100

4-160 Fuel types

Employers must notify HMRC of the type of fuel (or other power) used by an employer provided car by entering the appropriate 'key letter' on the forms P11D and P46(Car). The key letters in use are as follows:

Key letter	Fuel or power type description
A	All other cars
D	Diesel (all Euro standards)

4-180 Advisory fuel rates for company cars: recent rates

(Tax Reporter: ¶416-040)

HMRC publish rates that can be used by employers wishing to pay their employees the cost of fuel for business journeys in company cars (or, where the employer initially pays for all fuel, for reimbursement of private mileage by company car drivers to their employers). Passenger payments may be made for company cars as for private cars (see ¶4-220). Hybrid cars are treated as either petrol or diesel cars for this purpose.

HMRC now review the rates four times a year – on 1 March, 1 June, 1 September and 1 December. For one month from the date of change, employers may use either the previous or new current rates, as they choose.

	Cost per mile		
Engine size	**Petrol**	**Diesel**	**LPG**
Rates applying from 1 September 2017			
1400cc or less	11p	—	7p
1600cc or less	—	9p	—
1401cc to 2000cc	13p	—	8p
1601cc to 2000cc	—	11p	—
Over 2000cc	21p	12p	13p
Rates applying from 1 June 2017			
1400cc or less	11p	—	7p
1600cc or less	—	9p	—
1401cc to 2000cc	14p	—	9p
1601cc to 2000cc	—	11p	—
Over 2000cc	21p	13p	14p
Rates applying from 1 March 2017			
1400cc or less	11p	—	7p
1600cc or less	—	9p	—
1401cc to 2000cc	14p	—	9p
1601cc to 2000cc	—	11p	—
Over 2000cc	22p	13p	14p

Engine size	Cost per mile		
	Petrol	Diesel	LPG
Rates applying from 1 December 2016			
1400cc or less	11p	—	7p
1600cc or less	—	9p	—
1401cc to 2000cc	14p	—	9p
1601cc to 2000cc	—	11p	—
Over 2000cc	21p	13p	13p
Rates applying from 1 September 2016			
1400cc or less	11p	—	7p
1600cc or less	—	9p	—
1401cc to 2000cc	13p	—	9p
1601cc to 2000cc	—	11p	—
Over 2000cc	20p	13p	13p
Rates applying from 1 June 2016			
1400cc or less	10p	—	7p
1600cc or less	—	9p	—
1401cc to 2000cc	13p	—	9p
1601cc to 2000cc	—	10p	—
Over 2000cc	20p	12p	13p
Rates applying from 1 March 2016			
1400cc or less	10p	—	7p
1600cc or less	—	8p	—
1401cc to 2000cc	12p	—	8p
1601cc to 2000cc	—	10p	—
Over 2000cc	19p	11p	13p

Private vehicles

4-200 Mileage allowance payments

(ITEPA 2003, s. 230)

(Tax Reporter: ¶432-100ff.)

Statutory rates are set for mileage allowance payments. An employer may, of course, reimburse business mileage driven in a privately-owned car at more or less than the statutory rates but any excess is taxable. Any shortfall is tax deductible and the employee may claim relief accordingly.

Kind of vehicle	Rate per mile from 6 April 2011
Car or van	45p for the first 10,000 miles 25p after that
Motorcycle	24p
Cycle	20p

4-220 Passenger payments

(ITEPA 2003, s. 233)

(Tax Reporter: ¶432-150)

No liability to income tax arises in respect of an approved passenger payment made to an employee for a car or a van, whether the vehicle is privately owned or provided by the employer. The approved amount is 5p per passenger mile.

Company vans

4-300 Taxable benefit

(ITEPA 2003, s. 114, 154–164)

(Tax Reporter: ¶416-200ff.)

	£
2017–18	3,230
2016–17	3,170
2015–16	3,150
2014–15	3,090
2013–14 (from April 2007)	3,000

But nil if:

(1) the restricted private use conditions are met (available and used only for ordinary commuting and business travel);

(2) private use in the tax year is insignificant.

Zero-emission vans

For tax years to 2014–15, the cash equivalent of the benefit of a van was nil if the van could not produce any CO2 emissions under any circumstances by being driven (e.g. an electric van). From 2015–16, the charge for zero-emission vans is calculated as the 'relevant percentage' per the table below of the main rate as per the table above.

	Appropriate percentage
2015–16	20%
2016–17	20%
2017–18	20%
2018–19	40%
2019–20	60%
2020–21	80%
2021–22	90%

4-345 Fuel for company vans

(ITEPA 2003, s. 160ff.)

(Tax Reporter: ¶416-200ff.)

Tax Year	£
2017–18	610
2016–17	598
2015–16	594
2014–15	581
2013–14	564
2012–13	550
2011–12	550

But nil if:

(1) the restricted private use conditions are met (available and used only for ordinary commuting and business travel);

(2) private use in the tax year is insignificant.

Buses

4-360 Bus services

(ITEPA 2003, s. 242 and 243)

(Tax Reporter: ¶432-600ff.)

An exemption applies to:

(1) works transport services, which must be a bus or minibus:
- (a) available to employees generally;
- (b) used mainly for qualifying journeys; and
- (c) used substantially by employees or their children;

(2) support for public bus services:
- (a) available to employees generally;
- (b) used for qualifying journeys by employees of one or more employers; and
- (c) either:
  - (i) a local bus service; or
  - (ii) the bus must be provided to other passengers on terms that are as favourable as the terms on which the bus is provided to employees.

Used cycles

4-380 Used cycles: valuation table

(Tax Reporter: ¶419-090)

HMRC allow used cycles to be transferred to employees using disposal values as follows:

Age of cycle	Original price less than £500	Original price £500+
1 year	18%	25%
18 months	16%	21%
2 years	13%	17%
3 years	8%	12%
4 years	3%	7%
5 years	Negligible	2%
6 years & over	Negligible	Negligible

Beneficial loans

4-390 Beneficial loans threshold

(ITEPA 2003, Pt. 3, Ch. 7; s. 180)

(Tax Reporter: ¶417-000ff.)

A taxable benefit may arise where an employee (or a relative of an employee) is provided with a loan either interest-free or at a favourable rate of interest. A tax charge does not arise where the amount outstanding on the loan does not exceed the threshold at all times during the year. Threshold is as follows:

Period	Threshold £
2014–15 and subsequent years	10,000
2013–14 and earlier years (post-6 April 1994)	5,000

Official rates of interest

4-400 Official rate of interest

(ITEPA 2003, s. 181)

(Tax Reporter: ¶417-100)

The official rate of interest is used to calculate the cash equivalent of the benefit of an employment-related loan which is a taxable cheap loan. HMRC review the level of the official rate of interest on a quarterly basis but normally set a single rate in advance for the whole tax year in line with a commitment given in January 2000, that (following announcement of the rate for any given tax year) the official rate may be reduced but will not be increased in the light of interest rate changes generally.

Date	Rate %	SI No.
From 6 April 2017	2.50	SI 2017/305
6 April 2016 to 5 April 2017	3.00	—
6 April 2015 to 5 April 2016	3.00	SI 2015/411
6 April 2014 to 5 April 2015	3.25	SI 2014/496
6 April 2010 to 5 April 2014	4.00	SI 2010/415

The average official rates of interest are given at ¶4-405.

4-405 Official rate of interest: average rates

(ITEPA 2003, s. 181)

(Tax Reporter: ¶417-100)

Official rates of interest are given at ¶4-400. Average official rates of interest, given below, should be used if the loan was outstanding throughout the tax year and the normal averaging method of calculation is being used Average rates were last published by HMRC for 2013-14.

Year	Average official rate %
2013–14	4.00
2012–13	4.00
2011–12	4.00

4-420 Official rate of interest: foreign currency loans

(ITEPA 2003, s. 181; SI 1989/1297)

(Tax Reporter: ¶418-100)

Period	Switzerland[1] %	Japan[1] %
From 6 July 1994	5.5	3.9

Note

[1] These rates apply to loans made in the currency of a country or territory outside the UK, and to an employee who normally lives in that country or territory, and who has lived in that country or territory at some time in the tax year or in the previous five years. The intention of the rules is to give relief for employees working temporarily in the UK, where interest rates in the overseas country are lower than interest rates in the UK. The relief does not apply to employees who come to the UK and live here permanently.

Travel and subsistence

4-500 Subsistence scale rates

(Tax Reporter: ¶457-560)

The following 'day subsistence' rates may be used when applying for a dispensation for payments to employees away from home for work purposes:

Rate	Detail	£
Breakfast rate	Irregular early starters	5
One-meal rate	Away for at least five hours	5
Two-meal rate	Away for at least ten hours	10
Late evening meal rate	Irregular late finishers	15

4-520 Accommodation and subsistence – overseas rates

(Tax Reporter: ¶457-570)

Employers can reimburse subsistence to employees by making a scale rate payment. HMRC usually publish the rates in October or November every year.

Recent rates are available as follows:

From October 2014[(1)]: www.gov.uk/government/uploads/system/uploads/attachment_data/file/359797/2014_Worldwide_subsistence_rates.pdf;

Note

(1) The rates published in October 2014 will continue to apply for the year commencing October 2016.

4-540 Incidental overnight expenses and benefits

(ITEPA 2003, s. 240)

(Tax Reporter: ¶432-900)

Benefits, reimbursements and expenses provided by an employer for employees' minor, personal expenditure whilst on business-related activities requiring overnight accommodation away from home are not taxable provided that the total amount reimbursed, etc. does not exceed the relevant maximum amount(s) per night, multiplied by the number of nights' absence. If the limit is exceeded, the whole amount provided remains taxable.

	Authorised maximum per night	
From	In UK £	Overseas £
6 April 1995	5	10

4-550 Lorry drivers subsistence allowances

(ITEPA 2003, s. 337 and 338)

(Tax Reporter: ¶455-020; ¶455-040)

A subsistence allowance paid to long distance lorry drivers will not be taxed provided they are paid or reimbursed in an approved way and both of the following conditions are met:

(1) The payer, or another person, operates system for checking that the employees are in fact incurring and paying amounts in respect of expenses of the same kind and that a fully matching deduction would be allowed under ITEPA 2003, Pt. 5, Ch. 2 or 5 in respect of those amounts.

(2) Neither the payer nor any other person operating the system for checking knows or suspects, or could reasonably be expected to know or suspect, that the employee had not incurred an amount in respect of the expense, or that a deduction under ITEPA 2003, Pt. 5, Ch. 2 or 5 would not be allowed in respect of those amounts.

HMRC accept the following amounts as reasonable for nights in the UK.

	Payment per night	
Year ended	**Drivers with non-sleeper cabs** **£**	**Drivers with sleeper cabs**[(1)] **£**
31 December 2017	34.90	26.20
31 December 2013 to 2016	34.90	26.20

Note

[(1)] The mere fact that a lorry has a sleeper cab does not prevent the employer paying an amount tax free up to the limit shown for drivers with non-sleeper cabs (or locally agreed limits) provided that the employer is satisfied that the driver did incur expenses on overnight accommodation (for example by staying in a hotel) and meals. HMRC accept that a payment of 75% of the figure shown for drivers with non-sleeper cabs does no more than reimburse the expense incurred when the driver uses the sleeper cab overnight.

Shares and share incentives

4-600 Share incentive plans

(TCGA 1992, s. 236A, 238A, Sch. 7C, 7D, Pt. 1; ITEPA 2003, s. 488ff., Sch. 2)

(Tax Reporter: ¶468-000ff.)

	Free shares	**Partnership shares**	**Matching shares**	**Dividend shares**
Employment before eligibility[(1)]	Up to 18 months employment	Up to 18 months employment[(4)] where no accumulation period, up to six months with accumulation period	Only awarded to employees who buy partnership shares	Must be acquired with dividends from plan shares
Limits	Up to £3,600 per tax year	Up to £1,800 per tax year or 10% of salary, if less	Up to two matching shares for each partnership share bought	Dividends from shares in the plan reinvested: – no limit
Minimum amount if stated[(1)]	—	no more than £10 per month	—	—
Performance measures[(1)]	Yes	No	No	No
Holding period	At least three years from award[(2)]	None	At least three years from award[(2)]	Three years from acquisition
Forfeiture on cessation of employment[(1)]	Yes(5)	No	Yes(5)	No
Tax on award	None	None – tax relief for salary used to buy shares	None	None
Tax on removal of shares from plan within three years of award[(3)]	On market value when taken out	On market value when taken out	On market value when taken out	Original dividend taxable but in year when shares taken out of plan

	Free shares	Partnership shares	Matching shares	Dividend shares
Tax on removal between three and five years of award(2)	On lower of: – value at award – value on removal	On lower of: – salary used to buy shares – value on removal	On lower of: – value at award – value on removal	None
Tax on removal after five years	None	None	None	None
CGT on removal – any time	None	None	None	None

Notes

(1) These conditions can be included at the option of the company.

(2) The holding period may be up to five years at the option of the company.

(3) PAYE and NICs will be operated in relation to any income tax charge where the shares are readily convertible assets.

(4) Maximum accumulation period for partnership shares is 12 months.

(5) Restrictions apply to provisions for forfeiture that may be applied including a maximum forfeiture period of up to three years from award, that forfeiture provisions cannot relate to cesation of employment through injury, disability, redundancy, TUPE transfers, changes of control, retirement (at normal age), death, or be linked to the performence of any person.

(6) From 15 September 2016, rules for share incentive plans previously repealed will be reinstated to enforce the principle that shares with preferential rights cannot be issued to selected employees only (amendments by FA 2016, Sch. 3).

4-610 Company share option plan

(TCGA 1992, s. 238A, Sch. 7D, Pt. 3; ITEPA 2003, s. 521–526, Sch. 4)

(Tax Reporter: ¶467-000ff.)

Maximum options(1)(2)	£30,000

Notes

(1) This includes options granted under the scheme, or under any other approved CSOP scheme established by the scheme organiser or an associated company of the scheme organiser.

(2) The 'market value' of shares is calculated at the date of grant, or of each relevant option grant (if more than one grant); or if any agreement relating to any such shares has been made under ITEPA 2003, Sch. 4, para. 22, the earlier time or times stated in the agreement.

4-620 Enterprise management incentives (EMI)

(TCGA 1992, s. 238A, Sch. 7D, Pt. 4; ITEPA 2003, s. 527–541, Sch. 5)

(Tax Reporter: ¶466-000ff.)

Qualifying company	• Gross assets not exceeding £30m • Fewer than 250 employees (full-time or equivalent),
Maximum options	£250,000

Notes

[1] The above limits are qualified as follows:

(a) options held by the employee under a (HMRC-approved) Company Share Ownership Plan (CSOP), that are unexercised at the date of grant of an EMI option, are taken into account in applying the maximum figure above;

(b) by the 'three-year restriction period' rule; the grant of an option to an employee within three years from the most recent EMI option grant to him, cannot itself qualify as an EMI option if the value of the shares which were the subject of all previous EMI option grants, down to and including the most recent grant, amounted to £250,000 (or other applicable threshold figure in earlier periods). This applies whether or not any of such previously granted options have been exercised; and

(c) there is an overriding company limit; the total value (as defined) of shares in the company that are the subject of unexercised EMI options cannot exceed £3,000,000.

For purposes of (a) and (b) above, one takes into account all options granted by reason of the same employment, or employment by any member of the same group of companies.

4-635 SAYE

(TCGA 1992, s. 238A, Sch. 7D, Pt. 2; ITEPA 2003, s. 516–520, Sch. 3)

(Tax Reporter: ¶470-000ff.)

Limits	Savings periods	Monthly contributions
Minimum	36 months	£5–£10[1]
Maximum	60 months	£500

Notes

[1] Company may impose a minimum monthly payment of up to £10 per month; otherwise the minimum is £5 per month.

4-640 SAYE bonus rates: multiple of monthly payments

(ITEPA 2003, Sch. 3)

(Tax Reporter: ¶470-000ff.)

The bonus rate applicable to a scheme is set at the time the savings contract is entered into and is unaffected by any subsequent change to the rates. Current and historical rates are shown below. See ¶4-660 for details of the 'early leaver rate' applying for those who withdraw their funds after 12 monthly contributions, but before the three-year anniversary.

From	3-year	5-year	7-year[1]
27 December 2014	0.0	0.0	—
28 July 2014	0.0	0.6	—
1 August 2012	0.0	0.0	0.0
23 September 2011	0.0	0.0	1.6
12 August 2011	0.0	0.9	3.5
27 February 2011	0.1	1.7	4.8

Note

(1) The seven-year savings period of Save As You Earn (SAYE) Share Option Schemes was withdrawn with effect from 23 July 2013. Employees already saving under existing SAYE contracts before that date were not affected by the change.

4-660 SAYE 'early leaver rates'

(ITEPA 2003, Sch. 3)

(Tax Reporter: ¶470-000ff.)

The following 'early leaver rates' have applied for employees whose SAYE contracts are cancelled after 12 monthly contributions but before the maturity date:

Dates	Rates %
27 December 2014	0.00
28 July 2014	0.00
1 August 2012	0.00
23 September 2011	0.00
12 August 2011	0.00
27 February 2011	0.12

Note

The relevant date is that on which the employee starts saving under the contract, not the date on which the contract is cancelled.

4-680 SAYE effective interest rates

(ITEPA 2003, Sch. 3)

(Tax Reporter: ¶470-000ff.)

From	3-year	5-year	7-year[1]
27 December 2014	0.00	0.00	—
28 July 2014	0.00	0.39	—
1 August 2012	0.00	0.00	0.00
23 September 2011	0.00	0.00	0.58
12 August 2011	0.00	0.59	1.25
27 February 2011	0.18	1.10	1.70

Note

[1] The seven-year savings period of Save As You Earn (SAYE) Share Option Schemes was withdrawn with effect from 23 July 2013. Employees already saving under existing SAYE contracts before that date were not affected by the change.

4-690 Employee shareholder status

(ITEPA 2003, s. 226A–226D)

(Tax Reporter: ¶471-500ff.)

Finance Act 2017 removed the income tax relief in respect of employee shareholder shares received in return for entering into an employee shareholder agreement on or after 1 December 2016.

Previously, employees accepting a position under an employee shareholder employment contract could be awarded fully paid up shares in their employer or parent company, at no cost to the employee without incurring a liability to income tax (or National Insurance contributions).

See ¶5-050 for capital gains tax exemption on employee shareholder shares (also withdrawn for shares received on or after 1 December 2016).

	1 September 2013 to 30 November 2016. £
Minimum value of share award (market value on acquisition)	2,000
Income tax and NIC exemption[1] (market value on acquisition)	2,000

Note

[1] Employee was treated as having made a payment of £2,000 for the acquisition of shares and accordingly; any excess (of market value) over £2,000 was treated as earnings from the employment subject to income tax (and NIC as applicable).

4-695 Employee ownership trusts

(ITEPA 2003, s. 312A–312I)

An exemption from income tax is available for any relevant bonus payment made in a tax year to an employee by a qualifying indirectly employee-owned company that meets the relevant conditions (a trading company in which a controlling interest is held by an employee-ownership settlement). A relevant bonus will be a cash award other than regular salary or wages that is paid to all employees on equal terms, although bonuses can be set by an employer by reference to a percentage of salary or length of service or hours worked. The exemption is available from 1 October 2014 and subject to an annual cap per employee for each qualifying company as set out below.

Period	£
From 1 October 2014	3,600

National minimum wage

4-700 National minimum wage: from 1 October 2010

(SI 2016/953)

Period(1)	Workers aged 25 plus(2) £	Workers aged at least 21 but under 25 £	Workers aged at least 18 but under 21 £	Workers aged under 18 £	Apprentices aged under 19 or in the first year of apprenticeship £
From 6 April 2017	7.50	7.05	5.60	4.05	3.50
1/10/16–05/04/16	7.20	6.95	5.55	4.00	3.40
1/04/16–30/09/16	7.20	6.70	5.30	3.87	3.30
1/10/15–31/03/16	–	6.70	5.30	3.87	3.30
1/10/14–30/09/15	–	6.50	5.13	3.79	2.73
1/10/13–30/09/14	–	6.31	5.03	3.72	2.68
1/10/12–30/09/13	–	6.19	4.98	3.68	2.65
1/10/11–30/09/12	–	6.08	4.98	3.68	2.60
1/10/10–30/09/11	–	5.93	4.92	3.64	2.50

4-720 National minimum wage: accommodation offset

The maximum permitted daily and weekly rates of accommodation offset in relation to the national minimum wage are as follows:

Period	Daily offset £	Weekly offset £
From 6/4/2017	6.40	44.80
1/10/16–5/4/17	6.00	42.00
1/10/15–30/09/16	5.35	37.45
1/10/14–30/09/15	5.08	35.56
1/10/13–30/09/14	4.91	34.37
1/10/12–30/09/13	4.82	33.74
1/10/11–30/09/12	4.73	33.11
1/10/10–30/09/11	4.61	32.27

Flat-rate expenses

4-750 Fixed sum deductions for repairing and maintaining equipment

(ITEPA 2003, s. 367)

(Tax Reporter: ¶457-500)

A tax deduction is given for certain amounts 'representing the average annual expenses incurred by employees of the class to which the employee belongs in respect of the repair and maintenance of work equipment'. The term 'flat-rate expenses' is often used for these figures. The following table is from EIM32712.

Manual and certain other employees: flat-rate expenses deduction for tools and special clothing

Industry	Occupation	Deduction for 2008–09 onwards £	Deduction for 2004–05 to 2007–08 £
Agriculture	All workers	100	70
Aluminium	a. Continual casting operators, process operators, de-dimplers, driers, drill punchers, dross unloaders, firemen, furnace operators and their helpers, leaders, mouldmen, pourers, remelt department labourers, roll flatteners	140	130
	b. Cable hands, case makers, labourers, mates, truck drivers and measurers, storekeepers	80	60
	c. Apprentices	60	45
	d. All other workers	120	100
Banks and building societies	Uniformed doormen and messengers	60	45
Brass and copper	Braziers, coppersmiths, finishers, fitters, moulders, turners and all other workers.	120	100
Building	a. Joiners and carpenters	140	105
	b. Cement works, roofing felt and asphalt labourers	80	55
	c. Labourers and navvies	60	45
	d. All other workers	120	85
Building materials	a. Stone-masons	120	85
	b. Tilemakers and labourers	60	45
	c. All other workers	80	55
Clothing	a. Lacemakers, hosiery bleachers, dyers, scourers and knitters, knitwear bleachers and dyers	60	45
	b. All other workers	60	45

Industry	Occupation	Deduction for 2008–09 onwards £	Deduction for 2004–05 to 2007–08 £
Constructional engineering	a. Blacksmiths and their strikers, burners, caulkers, chippers, drillers, erectors, fitters, holders up, markers off, platers, riggers, riveters, rivet heaters, scaffolders, sheeters, template workers, turners, welders	140	115
	b. Banksmen labourers, shop-helpers, slewers, straighteners	80	60
	c. Apprentices and storekeepers	60	45
	d. All other workers	100	75
Electrical and electricity supply	a. Those workers incurring laundry costs only (generally CEGB employees)	60	45
	b. All other workers	120	90
Engineering	a. Pattern makers	140	120
	b. Labourers, supervisory and unskilled workers	80	60
	c. Apprentices and storekeepers	60	45
	d. Motor mechanics in garage repair shops	120	100
	e. All other workers	120	100
Fire service	Uniformed fire fighters and fire officers	80	60
Food	All workers	60	45
Forestry	All workers	100	70
Glass	All workers	80	60

Industry	Occupation	Deduction for 2008–09 onwards £	Deduction for 2004–05 to 2007–08 £
Healthcare staff in the National Health Service, private hospitals and nursing homes	a. Ambulance staff on active service (i.e. excluding staff who take telephone calls or provide clerical support)	185 (but £140 to 6 April 2014)	110
	b. Nurses, midwives, chiropodists, dental nurses, occupational, speech, physiotherapists and other therapists, healthcare assistants, phlebotomists and radiographers	125 (but £100 to 6 April 2014)	70
	c. Plaster room orderlies, hospital porters, ward clerks, sterile supply workers, hospital domestics, hospital catering staff	125 (but £100 to 5 April 2014)	60
	d. Laboratory staff, pharmacists, pharmacy assistants	80 (but £60 to 5 April 2014)	45
	e. Uniformed ancillary staff – maintenance workers, grounds staff, drivers, parking attendants and security guards, receptionists and other uniformed staff	80 (but £60 to 5 April 2014)	45
Heating	a. Pipe fitters and plumbers	120	100
	b. Coverers, laggers, domestic glaziers, heating engineers and their mates	120	90
	c. All gas workers, all other workers	100	70
Iron mining	a. Fillers, miners and underground workers	120	100
	b. All other workers	100	75

Industry	Occupation	Deduction for 2008–09 onwards £	Deduction for 2004–05 to 2007–08 £
Iron and steel	a. Day labourers, general labourers, stockmen, time-keepers, warehouse staff and weighmen	80	60
	b. Apprentices	60	45
	c. All other workers	140	120
Leather	a. Curriers (wet workers), fellmongering workers, tanning operatives (wet)	80	55
	b. All other workers	60	45
Particular engineering	a. Pattern makers	140	120
	b. All chainmakers; cleaners, galvanisers, tinners and wire drawers in the wire drawing industry; tool-makers in the lock making industry	120	100
	c. Apprentices and storekeepers	60	45
	d. All other workers	80	60
Police force	Police officers (ranks up to and including Chief Inspector)	140	55 (but £110 for 2007–08)
Precious metals	All workers	100	70
Printing	a. *Letterpress Section*: Electrical engineers (rotary presses), electrotypers, ink and roller makers, machine minders (rotary), maintenance engineers (rotary presses) and stereotypers	140	105

Industry	Occupation	Deduction for 2008–09 onwards £	Deduction for 2004–05 to 2007–08 £
	b. Bench hands (periodical and bookbinding section), compositors (letterpress section), readers (letterpress section) telecommunications and electronic section wire room operators, warehousemen (paper box making section)	60	45
	c. All other workers	100	70
Prisons	Uniformed prison officers	80	55
Public service	a. *Dock and inland waterways* – Dockers, dredger drivers, hopper steerers	80	55
	– All other workers	60	45
	b. *Public transport* – Garage hands (including cleaners)	80	55
	– Conductors and drivers	60	45
Quarrying	All workers	100	70
Railways	(See the appropriate category for craftsmen, e.g. engineers, vehicle, etc.)		
	All other workers	100	70
Seamen	a. Carpenters (Seamen) Passenger liners	165	165
	b. Carpenters (Seamen) Cargo vessels, tankers, coasters and ferries	140	130
Shipyards	a. Blacksmiths and their strikers, boilermakers, burners, carpenters, caulkers, drillers, furnacemen (platers), holders up, fitters, platers, plumbers, riveters, sheet iron workers, shipwrights, tubers, welders	140	115

Industry	Occupation	Deduction for 2008–09 onwards £	Deduction for 2004–05 to 2007–08 £
	b. Labourers	80	60
	c. Apprentices and storekeepers	60	45
	d. All other workers	100	75
Textiles and textile printing	a. Carders, carding engineers, overlookers and technicians in spinning mills	120	85
	b. All other workers	80	60
Vehicles	a. Builders, railway vehicle repairers and railway wagon lifters	140	105
	b. Railway vehicle painters, letterers, and builders' and repairers' assistants	80	60
	c. All other workers	60	45
Wood and furniture (formerly Wood)	a. Carpenters, cabinet makers, joiners, wood carvers and woodcutting machinists	140	115
	b. Artificial limb makers (other than in wood), organ builders and packaging case makers	120	90
	c. Coopers not providing own tools, labourers, polishers and upholsterers	60	45
	d. All other workers	100	75

Notes

'Workers' and 'all other workers' are references to manual workers or to workers who have to pay for the upkeep of tools and special clothing.

'Firemen' means persons engaged to light and maintain furnaces.

'Constructional engineering' means engineering undertaken on a construction site, including buildings, shipyards, bridges, roads and other similar operations.

'Particular engineering' means engineering undertaken on a commercial basis in a factory or workshop for the purposes of producing components such as wire, springs, nails and locks.

Miscellaneous

4-800 Mobile phones

(ITEPA 2003, s. 319)

(Tax Reporter: ¶437-700)

No tax charge on employer-provided mobile phones but exemption restricted to one phone per employee, with no exemption for phones provided for family members. Limited exemption for vouchers supplied for mobile phone use. The right of the employee to surrender the phone for additional pay does not trigger a tax charge.

4-805 Recommended medical treatment

(ITEPA 2003, s. 320C)

(Tax Reporter: ¶437-900)

No liability to income tax arises in respect of the provision to an employee of recommended medical treatment, or the payment or reimbursement, to or in respect of an employee of the cost of such treatment, if the provision, payment or reimbursement is not pursuant to relevant salary sacrifice arrangements or relevant flexible remuneration arrangements. The exemption does not apply if, and to the extent that, the value in the tax year exceeds the limit shown in the table below.

Period	Annual limit
From 1 January 2015	£500

4-810 Employer-provided childcare (workplace nurseries)

(ITEPA 2003, s. 318)

(Tax Reporter: ¶434-600)

No liability to income tax arises in respect of employer-provided childcare (workplace nurseries) provided certain conditions are met; including that the premises are made available by the employer alone, or that the care is provided under partnership arrangements by persons including the employer, one or more of whom makes the premises available, and under which arrangements the employer is wholly or partly responsible for financing and managing the provision of the care.

4-815 Employer-supported childcare

(ITEPA 2003, s. 270A, 318A)

(Tax Reporter: ¶434-800ff.)

A limited exemption is available for childcare vouchers and directly contracted childcare. Where the cash equivalent of the benefit falls above the limits set out in the table below, liability to income tax arises only in respect of so much as exceeds the exempt amount.

The Childcare Payments Act 2014 amends s. 270A and 318A to restrict the availability of the existing tax exemptions for employer-supported childcare where the employee has given their employer a 'chilcare account notice' to say that they no longer want to receive employer-supported childcare so that they or their partner can open a childcare account under the new scheme launched in 2017 (by gradual roll out) (see ¶10-560). At Budget 2016 it was announced that Employer Supported Childcare will remain open to new entrants until April 2018 to support the transition between the schemes.

	Basic rate[1] £	Higher rate £	Additional rate £
From 6 April 2013			
Weekly	55	28	25
Monthly	243	124	111
Annual	2,915	1,484	1,325
From 6 April 2011			
Weekly	55	28	22
Monthly	243	124	97
Annual	2,915	1,484	1,166

Note

(1) The restriction on the amount of the exemption available for higher rate and additional rate taxpayers from 6 April 2011 does not apply where an employee joined the scheme before 6 April 2011, has not ceased to be employed by the employer since that date and there has not been a continuous period of 52 weeks since that date throughout which vouchers were not, or care was not, being provided under the scheme and such employees continue to be entitled to relief at the rates that are otherwise available for basic rate earners only (FA 2011, Sch. 8, para. 8).

4-830 Relocation allowance

(ITEPA 2003, s. 271–289)

(Tax Reporter: ¶433-850)

Tax exemption for the provision by employers of removal benefits, or payment or reimbursement of removal expenses in connection with an employee's change of residence where the employee's job or place of work is changed is generally subject to a statutory maximum of £8,000. No tax relief is available for the employee where expenses are not reimbursed by the employer.

4-840 Payments and benefits on termination of employment

(ITEPA 2003, s. 401–416)

(Tax Reporter: ¶437-000ff.)

Period	Relief[(1)(2)]
From 1998–99	£30,000 exempt

Notes

(1) The exemption is not available for any payment or other benefit chargeable to income tax under other legislation (ITEPA 2003, s. 401(3)). There is therefore no exemption for any amounts already taxable as earnings (e.g. payments made under a contract of employment).

(2) Finance (No. 2) Act 2017 aligns the employer National Insurance contributions (NIC) treatment of termination payments with income tax and tightens the scope of the £30,000 exemption by making it clear that all payments in lieu of notice (PILONs), not just contractual PILONs, are taxable earnings. All employees will pay tax and Class 1 NICs on the amount of basic pay that they would have received if they had worked their notice in full, even if they are not paid a contractual PILON. The existing £30,000 income tax exemption is retained and employees will continue to benefit from an unlimited employee NICs exemption for payments associated with the termination of employment.

4-850 Scholarships and sandwich courses

(SP 4/86)

(Tax Reporter: ¶419-200)

Subject to conditions, employers may make tax-free payments up to a specified figure to employees who are attending certain educational courses. The specified amount for recent years has been as follows:

Period	Specified amount
From 1/9/07	£15,480

4-860 Trivial benefits

(ITEPA 2003, s. 323A)

No liability to income tax arises in respect of a benefit provided by, or on behalf of, an employer to an employee or a member of the employee's family or household provided the benefit is not cash or a cash voucher, is not a reward for work or performance, is not in the terms of the employment contract and falls within the limits set out below:

From	Maximum benefit cost £	Annual exempt amount £
6 April 2016	50	300

4-870 Sporting testimonials

(ITEPA 2003, s. 306B)

A one off exemption from income tax applies in respect of income arising from a non-contractual or non-customary sporting testimonial or benefit for an employed sportsperson. Testimonials granted or awarded under contract or custom are already subject to income tax and are not eligible for the exemption.

From	Exemption[(1)] £
6 April 2016(2)	300

Note

[(1)] Applies to income arising from relevant events held in a maximum period of 12 calendar months only, beginning with the date the first event is held in a 'testimonial year' (even if that year straddles more than one tax year). If the level of the income arising from the testimonial or testimonial year falls below the value of the exemption, the unused exemption cannot be carried forward to any future sporting testimonial/benefit matches, or against any other testimonial events held after that 12-month period.

[(2)] Events held on or after 6 April 2017 from a testimonial that is awarded or arranged for a sportsperson prior to 25 November 2015 will continue to fall within guidance previously published by HMRC on the tax treatment of sporting testimonials and benefits for employed sportspersons which afforded a concessionary exemption.

PAYE

4-900 PAYE thresholds

(SI 2003/2682)

(Tax Reporter: ¶493-240ff.)

	Amount	
Tax year	Weekly £	Monthly £
2017–18	221.00	958.00
2016–17	212.00	917.00
2015–16	204.00	883.00
2014–15	192.00	833.00
2013–14	182.00	787.00
2012–13	156.00	675.00
2011–12	144.00	623.00

Note

Under normal circumstances, employers need not deduct tax from employees who earn less than the above amounts.

The PAYE monthly and weekly thresholds are calculated arithmetically as 1/52 and 1/12 respectively of the personal allowance, rounded to the nearest pound (SI 2003/2682, reg. 9(8)).

4-920 PAYE codes

The PAYE code enables an employer or payer of pension to give the employee or pensioner the approved amount of tax-free pay.

L	Entitled to the basic tax-free personal allowance – 1150L for the 2017–18 tax year. Also used for 'emergency' codes
M	Marriage allowance: people who have received a transfer of 10% of their partner's personal allowance
N	Marriage allowance: people who have transferred 10% of their personal allowance to their partner
S	Income or pension taxed at Scottish rate of income tax
T	Tax code includes other calculations to work out the personal allowance (i.e. income-related reduction to the personal allowance)
0T	Allowances fully used up or reduced to nil and income is taxed at the relevant rates, may also be used for a new job where the employee does not have a P45 or has not completed a P46 before the first pay day
BR	All income is taxed at the basic rate, currently 20%, most commonly used for a second job or pension
SBR	Scottish taxpayer; all income taxed at the basic rate, currently 20%

D0	All income taxed at the higher rate, currently 40%, most commonly used for a second job or pension
SD0	Scottish taxpayer; all income taxed at the higher rate, currently 40%
D1	All income taxed at the additional rate, currently 45%, most commonly used for a second job or pension
SD1	Scottish taxpayer; all income taxed at the additional rate, currently 45%
NT	No tax to be deducted from income or pension
K	Untaxed income exceeds tax-free allowances (e.g. tax due for previous tax year, taxable state benefits or taxable employment benefits)

Emergency codes

W1, M1, X are emergency tax code indicators and denote the tax code is operating on a non-cumulative basis. Also issued where the tax code is adjusted during the tax year and the adjustment is to reduce net allowances/increase taxable benefits (so that the new collects on a non-cumulative basis for the remainder of the year). Emergency tax codes for the 2017–18 tax year are 1150L M1, 1150L W1, 1150L X.

4-925 PAYE coding out limits

Debts

(ITEPA 2003, s. 684; SI 2003/2682, reg. 14A–14C)

(Tax Reporter: ¶493-340)

HMRC may collect specified relevant debts up to the permitted limit through the PAYE system. The table below sets out the maximum amount that may be collected in this way (but see also the 'overall limit' and the 'overriding limit' below):

Tax year in which deduction made	Maximum deduction £
From 2015–16	17,000
2012–13 to 2014–15(1)	3,000

Note

(1) SI 2003/2682, reg. 14A which provides for determination of a tax code to recover a 'relevant debt' within the meaning of ITEPA 2003, s. 684 was introduced with effect from 6 April 2012.

To the extent that the payee does not object, HMRC may also determine a code to collect or repay income tax payable or overpaid in respect of the high income child benefit charge and, from 2015–16, to collect child or working tax credit debt.

Self-assessment balancing payments

(SI 2003/2682, reg.186)

(Tax Reporter: ¶493-330)

Payments due on or after	Maximum deduction £
6 April 2012	3,000

Overall limit

(SI 2003/2682, reg. 14D)

With effect for tax codes issued for the tax year 2015–16 onwards, and to coincide with the increase in the coding out limit above from £3,000 to £17,000, an overall limit on the total amount of 'relevant debt' (under SI 2003/2682, reg. 14A) and 'tax credit debt' (under SI 2003/2682, reg. 14C) that may be recovered from an employee in a tax year via their tax code will be introduced, based on the expected amount of the individual's PAYE income for the tax year and as set out in the table below (subject to the 'overriding limit' below):

Expected amount of PAYE income in the tax year for which the code is determined	Total amount of debt recoverable in that tax year
Less than £30,000	No more than £3,000
£30,000 or more but less than £40,000	No more than £5,000
£40,000 or more but less than £50,000	No more than £7,000
£50,000 or more but less than £60,000	No more than £9,000
£60,000 or more but less than £70,000	No more than £11,000
£70,000 or more but less than £80,000	No more than £13,000
£80,000 or more but less than £90,000	No more than £15,000
£90,000 or more	No more than £17,000

Overriding limit

(SI 2003/2682, reg. 2)

The 'overriding limit' is the limit on the amount of tax that may be deducted from a relevant payment and is an amount equal to 50% of the amount of the relevant payment. A relevant payment is defined as a payment of net PAYE income, except PAYE social security income, UK social security pensions, excluded relocation expenses, excluded business expenses, excluded pecuniary liabilities, and excluded notional payments (SI 2003/2682, reg. 4).

Additionally, HMRC will further not code out debts which result in the individual's liability for the year doubling, even though the debt might otherwise fall within the limits set out above (i.e. only debts that equate to less than the individual's expected liability for the tax year will be coded out) (see HMRC manuals, PAYE12070).

4-930 PAYE real time information returns

(SI 2012/822; SI 2003/2682)

(Tax Reporter: ¶493-015)

Since 6 April 2013 (or 5 April 2014 for businesses with 50 or less employees), reporting PAYE information in real time has been mandatory, unless HMRC have notified otherwise. Key RTI requirements are as follows:

Submissions	Deadlines	Details
Full Payment Submission (FPS)	On or before the day employees are paid Final submission by 19 April (cannot file an FPS after this date)	• include all employees that are paid (including those earning below the NIC lower earnings limit (e.g. students)) • information to be submitted includes: amounts paid, deductions (tax and National Insurance), starter and leaver dates (if applicable)
Employer Payment Submission (EPS)	19 April following tax year (by 19 May following tax year to avoid a penalty)	• to report a reduction in the amount you pay to HMRC or if you have not paid any employees in a pay period
Earlier Year Update (EYU)	Up to six years after original FPS or EPS filed (by 19 May following tax year to avoid a penalty)	• to correct, after 19 April, any of the year to date totals submitted in your final FPS for the previous tax year. This only applies to years after you started to send information in real time
National Insurance verification request (NVR)	—	• to verify or obtain an National Insurance number for new employees

4-932 PAYE RTI: forms no longer needed

Reporting PAYE pre-RTI	Reporting in real time
Forms P14 and P35 end of year returns – do not use after you have submitted your 2012–13 return	FPS each time you pay employees EPS each month for any adjustments to what you owe Earlier Year Update (EYU) to amend details for earlier years
P45 – do not send any parts to HMRC – only use for the employees own records after 6 April 2013	Include starters and leavers information on your FPS
P46, P46(Pen) or P46(Expat) – do not use these forms after 6 April 2013	Include starters and leavers on your FPS.
Form CA6855 to trace or check a National Insurance number – do not use after 6 April 2013	Use payroll software to issue a National Insurance number verification request (NVR) to trace or check a National Insurance number
Form P38(S) – do not use after 6 April 2013	Include on your payroll and in your FPS

4-935 PAYE RTI: procedures unchanged

- **PAYE** – remains the same, only reporting that changes;
- **Coding notices** – employers still choose how they receive coding notices as previously;
- **Reporting a change to HMRC,** e.g. updating employee's new name or address for HMRC records – a real time submission will not update HMRC records. It remains the responsibility of the individual employee to notify HMRC of changes to name, address, etc.;
- **HMRC messages to employers** – HMRC continue to use the Data Provisioning Services (DPS) and EDI outbound message services;
- **Payment dates** – remain unchanged;
- **Forms P60** – P60s remain the same;
- **Expenses and benefits** – real time reporting has not changed how expenses and benefits are reported. Employers continue to complete and file any forms P9D, P11D and P11D(b) due under existing arrangements;
- **The Construction Industry Scheme (CIS) payment and reporting process** – real time reporting has not changed the CIS process. Employers continue to complete and file monthly returns (CIS300) due under the existing CIS arrangements. But where a limited company acting as a subcontractor has suffered CIS deductions, amounts should be reported to HMRC on an EPS and, as existing practice, subtract these from the amounts of PAYE due to be paid to HMRC.

4-938 PAYE RTI: correcting errors

Error in a Full Payment Submission (FPS) or EPS in the current tax year

Submit an additional FPS or EPS in the week or month of discovery or include correction in the next FPS or EPS for the next payroll run.

Error in FPS or EPS for previous tax year

Errors can be corrected before 20 April by submitting an additional FPS or EPS.

After 20 April, it is not possible to submit an additional FPS and instead the correction must be made on an EYU, however, errors on an EPS may be corrected by submitting an additional EPS for the tax year even after 20 April.

4-939 PAYE RTI: collection of tax on benefits in kind and expenses

(ITEPA 2003, s. 289Aff. and 684(1ZA); FA 2015, s. 13; SI 2003/2682, Pt. 3, Ch. 3A; SI 2015/1948)

Finance Act 2015 included amending legislation to enable the voluntary payrolling of benefits in kind from the 2016–17 tax year. Where an employer opts to payroll benefits in kind for cars, car fuel, medical insurance and gym membership, they will no longer be obliged to make a return (form P11D) and employers will instead report the value of these benefits in kind through Real Time Information (SI 2003/2682, Pt. 3, Ch. 3A).

Payrolling benefits in kind is extended by *Finance Act* 2016 to allow for the payrolling of non-cash vouchers and credit tokens from 2017–18 (amendments to SI 2003/2682, Pt. 3, Ch. 3A by SI 2016/1137).

From April 2016, the £8,500 a year threshold for the taxation of benefits in kind was abolished (FA 2015, s. 13) (meaning all benefits in kind are liable to income tax and National Insurance contributions, whatever the level of the employee's earnings and benefits in kind); and, also with effect from 6 April 2016, the dispensation regime for expenses was also replaced with an exemption for paid and reimbursed expenses (ITEPA 2003, s. 289Aff. and SI 2015/1948).

4-940 PAYE deadlines

(Tax Reporter: ¶494-700)

Reporting deadlines

Forms	**Date**	**Provision**	**Penalty provisions**
P14, P35, P38 and P38A (non-real time employers only)	19 May following tax year	*Income Tax (Pay As You Earn) Regulations* 2003 (SI 2003/2682), reg. 73 and 74	TMA 1970, s. 98A
P60 (to employee)	31 May following tax year	*Income Tax (Pay As You Earn) Regulations* 2003 (SI 2003/2682), reg. 67	TMA 1970, s. 98A
P11D	6 July following tax year	*Income Tax (Pay As You Earn) Regulations* 2003 (SI 2003/2682), reg. 85	TMA 1970, s. 98
P46(Car)	3 May, 2 August, 2 November, 2 February	*Income Tax (Pay As You Earn) Regulations* 2003 (SI 2003/2682), reg. 90	TMA 1970, s. 98

Other deadlines	**Date**
Employee payments in return for benefits in kind (making good) for 2017–18 and subsequent tax years(1)	6 July following tax year

Note

(1) Finance (No. 2) Act 2017 introduces a date for 'making good' on benefits-in-kind which are not accounted for in real time through Pay As You Earn (PAYE). The date has effect for benefits-in-kind which give rise to a tax liability for the tax year 2017-18 or any subsequent tax year.

4-942 PAYE Late filing penalties

(FA 2009, Sch. 55)

RTI

Where payment information is not received as expected on an FPS, or HMRC have not been notified that no employees have been paid in a tax period by submission of an EPS, late filing penalties will apply. The rules apply to each PAYE scheme, rather than each employer.

Late filing penalties will apply on a monthly basis, however, no penalty will apply for the first month in each tax year that returns are filed late.

New employers will not be penalised if their first FPS is received within 30 days of making their first payment to an employee.

In August 2017, HMRC announced it will continue with a risk based approach to late filing PAYE penalties for the 2017-18 tax year. This include not charging penalties if FPSs are filed late but within 3 days of the payment date and there is no pattern of persistent late-filing.

Initial penalties

Number of employees[1]	**Monthly Penalty**[2] **£**
1–9	100
10–49	200
50–249	300
250 or more	400

Notes

[1] HMRC will use the latest information available to determine the number of employees, and the size of the filing penalty for each period where a return is late.

[2] Filing penalty notices will be issued quarterly in July, October, January and April, if appropriate, showing the amount of the filing penalty for each tax month identified in that quarter.

Additional penalties for returns over three months late

	Penalty
3 months late	5%[1]

Note

[1] Calculated as a percentage of the tax/NICs that should have been shown on the late return.

Key deadlines	**Penalty**
Final FPS submitted by 19 April (last date for submission of an FPS)	None
EYU submitted after 19 April but by 19 May	None
Final payments unreported at 19 May	£100 per 50 employees for each month return outstanding(1)

Note

[1] Penalty notices issued after 19 September (once return outstanding for four months) and again, the following January and May.

Penalties (fixed) imposed for delays (TMA 1970, s. 98A)

Forms	First 12 months	Thereafter
P14, P35, P38 and P38A	£100 per 50 employees per month	Additional penalty not exceeding 100% of the tax and NIC payable for the year but remaining unpaid by 19 April following end of tax year

Penalties (mitigable) that may be imposed for delays (TMA 1970, s. 98)

Forms	Initial	Continuing
P11D	£300 per return	£60 per day

4-945 PAYE penalties for incorrect returns

(FA 2007, Sch. 24)

(Tax Reporter: ¶184-850)

HMRC use a risk-based approach to identify employers they think may be submitting incorrect returns. Where HMRC discover careless or deliberate errors, the penalties that could apply will be based on the behaviour that led to the error and the amount of potential lost revenue for that return. Errors that arise despite taking reasonable care attract no penalty at all and penalties for errors due to failure to take reasonable care can be reduced to zero with full and unprompted disclosure to HMRC.

The maximum penalty for an incorrect return is 100% of the potential lost revenue (deliberate and concealed action), 70% (deliberate but not concealed) or 30% (careless action).

4-946 PAYE: late payment penalties

(FA 2009, s. 107 and Sch. 56)

(Tax Reporter: ¶184-975)

Late payment penalties will be charged in-year on a late payment of monthly, quarterly or annual PAYE, student loan deductions, CIS deductions or Class 1, 1A and 1B National Insurance Contributions. Late payment penalty notices are issued quarterly in July, October, January and April showing the amount of the penalty due for each tax month. The total penalty charged can be made up of:

- a default penalty, for failure to pay monthly/quarterly payments on time and in full; and
- • penalties for amounts still unpaid after six and 12 months.

Penalties for late monthly or quarterly PAYE payments

No penalty if only one PAYE amount is late in a tax year, unless that payment is over six months late.

No. defaults in a tax year	Penalty percentage	Amount to which penalty percentages apply
1–3[1]	1%	The total amount that is late in the relevant tax month (ignoring the first late payment in the tax year)
4–6	2%	
7–9	3%	
10 or more	4%	

Note

[1] The first failure to pay on time does not count as a default.

Additional penalties	Amount
6 months late	5%
12 months late	Further 5%

Amounts due annually or occasionally (Class 1A and 1B NIC)

Penalty date	5%
5 months after initial penalty date	further 5%
11 months after initial penalty date	further 5%

Penalty dates

The penalty date varies according to the type of payment. For payments such as Class 1A and Class 1B NICs, HMRC determinations, assessments and amendments, or corrections to returns the 'penalty date' is 30 days after the due date. In most other cases, the penalty date is the day after the due date.

4-948 Interest on certain PAYE paid late

(FA 2009, s. 101 and 102)

(Tax Reporter: ¶494-900; ¶494-910)

HMRC charge in-year, rather than annual, interest on all unpaid:

- PAYE tax, Class 1 National Insurance contributions (NICs) and student loan deductions, including specified charges (estimates HMRC make in the absence of a PAYE submission);
- Construction Industry Scheme charges;
- In-year late filing penalties; and
- In-year late payment penalties.

Interest will also be charged on underpayments that arise because of adjustments reported on Earlier Year Updates submitted.

For annual payments such as Class 1A and Class 1B NICs, HMRC will continue to charge interest on any amount which remains unpaid after the due date.

Interest is charged daily, from the date a payment is due and payable to the date it is paid in full.

Repayment interest will apply where a payment is made and the charge is then reduced resulting in an overpayment which is either reallocated to a later charge or repaid.

4-962 PAYE electronic communications penalty: form P45 (Part 1 or Part 3), P46 or P46(Pen)

(SI 2003/2682, reg. 210BA)

(Tax Reporter: ¶498-745;

2013–14 and subsequent years Table 9AA	
Number of items	**Penalty**
1–49	£100
50–149	£300
150–299	£600
300–399	£900
400–499	£1,200
500–599	£1,500
600–699	£1,800
700–799	£2,100
800–899	£2,400
900–999	£2,700
1,000+	£3,000

Note

[(1)] Number of items of specified information the employer has failed to deliver in the tax year. (Each item mentioned in reg. 207(1), para. (a)–(d) counts as a separate item of specified information.) An item of specified information counts even if it relates to the same employee as one or more other items.

4-965 PAYE electronic communications penalty: forms P35 and P14

(SI 2003/2682, reg. 210AA,)

(Tax Reporter: ¶498-745)

2010–11 and subsequent years Table 9ZA	
Number of employees	**Penalty**
1–5	£100
6–49	£300
50–249	£600
250–399	£900
400–499	£1,200
500–599	£1,500
600–699	£1,800
700–799	£2,100
800–899	£2,400
900–999	£2,700
1,000+	£3,000

Note

[(1)] Number of employees for whom particulars should have been included with the specified information.

4-975 PAYE monthly accounting periods

(SI 2003/2682, reg. 69)

(Tax Reporter: ¶494-510)

Period	Month no.	Payment due (electronic)	Payment due (other)
6 Apr to 5 May	1	22 May	19 May
6 May to 5 June	2	22 June	19 June
6 June to 5 July	3	22 July	19 July
6 July to 5 Aug	4	22 August	19 August
6 Aug to 5 Sept	5	22 September	19 September

Period	Month no.	Payment due (electronic)	Payment due (other)
6 Sept to 5 Oct	6	22 October	19 October
6 Oct to 5 Nov	7	22 November	19 November
6 Nov to 5 Dec	8	22 December	19 December
6 Dec to 5 Jan	9	22 January	19 January
6 Jan to 5 Feb	10	22 February	19 February
6 Feb to 5 Mar	11	22 March	19 March
6 Mar to 5 Apr	12	22 April	19 April

4-976 PAYE quarterly accounting periods

(SI 2003/2682, reg. 70)

(Tax Reporter: ¶494-570)

Period	Month no.	Payment due (electronic)	Payment due (other)
6 Apr to 5 July	1–3	22 July	19 July
6 July to 5 Oct	4–6	22 October	19 October
6 Oct to 5 Jan	7–9	22 January	19 January
6 Jan to 5 Apr	10–12	22 April	19 April

4-980 Payroll giving scheme

(ITEPA 2003, s. 713)

(Tax Reporter: ¶457-500)

Employees whose remuneration is subject to deduction of tax at source under PAYE can make unlimited tax-deductible donations to charity by requesting that their employers deduct the donations from their pay.

4-985 Student loan deductions

(SI 2009/470, reg. 29; SI 2016/606)

There are now three categories of student loans: Plan 1 loans (pre-2012 loans); Plan 2 loans (post-2012 loans) and Postgraduate Master's Degree loans. Each type of loan carries different repayment terms although all repayment provisions, in respect of both student loans and postgraduate master's degree loans in England and Wales, are now consolidated in the 2009 Regulations (SI 2017/831).

Postgraduate Master's Degree Loans[1]

Year	Percentage	Threshold [2]
From 6 April 2019	6%	£25,000

Notes

[1] Postgraduate Master's Degree loans are available to eligible students for postgraduate master's degree courses which begin on or after 01 August 2016. No repayment of a postgraduate master's degree loan is required until on or after 6 April 2019.

[2] Postgraduate Master's Degree Loans repayment threshold aligned with post-2012 repayment threshold by SI 2017/831, reg. 20(6), with effect from 5 September 2017.

Plan 2 (post-2012[1]) student loans

Year	Percentage	Threshold[2]
2018–19(2)	9%	£25,000
2017–18	9%	£21,000
2016–17	9%	£21,000

Notes

[1] Plan 2 loans are loans taken out by new students starting courses on or after 1 September 2012 (and as defined by SI 2009/470, reg. 3(2)). Repayment of post-2012 loans commenced from 6 April 2016.

[2] Rates announced by Department for Education in October 2017.

Plan 1 (pre-2012) student loans

Year	Percentage	Threshold[1]
2018–19(2)	9%	£18,330
2017–18	9%	£17,775
2016–17	9%	£17,495
2015–16	9%	£17,335
2014–15	9%	£16,910
2013–14	9%	£16,365
2012–13	9%	£15,795
2011–12	9%	£15,000

Notes

[1] Repayment threshold uprated by RPI for tax years ending after 6 April 2012 (SI 2009/470, reg. 29(7)).

[2] Rates announced by Department for Education in October 2017.

4-990 Apprenticeship levy

(FA 2016, Pt. 6)

Apprenticeship levy is charged where:

- a person has a pay bill for a tax year (beginning with 6 April 2017 or any subsequent year); and
- the relevant percentage of the pay bill exceeds the person's levy allowance (if any) for that tax year.

Amount of charge

The amount of the charge is equal to–

N – A

where–

N is the relevant percentage of the pay bill for the tax year; and

A is the amount of the levy allowance (if any) to which the person is entitled for the tax year.

From	Levy allowance[1] £	Relevant percentage %	Pay bill threshold[2] £
6 April 2017	15,000	0.5	3,000,000

Notes

[1] Two or more companies which form a 'company unit' share a single levy allowance.

[2] Paybill threshold is calculated as the amount by which the employer's pay bill must exceed in order for a positive charge to arise after deducting the levy allowance (i.e. equals the levy allowance divided by the relevant percentage).

4-992 Apprenticeship levy: monthly cumulative levy allowance

(SI 2003/2682, reg. 147E)

(Tax Reporter: 495-943)

The table below may be used for the purposes of calculating the apprenticeship levy charge for the relevant month (based on the cumulative amount of the monthly pay bill, multiplied by 0.5%, minus the monthly cumulative levy allowance).

Relevant month in the tax year	Penalty percentage
Month 1	£1,250
Month 2	£2,500
Month 3	£3,750
Month 4	£5,000
Month 5	£6,250
Month 6	£7,500
Month 7	£8,750
Month 8	£10,000

Relevant month in the tax year	Penalty percentage
Month 9	£11,250
Month 10	£12,500
Month 11	£13,750
Month 12	£15,000

Capital allowances

8-000 Plant and machinery: overview of allowances

(CAA 2001)

(Tax Reporter: ¶235-000ff.)

Plant and machinery allowances are normally given by way of:

- annual investment allowances: see ¶8-100;
- first-year allowances: see ¶8-200; or
- writing-down allowances: see ¶8-300.

In specified circumstances, balancing allowances may be due or balancing charges may be made.

8-100 Plant and machinery: annual investment allowances

(CAA 2001, s. 51A)

(Tax Reporter: ¶236-400ff.)

	Maximum (£)
1 January 2016	200,000
1/6 April 2014 to 31 December 2015	500,000[(1)]
1 January 2013 to 31 March/5 April 2014	250,000[(1)]
1/6 April 2012 to 31 December 2012	25,000
1/6 April 2010 to 31 March/5 April 2012	100,000

Note

[(1)] Temporary increase in the annual invesment allowance initially for the period of two years beginning with 1 January 2013 (FA 2013, s. 7 and Sch. 1) was extended to 31 December 2015 (and increased to £500,000) by FA 2014, s. 10 and Sch. 2.

This figure is adjusted pro rata for chargeable periods shorter or longer than one year.

Where a chargeable period spans the above dates of change (i.e. 1/6 April 2014, or 1 January 2016), the maximum AIA is calculated by splitting the chargeable period into separate periods falling before and after each of the dates of change. Transitional rules are then applied to determine the maximum AIA available in respect of the total chargeable period and the maximum AIA that may be allocated against qualifying expenditure incurred in each of the separate periods (FA 2014, Sch. 2; FA 2013, Sch. 1; FA 2011, s. 11).

Groups of companies, companies and qualifying activities carried on by individuals or partnerships, under common control which share premises and carry on similar activities are entitled to a single annual investment allowance only.

8-200 Plant and machinery: 100% first-year allowances

(CAA 2001, s. 52)

(Tax Reporter: ¶237-000ff.)

Subject to the general exclusions listed at ¶8-210, full 100% allowances are available for the following types of expenditure incurred by a business of any size. If full FYAs are not claimed, WDA is normally available on a reducing balance basis (see ¶8-300).

Nature of expenditure	**Authority (CAA 2001)**	**Notes**
Energy-saving plant or machinery	s. 45A–45C; Sch. A1	Loss-making companies may claim tax rebate until 31 March 2018[(1)].
Cars with low CO_2 emissions	s. 45D	On expenditure incurred until 31 March 2021. See also ¶8-500.
Zero-emission goods vehicles	s. 45DA	On expenditure incurred before 1 April 2018 (corporation tax) or 6 April 2018 (income tax).
Plant or machinery for certain refuelling stations	s. 45E	Expenditure incurred until 31 March 2018 (for both corporation tax and income tax).

Nature of expenditure	Authority (CAA 2001)	Notes
Plant or machinery for electric vehicle charging point	s. 45EA	On expenditure incurred from 23 November 2016 until 31 March 2019 (corporation tax) or 5 April 2019 (income tax).
Plant or machinery (other than a long life asset) for use by a company wholly in a ring fence trade	s. 45F	
Environmentally beneficial plant or machinery	s. 45H–45J	Loss-making companies may claim tax rebate until 31 March 2018(1)
Expenditure on plant and machinery for use in designated assisted areas	s. 45K	Initially due to end on 31 March 2017 but extended to 31 March 2020.

Notes

(1) First-year tax credits, for companies surrendering losses attributable to their expenditure on designated energy-saving or environmentally beneficial plant or machinery has been extended for a further five years until 31 March 2018 (SI 2013/464).

First-year allowance for cars with low carbon dioxide emissions extended for a further three year period ending on 31 March 2021 by SI 2016/984, art. 4(a) (and qualifying emissions threshold for the first-year allowance reduced from 75 grams to 50 grams per kilometre driven, in relation to expenditure incurred on or after 1st April 2018).

8-210 Plant and machinery: first-year allowances – general exclusions

(CAA 2001, s. 46(2))

(Tax Reporter: ¶237-150)

No first-year allowances are available for:

- expenditure incurred in the final chargeable period;
- cars (other than those with very low CO_2 emissions);
- items excluded from the long-life asset treatment only by virtue of the transitional provisions in CAA 2001, Sch. 3, para. 20;
- plant or machinery for leasing;
- in certain anti-avoidance cases where the obtaining of a FYA is linked to a change in the nature or conduct of a trade;
- where an asset was initially acquired for purposes other than those of the qualifying activity;

- where an asset was acquired by way of a gift; and
- where plant or machinery that was provided for long funding leasing starts to be used for other purposes.

8-300 Plant and machinery: writing-down allowances

(CAA 2001, s. 56)

(Tax Reporter: ¶238-050ff.)

	Standard rate (%)	Special rate (%)
From April 2012	18	8
April 2008 to April 2012	20	10

Note

Different rules apply for certain cars (see ¶8-500).

WDA for small pools

Main pool or special rate pool only where tax written down value brought forward plus expenditure added to the pool during the period minus disposal receipts deducted from the pool during the period totals less than or equal to £1,000 (apportioned for periods of more or less than one year), an allowance may be claimed for the former amount in place of the standard rates above (CAA 2001, s. 56A).

Pooling

Expenditure is allocated to the main pool unless it is allocated to either a single asset pool or single class pool. Single asset and single class pools are as follows:

Single asset pools

- short life asset (CAA 2001, s. 86);
- ship (CAA 2001, s. 127);
- assets with partial non-qualifying use (CAA 2001, s. 206);
- expenditure in relation to which a partial depreciation subsidy is received (CAA 2001, s. 211); and
- contribution allowances: plant and machinery (CAA 2001, s. 538).

Single class pools

- special rate expenditure (see below) (CAA 2001, s. 104A); and
- overseas leasing (CAA 2001, s. 107).

Special rate expenditure

Expenditure	Incurred on or after	Provision
Thermal insulation of buildings	1 April 2008 (corporation tax) or 6 April 2008 (income tax)	CAA 2001, s. 28
Integral features	1 April 2008 (corporation tax) or 6 April 2008 (income tax)	CAA 2001, s. 33A
Long life asset expenditure	26 November 1996, or 1 January 2001 in pursuance of a contract entered into before 26 November 1996 or incurred before 26 November 1996 but allocated to a pool in a chargeable period beginning on or after that date	CAA 2001, Ch. 10
Cars (excluding main rate cars (first registered before 1 March 2001, cars with low CO_2 emissions, electrically-propelled cars))	1 April 2009 (corporation tax) or 6 April 2009 (income tax)	CAA 2001, s. 104AA
Provision of cushion gas	1 April 2010	CAA 2001, s. 70J(7)
Solar panels	1 April 2012 (corporation tax) or 6 April 2012 (income tax)	CAA 2001, s. 104A(1)(g)

8-400 Plant and machinery: integral features

(CAA 2001, s. 33A)

(Tax Reporter: ¶243-400ff.)

The following assets are designated as integral features:

- electrical systems (including lighting systems);
- cold water systems;
- space or water heating systems, powered systems of ventilation, air cooling or air purification, and any floor or ceiling comprised in such systems;
- lifts, escalators and moving walkways; and
- external solar shading.

8-410 Plant and machinery: expenditure unaffected by statutory restrictions re buildings

(CAA 2001, s. 23)

(Tax Reporter: ¶245-550)

The restrictions in CAA 2001, s. 21 and 22 (buildings, structures and other assets) do not apply to the following categories of expenditure:

- thermal insulation of buildings (CAA 2001, s. 28);
- personal security (CAA 2001, s. 33);
- integral features (CAA 2001, s. 33A); and
- software and rights to software (CAA 2001, s. 71).

Note

Before 1 April 2013, expenditure on safety at designated sports grounds, safety at regulated stands at sports grounds and safety at other sports grounds was also included in the list of exclusions.

The restrictions in CAA 2001, s. 21 and 22 (buildings, structures and other assets) also do not apply to expenditure in List C at CAA 2001, s. 23. List C, as amended, is as follows:

(1) machinery (including devices for providing motive power) not within any other item in this list;

(2) gas and sewerage systems provided mainly:

(a) to meet the particular requirements of the qualifying activity;

(b) to serve particular plant or machinery used for the purposes of the qualifying activity;

(3) [omitted by *Finance Act* 2008];

(4) manufacturing or processing equipment; storage equipment (including cold rooms); display equipment; and counters, checkouts and similar equipment;

(5) cookers, washing machines, dishwashers, refrigerators and similar equipment; washbasins, sinks, baths, showers, sanitary ware and similar equipment; and furniture and furnishings;

(6) hoists;

(7) sound insulation provided mainly to meet the particular requirements of the qualifying activity;

(8) computer, telecommunication and surveillance systems (including their wiring or other links);

(9) refrigeration or cooling equipment;

(10) fire alarm systems, sprinkler and other equipment for extinguishing or containing fires;

(11) burglar alarm systems;

(12) strong rooms in bank or building society premises, safes;

(13) partition walls, where moveable and intended to be moved in the course of the qualifying activity;

(14) decorative assets provided for the enjoyment of the public in hotel, restaurant or similar trades;

(15) advertising hoardings, signs, displays and similar assets;

(16) swimming-pools (including diving boards, slides and structures on which such boards or slides are mounted);

(17) any glasshouse constructed so that the required environment (namely, air, heat, light, irrigation and temperature) for the growing of plants is provided automatically by means of devices forming an integral part of its structure;

(18) cold stores;

(19) caravans provided mainly for holiday lettings;

(20) buildings provided for testing aircraft engines run within the buildings;

(21) moveable buildings intended to be moved in the course of the qualifying activity;

(22) the alteration of land for the purpose only of installing plant or machinery;

(23) the provision of dry docks;

(24) the provision of any jetty or similar structure provided mainly to carry plant or machinery;

(25) the provision of pipelines or underground ducts or tunnels with a primary purpose of carrying utility conduits;

(26) the provision of towers to support floodlights;

(27) the provision of:

   (a) any reservoir incorporated into a water treatment works; or

   (b) any service reservoir of treated water for supply within any housing estate or other particular locality;

(28) the provision of:

   (a) silos provided for temporary storage; or

   (b) storage tanks;

(29) the provision of slurry pits or silage clamps;

(30) the provision of fish tanks or fish ponds;

(31) the provision of rails, sleepers and ballast for a railway or tramway;

(32) the provision of structures and other assets for providing the setting for any ride at an amusement park or exhibition;

(33) the provision of fixed zoo cages.

Items (1)–(16) of the above list do not, however, include any asset with the principal purpose of insulating or enclosing the interior of a building or of providing an interior wall, floor or ceiling that is intended to remain permanently in place (CAA 2001, s. 33A).

8-420 Assets treated as buildings

(CAA 2001, s. 21)

(Tax Reporter: ¶245-550)

Plant and machinery allowances are not available on expenditure on the provision of a building, including its construction or acquisition. Building includes:

- an asset incorporated in the building;
- although not incorporated in the building (whether because the asset is moveable or for any other reason), is in the building and is of a kind normally incorporated in a building; or
- is in, or connected with the building and is in list A as follows:
  - walls, floors, ceilings, doors, gates, shutters, windows and stairs;
  - mains services, and systems, for water, electricity and gas;
  - waste disposal systems;
  - sewerage and drainage systems;
  - shafts or other structures in which lifts, hoists, escalators and moving walkways are installed;
  - fire safety systems.

8-430 Excluded structures and other assets

(CAA 2001, s. 22)

Plant and machinery does not include expenditure on the provision of a structure or other asset within list B, or any works involving the alteration of land. List B is as follows:

(1) a tunnel, bridge, viaduct, aqueduct, embankment or cutting;

(2) a way, hard standing (such as a pavement), road, railway, tramway, a park for vehicles or containers, or an airstrip or runway;

(3) an inland navigation, including a canal or basin or a navigable river;

(4) a dam, reservoir or barrage, including any sluices, gates, generators and other equipment associated with the dam, reservoir or barrage;

(5) a dock, harbour, wharf, pier, marina or jetty or any other structure in or at which vessels may be kept, or merchandise or passengers may be shipped or unshipped;

(6) a dike, sea wall, weir or drainage ditch;

(7) any structure not within items (1)–(6) other than:

   (a) a structure (but not a building) within the meaning of 'industrial building';

   (b) a structure in use for the purposes of an undertaking for the extraction, production, processing or distribution of gas; and

   (c) a structure in use for the purposes of a trade which consists in the provision of telecommunication, television or radio services.

Note

Structure means a fixed structure of any kind, other than a building (as defined by s. 21(3) (see ¶8-420 above)). Land does not include buildings or other structures.

8-450 Fixtures

(CAA 2001, s. 187A)

From April 2012, purchasers of buildings which include fixtures on which capital allowances have previously been claimed will only be able to claim capital allowances on the fixtures if either:

(1) the fixed value requirement is met whereby the value of the fixtures transferred is agreed within two years of the transfer either:
   - between the seller and purchaser by joint election under CAA 2001, s. 198–199; or
   - by determination of the First-tier Tribunal; or

(2) the purchaser obtains a written statement from the seller that the fixed value requirement has not been met and is no longer capable of being met and the purchaser obtains from a past owner a written statement of the disposal value brought into account by that owner (this will apply in cases where the seller is an intermediate owner or lessee not entitled to claim allowances but who acquired the fixtures from a past owner who was entitled to claim allowances).

From April 2014, it will also be necessary to show that historic expenditure has been pooled, or that the past owner claimed a first year allowance on the expenditure (or any part of it) before a subsequent transfer to another person.

8-500 Plant and machinery: allowances for cars

(CAA 2001, s. 104A and 104AA)

(Tax Reporter: ¶238-500ff.)

	CO_2 emissions			
	2018–19 to 2020–21	**2015–16 to 2017–18**	**2013–14 & 2014–15**	**2012–13 (from 2009–10)**
100% FYAs (CAA 2001, s. 45D) (see also ¶8-200)	50g/km or less	75g/km or less	95g/km or less	110g/km or less
Main rate pool (18%)	Over 50g/km up to 110g/km	Over 75g/km up to 130g/km	Over 95g/km up to 130g/km	Over 110g/km up to 160g/km
Special rate pool (8%)	Over 110g/km	Over 130g/km	Over 130g/km	Over 160g/km

Cars with private use go to a single asset pool but still with WDA as above, but then adjusted for private use percentage.

8-550 Enterprise zones: 100% capital allowances

(CAA 2001, s. 45K–45N)

(Tax Reporter: ¶237-610)

First year allowances (at 100%) are available in respect of expenditure incurred by companies (not unincorporated businesses) on new and unsued plant and machinery for use primarily in designated assisted areas in enterprise zones. The allowances are available for expenditure incurred during the period of eight years beginning with the date on which the area is (or is treated as) designated by Treasury Order(1). Expenditure must be incurred for the purposes of a new or expanding business carried on by the company, must not be replacement expenditure and is limited to €125m per single investment project (as defined) (CAA 2001, s. 45K–45N). A full list of current zones and designated assisted areas is available at:

- http://enterprisezones.communities.gov.uk (see also maps at www.gov.uk/government/publications/enterprise-zones);
- http://business.wales.gov.uk/enterprisezones/enhanced-capital-allowances;
- www.scotland.gov.uk/Topics/Economy/EconomicStrategy/Enterprise-Areas/Incentives/Capital-Allowances.

Note

(1) The period of availability was originally introduced as five years beginnning with 1 April 2012 (FA 2012, s. 44 and Sch. 11, para. 3), extended to eight years from the same date by FA 2014, s. 64(5)(a) and has been further extended to eight years from the date of designation by FA 2016, s. 69.

8-650 Enterprise zones: industrial buildings, hotels, commercial buildings or structures

(Former CAA 2001, s. 271ff.; FA 2008, Sch. 27, para. 31)

(Tax Reporter: ¶250-950ff.)

No IBAs are given for any chargeable period beginning after 1 or 6 April 2011. For enterprise zone expenditure only, a balancing charge can still be incurred up to 5 April 2018.

8-800 Other allowances

Allowance	Date expenditure incurred (from)	Initial allowance (%)	WDA (%)	CAA 2001	Tax Reporter
[Business premises renovation[3]*]*	[11 April 2007 (to 31 March or 5 April 2017)]	[100]	[25]	[s. 360A]	¶252-500
[*Flat conversion*[1]]	[*11 May 2001 (to 31 March or 5 April 2013)*]	[*100*]	[*25*]	[former s. 393A]	¶254-000
Mineral extraction[4]	1 April 1986	—	25	s. 394	¶255-500
Research and development	6 November 1962	100	—	s. 437	¶256-000
Know-how[2]	1 April 1986	—	25	s. 452	¶257-000
Patents[2]	1 April 1986	—	25	s. 464	¶257-500
Dredging	6 November 1962	—	4	s. 484	¶258-000
Assured tenancy	10 March 1982 (to 31 March 1992)	—	4	s. 490	¶258-500

Notes

(1) Flat conversion allowances were abolished in respect of expenditure incurred on or after 1 April 2013 for corporation tax purposes and 6 April 2013 for income tax purposes (FA 2012, s. 227 and Sch. 39, para. 36 and 37). The entitlement to claim writing-down allowances on any residual expenditure is also withdrawn from that date.

(2) Capital allowances for know-how and patents still apply for income tax but were replaced for most corporation tax purposes by the intangible assets regime with effect from 1 April 2002.

(3) BPRA expired on 1 April 2017 (corporation tax) and 6 April 2017 (income tax), with effect in relation to expenditure incurred on or after those dates.

8-950 Time limits for elections and claims

(CAA 2001, s. 3; TMA 1970, s. 43; FA 1998, Sch. 18, para. 54–60)

(Tax Reporter: ¶235-050)

Capital allowances must be claimed in a tax return. However, the rules for claims outside a return for income tax (TMA 1970, s. 42) and corporation tax (FA 1998, Sch. 18, para. 54–60) apply in certain instances:

- special leasing plant and machinery allowance claims; and
- claims for patent allowances on non-trading expenditure (in income tax cases).

Provision	Time limit	Statutory reference
General claim to capital allowances under corporation tax self-assessment	Claims to capital allowances must be made (or amended or withdrawn) by the later of: (1) 12 months after the claimant company's filing date for the return for the accounting period covered by the claim; (2) 30 days after a closure notice is issued on the completion of an enquiry; (3) 30 days after HMRC issue a notice of amendment to a return following the completion of an enquiry (issued where the company fails to amend the return itself); or (4) 30 days after the determination of any appeal against an HMRC amendment (as in (3) above).	FA 1998, Sch. 18, para. 82

Provision	Time limit	Statutory reference
	'Enquiry' in the above does not include a restricted enquiry into an amendment to a return (restricted because the time limit for making an enquiry into the return itself has expired), where the amendment consists of making, amending or withdrawing a claim for capital allowances. These time limits have priority over any other general time limits for amending returns to the extent that an amendment makes, amends or withdraws a claim for capital allowances. A claim for capital allowances may be made, amended or withdrawn at a later time if an officer of HMRC allows it.	
Certain plant and machinery treated as 'short life' assets (income tax elections)	12 months from 31 January next following the tax year in which ends the chargeable period in which the qualifying expenditure was incurred	CAA 2001, s. 85
Certain plant and machinery treated as 'short life' assets (corporation tax elections)	Two years from end of the chargeable period in which the qualifying expenditure was incurred	CAA 2001, s. 85
Set-off of capital allowances on special leasing (corporation tax)	Two years from end of accounting period	CAA 2001, s. 260(3), (6)
Business successions: election between connected parties to transfer plant and machinery at tax written down value	Two years from date on which succession takes effect	CAA 2001, s. 266(4)

Provision	Time limit	Statutory reference
Transfer between connected parties of certain assets treated as being at market value; election for sale to be treated as being for an alternative amount value	Two years from date of sale	CAA 2001, s. 570(5)
Purchase of interest in land that includes a fixture – election to fix apportionment of disposal proceeds	Two years from the date of purchase	CAA 2001, s. 198, 201
Lease of interest in land that includes a fixture – election to fix apportionment of disposal proceeds	Two years from the date the lease is granted	CAA 2001, s. 199, 201

National Insurance contributions

9-000 NIC rates: general

(NIC Reporter: ¶305-000ff.)

There are six classes of National Insurance contributions (NICs) payable according to the individual circumstances of the payer.

Class 1 contributions

Class 1 contributions are earnings-related and payable by employer and employee on earnings above the earnings thresholds. The primary threshold (PT) applies for employees and the secondary threshold (ST) for employers. Employees pay at the main rate up to the upper earnings limit (UEL) and the additional rate above the limit.

The *Pensions Act* 2014 abolished the contracting-out for salary-related occupational pensions schemes (from 6 April 2016) and introduced a new single-component state pension to replace the existing state pension comprising basic state pension and additional state pension (from 6 April 2016).

Contracting out for money purchase schemes (COMPS), mixed benefit schemes (COMB) contracted-out on a defined contribution basis, appropriate personal pension schemes (APP) and APP stakeholder schemes was abolished on 5 April 2012.

The reduced rate applies to married women or widows with a valid certificate of election and affects only primary contributions.

Individuals over state pension age pay no primary contributions, though employers still pay the secondary contribution regardless of the previous category of contribution liability. Children under 16 and their employers pay no contributions.

Employer NIC for the under 21s and apprentices under 25

(SSCBA 1992, s. 9A and 9B)

From 6 April 2015, employers with employees under the age of 21 are no longer required to pay Class 1 secondary NICs on earnings up to the upper earning limit (UEL), for those employees.

From 6 April 2016, employers of apprentices under the age of 25 are no longer required to pay secondary Class 1 (employer) NICs on earnings up to the UEL, for those employees.

9-005 National Insurance rate ceilings

(NIC(RC)A 2015)

(NIC Reporter: ¶305-600)

The *National Insurance Contributions (Rate Ceilings) Act* 2015 sets a ceiling on the main and additional primary percentages, the secondary percentage and the upper earnings limit in relation to Class 1 NICs. The Act came into force on 17 December 2015, with effect for a tax years beginning after that date but before the date of the first Parliamentary general election after that day (i.e. from 2016–17 until the tax year starting before the next general election thereafter). The Act prescribes the following limits:

Contribution/limit	Ceiling
Class 1 main primary percentage	12%
Class 1 additional primary percentage	2%
Class 1 secondary percentage	13.8%
Upper earnings limit	HRT[(1)] / 52

Note

(1) HRT is the proposed higher rate threshold for the tax year calculated as the sum of the basic rate limit for income tax for the tax year as proposed in the pre-budget proposals for that year, and the personal allowance for income tax for the tax year as so proposed.

9-010 Class 1 NIC: 2017–18

(SSCBA 1992; NICA 2014, s. 1, 8–9; SI 2001/1004, reg. 10–11 and 131)

(NIC Reporter: ¶305-575ff.)

Class 1 contributions

Class 1 primary (employee) contributions 2017–18	
Lower earnings limit (LEL)[(4)]	£113 weekly £490[(2)] monthly £5,876[(2)] yearly
Primary threshold (PT)[(4)]	£157 weekly £680[(3)] monthly £8,164[(3)] yearly
Upper earnings limit (UEL)	£866 weekly £3,750[(3)] monthly £45,000[(3)] yearly
Rate on earnings up to PT[(1)]	0%
Rate	12% on £157.01 to £866 weekly 2% on excess over £866 weekly
Reduced rate	5.85% on £157.01 to £866 weekly 2% on excess over £866

Notes

(1) No National Insurance contributions (NICs) are actually payable but a notional Class 1 NIC is deemed to have been paid in respect of earnings between the LEL and PT to protect contributory benefit entitlement.

(2) Monthly and annual LEL and UAP figures are calculated as per SI 2001/1004, reg. 11.

(3) Monthly and annual PT and UEL figures are prescribed by SI 2001/1004, reg. 11 and amended by Statutory Instrument.

(4) These thresholds are uprated by CPI.

Class 1 secondary (employer) contributions 2017–18	
Secondary earnings threshold (ST)[4]	£157 weekly £680[1] monthly £8,164[1] yearly
Upper secondary threshold (UST) for under 21s[2]	£866 weekly £3,750[1] monthly £45,000[1] yearly
Apprentice upper secondary threshold (AUST) for under 25s[3]	£866 weekly £3,750[1] monthly £45,000[1] yearly
Rate	13.8% on earnings above ST/UST[2]/ AUST[3]
Employment allowance[5]	£3,000 per year, per employer

Notes

[1] Monthly and annual ST, UST and AUST figures are prescribed by SI 2001/1004, reg. 11 and amended by Statutory Instrument.

[2] Upper secondary threshold (UST) introduced from April 2015 for employees under the age of 21. The rate of secondary NICs for employees under the age of 21 on earnings between the ST and UST is 0%.

[3] Apprentice upper secondary threshold (AUST) introduced from April 2016. The rate of secondary NICs for employees under the age of 25 on earnings between the ST and AUST is 0%.

[4] The weekly secondary threshold is uprated by CPI.

[5] From 6 April 2016, companies where the director is the sole employee are longer be able to claim the allowance (NICA 2014, s. 2(4A)).

9-015 Class 1 NIC: 2016–17

(SSCBA 1992, NICA 2014, s. 1, 8–9; SI 2001/1004, reg. 10–11 and 131)

(NIC Reporter: ¶305-575ff.)

Class 1 contributions

Class 1 primary (employee) contributions 2016–17	
Lower earnings limit (LEL)[4]	£112 weekly £486[2] monthly £5,824[2] yearly
Primary threshold (PT)[4]	£155 weekly £672[3] monthly £8,060[3] yearly

Class 1 primary (employee) contributions 2016–17	
Upper earnings limit (UEL)	£827 weekly £3,583[3] monthly £43,000[3] yearly
Rate on earnings up to PT[1]	0%
Rate	12% on £155.01 to £827 weekly 2% on excess over £827 weekly
Reduced rate	5.85% on £155.01 to £827 weekly 2% on excess over £827 weekly

Notes

(1) No National Insurance contributions (NICs) are actually payable but a notional Class 1 NIC is deemed to have been paid in respect of earnings between the LEL and PT to protect contributory benefit entitlement.

(2) Monthly and annual LEL and UAP figures are calculated as per SI 2001/1004, reg. 11.

(3) Monthly and annual PT and UEL figures are prescribed by SI 2001/1004, reg. 11 and amended by Statutory Instrument.

(4) These thresholds are uprated by CPI.

Class 1 secondary (employer) contributions 2016–17	
Secondary earnings threshold (ST)[4]	£156 weekly £676[1] monthly £8,112[1] yearly
Upper secondary threshold (UST) for under 21s[2]	£827 weekly £3,583[1] monthly £43,000[1] yearly
Apprentice upper secondary threshold (AUST) for under 25s[3]	£827 weekly £3,583[1] monthly £43,000[1] yearly
Rate	13.8% on earnings above ST/UST[2]/ AUST[3]
Employment allowance[5]	£3,000 per year, per employer

Notes

(1) Monthly and annual ST, UST and AUST figures are prescribed by SI 2001/1004, reg. 11 and amended by Statutory Instrument.

(2) Upper secondary threshold (UST) introduced from April 2015 for employees under the age of 21. The rate of secondary NICs for employees under the age of 21 on earnings between the ST and UST is 0%.

(3) Apprentice upper secondary threshold (AUST) introduced from April 2016. The rate of secondary NICs for apprentices under the age of 25 on earnings between the ST and AUST is 0%.

(4) The weekly secondary threshold is uprated by CPI.

(5) From 6 April 2016, companies where the director is the sole employee are no longer able to claim the allowance (NICA 2014, s. 2(4A)).

9-020 Class 1 NIC: 2015–16

(NIC Reporter: ¶305-575ff.)

Class 1 contributions

Class 1 primary (employee) contributions 2015–16	
Lower earnings limit (LEL)[4]	£112 weekly £486[2] monthly £5,824[2] yearly
Primary threshold (PT)[4]	£155 weekly £672[3] monthly £8,060[3] yearly
Upper earnings limit (UEL)	£815 weekly £3,532[3] monthly £42,385[3] yearly
Upper accruals point (UAP)	£770 weekly £3,337[2] monthly £40,040[2] yearly
Rate on earnings up to PT[1]	0%
Not contracted-out rate	12% on £155.01 to £815 weekly 2% on excess over £815 weekly
Contracted-out rate	10.6% on £155.01 to £770 weekly 12% on £770.01 to £815 weekly 2% on excess over £815 weekly
Reduced rate	5.85% on £155.01 to £815 weekly 2% on excess over £815 (no rebate even if contracted out)

Notes

[1] Earnings from the LEL, up to and including the PT, count towards the employee's basic state pension, even though no contributions are paid on those earnings. Similarly, earnings between the LEL and the PT count towards the employee's entitlement to certain benefits including the second state pension (S2P). Employees in contracted-out employment earn no S2P rights and receive a rebate of contributions of 1.4%. This applies from the LEL to the UAP, so earnings from LEL to PT attract a 'negative' contribution of 1.4% and the rate for earnings from PT to UAP becomes 10.6%. Earnings from UAP to UEL are subject to the main not contracted-out rate.

[2] Monthly and annual LEL and UAP figures are calculated as per SI 2001/1004, reg. 11.

[3] Monthly and annual PT and UEL figures are prescribed by SI 2001/1004, reg. 11 and amended by Statutory Instrument.

[4] These thresholds are uprated by CPI.

Class 1 secondary (employer) contributions 2015–16	
Secondary earnings threshold (ST)[4]	£156 weekly £676[2] monthly £8,112[2] yearly
Upper secondary threshold (UST) for under 21s[3]	£815 weekly £3,532 monthly £42,385 yearly
Not contracted-out rate	13.8% on earnings above ST
Contracted-out rate[1]	10.4% for salary related (COSR) on earnings from ST to UAP (plus 3.4% rebate for earnings from LEL to ST), then 13.8% above UAP
Employment allowance[5]	£2,000 per year, per employer

Notes

(1) Although employer contributions do not per se give any benefit entitlements, earnings between the LEL and ST are those classed as relevant for S2P. Employers with contracted-out occupational pension schemes receive a rebate of contributions for scheme members of 3.4% (COSR). This applies from the LEL to the UAP, so earnings from LEL to ST attract a 'negative' contribution and the rate for earnings from ST to UAP is reduced as shown.

(2) Monthly and annual ST figures are prescribed by SI 2001/1004, reg. 11 and amended by Statutory Instrument.

(3) Upper secondary threshold (UST) introduced from April 2015 for employees under the age of 21. The rate of secondary NICs for employees under the age of 21 on earnings between the ST and UST will be 0%.

(4) The weekly secondary threshold is uprated by RPI.

(5) From 6 April 2015, the allowance is extended to care and support workers (NICA 2014, s. 2(3A)).

9-025 Class 1 NIC: 2014–15

(NIC Reporter: ¶305-575ff.)

Class 1 contributions

Class 1 primary (employee) contributions 2014–15	
Lower earnings limit (LEL)	£111 weekly £481[2] monthly £5,772[2] yearly
Primary threshold (PT)	£153 weekly £663[3] monthly £7,956[3] yearly
Upper earnings limit (UEL)	£805 weekly £3,489[3] monthly £41,865[3] yearly
Upper accruals point (UAP)	£770 weekly £3,337[2] monthly £40,040[2] yearly

Class 1 primary (employee) contributions 2014–15	
Rate on earnings up to PT(1)	0%
Not contracted-out rate	12% on £153.01 to £805 weekly 2% on excess over £805 weekly
Contracted-out rate	10.6% on £153.01 to £770 weekly 12% on £770.01 to £805 weekly 2% on excess over £805 weekly
Reduced rate	5.85% on £153.01 to £805 weekly 2% on excess over £805 (no rebate even if contracted-out)

Notes

(1) Earnings from the LEL, up to and including the PT, count towards the employee's basic state pension, even though no contributions are paid on those earnings. Similarly, earnings between the LEL and the PT count towards the employee's entitlement to certain benefits including the second state pension (S2P). Employees in contracted-out

employment earn no S2P rights and receive a rebate of contributions of 1.4%. This applies from the LEL to the

UAP, so earnings from LEL to PT attract a 'negative' contribution of 1.4% and the rate for earnings from PT to

UAP becomes 10.6%. Earnings from UAP to UEL are subject to the main not contracted-out rate.

(2) Monthly and annual LEL and UAP figures are calculated as per SI 2001/1004, reg. 11.

(3) Monthly and annual PT and UEL figures are prescribed by SI 2001/1004, reg. 11 and amended by Statutory Instrument.

Class 1 secondary (employer) contributions 2014–15	
Secondary earnings threshold (ST)	£153 weekly £663(2) monthly £7,956(2) yearly
Not contracted-out rate	13.8% on earnings above ST
Contracted-out rate(1)	10.4% for salary related (COSR) on earnings from ST to UAP (plus 3.4% rebate for earnings from LEL to ST), then 13.8% above UAP
Employment allowance	£2,000 (per year, per employer)

Notes

(1) Although employer contributions do not per se give any benefit entitlements, earnings between the LEL and ST are those classed as relevant for S2P. Employers with contracted-out occupational pension schemes receive a rebate of contributions for scheme members of 3.4% (COSR). This applies from the LEL to the UAP, so earnings from LEL to ST attract a 'negative' contribution and the rate for earnings from ST to UAP is reduced as shown.

(2) Monthly and annual ST figures are prescribed by SI 2001/1004, reg. 11 and amended by Statutory Instrument.

9-030 Class 1 NIC: 2013–14

(NIC Reporter: ¶305-575ff.)

Class 1 contributions

Class 1 primary (employee) contributions 2013–14	
Lower earnings limit (LEL)	£109 weekly £473[2] monthly £5,668[2] yearly
Primary threshold (PT)	£149 weekly £646 monthly £7,755 yearly
Upper earnings limit (UEL)	£797 weekly £3,454 monthly £41,450 yearly
Upper accruals point (UAP)	£770 weekly £3,337[2] monthly £40,040[2] yearly
Rate on earnings up to PT[1]	0%
Not contracted-out rate	12% on £149.01 to £797 weekly 2% on excess over £797 weekly
Contracted-out rate	10.6% on £149.01 to £770 weekly 12% on £770.01 to £797 weekly 2% on excess over £797 weekly
Reduced rate	5.85% on £149.01 to £797 weekly 2% on excess over £797 (no rebate even if contracted-out)

Notes

[1] Earnings from the LEL, up to and including the PT, count towards the employee's basic state pension, even though no contributions are paid on those earnings. Similarly, earnings between the LEL and the PT count towards the employee's entitlement to certain benefits including the second state pension (S2P). Employees in contracted-out employment earn no S2P rights and receive a rebate of contributions of 1.4%. This applies from the LEL to the UAP, so earnings from LEL to PT attract a 'negative' contribution of 1.4% and the rate for earnings from PT to UAP becomes 10.6%. Earnings from UAP to UEL are subject to the main not contracted-out rate.

[2] Monthly and annual LEL and UAP figures are calculated as per SI 2001/1004, reg. 11.

Class 1 secondary (employer) contributions 2013–14[2]	
Secondary earnings threshold (ST)	£148 weekly £641 monthly £7,696 yearly
Not contracted-out rate	13.8% on earnings above ST
Contracted-out rate[1]	10.4% for salary related (COSR) on earnings from ST to UAP (plus 3.4% rebate for earnings from LEL to ST), then 13.8% above UAP

Notes

[1] Although employer contributions do not per se give any benefit entitlements, earnings between the LEL and ST are those classed as relevant for S2P. Employers with contracted-out occupational pension schemes receive a rebate of contributions for scheme members of 3.4% (COSR). This applies from the LEL to the UAP, so earnings from LEL to ST attract a 'negative' contribution and the rate for earnings from ST to UAP is reduced as shown.

[2] From 22 June 2010 until 5 September 2013, qualifying businesses will be exempt (when a claim is made and accepted) from the first £5,000 of Class 1 NICs due in respect of the first ten qualifying employees hired in the first year of business (National Insurance Contributions Act 2011, s. 4).

9-350 Class 1A contributions

(SSCBA 1992, s. 10)

(NIC Reporter: ¶310-000ff.)

From 2016–17, employers (but not employees) pay NIC on an annual basis on benefits in kind provided to all employees (other than lower paid ministers of religion). Prior to 5 April 2016 (since 6 April 2000), NICs were payable only on benefits provided to employees earning at a rate of £8,500 p.a. or more or to directors (SSCBA 1992, s. 10). Contributions for the year are due by 19 July following the end of the tax year to which they relate (22 July for electronic payment). Rates applying are always the full Class 1 secondary (employer) rate for each year, as follows:

Period	%
2011–12 to 2017–18	13.8

For rates of interest on late paid Class 1A contributions, see ¶9-650.

9-400 Return deadlines for Class 1 and 1A contributions

(NIC Reporter: ¶310-425; ¶340-000ff.)

Forms	Date	Penalty provision
Real time employers (RTI) (see ¶4-930)	Each time a payment is made to an employee	FA 2009, Sch. 55 (see also ¶4-942) (previously TMA 1970, s. 98A)
Non-real time employers End of year returns P14, P35, P38 and P38A	19 May following year of assessment	TMA 1970, s. 98A
All employers P11D(b)	6 July following year of assessment	SI 2001/1004, reg. 81(2)

Note

In cases of PAYE and NIC default, there are provisions to prevent double charging. Class 1A contributions are recorded annually in arrears.

9-450 Class 1B contributions

(SSCBA 1992, s. 10A)

(NIC Reporter: ¶311-400ff.)

Class 1B contributions are payable by employers on the amount of earnings in a PAYE settlement agreement (PSA) that are chargeable to Class 1 or Class 1A NICs, together with the total amount of income tax payable under the agreement (SSCBA 1992, s. 10A). Class 1B contributions are charged at the same rate as Class 1A contributions (see above) and are payable by 19 October after the end of the tax year to which the PSA applies (22 October for electronic payment).

9-500 Class 2 contributions

(SSCBA 1992, s. 11)

(NIC Reporter: ¶315-000ff.)

Class 2 contributions are paid at a flat rate by a self-employed person. From 2015–16, the contributions are collected through self-assessment alongside income tax and Class 4 contributions and only those with profits at or above the small profits threshold (SPT) are liable to Class 2 NICs. Prior to 2015–16, a person had to pay Class 2 NICs unless he had applied for and been granted exception because his earnings were below the small earnings exception (SEE) limit. Persons with profits below the small profits threshold (or who were previously granted exception for earnings below the SEE limit) can (could) still pay voluntary contributions in order to protect entitlement to contributory benefits.

The Government has announced that Class 2 NICs will be abolished and self-employed contributory benefit entitlement will be accessed through Class 3 and Class 4 NICs. The changes are due to be legislated for in a NIC Bill. In November 2017, HM Treasury issued a written statement to the House of Commons announcing that the NIC Bill will be introduced in 2018 but the measures it will implement, including the abolition of Class 2 NICs, will now take effect from April 2019 (one year later than was originally announced).

Rates and small profits threshold

	Weekly contribution rate[1]			
Tax year	Rate £	Share fishermen £	Volunteer development workers £	Small profits threshold[2] £
2017–18	2.85	3.50	5.65	6,025
2016–17	2.80	3.45	5.60	5,965
2015–16	2.80	3.45	5.60	5,965
2014–15	2.75	3.40	5.55	5,885
2013–14	2.70	3.35	5.45	5,725
2012–13	2.65	3.30	5.35	5,595
2011–12	2.50	3.15	5.10	5,315

Notes

[1] These rates are uprated by CPI.

[2] The 'small profits threshold' replaced the 'small earnings exception' from 6 April 2015. This threshold is uprated by CPI.

9-550 Class 3 contributions

(SSCBA 1992, s. 13)

(NIC Reporter: ¶320-000ff.)

Class 3 contributions are paid voluntarily by persons not liable for contributions, or who have been excepted from Class 2 contributions, or whose contribution record is insufficient to qualify for benefits (i.e. Class 3 contributions allow people to fill gaps in their contributions record for basic state pension purposes). They are paid at a flat-rate. Class 3 contributions may not be paid where an individuals earnings factor (earnings on which primary Class 1 or Class 2 contributions have been paid) equals or exceeds the qualifying limit for the year.

Rate and earnings factor

Tax year	Weekly contribution rate[1] £	Earnings factor for each contribution in col. 2 £
2017–18	14.25	113.00
2016–17	14.10	112.00
2015–16	14.10	112.00
2014–15	13.90	111.00
2013–14	13.55	109.00

Note

(1) Rate is uprated by CPI.

9-570 Class 3A contributions

(SSCBA 1992, s. 14A–14C; PA 2014, Sch. 15, para. 4; SI 2014/3240)

(NIC Reporter: ¶321-500)

From 12 October 2015 until 5 April 2017, existing pensioners and those reaching state pension age before 6 April 2016 had the opportunity to gain additional state pension by paying Class 3A voluntary NICs. There were two conditions:

- contributors must have had entitlement to a UK state pension; and
- contributors must have reached state pension age before 6 April 2016.

The measure was in addition to Class 3 voluntary contributions (see above).

The maximum number of units of additional pension that a person could obtain was 25 and each unit equated to £1 per week of additional pension (i.e. a maximum of £25 per week of additional pension could be acquired).

Age at payment date (12 October 2015 to 5 April 2017)	Rate for each additional pension unit of £1 per week £	Age at payment date (12 October 2015 to 5 April 2017)	Rate for each additional pension unit of £1 per week £
62 (women only)	956	82	484
63 (women only)	934	83	454
64 (women only)	913	84	424
65	890	85	394
66	871	86	366
67	847	87	339
68	827	88	314
69	801	89	291
70	779	90	270
71	761	91	251
72	738	92	232
73	719	93	216
74	694	94	200
75	674	95	185
76	646	96	172
77	625	97	159
78	596	98	148
79	574	99	137
80	544	100	127
81	514		

9-600 Class 4 contributions

(SSCBA 1992, s. 15)

(NIC Reporter: ¶317-650ff.)

Self-employed people whose profits or gains are over a certain amount have to pay Class 4 contributions as well as Class 2 contributions. These contributions are earnings-related and paid at a main rate on trading profits (earnings) between the lower and upper annual limits (which are the same as the Class 1 earnings threshold and upper earnings limit), with an additional 2% on profits above the upper limit since 6 April 2011.

Tax year	Rate on profits between upper and lower limits %	Annual lower profits limit[1] £	Annual upper profits limit £	Rate on profits in excess of upper limit %	Maximum contribution £
2017–18	9	8,164	45,000	2	unlimited
2016–17	9	8,060	43,000	2	unlimited
2015–16	9	8,060	42,385	2	unlimited
2014–15	9	7,956	41,865	2	unlimited
2013–14	9	7,755	41,450	2	unlimited

Notes

(1) This threshold is uprated by CPI.

9-650 Rates of interest on National Insurance contributions

(NIC Reporter: ¶341-875ff.)

(SSCBA 1992, Sch. 1, para. 6(2))

The same rates of interest apply in relation to overdue and overpaid National Insurance as apply in relation to overdue and overpaid income tax (see ¶1-500).

From 15 September 2016, late payment interest rates and the special repayment rate for debts owed to or by HMRC under a court judgment or order are extended to National Insurance related debts (F(No.2)A 2015, s. 52) (see ¶1-500).

Interest on **overdue** National Insurance contributions is payable from the due date of payment:

- **Class 1:** from 2014–15, see ¶4-948: interest on certain PAYE paid late (previously 19 April, or 22 April (electronic payments) following end of the tax year in respect of which the NIC was due (SI 2001/1004, Sch. 4, para. 17(3))).
- **Class 1A:** 19 July, or 22 July (where payment is made electronically) following the end of the tax year in respect of which the NIC was due to the date of payment (SI 2004/1004, reg. 76(3)).
- **Class 1B:** 19 October, or 22 October (where payment is made electronically) following the end of the tax year in respect of which the NIC was due to the date of payment (SI 2004/1004, Sch. 4, para. 17(3)).

The qualifying period for repayment interest on **overpaid** National Insurance contributions is as set out below:

- **Class 1:** from 2014–15, see ¶4-948: interest on certain PAYE paid late (previously from 19 April following the end of the tax year in respect of which the NIC was paid to the date on which the order for the repayment is issued. Contributions paid late, i.e. after 19 April, and later repaid carry interest from the actual date of payment (SI 2001/1004, Sch. 4, para. 18(3))).
- **Class 1A:** from 19 April following the end of the tax year in respect of which the NIC was paid, or if the contribution was paid later, from the date of actual payment – usually 19 July in practice – to the date on which the order for the repayment is issued (SI 2001/1004, reg. 77(2)).
- **Class 1B:** from 19 October following the end of the tax year in respect of which the NIC was paid to the date on which the order for the repayment is issued. Contributions paid late, i.e. after 19 October, and later repaid carry interest from the actual date of payment (SI 2001/1004, Sch. 4, para. 18(3)).

Tax credits

9-700 Working tax credits

(SI 2002/2005)

Maximum rates 2012–13 to 2017–18

Element	2017–18[1] £	2016–17[1] £	2015–16 £	2014–15 £	2013–14 £
Basic element	1,960	1,960	1,960	1,940	1,920
Disabled worker element	3,000	2,970	2,970	2,935	2,855
Severe disability element	1,290	1,275	1,275	1,255	1,220
30-hour element	810	810	810	800	790
Couple and lone parent element	2,010	2,010	2,010	1,990	1,970
Childcare element:					
percentage of eligible costs covered	70%	70%	70%	70%	70%
• maximum eligible cost for one child (per week)	175	175	175	175	175
• maximum eligible cost of two or more children (per week)	300	300	300	300	300

Note

[1] Working age benefits, including tax credits and the local housing allowances (but excluding disability benefits which will continue to be indexed by CPI) frozen for four years from 2016–17 to 2019–20 (Summer Budget 2015).

9-720 Child tax credits

(SI 2002/2007)

Maximum rates 2012–13 to 2017–18

Element	Circumstance	2017–18[1] £	2016–17[1] £	2015–16 £	2014–15 £	2013–14 £
Family[3]	Normal case	545	545	545	545	545
Individual	Each child or young person[2]	2,780	2,780	2,780	2,750	2,720
	Each disabled child or young person	5,955	5,920	5,920	5,850	5,735
	Each severely disabled child or young person	7,245	7,195	7,195	7,105	6,955

Income thresholds and withdrawal rates 2012–13 to 2017–18

	2017–18[1]	2016–17[1]	2015–16	2014–15	2013–14
First income threshold	£6,420	£6,420	£6,420	£6,420	£6,420
First withdrawal rate	41%	41%	41%	41%	41%
First threshold for those entitled to child tax credit only	£16,105	£16,105	£16,105	£16,010	£15,910
Income rise disregard	£2,500	£2,500	£5,000	£5,000	£5,000
Income fall disregard	£2,500	£2,500	£2,500	£2,500	£2,500

Notes

[1] Working age benefits, including tax credits and the local housing allowances (but excluding disability benefits which will continue to be indexed by CPI) frozen for four years from 2016–17 to 2019–20 (Summer Budget 2015).

[2] Tax credits support to be limited to two children from 6 April 2017 (SI 2002/2007, reg. 7(2)).

[3] Not available to those starting a family after 6 April 2017 (SI 2002/2007, reg. 7(2A)).

State benefits and statutory payments

9-800 Taxable state benefits

(ITEPA 2003, s. 577, 660)

(Tax Reporter: ¶490-000ff.)

The following benefits are liable to income tax.

Rates were most recently updated by SI 2017/349.

Benefit	Weekly rate from April 2017[5] £	April 2016 £	April 2015 £	April 2014 £	April 2013 £
Bereavement					
Bereavement allowance[3])	113.70	112.55	112.55	111.20	108.30
Widowed parent's allowance[4]	113.70	112.55	112.55	111.20	108.30
Carer's allowance	62.70	62.10	62.10	61.35	59.75
Dependent adults					
with retirement pension[1]	66.35	65.70	65.70	64.90	63.20
with carer's allowance[1]	36.90	36.55	36.55	36.10	35.15
with long-term incapacity	61.80	61.20	61.20	60.45	58.85
with short-term incapacity (under pensionable age)	48.15	47.65	47.65	47.10	45.85
with short-term incapacity (over pensionable age)	59.50	58.90	58.90	58.20	56.65
Employment & support allowance					
Age 25+ contributions-based ESA	73.10	73.10	73.10	72.40	71.70
Industrial death benefit:					
Widow's pension					
Permanent rate:					
higher	122.30	119.30	115.95	113.10	110.15
lower	36.69	35.79	34.79	33.93	33.05
Widower's pension	122.30	119.30	115.95	113.10	110.15
Incapacity benefit (long-term)					
Rate	106.40	105.35	105.35	104.10	101.35
Increase for age:					
higher rate	11.25	11.15	11.15	11.00	10.70
lower rate	6.25	6.20	6.20	6.15	6.00
Jobseeker's allowance					
See ¶9-860.					

Benefit	Weekly rate from				
	April 2017[5] £	April 2016 £	April 2015 £	April 2014 £	April 2013 £
Incapacity benefit (short-term)					
Higher rate:					
under pensionable age[2]	95.00	94.05	94.05	92.95	90.50
over pensionable age[2]	106.40	105.35	105.35	104.10	101.35
Non-contributory retirement pension					
Standard rate[6]	73.30	71.50	69.50	67.80	66.00
Age addition (at age 80)	0.25	0.25	0.25	0.25	0.25
Retirement pension					
Standard rate	122.30	119.30	115.95	113.10	110.15
Age addition (at age 80)	0.25	0.25	0.25	0.25	0.25
SSP, SMP, SPP and SAP					
See ¶9-900ff.					
New state pension	159.55	155.65	—	—	—
Widow's pension[3]	113.70	112.55	112.55	111.20	108.30
Widowed mother's allowance[4]	113.70	112.55	112.55	111.20	108.30

Notes

(1) No new claims for adult dependency increases payable with the state retirement pension or the carer's allowance may be made on or after 6 April 2010. Adult dependency increases already in payment immediately before 6 April 2010 will be phased out between 2010 and 2020.

(2) A man born before 6 December 1953 still attains pensionable age at age 65, whilst a woman born before 6 April 1950 attained pensionable age at age 60. The date the pensionable age is attained by individuals born after those dates is set out in the tables at ¶3-175.

(3) Bereavement allowance replaced widow's pension from 9 April 2001 for all new claims by widows and widowers.

(4) Widowed parent's allowance replaced widowed mother's allowance from 9 April 2001 for all new claims.

(5) Working age benefits, including tax credits and the local housing allowances (but excluding SMA, SMP, SPP, SSP and disability benefits which will continue to be indexed by CPI) frozen for four years from 2016–17 to 2019–20 (Summer Budget 2015).

From April 2011, the consumer price index is used for the indexation of benefits.

9-820 Non-taxable state benefits

(ITEPA 2003, s. 677(1): see also EIM76100)

(Tax Reporter: ¶490-000ff.)

The following UK social security benefits are wholly exempt from tax, except where indicated otherwise.

- Attendance allowance
- Back to work bonus (see EIM76223)
- Bereavement payment (see EIM76171)
- Child benefit
- Child's special allowance
- Child tax credit
- Constant attendance allowance: see industrial disablement benefit
- Council tax benefit
- Disability living allowance
- Income related employment and support allowance (see EIM76186)
- Exceptionally severe disablement allowance: see industrial disablement benefit
- Guardian's allowance
- Housing benefit
- Incapacity benefit for first 28 weeks of entitlement, taxable thereafter (see EIM76180)
- Income support, certain payments (see EIM76190)
- Industrial injuries benefit, a general term covering industrial injuries pension, reduced earnings allowance, retirement allowance, constant attendance allowance and exceptionally severe disablement allowance
- Invalidity benefit, replaced by incapacity benefit from April 1995 but still payable where invalidity commenced before April 1995
- In-work credit, In-work emergency discretion fund payment, In-work emergency fund payment
- Maternity allowance (see EIM76361)
- Pensioner's Christmas bonus
- Personal independence payment
- State pension credit
- Reduced earnings allowance: see industrial disablement benefit
- Retirement allowance: see industrial injuries benefit
- Return to work credit and self-employment credit
- Severe disablement allowance

- Social fund payments – help with maternity expenses, funeral costs, financial crisis, community care grants and interest free loans.
- Universal credit
- War widow's pension (see EIM76103)
- Winter fuel payment (or 'cold weather payment')
- Working tax credit

With regard to wounds and disability pensions for service with the forces see EIM74302 and for allowances payable to civilians in respect of war injuries see EIM74700.

Certain foreign social security payments are exempt from UK tax (see EIM76009).

The new bereavement support payment, which is due to replace three current benefits paid in respect of bereavement from April 2017 (*Pensions Act* 2014) will be exempt from income tax (Autumn Statement 2014).

Benefit rates

	Weekly rate from				
Benefit	**April 2017[6]** **£**	**April 2016** **£**	**April 2015** **£**	**April 2014** **£**	**April 2013** **£**
Attendance allowance					
Higher rate	83.10	82.30	82.30	81.30	79.15
Lower rate	55.65	55.10	55.10	54.45	53.00
Child benefit[1]					
For the eldest qualifying child	20.70	20.70	20.70	20.50	20.30
For each other child	13.70	13.70	13.70	13.55	13.40
Guardian's allowance	**16.70**	**16.55**	**16.55**	**16.35**	15.90
Child dependency addition					
Payable with: state pension; widowed mothers/parents allowance; short-term incapacity benefit – higher rate or over state pension age; long-term incapacity benefit; carer's allowance; severe disablement unemployability supplement.	11.35	11.35	11.35	11.35	11.35
Reduced rate[2]	8.00	8.00	8.00	8.05	8.10

Benefit	Weekly rate from April 2017[6] £	April 2016 £	April 2015 £	April 2014 £	April 2013 £
Constant attendance allowance					
Exceptional rate	135.80	134.40	134.40	132.80	129.40
Intermediate rate	101.85	100.80	100.80	99.60	97.05
Normal maximum rate	67.90	67.20	67.20	66.40	64.70
Part-time rate	33.95	33.60	33.60	33.20	32.35
Exceptionally severe disablement allowance	67.90	67.20	67.20	66.40	64.70
Employment & support allowance – income-related based (ESA(IR)) Involves over 30 potential components					
Maternity allowances (where SMP not available)					
Standard rate	140.98	139.58	139.58	138.18	136.78
MA threshold	30.00	30.00	30.00	30.00	30.00
Disability living allowance (care component)[5]					
Higher rate	83.10	82.30	82.30	81.30	79.15
Middle rate	55.65	55.10	55.10	54.45	53.00
Lower rate	22.00	21.80	21.80	21.55	21.00
Disability living allowance (mobility component)(5)					
Higher rate	58.00	57.45	57.45	56.75	55.25
Lower rate	22.00	21.80	21.80	21.55	21.00
Incapacity benefit (short-term)[3]					
Lower rate:					
under pensionable age[4]	80.25	79.45	79.45	78.50	76.45
over pensionable age[4]	102.10	101.10	101.10	99.90	97.25

Benefit	Weekly rate from April 2017[6] £	April 2016 £	April 2015 £	April 2014 £	April 2013 £
Severe disablement allowance					
Basic rate	75.40	74.65	74.65	73.75	71.80
Age addition (from Dec 90)					
• Higher rate	11.25	11.15	11.15	11.00	10.70
• Middle rate	6.25	6.20	6.20	6.15	6.00
• Lower rate	6.25	6.20	6.20	6.15	6.00
Adult dependency increase	37.10	36.75	36.75	36.30	35.35
Pensions credit					
Standard					
Single	159.35	155.60	151.20	148.35	145.40
Couple	243.25	237.55	230.85	226.50	222.05
Additional amount for severe disability					
Single	62.45	61.85	61.85	61.10	59.50
Couple (one qualifies)	62.45	61.85	61.85	61.10	59.50
Couple (both qualify)	124.90	123.70	123.70	122.20	119.00
Additional amount for carers	**34.95**	**34.60**	**34.60**	**34.20**	33.30
Savings credit					
Threshold – single	137.35	133.82	126.50	120.35	115.30
Threshold – couple	218.42	212.97	201.80	192.00	183.90
Maximum award – single	13.20	13.07	14.82	16.80	18.06
Maximum award – couple	14.90	14.75	17.43	20.70	22.89
Polygamous marriage amounts					
Claimant and first spouse	243.25	237.55	230.85	226.50	222.05
Additional amount for additional spouse	83.90	81.95	79.65	78.15	76.65

Benefit	Weekly rate from				
	April 2017[6] £	April 2016 £	April 2015 £	April 2014 £	April 2013 £
Personal independence payment[5]					
Daily living component					
Standard rate	55.65	55.10	55.10	54.45	53.00
Enhanced rate	83.10	82.30	82.30	81.30	79.15
Mobility component					
Standard rate	22.00	21.80	21.80	21.55	21.00
Enhanced rate	58.00	57.45	57.45	56.75	55.25

Notes

[1] High income child benefit charge applies from 7 January 2013 (see ¶1-110).

[2] The rate of child dependency increase is adjusted where it is payable for the eldest child for whom child benefit is also paid. The weekly rate in such cases is reduced by the difference between ChB rates for the eldest and subsequent children.

[3] Incapacity benefit and contributory employment & support allowance (ESA(C)) are taxable, under the *Income Tax (Earnings and Pensions) Act* 2003, Pt. 10, Ch. 3, except for short-term benefit payable at the lower rate. It is not taxable, however, if the recipient started receiving invalidity benefit or sickness benefit before 6 April 1995 and has continued receiving long-term incapacity benefit since then.

[4] A man born before 6 December 1953 still attains pensionable age at age 65, whilst a woman born before 6 April 1950 attained pensionable age at age 60. The date the pensionable age is attained by individuals born after those dates is set out in the tables at ¶3-175.

[5] Personal independence payment (PIP) is replacing disability living allowance for claimants aged 16–64 (but not children under 16 or people aged 65 and over already in receipt of disability living allowance). PIPs were phased in between April 2013 and 2015.

[6] Working age benefits, including tax credits and the local housing allowances (but excluding SMA, SMP, SPP, SSP and disability benefits which will continue to be indexed by CPI) frozen for four years from 2016–17 to 2019–20 (Summer Budget 2015).

From April 2011, the consumer price index is used for the indexation of benefits.

9-840 Childcare accounts

(CPA 2014; SI 2015/448; SI 2015/522)

(Tax Reporter: ¶434-500)

The *Childcare Payments Act* 2014 introduces a new scheme which provides financial support to help working families with the cost of childcare. Once the scheme is implemented, the Government will make a top-up payment of £2 for every £8 which a person pays towards childcare. Government support will be capped at a maximum of £4,000 in the case of a disabled child and £2,000 in the case of any other child, per year, although there will be no restriction on the number of children for whom support is available. The scheme will be managed by HMRC and rolled out in 2017 following a trial which will run for six months from 14 November 2016 to 15 May 2017 (SI 2016/1083).

A person will be eligible to receive government support (referred to as a 'top-up payment') if they meet the eligibility conditions; provide information to demonstrate their eligibility in a declaration to HMRC, and HMRC agree, based on that information, that they are eligible; have a child who qualifies for support (broadly, a child under the age of 12 years old, or if disabled, 17 years old); have opened a childcare account in accordance with the scheme; and they, or another person, pay money into the childcare account.

Existing tax and NIC reliefs (see ¶4-815) will be withdrawn from employees and employers where the employee enters a childcare voucher or directly contracted childcare scheme after the new scheme has come into force, however, as part of the transition to tax-free childcare, employer-supported childcare will remain open to new entrants until April 2018 (Budget 2016).

A top-up payment made into a childcare account is not to be regarded as income of the account holder for the purposes of the Income Tax Acts (CPA 2014, s. 66).

9-860 Income support and jobseeker's allowance

(Tax Reporter: ¶490-250)

	Weekly rate from				
Benefit: Income support	**April 2017[1]** **£**	**April 2016** **£**	**April 2015** **£**	**April 2014** **£**	**April 2013** **£**
Single					
Under 25	57.90	57.90	57.90	57.35	56.80
25 or over	73.10	73.10	73.10	72.40	71.70
Lone parent					
Under 18	57.90	57.90	57.90	57.35	56.80
18 or over	73.10	73.10	73.10	72.40	71.70
Couple					
Both under 18	57.90	57.90	57.90	57.35	56.80
Both under 18 – higher rate	87.50	87.50	87.50	86.65	85.80
One under 18, one under 25	57.90	57.90	57.90	57.35	56.80
One under 18, one 25 and over	73.10	73.10	73.10	72.40	71.70
Both 18 or over	114.85	114.85	114.85	113.70	112.55
Dependent children	66.90	66.90	66.90	66.33	65.62

Benefit: Jobseeker's allowance	Weekly rate from				
	April 2017[1] £	April 2016 £	April 2015 £	April 2014 £	April 2013 £
Contributions based JSA – personal rates					
under 25	57.90	57.90	57.90	57.35	56.80
25 or over	73.10	73.10	73.10	72.40	71.70
Income based JSA – personal allowances					
under 25	57.90	57.90	57.90	57.35	56.80
25 or over	73.10	73.10	73.10	72.40	71.70
Lone parent					
Under 18	57.90	57.90	57.90	57.35	56.80
18 or over	73.10	73.10	73.10	72.40	71.70
Couple					
Both under 18	57.90	57.90	57.90	57.35	56.80
Both under 18 – higher rate	87.50	87.50	87.50	86.65	85.80
One under 18, one under 25	57.90	57.90	57.90	57.35	56.80
One under 18, one 25 and over	73.10	73.10	73.10	72.40	71.70
Both 18 or over	114.85	114.85	114.85	113.70	112.55
Dependent children	66.90	66.90	66.90	66.33	65.62

Premium: Income support and Jobseeker's allowance	Weekly rate from				
	April 2017[1] £	April 2016 £	April 2015 £	April 2014 £	April 2013 £
Family/lone parent	17.45	17.45	17.45	17.45	17.40
Pensioner					
Single (JSA only)	86.25	82.50	78.10	75.95	73.70
Couple	128.40	122.70	116.00	112.80	109.50
Disability					
Single	32.55	32.25	32.25	31.85	31.00
Couple	46.40	45.95	45.95	45.40	44.20
Enhanced disability					
Single	15.90	15.75	15.75	15.55	15.15
Disabled child	24.78	24.43	24.43	24.08	23.45
Couple	22.85	22.60	22.60	22.35	21.75

Premium: Income support and Jobseeker's allowance	Weekly rate from				
	April 2017[1] £	April 2016 £	April 2015 £	April 2014 £	April 2013 £
Severe disability					
Single	62.45	61.85	61.85	61.10	59.50
couple (lower rate)	62.45	61.85	61.85	61.10	59.50
couple (higher rate)	124.90	123.70	123.70	122.20	119.00
Disabled child	60.90	60.06	60.06	59.50	57.89
Carer	34.95	34.60	34.60	34.20	33.30

Note

[1] Working age benefits, including tax credits and the local housing allowances (but excluding SMA, SMP, SPP, SSP and disability benefits which will continue to be indexed by CPI) frozen for four years from 2016–17 to 2019–20 (Summer Budget 2015).

From April 2011, the consumer price index is used for the indexation of benefits.

9-880 Benefits cap

(SI 2006/213, reg. 75CA; SI 2013/376, reg. 80A)

The benefits cap limits the total amount of benefit that working age people can receive.

Benefit capped	Limits from		
	7 Nov. 2016		15 Apr. 2013
Housing benefit	**Annual £**	**Weekly[1] £**	**Weekly £**
Single claimants			
Greater London	15,410	296.35	350.00
Outside Greater London	13,400	257.69	350.00
Couples and lone parents			
Greater London	23,000	442.31	500.00
Outside Greater London	20,000	384.62	500.00
Universal credit	**Annual £**	**Monthly[2] £**	**Monthly £**
Single claimants with no dependent children			
Greater London	15,410	1,284.17	1,517
Outside Greater London	13,400	1,116.67	1,517
Joint claimants and single claimants with children			
Greater London	23,000	1,916.67	2,167
Outside Greater London	20,000	1,666.67	2,167

Notes

[1] Rates expressed as annual limits with weekly amount calculated as annual limit divide by 52, rounding up or down to the nearest whole penny (SI 2006/213, reg. 75CA).

[2] Ratesexpressedasannualrateswithmonthlyequivalentcalculatedasannualratesdivideby12(SI2013/376, reg. 80A(1)).

Benefits to which cap is applicable

The cap will apply to household income from the following:

- Bereavement Allowance
- Child Benefit
- Child Tax Credit
- Employment and Support Allowance (except where paid with support component)
- Housing Benefit
- Incapacity Benefit
- Income Support
- Jobseeker's Allowance
- Maternity Allowance
- Severe Disablement Allowance
- Widowed Parent's Allowance (or widowed mother's allowance or widow's pension)
- Universal credit

Note

Carer's allowance and Guardian's allowance added to list of excluded benefits from 7 November 2016 (SI 2013/376, reg. 83).

Households not affected by the cap

A partner or any dependant child qualifies for Working Tax Credit, or in receipt of any of the following:

- Armed Forces Compensation Scheme
- Armed Forces Independence Payment
- Attendence Allowance
- Carer's Allowance
- Disability Living Allowance
- Employment and Support Allowance
- Guardian's Allowance
- Industrial Injuries Benefit
- Personal Independence Payment
- Universal Credit (payments towards carer's costs or for 'limited capability for work and work-related activity')
- War pensions
- War Widow's or Widower's pension

9-900 Statutory sick pay (SSP)

Employers are liable to pay SSP in any period of incapacity for work to a maximum of 28 weeks at the SSP rate in force. Statutory sick pay is treated as wages and is subject to PAYE income tax and to National Insurance contributions. Statutory sick pay is not payable for certain periods in which statutory maternity pay is being paid.

The amount of SSP payable to an employee depends on the earnings band into which he or she falls. The earnings bands and the associated SSP payments are as follows:

Period (from)	Average gross weekly earnings £	Weekly SSP rate[(1)] £
6 April 2017	113.00 or more	89.35
6 April 2016	112.00 or more	88.45
6 April 2015	112.00 or more	88.45
6 April 2014	111.00 or more	87.55
6 April 2013	109.00 or more	86.70

Notes

(1) The daily rate of SSP is ascertained by dividing the weekly rate by the number of qualifying days in the week (beginning on Sunday), then multiplying by the number of qualifying days of incapacity in the week, rounded up to the nearest penny.

From April 2011, the consumer price index is used for the indexation of benefits.

Maximum entitlement

An employee reaches his maximum entitlement to SSP in one spell of incapacity when he has been paid 28 times the appropriate rate, i.e. £89.35 × 28 = £2,501.80.

9-920 Statutory maternity pay (SMP)

Women expecting a baby who satisfy the qualifying conditions are entitled to a maximum of 39 weeks' SMP. These include having 'average weekly earnings' of:

- £113 if their baby is due between 16 July 2017 and 14 July 2018;
- £112 if their baby is due between 19 July 2015 and 15 July 2017;

In other words, 'average weekly earnings' must reach or exceed the then-current NIC LEL in the eight weeks leading up to the fifteenth week before the expected week of childbirth (or placement of an adopted child).

Period (from)	First six weeks	Remaining weeks
6 April 2017	90% average weekly earnings	Lower of 90% average weekly earnings and £140.98
6 April 2016	90% average weekly earnings	Lower of 90% average weekly earnings and £139.58
6 April 2015	90% average weekly earnings	Lower of 90% average weekly earnings and £139.58
6 April 2014	90% average weekly earnings	Lower of 90% average weekly earnings and £138.18
6 April 2013	90% average weekly earnings	Lower of 90% of weekly earnings and £136.78

Note

From April 2011, the consumer price index is used for the indexation of benefits.

9-940 Statutory shared parental pay (ShPP)

Shared parental leave (SPL) and statutory shared parental pay (ShPP) is available in respect of:

- children with an expected week of birth ending on or after 5 April 2015;
- children placed for adoption on or after 5 April 2015.

SPL is available where both parents are eligible and one partner ends maternity or adoption leave or pay (or maternity allowance) early. The remaining leave will be available as SPL. The remaining weeks of pay will be available as ShPP.

The mother must take a minimum of two weeks' maternity leave following the birth (four if she works in a factory). Thereafter:

- the rest of the 52 weeks of leave (up to a maximum of 50 weeks) can be taken as SPL;
- the rest of the 39 weeks of pay or maternity allowance (up to a maximum of 37 weeks) can be taken as ShPP.

ShPP is paid at the rate of £140.98 (2017–18) a week or 90% of average weekly earnings, whichever is lower. This is the same as statutory maternity pay (see ¶9-920) except that during the first six weeks, SMP is paid at 90% of earnings (with no maximum).

9-980 Statutory adoption pay (SAP)

SAP was introduced in April 2003.

Employees who are adopting a child and are notified that they have been matched with a child or received official notification that they are eligible to adopt a child from abroad who satisfy the qualifying conditions are entitled to a maximum of 39 weeks' SAP. These include having average weekly earnings of:

Eligible to adopt on or after	Average weekly earnings
2 April 2017	£113.00
5 April 2015	£112.00
6 April 2014	£111.00
31 March 2013	£109.00

The weekly rate of statutory adoption pay is the same as the standard rate of statutory maternity pay (see ¶9-920). The adoptive parents are treated in effect as if they have had a baby and qualified for SMP.

9-985 Universal credit

(SI 2013/376)

(Tax Reporter: ¶490-670)

Universal credit is a new benefit that has started to replace six existing benefits with a single monthly payment. Universal credit will eventually replace all of the following tax credits and benefits:

- tax credits – both child tax credit and working tax credit;
- income-based Jobseeker's Allowance;
- income-related employment and support allowance;
- income support; and
- housing benefit.

Universal credit will not replace child benefit.

Universal credit started to be introduced in stages from April 2013. Existing claimants of the above benefits will be moved to universal credit during 2016 and 2017. Universal credit is exempt from income tax.

Universal credit	Per month				
	2017[1]	2016	2015	2014	2013
	£	£	£	£	£
Universal credit amounts					
Standard allowance					
– single under 25	251.77	251.77	251.77	249.28	246.81
– single over 25	317.82	317.82	317.82	314.67	311.55
– joint claimants, both under 25	395.20	395.20	395.20	391.29	387.42
– joint claimants, one or both 25 or over	498.89	498.89	498.89	493.95	489.06
Child element					
– first child(2)	277.08	277.08	277.08	274.58	272.08
– second/subsequent child[2]	231.67	231.67	231.67	229.17	226.67
Disabled child additions					
– lower rate	126.11	126.11	126.11	124.86	123.62
– higher rate	372.30	367.92	367.92	362.92	352.92
LCW and WRA elements					
– limited capability for work	126.11	126.11	126.11	124.86	123.62
– limited capability for work and work related activity	318.76	315.60	315.60	311.86	303.66
Carer element	151.89	150.39	150.39	148.61	144.70
Childcare costs element					
– max for one child	646.35	646.35	532.29	532.29	532.29
– max for two or more children	1,108.04	1,108.04	912.50	912.50	912.50
Non-dependants' housing cost contributions	70.06	69.37	69.37	68.68	68.00
Work allowances					
Higher work allowance (no housing element)					
– single claimant, no dependent children	Nil	Nil	111.00	111.00	111.00
– single claimant, one or more children	397.00	397.00	734.00	734.00	734.00
– single claimant, limited capability for work	397.00	397.00	647.00	647.00	647.00
– joint claimant, no dependent children	Nil	Nil	111.00	111.00	111.00
– joint claimant, one or more children	397.00	397.00	536.00	536.00	536.00
– joint claimant, limited capability for work	397.00	397.00	647.00	647.00	647.00
Lower work allowance					
– single claimant, no dependent children	Nil	Nil	111.00	111.00	111.00
– single claimant, one or more children	192.00	192.00	263.00	263.00	263.00

Universal credit	**Per month**				
	2017[(1)] £	**2016** £	**2015** £	**2014** £	**2013** £
– single claimant, limited capability for work	192.00	192.00	192.00	192.00	192.00
– joint claimant, no dependent children	Nil	Nil	111.00	111.00	111.00
– joint claimant, one or more children	192.00	192.00	222.00	222.00	222.00
– joint claimant, limited capability for work	192.00	192.00	192.00	192.00	192.00
Assumed income from capital (for every £250 or part thereof)	4.35	4.35	4.35	4.35	4.35

Notes

(1) Working age benefits (but excluding disability benefits which will continue to be indexed by CPI) frozen for four years from 2016–17 to 2019–20 (Summer Budget 2015).

(2) New claims from April 2017 limited to two children and first child premium also withdrawn for new claims from April 2017 (Welfare Reform and Work Act 2016, s. 13).

Scottish taxes

9-990 Scottish taxes

(*Scotland* Act 1998; Scotland Act 2012)

(Tax Reporter: ¶102-930)

The establishment of the Scottish Parliament and the Scottish Government was provided for in the Scotland Act 1998 (as amended by the Scotland Act 2012). The Scottish Parliament was officially convened on 1 July 1999.

The Scotland Act 1998 does not specify which matters are devolved to the Scottish Parliament, rather it specifies those matters that are reserved to the UK Parliament and those matters not reserved are devolved to the Scottish Parliament. Schedule 5 to the Act (as amended) sets out those matters which are reserved to the UK Parliament and all other issues are deemed to be devolved. The Scottish Parliament has primary legislative powers, i.e. the power to pass Acts.

The *Scotland Act* 2012 amended the *Scotland Act* 1998 to introduce a new power to set a Sottish rate of income tax, which took effect from 2016-17 (see below) and to fully devolve the power to raise taxes on land transactions and on waste disposal to landfill which took effect from

1 April 2015 and since then, the existing stamp duty land tax and landfill tax do not apply in Scotland. The Act also provides powers for new taxes to be created in Scotland and for additional taxes to be devolved.

Further devolution

The Scotland Act 2016 received Royal Assent on 23 March 2016 and is an enabling Act setting out further powers that are being transferred to the Scottish Parliament and or the Scottish Ministers. In particular, the Act provides the structure within which the Scottish Parliament may legislate to set the rates of income tax and the limits at which these are paid for the non-savings and non-dividend income of Scottish taxpayers, replacing the power of the Scottish Parliament to set, by resolution, a single Scottish rate of income tax, enabling it to instead set a basic rate and any other rates of income tax; makes provision for Scotland to control the first ten percentage points of the standard rate of VAT receipts and first two and a half percentage points of the reduced rate of VAT receipts; and provides that air passenger duty and aggregates levy will be fully devolved taxes.

Administration of devolved taxes

The devolved taxes are collected by Revenue Scotland, Scotland's new tax authority which started accepting returns and collecting taxes from 1 April 2015. Revenue Scotland was established by the *Revenue Scotland and Tax Powers Act* 2014 which received Royal Assent on 24 September 2014 and came into force on 1 April 2015 (to the extent not already in force). The RSTPA 2014:

- establishes Revenue Scotland and provides for its general functions and responsibilities (Pt. 2);
- makes provision about the use and protection of taxpayer and other information (Pt. 3);
- establishes the Scottish Tax Tribunals (the First-tier Tribunal for Scotland and the Upper Tribunal for Scotland) to exercise functions in relation to devolved taxes (Pt. 4);
- puts in place a general anti-avoidance rule (Pt. 5);
- contains provisions on the self-assessment system, the checking of tax returns by Revenue Scotland and claims for repayment of tax (Pt. 6);
- makes provision for Revenue Scotland's investigatory powers (Pt. 7);
- sets out the matters in relation to which penalties may be imposed (Pt. 8);
- makes provision about the interest payable on unpaid tax, on penalties and on tax repayments (Pt. 9);

- contains provisions on debt enforcement by Revenue Scotland (Pt. 10); and
- sets out the system for the review, mediation and appeal of Revenue Scotland decisions (Pt. 11).

Scottish Tribunals

The *Tribunals (Scotland) Act* 2014, which received Royal Assent on 15 April 2014 (and came into force on 1 April 2015 (so far as not already in force)), established the First-tier Tribunal for Scotland and the Upper Tribunal for Scotland. However, functions in relation to devolved taxes were initially exercised by the Scottish Tax Tribunals, as established under the RSTPA 2014, which were constituted on 1 April 2015. Functions of the First-tier Tax Tribunal and Upper Tax Tribunal for Scotland were subsequently transferred to the First-tier Tribunal for Scotland and Upper Tribunal for Scotland from 24 April 2017 and the earlier tax tribunals were abolished from the same date.

Opinions

In order to allow taxpayers to file with certainty, Revenue Scotland will, in certain circumstances, provide its opinion on the tax consequences of specific transactions.

Applications should be sent to:

Revenue Scotland Opinions

PO Box 24068

Victoria Quay

Edinburgh

EH6 9BR

For further information, see www.revenue.scot/help/revenue-scotland-opinions.

9-991 Scottish income tax

(Scotland Act 1998; ITA 2007, s. 6A and 11A)

(Tax Reporter: ¶148-160)

Scottish income tax: 2017–18

Scottish rates	Rate[(1)] %	Taxable income band[(1)] £	Tax on band £
Scottish basic rate	20	1–31,500	6,300
Scottish higher rate	40	31,501–150,000	47,400
Scottish additional rate	45	Over 150,000	

Note

(1) On 21 February 2017, the Scottish Parliament voted to freeze the basic rate of income tax of 20%, also freeze the higher and additional rates at 40% and 45% respectively, and maintain the higher rate of income tax threshold at £43,000 in 2017–18.

Scottish income tax: 2016–17

UK rate for England, Wales and Northern Ireland	Taxable income band £	UK rate paid in Scotland %	Scottish rate[(1)] %	Total rate for Scottish taxpayers %
Basic rate 20%	1–32,000	10	10	20
Higher rate 40%	32,001–150,000	30	10	40
Additional rate 45%	Over £150,000	35	10	45

Note

(1) Rate agreed by the Scottish Parliament on 11 February 2016.

Under the Scotland Act 2016 provisions, where the Scottish Parliament sets more than one rate of income tax, it must, by resolution, set out the limits at which those rates apply or make provision to determine which rates apply in relation to a Scottish taxpayer, however, a Scottish rate resolution may not provide for different rates to apply in relation to different types of income.

The Scottish basic, higher and additional rates of income tax will only apply to non-savings, non-dividend income of those defined as 'Scottish taxpayers' (ITA 2007, s. 11A, 13).

A 'Scottish taxpayer' is defined as an individual who in any tax year is treated as resident in the UK for income tax purposes for that year and who either:

- has a close connection with Scotland;
- does not have a close connection with England, Wales or Northern Ireland, and spends more days of that year in Scotland than in any other part of the UK; or
- is a member of Parliament for a constituency in Scotland, a member of the European Parliament for Scotland, or a member of the Scottish Parliament.

A close connection is defined by reference to where the individual has their only or main residence. If an individual has one residence and it is in Scotland, they are a Scottish taxpayer. Where an individual has more than one residence, they will need to determine which has been their main residence for the longest period in the tax year and if this is in Scotland, they are a Scottish taxpayer. Individuals who cannot identify a main place of residence will need to count the days spent in Scotland and elsewhere in the UK and if they spend more days in Scotland, they are a Scottish taxpayer. Scottish taxpayer status applies for a whole year and split year treatment is not available (it is not possible to be a Scottish taxpayer for part of a tax year). HMRC's detailed technical guidance on who, from 6 April 2016, will be a Scottish taxpayer is available at www.gov.uk/government/publications/scottish-taxpayer-technical-guidance.

Administration

Scottish income tax is administered by HMRC as part of the UK income tax system.

For employees and pensioners, the income tax change will be applied through PAYE. Scottish taxpayers have an 'S' prefix to their PAYE tax code.

Scottish law

9-993 Succession Scotland

Prior rights of surviving spouse, on intestacy, in dwelling house and furniture

(*Succession (Scotland) Act* 1964, s. 8–9; SSI 2011/436)

Prior rights apply where the deceased dies intestate leaving a spouse or civil partner. The surviving spouse or civil partner takes as follows:

Period	House £	Furniture £	Cash (children survive) £	Cash (no children) £
From 1/2/2012	473,000	29,000	50,000	89,000
1/6/2005–31/1/2012	300,000	24,000	42,000	75,000
1/4/1999–31/5/2005	130,000	22,000	35,000	58,000

Legal rights

(HMRC manuals: IHTM12221)

Legal rights vest in beneficiaries by force of law and apply whether the deceased dies testate or intestate. Accordingly, rights by any provision in the deceased's will or rules of intestacy can only take effect once legal rights have been met. Prior rights may reduce or extinguish the estate that would otherwise be available to settle legal rights. Legal rights apply to the deceased's moveable estate only (which includes money, shares, cars, furniture, jewellery but excludes heritable property (land and buildings)).

Surviving family	Right of surviving spouse or civil partner	Right of children	Deceased's part[(1)]
Spouse or civil partner and children	One-third	One-third	One-third
Spouse or civil partner but no children	One-half	N/A	One-half
Children but no spouse or civil partner	N/A	One-half	One-half
Neither spouse, civil partner or children	N/A	N/A	Whole moveable estate

Note

[(1)] The balance of the estate is the part which the deceased was free to dispose of by will, or which passes under the rules of intestacy.

Distributions under intestacy

(Succession (Scotland) Act 1964, s. 2)

After prior and legal rights have been satisfied, the remainder of the estate, both heritable and moveable devolves in the following order:

Surviving family	Beneficiaries take:
Children	Whole estate
Parents and brothers/sisters Either of, or both, parents and also by brothers or sisters, but not by any prior relative	Surviving parent(s) take half; Surviving brothers and sisters take half
Brother and sisters Brothers or sisters, but not any prior relative	Surviving brothers and sisters take whole estate
Parents Either of, or both, parents, but not survived by any prior relative	Surviving parent(s) take whole estate
Spouse Husband or a wife, but not any prior relative	Spouse takes whole estate
Uncles or aunts Uncles or aunts (being brothers or sisters of either parent of the intestate), but not any prior relative	Surviving uncles and aunts take whole estate
Grandparents A grandparent or grandparents (being a parent or parents of either parent of the intestate), but not any prior relative	Surviving grandparent(s) take whole estate
Great uncles or aunts Brothers or sisters of any of his grandparents (being a parent or parents of either parent of the intestate), but not by any prior relative	Surviving brothers and sisters (or grandparents) take whole estate
Other ancestors Where not survived by any prior relative, the ancestors of the intestate (being remoter than grandparents) generation by generation successively, without distinction between the paternal and maternal lines, shall have right to the whole of the intestate estate; so however that, failing ancestors of any generation, the brothers and sisters of any of those ancestors shall have right thereto before ancestors of the next more remote generation.	

Welsh taxes

9-995 Welsh taxes

(GoWA 2006, Pt. 4A; WA 2014, Pt. 2)

(Tax Reporter: ¶102-950)

The *Government of Wales Act* 1998 provided for the establishment of the National Assembly for Wales and for the transfer of all the powers of the Secretary of State for Wales to the new Assembly. The Assembly was established in 1999.

The *Government of Wales Act* (GoWA) 2006 led to the creation of a separate legislature (the National Assembly for Wales) and executive (the Welsh Government). The Assembly's enhanced legislative competence is set out in GoWA 2006, Sch. 7, Pt. 4 collectively known as the 'Assembly Act provisions'. These provisions enable the Assembly to legislate in relation to the subjects listed under the 20 headings in Sch. 7, as qualified by the exceptions and restrictions in that Schedule and in GoWA, s. 108.

The *Wales Act 2014*, which received Royal Assent on 19 December 2014, makes provision about the devolution of taxation powers to the Assembly and, in particular, makes provision about:

- elections to and membership of the National Assembly for Wales;
- the Welsh Assembly Government;
- the setting by the Assembly of rates of income tax to be paid by Welsh taxpayer; and
- borrowing by the Welsh Ministers.

The *Wales Act* 2017 received Royal Assent on 31 January 2017 and is an enabling Act with the majority of provisions setting out the powers that are being transferred to the National Assembly for Wales and or the Welsh Ministers. In particular, the Act:

- amends the *Government of Wales Act* 2006 by moving to a reserved powers model for Wales (the same model as underpins the devolution settlement in Scotland);
- includes a declaration that the Assembly and the Welsh Ministers are considered permanent parts of the UK's constitutional arrangements and will not be abolished without a decision of the people of Wales, and that the UK Parliament will not normally legislate in devolved areas

without the consent of the Assembly, whilst retaining sovereignty to do so.

- devolves further powers to the Assembly and in areas where there was a political consensus in support of devolution, including greater responsibility to run its own affairs (including deciding its name), responsibility for ports policy, speed limits, bus registration, taxi regulation, local government elections, sewerage and energy consenting (up to 350MW), marine licensing and conservation and energy consents in the Welsh offshore region, building regulations (including excepted energy building), power over all elements of Assembly elections and powers of the licensing of onshore oil and gas extraction.

"The Land Transaction Tax and Anti-avoidance of Devolved Taxes (Wales) Act 2017 received Royal Assent on 24 May 2017 and makes provision about the taxation of land transactions in Wales, amends the Tax Collection and Management (Wales) Act 2016 and makes provision about counteracting avoidance of devolved taxes. From April 2018, Land Transaction Tax (LTT) will replace UK Stamp Duty Land Tax (SDLT) in Wales.

Administration of devolved taxes

On 25 April 2016, the *Tax Collection and Management (Wales) Act* 2016 received Royal Assent. The purpose of this Act is to put in place the legal framework necessary for the future collection and management of devolved taxes in Wales. In particular, the Act:

- establishes the Welsh Revenue Authority and makes provision about its organisation and main functions (which will be the collection and management of devolved taxes) (Pt. 2);
- makes provision about the assessment of devolved taxes (Pt. 3);
- makes provision about the Welsh Revenue Authority's investigatory powers, including provision about notices requiring information and the inspection of premises (Pt. 4);
- makes provision for and in connection with the imposition of penalties in relation to devolved taxes (Pt. 5);
- makes provision for interest to be payable on late payments to the Welsh Revenue Authority and on repayments by the Welsh Revenue Authority (Pt. 6);
- makes provision about payments to the Welsh Revenue Authority and the recovery of unpaid amounts (Pt. 7);
- makes provision for and in connection with reviews of and appeals against decisions of the Welsh Revenue Authority (Pt. 8);
- confers powers to make subordinate legislation about the investigation of criminal offences relating to devolved taxes (Pt. 9);

- contains provision that applies generally for the purposes of the Act (Pt. 10).

9-997 Welsh rates of income tax

(WA 2014, s. 8–10; ITA 2007, s. 6B, 11B)

(Tax Reporter: ¶148-165)

The Wales Act 2014, which received Royal Assent on 17 December 2014, legislates for new Welsh rates of income tax by conferring on the Assembly a power to set, by resolution, a Welsh basic, higher and additional rate of income tax, for 'Welsh taxpayers'.

The Welsh basic rate, the Welsh higher rate and the Welsh additional rate for a tax year will be calculated under ITA 2007, s. 6B, as follows:

Step 1:

Take the basic rate, higher rate or additional rate.

Step 2:

Deduct ten percentage points.

Step 3:

Add the Welsh rate (if any) set by the National Assembly for Wales for that year for the purpose of calculating the Welsh basic rate, the Welsh higher rate or the Welsh additional rate (as the case may be).

The Welsh tax rates will only apply to non-saving, non-dividend income and applies for one tax year only, for the whole of that year.

A Welsh taxpayer is defined as an individual who is UK resident for income tax purposes for the tax year and who either:

- has a close connection with Wales;
- does not have a close connection with England, Scotland or Northern Ireland, and spends more days of that year in Wales than in any other part of the UK; or
- for the whole or any part of the year, is a member of Parliament for a constituency in Wales, a member of the European Parliament for Wales, or an Assembly member.

(GoWA 2006, s. 116E, as inserted by WA 2014, s. 8)

As with Scotland, the overall administration of Welsh income tax will remain with HMRC.

Northern Irish taxes

9-999 Northern Irish taxes

(*Northern Ireland Act 1998*)

(Tax Reporter: ¶102-910)

The Agreement reached on Good Friday 1998, often referred to as the Belfast or Good Friday Agreement, and the subsequent *Northern Ireland Act* 1998 (as amended a number of times since 1998, particularly following the 2006 St Andrews Agreement) continue to form the basis of the constitutional structure in Northern Ireland with the devolved institutions in Northern Ireland being constituted under the *Northern Ireland Act* 1998.

The Northern Ireland devolution settlement gives legislative control over certain matters (known as 'transferred matters') to the Northern Ireland Assembly. In the main, these are in the economic and social field. The NI Assembly may also, in principle, legislate in respect of 'reserved' category matters subject to various consents, but has not yet done so to any significant degree.

Matters of national importance which, in the normal course of events, it is expected will remain the responsibility of HM Government and Westminster, are known as 'excepted matters', and the NI Assembly does not have competence to legislate on these. The *Northern Ireland Act* 1998, Sch. 2 sets out these areas.

Many UK-wide issues such as broadcasting and genetic research are known as 'reserved matters'. The Northern Ireland Act 1998, Sch. 3 sets out which matters fall into the 'reserved' category.

Anything that is not explicitly reserved or excepted in Sch. 2 or 3 is deemed to be devolved and the Assembly has full legislative competence. It does not require consent from Westminster or HM Government to legislate.

Further details on devolution, including a full list of transferred, excepted and reserved matters can be found at www.gov.uk/devolution-settlement-northern-ireland.

Income tax generally

Legal background

Sources of tax law

10-000 The principal Acts

The levying of taxation in its many forms has been a constant source of friction throughout history. In 1688, when William and Mary, Prince and Princess of Orange were invited to assume the English throne as joint monarchs, it was conditional upon agreeing to a Declaration of Rights outlawing various acts of James II. They were also required by the Scottish Convention Parliament to agree to a similar declaration, the *Claim of Right* 1689, before assuming the Scottish throne.

The Declaration of Rights was later embodied in the *Bill of Rights* 1689, which is still on the statute book. In respect of taxation, it provided that:

> 'levying money for or to the use of the crown, by pretence of prerogative, without grant of parliament, for longer time, or in other manner than the same is or shall be granted, is illegal.'

As a result, taxation may only be levied by the authority of an Act of Parliament. Taxation measures are enacted in an annual Finance Act which either introduces new legislation or amends earlier legislation. From time to time, the opportunity is taken to consolidate, into a single Act, all current legislation relating to a particular tax or the administration of the tax system. The latest 'consolidated' Acts are:

- the *Income and Corporation Taxes Act* 1988 (ICTA 1988);
- the *Taxation of Chargeable Gains Act* 1992 (TCGA 1992);
- the *Capital Allowances Act* 2001 (CAA 2001);
- the *Inheritance Tax Act* 1984 (IHTA 1984); and
- the *Taxes Management Act* 1970 (TMA 1970),

though these have been substantially amended by subsequent Finance Acts.

The Tax Law Rewrite Project was charged with converting existing legislation into simpler language with a clearer, more logical, structure. As a consequence of its work, ICTA 1988 has been largely 'de-consolidated' by the removal of the provisions relating solely to income tax, which have been rewritten and now are to be found in the *Income Tax (Employment and Pensions) Act* 2003 (ITEPA 2003), the *Income Tax (Trading and Other Income) Act* 2005 (ITTOIA 2005) and the *Income Tax Act* 2007 (ITA 2007). Corporation tax provisions can be found in the *Corporation Tax Act* 2009 (CTA 2009) and the *Corporation Tax Act* 2010 (CTA 2010). International tax matters, including double tax relief, are now contained in the *Taxation (International and Other Provisions) Act* 2010, for both individuals and companies.

The *Scotland Act* 2012 gives the Scottish Parliament the power to set a separate income tax rate for Scottish taxpayers. The likely starting date for this is April 2016.

10-100 The annual Finance Acts

It comes as a surprise to many to learn that income tax is only a temporary imposition. It was introduced in 1798 to help pay for the Napoleonic wars, repealed in 1802 following peace with France and then re-imposed in 1803 when hostilities broke out again. It was repealed again in 1816 following Napoleon's final defeat, before being re-imposed again in 1842 due to the economic situation. This imposition was to be 'for a time to be limited' according to Sir Robert Peel and thus, to this day, income tax is imposed on a year by year basis; each Finance Act contains a section which says 'Income tax shall be charged for the year …' and sets out the rates to be applied.

The Finance Acts themselves are used to amend, repeal or expand existing legislation in other Acts, usually the principal Acts. Occasionally they will, in their own right, impose a new charge to tax or bring in a new relief.

10-200 Statutory instruments

Acts of Parliament often delegate powers to the Revenue and Customs Commissioners or the Treasury to make regulations or orders which themselves have statutory effect. Such regulations, etc. are known as 'subordinate', 'delegated' or 'secondary' legislation.

The main purposes of delegated legislation are:

- to set out detailed provisions in cases where parliamentary time for discussion of minutiae is short, or where the substance of the legislation is of a technical nature calling for specific expertise;

- to provide a commencement date for either the whole or part of an Act of Parliament, where that Act states it will come into force on a date 'to be appointed'; and
- to enable delegated bodies to amplify parliamentary legislation to provide for future contingencies.

10-300 Directions

A recent development in tax legislation has been the making of directions by the Revenue and Customs Commissioners. This is an element of their power under the parent Act to make regulations. The regulations themselves will provide that certain detailed matters will be prescribed by a direction of the Commissioners. The directions themselves are not statutory instruments and are therefore not subject to any parliamentary approval. Their attraction lies in their ability to allow HMRC to amend them speedily as circumstances change. To some extent, therefore, directions may be regarded as 'tertiary' legislation.

An example of directions are those in relation to the electronic filing of tax returns. *Finance Act* 1999 empowers HMRC to make regulations to facilitate the use of electronic communications for filing tax returns and for making tax payments. In exercise of those powers, HMRC made the *Income and Corporation Taxes (Electronic Communications) Regulations* 2003 (SI 2003/282). These provide that such communications must use 'approved' methods and provide that 'approved' means approved by means of a general or specific direction of HMRC. Those directions include the directions under SI 2003/282, reg. 3.

10-350 European legislation

The European Community has its own body of law which, subject to the provisions of the UK's withdrawal from the Union, takes precedence over the domestic legal systems of member states. For the purposes of the EC, the treaties are primary law, and regulations, directives and decisions of the Council and Commission are secondary. Within member states, the ranking of EC legislation as primary or secondary depends upon whether or not it has 'direct effect' in those states. Regulations of the Council and Commission are directly applicable in member states; they do not depend for their enforcement on the passing of national legislation.

Directives, on the other hand, are 'binding' on member states, to the extent that they must implement the provisions of directives in their domestic law; if a member state has failed to do so by the date provided for implementation, the directive has direct effect in that state to the extent that the obligations it creates are sufficiently clear and precise. Decisions are binding only on the member states to which they are addressed.

The UK became a member of the EC by virtue of the Treaty of Accession of 1972 and the *European Communities Act* 1972 (ECA 1972). Section 1 of that Act incorporates the treaties into UK law. Section 2(1) gives EC regulations direct force in the UK, where these are stated to be given effect without further enactment. Section 2(2) delegates to Her Majesty in Council, and to ministers and departments, power, whether by order or by regulation, to implement Community obligations of the UK. This does not include the power to impose or increase taxation.

Whilst the direct taxation systems of member states do not at present come within the scope of the European Community, the powers they retain must be exercised consistently with Community law. The Treaty of Rome, as amended by the Union Treaty signed at Maastricht in 1992 ('the Treaty'), established what have become known as the four freedoms:

(1) free movement of workers;

(2) freedom of establishment;

(3) freedom to provide services;

(4) free movement of capital and payments.

An overriding right guaranteed by the Treaty is the prohibition of discrimination on the grounds of nationality in any area covered by the Treaty. Subsequent case law has established that the prohibition includes both overt discrimination (i.e. clear discrimination on grounds of nationality) or covert (e.g. discrimination on grounds of residence, since non-residents of a member state are, mostly, non-nationals). The direct tax cases which have come before the European Court of Justice (ECJ) have principally concerned the free movement of persons, combined with the right of freedom from discrimination by the tax systems of member states.

Restrictions on free movement can be justified in tax terms by the need to maintain the coherence of the national tax system, e.g. where a member state's system linked the deductibility of insurance premiums with the taxability of the later payments, it was justified in taxing contributions paid by an individual to insurers established in another member state.

Tax Reporter: ¶103-890

10-400 Case law

Although the tax legislation is approved by Parliament, the actual interpretation of that legislation falls to the courts. In such cases where there is a dispute over the true meaning of a particular measure, the ultimate objective is to try and discern the intention of Parliament in enacting that measure.

Over the years a number of rules of interpretation have been established.

- 'The literal rule' where the words in the statute are to be given their ordinary and natural meaning even where this might produce an unjust, unreasonable or absurd result. However, there is often a departure from this rule where the words are ambiguous or ambivalent.
- 'The golden rule' where the words are to be given their ordinary and natural meaning only in so far as that does not lead to an absurdity or injustice. If normal usage provides for another interpretation which would not produce such a result, that interpretation may be adopted.
- 'The mischief rule' which can be applied where words are ambiguous or uncertain and allows the court to look beyond the measure concerned to its legislative background and the reasons which led to it being enacted, i.e. to ascertain what mischief the measure was intended to cure.
- 'The purposive rule' by which the court will seek to identify the purpose of measure and interpret it in a way that gives effect to that purpose, even if that means giving the words a wider meaning than under the strict 'literal rule'. In seeking to establish the intention of Parliament when it introduced a particular measure, the Courts are able to refer to parliamentary material, especially *Hansard*, but only where the measure itself is ambiguous or obscure or led to absurdity and where the parliamentary material relied on statements by a Minister or other promoter of a Bill, together with any other parliamentary material necessary to understand such statements and their effect; and the statements relied on were clear.

Case law is important not so much as for what has been decided, but more for why it has been decided, something lawyers term the *ratio decidendi*. For example, the capital allowances case of *Jarrold v John Good & Sons* held that, in that case, moveable partitions qualified as plant and machinery. However, the reason the court came to that decision was that the nature of the company's business was such that the partitions were used to enable it to cope with 'the varying vicissitudes' of that business.

Where a decision on a particular point of law has been decided by one court it is binding upon all lower courts and tribunals. Thus, in England and Wales, a decision of the High Court is binding on the First-tier and Upper Tribunals and a decision of the House of Lords binds the Court of Appeal, the High Court and the Tax Tribunals.

Case: *Jarrold v John Good & Sons Ltd* 40 TC 681

Tax Reporter: ¶104-000ff.

The legislative process

12-000 The Pre-Budget Report

A Pre-Budget Report (PBR) is delivered by the Chancellor to the House of Commons, usually in November each year. It is intended to provide a progress report on the state of the economy and public finances, and sets out the direction of government policy in the run up to the Spring Budget. It is also a vehicle to announce tax changes to be introduced in the Budget and where these are to be anti-avoidance measures, they will usually be effective from the date of the PBR even though the necessary legislation will not become law until the following summer.

The PBR is also an occasion when draft legislation is exposed for consultation prior to being included in the following Finance Bill.

12-100 Ministerial statements

Where, at any time of the year, HMRC become aware of a perceived abuse or of a new anti-avoidance scheme (see 66-050), an announcement will be made by a minister (usually the Paymaster General) that legislation blocking the abuse or scheme in a forthcoming Finance Bill, or statutory instrument, which will have effect from the date of the statement.

12-200 The Budget Statement

The Budget Statement is given by the Chancellor of the Exchequer to the House of Commons and its function is to provide an update on the state of the economy and the public finances and to present new forecasts for each, to set out the Government's economic and fiscal objectives, to report on the progress the Government has made toward achieving its objectives, and to set out the further steps the Government is taking to meet them. In reality, at least as far as taxation is concerned, it is of limited interest, being a public relations exercise focusing only on those aspects which the Chancellor of the day wishes to highlight.

Summaries of the Chancellor's proposal are to be found in the press releases and other documentation published immediately after the conclusion of the Budget Statement. However, for the real details one has to wait until the publication of the Finance Bill shortly afterwards.

12-300 The provisional collection of taxes

Because income tax is a temporary tax which is required to be re-imposed each year, a mechanism is needed to enable tax to be collected during the period from the beginning of the tax year until the date the re-imposition becomes law. This is achieved in the days following the Budget

Statement by the House of Commons passing a resolution providing for the re-imposition of income tax for the coming tax year with the detailed provisions remaining the same as for the current year. In the case of a Spring Budget, this resolution has statutory effect only until the following 5 August, by which time the Finance Bill should have become law.

Legislation: *Provisional Collection of Taxes Act* 1968, s. 1(2)

Tax Reporter: ¶103-150

12-400 The Finance Act

The Finance Bill is published shortly after the Budget Statement. It then has to pass through various stages before it can receive the Royal Assent and pass into law.

At the *first reading*, a dummy print is laid before the House, a clerk reads out the title of the Bill, a print is ordered and a date is fixed for the *second reading*.

The second reading involves a debate before the whole House on the general principles of the Bill. However, no amendment may be made at this stage.

There follows the *Committee stage* at which the Bill is debated clause by clause. A few selected clauses are debated by a Committee of the whole House and the remainder are delegated to a Standing Committee of between 16 and 50 members, selected from each party in proportion to the size of its representation in the House, and on the basis of their own particular expertise. Amendments are proposed and considered, and new clauses may also be proposed. There is often a tight schedule and use is sometimes made of parliamentary devices for cutting short debate, such as the 'guillotine'.

The Bill, as amended in Committee, is formally reported to the House (the *Report stage*). At this stage further amendments can be made and new clauses added, and a Bill can even be sent back to its Committee. However, it is usually given a *third reading* at which there is little or no debate, and if there are amendments they are of a minor nature.

The procedure in the Lords is similar except that Committee stage is before the whole House and debate cannot be cut short. Further, under the *Parliament Act* 1911 procedure, the extent to which the Lords can contribute to the final version of a Finance Bill is severely curtailed.

When a Bill has passed all its stages it is given the Royal Assent, it becomes an Act as opposed to a Bill, and its clauses become sections.

Tax Reporter: ¶103-250

12-500 Statutory instruments

Statutory instruments come into effect in various ways, depending on the provisions of the enabling statute. Those in relation to taxation normally come into effect by:

- being 'made' (and therefore having immediate effect). However, the instrument must be laid before Parliament, where it may be annulled by a resolution of the House of Commons (the 'negative' procedure). Such resolution must be passed within 40 days of the instrument being laid, otherwise it will cease to have effect, but without prejudice to anything done under it before annulment. The Treasury and HMRC usually make regulations and orders by means of a statutory instrument, which is subject to annulment by the House of Commons. This procedure does not apply in certain cases specified within the Taxes Acts, in particular where the statutory instrument does no more than bring into force a provision of an Act of Parliament (a 'commencement order'); or
- being laid in draft before Parliament (i.e. it is not 'made') and only taking effect by means of an *affirmative* resolution of the House of Commons within a specified period (the 'affirmative' procedure).

When existing legislation is consolidated, the consolidation Act often contains a provision which preserves the effect of existing delegated legislation.

Only in rare cases (for example, where the effect of the statutory instrument is favourable to the taxpayer) will the enabling provision allow delegated legislation to have retrospective effect.

Statutory instruments come into effect either when they are made, or on any other date specified in the instrument itself.

Legislation: ICTA 1988, s. 828; ITA 2007, s. 1014; CTA 2010, s. 1171

Tax Reporter: ¶103-500

HM Revenue and Customs

Organisation

14-000 Taxes under the care of HMRC

Following the merger of the Inland Revenue and HM Customs and Excise in April 2005, the range of taxes administered by the new HMRC comprises:

- income tax;
- capital gains tax;
- corporation tax;
- inheritance tax;
- National Insurance contributions;
- value added tax;
- excise duties;
- insurance premium tax;
- petroleum revenue tax;
- stamp duty land tax;
- landfill tax;
- climate change levy;
- aggregates levy; and
- betting duties.

In addition, it:

(1) administers and pays:

    (a) child tax credits;

    (b) working tax credits; and

    (c) child benefit;

(2) enforces the national minimum wage;

(3) collects repayments of student loans; and

(4) supervises specified business types for money laundering purposes, including accountancy service providers.

14-500 Current structure

Following a review that began in 2006, the whole structure of HMRC offices has changed. The concept of local tax districts went years ago and no doubt, with the pressure on costs, the structure could be even further streamlined going forward.

The basic idea is to improve efficiency and effectiveness, including by segmenting different types of operation. Thus, Local Compliance have a Large Business Service, which can affect businesses with more than 250 employees or turnover exceeding €50m and balance sheet asset value exceeding €43m. This covers both incorporated and non-incorporated businesses and so will include partnerships if they are that size. The proclaimed aim is to improve customer service and develop a more professional relationship with businesses.

There are also offices for Local Compliance, which have responsibility for small and medium-sized enterprises. This is organised into multi-functional geographical regions responsible for delivering the required operational activity. Within these regions there are many teams and staff with various functions, whose aim is to collect the right amount of tax and at the right time, improve compliance of those in legitimate business, support those businesses wishing to be compliant, and vigorously tackle deliberate non-compliance.

For the general public, there remains the Tax Enquiry Centres, whose aim is to provide a facility for tax payers to discuss their tax affairs on a face-to-face basis. An individual who is employed will be dealt with by the PAYE office of his or her employer. Anyone else without a tax reference, for example, can by inserting their postcode into the relevant page of HMRC's website, obtain details of their nearest tax office (which may be located many miles away from their home).

For the wealthy, there is the High Net Worth Unit. Their aim is to deal with the tax affairs of the wealthiest individual customers so as to build relationships to help them better understand these customers and better tailor service delivery for them through pro-active engagement. It is also stated that this unit will provide a single point of contact and a holistic approach to the tax affairs of these individuals.

There are many specialist offices. Thus, the Special Civil Investigations Unit continues to deal with large amounts of undeclared income and tax avoidance schemes. It is this unit that will consider prosecuting for fraud in appropriate cases, albeit that most cases are dealt with under the Code of Practice 9 procedure. There are separate divisions that deal with charities, trusts, shares and asset valuation and non-residence.

Publications

16-000 Statements of practice

Whilst legislation, and the interpretation of legislation by the courts, are the only sources of tax law, HMRC publish statements of practice which explain how, in practice, they will apply the law in particular situations. As such they are merely HMRC's interpretation of the law and are neither exhaustive nor authoritative.

It is of course open to the taxpayer to challenge the validity of the points expressed in such statements by referring cases to the courts; the judgment of the court then becomes authoritative and may either confirm, overturn, or modify the statement.

The statements of practice were previously published in a booklet IR 131 *Statements of Practice*, which has now been discontinued and replaced by a publication on the HMRC website.

Website: www.hmrc.gov.uk/practitioners/sop.pdf

16-100 Extra-statutory concessions

An extra-statutory tax concession (ESC) is a relaxation of the strict letter of the legislation which aims to avoid minor anomalies and cases of hardship which would otherwise arise under the statute. The justification for making such concessions has been claimed to be the power of 'care and management' of income tax granted to the former Inland Revenue under the *Taxes Management Act* 1970. That particular section was amended as a consequence of the formation of HMRC to read that the commissioners of HMRC are responsible for the 'collection and management' of income tax, but that they are also empowered to do anything which they thought was 'necessary' or 'expedient' or 'incidental or conducive' to enable them to carry out that responsibility.

Following clarification of HMRC's administrative discretion to make concessions, HMRC are reviewing their published concessions. Where appropriate, the effect of concessions will be put on a legislative basis as the House of Lords decision in the *Wilkinson* case has made it clear that HMRC's authority to depart from the strict statutory position is more restricted than previously thought. Statutory effect can be given to a concession by Treasury order.

Because an ESC is given at HMRC's discretion, there can be no right of appeal where they refuse to apply it. The only course open to a disgruntled taxpayer is to seek a judicial review of their decision (see 63-050).

ESCs were previously published in Booklet IR 1, *Extra-Statutory Concessions*, which has now been withdrawn. They can, however, be found on the HMRC website.

Legislation: TMA 1970, s. 1; CRCA 2005, s. 9(1); FA 2008, s. 160; *Enactment of Extra-Statutory Concessions Order* 2009 (SI 2009/730); *Enactment of Extra-Statutory Concessions Order* 2010 (SI 2010/157)

Cases: *R v HMIT, ex parte Fulford-Dobson* [1987] BTC 158; *R v IR Commrs, ex parte Wilkinson* [2005] BTC 281; *R (on the application of ELS Group Ltd) v R & C Commrs* [2015] BVC 508

Website: www.hmrc.gov.uk/specialist/esc.pdf

Tax Reporter: ¶103-520

16-200 Tax Bulletins

Tax Bulletins were published six times annually by HMRC until the end of 2006. They contained a number of articles giving the views of their technical specialists on particular issues. Items headed 'Interpretations' were statements of how HMRC interpreted certain areas of the legislation; these, they said, would normally be applied in relevant cases, but each case would turn on its facts and there could be circumstances in which an interpretation would not apply. There could even have been cases in which they would argue for a different interpretation in appeal proceedings.

Nothing in a Tax Bulletin article was to be taken as superseding a statement of practice nor did it affect the taxpayer's rights of appeal.

Tax Bulletins ceased to be issued at the end of 2006, to be replaced by Briefs. Bulletins issued may still be found on HMRC's website.

Website: www.hmrc.gov.uk/bulletins/index.htm

16-250 Revenue & Customs Briefs

These are publications which replaced *Tax Bulletins* with effect from 1 January 2007 and are only available on HMRC's website. They are not issued according to any fixed timetable, but as and when HMRC have news or views to impart and cover both direct and indirect taxes. By 31 July 2007, 53 Revenue & Customs Briefs had been issued, mainly in respect of indirect taxes.

Website: www.hmrc.gov.uk/briefs/index.htm

16-300 Codes of practice

HMRC have published a number of codes of practice explaining the approach and procedures which taxpayers may expect to be adopted in certain areas of work in addition to explaining the taxpayer's legal rights. A current list of those relevant to income tax is as follows.

(1) COP 8: *Special Compliance Office investigations. Cases other than suspected serious fraud.* [N.B. Special Compliance Office is now the Special Civil Investigations Unit.]

(2) COP 9: *Cases of suspected serious fraud.*

(3) COP 10: *Information and advice.*

(4) COP-AT: *Anti-Terrorism, Crime and Security Act 2001: Code of Practice on the Disclosure of Information.*

Copies of these publications may be downloaded from the HMRC website.

A number of codes of practice have been withdrawn and some replaced by other publications. In particular, COP 1 *Putting things right: how to complain* was withdrawn in April 2007 and replaced with a 'factsheet'.

Websites: www.hmrc.gov.uk/leaflets/c11.htm and www.hmrc.gov.uk/factsheets/complaints-factsheet.pdf

16-400 Internal manuals

For some years, HMRC have published their internal guidance manuals on their website and in conjunction with publishers such as CCH. These are available on disk and as a component of an online service.

The manuals are used in local tax and collection offices to guide staff on the interpretation of tax law and the operation of the tax system. HMRC claim that they have published most of the material in full or with only minor omissions, though certain material has been withheld from publication. This particularly relates to information which, if disclosed, could prejudice the assessment or collection of tax, duties or National Insurance contributions, or would assist tax avoidance or evasion. Over and above this, material concerning the affairs of particular taxpayers has not been made publicly available, and there may also be some omissions relating to material where someone other than HMRC owns the copyright.

These manuals are not in any way a substitute for the words of the legislation itself. They only provide a commentary, enabling the practitioner to understand why the HMRC officer is taking a certain line. It is important for practitioners to remember that the manuals are no more than HMRC's interpretation of the law, which may nevertheless be open to challenge.

A particular difficulty with relying on material in the manuals, is that HMRC have a tendency to amend them without notice and without leaving any trace of the original wording. A practitioner who advises his client on the basis of a statement in the manuals, may well find that if he needs to refer an HMRC officer to that statement, it can no longer be traced. Good practice is to print off a hard copy of the statement and place it on file.

The importance of being able to demonstrate a clear HMRC practice is illustrated by the judicial review decision in *Cameron v R & C Commrs*. In a published booklet, HMRC had set out their practice clearly in relation to seafarers' relief but changed their position. That change was not made in the official publication and, although mentioned in trade magazines, the High Court held that this was not sufficient to resist the taxpayers' claim that they had a legitimate expectation that HMRC should deal with their tax affairs in a particular manner.

Case: *Cameron v R & C Commrs* [2012] BTC 125

Website: www.hmrc.gov.uk/manuals

Taxpayers' rights

18-000 HMRC's Service Commitment

In 1999, the previous *Taxpayers' Charter* (see below) was replaced with a 'Service Commitment' setting out the principles by which taxpayers may expect to be dealt with by both the former Inland Revenue and HM Customs and Excise. The text of that commitment can be found on the HMRC website.

This service commitment is said to be a timeless, very broad based 'mission statement' of what taxpayers can expect to receive by way of service. It was claimed to be underpinned by two Charters, one for National Insurance contributors and the other for income tax payers. The income tax Charter was originally reproduced in booklet IR 167, but that booklet was withdrawn in 2003. Finding the text of the Charter on the HMRC website is not easy; nevertheless it can still be found at Appendix 1 of the *Pensions Schemes Instructions Manual*.

The Charter was first published in 1985. It was described as reflecting long-standing aims of the former Inland Revenue and its publication as representing a public commitment to those principles. This was followed in 1991 by a new version which set out the standard of service that people could expect to receive from both the Inland Revenue and Customs and Excise.

The 1991 Charter contained nothing that was not in the original one, but was presented in a format devoid of legalistic overtones. It is most notable for the things it changes and omits. The original undertaking (by both the Revenue and Customs) that 'you will be treated in the same way as other taxpayers in similar circumstances' was replaced by 'You are entitled to expect the Inland Revenue/Customs and Excise to be fair by treating everyone with equal fairness'. More importantly, the original undertaking that 'you will be presumed to have dealt with your tax affairs honestly, unless there is reason to believe otherwise' was replaced by the bald statement that 'we need you to be honest'. Questioned about the change in Parliament the then Financial Secretary to the Treasury said:

> 'Taxpayers will continue to be presumed to have dealt with their tax affairs honestly unless there is reason to believe otherwise. The omission of a statement to that effect from the 1991 taxpayer's charter does not constitute a change of policy in this regard.'

Following consultation, legislation has been introduced in the *Finance Act* 2009 requiring HMRC to prepare and maintain a Charter. The Charter will set out standards of behaviour and values to which HMRC will aspire when dealing with taxpayers. In addition, the legislation requires HMRC to report annually on how well they are doing in meeting the standards in the Charter. This provision is new, as although the former departments that merged to make up HMRC have had charters in the past, none of these has had a statutory basis.

Legislation: CRCA 2005, s. 16A; FA 2009, s. 92

Website: www.hmrc.gov.uk/manuals/psimanual/part02/psi2appendix1.htm

Tax Reporter: ¶184-000

18-100 Ex gratia payments and refunds of costs

HMRC will make an ex gratia payment of compensation to a taxpayer who has been financially prejudiced by an error on their part. Their attitude to the reimbursement of taxpayer costs is found in the complaints factsheet *Complaints and putting things right* (formerly Code of Practice 1, *Putting things right: how to complain*).

The current factsheet does not indicate the level of payments which might be expected. However they should be expected to be at, or perhaps slightly above those originally quoted in Code of Practice 1. Payments can be expected to be made in respect of:

- any extra costs incurred as a result of HMRC's mistake or unreasonable delay, such as postage, telephone calls, travel expenses, professional fees and financial charges;

- payments for worry and distress to acknowledge and apologise for the way in which the taxpayer has been treated. These payments, which are not intended to put a value on the distress suffered, will usually range from £25 to £500; and
- additional payments to compensate for continuing mistakes and delays following the initial complaint, also usually ranging from £25 to £500.

A source of contention is that where HMRC's mistakes or unreasonable behaviour have caused the taxpayer to incur additional professional fees, they insist on the fees being paid by the taxpayer to the adviser before they will make reimbursement.

Website: www.hmrc.gov.uk/factsheets/complaints-factsheet.pdf

18-200 Human rights

The *Human Rights Act* 1998 incorporates into domestic law the rights guaranteed by the European Convention on Human Rights and the body of jurisprudence created by the human rights institutions in Strasbourg (the European Court of Human Rights and the Commission). The Act requires the courts to give effect to primary and secondary legislation (including tax legislation) in a way which is compatible with the Convention. Thus the rights of individuals and companies under the Convention can be enforced without the necessity for reference to the court in Strasbourg.

It is unlawful for public authorities (a widely defined term, which includes courts and tribunals) to act incompatibly with Convention rights; and citizens who allege that a public authority has so acted can seek redress in the appropriate domestic court.

However, a public body may lawfully act in a way which is incompatible with Convention rights in two circumstances.

(1) Where, because of the provisions of the primary legislation, they could not have acted differently.

(2) Where the body is giving effect to primary legislation which cannot be read, or given effect, in a manner which is compatible with Convention rights.

Among the rights guaranteed by the Convention, those which are of greatest potential relevance in a tax context, are:

- the right of a person to peaceful enjoyment of his possessions. However, this is subject to the right of the state to enforce its laws to secure the payment of tax or other contributions or penalties;

- the right to a fair hearing in determination of a person's civil rights and obligations or of any criminal charge against him;
- the right to respect for a person's private and family life, his home and his correspondence; and
- the enjoyment of rights and freedoms without discrimination.

Apart from the right to 'peaceful enjoyment of possessions', the most relevant in a tax context is the right to a fair hearing in respect of a 'criminal charge'. The scope of criminality here is wider than may be thought.

The criteria for deciding whether a tax penalty was a criminal matter was established as:

- the classification of the proceedings in domestic law;
- the nature of the offence; and
- the nature and degree of severity of the penalty that could be imposed.

Certain penalties may be criminal even if they are not categorised as such by the laws of the contracting state, if the amount of the penalty makes it effectively criminal in nature.

The right to a fair trial includes a right of silence and a right not to incriminate oneself. In September 2002, the former Inland Revenue issued guidance to its staff on the approach to adopt in cases where penalties are likely to be considered (see 60-050).

Legislation: *Human Rights Act* 1998, s. 3(1), 6(1)

Tax Reporter: ¶103-970ff.

18-300 The Adjudicator

The Adjudicator's role is to provide an independent mechanism for investigating complaints about how HMRC have handled a taxpayer's affairs.

It is the *way* in which HMRC have handled a taxpayer's tax affairs which concerns the Adjudicator. The matters within his jurisdiction include excessive delay, errors and discourtesy on HMRC's part and the way in which they have exercised any discretion.

The Adjudicator will *not* deal with appeals on matters of law which lie within the jurisdiction of the tribunal nor, generally, with questions of fact which lie there. However, this is not to say that everything within appeal proceedings is 'off limits' to the Adjudicator; if, for instance, a taxpayer complains that information supplied to HMRC has been withheld from the commissioners, this is a complaint which might well be investigated.

The Adjudicator may not consider matters relating to a criminal prosecution instigated by HMRC until court proceedings have been completed, and will not investigate at all complaints which have already been investigated by the Parliamentary Ombudsman; on the other hand, if the Adjudicator has considered a complaint, there is no bar to a dissatisfied taxpayer referring his/her case to the Ombudsman.

Complaints may be in writing or by telephone, although in most cases it is likely that only a complaint in writing will be satisfactory, in order that no detail may be overlooked. The Adjudicator's Office has undertaken to provide assistance, on receipt of a telephone call from a taxpayer, in formulating a written complaint.

Generally, HMRC should be given the opportunity, through their own complaints procedures, to settle any complaint themselves before any approach is made to the Adjudicator. However, in practice, it is understood that the Adjudicator may, in appropriate cases, consider complaints where the full HMRC complaints procedure has not been followed.

When the Adjudicator decides that he is prepared to investigate a particular complaint, he will ask HMRC for a full report, and may then need to ask the taxpayer for more information. The Adjudicator will attempt to persuade HMRC and the taxpayer to come to an agreement to settle the dispute; in the absence of such an agreement, he will make a formal recommendation to HMRC as to how he considers the complaint should be dealt with (a copy of the recommendation being sent to the taxpayer).

HMRC have undertaken to follow the Adjudicator's recommendations 'in all but exceptional circumstances'. If HMRC do *not* follow a recommendation, the Adjudicator will want to know why and will publish each such case in an annual report (although this will be small consolation to an aggrieved taxpayer).

The very nature of the Adjudicator's function means that no guarantees can be given of the time within which a complaint will be settled, but if a case is complex, and takes more than a short time to deal with, the taxpayer will be kept informed of progress by the Adjudicator's Office.

The Adjudicator's Office has published a leaflet (A01) explaining generally which complaints will, and which will not, be dealt with by the Adjudicator and the procedures which will be followed once a complaint has been accepted for consideration. This leaflet can be found on the Adjudicator's website.

The address of the Adjudicator's Office is 3rd Floor, Haymarket House, 28 Haymarket, London SW1Y 4SP.

Website: www.adjudicatorsoffice.gov.uk

18-400 The Ombudsman

The remit of the Parliamentary and Health Service Ombudsman is to investigate any action taken by a government department or authority in the exercise of its administrative functions, where a member of the public claims to have 'sustained injustice in consequence of maladministration'.

Complaints about alleged maladministration cannot be made direct; they must be directed through an MP, who need not be the complainant's constituency MP, but the Ombudsman may accept cases directly from the public if an MP refuses to refer them.

The complainant must have brought the matter to the attention of an MP within a year of realising that he had a grievance. The Ombudsman may allow longer in exceptional cases. The complainant must be resident in the UK, or at least be present in the UK when the actions complained of took place, or the complaint must concern rights and obligations arising in the UK. The facts of the complaint should be set out in writing to the MP with supporting correspondence and other documentation. The complainant's professional adviser or a Citizens' Advice Bureau may formulate the complaint on his behalf.

The Ombudsman's investigative powers are distinct from any judicial proceedings, and he is not permitted to investigate any matter where a right of appeal lies to a tribunal, or where there is a remedy before a court of law, unless he is satisfied that in the particular circumstances it is unreasonable to expect the complainant to take that step. The cost of going to court is not on its own a good reason for not seeking judicial redress where appropriate. In practice, though, the Ombudsman appears to take a relaxed view of this restriction, and to investigate cases notwithstanding that they may be dealt with by way of judicial review. For instance, a decision by HMRC not to allow an extra-statutory concession is judicially reviewable yet the Ombudsman has been known to investigate such cases, particularly the application of ESC A19 (remission of tax in cases of official error). The Ombudsman will in all likelihood be more inclined to criticise any instances of maladministration in such cases than judges are to overturn administrative decisions which they regard as the province of the executive.

Examples of cases investigated by the Ombudsman include complaints about the processes of tax collection and repayment, the conduct of investigations, instances of confusion between tax offices and government departments which the taxpayer incurs expenses in sorting out, failure by HMRC to advise taxpayers of their rights or discouraging them from exercising such rights, alleged arbitrary and oppressive conduct by HMRC officials, and so forth.

The Ombudsman's powers are analogous to those of a court in his ability to require a minister, official or any person to give evidence and to compel attendance; nevertheless he cannot enforce his decisions. He can only make recommendations, which may include the payment of compensation where a complaint has been wholly or partly upheld, and he sometimes agrees with the department changes in its procedures to eradicate the cause of the complaint. His powers are reinforced by the readiness of the Select Committee to pursue any cases where the reluctance of a department to accept a remedy may be apparent. In practice, it is virtually unheard of for a department not to accept and act upon the Ombudsman's recommendations.

In many instances, neither the law nor administrative practice provide redress for a taxpayer who has sustained a loss as a result of maladministration by HMRC and in such cases, the Ombudsman often settles matters satisfactorily by recommending an 'ex gratia' payment equal to the loss borne, or the unnecessary expenses incurred.

The reference to the Ombudsman should be addressed to:

The Parliamentary and Health Service Ombudsman

Millbank Tower

Millbank

London

SW1P 4QP

Tel: 0345 015 4033

A leaflet entitled *A guide to making a complaint against the NHS, a government department or agency* can be obtained from the Ombudsman's website.

Website: www.ombudsman.org.uk/make-a-complaint

Calculation of IT liability

Taxable income

30-000 Nature of income

There is a well cited aphorism that income tax is a tax on income. However, there is no definition of income in the Taxes Acts. However, the courts have established principles whereby capital sums are not subject to income tax or capital expenditure allowed, but subject always to any statutory provision to the contrary. Thus, expenditure on plant and machinery although not as a rule deductible in arriving at trading profits is relieved under the capital allowances provisions. There are also statutory provisions that tax capital receipts as income. Examples are the premium provisions in relation to leases, particularly on the grant of a lease for less than 50 years, and the specific legislation governing the taxation of gains on land which, by its terms, taxes as income any gain of a capital nature where those provisions apply. However, unless there is a statutory provision to the contrary the default principle is that capital matters are not within the ambit of income tax.

Not all profits of an income nature are subject to tax as there must be a specific 'head of charge'. For most of its history, income tax was calculated and assessed under the various schedules but the schedular system as such was dispensed with in the tax law rewrite. Even so, the principles behind the schedular system still remain and so unless a source of profits is specifically charged to tax then there is no general right of HMRC to charge income tax.

Another principle of general application is that tax can only be charged on profits that arise in the form of money or money's worth. This means that profits must either be received in cash or in a form that can be converted into cash by, for example, selling an asset or right. For example, there is a well known case in relation to employment income where an employee who received a second-hand suit of clothes was taxed not on the cost to the employer but on the second-hand value that the employee could realise by selling it. Statute then countered this by bringing in a benefit in kind code which has been added to over the years to become itself a complex set of rules. Nevertheless, the principle remains wherever there is no statutory provision to the contrary. This raises the possibility that, in a trading context, as an example, a barter system might, in theory at least, avoid benefits being charged to income tax unless there was some tangible asset that could be sold or a right that could be assigned or surrendered for cash. Even then, there are not the same provisions as for employments and so the relevant amount for tax purposes would be the amount that could be received in cash for the asset or right.

In general, taxable income is usually derived from a transaction where there is a contractual or quasi contractual arrangement, so that any debt or other right can be enforced in the courts. Even that is not an immutable principle as the cases show, for example, that tips or gratuities received by an employee are taxable as employment income and gratuitous sums received by a trader can in appropriate circumstances be taxed as part of the trading profits. On the other hand, it has been held in the courts that gambling winnings in general are outside the scope of income tax unless the activity constitutes the conduct of a trade.

Legislation: ITA 2007, s. 756

Cases: *Partridge v Malandaine* (1886) 18 QBD 276; *Graham v Green* [1925] 2 KB 37; *Wilkins v Rogerson* (1960) 39 TC 34; *Burdge v Pyne* [1969] 1 WLR 364

Tax Reporter: ¶110-200

30-100 Introduction to income tax – some basic principles

In addition to the nature of income as discussed above, there are certain other principles that are important in creating the background against which income tax is assessed.

An individual who is resident in the UK is, in principle, liable to income tax on the whole of their taxable income whether arising in the UK or elsewhere. A person not resident in the UK is only subject to income tax on UK source income. There are also differences for an individual who, although resident in the UK, is not domiciled here. In certain circumstances, such taxpayers can restrict their chargeable overseas source income to the sums remitted to the UK in a particular year of assessment.

UK resident companies are not within the charge to income tax but to corporation tax. However, a non-resident company that has UK sources of income (other than from trading in the UK through a permanent establishment) is subject to income tax. For example, a company owning properties in the UK that are let is subject to income tax on the profits from the UK property business (and is also within the non-resident landlord provisions in the same way as a non-resident individual).

The treatment of husband and wife was quite different many years ago in that a husband was assessed on his wife's income and the wife had no obligation to complete a tax return. The introduction of the independent taxation of a wife's income changed this and so husband and wife are taxed broadly as separate individuals with their own personal allowance and tax bands. There are, however, special provisions dealing with husband and wife (and also civil partnerships with effect from 5 December 2005) whereby one spouse may be treated as having made a settlement for the benefit of the other and the income can, in certain instances, be treated as that of the settlor. There is also a special rule where property is owned jointly.

There is also a special regime for trusts. In principle, trustees are liable to income tax at the basic rate. They are not liable to income tax at the higher rate, which is particularly relevant for interest in possession trusts such as where the life tenant has a right to the income. However, in the case of trusts where the trustees have a discretion over the distribution of income, there is a separate regime so that non-dividend type income is subject to the trust rate. That rate is 45% for 2017–18. Dividends and other distributions are subject to income tax at the dividend trust rate, which is 38.1% for 2017–18. A beneficiary receiving income from a discretionary type trust is treated as if the amount received had tax deducted at 45%, which is potentially repayable to the extent that it exceeds the individual's liability to tax for the year in question. The fact that the income is paid out of sources that include UK dividends does not affect this. The rules for the taxation of trust income and distributions are quite complex and are dealt with in more detail at 150-250ff.

Certain persons are exempt from all taxes on income and gains whilst some persons are specifically exempt from income tax. Certain income is also exempt from income tax. The income which is excluded from the income tax charge is discussed at 30-200.

An individual, but not a trustee or personal representative, will be able to obtain an offset against income tax and capital gains tax by making a qualifying gift of 'pre-eminent property' to the nation. An agreement will be made to apply to up to five tax years and the total reduction will be 30% of the value of the property.

Legislation: FA 2012, Sch. 14; ITA 2007, s. 9

30-200 Exempt income

Certain categories of income are excluded from the charge to income tax including:

- statutory redundancy payments (and the corresponding amount of any other employer's payment);
- income which is awarded as a scholarship;
- certified contractual saving scheme terminal bonuses and interest. Only contracts linked to employee share option schemes are eligible for tax relief;

- wounds and disability pensions;
- government bounties and gratuities;
- war death pensions, annuities and additional pensions paid to holders of gallantry and distinguished conduct or service awards;
- interest on personal injury damages awarded by a court in the UK;
- income of an exempt approved retirement benefits scheme from deposits or investments;
- tax repayment supplement or repayment interest;
- national and war saving certificate accumulated interest;
- the first £70 on ordinary deposits with the National Savings Bank. Husband and wife have always each been able to claim this exemption, or a joint account qualifies for £140 exemption;
- some social security, including universal credit, and child benefits including 'jobfinders grant';
- benefit payments under certain government pilot schemes;
- most income of charities;
- interest on certain UK government securities beneficially owned by persons not resident in the UK;
- income from deposits and assets held in an Individual Savings Account (ISA);
- income from investments of up to the permitted maximum in qualifying Venture Capital Trusts; and
- compensation for National Socialist persecution.

Legislation: FA 1996, s. 151; ITTOIA 2005, s. 709; ITEPA 2003, s. 228, 638, 639, 641, 642

Tax Reporter: ¶132-400

30-400 Total income

Total income is an important concept in calculating a person's income tax liability. The statutory definition is brief, referring simply to the need to identify the amounts of income on which the taxpayer is charged to income tax for the year.

In simple terms, this means aggregating all the income that is subject to income tax including any income from which income tax is deducted at the basic rate.

Until 2005–06, the schedular system applied and so income usually fell into one of the Schedules (from A to F) and the various cases of Sch. D and (until April 2003) Sch. E. The schedular system was abolished for income tax purposes but the underlying principles remain, as the effect of the tax law rewrite is to express the same concepts in different language. There are now simply references in the legislation to the different types of income, such as trade profits and property business income. In principle, however, wherever income is subject to tax that income should be included in total income.

Legislation: ITA 2007, s. 23, Step 1

Tax Reporter: ¶148-400

30-450 Net income

'Net income' is defined in Step 2 of ITA 2007, s. 23, being the difference between total income and the sum of the reliefs and deductions set out in s. 24.

Examples of deductions from total income are:

- loss relief where available for set-off against total income – usually, this is for losses on trades, professions or vocations but can include certain property losses (for example, where broadly the losses arise from excess capital allowances) and amounts claimed under ITA 2007, s. 132 in relation to certain losses on unquoted shares;
- charges on income where allowable by deduction against total income (i.e. excluding Gift Aid payments as mentioned). These are now relatively few and not that common, but include, for example, UK patent royalties and partnership annuities (and income tax should be deducted at basic rate when paying such amounts). The legislation no longer uses the term 'charges on income' for such payments, but it continues in common use;
- pension payments where made gross;
- interest relief where deductible, such as on loans to buy interests in close companies and partnerships;
- allowable gifts of shares, securities and real property to charities and certain specified public bodies; and
- post cessation expenditure from trades, professions or vocations previously carried on, subject to meeting the conditions for relief.

Legislation: ITA 2007, s. 23–24

30-465 Adjusted net income

A further important concept is that of 'adjusted net income' as defined in ITA 2007, s. 58.

This is the figure that will dictate an individual's entitlement to certain reliefs and allowances, principally:

- income-related reduction to the personal allowance – where adjusted net income exceeds £100,000;
- the high income child benefit charge – where adjusted net income exceeds £50,000;
- with effect from 2016–17, the entitlement to the individual savings allowance.

An individual's adjusted net income is determined as follows:

- the starting point is the individual's net income as defined in s. 23;
- deduct the grossed up amount of any Gift Aid contributions;
- deduct the grossed up amount of pension contributions paid in accordance with FA 2004, s. 192 (where basic rate relief has been given at source);
- add back any relief under s. 457 or 458 (payments to trade unions or police organisations) that was deducted in calculating net income above.

Legislation: ITA 2007, s. 58

30-475 Personal allowances and tax reducers

It has been mentioned above that there is now a statutory definition of net income. The personal and blind person's allowances are then deducted to arrive at the amount on which income tax is actually charged (Step 3 of ITA 2007, s. 23).

Other tax reliefs are, however, given in various different ways as alternatives to a deduction from total income. Thus:

- the married couples, etc. allowance where available is given as an income tax reduction;
- relief under the enterprise investment scheme is given in terms of income tax with an overriding maximum of 30% for 2017–18. Relief for venture capital trusts is also given in a similar way, which is at 30% for 2017–18;

- relief for pension payments is given by extending the limit for the basic rate income tax band. However, where payments are still made gross (such as under old retirement annuity policies) relief is given by a deduction from total income;
- for payments to charities where allowable under the gift aid rules, relief is also given by an increase to the basic rate band, the increase being the gross amount that after deducting income tax at 20% equals the sum actually paid to the charity.

Where relief is given by reduction in the income tax liability (a 'tax reducer'), e.g. married couple's allowance, enterprise investment schemes and venture capital trusts, this relief cannot exceed the income tax payable. Indeed, in the case of payments to charities, if the individual does not have in charge sufficient allowable income tax and capital gains tax, the income tax deemed to have been deducted from the payment at the basic rate is payable to HMRC to the extent of the excess. However, in the case of pension payments payable under deduction of income tax, there is no such claw back.

A person's income tax liability where there are deductions from total income could be affected by the way in which the deductions are set off against total income. Statute provides that reliefs reducing a person's total income are to be made in the way which will result in the greatest reduction of his liability to income tax. However, it is also provided that where personal reliefs are given by way of a deduction from total income (now the personal allowance and blind person's allowance only), then these deductions are to be made after other deductions. One particular effect of this is that where a loss relief claim is made, it is not possible to restrict the losses to the income after notionally deducting the personal allowance. Thus, in this instance the priority works against the taxpayer whereas the general rule is in favour of the taxpayer.

A particular instance where the general priority of deductions will be relevant is where an individual has both dividend income and other income as it would not be in a person's interest to set deductions against dividend income, as the effect of this would result in a lower reduction in income tax liability compared to deducting from other income.

In addition to amounts that are deductible in arriving at total income, there are also, of course, various deductions that are made in arriving at the income from a particular source, where there are separate rules. Thus, in arriving at profits from a trade the expenditure incurred wholly and exclusively, etc. is deductible in computing the net sum that is then brought into charge as part of total income. Similarly, expenses allowable against rents are deducted in arriving at the profits of the property business.

Example

In 2017–18, Bob has income from a partnership trade and from a UK property business. He pays interest of £5,000 that is allowable on a partnership loan taken out by him. He also pays net pension contributions of £8,000 and gross contributions under old retirement annuity contracts of £3,000. His net income is as follows:

		£
Partnership profits		60,000
UK property business		8,000
'Total income'		68,000
Less: Interest on partnership loan	5,000	
Retirement annuity contributions	3,000	(8,000)
Net income		60,000
Less: Personal allowance		(11,500)
Taxable income		48,500

The basic rate band limit is extended by £10,000 from £33,500 to £43,500 to give higher rate relief for the pension contributions paid net of basic rate tax. The basic rate of 20% applies to the first £43,500 and the higher rate of 40% to the balance of £5,000.

Legislation: ITA 2007, s. 23, 24, 25, 65

Tax Reporter: ¶148-400

30-485 Savings, distributions and non-savings, etc. income

It is essential to understand the differences between each of the above classes of income as they are each eligible for their own allowances and are subject to subtly different tax rates. Summarised below are the principal components of each class.

Savings income

This comprises:

- interest chargeable under ITTOIA 2005, Pt. 4, Ch. 2, including foreign source interest;
- the income element of purchased life annuities unless excluded by ITTOIA 2005, s. 718(2). The logic behind this is that in consideration for the payment of a lump sum, a person receives an income for life. Based on life expectancy, the return is treated partly as a return of capital and the balance is income, which in economic terms is interest on the money;

- income chargeable under the accrued income scheme under ITA 2007, Pt. 2, Ch. 12;
- gains on life insurance and similar contracts (including, therefore, what are usually known as investment bonds) chargeable under ITTOIA 2005, s. 465. As explained elsewhere, in the case of UK policies, there is a deemed tax deduction at 20% given to the policyholder, which is not repayable;
- profits from deeply discounted securities charged under ITTOIA 2005, Pt. 4, Ch. 8.
- interest on UK government and other securities – interest on UK government securities is paid gross. Interest on quoted Eurobonds is also paid gross, including any security issued by a company and listed on a recognised stock exchange;
- interest on National Savings First Option Bonds (interest on other National Savings investments continues to be paid gross);
- interest distributions by authorised unit trusts;
- interest on cash deposits withdrawn from PEPS;
- other annual interest including such interest paid by an unquoted company; and
- the income element of purchased life annuities.

Interest paid by individuals is, as a rule, paid gross, the main exception being where a UK resident individual pays yearly interest to a non-resident person.

Dividends and other distribution type income

This expression includes:

- dividends and other matters treated as a distribution from UK companies. This will, therefore, include the appropriate element of a buy-back of shares where this cannot be treated as subject to capital gains tax under CTA 2010, s. 1033;
- dividends from non-UK resident companies, which are chargeable under ITTOIA 2005, Pt. 4, Ch. 4; and
- other distributions from non-UK resident companies where such a distribution would be chargeable if the company were resident in the UK. Part 4, Ch. 4 only deals with dividends. Other distributions, where taxable income, are within the residual charging provision under ITTOIA 2005, Pt. 5, Ch. 8. As explained elsewhere, receipts that are treated as income distributions from UK companies would not

necessarily be so treated as such for non-UK resident companies as it is necessary to analyse such a receipt according to the law of the country or state in which the foreign company is situated.

Non-savings income

This will encompass all other taxable income and will include income and profits arising from:

- trades, professions and vocations;
- employment;
- pensions;
- UK property business;
- overseas property business;
- post-cessation receipts;
- taxable social security income (including state pension);
- ITA 2007, s. 755 gains on land;
- residual income.

30-500 Savings income, savings nil rate and personal savings allowance

Finance Act 2008 introduced a 10% starting rate for savings income. This starting rate was reduced to 0% from 6 April 2015. For 2017–18, this applies on up to £5,000 of savings income. The application of the starting rate on savings income is dependent on the taxpayer's total income. To the extent that the person's non-savings income is less than his or her personal allowance plus £5,000, then some or all of their savings income will be tax free. If, however, the total of non-savings income exceeds the individual's personal allowance plus £5,000, then none of his or her savings income will benefit from the savings nil-rate band.

Independent of the savings nil-rate band, with effect from 2016–17, a taxpayer may also be eligible for the personal savings allowance. The use of the word 'allowance' in the legislation is unfortunate as it should more correctly be termed a zero rate tax band. A taxpayer's entitlement to this relief will be dictated by their adjusted net income (30-465).

Adjusted net income	Personal savings allowance
Up to £45,000	£1,000
£45,001–£150,000	£500
Over £150,000	No personal savings allowance

Savings income in excess of the savings nil-rate band and the personal savings allowance will be taxed at 20% up to the basic rate limit and at the higher rate of 40% where income is over the basic rate limit (and at the additional rate of 45% where appropriate, see 31-400).

Example 1

In 2017–18, Anthony has employment income of £9,000 and bank interest of £10,000. His tax liability is:

		Savings	Non-savings	Total
		£	£	£
Employment income			9,000	9,000
Bank interest		10,000		10,000
Taxable income		10,000	9,000	19,000
Less: personal allowance		(2,500)	(9,000)	(11,500)
Taxable income less personal allowance		7,500	0	8,000
Savings nil rate	0%	5,000		0
Savings allowance	0%	1,000		0
	20%	1,500		300
Income tax payable				300

Anthony's personal allowance is first used against the non-savings income of £9,000 so none of Anthony's non-savings income is taxable. The balance of the personal allowance is used against the savings income. All of Anthony's remaining taxable income is savings income.

The first £5,000 of taxable savings benefits from the savings nil rate band. The personal savings allowance gives a further £1,000 taxed at 0%. The balance of £1,500 is taxed at 20%.

Example 2

Ben has rental income of £30,000 and bank interest of £9,000. His tax liability is:

	Savings	Non-savings	Total
	£	£	£
Rental income		30,000	30,000
Bank interest	9,000		9,000
Taxable income	9,000	30,000	39,000

		Savings	Non-savings	Total
Less: personal allowance			(11,500)	(11,500)
Taxable income less personal allowance		9,000	18,500	27,500
	20%		18,500	3,700
Savings allowance	0%	1,000		0
	20%	8,000		1,600
Income tax payable				5,300

Ben's personal allowance is first used against non-savings income of £30,000 – £11,500 = £18,500. As the amount of non-savings income that is taxable is more than £5,000, none of Ben's savings income is subject to the savings nil-rate band. As he is a basic rate tax payer, then the first £1,000 of savings income benefits from the savings allowance and is taxed at 0%. The balance of savings income is taxed at 20%.

An individual's tax liability will ultimately depend on both the level of total income as well as the make-up of that income. Non-savings income will form the first tranche of taxable income. Personal allowances and reliefs and lower rate tax bands will typically be allocated to non-savings income. It is the taxation of savings and distribution income that is particularly complex.

- To the extent the total of savings and non-savings income is less than the sum of the personal allowance and £5,000, then savings income will be taxed at 0%.
- If an individual is a basic rate taxpayer, then the first £1,000 of savings income is taxed at 0%. The allowance is reduced to £500 for additional rate taxpayers and zero for additional rate taxpayers.
- If non-savings income exceeds the available savings nil-rate band and savings allowance, then it will be taxed at 20% in the basic rate, 40% in the higher rate and 45% in the additional rate.
- Distribution income is treated as the top slice of income. The first £5,000 of distribution income is taxed at 0%. Distribution income in excess of £5,000 is taxed at 7.5% to the extent it falls within the basic rate tax band, 32.5% in the higher rate band and 38.1% in the additional rate band.

Thus, the potential rates at which income is chargeable can be 0%, 7.5%, 20%, 32.5%, 38.1%, 40% and 45%.

30-550 Income already taxed when received

Prior to 6 April 2016, most interest was paid after deduction of basic rate tax. With effect from 6 April 2016, banks and building societies will no longer deduct basic rate tax from interest payments.

Income from trusts

Where a beneficiary, such as a life tenant, is entitled to the income of a trust, income received by the beneficiary preserves its nature. Income other than dividends will have tax deducted by the trustees at the basic rate, whilst dividend income will be taxed at 7.5%. The beneficiary includes in his total income an amount equal to the actual sum received plus the tax deducted, i.e. the grossed-up figure. In some circumstances if income is paid directly to the beneficiary, it may be paid gross.

For discretionary trusts, the trustees are liable for tax at the rate applicable to trusts (45%) or at the dividend trust rate (38.1%). Payments to beneficiaries are treated as made under deduction of tax at the rate applicable to trusts (even where made out of dividend income) and are grossed up accordingly. The beneficiary is entitled to a tax credit against total tax liability of an amount equal to the tax deducted by the trustees.

Wages and salaries

An employer deducts income tax from wages and salaries according to a code allocated to each employee by HMRC under the PAYE system. The amount received by the employee plus the tax deducted forms part of the employee's total income but he receives a tax credit for the tax deducted.

Trail commission

HMRC Brief 04/13 sets out HMRC's view on the tax treatment of, in particular, trail commission paid to investors. HMRC consider such payments to be taxable as annual payments, from which the payer should deduct income tax at the basic rate.

Tax Reporter: ¶117-000

The computation

31-000 Introduction

The principles to be applied in calculating income tax liabilities are set out in the previous paragraphs.

The first step, however, is always to determine the income assessable from a particular source. Thus, the profits from a trade should be established by arriving at the profits in accordance with generally accepted accounting principles, making such adjustments as are required by ITTOIA 2005. This would include disallowing expenditure not incurred wholly and exclusively for the purposes of the trade, but deducting capital allowances.

The net profit from each source should then be marshalled under the following headings:

- savings income (excluding dividends and other distributions);
- dividends and other distribution type income; and
- other income.

It is specifically provided that income received in a tax year is treated as part of the income for that year irrespective of the period of accrual. Similarly, dividends paid in a tax year are treated as income of that year.

Account should then be taken of the sums to be deducted or set off against total income. As explained in 30-450, the set off should be made in the order required to produce the lowest income tax liability but setting off the personal allowance and blind person's allowance last. As a general rule, deductions should be set against non-dividend distribution type income. In that way, the tax credit, where available, is not lost and relief is obtained at 40% for a higher rate taxpayer or 45% for an additional rate taxpayer as against 7.5%, 32.5% or 38.1% for dividends, etc.

The total of all these sums (less deductions) will then give the taxable income. It is then necessary to take account of the following:

- reliefs that are given by extending the basic rate limit band for a higher rate taxpayer. This includes pension payments paid net of income tax and gift aid payments to charities; and
- make deductions from the income tax charge by applying all the above rules for tax reducers, i.e. where relief is given in terms of an income tax reduction rather than a reduction in taxable income. This includes relief under the enterprise investment scheme, venture capital trusts and the married couple's, etc. allowance.

Tax Reporter: ¶148-400

31-100 Pro forma computation

The following pro forma computation sets out the main items that are likely to be met in practice under the various headings to illustrate how the principles set out above are applied.

Non-savings income

Trades, professions and vocations

UK property business

Overseas property business

Post cessation receipts

Employment income

Taxable social security income (including state pension)

ITA 2007, s. 755 gains on land

Residual income

Savings income

Non-dividend/distribution income

UK bank and building society interest

Other UK interest

Overseas interest

Purchased life annuity – income element

Accrued income scheme charges

Chargeable event gains on life policies, etc.

Dividend and other distribution income

UK dividends

Other qualifying UK distributions

Non-qualifying UK distributions

Foreign dividends

Foreign distributions (if of an income nature)

Total income

Less: Deductions

Annual charges – gross

Allowable interest payments

Post cessation expenditure

Trade, etc. losses

Property business losses if available

Pension contributions paid gross

Allowable gifts in specie to charities etc

Net income

Less: Personal allowance

Blind person's allowance

Taxable income

Income tax thereon

5,000	on non-dividend savings income (where the amount of earnings less the personal allowance is not more than £5,000) at 0%
1,000 or 500 or 0	0% on non-dividend savings income
	the basic rate limit 2017–18 is £33,500 plus the gross equivalent of net paid pension contributions and Gift Aid payments
A	at 20% being gross amount of pension contributions paid net and Gift Aid payments
B	at 20% on non-dividend income falling within basic rate limit
C	at 0% on first £5,000 of dividend income and at 7.5% on dividends falling within basic rate limit
D	at 40% – balance other than dividends, etc. up to higher rate limit
E	at 32.5% dividends in higher rate band (treating dividends, etc. as the highest part)
F	at 45% – balance other than dividends. etc, above higher rate limit
G	at 38.1% – dividends above higher rate limit (treating dividends as above)

Less: Income tax reducers

Venture Capital Trusts

Enterprise Investment Schemes

Community Investment Tax Relief

Interest on life annuity loan

Maintenance payments

Married couple's, etc. allowance	___	
		___
(treat as nil if a negative figure)		
Less: Double Taxation Relief		___
Add: Income tax deducted from charges		___
Less: Income tax paid or deemed paid at source		
PAYE		
Income tax deducted at source		___
Payable by self-assessment		£

31-200 Examples

The following examples illustrate the principles involved, particularly where savings income is included in total income.

Example 1

Tom has a salary of £23,000 in 2017–18 from which £1,625 was deducted under PAYE. He also receives bank interest of £1,500, interest of £400 on loan notes issued by a UK private company and dividends from UK companies totalling £6,000. His income tax liability for 2017–18 is:

		Dividends	Savings	Non-savings	Total
		£	£	£	£
Employment income				23,000	23,000
Bank interest			1,500		1,500
Loan note interest (gross equivalent)			500		500
Dividends		6,000			6,000
Total income		6,000	2,000	23,000	31,000
Less: personal allowance				(11,500)	(11,500)
Taxable income		6,000	2,000	11,500	19,500
	20%			11,500	2,300
Savings allowance	0%		1,000		0
	20%		1,000		200
Dividend nil rate band	0%	5,000			0
	7.5%	1,000			75
					2,575

		Dividends	Savings	Non-savings	Total
Less: PAYE					(1,625)
Tax deducted from company interest					(100)
Income tax payable					850

Had Tom's salary been £55,000, the savings allowance would have been restricted to £500 and the interest and dividends would have been taxed at the higher rate and dividend higher rate as follows.

Taxable income less personal allowance deducted from salary		6,000	2,000	43,500	51,500
	20%			33,500	6,700
	40%			10,000	4,000
Savings allowance	0%		500		0
	40%		1,500		600
Dividend nil rate band	0%	5,000			0
	32.5%	1,000			325
					11,625

Had Tom's salary been £157,000, he would have lost all of his personal allowance and the savings allowance would be reduced to zero. Interest and dividends would have been taxed at the additional rate and the dividend additional rate as follows.

Taxable income		6,000	2,000	157,000	165,000
	20%			33,500	6,700
	40%			116,500	46,600
	45%			7,000	3,150
Savings allowance	0%		0		0
	45%		2,000		900
Dividend nil-rate band	0%	5,000			0
	38.1%	1,000			381
					56,921

Example 2

Rebecca has taxable trading profits of £43,000 for 2017–18. In addition, she has bank interest of £2,250 and UK dividends of £1,500. She made a £10,000 investment qualifying for relief under the enterprise investment scheme. Her income tax liability for 2017–18 is:

		Dividends	Savings	Non-savings	Total
		£	£	£	£
Trading profits				43,000	43,000
Bank interest			2,250		2,250
Dividends		1,500			1,500
Total income		1,500	2,250	43,000	46,750
Less: personal allowance				(11,500)	(11,500)
Taxable income less personal allowance		1,500	2,250	31,500	35,250
	20%			31,500	6,300
Savings allowance	0%		500		0
	20%		1,500		300
	40%		250		100
	0%	1,500			0
					6,700
Less: EIS relief £10,000 × 30%					(3,000)
Income tax payable					3,700

As Rebecca is subject to higher rate tax, then the savings allowance is limited to £500.

Suppose now that Rebecca paid an allowable pension contribution of £4,000 net (i.e. £5,000 gross). Higher rate relief is given by extending her basic rate limit, so the computation becomes instead:

		Dividends	Savings	Non-savings	Total
		£	£	£	£
Trading profits				43,000	43,000
Bank interest			2,250		2,250
Dividends		1,500			1,500
Total income		1,500	2,250	43,000	46,750
Less: personal allowance				(11,500)	(11,500)
Taxable income less personal allowance		1,500	2,250	31,500	35,250
	20%			31,500	6,300
Savings allowance	0%		1,000		0

		Dividends	Savings	Non-savings	Total
	20%		1,250		250
	0%	1,500			0
					6,550
Less: EIS relief £10,000 × 30%					(3,000)
Income tax payable					3,550

Rebecca's pension contribution extends her basic rate tax band and this takes her out of the higher rate tax bracket. Her adjusted net income is £41,750 being £46,750 less £5,000 and as such her savings allowance is increased to £1,000.

It is noteworthy that if her dividend income had been £5,000, then despite the fact that the whole of the dividend would fall within the dividend allowance, it would still form part of her adjusted net income which would become: £45,250 (gross income of £50,250 less gross equivalent pension contribution of £5,000). As such, her savings allowance would be reduced to £500.

Rates of tax

31-350 Application of rates

The rates of tax are fixed each year by Parliament.

The income tax thresholds (which determine the bands of income which are subject to each rate) are linked to the consumer prices index (CPI); this was changed from the retail prices index (RPI) in *Finance Act* 2014. Parliament may determine not to use the CPI. Currently, there is the basic rate band, the higher rate and the additional rate. A 0% starting rate applies to savings income where taxable income is £5,000 (for 2017–18) or less after deducting the personal allowance from non-savings income. The personal savings allowance also gives a 0% tax rate. In addition, there are, as mentioned, special trust tax rates for trustees of trusts and settlements but these are not based on the bands of income.

With respect to the increase of the income tax thresholds based on the increase in the CPI, if the CPI for the September preceding the tax year (i.e. year of assessment) is higher than the CPI for the September previous to that one, then the percentage increase in the CPI is applied to the income tax thresholds. However, for 2017–18, legislation provides for the basic rate limit to be £33,500.

As income increases and exceeds each threshold, tax is charged on the excess amount at the rate appropriate to the next rate band – a progressive system. In addition, an individual has a tax-free level of income, i.e. a personal allowance, which is deducted from income in arriving at taxable income to which the rate bands then apply. A blind person's allowance is due to those who are registered blind at some time in the tax year. There are other personal reliefs, such as the married couple's allowance (i.e. where the elder spouse was born before 6 April 1935), which go to reduce the income tax liability directly rather than to reduce the taxable income.

Legislation: ITA 2007, s.21

Tax Reporter: ¶148-050

31-400 Basic and higher rate(s)

The basic rate is applied to taxable income up to the 'basic rate limit' (threshold). From 2008–09, the basic rate has been 20%.

The higher rate is then applied, as appropriate, to taxable income above the 'basic rate limit' and (from 2010–11 onwards) below the 'higher rate limit'. The additional rate applies to income above that limit. For 2017–18, the 'basic rate limit' is £33,500 and the higher rate 40%. The 'higher rate limit' is £150,000 and the additional rate 45%.

Special rules apply to certain types of taxable income ('savings income' and 'dividend income') (see 30-500).

The rates applicable for 2017–18 are summarised in the table below.

Taxable income band £	Tax rate %	Income tax on band £
0–33,500	20%	6,700
33,500–150,000	40%	46,600
Over 150,000	45%	–

The following example illustrates the use of the tax bands and rates.

Example 1

For 2017–18, Frederick has taxable income, after allowances, of either:

(a) £20,000;

(b) £50,000; or

(c) £160,000,

derived solely from his employment. His income tax liability in each situation is as follows:

(a) *Taxable income of £20,000*

	£	£
Basic rate tax	20,000 × 20%	4,000
Total tax		4,000

(b) *Taxable income of £50,000*

	£	£
Basic rate tax	33,500 × 20%	6,700
Higher rate tax	16,500 × 40%	6,600
Total tax		13,300

(c) *Taxable income of £160,000*

	£	£
Basic rate tax	33,500 × 20%	6,700
Higher rate tax	116,500 × 40%	46,600
Additional rate tax	10,000 × 45%	4,500
		57,800

Other income tax rates

From 6 April 2015, a 0% starting rate (the 'starting rate for savings') may only apply to non-dividend savings income, as explained in 30-500. Between 6 April 2008 and 5 April 2015, the starting rate was 10%.

From 6 April 2016, the personal savings allowance also gives a 0% tax rate on certain non-dividend savings income although the availability of this relief is dependent on the level of the individual's adjusted net income (30-500).

Where the starting rate for savings or personal savings allowance is not applicable, then non-dividend savings income falling:

- within the basic rate band is taxed at the basic rate;
- above the basic rate limit and below the higher rate limit is taxed at the higher rate; and
- above the higher rate limit is taxed at the additional rate.

Special dividend tax rates apply to dividends. Dividends falling:

- with effect from 6 April 2016, the first £5,000 of dividend income is taxed at 0%. Dividends above this amount and below the basic rate limit are taxed at the dividend ordinary rate (7.5%);
- above the basic rate limit and below the higher rate limit are taxed at the dividend upper rate (32.5%); and
- above the higher rate limit are taxed at the dividend additional rate (38.1%).

In the case of certain trustees, there is the trust rate (45% for 2017–18) which applies to income other than dividend income. Basically, dividend type income includes UK dividends, UK distributions and overseas dividends/distributions. Such trustees are subject to the dividend trust rate (38.1% for 2017–18) on the dividend type income.

In order to determine which of the four rate bands dividends fall within, and also to determine the extent to which a person's income below the £5,000 limit for the starting rate for savings actually consists of savings income, dividend income is taken as the highest part of income, savings income next, and other income last. Thus, as pointed out elsewhere in connection with the starting rate for savings, the personal allowance will be deducted first from other income.

It is important to appreciate that despite the use of the word 'allowance' that neither the savings allowance nor the dividend allowance actually operates as allowances and that they do not reduce taxable income. They are more correctly zero rate tax bands. As such, income falling within these 'allowances' will still form part of total income, net income and adjusted net income and it will also utilise the part of the tax bands in which it falls and this may have consequential impacts on the total tax liability.

Example 2

Stephen's income in 2017–18 consists of a gross salary of £38,000 (from which PAYE of £4,750 has been deducted), bank interest of £600 and UK dividends of £7,400. His tax liability will be:

	Dividends	**Savings**	**Non-savings**	**Total**
	£	**£**	**£**	**£**
Salary			38,000	38,000
Bank interest		600		600
UK dividends	7,400			7,400
Total income				46,000

		Dividends	Savings	Non-savings	Total
Less: personal allowance				(11,500)	(11,500)
Taxable income		7,400	600	26,500	34,500
	20%			26,500	5,300
Savings allowance	0%		500		0
Taxable savings income	20%		100		20
Dividend allowance	0%	5,000			0
Dividend lower rate	7.5%	1,400			105
Dividend higher rate	32.5%	1,000			325
					5,750
PAYE deducted					(4,750)
Income tax payable					1,000

Stephen's adjusted net income is £46,000 and as such his savings allowance is £500. Both the savings allowance and the dividend allowance utilise the part of his basic rate tax band and as such only £1,400 of the dividend is taxed at the dividend lower rate and the balance is taxed at the dividend higher rate.

Legislation: ITA 2007, s. 6–21, 479

Tax Reporter: ¶148-150; ¶148-200

31-450 Deduction of income tax at source

Income tax must be deducted at the basic rate for a tax year (i.e. currently 20%) when payments in the following categories are made:

- yearly interest paid to a person whose usual place of abode is outside the UK. Ordinarily, interest paid by individuals should be paid gross but this is the exception to this rule;
- yearly interest paid to individuals by companies. From 1 October 2013, this includes interest in respect of compensation;
- patent royalties where the payment arises in the UK (until 4 December 2012);
- royalties or sums payable periodically in respect of copyrights, design rights and book public lending rights where the usual place of abode of the owner is outside the UK;
- proceeds of the sale of patent rights where paid to non-UK residents where the non-resident is chargeable to tax on the amount; and

- qualifying annual payments by an individual made for a genuine commercial reason in connection with the individual's trade, profession or vocation. An example of this is an annuity paid to a partner who has retired from the partnership.

In the case of tax deducted from patent royalties and qualifying annual payments, the tax deducted is collected through the self-assessment return. In the case of the other deductions, an account must be delivered to HMRC without delay and HMRC may then make an assessment to collect the tax deducted.

These provisions for deduction of income tax can be overridden by an appropriate double taxation agreement, subject to HMRC agreeing that the treaty provision does apply. A treaty can exempt the income so that tax is not deducted or is deducted at a reduced rate.

In arriving at the income tax liability of the individual, the gross patent royalties or qualifying annual payment for genuine commercial reasons can be deducted in calculating net income and so by collecting the income tax deducted as declared in the self-assessment return relief at the appropriate rate is given in overall terms.

Legislation: ITA 2007, s. 874, 900, 903, 906, 910, 963 and 964

Tax Reporter: ¶117-000ff.

31-500 Rate applicable to trusts and dividend trust rate

Income received by the trustees of a discretionary trust is liable to tax at special rates. For most income, the special rate is known as 'the trust rate' and is 45% for 2017–18. For dividend income, the special rate known as the 'dividend trust rate' is 38.1% for 2017–18, subject to a 'standard rate' band which for 2017–18 is £1,000.

The trust rate and the dividend trust rate are not chargeable if:

- the trust is a charity and therefore exempt;
- the trust is an approved retirement scheme or superannuation fund; or
- the trust is not a discretionary or accumulation trust; because another person has an immediate interest or entitlement to the trust income as it arises.

Payments made out of the trust at the discretion of trustees are treated as net payments after deduction of tax at the rate applicable to trusts. This applies even where the payments are made out of dividend income.

Legislation: ITA 2007, s. 9, 479, 480, 481

Tax Reporter: ¶351-100

Personal reliefs

32-000 Introduction

All individuals who are resident in the UK in a particular tax year are entitled to a personal allowance, subject to rules which took effect from 2010–11 onwards under which the allowance is reduced, and eventually eliminated, for individuals with 'adjusted net income' in excess of £100,000. Other reliefs may be claimed in particular circumstances, although the availability of these other reliefs and their value have diminished.

In the case of married couples, for tax years after 1999–2000, a married couple's allowance is only available where the elder spouse was born before 6 April 1935.

All of the married couple's allowance may be claimed in the tax year in which one of the spouses died. The married couple's allowance is given by way of an income tax reduction at 10% of the relief (see below). For further details on the married couple's allowance, see 32-450.

An individual who is registered blind at any time in a tax year may also claim a blind person's allowance. The blind person's allowance is deducted from that individual's net income. Where the individual is married, any excess allowance (i.e. the amount of the blind person's allowance that cannot be deducted because of insufficiency of net income) can be transferred to the other spouse provided the registered blind person has given written notice for the transfer to HMRC not later that four years following the end of the tax year concerned. This notice is irrevocable. For further details, see 33-600.

A table of the various personal reliefs available is given in *Key data*.

If an individual's net income is less than his personal reliefs, he or she will not bear income tax on that income. Unused personal reliefs cannot be carried forward to the following year or back to an earlier year. A personal allowance cannot currently be transferred except under certain limited circumstances post-5 April 2015, see 32-400.

Other personal reliefs, such as married couple's allowance, are given by way of an income tax reduction. With respect to an income tax reduction, it is necessary first to compute the amount of the person's income tax liability apart from the income tax reduction concerned. This amount is then reduced by 10% of the specified amount of the relief but only so far as there is sufficient income tax from which to deduct it.

Allowances for married couples and civil partnerships

32-400 Transferable tax allowance

With effect from 6 April 2015, it is possible to transfer part of an individual's personal allowance to a spouse or civil partner provided the transferor's income is less than the personal allowance and the transferee is not a higher or additional rate taxpayer. The maximum amount that can be transferred for 2017–18 is £1,150. This facility is not available where the parties are eligible for the married couple's allowance 32-450.

Legislation: FA 2014, s. 11; ITA 2007, s. 55A–55E

Tax Reporter: ¶156-725

32-450 Married couple's allowance

A husband and his wife are treated as independent taxpayers and both are entitled to a 'personal allowance'. Prior to 2000–01, a married couple's allowance (MCA) was also available to all married couples. The MCA was abolished for 2000–01 onwards, unless at least one of the couple was born before 6 April 1935. The legislation now deals with civil partnerships by extending the MCA to such relationships.

In addition to the personal allowance (see 32-000) a 'married couple's allowance' is available to a claimant who, for the whole or any part of the tax year, is a married man whose wife is 'living with' him. The term 'wife' does not include a 'common law wife'. See below for the effects of the *Civil Partnership Act* 2004. Slightly different rules apply to marriages and civil partnerships entered into after 4 December 2005. This section indicates the position for pre-5 December 2005 marriages.

The amount of the allowance for 2017–18 is £8,455 if either the husband or wife was born before 6 April 1935. Where the husband's 'adjusted net income' (see 32-100) for the tax year exceeds £28,000, the allowance is reduced by half the excess, less any amount by which his personal allowance has been reduced for the same reason, as discussed at 32-550. The MCA may not, however, be reduced below a 'minimum amount' which, for 2017–18, is £3,260. Changes in the allowance are linked to the consumer prices index unless Parliament otherwise determines.

No more than one married couple's allowance is available in any tax year. For the computation of the married couple's allowance in the year of marriage, see 32-700.

The allowance is given initially to the husband, but all or one half of the minimum amount may be allocated to the wife and, furthermore, any excess allowance may be transferred to the other spouse.

The married couple's allowance can be disclaimed by the person giving HMRC notice that entitlement to the allowance is being given up in respect of a tax year. Provided the election is not revoked, the person will be treated as not being entitled to the married couple's allowance for the tax year concerned.

Relief for the allowance is given by way of an income tax reduction equal to 10% of the allowance. However, the income tax reduction cannot exceed an amount that reduces an individual's tax liability to nil.

Example

In 2017–18, Colin, aged 82, is living with his wife whom he married in 1990. He has pension income of £14,000. In the absence of other relevant factors, his tax liability will be as follows:

	£
Income	14,000
Less: personal allowance	(11,500)
Taxable income	2,500
Tax liability	£
Basic rate tax £2,500 × 20% =	500
Less: income tax reduction–	
married couple's allowance	
Lower of	
(i) amount reducing liability to nil, i.e. £500 and	
(ii) £8,455 × 10% = £845.50	(500)
Tax liability	Nil

As with the personal allowance, any unused married couple's allowance is lost, unless it can be transferred to and used by the other spouse. It cannot be carried forward or back to another tax year.

Civil partnerships

The *Civil Partnership Act* 2004 received Royal Assent on 18 November 2004. For tax purposes, the consequential changes are contained in the *Tax and Civil Partnership Regulations* 2005 (SI 2005/3229) which amend the relevant statutory provisions. The purpose of the legislation was to introduce a civil partnership scheme that, broadly, gives same-sex couples the same legal rights and obligations as married couples.

> 'A civil partnership is a relationship between two people of the same sex ... which is formed when they register as civil partners of each other.'

A valid civil partnership can be terminated only on death, dissolution or annulment. This means that same-sex couples who are registered within the civil partnership scheme are treated the same as married couples for all tax purposes (i.e. income tax, capital gains tax, inheritance tax, etc.).

Legislation: ITA 2007, s. 45, 48, 58

Case: *Rignell (HMIT) v Andrews* [1990] BTC 306

Tax Reporter: ¶155-000; ¶156-000

32-500 Transfer of married couple's allowance

In the first instance, the married couple's allowance (MCA) will go to the husband. But it is possible to transfer:

- the amount of the income tax reduction that exceeds his income tax liability; and
- one-half, or the whole, of the minimum amount.

Transfer of MCA income reduction in excess over income

For details on the transfer of the amount of the MCA income tax reduction that exceeds income tax liability, see 32-550.

Transfer of one-half, or whole, of the minimum amount of the MCA

If the couple wish, they may jointly elect that the whole of the 'minimum amount' of £3,260 should be transferred to the wife.

Alternatively, the wife alone may elect to claim one-half of the 'minimum amount' or, if the whole of that amount has been transferred to the wife as a result of a previous election, the husband may claim back one-half of the 'minimum amount'.

To reiterate, these claims are limited to the 'minimum amount'. Any allowance above that figure therefore remains with the husband (unless he has insufficient income to utilise it).

Since relief for the married couple's allowance is given as an income tax reduction rather than by way of a reduction in taxable income, the claim does not affect the total amount of the tax relief which may be obtained by the couple taken together. Apart from equality between the spouses, the main advantage may be by way of timing if, for example, one spouse can claim relief through PAYE.

Example

Ellie is in her late sixties and George is in his late eighties. They have been married for many years. Some years ago, Ellie made a claim for one-half of the married couple's allowance. In 2017–18, Ellie earns £14,000 and George has total pension income of £41,000. Neither has any other income. *Note*: George's higher personal allowance and married couple's allowance are fully abated to the minimum amounts due because the level of his adjusted net income substantially exceeds the income limit (£28,000 for 2017–18).

Their tax liabilities for 2017–18 are as follows:

				Ellie	*George*
				£	£
Salary				14,000	41,000
Less: personal allowance				(11,500)	(11,500)
Taxable income				2,500	29,500
Tax liability					
	£	£		£	£
Basic rate tax	2,500/	29,500	× 20%	500.00	5,900.00
Higher rate tax	Nil/	Nil/	–	–	
	2,500	29,500		500.00	5,900.00
Less: income tax reduction–					
married couple's allowance					
(£3,260 × 10% × ½)				(163.00)	(163.00)
Tax liability				337.00	5,737.00

An election should be made in writing to HMRC. A claim will normally be effective for the tax year following that in which it is made and will continue to apply for subsequent years until formally withdrawn or replaced by a new election; withdrawal will not be effective until the tax year following the year in which notice is given. Applications may be made on form 18. It should be noted that whilst either spouse may independently obtain half of the minimum amount, the full minimum amount may be given to one spouse only on the basis of a jointly signed election.

In two circumstances, the election will be effective for the year in which it is made. An election made in the year of marriage will be immediately effective. In addition, where HMRC have been given written notice in the previous tax year that it is intended that the election will be made, the election will apply provided it is made within the first 30 days of the tax year for which it is to be effective.

Legislation: ITA 2007, s. 47, 48

Tax Reporter: ¶156-100

32-550 Transfer of married couple's allowance where relief exceeds income

Where the husband is unable to take full advantage of his married couple's allowance because his income tax liability is insufficient, the unused part of the allowance may be transferred to the wife. This applies to the full amount of the allowance, and not simply to the minimum amount. Likewise, where the wife is unable to utilise fully any income tax reduction in respect of the married couple's allowance to which she may be entitled as a result of an election, the unused reduction can be transferred to her husband.

Notice of the transfer must be given to HMRC not more than four years after the end of the tax year to which it relates, and is irrevocable.

These transfers are made after taking into account any claims to transfer all or half of the basic married couple's allowance between spouses.

Example 1

Stephen and Claire have been married for 30 years. Stephen was born in January 1935 and Claire in 1947. Stephen received pension income of £5,800 during the tax year of 2017–18. Claire continues with her part-time job as a nurse and earned £17,080 in 2017–18. Stephen and Claire have no other taxable income for 2017–18.

No election has been made to transfer the benefit of the married couple's allowance to Claire.

As shown below, Stephen's tax liability for 2017–18 is nil. His income is insufficient to utilise fully his age-related personal allowance (for 2017–18: £11,500) and the unused balance of £5,700 is wasted. However, by giving notice to HMRC, the married couple's allowance income tax reduction of £845.50 (£8,455 × 10%), which he is unable to use, can be transferred to Claire.

	Stephen	*Claire*
	£	£
Income	5,800	17,080
Less: personal allowance	(5,800)	(11,500)
Taxable income	Nil	5,580

Claire's tax liability

	£	£
Basic rate tax	5,580 × 20% =	1,116.00
Less: income tax reduction –		
married couple's allowance		
transferred from Stephen		
£8,455 × 10% and Tax charge		(845.50)
Claire's tax liability		270.50

Example 2

Jimmy and Anne have been married for ten years. In 2017–18, both are 84 years of age. In January 2000, Anne claimed one-half of the married couple's allowance. In 2017–18, Anne receives a pension of £17,620 and Jimmy one of £8,000. Jimmy is unable to use all of his share of the income tax reduction in respect of the married couple's allowance. As Jimmy's total income is less than the income limit of £28,000, the married couple's allowance (for 2017–18: £8,455) is not subject to abatement. Provided Jimmy gives notice to HMRC, the unused portion of the MCA can be transferred to Anne. Initially, however, Anne's claim for half of the MCA is limited to one-half of the 'minimum amount' (for 2017–18: £3,260); the remainder of the MCA can only be transferred to her if Jimmy gives the required notice.

Their income tax liabilities for 2017–18 are as follows.

				Jimmy	*Anne*
				£	£
Income				8,000	17,620
Less: personal allowance				(8,000)	(11,500)
Taxable income				–	6,120
Tax liabilities					
	£	£		£	£
Basic rate tax	Nil/	6,620	× 20%	–	1,324
				Nil	1,324
Less: income tax reductions –					
married couple's allowance					
(£3,260 × 10% × 50%)				(163.00)	

lower of:		
(6,825[1] × 10%); and Nil	Nil	
unused reduction transferred from Jimmy		
(£682.50 – Nil)[2]	–	(682.50)
Tax liability	Nil	478.50

(1) £8,455 – (£3,260 x 50%) = £6,825.
(2) Both the unused half of the 'minimum amount' and the balance of the full allowance are transferred to Anne.

Example 3

John and Patricia have been married for a number of years. Patricia retired on her 60th birthday, which was in June 2008. In February 2009, John celebrated his 80th birthday. In March 2017, they jointly elected to transfer the whole of the basic married couple's allowance to Patricia. In 2017–18, Patricia received a pension of £10,125 and John one of £40,360. Neither has any other taxable income.

Note: John's married couple's allowance (for 2017–18: £8,455) is *fully abated* because of the level of his total income (which substantially exceeds the income limit for 2017–18: £28,000). Furthermore, Patricia is unable to utilise the full income tax reduction (being the minimum amount of MCA for 2017–18: £3,260 × 10%) and thus, provided Patricia gives notice to HMRC, the unused portion can be transferred to John.

Their tax liabilities for 2017–18 are calculated as follows:

				John	*Patricia*
				£	£
Salary				40,360	10,125
Less: personal allowance				(11,500)	(10,125)
Taxable income				28,860	0
Tax liabilities					
	£	£		£	£
Basic rate tax	28,860/	0	× 20%	5,772	0
Higher rate tax	Nil/	Nil	× 40%	–	–
	29,760/	0		5,772	0
Less: income tax reductions –					
married couple's allowance					
lower of: £3,260 × 10% and £0					(0)

reduction unused by Patricia		
(£326 − £0)	(326)	–
Tax liability	5,446	Nil

Legislation: ITA 2007, s. 551, 552, 553

Tax Reporter: ¶156-200

32-600 Position for post-4 December 2005 marriages and civil partnerships

The rules as set out above apply only to marriages before 5 December 2005. The creation of the concept of a civil partnership with effect from 5 December 2005 meant the need to recast the legislation as the previous rules were expressed in terms of a man living with his wife. It is now a question of considering whether for the whole or part of the relevant tax year the individual is married or in a civil partnership and is living with the spouse or civil partner.

The basic principles remain the same broadly, whether considering a marriage or civil partnership, so that one of the parties to a marriage or civil partnership must have been born before 6 April 1935. The main difference, however, is that the initial entitlement to the relief is only given to the spouse or civil partner having the higher income of the two whereas for marriages before 5 December 2005 the entitlement was given to the man. Clearly, for such earlier marriages, there is a possibility that the allowance could be given to a husband having a relatively low income compared to his wife with a high income. The new rule may, therefore, effectively restrict the cases where the allowance can be claimed. The provisions for one party to claim an allowance and joint election to transfer the allowance are the same for both marriages and civil partnerships. It is also possible for a joint election to be made so that a pre-5 December 2005 marriage is treated for the purposes of the allowance as if it had been made after that date. The election must be made before the first year of assessment for which it is to have effect and is irrevocable.

Legislation: ITA 2007, s. 44, 46

Tax Reporter: ¶134-375

32-650 Jointly held property

The law concerning ownership of property is beyond the scope of this publication. Suffice it to say that there is legal ownership and beneficial ownership of property. As the name suggests, a person with 'beneficial' ownership is entitled to enjoy the benefits (e.g. income and capital growth) flowing out of that ownership. A person may have both legal and beneficial ownership of the property. However, it may be that one person has legal ownership and another has beneficial ownership of the same property.

Where a person has a beneficial interest in the property, that person can enjoy the income. Where a person receives income but is legally forbidden to enjoy the income then that person does not have a beneficial interest (e.g. agent or bare trustee).

If a married couple (or parties to a civil partnership), who are living together, are beneficially entitled to income from property held in their joint names, each of them will normally be treated as entitled to half the income. This treatment of equality does not apply to UK qualifying furnished holiday accommodation, partnership income, and dividend income etc. derived from jointly held shares in a close company. If the beneficial ownership of the property, from which the income is derived, is unequal then they may make a joint declaration of their beneficial shares in the income.

The declaration has effect for income arising on or after its date, but is ineffective if:

- notice of it is not given to the inspector (on form 17), within 60 days of its making; or
- the beneficial interests of the spouses/civil partners in the property do not correspond to their beneficial interests in the income.

Once validly made, the declaration continues in effect unless and until the spouses', etc. interests in either the income or capital cease to accord with the declaration.

As mentioned, the deemed equality rule is disapplied inter alia where the jointly held property consists of close company shares and the income is any distribution from those shares. This means that dividends from such shares must be taxed on the basis of each party's *actual* beneficial entitlement.

Legislation: ITA 2007, s. 836, 837

Tax Reporter: ¶134-350

32-700 The year of marriage or civil partnership

The married couple's allowance is available for any tax year in which the parties to the arrangement are living together for at least part of the year in which it takes place. Thus, it is available in the year of marriage or entering into the civil partnership but is restricted on a time basis, unless a claimant was entitled to the allowance in the same year concerning another relationship. Subject to that, the allowance is reduced by one-twelfth for each complete month of the tax year ending before the date of marriage or entering into the civil partnership. Month for this purpose means the month beginning with the sixth day of a month for a calendar year. This restriction applies to the amount of the allowance as reduced (where appropriate) because income exceeds the £27,700 threshold.

Example

Richard, aged 84, marries Kathy, aged 73, on 22 June 2016. Richard has the higher income of the two and was not previously entitled to the allowance in 2017–18. For that year, his reduced maximum allowance is £6,963 (i.e. 10/12 × £8,355) with a minimum of £2,683 (i.e. 10/12 × £3,220), depending on his total income for the year.

Legislation: ITA 2007, s. 54

Tax Reporter: ¶156-300

32-750 Changing circumstances: separation

For tax purposes, a married woman and a civil partner are treated as 'living with' their husband or partner, unless:

- they are separated by court order or a deed of separation; or
- they are separated (although not necessarily under different roofs) in circumstances such that the separation is likely to be permanent.

In the tax year of separation, there is an entitlement to the full married couple's allowance (reduced as appropriate in view of the level of income) for that year. There is no apportionment similar to that made in the year of marriage (see 32-700). The rules for transferring the married couple's allowance, whether by election (see 32-500) or in the case of excess allowances (see 32-550), apply for the year of separation as for any other year.

Legislation: ITA 2007, s. 1011

Case: *Holmes v Mitchell (HMIT)* [1991] BTC 28

Tax Reporter: ¶156-400

32-800 Changing circumstances: divorce and annulment

For the purposes of personal reliefs, divorce or annulment have no additional consequences. This is because the rules for married couples and civil partnerships depend on the couple 'living together', so that it is the separation of the couple which, in most cases, affects the available reliefs.

If a marriage is annulled (treated as if it had never taken place), claims for the higher personal relief for a married man that applied before 1990–91 were nevertheless treated as valid for the years before annulment. The same presumably also applies with respect to the married couple's allowance.

For the tax treatment of makers and recipients of maintenance payments, see 33-700.

Case: *Dodworth (HMIT) v Dale* (1936) 20 TC 285

Tax Reporter: ¶156-500

32-900 Changing circumstances: death

Death does not cause the married couple's allowance to be reduced for the tax year of death. There is no apportionment similar to that made in the year of marriage (see 32-700).

If the income of the person entitled to the allowance is insufficient fully to utilise the allowance for the year of death, his or her executors may give notice that the excess should be transferred to the other partner.

Legislation: ITA 2007, s. 55

Tax Reporter: ¶156-500

Other reliefs

33-600 Blind person's allowance

An allowance of £2,320 for 2017–18 is given to a person who proves that he or she is a 'registered blind person' for all or part of a tax year.

A blind person who is 'living with' his or her spouse or civil partner (see 32-450) can transfer any excess allowance to that other party. In calculating how much of the allowance is excess, the allowance is treated as made after all other available deductions except pension scheme contributions where relief is given under FA 1994, s. 192, and after deducting the personal allowance due for the year.

Before these transfer provisions can apply, the person entitled to the allowance must have given to HMRC an irrevocable written notice, not later than four years from the end of the tax year to which it relates, that they should apply. The notice is also treated as a notice to transfer excess MCA (see 32-550).

A 'registered blind person' means a person registered as a blind person on a register kept under the *National Assistance Act* 1948 or who is ordinarily resident in Scotland or Northern Ireland and is unable to do any work for which eyesight is essential, because of blindness.

A person who becomes entitled to the blind person's allowance by being registered blind will also be granted the allowance for the previous tax year if, at the end of that year, that person had obtained the proof of blindness subsequently used to qualify for registration. This prevents people losing the benefit of the allowance because of delays in the registration process and represents the enactment of a previous concession.

Legislation: ITA 2007, s. 38, 39

Tax Reporter: ¶157-000

33-700 Maintenance payments

Apart from a relatively minor exception dealt with in the next paragraph, maintenance payments from one party to a marriage or former marriage to the other party are not eligible for any form of tax relief. On the other hand, the recipient is not subject to tax on the amount receivable and so clearly in agreeing payments of this nature, the parties need to take into account the lack of tax deductibility and absence of tax on the recipient. It does not matter whether the maintenance is directly to the other spouse or to a child of the marriage.

The exception relates to qualifying maintenance payments, which broadly are payments where the following conditions are met:

- one of the parties to the marriage must have been born before 6 April 1935;
- payments must be under a court order of a member state or under a written agreement which applies the law of such a state;
- the payment must be made by one of the parties to the marriage or former marriage either for the benefit and maintenance of the other party or of any child of the family;
- the payment must be due at a time when the parties are not living together and the party to whom the payment is made must not have remarried; and
- when the payments relate to a child of the family, that child must be under 21 years of age. Furthermore, payments made to the Child

Support Agency, etc. are treated as if made to the other party for maintenance of the children in question.

The relief is given in a similar way to the married couple's allowance, being a maximum tax reduction equal to 10% of, for 2017–18, £3,220 (i.e. the 'minimum amount' for the married couple's allowance). The relief is given as explained at 30-450 by way of a reduction in the tax liability, as calculated on 'net income'; less the personal allowance and blind person's allowance. An order of priority is set out in ITA 2007, s. 27 for deductions made at this stage. Qualifying maintenance payments come after various items such as EIS relief and VCT relief but before the MCA and double tax relief. These reliefs cannot exceed the amount which reduces a person's liability to nil, to ensure that the amount retained from any gift aid or pension payments paid net of basic rate tax is paid to HMRC.

Legislation: ITA 2007, s. 453–456

Tax Reporter: ¶115-650

Charges on income

34-000 Annual payments and royalties

Historically, these are known as charges on income and that expression is still used today, although it no longer appears in the legislation. From an income tax point of view, however, the essential question is whether an individual is required to deduct income tax from such payments at the basic rate. If such deduction is required, then as a general rule the gross payment is deducted in arriving at net income. Clearly, for a basic rate taxpayer the tax deducted is effectively the income tax relief but a higher rate taxpayer is entitled to the benefit of the difference between the basic rate and the higher rate.

The categories of payments that are dealt with in this way are now quite limited so that only the following, broadly, are both deductible in arriving at net income and require the deduction of income tax at the basic rate:

- patent royalties where the payment arises in the UK (but not after 4 December 2012); and
- payments made for commercial reasons in connection with the individual's trade, profession or vocation – this would include, therefore, annuities paid by a partnership to former members of that partnership. Again, the payment must arise in the UK and the recipient must be subject to UK tax on the amount.

The rate at which income tax should be deducted by a payer of such an amount is the rate in force for the tax year in which the payment is made.

In no case can an amount be treated as a deduction from total income if the payment is deductible in calculating the individual's income from any particular source.

In addition, the payments must be unaffected by the 'settlement' anti-avoidance provisions, and a payment made under a liability which is incurred for non-taxable consideration is to be made without deduction of income tax.

Legislation: ITA 2007, s. 899, 900, 903, 904

Tax Reporter: ¶115-900; ¶116-000

Reliefs for interest payments

35-000 Introduction to reliefs for interest payments

Income tax relief may be available for an interest payment that relates to a loan applied for one of the purposes specified below:

(1) to purchase machinery or plant (see 35-100);

(2) to acquire an interest in a close company (see 35-150);

(3) to acquire an interest in a cooperative (see 35-200);

(4) to acquire shares in an employee-controlled company (see 35-250);

(5) to acquire an interest in partnership (see 35-300);

(6) to pay inheritance tax (see 35-350); or

(7) to purchase a life annuity where the borrower is aged 65 or over (see 35-400).

Tax relief may be available effectively at the additional, higher or basic rate, or at a special rate in connection with (7) above. Apart from relief under (7) above, the allowable interest is set against total income (see 30-400).

Tax relief is not available more than once. Relief is also available for interest under the property business rules or as a deduction in computing trading profits, provided, as a general rule, the wholly and exclusively test is met. Otherwise there is no relief for mortgage interest.

Relief is not available under the present provisions for interest on an overdraft or under credit card arrangements.

Where the interest paid on a loan in a tax year exceeds a 'reasonable commercial' amount of interest on the loan for the 'relevant period', then interest representing the excess is not eligible for relief. The 'relevant period' is the tax year or part of the tax year for which the loan exists.

A 'reasonable commercial' amount of interest on the loan for the relevant period is an amount which, together with any interest paid before that period (other than unrelieved interest) represents a reasonable commercial rate of interest from the date the loan was made to the end of that period. Relief is also denied if the main purpose of the arrangements is to avoid tax.

In the case of joint loans taken out by a husband and wife where only one meets the qualifying conditions, HMRC will give the relief in full to the spouse meeting those conditions including where the joint liability is satisfied out of a joint account.

The level of tax relief for interest paid will be subject to the capping provisions outlined in 43-200.

Legislation: ITA 2007, s. 383, 384 and 387; TIOPA 2010, Sch. 7, para. 52

Other Material: HMRC Interpretation, IRInt. 15 (Tax Bulletin, February 1992)

Tax Reporter: ¶115-200

35-050 Form of relief

Most interest available for relief is set against the taxpayer's total income as discussed at 30-400. This means that tax relief on the interest paid is given at the taxpayer's highest marginal rate of tax.

Example

Christopher is a sole trader. In addition to this, he is a non-working shareholder in Exways Ltd, a close trading company. In the year 2017–18, his trading profits before deduction of interest were £52,000, he received a dividend of £9,000 from that company and bank interest of £2,400. He also owns a property in the UK, which he lets at an annual rent, net of running expenses, of £5,000 in 2017–18. He has three loans in connection with these interests, being: £50,000, which he used to buy the goodwill of his sole trader business; £40,000 to buy his shares in Exways Ltd; and £100,000 to purchase the let UK property. The interest rate on these loans is at 6% p.a.

His income tax liability is as follows for 2017–18:

		Dividends	**Savings**	**Non-savings**	**Total**
		£	**£**	**£**	**£**
Trading profits	52,000				
Less: interest on £50,000 loan	(3,000)				
				49,000	49,000
Property business	5,000				

		Dividends	Savings	Non-savings	Total
Less: interest on £100,000 loan	(6,000)				
Loss to carry forward	1,000				
Bank interest			2,400		2,400
Dividends		9,000			9,000
		9,000	2,400	49,000	60,400
Less: interest on £40,000 loan to buy shares				(2,400)	(2,400)
Net income		9,000	2,400	46,600	58,000
Less: personal allowance				(11,500)	(11,500)
Taxable income		9,000	2,400	35,100	46,500

The interest on the loans to acquire goodwill and the property purchase loan are deducted in arriving at the results of those particular sources and cannot be set against total income as such. The loan to purchase the shares in Exways Ltd is set off in the order which will produce the lowest income tax liability. This should, therefore, be by setting against the trading profits and the personal allowance will also be set off against that source, as can be seen:

		Dividends	Savings	Non-savings	Total
		£	£	£	£
Trading profits				49,000	
Less: Exways loan interest				(2,400)	
Less: personal allowance				(11,500)	
				35,100	35,100
Bank interest			2,400		2,400
Dividends		9,000			9,000
Taxable income		9,000	2,400	35,100	46,500
	20%			33,500	6,700
	40%			1,600	640
Savings allowance	0%		500		0
Taxable savings income	20%		1,900		380

		Dividends	Savings	Non-savings	Total
Dividend allowance	0%	5,000			0
Dividend higher rate	32.5%	4,000			1,300
Income tax payable					9,200

Had any of the deductions been set against, for example, the dividends, the tax payable would have been:

		Dividends	Savings	Non-savings	Total
Trading profits				49,000	
Less: personal allowance				(11,000)	
				37,500	37,500
Bank interest			2,400		2,400
Dividends		9,000			9,000
Less: Exways loan interest		(2,400)			
Taxable income		6,600	2,400	37,500	46,500
	20%			32,000	6,700
	40%			4,000	1,600
Savings allowance	0%		500		0
Taxable savings income	20%		1,900		380
Dividend allowance	0%	5,000			0
Dividend higher rate	32.5%	1,600			520
Income tax payable					9,200

This is reconciled with the lower liability of £9,020:

£2,400 × (40% – 32.5%) = £180

Claiming relief

Taxpayers must make a claim for interest relief. The borrower may be required by HMRC to provide a written statement from the lender that includes the following details:

- the date the debt was incurred;
- the amount of the debt when incurred;
- the interest paid in the tax year for which the claim is made; and
- the name and address of the debtor.

The borrower can insist that the lender supply these details. For lenders other than banks, the information is usually provided on form 38E-1. For bank loans, form 38E-2 is normally used. As well as asking the borrower for the purpose of the loan, this form also asks the bank to certify that the interest is on a loan other than an overdraft (since relief under ITA 2007, s. 383 cannot be claimed for overdraft interest).

The above forms do not have to be used, so long as the lender provides the required details in writing. However, written details are not needed in respect of interest paid to a building society or local authority as they supply information direct to HMRC.

Legislation: ITA 2007, s. 384, 412

Other Material: HMRC Interpretation, IRInt. 106 (Tax Bulletin, April 1995)

Tax Reporter: ¶115-200

35-100 Loan to purchase plant or machinery

Interest is eligible for relief where it is paid by an individual member of a partnership on a loan to buy plant or machinery if the partnership is entitled to capital allowances in respect of that machinery or plant under CAA 2001, s. 264.

An employee or director is entitled to similar interest relief if he is entitled to a capital allowance (or would be so entitled but for some contribution made by his employer) for plant or machinery belonging to him and used for the purposes of his office or employment (e.g. a van). From 6 April 2002, employees and directors are not entitled to claim capital allowances for a car used for the office or employment. Hence, relief is not available for interest on a loan taken out to purchase such a car.

In cases both of partnerships and employments, the relief is available for interest payable up to three years from the end of the tax year in which the debt was incurred.

Where the machinery or plant is used only partly for the purposes of the trade, etc. or the employment then a just and reasonable apportionment is made of the interest eligible for relief.

Where only part of a loan satisfies the necessary conditions, see 35-450.

Legislation: ITA 2007, s. 388–390

Tax Reporter: ¶115-250

35-150 Acquiring an interest in a close company

Interest may be eligible for relief if it is paid on a loan made to an individual ('the borrower') in the following circumstances:

- to acquire ordinary shares of a close company that is not a close investment-holding company (see below); or
- in making a loan to such a company where the loan is used wholly and exclusively for the business of the company or of any associated close company that is not a close investment-holding company; or
- in paying off an earlier loan, interest on which would have qualified for relief.

There are two further conditions, at least one of which must be satisfied (see below).

Close investment-holding company

A company (the 'relevant company') is a close investment-holding company in an accounting period if it does not exist throughout the accounting period wholly or mainly for any one or more of the following purposes.

(1) To carry on a trade or trades on a commercial basis.

(2) To invest in land, which is, or is intended to be, let to persons other than a person *either* 'connected with' the company *or* who is the spouse of an individual connected with it or a 'relative' (brother, sister, ancestor or lineal descendant), or spouse of a relative, of such an individual or such an individual's spouse.

(3) To hold securities of, or make loans to, one or more companies each of which either:

   (i) is a 'qualifying company' (see below); or

   (ii) is a company which is under the control of the relevant company, or of a company which has control of the relevant company, and which itself wholly or mainly exists to hold securities of, or make loans to, one or more qualifying companies.

(4) To coordinate the administration of two or more qualifying companies.

(5) For the purposes of a trade or trades carried out on a commercial basis by one or more qualifying companies or a company which has control of the relevant company.

(6) For the purposes of the making, by one or more qualifying companies or by a company which has control of the relevant company, of investments as mentioned in (2) above.

A company is a 'qualifying company' for (3) to (6) above if it:

(a) is under the control of the relevant company or of a company which has control of the relevant company; and

(b) exists wholly or mainly for at least one of purposes (1) and (2) above.

Further conditions

In addition, the following conditions must be satisfied at the time the interest is paid.

(1) The company is not a close investment-holding company.

(2) The borrower shows that he has not recovered any capital from the company (apart from any amount taken into account in reducing the interest eligible for relief; see 35-450).

(3) Either:

   (a) the borrower has a material interest in the company; or

   (b) the borrower holds ordinary shares of the company and during the period from taking out the loan to the time of payment of the interest he has worked for the majority of his time in the actual management or conduct of the company (or of an associated company). HMRC have stated that in their view the individual must be involved in the overall running and policy-making of the company as a whole. Managerial or technical responsibility for just one particular area will not be sufficient.

A person has a 'material interest' in a company if he, either on his own or with one or more 'associates', or if any associate of his (with or without any other associates):

- is the beneficial owner of, or able, directly or indirectly, to control, more than 5% of the ordinary share capital of the company; or
- possesses, or is entitled to acquire, rights giving an entitlement to receive more than 5% of the assets of the company in the event of a winding up of the company.

'Associate' means a relative (spouse, civil partner, ancestor, lineal descendant, brother or sister) or partner of the borrower, the trustees of a settlement of which the borrower or his relative was the settlor, and if the borrower has an interest in shares or obligations in the company under a settlement or estate, the trustees or personal representatives (but not the beneficiaries) of that settlement or estate.

If the company exists wholly or mainly to hold investments or other property, and the borrower uses property held by the company as a residence, relief will only be available if the borrower has spent the majority of his time in the management or conduct of the business of the company (or of an associated company). HMRC regard involvement in the actual management or conduct of a company as requiring participation in the overall running and policy making of the company.

For supplementary provisions, see 35-450.

The relief remains available even if the company ceases to be a close company after the loan proceeds have been applied provided the other conditions for relief are satisfied.

The relief is not available if the person who acquires the shares, or that person's spouse, claims income tax relief under the EIS scheme, or EIS deferral relief for capital gains tax.

Legislation: ITA 2007, s. 392–395

Other Material: SP 3/78

Tax Reporter: ¶115-300

35-200 Acquiring an interest in a cooperative

Interest paid by an individual ('the borrower') on a loan is eligible for relief if the loan is applied:

- in acquiring a share or shares in a 'cooperative'; or
- in on-lending to a cooperative money which is used wholly and exclusively for the cooperative's, or its subsidiary's, business; or
- in discharging an earlier loan which would have qualified for interest relief.

'Cooperative' means a 'common ownership enterprise' or a 'cooperative enterprise' as defined in *Industrial Common Ownership Act* 1976, s. 2.

A 'common ownership enterprise' is a company limited by guarantee or a registered industrial and provident society, certified by the Chief Registrar of Friendly Societies, whose memorandum and articles of association limit membership to employees and require that its assets may only be used to further its objects and that its assets on a winding up are transferred to a similar enterprise or fund for the benefit of such enterprise, or to charity. A 'cooperative enterprise' is one certified by the Secretary of State as such, being governed by a written constitution as to the application of its income to its members' benefit, and which is controlled by a majority of people working for it or its subsidiaries.

The following conditions must be satisfied if interest payments are to be eligible for relief.

- At the time the interest is paid, the cooperative continues to be a cooperative.
- The borrower has for the greater part of his time been an employee of the cooperative (or its subsidiary) from the time the loan is applied to the time of the interest payments.
- The borrower shows that he has not recovered any capital from the cooperative before the interest payment (apart from any amount taken into account in reducing the interest eligible for relief; see 35-450).

Legislation: ITA 2007, s. 401, 402

Tax Reporter: ¶115-350

35-250 Acquiring shares in an employee-controlled company

Interest is eligible for relief if it is paid on a loan made to an individual to:

- acquire ordinary shares in an employee-controlled company (see below); or
- pay off another loan, interest on which would have qualified for relief.

Qualifying conditions

For relief to be given, the following conditions must be satisfied.

(1) The company must be (from the date on which the shares are acquired to the date on which interest is paid):

 (a) an unquoted company resident only in the UK or in the European Economic Area; and

 (b) a trading company or the holding company of a trading group.

(2) The shares must be acquired before, or not later than 12 months after, the date on which the company first becomes an employee-controlled company.

(3) During the tax year in which the interest is paid, the company must either:

 (a) first become an employee-controlled company; or

(b) be an employee-controlled company throughout a period of at least nine months.

(4) The individual must be a full-time employee of the company from the date of buying the shares to the date on which the interest is paid. Relief will continue to be given for interest paid up to 12 months after the taxpayer has ceased to be a full-time employee.

(5) The taxpayer must not have recovered any capital from the company, unless that amount is treated as a repayment of the loan (in whole or in part); see 35-450.

Employee-controlled company

A company is employee-controlled at any time when more than 50%:

- of the issued ordinary share capital of the company; and
- of the voting power in the company,

is beneficially owned by persons who are full-time employees of the company. For this purpose, where an individual owns beneficially more than 10% of the issued ordinary share capital or controls more than 10% of the voting power in the company, the excess over 10% is not regarded as being owned by a full-time employee.

Example

The 20 employees and three directors of XYZ Ltd acquire 60% of the issued ordinary share capital of XYZ Ltd. The three directors each acquire 15% of those shares and the balance is divided equally among the 20 full-time employees. This is not an employee-controlled company as 15% of the shares (i.e. 5% for each director) are not regarded as being owned by a full-time employee.

For supplementary provisions, see 35-450.

Legislation: ITA 2007, s. 396, 397 and 410

Tax Reporter: ¶115-400

35-300 Acquiring interest in partnership

Interest paid on a loan to an individual is eligible for relief if the loan is used to defray money applied in:

- purchasing a share in a partnership;
- contributing capital to a partnership, or advancing money to it, where it is used wholly for the purposes of the trade, profession or vocation carried on by the partnership; or

- paying off another loan interest on which would have been eligible for relief.

For supplementary provisions, see 35-450.

For relief to be available the following conditions must apply.

- Throughout the period from the application of the loan until the interest is paid, the individual has been a member of the partnership. Although relief is generally available to members of limited liability partnerships registered under the *Limited Liability Partnership Act* 2000, it is not available to members of investment limited liability partnerships, nor to limited partners of limited partnerships registered under the *Limited Partnership Act* 1907. HMRC regard salaried partners in professional firms as qualifying for relief if they are indistinguishable from general partners in their relations with clients.
- The individual shows that, up to the date interest is paid, he has not recovered any capital from the partnership (apart from any amount taken into account in reducing the interest eligible for relief; see 35-450).

A former partner can continue to be eligible for relief where employed by the partnership in a senior capacity, allowed to act independently with clients and act in a way indistinguishable from the partners in relations with those clients.

If the partnership is replaced by another partnership to carry on the same undertaking, the relief may remain available.

Legislation: ITA 2007, s. 398, 399, 400, 409 and 410

Tax Reporter: ¶115-450

35-350 Loan to pay inheritance tax

Interest paid on a loan made to personal representatives of a deceased person is eligible for relief if the loan is applied:

- in paying (before the grant of representation) inheritance tax (and/or interest thereon) on the deceased's personal estate; or
- in paying off another loan, interest on which would have been eligible for relief under the bullet point above.

Only interest paid in respect of the first year from the making of the original loan is eligible for relief.

Where, in the year interest is paid, income is insufficient for full relief to be given, relief may be given against income of preceding tax years (taking the latest year first) and, if still unrelieved, relief may be given against income of succeeding tax years.

For supplementary provisions, see 35-450.

Legislation: ITA 2007, s. 403–405

Tax Reporter: ¶115-550

35-400 Loan to purchase life annuity

Interest paid on a loan to purchase a life annuity is eligible for relief if the following conditions are satisfied.

- The loan was taken out before 9 March 1999.
- At least 90% of the loan was applied in purchasing a life annuity ending on the death of the borrower or the survivor of the borrower and one or more other annuitants.
- At the time the loan was made the borrower and any other annuitant had reached the age of 65.
- The loan was secured on land in the UK or Republic of Ireland owned by the borrower, or one of the annuitants, and used as the annuitants' only or main residence immediately before 9 March 1999.
- The interest is payable by the borrower or by one of the annuitants.

Interest is only eligible for relief on up to £30,000 of the loan. If interest is payable by two or more persons, interest payable by each is eligible for relief on a proportion of the total eligible interest.

Example

In 2017–18, David and Ian are qualifying annuitants who pay respectively £2,000 and £3,000 interest on a loan of £40,000 taken in order to purchase the annuity.

David is entitled to interest relief of: $\frac{£30,000}{£40,000} \times £2,000 = £1,500$

Ian is entitled to interest relief of: $\frac{£30,000}{£40,000} \times £3,000 = £2,250$

In this case, the relief is not set against total income as discussed at 35-050. Instead, a deduction of 23% of the interest is given as a 'tax reducer', as discussed at 31-000.

Legislation: ICTA 1988, s. 353 and 365

Tax Reporter: ¶115-600

35-450 Supplementary provisions

Recovery of capital

If at any time after the application of a loan, the borrower recovers capital from a close company, employee-controlled company, cooperative or partnership (but does not use it in repayment of the loan) he is treated as if he had repaid the loan (in whole or in part). Subsequently the interest eligible for relief is reduced by an amount equal to the interest on the capital recovered.

The borrower is treated as having recovered capital if he receives consideration for the sale, exchange or assignment of his ordinary shares in the close company or of his shares in the cooperative or employee-controlled company or of his interest in the partnership. Capital is deemed to have been recovered if the company, etc. repays the loan or the partnership returns capital to the borrower.

However, a previous concession has now been enacted in ITA 2007 to continue relief where:

- the company, partnership or cooperative in question is involved in a transaction as a result of which the individual acquires shares in or makes a loan to another company or cooperative body;
- interest on the original loan for the period ending at the time of the transaction was eligible for relief; and
- had the original loan had been made at the time of the transaction and applied in acquiring the shares in, or making the loan to, the other company or cooperative it would have been within one of s. 392, 396 or 401.

Application of loan

For interest relief to be given, the loan concerned must be made in connection with the application of money for one of the qualifying purposes in 35-100 to 35-400 and the loan must be made at the time the money is applied or within a reasonable time therefrom.

What is a reasonable time is a question of fact but HMRC accept a period not exceeding six months without further enquiry.

Relief is not available if the loan is applied for some other purpose before being applied for the qualifying purpose.

Credit

The giving of credit to a purchaser under any sale is treated as the making of a loan to defray money applied by him in making the purchase.

> **Example**
>
> John buys a 10% shareholding in a close company for £50,000. £10,000 of the purchase price is left outstanding and John agrees to pay this sum over five years with interest at a commercial rate. Interest paid on the outstanding purchase price will be eligible for relief.

Part qualifying loans

Where only part of a loan satisfies the conditions for interest relief at the time it is made, only that proportion of the interest is eligible for relief. (This does not apply to a loan to purchase a life annuity where there is an overall £30,000 maximum: see 35-400.)

Legislation: ITA 2007, s. 385, 386, 406 and 410

Tax Reporter: ¶115-500

Charitable giving

40-000 Gift aid

Gift aid is the description given to donations to charity that attracts tax relief. It is not a statutory expression, the statute referring simply to donations to a charity and stating that tax relief applies to a qualifying donation. Until 6 April 2000, gift aid only applied to gifts of at least £250. For smaller gifts, tax relief was available where payments were made under a deed of covenant, which had to be capable of lasting for more than three years. If payments continued to be made under a deed of covenant, they would now attract tax relief in the same way as other donations to charity.

In broad summary, a payment made by an individual under gift aid is treated as if it were a net sum after income tax at the basic rate (currently at 20% therefore) had been deducted. The charity can then reclaim from HMRC this income tax deemed to be deducted and the payer, if a higher rate taxpayer, can obtain further income tax relief (see below).

Qualifying donations

To be a qualifying donation, a gift to a charity must meet the following conditions.

(1) The gift must be a sum of money (and so gifts in specie cannot be made). However, other provisions have been introduced to give relief for certain gifts of quoted investments and real property, as explained in 40-100. There is no minimum amount that need be paid.

(2) There must be no condition as to repayment.

(3) The gift must not be a sum falling within the payroll deduction scheme, ensuring therefore, that relief can only be given once.

(4) The gift must not be conditional on, or associated with, or part of an arrangement involving, the acquisition of property by the charity, otherwise than by way of gift, from the donor or a person connected with him.

(5) Neither the donor nor any connected person should receive a benefit associated with making the gift, the value of which exceeds the following limits, which are adjusted if, broadly, the benefits relate to a period of less than 12 months or a series of gifts are made at intervals of less than 12 months:
    - where the amount of the gift does not exceed £100, 25% of the amount of the gift;
    - where the amount of the gift exceeds £100 but is less than £1,000, the limit is £25; and
    - where the amount of the gift exceeds £1,000, the limit is 5% of the amount of the gift.

Legislation in *Finance Act* 2011 has increased the benefit limit for donations of more than £10,000. The existing rule that the benefit must not exceed 5% of the gift remains the same, but the overriding annual limit to the value of benefits a donor may receive is increased from £500 to £2,500. This change has effect for benefits received as a consequence of donations made on or after 6 April 2011.

However, certain rights of admission, whatever the value, are disregarded. The rules are quite complex having been tightened up with effect from 6 April 2006 and are dealt with in more detail in the next paragraph.

Rights of admission

Until 6 April 2006, certain rights of admission were disregarded. In some respects the relief was wide but also restrictive in that this was confined to charities whose sole or main purpose was the preservation of property or the conservation of wildlife, where for the public benefit. From 6 April 2006, the disregard of rights of admission was extended where a right is granted by a charity for the purpose of viewing property preserved, maintained, kept or created by a charity in pursuance of its charitable purposes. This includes buildings and grounds; plants; animals; works of art (but not performances); artefacts; and property of a scientific nature.

However, whereas previously it was possible because of the way in which the law was drafted for what was effectively an entrance fee to become a gift aid payment, from 6 April 2006 the benefit can only be disregarded if:

- the right of admission applies, during a period of at least one year, at all times at which the public can obtain admission (although this is treated as being met despite the fact that the right does not apply on up to five days specified by the charity, being days on each of which an event is to take place on the premises to which the right relates); or
- a member of the public could purchase the same right of admission and the amount of the gift is greater by at least 10% than the amount which he would have to pay. Thus, if the entrance fee is £10, someone would have to pay at least £11 for the payment to fall within the gift aid rules.

A right of admission is a right which:

- benefits either the person making the gift or that person and one or more members of his or her family;
- relates to premises or property to which the public are admitted on payment of an admission fee; and
- authorises admission without payment of such fee or on payment of a reduced fee.

The opportunity of both making the gift and receiving a right of admission in consequence thereof must be available to the public so that a right where the category of users is restricted would not qualify and would have to meet the usual benefit tests as set out above.

A donation giving a right of admission must not include any rights to full or partial refund in any circumstances.

Method of giving relief

As mentioned above, income tax relief at the basic rate is effectively given by the deemed deduction from the grossed up sum. Thus, a payment of £80 is deemed to be a gross payment of £100 from which income tax of £20 is deducted. The charity then reclaims the £20. A higher rate or additional rate taxpayer is then entitled to relief to bring the total up to his or her marginal rate of 40% or 45% (or, in certain cases, the dividend upper rate of 32.5% or the dividend additional rate of 38.1%). This is given by extending the basic rate band and the higher rate band by the grossed up amount of the gift and is not a deduction from total income as such. However, in arriving at 'adjusted net income' for the purposes of the age related personal allowances and the married couple's allowance, the gross sum is deducted.

> **Example 1**
>
> Peter is a higher rate taxpayer and makes a gift aid payment of £1,200 to a charity. This is treated as a gross payment of £1,500. His basic rate limit is increased for 2017–18 from £32,000 to £33,500 and his higher rate limit from £150,000 to £151,500.

In very broad terms, however, an individual must pay sufficient income tax or CGT to cover the basic rate income tax deemed to have been deducted, otherwise HMRC would be repaying to a charity tax that has not been collected.

A separate calculation is made for this purpose of the total amount of income tax to which an individual is charged for a tax year. Broadly, this is the figure before deducting any tax payments made (including, therefore, income tax deducted at source) and after deducting tax reductions at Step 6 of ITA 2007, s. 23 (referred to as 'income tax reducers' in the pro forma computation at 31-100) other than in respect of qualifying maintenance payments and double taxation relief.

Tax treated as paid under the following heads is then deducted to arrive at the income tax charge for this purpose:

(1) gains from contracts for life insurance;

(2) annual payments in respect of income from settlor-interested settlements.

It is possible to carry back a donation made in one year to the immediately preceding year as if it had been paid in that year. An election must be made in writing to HMRC on or before the date on which the donor files his tax return for that previous year of assessment and in any event not later than 31 January following the end of that year. An election cannot be made unless the grossed up amount of the gift would, had it been paid in the earlier year, be payable out of profits or gains brought into charge to income tax or capital gains tax.

> **Example 2**
>
> In 2016–17, Giles has total income of £60,000 but owing to a trading loss in 2017–18 has no income for that year. In August 2017, he makes a gift to a charity of £1,600. It is clearly in his interest to elect to carry back the payment to 2016–17. In that year, he is a higher rate taxpayer. Moreover, if the payment remained in 2017–18, he would be assessed for £400, being income tax deemed to be deducted from the gift, as he has no income tax or capital gains tax liability for the year. For 2016–17, he is given higher rate relief by increasing his basic rate limit from £32,000 to £34,000 (i.e. by £1,600 grossed up at 20%). The election should be made with the tax return for 2017–18 if not before. If for some reason he is late in filing his return, the carry back claim must be made by 31 January 2019 to be effective.

Tainted charity donations

The tainted charity donations provisions were introduced by *Finance Act* 2011 where, broadly:

- the donor or connected person (the 'linked person') has entered into arrangements and it is reasonable to assume that the donation would not have been made and the arrangements would not have been entered into independently of one another. The term 'arrangements' is widely drafted and includes any scheme or understanding whether or not it is legally enforceable;
- the main purpose, or one of the main purposes, of the linked person entering into the arrangements was to obtain a financial advantage, for itself or for a person connected with the donor.

The tainted charity donations provisions apply with effect for donations made on or after 6 April 2011.

Income tax will be charged where a person makes a tainted donation in a tax year, and:

- relief would have been available in respect of the 'gift aid donation'; and
- the charity to which the gift aid donation is made is entitled to claim a repayment of tax in respect of that donation.

The amount of tax charged is equal to the amount of the repayment of tax which the charity is entitled to claim in respect of the gift aid donation (whether or not such a claim is made).

Legislation: ITA2007, s. 413–430; FA2011, s. 41, 27 and Sch. 3; *Donations to Charity by Individuals (Appropriate Declarations) Regulations* 2000 (SI2000/2074)

Tax Reporter: ¶116–000

40-100 Gifts of shares, securities and real property to charity

Shares and securities

An individual who makes a gift of a qualifying investment to a charity is entitled to claim a deduction in calculating his total income.

Qualifying investments are:

- shares or securities which are listed or dealt in on a recognised stock exchange;
- units in an authorised unit trust;

- shares in an open-ended investment company; and
- an interest in an offshore fund.

The amount of the deduction is the excess of the 'relevant value' of the qualifying investments over the amount (if any) of consideration given by the charity. 'Relevant value' is the market value except where anti-avoidance provisions apply as below. Any incidental costs of disposal incurred by the donor may also be deducted, except that the deduction may be restricted in the case of a sale at an undervalue. In that case the deduction is limited to the excess of the deemed disposal proceeds for capital gains over the amount of the consideration received. This covers the situation where the charity has effectively contributed towards the incidental costs of disposal in the actual consideration.

Real property

Relief is extended to land in the UK by including qualifying interests in land in the list of qualifying investments. A qualifying interest in land is:

- a freehold interest; or
- a leasehold interest which is a term of years absolute.

Relief is only available if the charity provides a certificate which describes the interest in land, states the date of disposal, and confirms the charity's acquisition. In the case of land held jointly, each co-owner must dispose of the whole of his beneficial interest in the land to the charity.

Anti-avoidance

Anti-avoidance measures restrict the relief available to the donor where either the donor acquired the investments at less than market value as part of a scheme or arrangement, or the market value is artificially inflated at the date of the gift to the charity.

Legislation: ITA 2007, s. 431–446

Tax Reporter: ¶115-575

Anti-avoidance

41-000 Sale of income derived from personal activities

A professional individual may seek to exploit his earning capacity by selling the right to his earnings for a capital amount. If the main object, or one of the main objects, of the transaction is to avoid or reduce liability to income tax, the capital sum becomes taxable as income.

Capital amount is widely defined to include any amount, in money or money's worth, which is not treated as income for the purposes of income tax or corporation tax. Where the capital amount consists of property or rights (such as shares, or an option) liability only arises when the property, etc. is sold.

Liability may arise where a capital sum is derived either by the individual or by some other person in respect of the individual's activities.

Legislation: ITA 2007, s. 773–789

Tax Reporter: ¶269-000

Transactions in securities

41-100 Income charge on tax advantage from transactions in securities

This legislation was re-written by FA 2010 following an 'anti-avoidance simplification review'. The new rules apply to income tax advantages obtained on or after 24 March 2010.

Income tax may be charged to counteract income tax advantages arising from 'transactions in securities'. These rules apply to a person where:

- he or she is a party to a 'transaction in securities' or to two or more such transactions;
- the circumstances are covered by Condition A or Condition B in 41-150, and not within the exclusion for fundamental changes of ownership (see 41-150);
- the main purpose, or one of the main purposes, of the person in being a party to the transaction, or any of the transactions, is to obtain an 'income tax advantage' (see 41-200); and
- the person obtains such an advantage in consequence of the transaction or the combined effects of the transactions.

'Transactions in securities' means a transaction of whatever description relating to securities and, in particular, includes:

- the purchase, sale or exchange of securities;
- issuing or securing the issue of new securities;
- applying or subscribing for new securities; and
- altering, or securing the alteration of, the rights attached to securities.

Legislation: ITA 2007, s. 682–684

Tax Reporter: ¶339-550

41-150 Conditions A and B and the change of ownership exclusion

Condition A is that, as a result of the transaction in securities or any one or more of those transactions, the person receives relevant consideration in money or money's worth (and does not pay or bear income tax on it apart from these rules) in connection with:

(a) the distribution, transfer or realisation of assets of a close company;

(b) the application of assets of a close company in discharge of liabilities; or

(c) the direct or indirect transfer of assets of one close company to another close company.

Condition B is that:

(a) the person receives 'relevant consideration' in money or money's worth in connection with the transaction in securities or any one or more of those transactions;

(b) two or more close companies are concerned in the transaction or transactions in securities concerned; and

(c) the person does not pay or bear income tax on the consideration (apart from these rules).

'Relevant consideration', in the case of para. (a) or (b) of Condition A, means consideration which:

- is or represents the value of assets which are available for distribution by way of dividend by the company, or which would have been so available apart from anything done by the company;
- is received in respect of future receipts of the company; or
- is or represents the value of trading stock of the company.

In the case of para. (c) of Condition A, or any of the paragraphs of Condition B, 'relevant consideration' means consideration that consists of any share capital or any security issued by a close company, and which is or represents the value of assets which:

- are available for distribution by way of dividend by the company;
- would have been so available apart from anything done by the company; or
- are trading stock of the company.

The references in para. (a) and (b) of Condition A to 'assets' do not include assets which are shown to represent a return of sums paid by subscribers on the issue of securities, despite the fact that under the law of the country in which the company is incorporated, assets of that description are available for distribution by way of dividend.

So far as para. (c) of Condition A or any paragraph of Condition B relates to share capital that is not redeemable, it applies only so far as that capital is repaid, whether on a winding up or otherwise. For this purpose, any distribution made in respect of any shares on a winding up or dissolution of the company is treated as a repayment of share capital.

For the purposes of Conditions A and B and the provisions that interpret them, 'security' includes securities that do not create or evidence a charge on assets, and 'share' includes stock and any other interest of a member in a company. 'Close company', throughout these rules for transactions in securities, includes a company that would be close if it were resident in the UK.

The charge under these provisions does not apply where:

- immediately before the transaction in securities (or the first such transaction where there is more than one), the person who would otherwise be chargeable holds shares or an interest in shares in the close company; and
- there is a fundamental change of ownership of the close company.

Such a fundamental change is treated as occurring if the following three conditions are met as a result of the transaction or transactions in securities, and continue to be met for a period of two years.

(1) At least 75% of the ordinary share capital of the close company is held beneficially by a person or persons none of whom is connected with the person who would otherwise be chargeable, and none of whom has been so connected in the period of two years ending with the day on which the transaction, or first transaction, takes place.

(2) The shares in the close company held by that person, or those persons, carry an entitlement to at least 75% of the distributions that may be made by the company.

(3) Those shares carry at least 75% of the total voting rights in the company.

Legislation: ITA 2007, s. 685 and 686

Tax Reporter: ¶339-750ff.

41-200 Meaning of 'income tax advantage'

A person obtains an 'income tax advantage' if the amount of any income tax that would be payable by him or her in respect of the 'relevant consideration', if it were a qualifying distribution, exceeds the amount of the capital gains tax, if any, payable in respect of it; and the amount of that excess is the income tax advantage. For this purpose, there is left out of account any amount by which the relevant consideration exceeds the maximum amount that could in any circumstances have been paid to the person by way of a qualifying distribution at the time when the relevant consideration is received.

Legislation: ITA 2007, s. 687

Tax Reporter: ¶339-550

41-250 Cancellation of tax advantage

Once it is shown that a transaction in securities resulted in a tax advantage (see 41-200), HMRC may counteract the advantage by:

- raising a tax assessment;
- nullifying a right to repayment;
- requiring the return of a repayment already made;
- computing or recomputing profits or gains or a liability to tax.

There is no requirement to self-assess given that HMRC have to make a decision based on the facts.

Legislation: ITA 2007, s. 695–700

Tax Reporter: ¶339-750

41-300 Clearance procedure: tax advantage from transactions in securities

A procedure exists for advance clearance of transactions in which there is a potential tax advantage which may be challenged by HMRC (see 41-200). Where the taxpayer provides HMRC with details of the transactions concerned, HMRC must either give or refuse clearance, or request further details, within 30 days.

Legislation: ITA 2007, s. 701, 702

Tax Reporter: ¶340-700

41-350 Previous legislation

The main changes from the legislation which applied prior to FA 2010 are that:

- there is now a narrower definition of 'income tax advantage';
- the legislation now applies to all close companies (and companies that would be close if resident in the UK) rather than to a narrower class of 'relevant companies'; and
- there is now an exemption covering fundamental changes in ownership of affected companies.

Capital profits from land

41-900 Capital gains from land

A dealer or trader in land (one who buys and sells land as a business) will be assessed on profits or gains arising from that land as income, whereas one who sells land which he has held as an investment or sells any other investment property will pay tax on such profits or gains to the extent that they represent chargeable gains.

Shares are often held as an investment and if those shares were in a land-owning company it might be possible to avoid income treatment on transactions which, but for the fact that it is shares which are sold and not land, would otherwise be held to be trading transactions in land.

However, 'capital gains' from quasi-dealing transactions are charged to tax as income for the tax year or accounting period in which the gain is realised, wherever:

(1) land or buildings, or any property deriving its value from land, etc. (e.g. shares in a land-owning company), is acquired with the sole or main object of realising a gain from disposing of the land, etc.;

(2) land or buildings are held as trading stock; or

(3) land or buildings are developed with the sole or main object of realising a gain from their disposal when developed;

and any gain of a capital nature is obtained from the disposal:

(a) by the person acquiring, holding or developing the land, etc. or by any connected person; or

(b) where any arrangement or scheme is effected in respect of the land, etc. which enables a gain to be realised by any indirect method, or by any series of transactions, by any person who is a party to, or concerned in, the arrangement or scheme; and this is the case whether any such person obtains the gain for himself or for any other person.

The capital gains charged to income tax or corporation tax are computed on a just and reasonable basis, with relief only for limited expenses.

'Disposal' is widely defined for this purpose, and for the purposes of the indirect realisation of a gain includes various arrangements.

Exemptions

Where shares in a land-trading company (or, broadly, its 90% holding company) are disposed of, an exemption applies. However, it only applies where all the land (trading stock) held by the company is disposed of in the normal course of trade so that all gains and profits accrue to the company. This exemption does not affect the liability where there is a 'scheme or arrangement' as in (b) above.

There is also an exemption for a gain accruing to an individual from the sale of his 'principal private residence' (see *British Tax Guide: Capital Gains Tax* 220-500ff.).

Clearances

Except when land is held as trading stock, details of a proposed transaction may be submitted to HMRC for advance clearance, i.e. for HMRC to say whether or not they consider it will fall foul of the s. 776 provisions, above. Clearance will be binding on HMRC unless it transpires that the information supplied to them was incomplete or inaccurate, in which case the clearance will be void.

Legislation: ITA 2007, s. 755–772

Tax Reporter: ¶304-000

Transfer of assets abroad

42-000 Transfer of assets abroad

The overseas income of a person who is non-UK resident and non-UK domiciled is not liable to tax in the UK. Far-reaching anti-avoidance provisions exist to prevent an individual (or his spouse) who is resident in the UK from obtaining a tax advantage by transferring 'assets' abroad so that the income is paid to persons who are resident or domiciled abroad.

The income of any such transfer is regarded as that of the individual making the transfer, and is chargeable where he has 'power to enjoy the income' or 'receives a capital sum' in connection with the transfer.

For the purposes of the provisions, 'assets' include property or rights of any kind.

The provisions apply:

- whatever the residence of the individual when the transfer is made; and
- where a purpose of the transfer is to avoid any form of direct taxation (e.g. capital taxation).

Any 'benefit received' as a result by an individual other than the transferor may, if the individual is resident in the UK, also be charged (see below).

No duplication of charge

To avoid a double charge to UK tax, income which is caught by the above provisions and which is subsequently received by the transferor is ignored for other income tax purposes. Because the charges are made by reference to different criteria it would also be possible for the same income to be taxed twice under these provisions: this is specifically prevented.

Power to enjoy income

The transferor is deemed to have the power to enjoy the income if:

- the income is used for his benefit;
- the income increases the value of any assets held by or for him;
- he receives or is entitled to receive any benefit out of that income or money which represents that income;
- he may become entitled to enjoy the income through the exercise of any power; or
- he is able directly or indirectly to control the way the income is applied.

Receipt of capital sum

A transferor is liable to tax on the income of the assets transferred if he is entitled to receive any capital sum the payment of which is in any way connected with the transfer (see above). 'Capital sum' means:

- any sum paid or payable as a loan or repayment of a loan; and
- any other sum which is not income and which is not paid for full consideration in money or money's worth.

This is subject to any sum which a third person receives or is entitled to receive being treated as a capital sum which an individual receives or is entitled to receive if the third person's entitlement is at the individual's direction or is because of an assignment by the individual of his right to receive it.

Income is not deemed to be that of an individual for any tax year merely because he has received a loan if the loan is wholly repaid before the beginning of that tax year.

The House of Lords, in *Vestey v IR Commrs* accepted that the charge on transferors would apply to an individual who was not directly the transferor but was liable as transferor because he had procured the transfer. However, those provisions do not apply so as to treat a minority shareholder as procuring a transfer by a company and the section provides no machinery for attributing less than the whole of the relevant income to any one transferor, i.e. they do not apply where there is more than one transferor and the respective interests cannot be separated out so that an identifiable portion of the asset transferred can be attributed to any particular transferor (see *IR Commrs v Pratt*).

In *Vestey v IR Commrs*, the House of Lords held that the provisions applied only to the person (or that person's spouse) who made the original transfer of assets. HMRC had claimed that *anyone* who had power to enjoy the income could be caught by the anti-avoidance provisions. Additionally, HMRC contested that where there was more than one beneficiary, it could select whom it chose to tax and that it was entitled to apportion tax between the beneficiaries as it wished. The liability of any individual beneficiary could, therefore, depend on when HMRC chose to make an assessment. HMRC believed that the only constraint was that the total income could not be assessed more than once. These contentions were expressly disapproved by the House of Lords and, as a result, further provisions concerning the transfer of assets abroad were introduced to deal with non-transferors.

Liability of non-transferors

Further provisions apply where assets are transferred abroad (where the purpose or one of the purposes is to avoid tax) and:

- income becomes payable to a person resident or domiciled *outside* the UK; and
- an individual ordinarily resident *in* the UK (and who is not the original transferor) receives a benefit out of the assets transferred.

The amount of the benefit is treated as the income of the recipient and he is liable to income tax upon it in the year of receipt. This is so long as the amount received is not more than the relevant amount of income from the transferred assets which can be used for his benefit.

The relevant amount of income is the income up to and including the tax year in which the benefit is received (after 9 March 1981). Any part of the benefit received which exceeds this relevant amount of income is taxed as the income of the next or subsequent years when it is covered by income which can be used for his benefit.

HMRC have a discretion to apportion the income as they consider just and reasonable where there is more than one person liable under these provisions. The First-tier Tribunal has jurisdiction to review such a decision.

Defences

As an important safeguard, the above provisions do not apply where either:

- the transfer of assets is not made to avoid tax (see *IR Commrs v Willoughby*); or
- the transfer is a genuine commercial transaction not designed to avoid tax. For transactions effected after 5 April 2012, it is simply necessary to satisfy HMRC that a transaction is genuine where there would otherwise be an unjustified and disproportionate restriction on a freedom protected under the relevant part of the European Union Treaty, etc.

An individual who is domiciled abroad is not liable to tax on income deemed to be his under the above provisions if, had it in fact been his income, he would not have been liable to tax on it by reason of his domicile.

The provisions are not prevented from applying by the fact that an assessment might alternatively have been made under the transfers of income arising from securities provisions (*IR Commrs v McGuckian*).

Information

HMRC may request any person to supply them with such information as they think necessary for the purposes of the above provisions; however, solicitors' and banks' disclosure obligations are limited. For unsuccessful attempts to resist such requests, see *Royal Bank of Canada v IR Commrs* and *Clinch v IR Commrs*.

HMRC have published guidance on how they interpret various aspects of these anti-avoidance provisions. Even though at all times case law can overrule HMRC's interpretation, their guidance is useful for the purposes of particular advice.

Legislation: ITA 2007, s. 714–751

Cases: *Royal Bank of Canada v IR Commrs* (1971) 47 TC 565; *Clinch v IR Commrs* (1973) 49 TC 52; *Vestey v IR Commrs* (1979) 54 TC 503; *IR Commrs v Pratt* [1982] BTC 319; *IR Commrs v McGuckian* [1997] BTC 346; *IR Commrs v Willoughby* [1997] BTC 393

Other Material: HMRC Interpretation, IRInt. 192 (Tax Bulletin, April 1992)

Tax Reporter: ¶129-700

Child benefit charge

43-100 High income child benefit charge

Finance Act 2012 imposed an income tax charge on the child benefit, the broad effect being to reclaim the entirety of the child benefit where an individual's adjusted net income for a year is £60,000 or more. This charge will be collected through the same procedures as other income tax amounts, including an adjustment to a notice of coding where appropriate.

The reduction is phased in on a pro-rata basis for income between £50,000 and £60,000. The charge does not apply to the child benefit for weeks beginning before 7 January 2013. In the case of couples living together, whether as husband and wife or as civil partners, the effect of the provisions is to apply the new charge, where relevant, to the individual with the higher adjusted net income of the two. The partner bearing the charge does not need to be related to the child or have parental responsibility for the charge. If more than one person is entitled to child benefit at different times of the year it is necessary to apply the income test to each week but still by reference to the annual income of the partner with the higher adjusted net income.

It is possible for an individual entitled to child benefit and who reasonably expects that a high income child benefit charge would arise to elect not to receive the child benefit.

Legislation: ITEPA 2003, s. 681B–681H as inserted by FA 2012, Sch. 8

43-200 Limit on income tax relief

Finance Act 2013 introduced a limit on the deductions, as specified, that can be set against an individual's income. The total of those deductions must not exceed the greater of £50,000 and 25% of the adjusted total income for the relevant income tax year.

In principle, the deductions (in ITA 2007 unless stated otherwise) that this applies to are as follows (but there are exceptions as mentioned below):

- trade loss relief against general income under either s. 64 or 72;
- post cessation trade relief under s. 96;
- property and loss relief against general income under s. 120;
- post cessation property relief under s. 125;
- employment loss relief under s. 128;
- share loss relief under Pt. 4, Ch. 6;
- interest relief payments under Pt. 8, Ch. 1 (such as loans to acquire interests in close companies and partnerships);
- deduction for liabilities relating to former employment under ITEPA 2003, s. 555;
- relief for losses on strips of government securities under ITTOIA 2005, s. 446; and
- relief under ITTOIA 2005, s. 454 for loss relief on disposal of deeply discounted securities where the security has been held continuously since 26 March 2003.

However, the following reliefs are excluded from the above:

- business premises renovation allowances under CAA 2001, Pt. 3A;
- deductions for amounts of relief for trades and properties so far as made from the profits of the trade or business to which the relief in question relates;
- overlap relief arising from a trade which is given in the final tax year or on a change of accounting date; and
- share loss relief where the shares qualify for EIS or SEIS relief.

If the relief does not fall under the first listing above then there can be no question of any restriction. Thus, there is no restriction for payments to charities and pension contributions. In the case of pension contributions, there are separate restrictions in any event determining how much can be deducted in a given year.

The adjusted income to which the 25% percentage is applied is the total income after adding back payroll giving and pension scheme relief at source payments.

This rule applies for the tax year 2013–14 and subsequent tax years. However, if a loss, for example, arises in 2013–14 onwards but is carried back to the tax years before 2013–14, the amount of the claim is to be calculated as if this rule applied for those previous years.

The restriction does not apply where a trading loss is carried back or forward and offset against profits of the same trade.

> **Example**
>
> In the year to 31 December 2017, Jimmy has made a trading profit of £400,000 but in the next year to 31 December 2018 he makes a loss of £150,000 in the same trade. Assume he has no other income.
>
> He decides to claim that loss against his total income for 2017–18. The loss of £150,000 exceeds the 25% tolerance based on £400,000 but as this arises from the same trade the restriction does not apply.

Legislation: ITA 2007, s. 24A

Completion of IT return

Returns and obligations

Tax returns

50-000 Overview

The system of self-assessment requires individuals, trustees and partnerships to submit returns of income and capital gains for a tax year by 31 October (for paper returns, whether or not HMRC are to calculate the tax liability) following the end of that year. The return must also contain a calculation of their income tax, capital gains tax and Class 4 National Insurance liabilities for the year (the self-assessment).

For online returns, the deadline is 31 January following the end of the tax year.

The taxpayer is relieved of the obligation to self-assess if the return is submitted by 31 October following the end of the tax year. If the taxpayer chooses to self-assess, the deadline was 31 January following the end of the tax year.

The return is not only a submission of information, but also the means of creating a legal debt. The charge to tax is created by the self-assessment included in the return.

The return consists of a core section applying to all taxpayers, which is then customised by the addition of extra pages, according to the taxpayer's known circumstances. It is up to the taxpayer to request supplementary pages, if necessary.

The return does not require the submission of accounts as a matter of routine. Instead, the supplementary pages for self-employment contain a section requiring the submission of Standard Accounts Information (SAI). Even if submission of accounts is considered necessary for adequate disclosure, the standard information section must be completed for the return to be accepted.

Failure to submit a return by the prescribed filing date results in an automatic penalty (see 60-500ff.).

Failure to self-assess will result in HMRC making a determination of the taxpayer's liability for the year. Such a determination has statutory authority as if it was a self-assessment.

Obligation to report liability

There is a statutory duty on 'every person' who is chargeable to income tax or capital gains tax for a particular tax year and who has not received a notice to make a return of his total income and gains to give notice of his chargeability to HMRC not later than six months after the end of that. This obligation also applies to trustees.

Failure to notify liability can result in a penalty (see 61-550).

Prior to 6 April 2009, when an individual began to carry on a trade he had to register to pay Class 2 National Insurance contributions (NICs) within three months of commencing in business or face a penalty of £100.

A new penalty regime for failing to notify liability to Class 2 NICs was introduced from 6 April 2009 to mirror the new penalty regime for failing to notify liability to tax, introduced by FA 2008, Sch. 41 (see 61-550). Under the new regime:

- a person who becomes or ceases to be liable to pay Class 2 NICs must notify HMRC **immediately**;
- a person will be liable to a penalty if they do not notify their liability for Class 2 NICs by 31 January after the end of the tax year in which they become liable;
- no penalty is chargeable if there is a reasonable excuse for the failure to notify;
- any penalty is calculated as a percentage of the 'lost contributions', the percentage depending on the type of behaviour that led to the failure to notify:
  - (i) for a deliberate and concealed failure the penalty is 100% of the lost contributions;
  - (ii) for a deliberate but not concealed failure it is 70%;
  - (iii) for any other case it is 30%;
- the penalty can be mitigated if the person makes a disclosure.

The registration for Class 2 NICs is also effectively a registration for income tax purposes, but it does not absolve the taxpayer from informing HMRC of his source of earnings by 6 October following the tax year-end, if he has not received a tax return to complete.

The obligation to notify liability to tax does not arise if that liability is only because a person's income is derived from:

- income taxed under PAYE;
- benefits taken into account in PAYE codings; or
- income received with tax deducted at source or an attaching tax credit and the individual is not liable at the higher rate of tax.

It follows that a person, whose total income is from 'excluded' sources, is unaffected by the duty to notify liability: for example, an employee with a total income comprising, say, £15,000 gross earnings, building society interest of £150 and dividends of £225.

Employees receiving amended notices of coding in January can tell whether benefits received in the preceding tax year have been taken into account for PAYE and thus fall into the exclusion in (2) above. Published HMRC policy is to allow employees to assume that information on the form P11D submitted by their employer will be taken into account for PAYE purposes, and no separate notification of chargeability is necessary. This is subject to the qualification that the employee should have received a copy of the P11D from the employer and is not aware that the P11D is incorrect or that it has not been submitted.

Legislation: TMA 1970, s. 7(1); *Social Security (Contributions) Regulations* 2001 (SI 2001/1004), reg. 87

Other Material: SP 1/96

Tax Reporter: ¶180-325

50-025 Filing dates

Tax returns

The deadline will depend on the method by which the return is filed. For online returns, the date remains 31 January following the end of the tax year, but for returns filed on paper the deadline is 31 October following the end of the tax year (whether or not HMRC are to calculate the tax liability).

Where a return is issued after 31 July but before 31 October, the return must be filed within three months of the issue date if filed on paper, or by 31 January for online returns.

If the return is issued after 31 October, the deadline for both paper and online returns is three months from the date of issue.

A First-tier Tribunal has held that a partnership return submitted as a PDF file was a proper delivery of an 'electronic return'.

Legislation: TMA 1970, s. 8(1D)–(1G)

Case: *Fitzpatrick & Co Solicitors* [2012] TC 01932

50-050 Filing dates: when is the return 'received'?

Any returns received after the filing date are subject to a late filing penalty (see 60-500). HMRC policy as a result of a special commissioners' decision is that no penalty will be levied if the return is filed, or treated as filed, on the day immediately following the deadline, e.g. 1 November for paper returns. Paper returns for 2010–11 placed in the tax office post box before 7.30 a.m. on 2 November 2011 were treated as having been filed on 1 November.

In respect of online returns, HMRC policy is that returns must be received by midnight on 31 January or they would be considered late.

If a tax return is filed late, the period in which HMRC can open an enquiry ('the enquiry window') is extended by three months to the next quarter-day (see 58-050).

Case: *Steeden v Carver* (1999) Sp C 212

Other Material: HMRC *Income Tax Self Assessment Manual* SALF208; HMRC *Working Together*, Issue 7

Tax Reporter: ¶180-125

Reasonable evidence of submission of returns

HMRC offices do not issue receipts for self-assessment returns delivered by hand. However, should a penalty notice be disputed on the grounds that the return was filed on time, staff are instructed to accept 'reasonable evidence' held by the agent to show that the return was delivered before the deadline.

In order to satisfy the requirement for 'reasonable evidence', the professional bodies recommended the following procedure:

- that each batch of returns to be hand-delivered to HMRC should be accompanied by a list, date-stamped for the relevant date of delivery, and listing the name and UTR of each return in the batch;
- that each entry on the list should be checked back to the returns by a senior member of staff (for example, a manager), and this individual should sign the list to indicate that this has been done;
- that in all firms other than sole practitioners, each list should then be checked and countersigned by, for example, a partner;

- that a sole practitioner should mark the items clearly as having been checked, and sign to this effect;
- that a copy of the list (signed and dated) should be retained in case of subsequent problems; and
- that a copy of the signed and countersigned list should also be attached to each batch of returns handed in at Enquiry Centres.

Subsequently, HMRC confirmed that the 'audit trail' generated above will normally be accepted as 'reasonable' evidence of delivery.

HMRC have also confirmed that it is departmental policy to sign for items sent by recorded delivery.

50-075 Concession for 'unsatisfactory' returns

HMRC distinguish between a return which has some income omitted and is thus 'incomplete' and could be subject to an enquiry, and a return which is not signed and does not meet the statutory requirements and is thus 'unsatisfactory'.

Unsatisfactory returns will not be logged as received but will be sent back. Incomplete returns on the other hand can be logged as received and processed.

Where a return is delivered to HMRC on or before 31 October and is found to be unsatisfactory, it will be sent back to the taxpayer (or agent) for completion. If the return is sent back in the period from 18 October to 1 November, the taxpayer will be given a minimum of 14 days in which to complete the return and deliver it back to HMRC without incurring a late-filing penalty.

This practice is not established as a formal extra-statutory concession and the 14-day period may be extended in exceptional cases.

Other Material: HMRC *Self Assessment Manual* (Unsatisfactory individuals returns)

Tax Reporter: ¶180-050

50-100 Incomplete returns and use of provisional figures

In the view of HMRC, if a taxpayer submits an incomplete tax return by the due date, he has not complied with his statutory obligation. However, if the figures needed to complete the return are not available, perhaps because accounts have not been finished, it is possible to use provisional figures.

The published policy of HMRC is to accept that including provisional or estimated figures does not invalidate a self-assessment return, and they will not reject a return simply because provisional figures are not adequately explained, or because no date is given by which the final figure will be available. However, they emphasise that the use of provisional figures is a factor that will influence whether a return will be selected for an enquiry. Where there proves to be no good reason for the use of provisional figures, or they are not on a reasonable basis, HMRC consider this amounts to a lack of proper care in completing the return and penalties may be levied on the basis that the return is 'incorrect'.

Other Material: HMRC Tax Bulletin TB01/02–5; HMRC *Income Tax Self Assessment Manual*: Legal Framework SALF206

50-150 Filing by internet

By virtue of regulations, the returns and other information which may be provided over the internet currently comprise:

- individual's returns (see 50-600);
- trustees' returns (see 51-350);
- the amendment of return by taxpayer during an enquiry (see 58-200);
- the amendment of return by HMRC during an enquiry (see 58-200);
- partnership returns (see 51-000);
- partnership statements (see 51-050);
- notice of enquiry into partnership return (see 51-100);
- the amendment of a partnership return by taxpayer during an enquiry (see 51-100);
- claims not included in returns (see 55-200).

Agents are authorised to act for the taxpayer, either by a form 64-8 signed by the taxpayer or by an online authorisation given by the taxpayer on the government gateway website (www.gateway.gov.uk). To use filing by internet (FBI), the agent must register for FBI on the HMRC website and will need his agent code to do this. The agent code is the code allocated by HMRC to every tax agent who files tax returns for individuals, by whatever means. Requests for a new or amended agent code must be made in writing, on headed notepaper if appropriate. HMRC won't accept information provided on form 64-8 to create or amend a code.

It used to be the case that all agents who had registered to use the internet service for income tax self-assessment were automatically authorised to send an individual client's return over the internet, provided HMRC held a form 64-8 for that client. This included all forms 64-8 held at that date, as well as those completed and filed subsequently. However, the way that HMRC deal with self-assessment registrations and agent authorisations changed.

In December 2009, the Central Agent Authorisation Team (CAAT) stopped their informal practice that allowed tax agents and advisers to register a client for self-assessment using form 64-8 alone. Instead, agents must use the correct self-assessment registration form and send it to CAAT along with agent authorisation form 64-8. Forms for registering for self assessment can be viewed and downloaded from the HMRC website.

Up until 31 March 2011, if a form 64-8 was received without the appropriate self-assessment registration form, CAAT issued a letter telling agents and their clients that the 64-8 must be accompanied by the correct registration form. From 1 April 2011, these letters are no longer issued. It's important that all forms are sent to HMRC at the same time.

If form 64-8 is sent to HMRC before the client is registered for self assessment, HMRC will not be able to set up and update the client's self assessment record to include the agent details. The agent will not, therefore, be able to view the client on their online client list.

The agent must make a copy of the tax return and accompanying schedules, which needs to be approved by means of a signature by the taxpayer before it is sent by the agent. The software used by the agent to send the return over the internet must be approved by HMRC. A list of the approved software products is on HMRC's website.

HMRC have released a new version of form 64-8 which allows the agent to type all details directly onto the form on-screen. The form can then be printed and sent to the client for signature before posting to HMRC to process. All existing versions of the 64-8 form should be destroyed.

There is a network of some 40 HMRC Agent Account Managers (AAM) available to help agents resolve problems and find an escalation route through HMRC if they have been unable to obtain answers using the usual channels. The network can be accessed on the HMRC website. AAMs may telephone agents and advisers to explain the AAM team's services. Agents can register for AAM services during the call.

The services provided by the AAM teams include providing an AAM speaker to attend an agent event or meeting to deliver a presentation. HMRC have produced a guide that explains what AAMs do, what services they provide and how to register to use them, and the range of topics that tax agents and advisers can ask an AAM to cover at their meeting or event. The guide can be read on the HMRC website.

Agents can also use the Agent Dedicated Line, 0845 366 7855, a service for authorised agents that provides a service for personal self-assessment or PAYE for individuals queries.

Legislation: *Income and Corporation Taxes (Electronic Communications) Regulations* 2003 (SI 2003/282)

Websites: www.hmrc.gov.uk/efiling/sa_efiling/soft_dev.htm; www.hmrc.gov.uk/forms/64-8.pdf; www.search2.hmrc.gov.uk/kb5/hmrc/forms/selfassessmentforms.page#2020; www.hmrc.gov.uk/agents/aam.htm; www.online.hmrc.gov.uk/shortforms/form/AAMReg?dept-name=&sub-dept-name=&location=43&origin=http://www.hmrc.gov.uk

50-200 Record keeping

Persons who may be required to make returns are to keep records enabling them to make correct and complete returns, even if no notice to make a return is issued. Remember, however, that, in the absence of such a notice, they may be obliged to notify liability (see 50-000) and that notification will trigger the issue of a notice to make a return.

These records must normally be retained until:

- the fifth anniversary of the 31 January following the tax year, in the case of persons carrying on trades, professions or businesses (this applies to all records, not just business records);
- otherwise the first anniversary of the 31 January following the tax year;
- or (in either case) such earlier day as may be specified in writing by HMRC (and different days may be specified for different cases).

Where the return is issued at the normal time, or at any time before the above 'normal' retention dates, the retention period may be extended. In this case the records must be retained until the later of:

- the normal retention date described above:
- where enquiries are begun into the return, or any amendment to the return, the date those enquiries are completed (see 58-250); or
- where there are no enquiries into the return, or into any amendment of it, the date an officer of the Board may no longer initiate enquiries, normally 31 January following submission of the return (see 58-050).

If the return is issued after the end of the normal retention period, it is only those records as may still be in the taxpayer's possession that must be preserved. They must be then preserved until the later of:

- the date any enquiries are completed; and
- the date enquiries can no longer be initiated.

There is a separate, but similar, regime applying to records supporting claims made outside of a return (see 55-200).

For a person carrying on a trade, profession or business (whether in partnership or alone), the records to be kept are specified. It is specifically provided that, for these purposes, the letting of property is to be treated as a trade. The following must be recorded;

(1) all amounts received and expended and the matters concerning which the receipts and expenditures take place; and

(2) in the case of trades dealing in goods, all sales and purchases of goods.

HMRC may by regulations:

(a) provide that records required to be kept and preserved include, or do not include, records specified by regulation; and

(b) provide that those records include supporting documents so specified.

Finance Act 2009 aligns the record-keeping rules for environmental taxes (aggregates levy, climate change levy and landfill tax), insurance premium tax and stamp duty land tax from 1 April 2010.

Legislation: TMA 1970, s. 12B(1)–(3); FA 2008, s. 115 and Sch. 37

Website: www.hmrc.gov.uk/record-keeping

Tax Reporter: ¶180-250

Penalties

Failure to comply with the above requirements attracts a maximum penalty of £3,000.

HMRC have issued guidance on the requirement to keep records in support of returns. This includes:

- *Record keeping (individuals and directors)*;
- *Record keeping (self-employed)*;
- *Record keeping (partners and partnerships)*.

HMRC have said that they will allow a 'reasonable period' for taxpayers and their advisers to assimilate that guidance and change their systems if necessary, before seeking penalties for record-keeping failures (SAT 2).

A failure to maintain complete and reliable records is 'careless behaviour' (previously 'negligence') for the purposes of charging a penalty (see *Seafield General Store & Post Office v R & C Commrs* [2010] TC 00333). HMRC accept that if the standard of record-keeping has already been considered in the imposition of a penalty (e.g. incorrect returns in an investigation case), then a further penalty under this new legislation may not be appropriate. However, it may be appropriate in circumstances where, say, records have been deliberately destroyed in order to hamper an investigation.

Case: *Seafield General Store & Post Office v R & C Commrs* [2010] TC 00333

Legislation: TMA 1970, s. 12B(5)

Other Material: HMRC *Income Tax Self Assessment Manual*: The Legal Framework ITSA211, para. 2.103; *Record keeping (individuals and directors)* available on the HMRC website at www.hmrc.gov.uk/sa/record-keeping.htm; *Record keeping (self-employed)* available on the HMRC website at www.hmrc.gov.uk/sa/rec-keep-self-emp.htm; *Record keeping (partners and partnerships)* available on the HMRC website at www.hmrc.gov.uk/sa/rec-keep-part-partners.htm; *Keeping records* – an overview available on the HMRC website at www.hmrc.gov.uk/record-keeping/index.htm

Use of copies

The requirement for a taxpayer to keep the records which enable a return to be completed or a claim to be made can normally be satisfied by preserving the information contained in them, e.g. by taking copies of the information or recording it in the business books, and such copies are admissible in evidence before the commissioners. Whilst the rules may have been drafted with computer-held records in mind, the wording of the legislation does not specify any particular form of records which may be retained by preserving the information contained in them in another form.

Records which must be retained as originals are:

- vouchers relating to dividends;
- certificates showing the gross amount, tax deducted, and actual amount paid, in respect of payments made under deduction of tax (annual payments);
- certificates or other records in respect of the subcontractors' deduction scheme;
- any record required to enable a claim to be made in respect of foreign tax paid.

Failure to preserve dividend vouchers or tax deduction certificates in relation to annual payments does not attract a penalty, provided the taxpayer can provide alternative satisfactory evidence.

Legislation: TMA 1970, s. 12B(4), (4A), (5B); FA 2008, s. 115 and Sch. 37

50-300 Disclosure, etc. guidance

The Association of Taxation Technicians, the Chartered Institute of Taxation, the Institute of Chartered Accountants in England and Wales and the Institute of Indirect Taxation have issued guidelines on the subject of professional conduct in relation to taxation. The guidance includes a consideration of the requirements for disclosure in tax returns, computations and related correspondence with HMRC. The principal objective of the guidelines is to advise members of the steps they should take to ensure that their clients meet the requirements of revenue law and practice. The guidelines aim to help tax practitioners by providing them with greater certainty.

The section of the guidelines concerned with disclosure to HMRC includes the following headings:

- relevance of disclosure provisions;
- areas of doubt;
- discovery;
- practical considerations;
- relevant responsibilities;
- points on business accounts and related tax computations; and
- known HMRC practices.

The guidelines were reviewed by HMRC who, although not necessarily agreeing with all the views expressed, have acknowledged that they are an acceptable basis for dealings between Institute members and the Department.

The subject of disclosure is closely related to that of discovery assessments (see 59-500). For a taxpayer to have certainty that the liability for a particular year is final, there must have been sufficient disclosure to ensure that HMRC cannot make a discovery assessment.

Website: www.att.org.uk/attach.pl/76/244/ProfessionalConduct%2012A%20-%20Final.pdf

Tax Reporter: ¶180-350

50-350 Submission of accounts

For self-assessment returns made by individuals, the submission of accounts is not generally required (with the exception of large partnerships with annual turnovers in excess of £15m). Instead, the return form contains a section requiring standardised accounts information (SAI). This section must be completed even where accounts are provided as additional information.

Individuals and partnerships who are trading with an annual turnover below the VAT limit and people with gross rental income property below the same amount need only state their total turnover, total business purchases and expenses and the resultant net profit (three line accounts) when they submit tax returns. HMRC have stated that proper accounting records must be maintained to prepare the three line accounts and they will investigate any simplified accounts which are submitted if they believe profits may be understated. Despite the whole point of admitting simplified accounts in low turnover cases is to spend a minimum of official time on them, there is anecdotal evidence that the submission of such accounts is often the precursor to an enquiry.

Other Material: HMRC Tax help series: *Self Assessment – what you need to know about using the three line account* available on the HMRC website at www.hmrc.gov.uk/factsheet/three-line-account.pdf

50-400 Forms and substitute forms

HMRC are given power to prescribe the form in which returns must be made. Different forms are prescribed for returns by persons chargeable in different capacities. When prescribing return forms, HMRC must secure, so far as possible, that no person is required to make more than one return annually of the sources and amounts of his income.

Statement of Practice 5/87 makes it clear that HMRC are prepared to accept computer-produced returns and photocopies of returns and other tax forms. The statement lays down the criteria for the acceptance of facsimiles of tax returns and the circumstances in which returns and other HMRC forms filled out on a photocopy of a blank form will be accepted.

Computer-produced returns must:

- provide the same information as that on official returns;
- be readily recognisable as a tax return;
- have had HMRC approval before they can be used; and
- bear the correct reference number.

The circumstances in which photocopied returns and other HMRC forms will be accepted are as follows:

- they must be presented in numerical order;
- they must contain the explanatory notes shown on the original; and
- they must show the correct reference number.

Tax returns produced on a large scale for commercial gain will be subject to a copyright fee.

Legislation: TMA 1970, s. 113(1)

Other Material: SP 5/87

Tax Reporter: ¶180-450

Individuals

50-600 Individuals' returns

Individuals are to submit returns of income and capital gains when required by notice, which is normally contained on the first page of the self-assessment return itself. The notice may also, within reason, require accounts, statements and documents relating to information contained in the return. The return is to be submitted by 31 January following the tax year to which it relates, if filed online, or 31 October if made on paper (whether or not HMRC are to calculate any tax). The First-tier Tribunal in *Lorimer* decided that, in certain circumstances, a penalty for the late submission of a paper return may be avoided if an online return is filed before 31 January.

Where a return is issued after 31 July but before 31 October the return must be filed within three months of the issue date if filed on paper, or by 31 January if filed online.

If the return is issued after 31 October the deadline for both paper and electronic returns is three months from the date of issue.

A return is to be made in the form prescribed by HMRC. The prescribed form of return is the self-assessment return SA100, together with such supplementary pages as may be appropriate.

For 2012–13 and subsequent tax return years, an individual can request HMRC to withdraw a notice to complete a return. This request has to be made in the two years beginning with the end of the year of assessment to which the notice to complete relates unless HMRC agree otherwise where there are exceptional circumstances.

A tax repayment claim on form R40 is not a 'return' for these purposes. A taxpayer had realised a capital gain but was not within the self-assessment regime. She had personally completed an income tax repayment claim on form R40 but had not ticked the box to indicate she had made disposals of chargeable assets in the year. Subsequently, a self-assessment return was issued for the same year. However, the agents then acting only completed and returned the capital gains pages, relying on the fact that details of the taxpayer's income had already been returned on the R40. It was held that neither the R40, nor the capital gains pages in isolation, constituted a 'return'.

An individual's return is to include his share of any partnership income, losses, tax (i.e. tax deducted at source), tax credit or charge. These figures will be derived from the relevant partnership statement. A partnership statement is relevant if it is for a period which includes all or part of the tax year or its basis period. The requirement for a partnership statement is discussed at 51-050.

Employees are entitled to receive a copy of form P11D from their employer, and this must contain the cash equivalents of benefits provided. This, together with the P60, will enable them to complete a self-assessment.

Legislation: TMA 1970, s. 8

Cases: *Osborne (dec'd) v Dickinson (HMIT)* (2003) Sp C 393; *Lorimer* [2014] TC 03914

50-625 Returns to include self-assessment

Every return is to include a self-assessment consisting of:

- the amount of the individual's liability to income tax and capital gains tax for the year, taking into account claims for reliefs and allowances included in the return; and
- the amount of income tax payable, or repayable, after taking into account tax deducted at source and tax credits on distributions received.

In practice the self-assessment return, at box 18.3 on page 7, simply calls for the net amount of tax due for the year after taking into account tax already paid by deduction but before any payments made on account:

- release of close company loan;
- chargeable event gains on life policies;
- tax chargeable on the administrator of a registered pension scheme or the responsible person for an employer-financed retirement benefits scheme.

A person is not obliged to include a self-assessment in their tax return if they make and deliver their return:

- on or before 31 October following the end of the tax year; or
- if the notice is given after 31 August following the end of the tax year, within two months of the date on the notice is given.

Where the taxpayer does not include a self-assessment with the return, then HMRC will make an assessment on the taxpayer's behalf, and send it to him. This will be deemed to be a self-assessment for the purposes of the legislation.

Legislation: TMA 1970, s. 9(2)

Tax Reporter: ¶180-550

50-650 Amendments following submission

Amendments by taxpayer

If it comes to a person's notice that a return which he has made was incorrect, without fraud or negligence on his part, the error must be remedied. The taxpayer may amend his self-assessment tax return or the calculation of tax due within 12 months of the prescribed filing date. There is no prescribed format for the taxpayer to make his amendment. It may take the form of a letter, an amended return form, an additional supplementary page or an amended supplementary page.

Corrections after this period may be made by way of a combination of relief for overpayments (previously error or mistake relief) (see 57-000) or discovery assessments (see 59-000).

Where an error is careless or deliberate, the person submitting the return is liable to penalties (61-000).

A taxpayer is entitled to amend his return during an enquiry, but any such amendment does not restrict the enquiry but may itself be taken into account in the enquiry. Furthermore, any amendment does not take effect until the enquiry is completed, unless it is taken into account in the conclusions which HMRC issue at the end of the inquiry (see 58-200).

Legislation: TMA 1970, s. 9ZA, 9B

Other Material: HMRC *Self Assessment Manual* Returns, view and amend returns

Amendments by HMRC

HMRC may amend a self-assessment so as to correct any obvious errors or mistakes (whether errors of principle, arithmetical mistakes or other) and anything else in the return that the officer has reason to believe is incorrect in the light of information available to that officer. This must be done within nine months of delivery of the return, or within nine months of a taxpayer's amendment to the return, if HMRC's amendment is a consequence of the taxpayer's amendment. This is described as 'repairing' the return. The errors corrected under this process should be obvious: this is not a route for opening technical queries. The taxpayer has the right to reject such a correction within 30 days of it being issued.

If, during the course of an enquiry into a return, HMRC form the opinion that the tax liability stated in the self-assessment is insufficient and there is likely to be a loss of tax to the Crown, an amended assessment to make good the deficiency can be made by giving notice to the taxpayer (see 58-200).

Legislation: TMA 1970, s. 9ZB, 9C; FA 2008, s. 119

50-700 The 'short' tax return

Following a pilot project, a new, shorter tax return form ('SA 200') has been introduced. This is a four-page form with an accompanying guide which aims to use simpler language than the main self-assessment return and guidance notes. It does not have any facility to self-assess, nor, apart from capital gains, does it have any supplementary pages.

Because the form only contains a limited number of questions, it is only being issued to those whose affairs HMRC believe are straightforward. It is therefore being limited to certain employees, pensioners and the self-employed with annual turnovers below the VAT registration threshold. In contrast, it will not be applicable to beneficiaries of trusts or company directors. Those who are sent the short return will have to consult the guidance notes to confirm that they are eligible to complete that form and, if not, request a standard self-assessment return.

The limitations on the use of the short return are:

- taxpayers cannot use it unless it is issued to them and they fulfil the eligibility criteria; it will not be available from the Orderline, local offices or the website;
- there is no electronic version of the short return, nor any substitute form;
- taxpayers may choose not to use it if they prefer to send in a main return instead, either on paper or electronically;

- it is not issued to people who filed their previous return late;
- a short return issued to one person must not be used by another. The return carries a bar code, which identifies the person to whom it is addressed;
- all forms must be sent to a dedicated processing facility in Netherton, Merseyside;
- the actual short return form must be completed. A photocopy will not be acceptable;
- ideally, the form should be sent back without any attachments. The only exception is the capital gains supplement and computations, where appropriate. Where additional information is essential, it should be set out in a letter enclosed (not pinned or stapled) with the return; and
- the selection process to identify taxpayers eligible to receive the short return relies on the information from the completed tax return for one year being entered onto the HMRC's computer system before the selection for the following year's return is made. The selection run is carried out in February.

50-800 Taxpayers outside self-assessment

In April 2004, new guidelines were published in respect of taxpayers who should complete tax returns. The aim was to ensure that taxpayers whose affairs are straightforward or whose tax liability can be met through PAYE deductions will not normally be asked to complete self-assessment returns. The categories of taxpayers who were to be taken out of self-assessment were:

- employees paying tax at the higher rate (and without any other reason for a return);
- employees paying basic rate tax who claim professional fees and expenses below £2,500 per annum;
- employees with investment income below £10,000 per annum; and
- pensioners and people on low incomes with simple affairs.

Employees

HMRC identify those employees affected when a completed tax return is received and entered onto the system, by checking the entries on the return against the guidelines. Where a return is no longer needed, the taxpayer will be sent an 'exit' letter (SA251) and notes informing them that they no longer have to complete a return. The notes explain how the taxpayer's affairs will be handled within the PAYE system and what needs to be done if their circumstances change. Authorised agents will be sent copies of the letter. A signal will be set on the taxpayer's record to prevent returns being issued in the future.

Depending on the taxpayer's circumstances, adjustments are made in the following year's coding record to ensure that any additional tax is paid through PAYE. Any adjustment will be notified to the taxpayer in a coding notice before that year begins.

Where appropriate, the system will note the taxpayer's record to issue a one-page form, the tax review form (P810), the following April. This will be sent where the taxpayer, for example, makes claims to expenses or Gift Aid payments, or has items of income on which additional tax must be paid, such as untaxed interest, etc. On receipt of the completed tax review form, the previous year's liability will be reviewed and any overpayment repaid. Any additional liability will normally be included in the following year's coding record. The tax review form will also be used to update the coding record for income and allowances for the current year.

After the first tax review form the taxpayer will receive further forms, in a three-yearly cycle or, where the individual's affairs are more involved, annually. HMRC expect taxpayers to contact them if their affairs change and the coding record is no longer correct.

Low income and pensioner cases

Again, suitable cases are selected when processing a completed self-assessment return. Those selected are then manually reviewed to ensure they fit the criteria. Some of these taxpayers will be sent the tax review form (P810) in place of the return, although others may be set up as tax repayment cases, so the taxpayer will receive a form R40 to complete for the following year.

In all these cases, the taxpayer and their agent (if they have one) will receive an 'exit' letter and notes, as described earlier.

Returning to self-assessment

The purpose of the new guidelines is to reduce the compliance burden on taxpayers where possible. However, taxpayers may opt to continue to receive self-assessment returns and, if so requested, HMRC should set a signal on the computer system to ensure they are not automatically removed again in the future.

Taxpayers who return to self-assessment will receive an 'entry' letter (SA250) (copied to their agent, if they have one) explaining that they will be sent tax returns to complete in the future.

Obligations

Even if a self-assessment return is not issued, it remains the taxpayer's responsibility to inform HMRC of any changes to their financial circumstances, since the information given in their last tax return. New sources of income and gains should be notified within six months of the end of the tax year concerned (see 50-000).

If the taxpayer becomes self-employed, they have three months in which to notify HMRC. In any case where a self-assessment return has been issued it must be completed and submitted. Failure to do so will result in the fixed penalties being chargeable – limited, however, to the amount of tax payable with the return.

'Simple assessments'

With effect from 2016–17, HMRC may issue a simple assessment based on information that they hold without the need for the taxpayer to file a self-assessment tax return (see 59-025).

50-850 Incapacitated persons

The trustee or guardian, etc. who controls or manages the property or concerns of an 'incapacitated' person, is chargeable to any income tax or capital gains tax to which the incapacitated person would otherwise be chargeable. The trustee, etc. must make the necessary returns to HMRC, and, in the same way as an individual, must notify his liability to do so even if a return form is not issued (see 50-000ff.).

These provisions apply to infants (i.e. persons under 18) and the mentally handicapped.

The trustee, etc. may retain the tax out of the money he receives on the incapacitated person's behalf.

These special provisions have been removed by FA 2012 for 2012–13 and subsequent years such that a trustee is no longer assessable on an incapacitated person's income.

HMRC's view is that, despite the appointment of a trustee, etc., the return itself should be signed by the incapacitated person except where the person's health might suffer if he were obliged to provide a signature (see 50-900).

Legislation: TMA 1970, s. 72, 118(1); FA 2012, s. 222

Infant responsible for his own tax

An infant who does not have a trustee or guardian and who therefore controls his own affairs can be assessed and charged directly.

There is no minimum age at which an infant may be assessed to tax, but usually the assessment will only relate to earned income. This is because, in practice, much income taxed at source (e.g. trust income) is paid to the infant through his parent, guardian or trustee who is assessed to the tax on it. An infant is entitled to all the reliefs that an adult may claim.

If an infant was charged to income tax or capital gains tax, his parent or guardian was liable for the tax for years up to and including 2011–12.

Legislation: TMA 1970, s. 73; FA 2012, s. 222

Case: *R v Commissioners of Taxes for the Newmarket division of Suffolk, ex parte Huxley* (1915) 7 TC 49

The mentally incapacitated

If a person is unable to handle his own affairs, the court may appoint a receiver (a curator bonis in Scotland). Where that receiver has the direction and control of any property giving rise to income or capital gains, he is assessable on that income or those gains.

Legislation: TMA 1970, s. 75

50-900 Powers of attorney

Anyone of sound mind can grant to another a power of attorney to act on his behalf either in relation to certain specified matters or to matters generally. HMRC policy is not to accept returns signed by an attorney unless the taxpayer is unable to cope with the management of his affairs and his general health might suffer if he were to be troubled for a signature. In such cases, HMRC will 'consider the matter sympathetically and where possible accept the signature of an attorney who has full knowledge of the taxpayer's affairs'.

Other Material: SP A13; HMRC Relief Instructions RE3077

Partnerships

51-000 Partnership returns

A partnership is not treated as a tax-paying entity but the partners, whether individuals or companies, must include their partnership shares in their own returns and self-assessments.

In order to establish the amount chargeable to income tax on each partner, and the amount of tax due, HMRC may require a 'nominated partner' to complete a partnership tax return containing details of the partnership income for the year and a statement showing how that income is shared between the partners.

As with the return made by individuals, the amounts included must take into account any relief, allowance or repayment of tax for which a claim is made, as well as tax already deducted at source and tax credits on dividends.

The dates specified for the making of such returns may not be earlier than 31 October for paper returns and 31 January for online returns following the tax year to which they relate, or three months from the date of issue of the notice, if later. Where a partnership includes a company, the specified date is not to be earlier than 12 months after the end of the period for which the return is required, or three months from the date of the notice, if later.

Each return is to include the name, residence and tax reference of all partners involved in the period, and a declaration by the person making it that it is to the best of his knowledge correct and complete. In addition to the above, the returns are, if the notice so requires, to include details of capital gains on disposals of partnership property calculated as if the partnership were itself liable to tax, along with particulars relating to any acquisitions of partnership property.

Flexibility is permitted in the types of accounts and statements which may be required for different periods and from different types of partnership. Partnerships with a turnover in excess of £15m are required to submit full accounts and computations, rather than completing the standard accounts information on the return form.

Similarly to individuals' and trustees' returns, HMRC can be requested to withdraw a notice to deliver a partnership return.

Legislation: TMA 1970, s. 12AA

Tax Reporter: ¶180-700

The nominated partner

The nominated partner is one who is nominated by a majority of those who were partners in the period covered by the return (or their personal representatives). Nomination is only effective once it has been notified to HMRC. Similarly, a revocation of the nomination is only effective once notified. Where a partner is nominated a return is issued to the partners as a whole and is to be completed on their behalf by that nominated partner.

In the absence of such a nomination, HMRC have the option to choose the nominated partner and issue a return to that person. They also have the power to issue separate partnership tax returns to each partner if they think fit.

51-050 Partnership statement to be included

Every partnership tax return is to include a 'partnership statement' for the tax year, or for each period of account ending within the period covered by the return, comprising;

- the amount of the partnership's income or loss from each source on the basis of the information in the partnership return and taking into account claims to relief and allowances included in the return;
- the consideration received on each disposal of a partnership asset;
- the income tax deducted at source suffered by the partnership; and
- the partnership's charges on income.

The statement must also show each partner's share of the above amounts. Thus, a partner will be able to abstract the relevant figures in order to complete the personal return.

HMRC have nine months from the delivery of the statement to correct obvious errors. The nominated partner, or his successor, is also entitled to amend the partnership return within 12 months of the filing date. However, once it is amended or corrected, HMRC must make consequential amendments to the individual partners' return(s).

Legislation: TMA 1970, s. 12AB, 12ABA, 12ABB

51-100 Power to enquire into partnership return

HMRC have the same powers to make enquiries into partnership returns as they have in respect of individuals (see 58-050). Notice of the enquiry must be given to the person who made the return, or that person's successor (see 51-000). A special commissioner decided that a letter sent to the nominated partner stating an intention to enquire into a tax return constituted a valid notice and no 'formal' notice had to be given.

Where an enquiry is opened into a partnership return, enquiries are also deemed to be opened into the returns of the individual partners.

Legislation: TMA 1970, s. 12AC

Case: *Flaxmode Ltd v R & C Commrs* (2008) Sp C 670

51-150 Amendment following submission

Amendments by taxpayer

A partnership return may be amended by the nominated partner or his successor at any time up to 12 months following the filing date. Where this is done, HMRC are required to amend each of the partners' individual returns accordingly.

There is no prescribed format for the nominated partner to make his amendment. It may take the form of a letter or an amended return form.

Where the partnership return is amended during an enquiry, the amendment does not restrict the enquiry but may itself be taken into account in the enquiry. Furthermore, any amendment does not take effect until the enquiry is completed, unless it is taken into account in the conclusions which HMRC issue at the end of the enquiry (see 58-200).

However, where the original return was submitted carelessly or deliberately, a subsequent amendment by the taxpayer does not remove the risk of a penalty being charged for the incorrect completion of the original return.

Legislation: TMA 1970, s. 12ABA, 12AD

Other Material: HMRC *Self Assessment Manual:* Returns, view and amend returns

Amendments by HMRC

HMRC may amend a self-assessment so as to correct any obvious errors or mistakes (whether errors of principle, arithmetical mistakes or otherwise) and anything else in the return that the officer has reason to believe is incorrect in the light of information available to the officer. This must be done within nine months of delivery of the return, or within nine months of the nominated partner's amendment to the return, if HMRC's amendment is a consequence of that amendment. This is described as 'repairing' the return. The errors corrected under this process should be obvious: this is not a route for opening technical queries. The taxpayer has the right to reject such a correction within 30 days of it being issued.

If, during the course of an enquiry into a return, HMRC form the opinion that the tax liability stated in the self-assessment is insufficient and there is likely to be a loss of tax to the Crown, an amended assessment to make good the deficiency can be made by giving notice to the taxpayer (see 58-200).

Legislation: TMA 1970, s. 12ABB; FA 2008, s. 119

Trustees and personal representatives

51-300 Trustees' returns

The requirements for returns by trustees are similar to those for individuals: the time-limit is the same, as is the requirement to return net amounts and to include a self-assessment based on those amounts (see 50-600 and 50-625).

A notice to make a return may be given to any 'relevant trustee' or separate notices may be given to each trustee. A request can be made as with individuals to request HMRC to withdraw such a notice.

The amounts to be returned are net amounts. That is to say, the amounts chargeable to income tax and capital gains tax must take into account any claim or relief claimed in the return. Similarly, the amount payable by way of income tax must take into account tax deducted at source.

Different information and different accounts or statements (relating to information contained in the return) may be required for different periods, or different sources of income, or different settlements.

Every return must include a declaration that the return made by the person is 'to the best of his knowledge correct and complete'.

In the absence of a return, HMRC may determine the amount of the relevant trustees' liability (see 59-050). Similarly, an assessment may be made where a loss of tax is discovered (see 59-500).

The usual penalties apply for failure to make a return, or for making an incorrect return (see 60-500ff.). However, as with individuals and partnerships HMRC can withdraw a notice to complete a tax return from 2012–13 onward.

The relevant trustees are liable for any tax which falls due as a result of the self-assessment included in the return (see 50-625).

In common with individual's returns, a trustees return may be amended within 12 months of the filing date and HMRC have the power to 'repair' any obvious errors. HMRC may also open an enquiry into a trustee's return (see 50-650 and 58-050).

A 'relevant trustee' for income tax purposes is any person who was a trustee at or after the time when the income arose, although in the case of gains on life policies, the person has to have been a trustee in the year in which the gain arose, or any subsequent year.

Legislation: TMA 1970, s. 7(9), 8A

Tax Reporter: ¶181-000

51-350 Liability of relevant trustees

HMRC have the power to collect any income tax, penalty or interest in respect of trust income from any relevant trustee. However, the liability of any individual trustee may be limited because of the date of his appointment as a trustee or the availability of a reasonable excuse defence (see 60-800).

No amount of penalty or surcharge can be recovered from someone who did not become a relevant trustee until after the 'relevant time'.

The relevant time for surcharges (which apply to 2009–10 and earlier years) is the beginning of the day on which the surcharge is incurred. For the initial 5% surcharge, this will be the day following a 28-day period from the due date for the tax. For the additional surcharge, this will be the day following a six-month period from the due date for the tax. This date also affects liability to interest on the surcharge. If the person did not become a relevant trustee until after the relevant time, that person has no liability for interest on the surcharge. This is so even where interest continues to run after that time.

This can be contrasted with the position regarding the daily penalties for continued failure to make a return, and for continued failure to supply documents (see 60-500 and 61-500). The relevant time for each daily penalty, and for any related interest accruing on that day, is the beginning of that day. Thus, the new trustee's liability will run from the day following his or her appointment.

The relevant time for other penalties (failure to notify chargeability, failure to keep records, incorrect returns) is the time when the act or omission giving rise to the penalty occurred.

Legislation in *Finance Act* 2009 reformed the penalty regimes for the late filing of tax returns and for the late payment of income tax. The new regimes took effect from 6 April 2011 for 2010–11 tax returns and late payments of tax for 2010–11 and later years.

Legislation: TMA 1970, s. 107A; FA 2008, Sch. 36 and 40; FA 2009, Sch. 55 and 56

Tax Reporter: ¶181-000

51-400 Bare trusts

A 'bare trust' exists where the beneficial owner of the property held in trust is fully entitled to both the capital and the income from the property. Although the property is held in the trustee's name, the trustee has no discretion over what income to pay the beneficiary. The trustee is, in effect, a nominee in whose name the property is held.

Any income which is received gross by the trustees must be paid gross by them to the beneficiary. In addition, trustees of bare trusts are not required to complete self-assessment returns, or make payments on account. Beneficiaries must include income and gains from these trusts in their returns.

Other Material: HMRC *Trusts Settlements and Estates Manual* TSEM1030

51-450 Personal representatives' returns

Personal representatives (executors and administrators) of a deceased person are required to return estate income and gains on the trusts and estates return. They are also liable for the tax chargeable on the deceased on income up to the date of death.

The time-limit for enquiring into tax returns under self-assessment (see 58-050) means that personal representatives may not know for some time whether the deceased's tax affairs can be regarded as settled. As this could delay the winding up of an estate, HMRC will, on request, issue a tax return before the end of the tax year in which death occurred and give early written confirmation if they do not intend to enquire into that return. Personal representatives can also request such confirmation at any time before the expiry of the normal enquiry time-limit.

In the situation where the administration of a deceased person's estate is completed (or a trust is wound up) during a tax year, HMRC will, on request, adopt the same approach to the tax affairs of personal representatives and trustees.

The normal record-keeping obligations fall on the personal representatives throughout the period of administration (see 50-200). In respect of the years before death for which returns have been issued, those obligations fell on the taxpayer, though the personal representatives may be penalised for any failure by the deceased (see below). In respect of any period before death for which a return has not been issued, the personal representatives may be issued with the return. They accordingly have corresponding record-keeping obligations, which means that they must take reasonable steps to obtain and retain all the records which are available at the date of the death.

Where a taxpayer has died, HMRC cannot impose a penalty on the personal representatives of the deceased taxpayer for offences committed by the deceased before the date of death. TMA 1970, s. 100A(1) which had permitted HMRC to do so was repealed in *Finance Act* 2007 because it was not compatible with the Human Rights Act.

However, where an error or failure offence has occurred after the date of death in respect of the deceased's estate and this offence is attributable to the personal representatives, HMRC will seek to impose a penalty on the personal representatives.

Case: *AP, MP and TP v Switzerland* (1998) 26 EHHR 541

Other Material: HMRC press release, 4 April 1996; HMRC *Enquiry Manual* EM1395

51-500 Trustees in bankruptcy

A bankrupt's estate vests in his trustee at the time of the latter's appointment. This rule divests the insolvent taxpayer of any interest in assets owned (subject to some exceptions for personal chattels, etc.) and also any liabilities in respect of debts due. Thus, from the date of appointment, it is the trustee in bankruptcy who is responsible for continuing any existing legal proceedings (including tax-related matters) or for commencing new ones.

This point was confirmed by a special commissioner who held that, following a taxpayer's bankruptcy, it was the trustee in bankruptcy who had the authority and was responsible for agreeing and settling any tax assessments and appeals outstanding as at the date of the insolvency.

Legislation: *Insolvency Act* 1986, s. 306

Case: *Ahajot v Waller (HMIT)* (2003) Sp C 395

Returns from third parties

51-600 Overview

In addition to their powers to require returns of income, HMRC possess a wide range of powers to obtain information to enable them to identify income chargeable to tax. Many of these are powers to obtain information from persons who have made payments, such as income or rent, to persons who may be liable for tax thereon. These powers are backed up by penalties for failure to comply.

These powers were radically changed with effect from 1 April 2012 when a general data-gathering power which enables HMRC to require 'relevant data-holders' to provide information was introduced.

HMRC's power to call for documents from third parties is considered at 58-100.

51-980 Returns from third parties – penalties

TMA 1970, s. 98 imposes a penalty for failing to comply with a notice requiring a third party to make a return, etc., or for fraudulently or negligently providing false information on the return.

The section contains a table listing the sections in the *Taxes Management Act* 1970 and in the *Income and Corporation Taxes Act* 1988 to which it applies. Column 1 of the table applies to the provisions which require the returns from third parties referred to above (see TMA 1970, Pt. III). The sections in column 2 are those which include the duty of the taxpayer to notify the inspector of certain information without the need for the inspector to issue a notice.

For failures within column 1 or column 2, s. 98 provides for:

- an initial penalty of up to £300; and
- a further penalty of up to £60 per day for each day the failure continues after the initial penalty has been imposed (£50 and £10 respectively for failures beginning before the *Finance Act* 1989 was enacted, 27 July 1989).

Where incorrect information or documents are provided fraudulently or negligently, s. 98(2) provides for a penalty of up to £3,000. (For failures before 27 July 1989, £250 increased to £500 in the case of fraud.) This includes making a false declaration to receive interest without deduction of income tax, following the abolition of composite rate tax (*Finance Act* 1991, s. 82).

Payment of tax

Interim payments on account of liability

52-000 Normal due dates

The normal rule is that, for any given tax year, the taxpayer makes interim payments on account of his tax and Class 4 National Insurance contributions (NICs) based on the final amount due for the preceding year. These interim payments are due in two equal instalments on 31 January in the tax year and the following 31 July.

Final settlement, involving a further payment or a repayment, will be due on 31 January following the tax year which is also the normal filing date for the self-assessment return. It is therefore often the case that two payments fall due on that date, namely the final settlement for the previous year and the first payment on account for the current year.

The interim payments are calculated by taking the 'assessed amount', i.e. the total liability, for the previous year and deducting any tax deducted at source. This gives a figure termed 'the relevant amount', and each payment on account is to be 50% of that relevant amount.

However, a de minimis test applies and taxpayers are not required to make payments on account if:

- their total income tax and Class 4 NIC liability for the preceding year, net of tax deducted at source, is less than £1,000; or
- more than 80% of their income tax and NIC liability for the previous year was met by deduction of tax at source.

Example

Dwyer's self-assessment for 2017–18 shows profits of £50,000 (with no tax deducted) and interest from a UK company of £3,000 gross (tax deducted, £600).

His total tax and NIC liability turns out to be £13,463. His payment due for 2017–18 is therefore £12,863.

The £1,000 test does not relieve Dwyer of the need to make interim payments, so he has to consider the percentage test.

Dwyer has to make interim payments for 2018–19 because his tax deducted at source (£600) is not more than 80% of his total liability (£13,463).

Each payment on account for 2018–19 will be half of his liability for 2017–18, i.e. £6,431.50.

In addition to the above test, there is a power for HMRC to direct that interim payments are not required from specified persons for a particular tax year, and make any consequent adjustment. The time-limit for making this direction is 31 January following the tax year.

From April 2015, payments for Class 2 National Insurance contributions become due on 31 July and 31 January, the same as self assessment tax.

Legislation: TMA 1970, s. 59A; *Income Tax (Payments on Account) Regulations* 1996 (SI 1996/1654); *Income Tax (Payments on Account) (Amendment) Regulations* 2008 (SI 2008/838)

52-050 Late self-assessments

If the due date for an interim payment on account falls before a self-assessment has been made, then hindsight is used to establish the amount which should have been paid at that date. The payment on account will therefore be, *and will be assumed always to have been*, half of the liability of the preceding year, whenever that is established, and whether it is established by self-assessment or by amendment to that assessment. This is subject to a claim by the taxpayer to reduce or eliminate interim payments (see 52-100).

There are two important consequences of this:

(1) a payment on account may be due, even though a self-assessment is not in place by the due date for the payment (thus the amount may be unknown); and

(2) interest is running on the payment.

Legislation: TMA 1970, s. 59A(4A)

52-100 Claims to reduce interim payments

The taxpayer can make a claim at any time before 31 January following the tax year, stating his belief (with grounds for such belief) that either that there will be no *relevant amount* for that year (see 52-000) or that his actual liability will be less than the relevant amount. The claim should be made on form SA303 which can be downloaded from the HMRC website.

In either case, each of his interim payments are either deemed never to have been required or are deemed always to have been set at half that expected actual liability.

Where a claim is made, appropriate adjustments, including repayment if necessary, will be made to any interim payments already made, but if the taxpayer fraudulently or negligently makes an incorrect statement in connection with a claim, he becomes liable to a penalty amounting to a maximum of the difference between:

- the amount which would have been payable had he not made incorrect statements; and
- the amounts (if any) actually paid on account by him.

There may also be interest consequences (see 53-000).

Legislation: TMA 1970, s. 59A(3)–(6)

Website: www.hmrc.gov.uk/sa/forms/sa303.pdf

52-150 Impact of averaging claims

Where a taxpayer has made a claim to average profits from farming or the creative arts for two successive years or with effect from 6 April 2016 in the case of farmers (see 106-200), the liability for the earlier years are not amended. It therefore follows that the interim payments for the second year, being based upon the final liability for the first year, are not affected by an averaging claim.

The profits assessed for the final year are those produced by the averaging calculation. In respect of the tax underpaid or overpaid for the earlier years, a tax adjustment is made to the final year's liability. This adjustment is the difference between:

- the tax chargeable for the earlier year, before the averaging claim ('amount A'); and
- the tax liability which would arise for the earlier year if the profits were reduced or increased to the averaged amount ('amount B').

(In other words, the tax which would otherwise be overpaid or underpaid for that year as a result of the averaging claim, if the liability had been amended.)

Where there would have been an underpayment of tax for the earlier year, that amount is added to, but does not become part of, the liability for the final. Conversely, if there would have been an overpayment for the earlier year, that sum is treated as an interim payment on account of the liability for the final year.

The interim payments on account for the year following the claim will be based upon the final liability of the final year before the deduction of interim payments for that final year or any 'notional' interim payment referred to above. Thus, the revision of the final year's profits on to the averaged basis will affect the subsequent year's interim payments but the tax adjustment as a result of revision of the earlier year's profits will never have an effect.

> **Example**
>
> In 2016–17, a farmer's profit is £12,000 and his tax and Class 2 and 4 NIC liability is £593.24. In 2017–18, his profit is £50,000 and his liability would be £12,263.24. If a claim is made to average the two years, the profit figures for both years become £30,000.
>
> The liability which would have arisen for 2016–17 on a profit of £30,000 would have been £5,920.20 and additional tax of £5,326.96 would have become due. Instead of revising the 2016–17 liability, this amount is added to the 2017–18 liability.
>
> The 2017–18 liability is calculated on a profit of £30,000 and would be £5,813.44, to which would be added the £5,326.96 calculated above. The interim payments for 2017–18 would be £2,960.10 each being one-half of the 2016–17 liability ignoring the £5,326.96 adjustment.

Legislation: TMA 1970, Sch. 1B, para. 3; ITTOIA 2005, s. 221

52-200 Impact of discovery assessments

Where a discovery assessment is made for a particular year, then the interim payments due in the following year must be increased by 50% of the amount of the discovery assessment. This ensures that taxpayers whose returns are incorrect do not gain any advantage over other taxpayers. The increased amount is deemed always to have been the proper amount due, so interest will flow on that amount from the due date.

It may be that the interim payments for the year affected by the discovery assessment also need adjustment. This will be the case where there has been a claim to reduce the amount of the interim payments (see 52-100). Each interim amount will be treated as having always been the lower of:

- the amount due after the claim for reduction, plus 50% of the discovery assessment amount; or
- the amount which would have been due had the claim for reduction not been made.

Legislation: TMA 1970, s. 59A(4B)

Balancing payments

52-500 Normal due date

Any income tax and capital gains tax included in a person's self-assessment which is in excess of any interim payments and any amounts deducted at source is normally to be paid by 31 January following the end of the tax year concerned.

Where the interim payments and tax deducted at source exceed the amount of the self-assessment, that excess is repaid.

If the taxpayer has given notice of a liability to tax but has not received a notice to make a return until after 31 October following the tax year, the date of his final payment is deferred until three months from the date of issue of the notice.

Legislation: TMA 1970, s. 59B(1)–(4)

52-550 Payment after amendment or correction of return

As a general rule, an amount of tax payable or repayable as a result of an amendment (whether by the taxpayer or HMRC) or correction of a self-assessment is payable or repayable on or before the day following the end of the period of 30 days beginning with the day on which the notice of amendment was given. However if an amendment is made by the taxpayer during the course of an enquiry, that amendment is not to have effect, and no tax will be repayable/payable until 30 days from the date of the closure notice in respect of that enquiry.

Where the normal due dates (see 52-000 and 52-500) would give a later date, those normal dates apply instead.

In either case the amount payable is subject to the right to apply for postponement pending an appeal (see 62-550).

Legislation: TMA 1970, Sch. 3ZA

Tax Reporter: ¶180-250

52-600 Late payment of tax after 6 April 2011

Finance Act 2009, Sch. 56 introduced a new penalty regime for late payments under income tax self assessment. The new regime applies from 6 April 2011 to payments for the tax year 2010–11 and later years.

The following penalties are chargeable as follows.

- At 30 days late, there will be charged an initial penalty of 5% of the tax unpaid at that date.
- At six months late, there will be charged a further penalty of 5% of the tax that is still unpaid.
- At 12 months late, there will be charged a further penalty of 5% of the tax that is still unpaid.

These penalties will be issued automatically and are in addition to the interest that will be charged on all outstanding amounts, including unpaid penalties, until payment is received.

An appeal lies against any penalty on the grounds that there was a reasonable excuse for not complying on time and all penalty notices will include an appeal form and details on how to appeal.

Legislation: FA 2009, Sch. 56

Reasonable excuses for late payments of tax

The following are examples of what HMRC say they may accept as a reasonable excuse for missing the deadline for paying tax:

- loss of the cheque in the post or by HMRC (HMRC expect a prompt replacement cheque once the taxpayer becomes aware that the cheque is lost);
- dishonour of the cheque solely because of a bank error, followed by prompt payment after learning of the error;
- serious illness on or shortly before the due date for payment where arrangements to pay could not have been made;
- preoccupation with the serious illness of a close relative or domestic partner where arrangements to pay could not have been made; or
- death of a close relative or domestic partner at around the due date for payment (HMRC nevertheless expect payment within a reasonable time).

In contrast, the following are examples of what HMRC say they will not accept as a reasonable excuse for missing the deadline for paying tax:

- inconvenience on or around the date the payment was due;
- shortage of funds;
- cheque made out incorrectly;
- pressure of work;
- failure by the taxpayer's agent;
- not knowing exactly what to pay; or
- absence of reminders from HMRC.

The Upper Tribunal decided that a person who, on the evidence of a consultant psychiatrist, suffered from a mental state that caused and would have continued to cause 'avoidance symptoms', which covered areas such as her dealings with HMRC, had a reasonable excuse for late payment of her tax.

Similarly, where the taxpayer had a previous good record of compliance, there was evidence of poor state of health due to alcoholism and stress and the taxpayer's brother obtained authorisation to act and immediately contacted HMRC, the tribunal decided that the taxpayer had reasonable excuse for late payment due to illness through stress and alcoholism.

The question of reasonable excuse as a defence against a late payment surcharge was considered by a special commissioner in a case where the taxpayers posted a cheque on 28 February 2000 for the tax due on the previous 31 January. It was received by HMRC on 29 February. It was accepted that tax was unpaid on (part of) the day following the expiry of 28 days from the due date and accordingly the taxpayers were in principle liable to a surcharge. However, they argued that they had a reasonable excuse for paying the tax late, since they believed that they had until the end of February to pay the tax and 2000 was a leap year.

The special commissioner dismissed the appeals and confirmed the surcharge. The reasonable excuse for not paying the tax had to persist throughout the period of default, i.e. from 1 to 28 February and no such excuse had been put forward. The taxpayers were playing brinkmanship in paying the tax on the last possible date but they had not read the rules properly. A reasonable excuse implied that a reasonable taxpayer would have behaved in the same way. A reasonable taxpayer would at least have read the literature issued by HMRC which could not have been clearer: 'If it [the payment] does not reach us by 28 February you may also have to pay an automatic five per cent surcharge' (form SA324).

A tribunal held that the responsibility rests on the taxpayer to know the correct amount of tax due and to pay it on time. A lack of understanding of the online filing system and a lack of awareness of the liability to a surcharge for late payment is not a reasonable excuse for late payment.

A reasonable excuse must continue throughout the period of non-payment and the late payment must be remedied as soon as the excuse comes to an end. A failure to pay without further delay after HMRC have clearly stated that the tax is due would mean that the taxpayer would not have a reasonable excuse for late payment, even if such an excuse existed up to the date of HMRC's notification.

If a taxpayer experiences difficulty in paying the tax outstanding by the due date, they should contact HMRC's Business Payment Support Service with proposals for payment and a request for time to pay. Where this was not done, a tribunal found that the taxpayer did not have a reasonable excuse for non-payment throughout the period of default, despite their having made part-payment on time. Interest and a surcharge was payable on the balance paid late. It is recommended that any time to pay arrangements negotiated with HMRC should be confirmed in writing, although the First-tier Tribunal has acknowledged that a taxpayer may avoid the imposition of penalties where payment terms have been offered and not explicitly rejected by HMRC.

Legislation: FA 2009, Sch. 56

Cases: *Bancroft v Crutchfield (HMIT)* (2002) Sp C 322; *Sloots* [2011] TC 01013; *England (trustee of Mrs M E England Discretionary Will Trust)* [2010] TC 00477; *AZ v R & C Commrs* [2011] BTC 1,777; *Atkinson* [2011] TC 00909; *Pitt* [2011] TC 01073; *Campbell* [2014] TC 03628

Payment of tax generally

52-800 Methods of paying tax

HMRC accept payment of tax by a range of methods:

- cheque by post to an Accounts Office;
- bank giro or via the Post Office; or
- BACS/CHAPS.

However, they recommend that payment is made electronically by either:

- internet banking service;
- telephone banking;
- with a debit or credit card issued by a UK card issuer using the BillPay service provided by Santander Corporate Banking (previously Alliance & Leicester Commercial Bank). There is a transaction charge for payments by credit card and HMRC do not accept American Express or Diners Club cards.

If an electronic payment is not possible, the next recommended method is for payment to be made by Bank Giro or at the Post Office. Where payment is made by other than electronic means, it is very important that the taxpayer's payslip accompanies the payment. The encoded personalised details on the payslip issued with the taxpayer statement and the agent Client Account Information will ensure the payment is allocated quickly to the right account. HMRC ask that payments sent by post should not:

- enclose compliment slips or a courtesy letter; or
- use staples or paperclips to attach cheques and payslips.

Legislation: FA 2008, s. 136

Other Material: HMRC *Working Together*, Issue 7, December 2001

Website: www.billpayment.co.uk/hmrc/scripts/signup.asp

52-850 Statements of account

Each taxpayer has an account with HMRC, with liabilities (tax, interest and surcharges) being added as they arise, and payments deducted as they are made. A copy of the account is issued as a 'taxpayer's statement', which summarises liabilities arising and payments made, acts as a receipt for payments and also as an acknowledgment of the tax due shown on a self-assessment. Where tax is due, a payslip is included as part of the statement.

HMRC provide authorised agents with agents statements (clients' accounts) before the 31 January and 31 July payment dates giving details of the tax due by their clients. The clients' accounts are not a copy of the taxpayer's statement of account. They are produced at a slightly different time to the taxpayer's statement, so the tax due may have changed if the taxpayer has recently made a payment. Unlike the taxpayer's statement, the clients' account information does not include any interest which may have accrued to date on outstanding arrears.

Other Material: HMRC Booklet SA/BK8 *Self assessment: your guide*

52-900 Set off of payments against repayments

Following consultation, legislation in *Finance Act* 2008 gave a specific power to allow HMRC to set-off all repayments payable to a taxpayer against debts owed by the taxpayer and extended the principle of set-off across a wider range of debts administered by HMRC. The legislation also removed the requirement for HMRC to seek authority from taxpayers before the set-off takes place. However, HMRC must still advise the taxpayer in writing what has been done. A statement on the HMRC website explains how they will apply set-off following the new legislation. Repayments will be set only against 'established debt' defined as a quantifiable debt that is payable either based on a return from the taxpayer or which has been assessed and either the appeal has been determined, or the period for the appeal has passed. There will be no monetary limit to the amount of set-off, but HMRC may choose not to exercise set-off for small amounts. The legislation applies to England, Wales and Northern Ireland and has effect from 21 July 2008.

Legislation: FA 2008, s. 130

Website: www.hmrc.gov.uk/finance-bill2008/set-off-taxes.htm

52-950 Direct recovery of tax debts

Finance (No. 2) Act 2015 introduced 'Direct Recovery of Debt' (DRD) provisions that will allow HMRC to seek to collect tax debts directly from the banks or building societies accounts of a taxpayer. In order to be applicable, then all of the following conditions must be met:

Condition A: the total debt must be at least £1,000.

Condition B: it must be an 'established debt' from an assessment, determination or enquiry closure notice against which no appeal or further appeal can be made or as a result of an unpaid Advance Payment Notice.

Condition C: HMRC are satisfied that the taxpayer is aware that the sum is due.

The detailed provisions include a number of safeguards and protections to prevent undue hardship, for example, tax will only be collected in this manner provided the taxpayer's remaining balances does not fall below £5,000. HMRC have given assurances that these provisions will only be applied where all other means of collection have failed.

Legislation: F(No. 2)A 2015, Sch. 8

Interest on overdue tax

53-000 Overview

The interest regime falls naturally into four elements:

(1) Interest payable on routine payments, i.e.:

- (a) interim and balancing payments on account (see 52-000 and 52-500);
- (b) payments of tax where there is an appeal and postponement application (see 62-150);
- (c) payments due because of amendments to returns (see 58-200); and
- (d) the final, balancing payment for the year (see 52-500).

(2) Interest payable when a claim to reduce interim payments turns out to be unjustified (see 52-100).

(3) Interest where a discovery assessment has been made (see 59-500).

(4) Repayment of interest when tax is repaid.

Interest harmonisation

Legislation introduced in *Finance Act* 2009 created a harmonised interest regime for the first time for all taxes administered by HMRC with the exception of corporation tax and petroleum revenue tax. The legislation makes provision for the automatic setting and implementation of interest rate changes. This replaced the previous range of interest regimes. The new harmonised interest regime comes into force for the purposes of income tax self assessment amounts on 31 October 2011.

From 29 September 2009, a new formula for calculating interest on tax unpaid or overpaid was introduced. From that date, interest charged on unpaid tax will be base rate plus 2.5%. Interest earned on overpaid tax will be base rate minus 1%, but never less than 0.5%.

Legislation: FA 2009, s. 101, 102, 103 and Sch. 53; *Finance Act 2009, Sections 101 to 103 (Income Tax Self Assessment) (Appointed Days and Transitional and Consequential Provisions) Order* 2011 (SI 2011/701)

53-050 Interest on routine payments

Interest is due on what may be termed routine payments from the 'relevant date' until actual payment. The relevant date depends on the type of payment:

- for interim payments it is the due date for the payment: i.e. either 31 January in the tax year, or the following 31 July;
- for balancing payments and payments of tax where there is an appeal and postponement application (see 62-150), it is 31 January following the tax year. The one exception is where the notice requiring a return is not issued until after 31 October before the normal filing date (31 January following the tax year) when the due date of payment and the relevant date is three months from the day on which the notice was issued, provided there has been no failure to notify chargeability;
- for payments due as a result of a return being amended, it is 31 January following the tax year covered by the return.

The Upper Tribunal has held that a First-tier Tribunal does not have jurisdiction to waive interest payable under TMA 1970, s. 86.

Legislation: TMA 1970, s. 86(1), (2)

Case: *R & C Commrs v Gretton* [2012] BTC 1,656

53-100 Inaccurate claims to reduce interim payments

Interim payments are based on the preceding year's liability. A claim may be made to reduce interim payments because the current year's liability will be lower, or non-existent, or covered by deduction at source (see 52-000). If such a claim is made, and is correct, it must follow that no balancing payment will be due. If the claim is incorrect, and a balancing payment has to be made, interest will be charged on the reduction in interim payments. This is achieved by treating each interim payment as if it has always been the lower of:

- the amount actually paid under the incorrect claim, plus 50% of the balancing payment; and
- the interim payment that would have been due had the claim not been made.

Example

Jane's liability to income tax for 2017–18 is £6,000. No tax has been deducted at source. Interim payments for 2018–19, due on 31 January 2019 and 31 July 2019, are therefore £3,000 each. Jane makes a claim to reduce interim payments to £2,000 each, and she pays these on time. It turns out that the final liability for 2018–19 is £5,000, the claim was inaccurate, and a balancing payment of £1,000 is due. She makes this payment on 25 February 2020.

Interest is due on the underpayment for each interim payment from the due date, calculating the underpayment on the assumption that the amount due for each interim payment is the lower of:

- £2,500 (amount actually paid plus half the balancing payment); and
- £3,000 (the amount that would have been paid if no claim had been made).

Therefore interest will be due on £500 for each of the interim payments up to the following 31 January, and on £1,000 from that date until payment:

- £500 for the 12 months from 1 February 2019 to 31 January 2020;
- £500 for the six months from 1 August 2019 to 31 January 2020;
- £1,000 for the period from 1 to 25 February 2020.

Two further assumptions must be made.

- The balancing payment is calculated for this purpose as if both interim payments *originally* due have been paid.
- Payments on account outside the self-assessment system, or payments of capital gains tax, are ignored.

Legislation: TMA 1970, s. 86(4)–(6)

53-150 Interest where discovery assessment made

Where a discovery assessment is made for a particular year, the payments on account due in the following year must be increased by 50% of the amount of the discovery assessment. This ensures that taxpayers whose returns are incorrect do not gain any advantage over other taxpayers. The increased amount is deemed always to have been the proper amount due, so interest will flow on that amount from the due date.

It may be that the interim payments for the year affected by the discovery assessment also need adjustment. This will be the case where there has been a claim to reduce the amount of the interim payments. Each interim amount will be treated as having always been the lower of:

- the amount due after the claim for reduction, plus 50% of the discovery assessment amount; and
- the amount which would have been due had the claim for reduction not been made.

Example

Eric's self-assessment for 2014–15 was £10,000. Based on this amount, his interim payments for 2015–16 were £5,000 each, due on 31 January and 31 July 2016. He made a claim to reduce these to £4,000 each, and paid the reduced amounts on the due dates.

His self-assessment for 2015–16 was £6,000. He therefore received a repayment of £2,000, representing £1,000 from each of his interim payments. He received repayment supplement on £1,000 from 31 January 2016, and on £1,000 from 31 July 2016. His interim payments for 2016–17 were £3,000 each, due on 31 January and 31 July 2017.

A discovery assessment was made on 30 July 2018 in respect of 2015–16 in the sum of £6,000. The consequences of the discovery assessment are as follows:

- the interim payments for 2015–16 are increased to the lower of the amount paid, plus 50% of the discovery assessment (£7,000) and the amount due if the claim had not been made (£5,000). Thus, interest will be payable on £1,000 from 1 February 2016 to 31 January 2017, and on £1,000 from 1 August 2016 to 31 January 2017;
- interest will be payable on £6,000 from 31 January 2017; and
- the interim payments for 2016–17 must be increased to £6,000 each (i.e. £3,000, based on original figures, plus 50% of the discovery assessment for 2015–16).

Legislation: TMA 1970, s. 86(4)

53-250 Rate of interest

From 29 September 2009, a new formula for calculating interest on tax unpaid or overpaid was introduced. From that date, interest charged on unpaid tax will be base rate plus 2.5%. Interest earned on overpaid tax will be base rate minus 1%, but never less than 0.5%.

The current and previous rates may be found in *Key data*.

Legislation: *Taxes (Interest Rate) Regulations* 1989 (SI 1989/1297)

53-300 Effective dates of payment for interest charging purposes

When tax is paid late, interest is charged on a daily basis from the due date to the effective date of payment. The effective date of payment for different methods of payment are set out below.

- Where tax is paid by cheque and the cheque is honoured on its first presentation, the payment is treated as received on the date of the receipt of the cheque.
- Where the payment of tax, etc. is received by post following a day when the tax office is closed (for whatever reason), the effective date of payment is the day the office was first closed. The effective date for payments received on Monday is the previous Saturday.
- Where payment is made by BACS or CHAPS (Clearing House Automated Payment System), payment is treated as made one working day immediately before the date that the value is received.
- Payment by bank giro or Santander Corporate Banking BillPay by debit card is treated as made three working days prior to the date of processing by HMRC.
- Where payment is made by Santander Corporate Banking BillPay using a credit card, payment is treated as made once the transaction has been successfully completed.

(HMRC will no longer accept payment of tax by cheque, cash or postal order handed in or received by post at the local tax office.)

Legislation: TMA 1970, s. 70A

Other Material: HMRC *Self Assessment Manual*, 'Jumps', 'Effective Date of Payment'

53-350 Disallowance of relief for interest

Interest charged in respect of late paid tax is not tax deductible.

Legislation: ITTOIA 2005, s. 869(3)

Repayment supplement

53-500 Overview

Repayment supplement is to be added to repayments of income tax, penalties, surcharges, etc. It is, in effect, interest on overpaid tax and is calculated at a rate fixed by the Treasury for the period running from the 'relevant time' to the date on which the order for repayment is issued.

The supplement is not to be regarded as income for tax purposes.

Legislation: ICTA 1988, s. 824(1)

53-550 Relevant times

The relevant times from which repayment supplement is calculated are as follows:

- interim payments on account (see 52-000), or repayments of income tax which has not been deducted at source – the date of the payment that is being repaid;
- where the repayment arises as a result of a claim to carry-back losses or to average the profits of farmers or creative artists – 31 January following the end of the later year in relation to that claim;
- repayments of income tax deducted at source – the 31 January following the tax year in which the income arose; and
- surcharges (see 52-600) and penalties – the date of payment of that surcharge or penalty.

Legislation: ICTA 1988, s. 824(3)

53-600 Matching of repayments

A repayment of income tax is matched with payments of tax in the following order:

(1) the final, balancing payment in respect of the year (see 52-500);

(2) equally between interim payments (see 52-000); and

(3) income tax deducted at source for the year.

Where the original payment was made in instalments, matching is on a 'Last In First Out' basis (i.e. with a later instalment before an earlier one).

Legislation: ICTA 1988, s. 824(4)

53-650 Income tax deducted at source

Income tax deducted at source is defined as including income tax deducted, or treated as deducted, or treated as paid on any income (thus including, for instance, deductions under the sub-contractors' scheme).

However, amounts deducted at source in the year under PAYE in respect of previous years are specifically excluded from the definition.

Example

Janice pays £2,000 income tax under PAYE for the year 2017–18. She also has trading income, and makes interim payments of £500 on 31 January 2018, and £500 on 30 May 2018 (due on 31 July 2018). She makes a balancing payment in respect of the year on 31 January 2019 of £200.

Assuming a subsequent repayment claim for £1,500 in respect of 2017–18, repayment supplement would run as follows:

- on £200 from 31 January 2019 (in respect of the final payment for the year);
- on £500 from 30 May 2018 (payment on account made early);
- on £500 from 31 January 2018 (payment on account made on due date); and
- on the remaining £300 from 31 January 2019 (in respect of PAYE tax).

Legislation: ICTA 1988, s. 824(4A)

53-700 Rate of repayment supplement

The rate of repayment supplement is set by a formula which reflects the average rate of return on deposits and is considerably less than the rate payable on overdue tax.

Finance Act 2009 introduced legislation to create a harmonised interest rate regime (see 53-000). From 29 September 2009, repayment supplement on overpaid tax will be base rate minus 1%, but never less than 0.5%.

The current and previous rates of repayment supplement may be found in *Key data*.

Legislation: *Taxes (Interest Rate) Regulations* 1989 (SI 1989/1297), reg. 3AB; FA 2009, s. 103

53-800 Recovery of overpaid tax

Finance Act 2009 introduced legislation to provide a means of reclaiming overpayments of tax where there is no statutory route. The legislation removed the requirement that an overpayment must be made as a result of a mistake in a return and that it must be made under an assessment. The changes have effect for claims made on or after 1 April 2010. (See 57-000.)

Legislation: FA 2009, s. 100 and Sch. 52

Claims

Claims generally

54-000 Form of claims

Claims to allowances and reliefs will normally be made within the self-assessment return or by an amendment to that return (see 55-100). Where this is not possible, either because the time-limit for amending the return has passed or because the taxpayer is not within self-assessment, then the claim is made 'outside the return' (see 55-200).

Where a claim is made outside of a return, it should be made on the form prescribed by HMRC where such exists. However many types of claim, such as claims for loss reliefs and pension contributions, do not have a prescribed form and in such cases it is necessary to ensure that the claim contains sufficient information to identify the type of relief being claimed, the quantum of the claim, the tax year involved and, where appropriate, the source of the loss and the period in which it arose.

Claims are normally required to be in writing but see 55-050 for claims that may be made by telephone.

Other Material: HMRC Manual *Income Tax Self Assessment*: The Legal Framework SALF603, SALF605

54-050 Claims for relief involving two or more years

The claims affecting two or more years are:

- carry back of losses;
- an averaging claim in respect of profits of farmers and creative artists;
- carry-back of post-cessation, etc. receipts (where a claim is made to treat the receipt as received on the date of discontinuance).

Where such a claim is made the liability for the earlier year is not re-opened. Instead where the earlier year's liability would otherwise have been reduced as a result, a 'free-standing' credit is given in the taxpayer's statement to set against outstanding liabilities or to be repaid as appropriate. This credit is an amount equal to the tax repayment which would otherwise arise for that earlier year, if that year's liability had been recalculated.

Conversely, where claim would have resulted in an increase in the earlier year's liability, an amount is debited to the taxpayer's statement, and this becomes tax payable, representing that additional tax.

The amount of the debit or credit is the difference between:

- the liability for that earlier year; and
- the 'notional' liability for that year if it was recalculated as a result of the relief.

The special commissioners have held that, as the earlier year's liability is not amended, any surcharge or interest imposed on late payment of that year's tax is not affected by a claim.

For commentary on the impact of averaging claims on interim payments for the years involved, see 52-150.

Legislation: TMA 1970, Sch. 1B

Cases: *Norton v Thompson (HMIT)* (2004) Sp C 399; *R & C Commrs v Cotter* [2013] BTC 837

Other Material: HMRC Interpretation, IRInt. 211 (Tax Bulletin, August 2000)

54-100 General time-limit for making claims

Claims made on or after 1 April 2010

Finance Act 2008, Sch. 39 introduced a four-year time limit for assessments and claims in respect of capital gains tax, corporation tax, income tax, PAYE and VAT. For direct taxes, the new time limit came into effect on 1 April 2010, from which date the normal time limit decreased from six years, or five years from the 31 January immediately following the tax year, to four years from the end of the tax year.

The new time limit applies to assessments and claims for direct taxes made on or after 1 April 2010, regardless of the period the assessment or claim relates to.

Claims made before 1 April 2010

Subject to any provisions of the Taxes Acts prescribing a longer or shorter period, a claim for relief under the Taxes Act made before 1 April 2010 will only be allowed if it is made within five years of the 31 January next following the year to which it relates. For companies, the time limit is six years from the end of the accounting period to which the claim relates (TMA 1970, s. 43(1)).

Assessment made after year of assessment

A claim (including a supplementary claim) which could not have been allowed but for the making of an assessment to income tax or capital gains tax after the year of assessment to which the claim relates may be made at any time before the end of the year of assessment following that in which the assessment was made (TMA 1970, s. 43(2)).

The normal assessing time limit is four years. For direct taxes, it is six years where the loss of tax is brought about carelessly. For all taxes, it is 20 years where the loss of tax is brought about deliberately or where there is a failure to notify liability or disclose avoidance arrangements.

Finance Act 2009 makes corresponding changes to the limits that apply to claims and assessments for insurance premium tax, inheritance tax, stamp duty land tax, petroleum revenue tax, aggregates levy, climate change levy and landfill tax.

Legislation: TMA 1970, s. 43; FA 2008, s. 118 and Sch. 39; FA 2009, s. 99 and Sch. 51

54-150 Claims following HMRC amendments or discovery assessments

Following an enquiry into a self-assessment return for an individual, partnership or body of trustees, HMRC may amend the self-assessment for that year. They may also issue a 'discovery' assessment (see 59-500) for an earlier year if the enquiry suggests that tax has been under-assessed for that earlier year.

Where either an amendment or a discovery assessment is made, the taxpayer is given a fresh opportunity to make, amend or withdraw a claim for that year, though the extent of that opportunity depends upon whether the amendment or assessment is to recover a loss of tax brought about carelessly or deliberately.

Legislation: TMA 1970, s. 36(3), 43(2)

Other Material: HMRC Manual *Income Tax Self Assessment*: The Legal Framework SALF 407A

Amendments and assessments on other grounds

Where the amendment or assessment is not by reason of the taxpayer's careless or deliberate conduct, the steps he can take are slightly wider in that the ability to make a late claim extends to 'elections', 'applications' and the giving of 'notices'. In general terms elections, applications and notices are the means by which a taxpayer is able to exercise a choice in either treatment or in the year in which a relief is given.

Unless, by statute, it is irrevocable, he may make, vary or revoke a claim, an election, an application or give, revoke or vary a notice at any time up to one year from the end of the year in which the amendment or discovery assessment is made. However, the effect of the claim, etc. is limited to the amount of the additional tax charged by the amendment or assessment, so that, again, it cannot affect the original liability.

The claim, revocation or variation in point must either:

- relate to the year *in respect of which* the assessment is made;
- refer to an event occurring in that year;
- reduce the additional tax charged by the assessment; or
- reduce that person's tax for any tax year between that *in respect of which* the assessment is made and that last finishing within one year of the end of the tax year *in which* the assessment is made.

Legislation: TMA 1970, s. 43A(1), (2), 43B(3), 43C(2)

54-200 Claims 'out of time'

A late claim may exceptionally be accepted, but this should not be relied upon. HMRC will, by concession, accept late repayment claims where the overpayment arises as the result of an error by HMRC or another government department and where the facts are not disputed or in doubt. Therefore repayments made under the concession will not be subject to the statutory appeals procedure.

Other Material: ESC B41

54-250 Error or mistake in a claim

Where a claim has been made and the taxpayer subsequently discovers an error or mistake in the claim he may make a supplementary claim within the normal time-limit for the making of the original claim. This applies both to claims made in a return, and to claims made outside a return. See 57-000.

Legislation: TMA 1970, s. 42(9)

Procedures for making claims

55-000 Overview

Claims fall into two categories:

(1) claims included in returns (see 55-100);

(2) claims made outside the return form (see 55-200).

Whilst the legislation specifies that claims should be in writing, certain claims, which by definition are outside of the return, may be made by telephone (see 55-050).

55-050 Claims by telephone

HMRC are able to accept a range of claims from individuals in respect of their personal income tax affairs by telephone and, in due course, other electronic communications systems.

Power was given to HMRC to make directions as to the manner in which claims may be made by telephone and other electronic means. If claims are made in accordance with those directions, there will be no need to make them in writing even if the terms of any other legislation might otherwise require a written claim.

The directions cannot cover claims involving more than one year (such as loss relief and farmers' averaging claims), or any claim for capital allowances. Nor can they modify any time-limit fixed by statute for making a claim or amend any requirement as to what the claim must contain, though they can prescribe how any such requirement is to be fulfilled when the claim is not made in writing.

The 'directions' which HMRC have issued under these powers are not statutory instruments, as is usually the case with delegated authority, but Annexes to statements of practice, which are themselves non-statutory. There are two current statements of practice. The first is applicable to those taxpayers described as 'non-contact centre customers', that is callers to an HMRC office which is not linked to a call centre, whilst the second applies to taxpayers whose affairs are dealt with by an office which is linked to a call centre.

In summary, and subject to monetary limits, the following information, claims and requests will be accepted by telephone:

- personal details, e.g. contact details, changes in marital status;
- employment details;
- claims to personal allowances;

- claims for flat-rate and other expenses against employment income;
- claims for tax-deductible payments, e.g. professional subscriptions, gift aid, pension payments;
- notification of benefits, other earnings, investment income and pensions; and
- amendments to self-assessments in connection with personal and employment details plus minor corrections.

A claim in this context includes making an election, giving a notice or notification, amending a return, or amending or withdrawing any claim, election, notice or notification.

An individual may not make a claim in any capacity as trustee, partner or personal representative, though this does not preclude a person making a claim on behalf of another as that person's authorised agent.

The services are available to agents and other representatives of the taxpayer, provided HMRC hold written authority and can verify the identity of the caller. In addition, HMRC will provide certain information over the telephone to taxpayers or their representatives. For call centres only, HMRC will accept certain amendments to self-assessment returns by telephone.

Legislation: FA 1998, s. 118

Other Material: SP 2/03; SP 1/10 (which replaces SP 1/05)

55-100 Claims included in returns

Normally, where a notice requiring returns has been given and claims could be made in those returns, or they could at any subsequent time be included in returns, then they cannot be made in any other way. This rule does not however apply to claims given effect to by PAYE coding adjustments. This reflects the fact that most employees do not have to complete tax returns. If an employee wishes to have a code number adjusted during the course of a tax year the procedures relating to claims outside a return must be used (see 55-200).

The general time-limit for claims is four years. This time-limit applies from 1 April 2010. Prior to 1 April 2010, the time-limit was five years and ten months (see 54-100) means that many claims will be made after the return for a particular year has become final and must therefore be made under the procedure for claims outside returns.

Claims for a relief, an allowance or a repayment of tax must be quantified at the time the claim is made, although once again there is an exception for claims effected through the PAYE system. The intention of the legislation is to deny claims that anticipate a relief which may or may not arise in the future. However, it does not mean that estimated figures will always fail. For instance, if a loss has been established, but the amount not finalised, a best estimate will be acceptable as quantifying the claim. This is different from making a speculative claim to a loss because of an impression that the business is doing badly.

Legislation: TMA 1970, s. 42(2), (3)

55-150 Partnership claims

Partnership claims under specified provisions are to be made in partnership returns (see 51-000) where a notice to make a return has been issued, or otherwise by a nominated partner.

The specified claims include:

- gifts to educational establishments;
- claim for waste disposal preparation expenditure;
- valuation of work in progress at discontinuance of profession or vocation;
- letting of furnished holiday accommodation;
- disposal of know-how;
- delayed remittance of foreign securities;
- herd basis elections;
- trading profits: deduction for remuneration;
- claims and elections in connection with capital allowances;
- claims and elections in connection with expenditure on films.

Legislation: TMA 1970, s. 42(6), (7)

55-200 Claims outside of returns

Making claims

Claims are to be in such form as HMRC may determine, which will contain a declaration of the correctness of the claim, etc. according to the best of the information and belief of the signatory. The form *may* require the following:

- a statement of the amount of tax to be repaid or discharged;
- such information as is reasonably required to establish the correctness of the claim;
- such accounts, statements and documents in support of that information.

Repayment claims may not be made unless the claimant has documentary proof that the tax has been paid. However, in practice, UK residents are no longer required to submit tax vouchers of UK tax deducted with claims for repayment of tax (forms R40) which are made outside tax returns. Non-residents still have to send in vouchers, and the requirement for subcontractors to supply vouchers, even with tax returns, still remains.

Where a loss was claimed to be carried back to an earlier year, the Supreme Court held that the word 'return' for the purposes of TMA 1970, s. 8(1), 9, 9A, 42(11) has a very narrow meaning: 'a 'return' refers to the information in the tax return form which is submitted for 'the purpose of establishing the amounts in which a person is chargeable to income tax and capital gains tax' for the relevant year of assessment and 'the amount payable by him by way of income tax for that year'.' As a result, HMRC were not obliged to take into account the impact of a tax overpayment resulting from a loss relief claim carried back from one year to an earlier year when establishing the tax collectable for the earlier year.

In the case of a claim made by a non-resident or a person claiming to be non-resident, not ordinarily resident or not domiciled HMRC may require a statement or declaration in support of the claim to be made by affidavit.

Legislation: TMA 1970, Sch. 1A, para. 2(3)–(6)

Case: *Cotter v HMRC* [2013] BTC 837

Keeping and preserving records

There is a requirement to keep and preserve records supporting a claim which is not included in a return. This is very similar to the requirement to keep records supporting a return (see 50-200).

The records to be kept must be those required in order to make a correct and complete claim and the time for which they must be kept depends on whether there is an enquiry into the claim:

- if an enquiry is opened, records must be preserved until it is complete;
- if no enquiry is opened, records must be preserved until the deadline for opening an enquiry has passed (see 56-000).

With certain exceptions, it is sufficient to preserve only the information contained in records. A copy of any document forming part of the records will be admissible evidence before the commissioners to the same extent as the original records. The exceptions are:

- dividend vouchers and certificates of tax deducted from interest and annual payments;
- certificates required by regulations under the construction industry deduction scheme;
- any record required to enable claim to be made in respect of foreign tax paid.

Failure to keep adequate records can attract a penalty of up to £3,000 but does not apply in the case of these exceptions HMRC are satisfied that any facts reasonably required to be proved are proved by other documentary evidence.

From 1 April 2009, HMRC may specify by regulations the records and supporting documents that must be kept.

Legislation: TMA 1970, Sch. 1A, para. 2A; FA 2008, s. 115 and Sch. 37, para. 3

55-250 Giving effect to claims

HMRC are to give effect to a claim (or an amended claim) by discharge or repayment of tax as soon as practicable (unless there is a provision in the Taxes Acts which lays down an alternative treatment). There is a parallel provision with regard to partnership claims so that the discharge or repayment is in respect of each partner. This gives rise to the expression 'process now; check later'. Thus provided the claim is in the correct format, with the appropriate information, HMRC must either give effect to the claim or open an enquiry.

There are two exceptions from this treatment:

(1) claims can continue to be dealt with through the PAYE system, rather than by discharge or repayment of tax;

(2) HMRC need not give effect to a claim until enquiries are completed, but have the discretion to give whole or partial effect to the claim on a provisional basis.

Legislation: TMA 1970, Sch. 1A, para. 4

55-300 Amendments to claims

Within nine months of a claim being made, HMRC may amend the claim as to correct any obvious errors or mistakes. This parallels the 'repair' procedure for returns.

Within 12 months of a claim being made, the taxpayer may amend the claim by notice to HMRC. This right is suspended during the time between the opening of an enquiry and its completion.

Legislation: TMA 1970, Sch. 1A, para. 3

Enquiries into claims made outside a return

56-000 Power to enquire into claims

HMRC may enquire into claims or amendments of claims by giving notice to the person who made the claim, or, in the case of a partnership claim, any successor of that person. The notice must be given before the latest of:

- the next quarter day following the first anniversary of the claim being made (quarter days are 31 January, 30 April, 31 July and 31 October);
- if the claim relates to a tax year, the first anniversary of the 31 January following that year;
- if the claim relates to a period other than a tax year, one year from the end of that period.

A claim or amendment which has been subject to an enquiry cannot be subject to a further enquiry. This precludes HMRC issuing a further notice of enquiry, or picking up the claim again when it is subsequently included in a return.

Legislation: TMA 1970, Sch. 1A, para. 5

56-050 Power to call for information and documents

Legislation introduced with effect from 1 April 2009 enables an officer of HMRC to require a person to provide information or documentation where that information is reasonably required for the purposes of checking that person's tax position.

Where a notice is issued, the notice will specify the information or documents to be provided or produced. Additionally, the notice will specify the period for compliance, and the means and the form in which compliance should take place. Where documents are requested, copies can be provided unless the notice specifically requires original documents, or where a subsequent request for original documents is made.

Information and documents from a third party

HMRC may request information or documents from a third party if the information or document is reasonably required for the purposes of checking the tax position of another person.

Legislation: FA 2008, Sch. 36, para. 1 and 8; FA 2009, s. 95 and Sch. 47

Appeals

Where a taxpayer is given a notice, the taxpayer may appeal to the First-tier Tribunal against the notice or any requirement in the notice. Although the taxpayer may not appeal against a requirement to produce any documents, etc. that form part of the taxpayers' statutory records.

Legislation: FA 2008, Sch. 36, para. 29

Penalty provision

Finance Act 2009 provides for a penalty to apply where a person carelessly or deliberately provides inaccurate information or produces inaccurate documents in response to an information notice.

Legislation: FA 2008, Sch. 36, para. 40A; FA 2009, s. 95 and Sch. 47, para. 15

56-100 Completion of enquiry

An enquiry is completed when a 'closure notice' is issued to the claimant stating HMRC's conclusions.

In the case of a claim for discharge or repayment of tax, the closure notice must either:

- state that no amendment of the claim is required; or
- amend the claim so as to make good or eliminate any deficiency or excess. In the case of an enquiry into an amendment of a claim, this only applies so far as the deficiency or excess is attributable to the claimant's amendment.

In the case of a claim that is not a claim for discharge or repayment of tax, the closure notice must either:

- allow the claim; or
- disallow the claim, either wholly or partly as appears to be appropriate.

The claimant may apply to the tribunal for a direction requiring a closure notice to be issued within a specified period. The application is heard and determined in the same way as an appeal. The tribunal must give the direction applied for unless they are satisfied that there are reasonable grounds for not issuing a closure notice within that specified period. However, they can issue a closure notice only in relation to the whole enquiry, not one that is confined to particular aspects of the enquiry.

Legislation: TMA 1970, Sch. 1A, para. 7

Case: *Finnforest UK Ltd* [2011] TC 01202

56-150 Giving effect to amendment as a result of the enquiry

Any amendment arising from an enquiry is to be put into effect within 30 days of the issue of the closure notice, by either making assessments or by discharging or repaying tax (but in the latter case, proof of original payment will be required).

Legislation: TMA 1970, Sch. 1A, para. 8

Appeals

An appeal can be brought against any decision, conclusion or amendment made by a closure notice, by giving written notice within 30 days from its issue.

The period for bringing the appeal is extended to three months in any case where the matter concerns any of the following:

- claims for personal reliefs by non-residents;
- residence, ordinary residence or domicile;
- whether a tax exemption is due in respect of pensions from a fund established for those working wholly abroad.

On appeal, the tribunal can vary amendment, whether in favour of the claimant or otherwise. Where the amendment is varied by the commissioners or any court, it has to be given effect within 30 days and the provisions for giving effect to amendments resulting from enquiries described above are to apply to the variation.

Legislation: TMA 1970, Sch. 1A, para. 9

Overpayment relief/Relief for errors and mistakes

57-000 Recovery of overpaid tax etc

A new regime for recovering overpayments of tax was introduced by *Finance Act* 2009 to replace the relief previously provided by TMA 1970, s. 33 for overpayments of tax due to an error or mistake in a return.

A person may make a claim for repayment of income tax or CGT which they have paid but do not believe was due or discharge of an amount that has been over-assessed. For claims made before 1 April 2010, the 'error or mistake' has to be made in a return.

For claims made before 1 April 2010, the claim must be made within five years of the 31 January following the tax year to which the return relates. From 1 April 2010, the time limit for a claim is four years from the period in respect of which the payment or the assessment was made except where the claim arises from a mistake in a return. For mistakes in returns, the time limit runs from the end of the period for which the return was made. Claims are to be made outside a self assessment return.

No relief is available where the return was made on the basis, or in accordance with the practice, then generally prevailing. This prevents taxpayers reopening assessments following a tribunal or court decision that HMRC's basis of assessing profits in a particular class of case was erroneous.

Following a decision of the Court of Appeal, HMRC accept that, for the purposes of both error and mistake relief and overpayment relief, the 'practice generally prevailing' exception is to be read as subject to the limitation that it applies only if and to the extent that the United Kingdom can, consistent with its EU treaty obligations, impose such a restriction. The Court of Appeal concluded that practice generally prevailing does not affect a claim for repayment of taxes paid in breach of EU law.

Therefore, if a claim for error or mistake relief or overpayment relief relates to taxes paid in breach of EU law, HMRC will not seek to disallow it on the basis that the tax liability was calculated in accordance with the prevailing practice.

The relief is also not available in respect of claims included in returns for which different provisions apply (see 54-250).

For claims made before 1 April 2010, the error or mistake must have been *in a return*. In a special commissioners' case the taxpayer sought to make an error or mistake claim to obtain relief for bad debts in earlier years. When preparing the accounts for those years, no provision had been made against the debts as, at that time, they were considered 'good'; it was only subsequently that they proved to be bad. The special commissioner held that no error or mistake had occurred. The taxpayer was required to make a judgement of whether the debt was bad or doubtful, based on the facts known to him at that time. The fact that his commercial judgment had been proved wrong by subsequent events did not entitle him to go back and revise his tax computation for the earlier years. Instead, he could claim relief in the years when evidence came to light which substantiated a judgment that the debts had become bad.

For claims made on or after 1 April 2010, the requirement that the overpayment must be the result of a mistake in a return and that it must be made under an assessment are removed.

A claim will be possible only if no other statutory steps are available to recover an overpayment when a person first becomes aware, or might reasonably be expected be aware, that they have overpaid.

On a claim being made, HMRC have a very wide discretionary power to make such repayment as is 'reasonable and just'. They must have regard to all the relevant circumstances of the case and, in particular, must consider whether the granting of relief would result in the exclusion from tax of any part of the claimant's profits. For this purpose, they may look at other years than that to which the claim relates. Thus a person who previously benefited from a particular basis of assessing profits can expect no relief in respect of a chargeable period in which the same basis has disadvantaged him.

Before 1 April 2010, a right of appeal to the First-tier Tribunal is available if an error or mistake claim is rejected by HMRC. The tribunal has to determine the appeal in accordance with the principles set out above and the only appeal against their decision is on a point of law arising in connection with the computation of profits. There is therefore no appeal against the First-tier Tribunal's decision on such matters as:

- any other point of law;
- whether any repayment was 'reasonable and just'; or
- the practice generally prevailing at the time the return was made.

For claims on or after 1 April 2010, the current restrictions on the right of appeal will be removed, allowing an appeal to the courts on the same grounds as appeals against other matters.

Strictly an error or mistake claim will not be available where, instead of a formal assessment being made, an investigation settlement has been reached and it is subsequently discovered that the figures on which the settlement was based are incorrect. Moreover, because the settlement is a legally-binding contract, any revision of it is not possible. However

HMRC are prepared to re-open a settlement to allow a 'quasi' error or mistake claim where this would have been available had assessments been in place.

A claim in respect of a mistake in a partnership return must be made by a partner nominated by all the relevant partners.

Legislation: TMA 1970, s. 33, 33A and Sch. 1AB; FA 2009, s. 100 and Sch. 52

Cases: *Rose Smith & Co Ltd v IR Commrs* (1933) 17 TC 586; *Carrimore Six Wheelers Ltd v IR Commrs* (1944) 26 TC 301; *Arranmore Investment Co Ltd v IR Commrs* (1973) 48 TC 623; *Thompson v IR Commrs* (2005) Sp C 458; *Franked Investment Income Group Litigation v IR Commrs* [2012] BTC 312

Other Material: HMRC *Enquiry Manual* EM9025; HMRC Brief 22/10 *Overpayment relief and practice generally prevailing*

57-050 Overpayment/Error or mistake relief: point already agreed when appeal determined

A recovery of overpaid tax/error or mistake claim cannot be used to give the taxpayer a 'second bite at the cherry', allowing him a second chance to pursue arguments which should have been advanced on appeal. HMRC have said that relief will not be available where the substantive point was squarely in issue in the process of reaching an agreement by which an appeal was determined (see 62-250).

Legislation: TMA 1970, Sch. 1AB, para. 2(5)

Other Material: HMRC Interpretation, IRInt. 64 (Tax Bulletin, February 1994)

Tax Reporter: ¶183-700

57-100 Tax paid under an error of law

A claim is not valid if the return was made on the practice generally prevailing at that time.

Under English law there is a principle, established by the House of Lords, that it is possible to claim back money paid under a mistake in law, subject to the time limits imposed under the *Limitation Act* 1980.

There are two common law mechanisms whereby a taxpayer may seek to reclaim tax collected unlawfully or paid under a mistake in law.

- The 'Woolwich principle' (established in the *Woolwich Building Society case*) is that money paid by a citizen to a public authority in the form of taxes or other levies paid pursuant to an ultra vires demand by the authority is prima facie recoverable by the citizen as of right under common law, without the need to show a mistake of law. The *Limitation Act* 1980, s. 5 provides that the time limit for making such a claim is six years from the date of the payment.
- *Deutsche Morgan Grenfell* claims for restitution of tax paid under mistake of law. The House of Lords confirmed claims could be made to recover tax paid under mistake of law and that the claimant could opt for either a Woolwich or DMG restitutionary remedy. The limitation period for claims to recover payments made under mistake of law is extended by *Limitation Act* 1980, s. 32(1)(c) to a period of six years from the date the person making the payment discovered or could with reasonable diligence have discovered the mistake.

The Supreme Court ruled that where, under national law, a taxpayer has a choice between two possible courses of action as regards the recovery of tax levied, one of which benefits from a longer limitation period, then national legislation is precluded from curtailing that limitation period without notice and retroactively.

The High Court, in *Monro v R & C Commrs*, held that a claim for restitution of tax paid under a mistake of law failed because there was a statutory mechanism available in the form of an error or mistake claim under TMA 1970, s. 33. In that case such a claim was prevented by subs. (2A), which prohibits a claim where the return was made 'in accordance with the practice generally prevailing at the time'. The court held that it would be inconsistent with TMA 1970, s. 33 to recognise an alternative common law remedy in precisely the same circumstances but free of the limitation of subs. (2A). Such a conclusion was not permissible. This distinction between this case and the *DMG* and *Woolwich* cases was that s. 33 was not applicable in those cases because there were no valid assessments involved. Accordingly, the taxpayer's claim failed.

The Court of Appeal upheld the decision of the High Court that a claim for restitution of tax paid under a mistake of law failed because there was a statutory mechanism available in the form of an error or mistake claim under TMA 1970, s. 33. It was not possible to bring an action at common law for the recovery of money in circumstances where s. 33 applied. It was also not open to the court to rewrite the structure of s. 33 and treat it as not applying in this case.

Following a decision of the Court of Appeal, HMRC accept that, for the purposes of both error and mistake relief and overpayment relief, the 'practice generally prevailing' exception is to be read as subject to the limitation that it applies only if and to the extent that the United Kingdom can consistently with its EU treaty obligations impose such a restriction. The Court of Appeal concluded that practice generally prevailing does not affect a claim for repayment of taxes paid in breach of EU law.

Therefore, if a claim for error or mistake relief or overpayment relief relates to taxes paid in breach of EU law, HMRC will not seek to disallow it on the basis that the tax liability was calculated in accordance with the prevailing practice.

Cases: *Woolwich Building Society v IR Commrs* [1992] BTC 470; *IR Commrs v Deutsche Morgan Grenfell* [2005] BTC 126; *Monro v R & C Commrs* [2007] BTC 325; *Monro v R & C Commrs* [2008] BTC 188; *Franked Investment Income Group Litigation v IR Commrs* [2012] BTC 312

Enquiries

58-000 Overview

The self-assessment system works on the principle of 'process now, check later'. Until the changes introduced by *Finance Act* 2007 and 2008, HMRC had a window of opportunity in which they could make enquiries into a tax return. Once this window had closed, the only way the return could be challenged was through the 'discovery' provisions (see 59-500). Significant changes were introduced to the compliance checking regime in *Finance Act* 2007 and 2008, which formed part of HMRC's ongoing Review of Powers, Deterrents and Safeguards. HMRC have published a table summarising the legislation that has been enacted as a result of the Review of HMRC's Powers, Deterrents and Safeguards, identifying each relevant piece of legislation, its implementation date and the commencement order that brings it into force. The table is updated from time to time and can be found on the HMRC website.

Following the introduction of FA 2008, Sch. 36, HMRC refer to enquiries of any nature as compliance checks. Schedule 36, para. 58 states that '"checking" includes carrying out an investigation or an enquiry of any kind'. The new compliance checking regime was introduced in order to bring about consistency in the way HMRC handle compliance activity across all of the taxes they administer.

While all enquiries are compliance checks, not all compliance checks are enquiries. Compliance checks include examining business records and visiting business premises before a return has been received. If they suspect that there are irregularities, HMRC can use their information powers to check the person's tax position.

Only if the enquiry window is still open in respect of the last return received must HMRC start a formal enquiry. Otherwise they will use their information powers and the discovery provisions to make their check. The discovery powers are used, for example, when third party information does not reach HMRC before the statutory enquiry window closes. Under *Finance Act* 2008, Sch. 36, para. 21(6)) information can be requested in respect of historic, closed years if HMRC have reason to suspect that an amount of tax which ought to have been assessed may not have been assessed, that an assessment has, or may have, become insufficient or that a relief from tax may be or has become excessive. It is not necessary for HMRC to make a discovery assessment in order to obtain information in respect of a closed period.

Compliance Centres operate from three main sites in Newcastle, Bournemouth and Swansea with a smaller presence in Carmarthen. Generally, the work, which covers a wide range of duties, including income tax, pay as you earn (PAYE), value added tax (VAT) and National Insurance contributions (NICs), is additional to and/or supports (rather than replaces) activity carried out in HMRC's existing network of local and national offices. They deal with focused, single issue, non-complex intervention work based on third party information that indicates potential omissions from tax returns.

In May 2011, HMRC announced that they were bringing together specialist task forces from their compliance and enforcement teams to undertake intensive bursts of activity targeted at specific sectors and locations where there is evidence of high risk of tax evasion.

HMRC also run compliance projects aimed at encouraging voluntary disclosure by offering a lower penalty to those who come forward and admit to previously undisclosed income. These have included:

- people with undisclosed overseas bank accounts;
- doctors and dentists – the Tax Health Plan; and
- plumbing, heating or gas installation trades – the Plumbers Tax Safe Plan.

The Liechtenstein Disclosure Facility, running from 1 September 2009 until 31 March 2015, the agreement reached with Switzerland in August 2011, the creation of a new dedicated team of investigators to catch those hiding money offshore and ongoing work to put in place information sharing arrangements with other countries are further steps taken by HMRC to tackle offshore tax evasion.

If a compliance check is a full enquiry it must be carried out under the formal enquiry provisions. If the enquiry window is still open in respect of the last return received, HMRC must open a formal enquiry.

From 20 June 2011, HMRC started to contact businesses who have been selected for a single compliance process (SCP) pilot. In the trials, HMRC will use the new process for formal enquiries into SME business returns such as those made under TMA 1970, s. 9A. The trials will also include assurance work carried out for VAT and Employer Compliance. It will exclude pre-return compliance checks. The aim of the new process is to align HMRC's approach and to minimise the impact on the business by earlier contact and resolution and working multiple tax risks where necessary. It should not, for example, slow down the current process of conducting VAT visits nor add steps to that process.

The process will consist of five stages:

(1) planning;

(2) contact;

(3) process;

(4) resolve; and

(5) close.

The process is designed to concentrate solely on the risks or behaviours identified for the enquiry, using four different levels of intensity proportionate to those risks. The levels and the estimated time for the work required by the HMRC officer are shown below:

Level	**Estimated time required by HMRC staff**
1. The first level will be to carry out an enquiry where there is no need for a face to face meeting, for example by correspondence, and with minimum inconvenience.	1.5 days
2. The second level will adopt a simplified and faster route for those cases where a lower intensity face to face intervention approach is required.	2 days
3. The third level will address cases requiring a greater amount of time because the depth and breadth of the enquiry is more involved.	4 days
4. The fourth level will tackle the most demanding cases such as those indicating tax evasion characteristics or those highly complex in nature.	8 days

HMRC do not have to demonstrate prima facie grounds for dissatisfaction with a return before commencing an enquiry; the enquiry is initiated on the grounds of checking the accuracy of the return with no initial suggestion that anything is irregular.

Enquiries can only be initiated if HMRC issues a notice of intention to do so. Anything beyond a correction of an obvious error or omission (see 50-650) is an enquiry, and must be dealt with by way of a formal notice of enquiry.

HMRC may normally only open one enquiry into any particular personal or trustee's return but may open another enquiry in consequence of a taxpayer amendment (see 50-650).

For internal purposes, HMRC categorise enquiries into 'full enquiries' and 'aspect enquiries'. A full enquiry will involve a comprehensive review of the taxpayer's underlying records. An aspect enquiry is one which falls short of a full enquiry where only a particular aspect of a return will be examined, for instance the computation of a capital gain. HMRC will use their powers to obtain documents, etc. (see 58-150) to examine underlying records in aspect cases as well as in full enquiry cases.

An enquiry into a return covers anything contained in the return, including claims. There is a separate but similar enquiry regime for claims made outside of a return (see 56-000).

Enquiries conducted by local offices are governed by a published code of practice which is available in 'full' and 'short' versions. HMRC staff are required to issue a copy of the code to the taxpayer with the enquiry notice. In the majority of cases, the full version will be issued; the short version being intended for cases where the enquiry is expected to be brief, straightforward, where an extensive records examination is not anticipated and where no penalties are likely to arise.

The enquiry provisions relate to individuals and trustees and partnerships. In the case of partnerships, a notice of enquiry into the partnership return is also deemed to include a notice of enquiry into the individual or company return of each partner.

HMRC will not normally give a notice indicating that a return has been accepted and that no enquiries will be made. A notification that the return has been processed without any need for correction is no guarantee that an enquiry will not be raised. However, in order to facilitate the early settlement of a deceased's tax affairs, they will not only issue a return before the end of the tax year to which it relates, but also give early written confirmation that no enquiries are to be made into the return. A similar approach will be adopted where the administration of a deceased person's estate is completed, or a trust is wound up during a tax year.

Legislation: TMA 1970, s. 9A; FA 2008, Sch. 36

Other Material: HMRC Code of Practice COP11 *Enquiries into tax returns by local tax offices*; HMRC press release, 4 April 1996

Website: *Review of HMRC's Powers, Deterrents and Safeguards Implementation of legislation and related work* – www.hmrc.gov.uk/about/road-map.pdf

58-050 The power to enquire into a return

In order for HMRC to open an enquiry into a return for 2008–09 and subsequent years, a written notice of enquiry is to be given:

- within 12 months of the date the return was filed, where it is delivered on time; or
- if the return was filed late, on the first 'quarter day' following the first anniversary of the date on which the return was in fact filed. 'Quarter day' means 31 January, 30 April, 31 July or 31 October.

A new time-limit for the opening enquiries begins with any amendment by the taxpayer to the original return, if that amendment falls after the filing date for the return. The enquiry under this new time-limit is to be restricted to 'matters to which the amendment relates or which are affected by the amendment'. HMRC interpret this as allowing them to consider the whole return in cases where the amendment is so fundamental to the tax return that the whole return is considered for enquiry. An example given is where the original return contained a provisional figure. If the correction of that figure only altered a single entry in the tax return, any subsequent enquiry (after the end of the period for enquiring into the original return) would be limited to that entry. But if that correction altered a number of entries, or radically altered the overall self-assessment, it is possible that more of the tax return, and possibly the whole return, would be considered for enquiry.

Instances had been reported of enquiries being opened to ask for information that had already been provided with the return, either in the 'white space' or as an enclosure. This had arisen as a result of storage and retrieval problems in some of the local offices. HMRC have given an undertaking that these problems are being addressed and that full enquiries should not be opened without the officer concerned having a copy of the paper return and any attachments submitted with it.

Legislation in *Finance Act* 2008 enables HMRC to carry out compliance checks without reference to a particular tax return.

Where the self-assessment shows that a repayment of tax is due to the taxpayer, but before the repayment is made, an enquiry is opened into the return, the repayment is deferred until the enquiry has been completed, but HMRC have a discretionary power to make a provisional repayment to the extent that they see fit.

Legislation: TMA 1970, s. 9A, 59B(4A); FA 2008, Sch. 36

Other Material: HMRC *Enquiry Manual* EM404, para. 4.26; *Working Together*, Issue 14, September 2003

58-100 The power to call for documents or information

Legislation dealing with the provision of documentation and information has been repealed from 1 April 2009 and replaced by FA 2008, Sch. 36. The issue of an information notice is no longer related to the issue of a notice of enquiry. The notice is also no longer for the purposes of 'determining whether a return is incomplete' but merely for the purpose of 'checking the taxpayer's tax position'. This means that HMRC can inspect records before a return is filed.

The new legislation applies across all of the taxes administered by HMRC. It applied to IT, CT, CGT, VAT and PAYE from 1 April 2009 onwards and to other taxes from 1 April 2010 onwards (FA 2009, Sch. 48). It should be noted that there are no transitional powers in respect of the new powers. However, HMRC have indicated that, where enquiries straddle 1 April 2009, they will involuntarily commit to restricting the use of their powers under Sch. 36 so that they do not seek information or documentation which they would not have been entitled to under the previous regime.

The new provisions enable an HMRC officer to require a person to provide information or documentation where that information is reasonably required for the purposes of checking that person's tax position. An officer may also require a third party to provide information or documentation where that is reasonably required for the purposes of checking the tax of a person. Such a notice can only be issued if it has been approved by the First-tier Tribunal, or by an authorised officer. Legislation in *Finance Act* 2009 makes it clear that applications to the tribunal for approval of taxpayer or third party notices are heard without the taxpayer being present. From 1 April 2012, FA 2012 gives HMRC the power to require a person to provide information about another person whose identity is not known to HMRC if reasonably required and which cannot be ascertained from other information held.

Of particular importance to practitioners are the circumstances under which notices can be issued which are no longer restricted by reference to a particular enquiry. The key here is that the 'tax position' which can be subject to a notice includes a taxpayer's 'past, present and future' tax liabilities as well as penalties or other amounts which may be payable in connection with any tax. Therefore, notices under Sch. 36 can be issued before tax returns have been filed or for historic years when returns are closed.

Notices in respect of closed years can only be issued where an HMRC officer has reason to suspect that an amount of tax which ought to have been assessed may not have been assessed, that an assessment has, or may have become insufficient or that a relief from tax may be or has become excessive. It should be noted that it is not, therefore, necessary for an officer of HMRC to make a discovery assessment in order to obtain information in respect of a closed period.

A mechanism exists enabling HMRC to obtain the consent of the First-tier Tribunal to issue a notice. These provisions broadly mirror the previous provisions, under which an ex parte application for approval to the issue of a notice was made to the general or special commissioners. Also retained is the provision that HMRC must allow the taxpayer a reasonable period to produce the documents or information.

A taxpayer can only be required to produce a document if that document is within his 'possession or power'. Thus it follows that, if a document specified in the notice does not exist or is not in the taxpayer's possession or power, it cannot be produced and the taxpayer should communicate that fact to HMRC.

The requirement that documents or information is 'reasonably required' for the purpose of checking a tax position is similar in form to the restrictions which existed under the previous legislation. Consequently, case law on the previous legislation is likely to be instructive in considering how the tribunal and courts will interpret the new legislation.

A special commissioner expressed the view that a notice requiring the production of documents including those relating to the taxpayer's personal expenditure, was, in that case, intrusive and the taxpayer should not be required to divulge details of his personal expenditure if that could be avoided.

In a case before the special commissioners, a taxpayer appealed against a notice to produce documents on the grounds that he had already complied with an enquiry in respect of Working Families Tax Credit (WFTC) which covered part of the period covered by the notice. It was held that HMRC's powers to make enquiries into an application for WFTC and a self assessment return were governed by separate provisions and the computations involved in the two regimes were different. The fact that the taxpayer had complied with the WFTC enquiry was not grounds for challenging a notice.

Where a notice is issued, the notice will specify the information or documents to be provided or produced, and will indicate whether the notice is approved by the First-tier Tribunal. Additionally, the notice will specify the period for compliance, and the means and the form in which the compliance should take place. Where documents are requested, copies can be provided unless the notices specifically requires original documents, or where a subsequent request for original documents is made. HMRC are specifically empowered to take copies of documents where these are produced to or inspected by an officer. Additionally, where documents are produced or inspected, HMRC may remove the document and retain it for a reasonable time if it appears necessary for the officer to do so.

Amendments were made to *Finance Act* 2008, Sch. 36 by F(No. 3)A 2011, Sch. 24 to extend Sch. 36 to tax of other countries, to reflect international obligations. Some of the amendments took effect on and after F(No. 3)A 2011 received Royal Assent, while others only affect inaccuracies and failures on or after 1 April 2012. The effect of these amendments is as follows:

- F(No. 3)A 2011, Sch. 24, para. 2 amends FA 2008, Sch. 36, para. 5 so that all of the information powers in Sch. 36 may now be used to obtain information in relation to relevant foreign tax of a territory outside the UK;
- F(No. 3)A 2011, Sch. 24, para. 3 amends FA 2008, Sch. 36, para. 40A to introduce a new category for which a penalty may be charged, which is where a person knowingly provides information containing an inaccuracy but does not notify HMRC at the time;
- F(No. 3)A 2011, Sch. 24, para. 4 inserts new para. 49A–49C into FA 2008, Sch. 36 to allow for a daily penalty to be charged which is greater than that chargeable under FA 2008, Sch. 36, para. 40. This applies where there is a continuing failure to comply with a notice under Sch. 36, para. 5. Such an increased penalty must be approved by the tribunal and the person involved must be given prior warning and may attend the hearing. New para. 49B and 49C are administrative provisions about notification and payment of the penalty. The provision of an increased daily penalty corresponds to that introduced for F(No. 3)A 2011, Sch. 23;
- F(No. 3)A 2011, Sch. 24, para. 5 amends FA 2008, Sch. 36, para. 50 to clarify the relevant date for the purpose of charging a tax-related penalty.

In July 2011, HMRC launched a consultation on an amendment to FA 2008, Sch. 36 to bring HMRC's information powers into line with the international standard for the exchange of information for tax purposes. It concerned ways to ensure that HMRC can collect information in specific cases where the full identity of the taxpayer is not known but can be ascertained by reference to other available information.

Legislation: FA 2008, Sch. 36, para. 1, 3, 5, 8, 15, 21(6), 40A, 40, 49A–49C, 50; FA 2009, s. 95 and Sch. 47; FA 2011, Sch. 23; F(No. 3)A 2011, Sch. 24, para. 2, 3, 4, 5

Cases: *Guest House Proprietor v Kendall (HMIT)* (2004) Sp C 454; *Taylor v Bratherton* (2004) Sp C 448; *Low v HMRC* (2005) Sp C 510

Other Material: HMRC *Compliance Handbook* CH20200

58-125 Power to carry out inspections

In addition to the introduction of new information powers, *Finance Act* 2008 also introduced an inspection power enabling HMRC officers to inspect business premises, business assets that are on the premises and business documents that are on the premises. The provisions which authorise offers to carry out inspections, contains the same broad caveat as the information powers above, that the inspection must be 'reasonably required for the purposes of checking that person's tax position.'

Finance Act 2009 has extended powers to obtain information and inspect businesses to matters concerning insurance premium tax, inheritance tax, stamp duty land tax, stamp duty reserve tax, petroleum revenue tax, aggregates levy, climate change levy and landfill tax.

Legislation: FA 2008, Sch. 36, para. 10; FA 2009, s. 96 and Sch. 48

Tax Reporter: ¶184-925

58-150 Appeals against information or documentation notices

A person may appeal against a notice or any requirement in it. Appeal against the notice is to the First-tier Tribunal. However, where HMRC have obtained the consent of the tribunal to the issuing of the notice, there is no right of appeal. Additionally, a taxpayer cannot appeal against a notice to provide statutory records.

Where a third party notice has been issued, the recipient may appeal to the First-tier Tribunal on the basis compliance with the notice or any requirement of it is unduly onerous.

Notices of appeal must be made in writing, within 30 days of the date the notice is given to the HMRC officer by whom the notice was issued, stating the grounds of appeal. The tribunal may confirm, vary or set aside the information notice or a requirement of it. Where the tribunal directs that the notice or requirement is to be confirmed, the tribunal must specify a time period for compliance with that notice. If no time is specified, HMRC may specify a reasonable period for compliance. It should be noted that the decision of the First-tier Tribunal on an appeal on information is final.

Legislation: FA 2008, Sch. 36, para. 29, 32

Tax Reporter: ¶184-925

58-175 Penalties

Where a recipient of a notice fails to comply with the notice, including concealing, destroying or disposing of documents, or obstructs an HMRC officer in carrying out an inspection approved by the First-tier Tribunal, a penalty of £300 is chargeable.

Following the imposition of an initial penalty, further daily penalties of up to £60 are chargeable for each day on which the failure to comply or obstruction continues. Penalties are assessed by HMRC and an appeal can be lodged to the First-tier Tribunal in respect of either the imposition or the amount of a penalty.

A penalty will not be chargeable where the recipient of a notice, or a person subject to an inspection, can demonstrate that they have a reasonable excuse for non-compliance or obstruction or where the failure is a failure to comply within time limits but compliance took place within further time allowed by an HMRC officer.

Penalties for non-compliance or obstruction are payable within 30 days of notification of the penalty being given or within 30 days of an appeal against the penalty being determined. Penalties will be enforced as though they are amounts of income tax charged in an assessment.

A further significant penalty provision enables HMRC to charge a tax related penalty where there has been failure of obstruction and HMRC have reason to believe that the amount of tax that the person has paid, or is likely to pay, is significantly less than it would otherwise have been.

FA 2008, Sch. 36, para. 40A provides for a penalty of up to £3,000 where a person carelessly or deliberately provides inaccurate information or produces inaccurate documents in response to an information notice. If there is more than one inaccuracy, a penalty can be charged for each one. This penalty was previously provided by TMA 1970, s. 98(2).

Legislation: FA 2008, Sch. 36, para. 39–50

58-200 Amendment of return or self-assessment during enquiry

Taxpayer amendments

An amendment to a return or a self-assessment (which forms part of the return) does not take effect until the conclusion of the enquiry. The amendment may however be taken into account in the enquiry and if so, the HMRC officer may conclude that the amendment is incorrect, in which case it will not have effect at all.

Legislation: TMA 1970, s. 9B

HMRC amendments

Where the officer forms the opinion that the self-assessment is insufficient and that there is likely to be a loss of tax to the Crown unless it is amended immediately, he can amend that self-assessment by issuing a notice to the taxpayer. This is termed by HMRC a 'jeopardy amendment'. In the case of an enquiry which is limited to matters arising from the taxpayer's amendment of the return, the potential loss of tax must be attributable to that amendment.

This is not a power to increase the self-assessment simply because it is found to be insufficient. There must be a need for an *immediate* amendment because it is felt that any delay will prejudice the collection of that extra tax. HMRC officers are advised to make jeopardy amendments in situations such as where they suspect that the taxpayer may be planning to flee the country, file for bankruptcy or be imprisoned. They are also advised to consider a jeopardy amendment in cases where the taxpayer refuses to cooperate.

A jeopardy amendment is subject to a right of appeal, and a postponement application may be made (see 62-150). Although the issue of the postponement of tax may be dealt with immediately, the appeal cannot be heard until after a closure notice has been issued.

Legislation: TMA 1970, s. 9C, 31

Other Material: HMRC *Enquiry Manual* EM1953

58-230 Reference to First-tier Tribunal of matters in dispute

Any contentious question arising in the course of an enquiry can normally be the subject of appeal proceedings once HMRC have made the amendment they think necessary at the closure of the enquiry. However, if both sides wish, the question may be referred for determination by the First-tier Tribunal whilst the enquiry is still in progress.

Referral is by a written notice given jointly by the taxpayer and HMRC. The notice must specify the question(s) being referred, and more than one such notice can be given in relation to an enquiry. Either party may withdraw the notice by giving written notice to the other party and the commissioners before the first hearing in relation to the referral.

Regulations have been made which apply the normal appeal rules, with modifications, to ensure that there are similar rights of appeal from the special commissioners in relation to a determination on a referral as there are in relation to the determination of an appeal.

Whilst a referral is in progress, a closure notice cannot be issued in respect of the enquiry, nor can the taxpayer make an application for a notice to be issued.

The determination of a question by the tribunal binds the parties to the referral in the same way, and to the same extent, as a decision on an appeal and must be taken into account by HMRC in reaching their conclusions on the enquiry and in making the amendments necessary to give effect to those conclusions. Any right of appeal against those amendments may normally not be exercised so as to reopen the question already determined.

Legislation: TMA 1970, s. 28ZA–28ZE

58-250 Closure of enquiry

An enquiry is completed when HMRC issue a closure notice stating their conclusions and also that either stating that no amendment of the return is needed, or making any necessary amendments. The closure notice takes effect when it is issued.

To protect against HMRC unreasonably prolonging the enquiry, the taxpayer may apply to the tribunal for a direction that HMRC must issue a closure notice within a specified period. Unless they are satisfied that there are reasonable grounds for HMRC to continue the enquiry, the tribunal must direct that a closure notice be issued.

It should be noted that any direction that HMRC issue a completion notice is not a decision in favour of the original self-assessment. HMRC will issue the completion notice in the figures they think appropriate given the circumstances.

Provisions similar to the above apply as regards partnership returns.

Where an enquiry is kept open after the expiry of the period in which notice of enquiry had to be given, solely because of valuation negotiations, e.g. for capital gains tax purposes, HMRC will confine subsequent enquiries to matters relating to that unless matters come to light which, had the enquiry been closed, would have been a discovery (see 59-500).

Legislation: TMA 1970, s. 28A, 28B

Other Material: SP 1/99

58-300 Appeals

The taxpayer has a right of appeal against any amendments imposed by the closure notice. That appeal must be given by written notice within 30 days of the issue of the closure notice and must specify the grounds of appeal.

If the appeal cannot be settled by agreement, it will normally be heard by the First-tier Tribunal.

An appeal can be heard on grounds other than those set out in the closure notice. A closure notice completes an enquiry and states the inspector's conclusions as to the subject matter of the enquiry. Although the appeal against the conclusions is confined to the subject matter of the enquiry and of the conclusions, the jurisdiction of the First-tier Tribunal is not limited to the issue whether the reason for the conclusion was correct. Accordingly, any evidence or legal argument relevant to the subject matter might be entertained by the tribunal, subject only to the obligation to ensure a fair hearing.

However, this is not to say that HMRC officers should be free to draft every closure notice that they issue in wide and uninformative terms. In issuing a closure notice an officer is performing an important public function in which fairness to the taxpayer has to be matched by a proper regard for the public interest in the recovery of the full amount of tax payable. In a case in which it is clear that only a single, specific point was in issue, that point has to be identified in the closure notice. But if the facts are complicated and have not been fully investigated, and if their analysis is controversial, the public interest might require the notice to be expressed in more general terms. Unfairness to the taxpayer could be avoided by proper case management during the course of the appeal.

Legislation: TMA 1970, s. 31, 31A, 31B, 31D

Case: *R & C Commrs v Tower MCashback LLP1* [2011] BTC 294

58-350 Costs in relation to enquiries

Additional accountancy expenses, arising out of an enquiry into the accounts information in a particular year's return, will not be allowed in computing profits where the enquiry reveals discrepancies and additional liabilities for the year of enquiry, or any earlier year, which arise as a result of negligent or fraudulent conduct.

Where, however, the enquiry results in no addition to profits, or an adjustment to the profits for the year of enquiry only and that adjustment does not arise as a result of negligent or fraudulent conduct, the additional accountancy expenses will be allowable.

Other Material: SP 16/91

Assessments

59-000 Overview

Under the self-assessment system, as the name implies, it is for the taxpayer to make the assessment which imposes the charge to tax. HMRC then have the power to enquire into that self-assessment and if necessary amend it. The assessment nevertheless remains the taxpayer's self-assessment.

HMRC's powers to initiate a tax charge are limited to two situations:

(1) where the taxpayer fails to make a self-assessment at all, when they may 'determine' the tax liability; and

(2) where it comes to light that tax has been under-assessed, when they may issue a 'discovery' assessment. This is the only kind of assessment that HMRC can issue.

Discoveries will usually occur where, during the course of an enquiry into one year's return, information comes to light which suggests that the liability for an earlier year has been understated. Where the enquiry window for that earlier year (or an actual enquiry) has already closed, HMRC's only course of action is to issue a discovery assessment, an appeal against which will give them the opportunity to enquiry into that earlier year. However, where it is still possible to open an enquiry into the earlier year, they will do so in preference to a discovery assessment. An important practical distinction from the practitioner's point of view is that, in contrast to the opening of enquiries into a return, HMRC must give reasons for opening enquiries under the discovery provisions.

59-025 'Simple' assessments

With effect from 2016–17, HMRC have the power to issue a simple assessment to a taxpayer without that taxpayer being first required to complete a self-assessment return. The assessment will be based on information available to HMRC from the taxpayer and third parties.

The assessment must set out clearly the information used to arrive at a tax liability sufficient to enable the taxpayer to check that the information is accurate and complete. The taxpayer is under an obligation to notify HMRC in the event they believe the assessment to be incorrect.

Legislation: TMA 1970, s. 28H

Determinations

59-050 Determination of tax where no return received

Where an individual or trustee fails to submit a return by the prescribed filing date, an HMRC officer may make a determination of the tax due, to the best of his information and belief. With effect from 1 April 2010, the inspector may raise a determination within three years (previously five years) from the filing date of the return.

Notice of a determination is to be served on the taxpayer and is to be treated for all purposes as if it was a self-assessment and the tax determined is due and payable. There is no right of appeal against the determination. However, taxpayer can displace the determination by filing the outstanding return with a self-assessment before the later of:

- three years from the filing date;
- 12 months from the date of the determination.

In the event a taxpayer fails to displace a determination within the above time limits, then, with effect from 1 April 2011, their only recourse is to pursue a claim to 'special relief' (see 59-100).

Legislation: TMA 1970, s. 28C

59-100 Special relief

Prior to 1 April 2011, in the event a taxpayer failed to displace a determination by the submission of a tax return within the time limits outlined above, then there was no statutory remedy available to the taxpayer. Their only recourse would have been to rely on the concessionary application of 'equitable liability'.

For determinations issued after 31 March 2011, the above concessionary treatment was replaced by the statutory provisions of special relief.

In order to displace a determination through the application of special relief, the taxpayer must meet three conditions:

- Condition A: in the opinion of the Commissioners, it would be unconscionable for HMRC to seek to recover the amount which has been charged by a determination, or refuse to repay it if it has already been paid.

- Condition B: the person's tax affairs are otherwise up to date or arrangements have been made to the satisfaction of the Commissioners to bring them up to date as far as possible.
- Condition C: the person has not previously claimed special relief or sought equitable liability – whether or not relief was given.

Legislation: TMA 1970, Sch. 1AB, para. 3A

Discovery assessments

59-500 Conditions required

Where an HMRC officer 'discovers':

- profits which have not been assessed;
- an assessment to tax which has become insufficient; or
- excessive relief having been given,

then an assessment, termed a 'discovery assessment', can be made to recover the lost tax.

The word 'discovers' seems to mean simply 'comes to the conclusion' from any information he receives. It is not necessary to have legal evidence of undercharge, but there must be sufficient evidence to support a genuine discovery by the inspector.

Where the taxpayer has already filed a return for the year concerned, no discovery assessment can be made if the tax was lost due to an error or mistake in the return and the return was made on the basis of, or in accordance with the practice generally prevailing at the time it was made.

However, if a return has been made, a discovery assessment can be made if either:

(1) the loss of tax was brought about carelessly or deliberately by the taxpayer or his agent; or

(2) when either an enquiry could no longer be opened or having been opened, had been closed, the HMRC officer could not reasonably have been expected, on the basis of the information then 'available' to him, to have been aware of the loss of tax. An objection to an assessment on the grounds that neither of the above two relevant conditions is fulfilled can only be made by way of an appeal against the assessment.

It therefore follows that if the taxpayer has not filed a return, e.g. because he is not within self-assessment and has not been served with a notice to make a return, a discovery assessment can be made without either of the conditions having to be satisfied. For individuals, the prescribed form of return is the self-assessment return SA100, together with such supplementary pages as may be appropriate. A tax repayment claim on form R40 is not a return, thus in *Osborne (dec'd) v Dickinson* an appeal against a discovery assessment on the grounds that a return in the form of a repayment claim on a Form R40 was rejected.

In *Charlton v R & C Commrs*, the Upper Tribunal held that, although the validity of a discovery assessment did not depend on the emergence of any new fact, the taxpayers were protected from discovery assessments by TMA 1970, s. 29(5) since the notional inspector of taxes, at the point when the enquiry window closed, could in the circumstances reasonably have been expected to be aware that there was some insufficiency in the tax that ought to have been assessed. This judgment established that if a clear statement or analysis of the taxpayer's position is clearly stated in a return, enquiries can only be raised within the normal statutory time limits.

The Upper Tribunal found that a taxpayer's accountants adopting the wrong accounting practice in drawing up the taxpayer's trading accounts amounted to negligent conduct (now careless behaviour), entitling HMRC to raise discovery assessments.

It should be noted that whether behaviour is careless depends on the entries made in the return, not in any supporting documentation. Where a taxpayer deducted capital losses on investments from the bank interest and entered the net interest on his return, the Upper Tribunal held that his behaviour was careless even though the return was accompanied by additional sheets explaining how he had arrived at the net figure. The taxpayer's self-assessments were based not upon what he wrote on the additional sheets, but on what he entered in the boxes.

Parallel provisions apply in the case of partnerships. An assessment to recover tax lost as a result of fraudulent or negligent conduct may be made on any of the partners in the relevant tax year.

Note that the term 'fraudulent or negligent conduct' was replaced by 'was brought about carelessly or deliberately' from 1 April 2010.

Legislation: TMA 1970, s. 29, 29(2), 30B; FA 2008, Sch. 39, para. 1

Cases: *Osborne (dec'd) v Dickinson (HMIT)* (2003) Sp C 393; *Smith v R & C Commrs* [2011] BTC 1,742; *Moore v R & C Commrs* [2011] BTC 1,793; *Charlton v R & C Commrs* [2011] TC 01317

59-550 When information is 'available'

Information 'available' to the officer at the time includes any information in returns, documents submitted, claims, etc. It also includes any information the existence, or relevance, of which 'could reasonably be expected to be inferred by an officer of the Board' from the other information provided or which is notified in writing by the taxpayer to HMRC.

With regard to past information the HMRC officer is to look at the current and two preceding returns with supporting documents and 'to make reasonable inferences about the existence of other information from what he sees'. However, 'what is requested in practice is for taxpayers to cross-reference the current tax computation to earlier information that was provided'. In any event, the need to make inferences will provide significant protection against the discovery that HMRC had forgotten information that one would expect to find in a permanent note.

A change of opinion on the basis of information so made available will *not* be grounds for a discovery assessment.

Legislation: TMA 1970, s. 29(6), (7)

Other Material: HMRC *Enquiry Manual* EM409

59-650 Discovery and the Veltema decision

The *Veltema* case – a taxpayer was liable to income tax on the market value of a house transferred to him by his privately-owned company. A professional valuation of £100,000 was obtained and this was declared on his self-assessment return for the year concerned. No action was taken by HMRC to open an enquiry into that return. Subsequently the company submitted its return showing the same valuation as disposal proceeds but this time an enquiry was opened and the valuation was referred to the District Valuer. After negotiations, the value was agreed at £145,000. HMRC then raised a discovery assessment on the taxpayer in respect of the extra £45,000.

The taxpayer appealed successfully to the general commissioners on the basis that the deadline for opening an enquiry into his return had passed and that, the inspector having failed to open an enquiry, the liability had been finalised. HMRC argued that there had been negligent conduct by the taxpayer and therefore that a discovery assessment could be raised. This was rejected by the commissioners and not pursued before the High Court. HMRC's alternative argument was that the inspector was entitled to raise a discovery assessment since, when he ceased to be entitled to give notice of an enquiry, he could not have been reasonably expected, on the basis of the information before him, to be aware that the original assessment was insufficient.

The Court of Appeal held that the inspector was under no obligation to undertake an enquiry into a return. This was so even where it was clearly stated that a valuation had been used and therefore there was a possibility that tax may be underpaid. The inspector was only prevented from making a discovery assessment if he was 'reasonably aware' of the 'insufficiency' of the assessment. In other words, he had to be aware of an actual insufficiency, rather than just be aware that there might be a possible insufficiency. In this case, he was only in possession of information that the assessment was based on a valuation, not that the valuation was unreliable.

The *Veltema* decision highlighted the lack of certainty inherent in the self-assessment system and led the professional bodies to express concern as to how taxpayers whose liability was based on a valuation might obtain certainty that they would not be at risk of discovery assessments for the next six years. After pressure from the professional bodies, HMRC issued a statement, which subsequently was reproduced as a statement of practice.

The statement seeks to advise on how taxpayers may provide sufficient information to remove or reduce the risk of a future discovery in three situations:

- where liabilities are based on valuations (as in *Veltema*);
- where judgmental issues are involved (especially the tax deductibility of provisions and exceptional items); and
- where the taxpayer does not accept HMRC's stated interpretation of the legislation.

In essence, the advice is to make use of the 'white space' on the return to supply additional information over and above simply entering figures in relevant boxes. In valuation cases where a taxpayer states that a valuation has been used, indicates who has carried it out, and that it was carried out by a named independent and suitably qualified valuer, if that was the case, on the appropriate basis, he will be able to rely on that as protection from a later discovery assessment. In cases concerning judgmental issues, the advice is that details of the point on which a judgment has been made (e.g. the allocation of expenditure on a capital project between plant and machinery and construction costs) should be included in the white space. Where the taxpayer takes a different view of the legislation from that known to be held by HMRC, the suggestion is that a statement to that effect should be made.

Obviously, if any of these entries are made in the white space, they will alert HMRC to the need to open an enquiry and so the question of a discovery assessment will not arise anyway.

It should be noted that, although in 1983 the Keith Committee recommended that taxpayers should have to declare whether they had taken the benefit of any doubt about whether any item ought to be declared or any relief or deduction allowed, this was not adopted. There is therefore no specific statutory requirement to make such a declaration as is suggested by HMRC for situations where a different view of the legislation is taken. However, advisers need to consider this issue carefully and explain the situation and potential consequences to the client.

This is particularly important since a Court of Session decision that only if the taxpayer has made a return clearly alerting the officer to the insufficiency would it be considered adequate, preventing a discovery assessment. Whilst the taxpayer is not required to say there is an insufficiency, a reference to doubt or to the fact that it is a position contrary to HMRC's is required.

In a subsequent case the Court of Appeal decided in favour of the taxpayer. HMRC had enquired into a partnership return and the HMRC officer had made a note of a meeting at which the point in issue had been discussed. A copy of this note had been sent to the partnership and this was held to be sufficient to meet the requirement that there has to be something in writing regarding the relevant information. There was sufficient information given such that an inspector would realise that the profits could be understated.

Cases: *Langham (HMIT) v Veltema* [2004] BTC 156; *R (on the application of Pattullo) v R & C Commrs* [2009] CSOH 137; *R & C Commrs v Lansdowne Partners Limited Partnership* [2012] BTC 12; *Herbert* [2015] TC 04395

Other Material: SP 1/06

59-700 Discovery following the determination of an appeal

Where a taxpayer has lodged an appeal against an amendment to a self-assessment, and before any hearing before the tribunal, he may come to an agreement with HMRC, whether in writing or not, that the amendment should be varied or left unchanged. That agreement is final and conclusive, just as if the appeal had been determined by the tribunal (see 62-250).

If, in the determination of an appeal, whether by the tribunal or by agreement, a specific matter has been agreed by HMRC, they are precluded from reopening that matter by making a discovery assessment.

The particular point upon which HMRC now wish to raise a discovery assessment may not have been specifically agreed. However if the point is so fundamental to the computation of the liability and was clearly and fully described in the return so that its significance was readily apparent, it is reasonable to assume that the HMRC officer, in agreeing to determine the appeal, had decided to agree the point.

Protection from a discovery assessment will not be available where the information upon which the agreement was based was misleading or incorrect.

A statement of practice sets out HMRC's practice both in cases where there has been a specific agreement on a particular point, and in cases where the circumstances are such that it must be inferred that there was an agreement, even though the point at issue was not explicitly dealt with in exchanges between the taxpayer and the inspector. The practice set out in paragraphs 12 and 13 of the statement is extra-statutory.

Even though the case law on the topic does not strictly apply to cases where there has not been an appeal, HMRC will accept themselves as prevented from raising discovery assessments where there has been a specific agreement on the point (e.g. in the course of an enquiry). The principle is further extended to situations where there has been no specific agreement but the point accepted by HMRC was a tenable view, was fully and accurately disclosed and was so fundamental to the taxpayer's liability that the taxpayer could reasonably have believed that HMRC's decision was correct.

Legislation: TMA 1970, s. 54

Cases: *Cenlon Finance Co Ltd v Ellwood* (1962) 40 TC 176; *Scorer v Olin Energy Systems Ltd* (1985) 58 TC 592; *Gray (HMIT) v Matheson* [1993] BTC 76; *Yip* [2014] TC 03981

Other Material: SP 8/91

59-750 Time limits

The normal time limit for making assessments to income tax and capital gains tax from 1 April 2010 onwards is four years after the end of the year of assessment. Before 1 April 2010, the time limit was five years after the 31 January following the year of assessment to which it relates.

An objection that an assessment is invalid because it is made after the relevant time limit is only to be lodged by way of appeal against the assessment.

Fraudulent or negligent conduct – periods prior to 1 April 2010

If the assessment is made on the grounds of fraudulent or negligent conduct, the time limit is 20 years after the 31 January following the tax year. For corporation tax, the analogous time limit is 21 years after the accounting period to which it relates, applying in respect of accounting periods ending after 30 June 1999 (the advent of corporation tax self-assessment).

The person so assessed is permitted a relief or allowance for the chargeable period concerned as if he had made the claim within the statutory time limit.

Careless or deliberate conduct – periods after 1 April 2010

From 1 April 2010, HMRC's power to make discovery assessments on the basis of careless or deliberate conduct is limited to a period of six years from the end of the relevant year of assessment for careless conduct, while the assessment period for deliberate conduct is 20 years from the end of the year of assessment.

Taxpayer's death

For assessments on personal representatives before 1 April 2010, the maximum period for assessing income or gains of the deceased that arose before death is the end of the period of three years following the 31 January after the tax year in which death occurred. From 1 April 2010, assessments have to be made within four years of the end of the year of assessment in which the taxpayer died.

Assessments made before 1 April 2010 to recover tax lost as a result of *fraudulent or negligent conduct* on the part of the deceased, may go back only to years of assessment ending not earlier than six years before death. After 1 April 2010, the same time limit applies but the assessments must be to recover tax lost due to *careless or deliberate behaviour*.

Partnerships

There are also special provisions with regard to partnerships.

Where each partner is still alive, the extended time limit for assessments to recover a loss of tax brought about *carelessly or deliberately* (before 1 April 2010, due to *fraudulent or negligent conduct*) can apply in relation to persons other than the person in default and HMRC have an option either:

(1) to recover tax from fellow individual partners (effectively, by assessing the partnership) even if the person causing the neglect is no longer a partner, provided he was a partner at some time during the year for which the assessment was raised (any later incoming partner is exempted); or

(2) to recover tax from the particular individual in default.

If the partner concerned is dead, valid assessments can be made outside the four year time limit (before 1 April 2010, three years) but will be enforceable only against the surviving partner (*Harrison v Willis Bros* (1965) 43 TC 61).

Legislation: TMA 1970, s. 34, 36, 40; FA 2008, Sch. 39, para. 7(2), 9, 11; *FA 2009, Sch. 39 (Appointed Day, Transitional Provision and Savings) Order* 2009 (SI 2009/403)

Case: *Harrison v Willis Bros* (1965) 43 TC 61

Penalties

Overview

60-000 Overview

Until 1 April 2009, the *Taxes Management Act* 1970 (s. 93–107) contained the main provisions relating to the amount levied by way of penalties. FA 2007, Sch. 24 enacted a new regime charging penalties for the submission of incorrect documents, defined to include returns, claims and other documents, for all return periods ending after 1 April 2008 and due to be filed after 1 April 2009 (see 61-000). FA 2008, Sch. 41 introduced a new penalty regime for failure to notify liability to tax, which applies from 1 April 2010 (see 61-550). FA 2009, Sch. 55 and 56 introduced new penalty regimes for late filing (see 60-500) and late payment of tax (see 52-600), which apply from 6 April 2011 to returns and payments due for 2010–11.

Some penalties are fixed (see, for example, failure to make a return: see 60-500). Other penalties are 'tax-geared' (see, for example, failure to notify chargeability to income tax 61-550). Where two or more penalties are imposed in respect of the same tax, the total payable is limited to the highest penalty imposed.

Legislation: FA 2007, Sch. 24; FA 2008, Sch. 41; FA 2009, Sch. 55 and 56

60-050 Human rights

In October 2002, an interpretation was published in Tax Bulletin on human rights and penalties which contained a statement to the effect that the question of whether any penalties were 'criminal' for the purposes of art. 6 of the European Convention on Human Rights 'remains in issue'. It went on to explain that guidance had been issued to staff on what should be said to taxpayers when it becomes clear that penalties are likely to be considered.

That statement is curious given the decision in *King v Walden* which was released in May 2001, over a year earlier than the publication of Tax Bulletin. In that case, it was held that the system of imposition of penalties for fraudulent or negligent delivery of incorrect returns or statements was 'criminal' for the purposes of the Convention, following earlier decisions by the European Court of Human Rights (ECHR) especially *Georgiou (t/a Marios Chippery) v United Kingdom*. That case was concerned with whether penalty assessments in respect of VAT and the hearing of appeals from these were 'criminal'. The ECHR held they were. It said that the criteria for establishing whether a 'criminal charge' has been determined are the domestic classification of the 'offence', and the nature and degree of severity of the potential and actual penalty. As the penalty was intended as a punishment to deter re-offending, its purpose was both deterrent and punitive. Additionally, the penalty itself was substantial. These factors taken together indicated that the penalty imposed in that case was a 'criminal charge' within the meaning of the Human Rights convention.

The interpretation in Tax Bulletin referred to guidance issued to HMRC staff which is now incorporated into the *Enquiry Manual*. It also referred to a 'public funding leaflet' which was published by the Legal Services Commission in January 2002 and announced that 'legal aid' was available to fund appeals to the general and special commissioners where penalties are involved which would be regarded as 'criminal' under the Human Rights Convention. This leaflet is to be issued by HMRC in all cases where a tax-geared penalty may be involved or if a taxpayer argues that a fixed penalty is 'criminal', despite the fact that the official line of HMRC is that none of the penalties are 'criminal'.

For commentary of the Human Rights Act and penalties imposed on personal representatives in respect of acts of the deceased, see 51-450.

Case: *King v Walden* [2001] BTC 170

Other Material: HMRC Interpretation, IRInt. 237 (Tax Bulletin, October 2002); HMRC *Enquiry Manual* EM1362

Tax Reporter: ¶103-970; ¶186-650

60-100 Determination of penalties

HMRC officers themselves make a formal determination of a penalty. However, the taxpayer has a right to challenge the penalty before the First-tier Tribunal.

Any *authorised* HMRC officer may make a determination imposing a penalty in such amount as he considers correct or appropriate, except where the penalty is in respect of a failure to notify details of a tax avoidance scheme (see 66-900).

Where a penalty has been determined, a notice of determination must be served on the taxpayer, showing the date of issue and the time-limit for appeal. The notice cannot then be altered except on appeal.

Penalties may be determined by the courts where, in the opinion of HMRC, the liability for a penalty arises by reason of fraud. Where the court does not find fraud proved it is nevertheless empowered to impose such penalty (if any) as it considers appropriate even though the matter would not have come before it but for HMRC's opinion that there was fraud.

Legislation: TMA 1970, s. 100, 100C, 100D

60-150 Appeals against determinations

An appeal can be made against a penalty determined by HMRC and the provisions relating to appeals against assessments, etc. generally apply. The tribunal is empowered;

- to set the determination aside;
- to confirm it;
- to revise it to the correct amount (where the penalty is fixed); or
- to reduce it (even to nil) or increase it up to the statutory maximum, as they consider appropriate (in the case of a variable penalty).

The automatic penalties for late personal, trustee and partnership returns may not be varied by the tribunal, only confirmed, or set aside where a reasonable excuse applied throughout the default period.

There are also modifications of the appeals procedure where penalties are imposed on each partner as a result of an incorrect partnership. The modifications provide for proceedings to be in respect of the representative partner.

The person liable, but not HMRC, can appeal to the court against the decision of the tribunal as to the *amount* of penalty and the court is given to same powers of revision or discharge as the tribunal.

Legislation: TMA 1970, s. 93(8), 93A(7), 95A(3), 100B

60-200 Interest on penalties

Prior to 1 April 2008, interest was payable on penalties from the due date to the date of payment. The due date is 30 days after the notice of determination of the penalty.

Penalties assessed under FA 2007, Sch. 24 are to be treated for procedural purposes as though they are an amount of tax.

Legislation: FA 2007, Sch. 24, para. 13(2)

Late filing of return

60-500 Late filing and late payment penalties for 2010–11 and later years

Finance Act 2009, Sch. 55 and 56 reformed the penalty regimes for late filing of self assessment tax returns and late payment of tax. The new regimes replaced the previous variety of penalties and surcharges. It also removed late payment penalties where taxpayers have agreed a time to pay agreement with HMRC.

The new penalties are charged as follows:

- £100 penalty immediately after the due date for filing (even if there is no tax to pay, and whether or not the tax has been paid by the due date);
- daily penalties of £10 per day for returns that are more than three months late, running for a maximum of 90 days;
- if the return is still outstanding six months after the filing date, a further penalty of 5% of tax due for the return period or £300, whichever is the greater;
- if the return is still outstanding 12 months after the filing date, a further penalty of 5% of tax due for the return period or £300, whichever is the greater; and
- higher penalties of 70% of the tax due where a person fails to submit a return for over 12 months and has deliberately withheld information necessary for HMRC to assess the tax due (increasing to a 100% penalty if deliberate with concealment).

The penalties chargeable for late payment are:

- penalties of 5% of the amount of tax unpaid 30 days after the payment due date;

- further penalties of 5% of any amounts of tax still unpaid at six months;
- further penalties of 5% of any amounts of tax still unpaid at 12 months.

HMRC can suspend late payment penalties where the taxpayer agrees a time to pay arrangement (where a tax debt is paid over time) with HMRC.

The new late filing and late payment penalties apply from 6 April 2011 (6 October 2011 for Construction Industry Scheme returns) to returns and payments in respect of 2010–11 onwards.

Penalties in connection with offshore asset moves

In order to dissuade taxpayers from seeking to avoid penalties by moving assets or funds between overseas territories 'relevant offshore asset moves', HMRC have the power to impose an additional penalty. This penalty will arise where the taxpayer is found to be subject to a penalty through a deliberate failure and has undertaken a relevant offshore asset move. The additional penalty is 50% of the penalty imposed for the deliberate failure.

Legislation: FA 2015, Sch. 21

60-625 Late filing for 2009–10 and earlier years

The old penalty regime for late filing contained in TMA 1970, s. 93 and surcharges for late payment ceased to apply from April 2011. The old penalty regime for late filing, which continues to apply to returns for 2009–10 and earlier years, consisted of a fixed penalty, daily penalties and tax-geared penalties.

Fixed penalty

A fixed penalty of £100 automatically applies for individuals or trustees failing to make a return by the deadline (31 October for paper returns and 31 January for online returns). Where the failure extends beyond six months after the filing date the penalty increases by another £100, unless HMRC have applied to the First-tier Tribunal for a daily penalty to be imposed.

Where the liability to tax is less than the fixed penalties incurred, the penalties are limited to the amount of tax due. The tax liability cannot however be known until the return has in fact been submitted so situations often arise where a penalty is imposed and may later have to be reduced to the amount of the liability. HMRC have a power to revise the penalty where an officer discovers that it has become excessive.

An appeal against a fixed penalty may be made to the First-tier Tribunal on the basis that the taxpayer had a 'reasonable excuse' for the late filing of the return which lasted throughout the period of default. The tribunal can then either confirm the penalty or set the determination aside.

Daily penalty

In addition to the fixed penalty, an HMRC officer may request the First-tier Tribunal to make a direction allowing him to impose an additional penalty of up to £60 per day for each day the failure continues following the date of the direction. The penalty cannot be imposed once the return has been submitted.

Initially HMRC rarely sought daily penalties. However, following criticism by the National Audit Office of the ineffectiveness of the fixed penalties in 'encouraging' submission of returns on time, HMRC began increasingly to seek daily penalties.

Before an application is made to the First-tier Tribunal, a warning letter should be sent to the taxpayer and his agent, giving at least 30 days' notice. The taxpayer has a right of appeal against the penalty determination.

The actual daily rate is fixed by the HMRC officer. The factors to be taken into account include the previous compliance history, co-operation and attitude of the taxpayer and the likely amount of tax at stake. The suggestion is that most penalties should fall within the middle of the range with the highest levels being reserved for the more serious cases.

Although the determination of the penalty and therefore its daily rate is the responsibility of the HMRC officer, the tribunal on an appeal has the power to vary the rate.

Tax-geared penalties

In addition to the fixed and daily penalties, if the failure to make a return extends beyond the anniversary of the filing date and there would have been a liability to tax shown in the return, the taxpayer is liable to a penalty up to the amount of tax which would have been shown.

Legislation: TMA 1970, s. 93, 93(3), (5), (6), 100(6), 100B(2)

Other Material: HMRC *Enquiry Manual* EM4561

60-700 Partnership returns

The conditions for penalties on individuals are repeated with respect to failures to make partnership returns, with the following modifications:

- failure of the representative partner in submitting the return generates the penalties;
- each and every partner is liable for a penalty as shown in the preceding paragraph (i.e. £100 and up to £60 per day, etc.) even though each partner individually may have submitted their own personal return on time; and
- any appeal against penalties can only be brought by the representative partner as a composite appeal.

Legislation: FA 2009, Sch. 55, para. 25; TMA 1970, s. 93A

60-800 Reasonable excuse

The penalty for failing to make a return under self-assessment can be avoided should the taxpayer have a 'reasonable excuse'. The legislation states that the following will not be accepted as providing a reasonable excuse:

- an insufficiency of funds;
- reliance on another person to do something, unless reasonable care was taken to avoid the failure; or
- where there was a reasonable excuse but when it came to an end the failure was not remedied without unreasonable delay.

Apart from this, the legislation gives no guidance on what may or may not constitute a reasonable excuse. HMRC's policy is set out below, but in the end the taxpayer has a right of appeal to the commissioners. He will have to show that, not only was the excuse 'reasonable' but also that it existed *throughout* the period of default, i.e. from the statutory filing date to the date the return was actually delivered.

HMRC's general view is that a taxpayer only has a reasonable excuse where some exceptional event, beyond his control, prevents him from meeting the deadline in question. They point out that, in partnership cases, as only the representative partner can have a reasonable excuse for failing to make a return, the circumstances of the other partners are normally irrelevant.

The following are examples of what HMRC say they may accept as a reasonable excuse for missing the deadline for a return:

(1) where the deadline was not met because the taxpayer did not receive the return;

(2) where the return was posted in good time but an unforeseen event disrupted the postal service (e.g. prolonged industrial action within the Post Office) and led to the loss or delay of the return. The taxpayer in

Kestrel Guards Ltd [2014] TC 03324 was successful at the First-tier Tribunal where he was able to demonstrate that eight late payments of PAYE had been posted first class and should therefore have reached HMRC the following day. The fact that the payments had all arrived late was not the responsibility of the taxpayer;

(3) where the taxpayer or tax adviser lost his records as a result of fire, flood or theft;

(4) where serious illness prevented the taxpayer from controlling his business and private affairs immediately before the deadline;

(5) where a close relative or domestic partner died shortly before the deadline, provided that the taxpayer had already taken any necessary steps to have the return ready on time; or

(6) where the taxpayer's time and attention were preoccupied by the serious illness of a close relative or domestic partner during the period from the deadline to despatch of the return, provided that the taxpayer had already taken any necessary steps to have the return ready on time.

(7) where the individual was in prison. In the First-tier Tribunal case of *Richter*, this was found to be a reasonable excuse despite the fact that his incarceration commenced shortly after the filing deadline. This case was particularly interesting in that the judge pointed out that the six and 12-month late filing penalties should be levied based on 'information and belief'. This test could not be met where, as in this case, the penalty is issued automatically by computer.

The Upper Tribunal decided that a person who, on the evidence of a consultant psychiatrist, suffered from a mental state that caused and would have continued to cause 'avoidance symptoms', which covered areas such as her dealings with HMRC, had a reasonable excuse for filing her return late.

Similarly, a taxpayer who failed to submit an employer's annual return following the closure of the business had a reasonable excuse because HMRC failed to send the filing notice to the taxpayer's new address. The tribunal said that a reasonable excuse does not require exceptional circumstances.

In contrast, the following are examples of what HMRC say they will not accept as a reasonable excuse for missing the deadline for a return:

- the return is too difficult to complete;
- pressure of work;
- failure by the taxpayer's agent (although not in the case of *Taylor*);

- the unavailability of certain information; or
- absence of reminders from HMRC.

The onus is on the taxpayer to provide sufficient detail to determine that the reasons existed throughout the period of default and to show a causal link to the failure to file on time.

Various tribunal decisions have illustrated situations where the taxpayer had no reasonable excuse for the failure to file their return online, including:

- reliance on accountants who failed to procure the third party software necessary for online submission;
- no evidence to support the taxpayer's claim that a return was filed on time and a lack of cogency in the taxpayer's assertions to show that, on the balance of probabilities, it was; and
- lack of facility to file online and the fact that the taxpayer had no income.

Legislation: FA 2009, Sch. 55, para. 23

Cases: *AZ v R & C Commrs* [2011] BTC 1,777; *Joy* [2011] TC 01006; *Amelie Partnership* [2011] TC 01032; *Riaz* [2011] TC 01096; *Somercombe OTS No 39 Ltd* [2011] TC 01108; *Fisher (t/a Crispin)* [2011] TC 01100; *Kestrel Guards Ltd* [2014] TC 03324; *Taylor* [2015] TC 04375; *Kaczmarczyk* [2017] TC 05744; *Richter* [2017] TC 05816

Filing incorrect return

61-000 Incorrect return filed for periods commencing on or after 1 April 2008 and due on or after 1 April 2009

Finance Act 2007 introduced a new regime for all taxes administered by HMRC in respect of incorrect documents.

The regime applies where any person provides HMRC with a document of a kind listed in the schedule which contains an understatement of their liability to tax, a false or inflated statement of a loss, or a false or inflated repayment claim, and the inaccuracy is 'careless' or 'deliberate'. Where there is more than one inaccuracy in the document, a penalty is chargeable in respect of each inaccuracy.

'Document' includes any form of return, statement, account or claim. The definition is further widened to include: 'Any document which is likely to be relied upon by HMRC to determine, without further enquiry, a question about–'

'(a) [the person's] liability to tax
(b) payments by [the person] of or in connection with tax
(c) any other payment by [the person] (including penalties); or
(d) repayments or any other kind of payment or credit to [the person].'

The term is therefore extremely broad in scope and not restricted to the documents on which HMRC would previously have considered charging a penalty for inaccuracy.

Errors attributable to another person

Where an inaccurate document is submitted and a third party has deliberately supplied false information or deliberately withheld information from a taxpayer with the intention of the document containing an inaccuracy, that third party will also be liable to a penalty under the schedule whether or not the taxpayer is also liable to a penalty in respect of the same inaccuracy.

Where a penalty is incurred in respect of an inaccurate document, and that inaccuracy or failure is on a taxpayer's behalf by someone acting as their agent, the taxpayer is not liable to a penalty where they are able to satisfy HMRC that they have taken reasonable care to avoid the inaccuracy. Additionally, where a penalty is incurred for a failure to notify HMRC of an under-assessment, a taxpayer is not liable to a penalty where that failure is attributable to someone acting as their agent and they have taken reasonable care to avoid the failure.

Mitigation of penalties

The regime in FA 2007, Sch. 24 includes a statutory basis for determining the quantum of penalties. The standard amount for penalties is as follows.

- Where the document is incorrect as a result of a failure to take reasonable care, the standard amount is 30% of the potential of lost revenue.
- Where the inaccuracy is deliberate but not concealed, the standard amount of the penalty is 70% of the potential lost revenue.
- Where the inaccuracy is deliberate and concealed, the standard amount of the penalty is 100% of the potential lost revenue.

The standard amount of a penalty for failing to notify HMRC of an inaccuracy in an assessment is 30% of the potential lost revenue.

The three behaviours

In addition to harmonising penalties for inaccuracies across the range of taxes, HMRC's intention in establishing the new penalty regime was to establish a clearer distinction between the different types of behaviour which led to the submission of incorrect documents than had been the case under the previous regime. The three categories of behaviour are: failure to take reasonable care, deliberate understatement and deliberate understatement with concealment.

The onus of proof in establishing the type of behaviour leading to the inaccuracy rests with HMRC. The standard of proof required is the balance of probabilities, although HMRC accept that a higher quality of proof is likely to be required to establish a more serious type of behaviour.

Failure to take reasonable care

HMRC consider that failure to take reasonable care can be equated to negligence, the previous test for the application of incorrect return penalties.

Practical examples of failing to take reasonable care provided in HMRC's guidance include:

- failing to keep appropriate records required in order to complete a self assessment return;
- failing to take appropriate advice in respect of the treatment of particular items where these are in doubt;
- failing to adopt appropriate tax reporting processes and procedures;
- failing to obtain appropriate information to make a correct return;
- failing to take due care in reviewing a return prepared by a third party.

Case: *Kolek* [2015] TC 04253

Deliberate understatement

A deliberate understatement is considered to arise when a taxpayer submits a document which they know to be incorrect. Examples of deliberate understatements are given in the HMRC guidance and include:

- systematically paying wages without accounting for PAYE or Class 1 NICs;
- knowingly failing to record all sales, especially where there is a pattern to the under-recording;

- deliberately describing transactions inaccurately or in a way likely to mislead;
- claiming a deduction for personal expenses of such a size or frequency that the inaccuracy **must** have been known.

Deliberate understatement with concealment

This category of behaviour is considered to be the most serious form of evasion. This category of behaviour involves deliberately submitting a document known to be incorrect and then taking active steps to conceal the inaccuracy.

Potential lost revenue

The amount of potential lost revenue is defined as the additional amount of tax due and payable to correct the inaccuracy. Where there is more than one inaccuracy which impacts on the tax payable in a tax year, the amount of potential lost revenue is calculated on the basis that careless inaccuracies are corrected before deliberate inaccuracies, and deliberate inaccuracies with concealment are corrected after deliberate inaccuracies.

Reductions for disclosure

A reduction from the standard amount of a penalty is given for disclosure, based on whether the disclosure is prompted or unprompted. An unprompted disclosure is made where the person making it has no reason to believe that HMRC have discovered or are about to discover the inaccuracy or under-assessment. The standard amounts for each category of behaviour are:

- where a penalty is in respect of a failure to take reasonable care, the penalty may be reduced to a minimum of 15% for a prompted disclosure, but may be reduced to 0% where the disclosure is unprompted;
- where the penalty is in respect of a deliberate understatement, the penalty will fall into a range between 20% and 70% where the disclosure is unprompted. Where the disclosure is prompted, the range is between 35% and 70%;
- where a penalty is in respect of a deliberate understatement with concealment, the penalty falls within a range between 30% and 100%. Where the disclosure is prompted, the range is between 50% and 100%.

The amount of the disclosure reduction calculated is determined by allocating the following weightings to each of the three categories:

- telling – 30%;
- helping – 40%;
- giving access – 30%.

HMRC may allow a special reduction to reduce a penalty where there are special circumstances. Special circumstances do not include an inability to pay, or that potential lost revenue in respect of one taxpayer is balanced by an overpayment by another. There is no specific appeal against a failure to allow a special reduction, although an appeal mechanism exists under which the tax tribunal can determine the appropriate amount of any penalty. An example of the First-tier Tribunal approach can be seen in *White*, where the officer had given no reasons for refusing the taxpayer's claim. That meant the decision of the officer was flawed, enabling the tribunal to consider the claim. On the facts the penalty was reduced by 60% such that the effective rate was only 6%.

Calculating the penalty

The quantum of any penalty is determined by reference to the range within which the penalty falls, taking into account the behaviour which gives rise to the penalty and whether a disclosure is prompted or unprompted. The disclosure reduction is then applied to the range to determine the amount of the penalty charged. For example, where a penalty is to be charged for a deliberate understatement which was not the subject of an unprompted disclosure, the penalty will fall within the range of 20% and 70% and the maximum reduction for disclosure is therefore 50%. It is determined that the appropriate disclosure reduction is 65%, so the disclosure reduction is 65% × 50% = 32.5%. The penalty chargeable is therefore 70% – 32.5% of the potential lost revenue.

Suspension of penalties

HMRC have the power to suspend all or part of a penalty charged for careless inaccuracy. Conditions for suspension must be given, which can include actions to be taken and a period within which this should be done. It is necessary to demonstrate the conditions of suspension would help the taxpayer to avoid future penalties for careless inaccuracy. HMRC have argued that this criteria cannot be met where the inaccuracy is 'one-off' such as an error in a capital gains tax computation but tribunal decisions have consistently found in favour of the taxpayer where they can demonstrate that processes or procedures have or can be put in place to avoid further errors not directly linked to the initial error.

A penalty must be assessed before suspension can be agreed.

HMRC use a penalty suspension flowchart to assist in establishing whether a penalty should be suspended.

Legislation: FA 2007, Sch. 24, para. 14

Case: *Duncan* [2016] TC 05438

Other material: HMRC Manuals CH405070 and CH83100

Reasonable excuse

A penalty can be avoided where the taxpayer can demonstrate reasonable excuse for the error or omission. The criteria to be met is identical to that for a failure to make a return detailed in 60-800.

In the First-tier Tribunal case of *Pandey*, the taxpayer was able to demonstrate that, although she had been careless in not spotting that employment income had been omitted from her return, the error was primarily that of her accountant and that any potential loss of tax was due to her employer's failure to correctly apply PAYE codes. Had the codes been correctly applied, then there would have been no loss of tax and therefore no penalty.

Legislation: FA 2007, Sch. 24

Case: *Pandey* [2017] TC 05706

Offshore income and gains

Finance Act 2010, s. 35 and Sch. 10 amended the level of penalties that may be charged under FA 2007, Sch. 24 in cases where certain offshore income, gains or assets have not been declared to HMRC. The existing penalty levels continue to apply to domestic matters and where the offshore matter concerns a jurisdiction which automatically exchanges information with the UK. For other jurisdictions, for income tax and capital gains tax only, the penalties are increased by a factor of between 1.25 and 2, depending on the tax transparency of the jurisdiction concerned.

The level of the penalty and the reductions permitted for disclosure depend on which of three categories the inaccuracy falls into. If a single inaccuracy is in more than one category it is treated as if it were separate inaccuracies, one in each relevant category according to the matters that it involves, and the potential lost revenue is calculated separately in respect of each separate inaccuracy.

The new regime came into force on 6 April 2011.

As part of their Learning Together programme, HMRC have published a video entitled *Penalties for inaccuracies in documents and returns (part 1 of 2)* covering:

- when a penalty is chargeable;
- types of behaviours associated with the penalty regime;
- prompted and unprompted disclosures;
- reductions and quality of disclosures;
- penalty calculations; and
- suspensions and appeals.

Penalties in connection with offshore asset moves

In order to dissuade taxpayers from seeking to avoid penalties by moving assets or funds between overseas territories ('relevant offshore asset moves'), HMRC have the power to impose an additional penalty. This penalty will arise where the taxpayer is found to be subject to a penalty through a deliberate failure and has undertaken a relevant offshore asset move. The additional penalty is 50% of the penalty imposed for the deliberate failure.

Legislation: FA 2015, Sch. 21

Website: www.hmrc.gov.uk/news/offshore-penalties.pdf

Asset based penalties for offshore tax matters

Where one or more offshore tax penalties have been applied and the potential lost revenue exceeds £25,000, then HMRC may also apply a further penalty based on the value of the asset that generated the omitted income or gain.

The level of the asset based penalty is set at the lower of:

(a) 10% of the value of the asset; or

(b) ten times the potential lost offshore revenue.

These provisions apply with effect from 6 April 2016.

Legislation: FA 2016, Sch. 22

HMRC toolkits to help minimise common errors

HMRC have produced toolkits to provide guidance on areas of error that they frequently see in returns and to set out the steps that can be taken to reduce those errors. They are intended to help to:

- ensure that returns are completed correctly, minimising errors;
- focus on the areas of possible error that HMRC consider key; and
- demonstrate reasonable care.

It will be seen from this that an error in a return that could have been avoided by using one of the toolkits will be treated as arising due to careless behaviour.

The toolkits are available on the HMRC website.

Legislation: FA 2007, s. 97 and Sch. 24; FA 2008, Sch. 40; FA 2010, s. 35 and Sch. 10

Cases: *White* [2012] TC 02050; *Sheard* [2014] TC 04027; *Martin* [2014] TC 04117

Other Material: HMRC *Enquiry Manual* EM5105; HMRC Interpretation IRInt. 186 (Tax Bulletin, October 1998)

Websites: www.youtube.com/user/hmrcgovuk; www.hmrc.gov.uk/agents/It-video-transcript.pdf; www.hmrc.gov.uk/agents/prereturn-support-agents.htm

61-025 Incorrect return or accounts – returns for periods commencing prior to 1 April 2008 and due before 1 April 2009

Where a person 'fraudulently or negligently':

- delivers an incorrect personal or trustee return;
- makes an incorrect statement, etc. in connection with a claim for an allowance, deduction or relief in respect of income tax or capital gains tax; or
- submits incorrect accounts,

he is liable to a penalty not exceeding the difference between the amount of tax actually payable by him (including amounts deducted at source and not repayable) and the amount of tax which would have been payable had the return, etc. been correct. The penalty is in addition to the normal charge to tax. Interest may also be chargeable.

'Negligence' is simply a failure to take the requisite amount of care and includes any error which is not rectified without unreasonable delay after discovery. The term 'fraud' implies an active intention to deceive as opposed to a failure to take due care. In practice the distinction between the two terms is academic as there is no differentiation in the level of penalties. HMRC are normally content to collect penalties on the basis of negligence.

HMRC have confirmed that amending a self-assessment or a partnership statement does not preclude penalty charges being imposed for the incorrect completion of the original return.

61-050 Incorrect partnership returns

Where the representative partner fraudulently or negligently makes any returns or statements or submits incorrect accounts for periods commencing prior to 1 April 2008 and due before 1 April 2009, or his doing so is attributable to fraudulent or negligent conduct on the part of another partner, every person who was a partner in the tax year concerned is liable to a penalty of an amount of up to the tax which would have been lost as a result of the negligence, etc.

Where these penalties are levied, the only appeal permissible is by the representative partner, and is to be treated as a composite appeal against all penalties imposed on the partners.

In view of the fact that it is possible for an innocent partner to be penalised for the wrongdoing of another, it would seem arguable that a human rights violation is possible. The penalty could be regarded as 'criminal' under the Human Rights Convention (see 60-050) and the European Court of Human Rights has held that to impose criminal penalties on the innocent heirs to a deceased's estate due to the conduct of the deceased, is an infringement of their human rights (see 51-450). It would therefore not be stretching the principle by applying it to partnerships.

The new penalty regime (61-000) will apply to incorrect partnership returns or accounts where the return is filed on or after 1 April 2009.

Legislation: TMA 1970, s. 95A; FA 2007, s. 97 and Sch. 24

61-500 Failure to comply with notices issued before 1 April 2009

Failure to comply with a notice to produce documents, etc. issued prior to 1 April 2009 attracts an initial penalty of £50, and if the failure continues, to a further daily penalty of £30 or £150.

These penalties do not apply in respect of enquiry notices issued on or after 1 April 2009 (see 58-175).

Legislation: TMA 1970, s. 97AA(1)

61-550 Failure to notify liability to tax

If for any tax year a person is liable to tax but has not been sent a tax return for completion, he is obliged to notify HMRC within six months after the end of that year that he is chargeable (see 50-000). For obligations arising on or after 1 April 2009, there is an amended penalty regime for failing to notify chargeability to tax, based on the same principles as those contained in FA 2007, Sch. 24 for penalising incorrect returns. This now includes an obligation to notify liability to the high income child benefit charge.

For a deliberate and concealed act or failure the penalty is 100% of 'potential lost revenue', for deliberate but not concealed act or failure the penalty is 70% of potential lost revenue, and for any other case it is 30%.

'Potential lost revenue' is defined as any income tax or capital gains tax to which the person is liable in respect of the tax year and is unpaid on 31 January following the tax year.

There are reductions for disclosure: unprompted – where the person has no reason to believe that HMRC have discovered or are about to discover the act or failure; prompted – all other disclosures. The percentage reduction available depend on the disclosure.

- For an 'unprompted disclosure ' of a deliberate and concealed act or failure, the penalty may be reduced from 100% to no less than 30%.
- For a prompted disclosure of a deliberate and concealed act or failure, the penalty may be reduced from 100% to no less than 50%.
- For an unprompted disclosure of a deliberate act or failure without concealment, the penalty may be reduced from 70% to no less than 20%.
- For a prompted disclosure of a deliberate act or failure without concealment, the penalty may be reduced from 70% to no less than 35%.

Greater reductions will be given where the disclosure is made within 12 months of the time that the tax first becomes unpaid and the behaviour is not classed as deliberate. For an unprompted disclosure of a failure to notify where HMRC became aware of the failure less than 12 months after the time when tax first became unpaid by reason of the failure, the penalty may be reduced from 30% to a percentage which may be nil.

Appeals

Overview

62-000 Overview

The appeals system provides a formal mechanism for the resolution of certain disputes between taxpayers and HMRC. The way in which appeals against HMRC decisions were handled was inherited from the two departments, namely the Inland Revenue and Customs & Excise. When the two departments merged in 2005, HMRC looked at aligning and modernising the administration of appeals. This review has, broadly, resulted in the general and special commissioners being replaced with a new tribunals system from 1 April 2009.

From 1 April 2009, appeals go, almost invariably, to the First-tier Tribunal. In very rare cases, appeals will be fast-tracked by the First-tier Tribunal so as to be heard by the Upper Tribunal. For most tax matters, 1 April 2009 saw a seamless transition to the new rules, and the special commissioners will cease to exist from that date.

Late appeals

A late appeal can be made but the onus is on the taxpayer to show why it should be accepted. If HMRC do not accept that there are grounds for a late appeal, the matter must be heard by the tribunal. The tribunal will consider whether there was a reasonable excuse for the lateness of the appeal and whether it existed throughout the period ending with the making of the appeal. Where there is no reasonable excuse, as there was not in a case where there was a 13-month delay in appealing, they will dismiss the application.

Where a fault on the part of HMRC leads to an appeal being made late, the tribunal is likely to consider the application for a late appeal sympathetically. A tribunal decided that a faxed communication to HMRC notifying the accountant's intention to submit an appeal and postponement notifications was sufficient communication to amount to a valid appeal after the accountant had made several honest attempts to communicate the appeal. That, together with evidence of confusion between tax offices, resulted in the taxpayer's application for a late appeal to be granted.

The Upper Tribunal has held that in considering a late appeal the lower tribunal should have taken all relevant factors and circumstances into account. The tribunal is not limited to the same conditions that apply to HMRC in exercising their discretion in the first place and there is no requirement for exceptional circumstances.

Legislation: *Tribunals Courts and Enforcement Act* 2007; *Transfer of Tribunals Functions and Revenue and Customs Appeal Order* 2009 (SI 2009/56)

Cases: *MacDonald* [2010] TC 00476; *Greenoaks Pharmacy Ltd* [2011] TC 01118; *O'Flaherty v HMRC* [2013] BTC 1,814; *Singh* [2017] TC 05647

62-050 The two tribunals

One of the most important changes introduced by the new system is the fact that the new system introduces two different tribunals into the tax litigation process. These two new tribunals are known as:

- the First-tier Tribunal; and
- the Upper Tribunal

The persons hearing cases in the tribunals are referred to as judges or other members (collectively, referred to as 'members'), depending on their qualifications.

The vast majority of cases will be first heard by the First-tier Tribunal, which should therefore be considered as the successor to the general and special commissioners.

Under the new system, appeals from the First-tier Tribunal will invariably be heard by the Upper Tribunal. The Upper Tribunal is a superior court of record and will therefore have the same status as the High Court itself. Indeed, it is expected that the Upper Tribunal will often be presided over by High Court judges or (in Scotland) judges of the Court of Session.

Furthermore, the Upper Tribunal may exercise the same authority, powers and privileges and rights as those Higher Courts in relation to:

- the attendance and examination of witnesses;
- the production and inspection of documents; and
- all other matters incidental to the Upper Tribunal's functions.

Appeals from the Upper Tribunal will be heard by the Court of Appeal (in England and Wales and in Northern Ireland) or the Court of Session (in Scotland) .

Chambers in the First-tier Tribunal

Tax matters are handled by a specialist tax chamber of the First-tier Tribunal (the 'Tax Chamber'). However, it should be noted that tax credit appeals are dealt with in the Social Entitlement Chamber.

Chambers in the Upper Tribunal

In the Upper Tribunal, there will be fewer chambers. Appeals from the Social Entitlement Chamber of the First-tier Tribunal will all be dealt with by the Administrative Appeals Chamber of the Upper Tribunal. Again, tax matters are heard by a specialist finance and tax chamber of the Upper Tribunal.

Judicial review

Another major change is that judicial review powers (previously the preserve of the High Court and the Court of Session) can now be exercised by the Upper Tribunal.

Legislation: TCEA 2007, s. 3, 5, 11, 13

62-100 Bringing cases to the tribunal

One of the changes that will be introduced is the giving to taxpayers of a greater control over the listing of a hearing before a tribunal, particularly in direct tax cases. Historically, the request for a hearing was generally made by the tax office when negotiations reached an impasse. Whilst this definitely simplified matters for taxpayers (as it removed one level of bureaucracy from them), there was often a perceived 'closeness' between the tax authorities and the independent appeal Commissioners.

Once a taxpayer appeals against a decision by HMRC (in writing to HMRC), there are now three possible courses of action.

Either:

(1) the taxpayer can make a formal request that HMRC review the matter in question;

(2) HMRC may offer a review of the matter to the taxpayer; or

(3) the taxpayer may notify the appeal directly to the First-tier Tribunal.

Whichever approach is taken, it does not prevent the parties from settling the dispute by mutual agreement.

62-150 Statutory review

The statutory review provisions represent a completely new procedure in the context of direct tax disputes. They existed previously for some indirect taxes and, informally, for VAT purposes.

Request that HMRC review matter

If a taxpayer requires HMRC to review the matter, HMRC must set out their initial view of the matter within:

- 30 days of their receipt of the request for the review; or
- such longer period as is reasonable.

A request may not be made (and HMRC may not be required to conduct a review) if either:

- the taxpayer has already requested a review in relation to the matter;
- HMRC have already offered a review in relation to the matter; or
- the taxpayer has already notified the First-tier Tribunal of the appeal.

HMRC offer of review

When HMRC offer a review to the taxpayer, the offer must include HMRC's view of the matter in question.

The taxpayer then has 30 days (starting with the date stated on HMRC's offer of a review) to request that HMRC conduct a review.

It is imperative that taxpayers note this time limit carefully, because failure to accept the offer of a review will mean that the dispute will be treated as settled (in accordance with HMRC's views of the matter).

HMRC may not offer a review (and HMRC may not be required to conduct a review) if either:

- the taxpayer has already requested a review in relation to the matter;
- HMRC have already offered a review in relation to the matter; or
- the taxpayer has already notified the First-tier Tribunal of the appeal.

Nature of a review

There are three outcomes of a review: the original HMRC view will be either upheld, varied or cancelled. The nature and extent of the review will depend on what appears to be appropriate to HMRC in the particular circumstances. However, HMRC must bear in mind the steps taken by HMRC in first deciding the matter and any steps taken by any person seeking to resolve the disagreement.

The review must also take into account any representations made by the taxpayer, provided that they are made sufficiently early to give HMRC a reasonable opportunity to consider them. To avoid difficulties with this hurdle, it is therefore suggested that the representations be included in the request for a review (or the acceptance of the offer of the review).

Time scale for review

HMRC must notify the taxpayer of their conclusions of the review and their reasoning within a 45-day period (unless the parties agree a different timescale). That 45-day period runs:

- in a case where the taxpayer requested the review, from the day on which HMRC notified the taxpayer of their initial view of the matter; and

- in a case where the taxpayer accepted HMRC's offer of a review, from the day on which HMRC received the acceptance of the offer.

The conclusions reached by the review are then deemed to stand (as a TMA 1970, s. 54(1) agreement) and the taxpayer is unable to withdraw from this deemed agreement.

If HMRC fail to give their conclusions within the 45-day period (or such other period as agreed), then the initial HMRC view is deemed to stand and the taxpayer is unable to withdraw from this deemed agreement. HMRC are required to notify the taxpayer of the conclusion that is deemed to have been reached.

This provision begs the question: what is the point of asking HMRC for a review? Not only are there concerns about the effectiveness of a review, especially, if HMRC reviewers will not be able to diverge from HMRC policy; however, if HMRC fail to meet their own 45-day time limit, then the parties are deemed to have agreed to the original HMRC position that was subject to the review in the first place. If taxpayers wish to avoid this 'Catch 22' situation, then they should try to agree with HMRC for an extension of the 45-day period so that HMRC cannot argue that they have run out of time.

In either case, however, the matter may still be taken on appeal to the First-tier Tribunal.

For appeals made to HMRC before 1 April 2009, where no appeal had been lodged with the general or special commissioners, any review that is offered or requested before 1 April 2010 will be subject to a 90-day review period, rather than the 45-day period. This is subject to any agreement between the parties to vary the review period.

Notification of appeal to the Tribunal

Once HMRC have been notified that their decision is to be appealed against, the taxpayer may notify the First-tier Tribunal of the appeal. Once this is done, it will be for the tribunal to decide the matter.

However, different procedures apply if either:

- HMRC have given their view of the matter following a review under TMA 1970, s. 49B; or
- HMRC have given their view of the matter when offering a review under s. 49C.

Notification of appeal to the tribunal (after review)

Once a review has been concluded (or once the period for the review expires without HMRC notifying the taxpayer of their conclusion), the taxpayer may notify the First-tier Tribunal of the appeal. This generally should be done within a 30-day period (see below).

If the taxpayer is late in notifying the First-tier Tribunal of the appeal then the appeal may not proceed unless the Tribunal gives permission.

Once the tribunal has been notified of the appeal, the tribunal will decide the matter in question.

The operation of the period for notifying the tribunal depends on the circumstances of the case:

(1) if HMRC have notified the taxpayer of their conclusions following the review, the period to appeal runs for 30 days starting with the date on the notice on which HMRC state their conclusions of the review;
(2) if HMRC have failed to conclude the review in time (usually within 45 days), the taxpayer may notify the tribunal of the appeal at any time between:
    (a) the conclusion of the review period (usually 45 days); and
    (b) the 30th day following HMRC giving the document under TMA 1970, s. 45E(9) – the deemed conclusion of the review (being in accordance with the original decision).

Notification of appeal to the tribunal (after review offered but not accepted)

Although the review procedures are likely to catch out many taxpayers, the option of not accepting an offer of a review could be even more troublesome.

As previously noted, an offer of a review must be accompanied by a statement of HMRC's position. Furthermore, a taxpayer's failure to accept the offer of the review within 30 days will mean that the HMRC view will be deemed to have been accepted by both parties as their settled position from which the taxpayer cannot withdraw.

The taxpayer will, however, have the opportunity to notify the First-tier Tribunal of the appeal in such circumstances and the tribunal will decide the matter. Nevertheless, the timing will be critical.

If the notification to the tribunal is within the 30-day period (i.e. within the 30 days after the date of the document by which HMRC sends the offer of a review), then the matter can be heard by the tribunal without any additional hurdle.

However, if the tribunal is notified later (for example, because the taxpayer is unaware of the consequences of not accepting the offer of a review), then the appeal may not proceed to the tribunal unless the tribunal gives permission.

Procedure if no review offered or accepted

In direct tax cases, the taxpayer will usually have the opportunity to request a review at the same time as notifying HMRC of the appeal against the decision. However, the taxpayer may not necessarily do this and there is no obligation on HMRC to offer one. In such circumstances, the parties will be able to continue to discuss matters until such time as the taxpayer either requests a review or applies directly to the Tribunal or HMRC formally offers a review. Then, the procedures discussed above will be triggered.

Legislation: TMA 1970, s. 49A, 49B, 49C, 49D, 49E, 49G, 49H

62-200 Allocation of cases to categories

In order to streamline the tribunal's handling of cases, they will be allocated to one of four categories when the tribunal receives a notice of appeal, application notice or notice of reference:

- default paper cases;
- basic cases;
- standard cases; and
- complex cases.

Default paper cases

A default paper case will usually be disposed of without a hearing. It is proposed that this category will generally apply to appeals against:

- fixed penalties for late filing of tax returns;
- fixed penalties for late filing of employer returns (P35s);
- fixed penalties for late filing of returns under the construction industry scheme;
- Class 2 NICs late notification penalties;
- income tax surcharges (for late payment of tax under self-assessment); and
- applications by HMRC for the imposition of daily penalties in relation to late self-assessment tax returns.

Basic cases

Basic cases are those which will usually be disposed of after a hearing, but with minimal exchange of documents beforehand.

It is proposed that the basic case category will generally apply to appeals against:

- tax-geared penalties for late filing of tax returns;
- most tax-geared penalties for incorrect returns (but not where the penalty is for deliberate and concealed action, nor where there is also an appeal against the assessment itself);
- mitigation and reasonable excuse appeals against indirect tax penalties;
- appeals against CIS gross payment status decisions;
- appeals against information notices.

Standard cases

Standard cases are those which will usually be disposed of after a hearing, and subject to more detailed case management.

Complex cases

The tribunal may not direct that a case be allocated as a complex case unless the tribunal considers that the case:

- will require lengthy or complex evidence or a lengthy hearing;
- involves a complex or important principle; or
- involves a large financial sum.

Legislation: *Tribunal Procedure (First-tier Tribunal) (Tax Chamber) Rules* 2009 (SI 2009/273), r. 23

62-250 Respondent's statement of case

Except where the case has been allocated as a basic case, there is an obligation on the respondent (or respondents) to send or deliver to the tribunal (and the other parties) a statement of case so that their side of the argument can be considered in advance of any hearing (or, in default paper cases, before the determination of the appeal).

Time limit for providing a respondent's statement of case

In default paper cases, the respondent must send or deliver the statement of case within 42 days after the tribunal sent the notice of the appeal (or the copy of the application notice or notice of reference).

In standard or complex cases, the respondent must provide the statement of case within 60 days of the tribunal sending the notice of the appeal (or the copy of the application notice or notice of reference)

If the respondent's statement of case is sent to the tribunal after the relevant time limit (and after any extension of the time permitted under r. 5(3)(a), there are additional requirements on the respondent when sending or delivering the statement of case. In such cases, the statement of case must include:

- a request for an extension of time; and
- the reason why the statement of case was not provided in time

A statement of case must set out the respondent's position in relation to the case. Respondents may also request in their statement of case that they would prefer that the case be dealt with at a hearing or without a hearing.

Legislation: *Tribunal Procedure (First-tier Tribunal) (Tax Chamber) Rules* 2009 (SI 2009/273), r. 25

62-300 Default paper cases

The appellant may (but need not) send or deliver a written reply to the tribunal. Such a reply should be sent or delivered to the tribunal within 30 days after the date on which the respondent sent the relevant statement of case to the appellant. Copies of the reply should be sent or delivered to the other parties at the same time.

The reply may contain:

- arguments setting out the appellant's response to the respondent's statement of case;
- further information (including, where appropriate, copies of documents containing such information) not yet provided to the tribunal that is relevant to the case; and
- a request that the case be dealt with at a hearing.

The tribunal will not usually consider replies by an appellant once the time limit for reply has expired (unless an extension has been sought and that extended time limit has not expired).

This is because, once the appellant replies (or once the relevant time limit has expired), the tribunal must (subject to the two exceptions below) proceed to determine the case without a hearing.

However, the case will not proceed direct to a hearing if either:

- the tribunal directs otherwise; or
- a party has made a written request to the tribunal for a hearing, in which case the tribunal must hold a hearing before determining the case.

Legislation: *Tribunal Procedure (First-tier Tribunal) (Tax Chamber) Rules* 2009 (SI 2009/273), r. 26

62-350 Standard and Complex cases

The parties must (subject to any direction to the contrary) send or deliver a list of documents to the tribunal and each other party. Such a list should be sent or delivered within 42 days of the respondent sending its statement of case. Where there is more than one respondent, the list should be sent within 42 days of the last statement of case.

For each party, the list must show those documents:

- of which the party has are possession, the right to possession or the right to take copies; and
- on which the party intends to rely or produce in the proceedings.

Legislation: *Tribunal Procedure (First-tier Tribunal) (Tax Chamber) Rules* 2009 (SI 2009/273), r. 27

62-400 Transfer of complex cases to the Upper Tribunal

Where a case is likely to be litigated to the Court of Appeal and beyond, it will often be appropriate for the case to omit one of the tribunal stages. Consequently, complex cases can sometimes be heard in the Upper Tribunal at first instance (i.e. the hearing in the Upper Tribunal will be the first time that a case would have been argued).

Conditions for a transfer of cases to the Upper Tribunal

As already noted, a case must not be transferred to the Upper Tribunal unless it has already been allocated to the complex case category.

Secondly, the transfer requires the consent of the parties.

Thirdly, the tribunal must refer the request to the President of the Tax Chamber of the First-tier Tribunal.

Fourthly, the President of the Finance and Tax Chamber of the Upper Tribunal (if that is a different person) must concur with the transfer request.

Legislation: *Tribunal Procedure (First-tier Tribunal) (Tax Chamber) Rules* 2009 (SI 2009/273), r. 28

62-450 Determination with or without a hearing

The general rule is that there must be a hearing before any decision that disposes of proceedings (or part of proceedings).

However, this is subject to four exceptions.

(1) determination of cases allocated to the default paper case category (where no request for a hearing has been made);

(2) cases where:

  (a) each party has consented to the matter being decided without a hearing; and

  (b) the tribunal considers that it is able to decide the matter without a hearing;

(3) decisions under Part 4 (reconsideration of a case once a decision has been made);

(4) where the tribunal disposes of proceedings (or part) under a strike-out (what is generally known as an 'Unless Order'). Such an order provides that the proceedings will be struck out (or a part of the proceedings will be struck out) unless a party complies with a particular direction.

Legislation: *Tribunal Procedure (First-tier Tribunal) (Tax Chamber) Rules* 2009 (SI 2009/273), r. 29

62-500 Notice of hearings

The tribunal must give each party entitled to attend a hearing reasonable notice of the time and place of any hearing. This must occur each time that the hearing is arranged or rearranged and applies to adjourned and postponed hearings as well as those being heard for the first time . Where the hearing is to deal with the disposal of proceedings, the notice must be at least 14 days.

However, shorter notice can be given if either:

- the parties consent; or
- there are urgent exceptional circumstances.

Legislation: *Tribunal Procedure (First-tier Tribunal) (Tax Chamber) Rules* 2009 (SI 2009/273), r. 31

62-600 Public and private hearings

It is now the general rule that court and tribunal hearings should be held in public.

However, the tribunal may direct that a hearing (or part of a hearing) may be held in private if the tribunal considers that a restriction on access to the hearing is justified:

- in the interests of public order or national security;
- to protect a person's right to respect for their private and family life;
- in order to maintain the confidentiality of sensitive information;
- in order to avoid serious harm to the public interest; or
- because not to do so would prejudice the interests of justice.

Publication of decisions where hearings held in private

It is widely expected that the decisions in the more technical cases, at least, will continue to be published by the tribunal. Where a case is heard in private (or partly heard in private), the tribunal must (so far as is practicable) ensure that any published report of the decision does not disclose information which was referred to only in a part of the hearing that was held in private. In particular, there should not be disclosed any information that enables the identification of any person whose affairs were dealt with in the part of the hearing that was held in private.

Legislation: *Tribunal Procedure (First-tier Tribunal) (Tax Chamber) Rules* 2009 (SI 2009/273), r. 32

62-650 Hearings in a party's absence

It could be unfair if a party decided not to attend a hearing and that automatically meant that the hearing has to be adjourned. Thus, the tribunal may proceed with the hearing even if a party fails to attend.

However, for this to occur, the tribunal must:

(1) be satisfied that either the absent party has been notified of the hearing; or reasonable steps have been taken to notify the party of the hearing; and

(2) consider it to be in the interests of justice to proceed with the hearing.

Legislation: *Tribunal Procedure (First-tier Tribunal) (Tax Chamber) Rules* 2009 (SI 2009/273), r. 33

62-700 Consent orders

There will be occasions on which the parties, despite their previous differences, reach an agreement concerning the disposal of the proceedings.

If the parties agree and if the tribunal thinks it appropriate, the tribunal may make an order (a consent order) which disposes of the proceedings in accordance with the parties' agreement. The consent order may also make any other appropriate provisions as agreed by the parties.

In such cases, the tribunal need not hold a hearing. Nor does the tribunal need to provide reasons for giving the consent order.

Legislation: *Tribunal Procedure (First-tier Tribunal) (Tax Chamber) Rules* 2009 (SI 2009/273), r. 34

62-750 Decision notices

The tribunal may give a decision orally at a hearing. After a final decision is made, disposing of all issues in the proceedings, the tribunal must provide a decision notice to each of the parties. This decision notice should be provided within 28 days of the decision being made or as soon as is practicable thereafter.

Although the parties may agree that the tribunal need not provide a full statement of reasons for the decision, a party may not appeal the decision without it.

Consequently, a party may apply to the tribunal for a full written statement of its findings and reasons. Such a request must be:

- made in writing;
- sent or delivered within 28 days after the tribunal sent or otherwise provided the decision notice to that party.

When such an application is made, the tribunal must send to each party a full statement of its findings and reasons. This should be sent within 28 days of receiving the application or as soon as is practicable thereafter.

Legislation: *Tribunal Procedure (First-tier Tribunal) (Tax Chamber) Rules* 2009 (SI 2009/273), r. 35

62-800 Right of review

If a party is unhappy with the decision, there are two statutory courses of action available: review or appeal. The tribunal has the right to review a decision that it has made unless the decision was itself:

- a decision to review (or not to review) an earlier decision of the tribunal;
- a decision to take no action (or not to take any particular action) in the light of a review of an earlier decision of the tribunal;
- a decision to refer (or not to refer) a matter to the Upper Tribunal;
- a decision of the tribunal that has already been set aside; or
- a decision of the tribunal of a type specified in an order made by the Lord Chancellor (see below).

Other excluded decisions

The Lord Chancellor has provided that certain decisions of the tribunal may not be subject to review (see the *Appeals (Excluded Decisions) Order* 2009 (SI 2009/275)).

Consequences of a review

If the tribunal has reviewed a decision, it may as a result:

- correct any accidental errors in the decision or in a record of the decision;
- amend the reasons for given in the decision;
- set the decision aside.

Although not explicitly stated, the tribunal may of course do nothing.

Legislation: TCEA 2007, s. 9, 11; *Appeals (Excluded Decisions) Order* 2009 (SI 2009/275)

62-850 Appeals to Upper Tribunal

A party's right to appeal to the Upper Tribunal is limited to appeals on points of law arising from the decision of the First-tier Tribunal.

Decisions that cannot be appealed against

The following decisions may not be subject to an appeal:

- a decision to review (or not to review) an earlier decision of the tribunal;
- a decision to take no action (or not to take any particular action) in the light of a review of an earlier decision of the tribunal;

- a decision to set aside an earlier decision;
- a decision to refer (or not to refer) a matter to the Upper Tribunal;
- a decision of the tribunal that has already been set aside; or
- a decision of the tribunal of a type specified in an order made by the Lord Chancellor (see the *Appeals (Excluded Decisions) Order* 2009 (SI 2009/275)).

Requirement for permission (or leave)

Unlike a party's unfettered right to appeal (on points of law) from the Commissioners or the VAT and Duties Tribunal, appeals from the First-tier Tribunal are subject to the appellant first obtaining permission (or, in Northern Ireland, leave).

Many commentators have complained that this permission requirement under the rules represents a significant curtailment of a party's rights to justice. However, it has been suggested by some commentators that permission will be given automatically, provided that a point of law is identified. Others have suggested that the permission process will weed out totally unmeritorious appeals. It remains to be seen whether the permission stage will also be used to exclude vexatious litigants and other cases where the tribunals consider that (irrespective of the legal arguments) justice would be best served by not permitting an appeal to proceed.

Applications to the First-tier Tribunal for permission (or leave) to appeal

In order to obtain permission, the party wishing to appeal the decision must make a written application to the tribunal.

That application must:

- identify the decision of the tribunal to which it relates;
- identify the alleged error or errors of law in the decision; and
- state the result that the applicant is seeking.

Timing of applications for permission (or leave) to appeal

The party's application to the First-tier Tribunal must be sent or delivered to the tribunal so that it is received within 56 days of the latest of:

- the tribunal sending the person seeking permission full written reasons for its decision;
- the tribunal sending notification of amended reasons for (or correction of) the decision following a review; or

- in cases where an application was made for the decision to be set aside within the 28-day period or within any period extended by the tribunal, the tribunal sending notification that the application has been unsuccessful.

Late applications

The wording suggests that applications will be considered to be made on time, even if the application is received late, provided that it was sent or delivered so that it is (i.e. with the intention that it is) received in time. Consequently, late applications in such cases might not require any formal extension of time.

However, there are procedures that do permit late applications for permission (or leave) to appeal.

If the application for permission (or leave) is sent to the tribunal late (and no extension of time has been made, the application must include:

- a request for an extension of time; and
- the reason why the application was not made in time.

If, despite the request, the tribunal does not extend time for the application for permission, then the application must not be admitted by the tribunal.

Legislation: TCEA 2007, s. 11; *Appeals (Excluded Decisions) Order* 2009 (SI 2009/275)

62-900 Costs

The new tribunals will operate a costs regime (referred to as 'expenses' in Scotland) that is different from that operated under the general and special commissioners and in the VAT and Duties Tribunal.

Costs orders for unreasonable conduct

The tribunal may make an order for costs if the tribunal considers a party or the party's representative to have acted unreasonably in bringing, defending or conducting the proceedings. This is a relaxation of the rule that applied in cases before the special commissioners. There, the conduct had to be 'wholly unreasonable' before a costs award could be made.

Costs in complex cases

A further change being heralded under the new rules is that, in certain cases, costs will generally follow the event (i.e. the winner will be awarded his/her/its costs against the other side), irrespective of the party's conduct of the case.

This reflects the previous legal position for VAT appeals but, historically, HMRC (and, previously, Customs) generally refrained from claiming their costs when they won an appeal. It has been stated that HMRC will now generally seek their costs in cases where they win at the tribunal, where permitted to do so.

Wasted costs orders

Wasted costs are those costs incurred by a party either:

- as a result of any improper, unreasonable or negligent act or omission on the part of any legal or other representative (or employee of such a representative) (being a person exercising a right of audience or the right to conduct proceedings on a party's behalf); or
- before such conduct but, in the light of which, the tribunal considers it unreasonable to expect that party to pay.

In such cases, the tribunal may disallow (in accordance with the rules) the whole or part of the wasted costs so that they cannot be recovered from the other side. Alternatively, the tribunal may order the representative to meet those costs.

Application for costs

The tribunal can issue a costs order on its own initiative. Alternatively, the parties can apply to the tribunal for such an order.

Procedures before a costs order can be made

A costs order must not be made against a person without that person being given an opportunity to make representations. If the person against whom the order is proposed to be made is an individual, the tribunal must first consider that person's financial means. (It should be noted that the equivalent Rule applying in the Upper Tribunal excludes this additional test in cases involving wasted costs orders.)

Transitional rules – proceedings commencing before 1 April 2009

In any case where proceedings were in existence before 1 April 2009 before the general or special commissioners or before the VAT and Duties Tribunal (and therefore transferred to the First-tier Tribunal), a costs order may be made only to the extent that it could have been made under the rules in existence before that date.

Legislation: TCEA, s. 29; *Tribunal Procedure (First-tier Tribunal) (Tax Chamber) Rules* 2009 (SI 2009/273), r. 10; *Transfer of Tribunal Functions and Revenue and Customs Appeals Order* 2009 (SI 2009/56), Sch. 3

62-950 The Upper Tribunal

A number of the procedural rules for the Upper Tribunal are similar (or identical) to those applying to the First-tier Tribunal set out above. The rules in the Upper Tribunal are governed by the *Tribunal Procedure (Upper Tribunal) Rules* 2008 (SI 2008/2698) (as amended by the *Tribunal Procedure (Amendment) Rules* 2009 (SI 2009/274)).

63-000 Costs awards in the Upper Tribunal

Although the procedural rules in the Upper Tribunal are similar to those in the First-tier Tribunal outlined above, costs awards are different than those in the First-tier Tribunal.

Under r. 10, the Upper Tribunal may make a costs award in the following cases:

- in proceedings on appeal from the Tax Chamber of the First-tier Tribunal;
- in proceedings referred to the Upper Tribunal from the Tax Chamber of the First-tier Tribunal to the extent and in the circumstances that the First-tier Tribunal could have made an order in respect of costs (principally, in cases allocated to the complex case category where the opt-out has not been exercised by all the taxpayers);
- in judicial review proceedings;
- in cases involving wasted costs; and
- where the Upper Tribunal considers that a party or its representative has acted unreasonably in bringing, defending or conducting the proceedings.

Consideration of the financial means of a person having to pay the costs of an appeal is required only where the order for costs is made under r. 10(3)(a), (b) or (d) of the Upper Tribunal Rules. However, r. 10(1)(a), (4) gives the Upper Tribunal the normal discretion a decision maker usually has on the question of costs. Where costs have been increased due to the dilatory and inefficient conduct of the successful party, the tribunal may make a substantial reduction to the costs awarded.

Legislation: *Tribunal Procedure (Upper Tribunal) Rules* 2008 (SI 2008/2698), r. 10

Case: *Colquhoun v R & C Commrs* [2011] BTC 1,783

63-050 Judicial Review

Judicial review is a process that citizens can use to challenge decisions made by Government, either by Ministers, Government Departments, local authorities or other agencies that are acting on behalf of the state. It is generally commenced by an action in the High Court (or, in Scotland, in the Court of Session) and it highlights the fact that the Executive does not have supreme powers – where the executive acts unlawfully, the courts can intervene.

In the context of tax cases, judicial review will be an option where HMRC has made a decision that affects a taxpayer but where the taxpayer has no right of appeal. For example, a taxpayer cannot appeal against an information notice under FA 2008, Sch. 36 if the notice has already had the approval of the First-tier Tribunal. However, if a taxpayer believes that HMRC have not presented the full facts to the First-tier Tribunal, the taxpayer can seek the quashing of the notice under judicial review. In *Foulser*, the Upper Tribunal has held that a First-tier Tribunal has jurisdiction to deal with alleged abuses of process but not matters of public law competency.

Judicial review can also be an option where a taxpayer is given an assurance by HMRC about a proposed transaction and then HMRC subsequently change their mind, by which time the taxpayer has already acted in accordance with the previous assurance; for example, if a taxpayer were to seek a ruling about the VAT rate applicable to a particular transaction and HMRC advised the taxpayer that the transaction were zero rated. If, on a subsequent visit, HMRC were now to assert that the transaction should have been standard rated, the taxpayer might be able to argue the matter before the tribunal following the issue of an assessment. However, given that any assessment would be a breach of the taxpayer's legitimate expectations – the taxpayer can legitimately expect to rely upon a ruling by HMRC on the assumption that full disclosure had been made – the taxpayer could seek the quashing of the assessment, rather than argue the substantive point as to the correct rate of tax.

The Upper Tribunal has the power to hear judicial review cases instead of the High Court or the Court of Session. Where an application is made to the High Court, but it should have been made to the Upper Tribunal, the application will be transferred to the tribunal.

It is understood that such cases will be heard in the Administrative Appeals Chamber of the Upper Tribunal, rather than the Tax Chamber. However, this detail will be of little procedural consequence because the procedures are the same for all chambers in the Upper Tribunal and there will be very fluid transfer of personnel between the chambers.

Applying for permission

Applications can be made directly to the Upper Tribunal. In such cases (as with appeals to the Upper Tribunal and beyond), judicial review applications are a two-stage process: the applicant must first obtain permission to make the application (leave in Northern Ireland).

If permission (or leave) is refused, the applicant can then reapply at the Court of Appeal. (In those circumstances, the Court of Appeal can decide the substantive application (or remit the case to the tribunal and/or the High Court).)

If permission is granted by the Court of Appeal, the substantive case can be remitted to the Upper Tribunal or it can be dealt with by the Court of Appeal itself.

Legislation: TCEA 2007, s. 15, 16, 20; *Tribunal Procedure (Upper Tribunal) Rules* 2008 (SI 2008/2698), Pt. 4

Case: *Foulser v R & C Commrs* [2013] BTC 1,583

Collection and recovery

63-500 Recovery of unpaid tax

Unpaid tax may be recovered by the Crown in the following ways:

- by levying distress upon the lands or goods of the person in default (see 63-550);
- by action to recover the debt through court proceedings (see 63-600);
- by insolvency proceedings (see 63-650).

Any tax mistakenly repaid may be recovered (together with any repayment supplement included with the repayment) as if it were unpaid tax. The assessment is subject to the normal time-limits for assessment but will not be regarded as out of time if made before the later of:

- the end of the tax year following that in which the amount assessed was paid or repaid as the case may be; and
- the date when an enquiry is completed.

In addition, the restrictions on discovery assessments to recover loss of tax are applied to these assessments.

For the purposes of recovery, any penalty, surcharge or interest charged on overdue tax is treated as though due and payable under the assessment to which it relates.

Where a tax payment exceeding £5,000 is due and is not paid on time HMRC will make one telephone call to the taxpayer before embarking on legal action to recover the debt. Any taxpayer claiming cash-flow problems will have his history reviewed and will be expected to show that the bank will not lend any money. It will also be harder in future to obtain acceptance by HMRC of payment by instalments.

In circumstances where an HMRC determination in the absence of a return has become final, they may be persuaded to accept less than the full amount due under the law. This practice, known as 'equitable liability', depends on acceptable evidence being provided that the true liability is lower, and on the taxpayer's tax affairs being brought up to date.

From 1 April 2011, the former equitable liability concession is replaced by a new, statutory, special relief. HMRC have published an introduction to the new relief in HMRC Brief 17/11, with a link to further guidance. The relief is introduced by way of amendments to TMA 1970 by FA 1998.

Legislation: TMA 1970, s. 30 and Sch. 1AB; FA 1998, Sch. 18

Other Material: HMRC Tax Bulletin TB08/95-7; HMRC Brief 17/11

Websites: www.hmrc.gov.uk/briefs/income-tax/brief1711.htm; www.hmrc.gov.uk/briefs/income-tax/brief1711.htm; www.hmrc.gov.uk/briefs/income-tax/brief1711-sacm.pdf; www.hmrc.gov.uk/briefs/income-tax/brief1711-sacm.pdf

63-550 Business Payment Support Service

The Business Payment Support Service was launched following the 2008 Pre-Budget Report. From 24 November 2008, businesses which, because of the economic conditions, are having difficulty meeting payments due to HMRC can contact the Business Payment Support line with a view to agreeing a payment plan which meets the individual business' circumstances. By 19 April 2009, over 110,000 agreements had been reached with businesses suffering temporary difficulties worth almost £2bn.

The scope of the service

The Service is aimed at self-employed people and companies but can be used by any person who is having difficulty in meeting their tax liabilities. All of the main taxes, including income tax, corporation tax, VAT and PAYE are covered. However, only new enquiries, and not enquiries already being dealt with by HMRC prior to 24 November 2008, will be considered. In addition, the taxpayer must meet the following criteria in order to qualify to use the service:

- they must be in genuine difficulty;
- they must be unable to pay their tax on time;
- they must be likely to pay if allowed more time.

From April 2010, where a business applies for time to pay a debt of £1m plus, HMRC may require the business to engage, at its own expense, a suitably qualified professional adviser such as an insolvency practitioner, to carry out an independent business review (IBR) in support of its request. The review will include the current trading and financial position, profit and cashflow projections, business and financial strategies, management systems, and funding and banking arrangements.

HMRC will agree 'Time to Pay' arrangements on a case-by-case basis in order to bring the taxpayer back up-to-date on a timescale that is appropriate to the situation. Additional late payment surcharges will not be charged on payments included in the arrangement, although interest will continue to be payable on those taxes where it applies.

HMRC have confirmed that the purpose is to provide support for viable businesses with short-term cash flow difficulties and not to prop-up businesses that are likely to fail, putting further tax at risk.

All enquiries must be made through the Business Payment Support line (0300 200 3835) which is open Monday to Friday 8.00 a.m. to 8.00 p.m. and at weekends from 8.00 a.m. to 4.00 p.m. Further information is available on the HMRC website.

Information for agents

An agent can call the Business Payment Support line to discuss a client's affairs if they have authority to act on behalf of the client, either through a form 64-8 or an online agent authorisation. HMRC can agree a payment arrangement with the agent but may have to contact the client to set up payments through direct debit. Further guidance is available on the HMRC website.

Reviewing or extending the arrangements

If the circumstances of the taxpayer changes and they become unable to make the payments covered by the agreement they need to contact HMRC before they miss any payment. Provided HMRC are satisfied that the business continues to be viable, they will consider amending and extending the agreement.

Extension to the service announced on 22 April 2009

From 22 April 2009, extra help is available for businesses which have been profitable in recent years but which now expect to be loss-making. Businesses which qualify to use the service, those due to make an income tax or corporation tax payment in respect of the previous year's profits and expect to make a trading loss in the current year, will have this taken into account when a payment plan is offered. The business must be genuinely unable to pay immediately or enter into a reasonable Time to Pay arrangement.

A compliance officer will contact the taxpayer or agent to discuss why a loss for the current year is expected. It may also be necessary to submit supporting documentation.

It should be noted that:

- the loss can only be taken into account when considering Time to Pay for income tax or corporation tax liabilities and does not extend to VAT or PAYE;
- where a business has losses but is unable to enter into a Time to Pay arrangement, HMRC will only defer collection of the tax until the normal filing date for the return in which the loss is expected;
- if the loss turns out to be less than anticipated, the balance of any debt suspended will become payable when the current year return is submitted and the loss claim finalised. It will carry interest from the date it should have originally been paid.

Further guidance and Q&As can be found on the HMRC website.

Websites: www.hmrc.gov.uk/pbr2008/business-payment.htm; www.hmrc.gov.uk/budget2009/bus-payment-support-582.htm

Tax Reporter: ¶193-025

63-600 Court proceedings

Court proceedings to recover unpaid tax may be in the magistrates' court (in England, Wales and Northern Ireland), in the county court (or the sheriff court, in Scotland), or the High Court (the Court of Session sitting as the Court of Exchequer, in Scotland).

Magistrates' court

Tax which is less than £2,000 is recoverable summarily as a civil debt by proceedings in the magistrates' court commenced in the name of the collector.

All tax due from one person to any one collector, and which is recoverable summarily, may be included in the same complaint, summons, order, warrant or other document required by law to be laid before the justices.

Proceedings for the recovery of tax may be brought in England and Wales at any time within one year from the time when the matter complained of arose (the usual time-limit for bringing summary proceedings is six months from the time that the tax became due).

Legislation: TMA 1970, s. 65

County Court, High Court proceedings

Tax may be sued for as a debt due to the Crown. Tax may also be sued for and recovered in the High Court as a debt due to the Crown; unpaid tax and arrears may also be recovered with costs as a Crown debt in the High Court. The amount of an assessment cannot be reopened in the High Court in proceedings to collect the tax.

Certain types of county court proceedings require the leave of the county court or Court of Appeal judge before an appeal can be made to the Court of Appeal. Where the appeal concerns proceedings for the recovery of tax leave of a judge must be obtained if the value of the appeal does not exceed £5,000.

Legislation: TMA 1970, s. 66, 68

Cases: *IR Commrs v Pearlberg* 34 TC 57; *Soul v IR Commrs* 51 TC 86

Northern Ireland

In Northern Ireland, the jurisdiction of the county court is restricted to the county court limits.

Legislation: TMA 1970, s. 66(4); *High Court and County Courts Jurisdiction Order* 1991 (SI 1991/724)

Scotland

The provisions as to proceedings in magistrates' courts and county courts do not apply to Scotland. In Scotland, where the amount of tax due and payable does not exceed the sheriff court limit it may be sued for as a debt due to the Crown by proceedings commenced, in the name of a collector, in the sheriff court.

Tax may also be sued for and recovered as a debt due to the Crown in the Court of Session sitting as the Court of Exchequer.

Legislation: TMA 1970, s. 67, 68

63-650 Insolvencies

HMRC's policy is to take bankruptcy, etc. proceedings only where all other attempts to encourage payments of tax debts have failed.

It is not HMRC's usual practice to prove for penalties in insolvencies, since to do so would prejudice outside creditors. However, where it is the only substantial creditor and the available assets may prove more than enough to meet the tax claimed, it may well prove for penalties. Penalties which are eventually awarded against an insolvent person in proceedings commenced before the relevant date are provable in the bankruptcy.

Other Material: *Hansard*, 10 December 1992

Tax Reporter: ¶193-600

63-700 Tax due in other member states

HMRC are given powers to enable them to use collection procedures to recover tax due in another EU member state where a request is received under the mutual assistance recovery directive. Similarly the authorities in other member states may be requested to assist in the collection of UK tax.

Legislation contained in F(No. 3)A 2011, Sch. 25 implements EU Directive 2010/24/EU, covering mutual assistance arrangements between member states. It replaces and repeals the existing UK legislation implementing the current mutual assistance Directive as it relates to national and local taxes in England and Wales, and agricultural levies in England, Wales and Northern Ireland. The new Directive modernises and expands the scope of mutual assistance, and comes in to force on 1 January 2012.

Legislation: FA 2002, s. 134 and Sch. 39; F(No. 3)A 2011, Sch. 25; EU Directive 77/799; EU Directive 2010/24/EU

Tax Reporter: ¶103-825

63-750 Follower notices and accelerated payments

Follower notices and accelerated payments

Finance Act 2014 (FA 2014) introduced a radical new approach to the timing of the collection of tax where a taxpayer was perceived to have used 'aggressive' tax avoidance to either mitigate or delay the payment of tax. It had been argued for many years that certain taxpayers had entered into avoidance schemes in the full knowledge that, even if unsuccessful, the often lengthy litigation process would offer significant cash flow advantages.

FA 2014, Pt. 4 introduced the concepts of Follower Notices and Accelerated Payments. These are two separate but related strategies applied by HMRC to ensure that tax under dispute is held in Government coffers rather the bank accounts of taxpayers.

The provisions may be applied where 'tax arrangements' have been entered into, these are arrangements where the obtaining of a tax advantage was the main, or one of the main purposes of the arrangements.

Detailed commentary on how HMRC will apply the provisions is provided in guidance issued on 17 July 2014.

Although notifications under these provisions may not be issued before 17 July 2014, they are potentially applicable to any extant appeal or dispute regardless of whether the arrangements took place before that date.

Legislation: FA 2014, s. 199–203

Guidance: www.gov.uk/government/publications/follower-notices-and-accelerated-payments

Follower notices

A particular avoidance scheme may have many, often subtly different, variations. HMRC have claimed that despite successfully challenging one scheme version in the courts, other taxpayers have argued that their own version is sufficiently different to require entirely independent litigation with all of the incumbent delays and cost that this involves.

In order to address this problem, with effect from 17 July 2014, HMRC may issue a follower notice. This does not remove the taxpayer's rights to continue to argue the efficacy of their tax planning but failure to comply with a follower notice will expose the taxpayer to penalties.

The follower notice may be issued where, in the opinion of HMRC, a judicial ruling is relevant to a taxpayer's own arrangements. The notice must be issued within 12 months of the later of:

- the receipt of the judicial ruling; or
- the date a return, claim or tax appeal has been made in relation to the disputed tax.

In order to be a relevant ruling, then a judicial ruling must be final. This means that it will either be a ruling of the Supreme Court or of a lower court where no appeal has been made or has been refused.

The taxpayer in receipt of a follower notice has 90 days to make representations to HMRC to argue that the notice is not appropriate to their circumstances. The decision as to whether the notice will stand rests entirely with HMRC.

Legislation: FA 2014, s. 204–207

Transitional Provisions

Where a relevant judicial ruling arose before the passing of FA 2014 (17 July 2014), then HMRC may issue a follower notice within 24 months of passing of the Act.

Legislation: FA 2014, s. 217

Penalties

In order to avoid the issue of a penalty notice, a taxpayer in receipt of a follower notice must make the necessary corrective action. In effect, the corrective action involves the withdrawal of the taxpayer's open appeal and notification by the taxpayer to HMRC of the resultant tax liability.

Where the taxpayer fails to take the necessary corrective action within the 90-day notice period, then they will be subject to a penalty of up to 50% of the tax in dispute. HMRC have the discretion to reduce this to as low as 10% where the taxpayer has co-operated through the appeal.

In the case of a partnership's failure to comply with a follower notice, then the penalty percentages are between 20% and 4% but are applied to the amount of the reduction in the taxable income rather than the tax avoided.

Any penalty arising from failure to comply with a follower notice must be paid within 30 days of the issue of the penalty notice. The taxpayer similarly has 30 days within which they may appeal to the First-tier or Upper Tribunals against a penalty notice. It is noteworthy that the only matter that may be subject to an independent appeal is the issue of the penalty notice, not the follower notice itself.

Legislation: FA 2014, s. 208–210 and Sch. 30, 31

Tax Reporter: ¶192-764

Accelerated payments

The second limb of HMRC's efforts to collect tax subject to alleged tax avoidance is the accelerated payments regime.

Again, with effect from 17 July 2014, HMRC may issue an accelerated payment notice where a tax enquiry or appeal is in process and:

- HMRC have issued a follower notice in relation to the dispute;
- the tax arrangement is subject to the DOTAS regime; or
- a GAAR counteraction notice has been given in relation to all or part of the arrangement.

The amount payable under an accelerated payment notice is the understated tax, as determined by an HMRC officer acting to the best of that officer's information and belief.

The taxpayer in receipt of a notice has 90 days to make representations to HMRC that the notice is not in accordance with the relevant provisions. It is HMRC that will determine whether the notice will stand or should be withdrawn.

If no representations are made, then the tax determined is payable within 90 days of the issue of the notice. If a representation is made and rejected, then the tax is due on the later of 90 days from the date of the issue of the original notice and 30 days from the rejection.

Finance Act 2014, Sch. 32 makes provision for accelerated partner payments.

Legislation: FA 2014, s. 219–223

Penalties

Where the taxpayer fails to make the payments due under an accelerated payment notice, then a penalty of 5% of the outstanding tax will apply. Further 5% penalties will be applied if the corrective action is not taken five months and 11 months from the due date. There is a statutory right of appeal against the penalty notice but not the accelerated payment notice.

Legislation: FA 2014, s. 226

Tax Reporter: ¶192-765

63-850 Serial tax avoiders

With effect from 6 April 2017, a regime of warnings and escalating sanctions will be imposed on taxpayers who persistently engage in tax avoidance schemes which are defeated by HMRC. Following the first defeat, HMRC will warn the taxpayer that participation in any unsuccessful tax avoidance scheme in the subsequent five years will result in a penalty charge of up to 60% of any understated tax and the possible withdrawal of the entitlement to participate in certain relief. The regime will apply to all schemes entered into after 16 September 2016 together with earlier schemes that where not fully disclosed to HMRC before 5 April 2017.

Legislation: FA 2014, s. 237A

Criminal prosecutions

64-000 Overview

The fact that a taxpayer has incurred or may incur a civil penalty in respect of a particular infringement is no bar to his conviction by the ordinary criminal courts in respect of the same matter. However, on 1 September 2005, HMRC announced a new Civil Investigation of Fraud procedure, to be applied for both direct and indirect taxes. The procedure is set out in a new code of practice 'COP 9 (2005)'. Where HMRC decide to deal with the investigation as a civil matter, the taxpayer will be given a copy of COP 9 and he will be guaranteed not to be prosecuted for the alleged fraud. However, HMRC will reserve the right to prosecute where the taxpayer makes intentional false statements or provides false documents in the course of their disclosure.

In appropriate cases, up to April 2005, the Inland Revenue could institute criminal proceedings as a prosecuting authority in their own right in England and Wales, or via the Director of Public Prosecutions in Northern Ireland or the Procurator Fiscal in Scotland. With the merger of the Inland Revenue and Customs and Excise to form Her Majesty's Revenue and Customs (HMRC) in April 2005, the Revenue and Customs Prosecution Office (RCPO) was set up as an independent prosecuting authority for all Revenue and Customs cases. From 1 January 2010, the RCPO was merged with the Crown Prosecution Service (CPS). At that date, the Director of Public Prosecutions (DPP) was appointed as the Director of Revenue and Customs Prosecutions under *Commissioners for Revenue and Customs Act* (CRCA) 2005, s. 34(1) to exercise the functions of that office alongside those of the DPP. At the same time, the Revenue and Customs Division (RCD) was set up within the CPS to deal with Revenue and Customs prosecutions. The Director of RCPO became the Director of RCD within the merged prosecution service. The RCD was staffed by designated Revenue and Customs Prosecutors (CRCA 2005, s. 37) and other former staff of the RCPO who transferred to the RCD.

Since then, there has been a further reorganisation so that the RCD has now become a specialist work group within the CPS, the Central Fraud Group.

HMRC remain responsible for the investigation of potentially criminal matters and the decision to seek a financial settlement in lieu of prosecution but the CPS will take the decision on prosecution. Before the merger with the CPS, HMRC and the RCPO entered into a memorandum of understanding in accordance with which they would consult on a regular basis. The memorandum recorded that the Paymaster General (on behalf of the Treasury) and the Attorney General (on behalf of the RCPO) would consult on the development of a general prosecution policy, including the use of alternatives to prosecution after the commencement of criminal proceedings. The memorandum now applies between HMRC and the CPS.

Legislation: TMA 1970, s. 104

64-050 Fraudulently evading income tax

A person commits an offence if he is knowingly concerned in the fraudulent evasion of income tax by himself or another person.

If the offence is tried summarily (e.g. in a magistrates' court in England or Wales), the maximum penalty is a fine of £5,000 or six months in prison, or both. If the offence is tried on indictment (e.g. in the Crown Court in England or Wales), the fine is unlimited and the prison term can be up to seven years.

It might have been expected that the Taxes Acts, in their application to England and Wales, would somewhere criminalise the fraudulent evasion of all taxes falling within their scope (Scotland has long had a comparable offence: see 64-100). However, this is still not the case, given the offence's restriction to income tax.

HMRC have traditionally prosecuted some of the most serious tax frauds in the Crown Court, usually for the offence of cheating the public revenue (see 64-150). Unlike that offence, the offence of fraudulently evading income tax is a 'result', not a 'conduct', offence. In other words, tax must actually be lost (probably not necessarily permanently) before there can be a conviction for the full offence, though the defendant's failure to succeed might still result in a conviction for *attempting* to commit the offence.

There are other notable features of the offence. For example, the offence can apply not only to an errant taxpayer, but also to anyone who is knowingly concerned with the fraud. That could include a professional adviser, banker, spouse or business partner. Limited companies are 'persons' in law and are thus also exposed to liability for the offence. Further, whilst the overwhelming majority of serious criminal offences are aimed at (dishonest, disorderly or violent) *acts*, this offence also apparently criminalises knowing *omissions* (resulting in income tax evasion).

Legislation: FA 2000, s. 144(1), (3)

64-100 False statements (Scotland)

In Scotland, if a person:

- for the purpose of obtaining, for himself or another, an allowance, reduction, rebate or repayment in respect of income tax, capital gains tax or corporation tax; or
- in a 'return' made with reference to income tax, etc.,

knowingly makes a false statement or false representation, he is liable, on summary conviction, to imprisonment for up to six months.

Unlike the offence of fraudulently evading income tax, this offence appears limited to *acts* of falsity.

Proceedings may be commenced at any time within three years from the time when the offence was committed.

Legislation: TMA 1970, s. 107

64-150 Cheating the Revenue

Over the years, the ancient common law offence, commonly termed 'cheating the Revenue', has been charged in scores of cases of tax evasion. Although much of the offence's scope is now replicated in the statutory offence of fraudulently evading income tax, it continues to have relevance to the evasion of other taxes.

Cheating the Revenue is a 'conduct', not a 'result', offence so that, probably unlike the offence of evading income tax, it is not necessary to prove an actual loss of revenue: it suffices to prove deliberately fraudulent conduct to prejudice, or take the risk of prejudicing, the Crown's right to the tax in question.

Although in practice the submission of a false 'certificate of disclosure' is the usual starting-point for a prosecution for cheating the Revenue, there can be others. Thus, like the offence of fraudulently evading income tax, but unlike most other serious criminal offences, cheating the Revenue can be committed by 'omission or concealment', without a positive *act* of dishonesty or deception. A person can be convicted of cheating the Revenue not only where he dishonestly understates his taxable income, etc. but also where he dishonestly makes no statement of it at all.

The common law accordingly appears effectively to impose an immediate duty on a person who knows he has a tax liability to reveal that liability to HMRC. Although a similar *statutory* duty exists (see 50-000), this is merely enforced by monetary penalty, and periods of grace are allowed. The bearing which the statutory period of grace may have on a person's successful prosecution at common law for cheating by concealment has not been tested, and it seems highly unlikely that HMRC would prosecute, for cheating, a person who had made no statutory return of income, etc. and who had had no opportunity of completing a certificate of disclosure before expiry of the applicable statutory period of grace.

In summary, to be guilty of cheating the Revenue, a person must have:

- incurred a liability to tax;
- concealed that liability from HMRC; and
- realised that he would be regarded as dishonest by the standards of ordinary decent people.

Following a criminal conviction, the court may, in certain circumstances, make a confiscation order. This is limited, in a case of cheating the public revenue where full disclosure of income has not been made, to the underpayment of tax and does not extend to the whole of the undeclared income.

Tax Reporter: ¶194-200

64-200 Statutory offences of general application

On a charge of cheating the Revenue contrary to common law it would be no answer that the facts permitted a charge for a statutory offence, even a less serious one. There exist a number of such statutory offences which could be invoked in response to tax frauds. The most important of these is that of fraudulently evading income tax.

Some available charges relate to offences of general application. Thus the *Perjury Act* 1911, s. 5(b), imposes a maximum term of imprisonment of two years, or a fine or both on a person for knowingly or wilfully making a false statement in a statutory return. There are also a number of offences in the *Theft Acts* 1968–1978 which can be used: e.g. 'false accounting', and 'by deception dishonestly obtaining exemption from or abatement of liability to make payment'. False accounting charges are in fact the normal ones to be brought in prosecutions relating to the submission of false accounts. The *Forgery and Counterfeiting Act* 1981 also contains a number of relevant offences, and it is perhaps noteworthy that, under the forgery law which the 1981 Act replaced, it was no answer to a criminal charge that the false document submitted to the Revenue by the defendant accountant related to a genuine claim.

64-250 Falsifying or destroying documents

The intentional falsifying or destroying of documents, called for by HMRC under its information powers, is a criminal offence.

A person is guilty of an offence if he *intentionally* falsifies, conceals, destroys or otherwise disposes of, or causes or permits the falsification, concealment, destruction or disposal of, a 'document' which he has been required to deliver or make available for inspection by virtue of a notice issued under various statutory provisions.

The offence prohibits possibly as many as 12 different activities.

One of those prohibitions consists of intentionally 'causing' the *falsification* of the document, another of 'causing' the document's *concealment*, and so on.

Another of the prohibitions consists of intentionally *permitting* the falsification of the document. The High Court has held that a person can only 'permit' an activity if he is in a position to forbid it.

It should be noted that any person who incites, aids, abets, counsels or procures, agrees to or attempts the commission of any of the above offences is himself guilty of an offence, under general principles relating to criminal liability.

The offence is punishable on summary conviction with a fine not exceeding £5,000 or, on conviction on indictment, imprisonment for up to two years and/or an unlimited fine.

A 'document' is widely defined as anything in which information of any kind is recorded.

Legislation: TMA 1970, s. 20BB(1)

64-300 Secondary participation in offences

A practitioner or other person who 'aids, abets, counsels or procures' the main offender's offence is liable to the same punishment, etc. as the main offender. Alternatively, each can be prosecuted for conspiring together to cheat and defraud HMRC, or to falsify accounts, or whatever.

It is also an offence for a practitioner or other person, without lawful authority or reasonable excuse, to do any act with intent to impede the apprehension or prosecution of any other person he knows or believes to be guilty of an 'arrestable' offence. An arrestable offence, broadly, is one carrying at least five years' imprisonment: an example would be cheating the Revenue.

Legislation: *Criminal Law Act* 1967, s. 4(1); *Police and Criminal Evidence Act* 1984, s. 24(1)

Disclosure of tax avoidance schemes

66-000 Background

Finance Act 2004 introduced an early warning system in respect of tax avoidance schemes. The objective is to give HMRC earlier and better intelligence on avoidance schemes in order that they can take action much earlier than before. 'Promoters' of avoidance schemes (see 66-600), and in some cases, the taxpayers themselves (see 66-750), are now obliged to make disclosure of specific information within five days of the scheme being made available by the promoter, or implemented by the taxpayer. HMRC will therefore be aware of the scheme before it has been put to any widespread use.

It should be stressed that nothing in these provisions will nullify the effect of the schemes notified; they will either succeed or fail on the basis of the legislation applicable at the time the transactions were effected. All these provisions achieve is to require a return of the transactions substantially earlier than the self-assessment return.

The regulations specify a number of descriptions or 'hallmarks' which, if possessed by an arrangement, will identify it as notifiable.

Other Material: HMRC Guidance: www.gov.uk/government/uploads/system/uploads/attachment_data/file/560047/dotas-guidance.pdf

66-050 The reporting requirement generally

Reporting obligations arise in respect of 'notifiable arrangements' which are defined as any arrangement:

- which will, or might be expected to, enable a person to obtain a tax advantage;
- where that tax advantage is, or might be expected to be, the main benefit or one of the main benefits of the arrangement;
- where it is a 'hallmarked' scheme by being a tax arrangement that falls within any of the hallmarks prescribed in the regulations.

Reporting obligations also arise in respect of proposals for such arrangements which, if implemented, would then become a notifiable arrangement.

There are four specific reporting obligations.

(1) Where an avoidance scheme falling within the regulations has been offered to an end-user, the promoter must supply 'prescribed information' (see 66-800) to HMRC within five days.

(2) The promoter must also provide that information within five days of first becoming aware that any transaction forming part of the scheme has been carried out.

(3) Where the promoter is not UK resident, the scheme user must provide the information within five days of entering into the first transaction that forms part of the scheme.

(4) Where there is no promoter either in the UK or elsewhere, the scheme user is charged with providing the information within 30 days of the scheme being implemented.

The regulations set out a series of hallmarks, any one of which, if possessed by any arrangement, will bring it within the scope of the disclosure regime. These hallmarks may be summarised as:

- Confidentiality: where promoters are involved (see 66-150);
- Confidentiality: large businesses designing 'in-house' arrangements (see 66-200);
- Where a 'premium fee' could be charged by a promoter (see 66-250);
- 'Standardised tax products' (see 66-350);
- Income tax and capital gains tax loss schemes (see 66-400);
- Leasing arrangements (see 66-450);
- Employment income (see 66-480);
- Financial products (see 66-490).

HMRC have published consolidated guidance on disclosure of tax avoidance schemes related to income tax, corporation tax, capital gains tax, National Insurance contributions (NICs), stamp duty land tax and inheritance tax. The guidance is available on the HMRC website.

Legislation: FA 2004, s. 306–310; *Tax Avoidance Schemes (Prescribed Descriptions of Arrangements) Regulations* 2004 (SI 2004/1863), reg. 4; *Tax Avoidance Schemes (Prescribed Description of Arrangements) Regulations* 2006 (SI 2006/1543)

Other Material: HMRC booklet, *Disclosure of Tax Avoidance Schemes*

Website: www.hmrc.gov.uk/aiu/dotas-guidance.pdf

66-150 The confidentiality hallmark: promoters

Arrangements will be notifiable if an element of the arrangements is expected to give rise to an intended tax advantage and either:

(a) there is a 'reasonable expectation' that a promoter (see 66-600) of the same or a similar scheme would wish to keep confidential from any competitors how that element of the arrangements gives rise to the expected tax advantage; or

(b) the promoter, if he was not otherwise obliged to disclose the arrangements, would wish to keep confidential from HMRC how that element gives rise to the tax advantage. The reason for that wish being to enable repeated use of that element in the future. (Where there is no promoter or the promoter is a non-resident, this test is whether the scheme user would wish to keep that element confidential from HMRC for the same reason.)

It needs to be noted that the first test, (a) above, is a question of what a hypothetical promoter would wish, whereas the second, (b) is a question of what the actual promoter would wish, in both cases in the absence of any compulsion to make early disclosure.

A common factor to both tests is that this desire for confidentiality has to exist at any point from the date of the first transaction forming part of the arrangements to the date when the end-user files the tax return reporting details of the arrangements.

Where the promoter requires the user or his advisers to sign a confidentiality agreement to prevent them disclosing details to its competitors, then the arrangement would likely to be notifiable. However, HMRC in their guidance notes have said that if notwithstanding any confidentiality undertaking the scheme is 'reasonably well-known in the tax community' and can be evidenced by reference to articles, textbooks, etc., then a confidentiality agreement would not be evidence of this hallmark.

Legislation: SI 2006/1543, reg. 6

66-200 The confidentiality hallmark: 'in-house' schemes

Where the scheme has been designed 'in-house' for use by a business which is not a small or medium-sized enterprise, the arrangements will be notifiable if that business wishes to keep confidential from HMRC details of how any element of the arrangements achieves the expected tax advantage for any part of the period from the date of the first transaction forming part of the arrangements until the time when it is required to report the arrangements to HMRC.

Application of the hallmark is limited to companies which have 250 employees or more, and have an annual turnover of at least €50m or, alternatively, net assets of at least €43m. Although this may seem a generous concession to smaller companies, it is probably unlikely that they would have an in-house tax department anyway and would source any tax avoidance schemes from a promoter which may be notifiable under the first hallmark.

Legislation: SI 2006/1543, reg. 7

66-250 The premium fee hallmark

An arrangement will be hallmarked under this heading if it 'might reasonably be expected' that a hypothetical promoter of the same or a similar scheme would be able to obtain a 'premium fee' from 'a person experienced in receiving services of the kind provided'. In other words, a sophisticated consumer of tax advice would happily pay a hypothetical promoter of the same or a similar scheme, a premium fee.

There is however no quantitative test of a premium fee for these purposes. It is defined by the regulations as one which is chargeable by virtue of any element of the arrangements which give rise to the tax advantage and must also be either attributable to that advantage to a significant extent (say, a percentage of the tax saving) or contingent on obtaining that advantage.

Legislation: SI 2006/1543, reg. 8

66-350 Standardised tax products

This hallmark applies to 'off-the-peg' arrangements having standardised documentation which is not tailored to any significant extent to any individual user. The arrangements must require the user to enter into specific standardised transactions and will be a 'tax product' if an 'informed observer' could reasonably conclude that main purpose of the arrangement was to obtain a tax advantage. Stated in such terms, this would catch a number of approved savings and investment schemes and therefore specific exemptions are granted for such arrangements as:

- EIS and VCT investments;
- leasing agreements for machinery and plant;
- ISAs;
- approved share incentive and share option plans;
- registered pension schemes;
- community investment tax relief.

Legislation: SI 2006/1543, reg. 10, 11

66-400 Loss schemes

This hallmark is aimed at arrangements marketed by promoters to individuals where the main benefit is expected to be the creation of tax losses, either for income tax or capital gains tax.

Legislation: SI 2006/1543, reg. 12

66-450 Leasing arrangements

This hallmark covers schemes involving the long-term leasing of major items of plant and equipment (costing over £10m for any single item or over £25m in total). Long term in this context is a period which exceeds or might be extended to exceed, two years. In view of the values mentioned, it is restricted to arrangements where the tax advantage accrues to a large business.

For the arrangement to be hallmarked, one of three additional conditions needs to be satisfied:

- one party to the lease is able to claim capital allowances and another (usually the lessor) is not within the charge to UK corporation tax;
- under the terms of the lease the lessor is relieved from the greater part of the risk of the lessee defaulting on payments; or
- the scheme includes a sale and leaseback or a lease and leaseback (subject to exemption where the plant and machinery is new or less than four months old at the time it is sold).

Legislation: SI 2006/1543, reg. 13, 14

66-480 Employment income

Effective from 4 November 2013, this hallmark covers arrangements that by way of the inclusion of one or more contrived or abnormal steps seek to reduce or eliminate income that would otherwise be treated as employment income under the anti-avoidance provisions of ITEPA 2003, Pt. 7 (disguised remuneration).

Legislation: *Tax Avoidance Schemes (Prescribed Descriptions of Arrangements) Regulations* 2006 (SI 2006/1543), reg. 18

66-490 Financial products

Effective from 23 February 2016, this hallmark will apply where conditions 1 and 2 below are met together with either of conditions 3 or 4. A 'financial product' in this context includes:

(a) a loan;

(b) a share;

(c) a derivative contract;

(d) a repo;

(e) a stock lending arrangement;

(f) an alternative finance arrangement.

Condition 1 is that the arrangement includes a financial product.

Condition 2 requires that the main benefit or one of the main benefits of the arrangements is to give rise to a tax advantage.

Condition 3 is that the financial product contains at least one term which is unlikely to be entered into were it not for the tax advantage.

Condition 4 is that the arrangements contain one or more contrived steps without which the tax advantage would not arise.

The potentially very wide range of this hallmark has been much criticised. HMRC's published guidance provides useful examples of where the provisions are likely to apply.

Legislation: *Tax Avoidance Schemes (Prescribed Descriptions of Arrangements) Regulations* 2006 (SI 2006/1543), reg. 19

66-600 Promoters

The initial responsibility for notification lies with a 'promoter'. As notifications are required for both the initial proposal and the arrangement when implemented, it is possible to be a promoter at either stage and, indeed, for there to be multiple promoters.

In summary, there are a number of categories of persons who are to be regarded as promoters (but subject to exclusions to be discussed later):

(1) designers of the proposal;

(2) anyone making a firm approach to another person with a view to making a notifiable proposal available for implementation by that other person or by anyone else;

(3) anyone making a scheme available for implementation by others;

(4) anyone organising or managing the implementation of the scheme.

In practice, promoters often market schemes through 'introducers', persons whose role is to introduce potential clients to the promoter.

FA 2004, s. 307(1A) therefore includes a definition of 'introducer' as someone who, in relation to a notifiable proposal makes marketing contact with another person in relation to the notifiable proposal.

The detailed definition of a promoter or introducer is someone who:

(1) carries on a 'relevant business', being:

   (a) a business which involves the provision of 'services relating to taxation'; or

   (b) a business as a bank or as a securities house;

(2) in the case of a notifiable proposal:

   (a) is to any extent responsible for the design of the proposal; or

   (b) makes it available to others (i.e. markets the proposal which has been designed by others);

(3) in the case of a notifiable arrangement:

   (a) is already a promoter of the original proposal by virtue of marketing it;

   (b) is to any extent responsible for the design of the arrangements; or

   (c) is to any extent responsible for the organisation and management of the arrangements;

(4) in the case of a proposal/arrangement in respect of which no notification has been received and where HMRC have reasonable grounds for believing a proposal/arrangement *may* be notifiable and have applied to the tribunal for an order to that effect, the person who would be regarded as the promoter if the proposal/arrangements were notifiable.

For these purposes, a person 'makes a firm approach' to another person in relation to a notifiable proposal if the person makes a marketing contact with the other person in relation to the notifiable proposal at a time when the proposed arrangements have been substantially designed. A person makes a marketing contact with another person in relation to a notifiable proposal if:

(a) they communicate information about the notifiable proposal to another person;

(b) the communication is made with a view to that person, or any other person, entering into transactions forming part of the proposed arrangements; and

(c) the information communicated includes an explanation of the tax advantages that might be expected to be obtained from the proposed arrangements.

This covers communication of a general nature both to persons who may wish to use the scheme, and to intermediaries or introducers who may in turn communicate it to a potential user.

Transactions have been 'substantially designed' if the nature of the transactions has been sufficiently developed for it to be reasonable to believe that a person who wished to obtain the tax advantage might enter into:

(a) transactions of the nature developed; or

(b) transactions not substantially different from transactions of that nature

(FA 2004, s. 307(1), (1A), (2), (6)).

However these categories are subject to a number of exclusions prescribed by regulations and which are discussed below under the heading 'Exclusions'.

Legislation: FA 2004, s. 307(1), (2); *Tax Avoidance Schemes (Promoter and Prescribed Circumstances) Regulations* 2004 (SI 2004/1865)

Exclusions

The regulations exclude from the definition of promoter:

(1) a company carrying on a relevant business providing services to a fellow group member; (a group in this context is the subject of a special definition);

(2) an individual who is an employee, or an office holder, of a promoter or of the person entering into any transaction forming part of the notifiable arrangements. Where the individual is an employee, etc. of a person connected with the promoter or end-user, they are treated for these purposes as an employee of that promoter/end-user and therefore within this exclusion. This exclusion will not apply where there are no other promoters resident in the UK;

(3) a person who would otherwise be a promoter by virtue of being a 'designer', if either:

   (a) he is not responsible for the design of any part of the tax avoidance element of the proposal or arrangement (termed by HMRC the 'benign tax adviser' test);

   (b) although carrying on a business which involves providing services in relation to taxation, he does not actually provide tax advice in relation to the proposal/arrangements (termed the 'non-tax adviser' test); or

(c) he was not responsible for the design of all the tax avoidance elements of the proposal/arrangements and could not reasonably be expected to have sufficient information to know that they were notifiable or to be able to supply the prescribed information (termed the 'ignorance' test);

(4) a person who would otherwise be a promoter by virtue of being responsible for the organisation/management of the arrangements but who is not connected with another person who is a designer or marketer of those arrangements, or substantially similar arrangements;

(5) any person who is prevented from providing all the required information because it is 'privileged information', as a result of legal professional privilege (in England and Wales) or confidentiality of communications (in Scotland).

HMRC's guidance notes set out their interpretation of these exclusions on p. 19–21. Their comments on the tests they term 'benign tax advice', 'non-tax adviser' and 'ignorance' will be of particular interest to tax advisers.

Legislation: FA 2004, s. 314; *Tax Avoidance Schemes (Promoter and Prescribed Circumstances) Regulations* 2004 (SI 2004/1865), reg. 3–6

Website: HMRC Guidance Notes: www.gov.uk/government/uploads/system/uploads/attachment_data/file/560047/dotas-guidance.pdf

66-650 Obligations of promoters

The promoter is charged with the obligation to supply HMRC 'prescribed information' (see 66-850):

- in respect of a notifiable proposal – within the five days following the earliest of the date on which the promoter first makes a firm approach to another person in relation to a notifiable proposal, the date he makes a notifiable proposal available for implementation by another person, or the date on which he first becomes aware that a transaction has taken place which forms part of the implementation of that proposal;
- in respect of notifiable arrangements – within the five days following the date on which he first becomes aware that a transaction has taken place which forms part of those arrangements. However, no notification is required if notification has been given in respect of a notifiable proposal which the arrangements are simply putting into effect.

Legislation: FA 2004, s. 308(1)–(3); *Tax Avoidance Schemes (Information) Regulations* 2004 (SI 2004/1864), reg. 4(2); *Tax Avoidance Schemes (Information) (Amendment) Regulations* 2009 (SI 2009/611)

Multiple promoters

Where more than one person is a promoter in relation to a notifiable proposal or arrangement, compliance by any one of them will discharge the duty of the others. In such a situation it is clearly advisable for the promoters to agree amongst themselves, if possible, who is to comply with the obligation. Failing such agreement, it is in their own interests to make independent notifications.

Finance Act 2008 amends the rule where more than one person is a promoter, so that a promoter (P2) will only be discharged of the duty to disclose a scheme to HMRC if:

- another promoter (P1) has disclosed the scheme, or a scheme substantially the same, to HMRC;
- P1 has notified HMRC of P2's identity and address, or P2 holds the scheme reference number allocated to the scheme by HMRC; and
- P2 holds a copy of P1's disclosure.

Legislation: FA 2004, s. 308(4); FA 2008, s. 116 and Sch. 38

Publication by HMRC

FA 2004, s. 316C provides HMRC with the power to make public specific information in relation to schemes and promoters. This includes details of the disclosed schemes, the number of participators in the scheme and the scheme promoter.

66-665 Information provided to introducers

As a result of changes introduced by *Finance Act* 2010, Sch. 17, where HMRC suspect that a person is an introducer (see 66-600) in relation to a proposal and that the proposal may be notifiable, they can require that person, by way of a written notice specifying the proposal to which it relates, to provide within the prescribed period or such longer time as HMRC may direct, prescribed information about each person who provided any information relating to the proposal.

The other person who has provided the introducer with information about the scheme is likely to be the promoter of the scheme, but in some cases may be a further intermediary.

'Prescribed' means as specified by HMRC by regulation.

Legislation: FA 2010, Sch. 17; FA 2004, s. 313C, 318(1)

66-680 Duty to provide details of clients

Finance Act 2010, Sch. 17 imposed a duty on promoters to provide details about clients in certain circumstances. The requirement applies where a promoter is providing (or has provided) services to any person ('the client') in connection with the notifiable arrangements and either the promoter:

(a) is subject to the reference number information requirement (that is, the requirement under s. 312(2) to provide to the client prescribed information relating to the reference number allocated to the notifiable arrangements); or

(b) has failed to comply with s. 308(1) or (3) in relation to the notifiable arrangements (or the notifiable proposal for them) but would be subject to the reference number information requirement if a reference number had been allocated to the notifiable arrangements.

Unless HMRC have given notice under s. 312(6) that the promoter is no longer required to provide clients with SRN information, the promoter must, within the prescribed period after the end of the relevant period, provide HMRC with prescribed information in relation to the client. The 'relevant period' is the period during which the promoter is or would be subject to the reference number information requirement as is prescribed.

'Prescribed' means prescribed by regulations made by HMRC. It is expected that:

- the 'prescribed information' will be the names and addresses of clients;
- the 'relevant period' will be each calendar quarter; and
- the 'prescribed period' will be 14 days.

Promoters will therefore be required to provide HMRC with lists of clients who have implemented a scheme and have been issued with a SRN each calendar quarter, and to do so within 14 days of the end of the quarter.

Section 11A of HMRC's guidance on the Disclosure of Tax Avoidance Schemes (DOTAS) provides more detail on how to submit client lists. The updated section is available on the HMRC website.

Legislation: FA 2010, Sch. 17; FA 2004, s. 308, 312, 313ZA, 318(1)

Website: www.hmrc.gov.uk/avoidance/client-lists.pdf

66-700 The scheme user

The obligations imposed on promoters apply regardless of whether they are UK resident or not. Arguably, however, the obligation is unenforceable against a non-resident who has no 'presence' in this country. Therefore where a non-resident promoter does not comply with his obligation, it is necessary to have some alternate upon whom the obligation can be placed and that is the scheme user.

Similarly where arrangements have been designed 'in-house', so that there is no promoter (and any group member who may otherwise be classed as a promoter is excluded from being one by regulations), the obligation again devolves onto the scheme user.

Legislation: FA 2004, s. 309, 310; *Tax Avoidance Schemes (Promoter and Prescribed Circumstances) Regulations* 2004 (SI 2004/1865), reg. 2

66-750 Obligations of scheme users

In a situation where either all persons who are promoters are resident outside the UK, or where there are no promoters at all (because the arrangements have been designed in-house), the obligation to notify devolves onto the scheme user. The date by which that notification has to be given depends upon why that obligation has devolved onto the scheme user:

(1) where the promoter(s) are non-resident, the 'prescribed information' has to be notified within the five days following the day the scheme user enters into the first transaction forming part of the arrangements. However if, despite being non-resident, a promoter gives notification of the proposal/arrangements, the scheme user's duty is considered to have been discharged;

(2) where, with effect from 14 October 2004, there is no promoter as a result of the real promoter being excluded from that definition because of legal professional privilege, the scheme user has to notify the 'prescribed information' within the five days following the day on which he enters into the first transaction forming part of the arrangements; and

(3) where no promoters are involved, the prescribed information has to be notified within 30 days of the day the scheme user enters into the first transaction forming part of the arrangements.

Legislation: FA 2004, s. 309, 310; *Tax Avoidance Schemes (Information) Regulations* 2004 (SI 2004/1864), reg. 4(4), (5); *Tax Avoidance Schemes (Information) (Amendment) Regulations* 2009 (SI 2009/611); *Tax Avoidance Schemes (Promoters and Prescribed Circumstances) Regulations* (SI 2004/1865), reg. 6

66-800 Entries to be made on returns

The scheme user is required to notify:

- the scheme reference number as notified by the promoter, or HMRC where there is no UK resident promoter; and
- the tax year or accounting period in which, or the specific date on which the tax advantage is expected to be obtained.

The information has to be notified in the self-assessment returns for:

- the tax year or accounting period (as appropriate) in which the scheme reference number was notified by the promoter (or HMRC, as the case may be), or, if earlier, the tax year or accounting period in which the tax advantage is expected to arise; and
- every subsequent year or accounting period until the tax advantage ceases.

In the case of partnerships, the information must be provided in both the partnership return and the self-assessment returns of the partners who are expected to obtain the tax advantage.

Where the advantage is expected to arise in respect of employment arrangements, the information has to be notified in the employer's end-of-year return:

- for the tax year in which the employer is notified of the scheme registration number by the promoter, or HMRC (as the case may be), or, if earlier, the tax year in which the advantage is expected to arise; and
- for each subsequent tax year until the advantage ceases.

Where a person is obliged to notify HMRC of the prescribed information, but is not otherwise required to submit a self-assessment return, partnership return or end of year return (as the case may be), that person must nevertheless supply that information by the date by which he would have had to file the appropriate return if he had been obliged to do so. In such a case, the required information is specified as:

- the name and address of the provider of the information;
- the NI number, tax reference number, PAYE reference number or any other personal identifier of the scheme user;
- the scheme reference number as provided by the promoter or the board;
- the name of the individual providing the declaration as to the accuracy and completeness of the notification; and
- the capacity in which that individual is acting.

HMRC have produced form AAG4 for reporting information in cases where the scheme user is not otherwise required to file an appropriate return. It is available on HMRC's website.

Whereas the self-assessment returns, partnership returns and forms P35 would be submitted to the usual offices, form AAG 4 should be submitted to:

Avoidance Intelligence Unit

1st Floor South

22 Kingsway

London WC2B 6NR

Provision is also made for the notification to be made by electronic delivery.

Legislation: *Tax Avoidance Schemes (Information) Regulations* 2004 (SI 2004/1864), reg. 8, 10; *Tax Avoidance Schemes (Information) (Amendment) Regulations* 2009 (SI 2009/611)

Website: www.hmrc.gov.uk/aiu.index.htm

66-850 The prescribed information

The prescribed information to be notified by a promoter has been specified as sufficient information as might reasonably be expected to enable HMRC to comprehend the manner in which the proposal, or arrangements, as the case may be, is, or are, intended to operate. In particular, the following information is required:

- the promoter's name and address;
- the regulations by virtue of which the proposal, or arrangements (as the case may be) is, or are, notifiable;
- a summary of the proposal or arrangements and any name by which it, or they, are known;
- an explanation of each element of the arrangement or proposed arrangements and the way in which they are structured, from which the tax advantage is expected to arise; and
- the statutory provisions on which the expected tax advantage is based.

Scheme users when required to provide prescribed information must supply all the above plus their own name and address.

HMRC have produced forms (AAG 1 for promoters together with AAG 2 and AAG 3 for scheme users), which are available on their website, for use in complying with these obligations.

HMRC advise that the forms should be sent to:

Avoidance Intelligence Unit
1st Floor South
22 Kingsway
London WC2B 6NR

Provision is also made for notification of the information to be made by electronic delivery.

Once HMRC have been notified of the prescribed information, they 'may', within 30 days, allocate a reference number to that proposal or arrangement and must notify the promoter of that reference; the HMRC guidance notes say they 'will' issue a reference number to a promoter within 30 days. The promoter then has a further duty to notify that reference to the end-user of the arrangements within 30 days of the later of the date on which HMRC notify him of the reference, or the date the promoter first becomes aware of any transaction forming part of the notifiable arrangements.

Finance Act 2008, s. 116 and Sch. 38 extend the duty of HMRC to notify not only the promoter but also any co-promoter who has been identified to HMRC (see 66-650).

The promoter's duty to notify the client to whom he is providing services in connection with notifiable arrangements will be extended to cases where the promoter has ceased to provide services by the later of the date on which the reference is notified to the promoter, or the date the promoter first becomes aware of any transaction forming part of the notifiable arrangements. This is to cover cases where the reference may be notified by another promoter rather than by HMRC.

The changes made by *Finance Act* 2008, s. 116 and Sch. 38 also imposed duties on a client of a promoter of a notifiable scheme to notify the reference to any other person he knows either is, or is likely to be, a party to the scheme who might be expected to obtain a tax advantage. This must be done within 30 days from the date the client becomes aware of any transaction involving the other party, or the date the reference is notified to the client if later.

Finance Act 2008 changes took effect on 1 November 2008. FA 2015, Sch. 17 stipulated that this obligation extended to the provision of information by employers implementing schemes on behalf of their employees.

The guidance notes also indicate that scheme users providing prescribed information will be told if no reference number is to be issued. In the case of in-house arrangements, no reference will normally be issued.

Legislation: FA 2004, s. 311(1), 312, 312A; FA 2008, s. 116 and Sch. 38; *Tax Avoidance Schemes (Information) Regulations* 2004 (SI 2004/1864), reg. 3(1)–(4), 10; *Tax Avoidance Schemes (Information) (Amendment) Regulations* 2009 (SI 2009/611)

Website: www.hmrc.gov.uk/aiu.index.htm

66-900 Penalties

The penalty provisions in TMA 1970, s. 98C for failing to comply with duties relating to disclosure of avoidance schemes were amended by FA 2010, s. 56 and Sch. 17. The new penalty regime came into effect on 1 January 2011.

The penalty regime post 1 January 2011

The penalties chargeable are as follows.

Failures to comply with s. 308–310

A person who fails to make a notification required by:

- section 308(1) and (3) (duty of promoter in relation to notifiable proposals and notifiable arrangements);
- section 309(1) (duty of person dealing with promoter outside United Kingdom);
- section 310 (duty of parties to notifiable arrangements not involving promoter),

will be liable for a penalty not exceeding:

- £600 for each day during the initial period (but see *Failure where order issued* below); and
- if the failure continues after a penalty is imposed for the initial period, to a further penalty not exceeding £600 for each day on which the failure continues after the day on which the penalty for the initial period was imposed (but excluding any day for which a penalty has already been imposed.

For these purposes, the 'initial period' means the period:

(a) beginning with the relevant day; and

(b) ending with the earlier of the day on which the penalty for the initial period is determined and the last day before the failure ceases.

The 'relevant day' is the day specified in relation to the failure in the following table.

Failure	Relevant day
A failure to comply with s. 308(1) or (3) in so far as the subsection applies by virtue of an order under s. 306A	The first day after the end of the period prescribed under s. 306A(6)
A failure to comply with s. 308(1) or (3) in so far as the subsection applies by virtue of an order under s. 308A(2)	The first day after the end of the period prescribed under s. 308A(5) and (6)(a) (as it may have been extended by a direction under subs. (6)(b) of that section)
Any other failure to comply with s. 308(1)	The first day after the end of the period prescribed under that subsection
Any other failure to comply with s. 308(3)	The first day after the end of the period prescribed under that subsection
A failure to comply with s. 309(1)	The first day after the end of the period prescribed under that subsection
A failure to comply with s. 310	The first day after the latest time by which s. 310 must be complied with in the case concerned

The amount of a penalty for the initial period is to be arrived at after taking account of all relevant considerations, including the desirability of its being set at a level which appears appropriate for deterring the person, or other persons, from similar failures to comply on future occasions having regard (in particular) to:

- in the case of a penalty for a person's failure to comply with s. 308(1) or (3), the amount of any fees received, or likely to have been received, by the person in connection with the notifiable proposal; and
- in the case of a penalty for a person's failure to comply with s. 309(1) or 310, to the amount of any advantage gained, or sought to be gained, by the person in relation to any tax prescribed under s. 306(1)(b).

If the maximum penalty for the initial period above appears inappropriately low after taking account of those considerations, the penalty can be increased to an amount not exceeding £1m as appears appropriate having regard to those considerations.

Failures to comply with s. 312–313C

A person who fails to make a notification required by:

- section 312(2) (duty of promoter to notify client of reference number);
- section 312A(2) (duty of client to notify parties of reference number);

- section 313ZA (duty of promoter to provide details of clients);
- sections 313A and 313B (duty of promoter to respond to inquiry); or
- section 313C (duty of introducer to give details of persons who have provided information),

will be liable for an initial penalty not exceeding £5,000. If the failure continues after an initial penalty has been imposed, there will be liability to a further penalty or penalties not exceeding £600 for each day on which the failure continues after the day on which the penalty was imposed (but excluding any day for which a penalty under this paragraph has already been imposed).

Failure where order issued
Where the failure is in respect of a proposal/arrangement in respect of which an order under FA 2004, s. 306A has been issued, the daily penalty is to be £5,000 per day.

Similarly, in a case where an order to disclose has been issued, the daily penalty for the days following the tenth day from the making of the order is to be increased to £5,000 per day.

Legislation: TMA 1970, s. 96C(4), 98C, 98C(2A) and 98C(2B); FA 2004, s. 313(4); FA 2010, s. 56 and Sch. 17; *Tax Avoidance Schemes (Penalties) Regulations* 2007 (SI 2007/3104), reg. 3; *Tax Avoidance Schemes (Information) (Amendment) (No. 2) Regulations* 2007 (SI 2007/3101)

Money laundering

67-000 Background

In Directive 91/308 of 10 June 1991 on 'the prevention of the use of the financial system for the purpose of money laundering', money laundering was defined as being four types of intentional conduct:

(1) the conversion or transfer of property knowingly derived from 'criminal activity', with a view to concealing its illicit origin or to assist another to avoid the legal consequences of his actions;

(2) the concealing of information relating to property which is know to be derived from 'criminal activity' or the disguising of the true facts about the property;

(3) acquiring, possessing or using property knowing that it was derived from 'criminal activity'; or

(4) aiding and abetting anyone to commit any of the actions mentioned above.

'Criminal activity' was narrowly defined as a crime specified in art. 3(1)(a) of the 'Vienna Convention' (the full title being the United Nations Convention Against Illicit Traffic in Narcotic Drugs and Psychotropic Substances), and 'any other criminal activity designated as such for the purpose of this Directive by each Member State'. Basically, therefore, 'criminal activity' was confined to drug trafficking. The directive required member states to oblige credit and financial institutions to obtain evidence of identity from new customers and to report to the authorities facts which might be indicative of money laundering. The directive was implemented into UK domestic legislation by the *Criminal Justice Act* 1993 by amendment to the *Criminal Justice Act* 1988.

As far as the tax adviser was concerned, this created criminal offences for assisting someone to retain the proceeds of criminal conduct or to conceal, disguise, convert or transfer those proceeds. As permitted by the directive, 'criminal conduct' was largely defined in terms of drug trafficking but also included offences relating to terrorism, pirate videos, sex establishments and unlicensed cinemas. The Act was supplemented by the *Money Laundering Regulations* 1993 (SI 1993/1933) which imposed obligations on persons engaged in 'relevant financial business' (defined in terms of financial services and banking). They were obliged to establish specified procedures for the purpose of forestalling and identifying money laundering and for reporting suspicions to the National Criminal Intelligence Service, now the Serious Organised Crime Agency (SOCA). Therefore, unless tax advisers were also handling and investing client moneys they were largely unaffected by these provisions, unless they suspected drug trafficking or terrorism, etc. The *Terrorism Act* 2000, subsequently amended by the *Anti-Terrorism, Crime and Security Act* 2001, made it an offence not to report information which a person came upon in the course of their trade, profession, business or employment, which led them to believe, or suspect, that another person had committed an offence under the Act. The reporting obligation was extended to those in the 'regulated sector', who should have had reasonable grounds for believing or suspecting that an offence had occurred. Initially the regulated sector was again defined in terms of financial services and banking but amendments made in 2001 brought the giving of tax advise, accounting and audit services within the sector from 1 March 2004. From that date tax advisers were liable to a maximum of five years imprisonment and a fine for failing to comply with the disclosure requirements under the Act.

In December 2001, the European Parliament and the Council of the EU adopted the second money laundering directive (Directive 2001/97) and required member states to implement this into their domestic law by 15 June 2003. This required two main changes in the UK's money laundering legislation:

- to extend the reporting requirement from suspicion of drug trafficking to suspicion of all serious offences; and

- to expand the definition of 'the regulated sector' to include, amongst others, auditors, external accountants and tax advisers.

In October 2005, the European Parliament and Council of the EU adopted the Third Money Laundering Directive (Directive 2005/60/EC) which had to be implemented by December 2007. It introduced the term 'customer due diligence' to cover the identification of customers and clients and provided for three levels of due diligence: 'simplified', standard and 'enhanced'. In addition requirements were also introduced for ongoing monitoring of customers throughout a business relationship and a more precise requirement to verify the real beneficial owner in potential nominee/trustee situations. Relaxations were introduced in the form of the ability to rely upon due diligence measures performed by certain third parties and to apply due diligence measure and monitoring on a 'risk-sensitive basis'.

The Third Directive also extended the definition of 'criminal activity' to specifically include terrorist acts. (The UK had already defined money laundering as including an offence under *Terrorism Act* 2000, s. 18 which had its own definition of money laundering.)

After a period of consultation on the detailed implementation of the Third Directive, the *Money Laundering Regulations* 2007 (SI 2007/2157) were laid before Parliament on 25 July 2007 and have effect from 15 December 2007. They revoke the 2003 Regulations from the same date.

The following commentary is intended to focus on the implications for tax advisers of the measures introduced to implement the EU Directives. Those measures are very wide ranging and can impact on an adviser in a number of ways.

The *Proceeds of Crime Act* 2002 (PCA 2002)

67-100 Definitions

The provisions of the Act, which deal with money laundering, introduce five offences:

- concealment of criminal property (see 67-150);
- being concerned in arrangements with regard to criminal property (see 67-200);
- acquiring, using or possessing criminal property (see 67-250);
- failure to disclose suspicions of money laundering (see 67-350); and
- 'tipping off' – disclosing that suspicions of money laundering have been reported to the authorities (see 67-400).

The first three offences carry a maximum penalty of 14 years' imprisonment or a fine or both, whilst, for the final two, the maximum is five years. It is therefore imperative that tax advisers are fully aware of their responsibilities under the Act and the defences available to them if charged with an offence.

Money laundering itself is defined as an act which constitutes one of the first three offences listed above, or is an attempt, conspiracy or incitement to commit such an offence or aiding, abetting, counselling or procuring the commission of such an offence.

The Act introduces the term 'criminal property' which is, or represents, the benefit derived by a person from his, or another's, 'criminal conduct', provided he is aware, or suspects, that it is derived from such conduct. It is important to note therefore that the possessor of the benefit who is unaware, and has no grounds to suspect, that it has derived from criminal conduct, is not in possession of criminal property and none of the following offences/obligations will apply in relation to that property.

'Property' in this context is widely defined as being all forms of property and interests in property, including money, land and buildings, chattels, choses in action and other forms of intangible property. 'Criminal conduct' is defined as conduct which constitutes an offence in any part of the UK or would do so if the conduct occurred here. Thus all offences, of whatever nature, are now within the scope of the money laundering legislation. However, to bring the legislation into play there clearly needs to be some monetary benefit arising from that offence. As far as tax is concerned, there will clearly be a benefit arising from a deliberate failure to declare a particular source of income, i.e. the tax which should otherwise have been paid.

In looking at the implications of the Act on tax advisers, the natural tendency would be to concentrate on the proceeds of tax evasion, but it is vital that advisers should be aware that they may come across, or have suspicions about, proceeds of other criminal activity. However, as far as tax is concerned, the distinction between 'negligence' and 'fraudulent conduct' needs to be borne in mind. Similarly, advisers need to keep clearly in mind that tax avoidance is legal and tax evasion is an offence, even if government ministers and civil servants think the terms are interchangeable. There is no definition of 'negligence' or 'neglect' in the Taxes Act; similarly there is no definition of 'fraud 'or 'fraudulent conduct'. The view of HMRC is that:

> 'The general term "fraud" has a wide significance and there is no simple definition which covers the full range of conduct to which it may be applied. Fraud (in relation to HMRC) includes, in its various forms, falsification with an intention to deceive and this may be present even as a mere conscious understatement in, or omission from, a return or accounts.'

Tax evasion can therefore be said to be fraudulent conduct; it is the deliberate, intentional, non-declaration of income or the over-claiming of a deduction. Any under-declarations which are unintentional are the result of neglect, not fraudulent conduct.

Legislation: PCA 2002, s. 340(2), (3), (9), (11)

Other Material: HMRC *Enquiry Manual* EM5105

67-150 The offence of concealment

Any person acting in whatever capacity, (therefore not just a tax adviser), commits an offence if he conceals, disguises, converts, transfers or removes criminal property from the UK. This includes concealing or disguising its nature, source, location, disposition, movement or ownership of the property or of any rights in relation to the property.

A tax adviser could conceivably be guilty of such an offence if he assists a client in using or investing the proceeds of tax evasion where he is aware or should be aware that the funds involved are the results of criminal activity. For example, bearing in mind that the evasion of foreign tax is also a criminal activity, an adviser might be at risk in advising on, or assisting in, the investment of funds from abroad for a client where no foreign tax has been paid on the source of the funds. It does however need to be remembered that property is not criminal property if the alleged offender does not know or suspect that the property is a benefit of criminal conduct.

Legislation: PCA 2002, s. 327, 340(3)(b)

67-200 The offence of being concerned in an arrangement

Again a person acting in what ever capacity is guilty of an offence if he 'enters into, or becomes concerned in, an arrangement which he knows, or suspects, facilitates (by whatever means) the acquisition, retention, use or control of criminal property by or on behalf of another person'.

This is a very wide ranging offence and one which advisers of all disciplines may commit unwittingly as was illustrated in High Court in a divorce case. The legal team acting for Mrs P were in negotiations with Mr P's lawyers seeking a financial settlement. Based on the evidence they had seen and a report from their own forensic accountant, Mrs P's lawyers became suspicious that some of the matrimonial assets might be 'criminal property' within the meaning of PCA 2002, as representing the proceeds of tax evasion. As a result they therefore approached the High Court for directions. Dame Butler-Sloss held that a legal professional might become 'concerned in' an arrangement in a number of ways. She agreed that the act of negotiating an arrangement would amount to being 'concerned in' that arrangement and that arrangement might possibly involve the acquisition, retention, use or control of criminal property. It would follow that a tax adviser could equally become concerned in an arrangement by giving advice in connection with the sale or purchase of a business, or a company, or indeed a divorce settlement if it is suspected that part of the funds for that transaction, or the assets which are the subject of the transaction, are criminal property.

Legislation: PCA 2002, s. 328(1)

Case: *P v P* [2003] EWHC 2260 Fam

67-250 The offence of acquiring using or possessing criminal property

This offence applies where any person, again in whatever capacity, acquires, uses or possesses criminal property. There is however a defence available where he can show that he acquired, used or possessed the property for 'adequate consideration'. That consideration must be not significantly less than the market value of the property, or the value of the use or possession of the property, as the case may be. An adviser who, perhaps, enjoys a rent-free holiday in a client's Spanish villa which has been purchased out of the proceeds of tax evasion, will therefore be guilty of an offence under this section.

Legislation: PCA 2002, s. 329(1)

67-300 The defence of disclosure

In each of the three offences discussed above, an adviser will be protected from committing an offence if he makes an 'authorised disclosure', or he intended to make such a disclosure but has a reasonable excuse for not doing so.

Legislation: PCA 2002, s. 327(2), 328(2), 329(2)

Authorised disclosures

An 'authorised disclosure' is one which:

(1) is made to a 'constable', customs officer or a 'nominated officer';

(2) is made in a prescribed form, and either:

  (a) the disclosure is made before the person commits the act which would trigger the offence; or

(b) if the act has already been committed, there is good reason why the disclosure was not made earlier and it is made on the person's own initiative as soon as it was practical to do so.

Such a disclosure is also treated as a 'protected disclosure' in that it is not to be treated as a breach of any restriction on the disclosure of information. Thus an authorised disclosure does not breach any duty of client confidentially.

In this context, a 'constable' includes an officer of the Serious Organised Crime Agency (SOCA) and a 'nominated officer' is someone nominated by a person's employer to receive disclosures from within that organisation and to act as a channel of communication with SOCA. The role of the nominated officer is discussed in more detail at 67-400 below.

The prescribed form and manner of an authorised disclosure is one which is specified in an order by the Secretary of State (PCA 2002, s. 339). To date no such order has been made, thus disclosure can be made in any form.

However, the *Serious Organised Crime and Police Act* 2005 amended the *Proceeds of Crime Act* 2002 to introduce an offence of making a disclosure otherwise than in the form and manner prescribed. The penalty on summary conviction is a fine not exceeding level 5 on the Standard Scale. The offence will not, however, become effective until an Order has been made specifying the prescribed form, and no offence will be committed if the person concerned had a 'reasonable excuse' for making the disclosure in another form of manner.

Meanwhile, pending the required order, SOCA has produced preferred disclosure forms which can be downloaded from its website. These comprise the 'Standard Disclosure Report Form', comprising up to six separate sheets or 'modules', and a 'Limited Intelligence Value Report Form', which is a single sheet.

The criteria for using the Limited Intelligence Value Report Form are contained in guidance notes available on the website. In summary, these are:

- Certain suspicious activity taking place outside the UK which is not a criminal offence in the jurisdiction where committed, and relates either to local differences in regulations or social and cultural practices.
- Minor irregularities where there is nothing to suggest that these are the result of dishonest behaviour. Balance discrepancies and minor credit balances not returned because of the administrative costs involved, or other small discrepancies which are judged to have resulted from a mistake rather than dishonest behaviour.

This is at odds with the whole concept of PCA 2002 under which reports are required for 'criminal conduct' and not mistakes. Arguably, a mistake in tax terms is merely negligence, not fraud. In the guidance SOCA confirms that if there is no 'criminal property' then no report would be needed; this criterion has been added to advise those who nevertheless wish to make a report to use the shorter reporting form.

- The perpetrator of the criminal activity is not known and cannot be traced. This would include acts of theft and various cheque and credit card frauds.

- Accountants and tax advisers may aggregate multiple instances of suspicion arising during one audit in to a single Limited Intelligence Value Report provided that, the reason for the aggregate report is summarised and the aggregate report relates to a single audit only.

  SOCA goes on to say that:

  > 'Reporters should note that a Standard Report is appropriate should the issue of a Hansard (CoP9) letter by HMRC, taken with such other information as may be available, cause (or provide reasonable grounds for) knowledge or suspicion of money laundering;'

- Where the reporter considering whether to disclose knows (as opposed to assumes) that a report has already been made and a further report would provide no additional information. An example is where a client in the regulated sector has filed a report and an auditor or accountant knows this. Provided the caveat of 'no additional information' is adhered to, a Limited Intelligence Value report is appropriate. Note that HMRC is not authorised to receive disclosures direct from the regulated sector under PCA 2002.

- Where a government agency is already aware of an offence that also happens to be an instance of suspected money laundering. This category is intended to capture a range of regulatory/procedural offences. Examples include health and safety offences, environmental offences, and failure to file annual returns with the Companies Registrar. Provided the caveat of 'no additional information' is adhered to, a Limited Intelligence Value report is appropriate. However, any knowledge or suspicion of money laundering relating to serious tax evasion, including cases covered by the *Hansard* procedure, should be reported in a Standard Report.

- For mistakes in VAT or customs returns where reporters feel obliged to make a disclosure. Although the submission of an incorrect VAT or Customs return, however innocent, is a criminal offence, SOCA takes the view that a disclosure is not required for innocent error in these circumstances. However where the person knows of the omission and does not rectify the situation there will be a duty to report. Where reporting institutions feel obliged to make a disclosure, a Limited Intelligence Value report is appropriate.

- Where a reporting institution is served with a court order, which prompts suspicion, a Limited Intelligence Value report is appropriate except where the suspicion and report relate to matters not covered by the court order letter.
- Where the benefit from criminal conduct is in the form of cost savings, such as breaches of employment law and the illegal copying or distribution of software licences within a company.

Notwithstanding these guidelines, SOCA reserves the right in all cases to call for a Standard Disclosure Report if it thinks fit.

If forms are submitted by post should be addressed to UK FIU, PO Box 8000, London SE11 5EN. Telephone enquiries should be made to the Economic Crime Branch on 020 7238 8282.

Where an authorised disclosure is made directly to SOCA before the act which would otherwise be a money laundering offence takes place they have a seven-day notice period in which to respond. If no response is received in that period, the person making that report may continue to be involved in the arrangements, etc. and is regarded as having received 'appropriate consent' to the proposed action. However, if SOCA respond within the seven days by refusing consent for the person to continue to act, no action can be taken by that person in relation to the proposed course of action for a further 31-day moratorium period starting with the date of that notice of refusal. Once the moratorium period has expired, the person has 'appropriate consent' and may proceed with the proposed action.

Legislation: PCA 2002, s. 334(3), 335(4), (5), (9), 337, 338, 339(1A), (1B), 340(13); *Serious Organised Crime and Police Act* 2005

Website: www.soca.gov.uk/financialIntel/disclosure.html

67-350 The offence of failing to report suspicions of money laundering

This is an offence which can only be committed by someone in the regulated sector (in contrast with the previous offences which are capable of being committed by anyone). In the original version of the Act, tax advisers and accountants were not regarded as carrying on business in the 'regulated sector'. However, that definition was amended so as to include:

> '(i) the provision by way of business of advice about the tax affairs of another person by a body corporate or incorporate or, in the case of a sole practitioner, by an individual.'

A similar amendment was made in respect of the provisions of accountancy services.

Subject to the defence available for 'relevant professional advisers' referred to later, a tax adviser will therefore commit an offence if:

- he has, as a minimum, reasonable grounds for knowing, or even suspecting, that another person is engaged in money laundering;
- the information on which his suspicion is based came to him in the course of his business in the regulated sector;
- he can identify, or it is reasonable to believe that the information he has may assist in identifying, either the person suspected of money laundering or the whereabouts of the laundered property; and
- he fails to disclose that information as soon as practical to the nominated officer of his firm (see 67-400) or directly to SOCA.

A defence is available where the alleged offender:

- has a reasonable excuse;
- is a professional legal adviser or a 'relevant professional adviser' and the information came to him in privileged circumstances;
- is employed by, or is in partnership with, a professional legal adviser or a relevant professional adviser to provide assistance and support, the information came to the adviser in privileged circumstances and came to the employee or partner in the course of that assistance or support; or
- had not been provided by his employer with the training to be specified in an Order by the Secretary of State and he does not know or suspect that the other person was engaged in money laundering; at the time of writing no such order has been made.

Privileged circumstances mean disclosure was made:

- to a client or a client's representative in connection with the giving of legal advice; or
- to any other person in connection with proposed or actual legal proceedings,

provided the disclosure was not made with the intention of furthering a criminal purpose.

A 'relevant professional adviser' is an accountant, auditor or tax adviser who is a member of a professional body which grants membership only after a test of competence and which imposes professional and ethical standards on its members, backed up by disciplinary procedures.

In considering whether an offence has been committed, the court must consider whether the person concerned followed any relevant guidance issued by his professional body which has been approved by the Treasury. The CCAB guidance that has been approved by the Treasury for accountants and tax advisers can be found on the CCAB website at www.ccab.org.uk/PDFs/Guidance%20Clean.pdf.

Legislation: PCA 2002, s. 330

Website: www.ccab.org.uk/PDFs/Guidance%20Clean.pdf

67-400 The role of the nominated officer

As indicated above, a nominated officer is someone within an organisation who is nominated to receive authorised disclosures from employees of that organisation.

He or she may give 'appropriate consent' to an employee to continue with a proposed course of action which would otherwise be a money laundering offence, but only if he, in turn, has made a disclosure to SOCA and one of three conditions are satisfied:

(1) SOCA have given 'appropriate consent'; or

(2) SOCA have not responded within the seven-day notice period to the effect that consent is refused; or

(3) SOCA have responded within the seven-day notice period that consent is refused and the 31-day moratorium period has expired.

A nominated officer is guilty of an offence which carries a five-year maximum prison sentence if he gives consent to an act which would otherwise be a money laundering offence when none of the above conditions are satisfied and he knows, or suspects, that the proposed act is a prohibited act.

An offence can be committed by the nominated officer if:

- the officer actually knows, or suspects, or he has reasonable grounds for knowing or suspecting, that another person is engaged in money laundering;
- that knowledge or suspicion is based on a disclosure made to him by an employee of the organisation;
- he can identify, or it is reasonable to believe that the information he has may assist in identifying, either the person suspected of money laundering or the whereabouts of the laundered property; and
- he does not make a disclosure to SOCA in the correct form, as soon as is practicable after the disclosure was made to him.

In effect, this is saying that even if a nominated officer in this sector did not know or suspect money laundering, but should have done so based upon the information he held, he is still guilty of an offence. This is a higher standard of conduct than that required from a nominated officer who is not in the regulated sector.

However, no offence will be committed if the nominated officer has a 'reasonable excuse' for not making the disclosure to SOCA.

In considering whether an offence has been committed, the court must consider whether the alleged offender has acted in accordance with Treasury approved guidance from his professional body. The CCAB guidance that has been approved by the Treasury for accountants and tax advisers can be found on the CCAB website at www.ccab.org.uk/PDFs/Guidance%20Clean.pdf

Legislation: PCA 2002, s. 331, 336(1)–(6)

Website: www.ccab.org.uk/PDFs/Guidance%20Clean.pdf

67-450 The offence of 'tipping off'

An offence is committed where a person:

- knows, or suspects that an authorised disclosure under the Act has already been made either to SOCA or to a nominated officer; and
- makes a disclosure to another person 'which is likely to prejudice any investigation' which might be conducted following the authorised disclosure.

However no offence arises if the person concerned either:

(1) did not know or suspect that the disclosure was likely to be prejudicial to any investigation;

(2) the disclosure was made in carrying out any obligation of his under the Act or any similar enactments; or

(3) he is a professional legal adviser and the disclosure was made:

   (a) to a client or a client's representative in connection with the giving of legal advice; or

   (b) to any other person in connection with proposed or actual legal proceedings,

   provided the disclosure was not made with the intention of furthering a criminal purpose.

In the divorce case referred to in 67-200, it was held by the President of the Family Division that:

> 'In general terms the professional duties in family proceedings do, in my view, appear to attract the protection of section 333(3) ... in order to permit a legal adviser to inform, for instance, the other side that a disclosure either will be, or has been, made to the [SOCA].'

It should of course be remembered that a tax adviser, per se, is not a professional legal adviser and not entitled to rely on the professional privilege defence.

Legislation: PCA 2002, s. 333

Case: *P v P* [2003] EWHC 2260 (Fam)

67-500 PCA 2002 and the tax adviser

It is suggested that the money laundering offences under PCA 2002 which should be of major concern to a tax adviser are those of:

- entering into or being concerned in arrangements which he knows or suspects facilitates the acquisition, retention, use or control of criminal property by or on behalf of another person (see 67-200); and
- failing to report suspicions of money laundering (see 67-350).

Being concerned in arrangements

If he is invited to advise/assist in a transaction and he becomes aware, or suspects, that the subject matter is, or represents, the proceeds of criminal activity then he has two options:

- to refuse to act. If he plays no part in the arrangement, then no offence has been committed;
- if he has already become involved before forming his suspicions, he should make an authorised disclosure, either to the nominated officer of his firm or, if none exists, directly to SOCA.

Where an authorised disclosure is made he must take no further part in the arrangements for at least seven days whilst waiting for a response from SOCA. If that body gives approval or fails to respond within the seven days, he may continue to act in relation to the arrangement, but should not disclose to any party the fact that an authorised disclosure has been made, for fear of committing the offence of 'tipping off' (see 67-450).

Where SOCA respond within seven days to the effect that consent to act is refused, the adviser must refrain from acting for a further 31 days. After the expiry of that period he is then free to resume acting, but again, should not reveal that an authorised disclosure has been made.

This delay of up to 38 days may prove to be a practical difficulty where the client is trying to push through a transaction. The agent is not permitted to act but cannot tell the client the reason why for fear of 'tipping off'. To alleviate this difficulty, a 'fast-track' system has been introduced – the disclosure form should be faxed to 020 7238 8286 with a note requesting fast-track treatment and explaining the reason for the urgency.

Reporting suspicions

Perhaps the most controversial and problematic obligation imposed by the legislation is that of reporting knowledge or suspicion of money laundering. For the tax adviser, the majority of cases will involve the filing of incorrect returns or accounts, but it should also be remembered that other non-tax offences fall to be reported also.

In the area of tax compliance, a tax adviser must of course not knowingly assist in the completion and submission of an incorrect return. However if it subsequently comes to light that the client has, for example, intentionally withheld details of income, or the adviser has reasonable grounds for suspecting that has happened, then an authorised disclosure must be made to SOCA (either directly or via the nominated officer). In addition, the adviser needs to act in accordance with the rules of professional conduct laid down by his professional body which may require him to ask the client for authority to report the under-declaration to HMRC.

In contrast to other authorised disclosures, there is no requirement to suspend work on the client's affairs, although, clearly, advisers must avoid becoming involved in arrangements which facilitate the retention or use of criminal property.

Whilst advisers should follow the guidance issued by their respective professional bodies, the following is a summary of the main points which should be borne in mind.

- It is not just suspicions of clients having been engaged in money laundering that must be reported; the requirement relates to 'any person', which would include clients of other firms, relatives of clients and employees of clients.
- The information upon which an adviser concludes, or suspects, that another person has been engaged in money laundering must come to him in the course of business in the regulated sector, i.e. in his role as a tax adviser. Information gleaned as a private individual, e.g. overheard in a pub or from friends and relations, does not give rise to an obligation to report.
- There is no obligation to report knowledge or suspicion of money laundering where the information upon which it is based was acquired before 1 March 2004.

- Money laundering, apart from terrorism offences, includes the concealment, facilitating the acquisition, retention, use or control or the use and possession of 'criminal property'. This is the benefit derived from a person's criminal conduct, i.e. from the commission of an offence but that person must be aware, or suspect, they have committed the offence from which the benefit derives. It must follow that if the person genuinely does not know they have committed an offence, there can be no criminal property.
- Also because the person concerned must know, or suspect, that they have committed an offence, an omission from a return which was negligent rather than fraudulent does not need to be reported to SOCA. (However it may still need to be reported to HMRC under the code of conduct laid down by the adviser's professional body.)
- There is no de minimis provision. All offences must be reported regardless of the sums involved. In the case of divorce case quoted earlier, Dame Elizabeth Butler-Sloss commented:

  'It is important for the legal profession to take into account, as [Counsel for NCIS] reminded us, that the Act makes no distinction between degrees of criminal property. An illegally obtained sum of £10 is no less susceptible to the definition of 'criminal property' than a sum of £1million. Parliament clearly intended this to be the case. Whatever may be the resource implications, the legal profession would appear to be bound by the provisions of the Act in all cases, however big or small. If this approach is scrupulously followed by the legal advisers, the result is likely to have a considerable and potentially adverse impact upon the [SOCA] and would create serious consequential delays in listing and hearing family cases, including child cases.'

The *Money Laundering Regulations* 2007

68-000 Introduction and definitions

The *Money Laundering Regulations* 2003 came into force on 1 March 2004 and were revoked with effect from 15 December 2007 by the *Money Laundering Regulations* 2007 (SI 2007/2157).

The aim of the commentary which follows is to highlight the implications of the Regulations for tax advisers in their practice and is therefore necessarily much condensed.

The 2007 Regulations abandon the term 'relevant business' which was in the 2003 Regulations in favour of 'relevant person'. Although the Second Directive had referred to categories of persons as being within its scope, the UK, in implementing the Directive, had defined the scope by reference to activities. Thus, whilst the 2003 Regulations referred to the provision, by way of a business, of advice about the tax affairs of another person, the 2007 Regulations refer specifically to a tax adviser, who is defined as *a firm or sole practitioner who by way of business provides advice about the tax affairs of other persons, when providing such services.* This suggests that he is only a tax adviser when providing tax advice and not for other services he may provide. However those other services may still result in him being a 'relevant person', e.g. a similar definition applies for accountants. Although the general focus of the Regulations is on the relevant person, it was felt to be necessary to refer to the activities in these instances as there was no widely held definition of either occupation.

The 2003 Regulations defined money laundering by reference to the money laundering offences under both the *Proceeds of Crime Act* 2002 and the *Terrorism Act* 2000. The 2007 Regulations now refer to both money laundering and 'terrorist financing', the latter being more extensive than money laundering: it also covers offences related to fund-raising, use and possession of money for the purposes of terrorism, entering into funding arrangements for those purposes as well as offences under other anti-terrorism legislation.

The regulations impose on tax advisers the requirement;

- to carry out 'customer due diligence measures' (in other words, to check identities; see 68-050);
- to carry out ongoing monitoring of customers (see 68-200);
- to maintain records of such measures (see 68-350);
- to establish and maintain appropriate risk-sensitive policies and procedures (see 68-400);
- to train staff in the use of those procedures (see 68-450);
- to be monitored by a supervisory authority (see 68-500).

68-050 The obligation to check identities/carry out due diligence

A tax adviser is required to apply customer due diligence measures whenever he:

- establishes a new 'business relationship' with a client; this is a professional or commercial relationship which, at the outset, the adviser expects to have an element of duration, i.e. to continue for an indefinite period of time;
- carries out an 'occasional transaction'; being a one-off transaction valued at less than €15,000, which is not carried out as part of a business relationship;
- suspects money laundering or terrorist financing; or

- has doubts about the evidence of identity he may have previously obtained.

Due diligence measures fall into three categories:

- identifying the client and verifying that identity by documents, data or information from a reliable independent source;
- identifying the beneficial owner (as defined) of the property which is the subject of the transactions, where the client is not the beneficial owner, and, on a risk-sensitive basis verifying that identity to the satisfaction of the adviser. Where a company or a trust is involved, the adviser must take steps to understand the ownership and control structure of that body;
- obtaining information on the purpose and intended nature of the business relationship.

In a change from the previous regulations which required verification to take place 'as soon as reasonably practical' after the first contact with the client, the 2007 Regulations require verification to be completed before the business relationship is established or the occasional transaction is carried out.

A derogation is allowed from the strict rule in that, where there is little risk of money laundering, verification can be completed whilst the business relationship is being established in order not to interrupt the normal course of business.

The obligations of consultants

As with the 2003 Regulations, the key question is 'who is the client?'. If the firm seeking the advice is the client, it is that firm which should be the subject of the due diligence measures. (Note that although that firm may also be a relevant person under these regulations, this does not relieve the consultant of his obligation to carry out due diligence measures on that firm.)

On the other hand, if the client is the client of the other firm, the consultant may be relieved of his obligation to carry out due diligence in respect of that client. If, as seems likely, the firm has already carried out those measures, the consultant may be able to rely upon the evidence obtained by that firm (see 68-250).

Legislation: *Money Laundering Regulations* 2007 (SI 2007/2157), reg. 7

68-100 Simplified due diligence (post 15 December 2007)

In the case of a new business relationship, an occasional transaction or doubts about earlier evidence of identity, customer due diligence may be dispensed with where;

- that customer is either a credit or financial institution, a quoted company or a public authority;
- the transaction is in respect of certain life insurance and pension contracts; or
- the product is a junior ISA within the meaning given by *Individual Savings Account Regulations* 1998, reg. 2B.

Legislation: *Money Laundering Regulations* 2007 (SI 2007/2157), reg. 13; *Money Laundering (Amendment) Regulations* 2011 (SI 2011/1781)

68-150 Enhanced due diligence (post 15 December 2007)

Enhanced customer due diligence has to be applied in a number of instances, in particular:

- where the customer has not been physically present for identification purposes; additional evidence is required to make up for the higher risk, for example, additional documentation or confirmatory certification by a credit or financial institution which is also a relevant person for the purposes of these regulations;
- where the customer is a 'politically exposed person', i.e. someone holding a prominent public office in the EU, an international body or a state other than the UK; in this case there must be approval from senior management before entering into the business relationship, measures should be taken to establish the source of the customer's wealth and income and there must be 'enhanced ongoing monitoring' of the relationship.

Legislation: *Money Laundering Regulations* 2007 (SI 2007/2157), reg. 14

68-200 Ongoing monitoring (post 15 December 2007)

Under the 2003 Regulations, due diligence measures were only required at the beginning of a business relationship. The 2007 Regulations now impose a requirement for ongoing monitoring throughout the duration of that relationship.

That monitoring involves scrutinising the transactions undertaken during the relationship and the source of any funds involved so as to ensure they consistent with the adviser's knowledge of his client. It should be undertaken on a 'risk-sensitive' basis and to an extent appropriate to the risks of money laundering and terrorist financing involved.

Legislation: *Money Laundering Regulations* 2007 (SI 2007/2157), reg. 8

68-250 Reliance on third parties (post 15 December 2007)

A new feature is that a relevant person can now rely on certain other relevant persons to have carried out the customer due diligent measures on the same customer, provided that other relevant person consents. Those persons whose due diligence can be relied up are, basically, credit and financial institutions and auditors, insolvency practitioners, accountants in practice, tax advisers and solicitors in practice who are regulated for Money Laundering purposes by one of the following:

- Association of Chartered Certified Accountants;
- Council for Licensed Conveyancers;
- Faculty of Advocates;
- Bar Council;
- Bar Council of Northern Ireland;
- Institute of Chartered Accountants in England and Wales;
- Institute of Chartered Accountants in Ireland;
- Institute of Chartered Accountants of Scotland;
- Law Society;
- Law Society of Scotland;
- Law Society of Northern Ireland.

It should be noted that neither the Association of Taxation Technicians nor the Chartered Institute of Taxation appear in that list, even though they are both supervisory authorities for money laundering purposes (see 68-500). It follows that a member of those bodies may not, rely upon a fellow member unless that other member also happened to be a member of one of the bodies listed above and subject to monitoring by that body.

Legislation: *Money Laundering Regulations* 2007 (SI 2007/2157), reg. 17

68-300 Consequences of failure to verify identity, etc. (post 15 December 2007)

If the relevant person is unable to apply the required due diligence measures, there is now a specific obligation:

- not to conduct any transaction with or for the client via a bank account;
- not to establish a new business relationship with the client;
- to terminate any existing business relationship; and
- to consider whether a disclosure should be made under the Proceeds of Crime Act.

An exemption applies in the case of a lawyer, or an auditor, accountant or tax adviser who is regulated by a professional body appointed as a supervisory authority. However this is limited to situations where the lawyer, etc. is acting to ascertain the legal position of his client or acting for that client in any actual or potential legal proceedings.

Legislation: *Money Laundering Regulations* 2007 (SI 2007/2157), reg. 11

68-350 The obligation to retain records

The regulations require the retention of:

- copies of the evidence of the client's identity obtained as part of the due diligence measures, enhanced due diligence or ongoing monitoring, or references as to where that evidence may be found. These have to be retained for five years from the date on which the business relationship ends or the occasional transaction is completed;
- the supporting records of the business relationship or the occasional transaction which is the subject of due diligence or ongoing monitoring. These may be the original documents or copies and must be retained for a five year period. In the case of a specific transaction, that period runs from the completion of the transaction whilst for a business relationship it runs from the end of that relationship.

Similarly where a 'third party' relevant person has been relied upon by another relevant person (see 68-250), that third party must retain the evidence of the customer's identity for five years from the date on which he has been relied upon for the purposes of due diligence or enhanced due diligence.

Legislation: *Money Laundering Regulations* 2007, reg. 19

68-400 The obligation to establish policies and procedures

A tax adviser has to establish and maintain policies and procedures relating to:

- due diligence measures and ongoing monitoring;
- reporting, record keeping and internal controls;
- risk assessment and management; and
- the monitoring of compliance with those procedures and the communication of the procedures within his firm.

Those policies must be 'risk-sensitive' and appropriate to the aim of preventing activities relating to money laundering and the financing of terrorism. In the consultation document issued in July 2006, the Treasury made the point that firms will need to 'use intelligence and judgement rather than a tick-box approach'. They must specifically include procedures:

- which identify and scrutinise complex or unusually large transactions, unusual patterns of transactions with no apparent economic or legal purpose or any other activity which the tax adviser feels is particularly likely to be related to money laundering or terrorist financing;
- to identify whether a client is a 'politically exposed person' and therefore the subject of enhanced due diligence (see 68-150);
- under which a nominated officer ('Money Laundering Reporting Officer' or 'MRLO') is appointed within his firm, everyone within the firm is required to report to the MLRO suspicions of money laundering or terrorist financing and the MLRO to consider whether, in the light of the information available, there are reasonable grounds for knowledge or suspicion of money laundering or terrorist financing.

This final requirement does not however apply to a sole practitioner who has no employees and who does not act in associate with any other person.

Legislation: *Money Laundering Regulations* 2007, reg. 20

68-450 The obligation to train employees

A tax adviser must take appropriate steps to ensure that all relevant employees, i.e. client handlers, are made aware of the law relating to money laundering and terrorist financing and given training on a regular basis so that they may recognise transactions and activities which may be related to money laundering etc. and deal with them appropriately.

Legislation: *Money Laundering Regulations* 2007 (SI 2007/2157), reg. 21

68-500 Supervisory authorities

A requirement imposed by the Third Directive was that all those charged with carrying out due diligence measures should themselves be the subject of monitoring by a supervisory authority to ensure compliance with anti-money laundering controls.

This requirement is incorporated into UK law by the 2007 Regulations which appoint a number of supervisory authorities to cover the range of relevant persons within the scope of the regulations. In the case of auditors, accountants and tax advisers, the position is that those who are members of one of a list of designated professional bodies are to be monitored by that body. Those who are not members of any of those bodies are to be monitored by HMRC.

The bodies designated as supervisory bodies are;

- Association of Accounting Technicians;
- Association of Chartered Certified Accountants;
- Association of International Accountants;
- Association of Taxation Technicians;
- Chartered Institute of Management Accountants;
- Chartered Institute of Public Finance and Accountancy;
- Chartered Institute of Taxation;
- Council for Licensed Conveyancers;
- Faculty of Advocates;
- Faculty Office of the Archbishop of Canterbury;
- General Council of the Bar;
- General Council of the Bar of Northern Ireland;
- Insolvency Practitioners Association;
- Institute of Certified Bookkeepers;
- Institute of Chartered Accountants in England and Wales;
- Institute of Chartered Accountants in Ireland;
- Institute of Chartered Accountants of Scotland;
- Institute of Financial Accountants;
- Law Society;
- Law Society of Scotland;
- Law Society of Northern Ireland.

Where a person is a member of more than one body, the bodies concerned may agree which of them will act as the supervisory authority in relation to that person and advise him accordingly. They may also come to a blanket agreement covering all joint members in which case that agreement must be given appropriate publicity. Where no agreement of any kind is made, the bodies must 'cooperate' in the performance of their functions under the regulations.

All of the main accounting and tax bodies have issued guidance on their websites explaining how they will implement monitoring of their members.

HMRC maintain a register of auditors, accountants and tax advisers who are not supervised by any of the designated professional bodies and may make all or part of that register available for public inspection. Those who are not supervised by any of the designated professional bodies must register with HMRC. Penalties will be charged on those who fail to do so. If they continue to carry on business without registering with HMRC, they will be committing an offence (see 68-550). HMRC charge an annual fee for businesses registered with them. They have maintained this at £110 until 31 May 2012.

Legislation: *Money Laundering Regulations* 2007 (SI 2007/2157), reg. 23, 24, 32 and 33

68-550 Penalties

A failure to comply with any of the obligations imposed by the Regulations carries a potential fine equal to the statutory maximum or two years imprisonment or both.

In deciding whether an offence has been committed, the court is required to take into account whether the tax adviser has followed any guidance issued by a supervisory authority which regulates, or is representative of, the profession carried on by the relevant person, where that guidance has been approved by the Treasury both in terms of its content and its manner of publication.

It is specifically provided that a person is not guilty of an offence if he took all reasonable steps and exercised all due diligence to avoid committing the offence.

Legislation: *Money Laundering Regulations* 2007 (SI 2007/2157), reg. 45

69-000 Tax agents' dishonest conduct

Finance Act 2012 introduces a new offence in relation to the dishonest conduct of tax agents. This gives HMRC the power to impose a penalty on an individual involved in such conduct and there are also provisions enabling HMRC to obtain a tax agent's files.

A tax agent is broadly defined as an individual who, in the course of business, assists other persons with their tax affairs. Such an individual could be engaged on their own account or as an employee. Both acting (or purporting to) act as agent on behalf of a client and advising a client in relation to tax amounts to giving assistance with a client's tax affairs.

The word dishonest is not defined and so will carry its normal meaning requiring, therefore, some degree of impropriety. Dishonest conduct must, though, be in the course of acting as a tax agent with a view to bringing about, or attempting to bring about, a loss of tax revenue. Tax is very widely defined to include just about every tax in the UK system. Dishonesty, as would be expected, includes both acts of commission and omission.

Procedure to establish a penalty

HMRC will first establish whether they believe an individual is or has been engaged in dishonest conduct. An authorised officer of HMRC may then notify the individual of that determination setting out the grounds. An individual may appeal against such a conduct notice within 30 days, stating the grounds of appeal. That appeal then falls in the jurisdiction of, usually, a First-tier Tribunal that may confirm or set aside the determination, applying the usual provisions for appeal. If further evidence emerges in relation to the same conduct HMRC may issue a further conduct notice.

Assuming either that there is no appeal or the determination is confirmed by the tribunal, HMRC can then go to the next stage of assessing the penalty. There are time limits in which they must do this. In broad terms, this is the later of the end of the twelve months beginning with the expiry of the appeal notice, withdrawal or determination by the tribunal and the end of the appeal period for the assessment or other ascertainment of tax revenue lost (or, if no loss of tax revenue has in fact resulted, when HMRC ascertain that fact).

The penalty will be set be somewhere between £5,000 and £50,000. Where HMRC have determined the initial penalty at £5,000 they do have the power, in special circumstances, to reduce the penalty to below £5,000 (including nil), stay the penalty or agree a compromise. Special circumstances do not include inability to pay or the fact that there is no net loss of tax revenue by taking into account the circumstances of another person.

An individual may appeal in writing within 30 days against the amount of a penalty, stating the grounds of appeal. The tribunal has a wide power to confirm the decision or substitute another decision that HMRC had power to make. This can include the special circumstances provisions so as to reduce the amount below £5,000 but as a general rule will only do so if HMRC's judgment was flawed.

Power to obtain tax agent's files, etc.

An authorised officer of HMRC may make an application to the tribunal for approval to obtain relevant documents in the following circumstances:

- where a conduct notice as above has been given and there has been no appeal within the time limit or such an appeal has been withdrawn or determined by a tribunal; or
- an individual has been convicted of a tax offence involving fraud or dishonesty which was committed after the individual became a tax agent. In this instance HMRC have 12 months from the expiry of the time allowed to appeal against a conviction or the date the conviction is upheld on appeal.

There can be no appeal against such a notice. The tribunal, before approving such a file access notice, must be satisfied that HMRC's officer is justified in giving that notice and the tax agent has been given a reasonable opportunity to make representations.

The documents that can be obtained in this manner are only those which are in the document holder's possession or power and can be obtained not only from the tax agent but also any other person believed to hold them. The documents could include a tax agent's working papers when acting in the capacity of tax agent and any other documents received, created, prepared or used by the tax agent for the purposes or in the course of assisting clients with their tax affairs. This can relate to any clients of the tax agent, not just those involved in suspected tax evasion.

There is no time limit specified for this except that the period within which to provide the documents. The method and place of delivery must be such as is reasonably specified in the notice. Unless otherwise specified, copies of the relevant documents are sufficient to comply with the notice.

Documents which are the subject of claim to legal professional privilege are exempt from disclosure and so too are documents where no part relates to a period ending prior to the period of 20 years ending with the date on which the file access notice is given.

If the document holder is a person other than the tax agent, they can appeal within 30 days on the grounds that it would be unduly onerous to comply with the notice and it is then up to the tribunal to consider the matter.

Concealment, etc. of documents

It is a criminal offence liable on summary conviction to a fine and on conviction on indictment to imprisonment for two years or less (and possibly a fine as well) if an individual conceals, destroys or otherwise disposes of a material document. This can be either after the giving of a conduct notice or in relation to a file access notice.

A person who fails to comply with a file access notice is liable to a penalty of £300 which also includes concealing, destroying, etc. the required document. If the failure continues after a notification of such a penalty a daily penalty not exceeding £60 for each day can also be imposed. The defence of a reasonable excuse can be made that satisfies HMRC or a tribunal on appeal. A reasonable excuse cannot include insufficiency of funds unless outside the person's control or relying upon another person without taking reasonable care.

Legislation: FA 2012, Sch. 38

69-050 Civil penalties for enablers of offshore tax evasion

Civil penalties may be imposed on parties found to have deliberately enabled offshore tax evasion or non-compliance. In order to impose such a charge, the individual must be shown to have been aware that his actions would facilitate offshore avoidance or non-compliance that has subsequently resulted in an end user being found guilty of an offence of offshore tax avoidance or non-compliance and the sanctions to be applied can be up to 100% of the tax potentially lost together with the likelihood that the enabler's details will be made public.

Legislation: FA 2016, Sch. 20

General anti-abuse rule

69-100 General anti-abuse rule

General principles

Tax avoidance schemes, many of them of an aggressive nature, came under attack with the Disclosure of Tax Avoidance Schemes (DOTAS) reporting requirements, not to mention decisions of the tribunals and courts that in the vast majority of instances have found against the schemes. After many years of debate there is now a general anti-abuse rule (GAAR). The statutory provisions are contained in FA 2013, which came into effect on Royal Assent.

This applies to most UK taxes, including income tax. The broad thrust is to counteract tax advantages arising from tax arrangements that are abusive. Thus, it will be observed that this is not a general anti-avoidance rule and so conventional tax mitigation steps ought not to be affected by this. The difficulty in practice will be in determining where the cut off line is situated.

If an arrangement is caught by the GAAR then such adjustments are required to be made to counteract the tax advantages on a just and reasonable basis, the adjustment to be made by making an assessment. However, there are certain procedural requirements set out in FA 2013, Sch. 43 that must be complied with.

The important point is that, unlike transactions in securities, where the obligation is upon HMRC to instigate an adjustment by assessment, the GAAR rules are effectively part of the self-assessment system. Thus, if a person becomes subject to tax because a scheme does not work then in addition to the scheme having to be notified under the DOTAS rules (in all probability) an adjustment will be made to the self-assessment return. If a self-assessment return is not adjusted accordingly then clearly HMRC will in all probability be able to make a discovery with the potential for not only interest but also penalties.

Meaning of tax arrangements and 'abusive'

Essentially, if having regard to all the circumstances it would be reasonable to conclude that the obtaining of a tax advantage was a main purpose of the arrangements, then the first hurdle is met. If the tax arrangements form part of any other arrangements then regard has to be had to those other arrangements as well.

The second hurdle that has to be met is that the arrangements are abusive. This is widely defined as entering into or carrying out anything that cannot reasonably be regarded as a reasonable course of action in relation to the relevant tax provisions having regard in particular to:

- whether the substantive results of the arrangements are consistent with any principles on which those provisions are based, whether express or implied, and the policy objectives of those provisions;
- whether the means of achieving those results involves one or more contrived or abnormal steps;
- any intention to exploit any shortcomings in the tax provisions.

Three specific types of arrangements are then set out as being abusive where the arrangements:

- result in an amount of income, profit or gains for tax purposes significantly less than the economic result;

- result in deductions or losses for tax purposes significantly greater than the corresponding economic amount;
- result in a claim for the repayment or crediting of tax, including foreign tax, that has not been and is unlikely to be paid.

It must be the case, though, that the result claimed by the planning was not the anticipated result when the relevant tax provisions were enacted. Moreover, if tax arrangements accord with established practice where HMRC had indicated their acceptance of such practice, then the arrangements will not be regarded as abusive.

These are very wide definitions and only time will tell how they are interpreted both by HMRC and the tribunals and courts on appeal.

HMRC's GAAR guidance

HMRC have published this guidance, which sets out a broad summary of the GAAR rules and gives the particular features of the GAAR with examples. The guidance has been approved by the GAAR Advisory Panel. The guidance is for practical purposes mandatory reading for anyone considering whether or not the GAAR does apply to arrangements. As far as the examples are concerned, there are only five that apply to income tax and are fairly obscure including vaccine research, exploitation of double taxation agreements and schemes to exploit the drafting of the relevant discounted security legislation. All of the five schemes are regarded by HMRC as within the GAAR.

GAAR Advisory Panel

The purpose of this Advisory Panel is to act as a buffer between the taxpayer and HMRC on the one hand and the tribunal and courts system on the other. There are various procedural rules as explained below that must be met and which involve the panel.

HMRC must appoint designated HMRC officers for the purposes of the GAAR and it is those individuals who instigate the counteraction notice. In doing this the detailed provisions of FA 2013, Sch. 43 must be met so that in summary:

- written notice must be given to the taxpayer setting out the specified details so that broadly that person will be aware of the matter in hand and the reasons why the GAAR is in point;
- the notice must set out the steps that the taxpayer may take to avoid the counteraction notice; and
- the taxpayer has 45 days from the day of the notice to give written representations.

If the officer comes to the conclusion that the tax advantages should be considered the matter must then be referred to the Advisory Panel, having given proper consideration to any representations made by the taxpayer. Full details must be given to that panel and the taxpayer has the right within 21 days to make written representations (which can be extended by the Panel on request).

The Chair of the Advisory Panel must then arrange a sub-panel who can invite either side to supply further information. That sub-panel will then consider the matter and they must give a copy of their opinion notice or notices to the designated HMRC officer and the taxpayer. That notice will effectively conclude whether a tax arrangement falls within the GAAR with reasons.

Following this, the designated HMRC officer must then give the taxpayer a written notice setting out whether a tax advantage will be counteracted including the adjustments required and the steps that the taxpayer must take to give effect to it. It is quite clear from the legislation that the view of the Advisory Panel is simply advisory and HMRC are not bound by it. However, given that the onus before a court or tribunal is on HMRC to show that the arrangements are abusive such an appeal body must take into account HMRC's guidance referred to above where approved by the Advisory Panel and the opinion of that panel on those particular arrangements in hand. The court or tribunal is permitted (but not required) to take into account material produced by HMRC or a Crown department which is in the public domain at the time the arrangements are entered into and any evidence of the established practice at that time.

Other points

The effect of a counteraction notice could be to impose double taxation to some extent. There are provisions whereby within 12 months of the day on which the counteraction becomes final for a person to make a claim for consequential adjustments. Such adjustments are to be on a just and reasonable basis and can affect any period and any person whether or not a party to the tax arrangements.

No doubt to avoid any doubt it is specifically provided that any priority rule has effect subject to the GAAR notwithstanding the terms of the priority rule. Broadly, a priority rule is one that has the effect that particular provisions have effect to the exclusion of, or otherwise in priority to, anything else.

Legislation: FA 2013, s. 206–215 and Sch. 43

69-200 Promoters of tax avoidance schemes

Finance Act 2014 (FA 2014) introduced provisions aimed specifically at tackling the activities of individuals or organisations actively involved in the promotion of tax avoidance schemes.

A person is said to be a promoter where, in the course of their business activities, they either design or seek to promote arrangements where the main, or one of the main purposes is to achieve a tax advantage.

Where that person has, in the previous three years, met one of the long list of threshold conditions in FA 2014, Sch. 34, then an officer of HMRC will issue a conduct notice.

The threshold conditions will be breached not only where the person has been the subject of a notice under various serious regulatory provisions such as deliberate tax defaulters and dishonest tax agents but also where they have been subject to an adverse ruling by the GAAR advisory panel or have been penalised by certain regulatory or professional bodies.

Legislation: FA 2014, s. 234–237 and Sch. 34, 36; *Finance Act 2014 (Schedule 34 Prescribed Matters) Regulations* 2015 (SI 2015/131)

Tax Reporter: ¶192-770

Contents of a conduct notice

The conduct notice will specify conditions that the recipient must comply with. Before issue of the notice, the HMRC officer must give the recipient an opportunity to comment on the terms of the notice.

The principal conditions to be stipulated in a conduct notice will seek to ensure that the subject of the notice provides adequate information to clients about any proposals or arrangements they promote and that they cease to promote any scheme or arrangement that involves a proposal to rely on one or more contrived steps seeking to produce a tax advantage. Adequate information includes ensuring that clients are made fully aware of the risk involved in undertaking an action and that the promoter does not falsely give the impression that a particular arrangement has been approved by HMRC.

A conduct notice may also be used to ensure that a person complies with a ‘stop notice’ (see below).

Legislation: FA 2014, s. 238–241

A stop notice

An HMRC officer may issue a stop notice to a person where that person is a promoter of a scheme or arrangement that has been subject to a follower notice under FA 2014, s. 204.

The stop notice must specify the particular arrangements subject to the follower notice, the judicial ruling identified in the follower notice and it must also explain the effect of the stop notice.

Legislation: FA 2014, Sch. 34, para. 12(3)

Monitoring notice

Where a person is found to have failed to comply with a conduct notice, then HMRC may apply to the tribunal for authority to issue a monitoring notice. At the same time, the authorised HMRC officer must also notify the intended recipient of the monitoring notice and detail the alleged breaches of the conduct notice.

HMRC have the power to publish the details of any person subject to a monitoring notice and that person must inform any client that they are subject to the notice.

A person receiving a monitoring notice will be subject to a range of serious restrictions and disclosure obligations including a requirement to make clear to any new client that they are subject to the monitoring notice and may be required by HMRC to provide client information or product documentation. Although these powers are wide ranging, they do not override the normal limitation of legal professional privilege.

Failure to comply with these provisions may result in fines of up to £1m together with daily penalties of up to £10,000 where non-compliance continues.

Legislation: FA 2014, s. 242–249 and Sch. 35

69-300 Serial tax avoidance

Serial tax avoidance legislation was introduced on 15 September 2016. The aim is to deter taxpayers from entering into multiple tax avoidance schemes.

In the event a scheme is defeated in the courts, then HMRC will issue a warning notice which will be effective for five years. During this period, the taxpayer must notify HMRC of any avoidance schemes entered into. If a scheme is defeated that was entered into during a warning period, then HMRC may impose sanctions. Schemes entered into before 16 September 2016 and fully disclosed to HMRC before 5 April 2017 will be ignored under these provisions.

Tax avoidance schemes for these purposes are those schemes that are disclosable under DOTAS or are subject to a counteraction notice under the GAAR.

Sanction

Where a scheme is defeated whilst the taxpayer is in a warning period, then a penalty equivalent to 20% of the tax payable as a result of the defeat of the scheme will be charged. This increases to 40% for a further offence and 60% where a third scheme is defeated.

In the event three schemes are defeated then the taxpayer's name will be published and if each of these schemes relied on the exploitation of direct tax reliefs, then HMRC will issue a 'relief restriction notice' preventing them from taking advantage of these reliefs.

Investment income

Income from land

Taxation of property businesses

70-000 Introduction

The taxation of income from land (rents, premiums, etc.) is principally dealt with in *Income Tax (Trading and Other Income) Act* 2005, Pt. 3.

The legislation refers to 'property businesses' and there are two kinds of property business:

- a 'UK property business' covers all land in the UK; and
- an 'overseas property business' covers all land outside the UK.

If a person has property income both from land in the UK and from land outside the UK, there will be two property businesses, with profits and losses computed in the same way for each business. The two businesses are kept separate, so that for instance a loss in one of the businesses cannot be set against profits in the other business.

HMRC have published their 'Property Rental Toolkit', which in common with other toolkits contains a checklist of basic points, with some amplification. Similarly, HMRC publish a general guide to taxation of rental income at http://tinyurl.com/qfvf8ax.

Legislation: ITTOIA 2005, s. 264–265 and 831

Tax Reporter: ¶300-000

70-050 Property business or trade?

No trade of letting

It is a long-established principle that for the purposes of UK taxation the letting of land for rents or similar receipts does not of itself constitute a trade. The letting may be under formal leases or under less formal tenancy agreements or even under so-called 'licences to occupy' that do not amount to a lease; the important element is that the landlord gives up the legal right to occupy the land or premises concerned, ceding it to the tenant.

The leading case on the distinction between trading profits and rental income as wholly separate sources for tax purposes is *Salisbury House Estates Ltd v Fry (HMIT)*. The key element in the distinction between trading income and property business income is that where the owner of land or buildings exploits any of the rights to occupy the land *without parting with the legal occupation of the property*, any profits derived from that exploitation may be taxed as trading profits. Conversely, where the exploitation of property rights results in a loss of legal occupancy of the property the profits will be treated as property income. It was also established that the small-scale provision of some services incidental to letting does not convert the letting into a trade, although the income from the provision of those services may be taxed as trading profits.

Cases: *Salisbury House Estates Ltd v Fry (HMIT)* (1930) 15 TC 266; *Webb v Conelee Properties Ltd* [1982] BTC 368

Furnished holiday lettings

Cases in which the distinction between property income and trading income was a fine one provoked interesting comment, especially where the owner/landlord provided extensive services to the tenants occupying the property. In *Griffiths v Jackson; Griffiths v Pearman*, where Vinelott J said:

> 'The distinction between a hotelier or a lodging house keeper, on the one hand, and the owner of property who lets furnished rooms and provides services is no doubt in practice a narrow one, more particularly in these days of self-service hotels and motels, but the principle is clear and in the present case there can be no doubt on which side of the line the taxpayers' activities fall. It is quite clear from the terms of the tenancy agreements and the taxpayers' form of letter that they let rooms furnished to tenants, albeit with shared facilities and some services.
>
> [...]
>
> I may perhaps be permitted to add that I am not without sympathy for the taxpayers. It is a peculiar feature of United Kingdom tax law that the activity of letting furnished flats or rooms, while it may be a business and, in this case, a demanding and time-consuming business, is not a trade [...] and the rule operates to the disadvantage of the taxpayer; his income is not earned income and he is not entitled to capital allowances and to the rollover relief for capital gains tax purposes afforded to a person carrying on a trade. The business may, as in this case, occupy much of the taxpayer's free time or even be one which required his whole time attention [...] It is not too easy to see why in the modern world a business consisting of the exploitation of the right of property in land should be treated differently from a business consisting of the exploitation of other assets. However, the principle is now too deeply embedded in the law to be altered except by legislation.'

Following this case (which did not deal with holiday lettings, but rather with lettings to university students), specific rules relating to commercial furnished holiday lettings were enacted. In brief, these rules allow the profits from 'the commercial letting of furnished holiday accommodation' to be treated as if they are derived from a trade for most income tax and CGT purposes; see 71-200.

Cases: *Gittos v Barclay* [1982] BTC 197; *Griffiths v Jackson; Griffiths v Pearman* [1983] BTC 68

Priority rules

There are a number of situations where income derived from property is associated with a trading activity (which may be a 'deemed' trading activity). There are also possible conflicts between how profits that are not covered by the rules for the specific activities dealt with in 70-100 should be taxed. Where the specific rules do not cover the particular situation, there are priority rules.

When income could potentially be charged on two different bases, the following rules apply.

- Where rents arise in connection with mines, quarries and other extractive industries, canals, railways and rights of fishing, markets and tolls, they are to be charged, not as a UK property business under the normal property business, but as a separate source calculated on the amounts arising in the year subject only to the deduction of management expenses.
- Where the rents are receivable for UK electric line wayleaves, they are again to be charged as a separate source of income and not as part of a UK property business.
- Rents which could be chargeable under either of the first two bullet points are to be chargeable under the second.

Where the rents could be treated as deriving from a trade, profession, etc., they will be charged as such and not as part of a UK property business or as rents within the first two bullet points above.

Legislation: ITTOIA 2005, s. 12(4), 261 and 262

Tax Reporter: ¶300-005

70-100 Commercial occupation of land

There are a number of trades in which the conduct of the trade is closely associated with the occupation of land and which may derive profits from various methods of exploiting rights and interests in and over the land. It is often difficult to draw a clear distinction between trading activities and the activities of a property business. In order to avoid doubt, and in some cases to preserve long-standing arrangements, some business activities are treated by the legislation as trades and so are excluded from any property business (and in some cases are excluded from the charge to tax altogether). They are set out below.

Farming and market gardening

All 'farming' and 'market gardening' in the UK is regarded as a trade or part of a trade. It does not matter whether the land is managed on a commercial basis with a view to the realisation of profits. The term 'farming' means the occupation of land for the purposes of husbandry (which includes, for example, hop growing and the breeding and rearing of horses). The cultivation of short-rotation coppice is treated as farming and not as forestry. 'Market gardening' means the occupation of land as a garden or nursery for the purposes of growing produce for sale.

Legislation: ITTOIA 2005, s. 9

Commercial occupation of land

If land in the UK is occupied and managed on a commercial basis with a view to the realisation of profits then that commercial occupation is to be treated as a trade or part of a trade. If land is commercially occupied by a person and the activities fall short of being a trade by first principles, the charge is established by the legislation. Note that if the occupation of the land is clearly ceded to another person (a tenant) the profits will be part of a UK property business.

This rule does not apply to farming, and does not apply if the land is being prepared for forestry purposes or comprises woodlands.

Legislation: ITTOIA 2005, s. 10

Woodlands

The commercial occupation of woodlands in the UK is not a trade or part of any trade. The profits are exempt from tax, and any losses cannot be relieved.

Legislation: ITTOIA 2005, s. 11

Mines, quarries, etc.

Special rules require the profits and losses of certain types of business or concern to be calculated as if the concern were a trade. Most of these concerns exploit land for resources and if the activities amount to a trade on first principles the special rules will not apply. The concerns are:

(1) mines and quarries, including sand pits, gravel pits and brickfields;

(2) ironworks, gas works, salt springs or works, alum mines or works, waterworks and streams of water;

(3) canals, inland navigation, docks and drains or levels;

(4) rights of fishing;

(5) rights of markets and fairs, tolls, bridges and ferries;

(6) railways and other kinds of way; and

(7) a concern of the same kind as mentioned in (2) to (5) above.

Legislation: ITTOIA 2005, s. 12

Tied premises

Where:

- a trader supplies goods that are sold or used on premises that are occupied by another person; and
- that trader has an estate or interest in those premises, which are employed for the purposes of that trade,

the receipts and expenses are brought into account as part of the trade, if they would apart from this rule be counted as the receipts and expenses of a property business.

This rule typically affects traders such as brewers who let out tied premises and supply goods to the publicans. The brewer is able to include all of the receipts and expenses from the premises that would normally relate to a property business in the computation of trading profits.

Legislation: ITTOIA 2005, s. 19

Caravan sites

A person who carries on material trading activities associated with the operation of a caravan site (for example, the provision of a site shop, sales of gas, etc.) may bring into account in calculating the profits of that trade the receipts and expenses relating to pitches or caravans that would otherwise be property business receipts and expenses.

Legislation: ITTOIA 2005, s. 20

Surplus business accommodation

Strictly, rent receivable from letting temporarily surplus business accommodation should be taxed as property business income. But provided the accommodation is not held as trading stock and is part of a building used for trading, and provided the rents are relatively small, then the rents (and associated expenses) can be brought into account in calculating trade profits. The letting must be for less than three years, and the trader must have used the accommodation for trade purposes before the letting and must intend to use it for trade purposes after the letting.

Legislation: ITTOIA 2005, s. 21

Wayleaves

Where certain wayleaves (easements, servitudes, rights in or over land) relate to land that is used as part of a trade carried on by the recipient of the wayleave payments, the trader may bring the payments and any associated expenses into account in calculating trading profits rather than treating them as property business receipts and expenses. If there are any other receipts or expenses that relate to the land and are property business receipts and expenses (for example where some of the land is tenanted), this special treatment for wayleaves does not apply and they are treated as being part of the property business.

The wayleaves affected are those relating to:

- electric, telegraph or telephone wires or cables;
- poles, pylons and apparatus relating to those wires or cables;
- any pipelines used to convey anything; and
- any apparatus used in connection with those pipelines.

Legislation: ITTOIA 2005, s. 22

Tax Reporter: ¶300-010

70-150 The charges to tax on property income

The legislation contains several charges, each applying to a different kind of property income.

The main charge is applied to the profits of a 'property business', which can be either a 'UK property business' or an 'overseas property business'.

There are special charges on:

- 'adjustment income', arising from changes in accounting basis;
- rent receivable in connection with mines, quarries, etc.;
- rent receivable in connection with UK electric-line wayleaves; and
- post-cessation receipts from a UK property business.

Legislation: ITTOIA 2005, s. 260

Tax Reporter: ¶300-020

70-200 Property income: scope of tax charge

UK and overseas property businesses

Income tax is charged on the full amount of the profits arising in a tax year of a property business. A 'property business' means a 'UK property business' or an 'overseas property business'. The person subject to the tax charge is the person entitled to or receiving the profits.

The terms 'UK property business' and 'overseas property business' share the same essential definition.

- A 'UK property business' consists of every business which a person carries on for 'generating income from land' in the UK *and* every transaction which the person enters into for the purpose of generating income from such land, otherwise than in the course of such a business.
- An 'overseas property business' consists of every business which a person carries on for 'generating income from land' outside the UK *and* every transaction which the person enters into for the purpose of generating income from such land, otherwise than in the course of such a business.

It is clear from the above definitions that casual receipts obtained from outside the normal range of receipts that might be expected of a business are to be included as part of a person's property business. It is also clear that a 'UK property business' and 'overseas property business' should include every separate activity that a person carries on that might comprise 'generating income from land', in and outside the UK respectively. An individual who lets a range of different properties and property rights in the UK on various terms will have a single UK property business, for which a single set of accounts will be needed. All of an individual's overseas properties will similarly be aggregated into a single overseas property business.

Investment income

'Generating income from land' is a concept that covers the most fundamental aspects of the charge on a property business. The basic concept of 'generating income from land' is that it is the:

> 'exploiting [of] an estate, interest or right in or over land as source of rents or other receipts.'

It is expressly provided that the right to use a static caravan or houseboat at a single location is to be treated as a right deriving from an estate or interest in land.

Rents

The word 'rents' is not exhaustively defined in the legislation (which does, however, provide that 'rents' includes payments made by a tenant for work to maintain or repair leased premises which the lease does not require the tenant to carry out). So 'rents' generally takes its ordinary meaning of 'payments reserved by the lessor on the demise of land' (as stated in *Duke of Westminster v Store Properties Ltd*). Rent which is rendered in kind is nonetheless rent. If a payment or receipt is not rent it is still likely to be covered by the inclusion of 'other receipts' in the definition of 'generating income from land'.

The *Law of Property Act* 1925 does contain a definition of 'rent', for the purposes of that Act, that can assist in providing some scope to the term:

> "Rent' includes a rent service or rent charge, or other rent, toll, duty, royalty or other annual or periodical payment in money or money's worth, reserved or issuing out of or charged upon land, but does not include mortgage interest;'

A dictionary definition of the term 'rent' sets out the general range of meaning that can be ascribed to the term. The *Oxford Dictionary of Law* definition includes:

> 'Payment by a tenant to his landlord under the terms of a lease or tenancy agreement ... If the parties wish the rent may not be paid in money; it may be in the form of service to the landlord or payment in kind.'

Although the legislation for property businesses does not give a full definition of 'rents', the income clearly needs to be derived from land or an interest, estate or right in or over land. So if there is a separate agreement or arrangement that can be identified as the immediate source of income, it cannot be rent if it is not for exploiting an estate, interest or right in or over land use or occupation of land.

Other receipts

In the definition of 'generating income from land', the term 'other receipts' is, like 'rent', not exhaustively defined in the legislation, although it is specified to include:

- payments in respect of a 'licence to occupy' or otherwise use land;
- payments in respect of the exercise of any other right over land; and
- rent charges and other annual payments reserved in respect of land or charged on or issuing out of land.

A 'licence to occupy' land is usually held to be a permission to enter or occupy another person's land, for a specified purpose. It does not, usually, confer a right to exclusive possession of the land and such a licence does not transfer any estate in or rights over the land since it is essentially a personal agreement between the licensor and licensee. Many licences are informal, with few (if any) of the terms and conditions clearly set down in writing. For this reason, a licence to occupy can often be revoked at the discretion of the licensor and it is not capable of being assigned by the licensee. Where a contractual licence specifies a period or term it cannot be revoked at will, although the terms of any contractual licence will not necessarily bind a third party who acquires the land from the licensor.

Land

The expression 'land', which is fundamental to the concept of 'generating income from land' is not defined in the legislation for property income, but is defined in the *Interpretation Act* 1978, Sch. 1, which provides that land 'includes buildings and other structures, land covered with water, and any estate, interest, easement, servitude or right in or over land'.

Caravans and houseboats

'Caravan' means:

- a structure designed or adapted for human habitation which is capable of being moved, either by being towed or by being transported on a motor vehicle or trailer; or
- a motor vehicle designed or adapted for human habitation.

'Caravan' does not include tents or rail-mounted railway rolling stock that is part of any railway system.

A larger mobile home can be a 'caravan' if it is made up from two sections that, although separately constructed, are designed to be put together on site by means of bolts, clamps etc., even if the assembled structure could not lawfully be moved along the highway (or road) by being towed or by being transported on a motor vehicle or trailer. So, a static mobile home can be a 'caravan'. It should be noted, however, that this rule is apparently restricted to larger structures that are built up from two sections. A mobile home assembled from three or more units would not necessarily be within the definition of 'caravan'. This should not cause a problem, given any structure that is comprised of three or more sub-units and that is of such a size, when assembled, that it cannot be transported on the highway would probably be regarded as a 'building' for the purposes of the charge on property income, but the matter is not entirely free from doubt.

The term 'houseboat' means 'a boat or similar structure designed or adapted for use as a place of human habitation'.

Legislation: *Law of Property Act* 1925, s. 205(1); *Interpretation Act* 1978, Sch. 1; ITTOIA 2005, s. 264–266, 875 and 878(1)

Cases: *IR Commrs v Exors of Lord Hatherton* [1936] 2 KB 316; *Duke of Westminster v Store Properties Ltd* [1944] Ch 129

Furnished lettings

In calculating the profits of a property business which includes a furnished letting, amounts payable for the use of the furniture must be brought into account as receipts of the property business. Without this provision, receipts in relation to furniture would not fall within the scope of 'property income' since they do not derive from an estate or interest in land.

Where receipts (and related expenses) for the use of furniture are not incidental to the letting of land but are instead related to a trade that involves making furniture available for use in premises, those receipts are not to be included as part of the profits of a property business.

A 'furnished letting' is defined as a lease or other arrangement under which a sum is payable for the use of the premises and the person entitled to use the premises is also entitled to the use of furniture in those premises.

In this context, 'premises' includes a caravan and a houseboat (see above).

See 70-340 for detail of relief for 'wear and tear' and replacement of furniture.

Legislation: ITTOIA 2005, s. 308

Income from Real Estate Investment Trusts (REITs)

UK-resident property holding companies that meet certain conditions may elect to be treated as Real Estate Investment Trusts (REITs). The profits of the property rental business of a REIT are exempt from corporation tax and any gains arising from the disposal of land and buildings used in the property rental business are not chargeable gains. Where a REIT pays dividends that derive from its tax-exempt property rental activities, those dividends are treated in the hands of shareholders as if they were the profits of a UK property business.

A REIT is required to deduct income tax at the basic rate from such dividend payments and pay it over to HMRC.

Although the dividends are treated for tax purposes as if they were profits of a property business, they must be reported separately from other property business income, in the main body of the self assessment return rather than in the supplementary pages dealing with land and property.

Legislation: FA 2006, s. 121

Tax Reporter: ¶300-020

70-260 Rent factoring: anti-avoidance

The charge to income tax is on the full amount of the profits arising in the property business in the tax year, and those profits are calculated in the same way as trading profits. So generally capital gains on property are not within the charge; they will be subject to capital gains tax if they constitute chargeable gains.

However, there is legislation on structured finance arrangements that counters, amongst other things, schemes attempting to convert rent into a capital receipt ('rent factoring').

In a basic rent-factoring scheme, a person (the 'borrower') temporarily transfers the right to an income stream (rent) in return for a lump sum from a third party (the 'lender'). The income stream acquired by the lender will be sufficient both to repay the lump sum itself and to cover an amount equivalent to any interest charges that would have arisen on a loan equal to the lump sum. The borrower will usually have to account for the arrangement as a loan (under generally accepted accounting practice), so that the effective finance costs will be treated as an expense. The income arising from the asset or rights that are transferred to the lender during the period of the arrangement is not taxable on the borrower, and the lump sum received is either a capital receipt or is not taxable at all. The net effect of the arrangement is for the borrower to have tax relief for the finance charge (which effectively represents both interest on a loan and the repayment of the principal of the loan), while being charged to no (or low) tax on the lump sum.

Effects of the anti-avoidance rules

The anti-avoidance rules apply where an arrangement would, apart from those rules:

(1) allow income or receipts (in this case rents) that would have been charged on the borrower (or a person connected with the borrower) for tax purposes not to be brought into account; or

(2) allow the borrower to become entitled to a deduction in computing income or profits for tax purposes.

Where the anti-avoidance rules apply the arrangement is deemed for tax purposes not to have either of the above effects.

The anti-avoidance rules do not apply where the whole of the lump sum received is brought into account when taxing the income of the borrower.

Legislation: ICTA 1988, s. 774A–774G

70-300 Calculating the profits of a property business

Special rules

There are a number of rules that are specific to the calculation of certain kinds of property business income and expenses/deductions. These cover:

- rental allowance exemption up to £1,000: see 70-310;
- restricted relief for interest payments: see 70-320;
- replacement of capital items in domestic property: see 70-340;
- expenditure on energy-saving items: see 70-350;
- expenditure on sea walls: see 70-400;
- lease premiums: see 70-550;
- furnished holiday lettings: see 71-100;
- the 'rent a room' rules: see 71-000.

The general rule

The general rule for a property business is that tax is chargeable on the 'full amount of the profits arising in the tax year' (subject to rules concerning the remittance basis for foreign income).

Those profits must be calculated in the same way as the profits of a trade. This requirement is explicitly linked in the legislation to particular computational rules for trades; some rules for trades are unnecessary (for example, the herd basis rules or the rules relating to films and sound recordings).

The applicable 'trading profits' rules

The trading profits rules that are applied to the calculation of the profits of a property business are limited to the following:

- profits to be calculated in accordance with generally accepted accounting practice;
- losses to be calculated on same basis as profits;
- 'receipts' and 'expenses' in Tax Acts are equivalent to accounting 'credits' and 'debits';
- charges and allowances under the *Capital Allowances Act* 2001 treated as receipts and expenses;
- interest is always a revenue (as opposed to capital) item;
- restrictions apply to tax relief on interest payments for individual residential landlords. Relief is restricted to just basic rate (the restriction is being phased in over a four-year period from April 2017 and will not apply to Furnished Holiday Accommodation) (see 70-320);
- no expense deduction for capital expenditure;
- expenses not incurred wholly and exclusively for trade purposes and unconnected losses not allowed;
- types of bad and doubtful debt that may be deducted;
- limits on the allowability of unpaid remuneration;
- deductibility of employers' payments that rank as 'employee benefit contributions' (for example, pension contributions);
- prohibition on relief for expenses relating to business entertaining and gifts;
- restriction on allowable costs of hiring cars and motorcycles exceeding specified emission levels;
- disallowance of patent royalties paid;
- exclusion of double relief for interest;
- prevention of relief for payments in respect of the taxpayer's own National Insurance contributions (other than for payments in respect of employees);
- prevention of relief for payments of penalties, default interest and VAT surcharges;

- prevention of relief for crime-related payments;
- relief for expenses incurred for the purposes of the business in the seven years prior to its commencement (pre-trading expenses);
- relief for the incidental costs of obtaining loan finance (subject to the potential restrictions from April 2017 noted above in the context of tax relief on finance costs in general);
- relief for the replacement and alteration of trade tools (the 'renewals basis');
- relief for payments made to employees for restrictive undertakings;
- relief for the costs associated with seconding an employee to a charity or educational establishment;
- relief for contributions to an agents' expenses for the operation of a payroll deduction scheme;
- relief for the costs associated with the provision of counselling and retraining for employees;
- relief for redundancy payments and other similar contractual payments;
- relief in respect of payments related to meeting threats to the personal security of the proprietor of the business;
- relief for contributions to local enterprise organisations or urban regeneration companies;
- relief for expenses connected with qualifying research and development, etc.;
- relief for expenses connected with patents, designs and trade marks;
- relief for payments to the Export Credits Guarantee Department;
- prohibition against bringing capital receipts into account in calculating the chargeable profits;
- bringing into account the amount of any debt incurred by the business that is released;
- bringing into account the amount of any distribution of assets of a mutual concern where deductions have been previously allowed for contributions to such a concern;
- bringing into account certain industrial development grants;
- bringing into account certain sums recovered under insurance policies or indemnity contracts;
- bringing into account the receipt by the donor (or connected person) of any benefit attributable to the making of certain gifts to charities, educational establishments, etc.;

- relief for any levies paid and the bringing into account of any repayments obtained under FISMA 2000; and
- relief for amounts that are unremittable to the UK due to foreign exchange restrictions.

If a rule for the computation of trading profits does not appear on the above list it is not to be applied in calculating the profits of a property business. For commentary on the above computation of trading profits rules, see 92-000 to 96-440.

Legislation: ITTOIA 2005, s. 272

Conflicts between deduction rules

In some cases where there is an overlap in the nature or type of a possible deduction, there may be a conflict between rules permitting a deduction and rules prohibiting a deduction. To avoid such conflict, the legislation specifies that any rule permitting a deduction in calculating the profits of a property business has priority over any rule prohibiting or restricting the deduction.

Legislation: ITTOIA 2005, s. 274

Tax Reporter: ¶300-045

70-310 'Rental allowance': tax exemption for property income up to £1,000

With effect from 6 April 2017, an individual may receive miscellaneous rental income of up to £1,000 free of tax (the rental allowance). A similar exemption extends to trading income (trading allowance (92-220)).

Where the allowance covers all of the individual's income, then they will have no requirement to declare the income. Where income exceeds the allowance, then the individual may elect to calculate their taxable income simply by deducting the allowance from their receipts rather than providing details of actual expenditure incurred.

This allowance cannot be used in conjunction with rent-a-room relief.

Legislation: ITTOIA 2005, s. 783B

70-320 Restricted relief for interest payments post 5 April 2017

Finance Act 2015 introduced provision to restrict relief on interest claimed as a deduction against rental income. Over a four-year period from 5 April 2017, relief will be progressively reduced until it is limited to the basic rate of income tax. The phasing is achieved by restricting the full deduction for finance costs when calculating the profits of a residential property business to:

- 75% for 2017–18;
- 50% for 2018–19;
- 25% for 2019–20;
- 0% for 2020–21 and following years.

The proportion of finance costs not qualifying for full tax relief above will be restricted to relief at just the basic rate on income tax.

The restriction is limited to residential letting but will not apply to Furnished Holiday Accommodation.

Finance costs will include interest or sums equivalent to interest together with the incidental costs of obtaining loan finance.

Example 1

Jackson earns a salary of £35,000 and receives a rental profit of £20,000 after expenses but before the deduction of mortgage interest of £12,000.

The restriction on mortgage interest relief will have the following impact on Jackson's taxable income (2016–17 allowances and tax bands are used throughout for illustrative purposes):

	2016–17	2017–18	2018–19	2019–20	2020–21
	£	£	£	£	£
Salary	35,000	35,000	35,000	35,000	35,000
Rental profit	20,000	20,000	20,000	20,000	20,000
Allowable loan interest	(12,000)	(9,000)	(6,000)	(3,000)	
Adjusted total income	43,000	46,000	49,000	52,000	55,000
Personal allowance	(11,000)	(11,000)	(11,000)	(11,000)	(11,000)
Taxable income	32,000	35,000	38,000	41,000	44,000
Tax liabilities:					
• £32,000 @ 20%	6,400	6,400	6,400	6,400	6,400
• £3,000 @ 40%	–	1,200	–	–	–

	2016–17	2017–18	2018–19	2019–20	2020–21
	£	£	£	£	£
• £6,000 @ 40%	–	–	2,400	–	–
• £9,000 @ 40%	–	–	–	3,600	–
• £12,000 @ 40%	–	–	–	–	4,800
Total	6,400	7,600	8,800	10,000	11,200
Finance cost deduction(1)		(600)	(1,200)	(1,800)	(2,400)
Tax payable	6,400	7,000	7,600	8,200	8,800

(1) The finance cost tax deduction is limited to the lower 20% of:
- the finance costs not relieved directly against rental income;
- property profits;
- adjusted total income after deduction of personal allowances.

In addition to increasing the overall tax liability, it is important to note that adjusted total income is increased and this may have other implications such as the high income child benefit charge, loss of personal allowances at incomes over £100,000, restrictions to pension contribution annual allowances, etc.

Where finance costs contribute to a property income loss, then similar restriction will apply in the carry forward and offset of the loss against subsequent year's profits.

Example 2

Stephanie's income in 2020–21 consists of a pension of £16,000 and rental profits of £12,000 before deduction of mortgage interest of £14,000. Her taxable income for the year will be:

	£	£
Pensions	16,000	
Rental profit	12,000	
Adjusted total income		28,000
Personal allowance (estimated)		(15,000)

Taxable income		13,000
Tax liability		
£13,000 × 20%		2,600
Finance cost deduction[2]		(2,400)
Tax payable		200

The £2,000 of finance costs that have not been used are carried forward and used to calculate the basic rate deduction in subsequent years.

In 2021–22, Stephanie's income consists of pensions of £16,300, rental profits of £18,000 and her mortgage interest payments were again £14,000. Her taxable income and finance costs relief in the year will be:

	£	£
Pensions	16,300	
Rental profit	18,000	
Adjusted total income		34,300
Personal allowance (estimated)		(15,000)
Taxable income		19,300
Tax liability		
£19,300 × 20%		3,860
Finance cost deduction[3]		(3,200)
Tax payable		660

(2) The finance cost deduction is the lower of:
- 20% × finance cost (£14,000);
- 20% × property profits (£12,000);
- 20% × adjusted total income less personal allowances (£13,000).

(3) The finance cost deduction is the lower of:
- 20% × finance cost (£14,000 plus £2,000 brought forward);
- 20% × property profits (£18,000);
- 20% × adjusted total income less personal allowances (£19,300).

Legislation: ITTOIA 2005, s. 272A and 272B; ITA 2007, s. 399A and 399B

70-340 Wear and tear allowances and replacement allowances

Until 5 April 2016, landlords providing furnished accommodation have been able to claim tax relief by way of a 'wear and tear' allowance. This is a flat-rate tax deduction equivalent to 10% of the 'relevant rental amount'. The relevant rental amount is defined as the gross receipts from furnished residential letting less any expenses borne by the landlord that would normally be borne by the tenant, for example utility bills.

This allowance is meant to cover costs relating to items such as:

- movable furniture or furnishings, such as beds or suites;
- televisions;
- fridges and freezers;
- carpets and floor-coverings;
- curtains;
- linen;
- crockery or cutlery;
- beds and other furniture.

With effect from 5 April 2016, the wear and tear allowance will no longer be available and landlords will be able to claim relief on a replacement basis. This relief will cover the same types of expenditure as was relieved by the wear and tear allowance, but under the replacement relief no relief will be given for the initial expenditure, only for the actual cost of replacing such assets. Where the replacement is the same or substantially the same as the old item, then full relief for the cost of the replacement will be given. In the event the replacement item is not the same or substantially the same as the old item, then relief will be limited to an amount that would have been incurred to replace the original item.

Neither the wear and tear allowance nor the replacement allowance gave relief for expenditure incurred on fixtures integral to the building such as sanitary wear, immersion heaters, etc. The replacement of such items would continue to be a deductible expense as a repair to the property.

Landlords providing furnished holiday accommodation will not be affected by these changes and they will continue to receive relief under the capital allowance regime.

Legislation: ITTOIA 2005, s. 308C, 311A

70-350 Expenditure on energy-saving items

Capital expenditure on fixtures and fittings in a residential property is not eligible for capital allowances. However, capital expenditure on acquiring and installing certain energy-saving items may be deducted in calculating the profits of a property business. Formal claims for this relief are not needed, the relevant amount is simply deducted. The relief was introduced as a temporary measure and only cover expenditure incurred up to 5 April 2015.

The energy-saving items that qualify for relief are:

- cavity wall insulation;
- loft insulation;
- hot water system insulation;
- draught proofing;
- solid wall insulation; and
- floor insulation.

The amount of the capital expenditure that may be deducted in a tax year is limited to £1,500 per property ('dwelling house'). The item can be installed either in the property itself or in a building containing the property, provided it is for the benefit of that particular property (so, for example, expenditure of up to £4,500 in a building containing three flats may qualify). Expenditure on an item that benefits several properties must be apportioned on a just and reasonable basis between the properties. This can mean that some expenditure will not qualify, even though the total expenditure on the building, divided by the number of properties, is less than £1,500.

Example

Sophia owns a building that contains three flats, all of which she lets. Prior to 5 April 2015, she installs an energy-saving item in the building which benefits all the flats.

The cost of the item is £4,000 (i.e. less than 3 × £1,500).

On a just and reasonable apportionment, the expenditure is allocated to each flat as follows:

- £600 to Flat A;
- £2,400 to Flat B; and
- £1,000 to Flat C.

A full deduction is available for the expenditure allocated to Flats A and C. The deduction for Flat B is limited to £1,500, so that £900 of the total expenditure cannot be deducted in calculating the profits of Sophia's property business.

The £1,500 limit applies no matter how many possibly eligible claimants there might be for the property. Any contributions (from any source) towards the qualifying items that are received by the person making the deduction will reduce the amount deductible.

The person making the deduction must have an interest in the property in question. The expenditure must be incurred wholly and exclusively for the purposes of the property business, and must be of a capital nature that is not otherwise deductible in computing profits, and in particular the expenditure must not be eligible for capital allowances.

There is no relief if the property in question is:

- in the course of construction;
- furnished holiday accommodation (see 71-200); or
- wholly or partly within the 'rent-a-room' scheme (see 71-000).

If more than one person has an interest in the property in question, then both the amounts of shared expenditure and the £1,500 limit (if it is exceeded in a year) must be apportioned on a 'just and reasonable' basis.

The usual rules relating to pre-trading expenditure are modified so that expenditure only qualifies as pre-trading if it is incurred within the six months (rather than the seven years) before the commencement of the property business.

Legislation: CAA 2001, s. 35; ITTOIA s. 312–314; *Energy-Saving Items (Income Tax) Regulations* 2007 (SI 2007/3278)

Tax Reporter: ¶300-050

70-400 Expenditure on sea walls

Under general principles, there would be no deduction for capital expenditure incurred in the making of a new sea wall or embankment. But special rules apply so that such costs may be deducted in computing the profits of a property business.

Where the owner or tenant of any premises incurs capital expenditure on making a sea wall or other embankment necessary to preserve or protect the premises against the encroachment or overflowing of the sea or any tidal river, a deduction of 1/21 of the expenditure incurred may be made from the rent receivable in respect of those premises for that year and for the next 20 tax years.

This relief is not available if capital allowances have been made in respect of the expenditure.

If the wall, etc. is needed to improve the land and to change its character, the expenditure is not deductible.

There are apportionment provisions covering the case where, in the 21-year period during which relief is due, an interest or part of an interest in the premises is transferred from one person to another.

Legislation: ITTOIA 2005, s. 315–317

Case: *Hesketh v Bray* 2 TC 380

Tax Reporter: ¶300-055

70-500 Property business losses

Losses of a property business are calculated in the same way as profits, and all the losses and profits on individual properties in the business will be netted off automatically to give either a profit or a loss for the whole business for a tax year. If a person has both a UK property business and an overseas property business (see 70-200), the losses of one cannot be set against the profits of the other.

There are three types of relief available for property business losses:

- carry-forward relief (UK or overseas property business);
- relief against general income (UK or overseas property business); and
- post-cessation relief (UK property business only).

If a loss arises on a furnished holiday lettings business, it is treated as a trading loss (with some modifications; see 71-200).

Carry-forward relief

The default treatment for a property business loss is to carry it forward against future profits of the same (either UK or overseas) business. This happens automatically, unless the person makes a claim for general income relief or post-cessation relief. The loss is carried forward and set against the first available profits of the business, with any excess not relieved continuing to be carried forward, and with any other losses incurred along the way being added to the amount carried forward. So there is a 'pot' of losses carried forward, with amounts being added or removed to set against profits as the years go by.

Example 1

Lisa owns and lets several properties in the UK. Her results and her carry-forward loss relief are as follows:

Year	Profit or (loss) in year	Loss b/fwd	Chargeable for year	Loss c/fwd
	£	£	£	£
Year 1	(6,000)	0	0	(6,000)
Year 2	4,000	(6,000)	0	(2,000)
Year 3	(1,000)	(2,000)	0	(3,000)
Year 4	5,000	(3,000)	2,000	0
Year 5	(8,000)	0	0	(8,000)
Year 6	(3,000)	(8,000)	0	(11,000)
Year 7	6,000	(11,000)	0	(5,000)

Legislation: ITA 2007, s. 118

Tax Reporter: ¶300-085

Relief against general income

In certain circumstances an individual or partner may claim to have a loss of a property business (UK or overseas) set against the person's general income for the loss-making year and/or the following year.

The conditions for the business are that:

- capital allowances treated as expenses in the year exceed any balancing charges in the year; and/or
- the business has a 'relevant agricultural connection' and has 'allowable agricultural expenses' in the year.

A business has a relevant agricultural connection if, broadly, the land includes land managed as one estate which includes land occupied wholly or mainly for the purposes of husbandry.

Allowable agricultural expenses are expenses (other than loan interest) that are deductible in respect of maintenance, repairs, insurance or management of the estate and are directly attributable to the land used for husbandry. For parts of the estate with mixed use, expenses must be apportioned.

Amount of loss eligible for relief

The amount of the loss eligible for relief is the smaller of:

(1) the loss itself; and

(a) the amount of capital allowances after netting off allowances and any balancing charges;

(b) the amount of the allowable agricultural expenses; or

(c) in a case where there are both net capital allowances and allowable agricultural expenses, the sum of these two.

Claims and interactions

The person who makes the loss can claim to have it set against:

- general income of the loss-making year; or
- general income of the following year.

If the loss is not fully used up in the chosen year, the person may (but is not obliged to) make a separate claim for relief in the other year. Any unused loss is then carried forward under the normal rules.

The claim must be made by the first anniversary of the normal self-assessment filing date for the year in which the set-off is to be made. So if a person has a loss in 2015–16 and wishes to have it set against general income of 2017–18, the deadline for making the claim is 31 January 2019. But the deadline for making a claim for a set-off against general income of 2015–16 is 31 January 2018.

If a person makes claims to have losses from two different years set off against the same year's income, the claim for the prior year's loss takes priority. It does not matter which claim is made first.

Example 2

Bart has a property business that makes losses of £10,000 in 2016–17 and £5,000 in 2017–18. The full amount of each loss is eligible for relief against his general income. In May 2018, Bart makes a claim to set the 2017–18 loss against his general income for that year. In August 2018, he makes a claim to set the 2016–17 loss against his general income of 2017–18.

Bart has available income in 2017–18 of £12,000. Under the priority rule, the losses are used as follows:

- first, the £10,000 loss from 2016–17 is set off; and
- then £2,000 of the £5,000 loss from 2017–18 is set off.

The remaining £3,000 of the 2017–18 loss can then be carried forward to set against future profits of the same property business, or Bart can, at any time before 1 February 2021, make a claim to set it against his general income of 2018–19.

Legislation: ITA 2007, s. 120–124

Tax Reporter: ¶300-090

Restriction on relief against general income

In order to claim property loss relief against general income the loss must have either an agricultural connection or a capital allowances connection. In respect of the latter condition, FA 2010 introduced an anti-avoidance provision which seeks to ensure that no relief for a property business loss is available against general income to the extent that it is attributable to an annual investment allowance (see 111-875) in circumstances where tax avoidance arrangements are involved. This provision does not, however, prevent the property business loss from being carried forwards to set against future profits.

The restriction applies where, in a tax year a property business loss arises which is attributable to some extent to an excess of annual investment allowances over balancing allowances and it arises as a consequence of, or in connection with, 'relevant tax avoidance arrangements' one of the main purposes of which is to obtain an annual investment allowance to be able to claim property loss relief against general income.

Where the restriction applies, the amount of the loss available for relief is reduced by the amount of the annual investment allowance claimed, thus where the allowance exceeds the amount of the loss, the loss available for relief is reduced to nil.

This restriction applies where the relevant tax avoidance arrangements or transactions forming part of those arrangements are entered into on or after 24 March 2010 except where these are in pursuance of an unconditional obligation made before that date.

A similar anti-avoidance provision was introduced by FA 2012 in relation to tax-generated agricultural expenses where the arrangements are entered into after 12 March 2012 with a similar exception for unconditional obligations made before that date.

Legislation: ITA 2007, s. 127A, 127B

Tax Reporter: ¶300-092

Post-cessation relief

Certain payments and events relating to debts will qualify for post-cessation relief against a person's general income if they occur within seven years of the cessation of a UK property business. (The prohibition of a similar relief in respect of an overseas property business could well be said to be in breach of EU law by being a restriction in the free movement of capital.)

The amounts that qualify are:

(1) any payment made to remedy defective work or defective services, meeting legal expenses in connection with a claim regarding such defects, or insuring against liabilities in relation to either of these; and

(2) the amount of an unpaid debt that was taken into account in calculating the profits or losses of the property business and that either:

    (a) is released as part of a statutory insolvency arrangement; or

    (b) proves to be bad.

A qualifying payment is set against the person's general income of the tax year in which the payment is made. The amount of a released debt is set against the person's general income of the tax year in which it is released. The amount of a bad debt can be set against general income of the year in which it proves to be bad or any later tax year that begins within seven years from the date of cessation.

If there are any expenses of the property business that were taken into account in calculating profits or losses of the business but were never paid, these will reduce the amount of post-cessation relief available.

The relief must be claimed and the deadline for making the claim is the first anniversary of the self-assessment filing date for the tax year in which the relief is available.

Example 3

Maggie permanently ceased to carry on her property business on 15 September 2012.

On 2 September 2017, a debt of £12,000 owed to Maggie, which was taken into account in computing the profits of her property business, is released as part of a statutory insolvency arrangement. In her property business profit calculation for 2012–13, Maggie made a deduction for expenses of £3,000 which she has never in fact paid.

Maggie has available income in 2017–18 of £7,000.

In principle relief against general income for 2017–18 is available for £12,000 less £3,000, i.e. £9,000, if Maggie makes a claim by 31 January 2020. Maggie makes the claim but she can only use £7,000 of the amount against her general income for 2017–18.

This leaves £2,000 unrelieved. It cannot be carried forward. But relief may be available by setting the amount against chargeable gains.

Relief against chargeable gains

In Example 3 above, Maggie has an amount of £2,000 that in principle qualifies for relief against general income, but which has not been used in this way because Maggie does not have enough income to absorb it in 2017–18.

A person can claim to have such an unrelieved amount treated as an allowable loss for capital gains tax purposes. The relief is available only for amounts that cannot be relieved against general income. Again the time-limit for making the claim is the first anniversary of the normal self-assessment filing date for the year in which the relief is available, i.e. the for the year in which the qualifying payment was made or in which the debt was released, or, in the case if a bad debt, for the year in which it is proved to be bad or any subsequent tax year that starts within seven years of the cessation of the business.

The amount that can be relieved in this way is limited to the amount on which the person would be chargeable to capital gains tax in the year, ignoring any allowable losses brought forward, the annual exemption, and any other post-cessation property business or trading amounts treated as allowable losses for capital gains tax purposes in the year.

Example 4

The facts are as in Example 3 above, but Maggie has chargeable gains in 2017–18 of £15,000 and allowable losses brought forward at 6 April 2017 of £5,000. She makes a claim before 1 February 2020 to have the unrelieved post-cessation amount of £2,000 treated as an allowable loss, leaving her chargeable gains position for 2017–18 as follows.

	£
gains before set-offs	15,000
post-cessation relief	(2,000)
	13,000
annual exemption	(11,300)
	1,700
allowable losses b/fwd at 6/4/16	1,700
chargeable gains	Nil

	£	£
allowable losses c/fwd at 5/4/18	5,000	
	(1,700)	
		3,300

Legislation: TCGA 1992, s. 261D; ITA 2007, s. 125 and 126

Tax Reporter: ¶300-092; ¶524-125

Premiums and other receipts

70-550 Premiums and other receipts: introduction

A person who grants a lease in respect of land or property may charge a premium for the grant. Under general principles the premium would be a capital sum and not chargeable to income tax (it would, however, be chargeable to capital gains tax, but the liability would be lower). But, in the case of a 'short-term lease' (a lease lasting 50 years or less), special rules treat a proportion of the premium as *income* of a property business. The balance of the premium is the consideration for the disposal of an interest in land for capital gains purposes. This counters attempts to avoid income tax by converting what would otherwise be rent into a premium.

The amount charged as income is inversely proportional to the length of the lease, reflecting the fact that charging a premium for the grant of a very short lease is more 'artificial' than charging a premium for the grant of a much longer lease.

The lease premium rules apply to the simple grant of a short-term lease (see 70-650) and also to the essentially similar cases where:

- a premium is paid in lieu of rent for a period of 50 years or less (see 70-650);
- an amount is payable for the surrender, variation or waiver of a short-term lease (see 70-700);
- a short-term lease which was granted at undervalue is assigned at a profit (see 70-720);
- an estate or interest in land is sold subject to a right to reconveyance at a later date (see 70-720); or
- an estate or interest in land is sold subject to a right to a leaseback at a later date (see 70-720).

Legislation: ITTOIA 2005, s. 276

Tax Reporter: ¶300-110

70-600 Meaning of terms

Leases

The legislation provides that the word 'lease' includes an agreement for a lease (so far as the context permits), and any tenancy, but does not include a mortgage.

That is not particularly helpful and therefore the normal meaning of the word will be applicable. This is essentially a written contract whereby the owner of a property allows another person exclusive use of the property for an agreed period of time in return for the payment of rent. A lease may, in certain circumstances, also be a 'parol lease' which is verbal agreement.

The term 'tenancy' is also not defined in the legislation and again it has its normal meaning, which generally includes both formal and informal agreements relating to property.

Generally speaking, the lease premium charging provisions only apply if the lease lasts for 50 years or less. If the lease premium charging provisions were left that simple, they would be easy to sidestep. One way of doing this would be to grant a lease which was stated by the parties to be for more than 50 years but which in fact would become so expensive after, say, ten years that the lessee would have no alternative but to abandon the lease, so that in fact, for all practical purposes, the lease would only be one for ten years. This premium would, unless there were provisions to the contrary, escape the charge to income tax.

The legislation therefore defines the 'effective duration' of a lease, with three rules that apply for lease premiums and similar receipts.

(1) If the terms of the lease (or any other circumstances) make it unlikely that the lease will carry on beyond a certain date, and if the amount of the premium is not substantially greater than it would have been had the lease actually ended on that date, then the effective duration of the lease ends on that date.

(2) If the lease can be extended in duration, by way of a notice given by the tenant, and if there are any circumstances that make it likely that such a notice will be given, then those circumstances must be taken into account in determining the effective duration of the lease.

(3) If the tenant (or anyone connected with the tenant) is entitled or may become entitled to a further lease (or the grant of a new lease) of the same premises (or of premises comprising the whole or part of the same premises), then the initial lease may be treated as continuing until the end of the further lease. It is not necessary for the further lease to begin immediately after the end of the initial lease.

The above rules are applied by reference to the facts known or ascertainable at the time of the grant of the lease or, in the case of a variation or waiver of a lease, the facts known or ascertainable at the time of the waiver, etc. It is also to be assumed that all the parties involved act as if they are at arm's length, irrespective of their actual relationships.

The above rules dealing with the ascertainment of the duration of leases are widely phrased in the legislation, in order to prevent tax avoidance schemes where a short-term lease is dressed up to look as though it has a longer duration. But it is important to note that these rules will apply whether or not there is an avoidance motive.

Where HMRC have reason to believe that a person has information relevant to ascertaining the length of a lease, they may issue a notice requiring that person to give the information within a specified time. But a solicitor cannot be required to do more, in relation to anything which he or she has done on behalf of a client, than state that he or she is or was acting on behalf of that client, and to give the client's name and address.

Legislation: ITTOIA 2005, s. 303–305 and 364(1)

Tax Reporter: ¶300-115

Premiums

The term 'premium' is not exhaustively defined in the legislation, but it is stated to be a sum paid on or in connection with the granting of a tenancy, and to include any 'similar sum', payable to the immediate or a superior landlord or to a person connected with the immediate or a superior landlord. The term 'sum' includes the value of any consideration and therefore includes the transfer of value via assets, etc.

The word 'premium' has been stated in the courts to mean, 'where a lease is granted, part of the whole of the rent which is capitalised and paid in a lump sum at the time of the grant of the lease'. In this context any sum, other than rent, paid on or in connection with the granting of a tenancy is presumed to have been paid by way of premium, except in so far as other sufficient consideration for the payment can be shown to be given.

In Scotland, a premium includes a grassum payable to any landlord or any intermediate landlord on the creation of a sub-lease.

Legislation: ITTOIA 2005, s. 307

Case: *Clarke (HMIT) v United Real Moorgate Ltd* [1988] BTC 49

Tax Reporter: ¶300-115

70-650 Premiums paid in respect of short-term leases and similar amounts

Where the payment of any premium is required under a 'short-term lease' (i.e. any lease lasting 50 years or less), or otherwise under the terms subject to which a short-term lease is granted, the landlord is treated as entering into a 'UK property business' or an 'overseas property business' transaction, receiving (in the tax year in which the lease is granted) an amount calculated by a formula. The effect of the formula is to treat as an income receipt the amount of the premium, less one fiftieth of that amount for each year (except the first) of the lease's duration. So, for example, only one fiftieth of a premium paid for a 50-year lease will be chargeable as income, whereas the full amount of a premium paid for a one-year lease will be chargeable as income. The formula gives the amount of the income receipt as:

$$P \times \frac{50 - Y}{50}$$

P is the amount of the premium; and

Y is the number of whole years (other than the first year) in the effective duration of the lease.

The balance of the premium is taken into account for capital gains purposes.

Legislation: TCGA 1992, Sch. 8, para. 5(1); ITTOIA 2005, s. 277

Tax Reporter: ¶300-120

Amount treated as premium where tenant pays for works

There are rules to prevent avoidance of the main charge by the tenant incurring expenditure on behalf of the landlord instead of paying a premium. Where, under the terms subject to which the lease is granted, there is imposed on the tenant an obligation to carry out any work on the premises, there is a deemed premium, equal to the amount by which the value of the landlord's estate or interest immediately after the commencement of the lease exceeds what its then value would have been if there had been no such obligation on the tenant.

This does not apply to the extent that the expenditure would have been an allowable deduction from the rent, if it had been incurred by the landlord. So expenditure on repairs, maintenance and other allowable items is not treated as a premium.

> **Example 1**
>
> Sheila lets a plot of waste land to Construction Ltd on a 49-year lease that requires the company to build a road on the site. The value of Sheila's interest under the lease as granted is £500,000, but it would only be have been £200,000 without the obligation to construct the road. The company is treated as paying a premium ('P' in the above formula) of £300,000 (i.e. £500,000 less £200,000).
>
> Applying the formula above, £12,000 is taxed as rent and £288,000 is taken into account for capital gains purposes.

Legislation: ITTOIA 2005, s. 278

Tax Reporter: ¶300-120

Payments instead of rent

There is a charge where, under the terms of the grant of a lease, a lump sum becomes payable in place of the whole or part of the rent for a period of less than 50 years. It does not matter if the effective duration of the lease is more than 50 years; the period that is important here is the period for which the payment instead of rent is made. Where any part of the period covered by the lump sum falls after the end of the effective duration of the lease, that part of the period is not included in determining the duration of the period.

The landlord is treated as receiving property business income (in the tax year in which the lease is granted) the amount being calculated under the following formula:

> **Example 2**
>
> On 1 June 2015, Stephen grants a 70-year lease to Mark. In accordance with the terms of the lease, Mark pays £500,000 to Stephen on 1 June 2017. This payment is in lieu of rent for the period 1 June 2017 to 31 May 2037 (20 years). Stephen will have a deemed income receipt of £190,000 in 2017–18, calculated according to the above formula, where 'S' is £500,000 and 'Y' is 19.
>
> Stephen will also be treated as making a part disposal of the freehold or other asset out of which the lease is granted, the disposal consideration for which is £310,000 (£500,000 less £190,000).

Legislation: ITTOIA 2005, s. 279; TCGA 1992, Sch. 8, para. 2(1), 3(2) and 5(1)

Tax Reporter: ¶300-120

70-700 Surrender, variation or waiver of a short-term lease

Surrender

Where the payment of any sum by a tenant is required under the terms of a short-term lease (i.e. any lease with an effective duration of 50 years or less) for the surrender of the lease, the landlord is treated as receiving (in the tax year in which the sum becomes payable) an amount as income from a property business. The amount is calculated by the following formula:

Variation or waiver

Where a tenant makes a payment for the variation or waiver of any of the terms of a lease, and the period for which the variation or waiver takes effect is 50 years or less, there is a deemed property income receipt in the tax year in which the contract for the variation or waiver is executed. Note that it does not matter if the effective duration of the lease itself is more than 50 years; what matters is the length of the period of the variation or waiver. Where any part of the period of the variation or waiver falls after the end of the effective duration of the lease, that part of the period is ignored.

The deemed receipt is calculated using the following formula:

The issue of what amounts to a 'waiver' for these purposes has been considered in the House of Lords. A tenant sublet premises in breach of covenants against subletting. These breaches of covenants entitled the landlord to terminate the lease and re-enter the premises. However, in return for the payment of a sum of money, the landlord agreed not to enforce that power. It was held that the payment was in consideration for the waiver of a term of the lease even though the lease itself was not amended in any way and the landlord's right to terminate the lease in the case of future breaches remained in force.

Example

A tenant, Construction Ltd, pays £20,000 to Sheila, the landlord, for adjustment in the company's favour of the terms of the next rent review provided for by the lease. The contract is executed on 30 April 2017. The review period in respect of which the variation is agreed is four years from 1 May 2017. Sheila is treated as receiving property income in respect of the variation amounting to £18,800 in 2017–18 (£20,000 × 47/50 = £18,800; where the numerator is 50 minus (4 less 1)).

Legislation: ITTOIA 2005, s. 280 and 281

Case: *Banning v Wright* (1972) 48 TC 421

Tax Reporter: ¶300-130; ¶300-140

70-720 Other lump sums treated as income under the lease premium rules

The legislation covers three other circumstances in which a proportion of a lump sum is treated as a receipt of a property business:

- assignments for profit of a lease granted at undervalue;
- sales with a right to reconveyance; and
- sale and leaseback transactions.

Assignment at a profit

An individual may wish to benefit a member of his family by granting them a lease at an undervalue, which the family member could then assign at full value to a third party. To counter such a device, a specific provision applies where a tenant assigns a lease, which was granted at undervalue and the assignment is at a profit, the tenant who assigns the lease is treated as receiving an amount as income of a property business in the tax year in which the consideration for the assignment is payable. The amount is given by the following formula:

The description of 'P' ensures that the deemed income of the assignor is not calculated by reference to an amount that is not representative of the undervalue, and that the calculation excludes amounts already been brought into charge.

Example 1

Alice grants a lease worth £200,000 to Ben for £100,000. Ben assigns the lease to Carol for £150,000. Carol assigns the lease to David for £220,000.

In calculating Ben's deemed income, 'P' will be £50,000 (i.e. £150,000 less £100,000).

In calculating Carol's deemed income, 'P' will be not £70,000 or £120,000, but rather £50,000 (i.e. the amount by which the original undervalue of £200,000 less £100,000 = £100,000 exceeds Ben's profit of £50,000).

Legislation: ITTOIA 2005, s. 282 and 283

Tax Reporter: ¶300-150

Sale with a right to reconveyance

If:

- an interest in land is sold and the terms of sale are that it is or may be required to be re-conveyed to the seller (or a connected person) at a future date; and

- the period between the sale and the earliest date on which the interest would fall to be re-conveyed is 50 years or less; and
- the interest is to be re-conveyed at a lower price than that at which is was sold,

then the seller is treated as receiving an amount as income of a property business in the tax year in which the interest is sold. The income amount is calculated using the following formula:

Example 2

On 20 June 2017, Emma sells a plot of land to Frank for £100,000, on the condition that Emma may require Frank to re-convey the land to her at any time after 30 August 2030, for £60,000.

The period from 20 June 2017 to 30 August 2030 is 13 complete years.

Emma will have a deemed income receipt in 2017–18, calculated using the above formula, where 'E' is £40,000 and 'Y' is 12.

It is worth noting that there is little difference in reality between this transaction and a transaction under which Emma grants a 13-year lease to Frank for a premium of £40,000 (i.e. £100,000 less £60,000). Had she granted such a lease, the formula for the simple grant of a lease (see 70-650) would have given the same amount of deemed income.

Legislation: ITTOIA 2005, s. 284 and 286

Tax Reporter: ¶300-160

Sale and leaseback

If:

- land is sold and the terms of sale provide for a lease of that property to be granted to the seller (or a connected person);
- the period between the sale and the earliest date on which the lease would fall to be granted is 50 years or less; and
- the selling price exceeds the sum of the premium for the lease and the value at the date of sale of the right to receive a conveyance of the reversion immediately after the lease begins to run,

then the seller is treated as receiving an amount as income of a property business in the tax year in which the sale takes place. The income amount is calculated using the following formula:

Legislation: ITTOIA 2005, s. 285 and 286

Tax Reporter: ¶300-170

70-750 Reduction in the amount of a premium charged

It is possible to reduce the amount of a premium or other receipt that is brought into account as property income, if the landlord who is charging the premium, etc. is also a tenant whose own landlord has charged a premium, etc. The lease subject to the original charge is a 'taxed lease'.

This relief is not available for amounts charged on sales with a right to re-conveyance or on sale and leaseback transactions, but it is available for the other amounts charged under these lease premium rules (as discussed in preceding paragraphs).

The relief is determined by a statutory calculation, which is:

The amount calculated under these provisions is deducted from the amount charged under the lease premium rules, but it cannot reduce a receipt below zero.

Where a lease that may be eligible for relief does not extend to the whole of the premises covered by the taxed lease, a just and reasonable apportionment must be made.

Example

Geraldine grants a 21-year lease to Harry for a premium of £100,000. Geraldine is treated under the lease premium rules (see 70-650) as receiving income of £60,000 (i.e. £100,000 × 30/50).

Harry later grants an 11-year sublease to Ian for a premium of £70,000. Harry is treated under the same lease premium rules as receiving £56,000 (i.e. £70,000 × 40/50).

But relief is available to Harry because he grants the sublease out of a taxed lease. Under the above formula, the amount of the relief is £31,429 (i.e £60,000 × 11/21).

So when Harry grants the sublease, his deemed income will be £24,571 (i.e. £56,000 less £31,429).

Legislation: ITTOIA 2005, s. 287–289

Tax Reporter: ¶300-180

70-800 Relief for payment of premiums

If a tenant has paid a premium to the landlord and is using the leased land or premises as part of a property business or in the course of a trade, relief may be available for the tenant as a deduction in computing the profits of that business or trade. The deduction is a proportion of the premium paid to and charged on the landlord.

The amount of the relief is the amount charged in the landlord's hands, divided by the total number of days in the 'receipt period' of the lease (i.e. Y in the charging formula, plus 1).

This daily amount is then relieved as if it were a revenue expense of the tenant, incurred in respect of the premises (that may be either used in the management, etc. of the property business or sublet as part of that business), accruing on a daily basis. In this way the tenant can, over the full course of the lease, benefit from deductions that add up to the amount originally charged on the landlord.

For leases granted after 5 April 2013, this relief is not available if the landlord would not have been taxed on any premium but for the rule that deems a lease to be granted for a shorter period than it actually is.

Legislation: ITTOIA 2005, s. 60 and 291–294

Tax Reporter: ¶300-180

70-850 Appeals involving premiums and similar lump sums

Where it appears that the determination of an amount taxable under the lease premium rules may affect the income tax, corporation tax or CGT liabilities of another person or persons (for example, the tenant), an HMRC officer may (but does not have to) notify the other person or persons of the proposed determination in relation to the premium or other receipt and of their appeal rights. The notice may, notwithstanding HMRC's duty of confidentiality, state the grounds on which the proposed determination is based.

A person receiving such a notice may, within 30 days of the date on which it was given, object to the proposed determination by written notice to the inspector. If the person does not do this, he or she cannot later contest the determination.

Legislation: ICTA 1988, s. 42

Tax Reporter: ¶300-190

70-900 Premiums: payment by instalments

Where there is a receipt of:

- a lease premium;
- any amount payable in lieu of rent;
- any amount paid for the surrender, variation or waiver of a lease,

and the receipt is payable by instalments, the person liable to pay the tax due may request to pay the tax by instalments. The instalments are as permitted by an HMRC officer and there is no statutory limit on the number of instalments. However the period over which the agreed instalments of tax must be paid is specified to be eight years or less and must, in any case, end before (or at the same time as) the instalments of the taxable receipt.

Legislation: ITTOIA 2005, s. 299

Tax Reporter: ¶300-210

Reverse premiums

70-950 Reverse premiums

Where a landlord pays a premium or other amount as an inducement to take out a lease, the tenant may be treated as receiving an amount as a receipt of its trade or of a property business. For commentary on reverse premiums, see 97-420ff.

Legislation: ITTOIA 2005, s. 99–103 and 311

Tax Reporter: ¶222-200; ¶300-500

Rent-a-room relief

71-000 Introduction to rent-a-room relief

If an individual receives income from the letting of furnished accommodation at his or her only or main residence in the UK and that income can be classified as 'rent-a-room receipts' for a tax year, receipts of up to £7,500 (£4,250 prior to 2016–17) may be left out of account when computing that individual's taxable income.

Rent-a-room relief is available to an individual for a tax year where:

- the individual receives income during that year from the letting of furnished accommodation in a residence in the UK;
- receives income in respect of goods and services (such as the provision of meals, cleaning and laundry) supplied in connection with the use of such furnished accommodation; and
- for at least some time during the year, the residence was his or her only or main residence.

The receipts are 'rent-a-room receipts'.

A 'residence' for these purposes is defined as 'a building, or part of a building, occupied or intended to be occupied as a separate residence' and it includes a caravan or houseboat (see 70-200 for definitions of caravan and houseboat). Where a building or part of a building is designed for use as a single residence but is temporarily divided into two or more residential units it will be treated as a single residence for these purposes and so will only attract a single relief.

This relief does not have to be claimed; it applies automatically where the conditions are satisfied. It is possible to elect for the relief not to apply. The election will usually only be used where there are losses to claim in respect of the lettings.

Total rent-a-room amount

The total rent-a-room amount for an individual for a tax year is the total of:

- the rent-a-room receipts for the year; *plus*
- any balancing charges in respect of plant or machinery provided for the purposes of the letting (or trade) from which the rent-a-room receipts derive.

So the rent-a-room amount is the gross income (including balancing charges) with no relief for any expenses associated with the letting.

Trades

If an individual's activities in letting furnished accommodation with services amounts to a trade it is eligible for the relief on the same basis as letting activities that are treated as a UK property business.

Legislation: ITTOIA 2005, s. 784–788

Tax Reporter: ¶303-000

71-050 The amount of rent-a-room relief

Provided no other person is entitled to any of the rent-a-room receipts at a time when the accommodation is the individual's only or main residence, then he will be entitled to relief based on the exclusive receipt of the income. This is known as the 'basic amount' and is £7,500 (£4,250 prior to 2016–17) per year.

If other individuals are entitled to any part of the income then the basic amount is halved (to £3,750). This means that each person entitled to claim rent-a-room relief in respect of the shared income from the letting of the accommodation will get half of the basic relief available, even if the total number of individuals sharing the relief is three or more.

If an individual who qualifies for rent-a-room relief in a tax year has a total rent-a-room amount that is equal to or less than the individual's limit (i.e. £7,500 or £3,750), then all of the gross receipts from the letting are excluded from the charge to tax and there is no relief for expenses.

Legislation: ITTOIA 2005, s. 788–794

Tax Reporter: ¶303-010

The alternative basis

Where an individual's total rent-a-room amount exceeds his limit, the basic relief is not available and a normal computation (i.e. calculating profits using generally accepted accounting practice, etc.) will be needed to determine the profits of the UK property business. In other words the taxable profits are calculated in the same way as for any other forms of rental income. But it is possible to elect for a special 'alternative basis' to apply. The election must specify the year from which this alternative basis is to apply, and will have effect for that year and all subsequent years unless and until it is withdrawn by the individual.

The effect of the alternative basis is to bring into the charge to tax only those rent-a-room receipts for a year that are in excess of the individual's limit for the year. As with the basic relief, no deductions for expenses are permitted, so the taxable profits are equal to the difference between the gross receipts and the individual's limit.

An election or withdrawal must be made to an HMRC officer on or before the first anniversary of the normal self-assessment filing date for the tax year specified in the election or withdrawal notice. Where an election or withdrawal is made, any assessment to adjust an individual's tax liability must be made on or before the first anniversary of the normal self-assessment filing date for the tax year concerned.

Example

Duncan has a total rent-a-room amount for 2017–18 of £8,100. He is not eligible for the basic relief and so will have to prepare an account for his property business, unless he elects for the alternative basis to apply. He has until 31 January 2020 to make the election for 2017–18. He makes the election and so his taxable profit for 2017–18 will be £600 (i.e. £8,100 minus £7,500). The alternative basis will be applied for each subsequent year in which his rent-a-room income exceeds the limit, until he formally withdraws the election.

Legislation: ITTOIA 2005, s. 795–801

Tax Reporter: ¶303-000

Furnished holiday lettings

71-100 Introduction to furnished holiday lettings

Where lettings within the UK or the European Economic Area (EEA, i.e. the other member states of the EU plus Norway, Iceland and Liechtenstein) qualify as being the 'commercial letting of furnished holiday accommodation' the profits are to be treated for certain purposes as if they derived from a trade even though they are in fact part of the profits of a property business.

Treatment of profits and losses

The special treatment of furnished holiday lettings means that:

- capital allowances are available on plant and machinery used in the accommodation;
- accordingly there are no deductions for energy-saving items (see 70-350);
- the income is 'relevant UK earnings' for pension purposes;
- the letting is treated as a trade for the purposes of some capital gains tax reliefs, including rollover relief and entrepreneurs' relief;
- the losses are treated as the losses of a trade so that trading loss relief is applicable, with some restrictions (see below);
- married couples and civil partners are not automatically regarded as beneficially entitled to income from jointly-held property in equal shares.

If a property business includes both furnished holiday lettings and other types of letting, the profits and losses of the furnished holiday lettings part of the business must be calculated separately, because of the different treatment of profits and losses. If there is any accommodation that is only partly let as furnished holiday accommodation, amounts will need to be apportioned.

Although the special regime applies to furnished holiday lettings in both the UK and the EEA (excluding the UK), they are to be treated as two separate property businesses. The legislation effective from 6 April 2011 contains parallel provisions for each type of business and the results of each will need to be separately calculated.

Legislation: ITTOIA 2005, s. 322 and 327–328B; ITA 2007, s. 836(3); Exceptions D and DA

Tax Reporter: ¶303-100; ¶303-110

Loss relief: restrictions

With effect from 6 April 2011, relief for losses generated by a furnished holiday lettings business may only be used to carry forward against profits of subsequent tax years arising from the same business in which the loss arose (ITA 2007, s. 127(3A) and 127ZA(4)). Consequently the profits and losses of a UK business and an EEA business need to be calculated separately.

Legislation: ITA 2007, s. 127, 127ZA

Tax Reporter: ¶303-110

71-250 Furnished holiday lettings: conditions

For lettings to be treated as furnished holiday lettings, they must constitute 'the commercial letting of furnished holiday accommodation' in the UK or in the EEA (see 71-100).

'Letting' means a lease or other arrangement under which a person is entitled to use property.

'Commercial letting' occurs if the letting is on a commercial basis and with a view to the realisation of profits. This wording is similar to the wording of the anti-avoidance provisions which apply for income tax loss reliefs.

Letting a property to a friend or relation at a low rent will not be a commercial letting.

Following a Special Commissioners' decision regarding the availability of loss reliefs for a furnished holiday letting case regarding losses, HMRC published an interpretation in Tax Bulletin which set out their views. In brief:

- 'profits' means the 'commercial' and not the 'tax adjusted' profits;
- a taxpayer's expressed intentions are not necessarily conclusive. There may be evidence which points to a motive other than the income profit motive (such as a holiday or retirement home, or a long-term capital profit on the disposal of the property);
- where there is evidence to suggest that a property or caravan was acquired primarily as a holiday or second home, the letting activity is likely to be carried on with a view to generating income to offset costs rather than with a view to the realisation of profits;
- if the size of the mortgage used to purchase the property or caravan is so large that the projected profitability is jeopardised, then the commercial credibility of the scheme as a whole is, consequently, questionable even though individual lettings may be on a commercial basis.

Legislation: ITTOIA 2005, s. 323

Case: *Brown v Richardson (HMIT)* (1997) Sp C 129

Other Material: *Tax Bulletin*, Issue 31, October 1997

Tax Reporter: ¶303-140

Holiday accommodation

Accommodation is 'furnished holiday accommodation' if:

- the person entitled to the use of the accommodation is entitled to the use of furniture (the rules do not specify a minimum amount of furniture); and
- three conditions regarding the letting and the pattern of occupation are met.

The three conditions work by reference to a relevant period. Usually this will be the tax year, but in a case where accommodation is first let as furnished accommodation it is the 12 months starting from that time and in the case where accommodation ceases to be let as furnished accommodation it is the 12 months ending with the date of cessation.

The three conditions are that:

(1) *'the availability condition'*: the accommodation must be available for commercial letting to the public generally as holiday accommodation for a minimum number of days during the 'relevant period'. Where the 'relevant period' is a tax year from 2012–13 onwards or begins on or after 6 April 2012, the requirement is 210 days. For relevant periods which are tax years up to and including 2011–12 or which begin before 6 April 2012, the requirement was 140 days;

(2) *'the letting condition'*: the accommodation must actually be commercially let as holiday accommodation for a minimum number of days during the 'relevant period'. Where the 'relevant period' is a tax year from 2012–13 onwards or begins on or after 6 April 2012, the requirement is 105 days. For relevant periods which are tax years up to and including 2011–12 or which begin before 6 April 2012, the requirement was 70 days; and

(3) the *'pattern of occupation condition'*: during the 'relevant period', there must not be more than 155 days falling in 'periods of longer term occupation'.

A 'period of longer term occupation' is a continuous period of more than 31 days during which the accommodation is in the same occupation, unless there are abnormal circumstances. No guidance is provided for the exclusion to the rule on continuous occupation, otherwise than in circumstances that are not normal. There is no guidance on what constitutes 'not normal', but it is likely that this will cover unexpected situations such as where a tenant exceeds the 31-day limit due to illness etc.

As far as the letting condition is concerned, a period of longer-term occupation will not (unless covered by the exception for abnormal situations) count as letting for holiday accommodation.

Subject to the 'averaging election' (see below), every furnished property must meet all the conditions in order to be treated as qualifying holiday accommodation. Where properties which have previously met the letting condition, fail it in the following year or two despite a genuine intention on the part of the taxpayer to meet that condition, an election may be made to treat that property as qualifying holiday accommodation.

Example 1

James has a furnished flat in central London.

In 2017–18, the flat is available for holiday letting for the whole year. It is commercially let as furnished holiday accommodation as follows:

to Alan from 5 May to 18 May (14 days);

to Barbara from 26 May to 1 June (seven days);

to Carl from 9 June to 29 June (21 days);

to David from 30 June to 13 July (14 days);

to Alan again from 14 July to 3 August (21 days);

to Emma from 8 August to 12 September (36 days);

to Fiona from 15 September to 21 September (seven days);

to Alan again from 22 September to 2 November (42 days);

to Guy from 3 November to 7 December (35 days);

to Hugo from 8 December to 25 January (49 days);

to Imogen from 24 February to 7 March (14 days).

The 210-day availability condition is clearly met for the year. And, as the flat is actually let for 259 days, the 105-day lettings condition is also clearly met.

But the flat is let for continuous periods of more than 31 days for a total of 162 days, exceeding the 155-day limit, and so the lettings for the year will not qualify for furnished holiday lettings treatment.

Legislation: ITTOIA 2005, s. 325

Tax Reporter: ¶303-150

The averaging election

If a person has more than one property let as holiday accommodation, and if one or more of the properties would qualify for furnished holiday lettings treatment except that the letting condition is not met for the year, then the person may make an averaging election for that year. The election must be made on or before the first anniversary of the normal self-assessment filing date for the year covered by the election, and it can apply to as few or as many properties as the person wishes.

Example 2

Kathryn owns three cottages in Cornwall, all of which are available for holiday lettings in 2017–18 for a period of 215 days from early spring to late autumn. In a particular tax year, the cottages are commercially let as furnished holiday accommodation as follows:

Wren Cottage is let for 34 days;

Little Owl Cottage is let for 152 days; and

Teal Cottage is let for 72 days.

Without an election, only Little Owl Cottage would qualify for furnished holiday lettings treatment.

Averaging all three cottages would give a deemed letting period for each cottage of (34 + 152 + 72)/3 = 86 days, meaning that all properties would fail the letting condition.

Averaging Wren Cottage and Little Owl Cottage would give a deemed letting period for each of those cottages of (34 + 152)/2 = 93 days, meaning again that all three properties would fail the letting condition.

Kathryn chooses to make an averaging election for Little Owl Cottage and Teal Cottage, so that there is a deemed letting period for each of those cottages of (152 + 72)/2 = 112 days, meaning that both Little Owl Cottage and Teal Cottage qualify for furnished holiday lettings treatment. Wren Cottage cannot qualify for furnished holiday lettings treatment in that year.

Legislation: ITTOIA 2005, s. 326

Tax Reporter: ¶303-150

Non-resident landlords

71-400 Non-resident landlords: tax deduction scheme

Where a non-resident landlord has income from a UK property business, it is usually subject to deduction of tax at source. The tax is deducted and paid over to HMRC by the letting agent or, where there is no agent, by the tenant.

The scheme provides for letting agents or, where there is no letting agent, the tenants of a non-resident landlord, to:

- deduct tax at the basic rate from the landlord's UK rental income;
- pay the tax quarterly to HMRC; and
- submit annual information returns of details relating to income, expenses and tax deducted for each non-resident landlord.

Legislation: ITA 2007, s. 971

Website: www.hmrc.gov.uk/cnr/nr_landlords.htm

Tax Reporter: ¶303-200

71-450 Letting agents and tenants

Letting agents and tenants are defined in the primary legislation (which refers to them both as 'non-resident landlord representatives') as persons:

- by whom amounts are payable to a non-resident landlord, which are treated as income of a UK property business in the landlord's hands; or
- who act on behalf of the non-resident landlord in the management or administration of the business.

Letting agents

The above definition is very wide; potentially all sorts of persons could be letting agents. But HMRC guidance and the secondary legislation effectively narrow the definition by telling us that a letting agent is a person whose usual place of abode is in the UK and who has power to receive, or control over direction of, the rental income.

Friends and relatives of the landlord can be letting agents, as can persons acting in a professional capacity such as estate agents, solicitors or accountants. But persons who do no more than provide legal advice or services to the landlord (for example, a solicitor who receives apportioned rental income as a one-off on a conveyance) are not letting agents. Neither are banks and building societies who simply provide an account into which the rent is paid and from which withdrawals may be made, or persons who find tenants but do not generally handle or control rental income.

A letting agent must:

- produce a quarterly tax calculation for each non-resident landlord for whom he or she acts, submit to HMRC a quarterly return reflecting the calculations and pay the tax over to HMRC within 30 days of the end of the quarter;

- by 5 July after a tax year, provide each landlord for whom he or she acts with a certificate showing the tax payable to HMRC by the agent; and
- by the same date, submit to HMRC a yearly return summarising the income and expenses for the year.

The tax calculation applies basic rate tax to:

- property business income received in the quarter; plus
- other property business income paid away by the tenant in the quarter at the letting agent's direction; less
- expenses paid in the quarter by (or at the direction of) the letting agent which the agent can reasonably be satisfied are allowable expenses of the property business.

HMRC give extensive guidance on the 'reasonably satisfied' requirement and on the kinds of expenses that will usually be deductible, on their website.

Tenants

Tenants have similar quarterly and annual obligations where there is no letting agent. In this case, the calculation of tax deductible and due is based on:

- property business income paid in the quarter to the non-resident landlord; plus
- property business income paid to a third party in the quarter, unless the tenant can be reasonably satisfied that this represents an allowable expense of the business (see above with regard to HMRC guidelines).

This is subject to HMRC issuing a notice requiring the scheme to be operated.

There is an important de minimis exception for tenants paying rent or other sums for the occupation of the premises of £5,200 or less per year.

Legislation: ITA 2007, s. 972; *Taxation of Income from Land (Non-residents) Regulations* 1995 (SI 1995/2092), reg. 2–15

Tax Reporter: ¶303-250

71-500 Landlords

Where tax is deducted, the non-resident landlord should receive a certificate from the letting agent or tenant showing the amount of tax deducted in the year to 31 March. This amount can be set off against the landlord's self assessment liability for the tax year ended 5 April.

Non-resident landlords can apply to HMRC for approval for rents to be paid gross. Where approval is not given, or earlier approval is withdrawn, the landlord may appeal to the Tax Chamber of the First-tier Tribunal (see 62-050). Approval may be given where:

- the non-resident landlord's UK tax affairs are up to date; or
- the non-resident landlord has never had any UK tax obligations; or
- the non-resident landlord does not expect to be liable to UK income tax for the year in which the application is made.

The landlord must also undertake:

- where the basis of the application is that no UK tax liability is expected to arise, to notify HMRC if any liability does in fact arise or the landlord expects one to;
- to comply fully with all UK tax obligations; and
- to notify HMRC if the landlord's normal place of abode ceases to be outside the UK.

Legislation: ITA 2007, s. 972; *Taxation of Income from Land (Non-residents) Regulations* 1995 (SI 1995/2092), reg. 17–21

Savings and investment income

72-000 Savings and investment income

Savings and investment income is charged to income tax under ITTOIA 2005, Pt. 4, which covers a wide range of different types of savings and investment income, from interest to sales of foreign dividend coupons. This chapter will mainly focus on interest and dividends. It includes commentary on deeply discounted securities and the accrued income scheme.

Legislation: ITTOIA 2005, s. 365

Tax Reporter: ¶327-000

Interest

72-100 Meaning of interest

Tax is charged on 'interest'. There is no helpful statutory definition of the term 'interest' for this charge.

As a starting point, *The Concise Oxford Dictionary* defines 'interest' as 'money paid for use of money lent' or for not requiring repayment of debt. Other definitions, for instance that interest is 'payment by time for the use of money' derive from case law. In the Courts it has been held that:

> 'the essence of interest is that it is a payment which becomes due because the creditor has not had his money at the due date. It may be regarded either as representing the profit he might have made if he had had the use of the money, or, conversely the loss he suffered because he had not that use. The general idea is that he is entitled to compensation for the deprivation.'

Interest is generally held to accrue from day to day even if payable only at intervals and can therefore be time-apportioned where the amount of money on which interest arises is assigned from one person to another.

HMRC's view on the meaning of 'interest'

Following a number of cases involving the payment of compensation for the mis-selling of certain financial products, such as mortgage endowment policies, HMRC commented in a Tax Bulletin on the nature of interest, both generally and in the context of interest being included in compensatory payments.

The Tax Bulletin article emphasises that the particular facts of each case must be examined carefully to determine the nature of each element of any payment and that, in general, for a particular amount to be 'interest', 'there must be a sum of money by reference to which the payment is to be ascertained' and there must be an 'entitlement' to the interest. The article endorses the views on 'interest' expressed by judges as quoted above.

The article also notes that there are clear, statutory exemptions from tax in respect of interest included as a component in:

- compensation payments for mis-sold pensions: whilst these financial products are similar in nature to, say, endowment policies, they are distinct and the specific exemption from income tax for mis-sold pensions is not extended to compensation for other financial products that are mis-sold; and
- compensation payments for personal injury (which may include injury to feelings and other psychological impairments as well as physical injury): interest on such payments is exempt from income tax and is distinct from interest related to the mis-selling of financial products.

  See in this connection 72-300.

Legislation: FA 1996, s. 148; ITTOIA 2005, s. 369 and 751

Case: *Westminster Bank Ltd v Riches* (1947) 28 TC 159

Other Material: HMRC *Tax Bulletin* TB08/04-1

Tax Reporter: ¶327-075

72-150 The tax charge

Income tax is charged on the full amount of the interest arising in the tax year. The person liable to tax is the person entitled to or receiving the interest.

With effect from 6 April 2016, the obligation for most deposit takers (principally banks), Building Societies and National Savings & Investments to deduct basic rate tax from interest was removed. This obligation continues for other interest payments such as those arising on interest paid by a limited company to an individual.

A person who is UK resident is chargeable to income tax on savings and investment income on both UK source income and non-UK source income.

A person who is not UK resident is chargeable only if the source is in the UK.

Where income does not have a source, then it is treated as UK income if it has a 'comparable connection' to the UK.

Legislation: ITTOIA 2005, s. 368 and 369

Tax Reporter: ¶327-175

Extending the scope of the charge

There are a number of sources of income that, although not strictly 'interest', are to be treated as interest for the purposes of the charge to tax. These are as follows.

Building society dividends

Any dividend paid by a building society is to be treated as interest. 'Dividend' in this context includes any distribution, whether or not described as a dividend.

OEIC distributions

Where the distribution accounts of an open-ended investment company (OEIC) show the total amount available for distribution to owners of shares as yearly interest, for income tax purposes a payment of interest is treated as being made to owners of shares in the OEIC. The total payment to each share owner is to be taken as being an amount that is proportionate to the owner's share in the OEIC. The date on which payment is treated as made for a distribution period is either the date specified in the OEIC's instrument of incorporation and prospectus or, if no such date is specified, the last day of the distribution period.

Authorised unit trusts

Where the distribution accounts of an authorised unit trust show the total amount available for distribution to the unit holders as yearly interest, for income tax purposes payment of yearly interest is treated as being made to unit holders. The total payment to each unit holder is to be taken as being an amount that is proportionate to the unit holder's rights. The date on which payment for any distribution period is treated as made is either the date specified in the trust's terms or, if no such date is specified, the last day of the distribution period.

Industrial and provident societies

Any dividend, bonus, or other sum payable to a shareholder in a registered Industrial and Provident Society or a UK agricultural or fishing cooperative is treated as interest (provided that it is payable by reference to the shareholder's holding of share capital).

Funding bonds

Where any 'funding bonds' are issued to a creditor in respect of a liability to pay interest on a debt, whether in respect of any money borrowed or otherwise, by any government, public authority or public institution, or by any body corporate, the following rules will apply:

- the issue of the bonds is treated as if it were an interest payment equal to the value of the bonds when they were issued; and
- when the bonds are redeemed it is not treated as a payment of any interest for tax purposes.

Funding bonds include any bonds, stocks, shares, securities or certificates of indebtedness.

Amounts paid by the Financial Services Compensation Scheme (FSCS)

A tax charge is imposed on amounts paid by the Financial Services Compensation Scheme (FSCS) after 5 October 2008, which represent accrued interest, arising out of a default by a financial institution. The FSCS exists to compensate customers of defaulting financial institutions and part of that compensation may comprise an amount in respect of interest which should have been paid by the institution. The amount is calculated as if it had been paid after deduction of tax at source. The tax charge will be on the corresponding gross amount of the payment with the taxpayer being treated as if tax had actually been deducted.

Disguised interest

FA 2013 introduced an anti-avoidance provision dealing with disguised interest. Where there is an arrangement which produces a return economically equivalent to interest, then income tax is charged on that amount. To avoid double taxation an adjustment can be made on making a claim. There is an exception for certain shares which are trading on a regulated market and issued before 6 April 2013 or where it is reasonable to assume their main purpose was not to produce a return economically equivalent to interest.

Interest not paid in cash

Where interest is paid in the form of goods or services or a voucher a payment of the amount of interest paid is treated as equal to the market value of the goods or services. In the case of a voucher, this is the higher of the face value, the encashment value and the market value of goods or services for which the voucher is capable of being exchanged. Statements about interest paid in this form must be given to the recipient in broadly the same way as a payment of cash.

Discounts

See 72-400 for commentary on 'discounts'.

Legislation: ITTOIA 2005, s. 370A, 372–381, 381A–381E

Tax Reporter: ¶327-175

Exemptions from the charge

The principal exemptions from the charge to tax as interest are:

- income from authorised Savings Certificates issued by National Savings & Investments and Ulster Savings Certificates;
- income from Individual Savings Accounts (see 79-000ff.);
- interest arising in respect of certified Save As You Earn arrangements;
- income from government securities that are free of tax for residents abroad (FOTRA);
- interest on repayment supplement, tax reserve certificates, damages for personal injury, repayments of student loans, redemption of funding bonds, some foreign currency securities and interest on monies deposited by or on behalf of victims of Nazi persecution where the interest is paid under a compensation scheme; and
- tax treaties with the UK can exempt interest or apply a reduced rate of tax.

Legislation: ITTOIA 2005, s. 691–694, 702, 713 and 749–756A

Tax Reporter: ¶327-725; ¶327-750; ¶343-150ff.; ¶344-500

72-175 Peer-to-peer lending and loss relief on irrecoverable loans

Interest earned on peer-to-peer 'P2P' lending is taxable under basic principles. *Finance Act* 2016 introduces provisions to allow lenders to offset losses arising on irrecoverable loans against the P2P interest that they receive. Subject to a claim by the lender, then relief will be applicable on loans that become irrecoverable from 6 April 2015. For loans that become irrecoverable after 5 April 2016, the offset against P2P interest will be automatic. Initially, any loss may only be offset against interest arising on the loan that has become irrecoverable or on loans arranged through the same operator, but in the event this does not utilise the whole of the loss, then it may be extended to be offset against interest arising on other P2P loans.

Unused relief may be carried forward and offset against P2P interest arising in subsequent years.

In order to fall within these provisions, the loan must have been made on commercial terms and must not be part of a scheme or arrangement to obtain a tax advantage.

Legislation: ITA 2007, s. 412A–412J

72-200 When interest arises

Tax on interest is chargeable on the person 'receiving or entitled to' it, and interest is taxable by reference to the tax year in which it 'arises'.

For interest to have 'arisen', it must be at the disposal of the recipient. Interest has not arisen if it is receivable but not received.

Interest has been held to have been received where assets were received in lieu of the interest itself.

Bank interest is usually regarded as received when it is credited to an account in the recipient's name. However, interest paid by cheque sent to the a person does not 'arise' until the cheque is honoured and the funds are at the person's disposal at his or her bank, since a cheque represents only a promise to pay rather than an actual payment.

Legislation: ITTOIA 2005, s. 370–371

Cases: *Leigh v IR Commrs* [1928] 1 KB 73; *Cross v London & Provincial Trust Ltd* (1938) 21 TC 705; *Parkside Leasing Ltd v Smith* [1990] BTC 406

Tax Reporter: ¶327-200

72-250 Capitalisation of interest

Interest does not lose its character as interest by reason of being added to the principal sum and so bearing interest itself. In the case of *IR Commrs v Oswald*, the trustees of a creditor's estate exercised an option under the loan agreement to capitalise overdue interest. The House of Lords held that unpaid interest never ceased to retain its character of interest, although it had been added to capital indebtedness and had, in turn, carried interest. This meant that under the relevant legislation at the time a deduction of tax was required to be made on payment of so much of the total indebtedness as represented accumulated interest:

> 'Capitalisation means no more than that interest which continues to be interest shall be treated together with the capital sum due as itself interest-bearing but does not alter its quality as interest.'

Case: *IR Commrs v Oswald* (1945) 26 TC 435

Tax Reporter: ¶327-225; ¶327-250

72-300 Interest on damages, etc.

Where courts award interest on debts or damages for a period, the interest is annual interest which arises in the year in which it is received, even though it may relate to a period of more than one year.

Case: *Jefford v Gee* [1970] 2 QB 130

Personal injury

Interest is exempt from income tax if it is interest on damages in respect of personal injuries awarded by a court to a plaintiff or any other person, or in respect of a person's death, included in any sum for which judgment is given. 'Personal injuries' include any disease and any impairment of a person's physical or mental condition. Where such damages are paid by way of an annuity, the sum is paid without deduction of tax. This also applies to criminal injuries compensation paid by way of an annuity.

Legislation: ITTOIA 2005, s. 751

Mis-sold personal pensions, etc.

Any compensation paid in respect of certain mis-sold personal pensions, buy-out contracts and retirement annuity contracts is exempt from income tax and capital gains tax. The exemption applies where an individual who, acting in reliance on 'bad investment advice' given between 29 April 1988 and 30 June 1994, transferred from, opted out of or did not join an occupational pension scheme and instead took out a personal pension scheme, buy-out contract or retirement annuity contract.

A payment of interest also qualifies for exemption from income tax provided it is interest:

- on the whole or any part of a capital sum comprising compensation, as above;
- in respect of a period ending on or before the date on which the amount of that capital sum is agreed or determined (whether or not it is varied in subsequent legal proceedings).

HMRC commentary on whether payments are, or include, interest

A Tax Bulletin article sets out the principles that HMRC apply in considering whether a payment is, or includes, interest in the context of receipts, by individuals, of compensation for the 'mis-selling' of certain financial products, such as mortgage endowment policies. The status of a particular amount (i.e. whether it is interest or not) can only be answered by reference to principles of common law.

Whilst noting that detailed approaches to compensation awards may vary, the broad aim is to put investors back in the position they would have been in had they not bought, or put money into, the product. One way of doing this is to refund the premiums (or other amounts) paid by the investor together with an additional amount to compensate for the time he or she did not have use of the money. Where this approach is adopted, HMRC consider that in almost all cases the additional payment is interest. The interest component of any compensatory payment is usually calculated by reference to the sum of money which the aggrieved investor is entitled to be repaid, and effectively compensates him or her for being deprived of the use of that money.

A number of subsidiary issues are also covered in the article. The use of terminology such as 'damages', according to HMRC, often simply explains the reason why interest is being paid and does not alter its nature as interest.

Whilst accepting that a truly voluntary payment cannot be interest, even if described as such, because the essential feature of an entitlement to it is absent, HMRC consider it will be extremely rare for any payment arising from claims that a financial product has been mis-sold to be truly voluntary, since the redress is given in consideration of the complainant giving up a right of action.

Interest on compensation payments for mis-sold pensions is specifically exempt from income tax. There is also specific relief from tax where settlements include payment for personal injury. For example, damage to feelings. Such payments are exempt from income tax by statute. In the absence of specific provisions the general principle, that interest on compensation for the 'mis-selling' of other financial products is taxable, will apply.

Legislation: FA 1996, s. 148; ITTOIA 2005, s. 731–734

Other Material: HMRC *Tax Bulletin* TB08/04-1

Tax Reporter: ¶327-050

72-400 Discounts

Discounts (other than discounts in deeply discounted securities; see 72-450) are charged to income tax as interest. The legislation does not define 'discount', and the courts have interpreted the word over the years. A suitable starting point in attempting a definition is the *Oxford English Dictionary* which states that a discount means:

> '(1) a deduction from a bill or amount given esp. in consideration of prompt or advance payment or to special class of buyers.
>
> (2) a deduction from the amount of a bill of exchange etc. by a person who gives value for it before it is due ...'

A discount will not be chargeable to income tax just because it is described as such. It must represent an income profit if it is to fall within the charge.

The distinction between interest and a discount was analysed in the House of Lords :

> 'In my opinion there is an essential difference between interest and discount, so much so that to speak of "earning" discount, seems to me wrong. Interest accrues from day to day, or at other fixed intervals, but discount does not. Two consequences follow. First, when periodical interest is received (or is due to be received) the profit or gain on the loan is realised from time to time. But when a bill is discounted nothing is realised until the bill matures or is sold, and the whole profit is postponed or rolled up until one of these events occurs ... Secondly, it is possible to calculate, if necessary in advance, the interest that is, or will be, due at any date while the bill is outstanding, and therefore to calculate the profit as at that date. But when a bill is discounted no such calculation is possible ...'

Legislation: ITTOIA 2005, s. 381(1)

Cases: *Lomax (HMIT) v Peter Dixon & Son Ltd* (1943) 25 TC 353; *Willingale (HMIT) v International Commercial Bank Ltd* (1978) 52 TC 242

Tax Reporter: ¶327-475ff.

Deeply discounted securities

72-450 Deeply discounted securities

Profits from deeply discounted securities (DDSs) are subject to a special charge.

Meaning of 'deeply discounted security'

The general rule is that a security is a DDS if, at the time of issue, the amount payable on redemption or maturity exceeds the issue price by more than 0.5% of the amount payable on redemption for every year (or part year) of the security's life, or 30 years if that is less.

The security's life is the time between its issue and its redemption.

> **Example**
>
> Arcturus plc issues a security at a price of £300 per unit. It is redeemable after 25 years at £380. The difference between the issue and redemption prices is £80, which is more than £47.50 (0.5% × 25 × £380). The security is therefore a DDS.

Securities expressly excluded

The following are expressly *not* DDSs:

- shares in a company;
- gilts that are not strips;
- life assurance policies;
- capital redemption policies;
- securities (which might otherwise be DDSs) issued under the same prospectus where the most of the securities so issued are not DDSs; and
- 'excluded indexed securities'.

'Excluded indexed securities' are securities where the amount payable on redemption is to be determined by applying to the issue price a percentage change (over the redemption period) in the value of some specified chargeable assets or some index of the values of such assets. For these purposes any interest payable on redemption is ignored when determining the redemption amount payable.

Legislation: ITTOIA 2005, s. 427–433

Tax Reporter: ¶337-050

72-500 Deeply discounted securities: the charge to tax

Profits realised from the discount on a DDS are charged to income tax. In the case of securities that are outside the UK, the remittance basis may apply for certain taxpayers.

Subject to this, the income tax charge is on the full amount of the profit which arises on the disposal of a DDS. The person liable is the person making the disposal.

If the person acquiring a DDS becomes entitled to the security at the time of making the agreement for the transfer, the transfer is treated as occurring at the time of the agreement. Any conditional agreement is treated as being made when the condition is fulfilled.

The 'disposal' of a DDS includes:

- its redemption;
- its transfer by sale, exchange, gift or otherwise; and
- its conversion into shares or other securities (which may themselves be DDSs).

If a person entitled to a DDS dies, the security is treated as if it is transferred to the personal representatives immediately before the death.

The person who is treated as making a disposal of a DDS is:

- in the case of redemption, the person entitled as the holder of the security to any payment;
- in the case of a transfer by sale, exchange, gift, etc., the transferor; and
- in the case of the conversion of the security, the person who would be entitled to any payment on a disposal, were such payment to be made.

The measure of a person's profit on the disposal of a DDS is the difference between the amount payable on disposal and the amount paid to acquire the security. No account is taken of any incidental expenses incurred in connection with the disposal or acquisition.

Where a person re-acquires a security, any amounts paid for it (including incidental costs) on the previous purchase are ignored.

Legislation: ITTOIA 2005, s. 427–429 and 437–439

Tax Reporter: ¶337-100

The accrued income scheme

72-600 Accrued income scheme – introduction

It is possible for a person to buy an interest-bearing security just after an interest payment, when the security has little or no accrued interest attaching to it, and then sell it just before an interest payment, when the security has a large amount of accrued interest attaching to it. The sale price will contain an element that represents the interest which accrued in the seller's hands but will be received by the buyer. Effectively, the seller is selling interest but, without the special rules discussed in this and later paragraphs, the part of the sale price representing interest would be a capital receipt rather than an income receipt. The special rules (usually referred to as the accrued income scheme, or AIS) were introduced to counter the avoidance of income tax on interest-bearing securities via transactions such as this, where the interest was effectively converted to capital (and the capital receipt might be covered, for example, by the seller's annual exemption and so would escape the charge to tax altogether).

Legislation: ITA 2007, s. 615

Website: *Accrued Income Scheme-Taxing Securities on Transfer*, www.hmrc.gov.uk/guidance/ais.htm

Tax Reporter: ¶331-500ff.

72-650 Outline of the accrued income scheme

Although the details of the accrued income scheme are complex, the concept at the heart of the scheme is simple. Essentially, of the interest that accrues on a fixed interest stock between one interest payment date and the next, that part which accrues within the ownership period of the seller of that security is charged on the seller as income, and that which accrues within the ownership period of the buyer is charged on the buyer as income.

Where securities (widely defined) are transferred with accrued interest, the transferor is taxable on an amount equal to the interest accruing on those securities during his or her period of ownership and the transferee is entitled to relief of the same amount. Where securities are transferred without accrued interest, the transferee is taxable on the 'rebate amount' and the transferor is entitled to relief of the same amount.

For these purposes, interest includes dividends and any other form of return.

A charge will arise in respect of the adjustment for accrued interest not actually received in the following circumstances.

- Where securities are bought *without* the accrued interest (ex-dividend): the charge is on the buyer and the amount charged will be the amount by which the purchase price was reduced on account of the interest not received by the buyer.
- Where securities are sold *with* the accrued interest (cum-dividend): the charge is on the seller and the amount charged will be the amount by which the sale price was increased on account of the interest not received by the seller.

Matching relief will be due in respect of the adjustment for the amount of extra interest received in the following circumstances.

- Where securities are purchased *with* accrued interest (cum-dividend): the amount of the relief (for the buyer) will be the amount by which the purchase price was increased (and will correspond to the amount charged on the seller).
- Where securities are sold *without* accrued interest (ex-dividend): the amount of the relief (for the seller) will be the amount by which the sale price was decreased (and will correspond to the amount charged on the buyer).

Where, under the rules, a person is treated as entitled to a sum, it is treated as received on the last day of the interest period in question. An interest period ends on the day on which interest is paid, or 12 months after the last payment date (or issue date) if this is earlier. The charge is on the full amount treated as received in the year.

The application of the scheme is excluded in a number of situations. In these circumstances, there is no deemed income for the person concerned. Special rules apply in a number of cases, for example, nominees and trustees, death, foreign currency, appropriations to trading stock, most especially to underwriters.

The net charge or relief

Securities are treated as being of the same kind if they are treated as such by a recognised stock exchange or would be so treated if they were listed on a recognised stock exchange. For each kind of UK security, charges and reliefs should be netted off. Where there is a net charge (an 'accrued income profit'), it is subject to income tax. Where there is a net relief (an 'accrued income loss'), it is carried forward to set against future charges.

Legislation: ITA 2007, s. 615–635 and 671

Tax Reporter: ¶331-600

72-700 Holding and transferring securities

Holding securities

A person holds securities at a particular time if the person is entitled to them at that time, and a person acquires securities on becoming entitled to those securities. A person is regarded as holding securities on a particular day if either:

(1) the person is entitled to them throughout the day; or

(2) the person becomes entitled and does not cease to be entitled to them on that day.

This means that if a transfer is made on Wednesday afternoon, the seller is treated as holding the securities up to and including Tuesday, and the buyer is treated as holding them from Wednesday onwards.

Transferring securities

A transfer in relation to securities means a transfer by way of sale, exchange, gift or otherwise, but does not include the vesting of securities in a person's personal representatives on death and does not generally include any transaction forming part of an exchange of a gilt-edged security for strips, or vice versa. And the accrued income scheme does not apply to transfers of securities to which the deeply discounted securities rules apply (see 72-450).

Where an agreement is made for the transfer of securities, those securities are regarded as being transferred on the day on which the agreement is made and not when the actual transfer under the agreement takes place, if that is different. In such circumstances, the transferee under the agreement becomes 'entitled' to the securities when the agreement is made.

Legislation: ITA 2007, s. 619–620 and 675

Tax Reporter: ¶331-800

72-750 Chargeable and excluded securities

Chargeable securities

The term 'securities' includes any loan stock or similar security issued by a government (including governments of countries outside the UK) or a public or local authority (whether in the UK or not) or by any other company or body. It does not matter whether such a security:

- is or is not secured;
- does or does not carry a right to interest of a fixed amount or at a fixed rate per cent of the nominal value of the securities; or
- is or is not in bearer form.

The term 'securities' therefore includes both fixed and variable rate stocks and bonds (including those in bearer form), whether UK or foreign, in sterling or another currency, issued by governments, companies, local authorities or other institutions and whether secured or unsecured.

Excluded securities

Some securities are specifically excluded from the accrued income scheme. These are:

(1) shares in a company (although certain shares in a building society are not excluded);

(2) national savings certificates (including Ulster savings certificates);

(3) certificates of deposit;

(4) war savings certificates;

(5) uncertificated eligible debt security units;

(6) any security which is an uncertificated right to receive a principal amount, with or without interest, as a result of depositing money at the time the transfer occurs;

(7) any redeemable security which has no return other than the fact that the amount payable on redemption exceeds its issue price; and

(8) any security that is a deeply discounted security (see 70-450), although certain listed securities held since 26 March 2003 are not excluded.

Legislation: ITA 2007, s. 619

Tax Reporter: ¶331-950

72-800 Exemption and reliefs

There are various exemptions from the accrued income scheme. A person who falls within a particular exemption will be treated neither as receiving taxable income nor as entitled to any relief. The exemptions apply to the transferor and/or the transferee, not to the transfer itself. So if a transferor is not taxable on an accrued amount by virtue of an exemption, the transferee may still be eligible for relief on that amount.

The principal exemptions are as follows.

(1) Where the transferor carries on a trade and the transfer is taken into account in computing his trading profits or losses.

(2) Where the transferor is:

  (a) an individual;

  (b) a personal representative and the securities transferred form part of the estate of the deceased person; or

  (c) a trustee and the securities transferred are held on a disabled person's trust,

  and the nominal value of securities held by the transferor in that capacity at no time exceeds £5,000, both:

  (i) in the tax year in which the interest period ends; and

  (ii) in the previous tax year.

(3) Charities, in most circumstances.

(4) Where the transferor:

  (a) is not resident in the UK for any part of the tax year in which the transfer occurs; and

  (b) in the case of securities in the UK, does not carry on a trade in the UK through a branch or agency in for the purposes of which the securities have been held or acquired.

(5) Where a transferor who is an individual would be taxable on any interest on the securities transferred on the remittance basis.

(6) Where the securities concerned are held for the purposes of a registered pension scheme.

The categories of exemption above applicable to transferors apply equally to transferees, with the modification that the trading requirement refers to the charge in respect of a deemed transfer at the time of acquisition.

Legislation: ITA 2007, s. 638ff.

Tax Reporter: ¶333-450ff.

72-850 Trustees

Nominees and bare trustees

Where a person beneficially owns securities, but their legal title is in the name of a nominee or bare trustee, any transfers of those securities by the nominee or bare trustee are treated as having been made by the beneficial owner. Consequently, any transfers between the nominee or bare trustee and the beneficial owner are ignored for the purposes of the accrued income scheme.

Legislation: ITA 2007, s. 666

Trustees (other than bare trustees)

On the creation of a settlement, there will be a transfer of securities from the settlor to the trustees and, consequently, an accrued income charge may arise.

Where securities are held by trustees, any deemed interest arising by virtue of the accrued income scheme is assessed to income tax at the trust rate. In these circumstances, the trustees of a discretionary trust may set off the tax paid against the tax payable in respect of payments made to beneficiaries.

Accrued income charges which arise to the trustees, in respect of transfers they make, do not form part of the income of any beneficiary of the trust, even a life tenant, whose income is measured by reference to the amount of income arising to the trustees. Conversely, an accrued income loss reduces both the measure of trustees' income and that of the life tenant. As a result, the amount paid to the life tenant could be greater than his income for tax purposes.

Legislation: ITA 2007, s. 482

Other Material: *Savings and Investments Manual* SAIM4320

Tax Reporter: ¶334-350

Settlor-interested settlements

Any amount falling to be charged under the accrued income scheme is treated as income from, or arising under, the settlement. In the case of a settlor-interested settlement, therefore, (see 151-000) the charge can then be assessed on the settlor.

Dividends and other distributions

73-000 Introduction

When a shareholder receives a dividend or other distribution from a company, it is generally chargeable as savings and investment income, unless it is exempt from tax (for example, because it is a dividend from a venture capital trust).

'Distribution' is widely defined and includes any distribution (whether in cash or otherwise) out of the assets of the company, except for any element that represents repayment of share capital.

The following paragraphs deal with:

- dividends, etc. from UK resident companies (73-200);
- dividends from non-UK resident companies (73-400);
- stock dividends (73-600); and
- choice of capital or income (73-700).

See 30-500 and 30-550 for commentary on the calculation of the shareholder's tax liability.

Building society dividends are taxed as interest rather than as dividends (see 72-150).

'Property income dividends' received from Real Estate Investment Trusts are chargeable as income of a property business rather than as savings and investment income (see 70-200).

There are special rules dealing with shares in approved share incentive plans (SIPS): see 147-000ff. for commentary on these plans.

Legislation: ITTOIA 2005, s. 382, 392, 402, 405 and 409; ITA 2007, s. 989; CTA 2010, s. 1000

Tax Reporter: ¶328-000

73-200 Dividends, etc. from UK resident companies

For most distributions from UK companies, the charge for a tax year is on the value of the dividend paid (or the distribution made) in the tax year (see 30-550). The amount is treated as income for tax purposes, even if it would otherwise be capital.

Open-ended investment companies

If the distribution accounts of an open-ended investment company (which is not an approved personal pension scheme) show the total amount available for distribution to owners of shares in the company as available for distribution as dividends, a particular owner's proportional share of that amount is treated as a dividend, paid on the date specified in the company's instrument of incorporation and prospectus for the distribution period or, if no date is specified, on the last day of that period.

Authorised unit trusts

If the distribution accounts of an authorised unit trust show the total amount available for distribution to owners of units as available for distribution as dividends, a particular unit-holder's proportional share of that amount is treated as a dividend, paid on the date specified in the trust's terms for the distribution period or, if no date is specified, on the last day of that period.

Real Estate Investment Trusts

A Real Estate Investment Trust ('REIT') is a listed company which invests substantially in real property held as part of a property rental business and which is entitled to tax exemption of the profits of that rental business.

Liability to income tax falls on the shareholder in respect of the distributions they receive from the REIT. When distributions are made out of the tax-exempt profits, the shareholders are charged to tax as if the distributions were profits of a UK property business.

Income tax is required to be deducted at source from these distributions.

REITs may now issue a stock dividend in respect of profits and gains from its property rental business, either as an alternative or in addition to a cash dividend. The REIT must deduct tax from the stock dividend, which may create practical problems if there is no cash dividend being paid at the same time. The investor is regarded as receiving profits of a UK property business equal to the cash equivalent of the shares issued. This amount is initially the amount of the cash alternative, but there is provision for the market value of the shares to be substituted where that value has changed significantly between the offer date and the date the shares are issued.

The deemed UK property business of the shareholder is separate from any other property business he may carry on. In the case of LLPs and Scottish partnerships, this rule applies to each partner .

Where the shareholder is non-UK resident, the distribution is not liable to the deduction of tax at source under the non-resident landlords' scheme (see also 71-400).

Distributions received by the following persons, are treated as trading income and not as income from a UK property business:

- dealers in securities;
- individual members of Lloyd's but only in respect of income from premium(s) trust funds or ancillary trust funds.

Legislation: ITTOIA 2005, s. 382–391; FA 2006, s. 121

Tax Reporter: ¶328-100ff.; ¶328-450

73-400 Dividends from non-UK resident companies

Dividends and distributions other than dividends from non-UK resident companies are brought within the charge to income tax. For years up to 2007–08 inclusive, the recipient of a distribution from a non-UK company was chargeable to income tax on the gross amount of the dividend. No relief in any form was available to recognise the fact that it was paid out of profits which had already borne tax in the paying company's home state; no tax credit was available and only corporate shareholders in certain circumstances could claim relief for the 'underlying tax' paid by the foreign company on its profits. This discrimination was contrary to EU Law and a tax credit was introduced in FA 2008 in respect of minority shareholdings. This was extended by FA 2009 to cover larger holdings in certain companies.

Legislation: ITTOIA 2005, s. 402–403, 687(1)

Tax credits

In respect of dividends and distributions arising on or after 22 April 2009 and prior to 6 April 2016, a UK resident or an eligible non-resident is entitled to a tax credit of one-ninth of the amount or value of a 'relevant' distribution from a non-resident company, provided one of three conditions are satisfied:

(a) the relevant distribution is made by a company which has issued share capital and, at the time of the distribution, the recipient holds less than 10% of that share capital;

(b) the distributing company is an offshore fund (However, where a dividend is paid by an offshore fund which holds more than 60% of its investments in interest-bearing assets, the dividend will be treated as interest in the hands of the investor and therefore no tax credit will be available.); or

(c) the distributing company is resident at that time in a qualifying territory (and not also resident in any other territory) which is one which has a double taxation agreement with the UK which contains a non-discrimination provision.

As with the tax credit in respect of UK dividends:

- it serves to increase the amount of the distribution;
- it is only available to the extent that the aggregate of the distribution and tax credit is within the charge to tax. Therefore, it is also non-repayable; and
- it may be set against the income tax due on the distribution which is now to be charged at the appropriate dividend rate.

Legislation: ITTOIA 2005, s. 378A(1)–(3), 397A(1)–(4), 397AA and 397BA

Tax Reporter: ¶328-750

Relevant distributions

These comprise:

- a qualifying distribution;
- a cash dividend in respect of shares held under an approved share incentive plan, which is not required to be reinvested; and
- a dividend treated as having been paid to a participant in an approved share investment plan when dividend shares cease to be subject to the plan within three years.

Legislation: ITTOIA 2005, s. 397A(7)

Exclusions (relevant prior to 6 April 2016)

A tax credit is not given in respect of:

- distributions in respect of assets held in a Lloyds member's premium trust fund;
- distributions received by unauthorised unit trusts (which are deemed to have been received by the unit-holders);
- distributions received by borrowers under stock-lending arrangements; and
- distributions received by either the original holder or the interim holder under a repo.

Legislation: ITTOIA 2005, s. 397A

Provisions re shareholdings

For a person to be eligible for a tax credit under condition A, they must be a minority shareholder at the time the distribution is received (there is no shareholding condition under conditions B or C). That means a holding of less than 10% of the distributing company's issued share capital (ITTOIA 2005, s. 397C(1)). A person is to be regarded as holding shares in the company:

- where he or she is the beneficial owner of the shares and/or a distribution arising from the shares;
- where the shares are held by a settlement of which he or she is a settlor and the income arising from those shares is treated as his or hers for income tax purposes;
- where the shares are held by a connected person to whom they were transferred by him or her, or where he or she arranged for the connected person to acquire them, and that transfer or arrangement had a tax avoidance motive; and
- where he or she has transferred them to another person under a repo or stock-lending arrangement.

Legislation: ITTOIA 2005, s. 397C(2)–(6)

73-600 Stock dividends

Broadly, a 'stock dividend' is share capital issued to shareholders by a UK resident company, either instead of a dividend or as a bonus issue (where the class of shares carries the right to receive bonus share capital under its issue terms or any variation).

The income tax charge is on the 'cash equivalent' of the share capital issued. The cash equivalent of the share capital depends on whether it is issued instead of a dividend or is a bonus issue.

Where the share capital is issued instead of a dividend, the cash equivalent is:

- the amount of the cash dividend alternative; or
- the market value of the share capital, if the cash dividend alternative is at least 15% greater than the market value.

Where the share capital is a bonus issue, the cash equivalent is the market value of the share capital.

Legislation: ITTOIA 2005, s. 409–414

Tax Reporter: ¶328-500

73-700 Stock dividends, choice of income or capital

With effect from 5 April 2015, where a person is able to choose between what would otherwise be a distribution subject to income tax or some other form of receipt, then, regardless of the choice, the receipt will be subject to income tax as if they had received a dividend.

In the event they chose the alternative receipt which is itself subject to tax, typically capital gains tax, then the taxpayer may claim relief for that tax paid against the income tax liability on the distribution.

Legislation: ITTOIA 2005, s. 396A

Pensions

Introduction

74-000 Introduction

A new simplified tax regime for pensions applies from 6 April 2006. From that date, known as A-Day, a single unified tax regime applies in place of the eight previous regimes. The post A-Day rules apply to all types of schemes and to all members of those schemes, regardless of when they joined. Under the unified regime there are no limits on the amount that an individual can save in a pension scheme. However, there are limits on the amount of pension savings that qualifies for tax relief and tax charges where the annual allowance or lifetime allowance is exceeded.

The tax advantages apply only to registered pension schemes.

An individual who is a UK taxpayer is entitled to tax relief on contributions of up to 100% of UK earnings. Non-taxpayers benefit by having their contributions of up to £2,880 per year grossed up at the basic rate (i.e. £3,600 gross). Thus, for each £100 contributed, an extra £25 is invested by means of a 'tax credit'. Employers are also entitled to tax relief on contributions that they make to a pension scheme.

Under the unified regime, there are two controls on an individual's tax-relieved pension savings. The first is the annual allowance, set at £40,000 for 2014–15 onward (previously £50,000). If in the tax year the increase in the value of an individual's pension savings, or their contributions, (including any employer contributions) exceeds the annual allowance, together with any unused relief brought forward (see 74-880), the excess is charged to tax at the individual's marginal rate (see 74-850). With effect from 6 April 2016, the annual allowance is gradually reduced down to £10,000 where an individual's total income exceeds £150,000. The rate of reduction is £1 for every £2 of income above £150,000. The second control is the lifetime allowance, set at £1m from 2016–17 (reduced from £1.25m). It applies to total benefits taken from a pension scheme; the excess over the limit is subject to a tax charge of 55% or 25%, depending on the nature of the benefits (see 74-800).

Rules apply to determine when a person can take pension benefits. Every pension scheme must have an age limit of 55. The rules allow scheme members to take a proportion of overall benefits in the form of a tax-free lump sum. Subject to the scheme rules, this can be up to 25% of the pension fund subject to the amount of the lifetime allowance at the time.

Legislation: FA 2004, s. 149–284 and Sch. 28–36; FA 2005, s. 101, 102 and Sch. 10; FA 2013, Sch. 21; FA 2014, s. 41 and Sch. 6

Tax Reporter: ¶375-000ff.

74-010 Meaning of 'pension scheme'

A pension scheme is defined as a scheme or other arrangements, comprised in one or more instruments or agreements, having or capable of having effect so as to provide benefits to or in respect of persons:

- on retirement;
- on death;
- on having reached a particular age;
- on the onset of serious ill-health or incapacity; and
- in similar circumstances.

Registered pension scheme

A registered pension scheme is a pension scheme that is registered under FA 2004, Pt. 2.

An application for registration must be made to HMRC, contain such information as they reasonably require and be in the specified form. It must be made by the scheme administrator and accompanied by a declaration to that effect and by such other declarations by the scheme administrator which are reasonably required. These may include a declaration that the instrument or agreement by which the pension scheme is constituted does not entitle any person to unauthorised payments.

Once an application for registration has been made, the decision as to whether to register the scheme or not rests with HMRC. However, they can only decide not to register the scheme if it appears that the information contained in the application is incorrect or any declaration accompanying it is false. HMRC must notify the scheme administrator of the decision and, unless the decision is not to register the scheme, the notification must state the date from which the registration is effective.

In the event that HMRC decide not to register a pension scheme, the scheme administrator can appeal. The time limit for making an appeal is 30 days from the date on which the scheme administrator was notified of the decision. The tribunal must decide whether the scheme should be registered. If they decide it should not, they must dismiss the appeal. However, if they decide the scheme should be registered, it is treated as being a registered pension scheme from the date of the tribunal's determination.

Legislation: FA 2004, s. 153, 156

Tax Reporter: ¶375-050

Occupational pension scheme

An occupational pension scheme is a pension scheme that is established by an employer or employers and can provide benefits to, or in respect of, any or all of the employees of that employer or of any other employer. It does not matter whether or not it can also provide benefits in respect of other persons.

An occupational scheme will have a 'sponsoring employer', who is the employer, or any of the employers, whose employees can receive benefits from the scheme.

The National Employment Savings Trust (NEST) is a pension scheme established by the Secretary of State for Work and Pensions under powers given by *Pensions Act* 2008, s. 67. The scheme is aimed at employees who do not have access to a qualifying workplace pension. The scheme was launched in April 2011. NEST is to be a registered pension scheme for the purposes of the tax legislation and under the *Finance Act 2011*, the Treasury are given powers to make regulations in connection with the application of taxes to NEST and any other similar schemes which may be set up in the future. These regulations will ensure any individual and employer contributions to NEST receive the appropriate tax relief.

Legislation: FA 2004, s. 150(5)–(6); FA 2011, s. 70

Tax Reporter: ¶375-350

Overseas pension scheme and recognised overseas pension scheme

An overseas pension scheme is a pension scheme (other than a registered pension scheme) that is established in a country or territory outside the UK and which satisfies any of the requirements prescribed by regulations made by the Board for this purpose.

An overseas scheme can then be:

- a 'recognised' overseas pension scheme, from which a transfer to a registered pension scheme will enable an individual to benefit from a lifetime enhancement factor (see 74-800);
- a 'qualifying' overseas pension scheme, where contributions by members and employers are eligible for 'migrant member relief' (see 74-060); and/or
- a 'qualifying recognised' overseas pension scheme, which is one to which a registered pension scheme may transfer sums and/or assets as part of a 'recognised transfer', which is an authorised member payment (see 74-450).

Legislation: FA 2004, s. 150; *Pension Schemes (Categories of Country and Requirements For Overseas Pension Schemes and Recognised Overseas Pension Schemes) Regulations* 2006 (SI 2006/206)

Tax Reporter: ¶375-450

74-020 Meaning of 'member' and 'arrangement'

'Member'

'Member' means any active member, pensioner member, deferred member or pension credit member of the pension scheme.

A person is an active member of a pension scheme if arrangements are in place under the pension scheme for the accrual of benefits to or in respect of that person.

A person is a pensioner member of a pension scheme if that person is entitled to the present payment of benefits under the pension scheme and is not an active member.

A person is a deferred member of a pension scheme if that person has accrued rights under the pension scheme and is neither an active member nor a pension member.

A person is a pension credit member of a pension scheme if the person has rights under the pension scheme which are attributable (directly or indirectly) to pension credits.

Legislation: FA 2004, s. 151

Tax Reporter: ¶375-650

'Arrangement'

The legislation uses the term 'arrangement'. This refers to the type of arrangement a pension scheme has in relation to a member. The arrangements may be:

- cash balance arrangements;
- money purchase arrangements;
- defined benefits arrangements (i.e. final salary schemes); or
- hybrid arrangements, which are a combination of the above.

Legislation: FA 2004, s. 151–152

Tax Reporter: ¶375-700ff.

Tax relief for pension contributions

74-030 Relievable members' contributions

An individual who is an active member of a registered pension scheme is entitled to tax relief in respect of relievable pension contributions paid during a tax year, if the individual is a relevant UK individual during that year. An active member is one who is accruing benefits under one or more arrangements in a pension scheme.

Relievable pension contributions

'Relievable pension contributions' are contributions made by or on behalf of the individual under the pension scheme other than:

- any contributions paid after the individual reaches the age of 75;
- any contributions that are life assurance premium contributions;
- any contributions paid by an employer of the individual; and
- any amounts paid by the Board of HMRC under the *Pension Schemes Act* 1993, s. 42A(3) or 43 (or Northern Ireland equivalent), which deals with rebates and minimum contributions.

Legislation: FA 2004, s. 188(2), (3)

Tax Reporter: ¶376-000; ¶376-050

Payments treated as contributions

The following payments are treated as contributions paid by or on behalf of a member:

- pension credits from a non-registered pension scheme;
- any amount recovered from a member by his or her employer in respect of minimum payments made to a registered pension scheme in accordance with the *Pensions Schemes Act* 1993, s. 8(3) (or Northern Ireland equivalent); and
- transfers of certain shares in SAYE option schemes or share incentive plans.

A pension credit is the amount that corresponds to the amount of a pension debit (i.e. the amount by which the value of a person's shareable rights in a pension arrangement is reduced by a pension sharing order).

Legislation: FA 2004, s. 188(4), (6)

Tax Reporter: ¶376-000; ¶376-100

Payments not regarded as contributions

The following payments are not treated as contributions paid by or on behalf of the member:

- a transfer of any sum held for the purposes of, or representing accrued rights under, a pension scheme so as to become held for the purposes of, or to represent rights under, another pension scheme; and
- a pension credit received from another registered pension scheme.

Legislation: FA 2004, s. 188(5)

Tax Reporter: ¶376-000

Relevant UK individual

An individual is entitled to tax relief only if he or she is a 'relevant UK individual'. An individual is a relevant UK individual for a tax year if:

- the individual has relevant UK earnings chargeable to income tax for that year;
- the individual is resident in the UK at some time during that year;

- the individual was resident in the UK both at some time during the five years immediately before that year and when the individual became a member of the pension scheme; or
- the individual, or the individual's spouse or civil partner, has for the tax year general earnings from overseas Crown employment subject to UK tax.

For these purposes, 'relevant UK earnings' means employment income, trading income, income from furnished holiday lettings in the UK or the European Economic Area and certain patent income chargeable to income tax. Relevant UK earnings that are not taxable in the UK by virtue of a double taxation agreement are treated as not being chargeable to income tax.

Legislation: FA 2004, s. 189

Tax Reporter: ¶376-150

74-040 Annual limit on relief

The maximum total individual and employer contribution on which an individual may claim income tax relief is fixed on an annual basis. With effect from 6 April 2014, the annual limit was reduced from £50,000 to £40,000. With effect from 6 April 2016, the annual allowance is gradually reduced down to £10,000 where an individual's total income exceeds £150,000. The rate of reduction is £1 for every £2 of income above £150,000.

From 5 April 2015, an individual's annual allowance has been limited to £10,000 where they have already flexibly accessed their pension benefits (money purchase annual allowance). This limit is further reduced to £4,000 with effect from 5 April 2017.

In the event contributions are lower than the annual limit, then any unused relief may be carried forward up to three years. In order to carry forward relief, the individual must have been a member of a qualifying pension scheme during the year although they are not required to have made any contributions (see 74-850).

Subject to the above overriding limits, an individual's (but not employer's) personal contribution are further restricted to the greater of:

- the basic amount – set at £3,600; and
- the amount of the individual's relevant UK earnings that are chargeable to income tax for that year.

This means that where an individual has relevant UK earnings for a tax year of more than £3,600, he or she is entitled to relief for contributions to a registered pension scheme up to 100% of earnings subject to the annual contribution limit and any unused relief brought forward. An individual with relevant UK earnings of less than £3,600 is entitled to tax relief on individual contributions to a maximum of £3,600 (gross). This basic amount may be changed by Treasury order.

Money purchase annual allowance

The normal annual allowance outlined above is significantly restricted where individuals have already flexibly accessed their money purchase pension savings. The objective of these provisions is to prevent an individual extracting monies from their pension funds and using these to make further pension contributions and thereby securing additional tax relief.

With effect from 5 April 2017, the annual allowance in these circumstances is limited to £4,000 (previously £10,000). Unlike the normal annual allowance, there are no provisions to allow for the carry forward of unused relief from one year into a subsequent year.

Legislation: FA 2004, s. 227ZA

Contributions that do not count towards the annual maximum

Certain contributions do not count towards the annual limit set out above. Where an employer recovers from an employee minimum contributions paid by that employer under the *Pension Schemes Act* 1993, s. 8(3) that amount does not count towards the limit on tax relief. Relief is always given on these amounts, regardless of whether tax relief has already been given on contributions to the annual limit. This means that it is possible for tax relief to be given in a year on more than 100% of relevant UK earnings.

Legislation: FA 2004, s. 190(5)

Tax Reporter: ¶376-200

Transfer of certain shares treated as a payment of contribution

The transfer by an individual of eligible shares in a company within the 'permitted period' are treated as a payment of contributions eligible for relief. Eligible shares for this purpose are shares that the individual has exercised a right to acquire in accordance with the provisions of a SAYE option scheme or which have been appropriated to the individual in accordance with the provisions of a share incentive plan.

For these purposes, the permitted period is the period of 90 days following the exercise of the right or 90 days following the individual's direction to the trustees of the share incentive plan to transfer ownership to the individual.

Legislation: FA 2004, s. 195

Tax Reporter: ¶376-100

74-050 Methods of giving relief

There are three methods by which a member can receive tax relief for contributions made to a registered pension scheme:

- relief at source;
- net pay arrangements; and
- relief on making a claim.

Relief at source

Relief at source operates by allowing an individual to make a relievable pension contribution net of basic rate tax. The pension scheme administrator then reclaims a repayment from HMRC of the sum deducted. If the member is a higher-rate taxpayer, the difference between basic-rate relief given at source and higher-rate relief due is claimed in the individual's self-assessment return.

Example

Rupert wishes to make a contribution of £100 to a registered pension scheme. Relief is given at source, so Rupert deducts the basic rate amount of £20, paying £80 to the pension scheme. The scheme administrators then reclaim the £20 deducted from HMRC.

As Rupert is a higher rate tax payer, he is entitled to a total of 40% relief. The extra £20 of tax relief due is claimed through his self-assessment return.

A £100 contribution to a registered pension scheme thus costs a basic-rate taxpayer £80 and a higher-rate taxpayer £60.

Where members have no relevant UK earnings or their relevant UK earnings are less than the basic amount of £3,600, relief at source is the only mechanism by which relief can be given for contributions.

Example

Anna wishes to make the maximum possible tax-relieved contribution to a registered pension scheme. She has no earnings for the year. She makes a payment of £2,880 and HMRC will pay £720 to the scheme, so that Anna's total contribution is £3,600. The amount paid by HMRC is equal to basic rate tax at 20% on the gross amount of £3,600.

A registered pension scheme must operate relief at source unless it falls within the net pay arrangements (see below) or can accept contributions gross from members.

Any member making a contribution to a registered pension scheme that operates relief at source can deduct basic rate tax from that contribution. A third party who makes a contribution on behalf of that member can also deduct basic rate tax. However, only the member can claim any higher rate relief that is due in respect of a contribution by a third party.

Any member can make relievable pension contributions to a registered pension scheme using the relief at source method, except where:

- the member is an employee and the scheme has chosen to operate net pay arrangements for all its employee members;
- the member is a member of a public service pension scheme or marine pilots benefit fund and the scheme does not operate net pay on the contributions and does not choose to operate relief at source; or
- the provider of a retirement annuity contract does not wish to operate relief at source.

If a member is entitled to an age-related personal allowance, his or her total income for the purpose of the abatement of age-related allowances is reduced by the grossed up amount of a contribution.

Legislation: FA 2004, s. 192

Tax Reporter: ¶376-300

Net pay arrangements

Under net pay arrangements, the employer deducts the relievable pension contributions from an employee's taxable income before operating PAYE. In this way, the individual receives tax relief at his or her marginal rate of tax. So if an individual wishes to contribute £100 to a registered pension scheme under net pay arrangements, the employer would deduct £100 from his or her salary *before* applying PAYE and pay £100 into the registered pension scheme.

A registered pension scheme can only accept contributions that have been relieved through net pay arrangements in specific situations.

Only an individual entitled to tax relief who is both a member of an occupational scheme and an employee of a sponsoring employer for that scheme (or an employee member of a public service pension scheme or an employee member of the marine pilot's benefit fund) can have pension contributions relieved via net pay arrangements. If a contribution is made by a third party in respect of the member, relief cannot be given under the net pay arrangements. Instead, it will normally be given on the making of a claim, usually via the self-assessment return.

A member can pay contributions to a pension scheme under the net pay arrangements only if all the other members who are employees of the employer are also paying contributions under the net pay arrangements; an employer cannot choose to let some employees pay contributions under net pay arrangements and operate relief at source for another group of employees.

Legislation: FA 2004, s. 193

Tax Reporter: ¶376-350

Relief on making a claim

The third and final method of granting relief is on the making of a claim. No relief is given when the contribution is paid. Instead the tax relief is claimed from HMRC. This means that if a member wishes to contribute £100 to a registered pension scheme, he or she actually pays £100 to the pension scheme. The member then claims relief from HMRC, usually in the self-assessment return. The relief is normally given by a deduction from the member's total income, so that a basic rate taxpayer will have relief of £20 in respect of a £100 contribution and a higher rate taxpayer will have relief of £40 in respect of a £100 contribution.

Relief may be given on the making of the claim if it is not possible to claim relief either through net pay arrangements or under the relief at source provisions (see above). Relief by making a claim is available:

- to the holder of a retirement annuity contract where the contract does not operate relief at source;
- to a member of a public service pension scheme or a marine pilots' benefit fund where the member is not an employee;
- where contributions are made by a third party on behalf of an occupational scheme operating net pay arrangements; or
- where the full amount of relief has not been given via the net pay arrangements, for example if the member makes a relievable pension contribution in excess of the employment income or if the sponsoring employer is not able to deduct the contribution from the member's earnings.

Legislation: FA 2004, s. 194

Tax Reporter: ¶376-400

74-060 Migrant member relief

An individual who is a 'relevant migrant member' of a qualifying overseas pension scheme is entitled to tax relief in respect of relievable pension contributions during a tax year if:

- his relevant UK earnings are chargeable to tax for that year;
- he is resident in the UK when contributions are paid; and
- he has notified the scheme manager of an intention to claim relief for contributions.

The annual limit on relief applies as for contributions to a registered scheme. The relief must be claimed; it is not given by way of relief at source nor under a net-pay arrangement.

A relevant migrant member is a member of an overseas pension scheme who:

(1) was not UK resident when first a member of the scheme;

(2) was a member of the pension scheme at the beginning of the period of residence in the UK, which includes the time when the contributions are paid;

(3) either:

 (a) was, immediately before the beginning of that period, entitled to tax relief in respect of contributions paid under the law of the country or territory in which he was resident; or

 (b) was, at any time in the ten years before the beginning of that period, entitled to such tax relief;

 and

(4) has been notified by the scheme manager that information concerning events that are benefit crystallisation events (see 384-100) in relation to the individual will be given to HMRC.

The rules in respect of relief for employer contributions to a registered scheme are mirrored in relation to 'relevant migrant member contributions' paid by an employer.

Relevant migrant member contributions are contributions paid under a qualifying overseas pension scheme in respect of an individual who is a relevant migrant member.

No taxable benefit arises in respect of any such employer contributions.

Legislation: FA 2004, Sch. 33, para. 1–4; ITEPA 2003, s. 308A; SI 2006/212, reg. 2(2)

Tax Reporter: ¶391-050–391-150

74-080 Relief for employers' contributions

Employers are entitled to tax relief on contributions that they make to a registered pension scheme. The relief is given by deducting the contribution as an expense in computing the profits of the trade, profession or investment business. In this way, the contributions paid reduce the employer's taxable profits.

Employer contributions are deductible only if they are brought into account in the employer's profit and loss account. If the employer is operating a trade or profession, pension contributions must also be wholly and exclusively incurred for the purposes of that trade or profession in order for the deduction to be permitted in accordance with the normal rules for deductions.

The pension tax legislation adopts the normal rules for deductibility of expenses and amends them slightly as regards what constitutes an allowable deduction and the timing of that deduction.

Employers carrying on a trade or profession

The normal rules for deductibility of expenses are amended slightly for pension contributions. Where the employer is carrying on a trade or profession:

- pension contributions are not treated as payments of a capital nature to the extent that they otherwise would be; and
- if they are allowed to be deducted in computing the amount of profits of the employer, they can only be deducted in the period in which they are paid. It is not possible to carry contributions back or forward to other periods, other than indirectly where a trading loss arises.

Employers with investment business

Where the employer operates an investment business, employer contributions to a registered pension scheme are deductible as an expense of management of the employer's investment business. However, the rules are slightly modified as regards their application to deductible pension contributions:

- the contributions are treated as being expenses of management to the extent that they otherwise would not be; and
- the contributions are referrable to the accounting period in which they are paid.

Relief for contributions paid

Tax relief for employer contributions to registered pension schemes can only be given when those contributions have been paid. In a defined benefit scheme, the amount that is shown in the profit and loss account in respect of obligations in respect of defined benefits may be substantially different from the contributions made to the scheme. However, it is only the amount actually paid that qualifies for tax relief.

Relief for minimum contributions

Minimum payments made by an employer to a contracted-out money purchase occupational pension scheme under the *Pension Schemes Act* 1993, s. 8 are contributions and as such may qualify for tax relief. The relief does not extend to any amount recovered by the employer from the member in respect of the minimum contribution.

No taxable benefit on employees

A contribution by an employer to a registered pension scheme does not constitute earnings of the employee in respect of whom the contribution is made.

Restriction of relief

For contributions after 28 November 2011, relief for an employer's contribution is not to be given where there is an asset-backed arrangement as set out in legislation introduced by FA 2012. HMRC also have the power to restrict tax relief on employer contributions paid in respect of a member in certain circumstances. Relief may be restricted where:

- any of the benefits that the member may receive from a registered pension scheme are dependent on the non-payment of a benefit that the member was expecting to receive from an employer-financed retirements benefit scheme; and/or
- payment of benefits to the member from an employer-financed retirements benefits scheme would reduce the transfer value of any rights in a registered pension scheme.

Legislation: ITEPA 2003, s. 308; FA 2004, s. 196–196A and 196B–196J

Tax Reporter: ¶376-500–376-600

74-090 Spreading of employers' tax relief

Where an employer makes a large one-off contribution to a registered pension scheme, the relief may not be given in full in the period in which the contribution is made. Instead, the rules require that relief is spread forward into future chargeable periods.

The spreading rules operate where an employer makes a contribution to a registered pension scheme in two consecutive chargeable periods ('the previous chargeable period' and 'the current chargeable period') and the amount of the contribution paid in the current chargeable period, otherwise than for an 'excepted purpose', exceeds 210% of the amount of contributions paid in the previous chargeable period.

For these purposes, a chargeable period is a period of account or accounting period, depending on the nature of the employer.

The amount that is spread is the amount of the 'relevant excess'. This is the amount by which the current chargeable period's contribution exceeds 110% of the previous chargeable period's contribution. However, if the relevant excess is less than £500,000, spreading does not apply and relief is given in full in the period in which the contributions are paid.

If there is no contribution in the previous chargeable period, for example because the scheme has only just been set up, spreading does not apply, irrespective of the size of the contribution in the current chargeable period.

Where spreading is in point, the number of years over which relief is spread depends on the amount of the relevant excess contributions. The legislation provides a table that gives the amount to be spread and the period of spreading, which may be up to four chargeable periods.

When the chargeable periods are not of equal length, an adjustment is required to ensure that like is compared with like.

Contributions paid for an excepted purpose are ignored when working out whether spreading applies. Contributions are paid for an excepted purpose if they are paid with a view to funding:

- an increase in the amount of pensions paid to pensioner members of the pension scheme to reflect an increase in the cost of living; or
- benefits that may accrue under the pension scheme to or in respect of individuals who become members of the pension scheme in the current chargeable period as a result of future service as employees of the employer.

Once spreading of relief has been determined, it will not normally be adjusted. The exception to this general rule is on the cessation of the business.

Legislation: FA 2004, s. 197

Tax Reporter: ¶376-650; ¶376-750

Cessation of the business

The spreading rules are modified if the employer ceases to carry on the business during the spreading period and would otherwise not get full relief because of the cessation.

Relief for contributions that would otherwise be unrelieved can be given in one of two ways:

- by allowing the unrelieved balance of the relevant excess against profits in the chargeable period in which the business ceases; or
- by treating the unrelieved balance as if it had been carried back and paid in equal daily instalments beginning with the day of cessation and ending on the first day of the chargeable period in which the contribution was paid.

Example

An employer makes a large contribution to a registered pension scheme in the chargeable period ending 30 June 2016. The relevant excess is £1.2m, which is spread over three years such that £400,000 is relieved in each of the chargeable periods to 30 June 2016, 30 June 2017 and 30 June 2018.

The business ceases on 31 December 2016 (i.e. in the period to 30 June 2017). This means that the employer would not receive full relief for the spread contributions. The employer either can opt to have the contributions of £400,000 that would have been relieved in the period to 30 June 2018 carried back to the final period ending on 30 June 2017, or can opt for the unrelieved balance to be treated as carried back in daily instalments. If the second option is chosen, the unrelieved amount of £400,000 is spread over the period from 1 July 2015 to 31 December 2016. The number of days in this period is 550, giving a daily amount of £727.27. This allows relief for £266,181 to be given in the year to 30 June 2016 and the balance of £133,819 to be given in the final chargeable period.

Legislation: FA 2004, s. 198

Tax Reporter: ¶376-700

Taxation of pension income and other charges

74-400 Introduction

Payments made by a registered pension scheme are either authorised payments or unauthorised payments. There are four types of payment:

- authorised member payments;
- authorised employer payments;
- unauthorised member payments; and
- unauthorised employer payments.

For these purposes, the term 'payment' includes a transfer of assets and any other transfer of money's worth.

The distinction between the types of payment is important, as the tax treatment of any particular receipt depends on whether the payment is authorised or unauthorised (see 74-700 and 74-750).

Legislation: FA 2004, s. 160, 161

Tax Reporter: ¶378-000

74-410 Tax free pension advice

With effect from 5 April 2017, an individual with a defined contribution scheme will be able to access tax free funds from their pension scheme provided the funds are applied towards the costs of pension and retirement advice. This is limited to a maximum of three separate withdrawals of up to £500 each. Each individual withdrawal is to be made in different tax years.

74-420 Payments from the Financial Assistance Scheme ('FAS')

The Financial Assistance Scheme is a Government-funded scheme, set up by regulations made under the *Pensions Act* 2004, s. 286. Its aim is to provide financial assistance to members of final salary occupational pension schemes who have lost pension rights because the scheme was wound up. The FAS only covers those pension schemes which were wound up in the period from 1 January 1997 to 5 April 2005, when its role was taken over by the Pension Protection Fund. In the past, this assistance has been limited to topping up existing pensions to 90% of the pension entitlement, but from 2009, the FAS was also able to make lump sum payments.

Because the FAS is not a registered pension scheme, these lump sums would not be authorised member payments (see 74-450) and a tax charge would arise on the member. To avoid this unintended situation, the Treasury were given the power to make regulations to prescribe the tax treatment of payments made by FAS.

Legislation: FA 2009, s. 73; *Financial Assistance Scheme (Tax) Regulations* 2010 (SI 2010/1187)

74-430 Payments made by the Financial Services Compensation Scheme ('FSCS')

The FSCS is a scheme, established under the *Financial Services and Markets Act* 2000, which exists, inter alia, to provide assistance to insurance companies who are unable to meet their obligations under registered pension schemes for which they act as trustees. This could include paying compensation to a member of the pension scheme or facilitating the transfer of the member's rights to another insurer.

As in the case of the FAS, the FSCS is not a registered pension scheme and to avoid any payments it makes being regarded as 'unauthorised', the Treasury were given the power to make regulations covering the tax treatment of any *relevant interventions* by the FSCS. Such interventions are those concerned with securing the continuation of insurance in connection with the registered pension scheme, safeguarding the members and paying compensation in connection with that scheme. As yet, no regulations have been made under this power. However, a payment of compensation by the FSCS will be an authorised member payment (see 74-450) if the payment is less than £2,000 and extinguishes the member's entitlement to benefits under the registered pension scheme.

Legislation: FA 2009, s. 74; *Registered Pension Schemes (Authorised Payments) Regulations* 2009 (SI 2009/1171), reg. 8

74-450 Authorised member payments

Authorised member payments are the payments that a registered pension scheme is authorised to make to or in respect of the members or ex-members of the pension scheme. Authorised payments are:

- pensions permitted by the pension rules or the death benefit rules;
- lump sums permitted by the lump sum rule or the lump sum death benefit rule;
- recognised transfers (i.e. transfers between one pension scheme and another);

- scheme administration member payments (for example a salary paid to a person who is involved in the management or administration of the scheme);
- payments pursuant to a pension sharing order or provision; and
- various other payments, as prescribed in regulations made by the Board, and including: transfers to the Board of Pension Protection Fund; payments made in connection with the demutualisation of an insurance company; payments made in connection with state pension scheme premiums or rights; and payments of arrears of pension.

Legislation: FA 2004, s. 164; *Registered Pension Schemes (Authorised Payments) (Transfers to the Pension Protection Fund) Regulations* 2006 (SI 2006/134); *Registered Pension Schemes (Authorised Member Payments) Regulations* 2006 (SI 2006/137); *Registered Pension Schemes (Authorised Payments) Regulations* 2006 (SI 2006/209); *Registered Pension Schemes (Authorised Payments) (No. 2) Regulations* 2006 (SI 2006/571); *Registered Pension Schemes (Authorised Payments – Arrears of Pension) Regulations* 2006 (SI 2006/614)

Tax Reporter: ¶378-050

74-500 Authorised employer payments

Authorised employer payments are the payments that an occupational pension scheme is authorised to make to or in respect of a sponsoring employer. The following are authorised employer payments:

- public service scheme payments;
- authorised surplus payments;
- compensation payments;
- authorised employer loans;
- scheme administration employer payments; and
- payments of a description prescribed by any regulations made for these purposes.

Legislation: FA 2004, s. 175

Tax Reporter: ¶380-500

74-600 Unauthorised member payments

The legislation states that if a payment is not an authorised payment it is an unauthorised payment. In addition, certain payments are specified as unauthorised member payments. These include:

- an assignment or surrender of a person's benefits or rights under a scheme (with certain exceptions);
- an increase in the pension rights of a person which is attributable to the death of a member with whom the person was connected;
- certain reallocations of funds and increases in benefits in cases where the beneficiary and employer are connected;
- certain benefits in kind provided to a member (or ex-member) of an occupational scheme or to that person's family or household, where the recipient is a director of the sponsoring employer;
- certain events connected with value shifting; and
- the acquisition by an investment-regulated pension scheme of taxable property in connection with an arrangement relating to a member.

Legislation: FA 2004, s. 160(2) and 172–174A

Tax Reporter: ¶381-500

74-650 Unauthorised employer payments

The legislation states that if a payment is not an authorised payment it is an unauthorised payment. In addition, certain payments are specified as unauthorised employer payments. An employer payment is a payment by an occupation pension scheme to or in respect of a sponsoring employer.

There is an unauthorised payment if, in connection with certain specified value-shifting events or a change in the value of a currency:

- the value of an asset held for the purposes of the pension scheme is reduced or a liability of the scheme is increased; and
- the value of an asset held by or for the benefit of the employer is increased and there is a reduction in the employer's liability.

The amount of the unauthorised payment is the amount by which the reduction in value of the asset held for the purposes of the pension scheme, or the increase in the liability of the pension scheme, exceeds that which might be expected if the parties to the transaction were at arm's length.

Legislation: FA 2004, s. 160(4), 181

Tax Reporter: ¶381-550

Borrowings

A registered pension scheme is not authorised to borrow an amount in respect any arrangement (whether a money purchase arrangement or another kind of arrangement) unless the borrowing meets certain conditions.

Legislation: FA 2004, s. 182–185

Tax Reporter: ¶381-800; ¶381-850

74-700 Tax charges on authorised payments

For commentary on what constitutes an authorised payment, see 74-450 and 74-500.

Pensions

The rules set out below apply to any pension under a registered pension scheme, except to any extent that, when it is paid, a liability to the unauthorised payments charge arises. The taxable pension income for a tax year is the full amount of the pension accruing in that year, irrespective of what is actually paid. The person who is liable is the person receiving or entitled to the pension.

For the purposes of this charge, a pension under a registered pension scheme includes:

- an annuity under, or purchased with sums or assets held for the purposes of, or representing acquired rights under, a registered pension scheme; and
- income withdrawal or dependants' income withdrawal under a registered pension scheme.

Temporary non-residents

Because a scheme established within another state in the European Economic Area may apply for registration, it would be possible for a UK resident member of such a scheme to become non-resident, receive substantial flexible drawdown payments during the period of non-residence and then take up residence again. During that period of non-residence, no UK tax would be due because the pension would be from a non-UK source. If certain residence requirements are satisfied, any payments during the period of non-residence are treated as having been received in the tax year in which he becomes UK resident again.

The residence requirements are that;

- the individual must be UK-resident in any part of a tax year, termed the 'year of return';
- he was not resident in the UK for one or more tax years immediately before that year but was resident in a year prior to those years of non-residence;
- the gap between last year of UK residence, termed the 'year of departure' was four tax years or less; and
- immediately prior to the year of departure, he was UK resident in at least four of the last seven tax years.

The term 'UK-resident' also requires that the individual must also be not 'treaty non-resident' at any time in that tax year, (i.e. despite being resident under UK domestic law, he is treated as being resident in another jurisdiction under a double taxation treaty). It is also provided that no provision in any double tax treaty is to prevent a charge to income tax under this provision, thus domestic legislation overrules the treaty in this situation.

Legislation: ITEPA 2003, s. 579A–579D

Tax Reporter: ¶383-000; ¶383-010

Lump sums

Certain lump sums may be paid by a registered pension scheme without giving rise to a liability to income tax. The exemption from income tax applies to:

- a pension commencement lump sum;
- a serious ill-health lump sum, paid to a member under the age of 75;
- a refund of excess contributions lump sum;
- a defined benefits lump sum death benefit, paid in respect of a member who died under the age of 75; or
- an uncrystallised funds lump sum death benefit, paid in respect of a member who died under the age of 75.

A lump sum under a registered pension scheme is however chargeable to tax (but not as income) if it is:

- a pension protection lump sum death benefit;
- an annuity protection lump sum death benefit;
- a drawdown pension fund lump sum death benefit;
- a short service refund lump sum;

- a lifetime allowance excess lump sum;
- a serious ill-health lump sum paid to a member over 75;
- a defined benefits lump sum death benefit, paid in respect of a member who died under the age of 75; or
- an uncrystallised funds lump sum death benefit, paid in respect of a member who died under the age of 75.

Legislation: ITEPA 2003, s. 636A

Tax Reporter: ¶383-050

Trivial commutation and winding up lump sums

In certain limited circumstances, a lump sum may be paid from a pension scheme that will qualify as a trivial commutation lump sum. The individual must be over 60 years of age and the total value of their pension rights must not exceed £30,000. Where a trivial commutation lump sum or a winding up lump sum is paid to a member of a registered pension scheme, the lump sum is taxable pension income for the year in which the payment is made. But if, immediately before the lump sum is paid, the member has not become entitled to any of the benefits under the pension scheme, the amount of the taxable pension income is 75% of the lump sum, with the remaining 25% being tax-free.

Any trivial commutation lump sum death benefit or winding-up lump sum death benefit paid to a person under a registered pension scheme is treated as the person's pension income for the year in which it is paid.

Legislation: ITEPA 2003, s. 636B, 636C; FA 2004, Sch. 29, para. 7

Tax Reporter: ¶383-050

Short service refund lump sum charge

A short service refund lump sum is not treated as income. However, a short service refund lump sum charge arises where a short service refund lump sum is paid by a registered pension scheme. The person who is liable is the scheme administrator, irrespective of whether the scheme administrator and the person to whom the short service refund lump sum is paid are resident, ordinarily resident or domiciled in the UK.

The rate of this tax charge is:

- 20% on the first £20,000; and
- 50% on any excess.

The rates and limits may be amended by Treasury order.

The scheme administrator may deduct the tax that they are liable to pay in respect of the short service refund lump sum before making payment of the sum to the member if the scheme rules allow for this to be done.

Legislation: FA 2004, s. 205

Tax Reporter: ¶383-100

Special lump sum death benefits charge

A charge to income tax, known as the special lump sum death benefits charge, arises where any of the following amount are paid by a registered pension scheme:

- a pension protection lump sum death benefit;
- an annuity protection lump sum death benefit;
- an unsecured pension fund lump sum death benefit;
- a defined benefits lump sum death benefit, paid in respect of a member who died over the age of 75; or
- an uncrystallised funds lump sum death benefit, paid in respect of a member who died over the age of 75.

The scheme administrator is liable to pay the tax arising in respect of the charge, irrespective of whether the scheme administrator and the person to whom the lump sum death benefit is paid are resident, ordinarily resident or domiciled in the UK.

The rate of tax in respect of the lump sum death benefit is 45% from 6 April 2015 (previously 55%). This rate may be changed by Treasury order and from 5 April 2016, such payments will be taxed at the marginal rate of the recipient. If the rules of the scheme permit, the scheme administrator may deduct the tax before making the payment of the lump sum to the member. None of the above-mentioned lump sums is treated as income.

Legislation: FA 2004, s. 206

Tax Reporter: ¶383-150

Authorised surplus payments charge

An authorised surplus payment charge arises where an authorised surplus payment is made to a sponsoring employer by an occupational pension scheme that is a registered pension scheme. The person who is liable is the scheme administrator, irrespective of whether the scheme administrator and the sponsoring employer are resident, ordinarily resident or domiciled in the UK.

The charge does not apply to any authorised surplus payment to the extent that, in the absence of this charge, the sponsoring employer would have been exempt, or entitled to claim exemption from income tax or corporation tax, in respect of it or if the sponsoring employer is a charity.

The rate of tax for the charge is 35%. The rate may be changed by Treasury order. An authorised surplus payment in respect of which income is charged under the surplus authorised payments charge is not treated as income.

Legislation: FA 2004, s. 207

Tax Reporter: ¶383-250

Serious ill-health lump sum charge

This charge arises where a serious ill-health lump sum is paid to a member over the age of 75. Tax is charged at the rate of 45% (55% before 6 April 2015) of the amount of the lump sum and is payable by the scheme administrator, regardless of the residence or domicile status of the member or the administrator. The amount of the lump sum is not treated as income of the member for tax purposes.

Tax is also chargeable under this heading in respect of a lump sum paid to a 'relieved member' or a 'transfer member' of a 'relevant non-UK scheme'. In such a case, the tax is payable by the member, rather than the administrator.

The Treasury have power to vary the rate of tax.

Legislation: FA 2004, s. 205A and Sch. 34, para. 5

Tax Reporter: ¶383-120; ¶391-320

74-750 Tax charges on unauthorised payments

The making of an unauthorised payment can generate up to three tax charges:

(1) the unauthorised payments charge;

(2) the unauthorised payments surcharge; and

(3) the scheme sanction charge (chargeable on the scheme administrator).

For commentary on what constitutes an unauthorised payment, see 74-600 and 74-650.

Unauthorised payment charge

The nature of the unauthorised payment determines who is liable for the unauthorised payments charge:

- if the payment is an unauthorised member payment made before the member's death, the tax liability falls on the member to or in respect of whom the payment is made;
- if the payment is an unauthorised member payment made after the member's death, the tax liability falls on the recipient of the payment; and
- if the payment is an unauthorised employer payment, the tax liability rests with the sponsoring employer to or in respect of whom the payment is made.

If the liability falls on more than one person, those persons are jointly and severally liable. A person is liable for the unauthorised payments charge irrespective of whether that person, or any other person with liability for the charge and the scheme administrator are resident, ordinarily resident or domiciled in the UK.

The rate of the charge is 40% of the unauthorised payment amount. The rate may be changed by Treasury order. An unauthorised payment is not treated as income for any purposes of the Tax Acts. The scheme administrator should report details of any unauthorised payment made.

Legislation: FA 2004, s. 208

Tax Reporter: ¶383-550

Unauthorised payments surcharge

An unauthorised payments surcharge arises where a 'surchargeable unauthorised member payment' is made. A surchargeable unauthorised member payment is an unauthorised payment that together with any other unauthorised member payments made in a 12-month period reaches surcharge threshold.

The surcharge threshold is exceeded if the total unauthorised payments in the period uses up 25% of the pension fund. The rate of charge is 15% of the payment. The rate may be changed by Treasury order.

Legislation: FA 2004, s. 209–212

Tax Reporter: ¶383-600

Scheme sanction charge

The scheme administrator is liable to a charge to income tax, known as the scheme sanction charge, where in any one tax year, one or more scheme chargeable payments are made by a registered pension scheme. If the scheme is treated as having been wound up, the liability falls on the person who was the scheme administrator immediately before the winding up.

The charge is 40% of the aggregate of scheme chargeable payments.

Legislation: FA 2004, s. 239–241

Tax Reporter: ¶383-700

74-800 The lifetime allowance charge

The lifetime allowance is one of the controls on the amount of tax-free pension savings to which an individual is entitled. Each individual has a set level of benefits that can be drawn from the registered pension scheme without triggering a tax charge. This limit is known as the lifetime allowance. If it is exceeded, there will be a charge of 55% on the excess (for a lump sum) or 25% (for amounts taken as pension; see below).

The lifetime allowance charge is a charge to income tax. It arises where a benefit crystallisation event occurs in relation to an individual who is a member of one or more registered pension schemes and either of the two lifetime allowance charge conditions are met. The two conditions are that:

(1) at least part of the individual's lifetime allowance is available on the benefit crystallisation event, but the amount crystallised exceeds the available amount; or

(2) none of the individual's lifetime allowance is available.

The lifetime allowance is expressed as a capital value, which is set at a particular level for each tax year. The amount set is known as the standard lifetime allowance. The standard lifetime allowance was £1.8m for 2011–12 and fell to £1.5m from 6 April 2012. From 6 April 2014, the allowance was reduced to £1.25m and it was further reduced to £1m from 6 April 2016.

The standard lifetime allowance may be reduced in certain circumstances where the individual is permitted to draw the pension before normal retirement age.

Legislation: FA 2004, s. 218

Tax Reporter: ¶384-000

Benefit crystallisation events

The lifetime allowance and related charge work by reference to 'benefit crystallisation events'. A benefit crystallisation event can take different forms and is defined in detail in the legislation. Broadly, it occurs when a person becomes entitled to a benefit from the scheme. There are special rules to determine the amount to be treated as a crystallised benefit, depending on the nature of the crystallisation event.

Legislation: FA 2004, s. 216

Tax Reporter: ¶384-100–384-700

Availability of the lifetime allowance

If no benefit crystallisation event has occurred in relation to an individual before the current benefit crystallisation event, the whole of the individual's lifetime allowance is available on that benefit crystallisation event.

Example 1

Ben crystallises a benefit with a capital value of £900k in 2017–18, when the standard lifetime allowance is £1m. There have been no previous benefit crystallisation events. The whole lifetime allowance is available and covers the crystallised benefit. As a result no lifetime allowance charge is payable.

If one or more benefit crystallisation events have occurred prior to the current benefit crystallisation event, the position depends on whether the value of previously crystallised benefits is more or less than the lifetime allowance. If the previously used amount is greater than or equal to the amount of the lifetime allowance, none of the allowance is available in relation to the benefit crystallisation event, so that the lifetime allowance charge applies to the crystallised benefit.

If the lifetime allowance has not been fully used up by previous benefit crystallisation events, the amount that remains available is so much of the allowance as is left after deducting the previously used amount. The calculation of the previously used amount depends on the number of previous benefit crystallisation events.

Example 2

In 2017–18, Mark crystallises a benefit with a value of £50,000. Previous crystallised benefits were valued at £985k so only £15,000 of the lifetime allowance is available. The £50,000 crystallisation triggers a lifetime allowance charge on £35,000, if the sum is taken as lump sum (£19,250).

If there is more than one previous benefit crystallisation event, the lifetime allowance available is the amount remaining after deducting the aggregate of the previously used amounts. If the lifetime allowance limit was set at a different level when the previous benefit crystallisation events occurred, then for the purposes of the calculation, their amounts are increased by reference to the increase in the lifetime allowance limit; it is the *proportion* of the lifetime allowance previously used up that is important.

Example 3

Lucy crystallises a benefit with a value of £800,000 at a time when the standard lifetime allowance is £1.8m. She previously crystallised a benefit of £500,000 when the standard lifetime allowance was £1.75m and a benefit of £200,000 when the standard lifetime allowance was £1.6m.

The adjusted previously used amount in relation to the first benefit crystallisation event is £514,285 (£500,000 × 1.8/1.75).

The adjusted previously used amount in relation to the second benefit crystallisation is £225,000 (£200,000 × 1.8/1.6).

The total of the previously used amounts is £739,285, leaving £1,060,715 of the £1.8m lifetime allowance to set against the crystallised benefit of £800,000. As this is covered by the remaining lifetime allowance, no lifetime allowance charge is payable in respect of that benefit crystallisation event.

Legislation: FA 2004, s. 214

Tax Reporter: ¶384-050; ¶384-800

Lifetime allowance enhancement factors

The standard lifetime allowance may be enhanced in certain circumstances. These lifetime allowance enhancement factors include cases involving:

- pension credits in relation to previously crystallised rights (e.g. pension sharing on divorce);
- pre-commencement pension credits, acquired prior to 6 April 2006: an enhancement factor known as the pre-commencement pension credit factor provides parity of treatment where pension credits were

awarded before A-Day; the pension credit is increased in line with the RPI from the month in which it is awarded;

- periods of non-residence;
- transfers from recognised overseas pension schemes; and
- primary protection: members with rights of more than £1.5m as at 6 April 2006 are entitled to apply for the primary protection lifetime enhancement factor that recognises the extent to which the rights valued as at 5 April 2006 exceed the standard lifetime allowance for 2006–07.

In certain circumstances, more than one lifetime allowance enhancement factor may be present. It is the responsibility of the individual to notify HMRC if they believe an enhancement factor is present and if HMRC agree, they will provide a certificate confirming this is the case.

Legislation: *Registered Pension Schemes (Enhanced Lifetime Allowances) Regulations* 2006 (SI 2006/131)

Tax Reporter: ¶384-850–384-975

Amount of the charge

The charge is on the 'chargeable amount'. The charge applies at the rate of 55% on any part of the chargeable amount, that constitutes a lump-sum amount, and it applies at the rate of 25% any part of the chargeable amount that constitutes the retained amount (see below).

The chargeable amount comprises the aggregate of the basic amount and any amount that is treated as forming part of the lump sum amount or the retained amount. For these purposes, the basic amount depends on whether the first lifetime allowance charge condition or the second lifetime allowance charge condition is met in relation to the crystallisation event:

(1) if the first condition is met, the basic amount is the amount by which the amount crystallised exceeds the amount of the individual's lifetime allowance available; and

(2) if the second condition is met, the basic amount is the amount that is crystallised.

The lump sum amount is the element of the basic amount that is paid as a lump sum to the individual or a lump sum death benefit in respect of the individual. Where any tax that is payable as a result of the lifetime allowance charge on the lump sum amount is covered by a scheme-funded payment, it is itself treated as forming part of the lump sum amount.

The retained amount is the element of the basic amount that is not paid as a lump sum to the individual or a lump sum death benefit in respect of the individual. Where any of the tax that is payable as a result of the lifetime allowance charge on the retained amount is covered by a scheme-funded payment, it is itself treated as forming part of the retained amount.

The chargeable amount is not treated as income for any purpose of the Tax Acts.

Legislation: FA 2004, s. 215

Tax Reporter: ¶384-050

Person liable for the lifetime allowance charge

Generally, liability for the lifetime allowance charge falls on the individual and the scheme administrator, and their liability is joint and several (although it will usually be the scheme administrator who pays it). But where the liability arises by the payment of a lump sum death benefit, the liability falls on the person to whom it is paid.

If more than one lump sum death benefit is paid in respect of an individual and tax is not chargeable on the whole amount of all of them, the total amount of tax payable is apportioned on a just and reasonable basis between the recipients of the lump sum death benefits.

Liability to the lifetime allowance charge arises irrespective of when the person, any other person who is liable and the scheme administrator (if so liable) are resident, ordinarily resident or domiciled in the UK.

Legislation: FA 2004, s. 217

Tax Reporter: ¶384-050ff.

74-820 Lifetime allowance charge: transitional protection from 6 April 2012

As a consequence of the reduction in the lifetime allowance from 6 April 2012, a transitional measure will provide protection from the charge for those individuals who became members of a registered pension scheme after 6 April 2006 but before 6 April 2012.

Where a member gives notice to HMRC, in a form to be determined by regulations, that he intends to rely on this protection, the standard lifetime allowance used to determine a lifetime allowance charge is to be the greater of £1.8m or the actual allowance for the tax year in which the benefit crystallisation event occurs

This protection will however cease to apply where, on or after 6 April 2012, one of the following events occurs;

- a 'benefit accrual';
- an 'impermissible transfer';
- a 'non-permitted transfer'; or
- a new arrangement is made in 'non-permitted' circumstances.

Fixed protection was also available when the lifetime allowance reduced to £1.25m from 6 April 2014. If an individual elects for this so as to retain the lifetime allowance of £1.5m it will be lost if a pension contribution is paid after 5 April 2014 or there is an increase in the value of the individual's pension rights after that date.

Similar provisions were introduced in relation to the further reduction of the lifetime allowance from £1.25m to £1m effective from 5 April 2016.

Legislation: FA 2011, Sch. 18, para. 14; FA 2013, Sch. 21

Tax Reporter: ¶384-070

74-850 The annual allowance charge

The annual allowance is the second control on tax relieved pension savings. An annual allowance charge arises where the total pension input for a tax year in respect of a member of one or more registered pension schemes exceeds the annual allowance for that year. The charge also applies, with modification, in the case of certain non-UK pension schemes.

The annual allowance for 2017–18 is £40,000 (£50,000 for 2014–15 and earlier years).

The charge is on so much of the 'total pension input amount' as exceeds the annual allowance for that year. This excess is not treated as income for any purposes of the Tax Acts. However, the charge is amended where the individual meets the 'flexible drawdown conditions' (see 74-925).

From 2011–12 onwards, the rate of tax to be charged on the excess is to be the 'appropriate rate', that is the rate or rates which would be charged on the excess if it was to be added to the individual's income for the tax year concerned. Any increase in the basic rate or higher rate bands due to pension contributions made under deduction of tax or gift aid payments, is also taken into account for this purpose.

Liability for the annual allowance charge normally falls on the member but, in certain circumstances, some part may fall on the scheme administrator (see 74-875).

The annual allowance charge does not apply for any tax year to an individual who was a member of a scheme at 6 April 2006 and who has registered to have enhanced protection of pension rights and that protection applies throughout that year.

Legislation: FA 2004, s. 227(1), (4)–(5) and Sch. 36, para. 49

Tax Reporter: ¶386-000

74-860 Pension input amounts

This is the aggregate of the pension input amounts in respect of each arrangement relating to the individual under a registered pension scheme during the pension input period ending within the tax year. Until changes introduced in 2015–16, the pension input periods for a particular scheme were consecutive periods of 12 months starting on the date on which contributions were first made or rights begin to accrue in respect of the individual. With effect from 8 July 2015, the pension input period of all taxpayers was aligned with the tax year. However, no pension input amount is taken into account if, before the end of the tax year, the individual either dies or satisfies the following 'severe ill-health condition':

- he becomes entitled to all his benefits under the scheme as a result of evidence from a registered medical practitioner that his health is such that he is unlikely to be able to carry on in gainful employment;
- he becomes entitled to a serious ill-health lump sum; or
- he is a member of the armed forces entitled to a tax-exempt wounds and disability pension.

Legislation: FA 2004, s. 229(1)–(4)

Tax Reporter: ¶386-000; ¶378-750

Cash balance arrangements

The pension input amount in respect of a cash balance arrangement is the amount of any increase in the value of the individual's rights under the arrangement during the pension input period of the arrangement that ends in the tax year.

There is an increase in the value of the individual's rights under the arrangement during the pension input period if the opening value of the individual's rights is exceeded by the closing value of the individual's rights. The amount of the increase in the value of the individual's rights under the arrangement during the pension input period is the amount of that excess.

The opening value of the individual's rights under the arrangement is the amount which would, on the valuation assumptions, be available for the provision of benefits to or in respect of the individual under the arrangements, on the assumption that the individual became entitled to the benefits at the end of the immediately preceding pension input period. (If there is no such preceding period, the value is nil.)

The closing value of the individual's rights under the arrangement is the amount which would, on the valuation assumptions, be available for the provision of benefits to or in respect of the individual under the arrangements, if the individual became entitled to the benefits at the end of the pension input period.

The valuation assumptions are that the person has not reached such age, if any, as must have been reached to avoid any reduction in the benefits on account of age, that the person reached that age on that date, and that the person's right to receive the benefit had not been occasioned by physical or mental impairment.

The pension input amount is reduced by the amount of any minimum payments under the Pension Schemes Acts and is taken as nil in cases where the individual:

- is a deferred member throughout the pension input period; or
- is a deferred member for part of that period and a pensioner member for the other part,

and the value of his rights does not increase during the period by more than the 'relevant percentage' which is:

- the percentage specified in the scheme rules as at 14 October 2010, where throughout the period, the arrangement provides for the individual's rights to increase by that percentage (unless it is one which can be determined at the discretion of any person); or
- in other cases, the percentage increase in the Consumer Prices Index for the 12-month period ending with a month in the pension input period nominated by the scheme administrator.

The rights of the individual for this purpose do not include the right to a guaranteed minimum pension as defined by the Pension Schemes Acts.

The opening balance is automatically increased by the percentage increase in the Consumer Prices Index for the 12 months ending in September in the preceding tax year.

The closing value may also be adjusted in certain situations.

Legislation: FA 2004, s. 230–232

Tax Reporter: ¶386-050

Money purchase arrangements

The pension input amount in respect of a money purchase arrangement is the total of any relievable pension contributions paid by or on behalf of the individual and contributions paid in respect of him by an employer during the pension input period ending in the tax year. For these purposes, contributions do not include minimum contributions under the Pension Schemes Acts.

Employers may pay contributions to a pension scheme which are not immediately allocated to specific individuals. It is only when that allocation takes place that they are treated as contributions in respect of the individual under the arrangement and as having been paid at the time of the allocation

Legislation: FA 2004, s. 233

Tax Reporter: ¶386-100

Defined benefits arrangements

The pension input amount in respect of defined benefits arrangements is the amount of any increase in the value of the individual's rights under the arrangements during the pension input period of the arrangement that ends in the tax year.

The opening value of the individual's rights is determined at the end of the immediately preceding pension input period (if there was no such preceding period, the value is nil), whilst the closing value is determined at the or end of the current pension input period. The value at those times is the sum of:

- the annual rate of pension to which the individual would be entitled at that time on the valuation assumptions (the 'pension entitlement'), multiplied by a factor of 16; and
- the amount of the lump sum to which he would become entitled at that time, again on the valuation assumptions (the 'lump sum entitlement').

The valuation assumptions are that the person has not reached such age, if any, as must have been reached to avoid any reduction in the benefits on account of age, that the person reached that age on that date, and that the person's right to receive the benefit had not been occasioned by physical or mental impairment.

The pension input amount thus calculated is reduced by the amount of any minimum payments under the *Pension Schemes Act* 1993, s. 8 or the *Pension Schemes (Northern Ireland) Act* 1993, s. 4, in relation to the individual and in connection with the arrangement.

The pension input amount is taken as nil in cases where the individual is a deferred member under the scheme, by virtue of that arrangement throughout the pension input period (or is a deferred member for part of that period and a pensioner member for the rest) and the value of his relevant rights does not increase during the pension input period by more than the 'relevant percentage'.

The relevant percentage is:

- the percentage specified in the scheme rules (or those of a predecessor registered pension scheme) as at 14 October 2010, where throughout the pension input period, the arrangement (or a predecessor arrangement) provides for the individual's relevant rights to increase by that percentage (unless that percentage is one which can be determined at the discretion of any person); or
- in other cases, the percentage increase in the Consumer Prices Index for the 12-month period ending with a month in the pension input period nominated by the scheme administrator.

The relevant rights of the individual do not include the right to a guaranteed minimum pension as defined by *Pension Schemes Act* 1993, s. 8(2) and *Pension Schemes (Northern Ireland) Act* 1993, s. 4(2).

Uprating of opening value

For pension input periods ending within 2011–12 and subsequent years, the opening balance is increased by the percentage increase in the Consumer Prices Index over the 12 months ending in September of the previous tax year.

Legislation: FA 2004, s. 235

Tax Reporter: ¶386-150

Adjustment of closing value

The closing value may be adjusted where, during the pension input period:

- the individual's rights have been increased or reduced as a result of a pensions sharing order the amount of any pension credit is deducted from the value of the pension or lump sum entitlement, whilst any pension debit is added;

- the rights have been reduced by a transfer of assets, etc. to another registered pension scheme; the amount of that reduction is added to the value;
- the rights have been increased by a transfer of assets, etc. from any other pension scheme; the amount of that increase is deducted from the value;
- the individual has exercised an option to surrender any part of his rights in return for any other rights; the reduction is to be added to the value to the extent that it is not already reflected in the amount added under the following bullet point;
- a particular benefit crystallisation event (see 74-800) occurs; the relevant amount crystallising is added to the value;
- the scheme administrator has been made liable for tax charged on an annual allowance charge (see 74-875), and a consequential adjustment is made to the amount available to provide the individual's benefits, that adjustment, to the extent that it is reflected in the closing balance, is to be added back to that balance. However, no such addition is to be made where, in that year, the individual becomes entitled to all his benefits or certain benefit crystallisation events occur.

Legislation: FA 2004, s. 236

Tax Reporter: ¶386-150

74-870 Liability for the charge

The general rule is that liability for the annual allowance charge falls on the individual, regardless of his residence and domicile status or that of the scheme administrator.

However, in certain circumstances, the individual may make the scheme administrator jointly and severally liable for the tax by serving notice on that administrator. Where the administrator settles the liability, a consequential adjustment is made to the individual's benefits under the scheme on a just and reasonable basis, having regard to normal actuarial practice. HMRC have the power to make regulations to modify the rules of registered pension schemes to facilitate these provisions.

This option is available to an individual where:

- the tax due in respect of the charge is greater than £2,000; and
- the aggregate of all pension input amounts in respect of arrangements under that scheme are in excess of the annual allowance.

The amount of the tax for which liability can be imposed on the scheme administrator in this way is limited to tax on the excess which arises from that pension scheme, taking it as the top slice of the combined income and annual allowance charge.

> **Example**
>
> Sir Fred is a member of two pension schemes, AB and YZ. For 2017–18, his pension input amounts are £55,000 for scheme AB and £6,000 for scheme YZ. His net reduced income for the year is £89,000. He has no unused relief brought forward.
>
> The annual allowance charge is therefore the excess of £61,000 over the annual allowance for that year, i.e. £40,000.
>
> The tax charge at the appropriate rate would be £8,400, being 40% on £21,000.
>
> Fred cannot serve notice on the administrator of scheme YZ as the pension input amount in respect of that scheme did not exceed the annual allowance. He can however serve notice on the administrator of scheme AB. In that case, the tax to which the administrator will become jointly and severally liable will be calculated as 40% on £15,000, a total tax liability of £6,000.
>
> The tax due in respect of the excess attributable to the pension input amount relating to scheme YZ, £2,400, will remain the liability of Sir Fred.

The notice, which must specify the 'joint liability amount', must be given not later than 31 July following the end of the tax year concerned. However, where in the tax year:

- the individual becomes entitled to all the benefits under the scheme;
- certain benefit crystallisation events occur,

the notice must be given before the date on which that entitlement arose or the benefit crystallisation event occur. The scheme administrator's liability will then arise regardless of his residence or domicile status or that of the individual.

Legislation: FA 2004, s. 237A–237B, 237E–237F

Tax Reporter: ¶386-010

Exceptions

The scheme administrator cannot be made jointly and severally liable at any time during an 'assessment period' for the purposes of the Pension Protection Fund. In addition, an administrator who has been made liable and has not yet satisfied that liability, will cease to be liable when such an assessment period begins.

An administrator is also not liable on any amount of the charge to the extent that the consequential adjustment to the individual's benefits would result in those benefits being reduced below the amount of the statutory Guaranteed Minimum Pension under the Pension Schemes Acts.

Legislation: FA 2004, s. 237C

Applications for discharge from liability

The administrator may also be relieved of liability by applying to HMRC for a discharge on one of two grounds;

- that the liability would be to the substantial detriment of the scheme members; or
- that, in all the circumstances, it would not be just and reasonable for the administrator to be liable for that amount.

The Treasury have power to alter the grounds on which such an application can be made and HMRC can make regulations supplementing this provision and prescribing time limits for applications.

Legislation: FA 2004, s. 237D

74-880 Carry forward of annual allowance

Where the annual allowance for a tax year exceeds, the pension input amount for that year, a limited form of carry-forward is available. Where, in a 'current year' (being 2011–12 or subsequent years) there is an excess of pension input amount over the annual allowance, that allowance may be increased by the 'unused' annual allowance of the three immediately preceding years.

However, where the current year is 2011–12, 2012–13 or 2013–14, in determining the unused allowance for tax years ending prior to 6 April 2011, the annual allowance for those years is to be taken as £50,000 rather than the actual allowance.

An amount of annual allowance is 'unused' to the extent that, ignoring the effect of any carry-forward, it exceeds the pension input amount for that year and, where that excess arises in the penultimate or the antepenultimate year to the current year, that excess has not been 'used up'. An excess is 'used up' if there is an excess of pension input amount for an 'intervening year' (i.e. one between the year in which the excess arose and the 'current year') and that excess has been used under these provisions to reduce an annual allowance charge for that intervening year. Where the intervening year is 2009–10 or 2010–11, this set off is applied on a notional basis only, i.e. it cannot reduce any actual annual allowance charges which may have arisen for those years.

For any part of a year's annual allowance to be available for carry-forward, the individual must have been a member of a registered pension scheme at some time in that year, even if there were no pension input amounts for that year.

Where unused annual allowance is brought forward to a current year, it is regarded as being set against the current year's pension inputs on a 'first in, first out basis', i.e. the allowance for earlier years is used in priority to that for later years.

No claim is required; the carry-forward is mandatory. As a result, unused annual allowance is automatically set off against the next available year's pension input amount.

Example

Year	Input amount	Annual allowance	Unused allowance
2012–13	30,000	50,000	20,000
2013–14	65,000	50,000	–
2014–15	20,000	40,000	20,000
2015–16	65,000	40,000	–

For 2012–13, the unused allowance is deemed to be £20,000.

For these purposes an annual allowance charge of £15,000 is deemed to have arisen for 2013–14. The notional unused allowance from 2012–13 is used to cover the notional annual allowance charge, leaving £5,000 to carry forward to 2014–15 or 2015–16.

In 2015–16, an annual allowance charge of £25,000 would normally arise. It is however eliminated by the balance of the notional unused allowances of £5,000 from 2012–13 and £20,000 from 2014–15.

Legislation: FA 2004, s. 228A; FA 2011, Sch. 17, para. 30

Tax Reporter: ¶386-030

74-890 Accessing pension funds post 5 April 2015

In his 2014 Budget speech, the Chancellor announced the Government's intention to remove all restriction on an individual's ability to withdraw funds from a defined benefit pension scheme albeit that such withdrawals will, to the extent they exceed the 25% tax free threshold, be subject to tax at the individual's marginal rate. These provisions came into effect from 6 April 2015.

Flexible drawdown prior to 6 April 2015

Previously, on reaching the age of 75, individuals were obliged to use their pension funds to buy an annuity. Since 6 April 2011, individuals have been able to leave their funds in a 'drawdown arrangement' and make withdrawals from those funds, subject to an annual cap being the maximum annuity that could have been purchased with the fund. For pension years beginning after 25 March 2013, the cap is 120% of that maximum annuity, increasing to 150% from 27 March 2014. This cap did not apply to individuals who can show that they had a secure pension income of at least £12,000 p.a. (£20,000 prior to 27 March 2014) and who made a declaration to that effect in a year when no tax-relieved contributions were made and when he was not an active member of any scheme under which there were either defined benefits or cash balance arrangements relating to him. With effect from 6 April 2015, the requirement to demonstrate any level of secure pension income was removed.

In the case of an individual who qualifies for this 'flexible drawdown', any further pension contributions into a money purchase arrangement will be chargeable in full without any deduction for the annual allowance which will be set against any input amounts in respect of defined benefits or cash balance arrangements. This applies for all the tax years (other than the first) in which such an arrangement is in force.

Legislation: FA 2004, s. 165, 227A

Tax Reporter: ¶378-300; ¶386-040

Compliance

74-900 Compliance obligations: members

The registered pension schemes regime imposes compliance obligation requirements on scheme administrators, members and employers. Most of the obligations fall on the scheme administrators, but members and employers are also obliged to provide certain information.

Members of registered pension schemes are required to meet certain information and administration requirements.

Information to be provided to HMRC

HMRC can require a person who is or has been a member of a registered pension scheme to provide them with certain information. By issuing a notice, HMRC can require that the member produces, or makes available for inspection, documents that the member either has in his or her possession or has the power to obtain, which relate to any of the following matters:

- any matter relating to a registered pension scheme;
- any matter relating to a pension scheme that has ceased to be a registered pension scheme; or
- any matter relating to a pension scheme that has applied to be a registered pension scheme.

HMRC can also require a member to produce additional information relating to those matters as may reasonably be required.

Where the member has consented to the use of electronic communication, such notices may be issued electronically.

The notice will state the time limit by when the required information must be produced. This will be a minimum of 30 days from the date of the notice.

Copy documents can be supplied, although where a copy is provided HMRC may request the original document.

A right of appeal exists against a notice requiring information. An appeal must be lodged within 30 days of the date of the notice.

Legislation: FA 2004, s. 252 and 253

Tax Reporter: ¶309-000

74-950 Compliance obligations: employers

The registered pension schemes regime imposes certain information and administration obligations on employers.

Provision of information to HMRC

Where a registered pension scheme makes an unauthorised employer payment to a company, that company is required to provide HMRC with the following information no later than 31 January following the tax year in which the unauthorised payment was made:

- details of the scheme that made the payment;
- the nature of the payment;
- the amount of the payment; and
- the date on which the payment was made.

The report should be sent to the tax office dealing with the employer's affairs.

HMRC can also issue a notice requiring a sponsoring employer to provide documents or particulars in relation to any of the following matters:

- any matter relating to a registered pension scheme;
- any matter relating to a pension scheme which has ceased to be a registered pension scheme;
- any matter relating to a pension scheme in relation to which an application for registration has been made; or
- any matter relating to an annuity purchased with sums or assets held for the purposes of a registered pension scheme.

The notice can be issued up to six years after the event in question. The notice will state the time-limit by which the information must be provided. This will be a minimum of 30 days from the date of the notice. If the sponsoring employer has consented to the use of electronic information, such a notice may be issued electronically.

A right of appeal exists against requests for information issued to the sponsoring employer or a non-sponsoring employer. The appeal must be lodged within 30 days of the date of the notice.

Records

A person who is or has been the sponsoring employer in relation to an occupational pension scheme or the director of an employer company is required to keep records of:

- any moneys received or owing to the scheme;
- any investments or assets held by the scheme;
- any payments made by the scheme;
- any contracts to purchase a lifetime annuity in respect of a member of the scheme; and
- the administration of the scheme.

The records must be retained for the tax year to which they relate and the following six years. In the event that a person has ceased to act for a scheme, they are not required to retain the documents if another person has succeeded them in their duties and the documents have been transferred to that person.

Legislation: FA 2004, s. 252 and 253; *Registered Pension Schemes (Provision of Information) Regulations* 2006 (SI 2006/567)

Tax Reporter: ¶309-050

Life assurance relief

75-200 Gains arising from life policies, etc.

Gains arising from life insurance policies, life annuity contracts and capital redemption policies may give rise to a higher rate income tax charge on the happening of a 'chargeable event'.

Subject to the matters below, a chargeable event generally arises on:

- the death of the person whose life is insured;
- the maturity of the policy;
- the surrender of rights under the policy;
- the assignment of rights for money or money's worth; or
- the excess of annual withdrawals over a permitted 5% annual level, as far as is relevant to the type of investment in point.

Policies taken out before 20 March 1968 are exempt, as are 'qualifying' policies, i.e. those taken out after that date once the premiums have been paid for ten years or, if less, three-quarters of the term for which the policy is to run (in the case of an endowment policy).

The First-tier Tribunal decision in *Lobler* illustrates the care that must be taken in withdrawing funds from policies, as in that case the individual had taken partial withdrawals that produced a significant gain for tax purposes when there was no economic gain.

Where changes are made to a qualifying policy, the exemption may be lost. However, by concession, there will be no tax charge on benefits arising on subsequent maturity or surrender, provided a number of specific circumstances apply. It is uneconomical for insurers to collect premiums on policies made at least 20 years ago because of the small sums involved, and they can now stop collecting these amounts without loss of tax exemption to policyholders.

Where there is recourse to the courts on divorce, and a court makes an order:

- for ancillary relief under the *Matrimonial Causes Act* 1973 (or for financial provision under the *Family Law (Scotland) Act* 1985) which results in a transfer of rights under a life insurance policy from one spouse to another; or
- formally ratifying an agreement reached by the divorcing parties that deals with the transfer of assets including a life insurance policy,

the spouse to whom the rights under the life insurance policy are transferred does not give money or money's worth, in the form of surrendered rights, for their transfer. A court order made in these circumstances reflects the exercise by the court of its independent statutory jurisdiction. A consequence of this is that transferring ownership of the rights conferred by a life insurance policy under a court order is not for money or money's worth and so no gain can arise because of it.

Gains from life policies, capital redemption policies and life annuities that arise as a result of 'chargeable events' are taxed as income. Such gains on UK policies are treated, in the hands of individuals and trustees, as if basic rate tax has been paid on the gain, which is then subject to higher rate or additional rate tax or the trust rate.

Where a gain arises on a policy issued by a non-UK insurer, no credit is given for basic rate tax unless the insurer is in the European Economic Area and satisfies certain conditions.

In practice, the insurance company concerned will issue the individual or trustees with a 'chargeable event certificate' notifying the amount of the gain realised and the annual equivalent (see 75-220) applicable.

It has been common practice to divide an investment into separate policies so as to give more flexibility on withdrawing sums from time to time. Where such policies are issued on different terms and which would not be the case if they were not linked then for policies issued or varied after 20 March 2012 they will be treated as a single policy.

Where an individual has been non-UK resident for part of the period of ownership of a policy then the part attributable to the non-resident period (on a time basis) is not subject to tax under these rules. It does not matter whether the policy is UK or foreign where issued after 5 April 2013 but before then this time apportionment only applied to foreign policies. For policies issued after 5 April 2013, there is also an extension of this relief to trustees if the absent settlor has died, having been non-UK resident for part of the period.

Legislation: ICTA 1988, s. 461, 484 and Sch. 15; ITTOIA 2005, s. 473A, 528, 528A and 530–532

Case: *Lobler v HMRC* [2013] TC 02539

Other Material: HMRC Interpretation, IRInt. 257 (Tax Bulletin, December 2003)

Tax Reporter: ¶343-500; ¶311-350

75-220 Top-slicing relief

Where an individual claims, he may obtain 'top-slicing relief', the effect of which may be to reduce the liability on the gain. Where there is only one chargeable event involved, the relief is the difference between:

- the tax chargeable at the individual's marginal rate of tax on the full amount of the gain less the amount of basic rate tax deemed to have been deducted; and
- the tax which would otherwise be chargeable at that marginal rate on the 'annual equivalent' of the gain, less an amount equal to the basic rate in respect of that annual equivalent.

(The annual equivalent is simply the amount of the gain divided by the number of complete years that the policy or contract has run before the chargeable event, or, if there has been a previous chargeable event in relation to that policy, the number of complete years since that policy.)

If there are two or more chargeable events, the gains will be added together, but with the annual equivalent of the whole is calculated by adding together the annual equivalents of the individual amounts.

It will be seen therefore that relief will only be of use where, if the full amount of the gain was included as income, it would take an individual into the next highest income tax rate band.

In calculating the individual's final liability under the method prescribed in ITA 2007, s. 23, the full amount of the gain is included as income at Step 1, with the top-slicing relief being given by means of a tax reduction at Step 6.

In the case of certain non-qualifying policies by non-resident companies and offshore capital redemption policies, the annual equivalent may be modified by reducing the number of complete years the policy ran by the number of complete years during that period when the policy holder was not resident in the UK. The effect of this may be to reduce the relief.

Also, the provisions are modified in the case of non-resident policies or offshore capital redemption policies issued or made after 17 November 1983 in that the number of complete years taken into account always goes back to the start of the policy, even if more than one chargeable event occurs on one policy.

Legislation: ITTOIA 2005, s. 535–537

Tax Reporter: ¶344-500

75-250 Relief for deficiencies

Where, instead of a gain arising on the final chargeable event in relation to a policy, there is a loss, relief may be claimed for that 'corresponding deficiency'.

A corresponding deficiency occurring at the end of the final year gives rise to a tax reduction for that year. The deficiency is subject to a limit of the amounts previously treated as gains. This reduction is equal to an amount of tax on the deficiency at the difference between either the dividend higher rate and the dividend ordinary rate or the higher rate and the basic rate. (The deficiency being regarded as identified with dividend income charged at the dividend higher rate in preference to other income charged at the higher rate.) In the first Budget of 2010, it was announced that relief would be extended to cover individuals who would be liable to tax at the additional rate or the dividend additional rate coming into effect from 6 April 2010.

With effect for policies made on or after 3 March 2004, any deficiency relief is further restricted by the condition that only gains that formed part of the claimant's total income in an earlier year can be brought into account. This measure prevents relief from being obtained on purchased policies where the original owner crystallised a chargeable event. Where policies existed pre-3 March 2004, this new restriction will apply if any of the policy rights or benefits have been assigned, used as security, or increased on or after that date.

Because the deficiency relief is limited to the amounts already charged to tax on earlier chargeable events, it simply withdraws previous charges; it is not a means of giving relief for an overall loss. Schemes had been designed, which sought to claim relief for an overall loss under the provisions relating to losses from miscellaneous transactions. To put the question beyond doubt, an amendment was made by FA 2009 to the effect that no relief could be granted for losses on life policies.

Legislation: ITTOIA 2005, s. 484, 487 and 505; ITA 2007, s. 152

Tax Reporter: ¶344-700

75-300 Personal portfolio bonds

A personal portfolio bond (PPB) is a policy of life assurance where the assets backing the policy and giving rise to the benefits under the policy are personal to the individual policy holder, who may have significant control over those assets. The Treasury believe that many of the benefits of direct investment are retained by such policies, whilst the policy holder is able to defer taxation of investment income and gains by choosing the date of surrender, or to escape taxation altogether by becoming non-resident before the policy is surrendered. Following the case *IR Commrs v Willoughby*, regulations were brought in, from 6 April 1999, to levy an annual charge on the deemed return from the bond. They give details of the yearly charge on PPBs and define which policies are PPBs.

Legislation: *Personal Portfolio Bonds (Tax) Regulations* 1999 (SI 1999/1029)

Case: *IR Commrs v Willoughby* [1997] BTC 393

Tax Reporter: ¶343-600

Enterprise investment scheme

76-000 Introduction to the enterprise investment scheme

The enterprise investment scheme (EIS), a scheme designed to encourage new equity investment in companies, allows individuals to buy shares in certain companies and obtain income tax relief for the amount invested. There is also capital gains tax relief when the investor disposes of the shares.

Any company which carries on a qualifying activity (certain kinds of trade or research and development) can potentially issue shares under the EIS. (In respect of shares issued prior to 6 April 2011, the qualifying activity had to be carried on wholly or mainly in the UK.) There is no requirement for the company to be incorporated here. Additionally, any investor with a UK tax liability qualifies for EIS relief regardless of the investor's residence status.

An investor who becomes a paid director may qualify for relief provided, broadly, that he or she was not 'connected with' the company or its trade prior to his or her first acquisition of eligible shares. This is to attract investment from 'business angels' (individuals with business experience and funds to invest) who provide management skills in addition to new capital. Also, relief may be available if an issuing company acquires a company, or the trade of a company, previously controlled by a group of persons which included the director concerned. These measures should enable business angels to provide companies with capital and to take an active part in the management of the company concerned.

Legislation: ITA 2007, Pt. 5

Website: www.hmrc.gov.uk/eis/

Tax Reporter: ¶323-000ff.

76-050 Tax reliefs

An investor may qualify for both income tax relief and capital gains tax relief in respect of an EIS investment. Capital gains tax reliefs are dealt with in *CCH British Tax Guide: Capital Gains Tax* at 225-050ff.

Income tax relief

Subscriptions for EIS shares of up to £1m per year may qualify for income tax relief. The limit was £500,000 prior to 6 April 2012.

It is not possible to carry forward unused relief, but there is a carry-back facility. Subject to the overall annual limit of £1m, an individual may claim relief in a tax year for the whole of any amount invested in qualifying shares in the following year. The amount of the subscription carried back is treated as though it related to a share issue made in the previous tax year.

Until 2012–13, relief was available only if an individual subscribes an amount of at least £500 in the tax year for shares in the company concerned (including amounts carried back to the previous year). There is no longer a minimum subscription requirement.

From 2011–12 onwards, the rate of relief for qualifying EIS investments was increased from 20% to 30% in respect of shares issued on or after 6 April 2011. A taxpayer obtains relief as a reduction to his or her total income tax liability. This reduction takes place before any other available reduction. It cannot create a repayment of tax.

Example 1

John was born on 2 October 1934. He is married and has an income tax liability, before any EIS relief, of £18,275 for 2017–18. During the year, he invests £30,000 in shares qualifying for EIS relief.

The income tax relief for the EIS subscription will be £9,000 (£30,000 at 30%) and his total income tax liability will be reduced to £9,275 (£18,275 *less* £9,000).

Example 2

Assume that in the previous example John invests £100,000 in EIS shares. The maximum reduction from his income tax liability in respect of the EIS investment is now the lower of:

(1) 30% of the amount of the subscription, i.e. £30,000; and

(2) the amount that reduces his tax liability of £18,275 to £nil, i.e. £18,275.

The excess of the EIS relief (i.e. £11,725 being £30,000 – £18,275) remains unrelieved. If appropriate, he may elect to carry back this relief to the previous tax year.

Pre-arranged exits

Relief cannot be given where, at the time of an investment, certain exit arrangements are in place which guarantee the investor a way of disposing of the shares at a later date, effectively turning the whole investment into a low-risk venture. Broadly, relief is denied where the terms of the issue include, or there already exist at the time of issue, arrangements for repurchasing or exchanging the shares, ceasing the trade, disposing of assets of the company or otherwise providing some form of protection or guarantee for the investor.

Attribution of relief to shares

If, in any tax year, an individual claims EIS relief in respect of two share issues, the total relief obtained is apportioned between them. If there is a subsequent bonus issue, the relief is also apportioned across the increased holdings.

Avoidance motive

Relief is available only if the investor subscribes for the shares for genuine commercial reasons and not as part of a scheme or arrangement with a main purpose of avoiding tax.

Legislation: ITA 2007, s. 156–158, 165, 177 and 201

Tax Reporter: ¶323-050

76-100 Claiming EIS relief

EIS relief must be claimed. In general, an investor is not eligible for relief unless and until the company's qualifying trade (see below) has been carried on for four months. However, relief is available if the company concerned is wound up or dissolved before the end of the four-month period. The dissolution or winding up must take place for bona fide commercial reasons and not as part of a scheme or arrangement in which one of the main purposes is to avoid tax. The relief must be claimed within five years of the 31 January following the end of the tax year in which the shares were issued.

The four-month period can be satisfied by either the EIS company or a 90% subsidiary of the company or by both the company and its subsidiary.

Individuals who claim relief under EIS for investment in a close company cannot claim for interest relief on loans taken out to acquire those shares.

The issuing company must give an officer of HMRC a statement in respect of the issue of shares (a 'compliance statement' EIS 1), to the effect that it satisfies the conditions for relief so far as they apply in relation to the company and its trade, and has done so since the share issue. The compliance statement must be submitted to the inspector within two years of the end of the tax year in which the shares were issued or, if later, within two years of the end of the tax year in which the above four-month period ended.

Once the officer of HMRC has examined the compliance statement he or she may authorise the company to issue a certificate (a 'compliance certificate' EIS 3) to investors. This certifies that the conditions for relief, so far as applying to the company and the trade, are satisfied in relation to those shares.

Legislation: ITA 2007, s. 161, 164, 176, 202 and 205

Tax Reporter: ¶323-100

76-150 Investors who qualify for relief

General requirements

An individual who subscribes on his or her own behalf for eligible shares, and satisfies the conditions for investors, qualifies for EIS relief. It is not necessary for the individual to be resident in the UK; any investor subject to UK tax can obtain EIS relief.

Trustees can make a subscription on behalf of two or more individuals if they hold the shares issued on trust for the individuals absolutely. Although the trustees subscribe for the shares, the individuals concerned own the shares beneficially and are treated as having subscribed for the shares as individuals. The total amount subscribed is divided by the number of beneficiaries and allocated to the individuals concerned accordingly.

Connected persons

An investor does not usually qualify for EIS relief if he or she is connected with the issuing company at any time during the period that begins two years before the share issue and ends three years after the issue. The exception to this general rule is in the case of a paid director, who may obtain relief if certain conditions are satisfied (see below).

Under the EIS scheme an individual is connected with a company if the individual, or an associate of the individual's:

- is an employee of, or of a partner of, the company or any subsidiary;
- is a partner of the company or any subsidiary;
- is a 'paid' director (see below) of, or of a company that is a partner of, the company or any subsidiary;
- owns or can acquire more than 30% of the company or any subsidiary; or
- (with effect from Royal Assent to FA 2015) any individual who owns shares in the company other than those acquired as 'risk finance investment'. Risk finance investments are share subscribed for under EIS, SEIS or SITR.

'Subsidiary' for these purposes includes any company that was, is, or becomes, a 51% subsidiary of the issuing company at any time during the individual's relevant period.

Directors

A director is connected with the company only if the director, or an associate, or a partnership of which the director or an associate is a member, receives, or is entitled to receive, any payment within the period that begins two years before the share issue and ends three years after the issue. 'Payment' includes direct and indirect payments made by the issuing company, but excludes items such as reimbursement of allowable expenses and dividends.

There is one important exception to the rule that denies relief to paid directors. An individual connected with a company only because either the individual, or an associate, is a 'paid' director, may obtain EIS relief in one important circumstance. Relief is available provided that the subscriber was not at any time prior to the share issue either connected with the company, or an employee of any person who carried on the trade subsequently carried on by the issuing company. This is intended to allow 'business angels' to take an active part in the management of a company as a paid director without losing entitlement to relief. The director concerned must not receive remuneration in excess of an amount that is reasonable for the services performed.

Persons interested in capital, etc. of company

The provisions that determine whether an individual owns, or can acquire, more than 30% of a company are widely drawn and broadly include any direct or indirect legal interest in the shares, capital, voting rights or assets of the company. From 6 April 2012, loan capital is excluded in assessing this 30% test.

In the case of *Cook (HMIT) v Billings*, which concerned the business expansion scheme (the predecessor of EIS), it was found that seven individuals who were in partnership with each other and who held the company's issued share capital in equal proportions, were associates and were each treated as possessing more than 30% of the company.

An investor who acquires subscriber shares in a company from a formation agent can qualify for EIS relief even though he or she held more than 30% of the company for the period until further shares were issued.

Legislation: ITA 2007, s. 157, 163, 166–170, 250 and 256

Case: *Cook (HMIT) v Billings* [2001] BTC 3

Tax Reporter: ¶323-150

76-250 Loan-linked investments

An investor cannot obtain EIS relief in respect of shares if, at any time in the period beginning with the incorporation of the company (or two years before the shares were issued, if later) and ending three years after the shares were issued, the investor or an associate takes out a loan which is linked to the shares. A linked loan is one that would not have been made, or would not have been made on those terms, if the individual had not subscribed for the shares.

HMRC interpretation of the rules is set out in a statement of practice. When applying this rule in practice, HMRC are primarily concerned with the motive of the lender in making the loan, rather than the borrower's reasons for applying for it. The crucial test is whether the lender would have made the loan on the same terms if the eligible shares had not been involved.

Legislation: ITA 2007, s. 164

Other Material: SP 6/98

Tax Reporter: ¶323-250

76-300 Requirements to be met by the company, etc.

There are various conditions that must be met by the company itself, its activities and the share issue if the shares are to qualify for EIS relief. The rules are complex and detailed. In brief, they include the conditions set out below.

The shares must not be issued nor money raised by the issue in connection with disqualifying arrangements. Broadly, these are arrangements where in their absence it would have been reasonable to expect that the whole or greater part of the component activities of the EIS company would have been carried on as part of another business by a person who is a party to the arrangements or a connected person.

The company itself

The company must satisfy the following conditions, most of them by reference to the period starting with the issue of the shares and ending three years later.

- In respect of shares issued on or after 6 April 2011, the company must have a permanent establishment in the UK throughout the period. The definition of a permanent establishment is based upon art. 5 of the OECD Model Treaty.
- Also in respect of shares issued on or after 6 April 2011, the company must not, at the beginning of the period, be 'in difficulty'. The European Commission regards a firm as being in difficulty where it is unable, whether through its own resources or with the funds it is able to obtain from its owner/shareholders or creditors, to stem losses which, without outside intervention by the public authorities, will almost certainly condemn it to going out of business in the short or medium term.
- Throughout the period, the company must exist wholly for the purpose of carrying on one or more 'qualifying trades', or must be the parent of a group whose business does not consist substantially in the carrying on of non-qualifying or non-trading activities (see below).
- At the beginning of the period, the company must be unquoted.
- The value of the company's gross assets must be no more than £15m immediately before the share issue and no more than £16m immediately afterwards. Prior to 6 April 2012, these limits were £7m and £8m respectively.
- The company must not at any time during the period, either alone or with connected persons, have control over companies that are not 51% subsidiaries. Also, there must not be any arrangements in place under which the company could fail this condition.

- The company must not at any time during the period be a 51% subsidiary of another company, or under the control of another company and any person connected with that company, and there must not be any arrangements in place under which the company could fail this condition.
- At the beginning of the period the company itself and any subsidiaries must have no more than 250 full-time employees or equivalent in total, or 50 employees in relation to shares issued before 6 April 2012.
- In the year ending with the issue of the shares, the company must not have raised more than £5m via venture capital trusts, the corporate venturing scheme, or EIS subscriptions. In respect of shares issued before 6 April 2012, this limit was £2m.
- With effect from Royal Assent to FA 2015, the maximum total amount that may be raised by a company under 'relevant investments (EIS, SEIS, SITR)' is £12m (£20m for knowledge based companies).

Legislation: ITA 2007, s. 173AA and 180–191A

Other Material: *Community Guidelines for Rescuing Restructuring Firms in Difficulty* (2004/C244/02)

Tax Reporter: ¶323-310ff.

Qualifying trades

A qualifying trade is a trade which is not excluded by statute as a non-qualifying activity, and which is conducted on a commercial basis with a view to the realisation of profits.

Excluded activities include the following:

- dealing in land, in commodities or futures or in shares, securities or other financial instruments;
- dealing in goods otherwise than in the course of an ordinary trade of wholesale of retail distribution;
- banking, insurance, money-lending, debt-factoring, hire-purchase financing or other financial activities;
- leasing assets (including ship chartering and letting assets on hire) or receiving royalties or licence fees;
- providing legal or accountancy services;
- property development;
- farming or market gardening;

- holding, managing or occupying woodland, any other forestry activities and timber production;
- shipbuilding, coal or steel production (in respect of shares issued on or after 6 April 2008);
- operating or managing hotels or comparable establishments, or property used as such (see below);
- operating or managing nursing or residential care homes, or property used as such (see below);
- providing services or facilities for any trade carried on by another person (other than a company of which the company providing the services or facilities is the subsidiary), which consists to any substantial extent of the above activities, and in which a 'controlling interest' is held by someone who also has a controlling interest in the trade carried on by that company;
- electricity generation which receives Feed-in Tariffs or other subsidies where commercial generation does not begin before 6 April 2012 and where shares are issued on or after 23 March 2011; and
- making reserve electricity generating capacity available (in relation to shares issued on or after 30 November 2015).

The above restriction excluding certain subsidised energy generation was, for investments made after 5 April 2016, extended to all energy generating activities.

The exclusions for hotels and comparable establishments, and nursing and residential care homes, do not apply unless the person carrying on the activity has an estate or interest in the hotel or home, or is in occupation of it.

The share issue

There are some very detailed rules relating to the share issue. Very broadly:

- the shares must be new ordinary shares which for three years following the issue do not carry preferential rights and are not redeemable (for shares issued after 5 April 2012 a preferential dividend right is not caught by this rule unless dependent on the decision of another person). In the case of *Abingdon Health Ltd* [2016] TC 05525, the issue of ordinary shares that did not enjoy preferential rights on a liquidation that were part of the rights of earlier EIS shares meant that the earlier shares lost their qualifying status;
- the shares must be issued to raise money for a qualifying trade or for research and development;

- at least 80% of the funds raised by the issue must be intended for use in the qualifying activity;
- where shares are issued after 5 April 2012, the acquisition of shares or stock in a company is not recognised as employing the money for the purposes of a qualifying business activity; and
- where the shares were issued prior to 6 April 2011, that qualifying activity has to be carried on wholly or mainly in the UK.

Legislation: ITA 2007, s. 192–200

Tax Reporter: ¶323-400ff.

Withdrawal of EIS relief

76-450 Disposal of shares

Income tax relief is withdrawn if, within two years before or three years after the share issue, an investor makes a non-arm's length disposal of EIS shares or is granted an option that entitles the investor to dispose of the shares. The withdrawal does not apply where the disposal is made to the investor's spouse or civil partner.

Relief is also withdrawn if an investor makes an arm's length disposal during the same period. If the investor obtained full income tax relief on the acquisition of the shares, the relief withdrawn is equal to the consideration received for the disposal multiplied by the savings rate of tax applicable in the year for which relief was obtained, or, if lower, the amount of the relief given. If the income tax relief obtained on the acquisition of the shares was restricted, the relief withdrawn is restricted by the same proportion.

This means that if the sale proceeds exceed the issue price of shares, the relief is withdrawn in full, but that if the proceeds are less than the issue price, there is only partial withdrawal.

Example

Sue invests £100,000 in 80,000 EIS shares. She obtains income tax relief for the investment equal to her income tax liability for the year of £15,000 (the maximum relief being £30,000). Less than three years later, she sells all of the shares for £90,000.

Although Sue's investment was eligible for income tax relief of £30,000 (£100,000 at 30%) she obtained relief of only £15,000. The amount of the relief withdrawn is therefore £9,000 (30% × £90,000 × £15,000/£30,000).

> If instead she had sold the shares for £100,000 or more, the full relief given of £15,000 would be withdrawn.
>
> If the disposal is made at a loss, the loss may in certain circumstances be set against the investor's income (see 78-000ff.).

Identification of shares sold

If an investor acquired shares of any particular class at different times, he or she is treated as disposing of shares on a first in, first out basis. If shares were acquired on the same day, the disposal is made in the following order:

- first, from shares on which no reliefs were given;
- next, from shares on which only CGT deferral relief was given;
- then from shares on which only income tax relief was given; and
- finally, from shares on which both CGT deferral relief and income tax relief was given.

Legislation: ITA 2007, s. 209–211 and 246

Tax Reporter: ¶323-650

76-500 Value received from the company

Receipt of value by the investor

Income tax relief is withdrawn if, during the period of one year before to three years after the issue of the shares, the investor receives value from either the issuing company or a person connected with the issuing company. The relief withdrawn is an amount equal to the value received multiplied by the lower rate of tax for the year the relief was given, or, if lower, the amount of the relief.

The following actions by the company are treated as payments of value:

- repayment, redemption or repurchase of share capital or securities belonging to the investor, or payment for giving up any rights, payment or assets on the cancellation of the shares;
- repayment of a debt owed to the investor if it was incurred before the subscription date or if it replaced another debt incurred before then. Where a company had previously issued convertible loan notes to certain shareholders, the subsequent conversion into ordinary shares was a repayment by the company of its indebtedness under the loan notes.

Where a payment had been made to or on behalf of the company before there had been any resolution to allot shares, the question arose whether the amounts paid constituted a loan to the company which was then repaid by the issue of the shares, thus giving rise to a receipt of value. In the case of the first of a number of share issues, that payment was held to be repayable by the company as a debt and the issue of shares in satisfaction was a repayment of that debt. There has been no evidence to show that, at the time of the payment, there was any intention that it should be a subscription for shares.

However, in a case of a number of subsequent share issues, in similar circumstances, the shares were held to be eligible shares, relying on a decision of the Privy Council that where shareholders of a company agree to increase capital without a formal allocation of shares, that capital becomes like share premium and part of the owner's equity. Accordingly, a payment made to or on behalf of a company, other than by way of payment of shares or a gift, was not repayable; the funds were not a loan. By the time of these subsequent share issues, the investor had established a track-record of subscribing for share capital every time the company needed additional capital. Although he had not formally applied for additional shares, the monies were paid by the investor and accepted by the company on the clear implied agreement, that it would allot shares to him at par. In those circumstances, the payments did not give rise to a 'debt'. The investor had paid the monies 'conditionally' on shares being issued to him;

- payment for giving up a right to a debt (other than a trade debt or a debt for expenses incurred in the performance of director's duties) on its extinguishment;
- release or waiver of a liability of the investor to the company, or discharge of the investor's liability to a third party;
- loans or advances to the investor, unless they were repaid in full before the share issue;
- provision of a benefit or facility for the investor;
- transfer of an asset to the individual for no or insufficient consideration or the acquisition of an asset from the individual for excessive consideration;
- any other payment, other than dividends, reasonable expenses, etc. or payments in respect of a trade debt.

An investor does not suffer a withdrawal merely because of receiving reasonable remuneration for services as a director or employee.

The value received is the amount of any payment, debt or loan in question. Where a benefit or facility is provided, the value of it is measured by the cost to the company of its provision. Assets are valued at market value less any consideration given.

Receipts of value may be disregarded if they are insignificant in relation to the amount subscribed for the shares. Receipts of £1,000 are regarded as insignificant, regardless of the subscription amount. If there are several receipts which are insignificant if regarded individually, they are not disregarded unless they are also insignificant when regarded in total. There are also anti-avoidance provisions which prevent any receipt from being treated as insignificant if arrangements were made in the year before the share issue under which the investor could become entitled to receive value within the period ending three years after the share issue.

There are also provisions which enable receipts of value to be ignored if, as soon after the receipt as is reasonably practicable, an equivalent amount is paid back to the company.

Receipt of value by persons other than the investor

Similarly, an investor's EIS relief may be withdrawn if any other member (other than a person who has received EIS relief) receives a capital repayment during the individual relevant period. The repayments that cause withdrawal of relief are:

- repayment, redemption or repurchase of share capital by the issuing company or any company that is, or becomes, a 51% subsidiary at any time during the period; and
- payment of any sum to a member in consideration for the giving up of rights to any share capital on its cancellation or extinguishment.

There are relieving provisions that apply where both the amount paid and the market value of the shares concerned are insignificant in relation to the market value of the remaining issued share capital.

Legislation: ITA 2007, s. 213–225

Cases: *Domain Dynamics (Holdings) Ltd v R & C Commrs* (2008) Sp C 701; *Blackburn v R & C Commrs* [2009] BTC 39

Tax Reporter: ¶323-850

76-600 Transfers between spouses and civil partners

EIS relief is not withdrawn as a result of a transfer of shares between spouses or civil partners if the individuals concerned live together at the time of the transfer. The recipient spouse or civil partner is treated as having subscribed for the shares on the date of the original issue and as having received the EIS relief obtained by his or her spouse or civil partner. The recipient is assessed on any tax due as a result of a subsequent withdrawal of relief.

Legislation: ITA 2007, s. 245

Tax Reporter: ¶324-000

76-650 Anti-avoidance: replacement capital

The objective behind EIS is to give relief for 'new investment'. Hence there was a need to prevent existing business proprietors from transferring that business into an EIS company and claiming relief for what was an old investment re-packaged. As a result, relief is withdrawn where either a business and its assets or the shares in an existing trading company are transferred to the EIS company where the investor previously satisfied an ownership/control test.

Transfer of trade

EIS relief is withdrawn in respect of all of the shares held by an investor in the company if at any time in the period beginning with the incorporation of the company (or two years before the issue of shares, if later) and ending with the third anniversary of the share issue (termed 'period A'), the following conditions are satisfied;

- the company or any qualifying subsidiary either:
  - begins to carry on, whether as the whole or part its trade, a trade which was previously in existence; or
  - acquires all, or most, of the assets previously used for the purposes of such a trade;
- that trade was previously carried on by someone other than the company or any of its qualifying subsidiaries;
- the investor satisfies specific ownership/control conditions

(ITA 2007, s. 232(1)).

Those specific conditions are, that at any time in period A, he or she, either in his or her own right or as one of a group of persons:

- owned more than 50% of both the previous trade and the trade subsequently being carried on by the EIS company (determined on the basis of profit sharing or ordinary share capital as appropriate, with the interests of associates being taken into account; ITA 2007, s. 232(4), applying ICTA 1988, s. 344(1), (2)); or
- controlled both the company that previously carried on the trade and the EIS company

(ITA 2007, s. 232(2), (3)).

The ownership of the trades and control of the companies as mentioned above do not have to occur simultaneously.

Acquisition of shares

Relief in respect of the whole of the investor's shares is also withdrawn if at any time during period A:

- the company acquires all of the issued share capital of another company; and
- the investor himself or herself, or as one of a group of persons, controlled the EIS company and the acquired company whether or not both companies were controlled at the same time

(ITA 2007, s. 233(1), (2)).

'Paid directors'

The above provisions require all the various conditions to be satisfied 'within period A'. As indicated above, this could be a period of between three and five years depending upon the dates of incorporation of the EIS company and the issue of the shares. In circumstances where the conditions are satisfied either *before* the beginning or after the end of that period, (but not during) relief will not be withdrawn in most cases. Where, however, the investor is also a director of the EIS company, or of one of its partners or qualifying subsidiaries, and who receives or is entitled to receive reasonable remuneration for his or her services, relief will be withdrawn if the conditions are satisfied at any time *before the end* of the period. In other words, there is no earlier cut-off date so that if, for example, the investor/director owned the trade many years before the incorporation of the EIS company, he or she would not be entitled to relief.

Legislation: ITA 2007, s. 232 and 233

Tax Reporter: ¶324-050

76-700 Assessments

Where relief is withdrawn an investor is assessed to income tax.

An officer of HMRC cannot withdraw EIS relief on the grounds that the company is not a qualifying company or that the individual is not eligible for relief, unless either:

(1) the company has given the officer notice of that fact; or

(2) an officer has given notice to the company stating that, by reason of that ground, EIS relief previously given is not in his or her opinion due.

For the purpose of making an appeal under the *Taxes Management Act* 1970, a notice issued by an officer as described in (2) above is taken to be a decision refusing a claim made by the company.

Neither of the above notices, nor an assessment withdrawing EIS relief, can be made after the later of:

- seven years after the end of the tax year in which the share issue occurred;
- seven years after the end of the tax year in which the trade commenced; or
- six years after the tax year in which the event by reason of which the investor ceases to be eligible for relief occurred.

Interest

Interest on overdue tax arising as a result of withdrawal of relief generally accrues from the date of the event that causes the withdrawal of relief.

Legislation: ITA 2007, s. 234–239

Tax Reporter: ¶324-100; ¶324-150

76-800 Seed enterprise investment scheme

Finance Act 2012 introduced a new relief called the seed enterprise investment scheme (SEIS).

As this name suggests, its purpose is to encourage investment in small companies. It applies where shares are issued after 5 April 2012 and is planned to end on 5 April 2017 but the Treasury has the power to substitute a later date.

Many of the detailed rules follow those for the enterprise investment scheme (EIS) and in particular the definition of substantial interest. As with EIS, no individual can hold more than 30% of the ordinary share capital, issued share capital, voting power or the assets on winding up.

The main differences compared to EIS are the following.

(1) The tax reduction is 50% instead of 30% on the amount invested. The maximum that can be allowed in a tax year is an investment of £100,000 but there is, as with EIS, a carry back provision to the previous year.

(2) An investor cannot be an employee in the three years after issue but a director is not treated as an employee.

(3) The company must not have carried on non-qualifying activities since incorporation and cannot be a member of a partnership.

(4) The gross assets must not exceed £200,000 both immediately before and immediately after the investment.

(5) Employees on a full-time equivalent basis must number fewer than 25 at the date of issue of shares.

(6) Any investment in the issuing company carrying EIS or venture capital trust relief before the issue of shares will deny SEIS relief.

(7) The amount raised by the issue must not exceed £150,000 and this includes all investments on the same day or three years before the issue of shares. Any other aid other than de minimis aid as defined is also taken into account arriving at this limit.

    There is a form of marginal relief where the amount raised on the same day is less than £150,000 but other amounts when included would bring the total above £150,000.

(8) The definition of trades follows the same as for EIS but the legislation refers to a 'new qualifying trade'. The meaning of this is that the trade carried on by the company must not have been begun by anyone before the two years ending with the date of issue of shares. There is also a requirement that no other trade should have been carried on by the issuing company or a 51% subsidiary company before the trade in question commences. This is consistent with the aim of encouraging investment in small trading operations.

(9) The company must not since incorporation have been under the control of another company, ignoring an 'on-the-shelf period' when only subscriber shares had been issued and the company has not otherwise begun preparatory activities.

Legislation: ITA 2007, Pt. 5A as added by FA 2012

Venture capital trusts

77-000 Venture capital trusts: the tax reliefs

Introduction

Venture capital trusts (VCTs) are intended to encourage investment in unquoted trading companies.

To qualify for relief, the VCT (which is actually a form of investment company, whose ordinary shares are listed on the Stock Exchange) must satisfy various conditions. To encourage investment in VCTs, specific income tax and capital gains tax reliefs are given.

There are two income tax advantages associated with making a VCT investment:

- there is income tax relief at 30% for subscriptions of up to £200,000 per tax year; and
- dividends from up to £200,000 of VCT investments are not regarded as income for any income tax purposes.

Website: www.hmrc.gov.uk/guidance/vct.htm

Income tax relief for VCT subscriptions

Relief is given to an individual on the amount subscribed for eligible shares in a VCT, up to a limit of £200,000. The relief is withdrawn if the shares are held for less than the minimum period of five years (three years for shares issued between 6 April 2000 and 5 April 2006). The individual must be aged 18 or over at the time of issue of the shares.

The maximum relief which can be given is an amount which reduces the individual's liability to nil and, in determining an individual's liability, this relief is given before any reliefs given by way of an income tax reduction.

If, before relief is claimed, circumstances arise under which the relief would be withdrawn, the relief will not be given in the first place. Also, relief is not available unless the shares were both subscribed for and issued for bona fide commercial purposes, and not as part of any tax avoidance scheme.

Tax relief is denied in certain circumstances in which the issue of shares is related to the making of loans, or any equivalent act such as the giving of credit or the assignment of a debt.

Eligible shares for this purpose are new ordinary shares which, for the five (previously three) years from the date of issue, carry no present or future preferential rights to dividends or to a company's assets on its winding up, and no present or future preferential right to redemption.

Legislation: ITA 2007, s. 261–265

Tax Reporter: ¶326-010

Income tax relief for distributions

If an investor aged 18 or over becomes beneficially entitled to a dividend in respect of VCT shares, then the dividend is not regarded as income for any income tax purposes.

The dividend must be paid in respect of ordinary shares (i.e. shares forming part of the company's ordinary share capital) where the shares:

- were acquired by the investor at a time when the company was a VCT;
- are not shares in excess £200,000 value for any year of investment; and
- were acquired for bona fide commercial purposes, and not as part of a scheme or arrangement the main purpose of which, or one of the main purposes of which, was the avoidance of tax.

A dividend does not qualify if it is paid in respect of profits or gains arising in an accounting period at the end of which the company was not a VCT.

This relief is available in respect of all shares in a qualifying VCT, whether acquired by subscription or purchase, and regardless of whether any income tax relief was given on subscription.

The £200,000 limit applies to the value of all ordinary shares in a VCT acquired for bona fide commercial purposes (not as part of a tax avoidance scheme), whether held directly or via a nominee. The value of shares acquired is taken to be market value as at the time of acquisition.

Where there is a takeover or reorganisation so that the investor acquires new shares in a VCT in exchange for shares in another VCT, then the value of the new shares is ignored for the purposes of the £200,000 limit for the year in which the new shares were acquired. The new shares fall within the limit (and so qualify for dividend relief) if, and to the extent that, the old shares did.

Where shares are acquired in excess of the limit, special rules apply, broadly, to give relief on the first £200,000 acquired in any year. This can mean that the shares in respect of which tax relief on distributions is given may not be the same shares on which tax relief on investment is given.

Example

During 2017–18, John buys existing VCT shares for £160,000 and subscribes £80,000 for other new VCT shares. John receives dividends of £1,000 in respect of the shares bought and a dividend of £500 in respect of the shares subscribed for.

Dividends received on the £160,000 *purchase* are exempt from income tax. In addition, dividends received on half (£40,000) of the shares subscribed for are exempt from income tax (i.e. limit is £200,000 = £160,000 plus £40,000). An income tax reduction is available for 30% of the £80,000 shares *subscribed* for.

There had developed a form of recycling whereby an individual would sell shares in a VCT that had been held for the required minimum period and then the proceeds, or part of them, would be reinvested in a new issue of shares in the same VCT. The 'linked sales' provisions introduced by *Finance Act* 2014, Sch. 10, mean that where shares are issued after 5 April 2014 VCT relief will be restricted where the sale of the shares and the subscription for the new shares occur within six months of each other (and irrespective of the order in which the transactions take place). A similar restriction also applies where the transaction takes place outside the six-month period where the purchase of the shares is conditional upon a new subscription for VCT shares or vice-versa. The restriction will also apply where there is a new VCT in which shares are subscribed which is a successor or predecessor of the original VCT, whether this arises on a merger or reconstruction. The reinvestment of dividends for new shares in the VCT is not prevented by this recycling rule.

Legislation: ITTOIA 2005, s. 709–712

Tax Reporter: ¶326-080

Regulations

The detailed administrative rules for VCTs are laid down by regulations, which include provisions about:

- applications for approval;
- the Board of HMRC's approval of a company and refusal or withdrawal of approval;
- appeals to the special commissioners against decisions of the Board;
- breach of conditions for approval;
- the issue of certificates to investors;
- provisions regarding tax credits on dividends for periods before 6 April 1999; and
- returns to be made and records to be kept by the VCT.

Other regulations deal with specific aspects of VCT administration, such as making provision for the winding up of a venture capital trust, for mergers between venture capital trusts and for the tax treatment of a 'further issue' of shares by a venture capital trust.

Legislation: *Venture Capital Trust Regulations* 1995 (SI 1995/1979); *Venture Capital Trust (Exchange of Shares and Securities) Regulations* 2002 (SI 2002/2661); *Venture Capital Trust (Winding up and Mergers) (Tax) Regulations* 2004 (SI 2004/2199)

Tax Reporter: ¶326-240; ¶326-260; ¶326-320; ¶326-340; ¶326-760

77-050 Withdrawal of VCT relief

There is a withdrawal of relief if the individual to whom relief was given disposes of the shares in the VCT within the period of five years from the issue of those shares (the period is three years for shares issued between 6 April 2000 and 5 April 2006). If the original subscriber makes a disposal to his or her spouse or civil partner, relief is not withdrawn and the spouse or civil partner is treated as if he or she were the original subscriber for the shares.

If the disposal within the five-year time limit is by way of a bargain not at arm's length, then the relief is withdrawn in full. If the disposal is at arm's length, then the amount of relief withdrawn is calculated by reference to a percentage of the consideration for the disposal.

Where shares have been acquired at different times, shares acquired on different days are deemed to be disposed of on a first in, first out basis. Where shares were acquired on the same day and only some qualified for relief, then the shares which did *not* qualify for relief are deemed to be disposed of first.

If a VCT loses its approved status, then any person holding shares in that VCT is deemed to have disposed of them immediately prior to that time by way of a bargain not at arm's length. As a result, all the relief previously granted is withdrawn.

Assessment on withdrawal or reduction of relief

If relief, once given, needs to be withdrawn, it is withdrawn by way of an income tax assessment for the tax year in which relief was originally given. No assessment will be made to withdraw or reduce relief as a result of an event occurring after the subscriber's death.

Provision of information

An individual investor should inform HMRC within 60 days after becoming aware of an event which would cause relief to be reduced or withdrawn. An officer of HMRC may require an individual to supply any information (within a period of not less than 60 days) which the officer believes may be reasonably required regarding an event which may cause relief to be reduced or withdrawn.

An officer may, without breaching confidentiality, inform a VCT that relief given by reference to a number or proportion of its shares has been given or claimed.

Legislation: ITA 2007, s. 266–271

Tax Reporter: ¶326-040ff.

77-100 Requirements to be met by the VCT

A VCT is a non-close company that has been approved by the Board as a VCT. There are detailed rules on the conditions that must be met by a company, which are examined in broad terms below.

Conditions that must be met for approval

In order to obtain approval as a VCT a company must have satisfied the following conditions in its most recent complete accounting period, and must also satisfy them in the accounting period in which the application for approval is made:

- the company's income must be wholly or mainly derived from shares or securities;
- at least 70% of its investments be in shares or securities in 'qualifying holdings' (see below);
- at least 70% of the qualifying holdings must be in holdings of ordinary shares carrying no preferential rights (in respect of shares issued prior 6 April 2011, 30% is required;
- no holding in any company, other than another VCT (or a company which would qualify as a VCT if its ordinary shares were quoted), may amount to more than 15% of the company's investments;
- the company's ordinary share capital must be quoted; and
- the company does not retain more than 15% of the income it derives from shares or securities.

The grant of approval can be made retrospectively, but will not apply for any time before the application for approval was made.

Provisional approval

If not all of the conditions outlined above are satisfied for the company's most recent complete accounting period, HMRC may nevertheless grant approval to a company, if they are satisfied that certain conditions *will* be met within a certain time limit.

Withdrawal of approval

HMRC may, at any time, withdraw approval of a company as a VCT if they believe that the necessary conditions were not fulfilled at the time of granting of approval, or, in a case where provisional approval was given, the conditions were not met within certain time limits in accordance with the terms of that approval.

If approval as a VCT is withdrawn, the withdrawal will normally take effect at the time when the notice of withdrawal is given to the company. However, the withdrawal of provisional approval may, if the conditions were never completely satisfied, take effect as if the provisional approval had never been given.

Legislation: ITA 2007, s. 274–285

Tax Reporter: ¶326-140ff.

Qualifying holdings

Shares or securities cannot be part of a 'qualifying holding' unless the VCT acquired them when they were first issued and has held them ever since. The shares can form part of a qualifying holding of a VCT only if they carry no right to redemption.

In addition, any company (the 'relevant company') whose shares or securities are held by a VCT must satisfy various conditions if its shares or securities are to form part of the 'qualifying holdings'.

Conditions to be met by the relevant company

A relevant company must be unquoted.

If a VCT holds shares in a relevant company, and the relevant company subsequently becomes quoted, any shares or securities previously acquired by the VCT will continue to be treated as qualifying holdings for a period of five years from the time at which the relevant company becomes quoted.

In addition, a relevant company must satisfy one of the following conditions. It must:

- exist wholly for the purpose of carrying on one or more 'qualifying trades' (see below; although the carrying on of other activities which are no more than incidental will not mean that this condition is not satisfied); or
- be the parent company of a trading group.

Although the relevant company need not be UK resident;

– in respect of shares issued on or after 6 April 2011, it must have a UK permanent establishment; and

- in respect shares issued before that date, it (or a 90% subsidiary) had to carry on, or have been preparing to carry on, a qualifying trade wholly or mainly in the UK,

at the time when the relevant holding was issued, and at all times since.

The definition of 'permanent establishment' is based upon art. 5 of the OECD Model Tax Convention

A company is a parent company of a trading group if all its subsidiaries are 51% subsidiaries and the business of the group as a whole is the carrying on of one or more 'qualifying trades' (although the carrying on of other activities which are not substantial will not mean that this condition is not satisfied).

In respect of shares issued on or after 6 April 2011, the company must not, at the time of the issue, be 'in difficulty'. The European Commission regards a firm as being in difficulty where it is unable, whether through its own resources or with the funds it is able to obtain from its owner/shareholders or creditors, to stem losses which, without outside intervention by the public authorities, will almost certainly condemn it to going out of business in the short or medium term.

There are detailed rules about the use by the relevant company of the money raised.

Legislation: ITA 2007, s. 286–302A

Other Material: *Community Guidelines for Rescuing Restructuring Firms in Difficulty* (2004/C244/02))

Tax Reporter: ¶326-360ff.

Qualifying trades

A qualifying trade is any trade not excluded by statute that is conducted on a commercial basis with a view to the realisation of profits. The trade must not consist of one or more of the following excluded activities if it forms, or they form together, a substantial part of the trade:

- dealing in land, in commodities or futures or in shares, securities or other financial instruments;
- dealing in goods otherwise than in the course of an ordinary trade of wholesale or retail distribution;
- banking, insurance, money-lending, debt-factoring, hire-purchase financing or other financial activities;
- leasing or receiving royalties or licence fees (subject to the some exceptions);

- providing legal or accountancy services;
- property development;
- farming or market gardening;
- forestry activities and timber production;
- operating or managing hotels or comparable establishments, or property used as such;
- operating or managing nursing or residential care homes, or property used as such;
- providing services or facilities for any trade carried on by another person (other than a company of which the company providing the services or facilities is the subsidiary), which consists to any substantial extent of the above activities, and in which a controlling interest is held by someone who also has a controlling interest in the trade carried on by the providing company;
- shipbuilding and coal and steel production (for shares issued after 5 April 2008);
- electricity generation which receives Feed-in Tariffs or other subsidies where commercial generation does not begin before 6 April 2012 and the shares are issued on or after 23 March 2011;
- making reserve electricity generating capacity available (in relation to shares issued after 30 November 2015).

The above restriction excluding certain subsidised energy generation was, for investments made after 5 April 2016, extended to all energy generating activities.

The exclusions for hotels and comparable establishments, and nursing and residential care homes, do not apply unless the person carrying on the activity has an estate or interest in the hotel or home, or is in occupation of it.

Research and development activities constitute a qualifying trade if the company intends to derive from them a qualifying trade. For shares issued before 6 April 2011, the requirement was that the trade was intended to be carried on wholly or mainly in the UK.

A relevant company which goes into administration or receivership does not cease to be a qualifying holding for the VCT.

Restriction on the amount of capital held in any company

The relevant holding, at the time of its issue, must not represent an investment which exceeds £1m per relevant company, in the period starting with the beginning of the tax year in which the issue takes place (or six months before the issue, if earlier) and ending with the issue itself.

If a VCT holds an investment which exceeds the maximum, it is treated as split into two separate holdings: one of the maximum and the other of the excess. If any shares are disposed of, the disposal is treated as being made from the excess holding first.

Assets of the relevant company

At the time of issue of the relevant holding, the relevant company's gross assets (together with those of its subsidiaries, if any) must not exceed £15m immediately before the issue and £16m immediately after the issue. A statement of practice sets out HMRC's general approach in applying this gross assets rule. Before 6 April 2012, these limits were £7m and £8m respectively.

Other requirements

Other requirements include the following:

- there must be no securities in the VCT's holding which are supported by a guaranteed loan;
- at least 10% of the VCT's investment must be in the form of ordinary non-preference and non-redeemable shares;
- at the time of the issue the relevant company itself and any subsidiaries must have no more than 250 full-time employees or equivalent, raised from 50 employees in respect of shares issued prior to 6 April 2012; and
- in the year ending with the issue, the relevant company must not have been invested in to a level of more than £5m (£2m prior to 6 April 2012) via VCTs, the corporate venturing scheme or enterprise investment scheme subscriptions.

With effect from Royal Assent to FA 2015, the maximum total amount that may be raised by a company under 'relevant investments (EIS, SEIS, SITR)' is £12m (£20m for knowledge based companies).

Legislation: ITA 2007, s. 303–310

Other Material: SP 2/00

Tax Reporter: ¶326-860ff.

Relief for losses on unlisted shares

78-000 Form of relief

An individual who has made an allowable loss for capital gains tax purposes on a disposal of certain shares may claim income tax relief for the loss, effectively setting a capital loss against income.

In general, given that the maximum rate of capital gains tax is 28%, an income tax claim will be more beneficial for higher rate taxpayers.

To the extent that income tax share loss relief is given, the loss is not available for relief against capital gains.

Relief is not available unless the disposal is:

- made by way of a bargain at arm's length;
- made by way of a distribution on a dissolution or winding up; or
- a deemed disposal due to shares becoming of negligible value, etc.

The shares must be 'qualifying shares'. Qualifying shares are either:

- shares to which enterprise investment scheme (EIS) relief is attributable (see 76-000ff.); or
- shares in a 'qualifying trading company' (see 78-150) that the individual has subscribed for.

Legislation: ITA 2007, s. 131

Tax Reporter: ¶321-030

78-050 The relief

An individual may claim to set the loss (computed as for CGT purposes) against income in:

(1) the tax year of the loss;

(2) the preceding year; or

(3) (if there is not enough income in one year to absorb the loss) both of those years.

If the claim is made for both years, it must state which year is to take priority.

Relief must be claimed within 12 months from the normal self-assessment filing date for the loss-making tax year.

The relief takes priority over trade loss relief against general income (see 105-100) and over early trade loss relief (see 105-250).

There are priority rules that apply to the claims themselves:

(1) if the individual claims to have a Year 2 loss set against the income of both Year 1 and Year 2, the claim must state which year's income the loss is to be deducted from first (this is referred to below as Rule 1); and

(2) if the individual has a loss in Year 1 and a loss in Year 2 and claims to have both losses set against income of Year 1, the claim relating to the Year 1 loss takes priority over the claim relating to the Year 2 loss (this is referred to below as Rule 2).

Rule 2 above ensures that relief is given first in respect of the loss whose claim deadline passes first.

The decision made under Rule 1 above will only be important if the loss is smaller than the total available income in both years. The decision will often depend on whether the individual has a loss in Year 3. If there is a loss in Year 3, it will in principle make sense to choose to have Year 2's loss set against Year 1 first, leaving some income in charge in Year 2, as there will then still be the option to set at least some of Year 3's loss against Year 2's remaining income, whereas if the set-off is made in the other order, there will be some of Year 1's income that is not relieved by the Year 2 loss and cannot be relieved by the Year 3 loss.

Example

John has the following available income and makes the following losses on qualifying shares:

	Income	*Loss*
	£	£
Year 1	45,000	–
Year 2	30,000	50,000
Year 3	40,000	60,000

John has no capital gains in any of the three years and is not expecting to make any capital gains for some years to come.

John must make a claim in respect of the Year 2 loss by 31 January in Year 4 and he must make a claim in respect of the Year 3 loss by 31 January in Year 5.

Rule 2 says that, for relief in Year 2, the loss of Year 2 takes priority over the loss of Year 3.

John needs to decide, for both losses, which year's income is to be relieved first.

John claims as follows:

- the Year 2 loss is to be set first against income of Year 1 and then against income of Year 2; and
- the Year 3 loss is to be set first against income of Year 2 and then against income of Year 3.

As a result, John's relief is as follows:

Income of year	Income before relief	Year 2 loss set-off	Year 3 loss set-off	Income after relief
	£	£	£	£
Year 1	45,000	(45,000)	–	–
Year 2	30,000	(5,000)	(25,000)	–
Year 3	40,000	–	(35,000)	5,000
Totals	115,000	(50,000)	(60,000)	5,000

Had John chosen to reverse the order of set-off for the Year 2 loss, his relief would have been as follows.

Income of year	Income before relief	Year 2 loss set-off	Year 3 loss set-off	Income after relief
	£	£	£	£
Year 1	45,000	(20,000)	–	25,000
Year 2	30,000	(30,000)	–	–
Year 3	40,000	–	(40,000)	–
Totals	115,000	(50,000)	(40,000)	25,000

Clearly John has made the right decision is claiming to have the Year 2 loss set off in the earlier relevant year first. Both losses have been relieved in full and only £5,000 income remains in charge for the three years.

Had he claimed to have the Year 2 loss set off in the later relevant year first, he would have been left with £25,000 income in charge and he would also have been left with £20,000 of the Year 3 loss unrelieved for income tax, with no prospect of relieving it against capital gains in the near future.

Legislation: ITA 2007, s. 132 and 133

Tax Reporter: ¶321-060

78-100 Qualifying shares

The relief applies to EIS shares and to non-EIS shares for which an individual has subscribed (and for any bonus shares that correspond to the subscribed-for shares). The individual is treated as having subscribed for shares if his or her spouse or civil partner did so and transferred them to the individual during their lifetimes.

Because an individual may have a holding that includes both shares that qualify for relief and shares that do not qualify (for example shares acquired under a will or shares in respect of which the company has failed to meet necessary conditions), it is important to be able to identify the shares in the holding.

If income tax relief or CGT deferral relief was given under EIS, the EIS identification rules (see 76-450) are used. If business expansion scheme (BES) relief was given on some of the shares before BES was replaced with EIS, those shares are treated as disposed of first. Otherwise disposals are identified in line with capital gains tax identification rules (i.e. usually on a last in, first out basis).

Legislation: ITA 2007, s. 135 and 148

Tax Reporter: ¶321-100

78-150 Qualifying trading company

For non-EIS shares subscribed for on or after 6 April 1998, the relief is available for shares in companies that meet much the same conditions as those that apply for EIS companies (see 76-300).

For shares subscribed for before 6 April 1998 the company must have had no shares listed on the Stock Exchange or on a designated foreign stock exchange in the period beginning on the date the company was incorporated, or one year before the shares were subscribed for if later, and ending on the disposal date.

For shares subscribed for on or after 7 March 2001 the requirement that the company should not be listed was relaxed under the changes to the EIS scheme. The company must have been unquoted at the time of the subscription, and there must then have been no arrangements in place under which it could cease to be unquoted. A quoted company is one whose shares could be marketed to the general public.

If shares were subscribed for between 6 April 1998 and 7 March 2001 and were not listed on 7 March 2001 relief will be available if the company thereafter becomes a quoted company.

Other conditions which must be satisfied for a company to be a qualifying trading company are that the company:

(1) either:

   (a) is a trading company on the date of disposal; or

   (b) ceased to be a trading company not more than three years before the date of disposal and has not since then been an 'excluded company' or an investment company; and

(2) either:

   (a) has been a trading company for a continuous period of six years ending on the date of disposal or when it ceased to be a trading company; or

   (b) has been a trading company for a continuous period of less than six years ending on the date of disposal or when it ceased to be a trading company and has not been before the beginning of that period an 'excluded company' or an investment company.

An excluded company is a company:

(1) which has a trade which consists wholly or mainly of dealing in land, in commodities or futures, or in shares, securities or other financial instruments, or is not carried on on a commercial basis and in such a way that profits in the trade can reasonably be expected to be realised;

(2) which is the holding company of a group other than a trading group; or

(3) which is a building society, or a registered industrial and provident society.

Legislation: ITA 2007, s. 134, 151 and Sch. 2, para. 38

Tax Reporter: ¶321-300

Individual saving accounts

79-000 Introduction to individual saving accounts (ISAs)

The scheme for the individual saving account (ISA) became operational on 6 April 1999.

The main points to note are listed below.

- ISAs are available to individuals aged 18 or over (or 16 or over for cash ISAs) who are resident and ordinarily resident in the UK for tax purposes (see also Junior ISAs at 79-050 below).

- There is no minimum level of saving, and no requirement to hold the investment for a minimum period.
- An ISA is completely free of tax. There is no income tax or capital gains tax to pay in respect of investments or income in the account.
- ISAs can hold cash, certain stocks and shares, certain collective investment scheme units, certain life insurance policies, certain stakeholder products and National Savings.
- For 2017–18, there is an overall annual investment limit of £20,000 per individual investor.
- From 5 April 2015, there are no restrictions to how the annual investment limit is split between cash and share ISAs. For years prior to 2015–16, no more than one half of the annual allowance may be paid into any ISA investment where it is to be held as cash.
- There is no 'lifetime' investment limit.
- Subscriptions to PEPs (personal equity plans, roughly equivalent in nature to the stocks and shares component of ISAs) could be made until 5 April 1999. Existing PEP investors at 5 April 1999 were able to keep their PEPs outside the ISA if they so chose, but still benefit from the same tax advantages as ISA investors. (Many investors still have PEPs. They continue to provide a tax-free environment for investments for assets and for income and gains that are reinvested in the PEP.)
- ISAs are run by an ISA manager. They can be marketed either by financial institutions (selling their own products) or independent financial advisers (offering other people's products). Different accounts may be offered using a wide range of savings methods (cash, stocks and shares, life insurance and National Savings). Each year, the investor can choose which type of manager to opt for. A single manager can be used or, alternatively, a manager can be used for the stocks and shares ISA and a different manager for the cash ISA.
- ISAs are intended to be as accessible as possible; the introduction of 'stakeholder products' and their applicability to ISAs is intended to widen their appeal.

Legislation: ITTOIA 2005, s. 694; *Individual Savings Account Regulations* 1998 (SI 1998/1870)

Website: www.hmrc.gov.uk/isa/

Tax Reporter: ¶321-500

79-050 Types of individual savings account

A 'qualifying individual' (see 79-150) may invest in a stocks and shares ISA and/or a cash ISA, subject to the overall limit.

An investor may not subscribe to two or more cash ISAs or two or more stocks and shares ISAs in the same tax year, but from 6 April 2014, he can transfer sums in a cash ISA to a stocks and shares ISA and vice versa. Previously, transfers could only be made from a cash to a share ISA.

In general, subscriptions must be made in cash, although there are provisions for the transfer of shares from an approved SAYE share option scheme or share incentive plan to be transferred within 90 days of the exercise of option date. Otherwise, if an individual wishes an ISA to hold the same stocks that he owns in his own right, he would have to sell those shares, with potential capital gains tax, and subscribe the cash proceeds into an ISA.

Prior to 5 April 2015, the annual investment limits apply to amounts subscribed in a year and were not increased if an investor subsequently withdrew sums. Thus, if an individual invested, say, £6,000 in a stocks and shares ISA and the same tax year withdraws £3,000, only the balance of that year's limit could be the subject of a further ISA investment in the same tax year. The individual could not top up the amount withdrawn. With effect from 6 April 2015, these restrictions will no longer apply.

In addition, for deaths occurring after 3 December 2014, a surviving spouse will inherit an additional ISA allowance equivalent to the of their deceased partner's ISA holding at death.

Junior ISAs

These are available for individuals under the age of 18. The maximum investment limit for 2017–18 is £4,128. Until 5 April 2015, it was only possible to hold a Junior ISA if the child did not also hold a Child Trust Fund account.

Help to buy ISAs

Finance Act 2015 introduced provisions to allow individuals over the age of 16 to invest in a 'Help to Buy' ISA. The maximum investment is £200 per month together with a maximum initial one-off investment of £1,200.

Provided the funds are applied as part of a deposit to acquire the individual's first home in the UK, then the Government will add a bonus of 25% of the amount saved, plus accumulated interest, up to a maximum of £3,000. The maximum price of the property being acquired is £250,000 outside London and £450,000 in London.

Lifetime ISAs

A new form of ISA is to be introduced from 6 April 2017 to be known as a 'Lifetime ISA'. It will be possible for individuals aged between 18 and 40 to save up to £4,000 per annum and receive a Government bonus of 25% of the sum invested. The funds must be used either to purchase a first home or it may be retained until at least age 60.

Individuals with Help to Buy ISAs may elect to transfer these funds into the Lifetime ISA but, if they continue to invest in the former, then it will only be possible to use the bonus from one scheme to assist in the purchase of a property.

If funds are withdrawn other than to purchase a first property or after age 60, then the Government bonus will be lost (and accrued interest on this element) and there will be a 5% penalty charge.

Miscellaneous points

Joint accounts are not allowed: only one qualifying individual may subscribe to an account.

ISA account investments remain in the beneficial ownership of the investor. If required by the investor, the account manager can arrange for the ISA investor to receive a copy of the annual reports and accounts, attend any investors meetings, vote and receive other information in relation to stocks and shares held.

Where an investor does not subscribe the maximum amount in a tax year, the unused balance is lost and cannot be used in a later tax year.

Stakeholder standards

'Stakeholder' investment products were introduced to create a range of simple, price-controlled and regulated investment products that can be sold through a basic sales process and which may be particularly useful for people on moderate incomes.

Legislation: *Individual Savings Account Regulations* 1998 (SI 1998/1870), reg. 4, 5 and 7

Tax Reporter: ¶321-550

79-100 Subscribing to an ISA

Applications to subscribe to an account

An application must be made to an authorised ISA account manager, in writing, electronically or by telephone.

ISA account managers have to meet various detailed conditions in order to be authorised; HMRC publish a regularly updated list of authorised ISA account managers on their website, at www.hmrc.gov.uk/isa/pep-isa-managers.pdf.

The application must state the first year to which it applies. It will remain valid for subscriptions made in later years. This means that it is possible for the investor to make annual subscriptions by direct debit or standing order without having to make a fresh application each year. But where there is a gap of one year in making subscriptions, a fresh application will need to be made for later subscriptions.

An application must:

(1) state the first year to which the application relates;

(2) include a declaration:

  (a) stating whether the application is to subscribe to a stock and shares ISA or a cash ISA;

  (b) that cash subscriptions made to the account are the applicant's cash;

  (c) in the case of a stocks and shares ISA, that the applicant has not, and will not, subscribe to any other such account in the same tax year;

  (d) in the case of a cash ISA account, that the applicant has not, and will not, subscribe to any other such account in the same tax year;

(3) declare that the applicant is at least 18 years old (16 years old for a cash ISA), and is resident and ordinarily resident in the UK, or is either a Crown employee or the spouse of a Crown employee who is treated as performing duties in the UK;

(4) authorise the account manager to act on behalf of the investor in relation to the cash subscription, tax relief claims, investments and income arising; and

(5) contain the applicant's full name, address, National Insurance number and date of birth.

If the account manager has reason to believe that the applicant may not be a qualifying individual or that there may be untrue information in the application, the account manager must not accept the application.

Transferring an account

An investor is able to transfer the whole of subscriptions made for the current year, and previous years' investments in whole or in part, to another ISA manager. The investments and cash transferred are not treated as new subscriptions and will not affect the subscription limits for the year in which the transfer takes place. All tax benefits are preserved on the transfer of an ISA account which is made at the request of the investor or because the old ISA manager is no longer offering ISA accounts.

Closing an ISA account

An investor is able to close an ISA account at any time, without loss of tax exemptions. On the death of an investor, income and gains arising after that date are not exempt from tax. There may be practical problems for the ISA account manager who is not notified of the death at an early date.

Legislation: *Individual Savings Account Regulations* 1998 (SI 1998/1870), reg. 4, 7, 12 and 21

Tax Reporter: ¶321-550

79-150 Qualifying individuals

To be eligible to subscribe to an ISA account, an investor must be:

- an individual aged 18 years or older (or 16 or older for cash ISAs); and
- resident and ordinarily resident in the UK, or if not so resident, must perform duties as a Crown employee serving overseas and be paid out of the UK public revenue (usually a member of the armed forces or a diplomat), or be the spouse or civil partner of such a non-resident person.

If parents have provided funds for their child's cash ISA, the income can still be treated as that of the parents under the settlements legislation whilst the child is under 18 years of age.

Death of an investor

Prior to 6 April 2015, the income and capital gains tax free status of an ISA was lost on the death of the investor. *Finance Act* 2015 introduced provisions granting the spouse or civil partner of a deceased ISA investor the right to make an additional ISA investment equal to the value of the ISA held by the deceased individual. *Finance Act* 2016 further extended these provision to the personal representatives of an estate in administration with effect from 5 April 2016.

Legislation: *Finance Act* 2016, s. 27

Account investor ceases to be a qualifying individual

An individual who ceases to be UK resident and ordinarily resident, or who ceases to perform duties as a Crown employee serving overseas or ceases to be the spouse or civil partner of such a non-resident person, is not able to subscribe further to an ISA. However, he or she retains the benefit of tax exemption on any existing ISA investments.

Legislation: *Individual Savings Account Regulations* 1998 (SI 1998/1870), reg. 10 and 11

Tax Reporter: ¶321-600

79-200 Permitted investments

ISA managers must buy and sell ISA investments at the open market value. Purchases are to be made out of cash held in the ISA and generally, the ISA must not be allowed to go into deficit as a result of purchases. The ISA manager is not allowed to purchase investments from the account investor nor the spouse or civil partner of the investor. Where the account manager is a European institution, the cash subscription and any other cash held can be held in an account in the currency of the EEA state.

Subject to that exception, the cash subscription and any other cash held by the account manager in respect of an account generally has to be held in sterling and deposited with a deposit-taker or building society. Cash received by way of dividends, interest, distributions, etc. must be recorded separately and can only be invested in qualifying investments for the same component or by way of a cash deposit.

There are some very detailed rules regarding the permitted investments for the stocks and shares ISA and for the cash ISA. Insurance investments will fall to be treated as part of the stock and shares ISA or part of the cash ISA, depending on the nature of the investments. Broadly:

- the stocks and shares ISA may include: shares and corporate bonds issued by companies listed on a recognised stock exchange anywhere in the world; gilts issued by governments in the EEA; units or shares in certain authorised unit trusts, open-ended investment companies, approved investment trusts and UCITs (undertakings for collective investments in transferable securities); and insurance policies and other stakeholder medium-term products that do not have the nature of cash;

- the cash ISA may include: cash deposited in designated ISA accounts with building societies, with institutions authorised under the *Banking Act* 1987 and with certain European institutions; units in a money market fund; and insurance policies and other stakeholder medium-term products that have the nature of cash.

Legislation: *Individual Savings Account Regulations* 1998 (SI 1998/1870), reg. 2, 6, 7, 8 and 9

Tax Reporter: ¶321-700ff.

Child trust funds

79-600 Child trust funds

The child trust fund (CTF) was intended to be a savings and investment account for children. The Government were to make payments into the account initially at a child's birth and again at age 7 to help build up a fund for the child's use when he or she reaches the age of 18.

CTF accounts were for eligible children born on or after 1 September 2002. In the June 2010 Budget, it was announced that legislation was to be introduced to end the scheme. Payments at age 7 were discontinued from 1 August 2010 and the initial contributions were reduced from that date before being finally discontinued from January 2011.

Although the Government's contributions have ceased, any accounts already in existence will remain until maturity.

With effect from 6 April 2015, it is possible to transfer the balance of a CTF to a Junior ISA.

A CTF is an investment account managed for a child in accordance with the CTF regulations under terms agreed between the provider and the registered contact (usually, the person with parental responsibility, at least until the child is 16 years old). Providers have to operate 'stakeholder accounts' that use standardised terms and conditions (see below). The child's parents and others can also subscribe to the CTF on behalf of the child.

The only amounts that can be withdrawn from a CTF prior to the child's 18th birthday are those used to meet certain provider management charges and other specific expenses. There is no access to the money until then. The account and the money in it belongs to the child, although it is managed by a person with parental responsibility until the child is 16. When children reach 16, they will manage their own CTF accounts. Should the child die before they reach 18, the investments in the CTF become part of the child's estate.

Legislation: *Child Trust Funds Act* 2004; ITTOIA 2005, s. 629 and 631; *Child Trust Funds Regulations* 2004 (SI 2004/1450)

Tax Reporter: ¶351-450

79-650 CTFs: contributions and tax treatment

The initial contribution into a child's CTF did not need to be claimed; it was triggered by a child benefit award. Once a child benefit award had been made and eligibility for the CTF accepted, a voucher worth £250 for the initial government payment was sent to the child benefit claimant (usually the child's mother). Any person with parental responsibility for the child could then use the voucher to open a CTF account for that child. If an account was not opened before the voucher expired (usually 12 months from issue) HMRC would open a stakeholder CTF account (see below) for the child. Parents, family and friends are able to contribute up to £1,200 per year (in total) to a child's CTF account. This annual limit runs to the child's birthday and cannot be carried forward to a later year if it is not fully used.

Income and gains generated by CTF investments are exempt from income tax and capital gains tax. In particular, the income generated from parental subscriptions to the CTF does not count toward the parent's income under the settlements legislation. The provider holds investments on behalf of the child, and submits repayment claims for income tax deducted at source.

The CTF account and the income and gains from that account will not affect family benefit and tax credits during the time the CTF account is open.

Types of CTF

A CTF can either be a stakeholder or a non-stakeholder account. A child cannot have a mix of the two types. All providers must offer a stakeholder CTF. They can choose to offer non-stakeholder CTFs as well, if they wish.

A stakeholder CTF may hold a variety of investments but not:

- shares or securities in investment trusts;
- with-profits endowment or insurance policies;
- units or shares in dual-priced collective investment schemes;
- rights in dual-priced contracts of insurance; or
- depositary interests representing any of the above.

CTF providers are permitted to make charges for management and other expenses up to a maximum of 1.5/365% of the value of the stakeholder CTF for each day in which the CTF is held.

Non-stakeholder CTF accounts are not subject to these restrictions and may invest more widely, e.g. a cash only non-stakeholder account could be offered, as an alternative, alongside a stakeholder account.

Legislation: *Child Trust Funds Act* 2004; ITTOIA 2005, s. 629 and 631; *Child Trust Funds Regulations* 2004 (SI 2004/1450)

Tax Reporter: ¶351-450

Community investment tax relief

80-000 Introduction

Community investment tax relief (CITR) is available to an individual who invests in an accredited community development finance institution (CDFI). The investment may be in the form of a loan to the CDFI, or in the form of shares in or securities of the CDFI for which the individual has subscribed.

The total tax relief is 25% of the amount invested, but the relief is spread over five years, at a rate of 5% per year. The tax relief reduces the investor's tax liability, and is limited by the amount of that liability. If the investor receives any significant value from the CDFI within a six-year period starting one year before the date of the investment, the tax relief is withdrawn.

Legislation: ITA 2007, s. 333–336 and 359

Tax Reporter: ¶325-000

80-020 The community development finance institution

For the relief to operate, the CDFI must be an accredited CDFI.

The rules governing CDFIs are detailed; they are contained in primary tax legislation, secondary legislation, and official guidance published by the Secretary of State for Business, Enterprise and Regulatory Reform, which has statutory effect.

Broadly, a CDFI must satisfy the following conditions:

- it must have as its main objective the provision of finance and business advice to enterprises for disadvantaged communities, which include enterprises in disadvantaged areas and enterprises run by or for disadvantaged groups; and

- enterprises in which the CDFI invests must be small or medium-sized enterprises (SMEs) as defined by the European Commission Recommendation 2003/361/EC of 6 May 2003, and must be enterprises or disadvantaged communities;
- finance provided by the CDFI to an SME must be in the form of a loan or shares that the CDFI has subscribed for, or a combination of the two.

'Wholesale CDFIs' invest in other CDFIs as well as in relevant enterprises; 'retail CDFIs' primarily invest directly in enterprises.

Accreditation

The granting and monitoring of the accreditation process is delegated to the Director of Enterprise Environment at the Department of Business, Energy and Industrial Strategy (BEIS).

Each CDFI will only be granted accreditation for a period of three years and it will have to apply before the end of that period for a further period of accreditation.

In order to keep its accreditation status even within the accreditation period, the CDFI must submit an annual report to BIS, which can remove the accreditation of any CDFI which deviates from its business plan in such a way that it no longer meets the objectives of the scheme.

Legislation: ITA 2007, s. 340–342 and 356; *Community Investment Tax Relief (Accreditation of Community Development Finance Institutions) Regulations* 2003 (SI 2003/96)

Other Material: HMRC's *Community Investment Tax Relief Manual* (CITM)

Tax Reporter: ¶325-575

80-050 The investor

An investor in the CDFI must not control the CDFI at any time during the five years immediately following the investment date. Where the CDFI is an unincorporated body, the test of control is based on voting power and other powers granted by the constitution of the body.

Legislation: ITA 2007, s. 350

Tax Reporter: ¶325-200

80-100 The investment

The investment in the CDFI can be in the form of a loan or in the form of shares or securities for which the investor subscribes, but no tax relief is available if there are arrangements that reduce the risk of that investment, such as a guarantee or insurance. Such prohibited arrangements do not include normal commercial arrangements which would be made by a bank when lending as part of its business, such as a charge on property taken as security for a loan.

Loans

The investment in the CDFI may be in the form of a loan that either is drawn down by the CDFI in full on the investment date, or is drawn down in stages over a period of up to 18 months after the investment date. Tax relief will only be given on the capital balance of the loan that has been drawn down.

The loan must not be convertible into shares or securities that have rights to allow redemption within five years of the investment date, but the loan may be repayable in stages, as follows:

- nothing repayable in the first two years after investment;
- in the third year, up to 25% of the capital outstanding after two years;
- in the fourth year, up to 50% of the outstanding loan; and
- in the fifth year, up to 75% of the outstanding loan.

Shares or securities

Any shares or securities received as part of an investment in a CDFI under this scheme must be subscribed for in cash and fully paid up on the date of the investment. They must also not have any rights to allow redemption within five years, or conversion into a loan or other shares or securities which could be redeemed within five years of the investment date. The shares or securities must not be jointly subscribed for, as the investor must be the sole beneficial owner of the shares at the date of the investment.

Legislation: ITA 2007, s. 344–349 and 351

Tax Reporter: ¶325-150; ¶325-175

80-150 The tax relief

Tax relief under this scheme must be claimed on an annual basis and is given at the rate of 5% of the 'invested amount' (see below) for the tax year in which the investment date falls and the four subsequent tax years. If the investment was by way of a loan, the 'invested amount' will not necessarily be the amount of the loan made available at the beginning of the five-year investment period (see below). The tax relief due under this scheme is a tax reducer rather than an allowance, so it cannot reduce the taxpayer's tax liability below zero for any single tax year. If the tax reduction relief cannot be given effect to in a tax year, then for investments made after 5 April 2013 the excess can be carried forward for the specified period.

As an investment made as a loan may be drawn-down over an 18-month period and may be repaid in stages (see 80-100), the 'invested amount' for a tax year is:

- for the tax year in which the investment date falls, the average capital balance for the first 12 months from the investment date;
- for the second tax year, the average capital balance for 12 months starting with the first anniversary of the investment date; and
- for the third, fourth and fifth tax years, the average capital balance for the 12 months starting with the anniversary of the investment date that falls in the tax year concerned or, if less, the average capital balance for the 6 month period that starts 18 months after the investment date.

The investor must receive a tax relief certificate from the CDFI before any tax relief can be claimed in respect of an investment. The tax relief cannot be claimed in advance, as the investor must also judge for each tax year whether the conditions for the relief still applied throughout that year.

The tax relief given under this scheme is only available after any relief due under the EIS and VCT schemes has been taken, and before any double taxation relief due. Individuals must also retain sufficient income tax to cover any gift aid donations made.

Legislation: ITA 2007, s. 27, 334–335A and 337

Tax Reporter: ¶325-025

80-200 Withdrawal or reduction of tax relief

When CITR tax relief must be reduced, for example because of a sale of the investment (see below), or it is found not to be due, the tax relief will be clawed back by way of a 'free standing' assessment to income tax for the tax year in which the relief was obtained. However, no tax relief will be clawed back if the event triggering the tax relief reduction occurs after the investor's death.

Loss of accreditation

If the CDFI loses its accreditation, or fails to renew its accreditation, within the five-year period, its investors also lose their tax relief. If accreditation is lost in the tax year in which the investment is made, relief is lost for that year onwards. If accreditation is lost in later years, investors lose their tax relief by reference to the anniversaries of the investment date; relief is lost from the tax year of the most recent anniversary when accreditation is lost.

> **Example**
>
> Frank invests £10,000 in a CDFI on 1 June 2007. The CDFI was accredited with effect from 30 April 2007, but fails to renew its accreditation from 30 April 2010.
>
> The most recent anniversary of the investment date when accreditation is withdrawn is 1 June 2009. This falls in 2009–10, so no tax relief can be claimed for that tax year or a later year. The tax relief given for the earlier years is not removed.

Receipts of value

The investor will suffer a reduction or complete withdrawal of CITR tax relief if the investor (or a connected person) receives an amount that is not an amount of 'insignificant value' from the CDFI (or a person connected with it) during the six-year period that starts one year before the investment date.

An 'amount of insignificant value' is defined as a sum of no more than £1,000, or if greater:

- in the case of an investment in shares or securities, an amount that is insignificant in relation to the amount originally subscribed by the investor; or
- in the case of an investment in the form of a loan, the amount that is insignificant compared to the average capital balance of the loan for the year in which the value is received.

If the investor receives several insignificant amounts from the CDFI during the six-year period, those amounts are added together and the total may be considered to be a significant amount.

The investor is treated as receiving value from CDFI when any payment is received from the CDFI that which is not a 'qualifying payment'. A 'qualifying payment' is in essence a commercial transaction undertaken at or below market rates, including the payment of dividends or other distributions that which do not exceed a normal return on any investment in the shares or other securities of that company. Qualifying payments include the discharge of an ordinary trade debt, provided the credit given is not for more than six months.

How is the investor's tax relief reduced?

For shares or securities – if the investment in the CDFI was as shares or securities, the investor is allowed to receive some value (ignoring insignificant amounts) from the CDFI before tax relief is reduced. The permitted levels of those receipts in the six-year period that starts one year before the investment date are as follows :

- during the first three years, zero;
- during the fourth year, up to 25% of the invested capital;
- during the fifth year, up to 50% of the invested capital; and
- during the sixth year, up to 75% of the invested capital.

If the value received exceeds these permitted levels, all the tax relief in respect of the investment must be withdrawn.

If the value received is significant but does not exceed these permitted levels, the 'invested amount' is treated as reduced by the value received, in respect of the tax year in which the value was received and any later periods. This reduces the tax relief due for those tax years.

For loans – if the investment in the CDFI was a loan, any receipt of value (other than an amount of insignificant value) is treated as being a repayment of the loan made at the beginning of the year in which the value was received. However, if the value was received in first or second year of six-year period, the deemed loan repayment is treated as being made at the beginning of the second year, i.e. on the investment date.

Early loan repayment

An investment in a CDFI made in the form of a loan may be partially repaid within the five-year investment period within prescribed limits (see 80-100). If the loan repayments, calculated by reference to the average capital balances, exceed those limits by more than £1,000, or by an amount that is not an insignificant amount (see above), all of the tax relief must be withdrawn.

However, any non-standard loan repayments are disregarded when calculating the average capital balance for this purpose. 'Non-standard repayments' are those which are:

- made at the CDFI's discretion and not part of the loan agreement; or
- made as a consequence of commercial loan default provisions in the loan agreement.

Disposal of investment

Generally, if an investor disposes of all or part of an investment (whether a loan or shares and securities) in a CDFI within the five-year investment period, all the tax relief due on that investment will be lost unless the disposal happens:

- (for loans) as part of the winding up or dissolving of the CDFI;
- (for loans) as a deemed disposal under CGT rules for situations where the investment becomes of negligible value or is lost completely;
- (for both kinds of investment) after the CDFI has lost its accreditation; and
- (for shares or securities) as part of an arm's length bargain.

Where shares or securities are sold at arm's length, the tax relief given for each tax year is reduced (but not below zero) by 5% of the sale proceeds. If the tax relief attributed to the shares is less than 5% of the invested amount, say because the tax relief has been limited by the total tax liability of the investor, the reduction in the tax relief due to a sale is also proportionately reduced.

Identification

When an investor disposes of shares or securities in a CDFI, the shares or securities are treated as being disposed of on a first-in, first-out (FIFO) basis.

Legislation: ITA 2007, s. 356, 363–372 and 377

Tax Reporter: ¶325-225ff.

80-250 Information requirements

If an investor disposes of the investment in the CDFI within the five-year investment period or receives a loan repayment or receipt of value that would create a clawback or restriction of tax relief, the investor must inform HMRC of the circumstances by the normal self-assessment filing date for the tax year in which the event occurred.

If a person connected to the investor receives value from the CDFI, the investor must inform HMRC within 60 days of becoming aware of the event.

Legislation: ITA 2007, s. 373

Tax Reporter: ¶325-550

Tax relief for social investment

85-000 Introduction

Finance Act 2014 introduced provisions which allow individuals to claim income tax relief on making a qualifying investment into a 'Social Enterprise', to be known as 'SI relief'. A Social Enterprise is defined as:

(a) a community interest company;

(b) a community benefit society that is not a charity;

(c) a charity;

(d) an accredited social impact contractor;

(e) any other body prescribed by Treasury order.

The relief available

Relief is given as a tax reduction in exactly the same manner as EIS and VCT relief. An individual may make a qualifying SI relief investment of up to £1m per annum and will be eligible for a tax reduction of 30% of the qualifying investment.

The relief will be given against the tax liability in the year of investment or, subject to election, against the tax liability of the previous year.

It is also possible to elect to roll-over certain capital gains into a qualifying investment in a Social Enterprise on the same basis as the familiar EIS roll-over provisions.

Qualifying investments

A qualifying investment must be made after 5 April 2014 and before 6 April 2021. Gains subject to a roll-over relief claim must similarly be realised during this qualifying period.

Investment may be made by way of subscription for new shares or as a 'qualifying debt investment'. A 'qualifying debt investment' means any debentures of the social enterprise in respect of which the following conditions are met:

(a) neither the principal of the debt concerned, nor any return on that, is charged on any assets;

(b) the rate of any such return is not greater than a reasonable commercial rate of return; and

(c) in the event of the winding-up of the social enterprise and so far as the law allows.

Any sums due in respect of the debt are essentially subordinated to all other debts of the social enterprise.

The restrictions and qualifications in order to benefit from SI relief are essentially the same as those for a qualifying EIS investment; including the gross asset test, exclusion of individuals who are connected to the Social Enterprise, the preclusion of linked loans and guaranteed exits, etc. (see 76-150 to 76-650).

The amount raised from investments potentially eligible for relief

With effect from 6 April 2017, the maximum sum that an organisation may raise under these provisions is £1.5m. Relief is limited to investments made in the first seven years.

Entitlement to claim

The investor is entitled to make a claim for SI relief in respect of the amount invested in a social enterprise only if a compliance certificate has been issued in respect of the investment.

Legislation: FA 2014, Sch. 11, 12; ITA 2007, s. 257J

Tax Reporter: ¶3-430; ¶322-000

Business income

Introduction

90-000 Scope of this commentary

This chapter is concerned with the income tax regime for trades, professions and vocations.

The *Income Tax (Trading and Other Income) Act* 2005 (ITTOIA 2005) came into effect on 6 April 2005 and first had effect, for income tax purposes, for the tax year 2005–06. The Act was created as part of the ongoing Tax Law Rewrite project. The aim of that project, as stated on the HMRC website, is 'to rewrite the United Kingdom's primary direct tax legislation to make it clearer and easier to use, without changing the law'. This last principle is modified, however, where 'minor changes ... would further improve the rewritten legislation'.

It follows that the enactment of ITTOIA 2005 did not in itself change the law fundamentally. In addition to clearer presentation, however, the main effects of the 2005 legislation were:

- to abolish the long-established concept of imposing income tax by reference to Schedules (where trading profits, for example, were taxed under Sch. D, Case I); and
- to create a separate set of statutory rules for income tax, distinct from those applying for corporation tax (though the latter have now also been re-written, often mirroring the income tax rules where similar principles apply).

Legislation: ITTOIA 2005, s. 853

Further new income tax legislation was added in the *Income Tax* Act 2007 (see 105-000ff.).

90-050 Overview

The profits of a trade, profession or vocation are charged to income tax. The person liable to tax on trading income is the person who receives or is entitled to the profits. As originally enacted, ITTOIA 2005 had ten 'Parts', 886 sections and four schedules. The Parts, which vary considerably in length, are as follows.

- Part 1: Overview.
- Part 2: Trading income.
- Part 3: Property income.
- Part 4: Savings and investment income.
- Part 5: Miscellaneous income.
- Part 6: Exempt income.
- Part 7: Rent-a-room and foster-care relief.
- Part 8: Foreign income: special rules.
- Part 9: Partnerships.
- Part 10: General provisions.

Whilst the taxation of business income is an important part of what is covered in the Act, it can be seen from this list that the legislation also covers some other key areas, notably property income and investment income.

For present purposes, however, Pt. 2 is of the greatest interest. This part is in turn divided into the following 'chapters'.

- Chapter 1 (s. 3 and 4): Introduction.
- Chapter 2 (s. 5ff.): Income taxed as trade profits.
- Chapter 3 (s. 24ff.): Trade profits: basic rules.
- Chapter 3A (s. 31Aff.): Trade profits: cash basis.
- Chapter 4 (s. 32ff.): Trade profits: rules restricting deductions.
- Chapter 5 (s. 56ff.): Trade profits: rules allowing deductions.
- Chapter 5A (s. 94Bff.): Trade profits: deductions allowable at a fixed rate.
- Chapter 6 (s. 95ff.): Trade profits: receipts.
- Chapter 6A (s. 106Aff.): Trade profits: amounts not reflecting commercial transactions.
- Chapter 7 (s. 107ff.): Trade profits: gifts to charities, etc.
- Chapter 8 (s. 111ff.): Trade profits: herd basis rules.
- Chapter 9 (s. 130ff.): Trade profits: sound recordings.
- Chapter 10 (s. 144Aff.): Trade profits: certain telecommunication rights.

- Chapter 10A (s. 148ZAff.): Leases of plant or machinery: special rules for long funding leases.
- Chapter 11 (s. 148Kff.): Trade profits: other specific trades.
- Chapter 11A (s. 172Aff.): Trade profits: changes in trading stock.
- Chapter 12 (s. 173ff.): Trade profits: valuation of stock and work in progress on cessation of trade.
- Chapter 13 (s. 187ff.): Deductions from profits: unremittable amounts.
- Chapter 14 (s. 191Aff.): Disposal and acquisition of know-how.
- Chapter 15 (s. 196ff.): Basis periods.
- Chapter 16 (s. 221ff.): Averaging profits of farmers and creative artists.
- Chapter 16ZA (s. 225ZAff.): Compensation for compulsory slaughter of animals.
- Chapter 16A (s. 225ZHff.): Oil activities.
- Chapter 17 (s. 226ff.): Adjustment income.
- Chpater 17A (s. 240Aff.): Cash basis: adjustments for capital allowances.
- Chapter 18 (s. 241ff.): Post-cessation receipts.
- Chapter 19 (s. 258 and 259): Supplementary.

Legislation: ITTOIA 2005, s. 5, 8

Capital allowances

The capital allowances legislation was not much affected by ITTOIA 2005 as the Capital Allowances Act was itself rewritten (CAA 2001) under the same rewrite project. Coverage of all UK capital allowances is given at 110-000ff.

Losses

The revised rules for income tax losses were not included in ITTOIA 2005 but have since been rewritten in the *Income Tax Act* 2007. See 105-000ff. below.

90-075 Trading and other income: priorities of charge

Trading income or income of a UK property business

On occasion, a receipt may be such that it could be taxed either under ITTOIA 2005, Pt. 2, Ch. 2 (as the receipt of a trade, profession or vocation) or under ITTOIA 2005, Pt. 3, Ch. 3 (as relating to a UK property business). Such a receipt is dealt with under ITTOIA 2005, Pt. 3 (property income) (ITTOIA 2005, s. 4(1) except, as noted below, where the property income derives from overseas letting or UK electric line wayleaves).

Trading income or income taxed under ITEPA 2003

If a receipt falls within both ITTOIA 2005, Pt. 2 (trading income) and ITEPA 2003, Pt. 2, 9 or 10 (respectively employment income, pension income or social security income) then the provisions of ITEPA 2003 take priority (ITTOIA 2005, s. 4(2)).

Trading income or certain other income taxed under ITTOIA 2005

If a receipt falls within both ITTOIA 2005, Pt. 2, Ch. 2 (trading income) and ITTOIA 2005, Pt. 3, Ch. 3 (overseas property income or UK electric line wayleaves) then the trading income provisions take priority (ITTOIA 2005, s. 261).

Trading income or savings or investment income

If a receipt falls within both ITTOIA 2005, Pt. 2, Ch. 2 (trading income) and ITTOIA 2005, Pt. 4 (savings and investment income) then the trading income provisions take priority (ITTOIA 2005, s. 366). However, this provision does not apply to prevent gains from life insurance, etc. contracts from being counted both as income for the purposes of ITTOIA 2005, Pt. 4, Ch. 9 and as a receipt to be taken into account as income for the purposes of other Parts of ITTOIA 2005.

In the case of *Barnetts (a firm)* [2010] TC 00575, it was held that certain interest received by a solicitors' partnership on its clients' account was to be taxed as trading income as it was money received from clients in return for professional services, even if it was indirectly received.

Trading income or other miscellaneous income

If a receipt falls within both ITTOIA 2005, Pt. 2, Ch. 2 (trading income) and ITTOIA 2005, Pt. 5 (miscellaneous income), then the trading income provisions take priority (ITTOIA 2005, s. 575(1)).

90-100 Territorial scope of charge to tax

The charge to tax under ITTOIA 2005, Pt. 2 applies to those resident in the UK and to those who are not resident in the UK, but non-UK residents are in some circumstances charged to tax only on income arising in the UK. Specifically:

(1) a UK resident is charged to tax on the profits of a trade, profession or vocation wherever in the world that trade is carried on; whereas

(2) a person who is not resident in the UK is charged to tax under Ch. 2 on the profits of a trade, profession or vocation only if they arise from:

  (a) a trade carried on wholly in the UK; or

  (b) the part of the trade carried on in the UK if the trade is carried on partly there and partly elsewhere.

Although a UK resident is taxable on income wherever in the world it arises (even if the trade is carried on wholly abroad), the full force of this initial principle is mitigated in several ways:

(1) an alternative basis of calculating the taxable profit may be used for certain 'relevant foreign income';

(2) where that alternative basis does not apply, certain deductions may be made in calculating 'relevant foreign income'; and

(3) there is a form of relief where a person is prevented from remitting income to the UK.

A person with relevant foreign income may claim to be taxed on a 'remittance basis' if that person is not domiciled in the UK. This broadly means that tax is based on amounts brought into the UK rather than simply on amounts of income arising. The chance to claim this relief does not apply, however, to relevant foreign income arising in the Republic of Ireland.

Legislation: ITTOIA 2005, s. 3(4), 6, 189, 829

Tax Reporter: ¶200-150

Defining a trade

91-000 Introduction

The term 'trade' is defined for the purposes of the income tax legislation to include 'any venture in the nature of trade'. It follows that a one-off venture, which might not be thought to amount to a trade in the everyday use of that word, may nevertheless constitute a trade for tax purposes (and therefore be taxed as such).

Legislation: ITA 2007, s. 989

Professions and vocations

The Taxes Acts offer no definitions of profession or vocation. Thus there is no strict counterpart to the charge to tax on an isolated 'venture in the nature of trade'. Nevertheless, case law suggests that a tax charge will be imposed on such an isolated transaction.

Although, in the recent past, the distinction between a trade and a profession has been of no practical interest, it now has a renewed importance in the context of limited liability partnerships incurring losses. In general, a person in a profession will be either using his intellect to obtain the end product; for example, a solicitor, or using a manual skill which is controlled by the intellect, such as a surgeon. A self-employed actress was held to be in a profession (*Davies v Braithwaite*) but an insurance broker was not (*Durant v IR Commrs*).

Cases: *Durant v IR Commrs* (1921) 12 TC 245; *Davies v Braithwaite* (1933) 18 TC 198; *Billam v Griffith* (1941) 23 TC 757; *Hobbs v Hussey (HMIT)* (1942) 24 TC 153

Tax Reporter: ¶200-500ff.

91-030 Mutual trading

Where a trade is carried on in such a way that the only people with whom the trade has dealings are persons carrying on the same trade, then no profits or gains can be made for tax purposes, provided that surpluses produced are returnable in some way to the contributors. The persons involved are merely contributors to a common fund, and the surplus produced is in excess of that which is needed to achieve their aims and belongs to those who contributed. All the members of the group must be contributors and all contributors must participate in the 'profit sharing'.

This principle was established in the early case of *New York Life Insurance Co v Styles*. The assets of the mutual life insurance company were owned by its policy holders, who were its only members. Surpluses over expenses and estimated liabilities were distributed yearly, either by way of dividend, cash reduction or future premiums, or by addition to the amount of the policy held. However, amongst the surplus so distributed was an amount of profit which was earned from ordinary business dealings by the company with non-participators in the mutual trade. By majority, the House of Lords held that such part of the profit arising from an excess of contributions by policyholders as was distributed to them was not profit assessable to income tax. (It should be noted that an insurance company's profits reserved for its policyholders may now be exempt by statute.)

Where payments to the mutual trade are made by, or dealings take place with, an outsider, the profits resulting from such dealings are assessable (*Cornish Mutual Assurance Co Ltd v IR Commrs; National Association of Local Government Officers v Watkins*).

When the case of *Municipal Mutual Insurance Ltd v Hills* came before the House of Lords, the essence of the principle of 'mutuality' was explained by Lord Macmillan as follows:

> 'The cardinal requirement is that all the contributors to the common fund must be entitled to participate in the surplus and that all the participators in the surplus must be contributors to the common fund; in other words, there must be complete identity between the contributors and the participators. If this requirement is satisfied, the particular form which the association takes is immaterial.'

Cases: *New York Life Insurance Co v Styles* (1889) 2 TC 460; *Cornish Mutual Assurance Co Ltd v IR Commrs* (1926) 12 TC 841; *Municipal Mutual Insurance Ltd v Hills* (1930) 16 TC 430; *National Association of Local Government Officers v Watkins* (1934) 18 TC 499

Tax Reporter: ¶203-750ff.

Badges of trade

91-050 Badges of trade: overview

In most day-to-day transactions it is clear whether or not a trade is being carried on by a person. However, where a person buys and sells something either once only or a limited number of times it may be difficult to decide whether the article or articles were bought as an investment, thereby attracting tax on capital gains, or whether they were bought as stock in trade, profits on the sale of which would attract an income tax charge. The decision becomes more difficult where there is a single transaction unrelated to any other business interests of the taxpayer. If the particular article is one from which aesthetic enjoyment or income may be derived, this may be one factor indicating that it was not bought for trading purposes.

If an asset is an investment then it cannot be recategorised as trading stock just because it is sold and replaced with a different investment; selling one investment to buy another is not trading. An investment may become trading stock, or vice versa, but an asset must be one or the other at any given moment: it cannot be both or have an indeterminate status.

The definition of 'trade' to include 'every trade, manufacture, adventure or concern in the nature of a trade' is of limited assistance apart from declaring that the concept may include a one-off transaction. The only way to test for the existence of a trade, according to Lord Denning in *J.P. Harrison (Watford), Ltd. v Griffiths* is to look at the characteristics of a trade and see how the transaction in question measures up to them. There have been several attempts to identify these characteristics, or 'badges' of trade.

Nine such 'badges of trading' were enumerated by Sir Nicolas Browne-Wilkinson V-C, in *Marson (HMIT) v Morton*. Those badges are referred to in the HMRC Manuals and are likely to be used by an HMRC officer in any dispute on the question of trading. The manuals present them in the following order and with the following initial comments.

(1) Profit-seeking motive: 'An intention to make a profit supports trading, but by itself is not conclusive.'

(2) The number of transactions: 'Systematic and repeated transactions will support "trade".'

(3) The nature of the asset: 'Is the asset of such a type or amount that it can only be turned to advantage by a sale? Or did it yield an income or give "pride of possession", for example, a picture for personal enjoyment?'

(4) Existence of similar trading transactions or interests: 'Transactions which are similar to those of an existing trade may themselves be trading.'

(5) Changes to the asset: 'Was the asset repaired, modified or improved to make it more easily saleable or saleable at a greater profit?'

(6) The way the sale was carried out: 'Was the asset sold in a way that was typical of trading organisations? Alternatively, did it have to be sold to raise cash for an emergency?'

(7) The source of finance: 'Was money borrowed to buy the asset? Could the funds only be repaid by selling the asset?'

(8) Interval of time between purchase and sale: 'Assets which are the subject of trade will normally, but not always, be sold quickly. Therefore, an intention to resell an asset shortly after purchase will support trading. However, an asset, which is to be held indefinitely, is much less likely to be a subject of trade.'

(9) Method of acquisition: 'An asset which is acquired by inheritance, or as a gift, is less likely to be the subject of trade.'

These badges should not be applied too rigorously, however. As the judge himself said in the *Marson (HMIT) v Morton* case:

> 'I believe that in order to reach a proper factual assessment in each case it is necessary to stand back, having looked at those matters, and look at the whole picture and ask the question – and for this purpose it is no bad thing to go back to the words of the statute – was this an adventure in the nature of trade?'

It should in any case be noted that the badges only help when a person sells things, rather than provides a service.

Cases: *J.P. Harrison (Watford), Ltd. v Griffiths* (1962) 40 TC 281; *Marson (HMIT) v Morton* [1986] BTC 377

Other Material: HMRC *Business Income Manual* BIM20200ff.

Tax Reporter: ¶200-600

91-100 Badges of trade: profit-seeking motive

Evidence that an asset was acquired with the intention of reselling it at a profit, without any view of holding it as an investment, is a good indication that a trade is being carried on, but is not decisive. The HMRC view is that the motive will carry less weight in the case of those assets (such as shares) that are more likely to be held as investments:

> 'Shares may be bought with the intention of making a profit. However, because of the inherent investment nature of shares, in the absence of enough of the other badges of trade, the purchaser will be making and realising capital investments and not trading.'

A desire to make a profit is therefore not in itself sufficient evidence to support a finding of trading; a desire to make a profit is uppermost in the minds of all who buy for investment. However, where that desire is not coupled with an intention to hold the item as one would hold an investment, it will assist the court in a finding of trading. Conversely, the absence of an intention to acquire the asset as a permanent investment will tend to lead to the conclusion that the asset was acquired as trading stock, even where there is no direct indication of a profit motive.

Other Material: HMRC *Business Income Manual* BIM20210

Tax Reporter: ¶200-625

Change of intention

The question of motive becomes more important where the taxpayer buys for investment and quickly thereafter changes his mind and decides to sell. Providing that there is clear evidence that the asset was bought for investment, a quick resale will not make the transaction an adventure in the nature of trade. The reason for sale will rather be looked upon as an unforeseen contingency. To be unexpectedly offered a good price for the asset could be an unforeseen contingency, but enjoyment derived from an expectation of price rise will not assist in a finding that the asset is held for investment.

If, on the other hand, the taxpayer intends to sell as soon as possible, but cannot find a buyer for a considerable time, he is still likely to be held to be trading.

Tax Reporter: ¶200-625

91-110 Badges of trade: number of transactions

As a general rule, the greater the number of similar transactions, the more likely it is that there will be trading.

This statement is well illustrated by the case of *Leach v Pogson*. The taxpayer started a driving school and later sold it at a profit. He then set up and sold some 30 driving schools. In isolation, the first transaction would almost certainly have been treated not as trading but as the sale of a capital asset, but the High Court held that the subsequent sales had tainted the first, so that it too was a trading transaction. It would appear that there may not have been, initially, any intention to sell the first driving school from the outset but the subsequent sales led the court to believe that there must have been.

Conversely, there are numerous cases in which a single transaction has been held to be an adventure or concern in the nature of trade (see 91-000).

Case: *Leach v Pogson* (1962) 40 TC 585

Tax Reporter: ¶200-650

Trading in shares

Individuals buying and selling shares provide an exception to the general principle that a large number of transactions tends to be indicative of trading. HMRC take the view that 'transactions by individuals in shares and securities are not generally trading transactions'. As such, HMRC will normally seek to tax profits from share dealing as capital gains, but will deny tax relief against other income for any losses made by buying and selling shares. This HMRC stance was affirmed in the case of *Dr K M A Manzur*. A retired surgeon claimed relief against general income for losses incurred on buying and selling shares, having carried out 'thousands of transactions' in a single year with a claimed maximum two week period of ownership (though HMRC said that there were in fact under 300 transactions in one of the years reviewed, some being held for six months or more). The tribunal concluded that the transactions were more in the nature of an investment portfolio which necessitated a balance between shorter and longer periods of holding investment stock.

Case: *Dr K M A Manzur* [2011] TC 00830

Other Material: HMRC *Business Income Manual* BIM65701

Tax Reporter: ¶200-850

91-120 Badges of trade: nature of asset

The issue here was well summarised by the Royal Commission on the Taxation of Profits and Income back in 1954:

> 'While almost any form of property can be acquired to be dealt in, those forms of property, such as commodities or manufactured articles, which are normally the subject of trading, are only very exceptionally the subject of investment. Again property which does not yield to its owner an income or personal enjoyment merely by virtue of its ownership is more likely to have been acquired with the object of a deal than property that does.'

In other words, the nature of the asset may point to the question of whether there was a profit-seeking motive. In the view of HMRC, 'the nature of the asset can be of great, even decisive, importance'. It perhaps also ought to be added that if the quantity of the particular commodity acquired is too large for any non-trading purpose, there will be a strong inference of trading.

The classic case to illustrate this was *Rutledge v IR Commrs*, in which a film director on business abroad bought one million rolls of toilet paper. He sold the toilet paper to a single purchaser on his return to the UK and made a profit of £11,000. In the Court of Session, in holding that the taxpayer was engaged in an adventure in the nature of a trade, it was said that he 'made himself liable for the purchase of this vast quantity of toilet paper obviously for no other conceivable purpose than that of reselling it at a profit'.

Case: *Rutledge v IR Commrs* (1929) 14 TC 490

Other Material: HMRC *Business Income Manual* BIM20245

Tax Reporter: ¶200-675

91-130 Badges of trade: existing interests or trade

If the person buying and selling the asset has a related interest or expertise then this may be indicative that he knows what he is doing and is buying with a view to selling at a profit. In *Marson (HMIT) v Morton*, for example, the court commented that 'a one-off purchase of silver cutlery by a general dealer is much more likely to be a trade transaction than such a purchase by a retired colonel'.

Case: *Marson (HMIT) v Morton* [1986] BTC 377

Tax Reporter: ¶200-700

91-140 Badges of trade: modifying the asset

If a great deal of work is done to an asset before it is sold then this may be at least mildly indicative of trading. The factor will have greater significance if it involves setting up a quasi-business to promote the sale, perhaps involving the setting up of an office or extensive advertising (see 91-150).

In *IR Commrs v Livingston*, for example, a ship repairer, a blacksmith and an employee of a fish salesman bought a cargo ship and converted it into a steam drifter which was then sold at a profit. Lord Clyde, in the Court of Session, said that this was more than just a purchase and resale; they had actually spent money on making the asset more marketable: 'the profit made by the venture arose, not from the mere appreciation of the capital value of an isolated purchase for resale, but from the expenditure on the subject purchased of money laid out upon it for the purpose of making it marketable at a profit. That seems to me of the very essence of trade'.

On the other hand, simply taking steps to improve the value of an asset before sale does not indicate a trading transaction. As elsewhere, it is largely a matter of degree.

Case: *IR Commrs v Livingston* (1926) 11 TC 538

Tax Reporter: ¶200-725

91-150 Badges of trade: manner and circumstances of sale

A quick resale leads to an inference of trading, but if the asset is sold in response to an unforeseen contingency (e.g. a forced sale) then it is probable that the taxpayer will not be held to be trading.

Cases: *Californian Copper Syndicate Ltd v Harris* (1904) 5 TC 159; *West v Phillips* (1958) 38 TC 203

Tax Reporter: ¶200-750

91-160 Badges of trade: source of finance

If a person borrows money to buy an asset, the overall circumstances of the loan may make it clear that there was an intention to sell the asset on at a profit as soon as possible: an indicator of likely trading. This will be the case, for example, where the borrower would clearly struggle to make the required repayments without realising the value of the asset.

In *Wisdom v Chamberlain*, the taxpayer bought silver bullion. The general commissioners found that the bullion was not income-producing and that the taxpayer had financed its purchase by raising high-interest loans. The Court of Appeal upheld the commissioners' finding that the purchase and sale constituted trading transactions.

Case: *Wisdom v Chamberlain* (1968) 45 TC 92

Tax Reporter: ¶200-775

91-170 Badges of trade: interval between purchase and sale

Property that is bought and quickly re-sold is more likely to be treated as a trading asset. If the purchase is funded through short-term borrowings that are not sustainable over an extended period, then this may demonstrate a need to realise the asset quickly, which will tend to point to a trading motive: see 91-160.

Conversely, a long period of ownership may overturn a natural assumption of trading, a point illustrated in the case of *Waylee Investment Ltd v IR Commrs (Hong Kong)* where the acquisition of shares in a customer was held to be a capital transaction, largely because the shares were not sold immediately the company became profitable, but were held for four years and paid dividends.

A relatively long period of ownership was also a determining factor in the case of *Parveen Azam*, in which loss relief against general income was denied on the basis that the individual was not trading in property. Even if the appellant's original aim was to sell the properties quickly for a profit, that intention must have changed quickly, with most of the later properties acquired at a time when she knew that she would have to rent them out for a period of at least several years.

Cases: *Waylee Investment Ltd v IR Commrs (Hong Kong)* [1990] BTC 543; *Parveen Azam* [2011] TC 00928

Tax Reporter: ¶200-800

91-180 Badges of trade: method of acquisition

The HMRC view is that where an asset is acquired by way of gift or inheritance, 'it will be difficult, although not impossible, to show that a subsequent sale is by way of trade'. If an asset is acquired otherwise than by way of trading stock, its subsequent sale will only be a trading transaction if, at some point before the date of sale, it has changed its nature to become trading stock, a process HMRC label 'supervening trading'.

Any switch from fixed asset to trading stock may itself have tax implications.

Legislation: TCGA 1992, s. 161

Case: *Taylor v Good* (1974) 49 TC 277

Tax Reporter: ¶200-825

91-190 Car boot sales, eBay, etc.

At the end of 2006, HMRC released a 'guide for people who sell items online, through classified advertisements and at car boot sales'. Essentially, it is a re-working of the concept of the badges of trade but in seeking to be clear it cuts quite a few of the complexities out altogether. Indeed, it is arguably misleading in places, so care is needed. The article may be viewed at www.hmrc.gov.uk/guidance/selling/income.htm and at surrounding pages.

HMRC have also issued guidance under the general heading of 'Finding out about tax regulations' at www.hmrc.gov.uk/findout. This site addresses, in a fairly simplistic way, the question of whether a person needs to declare taxable income. It includes a heading 'Are you selling on sites like eBay?' and there is an online registration form for those wishing to register as newly self-employed.

Tax Reporter: ¶200-940

Legal basis for determining existence of trade

91-200 Deciding whether or not there is a trade

The question of whether a trade is being carried on is one of fact; as such, it is for the appeal tribunal to reach a decision. If, in arriving at their decision, they fail to take a properly balanced view of the facts or if the decision to which they come is one which could not be reached by properly constituted commissioners acting reasonably, then the courts may set aside their decision.

Those principles were at issue in *Edwards (HMIT) v Bairstow & Harrison*. Lord Radcliffe stated that the court may intervene where the facts found are such that:

> 'no person acting judicially and properly instructed as to the relevant law could have come to the determination'

reached, whether or not any misconception of law appears on the face of the case stated. In other words, if the tribunal infers a perverse conclusion from the facts, the court may then substitute its own conclusion.

Case: *Edwards (HMIT) v Bairstow & Harrison* (1955) 36 TC 207

Tax Reporter: ¶200-500ff.

91-250 Statutory trades

Certain activities are deemed by the legislation to be trades if they would not otherwise be so, and vice versa.

Farming

Farming and market gardening in the UK are two such activities, treated for income tax purposes as the carrying on of a trade or part of a trade, whether or not the land is managed on a commercial basis with a view to the realisation of profits (though the use of losses is restricted where there is no such basis).

Legislation: ITTOIA 2005, s. 9

Tax Reporter: ¶201-000

Woodlands

The commercial occupation of UK woodlands (i.e. where they are managed on a commercial basis with a view to the realisation of profits) is not a trade for any income tax purpose. Profits or losses arising from such occupation are therefore ignored for income tax purposes.

Legislation: ITTOIA 2005, s. 11, 267, 768

Other activities

Profits from the following concerns are also calculated as if the concern were a trade. Such profits are then charged to income tax as if the concern were a trade carried on in the UK (but not so as to impose a charge to tax on a person not resident in the UK where the concern is carried on outside the UK). Losses are treated as if they were losses of a trade carried on in the UK:

(1) mines and quarries (including gravel pits, sand pits and brickfields);

(2) ironworks, gasworks, salt springs or works, alum mines or works, waterworks and streams of water;

(3) canals, inland navigations, docks, and drains or levels;

(4) rights of fishing;

(5) rights of markets and fairs, tolls, bridges and ferries;

(6) railways and other kinds of way; and

(7) other concerns of the like nature as any of the concerns specified in paragraphs (2)–(5) above.

Legislation: ITTOIA 2005, s. 12

Starting and ceasing to trade

91-300 Importance

The question of whether a trade has commenced and ceased, and the date of any such change, can have critical tax consequences. The following matters illustrate the importance of this topic (and the list does not claim to be comprehensive).

(1) Pre-trading expenditure is only a revenue expense if certain conditions are satisfied.

(2) Losses can, for income tax purposes, be carried back under certain special provisions only if they are incurred during the first four tax years.

(3) Terminal loss relief can only be claimed if the trade is permanently discontinued.

(4) Special rules govern the basis of assessment during the first tax years after the commencement of a trade.

(5) Trading losses can only be carried forward by an unincorporated trader if there is a continuity of both the trade and the ownership of that trade, except for relief against post-cessation receipts and on the incorporation of a trade.

(6) On a cessation, balancing adjustments may arise on plant and machinery.

(7) An accounting period of a company begins when it comes within the charge to corporation tax: for example, by acquiring a source of income on commencing to trade. An accounting period can cease when a company ceases to trade.

(8) Inheritance tax business property relief on certain assets is no longer available once the assets cease to be used for the purpose of a business following the cessation of that business.

Tax Reporter: ¶202-500

91-320 Date of commencement of trading

There is a distinction between preparing to trade and actually commencing trading. In *Birmingham & District Cattle By-Products Co Ltd v IR Commrs* a company was incorporated. For the first three months, the activities consisted of installing machinery, obtaining premises, engaging staff and arranging for the supply of by-products. However, it was only found to have commenced trading when the actual processing began. In *Todd v Jones Bros Ltd* a company acquired another trade. The date of the contract for the acquisition was held to be the date of commencement. The company unsuccessfully claimed that *de facto* the transfer took place earlier.

Generally, a trade or profession commences when the trader is in a position to supply the goods or services. This date may well be some time before a supply actually takes place. Also, an activity may initially be a hobby but at some date become a taxable trading activity. In *Vallambrosa Rubber Co Ltd v Farmer*, the taxpayer carried on the business of rubber planting. It takes about six years before the rubber trees yield rubber, and in the accounting period in question only one-seventh of the trees began to bear rubber. The Crown unsuccessfully argued that only one-seventh of the expenditure on superintendence, weeding, etc. for each year was a deductible revenue expense, the remainder being a capital expense for the formation of rubber plantations and the improvement of the estate. The balance of six-sevenths did not refer to the profits reaped during the year. However, the whole of such expenditure was held to be deductible as a revenue expense of the trade in the period in which the expense was incurred, notwithstanding that no fruit had yet been produced and no profits generated from the outlay.

The issues were further explored in *Mansell v R & C Commrs*, in which the following principles were enumerated.

(1) A trade could not commence until it had been set up (to the extent it needed to be set up), and acts of setting up were not the same as commencing or carrying on the trade.

(2) Setting up trade would include setting up a business structure to undertake the essential preliminaries, getting ready to face customers, purchasing plant, and organising the decision-making structures, the management and the financing.

(3) Depending on the nature of the trade, more or less than that might be required before it was set up.

(4) Before a trade could be said to commence, there had to be a fairly specific concept of the type of activity to be carried on.

(5) An activity which consisted merely of a review of the possibilities in the expectation or hope that information would be obtained to justify going into a business of some kind was not the carrying on of a trade.

(6) It is not always necessary that a sale should be made or a service supplied before a trade could be said to begin.

(7) A trade commenced when the taxpayer, having a specific idea in mind of his intended profit making activities, and having set up his business, began operational activities, i.e. dealings with third parties immediately and directly related to the supplies to be made which it was hoped would give rise to the expected profits, and which involved the trader putting money at risk: the acquisition of the goods to sell or to turn into items to be sold, the provision of services, or the entering into a contract to provide goods or services: the kind of activities which contributed to the gross (rather than the net) profit of the enterprise.

(8) Carrying on negotiations to enter into the contracts which, when formed, would constitute operational activity was insufficient. At that stage no operational risk had been undertaken. Such negotiations might be part of setting up the trade but they did not betoken its commencement.

Cases: *Vallambrosa Rubber Co Ltd v Farmer* (1910) 5 TC 529; *Birmingham & District Cattle By-Products Co Ltd v IR Commrs* (1919) 12 TC 92; *Todd v Jones Bros Ltd* (1930) 15 TC 396; *Mansell v R & C Commrs* (2006) Sp C 551

Tax Reporter: ¶202-525

91-340 Date of cessation of trading

Whether a person has ceased to trade is a question of fact. A cessation may occur by reason of a change in the nature of the trade being carried on, or a change in its ownership, or by reason of an actual cessation of the trade (including, of course, cessations brought about by the trader going out of business, or dying).

The scale of a trade's activities can fall by various extents and over various periods of time. A significant and sudden drop in the scale of activities may well result in the trade ceasing for tax purposes and a new trade commencing. Indeed, there may be completely dormant periods of activity. If over a long period of time the activities gradually decline, then this is less likely to result in a cessation followed by a commencement.

A 'demerger', such as when a partnership of, say, accountants breaks up and some or all of the ex-partners continue to practise, may well be a relatively large contraction. It may be that the former profession ceased on the partnership dissolution and two or more new professions began. In any event, only one person can strictly claim a continuation as there was only one profession that could continue. The ex-partners may dispute who continues for tax purposes.

In *Rolls-Royce Motors Ltd v Bamford*, only two out of a company's six divisions, which had been treated as one trade, were transferred to the appellant company. The scale of activities of the appellants was found to be much less than that of the transferor company. The appellants did not take over the trade, but began a new trade. The main consequence was that the appellants could not bring forward the large trading losses incurred by the transferor company because such losses could only be carried forward and set off against future profits from the *same* trade.

Walton J said (at p. 346):

> 'if there is in substance a complete division of the trade of the company into two separate parts, notwithstanding that trade of the same general nature is carried on thereafter by each of the two now separate entities, it appears to me that neither of them is carrying on the same trade as the composite whole formerly carried on.'

Trading activities may expand by increasing the scale of existing production, by mergers, by entering new markets or by introducing new products. The question whether there has been an expansion of an existing trade, or a discontinuance of a former trade and commencement of a new one, is primarily a question of fact.

Case: *Rolls-Royce Motors Ltd v Bamford* (1976) 51 TC 319

Tax Reporter: ¶202-550

91-360 Effect of becoming or ceasing to be UK resident

Special rules apply where an individual (other than as a partner) carries on a trade, profession or vocation wholly or partly outside the UK. If the individual becomes resident in the UK, or ceases to be resident in the UK, then he or she is treated for income tax purposes as permanently ceasing to carry on the trade at the date of change and, if applicable, as commencing a new trade immediately afterwards. This rule does not, however, prevent a loss made before the change from being set off, under ITA 2007, s. 83 (carry forward against subsequent profits), against profits arising after the change.

Legislation: ITA 2007, s. 83; ITTOIA 2005, s. 17

Tax Reporter: ¶203-150

91-400 Change in persons carrying on a trade

Where there is a complete change in the composition of the partnership, taxable profits are calculated as if the trade had been permanently discontinued. However, where there is only a partial change in ownership so that one or more persons carrying on the trade before the change (either alone or in partnership) continue to carry on the trade after the change (either alone or in partnership), there is no deemed discontinuance. There is no provision to elect for a deemed discontinuance.

This is conceptually different from the way the legislation worked in the past. There is no single statutory authority for the newer approach but it is stated in various places in relation to particular elements of the tax law. See, for example, ITTOIA 2005, s. 860(2) in relation to 'adjustment income'.

91-450 Death of trader

On the death of a trader his executors may well continue the trade. However, the carry-forward of trading losses (for example) requires not only continuity of the trade, but also continuity of the ownership of that trade. If at least one person carried on the trade both before and after the change, it will in any event be treated as continuing.

Tax Reporter: ¶202-850

91-500 Incorporation of a business

A transfer by an unincorporated taxpayer of the whole of his trade to a company will result in the cessation of the trade. HMRC have been known to argue, however, that the discontinuance of only one element of a trade may not result in a cessation if other elements continue; see, for example, the case of *Watts v Hart*.

Case: *Watts v Hart* [1984] BTC 343

Tax Reporter: ¶202-900

91-600 Successions

The concept of one person 'succeeding' to a business previously carried on by someone else continues to have significance for tax purposes, but less so than in the past. Provisions that still refer to the concept include the following:

- the deemed disposal value in determining capital allowances for the successor and the predecessor (CAA 2001, s. 266, 559); and
- the transfer to a successor of rights to receive post-cessation receipts (ITTOIA 2005, s. 98, 251; CTA 2009, s. 95).

The term 'succession' is not defined in any statute but its meaning has been considered by the courts. Key factors in determining whether one business has succeeded to another will include:

- the extent to which the alleged successor carried on a similar trade after the transfer;
- the interval between the cessation by the predecessor and the commencement by the successor;
- the intentions of the parties;
- whether or not goodwill and other intangible assets have been taken over; and
- whether the newer business operates with the same staff, premises, stocks, etc.

Tax Reporter: ¶203-600

Calculating business profits

General principles

92-000 Introduction

Income tax is charged, in relation to business profits, on 'the full amount of the profits of the tax year'. The charge to tax applies to those resident in the UK and to those who are not resident in the UK, but non-UK residents are in some circumstances charged to tax only on income arising in the UK (see 90-100).

For income tax purposes, the ancient concept of taxing business profits under Schedule D ceased to apply from 6 April 2005 (with the concept being similarly abolished for corporation tax purposes some years later). The change, though, was one of terminology; apart from very minor tweaking of the underlying rules, the enactment of the *Income Tax (Trading and Other Income) Act* 2005 did not change the way in which business profits are calculated or taxed.

Basic guidance is given by HMRC in their 'Business Profit Toolkit', the latest version being that published in June 2014. This includes a checklist referring to matters such as stock and work in progress, provisions and the accruals basis. An election to be taxed on the cash basis will have to be allowed for when reading this toolkit.

Legislation: ITTOIA 2005, s. 3–8

Tax Reporter: ¶205-000ff.

92-025 Accounting practice

The tax legislation states that:

> 'the profits of a trade must be calculated in accordance with generally accepted accounting practice, subject to any adjustment required or authorised by law in calculating profits for income tax purposes.'

The same principle is extended to the calculation of the profits of a profession or vocation.

The predecessor legislation was FA 1998, s. 42(1), which had required the profits to be computed so as to give a true and fair view (though the wording was changed before the enactment of ITTOIA 2005). The requirement for profits to be computed in accordance with 'generally accepted accounting practice' (GAAP) has not removed the true and fair view requirement.

For any entity which prepares accounts in accordance with international accounting standards (IAS), the term 'generally accepted accounting practice' is defined to mean 'generally accepted accounting practice with respect to such accounts'.

In any other case, the term 'generally accepted accounting practice' is stated to mean 'UK generally accepted accounting practice', a term itself defined as:

> 'generally accepted accounting practice with respect to accounts of UK companies (other than IAS accounts) that are intended to give a true and fair view.'

The legislation specifically requires that the same definition is applied to individuals and other entities, and to non-UK companies, as it is applied to UK companies.

Failure to apply appropriate accounting principles will mean that the taxable profits are likely to be incorrect. This was illustrated, for example, in the 2010 case of *Smith*, where failure to include proper year-end valuations of stock and work in progress meant that the accounts were not prepared in accordance with SSAP 9. This amounted to negligence and empowered HMRC to make discovery assessments.

Legislation: ITTOIA 2005, s. 25

Case: *Smith* [2010] TC 00403

Tax Reporter: ¶205-500ff.

92-050 Accounting practice according to HM Revenue and Customs

For a view of the HMRC perspective on the importance of accounting evidence, see the *Business Income Manual*, BIM46500ff. which has the following headings on this topic, dealt with under the paragraphs shown:

- Specific deductions: provisions: allowability for tax (BIM46510);
- Specific deductions: provisions: accounting standards and GAAP: (BIM46515);
- Specific deductions: provisions: accounting standards and GAAP: when a provision can be made (BIM46520);
- Specific deductions: provisions: accounting standards and GAAP: quantification (BIM46525);
- Specific deductions: provisions: accounting standards and GAAP: contingencies BIM46530);
- Specific deductions: provisions: accounting standards and GAAP: unacceptable provisions (BIM46535);
- Specific deductions: provisions: accounting standards and GAAP: onerous contracts (BIM46540);
- Specific deductions: provisions: examples of allowable provisions (BIM46545);
- Specific deductions: provisions: examples of the effect of GAAP (BIM46550);
- Specific deductions: provisions: allowability for tax: accuracy (BIM46555);
- Specific deductions: provisions: risk assessment: approach (BIM46560); and
- Specific deductions: provisions: allowability for tax: provisions affected by specific statutory timing rules (BIM46565).

Tax Reporter: ¶205-550

92-075 Change of basis of calculating profits

Special rules apply when, from one period of account to the next, a trader changes the basis on which the trading profits are calculated for tax purposes (as that term is defined) but they only apply if both the old and the new basis accord with the law or practice that are applicable in relation to the period of accounts respectively before and after the change. The rules do not apply to relevant foreign income charged on the remittance basis by virtue of ITTOIA 2005, s. 832.

Definition

A person is said to change the basis on which profits of a trade are calculated for income tax purposes if that person makes:

(1) a change of accounting policy, defined to include either:

  (a) a change from using UK generally accepted accounting practice to using generally accepted accounting practice with respect to accounts prepared in accordance with international accounting standards; or

  (b) a change from using UK generally accepted accounting practice with respect to accounts prepared in accordance with international accounting standards to using UK generally accepted accounting practice;

or

(1) 'a change in the tax adjustments applied', for which purpose a 'tax adjustment' means any adjustment that is either required or authorised by law in calculating taxable trading profits.

The concept of 'a change in the tax adjustments applied' does not include any change that is made to comply with amending legislation that did not apply to the earlier accounting period but does include a change resulting from a change of view as to what is required or authorised by law or as to whether any adjustment is so required or authorised.

The concept of 'practice applicable' is defined to mean 'the accepted practice in cases of that description as to how profits of a trade should be calculated for income tax purposes'. In other words, reference is made to industry norms, rather than to those of a particular business.

An election to adopt the cash basis introduced from 6 April 2013 brings these rules into play both on entering and ceasing to be taxed on that basis.

Adjustment on change of basis

The calculation of the adjustment on a change of accounting basis is divided into two steps. The first is to work out by how much profits were understated (or losses overstated) on the old basis. Account is to be taken of receipts, expenses, adjustments for stock or work in progress, and depreciation adjustments. It is then necessary to deduct the amount by which profits were overstated (or losses understated) on the old basis. Account is this time to be taken of receipts, expenses, and adjustments for stock or work in progress; there is no equivalent adjustment re depreciation.

Adjustment income (i.e. where the result of the two steps described above is a positive figure) is normally treated as arising on the last day of the first period of accounts for which the new basis is adopted. It is also deemed to be included in profits for the purposes of loss relief. If the result of the two steps described above is a negative figure, it is normally treated as an expense of the trade, profession or vocation arising on the last day of the first period of account under the new basis.

Legislation: ITTOIA 2005, s. 227, as amended by FA 2012 for periods beginning after 31 December 2011

Tax Reporter: ¶206-000ff.

92-100 Adjusting accounting profits for tax purposes

The starting point in calculating taxable business profit is the profit and loss account, part of the 'financial statements' or accounts that the business draws up. Adjustments, required or authorised by revenue law, are made to the profit to arrive at the profit or loss for tax purposes. The adjustments that are required or authorised may decrease or increase trading income and trading expenses.

The adjustments may fall within:

- specific statutory rules; or
- more general principles which are not specifically stated in the Acts but which are fundamental to the scheme of tax.

An example of the first of these is the rule in ITTOIA 2005, s. 34(1)(a), which specifies that no deduction is allowed for expenses that are not incurred wholly and exclusively for trading purposes.

An example of the second would be the cost of repairs to an asset. Such an expense is deductible in arriving at the accounting profit or loss but if the repair results in an improvement to the asset, this will then represent capital (as opposed to revenue) expenditure. It follows that no deduction as such is allowed (though certain types of capital expenditure may qualify for a different form of tax relief by way of 'capital allowances' as below).

Once the adjusted profit of a business has been ascertained, business reliefs may be available when it comes to taxing that profit. The most important reliefs are those for trading losses. Unless there is an explicit provision to the contrary, the rules used to compute profits for trades, professions and vocations must also be used to compute losses.

Capital allowances are deducted in calculating taxable profits.

Legislation: ITTOIA 2005, s. 7, 24, 25, 26

92-150 Cash basis if accounting for small businesses

Overview

Finance Act 2013, Sch. 4 allows small businesses that meet the specified conditions to compute their trading results on a cash rather than accruals basis. Thus, there will be no need to account for debtors, creditors and stock in work in progress. The treatment of capital expenditure is also different compared to the accruals basis.

The first year for this basis to apply is 2013–14, and the cash basis of calculation will apply to the relevant basis period for that year. Thus, if a business prepares accounts to 30 September, the first period to which this basis can apply is the year to 30 September 2013.

The rationale behind bringing in this change is presumably to simplify matters for small businesses. Unfortunately, the legislation is very detailed and complex making it difficult for the professional to fully comprehend let alone a lay business person. No doubt in due course HMRC will issue more detailed guidance as many practical issues will arise in interpreting the legislation.

Basic conditions to be met

Anyone (other than excluded persons as explained below) can elect for the cash basis provided their turnover is less than the VAT registration threshold at the end of the tax year, that VAT threshold being referred to in the statutory provisions as a relevant maximum. However, if an individual is a universal credit claimant the relevant maximum is twice the VAT threshold. That threshold is apportioned on a time basis where less than 12 months. The cash basis receipts are defined as receipts of the business which are received during the basis period and will be brought into account in calculating the profits of that business on the cash basis.

The word business is used here so as to include a trade, profession or vocation.

The election will then continue for every subsequent year until:

- the cash basis receipts are greater than twice the VAT threshold for the relevant year (or four times for a universal credit claimant);
- there is a change of circumstances relating to a trade etc carried on by the person which makes it more appropriate for its profits for a subsequent tax year to be calculated on the accruals basis and an election is made to do this.

If an individual carries on more than one business, then the total receipts of those businesses has to be considered to see if the relevant maximum is exceeded and which can include a firm that an individual controls or is controlled by.

Excluded persons

The *Income Tax (Trading and Other Income) Act* 2005, s. 31C sets out the persons who cannot make a cash basis election being:

- a firm where one or more of the partners is an individual;
- limited liability partnerships;
- Lloyd's underwriters;
- a person who has made a herd basis election where a farmer;
- a person who has made a claim to average fluctuating profits;
- any person who has obtained a business premises renovation allowance within the previous seven years;
- a person who has carried on a mineral extraction trade;
- a person who has obtained research and development allowances under CAA 2001, part 6 and owns an asset representing the expenditure.

Computational matters

The broad effect of making the election is, as mentioned, that the individual will simply bring in the cash receipts of the business and deduct the expenditure. The change of accounting principles which create adjustment income calculations under ITTOIA 2005, Ch. 17 apply, so as effectively to avoid double taxation on debtors at a point of change and over deduction for creditors.

On an ongoing basis, the following points are particularly relevant.

(a) Other than cars, capital expenditure is deductible on the cash basis. With the increase in particular in the annual investment allowance this is perhaps not a major advantage. Equally, the sale proceeds of capital assets that would have qualified for capital allowances will be brought in as receipts.

(b) In the case of cars, they will continue to be dealt with on the capital allowance basis.

(c) On commencement, the capital allowance pools (other than cars) will be allowed as an expense.

(d) Interest on loans is not deductible except for an amount of £500 and no relief is given for interest on loans to invest into a partnership (other than to purchase a share in the partnership) or to buy plant or machinery for partnership use.

(e) There is no sideways loss relief so that if an individual is likely to make a loss in the trade and has other income the election is not likely to be beneficial, at least for that year.

(f) There are special rules where an asset has not been fully paid for prior to entering the cash basis to ensure that there is an appropriate deduction or addition to profits to reflect any difference so as to ensure that there is no over or under deduction in respect of the asset (but these do not apply to a car).

(g) Where there is a difference between the amount brought into the accounts and the amount that would have been so brought in had the transaction been between persons acting at arm's length in the open market, then an adjustment must be made to bring in an amount that is just and reasonable in all the circumstances. This is presumably aimed at the *Sharkey v Wernher* principle that applies when there are appropriations from trading stock as a particular example. This does not apply to gifts to charities that would be allowable on the accruals basis.

Where a person ceases to carry on a trade to which the cash basis has applied the value of any trading stock is to be brought into account as a receipt in calculating the profits of the trade for the year of cessation on a just and reasonable basis. There is a special rule for the work in progress of professions or vocations to bring in a similar rule for the value of any work in progress at the time of cessation on a just and reasonable basis.

On leaving the cash basis (other than on a cessation as such), the adjustment of income rules of ITTIOA 2005, Ch. 17 will apply as mentioned above. In addition, s. 239A provides for adjustment income to be spread over the following six tax years on an equal basis unless an election is made under s. 239B to accelerate the charge.

Deductions for expenditure: general principles

92-200 Introduction

Income tax is charged on the 'profits' of a trade, profession or vocation. The concept of 'profits' implies that income is received and expenditure is incurred. It follows that rules are needed to determine which types of income need to be taken into account for tax purposes and which types of expenditure may be deducted in calculating profits for those purposes.

The starting point in calculating taxable profits is to use the profit figure as determined using accounting principles (see 92-050). The tax legislation then applies its own rules to convert those accounting profits to a figure of profit on which tax is imposed. As far as expenditure is concerned, those rules may either specify that a particular amount *is* deductible in calculating profits (a 'permissive rule') or that a deduction is not allowed (a 'prohibitive rule'). The general principle is (perhaps surprisingly) that a relevant 'permissive rule' has priority over a 'prohibitive rule', but this general rule is subject to numerous specified exceptions.

In reality, many of the deductions allowable against tax are so allowable by implication only, and generally through a statement of double negatives. Thus, for example, ITTOIA 2005, s. 34(1) now contains the familiar wording that prohibits a deduction for expenses that are not incurred wholly and exclusively for the purposes of the trade. Nevertheless, this is interpreted as meaning that expenses that *are* so incurred are *prima facie* deductible, though subject always to any other rule prohibiting a deduction for different reasons. For a particular item of expenditure to be deductible in calculating business profits, it must usually pass this general test and also steer clear of a number of specific disallowances.

The justification for converting the double negative to a positive rule is long established.

Legislation: ITTOIA 2005, s. 5, 31

Case: *Usher's Wiltshire Brewery Ltd v Bruce* (1915) 6 TC 399

Other Material: HMRC *Business Income Manual* BIM71025

Tax Reporter: ¶207-200ff.

92-220 'Trading allowance': tax exemption for trading and property income up to £1,000

With effect from 6 April 2017, an individual may receive miscellaneous trading income of up to £1,000 free of tax (the trading allowance). A similar exemption extends to rental income (rental allowance).

Where the allowance covers all of the individual's income, then they will have no requirement to declare the income. Where income exceeds the allowance, then the individual may elect to calculate their taxable income simply by deducting the allowance from their receipts rather than providing details of actual expenditure incurred.

Legislation: ITTOIA 2005 s.783A

92-250 Capital expenditure

Capital expenditure not normally allowable

No deduction is allowed, in calculating business profits for tax purposes, for 'items of a capital nature'. This statutory provision thus reinforces unambiguously the accounting principles that disallow capital expenditure in calculating the commercial profits of a business.

The prohibition of capital expenditure applies even if the expenditure passes the general 'wholly and exclusively' test of ITTOIA 2005, s. 34 and therefore might appear expressly deductible.

Depreciation charged in the accounts must be added back in the tax computation, but only to the extent that the cost has fallen in the year itself (*Small (HM Inspector of Taxes) v Mars UK Ltd*).

Legislation: ITTOIA 2005, s. 33

Case: *Small (HM Inspector of Taxes) v Mars UK Ltd* [2007] BTC 315

Other Material: HMRC *Business Income Manual* BIM33190

Tax Reporter: ¶224-000

HMRC toolkit

In a 'toolkit' issued by HMRC and republished in June 2014, the following checklist of questions is given to help identify areas of risk in connection with the distinction between revenue and capital expenditure:

(1) Has all capital expenditure on the purchase of assets been identified and allocated appropriately?

(2) Have all items of expenditure on the improvement or alteration of an asset been treated correctly?

(3) Has any expenditure on essential repairs to a newly acquired asset been treated correctly?

(4) Has any incidental expenditure incurred when acquiring or disposing of an asset been treated correctly?

(5) Has any expenditure on an unsuccessful attempt to obtain an asset or other advantage for the enduring benefit of the business been treated correctly?

(6) Has any expenditure incurred in connection with the capital structure of the business been treated correctly?

(7) Have any costs incurred on the recruitment of additional partners to a partnership been treated correctly?

(8) Have any costs incurred on training for the proprietor or a partner in the business been treated correctly?

(9) Where any financial payment includes a capital element has it been treated correctly?

(10) Have all payments made by a proprietor or partnership to acquire a franchise been treated correctly?

(11) Are the arrangement fees for any long term security correctly spread over the lifetime of the security?

(12) Has the cost of any computer software acquired been treated correctly?

(13) Has any expenditure incurred on website development been allocated correctly?

(14) Has the correct tax treatment been followed for any amortisation of goodwill acquired by a company?

(15) Has the correct tax treatment been followed for the transfer of an asset within the corporate intangible assets regime either to or from a related party?

(16) Has depreciation been added back to the accounts profit in the tax computation?

More detailed HMRC commentary on all of the above questions may be found at www.hmrc.gov.uk/agents/toolkits/capital-v-revenue.pdf.

Exceptions

The denial of a deduction for capital expenditure does not override such statutory provisions as the following, which authorise deductions of expenditure which would or might be of a capital nature:

- ITTOIA 2005, s. 58 (incidental costs of obtaining loan finance);
- ITTOIA 2005, s. 60ff. (taxable premiums, etc.);
- ITTOIA 2005, s. 76ff. (redundancy payments);

- ITTOIA 2005, s. 169ff. (capital expenditure of cemetery operators); and
- ITTOIA 2005, s. 165ff. (waste disposal).

Interest on loans or overdrafts incurred for the purposes of the business is generally deductible.

Legislation: ITTOIA 2005, s. 33

Case: *Beauchamp (HMIT) v FW Woolworth plc* [1989] BTC 233

Tax Reporter: ¶207-500

92-300 Wholly and exclusively

Introduction

When the profits of a trade are calculated, no deduction is allowed for expenses that are not incurred wholly and exclusively for the purposes of that trade. In principle, as would be expected, the rule means that expenditure is only deductible in calculating business profits if it is incurred for business purposes alone.

Thus, for example, expenditure incurred exclusively for a purpose other than that of the trade is not allowable, even though it may be impossible to carry on the trade without making the payment. This was illustrated in a case in which an incoming sub-postmaster was required to make an 'introductory payment' to Post Office Counters Ltd. (The remuneration in respect of the post of sub-postmaster was in law chargeable to tax under what was then Sch. E (i.e. as earnings from an employment) though it was, by concession, treated as taxable under what was then Sch. D (i.e. as business profits).) A special commissioner held that the payment was not deductible in computing the profits of the taxpayer's retail business: it was concerned exclusively with the Appellant's appointment as sub-postmaster and had nothing to do with his general retail trade. (Incidentally, the payment was also held to be capital in nature.)

A simpler example of a non-trade purpose is the travel cost of commuting to work. The travel is obviously essential if the work is to be carried out, but the expense is not treated for tax purposes as incurred for the purposes of the trade.

Legislation: ITTOIA 2005, s. 34

Case: *Dhendsa v Richardson (HMIT)* (1997) Sp C 134

Tax Reporter: ¶208-000ff.

Duality of purpose

In general terms, the 'wholly and exclusively' rule also means that no deduction will be given where an expense is incurred partly for business and partly for non-business purposes. Case law refers to this principle as 'duality of purpose'. A good case illustrating the principle was that of *Murgatroyd v Evans-Jackson*. The taxpayer, who required medical treatment, chose to be treated in a private nursing home because the facilities provided there would enable him to carry on his business. He claimed that 60% of the cost was incurred for business purposes. But by claiming only a proportion of the expenses he admitted duality of purpose and the whole sum was disallowed. Nor could the taxpayer have succeeded with a claim for the whole of the hospital expenses: he was clearly not there solely for business purposes.

In *Duckmanton*, the Upper Tribunal dismissed the taxpayer's appeal in relation to legal costs incurred in defending criminal charges. The First-tier Tribunal on the facts had determined that the taxpayer's object in incurring those costs must at least in part have been to avoid the personal consequences of a criminal conviction.

See below, however, for the rule permitting an allowance for an identifiable proportion of an expense.

Cases: *Murgatroyd v Evans-Jackson* (1966) 43 TC 581; *Duckmanton v R & C Commrs* [2013] BTC 1,933

Motive and purpose

The meaning of the two words 'wholly' and 'exclusively' was considered by the Court of Appeal in *Bentleys, Stokes & Lowless v Beeson*, a case concerning entertainment expenses which nowadays would be disallowed by specific provision. In that case, Romer LJ noted that it was conceded by the Crown that the word 'wholly' refers to the quantum of the money expended.

As regards the word 'exclusively', Romer LJ said at p. 503–504:

> 'The sole question is whether the expenditure in question was "exclusively" laid out for business purposes, that is: What was the motive or object in the mind of the two individuals responsible for the activities in question? It is well established that the question is one of fact ... Was the entertaining ... undertaken solely for the purposes of business, that is, solely with the object of promoting the business or its profit earning capacity?
>
> It is, as we have said, a question of fact. And it is quite clear that the purpose must be the sole purpose. [ITTOIA 2005, s. 34(1)(a)] says so in clear terms. If the activity be undertaken with the object both of promoting business and also with some other purpose, for example, with the object of indulging

> an independent wish of entertaining a friend or stranger or of supporting a charitable or benevolent object, then [ITTOIA 2005, s. 34(1)(a)] is not satisfied though in the mind of the actor the business motive may predominate. For the statute so prescribes. *Per contra*, if in truth the sole object is business promotion, the expenditure is not disqualified because the nature of the activity necessarily involves some other result, or the attainment or furtherance of some other objective, since the latter result or objective is necessarily inherent in the act.'

To the extent that these dicta rely upon the motive in the mind of the taxpayer, they must be considered in the light of the House of Lords decision in *Mallalieu v Drummond*. In that case, a practising barrister sought to deduct the cost of replacing and laundering black clothes which she wore in order to comply with standards set by the Bar Council. The general commissioners found as a fact that the preservation of warmth and decency was not a consideration in the taxpayer's mind when she bought the clothes, and also found that she would not have bought them but for the exigencies of her profession. The House of Lords held by a four to one majority that the expenditure was not wholly and exclusively incurred for the purposes of the taxpayer's profession. Delivering the judgment of the House, Lord Brightman emphasised that 'the purposes of the business' was a different concept from 'the intentions or objects of the taxpayer'.

Up to this point, his Lordship was in line with the *Bentleys, Stokes and Lowless* decision, above. However, he continued at p. 387:

> 'If it appears that the object of the taxpayer at the time of the expenditure was to serve two purposes, the purposes of his business and other purposes, it is immaterial to the application of [ITTOIA 2005, s. 34(1)(a)] that the business purposes are the predominant purposes intended to be served.
>
> I reject the notion that the object of a taxpayer is inevitably limited to the particular conscious motive in mind at the moment of expenditure. Of course the motive of which the taxpayer is conscious is of a vital significance, but it is not inevitably the only object which the Commissioners are entitled to find to exist. In my opinion the Commissioners were not only entitled to reach the conclusion that the taxpayer's object was both to serve the purposes of her profession and also to serve her personal purposes, but I myself would have found it impossible to reach any other conclusion.'

In the end his Lordship regarded the case as indistinguishable in principle from the (then) Sch. E case of *Hillyer v Leeke*, in which it was held that an employee's expenditure on a suit which he only bought and used for work purposes, was not incurred 'exclusively' in the performance of his duties: the employee also wore it for warmth and decency.

The question of subjective and objective motives was considered in relation to a partnership and its senior partner in *AB (a firm) v R & C*

Commrs. The payment of certain costs by the firm was made to discharge a personal liability and the taxpayer's only conscious motive at the time of the expenditure was not a business motive. Similarly, disbursements paid by the taxpayer were not made for the purpose of enabling the firm to earn profits but to discharge a personal liability.

In *McQueen v R & C Commrs*, on the other hand, it was held that certain motor rallying expenditure was incurred wholly and exclusively for the purposes of the trade. Mr McQueen ran a business by the name of Garelochhead Coaches, which had grown rapidly. He had a keen interest in motor sport and had for many years taken part in motor rallies, but on a small scale. Mr McQueen's evidence, accepted by the commissioners, was that he had then consciously started in 1999 to use motor rallying as a means of marketing the coach business. On the evidence, the commissioners accepted that the motor rallying activities were, from 1999 onwards, undertaken for the purposes of the coach business. The rallying complemented the business and vice versa. The private satisfaction of success on the rally circuit could properly be described as an incidental effect of the costs incurred on that rallying. The taxpayer had other interests (local councillor, sailing) and the object of this particular activity was to promote his business. As such, the expenditure was incurred wholly and exclusively for the purposes of the coach trade and was fully allowable.

Cases: *Bentleys, Stokes & Lowless v Beeson* (1952) 33 TC 491; *Hillyer v Leeke* (1976) 51 TC 90; *Mallalieu v Drummond* [1983] BTC 380; *AB (a firm) v R & C Commrs* (2006) Sp C 572; *McQueen v R & C Commrs* (2007) Sp C 601

Illustrative cases

Case law demonstrates that any non-business purpose often relates to food and drink, medical treatment and holidays. It follows that companies, which never eat, drink, fall sick or take vacations, are much less likely to fall foul of the dual purpose rule than individuals or partnerships of individuals. Nevertheless, trade expenditure by companies which indirectly benefits (for example) the family of a director, may be tainted. It is possible for a company to have a subconscious purpose through its directors.

Cases (a small sample from many cases on this issue): *Norman v Golder* (1944) 26 TC 293; *Bowden v Russell & Russell* (1965) 42 TC 301; *Caillebotte v Quinn* (1975) 50 TC 222; *Watkis v Ashford Sparkes & Harward* [1985] BTC 391; *Mackinlay (HMIT) v Arthur Young McClelland Moores & Co* [1989] BTC 587; *Prior (HMIT) v Saunders* [1993] BTC 336; *Powell v Jackman (HMIT)* [2004] BTC 336

Apportionment of expenditure

The enactment of ITTOIA 2005 clarified what was previously an uncertain and sometimes inconsistent application of the 'wholly and exclusively' principle. The Act now specifies that:

> 'If an expense is incurred for more than one purpose, this section does not prohibit a deduction for any identifiable part or identifiable proportion of the expense which is incurred wholly and exclusively for the purposes of the trade.'

Thus if an individual flies to the USA for both a business conference and a holiday, no part of the travel expense is allowable as the cost of the flight is an indivisible expense. See, in this respect, the case of *Murgatroyd v Evans-Jackson* referred to above. By contrast, if a self-employed person uses a car for both private and business journeys, it will be possible (if adequate records are kept) to demonstrate that a specific proportion of the car's use was for business purposes. That proportion of fuel costs may then be claimed as a deduction in calculating the profits of the trade. The treatment of other costs, such as servicing and repairs, is discussed further below.

HMRC's *Business Income Manual* lists the following types of expense as 'having an intrinsic duality of purpose' (such that no apportionment will normally be due):

- ordinary 'civilian' clothing;
- food for sustenance;
- having somewhere to live;
- wishing to enjoy good health;
- wishing to avoid a criminal conviction – especially if there is a custodial sentence; and
- helping one's nearest and dearest.

A useful example is the deductibility of telephone expenses, where the taxpayer uses his telephone both for business and for domestic purposes. As regards charges for calls, it is feasible to record accurately the proportionate expenditure as between the two purposes. In practice, the allowable proportion is negotiated between the taxpayer and the HMRC officer, thus avoiding the unproductive task of noting every call made. As regards the rental, strict application of the dual purpose principle precludes deduction of any of the cost.

The same point applies to motor vehicles used for business and domestic purposes. Again, in practice, a proportion of running costs is normally agreed with HMRC, although in strictness lump sum expenses such as servicing and insurance could be disallowed in full. Similarly, interest payable in respect of a vehicle used for business and domestic purposes is apportioned for income tax purposes. The HMRC guidance is explicit in allowing a proportion of the overhead costs of running a vehicle:

> 'You should allow the actual costs of any trade journeys (fuel, tolls, parking fees etc.). You should also allow a proportion of the licence, insurance (provided the insurance covers business use), repairs, finance costs, etc. You should not argue that such costs would be incurred in any event and only the marginal additional costs attributed to trade use are allowed.'

Legislation: ITTOIA 2005, s. 34(2)

Case: *Lucas v Cattell* (1972) 48 TC 353

Other Material: HMRC *Business Income Manual* BIM37600, BIM37900

Tax Reporter: ¶208-100

Expenditure incurred 'for the purposes of' the business

As already noted, an expense is only deductible in calculating trading profits if it is incurred wholly and exclusively *for the purposes of* the business in question.

In *Vodafone Cellular Ltd v Shaw*, the court derived the following propositions from the House of Lords decisions in *Mallalieu v Drummond* and *MacKinlay v Arthur Young McClelland Moores & Co*.

(1) The words 'for the purposes of the trade' did not mean 'for the benefit of the taxpayer'.

(2) The taxpayer's object in making the payment was to be discovered, i.e. the taxpayer's subjective intention at the time of the payment.

(3) The object of the taxpayer was to be distinguished from its effect. A payment might be made exclusively for the purposes of the taxpayer's trade, even if some other consequential and incidental benefit was secured.

(4) The taxpayer's subjective intentions were not limited to conscious motives. Some consequences would be so inevitably and inextricably involved in the payment that, unless merely incidental, they would have to be taken to be a purpose for which the payment was made.

(5) The Court of Appeal added a further proposition: the question did not involve an inquiry of the taxpayer whether a business or personal advantage was intended. The primary inquiry was to ascertain the particular object of the taxpayer in making the payment. Once that

was ascertained, its characterisation as a trade or private purpose was a matter for the commissioners.

Payments made to enable a business to be wound up are unlikely to have been made wholly and exclusively for the purposes of the business.

A distinction is drawn between expenses incurred in earning profits, which are deductible, and expenses representing the application of profits after they are earned, which are not deductible. The principle is that the taxation of a person's profits should not be affected by what he chooses to do, or is required to do, with them after they have been earned.

Cases: *Mallalieu v Drummond* [1983] BTC 380; *MacKinlay (HMIT) v Arthur Young McClelland Moores & Co* [1989] BTC 587; *Vodafone Cellular Ltd v Shaw (HMIT)* [1997] BTC 247

Payments in connection with the discontinuance of the business

Payments made to enable a business to be wound up are clearly not made in order to keep it going, and accordingly are not made wholly and exclusively for the purposes of the business. In *IR Commrs v The Anglo Brewing Co Ltd*, the taxpayer company ceased to trade, and decided to make *ex gratia* payments to its employees. Rowlatt J held that such payments were not deductible as trading expenditure.

Payments made by way of additions to redundancy payments are allowed as a deduction if they would have been allowable but for the discontinuance of the trade. However, the principle in the *Anglo Brewing Co* case continues to apply to payments not covered by that specific allowance: for example, expenses of returning stock to wholesale suppliers.

Legislation: ITTOIA 2005, s. 79

Case: *IR Commrs v The Anglo Brewing Co Ltd* (1925) 12 TC 803

Other Material: HMRC *Business Income Manual* BIM38300ff.

Tax Reporter: ¶208-200

92-350 Pre-trading expenditure

Expenditure for the purposes of a business which has yet to be commenced is in principle deductible if incurred up to seven years before the trade or business begins. The expenditure must be such as would have been allowable as a deduction in computing trading profits had it been incurred after the commencement of the business.

> **Example**
>
> Ned carries on a trade of market gardening. Within seven years before commencing trading, he incurred expenditure in respect of:
>
> (1) rent for his premises;
>
> (2) interest on a bank loan; and
>
> (3) improvements to the buildings on his premises to fit them out for the purposes of his trade.

Items (1) and (2) are relieved under these rules but not item (3), since that is capital, not revenue, expenditure. However, equivalent rules give relief by way of capital allowances for certain capital expenditure incurred before the start of trading.

Except in the case of expenditure on research and development, including certain vaccine research, allowable pre-trading expenditure is treated as incurred on the day on which the business is first carried on, and is deducted as a business expense accordingly.

Legislation: ITTOIA 2005, s. 57

Tax Reporter: ¶208-300

92-400 Statutory provisions allowing a deduction for particular expenses

The following items of expenditure are expressly allowed as a deduction when computing business profits, even though they might not have been incurred wholly and exclusively for business purposes or might otherwise have been disallowed:

- contributions to approved local enterprise agencies (ITTOIA 2005, s. 82ff.);
- contributions to training and enterprise councils, business link organisations and local enterprise companies (ITTOIA 2005, s. 82ff.);
- contributions to urban regeneration companies (ITTOIA 2005, s. 86);
- certain intellectual property fees and expenses (ITTOIA 2005, s. 89ff.);
- costs incurred by companies in establishing approved share option schemes, profit-sharing schemes or ESOTs (ITTOIA 2005, s. 94A(3), CTA 2009, s. 1000);
- expenditure on employees seconded to charities and educational bodies (ITTOIA 2005, s. 70);

- contributions to payroll giving scheme costs (ITTOIA 2005, s. 72);
- payments to the Export Credit Guarantee Department (ITTOIA 2005, s. 91);
- debts proving irrecoverable after events treated as business discontinuances (CTA 2009, s. 55(2));
- additional payments to redundant employees (ITTOIA 2005, s. 79);
- certain pre-trading expenditure (ITTOIA 2005, s. 57);
- building societies' costs of issuing permanent interest bearing shares, etc. (CTA 2009, s. 131);
- contributions paid, and losses, etc. sustained, under certified schemes for rationalising industry (ICTA 1988, s. 568(1), 570(2));
- statutory redundancy, etc. payments (ITTOIA 2005, s. 76ff.);
- reimbursements of employees' training course expenses (ITTOIA 2005, s. 74);
- expenditure on counselling services for employees (ITTOIA 2005, s. 76);
- payments to employees, directors, etc. in respect of restrictive covenants (ITTOIA 2005, s. 69);
- payments by companies to ESOTs (FA 1989, s. 67);
- provision for individuals of security assets and services (ITTOIA 2005, s. 81);
- expenditure on research and development, etc. (ITTOIA 2005, s. 87ff.);
- pools payments to support games, etc. (ITTOIA 2005, s. 121);
- certain film-related expenditure (ITTOIA 2005, s. 130ff., but these rules have been subject to numerous recent changes); and
- expenditure on flood and coastal defences (ITTOIA 2005, s. 86A).

As regards allowable capital expenditure, see 92-250.

Tax Reporter: ¶208-350

92-450 Statutory provisions denying a deduction for particular expenses

Some items of expenditure might be allowed on ordinary principles but are subject to a specific rule that denied a deduction. In other cases, there is specific legislation to remove any doubt about the tax treatment of a particular form of expenditure.

The main express or implied prohibited deductions may be summarised as follows.

- Capital expenditure (ITTOIA 2005, s. 33: see 92-250).
- Expenditure not wholly and exclusively laid out for purposes of the trade (ITTOIA 2005, s. 34(1)(a): see 92-300).
- Losses not connected with or arising out of the business (ITTOIA 2005, s. 34(1)(b)).
- Debts, other than as specifically allowed (ITTOIA 2005, s. 35).
- Remuneration (or certain 'employee benefit contributions', as defined) unpaid within nine months of the year end (though an allowance is given in a later period if paid after the nine-month deadline) (ITTOIA 2005, s. 36, 38ff.).
- Business entertaining expenses (ITTOIA 2005, s. 48).
- Certain expenditure on the hiring of motor cars (ITTOIA 2005, s. 45).
- Patent royalties (ITTOIA 2005, s. 51).
- Interest already allowed under other provisions (ITTOIA 2005, s. 52).
- Social security contributions, other than employer contributions (ITTOIA 2005, s. 53).
- Penalties, interest and VAT surcharges (ITTOIA 2005, s. 54).
- Crime-related payments (ITTOIA 2005, s. 55).
- Rent exceeding a notional commercial rent under sale and leaseback arrangements (ITA 2007, s. 681AE).
- Interest under a scheme or arrangements solely or primarily made to reduce tax liability (ITA 2007, s. 809ZG).

Tax Reporter: ¶208-400

Deductions for expenditure: expenditure with a private element

92-600 Private expenditure

The cost of private expenditure may not be deducted in calculating business profits. The legislation formerly contained an express provision to that effect by explicitly denying relief for 'any disbursements or expenses of maintenance of the parties, their families or establishments, or any sums expended for any other domestic or private purposes distinct from the purposes of the trade'.

HMRC's Private and 'Personal Expenditure Toolkit' for 2012–13 was published in May 2013 covering matters such as personal bills; travel and subsistence; entertaining and gifts; and drawings, etc. This includes a checklist on the same lines as other toolkits.

Legislation: old ICTA 1988, s. 74(1)(b)

Tax Reporter: ¶208-500

92-610 Deductions allowable at a fixed rate

FA 2013 makes amendments to ITTOIA 2005 to the effect that in calculating the profits of trades, professions or vocations a deduction can be allowable at a fixed rate instead of the actual expenses in the following instances:

- expenditure on vehicles;
- use of home for business purposes; and
- premises used both as a home and as business premises.

Vehicles

The broad effect of these provisions is to permit a deduction based on the same rate per mile as for employment income so that for a car or goods vehicle the rate per mile is 45p for the first 10,000 miles and 25p thereafter. For a motorcycle, the rate is 24p. Capital allowances are not available and the fixed rate basis cannot be applied in the case of vehicles on which capital allowances have been claimed or relief given on the cash basis.

Subject to that, the deduction can be made for any car, motorcycle or goods vehicle used for the purposes of the trade. This method must continue until the vehicle ceases to be used in the business.

Use of home for business purposes

Where a home of the individual is used for business purposes, it has been common practice to permit a deduction, which no doubt has varied from taxpayer to taxpayer and is sometimes challenged by HMRC. The following amounts can now be claimed without question and depend upon the number of hours worked at home in a month so that the deduction is as follows:

Hours worked in month	Deductible amount per month
	£
25 or more	10
51 or more	18
101 or more	26

If an individual has more than one home available, this provision applies as if those homes were a single home so as to avoid multiple claims. Where work is undertaken by more than one individual from the same home, then only one fixed deduction is allowed.

These amounts are likely to be somewhat less than many individuals are claiming but do give an indication of HMRC's view of the appropriate amount.

These provisions cannot apply to partnerships with one or more corporate partners.

Premises used as both a home and business premises

An example where this could apply is a hotel with accommodation for the proprietor, where the expenses attributed to the private element must be disallowed in arriving at the profits of the trade.

As with the use of home, to date this has been negotiated with HMRC if challenged and there is now a procedure for making a standard deduction depending upon the number of occupants of the living part.

The broad effect of this change is that the following amounts calculated over a year will be deducted from the expenses in relation to the premises to arrive at the net deductible amount.

Number of occupants per month	Monthly restriction of expenditure
	£
1	350
2	500
3 or more	650

According to HMRC, the flat rate includes all household goods and services, food and non-alcoholic drinks and utilities. It does not, though, include mortgage interest, rent, council tax or rates. A reasonable apportionment of these expenses will still have to be made, which seems in large part to defeat the object of the fixed rate system.

HMRC have withdrawn 'board and lodging' agreements entered into previously with small hotel and guest house businesses, who must now apply this statutory method or base the disallowance on a justifiable basis, with appropriate records. As a transitional measure a business applying an agreement with HMRC for 2012–13 can also apply it for 2013–14.

Legislation: ITTOIA 2005, s. 94B-I

92-620 Meals and accommodation

Day subsistence costs

The rules relating to subsistence costs incurred by the self-employed were changed from April 2009.

In practice, HMRC have for some time permitted a deduction for 'reasonable expenses' incurred either: 'where a business is by its nature itinerant' (such as a commercial traveller); or where a person makes 'occasional business journeys outside the normal pattern'.

The relaxation was put on a formal footing from 6 April 2009. Specifically, a deduction is now given in calculating trading profits for any reasonable expenditure incurred on food or drink for consumption by the trader either at a place to which the individual travels in the course of the trade, or while travelling in the course of carrying out the trade. Two conditions must be met:

- the travel costs, if incurred by the trader, must be tax deductible; and
- the trade must by its nature be itinerant or the trader must travel only occasionally to the place in question and (in that case) the travel must be outside the trader's normal pattern of work travel (if he or she has any such pattern).

Legislation: ITTOIA 2005, s. 57A

Other costs of food and drink

HMRC have long accepted reasonable claims for the cost of evening meals and breakfast taken in conjunction with overnight accommodation if the cost of the accommodation would otherwise be allowable as an expense in carrying on the trade or profession.

As regards living expenses abroad, HMRC adopt a more lenient approach according to SP A16 (15 June 1977, but still referred to at BIM47710).

As to circumstances in which the provision of meals and accommodation may constitute non-allowable 'business entertainment', see 94-020.

Case: *Caillebotte v Quinn* (1975) 50 TC 222

Other Material: HMRC *Business Income Manual* BIM37670, BIM47710

Hotel proprietors

Practical problems arise in respect of accommodation of and consumption by persons such as hotel proprietors (and their families), whose business it is to provide meals and accommodation. It is possible that no account will have been taken of these benefits in the profit and loss account of the business. For tax purposes, however, it is appropriate to make an adjustment to reflect the fact that the profit would not otherwise disclose the benefit obtained through own consumption by the proprietor and his family.

It is understood that local tax officers may agree scales for own consumption with advisers in the area, although it would still be open to HMRC or to the taxpayer to establish actual consumption in individual cases.

The scale would cover essential items such as rent, rates, electricity, food, telephone, home insurance, laundry, television, and repairs of a revenue nature; but not items such as alcohol, cigarettes or motor expenses, in respect of which a further adjustment would have to be made as these items vary significantly from case to case.

Self-employed lorry drivers

The circumstances in which HMRC will accept claims for the cost of meals and breakfast taken in connection with overnight accommodation, particularly by self-employed long-distance lorry drivers, are set out in an interpretation in HMRC Tax Bulletin, which includes the following:

> 'Long distance self-employed lorry drivers may claim a deduction for the reasonable cost of meals taken in conjunction with overnight accommodation. We have been asked whether this treatment can be extended to such drivers who spend the night in their cabs rather than take overnight accommodation. We have confirmed that it can.'

Other Material: HMRC Interpretation, IRInt. 51 (Tax Bulletin, August 1993)

Tax Reporter: ¶208-550

92-640 Clothing

Expenditure on clothing has a personal element in that it is bought for warmth and decency as well as any purposes incidental to the taxpayer's business. The duality of purpose disqualifies it: see *Mallalieu v Drummond*, in which it was held that the cost of black clothing purchased by a barrister to meet the requirements of the Bar Council was not deductible.

The HMRC approach in practice is now summarised as follows:

> 'You should allow a deduction in computing profits for the cost of replacing gowns and wigs and frock coats worn by Queen's Counsel. You should not, however, allow a deduction for expenditure on "normal clothes", for example, black coats and pin-stripe trousers worn by male barristers or black dresses and suits worn by female barristers.'

Legislation: ITTOIA 2005, s. 34(1)(a)

Case: *Mallalieu v Drummond* [1983] BTC 380

Other Material: HMRC *Business Income Manual* BIM51105

Tax Reporter: ¶208-600

92-660 Child-minding

Expenditure incurred in employing a child minder to enable the taxpayer to work is not deductible. This HMRC practice is based on the case of *Halstead v Condon*. This was an employment income case, but was concerned principally with the 'wholly and exclusively' part of the earnings provision in what is now ITEPA 2003, s. 336.

Case: *Halstead v Condon* (1970) 46 TC 289

Tax Reporter: ¶208-650

92-680 Use of home as office

An allowance may be claimed for expenditure incurred in connection with a part of the taxpayer's home used for business purposes, for example as an office or a workshop. Rent paid for the premises was formerly specifically restricted to two-thirds of the total rent for the premises, unless in the circumstances of a particular case it appeared that a greater proportion ought to be allowed. That provision has not been re-written into ITTOIA 2005, on the grounds that the issue is already covered by the general 'wholly and exclusively' restrictions.

In practice the deduction of a proportion of general expenditure, such as insurance or mortgage interest is permitted. It is not essential that the part of the house for which an allowance is claimed is used exclusively for business purposes. Thus a room may be used as, for example, an office and a dining room. Of course, only such expenditure as is attributable to its use as an office is allowable.

The onus is on the taxpayer to demonstrate that the expenditure claimed is reasonable. In *Muhammad*, the taxpayer originally claimed that all his household expenditure was incurred wholly and exclusively for the purposes of his trade. He failed to produce for HMRC any convincing evidence of what was actually allowable and the tribunal held that HMRC had been more than reasonable in allowing a deduction for some 20% of the expenses originally claimed.

If part of the house is used exclusively for business purposes then this may jeopardise part of the private residence exemption on a subsequent sale of the property.

FA 2013 has introduced a fixed rate deduction that can be adopted as mentioned in 92-610.

Council tax

HMRC make the following observations in respect of a possible deduction for council tax payments when calculating business profits:

> 'In the main, the person who is carrying on a trade, profession or vocation will pay non-domestic or business rates … There will however be exceptions. For example, bed and breakfast establishments with fewer than six tenants do not pay the business rate. And a home in which a trader sets aside a room as an office is likely to attract only a council tax charge. Thus whether premises to which the council tax is applied are used for business purposes should be regarded as a question of fact. If business use is established the appropriate proportion of the tax may be allowed under the normal rules for the deduction of expenses.'

By contrast, it is possible that parts of premises chargeable to business rates are (exceptionally) used for non-business purposes. In such a case, a proportion will fall to be disallowed on general principles.

Case: *Muhammad* [2010] TC 00262

Other Material: HMRC *Business Income Manual* BIM45750, BIM46840

Tax Reporter: ¶208-700

92-700 Medical costs

Medical and hospital expenses incurred by a trader, etc. in respect of himself are generally disallowed as a deduction. Such expenditure is disqualified as having a dual purpose. The point has been ruled in several cases, including *Murgatroyd v Evans-Jackson* and *Norman v Golder*.

A different conclusion was reached, though, in the much more recent *Parsons* case, in which a stunt performer successfully claimed tax relief for a variety of medical costs. The tribunal found as a fact that 'in terms of his requirements as an ordinary human being, he could have waited, and would have been content to wait, to have the operation on the NHS. The evidence was also that in a physically less demanding job he could have carried on working in the meantime, and that it was only because of the particular demands of the kind of work that he does that he could not carry on working until the operation was done'. As such, the tribunal concluded that the circumstances were 'of a special character dictated by the occupation' and tax relief was allowed for costs relating to a knee operation, to chiropractic and massage costs, and to dental treatment. In relation to health and fitness, however, the tribunal found that the expenditure served a dual purpose and could not be allowed.

Legislation: ITTOIA 2005, s. 34(1)(a)

Cases: *Norman v Golder* (1944) 26 TC 293; *Murgatroyd v Evans-Jackson* (1967) 43 TC 581; *Parsons* [2010] TC 00421

Tax Reporter: ¶208-750

92-720 Personal security assets

A deduction is allowed for certain expenditure on the provision for or use by an individual, including a member of a partnership, of a 'security asset' or 'security service'. HMRC interpret the rules very strictly, warning that:

> 'The conditions are intentionally tightly drawn and are intended for people whose work or trade exposes them to a very real threat to their physical safety from terrorists, extremists and others who may resort to violence.'

The asset or service must be provided or used to meet a special threat to the individual's *personal* physical security which arises wholly or mainly by virtue of his particular trade, etc. and the person incurring the expenditure must have as his sole object the meeting of the threat. Capital allowances are also available for self-employed individuals in respect of expenditure on security assets.

Legislation: CAA 2001, s. 33; ITTOIA 2005, s. 81

Other Material: HMRC *Business Income Manual* BIM47305

Tax Reporter: ¶208-800

92-740 Expenditure on training courses

Training courses undertaken by proprietors must meet the usual criteria if the cost is to be deductible in computing business profits.

Wholly and exclusively

The 'wholly and exclusively' condition is usually straightforward, though there may be borderline cases where it will not be easy to determine whether any residual benefit for the proprietor causes that condition to fail. In *Azam*, a deduction was claimed in calculating trading profits for more than £30,000 spent on training and counselling sessions. The costs were incurred in attending sessions linked to the Church of Scientology and the tribunal accepted that Mrs Azam expected her business to benefit from what she learned in those sessions. However, the tribunal also found as a fact that 'she had in mind, at least subconsciously, the personal benefits she derived'. This led the tribunal to conclude that the taxpayer had two purposes in mind when attending the sessions, one personal and the other business. Accordingly the expenses were not incurred exclusively for the purposes of Mrs Azam's business, and were not deductible from the profits of that business. The fact that Mrs Azam derived a personal benefit from the courses did not disqualify the expenditure but the fact that she had two purposes in mind when incurring the expenses did mean that the statutory test was failed.

Case: *Azam* [2011] TC 00895

Revenue or capital expenditure

An issue that arises more often in practice is the need to determine whether the expense should be disallowed as capital expenditure. Where attendance at a course is intended to give business proprietors new expertise, knowledge or skills which they lack, the HMRC view is that the course brings into existence an intangible asset which is of enduring benefit to the business. HMRC then take the view that such expenditure is therefore of a capital nature, and deduction is prohibited. On the other hand, where attendance is merely to update expertise, etc. which proprietors already possess, the expenditure is normally regarded as revenue in nature. In this case, it will be deductible if it satisfies the 'wholly and exclusively' test. This approach was approved in the case of *Dass v R & C Commrs*, in which the cost of acquiring a new qualification was disallowed as capital expenditure.

Cases: *British Insulated & Helsby Cables v Atherton* (1925) 10 TC 155; *Dass v R & C Commrs* (2006) Sp C 570

Other Material: HMRC *Business Income Manual* BIM35660

Tax Reporter: ¶208-850

92-760 Costs of recruiting new partners

In a 'toolkit' issued in 2010, entitled 'Capital v Revenue Expenditure Toolkit: 2009–10 Self Assessment and Company Tax Returns', HMRC commented that 'costs incurred by a partnership on recruiting new partners will normally be allowable as revenue expenditure'. That principle applies both to equity and salaried partners. Nevertheless, HMRC argue that the cost *may* (depending on the facts) need to be capitalised if:

- the admission of the partner has a fundamental impact on the structure of the firm's business, involving more than a mere expansion of the business;
- the partner is recruited as part of the acquisition of a business; or
- the new partner's capital contribution is a material factor in the recruitment.

Tax Reporter: ¶208-900

Deductions for expenditure: repairs and improvements

93-000 Introduction

The question of whether repairs expenditure qualifies for relief in calculating business profits must now be determined according to ordinary principles alone; the 2005 Act does not replicate the provisions which used to refer more specifically to 'repairs of premises occupied' and to amounts that were 'actually expended'. The decision not to replicate those provisions in ITTOIA 2005 does not represent any relaxation of the rules but is rather a recognition that the issue is adequately addressed under the more general provisions.

Courts will be influenced by accountancy practice as to the category into which an expense falls.

Legislation: ITTOIA 2005, s. 34

Cases: *Lothian Chemical Co Ltd v IR Commrs* (1926) 11 TC 508; *Odeon Associated Theatres v Jones* (1971) 48 TC 257

Tax Reporter: ¶210-000

93-020 Entirety or part

Repair or renewal of a part of an asset is a revenue expense, whereas renewal or reconstruction of the entirety is a capital expense. In *Lurcott v Wakely & Wheeler* (not a tax case), Buckley LJ said:

> 'Repair is restoration by renewal or replacement of subsidiary parts of a whole. Renewal, as distinguished from repair, is reconstruction of the entirety, meaning by the entirety not necessarily the whole but substantially the whole subject-matter under discussion.'

The question of what constitutes the 'entirety' for these purposes is an issue of fact rather than a legal matter and can turn on fine distinctions of fact. In two cases involving the replacement of factory chimneys, for example, it was held in one that the entirety was the chimney (with the result that the expenditure on replacing it was capital, and not allowable), and in the other that the entirety was the factory, with the result that the expenditure was considered revenue in nature and was allowed for tax purposes.

It is sometimes apparent that the expenditure has produced a new asset, which did not exist before. If so, it is likely to be disallowed as being a capital expense.

A recent application of the principles can be found in the First-tier Tribunal decision in *Cairnsmill Caravan Park Ltd*, where expenditure on resurfacing a grass area at a caravan park with hard-core was held not to be an improvement on the facts. Moreover, the tribunal decided that the entirety was the whole caravan park.

Cases: *Lurcott v Wakely & Wheeler* [1911] 1 KB 905; *O'Grady v Bullcroft Main Collieries Ltd* (1932) 17 TC 93; *Avon Beach & Cafe Ltd v Stewart* (1950) 31 TC 487; *Samuel Jones & Co (Devonvale) Ltd v IR Commrs* (1951) 32 TC 513; *Cairnsmill Caravan Park Ltd* [2013] TC 02580

Tax Reporter: ¶210-000

93-040 Dilapidations

A tenant may be liable not only for repairs but also for the cost of reinstating the property to its former condition at the end of a lease. If expenditure is incurred on such dilapidations, it will not be allowable for tax purposes if it is capital in nature. As the HMRC manuals put it:

> 'If a taxpayer achieves their end by means of capital expenditure then the cost is disallowed. That the same end could have been achieved by revenue expenditure does not convert actual capital expenditure into a revenue deduction.'

That principle was upheld in *Jacksons v Laskers Home Furnishers Ltd*. If, on the other hand, repairs have been delayed and are carried out after the lease has expired, the mere fact that they have been deferred will not cause tax relief to be denied.

If, at the end of the lease period, the lessee makes a 'composition payment' in lieu of carrying out the repairs, the tax treatment will be determined by the underlying costs that the payment is meant to make good. To the extent that the payment covers deferred repairs, it will be allowable. An apportionment should be made where appropriate. The deduction of a payment by way of composition with the lessor is not conditional on the dilapidations being made good.

Case: *Jacksons v Laskers Home Furnishers Ltd* (1956) 37 TC 69

Other Material: HMRC *Business Income Manual* BIM35620, BIM43265

Tax Reporter: ¶210-050

93-060 Apportionment of expenditure

Occasionally it will be possible to show that part of a bigger project is capital and part is revenue (see, for example, *Conn v Robins Bros Ltd* and *Mann, Crossman & Paulin Ltd v IR Commrs*). This is probably still best regarded as exceptional, though the approach was approved in the more recent *Wills* case, where substantial repair works were allowed as such rather than being treated as capital expenditure.

Where the expenditure is found to result in the creation of a new asset, however, no apportionment may be made, even though some of the work done might in other circumstances have been regarded as repairs.

Cases: *Margrett v Lowestoft Water & Gas Co* (1935) 19 TC 481; *Mann, Crossman & Paulin Ltd v IR Commrs* (1947) 28 TC 410; *William P Lawrie v IR Commrs* (1952) 34 TC 20; *Conn v Robins Bros Ltd* (1966) 43 TC 266; *Wills* [2010] TC 00479

Tax Reporter: ¶210-100

93-080 Renewals basis (withdrawn from 6 April 2016)

The term 'renewals basis' is used, rather confusingly, to describe both a statutory provision and a related concession that is given in certain circumstances.

The statutory provision related to expenses incurred on replacing or altering any 'tool' (defined to mean an implement, utensil or article). This treatment pre-dated the introduction of capital allowance and was withdrawn with effect from 6 April 2016.

Legislation: ITTOIA 2005, s. 68; FA 2016, s. 68

Other Material: HMRC *Business Income Manual* BIM46935

Tax Reporter: ¶210-150

93-100 Newly acquired assets

A particular problem arises in respect of expenditure on a newly acquired asset. If HMRC can show that the expense was necessary in order to put the asset into workable condition, then it may be disallowed as representing part of the capital acquisition cost. This is the principle in the case of *Law Shipping Co Ltd v IR Commrs*. A ship was purchased for £97,000, and shortly thereafter the purchasers incurred expenditure including nearly £40,000 which related to work needing to be done at the time of purchase. It was held that this expenditure was of a capital nature. The case of *Jackson v Laskers Home Furnishers Ltd* is another example of expenditure on property which was required to put it in such a condition as to be commercially viable.

The Law Shipping case was distinguished by the Court of Appeal in *Odeon Associated Theatres Ltd v Jones*. The taxpayers purchased cinemas at a time when expenditure on renovation was prohibited by building restrictions following the second world war. Some time later expenditure was incurred on repairs which the taxpayers claimed were of a revenue nature. The court held that the expenditure was allowable, distinguishing the Law Shipping case on the following grounds.

- The purchase price was not affected by the state of repair of the assets.
- The cinemas purchased were in a profit-earning state during the time between purchase and renovation.
- There was evidence that the treatment followed proper accounting principles.

The particular circumstances of each case will determine whether an expense is disallowed under the Law Shipping rule or allowed on the basis of *Odeon Associated Theatres*. The importance attached by the courts to evidence of current accounting practice should be borne in mind.

HMRC have given the following example to illustrate their approach:

> 'A business purchases a vehicle that has failed its MoT and cannot be used. Carrying out the repairs necessary to obtain an MoT certificate will not improve the vehicle. However it will contribute to the cost of acquiring an asset of lasting benefit to the business. In these circumstances the cost of the repairs constitute capital expenditure for tax purposes and a revenue deduction is not available in computing the taxable profits.'

The example is taken from a 'toolkit' issued in 2010, entitled 'Capital v Revenue Expenditure Toolkit: 2009–10 Self Assessment and Company Tax Returns'. It goes on to say that capital allowances may be due on the disallowed costs.

Cases: *Law Shipping Co Ltd v IR Commrs* (1923) 12 TC 621; *Jackson v Laskers Home Furnishers Ltd* (1956) 37 TC 69; *Odeon Associated Theatres Ltd v Jones* (1971) 48 TC 257

Tax Reporter: ¶210-200

Deductions for expenditure: bad and doubtful debts

93-400 General principle

There are only three circumstances in which a deduction may be claimed in calculating trade profits, in relation to bad debts:

- if the debt is in fact bad;
- if the debt is estimated to be bad; or
- if the debt is released wholly and exclusively for the purposes of the trade as part of a 'statutory insolvency arrangement' (as defined at ITTOIA 2005, s. 259).

Where only part of a debt is bad, or estimated to be bad, a deduction may be made for that part only.

For the purposes of the second of the above bullets, the whole of the debt is estimated to be bad if the debtor is bankrupt or insolvent, except so far as there is a reasonable expectation of recovery.

A key consequence of the above is that it is not possible to make a general provision for bad debts, even though such a reserve may accord with sound accounting practice. HMRC state this principle by saying that:

> 'a general reserve, for example one calculated as a percentage of total debts or of total sales, should not be admitted as a deduction if made without regard to the circumstances of the particular debtors.'

The extent to which debts are to be taken into account must be determined each year. If a new debt is incurred in the course of a tax year, it may be brought into the account at a discounted value, representing the possibility that it may become bad: *Absalom v Talbot*. Equally, if a debt originally presumed to be good turns out subsequently to be irrecoverable, it must be deducted in the year in which it becomes bad.

The principle that a debt must be valued each year on the basis of information available at the time is expressed thus by Rowlatt J in *Anderton & Halstead Ltd v Birrell*:

> 'What the statute requires … is an estimate to what extent a bad debt is bad, and this is for the purposes of a profit and loss account. Such an estimate is

> not a prophecy to be judged as to its truth by after events, but a valuation of an asset *de praesenti* upon an uncertain future to be judged as to its soundness as an estimate upon the then facts and probabilities.'

The mere fact that a particular customer or client is a slow payer will not mean that a bad debt provision is appropriate.

Legislation: ITTOIA 2005, s. 35

Cases: *Anderton & Halstead Ltd v Birrell* (1931) 16 TC 200; *Absalom v Talbot* (1944) 26 TC 166

Other Material: HMRC *Business Income Manual* BIM42701, BIM42710

Tax Reporter: ¶211-000

93-420 Bad debts and post balance sheet events

Sometimes an event will occur after the balance sheet date, but before the accounts are drawn up, that has a bearing on whether or not a debt is doubtful or bad. HMRC comment that:

> 'accountancy practice accepts that events arising after the balance sheet date and before accounts are finalised may need to be reflected in the provision for bad and doubtful debts if they furnish additional evidence of conditions that existed at the balance sheet date.'

In other words, HMRC accept that a deduction may be made for a given year if it is discovered, between the year end and finalisation of the accounts, that the debt was doubtful at the year end. By contrast, however, no allowance is made for the year in question if:

> 'at that date the debtor had the capacity to pay, but before the accounts were finalised, circumstances arose which rendered the debt doubtful.'

Other Material: HMRC *Business Income Manual* BIM42705

93-440 Debts subsequently recovered

If, after a debt is written off, it turns out to be good, then the sum recovered must be treated as a business receipt of the year in which it is paid (*Bristow v William Dickinson & Co Ltd*). No alteration is made to previous assessments.

Case: *Bristow v William Dickinson & Co Ltd* (1946) 27 TC 157

Tax Reporter: ¶211-150

93-460 Overseas debts

A form of relief is available where:

- a trader brings into account, in calculating his trading profits, an amount either received or owed;
- the amount is paid or owed in a country outside the UK; and
- some or all of that money cannot be remitted to the UK.

An amount that has been received by the trader is said to be unremittable if it cannot be transferred to the UK because of foreign exchange restrictions. An amount that is *owed* to the trader is treated as unremittable if one of the following applies:

- temporarily, it cannot be paid in the territory where it is owed and the only reason is the existence of foreign exchange restrictions; or
- it could be paid there, but if it were it would not be transferable to the UK and the only reason would be the existence of foreign exchange restrictions.

If a trader has profits in any given period of account, and an unremittable amount has been brought into account as a receipt for that period, a deduction is allowed of the unremittable amount. Relief can therefore be given only against profits of the trade that include the unremittable amount; it cannot be used to create or increase a loss. However, any excess relief is carried forward and may be set against future profits of the trade.

Relief will be restricted as appropriate if:

- the funds are used to finance expenditure or investment outside the UK;
- the funds are applied for some other purpose outside the UK;
- the trader has received an insurance recovery in respect of the debt; or
- the trader can make a claim under ITTOIA 2005, s. 842 that the income is unremittable.

Relief, once given, will be withdrawn to that extent in any of the following circumstances:

- the amount, or part of it, ceases to be unremittable;
- the amount, or part of it, is applied for some purpose outside the UK;
- the amount, or part of it, is exchanged for, or discharged by, an amount that is not unremittable;

- relief is given under the general rules of ITTOIA 2005, s. 35 re bad and doubtful debts; or
- an insurance recovery is received (in which case, the relief withdrawn cannot exceed the insurance payment received).

Legislation: ITTOIA 2005, s. 187–191

Tax Reporter: ¶211-100

Deductions for expenditure: entertaining, advertising and sponsorship

94-000 General principle

As stated clearly in the legislation, 'the general rule is that no deduction is allowed in calculating the profits of a trade for expenses incurred in providing entertainment or gifts in connection with the trade'.

There are exceptions to this rule, as noted below. However, the basic principle of disallowing entertaining costs is firmly engrained in the legislation.

Legislation: ITTOIA 2005, s. 45

Tax Reporter: ¶211-500

94-020 Meaning of 'entertainment'

The term 'entertainment' is defined to include 'hospitality of any kind' and the expenses incurred in providing entertainment or a gift are defined to include 'expenses incurred in providing anything incidental to the provision of entertainment or a gift'.

The question of whether expenses are incidental to the provision of entertainment was considered in the case of *Netlogic Consulting Ltd v HMRC*, in which the company held a function promoting its services to potential clients. The total cost of £2,481 consisted of two separate invoices: one for £1,800 paid to the caterers and another for £681 for room hire. The £681 (only) was held to be allowable on the grounds that 'the entertainment was incidental to the promotional purpose of the meeting, rather than the hire of the room being incidental to the provision of the entertainment'.

A similar definition of 'business entertainment' was considered in the context of VAT in *C & E Commrs v Shaklee International*. The taxpayers marketed products through distributors who were not their employees. The distributors received training at meetings, in connection with which they were provided free of charge with food and, when necessary, overnight accommodation. The Court of Appeal held that the supplies of meals and accommodation constituted 'business entertainment'. The provision of free meals and accommodation fell within the term entertainment, and this entertainment was provided in connection with the taxpayers' business. The taxpayers argued that this was not business entertainment because there was a previously established contractual relationship between the taxpayer and the distributors, but this was rejected by the court, which held that the contractual relationship merely emphasised that the meals and accommodation were provided in connection with the taxpayers' business.

The HMRC manuals acknowledge that there are differences between the VAT and direct tax legislation but nevertheless advise Inspectors:

> 'Although these differences exist, many of the conclusions reached in VAT cases are persuasive in establishing the meaning of business entertainment. Unless the facts or legal context of a particular case suggests otherwise you should take an analogous VAT decision into account when considering Section 577 [of ICTA 1988: see now ITTOIA 2005, s. 45(4)].'

After consideration of various VAT cases, the HMRC view is that an event that is subsidised, rather than provided free of charge, may nevertheless constitute entertainment. On the other hand, HMRC accept that 'if a trader has a contractual obligation (an obligation that requires the other party to provide something of value in return) to provide hospitality' then this will not normally constitute business entertaining. There will then be no denial of tax relief as long as the obligation is genuine and the trader is able to demonstrate 'a full and direct return for the entertainment'. HMRC illustrate the principle by reference to the VAT case of *Kilroy Television Company*, where members of a studio audience were given a buffet meal before the programme began. The VAT tribunal had found that the value of the service provided by the audience in participating in the programme was sufficient to cover the cost of the food and drink. As such, it did not constitute hospitality. The view was upheld in the High Court.

Legislation: ITTOIA 2005, s. 45(4)

Cases: *C & E Commrs v Shaklee International* (1981) 1 BVC 444; *C & E Commrs v Kilroy Television Company Ltd* [1997] BTC 2,152; *Netlogic Consulting Ltd v HMRC* (2005) Sp C 477

Other Material: BIM45011ff.

Tax Reporter: ¶211-525

94-040 Employees

There are two special rules in relation to employees.

First, there is no denial of relief where the entertainment is provided for employees of the taxpayer, unless its provision for them is incidental to its provision for others. It follows that a deduction will be allowed for the costs of holding a staff function to which some customers or clients are invited, but no deduction will be available where a function is held principally for customers, etc. but some employees are invited. For these purposes, employees include company directors and those engaged in the management of the business.

The second special rule for employees covers the situation in which an employee entertains on behalf of the trader. Without a special rule, the tax consequences could be very unfair: the employer pays a sum to the employee to entertain a customer; tax relief would be denied to the employer on the grounds that the payment was for entertaining; the employee would pay tax on the expenses payment as general earnings; the employee would be unable to claim a deduction for the costs when entertaining the customer, as this would be entertaining expenditure.

The effect of the legislation is normally to ensure that there is a single denial of tax relief, i.e. for either the employer or the employee but not both. To this end, the employer is denied tax relief if he pays a sum for or on behalf of the employee, or if he puts a sum at the disposal of the employee, *exclusively* for the purpose of meeting expenses incurred or to be incurred in providing the entertainment or gift. In this case, the employee is taxed on the receipt of the entertaining allowance or payment but may claim relief for the entertaining costs incurred. However, where an employee or director meets entertainment expenses from an inclusive salary, or from a round-sum allowance paid by his employer to cover expenditure besides entertaining, the disallowance is made in calculating the employee's taxable earnings, and the employer may deduct the amount of the business entertainment expenses.

Legislation: ITTOIA 2005, s. 46(3); ITEPA 2003, s. 357(1)

Tax Reporter: ¶211-550

94-060 Advertising and marketing

Expenditure shown in the business accounts as 'marketing' may for tax purposes fall within the meaning of 'entertaining', in which case a deduction will not be available. Care should be taken when preparing tax computations to check whether the expenditure needs to be disallowed on the grounds that it is 'hospitality of any kind'. Expenditure on advertising and marketing is unlikely to fall foul of the 'wholly and exclusively' rule although in some cases an expense may fail to qualify on the basis that it is capital expenditure: for example, where a durable asset is purchased.

Tax Reporter: ¶211-575

94-080 Sponsorship

Expenditure on sponsorship falls somewhere between advertising expenses and charitable or other benevolence. There is a risk that such expenditure may be disallowed on the duality principle. This issue was illustrated in *Executive Network (Consultants) Ltd v O'Connor*. The two special commissioners accepted that the payments were laid out for the purpose of the company's trade, but that could not displace the conclusion that personal benefits played a part in the decision to make the sponsorship payments.

To avoid this problem, a sponsorship agreement should make it clear that the sole purpose behind the negotiation of the agreement is publicity for the sponsor. In that case, the expenditure will in principle be deductible.

A further danger arises in connection with long-term agreements where it can be said that the sponsor has purchased an enduring capital asset to add to his profit-making apparatus; no relief would then be due. In practice it should be possible to frame an agreement in such a way that this argument does not arise.

If the sponsor provides any entertainment at the event, part or all of the deduction is likely to be disallowed, as discussed above.

A recent case dealing with sponsorship payments is *Interfish Ltd*. The individual in control of the company became heavily involved in a rugby football club. The club was in financial difficulties and in the company's accounting periods ended 31 January 2003, 2005 and 2006 a total of £1.2m was paid to the club as sponsorship. The First-tier Tribunal had decided that there was duality of purpose so the payment did not pass the wholly and exclusively rule. Birss J dismissed the company's appeal. There was no error of law and the following extract from his judgment explains his reasoning:

> 'The question is only whether the taxpayer's actual purpose was exclusively (i.e. solely) a business purpose. If not then the test is not satisfied …
>
> … [the controlling director's] conscious purpose of improving Plymouth Albion's financial position was so that Interfish's commercial interests would be furthered in consequence. That is plainly true on the judge's findings but it does not mean that the improvement of Plymouth Albion's finances could be relegated to something consequential and incidental. As the judge held,

improving Plymouth Albion's finances was not an unintended consequence of Interfish's payments, it was an intended consequence. Both purposes were in view and therefore the payments were not wholly and exclusively for the purposes of the taxpayer's trade. The decision of the FTT was correct.'

In the Court of Appeal, Lord Justice Moses agreed with the First-tier Tribunal judge that the expenditure would be deductible only if there was a rule that a purpose that is pursued with a view to an ulterior purpose somehow drops out of the picture, but such an approach would be inconsistent with the nature of the exercise prescribed by the authorities, namely, that of identifying the purpose or purposes being pursued. The appeal failed and the payments were not deductible.

Sponsorship payments without any involvement would not normally be a problem on the basis that there is a commercial reason for doing this. The difficulty here was the close involvement of the controlling director in the club even though he justified the payment on business grounds. It was accepted that a payment does not cease to be allowable under the wholly and exclusively rule simply because there is a private benefit, but that benefit has to be incidental. Here it was held that at least one of the purposes was to benefit the club, which was clearly not a business purpose of the company.

Cases: *Executive Network (Consultants) Ltd v O'Connor (HMIT)* (1995) Sp C 56; *Interfish Ltd v R & C Commrs* [2014] BTC 34

Tax Reporter: ¶211-600

94-100 Provision of gifts

The 'general rule' that denies relief for entertaining expenses (see 94-000) similarly ensures that no deduction may be claimed for 'expenses incurred in providing gifts in connection with the trade'.

Where the gift is provided through an employee but the cost is ultimately borne by the employer, the rules ensure that there is no double disallowance of the cost. This mirrors the principle applying to entertaining expenditure, as above.

The legislation lists four sets of circumstances in which the denial of relief for the cost of a gift does not apply, naming them 'Case A' to 'Case D'. The use of the double negative here is important: where these exceptions operate, they ensure that relief for the cost of a gift is not denied by virtue of the particular rule relating to business entertainment and gifts. Normal principles still apply, however, so relief will still be denied if the cost is caught by other rules, for example if it is not incurred wholly and exclusively for the purposes of the trade. Subject to this, the four 'Cases' (where relief may therefore be due) are as follows:

(1) Case A is where the gift is of an item which it is the trader's trade to provide, and the item is given away in the ordinary course of the trade in order to advertise to the public generally.

(2) Case B is where the gift incorporates a conspicuous advertisement for the donor.

However, this relaxation does not apply if:

(a) the item consists of food, drink, tobacco or of any token or voucher exchangeable for goods; or

(b) the cost of the gift to the donor, taken together with the cost to him of any other such articles given by him to that person in the same 'basis period', does not exceed £50. In calculating this total, the cost of such items as are referred to in (a) above (food, etc.) are ignored.

(3) Case C is where gifts are provided for the trader's employees, unless gifts are also provided for others and the provision for employees is incidental to the provision for others.

(4) Case D covers gifts given to a charity, or to certain educational, cultural, religious, recreational or benevolent bodies.

Legislation: ITTOIA 2005, s. 45(1), 47

Other Material: ESC B7

Tax Reporter: ¶211-650

Deductions for expenditure: cars and motorcycles

94-500 Restrictions on hire costs of cars (and formerly motorcycles)

Rules applying from 6 April 2009

For leases entered into between 6 April 2009 and 5 April 2013, there was a fixed 15% restriction for cars with CO_2 emissions above 160g/km. With effect from 6 April 2013, the restriction applies where the CO_2 emissions exceeds 130g/km.

> **Example**
>
> A car is hired in 2017–18 at a cost of £400 per month. The vehicle has emissions of 144g/km. Tax relief is denied on £60 per month (£400 × 15%).

The 15% restriction applies to the actual rent paid plus any element of unrelievable VAT. If, however, the rental agreement separately identifies charges for costs such as maintenance, then those costs should not be included when calculating the restriction and the restriction is only applied to the rental payment.

As with the capital allowance changes, the leasing restriction no longer applies for motorcycles (where the lease was entered into from April 2009).

Exclusions

The rules restricting the tax relief do not apply to cars with lower emissions, to electric cars, to cars first registered before March 2001 or to qualifying hire cars. The last category covers cars hired under a hire purchase agreement (as defined) under which there is no option to purchase, or under which there is an option to purchase exercisable on payment of a sum that does not exceed 1% of the retail price of the car when new. The category also includes a car purchased under a long-funding lease.

Legislation: ITTOIA 2005, s. 48ff.

Chains of leases

The rules only apply to one lessee in a chain of leases. This was explained as follows in the *Explanatory Notes* that accompanied the 2009 Finance Bill:

> 'Broadly, businesses will not be subject to a restriction of their allowable lease rental payments where the car is made available to them for a period of no more than 45 consecutive days. Also a business will not be subject to [a lease rental restriction] in respect of expenses it incurs in hiring a car where it makes the car available to a customer for a subhire period of more than 45 consecutive days (this exclusion does not apply, however, where a business makes cars available to its employees or the employees of a connected person).'

Legislation: ITTOIA 2005, s. 50A

Deductions for expenditure: payments in connection with employees

95-000 Introduction

For many businesses, the biggest single cost is that of employing staff. The tax treatment of employees themselves is considered in depth at 130-000ff. This section discusses the tax deduction available for employers or others making payments to, or in connection with, the employees of a business.

Tax Reporter: ¶213-000

95-020 Salaries, wages, etc.

The remuneration of employees and directors is allowable to the extent that it is wholly and exclusively incurred for business purposes. This includes bonuses, gratuities, payments in respect of removal, etc. expenses, benefits in kind, medical insurance premiums, etc.

No deduction was allowed for wages of £3,800 in the case of *Auksoraitus* as there was no evidence that the business had any employees. (The appellant did not turn up for the hearing and was not represented. The disallowance of wages was one of numerous amendments made to his self-assessment in the absence of evidence relating to the declared profits.)

Excessive remuneration is not deductible. This was illustrated, for example, in *Copeman v William Flood & Sons Ltd*; see also *Dollar v Lyon*. Subject to that qualification, remuneration paid to members of the employer's family is allowable in the same way as payments to other employees. In an employment tax case (*Evans*), where remuneration paid to other employees is rarely allowable, HMRC accepted that a secretarial salary paid to the employee's wife was incurred both 'necessarily' and 'in the performance of the duties', but HMRC were partially successful in reducing the quantum of the claim. It has to be shown, however, that the money claimed to have been paid was in fact paid to and received by the employee (*Abbott v IR Commrs*).

Earnings that would ordinarily be deductible but that are not paid within nine months of the end of the period of account are deductible only in the period of account in which they are actually paid. (For this purpose, the ordinary meaning of 'earnings' is extended to include amounts allocated in respect of particular offices and employments, and any amounts allocated generally, including amounts or benefits received in the accounts of an employer, or held by an intermediary, with a view to allocation. The term 'paid' has a wide meaning which includes any circumstances in which remuneration is treated as received by virtue of ITEPA 2003, s. 18, 19, 31 or 32.)

Where a business submits its accounts within nine months of the end of the accounting period, remuneration that is then unpaid is assumed to remain unpaid to the end of the nine-month period and is not deductible. However, if the salary, etc. is in fact paid before the end of the nine-month period a claim for adjustment can be made within two years of the end of the period of account. Special extensions of the deadlines are allowed for Lloyd's underwriting agents.

Legislation: ITTOIA 2005, s. 36ff.

Cases: *Copeman v William Flood & Sons Ltd* (1940) 24 TC 53; *Dollar v Lyon* (1981) 54 TC 459; *Abbott v IR Commrs* (1995) Sp C 58; *Evans* [2010] TC 00446; *Auksoraitus* [2011] TC 00800

Tax Reporter: ¶213-050

95-030 Transfer to employee of capital asset

Although remuneration for an employee is normally tax deductible, there is a potential pitfall if the remuneration is in the form of a transfer of a capital asset.

In *Lion Co v R & C Commrs*, expenditure written off on the transfer of a property to a director by way of a bonus was held to be on capital account and so not deductible. The Appellant company incurred expenditure of approximately £1.6m on the acquisition and improvement of a property with the sole purpose of later transferring it to the director. When the transfer took place, the property was valued at £1.2m. In its corporation tax return for that period, the company claimed relief for a bonus of £1.2m and for the write-off of expenditure incurred on the acquisition of a current asset of £0.4m. The tribunal found that although the asset was bought with a view to paying a bonus, the means adopted for the payment of that bonus was the acquisition and improvement of a capital asset. The purpose behind the transaction did not alter the character of the original expenditure. Therefore, only the value of the bonus (£1.2m) was on revenue account and so deductible in calculating the company's profits chargeable to corporation tax.

Case: *Lion Co v R & C Commrs* [2010] TC 00295

95-040 PAYE and National Insurance

Tax and National Insurance contributions, deducted by an employer under the Pay As You Earn system, in effect form part of the employee's remuneration, and are deductible on that basis. Deductibility does not, of course, extend to the unincorporated employer's personal income tax liability; that liability is an appropriation of profits as opposed to a deduction in computing those profits.

Secondary Class 1, Class 1A or Class 1B National Insurance contributions are part of the employment-remuneration costs for the employer that are deductible as an expense in computing the taxable profits or losses of the employer's trade, profession or vocation.

Interest paid by employers on overdue PAYE, etc. is not allowable in computing income or profits for tax purposes. Similarly, there is a specific disallowance of interest paid by employers in respect of late payments of:

- tax under the construction industry deduction scheme;
- National Insurance contributions; and
- student loan repayments (both under the *Social Security Contributions and Benefits Act* 1992 and under the equivalent Northern Ireland legislation).

Legislation: ITEPA 2003, s. 684(4); ITTOIA 2005, s. 54

Tax Reporter: ¶213-100

95-060 Non-approved pension schemes and other trust funds

Sums paid to non-approved retirement benefit schemes and other trust funds will normally be deductible, provided they are of a revenue nature and that the benefits are chargeable to income tax on the employee. A sum so paid is deductible as an expense of the trade, profession or vocation in computing the taxable profits of that trade, profession or vocation.

Restrictions apply to the deduction of certain payments to employee benefit trusts.

The pension rules changed radically from 6 April 2006, as discussed at 74-000ff. As before, however, employers may claim a deduction for contributions paid to registered pension schemes. The previous practice of spreading large contributions over two to four years has been put onto a statutory footing. To be deductible, employer contributions must have been actually paid, not merely provided for in their accounts.

The employer is allowed relief on the legal and other expenses of establishing and running a scheme in the chargeable period in which they are paid.

Tax Reporter: ¶213-150

95-080 Employee expenses

Where an employer reimburses an employee for expenditure incurred in the course of his employment, the sum reimbursed is deductible in calculating the employer's business profits.

An exception to this is reimbursement of an employee's business entertaining expenses, as discussed at 94-040.

Tax Reporter: ¶213-300

95-100 Counselling services for employees

An employer may incur expenditure in providing certain counselling services to an employee in relation to a termination of employment. Such expenditure is deductible as a business expense, even if the redundancy of the employee arises out of the closing down of the business.

It is immaterial whether the counselling services are provided before or after the termination.

Subject to certain conditions, there is no charge to tax under ITEPA 2003 in respect of the provision of counselling services which are deductible as above.

Legislation: ITEPA 2003, s. 310, 403; ITTOIA 2005, s. 73

Tax Reporter: ¶213-500

95-120 Retraining of employees

Relief is made specifically available for expenditure on retraining courses for redundant employees which might otherwise be disallowed under the 'wholly and exclusively' rule.

If the relief is to be available, it is necessary to meet both the 'course conditions' and the 'employment conditions'. Travel expenses must also meet the given conditions of ITEPA 2003. The employer has a duty to notify HMRC in writing within 60 days of the event giving rise to such a breach coming to his notice.

Legislation: ITEPA 2003, s. 311; ITTOIA 2005, s. 74

Tax Reporter: ¶213-550

95-140 Provision of leisure facilities

Expenditure incurred in providing leisure facilities for employees is likely to be allowed unless of a capital nature (in which case, though, it may attract capital allowances). Running costs of such facilities will normally be deductible in the same way as the cost of other benefits in kind paid to employees.

Tax Reporter: ¶213-600

95-160 Payments on commencement of service contract

Lump-sum payments ('golden hellos') made to individuals on becoming employees (or as inducements to do so) may need careful analysis. By their very nature most payments of this type will be made wholly and exclusively for business purposes, etc.; however, considerations similar to those relating to wages and salaries (see above) may apply.

Payments referable to the terms of a person's employment and in the nature of an advance of salary will generally be deductible.

The exact structure of any particular payment may bring into point the question of whether it is of a capital or revenue nature.

Tax Reporter: ¶213-800

95-180 Charities and educational establishments

If an employer makes available to a charity, on a temporary basis, the services of an employee, any expenditure by the employer (e.g. on the employee's salary) attributable to that person's employment is expressly deductible against profits. The same relief is available to employers who second employees on a temporary basis to certain approved educational bodies, whether or not those bodies are charities.

A deduction is made in calculating business profits for contributions made by an employer towards the administrative costs incurred by approved agencies in running payroll deduction schemes.

Legislation: ITTOIA 2005, s. 70, 72

Tax Reporter: ¶213-950

95-200 Payments for restrictive undertakings

A sum paid or consideration transferred by a person for the giving, or the total or partial fulfilment, of 'restrictive undertakings' by an employee or director, etc. is deductible as an expense in computing the taxable profits of the person's trade, profession or vocation.

A 'restrictive undertaking' is one which has the tenor or effect of restricting the employee or director, etc. as to his conduct or activities in connection with his current, future or past employment (for example, a covenant not to compete with the employer).

Legislation: ITEPA 2003, s. 225(1)(a); ITTOIA 2005, s. 69

Tax Reporter: ¶214-100

95-220 Payments connected with share sale

Particular difficulties can arise where a payment to a retiring director coincides with the sale by him of his shares in the employer company. The question may be raised of whether a payment in such circumstances is not somehow coloured by the contract relating to the share purchase, thus raising the possibility of a challenge on 'wholly and exclusively' grounds. The matter was considered in depth in *James Snook & Co Ltd v Blasdale*, in which the judge made the following comment:

> 'The mere circumstance that compensation to retiring directors is paid on a change of shareholding control does not of itself involve the consequence that such compensation can never be a deductible trading expense. So much is common ground. But it is essential in such cases that the company should prove to the Commissioners' satisfaction that it considered the question of payment wholly untrammelled by the terms of the bargain its shareholders had struck with those who were to buy their shares and came to a decision to pay solely in the interests of its trade.'

The above is an HMRC favourite, often quoted by officers as authority for disallowing payments to departing directors.

Cases: *Mitchell v BW Noble Ltd* (1926) 11 TC 372; *Morgan Crucible Co Ltd v IR Commrs* (1932) 17 TC 311; *Alexander Howard & Co Ltd v Bentley* (1948) 30 TC 334; *James Snook & Co Ltd v Blasdale* (1952) 33 TC 244

Other Material: HMRC *Business Income Manual* BIM42955

Tax Reporter: ¶214-050

95-240 Deferred salary

Certain lump-sum payments made to employees in return for the termination of service contracts may be deductible. It is necessary to show in particular that such payments are not of a capital nature, and that they are made wholly and exclusively for business purposes.

Where a series of payments on retirement is in the nature of a deferred salary, the expectation of which encouraged an employee to accept a lower salary during employment, the expense is deductible. If the series is commuted to a lump sum to avoid the continuing obligation, or if the payer hedges the obligation by providing for an equivalent income on payment of a lump sum, the deductibility is less clear.

95-260 Statutory redundancy payments

Redundancy payments made on the discontinuance of a business were once normally non-deductible for tax purposes. However, specific statutory provisions now grant a deduction for certain types of redundancy and related payments.

The rules apply to 'redundancy payments' and to certain 'approved contractual payments' made by an employer to an employee. The term 'redundancy payment' is defined as a redundancy payment made under *Employment Rights Act* 1996, Pt. 11 or *Employment Rights (Northern Ireland) Order* 1996 (SI 1996/1919), Pt. 12.

The term 'contractual payments' is defined to mean 'a payment which, under an agreement, an employer is liable to make to an employee on the termination of the employee's contract of employment'. The contractual payment is said to be approved if, in respect of that agreement, an order is in force under the *Employment Rights Act* 1996, s. 157 or, as the case may be, under *Employment Rights (Northern Ireland) Order* 1996, art. 192.

The relieving rule applies first where the employee's employment has been wholly in the employer's trade (and where no deduction would otherwise be due). In calculating the profits of the trade, a deduction is allowed where such a redundancy or other contractual payment is made. In the case of an approved contractual payment, the deduction cannot initially exceed the amount that would have been due if a redundancy payment had been made. However, relief is then given separately for additional payments, limited to three times the amount of the statutory payment or, in the case of an approved contractual payment, to three times the amount that would have been paid if a statutory payment had instead been made.

A payment made after the cessation of trade is treated as made on the last day on which the trade was carried on and the deduction is given accordingly. Where there is a change in the persons carrying on a trade, this deemed date of payment does not apply as long as at least one person carrying on the trade before the change continues to do so thereafter.

Where the employee's employment has been partly in the employer's trade and partly in one or more other capacities, any redundancy payment is to be apportioned on a just and reasonable basis.

Legislation: ITTOIA 2005, s. 76ff.

Tax Reporter: ¶214-150

95-280 Other payments on termination of employment

Other cases in which payments to terminate service contracts have been disallowed include the following.

- Compensation payment to an employee after discontinuance of the taxpayer's business (*Godden v A Wilson's Stores (Holdings) Ltd*).
- Compensation paid to retiring directors in pursuance of a vote taken by a board which included those resigning, on the basis that the decision could not have been taken exclusively in the interests of the business (*George J Smith & Co Ltd v Furlong*).
- Payments to retiring directors which were in substance a distribution of profits accrued up to the date of the takeover (*Overy v Ashford Dunn & Co Ltd*).
- Payments to a resigning director to maintain good relations with him and to put him under an obligation not to set up business in competition (*Deverell, Gibson & Hoare Ltd v Rees*).
- A lump sum payment made to commute a liability to pay an annuity, which was held to be a capital payment (*Parnalls Solicitors Ltd v R & C Commrs*).

Cases: *Overy v Ashford Dunn & Co Ltd* (1933) 17 TC 497; *Deverell, Gibson & Hoare Ltd v Rees* (1943) 25 TC 467; *Godden v A Wilson's Stores (Holdings) Ltd* (1962) 40 TC 161; *George J Smith & Co Ltd v Furlong* (1968) 45 TC 384; *Parnalls Solicitors Ltd* [2010] TC 00261

Tax Reporter: ¶214-050

95-300 Theft and misappropriation

Irrecoverable losses due to theft by employees are generally deductible in computing profits. However, a distinction must be drawn between petty theft, arising in the normal course of business, and default by a director with authority to disburse the business's money. The latter is not allowed for tax purposes.

Cases: *Bamford v ATA Advertising Ltd* (1972) 48 TC 359; *Roebank Printing Co Ltd v IR Commrs* (1928) 13 TC 864

Tax Reporter: ¶214-200

Deductions for expenditure: finance costs

95-500 Interest generally

Interest paid on loans to, or overdrafts of, a business is a deductible expense, provided the loan was made wholly and exclusively for business purposes. Interest paid out is always a revenue rather than a capital expense, whatever the nature of the loan.

Interest payable in respect of the acquisition of an asset (e.g. a car) used by an individual partly for business and partly for private purposes is apportioned for income tax purposes (but no interest relief is available for an employee using a privately-owned car for the purposes of his or her employment).

Legislation: ITTOIA 2005, s. 29, 52

Tax Reporter: ¶215-000

95-520 Interest paid on business loan to fund proprietor's overdraft

Interest paid on a loan used to fund the proprietor's overdrawn current or capital account is not deductible. However, the position is more complex where a business revalues assets, whether downwards (depreciation) or upwards.

Useful guidance is given by HMRC as follows:

> 'The only foolproof way of ascertaining how much of an overdraft or loan has funded private expenditure is to look at each individual entry. This is usually impracticable and it is necessary to use a reasonable basis as an approximation.
>
> An overdrawn capital account shown in the balance sheet is no more than an indication that a loan or overdraft is being used to fund private drawings. You must be able to demonstrate that it is private drawings which have caused the account to become overdrawn and that the overdrawn capital account has been funded by bank borrowings. You must look carefully at all of the components of the balance sheet to judge how the proprietor's drawings have been funded. When examining the proprietor's capital account transactions you should draw a distinction between accumulated realised profits, both capital and revenue, on which a proprietor is free to draw and unrealised profits or losses. Unrealised profits do not represent a cash item and may never be realised. They cannot affect the level of bank borrowings. You should disregard unrealised profits or losses in considering whether a proprietor's account is overdrawn.
>
> In many cases depreciation is charged in the profit and loss account and this reduces the net amount of profit credited to the capital account. A trader who

provides for depreciation lowers the amounts he or she can draw from the capital account without that account going into deficit compared to a trader in otherwise identical circumstances who does not provide for depreciation. You need to adjust for accumulated depreciation in calculating a revised balance on the account.'

Case: *Silk v Fletcher (HMIT)* (2000) Sp C 262

Other Material: HMRC *Business Income Manual* BIM45705ff.

Tax Reporter: ¶215-050

95-540 Incidental costs of obtaining loan finance

The incidental costs of obtaining loan finance are deductible. 'Incidental costs of obtaining finance' means expenditure on fees, commissions, advertising, printing and other incidental matters, wholly and exclusively incurred for the purpose of obtaining the finance, of providing security for it, or of repaying it. Stamp duty is not included. Expenditure on abortive applications is allowed if the expenditure would have qualified had the finance been obtained.

Income tax relief is not given under these rules for expenditure as a result of, or for obtaining protection against, fluctuations in currency exchange rates. Similarly, relief is not given for the cost of repaying a loan or loan stock so far as attributable to its being repayable at a premium or to its having been obtained or issued at a discount.

Life assurance premiums are not regarded by HMRC as 'incidental' to obtaining finance, even if they are taken out by a self-employed person and required as a condition of obtaining the finance.

Legislation: ITTOIA 2005, s. 58

Other Material: HMRC *Business Income Manual* BIM45525

Tax Reporter: ¶215-100

95-560 Hire-purchase charges

Hire-purchase charges, so far as attributable to use of the asset as opposed to purchase, are deductible. The allowable element is the difference between the total consideration paid and the cash value of the asset acquired.

Case: *Darngavil Coal Company Ltd v Francis* (1913) 7 TC 1

Tax Reporter: ¶215-200

Deductions for expenditure: travel costs

95-700 Travelling expenses generally

The legislation is almost silent on the treatment of this all-important category of business expenditure. The only references to travel costs in the *Income Tax (Trading and Other Income) Act* 2005 are in relation to foreign trades and to employee counselling and retraining. This is to be contrasted with the fairly detailed statutory provisions (and extensive official guidance) in relation to employee travel expenses. In practice, the most likely difficulty with travelling expenses is that they may be excluded from deduction by the principle of duality of purpose, thus failing to meet the 'wholly and exclusively' test (see 92-300).

The expense of journeys which a taxpayer makes from his home to his place of work is not deductible. This is on the grounds that it fails the 'wholly and exclusively' (duality of purpose) test. In *Newsom v Robertson*, a barrister lived outside London and travelled each day to his chambers in Lincoln's Inn. Since his base of operations was in London, his journeys to and from work were not made wholly and exclusively for the purpose of his profession. A similar decision was reached in *Sargent v Barnes*, in which a dentist had a laboratory which was located between his surgery and his home (though nearer his home); in spite of the laboratory visits, the trips between home and surgery retained a dual purpose which disqualified the expenditure. The facts were held to be similar in *Manders*, in which a market trader unsuccessfully claimed the cost of travel between home and the market place. The taxpayer was also unsuccessful in *Samadian*. This case concerned a consultant doctor who claimed the cost of travel to private hospitals from his home. It was accepted that his home was also a place of business although he did not as a rule see patients there. *Horton v Young* was distinguished as there the taxpayer's only place of business was his home. There was a mixed object in Mr Samadian's travelling between his home and the private hospitals, which had to cause the expenditure to fail the wholly and exclusively rule.

Where a person's home is genuinely his base of operations then all travelling expenses are generally deductible. More specifically, this has been held (in *Horton v Young*) to apply where:

> 'a person has no fixed place or places at which he carries on his trade or profession but moves continually from one place to another, at each of which he consecutively exercises his trade or profession on a purely temporary basis and then departs, his trade or profession being in that sense of an itinerant nature.'

Cases: *Newsom v Robertson* (1952) 33 TC 452; *Horton v Young* (1971) 47 TC 60; *Sargent v Barnes* (1978) 52 TC 335; *Jackman (HMIT) v Powell*

[2004] BTC 336; *Manders* [2010] TC 00600; *Samadian v R & C Commrs* [2014] BTC 504

Tax Reporter: ¶216-000

95-720 International travel

Expenses incurred on business travel abroad will be deductible if the business purpose is the sole purpose of the journey but not if the trip has a secondary social purpose.

See also *Sargent v Eayrs* where it was held that travelling expenses incurred by the taxpayer on a visit to Australia to investigate the possibility of buying a farm there and emigrating were not deductible as expenditure wholly and exclusively laid out for the purposes of the taxpayer's farming trade in the UK.

Cases: *Bowden v Russell & Russell* (1965) 42 TC 301; *Edwards v Warmsley, Henshall & Co* (1967) 44 TC 431; *Sargent v Eayrs* (1972) 48 TC 573

Tax Reporter: ¶216-000

95-740 Cars used by the business proprietor

The general principles outlined above apply to travel by private car. In practice, an agreement may be reached between an unincorporated proprietor and the HMRC officer as to the proportion of annual running costs which is attributable to business use. Although in strictness lump sum expenses, such as servicing and insurance, could arguably be disallowed on the dual purpose principle, these are generally allowed in the same proportion as expenses that are accurately ascertainable.

In certain circumstances, HMRC will allow taxpayers to use the (employee) authorised mileage allowance rates (see *Hardman's Tax Rates and Tables* at 3-475) to compute vehicle expenses, instead of recording all expenses. Taxpayers have the option to do this if the annual turnover of the business is less than the VAT registration threshold when they first use the vehicle. The mileage rate basis must be consistently applied from year to year. Taxpayers are only allowed to change to or from on this basis when a vehicle is replaced. If the turnover of the business increases and exceeds the VAT registration threshold, then the taxpayer should continue to use the mileage rate basis until the vehicle is replaced.

The mileage rate covers the costs of running and maintaining the vehicle, such as fuel, oil, servicing, repairs, insurance, vehicle excise duty and MOT. So no further claim may be made for these expenses. Nor can a capital allowances claim be made as the payment rates already contain an element to allow for depreciation.

The mileage rate does not cover costs that are specific to a particular journey such as tolls, congestion charges and parking fees. These will be allowable as a deduction in calculating business profits where they are incurred solely for business purposes. The taxpayer can also claim the business proportion of the interest on a loan used to purchase the vehicle.

Other Material: HMRC *Business Income Manual* BIM47700ff.

Tax Reporter: ¶216-000

95-760 Cars used by employees

For cars provided to employees, whether of an incorporated or unincorporated business, the full amount of the employer's cost in providing petrol, etc. is generally allowable. Tax relief for the capital cost of buying a car will be given by way of capital allowances. (For the employee's tax position if the car is a company vehicle, see 132-200ff.)

Tax Reporter: ¶216-000

Deductions for expenditure: property-related payments

96-000 Rent

Rent of business premises (or equipment) is deductible in computing business profits. A fair rent paid to a partner in the tenant firm has been held to be deductible.

In certain circumstances rent for unoccupied premises may be allowed as incurred for the purposes of the business. Relief is given as long as the obligation to pay rent has been entered into for trade purposes, including for periods before the premises are first occupied for trade purposes.

Rent for dwelling-houses and domestic offices is disallowed except where the house or office is used for business, in which case an appropriate proportion will be allowed.

The taxpayer in *Healy* was an actor who sought to claim a deduction for rent paid for accommodation and subsistence expenditure incurred whilst living in London and performing in a successful West End show. The First-tier Tribunal rejected his claim on the grounds that the expenditure had a duality of purposes.

Cases: *Heastie v Veitch & Co* (1933) 18 TC 305; *Strick v Regent Oil Co Ltd* (1965) 43 TC 1; *Healy* [2015] TC 04425

Other Material: HMRC *Business Income Manual* BIM46815

Tax Reporter: ¶216-300

96-020 Lease premiums

A tenant will sometimes be required to pay a one-off lease premium in addition to regular rental payments. In certain cases (generally where the lease does not exceed 50 years) the landlord will pay tax on that premium. The tenant may then obtain a form of tax relief for the payment of the premium, even though it would on normal principles be treated as a capital payment.

Example

Black is granted on 1 September a lease of offices by White Ltd for 21 years, at a premium of £70,000 and rental of £12,000 per annum. Black, who has calendar year periods of account, immediately occupies the offices for the purposes of his trade.

White Ltd pays tax on £42,000 (£70,000 – £28,000, where £28,000 is calculated as £70,000 × 20/50. The figure of 20 is used as it is the number of complete years for which the lease runs, apart from the first year.)

Black will get tax relief for £4,000 of actual rent paid in the first year, plus £668, calculated as £42,000 × 122 (days from 1 September to 31 December) over 7,670 (days in 21 years).

Legislation: ITTOIA 2005, s. 61

Other Material: HMRC *Business Income Manual* BIM46255

Tax Reporter: ¶216-350

96-040 General office expenses

Most general office expenditure is allowable as a deduction in computing business profits, unless of a capital nature. This includes record-keeping and secretarial expenses, office supplies (other than capital items), rates, water rates and the like, electricity and bank charges. Telephone charges in respect of business calls are deductible, and also rental if the telephone is used exclusively for business purposes.

Case: *Lucas v Cattell* (1972) 48 TC 353

Tax Reporter: ¶208-150

Deductions for expenditure – other payments

96-200 Accountancy expenses

In theory there is a distinction between expense incurred in drawing up accounts for business reasons, and in drawing up accounts for tax purposes: the former is incurred in the course of business but the latter is not. However, the two are so closely linked that it would be a difficult and artificial process to identify expenditure attributable to one or other purpose, and in practice HMRC allow the deduction of expenses incurred in preparation of accounts for tax purposes, and agreeing the computation with the tax officer.

This does not, however, extend to the costs of pursuing an appeal against assessment, which in the view of HMRC are not allowable (though there is a possible counter argument if failure to win the appeal would have a severe impact on the ability to carry on trading).

As far as accountancy expenses relating to self-assessment enquiries are concerned, HMRC guidance is as follows:

> 'Additional accountancy expenses arising out of an enquiry into the accounts information in a particular year's return will not be allowed where the enquiry reveals discrepancies and additional liabilities for the year of enquiry, or any earlier year, which arise as a result of negligent or fraudulent conduct.
>
> Where, however, the enquiry results in no addition to profits, or an adjustment to the profits for the year of enquiry only and that adjustment does not arise as a result of negligent or fraudulent conduct, the additional accountancy expenses will be allowable.'

If, during the enquiry, the taxpayer concedes even a token penalty, this would properly be interpreted as an admission of negligence, which could therefore cause the related accountancy costs to be disallowed.

Cases: *Smith's Potato Estates Ltd v Bolland* (1948) 30 TC 267, especially per Lord Porter at p. 520; *Meredith v Roberts* (1968) 44 TC 559

Other Material: SP16/91; HMRC *Business Income Manual* BIM46455

Tax Reporter: ¶217-700

Tax return costs

The question of how to treat the cost of preparing tax returns for sole traders or partners is not straightforward.

The legal position is that a cost is only allowable if it is incurred wholly and exclusively for the purposes of earning profits in a trade. The HMRC view is that the preparation of business accounts meets that test but that preparation of the business tax computation does not strictly do so. Nevertheless, the HMRC practice is to allow recurring accountancy costs incurred both in preparing the accounts and in 'agreeing the tax liability' (which is interpreted in reality to mean preparing the business tax computation). The courts have approved this fudge of the strict legal position. What it means in practice is that work in completing the business tax computation is allowed in full, unless there are exceptional circumstances.

The HMRC guidance goes on to say that 'the costs of completion of a tax return ... are not allowable in computing trading profits'. Strictly, therefore, every business tax computation should include an addback if the full cost of tax services, including a personal tax return (whether for sole trader or partner), has been charged in the accounts.

Having said this, the HMRC guidance goes on to add: 'But the additional personal costs are likely to be minimal where, apart from the computation of the tax liability on trading profits, an individual's personal tax affairs are straightforward'.

So if there are other complications in the personal tax returns, there should clearly be an addback. The position is less clear cut if the remaining tax affairs are straightforward (some bank interest and a few dividends, perhaps). The HMRC statement could be interpreted as either meaning 'we only expect a small addback' or 'the additional costs are minimal and not worth bothering with, so we do not expect any addback'. Practitioners will need to exercise judgement in deciding whether the costs are such as to make some sort of addback necessary.

Other Material: HMRC *Business Income Manual* BIM46450

96-220 Annuities and annual payments

Any annuity, or other annual payment (other than interest), payable out of profits or gains charged to tax is disallowed as a deduction for the purposes of calculating the profits of a business for tax purposes.

This used to be explicitly stated in the legislation (ICTA 1988, s. 74(1)(m)). It was not considered necessary to rewrite the rule in ITTOIA 2005, however, as amounts payable out of the profits cannot be relevant when calculating the profits themselves.

Tax Reporter: ¶217-400

96-240 Charitable and similar payments

Charitable payments are allowable if made wholly and exclusively for the purposes of the trade. According to HMRC, 'many subscriptions and donations however are made from motives that are too general or personal to justify a deduction'.

In practice, HMRC take a reasonably broad view of whether a donation is made wholly and exclusively for business purposes. Strictly, any element of philanthropy would disqualify the gift on the duality principle, but HMRC do not generally follow this line. However, a large, irregular payment may be disallowed.

The best approach in practice is almost certainly to make any charitable payments under the Gift Aid scheme.

A person carrying on a trade, profession or vocation may normally deduct the cost of expenses incurred in making any contribution (whether in cash or in kind) to a local enterprise organisation or to an urban regeneration company. A restriction applies, however, if a benefit is received in return.

Donations for political purposes are not generally deductible.

Legislation: ITTOIA 2005, s. 47

Other Material: ESC B7

Tax Reporter: ¶217-700

96-260 Computer software

The correct tax treatment of computer software used in a business follows normal principles and thus depends on whether the expenditure is classified as capital or revenue. If capital, machinery and plant allowances are appropriate; where revenue, the expenditure is deductible in computing the profits of the business.

HMRC accept that where a lump sum payment is made for the acquisition of a software licence, it can be treated for tax purposes as revenue expenditure if the useful economic life of the software is expected to be less than two years. If software is acquired under licence, and paid for by regular periodical payments, these should be treated as revenue expenditure and normally spread over the useful life of the software.

Tax Reporter: ¶217-550

96-280 Crime-related expenditure

In computing business tax profits, no deduction is allowed for a payment 'the making of the payment constitutes a criminal offence'. The provision covers such payments as bribes of public officials, which are prohibited at common law, as well as payments that would be illegal under specific legislation.

The prohibition now expressly applies where the payment would constitute a criminal offence in any part of the UK. The effect is to render non-deductible a payment made by, say, an English company to a Ruritanian company which constitutes a crime in Northern Ireland but nowhere else in the UK.

No deduction is allowed for expenditure incurred in making a payment induced by a demand amounting to blackmail, contrary to the *Theft Act* 1968, s. 21 (or the *Theft Act (Northern Ireland)* 1969, s. 20), or to the offence of extortion in Scotland. Blackmail consists of making an unwarranted demand with menaces for the purpose of financial gain for oneself or another person or financial loss to the person threatened.

Legislation: ITTOIA 2005, s. 55

Tax Reporter: ¶217-500

96-320 Franchise payments

Certain kinds of agreement, popularly known as 'franchises', typically require the payment of an initial fee for use of the franchisor's business format, trademark or goodwill, followed by a series of payments which might represent consideration for goods and services supplied by the franchisor on an ongoing basis, or simply royalties for access to the franchisor's trade systems during the term of the franchise.

The question may arise as to whether the initial payment constitutes revenue or capital expenditure by the franchisee. To the extent that the payment represents consideration for revenue items, such as trading stock or services such as training of staff (but not necessarily of the franchisee), it will be a deductible trading expense of the franchisee. In a 'toolkit' issued in 2010, entitled 'Capital v Revenue Expenditure Toolkit: 2009–10 Self Assessment and Company Tax Returns', HMRC warned that 'deductions should not be made on the basis that elements of the initial payment relate to allowable revenue expenditure for specific services, unless they are clearly supported by both the franchise agreement and the facts'. HMRC will wish to check that the agreement stipulates that those services are paid for by reference to the initial payment and not just the annual fees.

Ongoing payments under franchise agreements normally represent consideration for continuing goods or services, such as training and support, supplied by the franchisor. To that extent they are deductible trading expenses.

Other Material: HMRC *Business Income Manual* BIM57620

Tax Reporter: ¶216-950

96-340 Insurance

Business-related insurance premiums are, in general, deductible on general principles.

Life assurance premiums for employees and directors ('keyman' or 'key person' policies) are deductible provided:

- the sole relationship between the policy holder and the life assured is that of employer and employee;
- the insurance is intended to meet loss of profit resulting from the loss of services of the employee; and
- it is an annual or short-term insurance (*Hansard*, 27 July 1944, col. 890).

The HMRC view is that the cost of fee protection policies is not tax-deductible. The basis of this view is that whilst normal accountancy costs are allowable, no deduction is given for those relating to an enquiry that reveals discrepancies and additional liabilities for any year, arising because of fraudulent or negligent conduct.

Where medical or other professionals take out insurance to cover themselves against the cost of engaging a locum tenens, or other practice expenses, in the event of their own illness or incapacity, the HMRC treat premiums payable under such policies as allowable business deductions. Equally, benefits payable are taxable receipts, as they diminish allowable business expenses.

Other Material: HMRC Interpretation, IRInt. 247 (Tax Bulletin, June 2003); HMRC press release 30 April 1996

Tax Reporter: ¶217-650

96-360 Legal expenses

There are numerous reasons why a deduction may be denied for legal and other professional expenses: an expense may be regarded as attributable to capital; it may be regarded as not wholly and exclusively laid out for business purposes; or it may be seen as an application of profits already earned rather than as an expense in calculating those profits.

Allowable expenditure

The following expenditure has nevertheless been held to be deductible against business profits.

- Costs of renewal of licences, terminations and assignments of leases, complaints against tenants and advice as to thefts, all in connection with tied houses owned by brewers (*Usher's Wiltshire Brewery Ltd v Bruce*), but the cost of terminating or assigning a lease will not normally be deductible.
- Costs incurred in defending an action concerned with the promotion of companies, such an activity being part of the taxpayer company's business (*Golder v Great Boulder Proprietary Gold Mines Ltd*).
- Damages for defamation payable by a newspaper company (*Herald and Weekly Times Ltd v Federal Commr of Taxation*, High Court of Australia, approved by the House of Lords in *McKnight (HMIT) v Sheppard*). Such claims against a newspaper are, in the court's words, a 'regular and almost unavoidable incident of publishing it', and the damages are compensatory rather than punitive.
- A payment to settle a slander action, which was part of a larger agreement over recovery of a business debt (*G Scammell & Nephew Ltd v Rowles*).
- Costs incurred in defending a title to a capital asset, against a claimant with no title to the asset (*Southern v Borax Consolidated Ltd* (where this expenditure was contrasted with the capital expense of acquiring a new title)).
- Costs incurred in defending the taxpayer's rights under a loan agreement, where breach of contract was alleged (*IT Commr, Bihar and Orissa v Singh*).
- Expenses incurred by a company in obtaining a supplementary charter necessary for its business (*IR Commrs v Carron Co*).
- Expenses incurred in connection with an action brought against the company by a shareholder (*IR Commrs v Carron Co*).
- Expenses incurred in respect of disciplinary proceedings against a stockbroker for alleged breaches of the rules and regulations of the Stock Exchange (*McKnight (HMIT) v Sheppard*). Here, the House of Lords rejected HMRC's contention that the taxpayer fell foul of the duality of purpose principle by having had two purposes in incurring the expenses: to prevent the destruction of his business and to preserve his reputation. Their Lordships applied *Mallalieu v Drummond* and

said that the taxpayer's purpose had been to protect his business, despite the effect of the expenditure also having been to preserve his personal reputation.

- Expenses incurred to acquire certain film rights (*Icebreaker 1 LLP v R & C Commrs*). The Upper Tribunal largely reversed the decision of the lower tribunal as there was no proper evidence that the payment was capital in nature and it was wrong to look at what the company did with the money, rather than at the purpose of the expenditure from the taxpayer's point of view.

Cases: *Usher's Wiltshire Brewery Ltd v Bruce* (1914) 6 TC 399; *Herald and Weekly Times Ltd v Federal Commr of Taxation* (1932) 48 CLR 113; *G Scammell & Nephew Ltd v Rowles* (1939) 22 TC 479; *Southern v Borax Consolidated Ltd* (1940) 23 TC 597; *IT Commr, Bihar and Orissa v Singh* [1942] 1 All ER 362; *Golder v Great Boulder Proprietary Gold Mines Ltd* (1952) 33 TC 75; *IR Commrs v Carron Co* (1968) 45 TC 18; *Mallalieu v Drummond* [1983] BTC 380; *McKnight (HMIT) v Sheppard* [1999] BTC 236; *Icebreaker 1 LLP v R & C Commrs* [2011] BTC 1,579

Other Material: HMRC *Business Income Manual* BIM42955

Tax Reporter: ¶217-700

Expenditure not allowable

By contrast, the following expenditure has been disallowed.

- Fines or other penalties imposed in relation to illegal, etc. transactions (*IR Commrs v Alexander von Glehn & Co Ltd*; *McKnight (HMIT) v Sheppard*).
- Damages paid in an action for negligence (*Strong & Co v Woodifield* (not incurred by the taxpayer in his capacity of a trader but as a householder)).
- Costs incurred by an accountant in defending (successfully) criminal proceedings on a charge of conspiracy to defraud HMRC (*Spofforth & Prince v Golder* (not wholly and exclusively laid out for the purposes of the taxpayer's profession)).
- Cost of legal advice obtained by the partners of the accused in *Spofforth & Prince* (above), after a decision to obtain independent advice was made (same reason).
- Damages and costs paid as a result of a libel action (*Fairrie v Hall* (not incurred wholly and exclusively for business purposes)).
- Payments and indemnities to settle an action for damages (*Hammond Engineering Co Ltd v IR Commrs* (appeal commissioners entitled to

conclude that payments were not made wholly and exclusively for business purposes).

- Costs in connection with application to the Transport Tribunal for variation of a road haulage licence (*Pyrah v Annis & Co Ltd* (capital, not revenue expense)).
- Solicitors' fees relating to work carried out in connection with litigation in a dissolution action brought by one partner against the other (*C Connelly & Co v Wilbey (HMIT)*) (expenses incurred by the taxpayer to protect his interests in the partnership could not be regarded as an expense of the practice).
- Legal fees in connection with a series of planning appeals, where it was held that the expenditure did not relate to the maintenance of an existing capital asset (*Market South West (Holdings) Ltd*).

The HMRC view is that the following types of payment are unlikely to be deductible:

- a payment to facilitate the winding-up of a business;
- compensation for loss of office connected with a change of control;
- payment to a connected person on termination of an employment; and
- payment to compensate for illegal actions.

In a 'toolkit' issued in June 2014, entitled 'Capital v Revenue Expenditure Toolkit: 2013–14 Self Assessment and Company Tax Returns' (and the previous published for 2010–11 onwards), HMRC have warned that:

> 'Incidental expenditure incurred when acquiring or disposing of an asset should be treated as capital expenditure. The most common example of such expenditure is legal and professional fees incurred in acquiring or disposing of an asset. Incidental expenditure may also include the cost of such items as the transportation and installation of the asset.
>
> ...
>
> When a business incurs expenditure on an unsuccessful attempt to obtain an asset or other advantage that will be of enduring benefit to the business the expenditure is classified as capital for tax purposes, just as it would have been if the attempt were successful.'

The guidance also reminds readers that:

> 'Legal and professional fees incurred in connection with changes in how the ownership of a business is structured are generally regarded as capital for tax purposes and not allowable as a revenue deduction. For example, changing from a sole trader or partnership to a limited company is a change in the capital structure of a business, as is a change in the membership of a partnership.'

This is on the grounds that 'fees incurred in connection with the acquisition, alteration or enhancement of how the ownership of a business is structured should generally be disallowed'.

Cases: *Strong & Co v Woodifield* (1906) 5 TC 215; *Spofforth & Prince v Golder* (1945) 26 TC 310; *Fairrie v Hall* (1947) 28 TC 200; *Pyrah v Annis & Co Ltd* (1956) 37 TC 163; *Hammond Engineering Co Ltd v IR Commrs* (1975) 50 TC 313; *C Connelly & Co v Wilbey (HMIT)* [1992] BTC 538; *McKnight (HMIT) v Sheppard* [1999] BTC 236; *Market South West (Holdings) Ltd* [2010] TC 00432

Other Material: HMRC *Business Income Manual* BIM42955

Tax Reporter: ¶217-700

96-380 Patents

The rules relating to patents are scattered through various parts of the tax legislation. A summary of how the legislation works is as follows:

- a deduction is given for the cost of obtaining (i.e. establishing) a patent (ITTOIA 2005, s. 89);
- capital allowances are given for the cost of buying patent rights (CAA 2001, s. 464ff., though for companies, these rules are broadly superseded by the FA 2002 legislation relating to intangible assets);
- various taxation issues arise when patent rights are sold (ITTOIA 2005, s. 587ff.); and
- tax relief is granted for certain expenses by offsetting them against income from patents (ITTOIA 2005, s. 600ff.).

Tax Reporter: ¶216-900

96-400 Research and development costs

Overview

Research and development allowances are available for certain capital expenditure on research and development. Separate income tax relief, not under the capital allowances code, is available for qualifying revenue expenditure. The following paragraphs relate only to revenue expenditure.

Relief is given both for expenses incurred directly by a trader and for certain payments made to research associations, universities, etc. In each case, the relief is available only to traders and not to those carrying on a profession or vocation. The legislation specifically provides that the same expenses may not be brought into account in relation to more than one trade.

Expenditure meeting the conditions qualifies for tax relief in its own right: it is not then necessary to consider the general 'wholly and exclusively' test.

Legislation: ITTOIA 2005, s. 31, 87–88

Tax deduction

A deduction is allowed in calculating business profits for expenses of a revenue nature incurred on research and development that is 'related to the trade' and that is directly undertaken by or on behalf of the trader. Certain payments to research associations, etc. are also allowed.

Expenses incurred on R&D exclude expenses incurred in acquiring rights in, or arising out of, R&D but (apart from that) include all expenses incurred in carrying out, or providing facilities for carrying out, R&D.

R&D expenditure 'related to a trade' is defined to include R&D which may lead to or facilitate an extension of the trade. It also includes R&D of 'a medical nature which has a special relation to the welfare of workers employed in the trade'.

Revised guidelines on the meaning of research and development for tax purposes, effective from 1 April 2004, were issued by the Secretary of State for Trade and Industry. The full text of these revised guidelines is given at CIRD 81900. The newer guidelines emphasise that R&D relief applies to development work as well as to research work.

Legislation: ITTOIA 2005, s. 87–88

Enhanced relief

Small and medium-sized companies may claim additional or enhanced relief for qualifying research and development expenditure.

Tax Reporter: ¶217-950

96-420 Subscriptions to trade associations, etc

The difficulty regarding payments to trade associations lies in deciding whether the expense is incurred in earning profits or after profits have been ascertained. To the extent that payments fall within the former category, they are deductible. The test applied by the courts is whether or not the expenses which the association meets out of the subscriptions would have been deductible if incurred by the traders themselves.

Where the subscriptions are used by the association for a variety of purposes, some of which pass the test and some of which do not, a corresponding proportion of the subscription is deductible.

The payment of an annual subscription to a local trade association by a non-member is allowed, provided it meets the 'wholly and exclusively' criteria. Subscriptions to the National Farmer's Union are allowable in full. Some trade associations reach an agreement with HMRC under which all subscriptions paid are allowable and the association pays tax on any surplus. Ordinary annual subscriptions to a local trade association are normally allowable in full.

Fixed annual subscriptions to an association outside the UK are normally allowed as a deduction in the absence of any evidence of inadmissibility. Payments to a mutual insurance association for insurance only against trade risks are deductible.

Other Material: ESC B7; HMRC *Business Income Manual* BIM47420ff., BIM55280

Tax Reporter: ¶216-500

96-440 Taxes and penalties

Certain taxes and duties incurred by a trader may be set off against business profits, while others may not. Income tax itself, corporation tax, and capital gains tax are all disallowed on various grounds.

Taxes and duties which are not calculated by reference to profits are generally deductible. These may include:

- local rates, water rates and the like;
- vehicle excise duty, and other customs and excise duties;
- licences required for a particular business (e.g. the sale of liquor); and
- some foreign taxes and duties not levied by reference to profits.

Case: *Harrods (Buenos Aires) Ltd v Taylor-Gooby* (1964) 41 TC 450

Tax Reporter: ¶217-050

96-460 Website development costs

The correct treatment of such costs is not straightforward. In the 'toolkit' issued in June 2014, entitled 'Capital v Revenue Expenditure Toolkit: 2013–14 Self Assessment and Company Tax Returns' (and in the previous 2012–13 version), HMRC commented that 'the appropriate treatment of expenditure on developing a website is dependent on the nature of the expenditure and the function the website performs for the business. If the costs incurred create an enduring asset, consideration should be given to treating the expenditure as capital. If such costs are not identified, there is a risk that these may be incorrectly claimed as revenue expenditure'. The fact that expenditure on website development may be shown in the accounts as advertising or marketing costs does not necessarily mean that it is allowable as revenue expenditure. According to HMRC:

> 'Application and infrastructure costs, including domain name, hardware and operating software that relates to the functionality of the website should normally be treated as capital expenditure. Design and content development costs should normally be treated as capital expenditure to the extent that an enduring asset is created. One such indication may be an expectation that future revenues less attributable costs to be generated by the website will be no less than the amounts capitalised.
>
> A website that will directly generate sales, subscriptions, advertising or other income will normally be regarded as creating an enduring asset and consideration should be given to treating the costs of developing, designing and publishing the website as capital expenditure.
>
> Whilst a revenue deduction would not therefore be allowable, this capital expenditure will generally qualify as expenditure on plant and machinery for capital allowances purposes. Expenditure on initial research and planning, prior to deciding to proceed with development, is normally allowable as revenue expenditure.
>
> The cost of maintaining or updating a website (in relation to price changes, for example) should be treated as revenue expenditure.'

Post-cessation expenditure

96-700 Overview

Tax relief is given for certain expenditure incurred after a trade has ceased. The relief is available to individuals in respect of certain post-cessation expenses including expenses connected with remedying or paying compensation for defective work, collecting debts, and debts that go bad. Relief is given by way of a reduction of income and chargeable gains for the tax year in which the expense is paid. Expenses must be incurred within seven years of the business ceasing. Claims must be made within the specified time.

If a claim is made, certain connected receipts (mainly insurance receipts) are specified as being taxable as post-cessation receipts.

Relief is not given under these rules where it has been given, or is available, under any other provision of the Income Tax Acts.

Legislation: ITA 2007, s. 96ff.

Tax Reporter: ¶223-200ff.

96-720 Scope of the relief

Relief is available for payments made wholly and exclusively for the following purposes:

- remedying, or paying damages for, defective work, goods or services;
- paying legal or other professional expenses connected with claims that work, goods or services were defective;
- insuring against either of the above eventualities; and
- collecting a debt which has been recognised in the taxable profit of the former business.

HMRC guidance confirms that 'the expenses covered by the relief include for example the costs of remedying defective work done while the business continued, professional indemnity insurance and damages payments'.

Legislation: ITA 2007, s. 96ff.

Other Material: HMRC *Business Income Manual* BIM80715

Tax Reporter: ¶223-200ff.

96-740 Method of relief

The amount of the payment is set-off against income for the tax year in which the payment is made or treated as made. Any excess of the payment above the income of the year is treated as an allowable loss for capital gains tax arising in that year, though there is an upper limit on the amount which may be set-off in this way. The order of set-off in the chargeable gains calculation is not directly set out, but from the above rules the implied order is as follows:

(1) capital losses of the year;

(2) post-employment qualifying amounts;.

(3) relevant post-cessation expenditure;

(4) trading losses under TCGA 1992, s. 261B;

(5) the annual exempt amount;

(6) capital losses brought forward.

There is no provision to carry forward amounts unrelieved under these provisions against income and gains of future years. Therefore, such unrelieved expenditure can only be set against any future post-cessation receipts.

Relief is not available in respect of payments made or events occurring after 11 January 2012 where the main purpose or one of the main purposes is the obtaining of a reduction in tax liability. A payment is not caught if pursuant to an unconditional obligation in a contract made before 12 January 2012.

Legislation: ITA 2007, s. 96ff., 98A

Tax Reporter: ¶223-200ff.

Trading receipts: general principles

97-000 Introduction

As noted at 92-000, income tax is charged on the 'profits' of a trade, profession or vocation. It follows that rules are needed to determine which types of income need to be taken into account for tax purposes and which types of expenditure may be deducted in calculating profits for those purposes.

Subject to any express provision to the contrary, the concept of 'trading receipts' is to be interpreted as meaning any items brought into account as credits in calculating the profits, whether or not an amount has been actually received.

In general, capital allowance balancing charges are treated as trading receipts.

Legislation: ITTOIA 2005, s. 5, 27, 28

Other Material: HMRC *Business Income Manual* BIM71025

Tax Reporter: ¶220-000ff.

97-010 Non-monetary consideration and 'money's worth'

Finance Act 2016 made clear that trading (and property) income received in non-monetary forms should be brought into account at full open market value in calculating taxable profits. The provisions are effective for all transactions occurring after 16 March 2016.

Legislation: ITTOIA 2005, s. 28A

97-020 Capital and revenue receipts

There is a general rule that items of a capital nature are not taxed as trading receipts. This general rule is specifically stated in the legislation, thus reinforcing the application of normal accounting principles. Nevertheless, the statutory rule is subject to various exceptions as indicated later in this chapter.

Numerous cases have reached the courts concerning the correct treatment of a receipt, and in particular the issue of whether it is revenue or capital in nature.

There is some correlation with the *principles* applying to determine whether expenditure is revenue or capital, but a moment's thought makes it clear that the treatment of an individual item may be capital for one party but not for the other.

> **Example**
>
> A manufacturer of fizzy drinks spends £2m to have a new factory constructed. For the building company, the £2m is an ordinary trading receipt but for the drinks manufacturer the payment is self-evidently capital in nature.

Before the introduction of capital gains tax, the distinction between revenue and capital receipts was often fundamental – a high tax charge or no liability at all. Generally, that is less true now but the distinction is still important if the receipt is to be taxed in the correct way; for example, the deductions and allowances allowed when taxing a capital receipt are very different to those applying to a trading receipt.

Legislation: ITTOIA 2005, s. 96

Tax Reporter: ¶220-200ff.

Trading receipts: compensation and similar receipts

97-040 Compensation for loss of stock

An amount received by way of compensation for losses of trading stock would be trading income. See, for example, the cases of *J Gliksten & Son Ltd v Green* and *Rownson, Drew & Clydesdale Ltd v IR Commrs.*

The position is similar where stock is taken over by a Government authority. Thus, a sum awarded as a result of the compulsory taking over of a stock of rum by the Admiralty was held to be income (*IR Commrs v Newcastle Breweries Ltd*). In *London Investment & Mortgage Co Ltd v Worthington,* a property dealing company received value payments under the *War Damage Act* 1943 in respect of its properties damaged by enemy action. The company disposed of some of the properties but retained others as part of its stock-in-trade and either was having them rebuilt or would have them rebuilt. The House of Lords held that the payments were part of the taxpayer's trading receipts as they were money into which their stock-in-trade had been converted.

Cases: *J Gliksten & Son Ltd v Green* (1929) 14 TC 364; *IR Commrs v Newcastle Breweries Ltd* (1930) 12 TC 927; *Rownson, Drew & Clydesdale Ltd v IR Commrs* (1931) 16 TC 595; *London Investment & Mortgage Co Ltd v Worthington* (1956) 38 TC 86

Tax Reporter: ¶220-600

97-060 Compensation re land

There have been a number of cases where the question in dispute has been whether compensation in connection with freeholds, leaseholds or structural improvements is liable to tax as trading income. In general, it may be said that a lump sum payment by way of compensation for damage to freehold or leasehold property, or to structural improvements thereon, is a capital receipt. On the other hand, there may be instances where the temporary deprivation of the use of freehold or leasehold property is in the nature of compensation for the loss of profits (see below) or may even be in the nature of a rent or a fee for the use of property. Again, instead of a lump sum payment, compensation may take the form of periodical payments and the question would then arise whether the payments are fixed instalments of a lump sum or are a series of income payments.

In *Boyce v Whitwick Colliery Co Ltd*, the taxpayer at the request of a local authority erected plant and buildings for the purpose of pumping water from its mine and making it available for distribution. The local authority agreed to make annual payments to the taxpayer for water supplied, and to pay in addition 30 annual instalments totalling the capital expenditure incurred by the taxpayer in providing the plant and buildings. At the expiration of the agreement, the plant and buildings were to remain the property of the taxpayer. It was held that the annual instalments were not revenue receipts but were payments received by the taxpayer to reimburse it for the capital expenditure incurred by it at the instance of the local authority.

In *Watson v Samson Brothers*, the taxpayers owned part of their farmland and were tenants of the remainder. Part of their farm consisted of pasture land which was flooded by the sea in 1953 and, pursuant to the *Coastal Flooding (Emergency Provisions) Act* 1953, the taxpayers received two acreage payments in respect of the rehabilitation of the pasture land damaged by salt water. It was held that the primary purpose of the making of the acreage payments was to restore the pasture land to productivity, that the land was a capital asset and that the sums so received were capital receipts.

Cases: *Boyce v Whitwick Colliery Co Ltd* (1934) 18 TC 655; *Watson v Samson Brothers* (1959) 38 TC 346

Tax Reporter: ¶220-650

97-080 Compensation for loss of profits and sterilisation of assets

A lump sum payment may be received for compensation by way of damages in respect of loss of profit, or otherwise directly related to the business operations. Almost invariably, such amounts have been held to be taxable as trading receipts.

By contrast, amounts received for the 'sterilisation' of assets (such as in *Glenboig Union Fireclay Co Ltd v IR Commrs*) are of a capital nature. Similarly, compensation paid for some restriction upon the activities or operations of the recipient or upon the use of capital may also be of a capital nature. Many of the cases pre-date the introduction of capital gains tax and most of the amounts that escaped income tax would now be taxed under the CGT rules.

In *Glenboig*, the appellant company was lessee of certain fireclay fields over part of which ran the lines of the Caledonian Railway Co. The railway company exercised its statutory powers to require part of the fireclay to be left unworked on payment of compensation. The House of Lords held that the compensation was not a profit earned in the course of the company's trade, but was a capital receipt, being a payment for the sterilisation of a capital asset. The fact that, in determining the amount of compensation, consideration was given to the profits that would have been earned from the fireclay left unworked was held to be immaterial and the point to be determined was for what the compensation was paid.

After pointing out that a capital asset of the company had been sterilised and destroyed and that it was for this that the compensation was paid, Lord Buckmaster said at p. 463–464:

> 'It is unsound to consider the fact that the measure, adopted for the purpose of seeing what the total amount should be, was based on considering what are the profits that would have been earned.
>
> That, no doubt, is a perfectly exact and accurate way of determining the compensation, for it is now well settled that the compensation payable in such circumstances is the full value of the minerals that are to be left unworked, less the cost of working, and that is, of course, the profit that would be obtained

> were they in fact worked. But there is no relation between the measure that is used for the purpose of calculating a particular result and the quality of the figure that is arrived at by means of the application of that test. I am unable to regard this sum of money as anything but capital money ...'

However, there are a number of cases where amounts have been held to be received as compensation for the loss of profits (rather than for deprivation of assets) for the use of assets, or for some restriction upon the operations of the recipient. In such cases, the amount of compensation is of a revenue nature and is assessable as such.

Thus the *Glenboig* case may be contrasted with other cases where a capital asset has been rendered only partly inoperative for a period of time. Thus, in *Ensign Shipping Co Ltd v IR Commrs*, an amount received from the Government because ships had been compulsorily detained by it for periods of 15 and 19 days respectively, was held to be a trading receipt and assessable to tax. All that had happened from a business point of view was that the two vessels had arrived much later to the ports to which they were consigned, with the result that for the number of days they were late they could not make any earnings.

Similarly, in *Burmah Steamship Co Ltd v IR Commrs*, the amount received from ship repairers as compensation for a delay beyond the time stipulated for the completion of repairs to a ship, was held to be in the nature of income. Lord President Clyde distinguished the *Glenboig* case and said, in effect, that the amount recovered was to fill a 'hole' in the profits caused by the delay.

In *London and Thames Haven Oil Wharves v Attwooll*, the taxpayer owned several jetties at its oil installation. While coming alongside one of the jetties, a tanker was negligently steered and struck the jetty, causing it serious damage. Repairs for the physical damage amounted to £83,168 but, in addition, there was consequential damage quantified at £32,450 for the loss of use of the jetty for 380 days while it was being repaired (though the amount actually received was somewhat less). In what has come to be regarded as the authoritative statement of the applicable principles, Diplock LJ explained:

> 'Where, pursuant to a legal right, a trader receives from another person compensation for the trader's failure to receive a sum of money which, if it had been received, would have been credited to the amount of profits (if any) arising in any year from the trade carried on by him at the time when the compensation is so received, the compensation is to be treated for income tax purposes in the same way as that sum of money would have been treated if it had been received, instead of the compensation.
>
> The rule is applicable whatever the source of the legal right of the trader to recover the compensation. It may arise from a primary obligation under a contract, such as a contract of insurance, from a secondary obligation arising

> out of non-performance of a contract, such as a right to damages, either liquidated, as under the demurrage clause in a charterparty, or unliquidated, from an obligation to pay damages for tort, as in the present case, from a statutory obligation, or in any other way in which legal obligations arise.'

Cases: *Glenboig Union Fireclay Co Ltd v IR Commrs* (1922) 12 TC 427; *Ensign Shipping Co Ltd v IR Commrs* (1928) 12 TC 1169; *Burmah Steamship Co Ltd v IR Commrs* (1931) 16 TC 67; *London and Thames Haven Oil Wharves v Attwooll* (1966) 43 TC 491

Tax Reporter: ¶220-200ff.

Interruption of use

Compensation paid for the destruction or exhaustion of a source of profit may constitute a capital receipt but this will not apply where use of a capital asset is merely interrupted. In *Able (UK) Ltd v R & C Commrs* , compensation for the temporary interruption of the use of the company's land as a landfill site was held to be a trading rather than a capital receipt. It was not possible to identify any source of income, derived from the landfill site, that was exhausted or realised.

The value of the land depended upon its capacity to produce profits from the deposit of waste. That capacity was temporarily interrupted by the service of a compulsory purchase order, and during the period of interruption the market for household and general waste had reduced significantly. But the capacity of the land was not in any way exhausted. The landfill site continued to be licensed for the deposit of both general and special waste but its potential could not be fulfilled because of the change in the market. The cause of the taxpayer's inability to use it for the deposit of general waste was the alteration in market conditions. The temporary interruption to the use of the site had no permanent impact on the site as source of profit from the deposit of general waste.

Case: *Able (UK) Ltd v R & C Commrs* [2008] BTC 3

97-100 Financial loss allowances (e.g. jury service)

Where a payment is made to compensate for loss of trading, etc. (e.g. to an individual on jury service) the recipient must treat the payment as a trading receipt. This is confirmed in the *Business Income Manual*, which states:

> 'Financial loss allowances, sometimes known as payment for loss of earnings, are paid to members of various public bodies for loss of remunerative time and, in some cases, for additional expenses, incurred while engaged on the duties of those bodies.'

Where the recipient is self-employed, the amounts received are made for the purpose of filling a hole in the profits of the trade, profession or vocation and are taxable receipts of the business. This follows the principles set out in *London & Thames Haven Oil Wharves Ltd v Attwooll*.

Payments that do not fill 'a hole in the profits' of the trade, profession or vocation are not taxable receipts of the business. For example a day subsistence allowance is not a payment to make up for the loss of profits, nor does it cover additional expenses of the business. It covers additional personal expenses. It will not be a taxable receipt of the business.

Case: *London & Thames Haven Oil Wharves Ltd v Attwooll* (1966) 43 TC 491

Other Material: HMRC *Business Income Manual* BIM40475; see also www.hmcourts-service.gov.uk

Tax Reporter: ¶220-800

97-120 Deficient services

Utility companies (for example) may pay compensation to customers for interruptions and other deficiencies in the service provided. Such a receipt will need to be considered on ordinary principles:

- Does the compensation arise from the business activities?
- Is the compensation of an income nature or is it capital?

Where the compensation relates to specific services used wholly by the recipient for business purposes, the compensation will almost invariably be taxable as a trading receipt.

Tax Reporter: ¶220-750

97-140 Receipts for varying or cancelling contracts

Generally speaking, amounts received in connection with the cancellation or variation of trade or other commercial contracts made in the course of carrying on a business are in the nature of income and are subject to tax accordingly. This principle has been established by a long line of cases over many years.

In *IR Commrs v Northfleet Coal and Ballast Co Ltd*, a lump sum received by a quarry company for relieving a purchaser from his contract to purchase a quantity of chalk annually for a period of ten years and to build a wharf at which it could be loaded, was held to be a trading profit.

Again, in *Short Bros Ltd v IR Commrs and Sunderland Shipbuilding Co Ltd v IR Commrs*, sums received for the cancellation of contracts to build ships were found to be a receipt of income and in the ordinary course of the company's trade. See also *Sommerfelds Ltd v Freeman* (compensation for breach of contract received by purchaser of business via vendor, in which a £50,000 lump sum was held to be a revenue receipt).

Moreover, the fact that a contract is new and is concerned with an unusual line of business is not material to the question whether the amounts received under it are in the nature of income or capital (*Shove v Dura Manufacturing Co Ltd*).

See also *A Consultant v HMIT* (compensation for cancellation of consultancy contract), in which a special commissioner held that the termination of the agreement did not affect the whole structure of the [taxpayer's] profit-making apparatus'.

Cases: *Sunderland Shipbuilding Co Ltd v IR Commrs* (1926) 12 TC 955; *IR Commrs v Northfleet Coal and Ballast Co Ltd* (1927) 12 TC 1102; *Short Bros Ltd v IR Commrs* (1927) 12 TC 955; *Shove v Dura Manufacturing Co Ltd* (1941) 23 TC 779; *Sommerfelds Ltd v Freeman* (1966) 44 TC 43; *A Consultant v HMIT* (1998) Sp C 180

Tax Reporter: ¶220-200

97-160 Compensation by way of reimbursement of trading expenses

Where a sum of compensation which is not in itself a trading receipt is paid in reimbursement of trading expenses which are allowable as deductions, such expenses are treated as diminished to the extent of the reimbursement. HMRC will normally accept that effect may be given to this principle by crediting the reimbursement in the trader's accounts when the reimbursed amounts are received.

Other Material: HMRC *Business Income Manual* BIM40130

Tax Reporter: ¶220-900

97-180 Damage to goodwill

In *IR Commrs v David C MacDonald & Co*, it was claimed that (in addition to the loss of an agency agreement) the taxpayers had suffered damage to their goodwill. The question of damage to goodwill was also referred to in *Wiseburgh v Domville* where Lord Evershed MR said that if and in so far as damages were claimed because the taxpayer's goodwill had been impaired he could well conceive that such a sum of damages would not be taxable as a revenue receipt.

In *Beveridge v Ellam (HMIT)*, a special commissioner rejected the taxpayer's argument that annual payments made to him by the French government under a redundancy scheme, which precluded him from finding professional work while in receipt of the payments, were compensation for sterilisation of an asset, namely his qualifications, capabilities and experience. The annual payments were income of the taxpayer chargeable to income tax under what was then Sch. D, Case V (broadly, income from foreign possessions). See also 97-200 below.

Cases: *IR Commrs v David C MacDonald & Co* (1955) 36 TC 388; *Wiseburgh v Domville* (1956) 36 TC 527; *Beveridge v Ellam (HMIT)* (1995) Sp C 62

Tax Reporter: ¶220-300

97-200 Restrictive covenants

Amounts received in consideration of a restrictive covenant – whereby the recipient undertakes not to use specified assets or to trade only with the other party to the agreement – may be of a capital nature and not taxed as a revenue receipt. Nevertheless, in some circumstances, an amount received for limiting or restricting the operations of the recipient may be so taxed, e.g. where it is in the nature of an amount intended to replace profits which would otherwise have been made.

In *Margerison v Tyresoles Ltd*, the taxpayer company carried on in its own works the business of 'tyresoling', a process for renovating old tyres pursuant to a patent which it owned. It also entered into agreements with motor traders under which:

(1) the trader provided suitable premises in which the taxpayer company erected and operated plant to carry out the process, the trader paying a monthly rental for such plant; and

(2) the taxpayer company agreed not to introduce another tyresoling plant nor to canvass for orders within the prescribed territory of the trader but retained the right to tyresole tyres sent direct to its own works by persons within that territory (other than the trader) for their own use.

In return for the rights conferred under (2), the trader, on signing the agreement, made a lump sum payment to the taxpayer company based on the size and capacity of the plant itself. Each agreement was initially for five years but was to continue thereafter indefinitely, subject to six months' notice on either side. However, the agreement was determinable at any time by either side on specified grounds and, if determined by the taxpayer company in certain circumstances within the first five years, part of the lump sum was to be returned to the trader. All tyres processed on the trader's premises were to be invoiced by the company to him at a discount off current list prices and were to be sold by him at prices fixed by the company. The general commissioners found that, on the facts, the lump sum payments were receipts of a capital nature, and Wrottesley J held that there was evidence to support their finding and that they made no error in law.

In *Higgs v Olivier*, the recipient entered into a contract in September 1943 to produce the film 'Henry V' and, during the currency of the agreement, i.e. until September 1944, the recipient was to devote his whole time to the service of the film company. The recipient rendered those services and was paid for them. The film was produced at the end of 1944 and at first achieved limited success. In order to promote its success, the recipient entered into another agreement in July 1945 with the film company whereby, in return for £15,000, he covenanted that for 18 months he would not appear in any capacity in any film for any other film company. The special commissioners decided that the £15,000 did not come to the recipient as part of his income from his vocation as an actor but that it came to him for refraining from carrying on his vocation and was a capital receipt. Harman J agreed with the finding of the special commissioners.

On the other hand, in *Thompson v Magnesium Elektron Ltd*, the taxpayer company manufactured magnesium which required the use of large quantities of liquid chlorine. The taxpayer company proposed to erect its own plant for the production of the chlorine required, and the cost of making it would have been considerably reduced by the sale of caustic soda which is a by-product of the manufacture of chlorine. Before the erection of the plant a chemical company, the largest manufacturers of chlorine in the country, being anxious to avoid competition in the production of caustic soda, entered into negotiations with the taxpayer company which culminated in two agreements between the two companies. The agreements were made in December 1936, and were to remain in force for ten years.

Under the first agreement the taxpayer company was to purchase all the chlorine it required (subject to a certain maximum) from the chemical company at a basic price of £10 per ton. Under the second agreement, the taxpayer company covenanted not to engage in the manufacture of caustic soda or chlorine, except in certain circumstances to meet its requirements of chlorine in excess of that supplied by the chemical company, and the chemical company agreed to pay the taxpayer the sum of £6 and 15 shillings for every ton of caustic soda that the taxpayer company would otherwise have produced.

The special commissioners found that the taxpayer company was paid for refraining from making chlorine and caustic soda, that it was not part of the taxpayer company's trade not to deal with the by-products of the manufacture and that the payments were not trading profits. However, this finding was reversed and the Court of Appeal held that the two agreements of December 1936 could not be regarded as separate and distinct contracts but constituted a composite arrangement under which the taxpayer company was enabled to secure a firm contract for the supply of chlorine it required and that the sums received by it were trade receipts and assessable to tax. It will also be noted that the amount assessed to tax was not a lump sum but a payment for every ton of caustic soda which the taxpayer would otherwise have produced and perhaps could be said to be in the nature of continuing payments of compensation for the profit which it would thereby have made.

Cases: *Margerison v Tyresoles Ltd* (1942) 25 TC 59; *Thompson v Magnesium Elektron Ltd* (1943) 26 TC 1; *Higgs v Olivier* (1952) 33 TC 136

Tax Reporter: ¶220-350

97-220 Exclusivity agreements

The question whether amounts received for 'exclusive trade tie' agreements are assessable as income has arisen mostly in connection with service station proprietors who have entered into arrangements with oil companies whereby they have agreed to sell exclusively the products of the particular company with which they have made such an arrangement. Such service stations became known as 'one brand' service stations.

The agreement or arrangement between the oil company and the service station proprietor has taken a variety of forms but most commonly the service station proprietor has received a sum in consideration of entering into a covenant to sell exclusively the products of the other party to the agreement. In some instances the oil company has agreed to expend moneys on improvements to the premises of the garage proprietor but in other cases has agreed to expend moneys on revenue items on behalf of the service station proprietor.

Initially HMRC sought to treat amounts so received by the garage proprietor as assessable to tax as income but appeals against such assessments were often successful.

In *Evans v Wheatley*, the taxpayer, who was the proprietor of a garage and petrol filling station, entered into an agreement with the Regent Oil Co, whereby the latter undertook to reimburse him for sums expended by him on 'sales promotion, cooperative advertising and dealer display' in connection with the sale of Regent Oil Co's motor fuel at his garage. Wynn-Parry J held that an amount of £575 received under the agreement was a trading receipt and not a receipt of capital.

The decision in *Evans v Wheatley* was distinguished in *IR Commrs v Coia (Achilles Motor Co)*. In reaching the conclusion that certain receipts were capital in nature, the Lord President said that the case was in marked contrast to *Evans v Wheatley* where the expenditure was on sales promotion and advertising, matters essentially of a revenue nature; in the present case the expenditure was to reimburse the respondent for expenditure of a capital nature. Lord Patrick pointed out that the taxpayer had parted with a valuable asset of a capital nature, namely his right to obtain supplies of fuel oils from such sources as he might consider most advisable from the point of view of his business. A similar decision was reached in *McLaren v Needham*. See also *Walter W Saunders Ltd v Dixon*.

It is submitted that the cases which have been discussed clearly show that an amount received for a trade tie such as that given in relation to a 'one-brand' service station, if received in a lump sum or by way of effecting or as a contribution to capital improvements, is a receipt of capital, but where the consideration for the tie is in the nature of income (e.g. an annual payment) or is a reimbursement of revenue expenditure, it is assessable as income.

It is the practice of HMRC, in determining whether the sum paid is income or capital, to look at the purpose for which the payment was made. In doing so, they will look at the particular agreement and the correspondence and discussions which supplemented its terms. If the payer stipulates a particular capital purpose, and the funds are spent accordingly, the receipt will be regarded as a capital receipt. If no such purpose is specified and the recipient is free to spend the funds as he wishes, HMRC will regard the sum as a taxable trading receipt, on the authority of *Ryan (HMIT) v Crabtree Denims Ltd*.

Cases: *Evans v Wheatley* (1958) 38 TC 216; *IR Commrs v Coia (Achilles Motor Co)* (1959) 38 TC 334; *McLaren v Needham* (1960) 39 TC 37; *Walter W Saunders Ltd v Dixon* (1962) 40 TC 329; *Ryan (HMIT) v Crabtree Denims Ltd* [1987] BTC 289

Tax Reporter: ¶220-400

97-240 Franchise agreements

The tax treatment of a fee received by a franchisor depends upon the purpose for which it was paid. It is necessary, therefore, to apply established law to the facts of each case and to the terms of the particular agreement. A typical franchise arrangement might specify the elements to be attributed to the fee payable by the franchisee: for instance, a payment might represent consideration for the acquisition of goodwill or know-how, for training and ongoing management support, for equipment, items of fixed capital, alterations to premises, the franchisor's undertaking not to compete, and so on. The tax treatment of the payments in the hands of the franchisee does not in any way determine their correct tax treatment as receipts of the franchisor.

The main question is to determine whether the initial payment by the franchisee is capital or income in the hands of the franchisor. The test to be applied was succinctly stated by Bankes LJ in *British Dyestuffs Corporation (Blackley) Ltd v IR Commrs*:

> 'Is the transaction in substance a parting by the company with part of its property for a purchase price, or is it a method of trading by which it acquires this particular sum of money as part of the profits and gains of that trade?'

To the extent that the franchise fee receivable by the franchisor is attributable to the provision by the franchisor of goods and services in the course of carrying on a trade, it will be taxed in its hands as a trading receipt. However, a careful analysis may reveal that part of the payment relates to items of a capital nature.

Case: *British Dyestuffs Corporation (Blackley) Ltd v IR Commrs* (1924) 12 TC 586

Tax Reporter: ¶220-450

Other trading receipts

97-280 Bad debts

Where a trade debt for which a deduction has been allowed is subsequently released, the release is generally treated as a trade receipt arising on the date of the release, unless it takes place as part of a statutory insolvency arrangement.

Where the debt is released after the business has been treated for tax purposes as discontinued, the amount released is treated as a post-cessation receipt.

The HMRC view of the meaning of 'released' is as follows:

> 'The "release" of a debt must involve a contractual agreement. A debt is not deemed to be released because the debtor is bankrupt or in liquidation. Where the release is under seal no consideration is necessary. All other releases must involve the debtor giving consideration for the release. The consideration may be in non-monetary form, for example shares. A formal waiver of remuneration is also a release of a debt.'

The guidance also confirms that the section does not apply if there is no release as such, for example because the creditor 'merely writes off the debt, fails to invoice or demand payment, or fails to present a cheque for payment'. However, if proper accounting policy is to show a credit to the profit and loss account for a trade debt written back then that credit should not be adjusted out in the tax computation.

Legislation: ITTOIA 2005, s. 97, 259

Other Material: HMRC *Business Income Manual* BIM40265

Tax Reporter: ¶222-100

97-300 Government grants and subsidies

General principle

As a general rule, grants and subsidies that are intended to supplement trading profits, or to reduce trading losses, are taxable as trading receipts. On the other hand, grants designed as compensation for capital expenditure are not chargeable as trading receipts. Although in certain circumstances these rules are specifically laid down by statute, they are also in line with general principles relating to compensation, discussed above. Indeed, little normally turns on the fact that money is received from the government rather than from a private source.

The distinction may be illustrated by contrasting the cases of *Seaham Harbour Dock Co v Crook* and *Smart v Lincolnshire Sugar Co Ltd*. In the *Seaham Harbour* case a dock company received a grant in connection with the extension of a harbour and ancillary works. Although the amount of the grant was calculated by reference to interest which the company would otherwise have had to pay, the House of Lords held that since the money was received in respect of capital works, it was not a trading receipt.

By way of contrast, in the *Lincolnshire Sugar case*, the taxpayer company carried on the business of manufacturing sugar from beet grown in the UK. Because of a fall in the price of sugar, government aid was provided to manufacturers in the forms of 'advances' in respect of sugar manufactured by them. The relevant Act made provision for the 'advances' to be repayable in certain circumstances, but otherwise not to be repayable. In the event, the payments to the taxpayer company became irrevocable. The House of Lords held that the payments were in the nature of subsidies, intended artificially to supplement the company's trading receipts and enable it to maintain its trading solvency.

Cases: *Seaham Harbour Dock Co v Crook* (1931) 16 TC 333; *Smart v Lincolnshire Sugar Co Ltd* (1937) 20 TC 643

Tax Reporter: ¶221-000

Grant payments under the* Industrial Development Act *1982, etc.

Certain payments made to a trader (but not to a person carrying on a profession or vocation) are specifically taken into account as business receipts in computing trading profits. The grant is not, however, taxed if it is designated as made towards the cost of specified capital expenditure, or as made by way of compensation for the loss of capital assets. Similarly, there is no tax charge under this rule if the grant is for all or part of a corporation tax liability (including one that has already been met).

Subject to the above exceptions, payments will be treated as trading receipts if the payment is made by way of a grant under:

- the *Industrial Development Act* 1982, s. 7 or 8; or
- the *Industrial Development (Northern Ireland) Order* 1982 (SI 1982/1083), art. 7, 9 or 30.

Replying to a Parliamentary Question, the Financial Secretary to the Treasury said:

> 'The precise tax treatment will depend on the facts of each case, but, in general, regional selective assistance is taken into account in determining the taxable profits of a business.'

Legislation: ITTOIA 2005, s. 105

Other Material: *Hansard*, 20 January 1988 col. 727–728

Business start-up payments

These are taxable receipts. Special rules ensure that they are not taxed twice if received during an overlap period.

Legislation: ITTOIA 2005, s. 207

97-320 Insurance proceeds

General principle

A sum has to be brought into account as a trading receipt if:

- a deduction has been allowed in calculating trading profits for a loss or expense; and

- the trader, in relation to that loss or expense, recovers a sum under an insurance policy or contract of indemnity.

If the sum is of a revenue nature it will be brought into account on ordinary principles. In relation to a capital sum, the receipt is taxable by virtue of a specific statutory provision, but only to the extent that a deduction has been allowed.

Legislation: ITTOIA 2005, s. 106

Tax Reporter: ¶221-200

Insurance receipts from locum and fixed practice expenses policies

Some professional people who practise alone or in partnership, in particular medical professionals, take out insurance policies to indemnify themselves against the cost of engaging a *locum tenens*, or against other practice expenses, in the event of the policyholder's illness or other incapacity. HMRC's policy is to treat the benefits derived from such policies as taxable receipts of the profession. Equally, the premiums are treated as deductible expenses.

As the premiums are treated as a deductible business expense, the benefits do not fall within the exemption in ITTOIA 2005, s. 735 (health and employment insurance payments).

Other Material: HMRC *Business Income Manual* BIM45565

Tax Reporter: ¶221-250

Key man policies

In a case with fairly complex facts, it was held that the proceeds of some £586,000 from a series of key man insurance policies constituted a capital receipt (*Greycon Ltd v Klaentschi (HMIT)*).

It is suggested that this case does not provide a precedent for treating all key man insurance policy proceeds as capital in nature. The HMRC manuals are silent on the treatment, other than a few minor references that do not address the main question of how the proceeds should be treated. The *Pension Schemes Manual* refers to text on the subject that has been 'withheld under the Code of Practice on Access to Government Information'.

Case: *Greycon Ltd v Klaentschi (HMIT)* (2003) Sp C 372

Tax Reporter: ¶221-300

97-340 Surplus business accommodation

Where a business lets our surplus business accommodation, the rents received may often be treated as trading receipts rather than treated as a separate source of property income. This was previously a matter of practice rather than a strict application of the law but now has statutory force. For this treatment to apply for tax purposes, all of the following conditions must be met:

(1) the accommodation must be temporarily surplus to current business requirements;

(2) the accommodation must not be held as trading stock;

(3) the individual premises must be partly used for the business and partly let. The point of the provision is to avoid the need to apportion expenses between different premises. Thus 'the treatment cannot be applied to whole buildings which are let because there is no question of any apportionment of expenses being necessary';

(4) the rental income must be comparatively small;

(5) the receipts and expenses of letting are such as would otherwise be brought into account in calculating the profits of a property business carried on by the trader; and

(6) the rents must be for surplus business accommodation only (and not for land).

If the trader ceases to occupy the premises for business purposes then the rents will have to be taxed on a statutory basis from the end of the period of accounts in question.

Accommodation will only be treated as meeting the first condition above if it has been used for the purposes of the trade (or has been acquired) within the last three years, if the trader intends to use it for trading purposes in the future, and if the letting is for a period of not more than three years.

Legislation: ITTOIA 2005, s. 21

Other Material: HMRC *Business Income Manual* BIM41015

Tax Reporter: ¶222-300

97-360 Acquisition of trade: receipts from transferor's trade

A special rule ensures that receipts are not lost to the tax system when a trade is transferred from one person to another. Specifically, certain sums must be brought into account for tax purposes if:

- a person (the transferor) has permanently ceased trading;

- at the date of cessation, the transferor transferred to another person (the transferee) the right to receive sums arising from the carrying on of the trade; and
- the transferee subsequently carries on the transferor's trade.

The transferee must then bring into account any sums received as a result of the transfer to the extent that these are not brought into account by the transferor in calculating any profits (whether for income or corporation tax purposes) for a period before the cessation. The transferee must bring them into account when received. Any such sums as are mentioned in the second bullet point above, and as are only received after the cessation of the transferor's trade, are not treated as post-cessation receipts.

A question may arise as to whether particular receipts are properly taxable on the transferor or on the transferee. This point was tested in the special commissioner case of *Rafferty v R & C Commrs*, in which a self-employed sales associate sold his business to a company which thereafter received any commissions relating to policies sold before the transfer. The special commissioners decided that, when a taxpayer sold his business on his retirement, the part of the consideration which represented fees and commissions was not taxable on the taxpayer but on the transferee; the trade was treated as permanently discontinued by reason of a change in the persons carrying it on and the right to receive the renewal commissions was transferred to the transferee.

Legislation: ITTOIA 2005, s. 98

Case: *Rafferty v R & C Commrs* (2005) Sp C 475

Tax Reporter: ¶222-150

97-380 Rental receipts under finance leases

A lease is an agreement whereby one person (the lessor) agrees to hire an asset to another person (the lessee). At one end of the scale, a car might be leased for a few hours. At the other end, a property company might lease an extensive office block to another over a period of many years.

See 113-450 for commentary on the rules introduced by FA 2006.

Legislation was introduced in the *Finance Act* 1997 to counter a perceived abuse of the tax system. The principal purpose of the anti-avoidance provisions is to tax the lessor, over the term of the lease, on an amount equivalent to the income return under the lease as ascertained for accounting purposes in accordance with generally accepted accounting practice.

Legislation: CTA 2010, s. 900

Website: www.hmrc.gov.uk/ria/ria-leasingreform.pdf

Tax Reporter: ¶221-600ff.

97-400 Unclaimed moneys

When a business receives money on behalf of a customer and the customer forgets to claim it from the business, the unclaimed money is not a business receipt. The money never belonged to the business, was never part of its income and cannot subsequently become so. This principle was illustrated in *Morley v Tattershall*, in which a firm of auctioneers received money from sales which they held for vendors. Unclaimed sums were transferred to partners' accounts. These sums were clients' moneys and could not subsequently become trading receipts.

However, sometimes the money becomes that of the business by operation of law and in such cases it may be held to be a business receipt. This was the outcome of *Jay's The Jewellers Ltd v IR Commrs* in which unclaimed balances held by pawnbrokers became theirs by operation of statute. In this case, it was held that these were trading receipts because their character had altered by operation of law.

If the payment is strictly a deposit, which means that it goes towards the cost of whatever is ordered, then this would be a business receipt even though whatever was ordered was not collected *(Elson v Prices Tailors Ltd)*. In practice, HMRC advise that 'the deposit should be recognised either when the goods or services are provided or when it is reasonably certain that no goods or services will ever be provided and the deposit will be forfeited'.

It is relevant to determine the reason for an overpayment and to decide whether the retention of surpluses is part of the trading activities. Where it is, such sums will be taxable. In the special commissioners' case of *Anise Ltd & Ors v Hammond (HMIT)*, the overpaid sums were received by error of the customer or of the bank. They were not received as trading receipts and the nature of the sums could not change after receipt. Where the payments are received in consequence of a business carried on by the recipient, however, they will be taxable as income of that business. This was the outcome of *Pertemps Recruitment Partnership Ltd* where the appellant, a recruitment agency, had released to its profit and loss account monies paid to it in error by its customers. The tribunal found that the payments made in error had the same characteristics in the hands of the appellant as payments made for its services. The *Pertemps* tribunal also noted that the decision of the special commissioners in *Anise* was inconsistent with the later case of *Forbes v Director of the Asset Recovery*

Agency (a case concerning fraudulent trading) where it was found that the liability to make refunds did not prevent the receipts being treated as trading profits.

The principle of determining the status of an asset at the outset was confirmed in the *Gower Chemicals* case, where the commissioner commented that 'it must either be a trading receipt from the beginning or not at all'.

Cases: *Morley v Tattershall* (1938) 22 TC 51; *Jay's The Jewellers Ltd v IR Commrs* (1947) 29 TC 274; *Elson v Prices Tailors Ltd* (1962) 40 TC 671; *Anise Ltd v Hammond (HMIT)* (2003) Sp C 364; *Forbes v Director of the Asset Recovery Agency* (2007) Sp C 613; *Gower Chemicals Ltd v R & C Commrs* (2008) Sp C 713; *Pertemps Recruitment Partnership Ltd* [2010] TC 00519

Other Material: HMRC *Business Income Manual* BIM31110

Tax Reporter: ¶220-050

97-420 Reverse premiums

Introduction and overview

Financial inducements to take a lease made by landlords to potential tenants ('reverse premiums') are taxable as revenue receipts. If the recipient has entered into the property transaction for trading purposes then the reverse premium is brought into account in calculating trading profits. (In any other case, it is charged as a property business receipt in accordance with ITTOIA 2005, s. 311.)

The commercial background to the making of such reverse premiums can be complex. A payment will be made where a landlord wishes to encourage a tenant to take a lease at a particular rental value. In the case of a commercial shopping centre, for example, the landlord may wish to encourage a popular 'anchor tenant' to move in, thereby attracting shoppers and increasing the value of the remaining parts of the centre. If the landlord is a property investor, the payment of a reverse premium may lead to a higher monthly rental payment; this will in turn increase the value of the freehold should the landlord wish to sell it on.

Legislation: ITTOIA 2005, s. 101

Other Material: HMRC *Business Income Manual* BIM41050ff.

Tax Reporter: ¶222-200

Meaning of 'reverse premium'

Apart from certain 'excluded cases' (see below), a reverse premium is a payment or other benefit that meets the following conditions:

(1) a person receives the payment or other benefit by way of an inducement in connection with a transaction, whether that transaction is entered into by the recipient or by a person connected with the recipient;

(2) the transaction is one under which the recipient or connected person becomes entitled to an estate, interest or right in or over land; and

(3) the payment or other benefit is made or provided by:

    (a) the person ('the grantor') by whom the estate, interest or right is now granted, or was granted at an earlier time;

    (b) a person connected with the grantor; or

    (c) a nominee of, or person acting on the directions of, either of the above.

As to the meaning of 'payment or other benefit', HMRC comment that:

> 'the legislation charges only benefits procured by actually laying out money. It does not catch inducements which represent amounts foregone or deferred by the operator, such as rent free periods or reduced rents. The smaller deduction for rent payable will reflect such inducements in the tenant's chargeable profits.'

In addition to cash payments, though, the following are listed as examples of benefits that would be caught:

- a contribution specified to be towards the tenant's costs, such as start up, fitting out or relocation;
- assumption by a landlord of the tenant's liabilities under an existing lease, such as a continuing obligation to pay rent, or the payment of a lump sum to terminate it;
- other sums paid to third parties to satisfy some obligation of the tenant; and
- payment of cash by indirect means, for example writing off a loan which is a liability of the tenant.

Legislation: ITTOIA 2005, s. 99

Other Material: HMRC *Business Income Manual* BIM41075ff.

Excluded cases

There are various circumstances in which a payment or other benefit will not be a reverse premium:

- if (or to the extent that) the payment is brought into account under CAA 2001, s. 532 (the general rule excluding contributions) to reduce the recipient's expenditure qualifying for capital allowances;
- if the person entering into the transaction is an individual, and the transaction relates to premises to be occupied as that individual's only or main residence; and
- so far as the payment or other benefit is consideration for the transfer of an estate or interest in land which constitutes the sale in a sale and lease-back arrangement.

In practice, this legislation does not catch inducements to buy a freehold interest in land.

Legislation: ITTOIA 2005, s. 100

Other Material: HMRC *Business Income Manual* BIM41105

Anti-avoidance (arrangements not at arm's length)

The whole amount or value of the reverse premium is brought into account as a taxable receipt in the 'first relevant period of account' where:

- two or more parties to the 'property arrangements' are connected persons; and
- the terms of the arrangements are such as would reasonably have been expected had those person been dealing at arm's length.

The latter condition is met if the terms differ to a significant extent from those which would be regarded as normal and reasonable in the prevailing market conditions between persons dealing with each other at arm's length in the open market. The test is to be applied at the time the arrangements are entered into.

The first relevant period of account is that in which the property transaction is entered into. However, if the property transaction is entered into by the recipient, and for the purposes of a trade, etc. which is only commenced later, the first relevant period of account is that in which he carries on the trade, etc.

For these purposes, persons are treated as connected if they are connected at any time during the period when the property arrangements are entered into. The 'property arrangements' are the property transaction and any arrangements entered into (at whatever time) in connection with it.

Legislation: ITTOIA 2005, s. 102

97-440 Disposals of know-how

Introduction

A particularly difficult application of the distinction between income and capital receipts is the tax treatment of sums received for the sale of secret knowledge, usually referred to as 'know-how'. On the one hand, the seller may be giving up forever secret knowledge which has been the very foundation of a successful business. On the other hand, the seller may simply be imparting knowledge in circumstances where the loss of secrecy will have no adverse effect on his business. On general principles, one would regard the former as a sale of a capital asset, and the latter as an incident in the course of trade. However, statutory rules sometimes override those principles.

Tax Reporter: ¶221-400ff.

Disposal of know-how: trade continues

Where a trader receives consideration for the disposal of know-how that has been used in the trade, the tax treatment depends on whether or not the trade continues. Except so far as it is brought into account as a disposal value for capital allowance purposes, consideration will be treated as a trading receipt if:

- the person continues to trade after the disposal;
- ITTOIA 2005, s. 194 (disposal as part of disposal of trade) does not apply; and
- ITTOIA 2005, s. 195 (seller controlled by buyer, etc.) does not apply.

Where know-how is sold together with other property, a just and reasonable apportionment must be made to determine what figure applies to the disposal of the know-how. This rule applies even if the contract for sale shows specific figures for separate items of property, or even if 'there are, or purport to be, separate sales of separate items' of the property. Where two or more parties to a transaction are affected by an apportionment, there are procedural rules for deciding how the proceedings are to be conducted.

Legislation: CAA 2001, s. 563; ITTOIA 2005, s. 193ff.

Tax Reporter: ¶221-450

Disposal as part of disposal of trade

Where a person disposes of know-how as part of a disposal of his trade, or part of his trade, any sum received for the know-how is treated as a payment for goodwill, i.e. for a capital asset. This applies both to the seller and to the purchaser if they are within the charge to income tax.

The treatment as capital does not apply if both the parties to the transaction so elect; such an election must be made jointly within two years of the disposal. The person making the disposal must be within the charge to income tax but the person acquiring the know-how does not have to be. (It is possible for an equivalent election to be made under the corporation tax provisions (CTA 2009, s. 178). If the person making the acquisition is within the charge to income tax then those making the election under the CTA 2009 provisions are treated as making an election under ITTOIA 2005, s. 194, even though the person making the disposal is not in fact within the charge to income tax.)

The treatment as capital does not apply if the trade in question was carried on wholly outside the UK before the transaction.

Legislation: ITTOIA 2005, s. 194

Tax Reporter: ¶221-500ff.

Disposal to associated body

Where the seller and purchaser of the know-how are bodies controlled by the same person, or where one controls the other, then ITTOIA 2005, s. 193 (see above) does not apply; any sum paid is then treated as a payment for goodwill. For these purposes, a 'body of persons' includes a partnership. Similarly, no election under ITTOIA 2005, s. 194 (see above) may be made where the seller and purchaser of the know-how are bodies controlled by the same person, or where one controls the other.

Legislation: ITTOIA 2005, s. 195

Tax Reporter: ¶221-550

97-460 Gifts and voluntary receipts

A sole trader or partner may receive a gift that is in some way connected with the carrying on of the trade, profession or vocation. The tax treatment of such a gift is not clear cut.

The statutory position is simply that income tax is charged, in relation to business profits, on 'the full amount of the profits of the tax year'. The legislation is silent on the treatment of a gift received by a self-employed person, so general principles must be applied to determine the correct tax treatment.

HMRC guidance quoted in *Taxation* magazine of 11 January 2007 included the following statement:

> 'If a self-employed customer receives a gift as part of their professional activities, then the value of that gift is taken into account in calculating the profit on which they are taxed under Case I/II of Schedule D. The value of the gift is the amount that they could sell it for, not the retail price. If they cannot sell the item, for example a non-transferable holiday with no cash alternative, then there is no amount to be taken into account in arriving at the profit.'

If a person in business receives a gift from a close relative (which HMRC define for these purposes to include 'forebears, offspring, brothers and sisters'), then it will normally be accepted that the person receives it in that personal capacity rather than as a trading receipt (BIM41810).

If a voluntary payment is intended in some way to augment the consideration payable for goods or services (whether past, present or future) then it will be taxable. In support of this view, HMRC quote the cases of *Severne v Dadswell* and *CIR v Falkirk Ice Rink Ltd.*

A payment may escape tax, however, if it is considered a windfall. In *Simpson v John Reynolds & Co (Insurances) Ltd*, the taxpayer had acted for a client for many years but on the client's being taken over by another company, the trading relationship with the client ceased. The client made voluntary payments at the rate of £1,000 per year for five years. The Court of Appeal held that such payments were not trading receipts of an income nature, since they were not received in return for activities carried on by the taxpayer in its trade, but were rather received as a windfall in the nature of a gift.

Cases: *Severne v Dadswell* (1954) 35 TC 649; *CIR v Falkirk Ice Rink Ltd* (1975) 51 TC 42; *Simpson v John Reynolds & Co (Insurances) Ltd* (1975) 49 TC 693

Other Material: HMRC *Business Income Manual* BIM41800ff.

Tax Reporter: ¶222-400

Post-cessation receipts

97-600 Introduction

Certain receipts derived from a trade may not be received until after the trade has ceased. Although ordinary accounting principles will generally ensure that they are taxed, legislation is in place to ensure that such receipts are subject to tax if they have not already been brought into account in calculating trading profits. The person liable for any tax under these rules is the person who receives or who is entitled to the money. Tax is charged on the full amount of the receipts in the tax year but subject to certain allowable deductions and to the option of electing to treat the amount in question as received on the date of cessation.

The rules apply to professions and vocations as they apply to trades. Indeed, the rules in practice apply mainly to professions and vocations as the profits of a trade should invariably be calculated on an earnings basis which will normally take into account amounts received after the cessation of trade. (The profits of the profession or vocation should likewise be calculated on an earnings basis but there are exceptions for certain legal professionals and there is a chance to elect for a different treatment.)

Legislation: ITTOIA 2005, s. 241ff.

Tax Reporter: ¶223-000

97-620 Circumstances in which there is no tax charge

There are various circumstances in which the special rules relating to post-cessation receipts do not apply. No tax charge will be made under these rules if, or to the extent that:

- the receipt is brought into account in calculating trading profits for any period;
- it is otherwise chargeable to income or corporation tax;
- it is received by or on behalf of a non-UK resident who is beneficially entitled to it and it represents income arising outside the UK (see below); or
- it arises from a trade carried on wholly outside the UK.

In the case of a partner in a partnership, no charge arises under these rules if the receipt represents income arising outside the UK from a trade carried on by the firm and the partner's share of the firm's income arising out of the UK is treated as relevant foreign income by ITTOIA 2005, s. 857(3) (partners to whom the remittance basis applies).

The third bullet point above would apply to a trader who has become non-resident. When resident in the UK, all trading profits would have been liable to tax. For a non-resident trader, UK tax would be levied only on profits arising in the UK. The third bullet thus achieves an equivalent exemption for non-residents with post-cessation receipts arising abroad.

Legislation: ITTOIA 2005, s. 6, 243

97-640 Meaning of 'post-cessation receipt'

The legislation provides:

- an initial 'basic' definition of the term;
- an extended definition of amounts that 'count as' post-cessation receipts; and
- certain items that are specifically outside the definition.

The concept of 'post-cessation receipt' is initially defined as a sum which is received after a person permanently ceases to carry on a trade but which arises from the carrying on of the trade before the cessation. A partner will be treated as ceasing to trade if he ceases to be a member of a trading partnership and if his departure from the partnership is treated under ITTOIA 2005, s. 852 as the cessation of his notional trade.

Legislation: ITTOIA 2005, s. 246ff.

Tax Reporter: ¶223-100

97-660 Election for WIP valuation at cost

A person carrying on a profession or vocation immediately before a cessation may elect for work in progress to be valued at cost in calculating the profits of the final period immediately before the cessation. If a valid election is made, then only the amount by which any sums received for the transfer of the work exceed the cost will be treated as a post-cessation receipt.

Legislation: ITTOIA 2005, s. 185

97-680 Debts paid after cessation

A charge will arise if an allowance has been made for a bad or doubtful debt under ITTOIA 2005, s. 35, the trade ceases and a sum is received after the cessation. The legislation is oddly silent on the link needed between the deduction claimed and the sum received, but it must presumably be clearly received in settlement of the debt. The amount taxed cannot exceed the amount in respect of which a deduction was previously made.

As an extension of the above, relief may have been given in the case of a debt released as part of a statutory insolvency arrangement or in the case of a debt proving bad after the cessation of trade. If, in either case, a sum is subsequently received in payment of the debt, this will be treated as a post-cessation receipt up to the amount allowed as a deduction.

Legislation: ITTOIA 2005, s. 248

97-700 Debts released after cessation

There will be a post-cessation receipt where all of the following apply:

- a deduction has been allowed in calculating the trader's profits for an amount owed by him but unpaid;
- the trader has subsequently ceased to trade (or is treated as so); and
- after the cessation, all or part of the debt is released (but not as part of a statutory insolvency arrangement).

The amount so released will be treated as a post-cessation receipt.

Legislation: ITTOIA 2005, s. 249

97-720 Cars and motorcycles

In the case of cars and motorcycles costing over £12,000 there used to be a permanent restriction (of an amount that varied according to the cost) on the amount of the hire cost qualifying for tax relief. Now the £12,000 threshold has disappeared, but there is a 15% restriction for higher emission cars. Any rebate or release of the hire charge must be similarly restricted before being taxed as a post-cessation receipt.

See 94-500 for more detail about the restriction applying to cars (and formerly to motorcycles).

Legislation: ITTOIA 2005, s. 48(4)

97-740 Receipts relating to post-cessation expenditure

A tax charge may arise where relief has been given under ITA 2007, s. 96 in respect of certain post-cessation expenses and where amounts are recovered by way of contribution towards those expenses. Specifically, the following will be treated as post-cessation receipts:

- in the case of a payment to remedy defective work, etc. or to defray expenses of a claim, any insurance proceeds or other sum received by way of contribution to, or reimbursement of, the payment;
- in the case of a payment to insure against claims for defective work, etc. any refund of the premium, or other sum received in connection with the insurance; or
- in the case of a payment for the purpose of collecting a debt, any sum received towards the cost of collecting the debt.

If the reimbursement, etc. is received in a tax year before that in which the related payment is made, it is treated as if received in the later year.

Any necessary adjustment is made by amending an assessment or by discharge or repayment of tax.

Legislation: ITTOIA 2005, s. 250

97-760 Transfer of rights: transferee not trading

The legislation addresses the possibility that the trader ceases trading and transfers to a non-trading third party the right to receive sums subsequently arising from the trade. The former trader will be treated as having a post-cessation receipt of:

- the amount (or value) given for the transfer, if it was at arm's length; or
- the amount (or value) that would have been given for the transfer, if it had been at arm's length.

Any sums subsequently received by the third party are not taxed as post-cessation receipts.

Legislation: ITTOIA 2005, s. 251

97-780 Unremittable income

In certain circumstances, relief is given where income arising abroad cannot be remitted to the UK. If, following such a claim, the income ceases to be unremittable (or a payment is made under the Export Credit Guarantee Department scheme), the receipt will normally be brought into account at that time. If the business has since ceased, however, the income so arising is taxed as a post-cessation receipt. In this case, ITTOIA 2005, s. 243 is disapplied.

Legislation: ITTOIA 2005, s. 841, 844

97-800 Transfer of trading stock or work in progress

It is possible for a person to elect for work in progress to be valued at cost in calculating the profits of the final period immediately before the cessation. In such cases, only the amount by which any sums received for the transfer of the work exceed the cost will then be treated as a post-cessation receipt.

For these purposes, 'trading stock' is defined in accordance with ITTOIA 2005, s. 174 and 'work in progress' and 'transfer of work in progress' are defined in accordance with ITTOIA 2005, s. 183.

Legislation: ITTOIA 2005, s. 185

97-820 Assignment of copyright, etc

A professional author or other creative artist who receives lump sums from the sale of rights in artistic works will have to bring them into account in calculating the profits of the profession. After the death of the author, etc. however, there is no post-cessation receipt if the personal representatives receive a lump sum for assignment by them of the copyright or of the public lending right. This applies to the author of a literary, dramatic, musical or artistic work. The same principle applies where a lump sum is received by personal representatives for the assignment of design right.

In each case, the exemption applies whether the assignment is of the whole or of part of the right.

Legislation: ITTOIA 2005, s. 253

97-840 Post-cessation receipts: deductions

Certain limited deductions are allowed in calculating the amount charged to tax as a post-cessation receipt. More specifically, a deduction is allowed for any 'loss, expense or debit' which would have been allowable in calculating profits for income or corporation tax purposes before discontinuance, or would have been deducted from or set off against such profits.

Losses, expenses and debits arising directly or indirectly from the discontinuance itself are not deductible.

No deduction is allowed if an amount has already been allowed under any other provision of the Tax Acts or as a result of the rules giving CGT relief for post-cessation expenditure.

No deduction is due if a deduction for the same amount has already been made. Any deduction for losses must be made for an earlier year rather than for a later year, but a loss cannot be set against post-cessation receipts arising in a year earlier than the year in which the loss itself arose.

No deduction may be made from any amount treated as a post-cessation receipt under ITTOIA 2005, s. 248(4) (debts paid after cessation) or s. 250 (receipts relating to post-cessation expenditure).

Legislation: ITTOIA 2005, s. 254

Tax Reporter: ¶223-200

97-860 Post-cessation receipts: reliefs

Post-cessation receipts are treated as earned income or relevant UK earnings as long as the following conditions are met:

- the individual has permanently ceased to trade; and
- the trading income constituted relevant UK earnings (within FA 2004, s. 189(2)(b)).

A taxpayer may elect to have a post-cessation receipt treated as if it had been received in the year of cessation instead of in the actual year of receipt. This applies to a post-cessation receipt received in a tax year beginning no later than six years after the person ceased permanently to trade.

The election must be made before 31 January following the end of the tax year in which the amount is received. Effect will be given to the election in the tax year of receipt. There is nothing to prevent an election being made in respect of some post-cessation receipts and not others.

Legislation: TMA 1970, Sch. 1B, para. 5; ITTOIA 2005, s. 256

Tax Reporter: ¶223-300

Trading stock and work in progress: general principles

98-000 Significance

To present an accurate picture of the financial position of a business, the accounts drawn up annually, etc. must take in the trading stock held by the business at the date on which the accounts are prepared. The profit/loss for a given period should be adjusted so that the cost of stock brought forward from the last period is deducted, and the cost of stock carried forward to the next period is added back. Clearly, the method of accounting adopted by a business must be such as is capable of disclosing the stock position at the relevant date.

For the purposes of this topic, it is prudent to distinguish between trades on the one hand and professions and vocations on the other. The legislation makes a broad assumption that trades have trading stock and that professions and vocations have work in progress. There are subtle differences between the tax treatment of the two.

General provisions against the value of stock are disallowed whilst specific write-offs are, on the whole, allowable.

Tax Reporter: ¶224-000ff.

98-050 Definition of trading stock

The only statutory definition of 'trading stock' is in relation to a business cessation; the legislation provides detailed rules as to how such stock must be valued and brought into account when a business ceases. In relation to such a cessation of trade, 'trading stock' is for income tax purposes defined as being either:

- any property (whether land or other property) which is sold in the ordinary course of the trade or would be so sold if it were mature or its manufacture, preparation or construction were complete;
- materials used in the manufacture, preparation or construction of any property mentioned in the above paragraph;
- any services performed in the ordinary course of the trade where the services are wholly or partly completed at the time of the cessation, and where it would be reasonable to expect that a charge would be made for the services if there were no cessation and, in the case of partly completed services, their performance were fully completed; and
- any article produced, and any material used, in the performance of any such services.

The definition is 'an extended one ... not confined to property which is acquired with a view to resale at a profit nor even to property which is traded in, by which I mean property which is acquired to be re-sold at a profit or at a loss or at neither but with a view to a profit on sales as a whole' (per Nourse LJ in *General Motors Acceptance Corporation (UK) Ltd v IR Commrs,* a decision on the old stock relief provisions, which incorporated a similar definition of 'trading stock').

In addition to this statutory definition (with its limited application), certain other principles have emerged from case law precedents.

Legislation: ITTOIA 2005, s. 174

Case: *General Motors Acceptance Corporation (UK) Ltd v IR Commrs* [1987] BTC 71

Tax Reporter: ¶224-050

Items not traded may still be stock

Items in which the business does not trade may nevertheless form part of its trading stock. In *General Motors Acceptance Corporation (UK) Ltd v IR Commrs* (above), a finance company within the General Motors group arranged sales of cars to dealers who did not wish to purchase the cars outright. The company acquired the cars from Vauxhall, the manufacturers, and, before resale, delivered them to dealers for display. The company made its profit from the handling charge paid to it by the dealers.

HMRC contended that because the company did not trade in cars, it could not claim stock relief in respect of them, but the Court of Appeal, affirming the decision of the High Court, held that as the company sold the cars in the ordinary course of its trade as a financial dealer, they formed part of its trading stock. An alternative HMRC argument that the cars were let on hire to the dealers was also rejected.

Property acquired to gain tax relief

Property acquired with the sole objective of obtaining a tax relief is not acquired as trading stock. The cases of *Coates v Arndale Properties Ltd* and *Reed v Nova Securities Ltd* both concerned schemes to obtain group relief by converting a capital loss into a trading loss. In order for relief to be available, the assets in question (a lease in *Arndale*; shares and bank debts in *Nova*) had to be acquired by the respective taxpayer companies and immediately appropriated by them 'as trading stock'.

In the case of *Arndale*, the property was immediately sold on to another member of the group, at a price which left the taxpayer company with a paper profit of £10,000. The House of Lords held that this was merely a book entry with no real effect, and that the property had not been acquired by the taxpayer company as trading stock.

In the *Nova* case, the actual consideration paid for the bank debts was sufficiently realistic for the House of Lords to hold that they were acquired 'as trading stock' (in spite of the fact that the true advantage of the transaction was that the taxpayer company was deemed to acquire the debts for a very much higher price). However, the shares acquired were worthless, and it could not be said that they were acquired as trading stock.

Cases: *Coates v Arndale Properties Ltd* [1984] BTC 438; *Reed v Nova Securities Ltd* [1985] BTC 121

Trading stock or fixed capital

There may be doubt as to whether a particular item is part of the business's trading stock or part of its fixed capital. If the item is part of the stock, its cost may be deductible, but its sale will give rise to a taxable receipt. If the item is part of the fixed capital, neither the deduction nor the receipt will be taken into account in calculating trading profits.

A similar distinction exists between property acquired as stock and property acquired as an investment. Once again, sale of the latter will not give rise to a trading receipt, although it may give rise to a charge to tax on capital gains. Conversely, where an asset is sold at a loss, it is likely to be the taxpayer who will wish to argue that the asset in question was part of his trading stock. There have been many cases on this subject.

98-100 Time at which goods enter stock

The time at which assets are taken into or out of stock will affect the profit for tax purposes. As a general rule, it may be said that goods become part of stock not earlier than the time at which ownership passes to the purchaser, and not later than the time at which the purchaser obtains both ownership and possession. However, there may be circumstances in which a different method may be acceptable.

In the particular case of goods sold subject to reservation of title, HMRC have agreed that goods should be treated as entering the purchaser's stock, provided that the same approach is adopted by both parties to the transactions. Statement of Practice B6 (18 June 1979) includes the following:

> 'Certain traders sell goods on special terms whereby they retain the title to the goods until payment is made. The accountancy bodies have advised their members that, for accountancy purposes, if the circumstances indicate that the reservation of title is regarded by the parties as having no practical relevance except in the event of the insolvency of the buyer, the goods should, notwithstanding the strict legal position, normally be treated as purchases in the accounts of the buyer and sales in the accounts of the supplier.
>
> The Revenue has agreed that for sales subject to reservation of title the above recommended accountancy treatment will be accepted for tax purposes provided that both parties to the contract follow it.
>
> The sale of goods subject to reservation of title as described above is to be distinguished from the supply of goods as consignment stocks eg on a sale or return basis. Goods supplied as consignment stocks are normally to be treated as stock in the hands of the supplier until disposed of by the consignee.'

Tax Reporter: ¶224-200

98-150 Definition of work in progress

As with trading stock, 'work in progress' is defined only in relation to the cessation of a business. In that context, it means services performed in the ordinary course of the profession or vocation:

(1) the performance of which is wholly or partly completed at the time of the cessation; and

(2) for which it would be reasonable to expect that a charge would be made if the profession or vocation had not ceased and (in the case of partly completed services) if the performance of the services had been fully completed.

The term also specifically includes any article produced, and any material used, in the performance of any such services.

Legislation: ITTOIA 2005, s. 183

Tax Reporter: ¶224-100

Valuation of trading stock

98-500 Introduction

With the exception of the special case of discontinuance of trade, there are no statutory provisions governing the valuation of trading stock for tax purposes. As a consequence, the method adopted must be consistent with the ordinary principles of generally accepted accounting practice.

In *Whimster & Co v IR Commrs*, Lord President Clyde stated that the values of stock at the beginning and at the end of the accounting period should be entered at cost or market price, whichever is the lower. This principle has since been adapted to the lower of cost and net realisable value.

Hence, it is open to the trader to enter whichever of cost price or market value is used in the accounts irrespective of which produces the lower profit for tax, though it must be remembered that the same opening stock figure must generally be used if there is a change in the method of valuation in the following account.

It is not necessary that a trader adopt the same method of valuation in respect of all items of stock in the same period: as recognised in *Whimster* above, it is sound accounting practice to value individual items at the lower of the two figures. This method was put to the test in *IR Commrs v Cock Russell and Co Ltd*, in which the whole stock of a firm of wine and spirit merchants was valued at cost, except for a quantity of port whose value had fallen since it was purchased. HMRC argued that the port should be valued at cost along with the rest of the stock. However, the accountancy evidence was overwhelmingly in favour of the method adopted by the taxpayer company, and in absence of any statutory modification for tax purposes, it was held that the company was entitled to value the port at its market value. HMRC now accept this principle.

Cases: *Whimster & Co v IR Commrs* (1925) 12 TC 813; *IR Commrs v Cock Russell and Co Ltd* (1949) 29 TC 387

Tax Reporter: ¶224-500

98-520 UITF 40 – general

During 2005 and early 2006 some vigorous debate was prompted by the issue of 'UITF 40' (i.e. a release by the Urgent Issues Task Force, part of the Accounting Standards Board). The key statement that emerged for debate (contained in Application Note G to Financial Reporting Standard 5) was that:

> 'a seller may obtain a right to consideration when some, but not all, of its contractual obligations have been fulfilled. Where a seller has partially performed its contractual obligations, it recognises revenue to the extent that it has obtained the right to consideration through its performance.'

A typical argument illustrated the debate: if an accountant had completed half of a client's tax return at the accountant's year end, should half of the fee be brought into account (even though this includes both the proprietor's time and the profit element)?

On 1 February 2006, the Association of Taxation Technicians and the Association of Accounting Technicians published guidance for their members on the effect of UITF 40. The guidance was issued subject to the caveat that 'the role of the Task Force is to interpret the standards set by the Accounting Standards Board, and neither the Board nor the Task Force are in a position to endorse guidance which any professional body offers to its members'.

The key points made by the guidance were summarised as follows:

- there had been no change [i.e. as a result of the issue of UITF 40] to the basis of valuation of stocks, work in progress or debtors;
- to recognise revenue from an uncompleted contract, the entity must have reached a point where there is a right to consideration in respect of the work done to date;
- if the right to consideration does not arise until the occurrence of a critical event during the contract, then revenue is not recognised until that event occurs. The incomplete assignment is then valued as work in progress at the lower of cost or its net realisable value;
- however, for many entities there will be no ability to invoice until the immediate task is complete. In those circumstances an uncompleted contract will continue to be valued as work in progress.

Guidance was also provided by the ICAEW.

Where an additional tax charge arises as a result of following the principles outlined in UITF 40, there are now statutory provisions allowing the adjustment income to be spread over a period of up to six years (see 98-550).

98-540 HMRC practice

The current HMRC views on the valuation of stock include the following key principles.

(1) The normal basis of valuing stock and work in progress is to use the lower of cost and net realisable value. See 98-620 for commentary on 'net realisable value'.

(2) The only other basis generally acceptable for tax purposes is that of 'mark to market', whereby stock is valued at its market value, rather than at the lower of cost and net realisable value. The use of this method is, according to HMRC, 'only appropriate where there is a liquid market in the stock, so that the value could be realised easily'. Examples given are financial institutions and commodities dealers.

(3) Long term contracts are valued on a basis which brings in a profit/loss element.

(4) The valuation included in financial statements prepared in accordance with generally accepted accounting practice should be accepted as long as:

    (a) it reflects the correct application of the principles of normal accountancy;

    (b) the method pays sufficient regard to the facts; and

    (c) the basis does not violate the taxing statutes as interpreted by the courts.

(5) A valuation that pays insufficient attention to the facts will not be acceptable even if it is made on a recognised basis.

(6) Valuation policy should be consistent unless the reasons for change outweigh the need for consistency.

(7) Subject to that, HMRC do not have the right to substitute one basis which is valid for tax purposes for another such basis.

Other Material: HMRC *Business Income Manual* BIM33100ff.

98-560 Long-term contract work

At one time it was the practice never to anticipate a profit on a long-term contract. Work in progress was carried forward from year to year at cost. This was, broadly speaking, the approach that was approved by the House of Lords in *Duple Motor Bodies Ltd v Ostime*. Under that practice, the whole of the sum payable under the contract was brought in as a receipt when the contract was completed. Accordingly no profit was shown before that stage.

However, a practice grew up in the case of large companies having long-term contracts and sufficiently sophisticated budgeting systems, of including an element of profit in the valuation of work in progress. This principle is now established and SSAP 9 (revised) recognises that separate consideration needs to be given to long-term contracts (usually, but not invariably, lasting more than one year). In the absence of such treatment, the deferral of profit until completion may give a distorted profit figure by including only the results relating to contracts that have been completed in the year.

Where a business carries out long-term contracts, and the outcome of those contracts can be assessed with reasonable certainty before their conclusion, the attributable profit should therefore be included (calculated on a prudent basis) in the accounts for the period under review. No profit should be reflected in the earlier periods if it is not possible to assess the outcome of long-term contracts with reasonable certainty before the conclusion of the contract.

HMRC accept that 'profits and losses recognised during the currency of long term contracts are recognised for tax purposes'.

See also *Symons (HM Inspector of Taxes) v Weeks and Others* (also reported as *Symons v Lord Llewelyn-Davies' Personal Representative*), a case concerning a firm of architects the majority of whose professional engagements extended over periods of several years.

Cases: *Duple Motor Bodies Ltd v Ostime* (1961) 39 TC 537; *Symons (HMIT) v Weeks and Others* [1983] BTC 18

Other Material: HMRC *Business Income Manual* BIM33025

Tax Reporter: ¶224-550

98-580 Meaning of 'cost price'

Determining the cost price of an item of stock raises two separate issues.

First, the item must be identified with a particular purchase or set of purchases. Secondly, the extent of the expenditure attributable to the item must be ascertained.

In some cases, it is a straightforward matter to match purchases with current stock: an antiques shop, for example, will clearly be able to demonstrate that each item is unique and has its own purchase history.

In other cases such an approach will not be possible, as for example where the stock is purchased and sold by weight or volume, without any further identification (e.g. quantities of grain or oil). Certain accountancy principles have evolved to deal with such cases, and as a rule these are followed for tax purposes. The most common method of identification is 'first in, first out' (FIFO), presuming that stock acquired first is disposed of first. On this basis the stock held by a trader at the year end is deemed to have been acquired by his most recent purchases. In many circumstances, the FIFO method will correspond closely with the reality.

Other methods of valuation which might accord with sound accounting practice may be rejected for tax purposes. This would include the 'last in, first out' (LIFO) method, which identifies stock with the most recent purchases, thus keeping the value of closing stock low.

The 'discounted selling price' method of valuation (or 'retail method') is used in practice for valuing large quantities of small items of stock where it would be disproportionately time-consuming to value on a different basis. An example is the stock of a departmental store. HMRC comment on this valuation method as follows:

> 'In some cases, where such large numbers of rapidly changing individual items are held, the only practical method of arriving at a figure to represent cost is to value the items at current selling price less the normal gross profit margin. For example, in the case of a department store, a valuation by reference to the ticketed selling price of the stock reduced by the appropriate departmental mark-up. This method of valuation is acceptable if it can be demonstrated that it gives a reasonable approximation of the actual cost. Whilst this method may lead to some undervaluation where the original ticketed selling price has already been reduced, other stock may never reach its ticketed selling price and to that extent would be overvalued.'

As far as the meaning of 'cost' is concerned, HMRC give the following view:

> 'In general, the term "cost" should be interpreted as meaning the total historical cost of bringing the relevant stock to its existing condition and location; and where this is not precisely ascertainable, the aim should be to arrive at the closest approximation to historical cost that is practically attainable ...'
>
> "Overhead' charges, if any, should be included in the cost valuation to the extent that is appropriate having regard to recognised accounting practice and to the principle of consistency.'

Unless there is a statutory provision to the contrary, HMRC guidance should not, however, be allowed to override the principles of GAAP (see 92-025).

Case: *Minister of National Revenue (Canada) v Anaconda American Brass Ltd* [1956] AC 85

Other Material: HMRC *Business Income Manual* BIM33135

Tax Reporter: ¶224-600

98-600 Overheads

As noted at 98-580, the HMRC view is that overheads 'should be included in the cost valuation to the extent that is appropriate having regard to recognised accounting practice and to the principle of consistency'. The guidance goes on to state the following three principles:

- overhead expenses which vary directly with the volume of production are considered to be 'directly attributable' to the production process and should be included;
- the fact that an overhead accrues on a time basis is not in itself a reason for its exclusion from the stock valuation but generally the classification of such overheads is less certain; and
- overheads accruing on a time basis may be more remote from the production process. An accounts treatment that has consistently excluded such overheads from a stock valuation may be within the range of generally accepted accounting practice for the specific industry and may still be a valid basis in the particular circumstances.

The HMRC guidance warns that 'a valuation basis which excludes substantial costs which are clearly directly related to production is incorrect'.

Tax Reporter: ¶224-600

98-620 Meaning of 'net realisable value'

Generally speaking, net realisable value means the value which a given item of stock would be expected to fetch if sold on the date at which the accounts are drawn up.

It may be that if such a sale were made, the whole value would not be realised because of necessary expenses before and at the time of the sale. As such, the 'net realisable value' is lower than the gross value of the stock. However, it is unlikely that HMRC will allow the deduction of such expenses, other than identifiable expenditure directly connected with the sale itself. Thus, for example, commission may be allowed as a deduction, but costs of storage until sale will not.

It will be noted that this definition of net realisable value is not necessarily the same as the meaning of 'market value' as the latter term would generally be understood; the definition of net realisable value regards the trader as a hypothetical seller and not a hypothetical purchaser of the goods in question. The latter, equating market value with replacement cost, is not normally accepted by HMRC as an appropriate method of valuation, and was rejected by the House of Lords in *BSC Footwear Ltd v Ridgway*.

HMRC give the following guidance:

> 'The realisable value is the expected sale price of the relevant stock in the condition in which it is expected to be sold in the traders normal selling market. From that value are deducted the estimated further costs which will have to be incurred to get the stock into its normal sale condition to arrive at the net realisable value.'

The guidance goes on to acknowledge that 'net realisable value may be less than cost because of deterioration, obsolescence, or changes in demand'. If, at the accounting date, there are reasonable grounds to expect the sale proceeds to be less than cost then 'a loss on such stock should be recognised in the year under review by writing off the irrecoverable costs incurred'. For such purposes, however, the stock must not be valued as if there were a forced sale at the balance sheet date, perhaps of stock that is only partially manufactured.

As before, however, HMRC guidance should not be allowed to override the principles of GAAP (see 92-025) unless there is a statutory provision to the contrary.

Cases: *Brigg Neuman & Co v IR Commrs* (1928) 12 TC 1191; *BSC Footwear Ltd v Ridgway* (1970) 47 TC 495

Other Material: HMRC *Business Income Manual* BIM33140

Tax Reporter: ¶224-800

98-640 Events between balance sheet date and completion of accounts

Events may occur after the balance sheet date but before the accounts are completed. The issue will therefore arise of whether it is permissible to reflect those events in the accounts by revaluing the stock accordingly. SSAP 17 refers to such 'post balance sheet events' and the correct treatment is summarised in the HMRC guidance as follows:

- if the event provides additional evidence of *conditions existing at the balance sheet date* then the accounts should be adjusted accordingly; but
- if the event concerns conditions that did not exist at the balance sheet date then the accounts should not be changed (though they may justify a note to the accounts).

HMRC give an example of a farmer whose crops had, at the balance sheet date, an undetected disease. If evidence of the disease came to light after the accounting date but before the accounts were finalised then it would be appropriate to mark down the value of the crops, perhaps even to nil. If, on the other hand, a fire were to destroy the crops a day or two after the accounting date then no adjustment would be appropriate.

Other Material: HMRC *Business Income Manual* BIM33140

Tax Reporter: ¶224-850

98-660 Valuation of stock on cessation – general principle

As a general principle, trading stock and work in progress have to be valued, using statutory rules, when a person ceases to carry on a business.

In the case of trading stock, there is usually a statutory requirement to value trading stock when a person ceases permanently to carry on a trade. The value is to be determined in accordance with ITTOIA 2005, s. 175–178. There are, however, certain circumstances in which the stock does not need to be valued in this way:

- in certain cases involving transfer pricing;
- in the case of a partnership change where at least one partner from before the change continues to carry on the business after the change; and
- in the case of a sole trader whose business ceases because of the individual's death.

In any of these cases, stock would be valued on ordinary principles rather than by using the statutory provisions relating to the cessation of trade.

Legislation: ITTOIA 2005, s. 173ff.

Tax Reporter: ¶225-500

98-680 Valuation of stock on cessation – method

If trading stock is sold in isolation to an unconnected person then the value to be brought into account will simply be the sale value as long as the buyer is able to deduct the cost of the stock in calculating the profits of a UK trade for income tax or corporation tax purposes. This applies whether or not the buyer has yet begun to trade. Where the stock is sold together with other assets, a just and reasonable apportionment must be made to determine the value that is properly attributable to the stock.

The second scenario is where trading stock is sold to a connected person who is able to deduct the cost of the stock in calculating the profits of a UK trade for income tax or corporation tax purposes (whether or not the buyer has yet begun to trade). In such a case, the starting point is that the stock must be valued as the amount that would have been realised had the transaction been between independent persons dealing at arm's length. In determining the arm's length price, the only change to the constituents of the transaction are that the parties are independent and dealing at arm's length. Thus, if a wholesaler sells in bulk to another wholesaler, the wholesale price will be substituted, not the sum of the retail prices that could have been obtained for smaller lots.

It is possible, however, for the connected parties to elect for a different treatment if the value of the stock as above exceeds both the acquisition value of the stock (see below), and the amount actually paid for the stock by the purchaser. In such a case, the parties may elect to value the stock at the greater of its acquisition value and the amount actually realised on its sale. As both parties to the transaction have to agree on the value to place on stock, an HMRC officer dealing with one party's affairs is instructed to liaise closely with the officer dealing with the other party to ensure a consistent line is adopted.

The time limit for an election (changed in connection with the enactment of ITTOIA 2005) is the first anniversary of the normal self-assessment filing date for the tax year in which the cessation occurred.

'Acquisition value' is defined as the amount which would have been deducted in calculating the taxable profits of the transferor on an arm's length sale immediately before the discontinuance. Where the stock is sold together with other assets, a just and reasonable apportionment must be made to determine the value that is properly attributable to the stock.

In any case not covered above (and not connected with the farming 'herd basis'), the value of the stock at the time of cessation is to be the amount which it would have realised if sold in the open market at that time.

Legislation: ITTOIA 2005, s. 175ff.

Other Material: HMRC *Business Income Manual* BIM33495

Tax Reporter: ¶225-600

98-700 Valuation of work in progress on cessation – general principle

Similar but not identical rules apply to the valuation of work in progress where a person ceases to carry on a profession or vocation.

The legislation does not in itself impose a requirement to bring in a work in progress valuation; this therefore differs from the approach to trading stock. However, accounts must be drawn up in accordance with generally accepted accounting practice which will therefore require a valuation of work in progress. (This is subject to an exception, though, for barristers and advocates.)

Where work in progress is indeed valued at the time a person ceases to carry on a profession or vocation, the legislation imposes rules as to how that valuation is to be made. There are, though, two exceptions to the requirement to make any valuation under those rules:

- no such valuation is required in the case of a partnership change where at least one partner from before the change continues to carry on the business after the change; and
- no such valuation is required in the case of an individual who carries on a profession alone, or who carries on a vocation, and whose business (in either case) ceases because of the individual's death.

In either of these cases, work in progress would be valued on ordinary principles rather than by using the statutory provisions relating to the cessation of the profession or vocation.

Legislation: ITTOIA 2005, s. 25, 160, 182ff.

Tax Reporter: ¶225-750

98-720 Valuation of work in progress on cessation – method

There are three different ways in which work in progress may have to be valued for tax purposes when a business ceases.

First, a person who ceases to carry on a profession or vocation may elect to value at cost the work in progress at the date of cessation. This may therefore produce a lower taxable profit figure for the final period of accounts.

Where this is done, the person will be treated as receiving a post-cessation receipt if the amount subsequently received for any transfer of the work exceeds the cost figure brought into the final accounts. An election to this effect must be made by the first anniversary of the normal self-assessment filing date for the tax year in which the cessation occurred.

If a person transfers work in progress to another person (and no election is made as above) then the value to be brought into account in the cessation accounts will normally be the sale value. This will apply as long as:

- the buyer is able to deduct the cost of the work in progress in calculating the profits of a UK profession or vocation for income tax or corporation tax purposes (whether or not the buyer has yet begun to carry on the profession or vocation); and
- the transfer is made 'for money or other valuable consideration'. If the buyer pays £1, for example, then this rule will be triggered. If the buyer pays nothing then it may be necessary to bring in a much higher value, as discussed immediately below.

If work in progress has to be valued according to the statutory rules, but the method of valuation is not covered by either of the headings above, then the value to be included for tax purposes in the final tax computations of a ceasing business will be broadly market value. More specifically, it will be 'the amount which would have been paid for a transfer of the work at the time of the cessation as between independent parties dealing at arm's length'.

Legislation: ITTOIA 2005, s. 184, 185

Tax Reporter: ¶225-750

98-740 Determination of questions

Questions as to the basis of valuation of stock or work in progress are to be determined in the same way as a tax appeal.

Legislation: ITTOIA 2005, s. 186

Transfers to and from trading stock

99-000 Transfers at undervalue

Where goods leave a trader's accounts in return for no consideration, or for less than full consideration, the potential effect will be to reduce the taxable profits. Examples are:

- the appropriation of stock by a trader for his or her own use (the owner of the corner shop who takes a tin of beans off the shelf for his or her supper);
- the use of stock to make a gift to someone else (the florist who gives plants as presents to friends); or
- the sale of goods at an undervalue to a connected person (the builder who sells a new house to his or her daughter at less than it cost to construct).

The tax avoidance possibilities are manifest, and special rules exist to ensure that a trader obtains no tax advantage by choosing to dispose of stock at less than market value.

FA 2008 introduced provisions that put onto a statutory footing some principles that had been established more than half a century earlier in the case of *Sharkey (HMIT) v Wernher*. It has been suggested that the reason for enacting those principles after such a long period is that HMRC felt that there was some likelihood that the provisions would be overturned.

These provisions have effect in relation to appropriations of stock that occur from 12 March 2008, but in most cases this simply represents a continuation of the treatment that previously applied based on the then established case law principles.

Legislation: FA 2008, s. 37 and Sch. 15

Tax Reporter: ¶226-500

99-010 Changes in trading stock – overview

FA 2008 introduced provisions to determine the tax consequences of various transactions involving trading stock, with effect in relation to changes in stock that occur from 12 March 2008. The provisions give statutory effect to the principles established more than 50 years earlier in the case of *Sharkey (HMIT) v Wernher*.

The *Explanatory Notes* to the Finance Bill 2008 explained that:

> 'The tax treatment of changes to trading stock otherwise than by way of trade is one instance in which GAAP differs from tax law. Under GAAP, such a transaction should be credited to the accounts at either the cost price of the stock or at the price actually paid on the disposal. For tax purposes, however, the GAAP treatment is overridden and the tax computation needs to be adjusted to reflect the appropriation from stock at market value (the "market value" rule). The market value rule also applies where goods are acquired or appropriated into trading stock other than in the course of a trade. This rule is well understood and arises from long standing case law.'

Legislation: FA 2008, s. 37 and Sch. 15

Meaning of 'trading stock'

The concept of 'trading stock' is defined for these purposes. The definition, in relation to trades only, includes land or any other property that is sold in the ordinary course of trade or that 'would be so sold if it were mature or its manufacture, preparation or construction were complete'. The following, however, are specifically excluded from the definition.

(1) Materials that are used in the manufacture, preparation or construction of such land or other property.

(2) Any services performed in the ordinary course of the trade.

(3) Any article produced, or any material used, in the performance of any such services.

Statutory concepts

For income tax purposes, these statutory provisions are addressed as follows:

- trading stock appropriated by the trader: see 99-020;
- other disposals not made in the course of the trade: see 99-040;
- trading stock supplied by the trader: see 99-060;
- other acquisitions of stock not made in the course of the trade: see 99-080;
- interaction with transfer pricing rules: see 99-100.

Legislation: ITTOIA 2005, s. 172A

Case: *Sharkey (HMIT) v Wernher* (1955) 36 TC 275

Tax Reporter: ¶226-510

99-020 Trading stock appropriated by the trader

As explained at 99-010, statutory principles now govern the tax treatment of stock taken by a trader for his own use. The following provisions apply where trading stock of a person's trade is appropriated by that person for any other purpose. This therefore covers everything from the owner of the corner shop who takes a tin of beans home for supper to a large property developer who decides to use a prime parcel of land to build a house for his or her daughter.

A trading receipt is treated as arising at the time any trading stock is appropriated in this way. The value of anything received into the trading accounts (i.e. as payment for the item in question) is ignored in calculating the trading profits. In its place, it is necessary to bring in, as a trading receipt, the amount that the appropriated stock would have realised if it had been sold in the open market at the time of the appropriation.

Example

Arthur, a carpet trader, buys 50 carpets for £5,000 and enters it in his books as an expense. The selling price of the carpets is £10,000. At a later date Arthur takes five carpets home for his own use. These carpets cost him £500, but he could have sold them for £1,000. Even though Arthur has made no profit, he must enter £1,000 into his books as the selling price and this will form part of his taxable income.

The *Sharkey v Wernher* principle, and now the rules introduced by FA 2008, only apply if the disposal of stock is not a genuine trading transaction. As long as the disposal can be justified on commercial grounds the general principle remains that, subject to anti-avoidance rules such as those that impose market value (e.g. transfer pricing), a trader is free to charge what he likes for his goods.

The rule only applies, moreover, to items that have become part of the trading stock. If Arthur, in the above example, could demonstrate that the five carpets were always bought for his own use then the treatment is to charge the cost to drawings (i.e. as the purchase through the business of items for personal use). In this case, he would reduce the cost of purchases by £500 rather than increasing the sales figure by £1,000 (thus increasing his taxable profits by only £500 rather than £1,000).

See 99-040 for the treatment of other disposals of stock that are not made in the course of the trade.

Legislation: ITTOIA 2005, s. 172B

99-040 Disposals not in the course of trade

As explained at 99-010, statutory provisions govern the tax treatment of certain stock transactions. The following provisions apply where trading stock is disposed of otherwise than in the course of trade, but in circumstances that are not caught by the s. 172B rules described at 99-020. They would come into play, for example, if a builder had a stock of houses and gave one to his or her son. On the face of it, they could also apply if a trader – perhaps by way of protest – dumped an amount of stock.

Once more, a trading receipt is treated as arising at the time any trading stock is disposed of in this way. The value of anything received into the trading accounts is ignored in calculating the trading profits. In its place, it is necessary to bring in, as a trading receipt, the amount that the appropriated stock would have realised if it had been sold in the open market at the time of the disposal. In this case, however, the rules are subject to the transfer pricing legislation, which generally takes precedence, as explained at 99-100.

Legislation: ITTOIA 2005, s. 172D

99-060 Trading stock supplied by trader

As explained at 99-010, statutory provisions govern the tax treatment of certain stock transactions. The following provisions apply where something belonging to the trader becomes trading stock of the trade.

No deduction is given, in calculating the profits of the trade, for any amount that is paid for the item that is brought in as stock. Instead, the cost of the stock is for tax purposes taken to be the amount that it would have realised if it had been sold in the open market at that time of the transfer into the trade. The cost is treated as incurred on the date on which the goods become trading stock.

Legislation: ITTOIA 2005, s. 172C

99-080 Acquisitions of stock not made in the course of the trade

As explained at 99-010, statutory provisions govern the tax treatment of certain stock transactions. If a trader takes into the trade as stock an asset that he or she has owned personally, then the provisions of s. 172C apply (see 99-060). The following provisions apply where trading stock is acquired otherwise than in the course of trade, but in circumstances that are not caught by the s. 172C rules. They would come into play, for example, if stock was acquired from a relative of the trader.

Once more, no deduction is given, in calculating the profits of the trade, for any amount that is paid for the item that is brought in as stock. Instead, the cost of the stock is for tax purposes taken to be the amount that it would have realised if it had been sold in the open market at that time of the transfer into the trade. The cost is treated as incurred on the date on which the goods become trading stock. In this case, however, the rules are subject to the transfer pricing legislation, which generally takes precedence, as explained at 99-100.

Legislation: ITTOIA 2005, s. 172E

99-100 Interaction with transfer pricing rules

As explained at 99-010, statutory principles now govern the tax treatment of certain stock transactions. Some of the 2008 provisions potentially overlap with the transfer pricing rules in TIOPA 2010, Pt. 4, Sch. 1.

The transfer pricing legislation broadly takes precedence over the rules in ITTOIA 2005, s. 172D (disposals not made in the course of trade: see 99-040) and in s. 172E (acquisitions not made in the course of trade: see 99-080).

Tax Reporter: ¶226-540; ¶226-850

99-120 The rule in Sharkey v Wernher

As explained at 99-010, statutory principles now govern the tax treatment of certain stock transactions. The intention of the 2008 legislation was to put on a statutory footing the long-established principles that were established in *Sharkey (HMIT) v Wernher* (1955) 36 TC 275.

The *Sharkey v Wernher* case remains of historic interest, and may still be of direct relevance to transactions before 12 March 2008. It is also relevant in that it clearly and explicitly provides the basis for the principles enacted in FA 2008.

Following the *Sharkey v Wernher* decision, the Revenue issued a statement of practice (SP A32, January 1957 but subsequently updated). The principles outlined in that statement are now reiterated at BIM33630:

> 'The decisions in House of Lords in Sharkey v Wernher *Sharkey v Wernher* (1955) 36 TC 275, established the principle that where a trader takes stock from his business for private use or for use in another business which he owns, or where he transfers to his business stock which he owns in some other capacity than that of proprietor of that business, the transfer should be dealt with for taxation purposes as if it were a sale or purchase at market value. Thus, goods which a trader takes from his trading stock (for example, for the personal use and enjoyment of himself and members of his household) should be credited at market value. Inspectors should, however, take a reasonably broad view in applying this principle. Where a trader in the course of trade gives special terms, "market value" may be taken as the lowest price at which he sells the goods in comparable quantities in the ordinary course of trade.
>
> The decision does not apply to:
>
> a. services rendered to the trader personally or to his household, the costs of which should be disallowed in accordance with ICTA88/S74 (b);
>
> b. the value of meals provided for proprietors of hotels, boarding houses, restaurants etc and members of their families, which should also be dealt with on the basis that ICTA88/S74 (b), applies;

c. expenditure incurred by a trader on the construction of an asset which is intended from the outset to be used as a fixed asset in the trade.'

Subsequent case law has considered the application of *Sharkey v Wernher* in various circumstances. Various statutory provisions have also been introduced which override the *Sharkey v Wernher* principle in particular cases.

Tax Reporter: ¶226-550

99-140 Sharkey v Wernher and professions

The relevance of *Sharkey (HMIT) v Wernher* to the disposal of stock or work in progress by a person carrying on a profession or vocation was considered by the Court of Appeal in *Mason v Innes*. Hammond Innes, the author, assigned the copyright in a novel to his father without consideration. HMRC sought to tax him on the market value of the copyright (£15,425) at the time of the assignment. It was held that the rule in *Sharkey v Wernher* had no application to professional persons who keep their accounts on a cash (as opposed to an earnings) basis. Lord Denning MR gave the analogy of an artist who paints a picture of his mother and then makes a gift of the painting to her, or that of an artist who paints a picture and then destroys it. He regarded as unacceptable the proposition that tax should be charged in either of these instances, and concluded that *Sharkey v Wernher* should not be applied.

The decision gives rise to certain anomalies. It is unclear whether it should be applied to professional persons who keep their accounts on an earnings basis, though it would seem odd to maintain a distinction. On the other hand, it may be that to extend the effect of *Mason v Innes* to accounts on an earnings basis would be to exaggerate the difference between a trade and a profession. It has been suggested that it might be better in cases such as *Mason v Innes*, and those instanced by Lord Denning, to treat the whole transaction as being outside the taxpayer's profession; thus, no tax liability could arise, and no expenditure incurred would be deductible.

As explained at 99-010, statutory principles now govern the tax treatment of certain transfers of stock that occur from 12 March 2008. The 2008 provisions are applied only to trades and therefore preserve the case law distinction between trades (on the one hand) and professions and vocations (on the other).

Case: *Mason v Innes* (1967) 44 TC 326

Tax Reporter: ¶226-600

99-160 Gifts to charity

The rule in *Sharkey (HMIT) v Wernher* (see 99-020) does not apply to gifts of trading stock to certain charities or other bodies. (Parallel rules ensure that no disposal value of used plant and machinery donated for such purposes need be brought into account.)

Relief is available where a person carrying on a trade, profession or vocation gives to certain designated parties an article that is manufactured, or of a type sold, by the donor in the course of his trade, etc. The mechanics of the relief are that no amount is to be brought into account as a receipt arising from the disposal. This, therefore, overrides the *Sharkey (HMIT) v Wernher* principle referred to above.

Where relief is given under this rule, a receipt must be brought into account, equal to the value of the benefit, if the donor or any connected person 'receives a benefit which is in any way attributable to the making of the gift'. Any sum brought into account under this rule is treated as a trading receipt arising on the day on which the benefit is received. If the trade has by that time ceased, it is taxed as a post-cessation receipt.

The relief applies to gifts to:

- a charity;
- a registered club, as defined at CTA 2010, s. 658 (community amateur sports clubs);
- a designated educational establishment;
- the National Heritage Memorial Fund;
- the Historic Buildings and Monument Commission for England; and
- the National Endowment for Science, Technology and the Arts.

Legislation: ITTOIA 2005, s. 108ff.

Tax Reporter: ¶226-650

Basis periods

Introduction and first principles

100-000 Introduction

Income tax is charged, in relation to business profits, on 'the full amount of the profits of the tax year'. Few businesses draw their accounts up to a date that coincides with the tax year end (i.e. to 5 April) and it would cause difficulties if every calculation had to apportion the profits of two different sets of accounts. The legislation therefore operates a system of 'basis periods' whereby the profits arising in a defined basis period are treated as if they were the profits of the tax year.

The basis period rules for determining which profits are taxed in any given year can be complex, especially in relation to a business that is starting or ceasing, or one which changes the date to which it draws up its annual accounts. The system of basis periods operates for vocations and professions as it does for trades.

Legislation: ITTOIA 2005, s. 7, 196

Tax Reporter: ¶230-000

100-020 Accounting date

Before the correct basis periods can be established, it is essential to understand what is meant by 'accounting date'. Usually, this is simply the date in the tax year to which accounts are drawn up. There are, however, a few exceptions:

- if accounts are drawn up to more than one date in the same tax year then only the latest of such dates is treated as an accounting date for the purpose of working out basis periods;
- special rules apply if accounts are drawn up to a slightly different date each year but within a defined range (for example, to the last Friday in March); and
- special rules also apply in certain cases where there is a change of accounting date in the year.

Legislation: ITTOIA 2005, s. 197, 211, 214

Tax Reporter: ¶230-050

100-040 General rule re basis periods

The general rule is that the basis period for any given tax year is the 12-month period that ends with the accounting date in that tax year. In practice, the majority of basis periods are simply decided under this general rule.

Example

Anna draws accounts up to 31 July each year. The profits arising in accounts for the year ended 31 July 2017 will under the general rule be taxed as the profits for the tax year 2017–18.

Tax Reporter: ¶230-100

100-060 Exceptions to the general rule: overview

The general rule is overridden in a variety of circumstances. Different rules may apply to the following:

- first tax year;
- second tax year;
- a tax year with no accounting date;
- the final tax year;
- where the first accounting date falls near the end of the tax year; or
- where there is a change of accounting date.

Tax year in which trade starts

100-140 Business starts and ends in same tax year

It is possible that a business will both start and cease in the same tax year, perhaps because the venture was inherently short-lived or because the trader decides that going it alone was a bad option.

In this case, the basis period is simply the whole period of trading.

Example

Bill starts trading on 1 June 2017, but is then offered a good employment role and so he stops trading on 7 September 2017. He duly draws his accounts up for the whole period of trading and has made profit of £5,500 (after adjusting the profit figure in the accounts to reach the correct profit figure for tax purposes).

The first (and only) tax year in which he is trading is 2017–18, i.e. the year ended 5 April 2018. Bill's taxable trading profit for the tax year 2017–18 is therefore simply £5,500.

Legislation: ITTOIA 2005, s. 202(2)

Tax Reporter: ¶230-150

100-160 Accounts drawn up to 31 March or first four days in April

Special rules may apply in this case – see 100-380ff. (31 March) and 100-460 (first four days in April).

100-180 Business starts in the year and continues past 5 April

The basis period for the year in which a person starts to carry on a trade, profession or vocation is the period from the start of trading to 5 April at the end of the tax year. Thus the period may be anything from as little as one day (a person who starts trading on 5 April) to as much as one year (a person who starts trading on 6 April). This is subject to the exceptions referred to at 100-140 (business starts and ends in same tax year) and at 100-160 (accounts drawn up to 31 March or first four days in April).

The normal way of calculating the profit for the year will be to apportion the profits of the relevant periods of account. Any apportionment is in theory to be made on a daily basis but HMRC will in practice accept 'any reasonable time based apportionment basis that is consistently applied'.

Example

Carol starts trading on 1 February 2017 and draws her first accounts up to 31 December 2017, making a profit for tax purposes of £10,000.

The first tax year in which she is trading is 2016–17, i.e. the year ended 5 April 2017. The length of the period of accounts is 334 days. The number of days on which Carol is trading in the tax year 2016–17 is 64 (i.e. 1 February to 5 April, both dates inclusive). Carol's taxable trading profit for the tax year 2016–17 is therefore calculated as £1,916 ($^{64}/_{334}$ × £10,000).

Example

Debbie starts trading on 1 May 2017 and draws her first accounts up to 31 December 2017, making a profit of £60,000 (after adjusting the profit figure in the accounts to reach the correct profit figure for tax purposes). Her next accounts are drawn up to 31 December 2018 and show a reduced profit of £25,000.

The first tax year in which she is trading is 2017–18, i.e. the year ended 5 April 2018. The whole of the first period of trading (1 May to 31 December 2017) falls in Debbie's first tax year. It is also necessary to include, though, the part of her second period of trading that ends on 5 April; this will be 95 days (1 January to 5 April 2018) out of the 365 day period. Debbie's taxable trading profit for the tax year 2017–18 is therefore calculated as the sum of two figures:

- £60,000; and
- £6,507 ($^{95}/_{365}$ × £25,000).

As such, Debbie's taxable business profit for her first tax year 2017–18 will be £66,507.

Legislation: ITTOIA 2005, s. 199, 203(3)

Other Material: HMRC *Business Income Manual* BIM71025

Tax Reporter: ¶230-150

Second tax year

100-240 Overview

The basis of assessment for the second tax year is dependent on the choice of accounting date. Five possibilities arise, as follows, and each is considered in turn below:

- the business ends in year two;
- the accounting date in year two falls less than 12 months from commencement;
- the accounting date in year two falls not less than 12 months from commencement;
- there is a change of accounting date in year two; or
- there is no accounting date in year two.

As to the meaning of 'accounting date' for these purposes, see 100-020.

Tax Reporter: ¶230-200

100-260 Business ceases in year two

If a person starts trading in one tax year and ceases trading in the next, the basis period for that second year will be the period from 6 April at the start of the second year to the date of cessation of trading. This may be referred to as an 'actual basis'.

Example

Elton starts trading on 1 February 2017 and ceases trading on 31 May 2017. He makes a profit of £6,000.

Although the period of trading is only for four months, that period spans two tax years and each must be considered.

His basis periods will be as follows:

Year of assessment	Basis period
2016–17	1 February 2017 to 5 April 2017
2017–18	6 April 2017 to 31 May 2017

Accounting date of 1, 2, 3 or 4 April

100-460 Basis period: accounting date of 1, 2, 3 or 4 April

Many businesses draw accounts up to 31 March and it is also common to see a 5 April accounting date, chosen precisely to simplify matters. The special rules applying to accounts drawn up to 31 March are explained at 100-420. No special rules are needed for accounts drawn up to 5 April as they slot naturally and easily into the system of basis periods. Accounts may, of course, be drawn up to one of the first four days of April. Although such a date would be an unusual choice, it would be perverse to deny a special treatment for such accounts having allowed it for accounts ending on 31 March.

As such, the rules described at 100-420 apply equally to accounts that are regularly drawn up to any of the first four days of April. Exactly the same principles apply, modified only to take account of the difference of up to four days.

Legislation: ITTOIA 2005, s. 208(2)(a)

Tax Reporter: ¶230-275

Tax year with no accounting date

100-500 Basis period: tax year with no accounting date

As a general rule, if there is no accounting date in a tax year then the basis period is the period of 12 months following the end of the basis period for the previous tax year. This, however, is subject to several exceptions:

- the rules that apply specifically to the second tax year (see 100-240ff.);
- the rules that apply to a change of accounting date in the third tax year (see 100-660); and
- the rules that apply to a change of accounting date in a later tax year (see 100-680).

Legislation: ITTOIA 2005, s. 201

Tax Reporter: ¶230-300

Final tax year

100-540 Basis period: final tax year

See 100-140 where a person begins and ceases to trade in the same year.

With that exception, the basis period for the final year of trading begins immediately after the basis period for the previous tax year and ends on the date of the permanent cessation of the trade.

Example

Mark has been in business for many years making up accounts to 31 October. He ceases trading on 31 December 2017, making up a final set of accounts for a 14-month period. Basis periods for the final two years are as follows:

Year of assessment	Basis period
2016–17	1 November 2015 to 31 October 2016
2017–18	1 November 2016 to 31 December 2017

Example

Nigella starts to trade on 1 September 2016 and ceases to trade on 14 February 2018. Her basis periods will be:

Year of assessment	Basis period
2016–17	1 September 2016 to 5 April 2017
2017–18	6 April 2017 to 14 February 2018

Legislation: ITTOIA 2005, s. 202

Tax Reporter: ¶230-350

Slight variations in accounting date

100-580 Basis periods re slight variations in accounting date

Where there is a change of accounting date, fairly complex rules normally apply to determine the calculation of the resulting new basis periods (see 100-620ff.). HMRC have in the past allowed a relaxation of the strict position where the variation in possible dates is small, thus avoiding the need in some cases to apply those complex rules. With the enactment of ITTOIA 2005, this concessionary treatment was put on a statutory footing.

The rule may be useful, for example, for a school that always breaks up for the summer holidays on the second Friday of July and that draws its accounts up to that date.

A trader may elect for special treatment so that the normal rules governing a change of accounting date do not apply. An election may be made if accounts are drawn up to a particular day, as opposed to a particular date, and if that day is capable of falling on one of only seven consecutive dates (or eight, if that day is in February).

For a given tax year, a person may elect for the fourth of those dates to be treated as the accounting date in the tax year. This date is known as the 'middle date'. Broadly, the profits of each account will then be taxed as though they were for the 12 months to the constant middle date.

An election, which must specify both the day to which accounts are made up and the middle date, is made on a year-by-year basis, so must be renewed if necessary. The deadline is the first anniversary of the normal self-assessment filing date for the tax year in question.

Legislation: ITTOIA 2005, s. 211ff.

Tax Reporter: ¶230-400

Planning with basis periods

100-595 Choice of year end

Choosing a year end is an important issue for any business.

With steadily rising profits, there is a cash flow advantage in selecting a year end of 30 April rather than 31 March, for example. However, some care is needed here as there must inevitably be a pay back when the business ceases: under the current year basis of assessment, the profits taxed are equal to the profits earned.

Suppose, for example, that a business has steadily rising profits over the duration of its existence, a period of 20 years. It is quite possible that (on average) it will pay tax on say £3,000 less each year because of choosing a 30 April year end (i.e. as the profits to 30 April in any given year tend, in this business with its rising profitability, to be around £3,000 less than those to the following 31 March). When the business ceases, however, the full amount that has escaped taxation over the 20 years will be taxed, and any overlap relief is given simply at its original figure, without any indexing. The business will therefore have to pay tax on an additional £60,000 at the time of cessation.

Another way of illustrating this is as follows. Suppose that a business makes profits of £12,000 (£1,000 per month) in its first year to 30 April 2008 and that it makes profits of £100,000 (£5,000 per month) in its final period of trading from 1 May 2019 to 31 December 2020. The individual is trading for nine months in the final tax year, and notionally earns £45,000 in that period, but the taxable profit for that period is calculated as £89,000 (£100,000 less overlap relief of £11,000).

If the savings over the years have been treated with appropriate caution, and somehow the trader has been persuaded to retain the value of those savings against the future tax liability, then the choice of year end was clearly the correct option. The reality, of course, is often that a business is under financial pressures and is only too pleased to have additional cash funds in the early years to reinvest in the business.

This point was well illustrated by an article in *Taxation* magazine of 18 January 2007, written by Mike Thexton.

Apportioning profits

100-600 Apportioning profits

If a basis period does not exactly match a period of accounts it will be necessary to apportion profits, as seen in many of the examples above. In the same way, it will sometimes be necessary to aggregate the profits of more than one period, often adding them to the apportioned profits of another period.

Such apportionments and aggregations should in principle be calculated on a daily basis. The trader has the right to use a different basis consistently as long as the use of such an alternative is reasonable.

The question of whether or not HMRC can insist on a different approach from a daily apportionment is a moot point. The legislation clearly gives the taxpayer, but not HMRC, such a power. However, the statutory authority for apportioning or aggregating profits arises only where such steps 'are necessary in order to arrive at the profits or losses of the basis period'. In an extreme case, it might be possible to argue that an apportionment is unnecessary where other factors clearly indicate the profitability level. HMRC's *Business Income Manual* states that:

> 'Exceptionally, there will be circumstances in which a more accurate measure of the profit arising in any period can be obtained by reference to the actual transactions which took place during that period … Normally this will only be the case where there are relatively few identifiable transactions.'

Legislation: ITTOIA 2005, s. 203

Case: *Marshall Hus & Partners Ltd v Bolton* (1980) 55 TC 539

Other Material: HMRC *Business Income Manual* BIM71025

Tax Reporter: ¶230-450

Change of accounting date

100-620 Introduction and overview

Different rules are applied to calculate basis periods where there is a change in the date to which a business draws up its accounts. If, for example, a business has drawn accounts up to 31 December each year, special rules will operate if it changes to (say) 30 September or 31 March. The change will obviously result in at least one period of accounts that is shorter or longer than 12 months.

The technical issues to be considered include the following.

- When is the change treated as occurring (the answer to which is not as obvious as it may seem)?
- How is the change treated for tax purposes if it occurs in the third tax year of trading?
- How is the change treated for tax purposes if it occurs in a later tax year?

Tax Reporter: ¶230-500

100-640 When a change of accounting date occurs

Where there is a change from an old to a new accounting date, the change occurs in the earlier of the first tax year in which accounts are drawn up to the new date or the first tax year in which accounts are not made up to the old date.

This means that an accounting date change may be recognised in a tax year in which no accounts are made up. In such a case, the date corresponding to the new accounting date is treated as the accounting date in that tax year. This applies for the purposes of determining the basis period for the year in question and also for the year following an 'ineffective' change of accounting date (see 100-680).

Where a business draws accounts up to a particular day rather than a specific date each year, the tax rules may be applied as if the accounts were in fact drawn up to a constant date. This is explained at 100-580. To prevent profits from being either double counted or missed out altogether, a change from a date determined under those special rules to an actual accounting date is treated as if it were a change from one accounting date to another, even if the two dates are in fact the same.

Legislation: ITTOIA 2005, s. 214

Tax Reporter: ¶230-525

100-660 Change of accounting date in third year

A change of accounting date may occur in the third tax year even if no accounts are in fact drawn up to a date in that tax year – see 100-640.

A particular rule applies if there is a change of accounting date in the third tax year in which a business is carried on and if the accounting date (or deemed accounting date) falls more than 12 months after the end of the basis period for the previous (i.e. second) tax year. Where these conditions are met, the basis period for the third year will run from the day after the end of the basis period for the second year and will end on the new accounting date in the year.

This rule will not apply if, in that tax year, the person ceases permanently to carry on the trade (in which case, see 100-540).

Example

Oscar starts trading on 27 February 2015 and draws his first accounts up to 28 February 2016. He then decides to draw accounts up to 30 April thereafter and so has a 14-month period of accounts from 1 March 2016 to 30 April 2017.

The first tax year is 2014–15 (basis period 27 February 2015 to 5 April 2015).

The second tax year is 2015–16 (basis period 1 March 2015 to 28 February 2016).

The third tax year is 2016–17. No accounts are drawn up to a date in that tax year so there is a change of accounting date in the tax year. The date corresponding to the new accounting date (30 April) is treated as the accounting date in the tax year. But 30 April 2016 falls less than 12 months after the end of the basis period for year two (28 February 2015) so the special rule (in ITTOIA 2005, s. 215) cannot apply. Given that there is a deemed accounting date, it seems that s. 201 can similarly not apply and that the basis period is therefore determined under the general rule of s. 198 (see 100-040).

The next example illustrates the position where there is an actual new accounting date in the third year:

Example

Penny starts trading on 1 June 2015 and draws her first accounts up to 30 April 2016. She then decides to draw accounts up to 31 July thereafter and so has a 15-month period of accounts from 1 May 2016 to 31 July 2017.

The first tax year is 2015–16 (basis period 1 June 2015 to 5 April 2016).

The second tax year is 2016–17 (basis period 1 June 2015 to 31 May 2016).

The third tax year is 2017–18. This is the first tax year in which accounts are drawn up to the new date (31 July) so there is a change of accounting date in the tax year. As the accounting date (31 July 2017) falls more than 12 months after the end of the basis period for the second tax year (31 May 2016), the special rule in s. 215 applies. As such, the basis period for 2017–18 is 1 June 2016 to 31 July 2017. Overlap relief will in principle be due.

Legislation: ITTOIA 2005, s. 214, 215

Tax Reporter: ¶230-550

100-680 Change of accounting date in later year

Different rules apply where there is a change of accounting date after the third year, though these will not apply if, in that tax year, the person ceases permanently to carry on the trade (in which case, see 100-540).

There are three possible ways in which the basis period may need to be calculated.

Conditions not met

If the specified conditions (see below) are not met then the change of accounting date is ignored and the basis period will continue to be the 12-month period ending with the old accounting date. This would be the case, for example, if the trader failed to give due notice to HMRC of the change of accounting date (as this is one of the conditions for recognising a change).

Example

Queenie has been working as a freelance editor for some years, drawing accounts up to 31 July each year. In 2017, she changes her accounting date to 30 September (by having a 14-month period of accounts) as it was not convenient that the date fell during the summer holidays. She does not give notice of the change to the tax authorities (whether by accident or design).

Her basis period for 2017–18 will be the year ended 31 July 2017 and an apportionment of the profits of the period of accounts will need to be made.

In the following tax year, Queenie has another chance to switch the date for tax purposes to coincide with her new accounting date but she is not obliged to do this. If she does not do so, her basis period will be the year ended 31 July 2018 and her profits will once more be worked out by apportionment.

Legislation: ITTOIA 2005, s. 216(4), 219

Conditions met – new date less than 12 months from end of previous basis period

The second possibility is that the necessary conditions (see below) are met and that the new accounting date falls less than 12 months from the end of the basis period for the previous year.

Where this is the case, the basis period will be given by the general rule in ITTOIA 2005, s. 198 (see 100-040). As such, the basis period will be the 12-month period ending with the new accounting date.

Example

Rob draws accounts up to 31 May each year up to and including 31 May 2017. He then changes his accounting date to 30 April 2018 (and to 30 April each year thereafter). He meets all the necessary conditions for the change to be recognised.

His basis period for 2017–18 will be the year ended 31 May 2017.

His basis period for 2018–19 will be the year ended 30 April 2018.

The profits of the month of May 2017 are therefore counted twice and will generate overlap relief to be set against future profits.

Legislation: ITTOIA 2005, s. 216(2)

Conditions met – new date more than 12 months from end of previous basis period

The final possibility is that the necessary conditions (see below) are met and that the new accounting date falls more than 12 months from the end of the basis period for the previous year.

Where this is the case, the basis period will run from the day after the end of the basis period for the previous tax year and will end with the new accounting date.

Example

Steffi draws accounts up to 31 May each year up to and including 31 May 2017. She then changes her accounting date to 30 June 2018 (and to 30 June each year thereafter). She meets all the necessary conditions for the change to be recognised (see below).

> Her basis period for 2017–18 will be the year ended 31 May 2017.
>
> Her basis period for 2018–19 will be the 13-month period from 1 June 2017 to 30 June 2018.
>
> By definition, her previous accounting date of 31 May will mean that she will have overlap relief to set against these profits. She will be able to set one month's worth of overlap profits against the amount now taxed so that she is still taxed on 12 months' worth of profits.

Legislation: ITTOIA 2005, s. 216(3)

Conditions

As noted in the above paragraphs, a change of accounting date that takes place after the third tax year in which a business is carried on is only recognised if certain conditions are met. There are three such conditions (though one of these is in two parts, as explained below); all three must be met.

The first condition is that the person carrying on the trade must give notice to HMRC of the change. This notice must be given in the tax return, which must be submitted within the statutory time limit. It follows from this condition that a person may, if he or she so wishes, change the date for accounting purposes but retain the original date for tax purposes. This is illustrated with the first example ('Queenie') above.

The second condition is met if the period of account ending with the new accounting date is of 18 months or less. This test is normally applied to the period ending with the accounting date in the tax year in which the change of date takes place. If there is no accounting date in that year then the test is applied to the period of account ending with the new accounting date in the first tax year in which accounts are drawn up to the new date.

The third condition seeks to restrict unnecessary changes of accounting date for tax purposes. There are two ways in which this condition can be met. First, the condition is met if no change of accounting date has been recognised for these tax purposes in the five tax years preceding that in which the current change of date takes place. See 100-640 for details of when a change of accounting date occurs, which can have a bearing on this five-year rule.

If there has been such a condition in the previous five years, the condition can still be met if the change is made 'for commercial reasons' and the notice of change (see the first condition above) sets out those reasons. A change of accounting date is treated as meeting the 'commercial reasons' condition unless an officer of Revenue and Customs gives notice to the contrary. Such a notice, which must be given within the period of 60 days from the date on which the notice is received, must state that the officer is not satisfied that the change of accounting date is made for commercial reasons. The trader in turn then has 30 days in which to appeal if he or she wishes to do so.

The obtaining of a tax advantage is specifically stated not to be a commercial reason for these purposes.

Legislation: ITTOIA 2005, s. 217

Tax Reporter: ¶230-600

Overlap profits and losses

101-000 Introduction and definitions

One of the principles of self-assessment is that the profits taxed over the lifetime of a business should be equal to the profits (as adjusted for tax purposes) generated by that business. This may seem like a truism but this result was not achieved under the earlier rules applying up to 1996–97. The reason for the earlier failure to achieve this result was mainly to do with the rules then applying in relation to businesses that were starting or ceasing to trade.

As illustrated in the paragraphs dealing with basis periods, the profits of a given period may be assessed more than once; this typically arises, for example, where a business starts. To achieve the principle stated in the above paragraph, it follows that a deduction must be given at some later stage for those profits that have been double counted. This deduction may be made if the business changes its accounting date or (if not thereby exhausted) will be made when the business ceases (or is deemed to cease).

The legislation uses two key terms in this respect. The term 'overlap period' is defined to mean a period which falls in two basis periods, and the term 'overlap profit' is defined to mean a profit arising in such an overlap period. The overlap profit is not adjusted for inflation and therefore gradually loses its real value.

When self-assessment (or, more strictly, the current year basis of assessment) was introduced, transitional rules generated a second form of overlap relief. This 'transitional overlap relief' arose where a business with an accounting date other than 5 April started before 6 April 1994 and continued after 5 April 1997. The relief was calculated by reference to the profit in the period between the end of the basis period for 1996–97 and 6 April 1997.

Legislation: ITTOIA 2005, s. 204

Tax Reporter: ¶230-750

101-020 Deduction for overlap profit in final year

A deduction is allowed for overlap profits (transitional or other) where a person ceases permanently to carry on a trade. All available overlap relief may be deducted at this stage, calculated as the total of all overlap relief arising in all overlap periods, less any relief already given on a change of accounting date (see 101-040). The effect should be that a trader (who started in business since 6 April 1994) is taxed according to the number of years and months for which he has traded.

Example

Venus starts to trade on 1 February 2013 and draws her accounts up to 31 December 2013 and annually thereafter. She ceases trading on 30 June 2017, drawing up a final set of accounts for that last six-month period. Her total period of trading is therefore 53 months. Apportionments are made by reference to months rather than days.

Her basis periods will be as follows:

2012–13: 1 February 2013 to 5 April 2013

2013–14: 1 February 2013 to 31 January 2014

2014–15: 1 January 2014 to 31 December 2014

2015–16: 1 January 2015 to 31 December 2015

2016–17: 1 January 2016 to 31 December 2016

2017–18: 1 January 2017 to 30 June 2017

It follows that the profits of February and March 2013, and of January 2014, are counted towards more than one tax computation. It is often said loosely that such profits 'are taxed twice' but some care is needed with that concept. In each tax year, the number of months of profits that are taxed can be seen to equal the number of months actually worked in the tax year.

Without overlap relief, Venus would pay tax on six months of profits in her final tax year even though she only worked for approximately three months in that tax year (i.e. from 6 April to 30 June). She has three months of overlap relief to set against the six months, which has the effect that she pays tax on only three months, which is equal to the period during which she worked in the tax year.

Suppose that her profits in each period of trading are as follows:

1 February 2013 to 31 December 2013: £11,000

1 January 2014 to 31 December 2014: £14,400

1 January 2015 to 31 December 2015: £18,000

1 January 2016 to 31 December 2016: £15,000

1 January 2017 to 30 June 2017: £4,800

> Venus will therefore pay tax on trading profits as follows:
>
> 2012–13: £2,000
>
> 2013–14: £12,200 (generating overlap relief of £2,000)
>
> 2014–15: £14,400 (generating further overlap relief of £1,200)
>
> 2015–16: £18,000
>
> 2016–17: £15,000
>
> 2017–18: £1,600 (i.e. £4,800 less overlap relief of £3,200)
>
> The total profits to be taxed are therefore £63,200. (If the apportionments are made on a more strict daily basis, she will still pay tax on exactly the same figure of taxable profit but the allocation between years will be slightly different.)

Legislation: ITTOIA 2005, s. 205

Tax Reporter: ¶230-775

101-040 Deduction for overlap profit on change of accounting date

As noted at 101-020, all unused overlap relief will be available to set against taxable profits at the time a business permanently ceases. It is possible, however, that some overlap relief will be absorbed before the tax year of cessation; this will be by virtue of a change of accounting date.

Where a change of accounting date occurs in the tax year, with the result that the basis period is longer than 12 months, then a deduction has to be made for any overlap relief available at that time. Despite the use of the word 'may' in the Steps listed below, the taxpayer does not have the option of declining to use the relief (so that it is available against a later change of accounting date, or at the time of cessation).

The effect of offsetting overlap relief on a change of accounting date is to ensure that tax is paid on 12 months' worth of profits. If, for example, the basis period is 14 months long then the overlap relief of two months will be deducted. The legislation achieves this result by listing six 'steps' used to calculate the deduction, as follows:

- Step 1: add together the overlap profit arising in all previous overlap periods;
- Step 2: subtract from that the amount of any deduction already made under these rules; call the resulting figure 'the remaining overlap profit';
- Step 3: add together the number of days in all previous overlap periods, deduct the number of days already counted per Step 5 below

on any previous occasion; call the resulting balance 'the number of days on which the remaining overlap profit arises';

- Step 4: calculate 'one day's worth of remaining overlap profit' by dividing 'the remaining overlap profit' by 'the number of days on which the remaining overlap profit arises';
- Step 5: calculate the number of days by which the basis period exceeds the length of the tax year (ignoring 29 February if desired) and call the balance 'the number of days' worth of overlap profits that may be deducted on this occasion'; and
- Step 6: multiply the results of Steps 4 and 5 to calculate the amount of the deduction to be made.

Once the underlying logic is understood, the steps can normally be simplified in practice.

Example

Pluto started to trade on 1 September 2002 and made up accounts to 30 April 2003. He was taxed twice on the profits for the period 1 September 2002 to 5 April 2003, a period of 217 days. The amount of profits taxed twice was £3,000.

In a later year, Pluto shows profits of £15,000 for a period of 14 months to, say, 30 June 2017, a period of 426 days. Pluto can deduct from his 2017–18 taxable amount £843 calculated as follows:

426 – 365 = 61

(61/217) × £3,000 = £843

On a later calculation, the £3,000 would be reduced by £843 and the 217 by 61. If there were no later calculation but Pluto ceased to trade, in the year of cessation he could deduct £2,157 (i.e. £3,000 less £843) from his assessment.

Legislation: ITTOIA 2005, s. 220

Tax Reporter: ¶230-800

101-060 Losses

If an amount of loss would fall to be included in the computations of two years' profit, that amount must not be included in the computation for the second of the years. This prevents overlap losses from being used twice. In the calculation of the result of the second of the two years, the loss period will count as a 'nil' profit.

Legislation: ITTOIA 2005, s. 206

101-080 Business start-up payments

Special rules apply where a trader receives a 'business start-up payment' or 'enterprise allowance', as defined. If such a payment, not being a lump sum payment, is received by a trader in a period that falls within two basis periods then it is brought into account in calculating the profits of the first basis period only.

Legislation: ITTOIA 2005, s. 207

Tax Reporter: ¶230-850

Partnerships

Legal background

102-000 Legal definition

The *Partnership Act* 1890, s. 1 defines partnership as 'the relationship which subsists between persons carrying on business in common with a view to profit'. In this context, 'business' includes every trade, profession or vocation.

It follows that there must be two or more persons, though not necessarily individuals, to form a partnership. Thus, the partners may comprise individuals, companies, bodies of trustees and limited liability partnerships.

The requirement of partnerships to be carried on 'with a view to profit' means a profit to which the partners will be individually entitled.

The *Partnership Act* 1890, s. 2 provides that certain relationships will not, of themselves, create a partnership:

(1) the joint ownership of property, even where the profits from that property are shared by the joint owners;

(2) the sharing of gross receipts from a venture, even where the persons involved have a joint interest in any property from which, or from the use of which, the receipts are derived;

(3) whilst the receipt of a share of net profits of a business is prima facie evidence that the recipient is a partner, the receipt of such a share, or of an amount which is calculated by reference to such profits, does not, of itself, make him or her a partner.

Tax Reporter: ¶286-000

102-050 Partnership agreements

Unless a partnership exists under general legal principles, it cannot exist for tax purposes. Therefore, there must be an agreement between persons to form a partnership and this is largely a question of fact. The existence of a partnership agreement is not conclusive of the existence of a partnership, nor is it a requirement. For example, in *Dickenson v Gross*, a farmer entered into a partnership deed with his three sons. The deed recited that he had given his sons undivided quarter-shares in his farms and stock. Contrary to the agreement, no annual accounts were kept, nor had there been any distribution of profits. The appeal commissioners' finding that there was no partnership in fact was upheld.

Where matters have been conducted on the basis that a partnership exists, however, the onus is on the taxpayer if he wishes to assert that there was in fact no partnership. In *Phillips v R & C Commrs*, separate legal proceedings had been concluded on the basis that there was a partnership and tax returns had been made on the same basis. The taxpayer had failed on the balance of probabilities to displace the prima facie evidence that a partnership existed for the years in question. In *London & Essex Cleaning Services (Southern)*, also, some attempt was made to argue that there was no partnership but the evidence was clearly against the contention. Partnership accounts had been prepared (showing capital accounts for the four individuals concerned) and the tribunal had no hesitation in finding, as a fact, that the business was a partnership.

Similarly, a statement that an agreement does not constitute a partnership or that it begins or ends on a particular date, is not conclusive of the matter.

In *Waddington v O'Callaghan*, a partnership deed executed in May was expressed to be effective from the preceding January. It was held that the partnership constituted by the deed started at the date of the deed and that there was no evidence before the appeal commissioners that a partnership existed before that date.

Cases: *Dickenson v Gross* (1927) 11 TC 614; *Waddington v O'Callaghan* (1931) 16 TC 187; *Phillips v R & C Commrs* [2010] TC 00276; *London & Essex Cleaning Services (Southern)* [2010] TC 00309

Tax Reporter: ¶286-050

102-100 Joint transactions or ventures

Although joint transactions or ventures between two or more parties may constitute a partnership, each party might also be trading quite separately in its own right. Numerous cases have reached the courts in connection with the issue of whether or not there is a partnership for tax (or other) purposes. The following paragraphs refer to a selection of such cases.

Cases in which it was held that the relationship did *not* constitute a partnership include *Dodd and Tanfield v Haddock* (the general commissioners could not reasonably have concluded on the findings that a joint venture existed) and *Hawker v Compton* (the evidence presented to the court was inconsistent with the existence of a partnership and the appellant was the sole occupier of the farm).

Cases: *Hawker v Compton* (1922) 8 TC 306; *Dodd and Tanfield v Haddock* (1963) 42 TC 229

Tax Reporter: ¶286-100

102-150 Admission of family members

It is common for a partner to seek to admit his or her spouse or civil partner or children to the partnership. In many cases, this will reflect the contribution made by the individual to the running of the business. Subject to the considerations below, a partnership solely between husband and wife (or between the two members of a civil partnership) is treated for income tax purposes in the same way as any other partnership (Parliamentary Answer, 14 November 1988).

HMRC do now accept that it is relatively difficult for them to attack partnership profit shares between family members, as in this comment from the *Business Income Manual* at BIM72065:

> 'You cannot challenge the apportionment of profits, as you can a wage, by reference to the value of the partners' contribution to the firm's activity. It may be possible in these cases to challenge the spouse's status as a partner, but such a challenge is often very difficult to sustain. It is sometimes overlooked that there is no need for the spouse to contribute capital; or to participate in management; or, in a trading context at least, to be capable of performing the main activity of the business. Indeed to be a partner one need not take an active part in the business at all. Where the spouse has signed a deed declaring an intention to carry on the business and the deed gives a right to share in the profits, and subsequently accounts of the business show that that person has been allocated a share of the profits, there will not usually be much chance of mounting a successful challenge.
>
> It is worth emphasising that a partnership is not a sham merely because it is set up to save tax, as indeed the spouse who is deserted by a partner leaving that spouse to meet the firm's liabilities may find to their cost. There will always of course be some cases which will be worth you investigating and challenging, but these are more likely to be found among those where there is no current partnership deed, and particularly where there is a clear attempt to

> antedate the setting up of a partnership by more than a few months. Business Tax (Technical) will be happy to advise on worthwhile cases.'

The issue is arguably more complex where a profession or vocation is being carried out that is heavily dependent on the skill of one of the partners, though even here the position is not absolutely clear cut. Again, the HMRC guidance provides some useful insights:

> 'Difficult problems are posed where a taxpayer who is carrying on a profession or vocation (as opposed to a trade), which is dependent on their personal skills or qualifications, purports to take a spouse (who does not possess a like skill or qualification) into partnership. Some professions have internal rules that preclude this; but this is not always the case. You could argue that in such a case a partnership between the husband and wife to carry on the profession or vocation in question would not be possible, but in the light of the judgements in the case of [*Newstead v Frost*] (Entertainer entered into an agreement with a company to exploit his artistic talents. Held there was a valid partnership) that still leaves open the possibility that there might be a partnership between them to exploit the spouse's talents for the benefit of both. The Frost case involved a partnership with a company, but the principle is the same.'

In *Alexander Bulloch & Co v IR Commrs*, a partnership carried on the business of operating off-licence shops. At a partnership meeting, it was decided to invite the children of two of the partners, aged 15 and 14, to become partners, to accept responsibility for one shop each, and to share in partnership profits. A deed to this effect was executed. Thereafter, the two children did routine work in the shops but did not draw salaries or shares of profits, although their shares were credited to their respective capital accounts. The commissioners decided on the facts, including the inexperience and immaturity of the children, that they were not partners in the firm. The Court of Session held that the commissioners were entitled to reach this decision.

Similarly, in *Saywell v Pope*, the court refused to disturb a commissioners' finding that the wives of two partners were not members of the partnership. As in the *Alexander Bulloch* case, the wives were credited with shares of profit, but did not make any drawings. Neither wife introduced any capital, or was permitted to sign cheques on the firm account. No notice of the change was given to the bank or to creditors or customers of the firm. The taxpayers failed to discharge the burden of proving that the wives were partners in the firm.

Settlements legislation

A more likely line of HMRC attack is to rely on the settlement provisions now at ITTOIA 2005, s. 622ff. The income tax definition of a settlement is extremely wide and can encompass the admission of a spouse (or civil partner) to partnership where this involves an element of bounty, e.g. no requirement to contribute to the capital of the business or to play an active role in the running of the business. During the course of 2003, it became apparent that HMRC were looking much more closely than before at the settlement rules in these circumstances, as for example, in various *Tax Bulletin* articles. The process culminated in the *Arctic Systems* case of *Jones v Garnett (HMIT)*, which HMRC lost in the House of Lords overall, though not on all points of detail. That case is considered in more detail at 151-150.

The current HMRC view is that 'bounty entails giving something away without receiving any quid pro quo. Partnerships where the incoming partner receives a share of profits out of all proportion to the contribution made to the partnership will therefore include an element of bounty'. HMRC policy is to consider a challenge in cases 'where it is not possible to challenge the existence of the partnership and the amount of tax at risk is significant'.

Cases: *Alexander Bulloch & Co v IR Commrs* (1976) 51 TC 563; *Saywell v Pope* (1979) 53 TC 40; *Newstead v Frost* (1980) 53 TC 525; *Jones v Garnett (HMIT)* [2007] BTC 476

Other Material: HMRC *Business Income Manual* BIM72065

Tax Reporter: ¶286-300

Taxation of partnership income

102-500 Introduction

The special income tax rules affecting partnerships are contained in ITTOIA 2005, Pt. 9. Those rules introduce the term 'firm' to denote, for tax purposes, the persons carrying on a trade in partnership. The provisions apply 'expressly' to trades but (unless there is an express or implied indication to the contrary) also apply to professions and, for certain purposes, to other businesses. Those purposes are the calculation and allocation of profits and losses, partners to whom the remittance basis applies and the treatment of certain UK resident partners affected by double taxation agreements.

The general income tax rule, subject only to express or implied exceptions, is that a firm is not to be regarded as an entity that is separate and distinct from the partners. This is the case even where (as in Scotland) the partnership has its own legal identity. However, a partnership *is* treated as a separate entity for the purposes of taxing third party (agency) income.

Legislation: ITTOIA 2005, s. 846ff.

Other Material: HMRC *Business Income Manual* BIM72205

Tax Reporter: ¶287-000

Registering partners and partnerships for self-assessment

HMRC issued guidance in October 2010 re the process to be used by tax agents when registering partners and partnerships for self-assessment. In brief:

- form SA401 should be used for registering an individual partner for self-assessment and for paying Class 2 National Insurance contributions;
- form SA402 should be used for registering a partner for self-assessment where the partner is not an individual (e.g. a company or trust); and
- form SA400 should be used for registering a partnership for self-assessment, the form being completed by the nominated partner. However, Limited Liability Partnerships and Limited Partnerships which register with Companies House after 25 October 2010 will not need to complete form SA400 as they will be automatically registered for self-assessment.

The HMRC preference is for forms SA401 and SA402 to be sent in at the same time as form SA400 (also accompanied by form 64-8). However, this is not a statutory requirement and HMRC do warn that submission of the SA400 should not be delayed while waiting for the remaining forms to be completed. Registration forms and forms 64-8 should be sent, without a covering letter, to:

HM Revenue & Customs

Central Agent Authorisation Team

Self Employment and Self Assessment Registrations

Benton Park View

Longbenton

Newcastle upon Tyne

NE98 1ZZ

102-520 Calculation of partnership profits and losses

Where a partner in a trading firm is chargeable to income tax, the trading profits (or losses) are normally calculated as if the firm were a UK resident individual.

In the case of a non-UK resident partner, however, they are calculated as if the firm were a non-UK resident individual. The effect of this is to limit the charge on the non-resident to his share of the profits of the part of the trade carried on in the UK, where the partnership carries on a trade partly in the UK and partly outside the UK.

For tax years from 2009–10 onwards, no account is taken – when calculating the trading profits of any given period of account – of losses for any other period of account.

It follows from the above that if some partners are resident and others are not, then the profits of the trade will need to be calculated on two different bases. For partners who are resident in the UK, it will be necessary to include profits arising anywhere in the world. For non-resident partners, only profits arising in the UK are to be counted. The joint assessment will therefore consist of the shares of the worldwide profits of the UK resident partners and the shares of the UK profits of the non-resident partners.

Where a partnership is managed and controlled outside the UK and is trading wholly or partly outside the UK, then a partner who is a UK-resident individual may be taxed on a remittance basis if he is either not domiciled or not ordinarily resident in the UK, and makes a claim to that effect.

Legislation: ITTOIA 2005, s. 849, 857

Other Material: HMRC *Residence, Domicile and Remittance Basis Manual* RDRM33530

Tax Reporter: ¶287-050

102-540 Capital allowances for partnerships

Capital allowances are claimed by the partnership at partnership level. Allowances are available in respect of plant and machinery belonging to an individual partner and used by the partnership but the claim must be made by the partnership rather than by the individual partner.

Legislation: TMA 1970, s. 42(6); CAA 2001, s. 264

102-560 Expenses incurred by partners individually

As with capital allowances, expenditure incurred by the partners in respect of partnership business must be claimed on the partnership return; it is not possible for partners to make supplementary claims in their own tax returns for expenses. HMRC guidance goes on to make the following comment in this respect:

> 'This does not mean that expenditure incurred by a partner can only be relieved if it is included in the partnership accounts. You may accept adjustments for such expenditure in the tax computations included in the partnership

return providing the adjustments are made before apportionment of the net profit between the partners. But once the adjustments have been made the expenditure is treated, for all practical purposes, as if it had been included in the partnership's accounts.'

Legislation: TMA 1970, s. 42(6)

Other Material: HMRC *Business Income Manual* BIM72075

102-580 Director's fees received by partnerships

As a general rule, fees received by a partner in his capacity as a director of a separate limited company are assessed on him individually as earnings from an office or employment. However, if the fees are (under the partnership agreement) pooled to be shared amongst the partners and form only a small part of the partnership profits and the directorship is a normal incident of the profession and particular practice of the partnership, the fees may be treated as part of the partnership income and taxed accordingly. This treatment is by concession (and therefore not automatic) and the partners must give a written undertaking not to make a tax deduction under the PAYE system even if in the relevant year of assessment the partner is no longer a director or the director is no longer a member of the partnership.

Other Material: ESC A37; HMRC *Business Income Manual* BIM40351

Tax Reporter: ¶287-850

102-600 Corporate partners

Where one of the partners is a company, special rules apply. The profits allocated to the corporate partner are computed in accordance with corporation tax rules, whereas those allocated to individual partners are computed in accordance with income tax rules. It is therefore necessary to perform two separate computations for the purpose of allocating the income to the partners – one using corporation tax rules and one using income tax rules.

Legislation: CTA 2009, s. 1262ff

Tax Reporter: ¶289-300

102-620 Allocation of profits and losses

The profits of the partnership are computed at partnership level and are then allocated to the individual partners, the assessment being made on the partners individually. The basis of allocation is the commercial profit-sharing arrangements that are in force during the period of account.

Where the profit-sharing arrangements change during the basis period, this is reflected in the allocation for tax purposes.

Example

Ian and Peter have for several years traded in partnership. Their accounts for the year to 31 December 2017 show a profit of £16,000. Profits and losses are shared equally until 31 March 2017. From 1 April, profits and losses are shared in the ratio 7:9.

Profits for 2017–18 are allocated in accordance with the profit-sharing arrangements in force during the year to 31 December 2017 as follows:

Three months to 31 March 2017

Profits for period:

$^{3}/_{12} \times$ £16,000 = £4,000

Allocated 1:1 as follows:

	£
Ian ($^{1}/_{2}$ × £4,000)	2,000
Peter ($^{1}/_{2}$ × £4,000)	2,000
	4,000

Nine months to 31 December 2017

Profits for period:

$^{9}/_{12} \times$ £16,000 = £12,000

Allocated 7:9 as follows:

	£
Ian ($^{7}/_{16}$ × £12,000)	5,250
Peter ($^{9}/_{16}$ × £12,000)	6,750
	12,000

Thus, profits for 2017–18 (year to 31 December 2017) are allocated as follows:

	Ian	*Peter*	*Total*
	£	£	£
1/1/17 – 31/3/17	2,000	2,000	4,000
1/4/17 – 31/12/17	5,250	6,750	12,000
Total	7,250	8,750	16,000

Legislation: ITTOIA 2005, s. 850

Tax Reporter: ¶287-200

102-640 Treatment of salaries and interest on capital

In England and Wales (unlike Scotland), a partnership is not a legal entity. Therefore, a partnership cannot enter into a contract of employment with an equity partner and an equity partner cannot be the employee of the remaining partners. If, therefore, a partner is entitled (under the terms of the partnership agreement) to a salary or wage, he is merely entitled to an allocation of profits prior to the general division among the partners.

Salaries paid to an equity partner are therefore not deductible in determining the partnership profits (or losses). Rather, they are merely an allocation of profits prior to the general division among the partners in accordance with the other profit-sharing arrangements. Interest paid on partners' capital accounts is treated as an allocation of profit in the same way.

This does not cause a problem when all the individual partners' interests in the profit (or loss) show a surplus (or deficiency). However, the allocation process must not create a loss for some partners and a profit for others. If that process produces a mixture of profits and losses, then the actual partnership profit (or loss) is therefore reallocated between the profit-making (or loss-making) partners in proportion to the notional profit (or loss) originally allocated to those partners.

Example

George, Jack, Eileen and Ian set up in partnership in June 2003. They prepare accounts to 30 September each year. Profits and losses are allocated in the ratio 5:2:2:1. For the year to 30 September 2017, they made a profit of £6,000. George and Eileen each received salaries of £8,000.

The partnership profits for 2017–18 assessment are allocated as follows:

	George	Jack	Eileen	Ian	Total
	£	£	£	£	£
Salaries	8,000	–	8,000	–	16,000
Balance of profit distributed 5:2:2:1	(5,000)	(2,000)	(2,000)	(1,000)	(10,000)
Initial allocation	3,000	(2,000)	6,000	(1,000)	6,000
Reallocation of notional loss 1:2	(1,000)	2,000	(2,000)	1,000	–
Net allocated	2,000	Nil	4,000	Nil	6,000

Without the reallocation, the result would not be acceptable for tax purposes as there is no real loss to be allocated to any partner. The aggregate notional profit allocated to George and Eileen was initially £9,000, whereas an aggregate notional loss of £3,000 had been allocated to Jack and Ian. This notional loss is therefore reallocated between George and Eileen in proportion to the notional profit originally allocated to them, i.e. 3,000:6,000 or 1:2.

A similar situation arises if the partnership makes a loss and the initial allocation results in one or more partners being allocated a notional profit, the aggregate notional loss allocated to the remaining partners exceeding the actual loss made by the partnership.

This principle was upheld by a special commissioner in *PDC Copyprint (South)*. In that case, the partnership agreements provided for two of the equity partners, who were regarded as being the managers of the business, to be entitled to salaries expressed as a first charge upon the net trading profits. In the event, the salaries were paid regardless of the profitability. No PAYE was operated on the salaries. The other equity partners, who had little active involvement with the business, sought to increase their loss relief claims for certain years by the salaries paid. Although the report of the judgment is unclear, this claim was presumably on the grounds that the salaries were costs of operating the business. They could not have been appropriations of profit, for no profit arose in those years.

The special commissioner held that the losses must be computed in accordance with the Taxes Acts, which prohibit the deduction of partners' salaries in computing taxable profits. It was not open to partners to inflate their loss claims by the payment of salaries to one or more of their number.

Case: *PDC Copyprint (South)* (1997) Sp C 141

Tax Reporter: ¶287-250

Payments to outgoing partners

Two related cases addressed the question of how to treat certain payments made to partners who had been asked to withdraw from a firm of chartered accountants. The firm in question paid out the partners' shares of profits, calculated to the date of withdrawal, but also made a further payment equivalent to the share of profits to which the partners would be entitled for 12 months. The dispute concerned the tax treatment of those further payments, the retiring partners arguing that they were not payments of profits (*Morgan v R & C Commrs; Self v R & C Commrs*). The partners also argued that the payments should have been deducted by the partnership in computing its taxable profits.

The First-tier Tribunal rejected the taxpayers' argument. It was clear that the partners were carrying on business in partnership and that the terms of the partnership were binding on each partner. The constitutional documents indicated that payments made to partners leaving the firm could include both special allocations of profits as well as profits calculated by reference to the points basis and the accounts confirmed that the further payments made to retiring partners were in fact made out of profits. The further payments were made to the taxpayers in their capacity as partners and were payments of profits chargeable to income tax accordingly. They were not amounts which should have been deducted by the firm in computing its profits.

Case: *Morgan v R & C Commrs; Self v R & C Commrs* [2009] TC 00046

Tax Reporter: ¶287-050

102-660 Notional trades for individual partners

For each tax year in which a firm carries on an actual trade, each partner's share of trading profits (or losses) is treated as profits (or losses) of a notional trade carried on by the partner alone. This fictional trade created by the legislation has a number of consequences.

A partner is normally treated as starting to carry on the notional trade at the time of becoming a partner in the firm. However, the notional trade cannot begin before the start of the actual trade, but if the partner has been carrying on the trade as a sole trader before it is carried on by the partnership then the date on which the actual trade began is treated as the date on which the notional trade began.

A partner is normally treated as ceasing to carry on the notional trade at the time of ceasing to be a partner in the firm or (if earlier) at the time when the firm permanently ceases to carry on the trade. However, if the partner continues to carry on the trade as a sole trader after it is carried on by the partnership then the date on which the actual trade ceases is treated as the date on which the notional trade ceases.

Example

Mary and Albert set up in business in May 2010. In April 2017, Albert leaves the partnership and in July 2017, Elizabeth joins Mary in partnership. The same trade is carried on throughout. There is no discontinuance of the business in April 2017 when Albert leaves nor in July 2017 when Elizabeth joins, as, in both cases, Mary continues to carry on the business both before and after the change.

Albert's notional business ceases in April 2017 when he leaves the partnership and Elizabeth's notional business commences in July 2017 when she joins the partnership.

A special rule applies if the firm is carrying on the actual trade wholly or partly outside the UK and a partner starts or ceases to be resident in the UK. In such a case, the partner whose residence status changes is treated, at the time of change of residence, as permanently ceasing to carry on one notional trade and as beginning another.

This rule does not stop the partner from carrying forward a loss from before the change of residence and setting it against a profit arising after that change.

Legislation: ITTOIA 2005, s. 852

Tax Reporter: ¶287-450

102-680 Notional trades: basis periods

In computing the business profits of the partnership, the normal basis period rules for business profits (or losses) apply. Thus when a partner joins a partnership, for example, he is chargeable for the first year on his share of the profits for the period from the date he joined the partnership to the following 5 April.

Each partner will be entitled to his own amount of overlap relief, which will vary from partner to partner.

Where a partner leaves a partnership, the basis of assessment for the final year is the sum of his share of profits for the period from the accounting date in the previous year to the date he leaves the partnership.

Legislation: ITTOIA 2005, s. 853

Tax Reporter: ¶287-475

102-700 Change of partnership accounting date

Any change of accounting date or any accounting change of the partnership's trade also applies to each individual partner. Where there is a change of accounting date, the partnership must apply the rules for a change of accounting date as if it were an individual. If the partnership satisfies the relevant conditions in ITTOIA 2005, s. 217 (see 100-680) then the new accounting date will be effective for tax purposes. If those conditions are not satisfied, the new accounting date is not effective for tax purposes, and therefore the old accounting date continues to be applied. In the case of new partners, the commencement rules are applied in order to determine a basis period, with the modification that the accounting date is taken to be the old, rather than the new, accounting date.

Where a trader changes the accounting date, notice must be given to an officer of the Board. In the case of a partnership, one partner may be nominated to give the required notice and to appeal against a decision that the change is not made for bona fide commercial reasons.

The income (or loss) allocated to each partner is included on that partner's personal tax return. The figure returned must be the figure shown on the partnership statement.

Example

Alan and Brian are in partnership, having always made up their accounts to 31 December. On 1 March 2017, Charles is admitted to the partnership. Accounts are made up to 30 June 2017, and 30 June is then retained as the accounting date. All the necessary conditions of ITTOIA 2005, s. 217 are satisfied.

Alan and Brian's position is as follows:

Year of assessment	*Basis period*	*Statutory reference*
2016–17	year ending 31 December 2016	ITTOIA 2005, s. 198(1)
2017–18	12 months to 30 June 2017	ITTOIA 2005, s. 198(1)
2018–19	year ending 30 June 2018	ITTOIA 2005, s. 198(1)

Charles's position is as follows:

Year of assessment	*Basis period*	*Statutory reference*
2016–17	1/3/17–5/4/17	ITTOIA 2005, s. 199
2017–18	1/3/17–28/2/18	ITTOIA 2005, s. 200(2)
2018–19	year ending 30 June 2018	ITTOIA 2005, s. 198(1)

Thereafter, Charles's basis period will be governed by ITTOIA 2005, s. 198, unless there is a subsequent qualifying change of accounting date. He will also be entitled to overlap relief (see 101-000ff.) in respect of the profits which have been taxed more than once.

Legislation: ITTOIA 2005, s. 853

Tax Reporter: ¶287-475

102-720 Partner losses

Partners are entitled to loss relief in respect of their share of partnership losses in the same way as other traders (see 105-000ff.). Consequently, the loss relief provisions applying for the relief of business losses generally under the current year basis are in point.

Broadly, the options available to an individual partner are:

- relief against general income (ITA 2007, s. 64ff.);
- relief against future profits from the same business (ITA 2007, s. 83ff.); or
- relief against chargeable gains (ITA 2007, s. 71).

In the early years of the trade, relief may be available in accordance with ITA 2007, s. 72ff. Where a terminal loss arises, this may be relieved in accordance with ITA 2007, s. 89ff.

Once the partnership loss has been established and allocated among the partners, each individual partner must claim his/her own loss relief appropriate to his/her circumstances. However, ITA 2007, s. 102ff. places a restriction on the loss relief available to certain limited partners, members of LLPs and 'non-active' partners (see below).

Loss relief is also restricted in the case of partnerships who have exploited films (again, see below).

Tax Reporter: ¶287-600

Restrictions on trade losses for partners: overview

Restrictions on loss relief for certain partners are intended to 'tackle avoidance schemes that exploit relief for trading losses from partnerships'. The legislation identifies three types of partner that are potentially affected by the rules:

- limited partners;
- members of limited liability partnerships; and
- non-active partners.

In addition to these, loss relief may be restricted in relation to partners involved with the exploitation of films.

In certain circumstances, an income tax charge may be imposed in relation to the following (see 105-500ff.):

- partners claiming 'excess relief';
- individuals claiming relief for film-related trading losses; and
- partners claiming relief for licence-related trading losses.

Legislation: ITA 2007, s. 102, 115ff., 791ff.

Tax Reporter: ¶263-200

Restrictions applying to limited partners

Loss relief may be restricted where, in a given tax year ('the relevant tax year'), an individual sustains a loss in a trade he is carrying on as a limited partner in a firm. The restriction applies to 'sideways relief' (against the individual's other income) and to 'capital gains relief'. There is no restriction on the right to carry the loss forward and set it against future profits from the same trade.

The legislation then states that the sum of (a) the amount of relief given as a result of the loss claim and (b) the total amount of all other relevant relief given, less (c) the total amount of 'recovered relief' must not exceed the individual's contribution to the firm as at the end of the basis period for the relevant tax year.

Example

Smith is a limited partner in a farming partnership and has contributed a net £8,000 to the capital of the firm. His share of the firm's adjusted trading loss in the first year is £12,000. In a simple case, this is his contribution to the firm.

Thus, Smith can only claim a total of £8,000 of relief against other income. The balance of £4,000 (being £12,000 – £8,000) is available for carry-forward.

Legislation: ITA 2007, s. 104

Tax Reporter: ¶263-300

Restrictions applying to members of LLPs

Loss relief is restricted where, in a given tax year ('the relevant tax year'), an individual makes a loss in a trade ('the relevant trade') that he is carrying on as a member of a Limited Liability Partnership. The restriction applies to 'sideways relief' (against the individual's other income) and to 'capital gains relief'. There is no restriction on the right to carry the loss forward and set it against future profits from the same trade.

The maximum amount of relief that can be claimed for the loss made by the individual can be expressed as follows:

- the individual's contribution to the LLP as at the end of the basis period for the relevant tax year; plus
- the total amount (if any) of recovered relief; less
- the total amount (if any) of all other relevant relief given.

Where relief has been restricted under these provisions, the unrelieved loss may in certain circumstances be carried forward and treated as arising in a later year.

Legislation: ITA 2007, s. 107, 109

Tax Reporter: ¶263-350

Restrictions for non-active partners

Loss relief is restricted where, in a given tax year ('the relevant tax year'), an individual makes a loss in a trade ('the relevant trade') that he is carrying on as a non-active member of a firm. The restriction applies to 'sideways relief' (against the individual's other income) and to 'capital gains relief'. There is no restriction on the right to carry the loss forward and set it against future profits from the same trade.

The maximum amount of relief that can be claimed for the loss made by the individual can be expressed as follows:

- the individual's contribution to the firm as at the end of the basis period for the relevant tax year; plus
- the total amount (if any) of recovered relief; less
- the total amount (if any) of all other relevant relief given.

The term 'non-active partner' is used to describe an individual (other than a limited partner but including a member of an LLP) who carries on a trade as a partner in a firm at any time during the tax year in question but who does not devote 'a significant amount of time' to the trade in the 'relevant period for the year'. For these purposes, an individual is said to devote a significant amount of time to a trade if, in the relevant period, he spends an average of at least ten hours a week personally engaged in trading activities. The 'relevant period for the year' is normally defined to mean the basis period for the tax year in question but different rules apply if that basis period is less than six months.

In relation to relevant periods ending on or after 12 March 2008, the legislation specifies that the activities must be carried on on a commercial basis and 'with a view to the realisation of profits as a result of the activities'. If relief is given on the basis that the individual is expected to devote a significant amount of time to the trade in the relevant period, but he or she in the event fails to do so, then an income tax assessment is made to withdraw the relief.

Legislation: ITA 2007, s. 103B(2), 110

Tax Reporter: ¶263-400

102-730 Excess loss allocations

Schemes had evolved to exploit loss relief where there is a mixed membership partnership, such that losses are allocated to individuals. Loss relief is not available to individuals in circumstances where the main purpose, or one of the main purposes, is to secure that losses are allocated to an individual rather than to non-individuals, such as a company. This rule applies to both trading (including professional) businesses and property businesses and covers all types of loss relief, including both sideways and carry forward reliefs.

Legislation: ITA 2007, s. 116A, 127C

102-740 Partnership changes

Where there is a complete change in the composition of the partnership, taxable profits are calculated as if the trade had been permanently discontinued. However, where there is only a partial change in ownership so that one or more persons carrying on the trade before the change (either alone or in partnership) continue to carry on the trade after the change (either alone or in partnership), there is no deemed discontinuance. There is no provision to elect for a deemed discontinuance.

Commencement and cessation rules apply individually to partners who join or leave the partnership.

Tax Reporter: ¶287-650

102-760 Adjustment income for partnerships

The issue of adjustment income (where there is a change in the basis on which profits are calculated for income tax purposes) is addressed at 92-075. Where there is a change in the persons carrying on a trade, etc. this does not prevent the adjustment income rules applying as long as there is at least one person who carries on the trade both before and after the change. Similarly, a change where at least one person continues to carry on the trade does not constitute the permanent cessation of the trade for these purposes.

In the case of a firm, the amount of any adjustment income is to be calculated as if it were an individual who is resident in the UK.

Legislation: ITTOIA 2005, s. 860

102-780 Mergers and demergers

In *George Humphries & Co v Cook*, two sole traders merged their business and traded in partnership. One of the former sole traders had carried on the business of contracting with film companies for the processing of films, procuring orders, contracting out the processing for an agreed price, and making delivery of the processed films; the other had processed films. The court held that a new business had begun with the formation of the partnership and that the old business of the partners had ceased.

In any event it would seem that technically, on an amalgamation, only *one* of the partners could claim a continuation of his trade if only one trade is carried on after the merger. However, HMRC may in practice agree that there has been no cessation of either profession when professional persons such as accountants, estate agents or solicitors merge or amalgamate to form a new partnership. HMRC may ask for sight of the merger agreements to establish the facts.

The possibilities of treatment of a merger are essentially those applicable to any partnership as follows:

- one only of the old trades ceases and the other is continued by the new firm; or
- both of the old trades cease, and a new trade is commenced by the new firm.

Where a business is divided up between the persons carrying it on, it will be a question of fact as to whether any of those persons carries on the business previously carried on.

Where the purchaser of a business is already trading, his tax position will depend on whether he has acquired the new trade as a going concern or whether he has merely bought the assets. Where he has bought the assets for use in his old trade, his trading position is unaffected. Where, however, he has bought a business of the same kind as his existing business as a going concern, it may be that he is expanding his existing business or has begun a new trade.

Case: *George Humphries & Co v Cook* (1934) 19 TC 121

Tax Reporter: ¶287-700

Limited liability partnerships

103-000 Main principles

Unlike other partnerships, a limited liability partnership (LLP) is a separate legal entity from its members.

Despite this, the basic rule for tax purposes is that LLPs are treated as having tax transparency in that the activities are treated as being carried on by the members themselves and not by the LLP. As a result, the LLP itself normally has no liability to tax on its profits; each member is taxable on his or her share of profit.

There are restrictions on the amount of loss relief that can be claimed by a member against other income and on the relief available for interest on borrowings to lend to, or acquire an interest in, the LLP. Broadly, the restriction is made by reference to the contribution to the capital of the LLP as at the end of the tax year in which the loss is sustained or the interest is paid. Where a claim is restricted in this way, the unrelieved loss or payment of interest is carried forward to each subsequent year in turn and treated as a loss or payment for that year.

For as long as the LLP qualifies for tax transparency, it is not to be regarded as a company for tax purposes. However if the LLP permanently ceases to trade or a liquidator is appointed, the tax transparency is lost and it would become chargeable in its own right. In that event it would then become a 'company' resident in the UK.

The above-mentioned restrictions do not apply where the LLP is carrying on a profession rather than a trade.

Legislation: ITA 2007, s. 104ff.; ITTOIA 2005, s. 863

Tax Reporter: ¶289-750ff.

103-020 LLPs: anti-avoidance

To prevent the avoidance of tax through the use of LLPs, specific anti-avoidance measures identify two specific classes of LLP. The types of LLP singled out for special attention are:

- an 'investment LLP', being one whose business consists wholly or mainly in making investments and the income of which is principally derived from such activities; and
- a 'property investment LLP', being one whose business consists wholly or mainly in making investments in land and the income of which is principally derived from such activity.

Legislation: ITA 2007, s. 399(6), 1004; TCGA 1992, s. 288(1)

Tax Reporter: ¶289-950

103-050 Salaried members

Finance Act 2014 contains wide ranging provisions relating to salaried members with effect from 6 April 2014. Although the legislation refers to salaried members, in the heading to ITTOIA 2005, s. 863A, that status is not defined as such for the purposes of these new provisions.

The broad thrust of these provisions is that if all of three conditions are met, then an individual who is a member of an LLP will be treated for income tax purposes as employed under a contract of service. Thus, the LLP in question would be required to deduct income tax under PAYE and account for national insurance contributions in the same way as any other employee. The LLP would then be able to deduct the amounts deemed as employment income in arriving at its profits for tax purposes subject to, in particular, the wholly and exclusively rule in the same way as any other such business payment.

These provisions, which are complex to apply, came about because of the basic rule that if an individual is a member of an LLP, then they are deemed to be self employed and cannot be employed. A practice seems to have developed for employees to be members of an LLP but in reality they were rewarded in the same way as they would as an employee. The Government deemed the potential loss of tax to be substantial and hence these changes. These provisions only apply for tax purposes and so an individual member caught by them will not be an employee for employment law purposes.

The three conditions

Condition A

Condition A looks at the quality of the payments made to an individual and, very broadly, if it is reasonable to expect at the 'relevant time' that at least 80% of the total amount payable to the individual for the performance of services to the LLP is disguised salary, then this condition would be met. Disguised salary means that:

- the amount is fixed;
- is variable but is varied without reference to the overall profits or losses of the LLP; or
- is not in practice affected by the overall amount of the LLPs profits or losses.

importantly, the provision of any services involving any partner in the firm in addition to the company is to be ignored. Thus, it cannot be argued that through its directors or employees who are partners in a firm, that the company is deserving of a greater consideration for its services.

Cases involving individuals who are not partners

In the past, firms have been set up on the basis of having wholly corporate partners, the shareholders and directors being the individuals who, in a conventional structure, would have been partners in the firm. In this way, they could have effectively shared their income with a spouse and retain profits in the company at a lower rate of tax. For past arrangements, this appears to be effective going forward after 5 April 2014 subject to an anti-forestalling rule mentioned below. Apart from that, if the conditions as set out below are met, then an individual is treated for tax purposes as if they were a partner in the firm throughout the relevant period. Their profit share is, as determined on a just and reasonable basis, the amount of that individual's deferred profit or of which they have the power to enjoy (calculated on the same basis as for mixed partnerships).

The conditions to be met are:

- For the time during the period of account, an individual personally performed services for the firm in question.
- If that individual had been a partner in the firm throughout that period, there would have been a profit for the firm.
- A corporate member or other non-individual partner has a share of the profit of the firm.
- It is reasonable to suppose that the individual would have been a partner in the firm at a time during that relevant period of account (or in any earlier period) but for the new rules brought in from 6 April 2014 in relation to mixed membership partners (as set out above).
- Condition X or Y is met, which is that individual meets the deferred profit or power to enjoy conditions.

Thus, as with the mixed partnership rules, it is necessary to determine the company's appropriate notional profit where Condition Y (the power to enjoy) is met, calculated in the same way as for the corresponding condition in the mixed partnership rules. To avoid double taxation, provision is made to exclude from the charge to tax in the hands of the company any profit reallocated to an individual.

Having a sound commercial reason for an arrangement having only corporate members should be a valid defence to any suggestion that these provisions apply as an essential condition to be met is that the arrangement has been set up to effectively avoid the provisions of ITTOIA 2005,

s. 850C. This is all down to the facts of a particular case so as to be able to demonstrate the commercial as opposed to tax avoidance motive. The reasons must have some substance to them as HMRC will no doubt put these to the test where appropriate. It should also be borne in mind that this particular condition on the avoidance of s. 850C is deemed to be met if the individual is a member of a partnership which is a member of the firm in question or a member of the partnership which is associated with the firm.

Finally, anti-forestalling provisions were introduced which came into force on 5 December 2013 so as to be able to look through attempts made from that date to disapply the new legislation by means of avoidance arrangements.

Legislation: ITTOIA 2005, s. 850C–850E

Residence issues

103-300 Non-resident partners

The trading profits (or losses) of a partnership are normally calculated as if the firm were a UK resident individual. In the case of a non-UK resident partner, however, they are calculated as if the firm were a non-UK resident individual. The effect of this is to limit the charge on the non-resident to his share of the profits of the part of the trade carried on in the UK, where the partnership carries on a trade partly in the UK and partly outside the UK.

It follows that if some partners are resident and others are not then the profits of the trade will need to be calculated on two different bases.

Legislation: ITTOIA 2005, s. 849

Tax Reporter: ¶288-500

103-320 Partnerships to whom remittance basis may apply

Where a partnership is managed and controlled outside the UK and is trading wholly or partly outside the UK, then a partner who is a UK-resident individual may be taxed on a remittance basis if he is not domiciled in the UK, and makes a claim to that effect. The partner's share of profits arising in the UK is taxed in the ordinary way. Profits of such a partner arising overseas are treated as 'relevant foreign income' (per ITTOIA 2005, s. 830).

Legislation: ITTOIA 2005, s. 857

Tax Reporter: ¶288-550

103-340 Double taxation relief

A UK-resident partner's share of any profits or gains of a partnership which is controlled outside the UK cannot be relieved from tax under any provisions of a double tax treaty.

It is also provided that where the resident partner is entitled to a share of any qualifying distribution received from a UK resident company, he is also personally entitled to a share of the tax credit arising.

Legislation: ITTOIA 2005, s. 858

Tax Reporter: ¶288-600

103-690 Alternative investment fund managers

This is a specialist area and is touched on very briefly here. The changes made by FA 2014 recognise that AIFM firms are a special case where it has been customary for a partner's variable remuneration to be deferred. In that case, if the AIFM firm makes an election it is taxed at the additional rate of, currently, 45% and when the final allocation is made to an individual a credit is given for the amount of tax paid by the firm.

Legislation: ITTOIA 2005, s. 863H–863L

Losses

105-000 Business losses

Trading losses are calculated in the same way as profits and the rules for basis periods (see 100-000ff.) are the same.

Where a period of account is used wholly or partly in the computation for more than one year of assessment (e.g. as with the commencement provisions or on a change of accounting date), any loss is used in the first year of assessment only and not in any later year. This is to avoid giving relief more than once for the same loss.

Example

Steven starts in business on 1 January 2017. He makes up his first accounts to 30 November 2017 and thereafter to 30 November each year. His trading losses (including capital allowances) are:

- 11 months to 30 November 2017 – (£15,000); and
- 12 months to 30 November 2018 – (£1,500);

His tax losses are computed as follows:

Year	*Basis period*			*Allowable loss*
				£
2016–17	01/01/17 – 05/04/17	£15,000 × $^{3}/_{11}$		4,090
2017–18	01/01/17 – 31/12/17	£15,000 – £4,090	= 10,910	
		£1,500 × $^{1}/_{12}$	= 125	11,035
2018–19	01/12/17 – 30/11/18	£1,500 – £125		1,375

The loss of £4,090 which relates to the period from 1 January 2017 to 5 April 2017 would fall to be included in the computations for two years of assessment (2016–17 and 2017–18) and it is therefore allocated to the earlier year, and is excluded from the later year's loss calculation. The same principle applies to the loss of the period from 1 December 2017 to 31 December 2017 (£125) which forms part of the loss for 2017–18 and not 2018–19. In strictness the apportionments in the example should have done on a daily basis, but for illustration purposes a monthly basis has been used.

Business losses may be relieved in a number of ways:

- carry forward of losses to relieve trading profits (and in limited circumstances other types of income) in future years (105-050);
- using current year losses to relieve current year (or immediately preceding year) general income, sometimes referred to as 'carrying across' (105-100);
- carry back of losses to relieve income of earlier years where a trade either starts or ceases (105-300); and
- using surplus trading losses to relieve chargeable gains (105-350).

Double loss relief is never available. If relief has been claimed under one set of provisions it cannot be used again in any other claim (*IR Commrs v Scott Adamson*, *Westward Television Ltd v Hart*). In the first of these cases, it was also established that relief cannot be given to the extent that a loss has been set off against a profit in calculating an assessable profit for a year.

HMRC will in practice accept claims for loss relief on a best estimate basis once it has been established that a loss has arisen. The final figure for the loss must then be notified as soon as possible. This practice does not extend to loss relief claims submitted before the end of the loss making period as HMRC do not accept that a loss can be anticipated before the end of the accounting period.

Capital allowances are deducted as a trading receipt and thus are automatically taken into account when computing any trading loss.

HMRC's 'Income Tax Losses Toolkit' was published in May 2014, containing basis information on the use of losses, including a checklist and references to relevant HMRC manuals.

Legislation: ITA 2007, s. 61

Cases: *IR Commrs v Scott Adamson* (1932) 17 TC 679; *Westward Television Ltd v Hart* (1968) 45 TC 1

Tax Reporter: ¶260-000

HMRC toolkit

HMRC have issued a 'toolkit' on income tax losses (available at www.hmrc.gov.uk/agents/toolkits/income-tax-losses.pdf). That kit incorporates the following questions, which can act as a checklist of issues to consider.

(1) Have all relevant adjustments been made to arrive at the allowable trade loss for tax purposes?

(2) If a claim for trade loss relief is made, is the claim within the relevant time limit?

(3) Where trade loss relief is claimed against general income and/or chargeable gains of the same and/or previous year, do the claims meet the necessary requirements?

(4) Have any trade losses brought forward been used correctly and set in full against the first available profits of the same trade?

(5) Where trade losses are set against income that is not liable for Class 4 NICs, has the correct amount of loss been carried forward for Class 4 NICs purposes?

(6) Where a claim is made to set off trade losses from the first four tax years of a new trade against general income of earlier years, have all conditions been satisfied?

(7) If there are trading losses in overlapping basis periods, have they been correctly apportioned?

(8) Where the business has permanently ceased trading, has any terminal loss been calculated and utilised correctly?

(9) Have any capital losses arising in the year, or brought forward from an earlier year, been utilised correctly?

(10) If a partnership profit or loss allocated on a commercial basis produces a mixture of notional profits and losses, have all the appropriate re-allocations been made?

105-050 Carrying losses forward

A person who carries on a trade, profession or vocation and who makes a loss which has not been wholly relieved under other provisions can make a claim to carry the loss forward for set-off against trading income from the same trade in subsequent years. Relief is given as soon as profits are made, with any amount remaining unrelieved being carry forward for offset against later profits. Losses can be carried forward and set off only against profits of the same trade (*Gordon and Blair Ltd v IR Commrs*).

A claim is required for the unused loss itself to be carried forward to future years and set off. The subsequent use of the loss in reducing profits, etc. in a later year is automatic and does not require a further claim. The initial claim for carry forward must be made within five years of 31 January following the tax year in which the loss arises.

Example

Gemma made a trading loss of £10,000 in the year ended 31 December 2017. In the following two years she made profits of £4,000 and £14,000 respectively. She has no other income. If carry forward relief is claimed, her taxable profit will be:

		£
2017–18	Year to 31 December 2017	Nil
2018–19	Year to 31 December 2018	4,000
	Less: loss brought forward	(4,000)
		Nil
2019–20	Year to 31 December 2019	14,000
	Less: loss brought forward (10,000 – 4,000)	(6,000)
		8,000

The loss must be offset in 2018–19, even though this leads to the wastage of her personal allowance for that tax year.

Legislation: TMA 1970, s. 43; ITA 2007, s. 83ff.

Case: *Gordon and Blair Ltd v IR Commrs* (1962) 40 TC 358

Tax Reporter: ¶260-650

Transfer of a business to a company

Where an individual transfers a business into a company, losses sustained before incorporation which remain unrelieved may be carried forward and set against dividend or other income from the company (e.g. remuneration) provided:

(1) the business was transferred wholly or mainly for shares in the company;

(2) the taxpayer has a beneficial interest in the shares for the whole of the tax year in question;

(3) the company carries on the trade throughout the year in question.

Of course, in the year of transfer, (2) and (3) must only be satisfied for the part of the year after the transfer.

> **Example**
>
> On 1 January 2017, Hugh transfers his business to Y2 Ltd in return for shares. Hugh's business has an outstanding loss of £20,000. Hugh owns the shares in Y2 Ltd at all material times. In the year 2017–18, Hugh receives director's fees of £15,000 and a dividend of £1,500 (despite the fact that, with effect from 5 April 2016, the dividend may otherwise have been taxed at 0%). If the relief is claimed, the loss will be set off against both types of income. The £3,500 loss which remains outstanding is then carried forward and set off against income from the company (salary before dividends) in 2018–19 and so on until the loss has been set off completely.

Legislation: ITA 2007, s. 86

Tax Reporter: ¶261-650

105-100 Using losses against general income

Relief for a trading loss sustained for a tax year may be given against general income of the same tax year or for the preceding tax year (irrespective of whether the trade was carried on in that preceding tax year). A claim may be made for either or both years, in whichever order the taxpayer chooses, but a claim for the offset of current year losses takes precedence over losses carried back. The claim must be for the lower of the loss and the full amount of total income in the year. It is not possible to restrict the claim, e.g. to enable personal allowances to be used. A loss claim may thus lead to the wasting of other reliefs and allowances.

A claim must be made in writing not later than 12 months after the 31 January next following the end of the tax year in which the loss is sustained (i.e. approximately 22 months from the end of the year of loss).

To the extent that the loss cannot be relieved against general income it can be carried forward for relief against future profits from the same trade (see 105-050).

A temporary extension of income tax loss relief had effect for trading losses incurred in 2008–09 or 2009–10 (or both).

Legislation: ITA 2007, s. 64

Tax Reporter: ¶260-200ff.

Choice of relief

With the option to claim relief either against:

- total income for the same year as the year of loss; or
- total income for the year immediately preceding the year of loss,

the optimum claim that can be made in any situation will depend on the individual's circumstances. The wasting of personal allowances, the rates of tax being relieved and the likelihood of significant future profits arising in the trade will be some of the factors to be considered.

Example

Hugo has traded for many years. His recent results are as follows:

Period of account	*Trading profit/(loss)*	*Year of assessment/loss*	*Other taxable income*
	£		£
31 December 2015	5,000	2015–16	3,000
31 December 2016	(10,000)	2016–17	7,000
31 December 2017	(1,000)	2017–18	3,000

2015–16		£	
	Profits	5,000	
	Other income	3,000	
	Total income	8,000	
	Loss	(8,000)	Loss of 2016–17
		Nil	Personal allowances for 2015–16 wasted
2016–17			
	Profits	Nil	
	Other income	7,000	
	Total income	7,000	
	Loss (1)	(2,000)	Loss of 2016–17
	(2)	(1,000)	Loss of 2017–18

		4,000	Some personal allowances for 2016–17 wasted
2017–18			
	Profits	Nil	
	Other income	3,000	
	Total income	3,000	
Losses utilised			
2016–17 loss		£	
		10,000	(account period 31/12/16)
used 2015–16		(8,000)	
used 2016–17		(2,000)	
2017–18 loss			
		1,000	(account period 31/12/17)
used 2016–17		(1,000)	

Conditions for s. 64 relief

Losses are only available for relief against other income of the same or preceding year if it is shown that for the tax year in which the loss is claimed to have been sustained the trade was being carried on:

- on a commercial basis; and
- with a view to the realisation of profits in the trade (this includes a reasonable expectation thereof).

In *Wannell v Rothwell (HMIT)*, the High Court upheld a finding of fact that a taxpayer who left employment and set up as an independent fund manager, but who acquired no clients and made substantial losses, was not trading on a commercial basis within the meaning of the legislation. Similarly, in *Agnew*, the tribunal held that the taxpayer was not carrying on a trade in the years in question or, if he was, any such trade was not carried on on a commercial basis and with a view to the realisation of profits. The taxpayer claimed to be carrying on a trade and he paid amounts to his wife as an employee, seeking to set the resulting losses against his other income. HMRC argued that the wages should be disallowed as they were not paid for business purposes but merely represented a transfer of income between the taxpayer and his wife. The tribunal, in *Patel*, found that although a small element of the taxpayer's two businesses was profitable, it was not sufficient to demonstrate that as a whole they were run on a commercial basis and with a view to a profit.

By contrast, the tribunal found that there had been a reasonable expectation of profit in the case of *AW Kerr*, concerning a National Trust tenant who incurred losses for a variety of reasons. HMRC argued that during the year in question there was just a single commercial transaction and that in any case there was an onerous lease that restricted trading activities and that made it impossible to run a commercial business. The tribunal found, however, that the appellant had done all he could with the intention of making a profit. There had been a delay in obtaining the lease but the anticipated activities, when carried on as a trade, would clearly be and were in fact commercial.

Legislation: ITA 2007, s. 64 and 66

Cases: *Wannell v Rothwell (HMIT)* [1996] BTC 214; *Agnew* [2010] TC 00566; *AW Kerr* [2011] TC 00917; *Patel* [2015] TC 04225

Relief for farming losses

Any loss incurred in a trade of farming or market gardening is generally excluded from relief against other income if in each of the previous five years a loss was incurred in carrying on that trade (see 106-180).

105-200 Carrying losses back

In addition to the general rule allowing a loss to be carried back and set off against general income of the preceding year, the carry-back of losses is also permitted in the following cases:

(1) losses in the opening years of a new trade, etc. (see 105-250); and

(2) terminal year losses in the final year of a trade, etc. (see 105-300).

Where a loss is carried back for offset in an earlier year, the self-assessment for that year is not re-opened. Instead relief for the carry back of losses is given as follows:

- calculate the tax saving in the earlier year to which the loss relief is carried back; and

- give relief for the tax saving in the (later) year in which the loss actually arises, by means of a 'free-standing' credit to the taxpayer's self-assessment account.

Where there are no outstanding liabilities, the free-standing credit can be repaid if the taxpayer requests this. Otherwise, assuming the claim is made in the return for the later year (and both the required payments on account have been paid in full), the credit will be treated as increasing the total of the tax already paid by deduction and the tax due as payments on account for that year. The effect will be to reduce the balancing payment for that year or eliminate it entirely and perhaps give rise to a repayment of tax paid on account. Where a repayment is made, repayment supplement does not begin to accrue until the first anniversary of the statutory filing date for the later year.

If the credit is set against any unpaid tax of the later year, it is set off firstly against the balancing payment, then against the second payment on account and then against the first payment on account. For these purposes and those for setting against unpaid tax charges of any previous year, the 'effective date of payment' is the later of the date of the valid claim or the due date of the unpaid tax charge

These rules apply to any claim requiring losses incurred in one year to be relieved in an earlier year and they override the normal rules in TMA 1970, s. 42(2) that deal with claims to be included in a tax return.

Legislation: TMA 1970, Sch. 1B, para. 2; ICTA 1988, s. 824(2C)(a), (3)(ab)

Other Material: *Self Assessment Manual* SAM110085; *Self Assessment Claims Manual* SACM11020

105-250 Losses in opening years

If an individual who is carrying on a trade or profession sustains a loss in the tax year in which the trade is first carried on by him or any of the next three tax years, he can carry back that loss and set it off against other income. The set-off is against the income of the three tax years last preceding that in which the loss is sustained, earliest year first.

For the above loss relief to apply the taxpayer must show that he was carrying on the business throughout the period in which the loss was sustained on a commercial basis and in such a way that profits in the trade could reasonably be expected to be realised in that period or within a reasonable time thereafter.

Example

Elaine was employed for many years; her last three years' taxable earnings were:

- 2014–15: £25,000
- 2015–16: £28,000
- 2016–17: £29,000

She left employment on 31 March 2017 and commenced as a sole trader on 1 July 2017 making up her first accounts to 30 June 2018 (and to 30 June thereafter). Her tax adjusted trading loss for the 12 months to 30 June 2018 (including capital allowances) was £36,000. She has no other income sources apart from those indicated. Her trading activities are unlikely to show significant profits for several years. The claims available to her under s. 72 are as shown below.

(1) Determine the losses available

		£
2017–18	(1 July 2017 – 5 April 2018) $^{9}/_{12}$ × £36,000 =	(27,000)
2017–18	(1 July 2017 – 30 June 2018) £36,000 – £27,000 =	(9,000)

(2) The earliest year for carry-back is:

2017–18 carry-back to 2014–15

2018–19 carry-back to 2015–16

(3)

2014–15		£	
	Income (Earnings)	25,000	
	Less:		
	Loss of 2017–18	(25,000)	
		Nil	
2015–16		£	
	Income (Earnings)	28,000	
	Less:		
	Loss of 2017–18	(2,000)	(27,000 – 25,000)
		26,000	
	Loss of 2018–19	9,000	
		17,000	

(4) *Loss memorandum*

		£
(a)	loss of 2017–18	27,000
	used 2014–15	(25,000)
	used 2015–16	(2,000)
(b)	loss of 2018–19	9,000
	used 2015–16	(9,000)

> *Note:* Once a loss has been carried-back three years under these provisions, any unused portion *must* be carried forward and set against income of the next year (as in the example, where £2,000 of loss unused in 2014–15 is carried forward to 2015–16) even if it results in other allowances (e.g. personal allowance) being wasted.
>
> Alternative claims are available to Elaine should she wish to make them. For example, she could set the loss of 2017–18 (£27,000) against the income of 2016–17 (final year of employment; £29,000). Such a claim would have been advantageous if she had sufficient income in 2016–17 to make her liable at the higher rate. A claim to carry back the loss of 2018–19 (the second year of trade) would still have been possible if such a claim had been made. It is open to Elaine to choose the order in which to make the claims. However, where a claim is made under one provision, only the loss remaining unrelieved may be claimed under the other provision (*Butt (HMIT) v Haxby*).

A claim under these rules must be made within one year of the 31 January following the tax year in which the loss was sustained.

Legislation: ITA 2007, s. 72

Case: *Butt (HMIT) v Haxby* [1983] BTC 32

Tax Reporter: ¶261-000

Restriction for spouses and civil partners

There are provisions to prevent manipulation of the rules by spouses or civil partners. Loss relief will not be given under these provisions to a taxpayer if:

- at the time when the business was first carried on by him he was married to, or a civil partner of, another individual who has previously carried on the business; *and*
- the loss is sustained in a tax year later than the third tax year after that in which the trade was first carried on by the other individual.

Legislation: ITA 2007, s. 74(4)

105-300 Terminal year losses

Losses sustained by an individual in the final year of trading (terminal losses) can be carried back and set off against profits of that trade or profession for the final year and the three years preceding the final tax year (latest year first).

The 'terminal loss' is the loss which arises in the last 12 months of the trade (or profession or vocation). The basic calculation of the loss is the same as under other rules (e.g. capital allowances are included as a trading expense; overlap relief may increase or create a loss), but the normal rules for allocating an accounting period to a year of loss do not apply. The terminal loss is calculated in two parts, as the loss actually arising in:

(1) the year of assessment in which the trade ceases (i.e. from 6 April to the date of cessation) and may include overlap profit relief; and

(2) that part of the preceding year of assessment that begins 12 months before the date of cessation.

Any apportionments needed to determine the losses for the periods in (1) and (2), above, are normally made on a time basis. In determining (1) and (2) losses must be aggregated with profits; where the result is a (smaller) profit it will count as a 'nil' loss in determining the overall loss for the final 12 months.

Interest wholly and exclusively laid out for the purpose of the trade, etc. which is eligible for relief under ITA 2007, s. 383 but unrelieved because of an insufficiency of income, may be treated as a loss sustained when the interest was paid.

Example

Gordon has traded for many years, normally preparing accounts to 30 September each year; he ceases trade on 30 April 2017 producing seven month accounts to that date. Tax adjusted results (including capital allowance claims) for his final periods of trading are a profit of £12,000 for the 12 months ending 30 September 2016 and a loss of £3,500 for the seven months to cessation on 30 April 2017. He has transitional overlap profit relief of £1,000 available. His terminal loss is for the year 2017–18 and will be:

(1) *Loss arising in final year* (2017–18)			£
$^1/_7$ × (£3,500)			(500)
Overlap relief available			(1,000)
			(1,500)
(2) *Loss of preceding year* (beginning 12 months prior to cessation.)			
Period 1/5/16 – 5/4/17		£	
(a) 1/5/16 – 30/9/16 $^5/_{12}$ × £12,000 =		5,000	
(b) 1/10/16 – 5/4/17 $^6/_7$ × (£3,500) =		(3,000)	
	Profit	(2,000)	
An overall profit is treated as a 'nil' loss			0
			(£1,500)

> The terminal loss of 2017–18 is £1,500. It can be used against trading profits of 2017–18 (in this case there are none); then carried back to 2016–17 where the profit of £12,000 can be relieved. If the loss were greater than the 2016–17 profit further carry backs to 2015–16 and 2014–15 would be possible.
>
> The loss of £3,000 which was aggregated with profits for the period 1 May 2016 to 30 September 2016 is still available for relief against other income, since it has not been utilised in the terminal loss claim.

Legislation: ITA 2007, s. 89ff.

Tax Reporter: ¶261-100

105-350 Set-off against capital gains

Relief for trading losses which cannot be fully utilised against general income may be set off against capital gains (see 206-860 for commentary on this relief).

Legislation: ITA 2007, s. 71

Tax Reporter: ¶260-300

Avoidance involving trade losses

105-500 Overview

Imposition of tax charge

In certain circumstances, an income tax charge is imposed on individuals who have obtained tax relief for losses incurred. The charges are imposed on:

- partners claiming 'excess relief' (ITA 2007, s. 791ff: see 105-520);
- individuals claiming relief for film-related trading losses (ITA 2007, s. 796ff: see 105-540); and
- partners claiming relief for licence-related trading losses (ITA 2007, s. 804ff: see 105-560).

There is also a restriction for 'tax-generated losses' (see 105-585).

Denial of tax relief

These anti-avoidance rules, imposing a tax charge after the event, may be seen as complementary to the provisions of ITA 2007, Pt. 4, Ch. 3

('restrictions on trade loss relief for certain partners'), which restrict the amount of relief that can be given in the first place (see 102-720).

105-520 Partners claiming excess relief

Overview

If a partner claims loss relief but subsequently has his partnership contribution reduced, an income tax charge is made to recover the 'excess relief'. The individual partner is taxed on the amount of income he is treated as receiving under these anti-avoidance provisions.

The charge arises where partners (who must have been limited partners, members of a LLP or non-active partners) have claimed relief for trading losses sustained in periods beginning after 1 December 2004. The individual is treated as receiving non-trading income every time a 'chargeable event' occurs.

These provisions only apply where the relief is sideways relief claimed against income other than profits of the same trade, or capital gains relief.

Legislation: ITA 2007, s. 791ff.

Tax Reporter: ¶263-725

Chargeable events

A chargeable event occurs only if the individual's contribution to the firm is reduced as a result of the application of regulations made under s. 114. That reduction must immediately have the effect that:

- the total trade losses for which relief is claimed, less any relief that has been reclaimed, start to exceed the contribution; or
- there is an increase in the amount by which that net relief exceeds the contribution.

Special provisions apply where there is more than one trade.

Legislation: ITA 2007, s. 792(3)

Tax Reporter: ¶263-735

Amount of income treated as received

The amount of income charged to tax in these circumstances is broadly the reduction in the individual's contribution, as resulting from the regulations, but capped by reference to the amount of losses claimed and not reclaimed.

Legislation: ITA 2007, s. 793

Tax Reporter: ¶263-745

105-540 Film-related losses

Overview

If an individual claims certain types of loss relief for film-related losses, an income tax charge is made if there is a 'chargeable event'. The individual is taxed on the amount of income he is treated as receiving under these anti-avoidance provisions. Three key conditions need to be met if the charge is to be imposed:

(1) One of the following types of relief is claimed for a film-related loss (as defined):

  (a) sideways relief; or

  (b) capital gains relief.

  The term 'relevant claim' is given to such a claim.

(2) The second condition is that there is a disposal (a 'relevant disposal') of the individual's right to trading profits.

(3) Thirdly, an exit event must occur.

Legislation: ITA 2007, s. 796ff.

Tax Reporter: ¶263-800

Exit events

An exit event occurs in either of two ways:

(1) If the individual receives any 'non-taxable consideration' (i.e. consideration that is not otherwise chargeable to income tax) for a relevant disposal. If consideration is received after deduction of any costs relating to the disposal, or exit event, then the gross amount is treated as the non-taxable consideration.

(2) If there is either:

  (a) an increase in the individual's claimed film-related losses; or

  (b) a decrease in the individual's capital contribution,

  as a result of which the losses exceed (or further exceed) the contribution.

Legislation: ITA 2007, s. 797(2)

Tax Reporter: ¶263-800

Chargeable events

The individual is treated as receiving taxable income (but not trading profits) whenever there is a 'chargeable event', broadly involving a relevant claim, a relevant disposal and an exit event.

On the occurrence of a chargeable event, the individual is treated as receiving the amount (or value) of any non-taxable consideration received by the individual for relevant disposals, plus the amount (if any) by which the individual's claimed film-related losses exceed his capital contribution. The calculation is to be made immediately after the chargeable event has occurred.

Legislation: ITA 2007, s. 797(4), (5)

Tax Reporter: ¶263-810

105-560 Licence-related losses

Overview

If an individual claims certain types of loss relief for 'licence-related losses', an income tax charge is made if there is a 'relevant disposal'. The individual is taxed on the amount of income he is treated as receiving under these anti-avoidance provisions. The income is not treated as trading profits for tax purposes.

For the purposes of these rules, an agreement (or part of an agreement) is not prevented from being a licence merely because it imposes an obligation to do a thing (rather than merely gives authority to do it). References to exploiting a licence are interpreted accordingly.

Legislation: ITA 2007, s. 804ff.

Tax Reporter: ¶263-875

Occasion of charge

The tax charge arises (ITA 2007, s. 805) if:

- the individual carries on a trade as a 'non-active partner' during an 'early tax year';
- he makes a loss in the trade in that tax year;

- he claims 'sideways relief' or 'capital gains relief' (a 'relevant claim');
- the loss derives to any extent from expenditure incurred in the trade in exploiting a licence acquired in carrying on the trade; and
- there is a relevant disposal of the licence.

The individual is then treated as receiving an amount of income if there is at least one chargeable event in the year.

Legislation: ITA 2007, s. 805

Tax Reporter: ¶263-875

Calculation of tax charge

The income treated as received by the individual under these anti-avoidance provisions is calculated by using five statutory steps, as follows. If the result is a negative figure, the income is nil:

Step 1

At the end of the tax year, calculate the amount of claimed losses (so far as relating to the licence) made by the individual in the trade in any 'early tax year' during which the individual carried on the trade as a 'non-active partner'.

Step 2

At the end of the tax year, calculate the amount of the profits (so far as relating to the licence) made by the individual in the trade in any tax year.

Step 3

Deduct the total calculated at Step 2 from the total calculated at Step 1 to give 'the net licence-related loss'. If this figure is nil or negative then no income is treated as received in the tax year and the next two steps are ignored.

Step 4

At the end of the tax year, calculate the amount or value of all non-taxable consideration received by the individual for relevant disposals. In principle, this includes any consideration received in previous tax years but non-taxable consideration received before 10 February 2004 is excluded.

Step 5

Take the lower of the net licence-related loss, and the result of Step 4, and deduct from that lower figure the amount of all income treated under

s. 805 (and certain predecessor legislation) as received by the individual in previous tax years as a result of chargeable events.

Legislation: ITA 2007, s. 806

Tax Reporter: ¶263-890

105-585 Tax-generated losses

Certain restrictions apply on tax relief for artificial losses incurred from 21 October 2009 (but subject to commencement provisions). On that date, the Government published draft legislation, together with explanatory notes and other guidance material. According to that guidance, 'this measure targets those who enter into arrangements for the purpose of obtaining a reduction in tax liability by means of sideways loss relief. It does not impact on loss-makers who have not entered into avoidance arrangements'.

The 2010 legislation replaces the rules for tax-generated losses incurred by certain non-active traders from March 2008, but the newer rules have a broader impact. The effect of the rules is to deny completely any sideways relief or capital gains relief for losses incurred by an individual or partner where:

- the person carries on a trade, profession or vocation (the 'relevant activity') in the tax year, either alone or in partnership;
- he or she incurs a loss in the relevant activity in that tax year; and
- the loss arises (directly or indirectly) 'in consequence of, or otherwise in connection with, relevant tax avoidance arrangements'.

Legislation: ITA 2007, s. 74ZA

Tax Reporter: ¶261-350

105-590 Losses attributable to annual investment allowances

No relief is given in certain circumstances where a person makes a loss in a UK or overseas property business and where there are relevant tax avoidance arrangements. More specifically, the restrictions apply where:

- a person makes a loss (whether in partnership or not) in a UK property business or an overseas property business;
- the loss has a capital allowances connection (as defined); and
- the loss arises directly or indirectly in consequence of, or otherwise in connection with, relevant tax avoidance arrangements (again, as defined).

When the rules apply, no property loss relief is allowed against general income for so much of the 'applicable amount of the loss' as is attributable to an annual investment allowance.

Legislation: ITA 2007, s. 127A

Tax Reporter: ¶260-270

105-595 Investments to obtain sideways loss relief

HMRC issued a statement on 8 February 2010, under the heading 'Spotlight 8: Investments to obtain trade loss reliefs'. The opening paragraph of that statement, which summarises the issues, is as follows:

> 'We are aware of schemes seeking to exploit sideways loss relief by generating trade losses for individuals. Typically, a large loss is generated, either in partnership or alone, by accounting for the arrangement as a trade and either writing down the value of trading stock or claiming deductions or allowances for purported trading expenditure. Often these schemes are funded in part by borrowing and may include a mechanism that means repayment is guaranteed. The individuals claim the loss as sideways loss relief against their other tax liabilities. HMRC's view is that these schemes fail to meet the commercial and other fundamental requirements for sideways loss relief so that no relief is available to the participants.'

See also 105-585 regarding 'tax-generated losses'.

Tax Reporter: ¶261-375

Particular activities

Farmers and market gardeners

106-000 Introduction and definitions

Farming or market gardening in the UK is treated for income tax purposes as the carrying on of a trade or part of a trade (whether or not the land is managed on a commercial basis and with a view to the realisation of profits).

'Farming' is defined as the occupation of land wholly or mainly for the purposes of husbandry, but does not include market gardening. Husbandry includes hop growing, and the breeding and rearing of horses and the grazing of horses in connection with those activities. 'Market gardening' means the occupation of land as a garden or nursery for the purpose of growing produce for sale.

'Short rotation coppice' is regarded for tax purposes as farming rather than forestry. Consequently, the land on which it is undertaken is regarded as farmland or agricultural land and not commercial woodland. 'Short rotation coppice' means a perennial crop of tree species planted at high density, the stems of which are harvested above ground level at intervals of less than ten years.

'Farming' has different meanings in different contexts for tax purposes. For example, for the purposes of restricting certain loss reliefs which would otherwise be available to farmers or market gardeners 'farming' and 'market gardening' are interpreted as above, but with the difference that activities carried on outside the UK are included.

'Farm land' excludes 'market garden land'. 'Market garden land' means 'land in the UK occupied as a nursery or garden for the sale of produce (other than land used for the growth of hops) and "market gardening" is construed accordingly.'

Legislation: ITTOIA 2005, s. 876.

106-020 Trading

All farming (but not market gardening) which is carried on by a sole trader, persons in partnership or body of persons is treated as one trade. Accordingly, profits derived from more than one farm must be aggregated into a single chargeable source of income where the taxpayer operates more than one farm at the same time, whether the farms are in the same or in different parts of the country.

Where a farmer ceases to operate one farm and starts to operate another he is not treated as having ceased to carry on one trade and as having begun to carry on a new trade. In *Bispham v Eardiston Farming Co (1919) Ltd*, a farming company which bought one farm in Scotland and soon after sold a farm in England was (being engaged in a continuous trade) entitled to carry forward losses and unused capital allowances from the English farming business to the Scottish one.

However, where there has been a substantial lapse of time between the cessation of operations on one farm and the commencement of operations on another, HMRC are likely to treat the taxpayer as having ceased to carry on one trade and as having begun to carry on a new one. What amounts to a significant lapse of time is a question of fact to be decided in the light of all the circumstances of a particular case.

Case: *Bispham v Eardiston Farming Co (1919) Ltd* (1962) 40 TC 322

Tax Reporter: ¶270-500

106-040 Computation of profits

In general, profits from farming and market gardening are computed in the same way as profits from any other trade are computed.

There are, however, a number of special rules which apply in connection with farming and market gardening, including in particular:

- grants, subsidies, and compensation (see 106-060);
- livestock (see 106-100ff.); and
- farm stock valuation (see below).

The basis of valuation of farm stock which is acceptable to HMRC is explained in Business Economic Notes (BEN 19 *Farming: Stock Valuation for Income Tax Purposes*).

Tax Reporter: ¶270-550; ¶271-850

Farmhouse expenses

If the farmer's premises, such as a farmhouse, are used partly for farming and partly for domestic purposes, HMRC in practice allow a deduction for that part of the rent attributable to the farm business. The maximum amount allowable is usually one-third, but may be less where the extent or cost of the premises is out of proportion to the size of, or revenue obtained from, the farm land.

Tax Reporter: ¶272-100

Farm drainage

The conditions under which HMRC are prepared to treat certain farm drainage expenditure as a revenue expense, deductible in computing farm profits, are as set put in SP 5/81.

Tax Reporter: ¶272-150

106-060 Grants, subsidies and compensation

Terminology

Many schemes, statutes, or statutory instruments provide for grants, subsidies or compensation (collectively referred to from now on as 'grants, etc.' unless the context otherwise requires) to be paid to farmers and market gardeners (collectively referred to from now on as 'farmers, etc.' unless the context otherwise requires) against the cost of both revenue and capital assets.

A grant, where available, is usually made to a farmer to help him to improve his farming business in some way, for example for fencing or planting.

Subsidies are usually given to a farmer to compensate him for loss of production on one type of produce, in order either:

- to keep prices in the market place down; or
- to encourage him to enter into a new and possibly risky form of farming activity.

Compensation is usually paid to the farmer where an asset of his has been lost or destroyed.

However, for tax purposes the essential criterion is the purpose of the payment, not the label attached to it. For example, a payment which is actually a grant may be referred to as a subsidy. The courts would treat it as a grant.

More importantly, expenditure in respect of which a grant is made may be considered by the Department for Environment, Food and Rural Affairs to be capital expenditure whilst the courts may class it as revenue expenditure for tax purposes.

Tax Reporter: ¶270-600

Income or capital receipt?

Where compensation is received, the test is whether it is compensating:

- a mere restriction of the farmer's trading opportunities; or
- the depreciation of one of the capital assets of his business.

The character of a payment is not governed by the method of calculating the amount of the payment.

The tax treatment of any particular grant or subsidy depends on the purpose for which such grant or subsidy is made. If it is made to reduce the amount of the farmer's revenue expenditure, then it is treated as reducing his allowable deductions for income tax purposes. If, on the other hand, it is paid against the amount of any capital expenditure to be incurred, it is treated as proportionately reducing the amount of any capital allowance to which the farmer might otherwise have been entitled.

If a grant, etc. is paid to a farmer, etc. or to someone else on his behalf, towards a farming or other trading expense then it is income. Grants, etc. are generally treated, for tax purposes, as reducing the amount of expenditure in respect of which they were paid.

Cases: *Burmah Steam Ship Co Ltd v IR Commrs* (1931) 16 TC 67; *Higgs v Wrightson* (1944) 26 TC 73; *White v G & M Davies & Anor* (1979) 52 TC 597

Tax Reporter: ¶270-650

Payments under the single payment scheme

The Single Payment Scheme was introduced by Regulation 1782/2003 and replaced numerous earlier types of payment with effect from 1 January 2005. All SPS receipts are chargeable to income tax (subject to the usual exemptions, for example, for charities). The basis of charge will depend on the circumstances under which they are received.

The most straightforward situation is that of ordinary commercial farmers who continue to farm as they have for many years in that they grow and harvest crops and/or rear farm animals. In such a case, sums receivable are chargeable as revenue trade receipts for income tax purposes.

Under the SPS it is possible to receive an income without production by keeping the land in Good Agricultural and Environmental Condition (GAEC). Where there is no actual production then there can be no occupation for the purposes of husbandry and therefore no farming trade. The tax treatment may be different in such cases.

If it can be shown that additional expenditure has been wholly and exclusively laid out to secure the SP then such can be set off to reduce the tax charge but this is likely to be rare.

Other Material: HMRC *Business Income Manual* BIM55125ff.

Tax Reporter: ¶270-650

Capital allowances

The receipt of a grant is treated as proportionately reducing the amount of any capital allowance which would have been available to the farmer, etc. had it not been for such receipt.

106-080 Share farming

Share farming is a method of farming where two parties jointly farm the same land. Typically a share farming agreement involves the owner or tenant of farm land (the landowner) who enters into a contract with a working farmer (the share farmer).

Share farming enables a landowner to farm as a joint venture with a person who has farming expertise. Genuine share farming agreements fall short of creating a tenancy or partnership whilst ensuring that the landowner can still enjoy the inheritance tax, capital gains tax and income tax advantages of being treated as a farmer. The landowner may also be anxious to avoid creating a tenancy because agricultural tenants are hard to remove, and anxious to avoid creating a partnership because that would make him or her liable for the share of the farmer's debts.

Both parties to a genuine share farming agreement may be accepted as farming. They have concurrent rights to the land and both are contributing to an undertaking of husbandry thereon.

Share farming should not be confused with contract farming, in which a contractor carries out husbandry activities on behalf of the landowner. In such cases, the landowner is normally treated as the occupier of the land, who is therefore farming. The contractor is taxed not on farming profits but on the profits of the contracting activities.

Tax Reporter: ¶270-950

106-100 Livestock: general principles

Animals or other living creatures kept for the purposes of a trade are treated as trading stock if they are not kept wholly or mainly:

- for the work they do in connection with the carrying on of the trade;
- for public exhibition; or
- for racing or other competitive purposes.

In general, a farmer who keeps livestock for his farming purposes must treat them as trading stock but they are not so treated if they are part of a herd in relation to which a herd basis election has effect (see 106-120).

In this connection, the following points should be noted:

- if the farmer does nothing, any livestock which he keeps for his farming purposes are automatically treated as trading stock; and
- the tax treatment of livestock on the trading stock basis is exactly the same as the tax treatment of any trader's stock.

Legislation: ITTOIA 2005, s. 30

Tax Reporter: ¶271-000

106-120 Herd basis: introduction

Definitions

A farmer who has livestock which forms part of a 'production herd' can elect for the herd basis to apply to that herd and if he does so, then that basis will apply instead of the trading stock basis.

The expression 'the production herd' here means a herd of animals, or living creatures other than animals, of the same species, irrespective of breed, kept by the farmer wholly or mainly for the sake of the products which can be obtained from them when alive, for him to sell. The relevant 'products' are offspring, or any other product obtainable from the animal except a product only obtainable by slaughtering the animal itself.

Legislation: ITTOIA 2005, s. 30, 111ff.

Tax Reporter: ¶271-100

Immature animals

Immature animals kept in a herd are not, in general, treated as being part of their herd. There are, however, two exceptional cases in which immature animals are treated as being part of a herd. Those cases are when:

(1) the land on which the herd is kept is such that animals which die or cease to form part of the herd cannot be replaced except by animals bred and reared on that land; and

(2) the relevant animals are:

   (a) bred in the herd; and

   (b) maintained in order to replace animals which die or cease to form part of the herd.

There is, however, a proviso that no more immature animals can be treated as forming part of a production herd than are needed in order to prevent a fall in the number of animals therein.

Female animals are treated as becoming mature when they produce their first young, and laying birds are regarded as becoming mature when they first lay.

Legislation: ITTOIA 2005, s. 112–113

Tax Reporter: ¶271-100

106-140 Herd basis election

General rules

Any herd basis election must apply to all production herds of a particular class which the farmer keeps, including herds which he ceased to keep before he made the herd basis election or begins to keep after having made such election. Where a farmer farms more than one farm, or farms on more than one estate, any herd basis election which he makes applies to his production herds of the same class on all of his farms or estates.

Two conditions must be met in order for production herds to be deemed to be of the same class.

(1) All the animals kept in the relevant herds must be of the same species, irrespective of breed. If, for example a farmer has two dairy herds, one herd comprising Friesians and the other comprising Guernseys, they will be deemed to be of the same class, because, although they are not of the same breed, they are of the same species; the species being cattle.

(2) The products obtainable from the creatures which the farmer could sell and for the sake of which he keeps the herds (either wholly or mainly) must be of the same kinds in the case of all the herds. If, for example a farmer has two herds of dairy cattle which are of different breeds, the second condition is met since they both produce milk.

A herd basis election may apply to herds which the farmer:

- no longer has when he makes his election; or
- does not have at the time when he makes such election but acquires in the future.

Anti-avoidance rules prevent the exploitation of these rules. These have effect if all or part of the herd is disposed of otherwise than in a normal transaction, either to a connected party or in circumstances that point to a tax-saving motive.

Legislation: ITTOIA 2005, s. 124(6), 127

Tax Reporter: ¶271-150

Mechanics

The farmer must specify the class of production herds to which the election relates and must make the election (which is irrevocable) within the specified time limit. The time limit is the first anniversary of the normal self-assessment filing date for the tax year in which the first relevant period of account ends, or if that is the tax year in which the farmer starts to carry on the trade and the farmer is not a firm, on or before the second anniversary of the normal self-assessment filing date for that tax year. 'The first relevant period of account' means the first period of account in which the farmer making the election keeps a production herd of the class to which the election relates.

If the farmer is a partnership and there is a change in the persons who are partners in the firm any herd basis election made by the old firm ceases to have effect, and in relation to the new firm, 'the first relevant period of account' means the first period of account in which the new firm keeps a production herd of the class to which the election relates.

Where compensation is payable for compulsory slaughter, the farmer may be granted extra time for making an election.

Legislation: ITTOIA 2005, s. 124

Other Material: ESC B11

Tax Reporter: ¶271-750

Information

HMRC may by notice require the person carrying on a trade in relation to which a herd basis election is made to deliver a return of such information about the animals kept for the purposes of the trade, and the products of those animals. The return must be delivered to HMRC within the time reasonably specified in the notice.

Legislation: FA 2008, Sch. 36, Pt. 1

Tax Reporter: ¶188-000; ¶271-800

Effect of election

In general, a herd basis election takes effect for the farmer's first tax year and all subsequent tax years. Exceptionally, where the farmer receives compensation for the compulsory slaughter of a production herd, the herd basis has effect for the first tax year in which the compensation is taken into account for tax purposes and all subsequent tax years (subject to loss relief provisions).

A herd basis election is, in general, irrevocable, and it applies to all production herds of the same class which the farmer has kept in the past, keeps at present, or may keep in the future. However, there is one case in which such an election will cease to have effect and in which the farmer will have a new right to make a herd basis election. If the farmer:

- has kept a production herd of a particular class; and
- altogether ceases to keep herds of that class for at least five years,

he will be treated as if he had never kept any production herds of that class before the end of those five years as regards production herds of that particular class.

A newly constituted partnership, including a case in which there has been a change in an existing partnership, if it keeps a production herd of any class, will have a right of election in respect of herds of that class. Any election already made by an individual partner, or by the previous partnership, in respect of herds of that class will be of no effect in relation to the herds kept by the new partnership.

Once a herd basis election takes effect, the following tax consequences follow as regards any relevant tax year:

- all assessments and repayments of tax must be made as are necessary to give effect to the election; and
- any claim for relief for income tax by reason of the operation of the election must be made in writing to HMRC.

Legislation: ITTOIA 2005, s. 125–126, 129

Tax Reporter: ¶271-200

106-160 Effect of herd basis election on trading profits

Initial cost of the herd

The farmer cannot deduct the initial cost of the herd to him as a trading expense (ITTOIA 2005, s. 114). Equally, the value of the herd is to be ignored in computing trading profits or losses. These rules also apply, in general, to the cost of any animal which the farmer may periodically add to his initial herd (subject to replacement provisions).

Example

Farmer Brown buys a herd of cows for £10,000. He elects for the 'herd basis' to apply.

There is therefore no tax relief in respect of the initial cost of £10,000, either as revenue or capital.

The next year, he sells two cows for £1,500 and buys two more for £1,300. He is therefore assessable on the difference of £200 as trading receipt (ITTOIA 2005, s. 116).

In the following year, he retires and sells his whole herd for £12,000. This receipt is not subject to tax.

The following must be brought into Fiona's accounts as trading receipts:

- proceeds of sale of cattle sold (since this is not a 'substantial part' of the herd);
- proceeds of sale of dead cattle;
- initial cost (if immature animals bought in), and cost of rearing whichever of cattle maturing are not treated as replacements.

The following may be brought into Fiona's accounts as trading expenses:

- purchase price of whichever of the cattle purchased are treated as replacements, *restricted* to the amount which would have been spent on cattle of the same quality as those sold;
- cost of rearing whichever of the cattle maturing are treated as replacements.

Note that if Fiona also sold immature animals, which had not been added to the herd, the proceeds of sale would be taxable as trading receipts.

For the purpose of calculating the profits of the trade if, either all at once or over a period not longer than 12 months, the herd or a substantial part of the herd is sold, any profit arising from that sale is not brought into account as a receipt. Similarly, no deduction is allowed for a loss arising from such a sale. This provision does not, however, apply if the acquisition of a new herd, or replacement of the herd, commences within five years of the sale.

Legislation: ITTOIA 2005, s. 116, 119

Tax Reporter: ¶271-400

New herd acquired within five years of sale

Special rules apply if, within five years of the sale of a herd, the farmer acquires or starts to acquire another production herd of the same class. Broadly, any profit or loss which results from the sale (i.e. the difference between the sale proceeds and the value of the herd) is disregarded for tax purposes.

If, either all at once or over a period not longer than 12 months, a substantial part of the herd is sold, and the farmer acquires or starts to acquire animals to replace the part sold within five years of the sale, then special 'replacement of animals' provisions apply for the purposes of computing profits so far as the animals included in the part sold are replaced. Generally, the sale proceeds of an animal included in the part sold are not brought into account as a receipt until the animal that replaces it in the herd is acquired. The rule is adapted if the farmer is compelled to sell the part of the herd for reasons wholly outside his control.

Legislation: ITTOIA 2005, s. 121ff.

Tax Reporter: ¶271-450; ¶271-550

106-180 Trading losses: hobby farming

The rules which apply to the computation and assessment of the trading losses of a farmer or market gardener are, in general, the same as those which apply to any other trader.

A trader is normally entitled to set off his losses against his other profits in the year of the loss or in the preceding year. There are, however, special rules which apply exclusively to farmers and market gardeners, often referred to as the 'hobby farming' rules. The measure is aimed at, for example, high-earning individuals who dabble in farming and who wish to claim tax relief against their other income for the losses they incur as a result.

Relief is therefore unavailable to a farmer or market gardener if, in each of the previous five years of farming or market gardening, he made a loss. For the purpose of computing a loss in this context, capital allowances are ignored.

Relief is not denied if the farmer can show that in the following (sixth) year the business of farming or market gardening was being conducted in such a way as would have justified a reasonable expectation of future profits if it had been undertaken by a competent farmer or market gardener, but that, if such a person had taken on those activities at the beginning of the prior period of loss, he could not reasonably have expected the activities to become profitable until after the end of the sixth year. This qualification allows for the possibility that some forms of farming and market gardening may need more than five years in which to become profitable.

Where any loss is excluded from relief by the hobby farming rules, capital allowances are also excluded.

The restriction only applies to the set-off of losses and capital allowances against other income and does not prevent their being carried forward against future profits.

Legislation: ITA 2007, s. 67ff.

Tax Reporter: ¶272-850

106-200 Relief for fluctuating profits (averaging): introduction

Farming and market gardening profits often fluctuate substantially from year to year, partly as a result of the vagaries of international trade and partly as a result of the weather. Consequently, a farmer, etc. could suffer a severe tax charge in one particularly successful year because of the higher rate of income tax, whilst he may not enjoy any substantial relief in a subsequent, less successful year, unless there were provision to the contrary in the legislation.

In the situation outlined above, farmers and market gardeners are entitled to claim the right to average their farming profits in any two or, with effect from 2016–17, five consecutive tax years.

Years prior to 2016–17

Provided that the relevant profits in either of two consecutive tax years do not exceed a specified proportion of the profits for the other year. An averaging claim may be made in relation to the two years provided:

- the relevant profits of one of the tax years are less than 75% of the relevant profits of the other tax year; or
- the relevant profits of one (but not both) of the tax years are nil.

The relevant profits of a tax year are profits before making any deduction for a loss made in any tax year. If the taxpayer makes a loss in the qualifying trade, profession or vocation in a tax year, the relevant profits of the tax year for averaging purposes are nil.

The farmer, etc. is not entitled to profit averaging relief:

- in respect of any tax year before a year in respect of which a claim for profit averaging relief has already been made; or
- in respect of a tax year in which the trade is, or is treated as, set up and commenced or permanently discontinued.

Years subsequent to 2015–16

The above two-year averaging election continues but FA 2016 introduced an extended relief that would allow a taxpayer to average over a five-year period provided certain volatility conditions are met, these are:

- one of the following is less than 75% of the other:
  - the average of the relevant profits for the first four years to which the claim relates; and

  - the relevant profits of the last of the tax years to which the claim relates; or
- the relevant profits of one or more of the five tax years is nil.

Any of the first four tax years may also be a tax year in which a two-year averaging claim has been made.

A claim under these provisions may not be made in relation to a year of commencement or cessation of the farming business.

The claim must be made no later than the second 31 January following the end of the final year to which the claim relates.

Legislation: ITTOIA 2005, s. 221

Tax Reporter: ¶272-300

106-220 Farm averaging: computations

Tax years 2015–16 and earlier

'Full averaging'

If the claimant's profits for either year do not exceed 70% of his profits for the other year, or are nil, his profits for each such tax year are to be adjusted so as to be equal to 50% of his profits for the two years taken together or, as the case may be, for the year for which there are profits.

> **Example**
>
> Archer, a farmer, has assessable farming profits of £28,000 in 2014–15 and assessable profits of £13,800 in 2015–16. Since his profits in 2015–16 do not exceed 70% of his profits in 2014–15, if he makes a claim for profit averaging the result will be that his profits in each year are to be added together and his averaged profits for each year will become one-half of £28,000 plus one-half of £13,800, i.e. £20,900 in each year.

Legislation: ITTOIA 2005, s. 223

'Marginal averaging'

These provisions are only relevant for years up to 2015–16. Where the claimant's profits for either year exceed 70% but are less than 75% of his profits for the other year, his profits for each year are to be adjusted by adding to the profits that are lower and deducting from those that are higher an amount equal to three times the difference between them, less 75% of those that are higher. This can be expressed as:

Example

Fred, a farmer, has assessable farming profits in 2014–15 of £20,000 and assessable farming profits in 2015–16 of £14,600. Here, his farming profits for 2015–16 exceed 70% of his farming profits for 2014–15, but are less than 75% of his farming profits for 2014–15. If Fred elects to average his profits the result will be that each year's farming profits will be adjusted by adding to Fred's farming profits for 2015–16 and deducting from his farming profits for 2014–15 the following figures:

£16,200 (i.e. £20,000 – £14,600 = £5,400 × 3 = £16,200)

Less: 75% of Fred's profits in the more profitable year = £15,000.

The adjustment to be made in respect of each relevant tax year is therefore £1,200. Fred's new assessment for 2014–15 will now be £18,800 (i.e. £20,000 – £1,200 = £18,800) and his new assessment for 2015–16 will now be £15,800 (i.e. £14,600 + £1,200 = £15,800).

Legislation: ITTOIA 2005, s. 223

Tax Reporter: ¶272-400

106-225 Farm averaging: computations

Tax years 2016–17 and later

The concept of 'marginal averaging' is removed and full averaging will apply only where the 75% volatility thresholds are reached. Where the conditions are met, it is open to the taxpayer to make either a two-year or a five-year averaging claim. The effect of the claim is to simply tax the average profit over relevant years (treating a low making year as nil) and tax this profit in each year.

Example

Andy has the following assessable farming profits:

2015–16	£31,000
2016–17	£75,000
2017–18	£12,000
2018–19	(£4,000)
2019–20	£6,000

Since his profits in 2019–20 do not exceed 75% of the average of the profits of the previous four years (£29,500), then it is open to Andy to elect to apply the averaging provisions over the five years. The result would be taxable profits of £24,800 (the loss in 2018–19 being treated as nil) in each of the five years.

Legislation: ITTOIA 2005, s. 223A

106-240 Farm averaging: effect of adjustment

The adjusted profits are taken to be the relevant profits of the tax years to which the claim relates for all income tax purposes. This is subject to the following:

- if the relevant profits of one of the tax years are nil, it does not prevent the taxpayer from obtaining relief for a loss made by him in the tax year in question or any other tax year;
- for these purposes, the averaging claim is ignored.

The following points should therefore be noted.

(1) What are averaged in each tax year are the claimant's adjusted trading profits for income tax purposes, not his accounting profits. In other words, what are averaged are the assessable profits for each tax year before any deduction for losses.

(2) Any loss which the claimant suffers in a particular tax year is treated as neither a gain nor a loss in that year for averaging purposes. However, any rights to loss relief which the claimant may have are still preserved under the appropriate sections of the Taxes Acts (see example below).

(3) Once the averaging has been made there is a new assessment for the relevant tax years, and the revised profits after the averaging claim are treated as the profits for all tax purposes, except that losses are relieved in the normal way.

(4) After averaging, the revised profits of the second year will form the profits which may themselves be averaged if the rules are met by the two tax years of which that year is one. So, subsequent averaging will take the new assessment as the appropriate figure with which to work, not the pre-averaged assessment.

Legislation: ITTOIA 2005, s. 224–225

Tax Reporter: ¶272-600

106-260 Implementation of claims for averaging relief

An averaging claim must be made by the first anniversary of the normal self-assessment filing date for the second of the tax years to which the claim relates. However, where the profits for any of the years which are the subject of the averaging claim are adjusted, any further averaging claim will not be out of time as long as it is made on or before the first anniversary of the normal self-assessment filing date for the tax year in which the adjustment for the other reason is made.

Where the claim relates to the earlier year, it is given effect in the later year, either by an increase in the amount of tax payable, or by increasing the amount of any payments on account made in respect of that year. This approach avoids the need to reopen earlier years, so that tax due for each year can be finalised with certainty on the basis of events of that year and is not contingent on later events.

Legislation: TMA 1970, Sch. 1B, para. 3; ITTOIA 2005, s. 222(5), 225(4)

Tax Reporter: ¶272-750

Creative artists

107-000 Averaging of fluctuating profits

Certain individuals who derive profits from creative works may make a claim to 'average' the profits of two successive years. This can have tax advantages where, for example, there is a one-off year with exceptionally high income followed by several successive years of very low profits. Without the special rules, an individual might find that in the first year there is a substantial amount of income taxed at 40% but then in later years the basic rate band is not used up.

Prior to 2016–17, the tax rules for creative artists exactly mirrored those that applied for farmers. Although the farming rules have been in position for far longer, the two separate sets of legislation were merged into one when the *Income Tax (Trading and Other Income) Act* 2005 (ITTOIA 2005) was enacted. The direct mirroring of provisions for creative artists and farmers was ended in FA 2016 when the five-year averaging rules were introduced exclusively for farmers. The ability to average over five years was not extended to creative artists. With the exception of the above, all of the following apply in exactly the same way for creative artists as they do for farmers, and reference should be made in this commentary to the coverage of farming at 106-200ff.:

- the circumstances in which a claim may be made;
- the manner in which the adjustment is made;
- the tax effect of that adjustment; and
- the mechanics of giving relief where profits are adjusted for other reasons.

Definitions

For relief to be given in this way, an individual must make a claim. That individual must have been carrying on a trade, profession or vocation, either as a sole trader or in partnership. In the case of creative artists, the profits from the trade, etc. must derive 'wholly or mainly from creative works'. These are defined to include:

- literary, dramatic, musical or artistic works; or
- designs,

which (in either case) must be created personally by the individual or by one or more of the partners.

> **Example**
>
> When the averaging rules were first applied to creative artists, the Treasury supplied the following example of an author's profits, without averaging, of:
>
> Year 1 – £3,000; and
>
> Year 2 – £45,000.
>
> In Year 1, the author might have unused allowances, and in Year 2, he might be liable to tax at the higher rate of 40%. Averaging results in the tax bill being computed as if the profits were £24,000 in each year, so the personal allowances would all be used and the higher rate liability eliminated. Further, the averaged profit in Year 2 can be used in averaging a claim in Year 3. Thus, if the result for Year 3 was a loss (treated as a nil profit for averaging), it could be averaged with the profit of £24,000 for Year 2, so that the tax for Years 2 and 3 would be re-computed as if the profit was £12,000 for each year.

Legislation: ITTOIA 2005, s. 222–224

Tax Reporter: ¶268-300

Qualifying care relief

107-450 Introduction

A measure of tax relief is given to individuals who provide qualifying care (formerly, foster-care services) and who might be considered to be carrying on a trade, profession or vocation. The relief formerly given to foster carers was extended from April 2010 so that the relief is now available to 'qualifying shared lives carers'. As part of this change, 'foster care relief' is renamed 'qualifying care relief'.

For an individual whose receipts from providing the care do not exceed a given threshold, a complete exemption is given from income tax on those receipts.

Individuals with a higher level of receipts can elect for an alternative (simplified) method of calculating the taxable profits of their trade, profession or vocation. Special rules are then needed if accounts are not drawn up to 5 April each year. Special rules are also required to ensure that the capital allowances rules integrate fairly with the qualifying care relief.

Various key terms are defined for the purposes of this tax relief. Definitions of the following concepts are given at 107-480:

- qualifying care receipts;
- provision of qualifying care;
- provision of foster care;
- provision of shared lives care;
- residence.

Legislation: ITTOIA 2005, s. 803ff.

Tax Reporter: ¶281-800

107-460 Individuals qualifying for relief

Qualifying care relief is only available to individuals.

The test of whether an individual qualifies is made for a year of assessment. Subject to the concept of the 'placement cap' (see 107-470), the individual will qualify if:

- he has 'qualifying care receipts' for the year; and
- apart from the qualifying care receipts as such, the individual does not derive any taxable income from a 'relevant trade or arrangement'.

A 'relevant trade or arrangement' is defined to mean any trade, profession, vocation or arrangement from which he derives any other qualifying care receipts in that year. The inclusion of 'arrangement' is to catch any arrangements by which an individual provides foster care otherwise than as part of a trade, profession or vocation carried on by him.

Legislation: ITTOIA 2005, s. 804

Tax Reporter: ¶281-810

107-470 Placement cap

From 6 April 2010, an upper limit of three (the 'placement cap') is imposed on the total number of 'shared lives placements' that the carers in a household can provide simultaneously before they cease to qualify for qualifying care relief. The loss of relief applies if the placement cap is exceeded for any residences used by the individual to provide the care from which qualifying care receipts are derived.

The placement cap applies if, at any given time during the relevant period, shared lives care is provided in the residence for more than three people in total (whether or not by the individual in question). In relation to any given residence, the relevant period is the period for which the residence is the individual's only or main residence during the income period for the receipts.

Where there is more than one carer in the household, the cap applies to the total number of shared lives placements provided by all those carers.

Foster care placements are not counted as shared lives care placements. If the placement cap is exceeded, the qualifying care relief will not be available in respect of shared lives care but will continue to be available for foster care.

A group of siblings placed in the same household will count as one shared lives placement for the purpose of the placement cap, however many siblings are in fact placed within the household.

Legislation: ITTOIA 2005, s. 804A

Tax Reporter: ¶281-820

107-480 Definitions

Qualifying care receipts

The term 'qualifying care receipts' is defined to mean the receipts of an individual for any tax year arising from the provision of qualifying care:

- that would, but for this legislation, be brought into account in computing the profits of a trade, etc. or would otherwise be chargeable under ITTOIA 2005, Pt. 5, Ch. 8 (income not otherwise charged); and
- that accrue to that individual during the income period for those receipts.

For these purposes, the term 'income period' means, for receipts that would be taxed under ITTOIA 2005, Pt. 5, Ch. 8, the tax year. For trading income, it means the basis period for the trade.

In calculating an individual's 'total qualifying care receipts', no deductions of any sort are allowed.

Legislation: ITTOIA 2005, s. 807

Tax Reporter: ¶281-830

Provision of qualifying care

Qualifying care is said to be provided if an individual (either alone or in partnership) provides foster care or shared lives care or both.

Legislation: ITTOIA 2005, s. 805A

Tax Reporter: ¶281-830

Provision of foster care

Foster care is defined to mean the provision for a child of accommodation and maintenance by a foster carer. The legislation lists the various statutory provisions under which an individual may be treated, in different parts of the UK, as a foster carer for these purposes.

Exclusions

The relief does not apply to adult placement care. The following are also excluded individuals:

- any parent of the child;
- any individual who exercises parental responsibility (or, in Scotland, responsibilities) in relation to the child;
- (if the child is in care and there was a residence order in force with respect to the child immediately before the care order was made), an individual in whose favour the residence order was made;
- (in Scotland, if the child is in care and there was a residence order or contact order in force with respect to the child immediately before the child was placed in care), an individual in whose favour the residence order or contact order was made.

Legislation: ITTOIA 2005, s. 806

Tax Reporter: ¶281-830

Provision of shared lives care

An individual is said to provide shared lives care if he or she provides accommodation and care for an adult or child who has been placed with the individual, and certain conditions are met.

The care must be provided in the carer's own home on the basis that the child or adult will share the individual's home and daily family life during the placement. The placement must be made under a specified social care scheme (see below) and the care must not constitute the provision of foster care (see above). The care provider must not be an excluded individual (e.g. a parent).

The following definitions apply for the purposes of determining whether shared lives care is being provided:

- 'care' means personal care, including assistance and support;
- 'home' means an individual's only or main residence;
- 'social care scheme' means a scheme, service or arrangement for those who, by reason of age, illness, disability or other vulnerability, are in need of care.

Legislation: ITTOIA 2005, s. 806A

Tax Reporter: ¶281-830

Specified social care scheme

Secondary legislation specifies three different types of social care schemes, defined to mean a scheme or service or arrangement that provides:

- 'adult placement care';
- 'kinship care'; or
- 'staying put care'.

Detailed conditions are specified in the Order for each type of care.

Legislation: *Qualifying Care Relief (Specified Social Care Schemes) Order* 2011 (SI 2011/712)

Tax Reporter: ¶281-830

Residence

For the purposes of the rules governing qualifying care relief, the term 'residence' is defined to mean:

- a building, or part of a building, occupied or intended to be occupied as a separate residence; or
- a caravan or houseboat.

The legislation also provides that 'if a building, or part of a building, designed for permanent use as a single residence is temporarily divided into two or more separate residences, it is still treated as a single residence.'

Legislation: ITTOIA 2005, s. 806B

Tax Reporter: ¶281-830

107-490 Individual's limit

The individual's limit, used to determine whether there is to be any tax liability, consists of two elements:

- the fixed amount for the tax year (or, in certain circumstances, the individual's share of that amount) (see 107-500); and
- the amount per adult or child for the tax year (see 107-510).

Legislation: ITTOIA 2005, s. 808

Tax Reporter: ¶281-840

107-500 Fixed amount

The individual's limit consists of two elements.

The first such element, the fixed amount, is £10,000 (a figure that is subject to alteration by Treasury Order). In practice, this fixed figure is an amount per residence and 'is intended to broadly represent the fixed costs of a household in providing foster care, irrespective of the number of children cared for at any one time' (Finance Bill 2003 – Notes on Clauses).

The fixed figure is then also subject to alteration as follows.

Residence used by more than one carer

The fixed figure is reduced if the same residence is used by more than one individual who derives receipts from the provision of qualifying care in the same tax year. In these circumstances, the legislation takes a broad brush approach and requires that the fixed amount must be split equally between the two or more individuals receiving qualifying care receipts in relation to the same residence.

Legislation: ITTOIA 2005, s. 809

Tax Reporter: ¶281-845

Income period not a year

A second adjustment to the fixed amount will be needed if the income period is greater or shorter than 12 months. In such a case, the figure of £10,000 (or this figure as already adjusted for a shared residence) is adjusted pro rata. Strictly, this calculation is to be done to the day, applying the fraction D/365 where D is the number of days in the income period.

Example

Beth and Kath share a house. Beth has been a foster parent for some years and Kath starts to act as a foster parent. Kath's basis period for the year in question is 270 days.

Beth's share of the fixed amount is £5,000. Kath's share for the first period of her trade is £3,699 ((£10,000/2) × 270/365).

Legislation: ITTOIA 2005, s. 810

Tax Reporter: ¶281-845

107-510 Amount per adult or child

The second element of the individual's limit is an amount per adult or child.

For an individual providing qualifying care throughout the tax year, the amount per child is £200 per week for a child who has not yet reached his or her 11th birthday, and £250 per week for an older child or an adult. The £250 starts to apply from the week in which the child reaches 11. A week is a seven-day period starting on a Monday. The Treasury has the power to amend the weekly figures.

If care is provided by an individual for only a part of the tax year, then a weekly calculation is to be made. Part of a week is treated as a whole week for these purposes.

Where an income period begins or ends during a week, that week is treated as falling within the income period that ends during the week. (If there is no such period, then the week is treated as falling within the other income period.)

Legislation: ITTOIA 2005, s. 811

Tax Reporter: ¶281-800

Parent and baby schemes

In such schemes, only the parent is in foster care, but the local authority pays an amount to cover accommodation and care for both the parent and the baby. In such cases, HMRC treat both the parent and the baby as being in foster care and foster carers can claim a weekly amount for both when calculating their qualifying amount.

Legislation: ITTOIA 2005, s. 803

Tax Reporter: ¶281-850

Children with disabilities

HMRC recognise that carers dealing with children who are disabled or who have other special needs may incur exceptional expenditure (such as the provision of special equipment for a disabled child). HMRC have stated that such expenditure may be added to the qualifying amount if the carer needs to incur expenses that are 'different from normal maintenance costs'.

107-520 Full qualifying care relief

Where an individual's total qualifying care receipts do not exceed his limit, those receipts will be exempt from tax altogether for that year. Differing rules apply depending on whether or not the income would otherwise constitute trading profits.

Legislation: ITTOIA 2005, s. 812–814

Tax Reporter: ¶281-860

Trading profits

If the income would otherwise constitute trading profits, the mechanism for granting exemption is to treat the profits or losses of the trade as nil. The mechanism for relief is not optional in these circumstances – if the receipts are less than the income limit then it is not possible to claim relief for any loss actually incurred.

The method of calculation varies according to whether or not accounts are drawn up to 5 April. Where the accounting year end is 5 April, or where the profits are calculated simply by reference to the tax year, an individual's qualifying care receipts will be exempt from tax if his total care receipts do not exceed his limit. His limit for the tax year in question is calculated as his share of the fixed amount plus each amount per adult or child.

> **Example**
>
> Sue provides foster care from her home throughout the tax year. She fosters a seven-year-old boy for 30 weeks and a 14-year-old girl for 40 weeks during the year. Nobody else provides foster care or other qualifying care from her home.
>
> Her fixed amount is £10,000.
>
> The 'amount per child' for the boy is £6,000 (30 weeks at £200 per week) and for the girl is £10,000 (40 weeks at £250 per week).
>
> Sue's limit is therefore calculated as £26,000.
>
> If Sue draws accounts up to 5 April, and her total receipts are under £26,000, the foster income is exempt from tax.

Legislation: ITTOIA 2005, s. 813

Tax Reporter: ¶281-860

Period of account not ending on 5 April

The same principle is adapted where the individual's taxable profits for any given tax year are not calculated by reference to a 5 April accounting date. In this case, it is necessary to calculate the 'relevant limit' for the period of account in which the individual's qualifying care receipts accrue. This is found by adding together two amounts:

(1) The fixed amount (or the individual's share of the fixed amount, if appropriate) is that for the year in which the accounting period ends.

(2) (For each of the tax years in which the period of account falls), each amount per adult or child for the individual for each part of the period of account falling in that tax year. In other words, the accounting period is notionally split into two (or more) parts if different adult or child rates apply for the two (or more) tax years into which the accounting period falls. For those cared for in so much of the accounting period as falls before 6 April, the rates for the earlier year will apply; for later periods, the rates for the later year will be used.

As long as the individual's total qualifying care receipts do not exceed his or her limit, calculated on this basis, the profits or losses of the trade for that year are treated as nil. This is subject to the 'alternative calculation' as explained at 107-530 below.

Legislation: ITTOIA 2005, s. 821, 822

Tax Reporter: ¶281-860

Not trading profits

Different rules apply if the qualifying care receipts would have been taxed not as trading profits but under ITTOIA 2005, Pt. 5, Ch. 8 (income not otherwise charged to tax).

In these circumstances, the receipts received from each arrangement in the tax year, less any expenses associated with those receipts, is simply treated as nil.

Once more, though, an alternative calculation is available, as explained at 107-530.

Legislation: ITTOIA 2005, s. 814

Tax Reporter: ¶281-860

107-530 Alternative calculation

Where an individual qualifies for qualifying care relief for a given tax year, but the amount of his total qualifying care receipts exceed his limit for the year, a simplified method of computing profits is offered. The choice of method is important, not just to save administration time but potentially to save a considerable amount of tax. Once more, there is a variation in how the limit is calculated, depending on whether or not profits are calculated by reference to an accounting period ending on 5 April.

Accounting date to 5 April

An individual in these circumstances may elect to calculate taxable income from the provision of qualifying care by simply taking the excess of his or her total qualifying care receipts for the tax year over his or her limit for that year. If Sue, in the example at 107-520, had total foster care receipts of £28,000, she could therefore elect to pay tax on trading profits of £2,000, rather than calculating her profits following ordinary trading principles. The same calculation is used to calculate the taxable amount for an individual whose income would be charged other than as trading profits.

Legislation: ITTOIA 2005, s. 816, 817

Tax Reporter: ¶281-870

Mechanics of election

To claim the simplified treatment, an individual must make a written election on a year-by-year basis, specifying the year for which it is made. The deadline for the election follows self-assessment principles, and is set as 31 January following the tax year to which it relates (or such later date as an officer of Revenue and Customs may allow). The deadline is extended if an adjustment is made to the taxable profits to be assessed from the provision of qualifying care for that year. In such a case, the individual has until the first anniversary of the 31 January next following the tax year in which the adjustment is made (or, again, such later date as an officer of Revenue and Customs may allow).

HMRC have stated that 'completing your tax return using the simplified method and submitting it by the filing date will be accepted as notification', i.e. as an election to use that simplified method for the year in question.

Legislation: ITTOIA 2005, s. 818, 819

Tax Reporter: ¶281-870

Accounting date not 5 April

Where the period of account does not end on 5 April, an election may still be made if the individual's total qualifying care receipts for the period exceed his relevant limit for that period. The trading profits for the tax year are in that case taken to be the amount of those total receipts less the relevant limit for the period. Again, the election must specify the year for which it is made. The same rules apply as above to extend the time limit for the election if HMRC adjust the assessment.

Legislation: ITTOIA 2005, s. 823

Tax Reporter: ¶281-870

107-540 Capital allowances

The exemption and alternative calculation given for qualifying care relief together create a complication in relation to capital allowances. The qualifying care rules therefore take a number of steps to address the issue, the broad effect of which is to suspend the entitlement to capital allowances for any period in which qualifying care receipts are not taxed at all or are subject to the alternative calculation.

First, no capital allowances are given for any period for which either the profits are exempt or the alternative calculation is used.

Secondly, there are special rules that apply to prevent a balancing charge or allowance when the individual starts to benefit from either the exemption or the alternative method.

Thirdly, capital expenditure does not constitute qualifying expenditure for capital allowances purposes if incurred by an individual during a year in which he is benefiting from either the exemption or the alternative calculation. Such expenditure is referred to as 'excluded capital expenditure'.

Finally, there is a mechanism for renewing capital allowances for an individual who has either been exempt or has used the alternative calculation but who moves on to the standard basis of calculating profits in a subsequent year. Such an individual can then start to claim capital allowances once more in respect both of assets that were subject to the deemed disposal event and of new assets that have been excluded capital expenditure. In either case, it is a condition that the asset must still be owned at the start of the period in question.

Legislation: ITTOIA 2005, s. 825–827

Tax Reporter: ¶242-300

Adopters, special guardians, etc.

107-600 Introduction and overview

Most financial support provided to adopters in the UK is exempt from tax. The exemption applies to payments made under the *Adoption and Children Act* 2002 and to certain other payments to adopters. The declared intention of the original legislation (Finance Bill 2003 – Notes on Clauses) was to ensure that all contributions by local authorities and adoption agencies to adoption costs should be exempt from tax.

The exemption was extended from April 2010, so that the relief is now also available to qualifying guardians. Different rules apply under the legislation to different parts of the UK. In each case, however, the exemption applies to special guardians, and to any individual looking after a child under a residence order as long as the individual is not the parent or step-parent of the child. Differing regional rules apply for the various regions of the UK.

Legislation: ITTOIA 2005, s. 744ff.

Tax Reporter: ¶281-950ff.

Subcontractors in the construction industry

108-000 Introduction and overview

The special tax deduction scheme in the construction industry applies to payments made by contractors to subcontractors for work involving construction, installation, repairs, fitting, decorating and demolition. The scheme was changed quite radically from April 2007.

In essence, the scheme requires a contractor to make tax deductions at a prescribed rate from amounts ('contract payments') payable to subcontractors for services, unless HMRC have provided a verification reference number.

Legislation: FA 2004, Pt. 3, Ch. 3; *Income Tax (Construction Industry Scheme) Regulations* 2005 (SI 2005/2045)

Tax Reporter: ¶282-350

108-025 Employment status

Under the CIS rules as they have applied since April 2007, contractors must check or 'verify' new subcontractors with HMRC. Broadly, this means that HMRC will check the employment status of the subcontractor and ensure that he is properly registered for income tax and National Insurance contributions (NICs) purposes.

A worker's employment status, that is whether he is employed or self-employed, is not a matter of choice. Whether someone is employed or self-employed depends upon the terms and conditions of the relevant engagement. A worker's employment status will determine the charge to tax on income from that employment or self-employment. It will also determine which class of NICs must be paid.

HMRC provide an 'Employment Status Indicator (ESI) Tool' on their website (www.hmrc.gov.uk/calcs/esi.htm). Employers and contractors may use the tool to obtain a HMRC 'view' of the employment status of their workers. However, the tool is fairly limited and will at best provide a general guide which would not be binding on HMRC. To obtain a written 'opinion' of employment status in the construction industry, the contractor will need to telephone the New CIS Helpline on 0300 200 3210.

There are proposals – announced in July 2009 – to introduce a statutory test for employment status for some of those working in the construction industry.

For a much fuller discussion of employment status, and of the difficulties that arise in practice, see 131-250.

Tax Reporter: ¶282-425

108-050 Registration

A new subcontractor, starting working in the construction industry on a self-employed basis for the first time after 5 April 2007, or an existing subcontractor who last had a temporary registration card CIS4(T) that expired on or before March 2007, had to register for CIS from April 2007 if they did not want deductions at the higher rate made from their payments.

Contractors or subcontractors who incorporate or disincorporate their business need to re-register with HMRC. This point was made explicit in a 'Frequently Asked Questions' published on the HMRC website in January 2008.

Subcontractors who had a tax certificate CIS5 or CIS5(Partner) or CIS6 kept gross payment status only where their certificate was due to expire on or after April 2007. Otherwise, a fresh application was needed if they wanted to be paid gross under the amended CIS rules as they applied from April 2007.

HMRC will only authorise a contractor to make gross payments to a subcontractor where the following conditions are satisfied.

Tax Reporter: ¶283-525

The business test

To satisfy this condition, the subcontractor must provide evidence that he is carrying on a business in the UK which:

(1) consists of or includes the carrying out of construction operations or the furnishing or arranging for the furnishing of labour in carrying out construction operations; and

(2) is, to a substantial extent, carried on by means of an account with a bank.

Evidence prescribed to satisfy the business test is as follows:

- the business address;
- invoices, contracts or purchase orders for construction work carried out by the applicant;
- details of payments for construction work;
- the books and accounts of the business; and
- details of the business bank account, including bank statements.

Legislation: *Income Tax (Construction Industry Scheme) Regulations* 2005 (SI 2005/2045), reg. 27

Tax Reporter: ¶283-550

The turnover test

The applicant must satisfy HMRC that in the year following the making of the application:

- as an individual, his net business turnover from construction work (that is, after the cost of any materials used to earn that income) is £30,000 a year or more; or
- as a partnership or company, the net business turnover from construction work (that is, after deducting the cost of any materials) is £30,000 a year or more multiplied by the number of partners or directors.

In the case of 'close companies' (broadly, companies controlled by five or fewer individuals), the figure will be multiplied by the number of individuals who are directors and/or shareholders. For a husband and wife team, for instance, it would be £60,000.

An alternative test for partnerships and companies is that the business has an annual net turnover from construction work (after deducting the cost of materials) of £200,000 or more.

Legislation: *Income Tax (Construction Industry Scheme) Regulations* 2005 (SI 2005/2045), reg. 28

Tax Reporter: ¶283-575

The compliance test

The subcontractor must have kept all your tax affairs up to date during the period of 12 months ending with the date of the application. This means he must have paid all tax liabilities, including any PAYE and subcontractor deductions, and submitted all tax returns on time. HMRC will not accept an application from a subcontractor who brings his tax affairs up to date just prior to submitting that application.

Legislation: *Income Tax (Construction Industry Scheme) Regulations* 2005 (SI 2005/2045), reg. 32

Tax Reporter: ¶283-600

108-100 HMRC guidance on CIS

HM Revenue & Customs have published various online guidance in relation to the CIS rules as they have applied from April 2007. See, in particular, www.hmrc.gov.uk/cis/index.htm and booklet CIS340: *Construction Industry Scheme – guide for contractors and subcontractors* (which has been updated since it was first published).

HMRC have also published extensive FAQs in relation to CIS under the following broad headings (www.hmrc.gov.uk/new-cis/faqs-index.htm):

- CIS online;
- late returns;
- payments and returns;
- penalties for late submission of the CIS300 contractor monthly return;
- registration;
- The Scheduled Review (Ongoing TTQT);
- transition;
- verification.

Tax Reporter: ¶282-375

HMRC Factsheets

The following 'factsheets' are produced to help contractors (and employers) to understand the compliance processes exercised by HMRC:

- EC/FS1: Employers and contractors – reviewing your records;
- EC/FS2: Large employers and contractors – reviewing your records;
- EC/FS3: Compliance checks – what happens during and at the end of a check;
- EC/FS4: Compliance checks – types of penalty;
- EC/FS5: Employers and contractors compliance checks – your obligations.

Other Material: www.hmrc.gov.uk/leaflets/ecfs5.pdf

108-125 Meaning of 'subcontractor'

For the purposes of the special tax deduction scheme, a party to a contract relating to construction operations is a 'subcontractor' if, under the contract, he is:

(1) under a duty to the contractor to carry out the operations, or to furnish his own labour (in the case of a company, the labour of employees or officers of the company) or the labour of others in the carrying out of the operations or to arrange for the labour of others to be furnished in the carrying out of the operations; or

(2) answerable to the contractor for the carrying out of the operations by others, whether under a contract or under other arrangements made or to be made by him.

A subcontractor is, therefore, any business which has agreed to carry out construction operations for another business or body which is a contractor or deemed contractor – whether by doing the operations itself, or by having them done by its own subcontractors or employees, or in any other way. Subcontractors include concerns normally known as main contractors, where they are engaged by a client who is a contractor; for example, a local authority.

Some businesses may act solely as contractors or as subcontractors but many act as both. This means that they both pay businesses below them and are paid by businesses above them in a chain. So for some of their transactions they will have to follow the rules for contractors and for others, the rules for subcontractors.

The term 'labour-only subcontractor' includes arrangements where the subcontractor may be required to supply his own tools. A subcontractor may also be required to supply materials connected with the contract the cost of which will be deducted prior to the calculation of the deduction on account of tax made from payments to subcontractors.

Special rules apply to agency workers.

The contractor must meet its obligations under the scheme for a payment to a gang-leader. The contractor does not need to be concerned with the transactions between the gang-leader and the other members of the gang. Any deductions from payments to the members of the gang are the responsibility of the gang-leader.

Legislation: FA 2004, s. 58

Tax Reporter: ¶282-775

108-150 Meaning of 'contractor'

The term 'contractor' includes any person carrying on a business which includes construction operations. These are known as 'mainstream contractors'. It also includes a wide range of public bodies, housing corporations, etc.

Property developers are included within the meaning of mainstream contractors because their principal business activity is the creation of buildings or other civil engineering works. The same is true of a speculative builder. A property investment business is not, however, the same thing as a property developer. A property investment business acquires and disposes of buildings for capital gain or uses the buildings for rental. It need not be involved in the construction of buildings. Even so, if its property estate is substantial enough, its expenditure on construction operations may well cause it to fall within the meaning of 'deemed contractor'.

Businesses which would not normally be regarded as contractors because their trading activities are not in construction areas will be regarded as contractors if the average annual expenditure of the business on construction operations in the three years ending with its last accounting date exceeds £1m; if the business has been carried on for less than three years it will be regarded as a contractor for the purposes of the scheme if its total expenditure on construction operations during the period it has been trading exceeds £1m. A business which is so regarded as a 'contractor' because of its expenditure on construction operations will continue to be regarded as a contractor until it satisfies the Board that subsequently the expenditure on construction operations has been less than £1m in each of three successive years commencing in or after the period for which it is first so regarded.

Example

Egg Ltd commences a new trade, having built new multi-storeyed premises, in February 2010. In earlier years Egg Ltd had traded as a retail store but had no expenditure on construction.

Construction expenditure year ended	£
31/12/10	250,000
31/12/11	1,000,000
31/12/12	1,440,000
31/12/13	800,000
31/12/14	800,000
31/12/15	500,000
31/12/16	200,000

Egg Ltd will be required to comply as a 'contractor' with the provisions of the construction industry deduction scheme from January 2014 and will not be able to satisfy HMRC that it is no longer within those requirements until some time in the year ending 31 December 2017.

Deemed contractor status applies, strictly speaking, as soon as the conditions are met, though in practice HMRC will allow 'a certain period of grace' for the business to meet its obligations.

As it is more difficult for businesses outside the mainstream construction industry to gear their tax administration around the needs of the CIS, HMRC make concessions for small payments. HMRC can authorise deemed contractors not to apply the scheme to small contracts for construction operations amounting to less than £1,000, excluding the cost of materials.

Contractors wishing to request authorisation not to apply the scheme to small payments should contact HMRC on 0300 200 3210.

HMRC advise that businesses which have any doubts as to their status as 'contractors' under the scheme, should refer their cases to their local HMRC Office.

Legislation: FA 2004, s. 59

Tax Reporter: ¶282-700ff.

Other Material: HMRC *Construction Industry Scheme Reform Manual* CISR12060

108-200 'Construction operations'

'Construction operations' are defined to include:

(1) the construction, alteration, repair, extension, demolition or dismantling of buildings and structures (whether permanent or not);

(2) the construction, alteration, repair, extension or demolition of any works forming, or to form, part of the land;

(3) the installation in any building or structure of systems of heating, lighting, air conditioning, ventilation, power supply, drainage, sanitation, water supply or fire protection;

(4) the internal cleaning of buildings and structures, so far as carried out in the course of their construction, alteration, extension, repair or restoration;

(5) operations which form an integral part of, or are preparatory to, or are for rendering complete, any of the operations listed above, including (inter alia) site clearance, scaffolding, landscaping, the provision of roads; and

(6) the painting or decorating of the internal or external surfaces of any building or structure.

Excluded operations

Excluded operations include the following:

(1) manufacture and delivery of building equipment and materials, and specifically of components for systems of heating, lighting, air-conditioning, ventilation, power supply, drainage, sanitation, water supply or fire protection;

(2) the professional work of architects or surveyors, or of consultants in building, engineering, interior or exterior decoration or in the laying-out of landscape;

(3) artistic works and sign-writing, and erecting, installing and repairing signboards and advertisements; and

(4) the installation of seating, blinds and shutters, security systems, including burglar alarms, closed circuit television and public address systems.

The Treasury may, by an order approved by the House of Commons, extend the above list.

HMRC take the view that carpet fitting is an operation outside the scope of the scheme (SP 12/81).

Legislation: FA 2004, s. 74

Core business

In *Mundial Invest SA v Moore (HMIT)*, the High Court held that construction operations included only those operations forming part of a person's core business.

Case: *Mundial Invest SA v Moore (HMIT)* [2006] BTC 301

HMRC guidance

HMRC booklet CIS 340 lists the types of construction works which are, generally speaking, within or outside the scheme. The list is not comprehensive and, where doubts exist, a ruling should be obtained from the local HMRC Office. Note that where a single contract relates to a mixture of jobs, the total payment is considered by HMRC to be subject to the scheme even if only one of the jobs falls within the meaning of 'construction operations' (CIS 340, Appendix C).

HMRC take the view that carpet fitting is an operation outside the scope of the scheme (SP 12/81).

Tax Reporter: ¶282-800

108-250 Contractor obligations – overview

This Chapter explains what contractors must do before payments can be made to subcontractors and how payments are made. The following table summarises a contractor's obligations under the new CIS:

Action	Due date	Legislation
Monthly returns	Within 14 days of the end of the tax month (that is by the 19th).	SI 2005/2045, reg. 4(1)
	If no payments made, contractor obliged to make a nil return within 14 days of the end of the tax month, unless contractor has notified HMRC that he will make no further payments in next 6 months	SI 2005/2045, reg. 4(10), (11)
Subcontractor information to be provided	Information in writing to be provided within 14 days after the end of the tax month either in respect of the total payments made in that month or in respect of each payment made in that month.	SI 2005/2045, reg. 4(8)
Payment and recovery	The contractor must pay any amounts deducted from subcontractors to HMRC within 17 days after the end of the tax period, where payment is made by an approved method of electronic communications, or within 14 days after the end of the tax period, in any other case.	SI 2005/2045, reg. 7(1)
Quarterly payments	Contractors may use quarterly tax periods if there are reasonable grounds for believing that the average monthly amount will be less than £1,500.	SI 2005/2045, reg. 8

Tax Reporter: ¶283-000

108-275 Verification

Verification is the process HMRC use to make sure that subcontractors have the correct rate of deduction applied to their payments under the CIS. There are three main steps to the process:

- the contractor contacts HMRC with details of the subcontractor;
- HMRC check that the subcontractor is registered with them;
- HMRC tell the contractor what rate of deduction to apply, if any.

Before a contractor can make a payment for construction work to a subcontractor, they must decide whether they need to verify the subcontractor.

The general rule is that a contractor does not have to verify a subcontractor if they last included that subcontractor on a return in the current or two previous tax years.

If either of the two previous tax years was before 6 April 2007, transitional rules applied.

If a contractor does not have to verify a subcontractor they must pay the subcontractor on the same basis as the last payment made to them. This means that if the subcontractor was last paid under the standard rate of deduction, the current payment must also be made under the standard rate of deduction. If the last payment was made gross, because a deduction was not required, the current payment must also be made gross.

In order to verify a subcontractor, HMRC will require the following information.

About the contractor

- name;
- unique taxpayer's reference (UTR);
- Accounts Office reference; and
- employer's reference.

About the subcontractor

Type of subcontractor	**Information required**
Sole-trader	• Name • unique taxpayer's reference (UTR) • National Insurance number, if known
Partner in a firm	• firm's name • partner's name

Type of subcontractor	Information required
	• firm's unique taxpayer's reference (UTR) • if the partner is an individual: – partner's unique taxpayer's reference (UTR) or partner's National Insurance number • if the partner is a company: – company's unique taxpayer reference (UTR) or company registration number
Company	• name of company • company's unique taxpayer's reference (UTR) • company registration number

About the contract

Confirmation that a contract has been agreed with the subcontractor or that the contractor has formally accepted a tender for work under a contract.

Tax Reporter: ¶283-025

108-300 Deduction of tax

Verification reference number

Once HMRC have received the necessary information they will tell the contractor to pay the subcontractor in one of the following ways:

- gross, i.e. without any deductions taken from the payment;
- net of a deduction at the standard rate; or
- net of a deduction at the higher rate (because HMRC have no record of that subcontractor's registration, or are unable to verify the details for any other reason).

When HMRC verify a subcontractor, they will give the contractor a verification reference number. The verification reference number will be the same for each subcontractor that they have verified at the same time. If it is not possible to verify a subcontractor, HMRC will add one or two letters to the end of the number so that it is unique to that subcontractor.

Tax Reporter: ¶283-025

Rate of deduction

The rates of deduction to be made from subcontractors are:

- registered subcontractors: 20%; and
- non-registered subcontractors: 30%.

If HMRC need to change a subcontractor's payment status from gross payment to payment under deduction, they will write and tell the subcontractor giving 90 days' notice of any change to allow the subcontractor to appeal, if required.

Sometimes a subcontractor's payment status will change from payment under deduction to gross payment. If this happens, HMRC will tell the subcontractor and any contractors who have verified or used the subcontractor in the current or previous two tax years. The revised payment status should then be applied to all subsequent payments to the subcontractor as soon as it is practical for the contractor to do so.

Tax Reporter: ¶283-125

Payments under deduction

Deductions must only be made from that part of the payment that does not represent the cost of materials incurred by the subcontractor.

Any travelling expenses (including fuel costs) and subsistence paid to the subcontractor must, however, be included in the gross amount of payment and the amount from which the deduction is made.

The contractor will need to keep a record of the gross payment amounts so that these can be entered on the monthly return.

The contractor must provide a written statement to every subcontractor from whom a deduction has been made within 14 days of the end of each tax month. A tax month runs from the 6th of one month to the 5th of the next month so the statement must be provided by the 19th of the month.

Contractors may choose the style of the statements but they must include the following information:

(1) the contractor's own name and employer's tax reference;

(2) the following details of the subcontractor:

   (a) name;

   (b) unique taxpayer reference number (UTR);

(c) the personal verification number if the subcontractor could not be verified and a deduction at the higher rate has been made;

(d) the gross amount of the payments made to the subcontractor;

(e) the cost of any materials that has reduced the amount against which the deduction has been applied; and

(f) the amount of the deduction.

It is good practice for a contractor to give a subcontractor a payment statement where the payment has been made gross, but there is no obligation to do so.

HMRC announced in June 2008 that they will not routinely provide payment and deduction details for subcontractors or their agents. Subcontractors should always keep their tax certificates so that they can comply with their own tax obligations and, where appropriate, claim any repayment of tax that may be due.

Tax Reporter: ¶283-100

108-305 Withdrawal of gross payment status

Where a subcontractor does not pass the various tests, and where there is no reasonable excuse for the failure (see 108-310), HMRC may withdraw gross payment status. The subcontractor will then suffer a tax deduction from every payment received, a change that can sometimes have severe cash flow consequences.

If HMRC seek to cancel gross status under these provisions, there is a statutory obligation that they 'must without delay give the person notice stating the reasons for the cancellation'. This point was tested in the case of *Radford*, where the partnership was not immediately told why its status was being changed. Although full details were provided by HMRC some two months later, the tribunal found that notification of withdrawal from the gross payment scheme was not given 'without delay'. The business therefore retained its gross status.

Legislation: FA 2004, s. 66

Case: *Radford* [2010] TC 00345

108-310 Reasonable excuse

Numerous cases have reached the tax tribunals and courts concerning the granting or withdrawal of gross payment status. An obligation is imposed on subcontractors to comply with their tax obligations, failing which they will not be allowed to receive payments gross (FA 2004, s. 67(3)(b)).

There is, however, an opportunity for the person concerned to appeal against a refusal to grant gross payment status, or against a cancellation of such status. The appellant will need to demonstrate that there was a reasonable excuse for the failure (FA 2004, Sch. 11, para. 4).

Key principles to emerge from appeals on the question of reasonable excuse are as follows.

- An appellant must give grounds for any appeal if HMRC cancel a person's registration for gross payment status (*Westview Rail Ltd*).
- The fact that cancellation of gross status could have dire consequences for a business is not normally accepted as constituting a reasonable excuse. This was the conclusion in *Grosvenor v R & C Commrs*, *Ductaire Fabrications Ltd v R & C Commrs* and *Enderbey Properties Ltd*, where the tribunal considered itself bound by the Chancery Division case of *Barnes (HMIT) v Hilton Main Construction*. A similar view was taken in *GC Ware Electrics* and in *Chatterton*. Also in *Eurotec Services (GB) LLP*. On the other hand, a very different attitude was seen in *Bruns t/a TK Fabrications*, where the tribunal recorded that 'another relevant fact is that withdrawal of gross payment status from the Appellant would have very serious consequences indeed for his ability to continue in trade'. The tribunal went on to comment that 'an excuse can arguably be regarded as reasonable by reference to the consequences of the withdrawal of gross payment status'. The dire consequences from withdrawal of gross payment status were also allowed as a reasonable excuse in *S Morris Groundwork Ltd*. The tribunal accepted the factual assertion that the company might lose a contract worth more than £3m if it lost its gross payment status, and that this could risk the livelihoods of its 100 employees in a difficult economic climate. As such, the tribunal considered the judgments of both the *Grosvenor* case (where the consequences were not taken into account) and of the *Bruns* case (where they were). The tribunal took note of the experience of the tribunal judge in the latter case and preferred that decision to the *Grosvenor* one. It held that the consequences of losing gross payment status in the present appeal would be disproportionate to the late payment of under £8,000 of corporation tax and, as such, the tribunal decided that there was a reasonable excuse.
- The fact that the taxpayer was unaware of the consequences of filing his returns late did not constitute a reasonable excuse (*Pollard*).
- An insufficiency of funds is not of itself a reasonable excuse for late payments of tax (*Beard v R & C Commrs*).
- Cashflow problems do not by themselves amount to a reasonable excuse for paying tax late (*Munns v R & C Commrs* and *Strongwork Construction Ltd v R & C Commrs*), though a more lenient approach was taken in *Bruns t/a TK Fabrications*.

- A taxpayer's unexceptional trading problems, whether due to cash flow or losses, do not constitute a reasonable excuse for compliance failures (*A Longworth & Sons Ltd v R & C Commrs*).
- By contrast, a trader who dealt in a fair and business-like way with the demands on his available cash resources, in trading circumstances that suffered a sudden and severe deterioration, was held to have had a 'reasonable excuse' in the context of the CIS (*Mutch v R & C Commrs*).
- A company could be held to have a reasonable excuse where it could demonstrate an exceptional downturn in trade combined with 'the refusal of banks to assist customers which in more normal times might reasonably expect to be supported' (*Prior Roofing Ltd v R & C Commrs*).
- Personal circumstances may, in certain cases, be taken into account (*Cormac Construction Ltd v R & C Commrs* and *Bruns t/a TK Fabrications*). However, serious ill health was not accepted as a reasonable excuse in *Austin* as the taxpayer had failed to take responsibility for managing his affairs despite an awareness (if not a clear understanding) that matters remained outstanding. On the other hand, in *Daniel* the taxpayer was successful in circumstances involving unexpected financial difficulties and the death of his daughter.
- Reliance on a company officer may constitute a reasonable excuse (*Devon & Cornwall Surfacing Ltd*) though reliance on an accountant who was seriously ill was held not to do so, partly because the failure continued for several months (*Smith*). It was also held that there was no reasonable excuse where a plumbing and heating engineer fell short in his payments by minor amounts as a direct result of a change of agents (*Getty*). Again, in *Grayson*, it was held that reliance on an allegedly incompetent bookkeeper, while the taxpayer herself was on holiday, did not constitute a reasonable excuse.
- Where an informal payment arrangement had been made with HMRC, this was held to constitute a reasonable excuse for failing to pay according to the strict letter of the law (*Bannister Combined Services*).
- Where delays by HMRC were a factor, this too was a reasonable excuse (*Turner*).

Cases: *Barnes (HMIT) v Hilton Main Construction* [2005] BTC 568; *Westview Rail Ltd* [2009] TC 00215; *Grosvenor v R & C Commrs* [2009] TC 00227; *Beard v R & C Commrs* [2009] TC 00228; *A Longworth & Sons Ltd v R & C Commrs* [2009] TC 00230; *Mutch v R & C Commrs* [2009] TC 00232; *Munns v R & C Commrs* [2009] TC 00234; *Strongwork Construction Ltd v R & C Commrs* [2009] TC 00236; *Prior Roofing Ltd v R & C Commrs* [2009] TC 00246; *Ductaire Fabrications Ltd v R & C Commrs* [2010] TC 00288; *Cormac Construction Ltd v R & C Commrs*

[2010] TC 00315; *Bruns t/a TK Fabrications* [2010] TC 00371; *Enderbey Properties Ltd* [2010] TC 00396; *Chatterton* [2010] TC 00453; *Bannister Combined Services* [2010] TC 00463; *Smith* [2010] TC 00489; *GC Ware Electrics* [2010] TC 00499; *Devon & Cornwall Surfacing Ltd* [2010] TC 00501; *Getty* [2010] TC 00546; *Grayson* [2010] TC 00547; *Pollard* [2010] TC 00563; *Austin* [2010] TC 00599; *Eurotec Services (GB) LLP* [2010] TC 00608; *Turner* [2010] TC 00743; *S Morris Groundwork Ltd* [2011] TC 00835; *Daniel* [2013] TC02565

Tax Reporter: ¶283-625

108-325 Monthly returns

Each month, contractors must send HMRC a complete return of all payments made to all subcontractors within the CIS in the preceding tax month. This is regardless of whether the subcontractors were paid gross or net of either the standard or higher deduction. Monthly returns must reach HMRC within 14 days of the end of the tax month they are for. Returns may be made electronically or by post.

Contractors who have not paid any subcontractors in a particular month must submit a 'Nil return'. In *Bells Mills Developments Ltd*, for example, a contractor suffered substantial penalties even though there had been no loss of tax.

Contractors must pay the amount deductible from payments to subcontractors to HMRC Accounts Office monthly. They must pay deductions due to be made in each tax month within 14 days of the end of that month or within 17 days where payment is made electronically, whether or not these deductions have actually been made. This means that where a required deduction has not actually been made from the subcontractor's payment, for whatever reason, the contractor is still responsible for paying that amount over to HMRC.

Where reasonable care is taken and a failure to deduct tax is made in good faith a contractor can be relieved of the obligation to account for the tax not deducted. In *PDF Electrical Ltd*, the company was successful in arguing this in circumstances where there was a genuine error, being the only error made in 10 years.

There are no annual returns within the Construction Industry Scheme. Contractors who are required to submit an Employer's Annual Return on form P35 should, however, remember to include on that form the total amount of CIS deductions they are due to pay so they can reconcile the total payments made during the year. HMRC have issued guidance, available at www.hmrc.gov.uk/cis/complete/p35.htm to help contractors and subcontractors to complete forms P35 correctly where these are required.

HMRC have also produced a guide to help contractors complete and submit their monthly return (at www.hmrc.gov.uk/new-cis/contractor-monthly-return.htm).

Legislation: FA 2004, s. 70ff.; *Income Tax (Construction Industry Scheme) Regulations* 2005 (SI 2005/2045), reg. 7

Cases: *Bells Mills Developments Ltd* [2010] TC 00349; *PDF Electrical Ltd* [2012] TC 02375

Tax Reporter: ¶283-050

108-350 Penalties for late returns

HMRC will impose a penalty of £100 where a contractor fails to submit a monthly return on time.

If the contractor should have returned information about more than 50 subcontractors, the penalty will be a further £100 for each additional 50 subcontractors or part thereof. The penalty will be repeated for every month the return is outstanding.

If a contractor submits a monthly return that is incomplete or incorrect, HMRC may charge penalties where they believe the error or omission has been caused by negligence or intent on the part of the contractor.

Penalties of up to £3,000 may be charged where a contractor:

- fails to produce records relating to payments made under the CIS when asked to do so;
- fails to give statements to subcontractors registered for payment under deduction recording their payments and deductions; or
- negligently or deliberately provides incorrect information in such statements.

Legislation: FA 2004, s. 72

Tax Reporter: ¶283-300

Extent of penalties

HMRC publish the minutes of the 'Construction Industry Scheme Operational Forum (CISOF)' meetings. The minutes of the meeting of 20 November 2008 (see www.hmrc.gov.uk/consultations/cirip-201108.htm) reveal that the number of penalties imposed under these rules is very high:

'A total of 136,893 contractors (roughly three quarters of the contractor population) had received at least one penalty. However, of those receiving a penalty around three quarters had received three or fewer penalties.'

Another interesting revelation in the minutes is the admission that whilst £180m of penalties had been raised, 'around half of these had been remitted by HMRC, for various reasons, without an appeal and others had been discharged on appeal'.

New penalty regime

A new regime of penalties for late filing of CIS returns was implemented from October 2011. The rate of penalties under the new regime are as follows:

- a fixed penalty of £100 as soon as a return is late;
- a second fixed penalty of £200 if the return is still outstanding two months after the filing date;
- a tax-geared penalty for returns still outstanding six months after the filing date, which will be 5% of the deductions shown on the outstanding return or, if greater, £300; and
- a second tax-geared penalty for returns still outstanding after 12 months, the amount depending on the degree of culpability.

HMRC guidance confirms that 'in many cases, the new penalties will be less than what would be charged now'. An important aspect of the change is that any contractor who has already paid a penalty, or who is asked to pay a penalty in relation to any earlier period, may ask for it to be recalculated on the new basis if it will result in a lower charge. Where appropriate, penalties already paid will be reimbursed to the extent that the newly calculated charge is lower. HMRC have given three circumstances in which they are expecting that the penalties *may* be lower under the new regime:

> '• you have been charged more than one penalty in respect of any one monthly return;
>
> • you have been charged more than £100 in respect of any one monthly return; [or]
>
> • you are a new contractor who has been charged penalties for more than one late monthly return.'

Legislation: *Finance Act* 2009, Sch. 55

Tax Reporter: ¶283-300

Other Material: www.hmrc.gov.uk/cis/penalties-late-returns.htm

Reasonable excuse for failing to deliver return

The tax tribunal has the power to set aside a penalty determination if it appears that the taxpayer had a reasonable excuse for failing to deliver a CIS return on time. The fact that all the tax has been paid does not constitute a reasonable excuse for failing to deliver the return. In *Leeds Lifts Ltd*, it was held that the proper operation of the CIS scheme required compliance with both the payment of tax and the delivery of the return. As such, payment of the tax does not relieve the taxpayer from the obligation to complete and file a form CIS36 even if the return might have no bearing on the taxpayer's liability. The fact that HMRC had not lost out, as all the tax was paid on time, was again rejected as a reasonable excuse in *King*. Again, substantial penalties were charged in *GT Plasterers*, even though no tax was outstanding.

By contrast, an appeal based on the reasonable excuse provision of TMA 1970, s. 118(2) was partially successful where a contractor had relied on his accountant, and where the accountant had been unexpectedly detained abroad at the relevant time. Nevertheless, the contractor was still liable to penalties for later returns, as the penalty for the first failure should have alerted the taxpayer to the problem, and the taxpayer should have taken advice from HMRC or from another quarter at that time (*Jonathan David Ltd*). In the case of *Monitor Audio Ltd*, the taxpayer was successful in his appeal against a penalty for failing to deliver a return. He demonstrated that he had a reasonable expectation that these would have been dealt with by his accountant and he had provided his accountant with all relevant information.

One case identified a problem with the question of proportionality in relation to penalties for late filing of a return. A company ran a business and its accountants noted that the services of a subcontractor had been used. The accountants advised the company of its obligations and rang HMRC to register the company in the CIS scheme. HMRC issued penalty notices amounting to £2,800 and refused to reduce or waive them, even though the penalties were high in relation to the tax at stake of £3,483. The taxpayer was honest throughout and the problem was rectified as soon as the accountants spotted it. The tribunal expressed concern that neither HMRC nor the tribunal itself had the power to mitigate the penalty, and the tribunal questioned whether the situation satisfied the human rights principle of proportionality (*SKG (London) Ltd*). The appeal was therefore listed for further argument on the proportionality points that had been identified.

In *Bells Mills Developments Ltd*, the tribunal noted that certain staff difficulties had led to the failure to make returns, the fact that only one contractor payment was being made each month, the fact that the omission did not result in any loss of tax (as the subcontractor had gross payment status) and the fact that the failure was disclosed as soon as it became apparent. It was also noted that the taxpayer company was under financial pressure. However, none of these constituted a reasonable excuse (though the tribunal did mitigate those discretionary penalties where it had discretion to do so).

Where a person was warned by HMRC of the need to demonstrate the date of posting, but did not do so, he did not demonstrate to the tribunal that he had a reasonable excuse for failing to deliver his return on time. HMRC asserted that the return was received three days late and the appellant was not able to dislodge that assertion. His actions were not those of a prudent business person and the penalties for late delivery were therefore properly imposed (*Holland Kitchen & Bathroom Design*). Another business, which had repeatedly submitted returns late, was found not to have a reasonable excuse as a result of alleged postal delays. The proprietor had already been advised to obtain proof of posting (provided without charge by Royal Mail) but had not done so. Although he had said that he would provide a witness statement concerning the postage date, this was not in fact produced either to HMRC or to the tax tribunal (*O'Brien*).

Legislation: TMA 1970, s. 93(8)

Cases: *Leeds Lifts Ltd* [2009] TC 00231; *Jonathan David Ltd* [2009] TC 00233; *SKG (London) Ltd* [2010] TC 00282; *Bells Mills Developments Ltd* [2010] TC 00349; *King* [2010] TC 00391; *GT Plasterers* [2010] TC 00750; *Holland Kitchen & Bathroom Design* [2011] TC 00794; *O'Brien* [2011] TC 01026; *Monitor Audio Ltd* [2015] TC 04541

Tax Reporter: ¶283-250

108-360 Penalties for late payment

Late payment penalties have applied for all contractors who make CIS deduction payments for periods starting from April 2010. The penalties are broadly the same as those applying for late payments of PAYE. Penalties are charged as a percentage of the amount that is paid late, with the percentage determined according to the number of late payments in the year. The statutory rules are given in FA 2009, s. 107 and, particularly, Sch. 56.

Detailed coverage of the penalties for late payment can be found at 145-430 and following paragraphs. Although that commentary is written primarily for PAYE purposes, the same regime applies to late payments of CIS deductions, even if (exceptionally) the CIS contractor is not also an employer.

108-400 Online filing

Contractors can use HMRC's CIS Online service to file monthly returns and perform verifications over the Internet or using Electronic Data Interchange (EDI).

HMRC also provide an online registration service for subcontractors wishing to register for payment under deduction. Subcontractors wanting to use this service do NOT need to register and enrol beforehand.

Key features of the new online system include:

- aimed at smaller contractors (typically, those who pay 50 or fewer subcontractors a month);
- online completion of CIS300 monthly return forms and verification requests with the ability to save partially-completed returns;
- built-in guidance to help contractors complete only the necessary forms and questions, based on the information provided;
- immediate validation of data;
- provision of an initial pre-populated list of subcontractors the contractor has paid in the preceding three months (from the date that they register for the service);
- a history of monthly returns and verification requests made using the service; and
- the ability to print copies of submitted/saved monthly returns.

Tax Reporter: ¶283-750ff.

Share fishermen

108-800 Share fishermen

Share fishermen are classified as self-employed and receive a share of the profits or gross earnings of a fishing boat.

The Share Fisherman Scheme, set up by HMRC, therefore has the aim of helping its members to set aside 20% of money earned each month, helping them to pay tax and national insurance on time and automatically at the end of the tax year.

To sign up for the scheme, share fishermen need to sign a mandate allowing a bank account to be opened in their name. The boat owner will then pay 20% of earnings into the account each month and the fishermen sign a direct debit allowing HMRC to take money out of the account to fund tax and NIC liabilities.

Tax Reporter: ¶268-800

Particular types of occupation: further guidance

109-000 Tactical Information Packages

HMRC used to make available on their website a series of Tactical Information Packages (TIPs). These were trade/profession-based notes, supposedly for internal use by HMRC officers. However, they overlapped considerably with *CCH Business Focus* (see 109-010) and were withdrawn after a copyright dispute.

109-010 CCH Business Focus

CCH publish, in their *Business Focus* series, very detailed notes on a wide range of particular occupations. *CCH Business Focus* is a package of around 100 different business notes, grouped for ease of use into a number of modules, including Agriculture; High Street; Leisure; Professions; Services, and Trades. In addition to the individual trade sectors covered in these six modules, an Overview Module includes comprehensive sector overview notes on Manufacturing, Wholesaling and e-Commerce. Chronological coverage of key events and trends in the economy as a whole is also included.

109-020 Tax Reporter

Commentary of particular relevance to certain occupations, including those listed below, can be found in Volume 2 of the *Tax Reporter*.

- accountants;
- actors;
- advocates;
- agency workers;
- air crew;
- ambassadors;
- 'angels';
- architects;
- armed forces;
- artists;
- artists' models;

- athletes;
- authors;
- barristers;
- bloodstock breeders;
- casual workers;
- clergymen;
- composers;
- crown servants;
- dentists;
- designers;
- diplomats;
- directors;
- doctors;
- entertainers;
- farmers;
- fashion models;
- the film industry;
- fishermen;
- footballers;
- foster carers;
- hoteliers;
- inventors;
- justices of the Peace;
- lecturers (part-time);
- lifeboatmen;
- liquidators;
- lorry drivers;
- magistrates;
- market gardeners;
- miners;
- musicians;

- oil rig workers;
- politicians;
- religious communities;
- restaurateurs;
- sculptors;
- solicitors;
- sportsmen;
- stage managers;
- subcontractors in the construction industry;
- teachers;
- underwriters;
- volunteer drivers.

Capital allowances

General principles

110-000 Different codes of allowance

Capital allowances are given in respect of capital expenditure on the following types of expenditure:

- plant and machinery (see 111-000ff.);
- industrial buildings and structures (though these allowances are broadly no longer available), including hotels and commercial buildings or structures in enterprise zones (see 118-400ff.);
- renovation of business premises;
- agricultural buildings (though these allowances are broadly no longer available);
- flat conversions (though these were withdrawn from April 2013) (see 122-000ff.);
- research and development (see 123-000ff.);
- mineral extraction (see 125-000ff.);
- know-how (see 125-500ff.);
- patents (see 126-000ff.);
- dredging (see 126-500ff.).

The rates and methods of giving allowances for each of the above categories differ in detail. Tables of rates are given, *Hardman's Tax Rates and Tables* at 11-000ff. (plant and machinery) and at 11-700ff. (other allowances).

Capital allowances are given only for capital expenditure that is not otherwise deductible against income. Some capital expenditure is, however, specifically permitted as a deduction in computing taxable income (see 92-250). Capital allowances are not generally taken into account for capital gains tax purposes, except where a loss accrues on the disposal of the asset. If an election is made to adopt the cash basis available from 2013–14, a claim cannot be made for capital allowances except in relation to motor cars.

Generally speaking, the rules apply in the same way for corporation tax as for income tax purposes. The approach taken has been to include the fuller coverage in this income tax volume, with reduced coverage in the corporation tax part of the commentary. An exception is made for the treatment of payable tax credits arising from certain first-year allowances: these are available only for companies, and commentary is therefore included in the corporation tax volume only. Also, corporation tax relief for expenditure incurred by companies since 1 April 2002 on know-how and on patents will in practice be given instead under the regime applying for expenditure on intangible assets.

Legislation: CAA 2001, s. 1, 4

Other Material: ESC B1

Tax Reporter: ¶235-000

110-050 Giving effect to capital allowances

Capital allowances are given as a deduction in calculating profits for a 'chargeable period'. Any balancing charges are accordingly treated as trading receipts.

For income tax purposes, a chargeable period is a period of account, i.e. a period for which the accounts of a business are drawn up. For corporation tax purposes, a chargeable period is an accounting period.

For income tax purposes, where accounts are made up to a date more than 18 months after the previous accounting date, the first 12 months is taken as one period, with the remainder (up to a further 12 months) forming another period, and so on. The division of a period of account is not required where the length of a period of account does not exceed 18 months. Hence, for income tax purposes, provision has to be made for increasing or decreasing writing-down allowances in line with the length of the relevant chargeable period. The rate of a writing-down allowance is based on a 12-month period and so an increase or decrease in that rate is required when the length of the chargeable period is longer or shorter than 12 months. For example, in a 15-month period of accounting (relevant chargeable period), an 18% writing-down allowance becomes, effectively, a 22.5% allowance (i.e. 18% × 15/12).

The application of capital allowances according to a 'period of account' requires special provisions for opening and closing years or where there is a change in accounting date. Where two basis periods overlap, the period common to both is treated as falling in the first period only (as is the case before self-assessment). Similarly, where there is a gap period, the interval treated as part of the first period (unlike the situation before self-assessment).

For corporation tax purposes, the length of an accounting period cannot exceed 12 months. Hence, where the length of a period of account is greater than 12 months, the first 12 months is taken as one accounting period, with the remainder (up to a further 12 months) forming another accounting period, and so on. Again, the rate of the writing-down allowance, which is based on a 12-month period, will need to be decreased when the length of the accounting period is less than 12 months. For example, for corporation tax purposes, a 15-month period of account would normally break down into two accounting periods; namely, the first 12 months and the remaining three months. In this example, the writing-down allowance for the three-month accounting period becomes, effectively, a 4.5% allowance (i.e. 18% × 3/12).

Tax Reporter: ¶236-080

110-100 When expenditure is 'incurred'

General rule

Allowances are normally given when expenditure is 'incurred'. The general rule is that expenditure is incurred on the date when the obligation to pay becomes unconditional, whether or not a later date for payment is specified.

HMRC consider that whether an obligation to pay has become unconditional depends on the terms of the particular contract for the supply of the asset concerned and not simply on the date of the contract or on the issue of an invoice. Where a person buying goods is legally required to pay for them on or within a prescribed delivery time, the obligation to pay becomes unconditional, and therefore the expenditure is 'incurred' when the asset is delivered.

The taxpayer must also satisfy the conditions for obtaining the particular allowance, for example, in the case of plant and machinery, whether or not the taxpayer owns the asset in question in consequence of incurring the expenditure.

Legislation: CAA 2001, s. 5,11

Other Material: HMRC *Capital Allowances Manual* CA11800ff.

Payment due at special times

Where a payment is due more than four months after the date when the obligation to pay becomes unconditional, such payment will not be taken to be incurred until it is required to be paid.

Where an asset is constructed in stages and progress payment arrangements mean that the asset becomes the property of the purchaser as it is being constructed. Normally, the obligation to pay for a part of the asset which has been completed becomes unconditional when the work is certified (a 'milestone' contract). If the part of the asset which has been completed becomes the property of the purchaser before the end of his accounting date and the work is certified before that accounting date, the normal rules above apply, the accounting date is the last day of the accounting period. If the part of the asset which has been completed becomes the property of the purchaser before his accounting date and the work is certified within one month of that accounting date, then the expenditure which is certified is treated as incurred on the accounting date. If the part of the asset which has been completed becomes the property of the purchaser before his accounting date but the work is not certified until more than one month after that accounting date, the expenditure is treated as incurred when the work is certified.

Where a date is inserted solely or mainly to accelerate entitlement to a capital allowance, the date is disregarded and the allowance is given instead when payment is due.

Legislation: CAA 2001, s. 5

Hire purchase

Where plant or machinery is acquired by way of a hire purchase agreement any capital expenditure still to be incurred under the contract at the time when the asset is brought into use is treated as incurred on the date on which the asset is brought into use; see 115-350.

Legislation: CAA 2001, s. 67

Pre-trading expenditure

If expenditure is incurred before a trade begins, it is treated as incurred on the first day of trading (CAA 2001, s. 12 for plant and machinery; s. 306(4) for industrial buildings; s. 401 for mineral exploration and access; s. 434 for mineral extraction activities; and s. 468 for patent rights).

VAT capital goods scheme

Where, under the capital goods scheme for computers, computer equipment, land and buildings, an additional VAT liability is incurred (or a VAT rebate is due), the date that new expenditure is treated as incurred (or a disposal made) for capital allowance purposes is the last day of the VAT period of adjustment in which the change of use giving rise to the liability (or rebate) occurred. This is the period which HMRC use to make the computation which gives rise to the additional VAT payable or the VAT repayment; see 110-300.

Legislation: CAA 2001, s. 548

Tax Reporter: ¶235-100

110-200 Apportionment of sale proceeds, etc.

Where any property is sold together with other property, a 'just and reasonable apportionment' of the net sale proceeds (or insurance, salvage or compensation moneys where appropriate) between the items is to be made. All property that is sold as part of a single bargain, is deemed to be sold together (and thus subject to a just and reasonable apportionment) even if separate prices are identified in any contract and also if separate contracts are used for individual items.

Any dispute regarding the apportionment of net sale proceeds which appears to be material to the tax liability of two or more persons is to be decided by the appropriate tax tribunal. The cases of *Fitton v Gilders and Heaton* and *Wood (t/a A Wood & Co) v Provan (HMIT)* (decided under the broadly identical earlier legislation in the *Capital Allowances Act* 1968) both approved the view that under these rules sale agreements could be revised for tax purposes. In the latter case, Buckley J said:

> '... [those] who are responsible for considering that assessment must determine what is the proper value to be put upon the machinery and plant in respect of which the balancing charge arises. They are not to be bound by the consideration expressed in a sale agreement where the sale is a sale of a number of items of property including the machinery and plant in question. The consideration for the sale is to be aggregated and a just apportionment of it is to be made in order to discover how much of those proceeds of sale ought properly to be regarded as the sum which the taxpayer received in respect of the plant and machinery.'

Where the property disposed of includes fixtures contained within buildings or structures which are also disposed of, a joint election may be made apportioning the sale price between the fixtures and the property in amounts agreed by the vendor and purchaser. See 114-600ff.

Legislation: CAA 2001, s. 562, 563

Cases: *Fitton v Gilders and Heaton* (1955) 36 TC 233; *Wood (t/a A Wood & Co) v Provan (HMIT)* (1968) 44 TC 701

Other Material: HMRC *Capital Allowances Manual* CA12100ff.

Tax Reporter: ¶243-325

110-250 Subsidies and contributions

Contributions by certain public bodies

Expenditure is not regarded as having been incurred to the extent that it is met directly or indirectly by the Crown, other government, or public or local authority (whether or not in the UK). An exception to this rule is allowed for certain Northern Ireland regional development grants.

It apparently does not matter if a grant or subsidy is made as a matter of discretion rather than pursuant to some statutory or contractual obligation preceding or contemporaneous with the incurring of the relevant expenditure. In *Cyril Lord Carpets Ltd v Schofield*, a company incurred expenditure on plant and machinery for its textile manufacturing and warehousing business. Subsequently it received grants for that expenditure under the *Capital Grants to Industry (Northern Ireland) Act* 1954. It was held that the expenditure was 'met' by the grants either directly or indirectly.

Legislation: CAA 2001, s. 532ff.

Case: *Cyril Lord Carpets Ltd v Schofield* (1966) 42 TC 637

Meaning of 'public authority'

The term 'public authority' was held to have a wide meaning when considered by the Court of Appeal in the case of *McKinney v Hagans Caravans (Manufacturing) Ltd*. The criteria considered by the court as determining the status of a body as a public authority were:

- the public source of the constitution of the body;
- its performance of a public service for the wider good of the public;
- the degree of public control and accountability;
- the absence of profit for private citizens; and
- public funding, though not a necessary qualification, was a pointer towards classifying the body as a public authority.

It was not a requirement that the body in question should have executive powers.

Case: *McKinney v Hagans Caravans (Manufacturing) Ltd* [1997] BTC 402

Insurance and compensation

Insurance or other compensation moneys paid in respect of an asset which has been demolished, destroyed or put out of use do not reduce expenditure on which capital allowances will be granted, though such amounts may be treated as disposal proceeds (e.g. under CAA 2001, s. 61 in the case of plant and machinery).

Legislation: CAA 2001, s. 535

Wear and tear subsidies

If a subsidy is paid towards the wear and tear of plant or machinery and it is not a taxable receipt of the qualifying activity, allowances will be restricted to a 'just and reasonable' proportion of those otherwise available (or nil, if the subsidy covers the whole of the wear and tear). Where this applies the expenditure will be separately pooled in order to facilitate the necessary apportionments.

Legislation: CAA 2001, s. 37, 209ff.

Tax Reporter: ¶235-300

110-300 Interaction with the VAT capital goods scheme

The VAT rules provide for adjustments to recoverable VAT input tax, where there is a change in the extent to which assets are used in making taxable supplies, over a period of up to ten years. Accordingly, the capital allowances legislation provides amendments to be made to ensure that allowances given over the life of the assets concerned are based on the actual costs as adjusted for non-recoverable VAT.

The main businesses affected are those making *partly* exempt supplies. The assets to which the rules apply are:

- computers and items of computer equipment worth £50,000 or more (five-year adjustment period); and
- land and buildings (or parts of buildings) worth £250,000 or more (generally ten-year adjustment period).

The effects of the VAT adjustments are as follows.

- Additional non-recoverable VAT will be treated as expenditure incurred on the last day of the VAT period in which the change of use occurred. Any extra relief will be based on capital allowance rates, etc. applicable *at the time when the use of the asset changed.*
- VAT refunds are deemed to be made on the last day of the VAT period in which the change of use occurred.

The VAT period referred to here means one of the periods making up the overall adjustment period for the capital goods scheme. However, the payments or receipts are allocated to a chargeable period by means of a table. Capital allowance adjustments will, in practice, be generally straightforward, as no adjustment will be required to earlier computations. See also CA 11900ff.

Legislation: CAA 2001, s. 234–246 (plant and machinery), 446–449 (research and development) and 546–551 (interpretation); *Value Added Tax Regulations* (SI 1995/2518), reg. 112–116

Tax Reporter: ¶235-550

110-350 Successions to trade

General rule

Where any person takes over a trade, profession or vocation, that trade, etc. may be treated as having been permanently discontinued and a new trade having been commenced (see 91-400), but there is no permanent discontinuance where, for the purposes of income tax, at least one person continues carrying on the trade.

Assets of the old trade which continue to be used in the new trade which have not actually been sold to the successor are treated as if they have been sold to the successor, when the succession took place, at the open-market value of the assets. However, the successor is not entitled to claim any first-year allowances in respect of these assets. This would apply, for example, if a new company is incorporated and the sole trader gives all of the assets of the business to the company (but not if the asset is sold to the new company).

Legislation: CAA 2001, s. 265ff., 559

Tax Reporter: ¶241-720

Other Material: HMRC *Capital Allowances Manual* CA29050

Election

The general rule is subject to a joint election in relation to plant or machinery where the parties are connected (in broadly common partnership or under broadly common control). This plant and machinery election permits assets to be treated as if sold by the predecessor at a price that gives rise to no balancing adjustments (i.e. at the assets' tax written down value), again, the successor is not entitled to first-year allowances in respect of these assets. A similar election is available if the succession arises under a will – in which case the beneficiary can make the election.

Legislation: CAA 2001, s. 265ff., 559

Other Material: HMRC *Capital Allowances Manual* CA29050

Tax Reporter: ¶241-720

Partnerships

A change in the members of the partnership does not trigger a discontinuance of the business for tax purposes, provided at least one partner is common to the partnerships involved in carrying on the business before and after the membership change. This treatment is mandatory and not subject to election. The capital allowances continue to be given to the new partnership as if it were the same as the old.

Company reconstructions

In the case of certain company reconstructions, the trade is not treated as permanently discontinued. Capital allowances are generally given as if the successor and predecessor were the same person and no balancing adjustments arise because of the transfer.

Legislation: CTA 2010, s. 948

Tax Reporter: ¶235-450

110-400 Sales without change of control, avoidance, etc.

Anti-avoidance provisions deal with sales of property (or, for plant and machinery, hire purchase contracts or the assignment of the benefit thereof) between connected persons, with leasebacks or with tax-structured transactions.

For plant and machinery, the expenditure of the buyer, etc. eligible for allowances may be restricted to the disposal value to be brought into account by the seller, etc. However, the disposal value may be restricted in the case of a 'sale and finance leaseback'.

If, for plant and machinery, the seller is not required to bring into account any disposal value (e.g. there is no actual disposal value), then the expenditure of the buyer, etc. eligible for allowances will be restricted by the smaller of market value or the original expenditure. In the case of a 'sale and finance leaseback', the original expenditure is replaced by the notional written-down value of the seller's expenditure or the expenditure of a person connected with the seller, whichever is the case.

However, the parties to a sale and leaseback, or sale and finance leaseback arrangement, in respect of plant or machinery may elect to disapply the market value rule, provided certain conditions are met. An election must be made within two years after the date of the transaction and is irrevocable.

For other assets, there will be substituted for the actual price the property's market value. However, with respect to sales which are not tax-structured, the seller and buyer may jointly elect to substitute the tax written-down value for the market value. The right of election has been specifically extended to an industrial building or structure, a qualifying hotel or commercial building or structure and capital expenditure on scientific research. The election, which must be made within two years of the sale, is unavailable in certain specified circumstances.

No balancing allowance is allowed if it has arisen as a result of a tax avoidance scheme that has artificially depressed the market value of the asset (for example, by making it subject to a loan) prior to its transfer to a connected person; the low market value would then generate a balancing allowance. Not only is the balancing allowance disallowed, but the purchaser must base his capital allowances claim on the actual proceeds paid. This rule does not apply to plant and machinery capital allowances.

Legislation: CAA 2001, s. 213ff., 568ff.

Tax Reporter: ¶240-200

110-450 Exclusion of double allowances

Where a person receives a capital allowance under any of the provisions relating to industrial buildings and structures, dredging, agricultural land and buildings, scientific research, dwelling-houses let on assured tenancies, or mineral extraction, the person cannot claim allowances under any other provision. Nor can he or she claim writing-down allowances for plant or machinery.

There are specific prohibitions against claiming capital allowances on fixtures in buildings and structures, etc. that have been subject to other claims unless such claims were for industrial buildings allowance or scientific research allowance and claims under CAA 2001, s. 186 or 187 have been made to identify the allowable expenditure on fixtures. For further details, see 114-600.

HMRC issued guidance (HMRC Brief 12/09) at the end of March 2009 to remove any doubt about the matter, but the guidance did not change anything. The HMRC line is that 'a choice, once final, may not be changed'. The Brief also restates the existing guidance that 'once a choice has been made to claim one type of allowance the taxpayer cannot change to another in later years'. Specifically, HMRC do not accept that a claim may be made under what used to be the 'error or mistake' provisions of

TMA 1970 because s. 33(2A) of that Act made it clear that the provisions do not apply to a claim included in a return. The equivalent restriction since April 2010 has been for claims made for 'overpayment relief'.

Legislation: TMA 1970, Sch. 1AB; CAA 2001, s. 7ff.

Tax Reporter: ¶235-200

Plant and machinery allowances

First principles

111-000 Introduction

Subject to certain exceptions, writing-down allowances (WDAs) are available for capital expenditure incurred on plant and machinery for the purposes of a 'qualifying activity'. Enhanced first-year allowances (FYAs) are available in certain circumstances. Since April 2008, however, most plant and machinery allowances for the majority of businesses have been given by means of the annual investment allowance, discussed at 111-875ff. For rules applicable to capital allowances generally, see 110-000ff.

The qualifying activities are:

- a trade;
- an ordinary UK property business;
- a UK furnished holiday lettings business;
- an ordinary overseas property business;
- an EEA furnished holiday lettings business;
- a profession or vocation;
- certain mines, transport undertakings, etc. (per ITTOIA 2005, s. 12(4) or CTA 2009, s. 39);
- the management of an investment company;
- special leasing of plant or machinery;
- an employment or office,

but only to the extent that the profits or gains of the activity are within the charge to tax. The activity must be undertaken on a commercial basis with a view to making a profit.

An ordinary UK property business is a UK property business, except in so far as it is a UK furnished holiday lettings business.

Special leasing, in relation to plant or machinery, means hiring out, or letting of, the plant or machinery otherwise than in the course of any other qualifying activity.

Legislation: CAA 2001, s. 11 ,15ff., 44(1)

Case: *Beacon Estates (Chepstow) Ltd* [2014] TC 03808

Property businesses

Where a person carries on a qualifying activity consisting of an ordinary UK property business, an ordinary overseas property business or special leasing of plant or machinery, capital expenditure incurred in providing plant and machinery for use in a dwelling-house does not qualify for capital allowances. A just and reasonable apportionment applies to the capital expenditure where the plant or machinery is provided partly for use in a dwelling-house and partly for other purposes; capital allowances may be able to be claimed on the part of expenditure attributable to the other purpose, provided the other purpose relates, in fact, to a qualifying activity.

The restriction does not apply to other qualifying activities (e.g. ordinary trades). However, it follows that if a trader has living accommodation as part of the overall premises (such as staff accommodation in a hotel) there is no restriction in such a case.

There is no statutory definition of the term 'dwelling-house' for the purposes of the plant and machinery part of the capital allowances legislation. HMRC have revised their interpretation twice in recent years and the manuals (as amended from October 2010) state that the distinctive characteristic of a dwelling-house 'is its ability to afford to those who use it the facilities required for day-to-day private domestic existence'. Extensive guidance has been issued in relation to student accommodation.

HMRC have commented that:

> 'A person's second or holiday home or accommodation used for holiday letting is a dwelling house. The common parts of a building which contains two or more dwelling houses will not comprise a dwelling house, although the individual dwelling houses within the building will do so. A hospital, a prison, nursing home or hotel (run as a trade and offering services) are not dwelling houses.'

With effect from 6 April 2016, a landlord of a dwelling-house is entitled to tax relief on the replacement of certain domestic items including furnishings, appliances and kitchenware (70-340).

Legislation: CAA 2001, s. 35; ITTOIA 2005, s. 311A

Other Material: HMRC *Capital Allowances Manual* CA23060

Tax Reporter: ¶236-354

Private use of business assets

Where an asset is used partly for private purposes by a business proprietor, only a proportion of the full allowance may be claimed. This will not usually affect companies directly since they cannot normally incur expenditure for purposes other than the business being carried on, although since the proportionate disallowance does strictly extend to use otherwise than wholly for the purposes of the trade it is conceivable that if a non-business motivation influenced the acquisition of assets a disallowance could be made. Generally, however, the personal use by employees of company assets is not treated as a non-business use, but rather as part of their remuneration package. Full capital allowances would thus be available for motor cars provided to employees where personal, non-business use was permitted.

Building alterations and demolitions

Where plant or machinery, the expenditure on which is qualifying expenditure for capital allowances, has to be installed in an existing building, any expenditure on alterations to the building that are incidental to the installation is also treated as qualifying expenditure for plant and machinery allowances (see 114-200).

Where plant or machinery is demolished and it was last used for a qualifying activity, the net cost of demolition can be added to the cost of replacement plant or machinery.

Legislation: CAA 2001, s. 25, 26

Tax Reporter: ¶245-480

Renewals basis

Prior to 6 April 2013, expenditure on plant or machinery which had been subject to a 'renewals' deduction did not strictly qualify as capital expenditure for capital allowances purposes. 'Renewals allowance' permitted a revenue deduction for the full cost of *replacing* or *renewing* existing capital assets. No allowance or deduction was permitted for the original cost of acquiring new capital assets. The disposal proceeds (if any) of replaced assets were brought into account as trading receipts. By concession a taxpayer who changed from the 'renewals' basis could claim capital allowances in respect of that expenditure provided the change to the 'capital allowances basis' occurred in respect of all items in that class.

The above treatment was withdrawn with effect from 6 April 2013 and the 'renewals basis' was removed completely with effect from 6 April 2016.

Other Material: HMRC *Business Income Manual* BIM46990

111-050 Asset used only partly for qualifying activity

Qualifying expenditure must be incurred 'wholly or partly' for the purposes of the qualifying activity. The requirement is therefore satisfied where the provision of plant or machinery is only partly for the qualifying activity. In such a case, though, allowances and charges are apportioned so as to reflect the qualifying activity element.

To give effect to these rules, the plant or machinery is held in a single asset pool and the writing-down allowances are calculated in the normal way but then apportioned as necessary. First-year and annual investment allowances are in principle available for assets used for mixed purposes but, once more, the amount of the allowance will be restricted.

If an asset is initially used only for the purposes of a qualifying activity but then starts to be used partly for other purposes, its disposal value must at the date of change be taken into account in the pool into which the expenditure on the asset was allocated. At the same time, an amount equal to the disposal value is treated as expenditure on a new item of plant or machinery, the expenditure on which is allocated to a single asset pool, with allowances and charges apportioned as appropriate.

If the proportion of qualifying activity use changes (or, indeed, even if the plant or machinery begins to be used wholly for the purposes of a qualifying activity) the proportion of allowances given varies accordingly: when the plant or machinery is disposed of (if this is before the qualifying activity ceases) a balancing adjustment is made, to ensure that the net allowances given reflect the depreciation of the equipment subject to any just and reasonable apportionment.

If, instead, the plant or machinery begins to be used wholly for purposes other than those of a qualifying activity, then the taxpayer must at that date bring into account a disposal value.

Allowances are given in relation to the qualifying activity in question. Any reduced claim or disclaimer is made in respect of that qualifying activity and this is then reflected in the future calculations of capital allowances made in respect of that qualifying activity.

In general, the most common application of these rules will be in relation to private use of plant or machinery by a proprietor of an unincorporated business. It is likely that the private use will commence in the same period as the allowances are first available so that expenditure will go into a pool for which allowances and charges are always apportioned – no interim disposal and reacquisition will arise. The private use element will generally be agreed with the HMRC officer as a percentage based on whatever information is available as to the individual concerned and the type of business in which he is involved.

Example

Wendy has been in business for many years. Wendy bought a car for the purposes of her business. The car cost £9,000. She also uses the car privately and agrees a 70% business use with the HMRC officer. The car is subsequently sold for £3,000. The allowances will be as follows (assuming that the standard WDA rate of 18% applies):

	Private use asset	*Private use adj.*	*Allowances*
	£		£
Year 1			
Cost	9,000		
WDA (9,000 × 18%)	1,620	(1,620 × 30%)	1,134
WDV c/fwd	7,380		
Year 2			
WDA (7,380 × 18%)	1,328	(1,328 × 30%)	930
WDV c/fwd	6,052		
Year 3			
Disposal	3,000		
Balancing allowance	3,052	(3,052 × 30%)	2,136
			4,200

Note: the total allowances given are the loss on the car (£6,000) at the business percentage (70%).

Legislation: CAA 2001, s. 11(4)(a), 205ff.

Tax Reporter: ¶236-300

111-060 Assets used by employees

In the case of employees, the item of plant or machinery must be necessarily provided for use in the performance of the employee's duties. Capital allowances are not available on cars owned by employees.

In *Williams*, clothes bought by a BBC newsreader did not constitute 'plant or machinery ... necessarily provided for use in the performance of the duties of the employment or office'. The tribunal found that the clothing presented no special feature 'either in construction, purpose or position'. The tribunal was of the view that ordinary civilian clothing of the sort that is also worn off-duty (whether or not it is in fact so worn) would not qualify as plant bought by an employee.

Legislation: CAA 2001, s. 15, 36

Case: *Williams* [2010] TC 00397

111-065 Assets used for business entertainment

Expenditure on assets used for business entertainment does not qualify for capital allowances, except where it is the trader's business to provide entertainment. Where it is not the trader's business to provide entertainment, the entertainment activity is not a qualifying activity for the purposes of capital allowances. For a general discussion of business entertainment, see 94-000ff.

Legislation: CAA 2001, s. 269

111-070 Animals

Capital allowances may not be claimed in respect of animals on which the 'herd basis' is used to compute trading profits (see generally 106-120). Generally, with the herd basis, the initial cost of the herd is treated as capital expenditure, proceeds from the sale of a herd animal are treated as a trading receipt and the replacement cost for a similar or lower quality of animal is treated as a trading expense. Where the election for the herd basis has not been made and instead the normal trading stock basis applies, there is no capital expenditure on which to claim capital allowances. There are no capital allowances on revenue expenditure (e.g. purchases of trading stock).

Other animals – such as horses that are not trading stock – may qualify for plant and machinery allowances.

Legislation: CAA 2001, s. 38

111-075 Members of Parliament

Expenditure by a member of one of the following bodies is specifically excluded from being qualifying expenditure for the purposes of capital allowances if paid in connection with the provision or use of residential or overnight accommodation:

- the House of Commons;
- the Scottish Parliament;
- the National Assembly for Wales; or
- the Northern Ireland Assembly.

Legislation: CAA 2001, s. 34

111-080 Second-hand plant and machinery

In general, the fact that an item of plant or machinery is purchased second-hand does not affect the capital allowances which are given with respect to the expenditure incurred. The main exception is long life assets, where the expected life is ascertained when the asset is 'new'. In this context 'new' means 'unused and not second-hand'.

Legislation: CAA 2001, s. 91(2)

111-085 Long-funding leasing

Expenditure does not qualify for plant and machinery allowances if it is incurred on the provision of plant or machinery for leasing under a long funding lease. Allowances are instead normally given to the lessee. The provisions are complex but are summarised at 113-450.

Legislation: CAA 2001, s. 34A

111-100 The pooling basis

A business may buy many items of plant and machinery and it would be impractical to calculate allowances on each one separately. Qualifying expenditure is therefore 'pooled' for the purpose of determining a person's writing-down allowances and balancing adjustments. First-year allowances, where still given since April 2008, are normally but not necessarily at 100%. The remaining qualifying expenditure, or even the zero balance, then enters the pool for determining subsequent balancing charges (or possibly allowances, if less than the 100% allowance was taken).

If a person carries on more than one qualifying activity then expenditure relating to the different activities cannot be allocated to the same pool.

There are single asset pools, class pools and the main pool. A special rate pool (a new concept from April 2008) is a type of class pool.

For the rates of allowances to be applied to the appropriate pool and for the rates of first-year allowance, see *Hardman's Tax Rates and Tables* at 11-000ff.

Legislation: CAA 2001, s. 53, 54, 58, 104C

Single asset pool

As the name suggests, a single asset pool cannot contain qualifying expenditure relating to more than one asset. Each of the following types of qualifying expenditure is allocated to a separate 'single asset pool':

- a car bought before 1 or 6 April 2009 and costing more than the then cost threshold (£12,000) (former CAA 2001, s. 74);
- a short-life asset (CAA 2001, s. 86);
- a ship (CAA 2001, s. 127);
- plant or machinery provided, or used, partly for non-qualifying activities (CAA 2001, s. 206);
- plant or machinery for which a payment of a partial depreciation subsidy has been received by the person incurring the expenditure (CAA 2001, s. 211);
- plant or machinery on which the contributor claims contribution allowances (CAA 2001, s. 538).

Legislation: CAA 2001, s. 54

Class pool

A class pool can contain qualifying expenditure relating to more than one asset but only of the particular class. The following qualifying expenditure is allocated to a 'class pool':

- special rate expenditure (including integral features (see 115-000ff.), items formerly classified as long-life assets, cars bought from (broadly) the start of April 2009 with emissions exceeding 160g/km and expenditure after 5 April 2012 on solar panels) (CAA 2001, s. 104C); and
- plant or machinery provided, and used for a certain period, for overseas leasing (CAA 2001, s. 107) – the overseas leasing pool for all such plant and machinery.

Legislation: CAA 2001, s. 54 and 104A

(8) Has a property together with fixtures that are plant and machinery been acquired or disposed of?'

The checklist, together with notes on the questions posed, may be found at www.hmrc.gov.uk/agents/toolkits/ca-plant-machinery.pdf.

Meaning of 'plant and machinery'

111-150 Meaning of plant: introduction

There is no definition in the *Capital Allowances Act* 2001 of the word 'plant'. Some types of expenditure are specifically included, for example, the cost of thermal insulation and the expense of altering existing buildings in connection with the installation of plant and machinery. These, and other such items, are all subject to their own conditions and in each case the full details can be found elsewhere in this division.

Certain assets are excluded by statute from the definition of plant. All of these items are excluded on the grounds (broadly) that they are buildings or structures or parts thereof. The relevant legislation is fairly convoluted (though less so since the enactment of CAA 2001) and contains an array of exceptions which generally have little in common, other than that they happen to have been the subject of tax cases reaching the courts before the legislation was enacted.

For the most part, the definition of plant has been left to the courts, where many an intellectual battle has been fought in an attempt to pin down the concept.

The meaning of 'machinery' is a separate issue, and an item does not need to qualify as both plant and machinery. If it is machinery, then the question of whether it is also plant is irrelevant; it will qualify for allowances if all the other conditions are met.

Although the concept of 'plant and machinery' is of interest primarily for income tax and corporation tax purposes, the definition can also be relevant for CGT and, to a limited extent, for inheritance tax purposes. It is worth bearing in mind that for these other purposes the meaning of 'plant' will be based on case law definitions only; CAA 2001, s. 21–23 will not apply. Similarly, where expenditure is deemed to be plant (for example, building alterations connected with the installation of plant, thermal insulation, computer software, integral features, etc.) then these deeming provisions apply only for the purposes of the CAA 2001 and do not extend to CGT or inheritance tax legislation.

Tax Reporter: ¶244-500

111-175 Plant – statutory exclusions

Buildings

Expenditure on the provision of plant or machinery does not include any expenditure on the 'provision' of a 'building'. Building includes any asset which:

- is incorporated into the building; or
- is not so incorporated but is of a kind which is normally incorporated into buildings,

and in particular includes any asset in, or in connection with, the building included in any item in List A at CAA 2001, s. 21.

Structures, assets and works

Expenditure on the provision of plant or machinery does not include any expenditure on the 'provision' of 'structures', other assets or any works involving the alteration of 'land'. This is applied to any structure or other asset falling within List B at CAA 2001, s. 22. For these purposes, a structure is a fixed structure of any kind, other than a building, and references to the provision of a building structure or other asset include references to its construction or acquisition.

Expenditure unaffected by the exclusions for buildings and structures

Expenditure falling within List A or List B is not excluded from being expenditure on plant or machinery if it falls within List C at CAA 2001, s. 23 (see *Hardman's Tax Rates and Tables* at 11-400, though items 1 to 16 of list C are deemed not to include any asset whose principal purpose is to insulate or enclose the interior of a building and which is intended to be permanent).

It does not follow that such assets will necessarily qualify as plant; the legislation does not prevent them from so qualifying but the assets must still be considered on first principles.

In addition to the items falling within List C, the legislation identifies certain other categories of expenditure that qualify for plant and machinery allowances in their own right. These are considered at 111-200.

Legislation: CAA 2001, s. 23

Land

Expenditure on the provision of plant or machinery does not include any expenditure on the acquisition of any 'interest in land'. However, for this purpose, 'land' does not include buildings or other structures, or any asset that is so installed or otherwise fixed in or to any description of land as to become, in law, part of that land. The term 'interest in land' has the same meaning as in CAA 2001, s 175. The word 'land' includes land covered by water.

Legislation: CAA 2001, s. 24; *Interpretation Act* 1978, Sch. 1

Tax Reporter: ¶245-550

111-200 Specific qualifying expenditure

Expenditure falling within one of the following categories qualifies for plant and machinery allowances:

- thermal insulation (CAA 2001, s. 28: see 113-850);
- certain personal security expenditure (CAA 2001, s. 33: see 113-700);
- integral features (CAA 2001, s. 33A: see 115-000ff.);
- defined expenditure on safety at sports grounds (CAA 2001, s. 30–32: see 113-650); and
- computer software and rights thereto (CAA 2001, s. 71: see 113-600).

Legislation: CAA 2001, s. 23ff.

Tax Reporter: ¶245-400ff.

111-225 Plants and gardens

In the case of *Cole Brothers Ltd v Phillips*, the judge commented on the origin of the term 'plant' used in the business sense, and made an etymological link with the more general, botanical, sense of the word. The concluding words in the following quotation provide a useful background in the search for a definition:

> 'I think it worthwhile spending a moment's time in reflecting briefly on what the botanical analogy is. In the field of botany "plant" is used in three quite separate contexts. It can mean a vegetable organism synthesizing its nourishment from inorganic materials by the use of chlorophyll. In this sense an oak tree is a plant, whilst the Matterhorn is not. It can mean a vegetable organism with a soft stem. In this sense a bluebell is a plant, but an oak tree is not. Neither of these senses affords the analogy. But the word can mean a vegetable organism deliberately placed in an artificially prepared setting.

> A gardener can say "I am going to dig my flower beds in readiness for my plants" or, "I am going to buy some plants at my garden centre". It is this sense which gives it its analogical meanings, eg in medicine ("an organ transplant"), in crime ("it was planted on me"), or in industry, which is the sense we are now discussing, as the means by which a trade is carried on in an appropriately prepared setting. In each case, the contrast is between the thing implanted, ie the plant, and the prepared setting into which it is placed.'

As will be seen below, this distinction between 'the thing implanted' and 'the prepared setting' is fundamental to the issue of drawing the line between plant and premises.

Case: *Cole Brothers Ltd v Phillips* [1982] BTC 208

Tax Reporter: ¶244-575

111-250 Yarmouth v France – the beginnings of a definition

The starting point in the search for a definition of plant is not difficult to find. One case, concerned not with taxation but with compensation under the *Employers' Liability Act* 1880, has been quoted and referred to in nearly every judgment that has considered the meaning of plant. The case in question, *Yarmouth v France*, was heard by the Court of Appeal in 1887. The facts on which the decision was based have ceased to be of relevance but the following short quotation from the judgment of Lindley J has become the cornerstone in seeking to build the definition:

> 'There is no definition of plant in the Act: but, in its ordinary sense, it includes whatever apparatus is used by a business man for carrying on his business – not his stock in trade which he buys or makes for sale; but all goods and chattels, fixed or moveable, live or dead, which he keeps for permanent employment in his business.'

This definition has received judicial approval at the highest level, as by the House of Lords in, for example, the cases of *Maden & Ireland* and of *IR Commrs v Barclay, Curle & Co Ltd*. It was also used as the justification for overturning, after 50 years, the *Daphne v Shaw* decision which had held that a law library was not plant. That the definition is sound is therefore now beyond doubt but it in fact tells us little beyond what is seemingly rather obvious. The contrast with trading stock is uncontroversial, as is the reference to 'fixed or moveable'. (Certainly, the CGT legislation recognises that plant may or may not be fixed, as in the listing of assets that qualify for the relief for replacement of business assets, 'rollover relief'.) The concept that plant may be live or dead has not in practice exercised the courts, though the case itself concerned a horse and in recent times an inspector has been known to accept horses in a riding stable as plant for tax purposes.

Of the different aspects of the *Yarmouth v France* definition, however, it is undoubtedly the reference to 'apparatus used by a business man for carrying on his business' that has given rise to the greatest level of argument in the courts. The contrast has been drawn between the 'apparatus with which' and the 'setting within which' a business is conducted, as per the more recent quotation above.

It should be remembered, however, that all of the cases referred to in the above paragraphs predate the 1994 legislation which restricts the definition of plant. For an item to qualify as plant, it will have to satisfy two tests. First, it must be shown that the item in question does not fall foul of the legislation now in CAA 2001, s. 21 and 22. Second, it must be demonstrated that on the case law principles discussed above it is properly treated as apparatus.

A more recent analysis of the distinction between plant and premises was given in the *Wetherspoon* case, part of which concerned the treatment of decorative panelling in a pub. The Upper Tribunal took the view that the panelling turned the premises from an unpanelled room into a room that was mainly panelled, but was an unexceptional component of the type of premises (by contrast, for example, to the fixed but not easily removable metal sculpture, that was held to be plant in the *Scottish & Newcastle Breweries* case. Balancing all the considerations, the commissioners concluded that the panelling was more appropriately described as having become part of the premises than as having retained a separate identity. Therefore it did not qualify as plant.

Cases: *Yarmouth v France* (1887) 19 QBD 647; *Daphne v Shaw* (1926) 11 TC 256; *Hinton (HMIT) v Maden & Ireland* (1959) 38 TC 391; *IR Commrs v Barclay, Curle & Co Ltd* (1969) 45 TC 221; *JD Wetherspoon plc v R & C Commrs* (2007) Sp C 657; *JD Wetherspoon plc* [2010] TC 00312; *JD Wetherspoon plc v R & C Commrs* [2012] BTC 1,578

Tax Reporter: ¶244-800

111-275 The 'function' test

It is not possible to determine whether an asset is apparatus, and thus plant, without looking at the business and the function that the asset has in the business. That function may be an active or a passive one (see *Jarrold v John Good & Sons Ltd*).

The courts have distinguished between the 'plant' and the 'setting' into which that plant is placed, but the two are not mutually exclusive (see, e.g. *IR Commrs v Scottish Newcastle Breweries Ltd* and *Leeds Permanent Building Society v Proctor*). Further, the functional test itself raises the question 'is the functional purpose in providing the setting one for use in the trade?'

In distinguishing between the functional use and the setting, it must be noted that in some cases buildings and structures have been held to be plant in their entirety as the courts considered the structures to be performing an integral function with the plant and machinery contained within it (see *Schofield v Hall Ltd* (a grain silo), *IR Commrs v Barclay, Curle Co Ltd* (a dry dock), and *Cooke v Beach Station Caravans Ltd* (a swimming pool)). These examples are exceptions, however, and such treatment was described as applying in 'only extremely rare cases' in *McMillin*, where the tribunal firmly rejected the idea that some 'eco' cottages could be classified as plant and machinery.

Cases: *Jarrold v John Good & Sons Ltd* (1963) 40 TC 681; *IR Commrs v Barclay, Curle Co Ltd* (1969) 45 TC 221; *Schofield v Hall Ltd* (1974) 49 TC 538; *Cooke v Beach Station Caravans Ltd* (1974) 49 TC 514; *IR Commrs v Scottish Newcastle Breweries Ltd* [1982] BTC 187); *Leeds Permanent Building Society v Proctor* [1982] BTC 347; *Wimpy International Ltd v Warland (HMIT); Associated Restaurants Ltd v Warland (HMIT)* [1989] BTC 58; *McMillin* [2011] TC 00943; *Bowerswood House Retirement Home Ltd* [2015] TC 04299

111-300 Football League letter

Given the difficulties in determining what is or is not plant, it is very helpful to have from HMRC a list of items that are generally accepted as being plant. The following extract from HMRC *Capital Allowances Manual* gives details of a letter sent by the Revenue to the Football League in January 1991. It is of much wider interest than merely to football grounds. It must be noted that this represents the Revenue view before the enactment of FA 1994, introducing what is now broadly at CAA 2001, s. 21–26 (and of course well before the introduction in 2008 of the rules for integral features). Nevertheless, the declared intention of that legislation was to 'leave the present position unchanged'.

> 'Football clubs may incur expenditure on ground improvements in order to implement the recommendations of the Taylor report. The Inland Revenue had discussions with the Football League about what expenditure is likely to qualify for capital allowances. Following those discussions the Inland Revenue sent the Football League a letter on 25 January 1991 indicating what expenditure is likely to qualify. The letter listed as an appendix the sort of assets used by a football club in its trade which would normally qualify as plant or machinery. This is the list.
>
> (1) Advertising hoardings and perimeter boards which are not simply part of a perimeter fence or other structure.
>
> (2) Air conditioning plant, fans and ventilation machinery.
>
> (3) Automatic exit doors and gates.
>
> (4) Bicycle holders.

(5) Cameras, televisions, video recorders.

(6) Cars, coaches and vans.

(7) Computers, printers, photocopiers, typewriters and cash registers.

(8) Cookers, fridges, freezers, microwaves, dishwashing machines.

(9) Crush barriers securely fixed to the ground are not plant or machinery but they may come within the 1975 safety legislation and so qualify under Section 32 CAA2001.

(10) Electric scoreboards and visual displays.

(11) Fencing is not plant or machinery but it may come within the 1975 safety legislation and so qualify under Section 32 CAA2001.

(12) Fire alarm systems, fire extinguishers, sprinkler systems.

(13) Floodlighting.

(14) Floor coverings which are not part of the building or structure; for example, carpets (but not tiles which are stuck down).

(15) Goalposts and certain movable training equipment of a capital nature, for example, a vaulting horse (but not equipment which is part of the premises).

(16) Heating installations, boilers and water heaters.

(17) Lifts and hoists.

(18) Public address equipment – microphones, amplifiers and loudspeakers.

(19) Racking, shelving, cupboards and furniture.

(20) Telephones and telephone equipment, for example, private exchanges.

(21) Toilet sanitary ware, sinks and basins, baths and showers whether for staff or public (but not the mains water supply).

(22) Turnstiles and spectator counting equipment.

The letter gave some guidance on seats. It said that most modern types of seats are likely to qualify as plant or machinery, both plain plastic tip-up seats and more luxurious types of seat. It makes it clear that seating which is no more than an integral part of the stand will not qualify.

It says that the incidental costs of installing seats, or any other type of plant or machinery, may qualify under Section 25 CAA2001. It says that expenditure will not qualify as incidental if it creates an essentially new asset such as a stand or a terrace with an entirely new rake. It also says that we would not expect expenditure to qualify as incidental if it is large in proportion to the cost of the plant or machinery being installed.

Remember that not all expenditure incurred by clubs to comply with the requirements of the Football Spectators Act 1989 will qualify for capital allowances. The normal rules will apply.

> The letter states that expenditure on the fabric of a police control box will not qualify for capital allowances. We have now been advised that some local authorities take the view that they have the power under the Safety at Sports Grounds Act 1975 to require police control rooms to be installed. If that happens the expenditure will qualify under Section 32 CAA2001.'

Other Material: HMRC *Capital Allowances Manual* CA21230

Tax Reporter: ¶245-100

111-310 Farm expenditure

The plant and machinery legislation does not contain any rules relating specially to farms or farmers. With the demise of agricultural buildings allowances, however, it is more important than ever for a farming business to maximise its claims to plant and machinery allowances.

In February 2010, HMRC issued a guidance document in the form of HMRC Brief 03/10, entitled 'Guidance on plant and machinery capital allowances for the pig industry'. Some of this is general background information on how to claim plant and machinery allowances but the document also contains lists that are of potential interest to farmers and in some cases to other businesses as well. The introductory wording states the aim as being to 'illustrate the range of assets on which the pig industry might claim plant and machinery capital allowances' and the lists should certainly not be considered as comprehensive as there are many items of potential expenditure that are not listed. Subject to that principal caveat, the lists are as summarised below.

Outdoor items

Under this heading, HMRC have listed the following items of qualifying expenditure.

- Slurry storage systems, including slurry storage tanks (whether above or below ground) and any reception pit and/or effluent tank and/or channels and pipes used in connection with the slurry storage tank.
- Small scale slurry and sludge dewatering equipment (which may qualify for 100% allowances).
- Rainwater harvesting and filtration equipment (which again may qualify for 100% allowances).
- Gutters and associated piping for carrying rain water harvested for business uses.
- Sewerage systems designed to meet the particular requirements of the business.
- Silos for temporary storage.

- Concrete pad surrounded by low-level barriers for temporary storage of manure.
- Storage tanks.
- Moveable pig tents or pig arks.

See the general comment above about the need to view the list as illustrative rather than comprehensive.

Fixtures in buildings or structures qualifying for standard allowances

Under this heading, HMRC have listed the following assets as qualifying for allowances.

- Monitoring systems (including telemetry) for monitoring temperature, humidity, lighting, water and food levels.
- Water meters and monitoring equipment, including flow meters and water management software (which may qualify for 100% allowances).
- Computer and telecommunications systems (including their wiring or other links).
- Fire alarm, burglar alarm and surveillance systems (including their wiring or other links).
- Feed systems (whether or not automated).
- Slatted flooring areas (as internal parts of a slurry system).
- Farrowing crates.
- Moveable, adjustable pen dividers.
- Taps, sinks, basins and drinkers (and note that certain water efficient taps may qualify for 100% allowances).
- Fitted bathrooms, toilets, showers, kitchens and furnishings in office and staff accommodation used in the business (and note that certain water-efficient taps, toilets and showers may qualify for 100% allowances).

See the general comment above about the need to view the list as illustrative rather than comprehensive.

Fixtures in buildings or structures qualifying for special rate allowances

Under this heading, HMRC have listed the following assets as qualifying for allowances.

- All parts of a general electrical system (whether providing mains power or a lighting system) irrespective of whether or not the system is designed to be 'trade specific'.
- Certain lighting controls and Automatic Monitoring & Targeting (AMT) equipment designed to save energy (which may qualify for 100% allowances if certified by the Department for Energy and Climate Change (DECC)).
- All parts of air conditioning systems including, for example, ventilation shafts, (automatically controlled natural ventilation) shutters, and metal mesh and curtain arrangements for controlling airflow.
- Cold water, hot water and heating systems, including pipes, pumps, boilers, valves, etc. (but sinks or basins that are plumbed into the system qualify for standard allowances as above).
- Thermal insulation added to existing buildings or structures (and certain pipe work insulation may qualify for 100% allowances).

See the general comment above about the need to view the list as illustrative rather than comprehensive.

Non-fixtures qualifying for standard allowances

Expenditure qualifying under this heading includes cars (but subject to the special rules relating to these), and the following items listed by HMRC.

- Any agricultural or other machinery used for the purposes of the business. (As the guidance was aimed particularly at pig farmers, it goes on to list, by way of example, specialist equipment for the production, storage, handling and distribution of pig feed, pig transportation crates, pig weighing and handling equipment.)
- Lorries, vans, tractors, trailers, forklift trucks and other agricultural vehicles and machines.
- Computers and computerised equipment.
- Free-standing heaters and air conditioning units (and note that certain radiant heaters may qualify for 100% allowances).
- Office equipment and furnishings.

See the general comment above about the need to view the list as illustrative rather than comprehensive.

See also 111-325 re greenhouses.

111-325 Guidance re treatment of particular assets

- Moveable office partitions were held to be plant in *Jarrold v John Good & Sons Ltd* (1963) 40 TC 681.
- A stand at football club was held not to be plant in *Brown v Burnley Football and Athletic Co Ltd* (1980) 53 TC 357 (but special rules now apply to safety at sports grounds).
- Law books and law reports held by a barrister were held to be plant in *Munby v Furlong* (1977) 50 TC 491.
- A converted ship used as a floating restaurant was held not to be plant in *Benson v Yard Arm Club* (1979) 53 TC 67.
- A canopy over garage service area was held not to be plant in *Dixon v Fitch's Garage Ltd* (1975) 50 TC 509.
- False ceilings were held not to be plant in *Hampton v Forte's Autogrill Ltd* (1979) 53 TC 691.
- Lamps in tea-shops were held to provide general illumination and therefore not to be plant in *J Lyons & Co Ltd v A-G* [1944] 1 All ER 477 (but such lamps would, since April 2008, qualify as integral features).
- Free-standing decorative screens were held to be plant in *Leeds Permanent Building Society v Proctor* [1982] BTC 347.
- Special electric light fittings, decor, etc. for hotels and pubs were held to be plant in *IR Commrs v Scottish & Newcastle Breweries Ltd* [1982] BTC 187.
- A prefabricated laboratory and gymnasium in a school was held not to be plant in *St John's School v Ward* (1974) 49 TC 524.
- Acoustic ceilings and electrical installations were held not to be plant in *Imperial Chemical Industries of Australia and New Zealand Ltd v Federal Commissioner of Taxation* 120 CLR 396 (but the electrical installations would, since April 2008, qualify as integral features).
- Certain buildings used in mining operations were held to be plant in *Broken Hill Pty Ltd v Commrs of Taxation* 69 ATC 4028.
- Electrical installations for equipment were held to be plant, but ordinary lighting circuits were held not to be plant in *Cole Brothers Ltd v Philips* [1982] BTC 208. However, the lighting would now qualify as integral features.
- An inflatable tennis court cover was held not to be plant in *Thomas v Reynolds* [1987] BTC 147.
- A car wash site was held not to be plant in *Attwood v Anduff Car Wash Ltd* [1997] BTC 454.

- An underground electric substation was held not to be plant in *Bradley v London Electricity plc (No. 2)* [1996] BTC 451.
- Greens on a golf course were not 'plant' in *Family Golf Centres Ltd v Thorne* (1998) Sp C 150.
- 'Carpet' of synthetic grass for outdoor pitch at leisure centres was held to be plant in *IR Commrs v Anchor International Ltd* [2005] BTC 97.
- Expenditure on installing an artificial all-weather race track at a race course was held by the High Court in *Shove (HMIT) v Lingfield Park* [2003] BTC 422 to be expenditure on part of the premises instead of plant or machinery.
- A gazebo has been held to be plant in the context of a pub, even though it did not constitute a decorative asset, in *Andrew* [2011] TC 00799.

Greenhouses

In general, a simple greenhouse or glasshouse will not be eligible for plant and machinery allowances. However, this does not apply to certain glasshouses which are constructed so that the required environment (i.e. air, heat, light, irrigation and temperature) for growing plants is provided automatically by means of devices which are an integral part of its structure (List C, Item 17). This provision does not automatically class them as plant, rather they are not statutorily prevented from being plant simply because they are fixed structures.

In *Gray v Seymours Garden Centre (Horticulture) Ltd*, the Court of Appeal held that a glass house was a fixed structure to which plants are brought already in a saleable condition and thus was a building rather than plant.

HMRC take this exclusion from List A and B to cover only certain highly mechanised and computerised structures. To qualify for plant and machinery allowances such glasshouses must:

- be designed as one unit (i.e. the structure and the equipment) to operate as a single entity;
- incorporate extensive computer controlled equipment, without which the structure cannot operate to achieve the optimum artificial growing environment for the particular crops involved;
- have the equipment permanently installed during the construction of the greenhouse;
- have computer systems which control boiler, piped heating, temperature, humidity, ventilation and thermal or shade screens.

Depending on the crops grown, the equipment may include machinery for carbon dioxide enrichment of the greenhouse atmosphere; hydroponic culture; mobile benching; and lighting to control day length, etc.

See also 112-800 for glasshouses as long-life assets.

Case: *Gray v Seymours Garden Centre (Horticulture) Ltd* [1995] BTC 320

Other Material: HMRC *Capital Allowances Manual* CA22090

Platforms

In *Hunt (HMIT) v Henry Quick Ltd; King (HMIT) v Bridisco Ltd*, the High Court held that platforms erected in single-storey warehouses, to increase usable space and facilitating the handling of goods, were plant for the purpose of claiming capital allowances (but lighting installed beneath the platforms was not, though such lighting would now qualify under the rules relating to integral features).

Cases: *Hunt (HMIT) v Henry Quick Ltd; King (HMIT) v Bridisco Ltd* [1992] BTC 440

Cable television industry

It is believed that the cost of both the provision and the installation of ducting, in connection with the construction of cable television networks, is expenditure on the provision of plant and machinery. Other capital expenditure involved in setting up cable network systems, such as the studio and transmission equipment and the cable itself, is likewise expenditure on plant or machinery.

Other Material: HMRC *Capital Allowances Manual* CA21200

111-350 Assets used by directors or employees

There is a potential pitfall where an asset is provided for the private use of a director or employee. In these circumstances, HMRC accept that the asset may be a legitimate part of the remuneration package of the individual concerned (such that a liability on additional earnings will normally arise). However, it may be that the asset will not qualify as plant or machinery.

In practice, as long as the asset is a machine, HMRC instructions to inspectors say that the allowance should be accepted. Examples given include cars, aircraft, yachts, washing machines and dishwashers. However, if the asset is not machinery, then it will only qualify for capital allowances if it functions in the trade as plant. HMRC give as examples furniture or paintings provided for use in the director's home. Even though a benefit in kind charge will arise, the HMRC view is that the assets are not 'apparatus with which the company's trade is carried on' (see 111-200) and so allowances may be denied.

Other Material: HMRC *Capital Allowances Manual* CA27100

Tax Reporter: ¶245-175

111-360 Disability Discrimination Act

People providing services to the public have since October 2004 had certain statutory obligations, under the Disability Discrimination Acts of 1995 and 2005, to improve access to their premises for disabled people. Broadly, the law requires service providers to make 'reasonable adjustments' to their premises to remove obstacles that would prevent disabled people from using their services.

The cost of such adjustments may be treated for tax purposes as revenue expenditure, to be written off in full as it is incurred. HMRC give, as examples of such expenditure, the cost of printing large documents or of training staff on disability issues.

Other expenditure, however, will be capital in nature, in which case it will be necessary to consider whether or not it qualifies for plant and machinery allowances. The capital allowances legislation does not make special provision for such costs, so it is a question of applying general principles to the expenditure. However, HMRC have provided guidelines on the likely treatment of such costs and, in August 2008, updated those guidelines to take account of the changes introduced in FA 2008 (e.g. in relation to integral features). That guidance may be found at www.hmrc.gov.uk/specialist/disability-act-guidance.htm.

Tax Reporter: ¶245-765

First-year allowances

111-400 Rate changes

The standard rate of writing-down allowance was reduced from 25% to 20% from April 2008, with a 10% rate applying to certain expenditure. These rates were further reduced to 18% and 8% respectively from 6 April 2012.

For various reasons, Parliament has decided that it is appropriate, in particular circumstances, to allow tax relief at a faster rate. Since April 2008, this is normally by way of the annual investment allowance discussed at 111-875.

Prior to that date, accelerated relief was available only by way of first-year allowances (FYAs). FYAs were not abolished completely from April 2008, but the most common FYAs, giving relief at 40% or 50% for medium or

111-650 FYAs: expenditure on energy-saving plant or machinery

First-year allowances at 100% are available on first-year qualifying expenditure under the heading of energy-saving plant or machinery. Expenditure is first-year qualifying expenditure under this heading if:

- it is expenditure on energy-saving plant or machinery (as specifically defined) that is unused and not second-hand; and
- it does not fall within any of the general exclusions set out at 111-425.

The term 'energy-saving plant or machinery' is defined by the *Capital Allowances (Energy-saving Plant and Machinery) Order* 2001 (SI 2001/2541). In accordance with that Order, the plant or machinery is energy-saving plant or machinery if:

(1) it falls within a technology class specified in the Energy Technology Criteria List;

(2) it meets the environmental criteria set out in that List; and

(3) in the case of plant or machinery falling within any of the specified technology classes, it is of a type that:

  (a) is specified in, and has not been removed from, the Energy Technology Product List; or

  (b) has been accepted for inclusion in that List.

The Energy Technology Criteria List and the Energy Technology Product List are published by the Secretary of State for the Environment, Food and Rural Affairs. The lists are redefined annually. See the DEFRA website (www.defra.gov.uk/environment) for up-to-date details. See, also, the dedicated website www.eca.gov.uk.

Expenditure incurred after 5 April 2012 is not eligible for a first-year allowance if a payment is given under *Energy Act* 2008, s. 41 in respect of feed-in tariffs or after 5 April 2014 if a payment is made under s. 100 of that Act in respect of heat generated or gas or fuel produced by the plant or machinery.

A first-year allowance under this heading can be referred to as a 'section 45A allowance'. Such an allowance is available for all types of businesses, and is not restricted to small or medium-sized enterprises (incorporated or unincorporated).

Loss-making companies (only) may claim a tax repayment to the extent that losses are attributable to first-year allowances for energy-saving or environmentally beneficial plant and machinery: see the corporation tax commentary at 379-140.

Legislation: CAA 2001, s. 45A; *Capital Allowances (Energy-saving Plant and Machinery) Order* 2001 (SI 2001/2541) (as amended)

Tax Reporter: ¶237-400

Components

In the case of some (but not all) of the specified classes of technology, a component of the overall product may qualify for first year allowances in its own right (i.e. even though the product as a whole does not so qualify). The Energy Technology Product List specifies the amount for each qualifying component. That amount is the maximum expenditure on the component that can qualify for 100% first-year allowances under the energy-saving rules.

Legislation: *Capital Allowances (Energy-saving Plant and Machinery) Order* 2001 (SI 2001/2541), reg. 5

111-700 Cars with low carbon dioxide emissions

Expenditure on a car will attract a 100% first-year allowance provided:

- the expenditure is incurred before 31 March 2021;
- the car is unused and not second-hand; and
- the car is electrically propelled or has low CO_2 emissions.

The above is subject to the general exclusions set out at 111-425 except that the restriction specifically relating to cars does not apply.

A car has low CO_2 emissions if it has an official carbon dioxide emissions figure that does not exceed 75g/km (reducing to 50g/km from 1 April 2018) (95g/km between 6 April 2013 and 5 April 2015 and 110g/km before 6 April 2013). An electrically-propelled car is one that is propelled solely by electrical power and where that power is derived either from a source external to the vehicle or from an electrical storage battery that is not connected to any source of power when the vehicle is in motion.

Taxis are specifically included, motorcycles are specifically excluded.

Legislation: CAA 2001, s. 45D, 268B

Tax Reporter: ¶237-450

111-710 Goods vehicles with zero carbon dioxide emissions

First-year allowances are available for expenditure on new goods vehicles that cannot emit CO_2 by being driven (typically, electric vans). The 100%

first-year allowances apply to expenditure on unused, registered goods vehicles (though the registration may take place before or after the vehicle is bought). The expenditure must, for income tax purposes, be incurred after 6 April 2010 and before 6 April 2021. A goods vehicle is for these purposes to be defined as 'a mechanically propelled road vehicle which is of a design primarily suited for the conveyance of goods or burden of any description': broadly, a van.

Legislation: (proposed new) CAA 2001, s. 45DA

Exclusions and restrictions

General exclusions

The rules are subject to the general exclusions applying for the purposes of first-year allowances generally (CAA 2001, s. 46). This will, for example, exclude vehicles used for leasing.

Particular activities

First-year allowances for zero-emission vehicles are also denied for businesses engaged in fisheries or aquaculture (as covered by Council Regulation (EC) No. 104/2000) and for a qualifying activity 'relating to the management of waste of undertakings'. This last category does not exclude a business that is merely dealing with its own waste or that of a connected undertaking.

Firms in difficulty

No allowances will be due for any business considered to be in difficulty or subject to an outstanding recovery order (in terms of relevant European regulations).

Cap

The amount of expenditure on zero-emission goods vehicles qualifying for first-year allowances is to be capped at €85m per undertaking over the eight-year life of the measure. The limit applies per undertaking, but anti-avoidance measures take account of any partner enterprise or linked enterprise, as defined.

Legislation: (proposed new) CAA 2001, s. 45DA, 212T

111-725 Expenditure on plant or machinery for gas refuelling station

A 100% first-year allowance is available where expenditure is incurred on a 'gas refuelling station', defined to mean premises where vehicles are refuelled with natural gas or hydrogen fuel. The following conditions must be met:

- the expenditure is incurred before 31 March 2018;
- the plant or machinery is unused and not second-hand;
- none of the general exclusions set out at 111-425 apply.

The following items are specifically included:

- any storage tank for natural gas or hydrogen fuel;
- any compressor, pump, control or meter used for or in connection with refuelling vehicles;
- any equipment for dispensing the fuel to a vehicle.

Legislation: CAA 2001, s. 45E

Tax Reporter: ¶237-500

111-730 Expenditure on electric vehicle charging points

100% first-year allowance is available where expenditure is incurred on the provision of electric vehicle charging points. The following conditions must be met:

- the expenditure is incurred after 23 November 2016 and before 5 April 2019;
- the plant or machinery is unused and not second-hand;
- none of the general exclusions set out at 111-425 apply.

Legislation: CAA 2001, s. 45EA

111-750 Expenditure on plant and machinery for use wholly in a ring-fence trade

First-year allowances are available on plant and machinery provided for use in a ring-fence trade. Once again, this is subject to the general exclusions set out at 111-425. Allowances may be withdrawn if the plant and machinery is, within a five-year period from purchase, not used in the ring-fence trade or used for other purposes.

Legislation: CAA 2001, s. 45F, 45G

Tax Reporter: ¶237-550

111-800 Environmentally beneficial plant and machinery

First-year allowances are available at a rate of 100% on expenditure on new plant and machinery that falls into the category of 'environmentally beneficial'. The relief mirrors that for 'energy-saving plant or machinery' (see 111-650) but the term 'environmentally beneficial plant and machinery' is used for certain water technology products.

First-year allowances for environmentally beneficial plant or machinery are available to all businesses of whatever size. Expenditure must be on plant or machinery that is 'unused and not second hand' and relief is subject to the 'general exclusions' discussed at 111-425.

Meaning of 'environmentally beneficial plant or machinery'

The term 'environmentally beneficial plant or machinery' is defined by the *Capital Allowances (Environmentally Beneficial Plant and Machinery) Order*. In accordance with that Order, the plant or machinery is environmentally beneficial plant or machinery if:

(1) it falls within a technology class specified in the Water Technology Criteria List;

(2) it meets the environmental criteria set out in that List; and

(3) in the case of plant or machinery falling within any of the specified technology classes, it is of a type that:

   (a) is specified in, and has not been removed from, the Water Technology Product List; or

   (b) has been accepted for inclusion in that List.

The Water Technology Criteria List and the Water Technology Product List are published by the Secretary of State for the Environment, Food and Rural Affairs. The lists are redefined annually. See the DEFRA website (www.defra.gov.uk/environment) for up-to-date details. See, also, the dedicated website www.eca.gov.uk.

Loss-making companies (only) may claim a tax repayment to the extent that losses are attributable to first-year allowances for energy-saving or environmentally beneficial plant and machinery: see the corporation tax commentary at 379-140.

Legislation: CAA 2001, s. 45H, 45G; *Capital Allowances (Environmentally Beneficial Plant and Machinery) Order* 2003 (SI 2003/2076) (as amended)

Tax Reporter: ¶237-600

Environmentally beneficial components of plant or machinery

Special rules address the case in which qualifying plant or machinery is part of a larger item of plant or machinery that does not qualify for the 100% allowance. If figures are specified in the Treasury Order for one or more components, then the amounts qualifying for first-year allowances under this heading are restricted to those figures. If payments are made in instalments, then the proportion of each instalment qualifying for first-year allowances is equal to the proportion that the total qualifying expenditure bears to the whole expenditure incurred on the plant and machinery.

The normal apportionment rules of CAA 2001, s. 562(3) are disapplied where the special rules apply to environmentally beneficial components of plant or machinery.

Legislation: CAA 2001, s. 45J, 45G

111-850 Additional VAT liabilities and rebates

Additional VAT liability under Capital Goods Scheme

An additional VAT liability is subject to the same first-year allowances as the original expenditure which is first-year qualifying expenditure. The first-year allowance on the additional VAT liability is made for the chargeable period in which that additional VAT liability accrues.

An additional VAT liability can arise under the Capital Goods Scheme (for detailed commentary on the Capital Goods Scheme, see the *CCH Value Added Tax Reporter* ¶19-800). For the purposes of claiming plant or machinery allowances, the most likely assets for consideration are computers and computer equipment and possibly civil engineering works and parts thereof.

Broadly, the Capital Goods Scheme allows for the percentage of input tax which can be deducted from output tax to be adjusted in accordance with the extent of use of the item in question in making taxable supplies. This only affects those who make exempt (input tax on purchases, etc. to make exempt supplies generally cannot be deducted) and taxable supplies (input tax on purchases, etc. to make standard-rated, zero-rated or reduced-rated supplies, can be deducted) for VAT purposes.

The plant or machinery allowances which may be available are those existing when the original capital expenditure was incurred, but they are given for the chargeable period in which the additional VAT liability arose.

Any additional VAT liability on the plant or machinery in question will be eligible for first-year allowances at the appropriate rates in respect of the chargeable period in which the additional VAT liability arises. The balance of the additional VAT liability, after deducting the first-year allowance, will be brought into account as with any other qualifying expenditure, i.e. normally the balance is allocated to the appropriate pool in the following chargeable period.

Legislation: CAA 2001, s. 236; *Value Added Tax Regulations* 1995 (SI 1995/2518), Pt. XV

Tax Reporter: ¶241-300

VAT rebate under Capital Goods Scheme

Where:

- an additional VAT rebate arises under the Capital Goods Scheme (i.e. the item of plant or machinery is used to a greater extent in making taxable supplies);
- the rebate is made to the person who has incurred the original capital expenditure; and
- the person who incurred the original expenditure is the owner of the plant or machinery concerned at any time in the chargeable period in which the rebate is made.

the amount of the rebate is brought into account in respect of the plant or machinery concerned as a disposal value for the chargeable period in which the additional VAT rebate accrues.

Legislation: CAA 2001, s. 238

Tax Reporter: ¶241-350

Annual investment allowances

111-875 Introduction

Overview

In essence, the AIA gives full tax relief (similar in effect to a 100% first-year allowance) for the first £200,000 (formerly £500,000 prior to 1 January 2016) of annual expenditure on plant and machinery. Expenditure must be incurred by a 'qualifying person', defined to mean an individual, a partnership consisting only of individuals, or a company. Expenditure is said to be 'AIA qualifying expenditure' if it is incurred by such a person and is not subject to any of the general exclusions described at 111-900. The person claiming the allowance must own the plant or machinery at some time during the chargeable period for which the claim is made.

The declared purpose of the AIA is to 'target investment support on all businesses that are investing for growth and help alleviate the cash flow constraints which confront small and growing businesses'. The introduction of the AIA coincided with the withdrawal of most first-year allowances (see 111-400).

The AIA ceiling was reduced from £100,000 to just £25,000 per year from April 2012 and increased to £250,000 for the period to 5 April 2014 when it was increased temporarily to £500,000 for the period to 31 December 2015 and was set at £200,000 for expenditure incurred on or after 1 January 2016.

Legislation: CAA 2001, s. 38A, 51A

Tax Reporter: ¶236-400

Scope of the AIA

The AIA offers full and immediate tax relief, for all sizes of business, for (broadly) the first £200,000 (currently) of expenditure on plant and machinery in the year (but see 111-880). The AIA is made for the chargeable period in which the expenditure is incurred (but without the benefit of the pre-trading expenditure rules of CAA 2001, s. 12: see 111-410).

Cars and expenditure on 'green' technology continue to be treated separately, but the AIA is available for expenditure on most other plant and machinery, including long-life assets and integral features. Expenditure in excess of the annual allowance may attract writing-down allowances in the same accounting period.

Assets provided only partly for business use

Where an asset is provided partly for purposes other than those of the qualifying activity carried on by the person, AIAs may be given to the extent that is just and reasonable in relation to the proportion in which the expenditure was incurred for the purposes of the qualifying activity. So if an asset costs £20,000, and is used one-quarter for private purposes, AIAs can be claimed on £15,000.

Legislation: CAA 2001, s. 51A(11)(b), 205

Tax Reporter: ¶236-400

Other restrictions on relief

The AIA is subject to various 'general exclusions' described at 111-900, and to several targeted anti-avoidance measures (see 111-910).

Restrictions are also made under CAA 2001, s. 217 and 241 (additional VAT liabilities). See also CAA 2001, s. 236 with further measures about additional VAT liabilities.

111-880 Amount of annual investment allowance

The maximum amount of the AIA has been changed on an irregular basis since its introduction in April 2008; for income tax purposes, these can be summarised as:

6 April 2008 to 5 April 2010	£50,000
6 April 2010 to 5 April 2012	£100,000
6 April 2012 to 31 December 2012	£25,000
1 January 2013 to 5 April 2014	£250,000
6 April 2014 to 31 December 2015	£500,000
From 1 January 2016	£200,000

The present Government has indicated that the allowance of £200,000 will be fixed until the end of the current Parliament.

The figure of maximum allowance is proportionately increased or reduced if the chargeable period is greater or shorter than one year. This principle has important implications for periods of account spanning the introduction of the relief in April 2008, and also for periods spanning any date on which the maximum amount of relief is changed, as explained immediately below.

Legislation: CAA 2001, s. 51A(5)–(6)

Tax Reporter: ¶236-400

Transitional measures

The interaction between a taxpayer's basis period and changes in the level of AIA will have a significant impact on the maximum relief available. A point of change is known as a 'relevant date'.

Where a basis period spans the relevant date, an apportionment is to be made and in some circumstances a restriction is imposed. Suppose, for example, that a business draws accounts up for the year to 30 June 2016. In this case, the legislation requires that the period should be split into two notional periods for the purposes of calculating the entitlement to AIAs. The first notional period will run from 1 July 2015 to 31 December 2015 (a period of 183 days) and the second will run from 1 January 2016 to 30 June 2016 (183 days). The maximum overall allowance is then calculated by aggregating the two figures, as follows:

- £500,000 × 183/366 = £250,000; plus
- £200,000 × 183/366 = £100,000.

Thus the maximum overall allowance would be £350,000.

A restriction is imposed, however, on the maximum amount of AIA that may be claimed for expenditure incurred after the relevant date in December 2015: a maximum of only £100,000 of such expenditure may be subject to an AIA claim. If, for example, the business with accounts to 30 June 2016 incurred £290,000 of expenditure on plant and machinery, but this related to a single asset bought in January 2016, the AIA would be restricted to £100,000. If, on the other hand, the asset was bought in December 2015, then AIA would be given on the whole cost (even though this is more than the £250,000 figure above).

The same implications for the calculation of available relief has applied on each change in the relevant date. The calculation is particularly complex where the basis period spans more than one change in the AIA, as illustrated below.

Transitional measures (more than one change in AIA)

Assume a sole trader draws up accounts to 28 February 2013, which bridges 6 April 2012. Apportioning to the nearest month, the maximum allowance for that period is £68,750, calculated as follows:

	£
1 March 2012 to 5 April 2012 – 1/12 × £100,000	8,333
6 April 2012 to 31 December 2012 – 9/12 × £25,000	18,750
1 January 2013 to 28 February 2013 – 2/12 × £250,000	41,667
	£68,750

The complications that arise depend upon when expenditure is actually incurred, as the purpose of this temporary increase in AIA is to encourage investment in plant and machinery, not reward expenditure incurred before 1 January 2013 where the allowance was lower.

For example, assume the sole trader incurred expenditure on plant as follows:

	£
March 2012	20,000
November 2012	30,000
February 2013	25,000

The AIA claimable by that sole trader is:

	£
Period to 5 April (being within the maximum of £31,250 that could have been claimed ignoring the change)	20,000
Period from 6 April 2012 to 31 December 2012 (being restricted to £22,917 – (20,000 – 8,333))	11,250
Period 1 January 2013 to 28 February 2013 actual expenditure incurred (being less than £60,417)	25,000
	£56,250

The figure of £22,917 represents the maximum allowance that could have been claimed, ignoring the change, for the period from 6 April 2012 to 28 February 2013 (i.e. 11/12 × £25,000). It will be observed that for the total period to 31 December 2012, the AIA is £31,250, which is the maximum for the entire period had the allowance continued without change for the year to 28 February 2013 (i.e. 1/12 × £100,000 + 11/12 × £25,000). Whatever the actual computation, the AIA cannot exceed £68,750 for the whole year.

Legislation: FA 2010, s. 5; FA 2013, Sch. 1; FA 2014, Sch. 2

Tax Reporter: ¶236-410

111-890 Claiming the annual investment allowance

Subject to various 'general exclusions' (see 111-900), and to various other restrictions (see 111-910), a business may choose which expenditure to include as AIA qualifying expenditure. This will be relevant if costs have been incurred on assets that potentially attract writing-down allowances at different rates.

> **Example**
>
> At a time when the AIA limit is £200,000, a business spends £250,000 on general plant and machinery and £120,000 on integral features. It will wish to treat the whole of the latter as AIA qualifying expenditure so that the excess £170,000 (£250,000 plus £120,000, less £200,000) can attract allowances at the main WDA rate of 18% rather than at the lower rate of 8%.

A person entitled to the AIA may claim AIA on a reduced amount of qualifying expenditure if desired (perhaps so as to avoid or reduce a future balancing charge), in which case any remaining allowances given on the expenditure will be by way of writing-down allowances only.

There is no question of carrying forward any unused AIA.

Legislation: CAA 2001, s. 51A; FA 2008, Sch. 24, para. 23

Tax Reporter: ¶236-425

111-900 General exclusions

No AIA is available:

- for the chargeable period in which the qualifying activity is permanently discontinued;
- for cars (as defined: see below);
- for expenditure incurred for the purposes of a ring fence trade in respect of which tax is chargeable under CTA 2010, s. 330(1);
- where the provision of the plant or machinery is connected with a change in the nature or conduct of the trade or business carried on by someone other than the person incurring the expenditure, and the obtaining of the AIA was the main benefit (or one of the main benefits) that could reasonably be expected to arise from the making of the change;
- where existing plant (or plant received as a gift) is brought into use for the purposes of a qualifying activity; or
- where plant that has been provided for long funding leasing is brought into use for other purposes.

Legislation: CAA 2001, s. 38B

Tax Reporter: ¶236-450

Cars (and other vehicles)

As noted above, no annual investment allowances are given for 'cars'.

Until April 2009, a car was specifically defined to include a motorcycle, so no AIAs were given for expenditure on motorcycles. However, the definition was changed in FA 2009 and from April 2009 expenditure on a motorcycle is no longer treated as expenditure on a car.

More generally, the denial of AIAs for cars means that the distinction between a car and a van gains new significance. Some care is needed, as the definition for capital allowance purpose is not identical to that applying in the context of benefits in kind (see ITEPA 2003, s. 115(1)), but precedents in that context may still be helpful as both definitions use the concept of a vehicle 'of a type not commonly used as a private vehicle and unsuitable' 'to be so used' or 'for such use' (see 132-210).

111-910 Other restrictions on relief

Overview

The annual investment allowance (AIA) rules contain numerous anti-avoidance provisions, the main purpose of which is to prevent artificial multiplication of the annual investment limit, though many perfectly normal business structures – such as groups of companies – are also caught. These provisions relate mostly to companies but can also cover qualifying activities under common control (see below). A further restriction denies AIAs where arrangements have been entered into for a 'disqualifying purpose' (see 111-930).

The mechanics of restricting relief are complex, but they will in practice be needed only rarely in income tax cases.

Legislation: CAA 2001, s. 51K

Tax Reporter: ¶236-475

Qualifying activities under common control

Relief is restricted where, in a given tax year, two or more qualifying activities meet all of the following conditions:

- they are carried on, at the end of the chargeable period for the activity ending in the tax year, by a qualifying person other than a company;
- they are controlled by the same person (as defined); and
- they are related to one another (again, as defined).

In such a case, a person is entitled to just the one AIA. Where the qualifying activities are carried on by more than one qualifying person, those persons are entitled to a single AIA between them in respect of the relevant AIA qualifying expenditure.

However, from a strict reading of the legislation it appears that a sole trader, for example, and a company controlled by that individual cannot give rise to a sharing of the AIA.

Legislation: CAA 2001, s. 51H

Tax Reporter: ¶236-475

111-930 Further restriction on AIA

No annual investment allowance (AIA) is given where an arrangement is entered into wholly or mainly for a disqualifying purpose. Arrangements are said to be entered into for such a purpose if their main purpose, or one of their main purposes, is to enable a person to obtain an AIA to which the person would not otherwise be entitled. If the allowance has already been given, and such a purpose prohibits the giving of the AIA, then it is to be withdrawn.

Legislation: CAA 2001, s. 218A

Tax Reporter: ¶236-490

Writing-down allowances

112-000 Overview

Writing-down allowances are available at two rates: the standard rate being 18% and the lower rate being 8%. The latter being applicable for certain common types of expenditure ('integral features', discussed in depth at 114-600ff.).

The rate of relief on all qualifying expenditure prior to 5 April 2008 was 25%. This was reduced to 20% (together with the introduction of the 10% lower rate) with effect from 6 April 2008. The rates were reduced further from 6 April 2012 to 18% and 8%. Where the chargeable period bridges that date, an apportionment is made to produce a hybrid rate. For example, the hybrid rate for a trade for the year to 31 December 2012 is 18.53%, being 96/366 at 20% plus 270/366 at 18%.

The introduction of the annual investment allowance (see 111-875ff.) means that some businesses will not need to claim writing-down allowances at all.

The normal rule is that the writing-down allowance (WDA) is 18% of the amount by which the AQE exceeds the TDR. (Broadly, AQE is the qualifying expenditure, including any residual amounts brought forward from earlier years, and TDR is the amount of disposal proceeds received in the year for items of plant and machinery. However, see 112-550ff. for a fuller definition of these terms.)

Example 1

A business has expenditure brought down from the previous period of £20,000. An asset is sold for £6,000 and a replacement is bought for £10,000. For simplicity, it is assumed that the business is not entitled to any annual investment allowance (probably because that allowance has been fully allocated to a connected business: see 111-910).

AQE will be £30,000 and TDR will be £6,000. Therefore, the allowance available is 18% of the net figure of £24,000, so £4,320. The balance of £19,680 is carried forward to the following period of account.

Example 2

A trader has a value brought down from year one of £100,000. He incurs expenditure in year two of £25,000. He sells an asset in the year for £5,000 (which is less than the cost of the asset). Assume that no first-year allowances or annual investment allowances are due. His computation for year two is as follows:

	£
Unrelieved qualifying expenditure brought forward	100,000
Additional qualifying expenditure	25,000
Available qualifying expenditure	125,000
Total disposal receipts	(5,000)
	120,000
Writing-down allowance (18%)	21,600
Unrelieved qualifying expenditure carried forward	98,400

Example 3

Suppose, instead, that the trader from Example 2 can claim annual investment allowances.

This time, the new expenditure of £25,000 will be fully relieved by way of the AIA claim.

Writing-down allowances on the net £95,000 will be given at 18%, so £17,100.

The total claim will therefore be £42,100, with £77,900 carried forward.

The normal rule is modified in various circumstances, as follows:

- in the case of special rate expenditure, where the rate is restricted to 8% (CAA 2001, s. 102 – see 112-800). This category includes integral features (CAA 2001, s. 104D);
- in the case of certain assets used for overseas leasing, where the allowance is restricted to 10% (CAA 2001, s. 109);
- if the qualifying activity is carried on for part only of the chargeable period then the amount is proportionately reduced;
- a person claiming a writing-down allowance may choose to reduce the allowance to a specified amount. This could be beneficial, for example, where a full allowance would reduce the level of profits of a sole trader to the point where the person's personal allowances would not be fully used. By restricting the amount of allowances claimed, the trader may be able to make better use of the higher allowances that will be available in future years. For a company, it may be appropriate to restrict relief claimed to make use, for example, of group relief;

- no writing-down allowance is given in the final chargeable period (see 112-550);
- if the chargeable period is less or (for an unincorporated business) more than a year then the figure of 18% is proportionately increased or decreased;
- in the case of qualifying expenditure incurred wholly for the purposes of a ring fence trade in respect of which tax is charged under CTA 2010, s. 330(1), in which case the rate is 25% (CAA 2001, s. 56(1A)).

Example 4

The facts are as in Example 2 above but the trader carrying on the business has an accounting period of just nine months. In this case, allowances are calculated as follows:

	£
Unrelieved qualifying expenditure brought down	100,000
Additional qualifying expenditure	25,000
Available qualifying expenditure	125,000
Total disposal receipts	(5,000)
	120,000
Writing-down allowance (18% × 9/12)	16,200
Unrelieved qualifying expenditure carried forward	103,800

Legislation: CAA 2001, s. 56

Tax Reporter: ¶238-050

Basis periods

A little care is needed when considering the interaction of these rules with the general principles for determining the taxable profits for any given period.

Example 5

A sole trader has always drawn up accounts to 31 December each year, most recently to 31 December 2015. He then draws accounts up to 30 September 2017.

For income tax purposes, his basis period for 2017–18 will be the period from 1 October 2016 to 30 September 2017, with an accrual of overlap relief for the period from 1 October 2016 to 31 December 2016, as this period has been taxed twice. This is on the assumption that the sole trader chooses, and is able, to meet the conditions for recognising a change of accounting date.

As far as capital allowances are concerned, he will have a short period of account to 30 September 2017, so his writing-down allowances for that period will be restricted to 9/12 of what they would otherwise have been. Nevertheless, the capital allowances still merge in with the other deductions from the trading profits. Therefore, his tax liability will be on:

(1) one-quarter of the profit net of capital allowances for the year to 31 December 2016; plus

(2) the whole of the profit net of reduced capital allowances for the period to 30 September 2017.

A company can never have an accounting period in excess of one year. Under self-assessment, however, it is possible for an individual sole trader or a partnership to have a chargeable period of more than 12 months (but not more than 18 months).

Where the period of account does exceed 12 months then an increased writing-down allowance is made accordingly.

Legislation: CAA 2001, s. 6(6); CTA 2009, s. 10(1)(a)

Example 6

The facts are as in Example 2 above except that the business is carried on by a sole trader in the course of a 15-month period to 31 July 2017. In this case, allowances are calculated as follows.

	£
Unrelieved qualifying expenditure brought down	100,000
Additional qualifying expenditure	25,000
Available qualifying expenditure	125,000
Total disposal receipts	(5,000)
	120,000
Writing-down allowance (18% × 15/12)	27,000
Unrelieved qualifying expenditure carried forward	93,000

112-030 Small pools

For the great majority of businesses, most *new* expenditure on plant and machinery (but excluding, for example, cars) will be relieved by way of the annual investment allowance (AIA). Most businesses, though, will have pools of expenditure brought forward from times before the new rules were introduced. This is where the concept of a 'small pool' (introduced by *Finance Act* 2008) will eventually simplify future capital allowance computations. Once the value of the pool has reduced to the 'small pool limit', it will be possible to write off the whole remaining balance in one go, by way of a special writing-down allowance. The small pool limit is set at just £1,000, however, which means that many businesses will need to retain small and diminishing pools for many years.

The £1,000 threshold is applied to the pool value brought down, as adjusted for additional qualifying expenditure and total disposal receipts in the year. If, for example, there is a value of £1,100 brought forward then this in itself is too high to benefit from the small pool rules. However, if there were also disposal proceeds in the year of £120 then this would take the value down to £980, and the whole amount could be claimed by way of a special writing-down allowance in the year.

Example

A sole trader draws up her accounts to 31 December. She has a pool value brought down at 1 January 2017 of £1,400 and she incurs no expenditure on plant and machinery in the following few years.

She can claim WDAs of £280 for 2017–18, giving a pool value carried down of £1,120. In the following year, WDAs will be given of £224, with £896 carried forward. In the year after that, WDAs can be claimed – under the small pool provisions – of the whole amount of £896. The sole trader will then never again need to claim WDAs on her main pool, unless her expenditure exceeds the AIA threshold in the year or she buys an asset (such as a car) that does not qualify for annual investment allowances.

The rules relating to small pools apply to the main capital allowances pool and to the special rate pool. They do not apply, for example, to short-life assets.

Legislation: CAA 2001, s. 56A

Tax Reporter: ¶238-060

112-050 Assets treated as belonging to taxpayer

Tenants who incur expenditure on plant or machinery which on installation become a landlord's fixture, and therefore, as a point of general law, the property of the landlord, may claim writing-down allowances in respect of them. For further details, see 114-600ff.

Similarly, persons who contribute toward the capital expenditure of others may be treated as if the assets in point belong to them so as to enable them to receive allowances (see 110-250).

Under hire purchase or lease purchase agreements, the assets in point do not belong to the acquirer until the contract is fully performed, i.e. usually when the last instalment is paid. The acquirer is nevertheless treated as if the assets belong to him when he brings them into use (see 115-350).

112-100 Disposals and discontinuance

Disposals of assets may give rise to balancing adjustments (see 112-400), in which case no further WDAs are given in respect of those same assets.

No WDA is available in a chargeable period during which the trade is permanently discontinued.

Legislation: CAA 2001, s. 55, 65

112-150 Claiming/disclaiming writing-down allowances

Capital allowances must be claimed, and the claim must be included in a tax return, which includes an amended return.

There is no obligation for all capital expenditure on plant or machinery to be included in capital allowances computations. In such cases, the expenditure may be included as 'qualifying expenditure' in a subsequent period, but only if the taxpayer owns the asset at some time in that later period.

> **Example**
>
> Tom bought a computer for £1,200 on 4 July 2015. Due to trading losses, he decided not to include the expenditure in his capital allowances computations.
>
> He started to make profits in the year ended 30 April 2017 and decided then to claim capital allowances in respect of the computer.
>
> He is free to claim writing-down allowances in respect of the computer provided he still owns it at some time in the year ended 30 April 2017. No annual investment allowances or first-year allowances may be given on the expenditure in these circumstances, however.

Legislation: TMA 1970, s. 42(5); FA 1998, Sch. 18, para. 79; CAA 2001, s. 3, 52(2), 58(4)

Tax Reporter: ¶238-050

Balancing adjustments

112-400 Balancing allowances

A balancing allowance can only be obtained in the 'final chargeable period' as defined (see 112-550). For the main pool or for a special rate pool, this only arises when the qualifying activity is permanently discontinued. For single-asset pools (including, for example, short-life assets), the disposal will itself trigger the final chargeable period for capital allowances purposes.

The results can be surprising. Taking the main pool as an example, the important point to note is that a balancing allowance does not arise merely because all the assets in the pool have been sold.

A person will thus continue to obtain capital allowances for as long as he carries on trading, with the writing-down allowance reducing each year and the tax relief may therefore lag behind any accounting treatment of the asset concerned. The way around this disadvantage may be to make a short-life asset election (see 112-700), or to use the asset for occasional private journeys. In either of these cases, the asset will need to go into a single-asset pool and the disposal will then (if appropriate) trigger a full balancing allowance. Since April 2008, this issue has only tended to arise for larger businesses as the annual investment allowance will generally ensure that full relief is obtained at the outset for most assets. The 'small pool' rules will also ensure that any remnants of value may be written off once they drop below £1,000 (see 112-030).

Legislation: CAA 2001, s. 55(4)

Tax Reporter: ¶238-100

112-450 Balancing charges

Unlike the balancing allowance (see 112-400), a balancing charge can arise at any time. It will arise if the disposal value to be brought into account exceeds the qualifying expenditure (brought forward plus expenditure in the year). In statutory terms, a person will be liable to a balancing charge in any period, including the final period, if total disposal receipts (TDR: see 112-580) exceed available qualifying expenditure (AQE: see 112-575). The charge will be the amount of that excess (unless any adjustment is needed for private use).

The balancing charge in relation to any given asset can never exceed the allowances that have been obtained for that asset. In other words, the worst that a balancing charge can ever do is to take back the allowances that have already been given for an asset.

Example

Winston buys a van for £4,000, obtains allowances of £800 and then sells the van for £4,500. His balancing charge is restricted to £800 (rather than £1,300).

Tax Reporter: ¶238-125

Definitions

112-550 Final chargeable period

This concept is important to determine the timing of any balancing adjustments. The meaning varies according to the type of pool in question. For the main pool, and for the special rate pool, it is the chargeable period in which the qualifying activity is permanently discontinued. For a single-asset pool, it is defined as the first chargeable period in which any disposal event within CAA 2001, s. 61(1) occurs, but this is subject to certain exceptions (e.g. when an asset starts to be used for other purposes, or at the end of the four-year cut off period for short life assets).

Legislation: CAA 2001, s. 65

Tax Reporter: ¶238-150

112-575 Available qualifying expenditure

The general rule is that the available qualifying expenditure (AQE), for a particular pool, in the current chargeable period, consists of:

(1) any unrelieved qualifying expenditure carried forward in the pool from the previous chargeable period – i.e. unrelieved qualifying expenditure is the excess, in the previous chargeable period, of the AQE over the TDR, less any writing-down allowance for that previous chargeable period); plus

(2) any qualifying expenditure allocated to the pool in the current chargeable period.

Any amount of expenditure on which first-year allowances have been claimed in the year must be excluded. Any amount on which first-year allowances have been claimed for an earlier period must be limited to the balance left after deducting the first-year allowance.

A person's available qualifying expenditure in a pool for a chargeable period also includes any amount allocated to the pool for that period under a number of provisions listed in the legislation (e.g. certain demolition costs). The statute also lists a number of items that must specifically be excluded (e.g. in certain cases involving fixtures).

Legislation: CAA 2001, s. 57, 58

Tax Reporter: ¶238-150

112-580 Total of any disposal receipts

Overview

Although the legislation uses the concept of 'the total of any disposal receipts' (which it abbreviates to TDR) there is no definition of this term. However, there is a definition of 'disposal receipt'. In other words, disposal receipts are converted to TDR simply by an arithmetic process rather than by any sleight of legislation.

In most cases, the disposal value for capital allowances purposes will simply be the sale proceeds. The position can be more complex, however, and even in the rewritten legislation of CAA 2001, the sections dealing with disposal events and disposal values need to be considered with some care.

A disposal event includes any of the following events.

- The person ceases to own the plant or machinery.
- The person loses possession of the plant or machinery where it is reasonable to assume the loss is permanent.
- The plant or machinery has been in use for mineral extraction and access, and the person abandons it at the site where it was in use for that purpose.
- The plant or machinery ceases to exist as such (i.e. as a result of destruction, dismantling or otherwise).
- The plant or machinery begins to be used wholly or partly for purposes other than those of the qualifying activity.
- The plant or machinery begins to be leased under a long funding lease.
- The qualifying activity is permanently discontinued.

Legislation: CAA 2001, s. 61

Tax Reporter: ¶238-150

Disposal values

A disposal value must be brought into account in the chargeable period wherever an asset belonging to the person carrying on a qualifying activity is or has been used for the purposes of the qualifying activity and ceases to belong to him (e.g. on sale) or permanently ceases to be used for the purposes of the qualifying activity (e.g. on the permanent discontinuance of the qualifying activity, or appropriation by the person carrying on the qualifying activity). No disposal value is brought into account if the disposal is by way of a gift taxable under ITEPA 2003 as an employee benefit.

The disposal value is the proceeds of sale taken together with any insurance moneys received or any other compensation moneys received for an event which has affected the sale price of the asset. Where the asset is sold for less than market value, market value is substituted unless:

- the buyer's expenditure on acquiring the asset can be taken into account in making capital allowances to him under the plant and machinery or research and development rules; or
- the difference between the sale price and the open market value is chargeable to tax on an employee under ITEPA 2003.

Where plant or machinery is installed or fixed in or to a building or land such that it becomes, in law, part of the building or land special rules may fix the disposal value of such 'fixtures'.

At the commencement of the term of a long funding lease, the deemed disposal value will be as follows:

- in the case of a long funding *finance* lease, an amount equal to that which would be recognised as the lessor's net investment in the lease if accounts were prepared in accordance with generally accepted accounting practice on the date on which the lessor's net investment in the lease is first recognised in the lessor's financial records; and
- in the case of a long funding *operating* lease, an amount equal to the market value of the plant or machinery at the commencement of the term of the lease.

If the asset is not sold but is demolished or destroyed, the disposal value is the net scrap value (i.e. after deducting any demolition costs, etc.) together with any insurance or compensation moneys of a capital nature. If the demolition costs exceed any moneys received for the remains of the asset, that excess is added to the general pool of expenditure unless the asset is replaced, in which case the excess is treated as expenditure incurred on the replacement.

The 'disposal value' cannot exceed the capital expenditure incurred on providing the plant or machinery unless it was acquired in a transaction between connected persons in which case the transferor's expenditure will be substituted if it was greater.

Legislation: CAA 2001, s. 26ff., 61, 63

Tax Reporter: ¶238-150

Gifts to educational establishments

A nil disposal value is shown for plant and machinery used, wholly or partly, in a person's business; where such plant and machinery is donated to a 'designated educational establishment'. This relief must be claimed within normal time-limits for submitting income and corporation tax returns.

Legislation: CAA 2001, s. 63(2)

Tax Reporter: ¶238-150

Charities, etc.

A wide ranging relief exists for gifts of plant and machinery used, wholly or partly, in a person's business and subsequently donated either to a charitable trust (defined per ITA 2007, s. 519, to a charitable company (defined per CTA 2010, s. 467), to a registered community amateur sports club) or to one of the bodies listed in CTA 2010, s. 468. These include the British Museum, the Natural History Museum, the Historic Buildings and Monument Commission for England, the National Heritage Memorial Fund, and the National Endowment for Science, Technology and the Arts.

Legislation: CAA 2001, s. 63(2)

Tax Reporter: ¶238-150

Computer software

The grant of a right to use or otherwise deal with computer software for a capital sum is treated in the same way as a sale of plant or machinery.

The disposal value is generally the net proceeds to the grantor plus any insurance moneys, compensation or other capital payments. This does not apply where:

- the consideration is not wholly in money but equals an open market value; or
- there is no consideration or the consideration is less than the open market value,

in which case a market valuation is applied. Where there are a series of grants of leases in respect of the same software, the aggregate consideration is taken into account for the purposes of limiting any balancing adjustment.

Legislation: CAA 2001, s. 61

Tax Reporter: ¶238-350

Cars

112-600 Introduction and overview

General principles

The underlying principle has always been that a business should gain tax relief – at some stage – on the amount by which the value of a car has fallen over the period of ownership. If, for example, a business buys a car for £20,000 and sells it three years later for £7,500 then it will be able to reduce its taxable profits by £12,500 (albeit subject to a likely private use adjustment if the car is not owned by a company). What the tax system does not do, though, is to give tax relief on a timescale that mirrors commercial depreciation; rather, it contains its own fairly complex rules to determine the timing of the tax deductions.

The rate of relief is determined primarily by the level of engine emissions, the idea being to encourage businesses to buy cars that are more fuel efficient and that, therefore, have a less damaging environmental impact.

Summary of current rules

Key features of the rules as they have applied since April 2009 are as follows:

- The rate of tax relief instead depends on the level of the vehicle's CO_2 emissions.
- Qualifying expenditure is normally allocated to one of the two main pools for plant and machinery. Expenditure on 'main rate cars' (broadly, those with emissions of up to 130g/km (110g/km from 6 April 2018), but see 112-610) goes into the main plant and machinery pool, attracting allowances at 18%. Cars with higher emissions attract allowances at just 8% in the 'special rate' pool.
- Cars with private use are kept in a single asset pool, but the rate at which allowances are given is still determined by reference to the same emission principles.
- Certain hire cars (e.g. taxis) that were formerly exempt from the restrictions for expensive cars are now subject to the new rules. Conversely, motorcycles were previously classified as cars for capital allowance purposes, but are now excluded from the definition.
- 100% first-year allowance for cars with very low emissions (see 111-700).

Tax Reporter: ¶238-500

112-605 Definition of 'car'

Statutory definition

The capital allowance definition of 'car' covers any 'mechanically propelled road vehicle' except:

- a motorcycle;
- a vehicle of a construction primarily suited for the conveyance of goods or burden of any description, (e.g. a van); or
- a vehicle of a type not commonly used as a private vehicle and unsuitable for such use (e.g. a police car).

The definition is similar (but not identical) to that used for the purposes of determining benefits in kind on company cars. As a result, some of the case law that has helped to hone the definition in that area of the legislation may be applied equally to the capital allowance definition.

Legislation: CAA 2001, s. 268A

Tax Reporter: ¶238-520

Motorcycles

Motorcycles are treated for capital allowance purposes like any other asset, rather than being subject to the special rules applying for cars. One effect of this is that annual investment allowances are available for motorcycles.

Conveyance of goods or burden

As noted in the definition given above, a vehicle will not be treated as a car if it is 'of a construction primarily suited for the conveyance of goods or burden of any description'.

This condition will mainly exclude vans, pick-up trucks and heavy-goods vehicles, though in practice, it is not always clear what constitutes a van in any particular case. A key point is that the test is one of construction rather than the use to which the vehicle will be put. This principle was explored in the case of *Morris v R & C Commrs*, where a 'motor home' was held to be a car, even though it was in fact used for transporting goods. The judge emphasised that the construction of the vehicle was what counted and not the use to which it was in fact put. On the facts found, the motor home was of a type commonly used as a private vehicle.

Case: *Morris v R & C Commrs* [2006] BTC 861

Estate cars

HMRC view is that estate cars are not 'primarily suited for transporting goods' and that such vehicles are therefore cars rather than vans. For employment income purposes, though, HMRC do say that estate cars may nevertheless come within the exemption if they 'have been permanently and substantially modified to change their construction' (EIM23100).

Tax Reporter: ¶238-520

Other Material: HMRC *Employment Income Manual* EIM23100

Off road vehicles

Luxury off road vehicles, and four wheel drive recreational vehicles, are normally treated as cars for the purposes of the benefit in kind rules and the same principles will apply to classify them as cars for capital allowance purposes. The HMRC view is that such vehicles are not designed primarily for carrying goods or burden (and there is nothing about them that makes them unsuitable for private use).

Other Material: HMRC *Employment Income Manual* EIM23145

Pick-up trucks

There can be areas of doubt over such vehicles as double cab pick-up trucks. In the area of employment tax law, where the same principle applies, HMRC take the view that such trucks are suitable for private use (see below) but that it is more difficult to determine whether they are of a construction primarily suited for the conveyance of goods or burden.

As a pragmatic approach (which is, however, open to possible challenge as there is no specific statutory authority for it), HMRC interpret the legislation in line with the definitions used for VAT purposes. The practical effect of this is explained as follows:

> 'Under this measure, a double cab pick-up that has a payload of 1 tonne (1,000kg) or more is accepted as a van for benefits purposes. Payload means gross vehicle weight (or design weight) less unoccupied kerb weight (care is needed when looking at manufacturers' brochures as they sometimes define payload differently).
>
> Under a separate agreement between Customs and the Society of Motor Manufacturers and Traders (SMMT), a hard top consisting of metal, fibre glass or similar material, with or without windows, is accorded a generic weight of 45kg. Therefore the addition of a hard top to a double cab pick-up with an ex-works payload of 1,010 kg will convert the vehicle into a car (net payload reduced to 965 kg). Under this agreement, the weight of all other optional accessories is disregarded. HMRC has also adopted this treatment.'

Other Material: HMRC *Employment Income Manual* EIM23150

Not commonly used as a private vehicle and unsuitable to be so used

As noted in the definition given above, a vehicle will not be treated as a car if it is 'of a type not commonly used as a private vehicle and unsuitable for such use'. As such, there are two separate tests, both of which have to be satisfied if the vehicle is to fall outside the definition of 'car' for capital allowance purposes:

- it must be of a type not commonly used as a private vehicle; *and*
- the vehicle must be unsuitable to be so used.

HMRC accept that fire engines, agricultural tractors, buses, back-hoe loaders and diggers are 'not commonly used as a private vehicle'. By contrast, HMRC comment that:

> 'a vehicle that in itself is not of a common model because there are not very many of them, for example a luxurious sports car, is still of a type of vehicle that is commonly used as a private vehicle and suitable for that use. The type in that instance is a sports saloon.'

Tax Reporter: ¶238-520

Other Material: HMRC *Employment Income Manual* EIM23130

Types of vehicle

The mere fact that a car is usually kept loaded with goods or equipment will not take it outside the definition if simple unloading would make it suitable for private use. Similarly, painting a car (e.g. as an advertisement) is not sufficient to establish a different type of vehicle. HMRC accept that any of the following may change the 'type' of vehicle:

- adding fixed flashing blue lights;
- fitting dual controls, for example, on a driving school vehicle; or
- fitting a loudspeaker or a roof-top sign (e.g. for a taxi or driving school) on top of a car.

In *Gurney v Richards*, the judge held that:

> 'a vehicle which is altered so that, without being reconverted, it cannot be used lawfully on a road by a member of the public ... cannot be said to be of a type commonly used as a private vehicle.'

However, even though such alterations may change the nature of the vehicle, HMRC go on to warn that 'even if a vehicle has been modified so that it is of a different type, it will not necessarily follow that the vehicle is not a car'. In other words, if it can be successfully established that the vehicle is of a type not commonly used as a private vehicle then it must be considered whether the second half of the test can also be satisfied, by demonstrating that it is unsuitable to be so used.

Cases: *Gurney (HMIT) v Richards* [1989] BTC 326; *Bourne (HMIT) v Auto School of Motoring (Norwich) Ltd* (1964) 42 TC 217

Other Material: HMRC *Employment Income Manual* EIM23125

Unsuitable for private use

In the *Gurney v Richards case*, the judge recalled an earlier definition of 'suitable' as meaning 'fitted for, adapted or appropriate for'. The case concerned a fire officer's car which was equipped with a flashing light and with emergency equipment. Under the Road Traffic Acts, the car (being fitted with a flashing light) could not lawfully have been used by any member of the public.

Taxis

The special rules relating to 'qualifying hire cars' were abolished from April 2009. It follows that most new taxis are therefore now treated for capital allowance purposes exactly as any other cars, with allowances determined according to emission levels.

The treatment of black cabs (or 'taxicabs') and limousines is less clear cut. It is understood, but only unofficially, that at least some HMRC officers take the view that these vehicles are not commonly used as a private vehicle and are unsuitable for such use. If this is correct, then they will not be treated as cars for these purposes. The practical effect of this will be that annual investment allowances will be available (but also, for example, the temporary first-year allowances given for the year beginning in April 2009).

112-610 Other definitions

Main rate car

The rate at which writing-down allowances are given depends on whether or not the car is a 'main rate car'. In simple terms, a main rate car will be added to the main plant and machinery pool (and will, therefore, attract allowances at 18%), but any other car will go into the special rate pool, where allowances are given at just 8%.

A 'main rate car' is defined as including three categories of vehicle:

- any car first registered before 1 March 2001;

- a car with CO_2 emissions that do not exceed 130g/km (160g/km for expenditure incurred before 6 April 2013) falling to 110g/km from 6 April 2018; or
- an electric car.

Legislation: CAA 2001, s. 104AA

Tax Reporter: ¶238-560

Motorcycle

The definition of 'motorcycle' is given by reference to *Road Traffic Act* 1988, s. 185(1) (by virtue of CAA 2001, s. 268A(2)).

Electrically propelled vehicle

An electrically propelled vehicle is one that is propelled solely by electrical power and where that power is derived either from a source external to the vehicle or from an electrical storage battery that is not connected to any source of power when the vehicle is in motion.

Legislation: CAA 2001, s. 268B

112-615 Allowances

General principle

The general rule is now that cars are pooled with other expenditure for the purposes of calculating capital allowances.

Writing-down allowances

If a car is a 'main rate car' (broadly with emissions not exceeding 130g/km, but see 112-610), and if there is no private use of the vehicle (i.e. by a sole trader or member of a partnership) then the cost of the car is added to the main plant and machinery pool and allowances are given accordingly. There are no special rules to determine the treatment of such cars as they are not needed: in simple terms, the legislation has removed the requirement to allocate these cars to a single asset pool.

If the car is not a main rate car and if there is no private use, the cost of the vehicle will be added to the special rate pool, together with expenditure on long-life assets, integral features, etc. Allowances will be given accordingly, i.e. normally at 8% of the reducing balance of the pool.

Cars with private use

Cars that are used partly for private purposes (i.e. by a sole trader or partner, but not a company car used by a director or employee) will be kept outside the main pools. Such cars will attract writing-down allowances at 8% or 18%, according to their emission levels.

Example

John is a sole trader. He buys a car for £20,000 in May 2017. The car has emissions of 125g/km.

John estimates that three quarters of his use of the vehicle is for business purposes.

He initially calculates allowances for the year of £3,600 (£20,000 at 18%), but he then reduces this figure by one quarter to reflect his private use. The allowances available are £2,700 and the value carried down to the next period of accounts is £16,400 (as he still deducts the whole of the £3,600).

As vehicles with private use are isolated within their own single-asset pools, it follows that a balancing adjustment will be made when they come to be sold.

Annual investment allowances

No annual investment allowances (AIAs) are given for 'cars'.

The term 'car' was specifically defined, until April 2009, to include a motorcycle, so no AIAs were given for expenditure on motorcycles. However, the definition was amended, broadly from April 2009, to exclude a motorcycle. It follows that AIAs are now available for expenditure on motorcycles.

Legislation: CAA 2001, s. 38B

First-year allowances, low emission cars and goods vehicles

The general rule is that no first-year allowances are available for cars. An exception is made for a car that is 'electrically propelled' or that has 'low CO_2 emissions'. Both of these are technical terms with their specific definitions, discussed below.

To qualify for these first-year allowances, such a car must be 'unused and not second-hand'. HMRC accept that this condition is met 'even if it has been driven a limited number of miles for the purposes of testing, delivery, test driven by a potential purchaser, or used as a demonstration car'.

Legislation: CAA 2001, s. 45D, 45DA

Other Material: HMRC *Capital Allowances Manual* CA23153

Electrically propelled

An electrically-propelled vehicle is one that is propelled solely by electrical power. The power must be derived either from a source external to the vehicle or from an electrical storage battery that is not connected to any source of power when the vehicle is in motion.

Legislation: CAA 2001, s. 268B

Low emissions

A car is said, for these purposes, to have low CO_2 emissions if it has an official certificate of emissions with an emissions figure that does not exceed 75g/km (95g/km for vehicles acquired before 6 April 2015). This limit is set to fall to 50g/km with effect from 6 April 2018.

Legislation: CAA 2001, s. 45D(2)

Tax effect

Where the conditions are met, 100% first-year allowances are available for such vehicles. See 111-700 for a fuller discussion of these allowances.

Legislation: CAA 2001, s. 46(2)

112-620 Employees

Employees are not permitted to claim capital allowances on privately owned cars used for business purposes. Instead, they can claim mileage allowance relief under ITEPA 2003, s. 231 (see 140-625) or tax-free mileage allowance payments from the employer under ITEPA 2003, s. 229 (see 140-550).

There was no change to this principle from April 2009.

Legislation: CAA 2001, s. 36

112-625 Anti-avoidance measures

Need for anti-avoidance provisions

Allowances for higher emission cars are now given at a rate that is much slower than the actual rate of commercial depreciation. Anti-avoidance measures are therefore in place to try to prevent the exploitation of loopholes.

Companies only

One of these anti-avoidance measures is entitled 'special rate cars: discontinued activity continued by relevant company', and is concerned to counter the generation of artificial balancing allowances. This measure is aimed at groups of companies only.

Legislation: CAA 2001, s. 104F

More general measure

A separate measure seeks to prevent the artificial generation of balancing allowances for cars attracting allowances at the lower 'special' rate, where there is private use of the vehicle. This rule applies where allowances are already restricted under CAA 2001, s. 217 or 218 (restrictions on allowances for connected party transactions). In such a case, the disposal value to be brought into account is the market value of the car at the time of the disposal event, restricted to the cost incurred (or treated as incurred) by the person disposing of the vehicle. The person acquiring the car is then treated as having incurred capital expenditure on it of an equal amount.

Legislation: CAA 2001, s. 208A

112-660 Restriction of car hire costs

In certain circumstances, there is a restriction on the allowable amount of car hire costs. This issue is considered in greater depth at 94-500, but in brief, the disallowance is zero for cars with emissions not exceeding 130g/km (110g/km from 6 April 2018 and 160g/km to 5 April 2013), and 15% of the relevant payments for cars exceeding these mission levels.

Legislation: ITTOIA 2005, s. 49

Tax Reporter: ¶238-930

112-680 Qualifying hire cars: old rules

Some of the capital allowance rules for cars did not apply to 'qualifying hire cars'. Specifically, such vehicles:

- did not need to be allocated to a single asset pool (CAA 2001, s. 74(2)(a));
- did not have annual writing-down allowances restricted to £3,000 (CAA 2001, s. 75(1));
- did not suffer the restriction on part of the hire cost (ICTA 1988, s. 578A(2)(a)); and

- were not affected by: CAA 2001, s. 76 (expenditure partly met by another person), s. 78 (partial depreciation subsidy for cars), or s. 79 (anti-avoidance).

The fact that a car was a qualifying hire car did not, however, change the rules about first-year allowances – they remained unavailable for such vehicles (except for those with very low carbon dioxide emissions – see 112-615). Annual investment allowances were also unavailable for cars and (in the past) motorcycles.

Definition

A qualifying hire car was defined as a motor car provided wholly or mainly for hire to, or for carrying, members of the public in the ordinary course of a trade (e.g. a taxi cab) where:

- the hire or use by the 'same' person (including connected persons) was normally for less than 90 days in any 12-month period;
- it was hired to a person who would himself use it wholly or mainly for hiring to or carrying members of the public in the ordinary course of a trade, and the conditions in (1) above were fulfilled; or
- it was provided wholly or mainly for the use of a person receiving a disability living allowance or mobility supplement, etc.

Legislation: CAA 2001, s. 38B, 74, 81

Other Material: HMRC *Capital Allowances Manual* CA23510

Tax Reporter: ¶238-950

Other assets with special tax treatment

112-700 Short-life assets

Introduction

Use of the short-life asset legislation is voluntary. If a person chooses to make an election, the effect is to accelerate capital allowances on certain assets that are scrapped or sold at a low value within approximately eight years from the date of their purchase. This eight year deadline was increased from four years for expenditure incurred from 6 April 2011.

The introduction, from April 2008, of the annual investment allowance has often meant that it is unnecessary to consider short-life asset elections as full relief will be given in the year of expenditure. For those with expenditure that exceeds their AIA entitlement, however, the short-life asset election is now of greater value than before because of the slower rate at which writing-down allowances are now given.

Some care is needed as, in particular circumstances, it is possible that the effect of making an election will be the reverse of what is intended and will actually be to slow down the overall rate at which allowances are given. This may happen if an asset is sold within the first eight (or, formerly, four) years or so for more than its tax written-down value.

The only effect of making an election is one of timing. Most assets which are the subject of a capital allowances claim go into the main pool. In broad terms, the effect of this is that tax relief is given each year on 18% of the reducing balance. Thus, an asset costing £1,600 will attract allowances of £288 (£1,600 × 18%) in the first year.

In the second year the allowances due will be £236 (£1,600 less £288 already given, to leave £1,312, at 18% = £236. In year three, the allowance will be £205 and so on. Because of the effect of pooling, allowances may continue to be given on an annual basis even after an asset has been scrapped.

The effect of making the short-life asset election will be to ensure that the total allowances given *over the period for which the asset is held* are (normally) exactly equal to the net cost of the asset to the trader, calculated as the original cost less any disposal proceeds. Thus, an asset costing £1,600 in year one which is sold for £200 in year three will attract total allowances over the three-year period of £1,400. This is therefore more favourable than the total allowances of £718 given in the ordinary way as above (£288 + £236 + £194), even though the remaining £882 of allowances would eventually be due anyway.

Legislation: CAA 2001, s. 83ff.

Tax Reporter: ¶239-000

Conditions

The conditions for a short-life asset election may be summarised into three rules, as follows.

(1) Qualifying expenditure must have been incurred on plant and machinery.

(2) Treatment as a short-life asset must not be prohibited.

(3) The person incurring the expenditure must make a valid election.

Legislation: CAA 2001, s. 83

Tax Reporter: ¶239-050

Cases where short-life asset treatment is ruled out

Short-life asset treatment is denied in various circumstances, as follows.

- Where an asset that has been used for other purposes is brought into use for the purposes of a qualifying activity, or where plant or machinery received by way of gift is used for such a purpose.
- Where plant or machinery is hired out otherwise than in the course of any other qualifying activity ('special leasing').
- Where the item concerned is a car. Until April 2009, this restriction applied also to a motorcycle, but that is no longer the case. Certain cars hired out to persons receiving disability allowances may still qualify as short-life assets.
- For any special rate expenditure (i.e. including integral features).
- For any plant or machinery provided for leasing. Two exceptions are given in the legislation, however, as follows:
  (a) cars as referred to at (3) above (hired out to persons receiving disability allowances, etc.);
  (b) plant which is provided for leasing but which within (normally) a ten-year period will be used for certain qualifying purposes (as defined at CAA 2001, s. 122–125).
- For certain plant or machinery used for overseas leasing and which qualifies only for a 10% writing-down allowance.
- For certain plant or machinery leased jointly to two or more persons at least one of whom is not resident in the UK.
- For ships.
- For expenditure incurred on an asset provided or used only partly for a qualifying activity.
- For expenditure on an asset enjoying a partial depreciation subsidy.

Legislation: CAA 2001, s. 84

Tax Reporter: ¶239-050

Electing for short-life asset treatment

An election for such treatment is irrevocable. Once made, HMRC are required to make 'such assessments and adjustments of assessments' as are needed to give the election effect.

The election needs to specify:

- the plant or machinery that is the subject of the election;

- the amount of qualifying expenditure incurred on that item; and
- the date on which the expenditure was incurred.

For income tax purposes, the time limit is 31 January some 22 months after the end of the tax year in which the relevant chargeable period ends.

For these purposes, the relevant chargeable period is the chargeable period in which the qualifying expenditure was incurred or the first such period if the expenditure was incurred in more than one chargeable period.

Example

John, a sole trader, incurs expenditure of £10,000 during his accounts year ended 31 December 2017. Thus, the period of account ends in the tax year 2017–18. The time limit for making an election for treatment as a short-life asset will be 31 January 2020.

Legislation: CAA 2001, s. 85

Effect of making a short-life asset election

Once an election is made, then a balancing adjustment will be made on the basis of the ordinary capital allowances rules if the asset is disposed of within approximately eight years. This is because qualifying expenditure on a short-life asset is in principle always allocated to a single-asset pool.

Example

A business with qualifying expenditure of £160,000 brought forward buys a computer system costing £24,000 in year one. In year four it is scrapped. No other assets are bought or sold in the period in question. The annual investment allowance has been fully used by an associated business. For simplicity, it is assumed that the 18% rate applies throughout.

Without a short-life asset election, the position is as follows.

Main pool	£
Value brought forward	160,000
Additions	24,000
	184,000
Year 1 WDA	(33,120)
Value carried forward	150,880
Year 2 WDA	(27,158)
Value carried forward	123,732
Year 3 WDA	(22,272)
Value carried forward	101,460

Year 4 WDA	(18,263)
Value carried forward	83,197

With no election, the total allowances given over the period amount to £100,803.

If an election is made, the position is as follows.

	Main pool	SLA pool
	£	£
Value brought forward	160,000	–
Additions	–	24,000
	160,000	24,000
Year 1 WDA	(28,800)	(4,320)
Value carried forward	131,200	19,680
Year 2 WDA	(23,616)	(3,542)
Value carried forward	107,584	16,138
Year 3 WDA	(19,365)	(2,905)
Value carried forward	88,219	13,233
Year 4 WDA	(15,879)	
Proceeds		Nil
		(asset scrapped)
Balancing allowance		(13,233)
Value carried forward	72,340	Nil

With the election, the total allowances given over the period amount to £111,660, an increase of £10,857.

The legislation defines an 'eight year cut-off', meaning the eighth anniversary of the end of the chargeable period (or first chargeable period) in which the qualifying expenditure was incurred on the provision of the short-life asset.

There will be a 'final chargeable period' if the asset is disposed of before the cut-off date (see below), and this will trigger a balancing adjustment.

If the asset is still held at that date then it ceases to be a short-life asset and the value is transferred to the appropriate pool for the first chargeable period ending after the cut-off date.

To gain a fuller understanding of the position three points need to be considered.

(1) The effect of a short-life asset election is one of timing only. The increased allowances of £10,857 in the above example will eventually be offset by reduced allowances in future years. The carried forward value of £72,340 is therefore exactly £10,857 less than the figure of £83,197 where no election is made.

(2) The timing benefit of £10,857 all arises in the year of disposal (year four in the example). All that is happening is that a full balancing allowance is being given in that year instead of the standard 18% writing-down allowance.

(3) By looking at the position at the start of the disposal period it can be seen (in this case too late – the time limit for the irrevocable election has passed) whether or not the election will be beneficial. In the example, the brought forward value of the short-life asset is £13,233. As long as the asset is sold for less than 82% of this figure, then the election will prove beneficial. If it is sold for more, the election will be disadvantageous.

Tax Reporter: ¶239-100

Other issues

Special rules apply in various circumstances:

- where short-life assets are used for leasing (CAA 2001, s. 87);
- where there is a disposal for less than market value (CAA 2001, s. 88);
- for transactions with connected parties (CAA 2001, s. 89).

There can be difficulties in practice where there are many small assets, each of which should strictly be subject to a separate election. See, in this respect, HMRC Statement of Practice SP 1/86.

112-800 Long-life assets

Background

If a business acquires an asset with an expected useful economic life of 25 years or more, normal accounting practice would depreciate the asset on a straight line basis at perhaps 4% per annum. If the asset concerned was plant or machinery this accounting treatment would not match the taxation treatment which, broadly, provides for allowances on a reducing balance basis at an annual rate of 18%.

Subject to certain exceptions (such as the de minimis limit of £100,000) the long-life asset regime aims to bring the taxation treatment of such assets into line with accountancy practice. Expenditure on such 'long-life assets' is written-off at a reduced rate of WDA of 8% per annum, on a reducing balance basis, within the 'special rate pool'. That pool also contains expenditure on integral features (since April 2008; see 115-000ff.), higher emission cars (since April 2009; see 112-600ff.) and certain other assets.

Tax Reporter: ¶239-500

Meaning of 'long-life asset'

A 'long-life asset' is plant or machinery where it is reasonable to expect that the useful economic life of the plant or machinery, when new, will be equal to or will exceed (or would have been equal to or would have exceeded, for second-hand items) 25 years. HMRC have indicated that they will generally accept the accounting treatment accorded to the expenditure in question in determining whether or not it is long-life asset expenditure. It is conceivable that the expenditure that is incurred on improvements made to plant or machinery, on which the original expenditure is long-life asset expenditure, will not rank as long-life asset expenditure. In such cases, the expenditure on the improvements would need to be added to the general pool of plant and machinery. Any apportionments needed as a result of this treatment (e.g. of disposal receipts on a disposal of the long-life asset) would need to be made on a 'just and reasonable' basis.

Legislation: CAA 2001, s. 91, 562

Tax Reporter: ¶239-600

Exclusions

The following assets cannot be treated as 'long-life assets':

- plant or machinery which is a fixture in, or provided for use in, a building used wholly or mainly as, or for purposes ancillary to a dwelling-house, retail shop, showroom, hotel or office;
- motor cars (including taxis and hire cars);
- 'seagoing ships', where the expenditure was incurred on or before 31 December 2010;
- 'railway assets' which are to be used wholly and exclusively for the purposes of a 'railway business', where the expenditure was incurred on or before 31 December 2010;
- assets (which may otherwise be long-life assets) where the relevant monetary limit applies to the expenditure and where the expenditure upon them is within the de minimis limit of £100,000 in the chargeable period in which the expenditure is incurred (see below for further details); and

- second-hand assets (that would otherwise be long-life assets) acquired from a vendor who has previously made a claim for capital allowances in respect of the assets under the arrangements applying prior to the introduction of long-life asset rules.

WDAs at the usual rate (20% until April 2012) will continue to be given on these assets.

Offshore installations (as defined by the *Mineral Workings (Offshore Installations) Act* 1971) and sport or recreational craft are not 'seagoing ships'.

'Railway assets' includes track, stations, light maintenance depots (as defined by the *Railways Act* 1993) and apparatus installed therein as well as locomotives, trams, carriages, wagons and other rolling stock designed or adapted for use on a railway. The term 'railway' is extended (by the *Railways Act* 1993, s. 81) to mean tramways and other systems of guided transport.

Legislation: CAA 2001, s. 93–99 and Sch. 3, para. 20

Tax Reporter: ¶239-650

Particular assets

HMRC have published particular guidance in relation to glasshouses (greenhouses) (see HMRC *Capital Allowances Manual* CA23785). See also 111-325 for details of 'sophisticated' glasshouses which qualify for plant and machinery allowances.

In relation to printing equipment, the broad principle is now that HMRC will accept that 'modern printing equipment purchased new and unused is unlikely to have an expected useful economic life of 25 years of longer. This means that it will not be a long life asset' (CA23790). As regards aircraft, see HMRC *Capital Allowances Manual* CA23781ff.

In all these cases, the guidance seems to be in need of updating as past dates are still referred to in the future and the status of the current HMRC view is not always clear. Reference should be made to the links shown above and, as the guidance may be going out of date, it may be worth keeping a printed record on file, with the date on which the advice was printed.

LLA treatment only where monetary limit reached

If the relevant monetary limit applies to the expenditure incurred on long-life assets, and the expenditure incurred in a chargeable period is less than the 'relevant limit', the provisions restricting the rate of WDAs do not apply and normal WDAs are available.

The relevant monetary limit applies to expenditure incurred on plant or machinery (other than on the provision of a share in the plant or machinery, or as a contribution on which 'contribution allowances' are obtained, or on the provision of plant or machinery for leasing whether or not the leasing is in the course of a trade) for the purposes of a qualifying activity carried on by the person who incurred the expenditure. Furthermore, that person, in the case of an individual (e.g. sole trader), must devote substantially all of his or her time to the carrying on of that qualifying activity, and in the case of a partnership, the partnership must only consist of individuals where at least one-half of the partners devote the whole or a substantial part of their time to the carrying on of the qualifying activity concerned.

The relevant monetary limit is £100,000 for periods of 12 months, increased or decreased on a pro rata basis where the chargeable period is longer or shorter than 12 months. If amounts due under a contract could be treated as incurred in two or more chargeable periods the total amount due is deemed to be incurred in the earliest of the chargeable periods for the purposes of applying the relevant monetary limit.

Where companies are 'associated,' the relevant monetary limit is divided by the total number of associated companies.

Legislation: CAA 2001, s. 98ff.

Tax Reporter: ¶239-700

Anti-avoidance

Where it can be shown that the main or one of the main objects of a disposal is the acceleration of allowances, anti-avoidance measures operate. These ensure that if a long-life asset is sold for less than what its tax written down value would be (on the presumption that the asset disposed of is the only long-life asset held) a deemed disposal value equal to this notional tax written down value is to be used rather than the actual disposal value.

Legislation: CAA 2001, s. 104

Tax Reporter: ¶239-800

112-920 Cable television

The cost of providing and installing ducting in connection with the construction of cable television networks will be regarded as expenditure qualifying for capital allowances on plant or machinery.

The costs in question relate to the provision of protective ducting into which the cable is inserted, and the cutting and covering of trenches in which the ducting is to be laid in the ground. HMRC are prepared to treat the costs as allowable expenditure on the provision of plant or machinery. Therefore, they will qualify for the appropriate rate of writing-down allowances. The rates of allowances will be those generally in force at the time when the expenditure is incurred.

Capital expenditure on setting up cable network systems, e.g. studio and transmission equipment, and the cost of the cable itself will qualify for plant or machinery allowance on first principles.

Other Material: HMRC *Capital Allowances Manual* CA21200

Tax Reporter: ¶246-410

113-250 Leased assets

Whether leasing at all

Certain special rules apply to assets used for leasing out. The first issue is therefore to determine what is meant by leasing in this context.

The term 'leasing' includes letting a ship or aircraft on charter or letting any other asset on hire. However, a distinction must be drawn between leasing and certain distribution agreements. In *Barclays Mercantile Industrial Finance Ltd v Melluish (HMIT)*, a film company granted licences to other group members to show a film in their respective territories; the High Court held that this did not amount to leasing.

In a non-tax case, *Baldwins Industrial Services plc v Barr Late*, Baldwins hired a 50 tonne crane to Barr to be used in the building of stadium for Southampton Football Club. An incident arose which led to a dispute as to which party was responsible for repairs to the crane. An essential element of the claim was whether the provision of the crane and driver was part of a construction contract within the ambit of the *Housing Grants, Construction and Regeneration Act* 1996.

A construction contract is one under which construction operations are carried out. It was accepted that a contract for mere plant hire is not a construction contract. The labour element was held to be crucial.

The hire of the crane plus driver was held to be a contract for supply of plant and labour to be used as part of the operation to build the stadium. The contract for supply of the crane and driver was for an operation that formed an integral part of, was preparatory to, or was for rendering complete a work of construction.

Following the judgment in this non-tax case, HMRC accept that the supply of plant or machinery with an operator is the provision of a service, as opposed to plant hire, and therefore such supply is not leasing. See also the decision in *MGF (Trench Construction Systems) Ltd* where the First-tier Tribunal held that a design service provided with the use of equipment was not merely the leasing of plant.

Legislation: CAA 2001, s. 105(1)

Cases: *Barclays Mercantile Industrial Finance Ltd v Melluish (HMIT)* [1990] BTC 209; *MGF (Trench Construction Systems) Ltd* [2012] TC 02399

Other Material: HMRC *Capital Allowances Manual* CA23115

Tax Reporter: ¶240-000

Lessors using finance leases

The writing-down allowances that may be claimed by a lessor who provides plant or machinery under a finance lease are restricted to the appropriate proportion of the full amount for the chargeable period, reckoned from the date on which the expenditure was incurred to the end of the chargeable period. Thus, if expenditure is incurred three months before the end of a chargeable period, the writing-down allowance is restricted to three-twelfths of the annual rate.

The object of these provisions is to restore a level playing field between finance leasing and direct purchase by countering the exploitation by many finance lessors of the rules under which writing-down allowances are otherwise given in full through the pooling mechanism irrespective of when the expenditure was incurred. The arrangements used to exploit this rule involved setting up a number of leasing subsidiaries, all with different year ends, so that a full allowance could be accelerated and set off straight away against other profits in the leasing group.

A 'finance lease' for these purposes is any arrangement or set of arrangements which falls, in accordance with normal UK accountancy practice, to be treated as a finance lease or loan in the accounts of the lessor or persons connected with the lessor, including consolidated group accounts. However, account must also be taken of the rules relating to long funding leases: see 113-450.

For the restrictions applying in the case of sale and leaseback arrangements, see 110-400.

Legislation: CAA 2001, s. 219–220

Lease purchase

Lease purchase transactions are similar in nature to hire purchase, i.e. the lessee of the plant or machinery obtains immediately the use of the plant or machinery, and at some time in the future also acquires ownership. Provided the lessee does have an ultimate right to acquire the plant or machinery, the lessee is treated as owning the plant or machinery concerned for so long as the plant or machinery is used for the purposes of a qualifying activity, and, thus, capital allowances will be given to him and not to the lessor.

Legislation: CAA 2001, s. 67

Tax Reporter: ¶240-000

113-400 Plant or machinery leased in the UK: overview

Plant or machinery leased in the UK qualifies for standard writing-down allowances whether or not it is leased in the course of a trade.

Special rules apply to the leasing of items of plant or machinery which become landlord's fixtures (see 114-600).

Tax Reporter: ¶240-050

113-420 Leasing otherwise than in the course of a trade ('special leasing')

The term 'special leasing' is used to describe the hiring out of plant or machinery other than in the course of any other qualifying activity.

The special leasing begins when the item is first hired out. It comes to an end for capital allowances purposes when the lessor 'permanently ceases to hire out the plant or machinery otherwise than in the course of any other qualifying activity'. There is deemed to be a separate qualifying activity (and therefore a separate pool) for each item of plant or machinery that is hired out in this way.

Legislation: CAA 2001, s. 15, 19, 53

Cessation of leasing

At the time when the lessor permanently ceases to let the plant or machinery (or starts to let it in the course of a trade), its disposal value falls to be brought into account and a balancing charge or balancing allowance may result.

Legislation: CAA 2001, s. 65

Giving effect to the allowances

Where a capital allowance is made it will be made by way of a deduction from the income from the letting concerned. Where the plant or machinery is not in the period used wholly for the purposes of the lessee's trade, a proportionate part of the allowances will be given as a deduction. Any excess is available against letting income from the letting concerned of the next chargeable period and so on.

Legislation: CAA 2001, s. 258, 259

113-430 Plant or machinery leased outside the UK

Overview

Expenditure incurred on the provision of plant or machinery 'leased outside the UK' qualifies for writing-down allowances at 10% per annum, unless they are excluded (i.e. prohibited) from allowances altogether. More particularly, the 10% writing-down allowance applies where plant or machinery is, at any time within the designated period which is ten years after it is brought into use or within the period of the lessor's ownership if shorter, leased to a person who:

- is not resident in the UK; and
- does not use the asset exclusively for earning profits chargeable to tax.

'Profits chargeable to tax' includes profits chargeable to UK tax from exploration or exploitation of the sea-bed but excludes profits which although within the charge are excluded from charge by a double taxation agreement.

No first-year allowances are available.

Legislation: CAA 2001, s. 46 (general exclusion 6), 105, 109

Tax Reporter: ¶240-140ff.

Leasing in the course of a trade

If the leasing is in the course of a trade, all such items are held together in the class pool, called overseas leasing pool, for the qualifying activity (i.e. leasing trade) concerned, and writing-down allowances are calculated accordingly.

Allowances and charges are made in computing the profits of the qualifying activity for the chargeable period to which they relate.

Legislation: CAA 2001, s. 54, 258, 259

Leasing otherwise than in the course of a trade

Where plant or machinery is first let by any person otherwise than in the course of a trade, then, whether or not it is used for the purposes of a trade carried on by the lessee, the capital expenditure incurred by the lessor in providing each item of plant or machinery is allocated to a separate class pool, called 'the overseas leasing pool' unless the expenditure is long-life asset expenditure or it is required to be allocated to a single asset pool (e.g. expensive motor cars and contributions to the expenditure of others). Writing-down allowances are calculated accordingly.

Legislation: CAA 2001, s. 19

Exceptions for 'protected leasing'

There are exceptions to the restriction to 10% allowances where the leasing is protected leasing, which means 'short-term leasing' or where a ship, aircraft or transport container is leased and used for a 'qualifying purpose'. In these circumstances the special rules do not apply and the usual pooling arrangements and standard writing-down allowances apply instead.

Legislation: CAA 2001, s. 105(5)

Recovery of excess relief

Special rules apply where an item of plant or machinery for which standard allowances have been given comes to be leased outside the UK so that only 10% allowances are available.

Legislation: CAA 2001, s. 111

Expenditure disqualified from any allowances

In certain circumstances, no writing-down or balancing allowances at all are available in respect of plant or machinery leased outside the UK. This is where plant or machinery is both used for overseas leasing which is not protected leasing and not used for a qualifying purpose at any time in the designated period, and any of the various listed conditions applies.

Any allowance previously given is clawed back by a balancing charge. In calculating the balancing charge, it is assumed that the plant or machinery in question is the only one on which the lessor has received any allowances.

Legislation: CAA 2001, s. 110, 114

113-450 Long funding leases: overview

Background

Lengthy legislation was introduced in *Finance Act* 2006 to address a perceived anomaly between the tax treatment of loan finance and leasing finance. The commercial effect of the two methods of financing could be very similar (a business uses an asset which is financed by a third party) but there were often significant differences in the timing of tax relief for expenditure incurred. The view was, therefore, that commercial decisions were being distorted, and sometimes driven, by the differing tax treatments.

In essence, the rules aim to remove such distortions by transferring entitlement to capital allowances on leased plant and machinery from lessors to lessees, where the reality is that the leases are essentially financing transactions. No change was made to the tax treatment of leases which do not function as financing transactions.

The rules are complex but the core provision denies capital allowances to an entity that incurs expenditure on plant or machinery that is acquired for long funding leasing. The legislation then provides the mechanism for granting capital allowances to the lessee. Fairly complex rules then apply to determine the amount of capital expenditure on which the lessee can claim tax relief, including the treatment of additional expenditure incurred and there are also detailed rules to deal with disposals of assets that are subject to the long funding rules.

Various anti-avoidance provisions are built into the long funding lease rules. In particular, the legislation targets tax avoidance involving international leasing, where transactions are carried out to allow non-residents to benefit from UK capital allowances through transactions that have no commercial purpose.

Legislation: CAA 2001, s. 34A, 70Aff.

Tax Reporter: ¶240-220ff.

Meaning of 'long funding lease'

The rules introduced in *Finance Act* 2006 apply only to a 'long funding lease', defined as a 'funding lease' which is not any of the following:

- a short lease (of up to five years or, subject to conditions, up to seven years);
- an excluded lease of background plant or machinery for a building (but this is subject to anti-avoidance provisions); or

- a lease that is excluded under de minimis provisions (where relatively small amounts of plant or machinery are leased with land but are not excluded under the background rules as above).

Only leases of plant or machinery can be long funding leases. Where plant or machinery is leased with other assets (whether or not those other assets are also plant and machinery) then the legislation creates a fiction of different leases so that the rules can be considered separately for each deemed lease.

A lessee is only permitted to claim allowances under these rules if it treats the lease as a long funding lease in the accounts for the period in which the lease begins. If the lease is not so treated in those accounts, and the return has become final, the same treatment must then be followed in later periods.

Meaning of 'funding lease'

A funding lease is a lease of plant or machinery that meets at least one of the following tests at the time of its inception:

- the finance lease test (broadly, if the lease falls to be treated as a finance lease or loan under generally accepted accounting practice);
- the lease payments test (see below); or
- the useful economic life test (where the term of the lease is more than 65% of the remaining useful economic life of the leased plant or machinery).

The lease payments test requires a comparison of the present value of the minimum lease payments with the fair value of the leased plant or machinery; the test is met if, broadly, the present value is at least 80% of the fair value.

Hire purchase contracts are specifically excluded from the long funding lease provisions.

Legislation: CAA 2001, s. 70J

Extension of term of existing lease

The term of a lease that is not a long funding lease may be extended. In such circumstances, the lease may become a long funding lease at that point.

Legislation: CAA 2001, s. 70YC

113-500 Lessees under long finance leases

Tax relief is given to a person who, under a long funding lease, incurs expenditure (whether capital or not) on the provision of plant or machinery for the purposes of a qualifying activity. The plant or machinery is treated as owned by that person for capital allowance purposes for as long as the person is the lessee under the long funding lease. He or she is also treated as having incurred capital expenditure, at the start of the long funding lease term, on the provision of the asset in question.

Legislation: CAA 2001, s. 70A

Long funding operating lease

In the case of a long funding operating lease, the amount of the capital expenditure that is deemed to be incurred by the lessee is the market value of the plant or machinery at the start of the lease term (or, if later, at the date on which the asset is first brought into use for the purpose of the qualifying activity).

Legislation: CAA 2001, s. 70B

Long funding finance lease

The amount of the capital expenditure that is deemed to be incurred under these leases is more complex. These more complex rules apply to long funding finance leases but also to any lease which, under generally accepted accounting practice, falls (or would fall) to be treated as a loan.

The capital expenditure consists of either one or two parts, and is in certain cases subject to an overall restriction. The first part is known as 'commencement PVMLP' which is defined as the amount that would fall to be recognised as the present value, at the appropriate date, of the minimum lease payments (as further defined) if appropriate accounts were prepared. The appropriate date is the start of the lease or, if later, the date on which the asset is first brought into use for the purposes of the qualifying activity.

A further element has to be added in some cases where the person has paid rentals under the lease before the commencement of its term.

The restriction is an anti-avoidance measure that applies where there has been a deliberate attempt to obtain allowances in respect of an amount that materially exceeds the market value of the leased asset at the start of the term of the lease.

113-600 Software

Introduction

Where a person carrying on a trade incurs capital expenditure on a right to use or otherwise deal with computer software, the expenditure is treated as having been incurred on the provision of plant or machinery for the purposes of the trade. As long as the person is entitled to the right, the plant or machinery will be treated as his or hers.

Where capital expenditure is incurred on computer software which does not constitute plant or machinery – for example, software transmitted electronically from the owner to the person who incurs the expenditure – the software is treated as plant or machinery for capital allowances purposes.

Expenditure on computer software may be subject to a short-life asset election (see 112-700).

Legislation: CAA 2001, s. 71

Tax Reporter: ¶238-350

Disposals

The granting of a right to use or otherwise deal with computer software for a capital sum is treated as a disposal of plant or machinery, and a disposal value brought into account accordingly. This does not apply if the machinery, etc. has previously started to be used wholly or partly for non-trade purposes, or if the qualifying activity has permanently discontinued.

The disposal value to be brought into account is as follows.

- If the consideration for the grant is not wholly in money but equals an open market money value, or if any consideration is less than the open market value, then the value is the market value of the right granted at the time of the grant (subject to the two exceptions below).
- In other circumstances the value is the net proceeds to the grantor plus any insurance monies, compensation or other capital payments.

If the grant gives rise to a charge to tax as earnings from an employment – for example, because it is made to an employee free of charge or at less than its market value – then only the actual proceeds (if any) need to be brought into account. This is the case even if no tax is actually payable by the director or employee because of the £30,000 exemption applying to certain payments on the termination, etc. of an employment.

Similarly, market value does not have to be substituted if the grantee can claim capital allowances on the asset as plant or machinery or under the research and development allowance rules (though this exemption does not apply if the grantee is a dual resident investing company connected with the seller (see CTA 2010, s. 109). This is the case even if the buyer and seller are connected with each other.

Where there is a series of grants of leases in respect of the same software, the aggregate consideration received is taken into account for the purposes of limiting any capital allowances balancing adjustment.

The distinction between revenue and capital expenditure on software is not always straightforward. The matter was discussed in a Tax Bulletin article in November 1993, now superseded by material in the HMRC manuals.

Legislation: CAA 2001, s. 61, 72, 73

Other Material: HMRC *Capital Allowances Manual* CA23250

113-650 Sports grounds

Capital allowances are available for capital expenditure incurred in complying with safety requirements at sports grounds as well as sports stadia.

If tax relief is not otherwise available, capital expenditure will qualify for capital allowances if it relates to certain necessary safety work carried out to designated sports grounds. This special relief ceases to apply for expenditure incurred after 5 April 2013.

Capital allowances are given on the basis that the expenditure is plant and machinery. Allowances are therefore available at 20% (18% from April 2012) on a reducing balance basis. The disposal value is taken as nil.

Where a trader incurs expenditure in respect of a 'regulated stand' (i.e. one providing covered accommodation for 500 or more spectators) in order to comply with a local authority's safety certificate requirements, if the expenditure does not attract a deduction in computing the trader's profits, it will qualify for capital allowances on plant or machinery.

Legislation: CAA 2001, s. 30ff., 63(5)

Tax Reporter: ¶246-330

Other Material: HMRC *Capital Allowances Manual* CA22240

Football grounds

The Revenue released correspondence with the Football League, dated 25 January 1991, which considered what tax relief may be available for capital expenditure on football grounds. The Appendix to the letter indicates items that may be used by a football club in its trade which will normally qualify as plant or machinery and the letter itself gives particular guidance on seating.

Other Material: HMRC *Capital Allowances Manual* CA21230

113-700 Security assets

Income tax deductions are available to self-employed individuals who incur personal security expenditure in meeting special threats of violence from terrorists etc. arising from their business, and corresponding capital allowances are also available where:

- an individual, or partnership of individuals, pursues a relevant qualifying activity (defined as a qualifying activity consisting of a trade, an ordinary property business, a furnished holiday lettings business, an overseas property business, or a profession or vocation);
- expenditure is incurred on the provision for or use by the individual, or any of the individuals, of a 'security asset' (see below);
- capital allowances in respect of plant or machinery would otherwise be unavailable;
- the asset is provided or used to meet a special threat to the individual's *personal* physical security which arises wholly or mainly by virtue of the particular trade, etc. concerned;
- the person incurring the expenditure has as his sole object the meeting of that threat and intends the asset to be used to improve personal physical security (the fact that it facilitates a form of staff welfare is irrelevant: ICAEW Technical Release 759).

Where the above conditions are satisfied, the expenditure is treated as capital expenditure on the provision of plant or machinery wholly and exclusively for the purposes of the relevant qualifying activity. The allowance is calculated on the whole of the expenditure, and no balancing adjustment arises on disposal.

The provisions of CAA 2001, s. 21 and 22, whereby buildings, structures and land are excluded from the capital allowances regime for plant and machinery, do not apply to expenditure on personal security within these rules.

Legislation: CAA 2001, s. 23, 27, 33, 63(5)

Other Material: HMRC *Capital Allowances Manual* CA22240

Tax Reporter: ¶246-250

Meaning of 'security assets'

'Security assets' are assets which improve personal security. Expressly included are 'equipment and a structure (such as a wall)' which improve personal security. The Inland Revenue press release, *Income Tax: Expenditure on Special Security Measures* (13 April 1989), gave as examples of security assets alarm systems, bullet-resistant windows in houses and floodlighting. Expressly *excluded* are a car, ship, aircraft, dwelling or its appurtenant grounds.

Legislation: CAA 2001, s. 33(6)

Mixed use assets

Provided that the person incurring the expenditure on the security asset intends it to be used *solely* to improve personal physical security, the fact that it has another, incidental, use is ignored. Also ignored is the fact that the asset also improves such security of a member of the individual's family or household.

It is immaterial that the security asset may become affixed to land, albeit a dwelling.

Legislation: CAA 2001, s. 33

Other Material: HMRC *Capital Allowances Manual* CA22270; ICAEW Technical Release 759

113-800 Fire safety expenditure

Most expenditure incurred on fire prevention and safety is deductible as revenue expenditure or under other capital allowances provisions, including expenditure on fire extinguishers, signage, alarms and sprinkler systems.

CAA 2001, s. 29 previously provided relief on other expenditure, such as fire escapes and fire doors, that would not otherwise qualify for any tax relief. As a result of changes to fire safety legislation, relief was latterly only available to businesses that had not complied with such legislation and that had therefore required penal action by the Fire Authority to remove fire risks. FA 2008 therefore removed the special treatment, for expenditure incurred from 6 April 2008 (for income tax purposes).

Legislation: CAA 2001, s. 23, 27

Tax Reporter: ¶245-890

113-850 Thermal insulation expenditure

Expenditure on adding any insulation against loss of heat to an existing building or structure is treated as if it were capital expenditure on plant and machinery, with a nil disposal value.

Where the expenditure is by a lessor who lets the property other than in the course of a trade (i.e. the lessor is carrying on a qualifying activity consisting of an ordinary property business or an overseas property business), that expenditure is treated as being on the plant and machinery included in the leased property and relief is available primarily against the letting income derived from any building or structure, or any balancing charge in respect of any buildings or structures.

The requirement that the building should be an industrial building or structure was removed with effect from April 2008.

The provisions of CAA 2001, s. 21 and 22, whereby buildings, structures and land are excluded from the capital allowances regime for plant and machinery, do not apply to expenditure on thermal insulation within these rules.

Legislation: CAA 2001, s. 23, 28

Tax Reporter: ¶246-030

Incidental costs

114-200 Installation of plant and machinery

Expenditure on altering an existing building which is incidental to the installation of plant and machinery (e.g. machinery foundations, strengthening floors) in an existing building is treated as capital expenditure on the provision of that plant and machinery.

Relief is only due under this provision if the alterations are 'incidental to the installation of plant or machinery'. In the case of *JD Wetherspoon plc v R & C Commrs*, the commissioners (and subsequently the tribunal) drew a distinction between alterations *incidental to* the installation of plant and alterations *consequential on* such installation. The company had claimed the cost of constructing new walls, on the grounds that the exigencies of the taxpayer's trade, including statutory or regulatory requirements, required the kitchen walls to be constructed to enable the cooker to serve its proper purpose. However, the commissioners rejected this claim. By contrast, it was held that timber partitions and doors to individual toilets were properly treated as incidental to the installation of plant as the toilets could not be properly used without partitions or cubicles. The drainage items in both premises also qualified as a trade specific sewerage system or as incidental alterations. The Upper Tribunal rejected the company's appeal.

See the *Tax Reporter* commentary at ¶245-480 for specific details of the tribunal's comments on the following categories of expenditure.

- Splashbacks and tiling.
- Plastering.
- Cement flooring.
- Floor surfaces.
- Inclined floor.

The question of the link between the building work and the installation of the plant and machinery was also explored in the case of *B & E Security Systems Ltd*. The company operated sensitive surveillance and security equipment in Northern Ireland. It had a control room constructed to house the security equipment, spending around £61,000 (in addition to the equipment itself, costing over £78,000). The company did not seek to argue that the control room constituted an item of plant in itself, but claimed allowances on the basis that the control room expenditure was incidental to the installation of the equipment.

HMRC argued that the control room could not be incidental to the actual installation costs of the security equipment installed inside it, as the equipment would have functioned normally irrespective of whether reinforced walls or a special ceiling were built around them and enclosed them. The expenditure by the company on the construction of the control room was, in HMRC's view, no more than part of the overall cost to the company of it providing premises suitable to enable it to carry out its business. HMRC also referred to the fact that the construction works were carried out before, rather than after, the security equipment was acquired.

These HMRC arguments were rejected by the tribunal. The construction works were carried out only because the company had to undertake them in order to obtain two work contracts. The carrying out of the works became necessary and inevitable if the equipment was to be acquired and operated in accordance with the demands of those contracts. The relative timings of incurring expenditure on the equipment and on the building were driven by practical considerations and were of no assistance in determining the tax outcome. There was no issue here of disproportionality: the building works cost less than the equipment. In summary, there was a sufficient nexus as between the expenditure incurred by the company on the construction room and the expenditure incurred on the acquisition of the security equipment.

Legislation: CAA 2001, s. 25

Cases: *JD Wetherspoon plc v R & C Commrs* (2007) Sp C 657; *JD Wetherspoon plc* [2010] TC 00312; *B & E Security Systems Ltd* [2010] TC 00452; *JD Wetherspoon plc v R & C Commrs* [2012] BTC 1,578

Tax Reporter: ¶245-480

114-250 Professional fees

Professional fees (e.g. fees of architects, consultants, surveyors) allocated to plant and charged on a scale or percentage basis may not be allowed by HMRC as part of the cost of providing the plant. However, HMRC will generally allow professional fees where separate fee notes (or sometimes carefully itemised fee notes) are issued in respect of work done in connection with the building and with the provision of plant.

It is a question of fact as to how much of the cost relates to plant and machinery.

The question of preliminary costs was considered in the case of *JD Wetherspoon plc v R & C Commrs*. It was held in that case that preliminary costs could be apportioned in part to incidental building alterations qualifying under what is now CAA 2001, s. 25 (see 114-200). The case also made the point that projected overheads should be apportioned rateably over all the measured work, this view being confirmed by the Upper Tribunal on appeal.

Cases: *JD Wetherspoon plc v R & C Commrs* (2007) Sp C 657; *JD Wetherspoon plc* [2010] TC 00312; *JD Wetherspoon plc v R & C Commrs* [2012] BTC 1,578

Tax Reporter: ¶246-160

114-300 Interest charges and currency exchange costs

Capital allowances are not available in respect of interest charges on money borrowed to provide plant or machinery (*Ben-Odeco Ltd v Powlson*).

However, additional cost due to currency fluctuations has been allowed as part of the cost of providing machinery. In *Van Arkadie v Sterling Coated Materials*, a Swiss manufacturing company agreed to supply the taxpayer (SCM) with plant for 4.4 million Swiss francs payable by instalments. The Swiss company could not finance the construction of the plant from their own resources and made arrangements with a Swiss bank for finance, and SCM agreed to pay its instalments to the bank. SCM and the bank entered into a loan agreement pursuant to these arrangements, whereby the bank credited SCM with 3 million Swiss francs, repaid by SCM by seven instalments between April 1974 and December 1976. Due to the appreciation of the Swiss franc against sterling, the cost to SCM was greater than the original sterling price. It was agreed that if the loan agreement had not been entered into, the sterling cost of meeting the instalments would have been deductible in the years the instalments were paid. However, if the loan agreement had been entered into before the contract for the plant, the additional sums paid to purchase Swiss francs would not have qualified for relief. It was held that SCM was entitled to first-year allowances in respect of the additional cost of the instalments as the purchase price was payable by instalments.

Cases: *Ben-Odeco Ltd v Powlson* (1978) 52 TC 459; *Van Arkadie v Sterling Coated Materials* [1983] BTC 11

Tax Reporter: ¶245-880

Fixtures

114-600 Fixtures: background

For the rules relating to integral features, see 115-000. For the practicalities of buying and selling property, apportionments, fixture elections, etc. see 114-700ff.

For the purposes of making a claim for plant and machinery allowances, an obvious and key concern is the question of whether particular assets fall within the definition of plant or machinery. It is important, however, that a second fundamental condition for obtaining plant and machinery allowances is not overlooked. This is the condition that, as a result of the expenditure incurred, the asset must belong to the person incurring the expenditure.

In most cases, it will be obvious, when a person incurs capital expenditure on an asset, that the asset will then belong to him. However, there is one specific set of circumstances – concerning fixtures in property – where a complication arises. For these purposes, a fixture is defined as 'plant or machinery that is so installed or otherwise fixed in or to a building or other description of land as to become, in law, part of that building or other land'. (The legislation also specifically provides that a fixture includes 'any boiler or water-filled radiator installed in a building as part of a space or water heating system'.) If a tenant incurs expenditure on such an item, does it legally belong to the tenant or to the landlord and what effect does that have when determining entitlement to capital allowances?

The importance of the concept of belonging was brought out in the case of *Stokes v Costain Property Investments Ltd.* That case decided that the terms 'belong' and 'belonging' were ordinary English words to be interpreted in an ordinary sense. If somebody merely had the right to use an asset for a limited period then it could not be said that the asset belonged to him. It was not an apt use of language to say that landlords' fixtures belonged to a leaseholder: 'he cannot remove them from the building, he cannot dispose of them except as part of the hereditament and subject to the provisions of the lease and for the term of the lease'.

A distinction was made between such landlords' fixtures on the one hand and a tenant's fixture on the other. An example given was of a machine tool which might be fixed down for the better use of the tool rather than as an improvement to the premises. Such a tool could be removed by the tenant when the lease expired and could thus be said to belong to the tenant. The case had been primarily concerned, however, with the installation in leasehold buildings of major items of plant including lifts and central heating equipment amounting to nearly £500,000 out of a total construction cost of nearly £3,000,000.

It became clear from that case that the law was unsatisfactory. Firstly, there had been a perception that this was not an issue the Revenue had taken in practice. Secondly, a substantial amount of expenditure had been incurred and yet nobody would obtain any tax relief for that expenditure. As Fox LJ said in the Court of Appeal dismissing the company's case:

> 'I cannot, however, regard the state of the law as satisfactory. The purpose of the statutory provisions must be to encourage investment in machinery and plant. In this case very large sums were expended on such investment but, under the enactment as it stands, nobody will receive the tax allowance in respect of it. The freeholder will not, because the freeholder did not incur the expenditure and is not carrying on the trade and the taxpayer will not because the items did not belong to the taxpayer. The Revenue are unable to suggest any policy reason why a person in the position of the taxpayer should be refused relief. It is to be hoped that the ambit of the legislation will be reconsidered.'

The legislation was indeed reconsidered with new rules introduced in 1985 which are now contained, as subsequently amended, in CAA 2001, s. 172–204 under the heading of 'fixtures'. The rules apply 'to determine entitlement to allowances under this Part in respect of expenditure on plant or machinery that is, or becomes, a fixture'. The legislation contains special rules to determine when a person is treated for tax purposes as owning a fixture or as ceasing to own one.

Legislation: CAA 2001, s. 11, 173(1)

Case: *Stokes v Costain Property Investments Ltd* [1984] BTC 92

Tax Reporter: ¶242-800

114-650 Persons treated as owning fixtures

Overview

For the reasons outlined at 114-600, the legislation has to create a pretence of legal ownership so that capital allowances can be given for fixtures in an appropriate manner.

The legislation recognises various categories of person who may be deemed to own fixtures, as follows:

- persons with an interest in relevant land having fixtures for the purposes of a qualifying activity;
- equipment lessors;
- energy services providers;
- purchasers of land with fixtures;
- incoming lessees.

Tax Reporter: ¶242-950

Persons with interest in relevant land

A person is treated as owning a fixture as a result of expenditure he has incurred if the following conditions are met:

- he incurs capital expenditure on plant or machinery;
- the asset is for the purposes of a qualifying activity that he is carrying on;
- the plant or machinery in question becomes a fixture; and
- the person incurring the expenditure has an interest in the relevant land at the date on which the asset becomes a fixture.

This will typically apply where the tenant pays for the installation of a heating or air conditioning system in the property. These rules do not apply, however, where an equipment lessor and an equipment lessee jointly elect for different treatment, as discussed below.

It is possible for two or more people with different interests in the land to be treated under the above rules as owning the same fixture. In this case, only the person with the lowest interest, e.g. the leaseholder rather than the freeholder, is treated as owning the fixture.

Legislation: CAA 2001, s. 176

Tax Reporter: ¶242-950

Equipment lessors

There can be problems with the allowances available to equipment lessors where the plant or machinery in question becomes a fixture. In accordance with the principles outlined above, it might be the case that no allowances would be due without special legislation. The expenditure may have been incurred by the equipment lessor but he does not own the plant or machinery because, in law, it has become a fixture in a property in which the lessor has no interest. The lessee will not be able to claim capital allowances because he has not incurred the expenditure.

In certain circumstances, an election may be made whereby the equipment lessor may be treated as owning a fixture as a result of incurring capital expenditure on plant or machinery that is subject to an equipment lease (in which case the equipment lessee will be treated as not owning it).

Legislation: CAA 2001, s. 177

Energy services providers

In certain circumstances, the detail of which is quite complex, a provider of energy services will be treated as the owner of a fixture as a result of capital expenditure he has incurred on the provision of plant or machinery that has become a fixture. This will apply where there is a formal energy services agreement and where both the provider of the energy services and the client (who must not be connected persons) elect that this treatment should apply.

Legislation: CAA 2001, s. 180A

Purchasers of land with fixtures

A purchaser of an interest in relevant land is in certain circumstances treated as the owner of fixtures on that land. This is a very common situation in practice and one where the rules are poorly misunderstood and where full claims are often not made. The basic conditions are that:

- plant or machinery has become a fixture;
- a person acquires an interest in the relevant land; and
- that interest in the land was in existence before the purchaser acquired it.

The rules will not apply if any person has, immediately after the time of the acquisition, a prior right in relation to the fixture.

It may be necessary to apportion the overall capital sum between part relating to the fixture and part to the rest of the land. The parties can determine the matter by making an election. Failing this, a 'just and reasonable apportionment' will be made, irrespective of the wording of any documents relating to the purchase and sale. From April 2008, such an apportionment will also need to consider which of the assets qualifies/ constitutes integral features.

Where property is acquired from a previous owner who has used a building for a taxable purpose, there are more detailed rules that now apply with effect from 6 April 2012 for the purchaser. The broad effect of these new provisions is that the new owner can only claim allowances on fixtures where:

- the expenditure of a previous owner has been allocated to a capital allowances pool or a first year allowance claimed;
- either a tribunal determines the sum apportioned to fixtures or the two parties make an election under CAA 2001, s. 198 (which is likely to be the most practical solution); and
- the previous owner has, not later than two years after the date of disposal, made a written statement of the amount of the disposal value to be brought into account and the original or a copy is supplied to the new owner.

Legislation: CAA 2001, s. 181, 187A, 187B, 198, 562

Incoming lessees

In certain circumstances, where a lease is granted after plant or machinery has become a fixture, the lessee will be treated as if he were the owner of the fixture as a result of incurring expenditure. The rules for this treatment to apply depend on whether or not the lessor is entitled to an allowance in respect of the fixture for the chargeable period in which the lease is granted (or would be entitled to such an allowance if he were within the charge to tax).

Where the lessor is not (or would not be) entitled to allowances, the lessee is automatically treated as owning the fixture as long as the fixture has not previously been used for the purposes of a qualifying activity by the lessor or by any person connected with him. The HMRC manuals explain that 'the sort of case where this can happen is where the interest held by the lessor is held on trading account'. The lessee is not entitled to allowances in these circumstances if, when the interest is acquired, any person has a prior right in relation to the fixture.

Where the lessor is (or would be) entitled to allowances, the lessor and lessee can in some circumstances make an election to transfer deemed ownership, and therefore capital allowances, from lessor to lessee. The election must be signed by both lessor and lessee and must be submitted within two years of the date on which the lease takes effect. The other conditions for an election in these circumstances are as follows:

- a person ('the lessor') with an interest in the relevant land grants a lease after plant or machinery has become a fixture;
- the consideration given by the lessee for the lease includes a capital sum that (in whole or in part) is treated as expenditure on the provision of the fixture; and
- the lessor and the lessee are not connected persons.

Ownership of the fixture is then deemed to pass to the lessee from the time when the lease is granted.

Legislation: CAA 2001, s. 183–184

Other Material: HMRC *Capital Allowances Manual* CA26350

114-660 Restrictions on qualifying expenditure

Qualifying expenditure on fixtures is restricted if a claim has already been made under the plant and machinery rules, the IBA rules or the research and development rules.

In the case of fixtures on which plant and machinery allowances have been claimed, the broad effect of the legislation is to restrict the allowances available on a fixture to the original cost of that fixture plus any allowable installation costs. The HMRC view is that 'it is the responsibility of the taxpayer to obtain and provide details of the past owner and the disposal value'. If necessary, HMRC will deny all allowances where it seems likely to the HMRC officer that this restriction will apply.

Legislation: CAA 2001, s. 185–187

Other Material: HMRC *Capital Allowances Manual* CA26400

Tax Reporter: ¶243-025

114-670 Cessation of ownership of fixtures

A disposal value must be brought into account by a person who has been eligible for allowances in respect of it if the fixture is sold or otherwise disposed of, is permanently lost, ceases to exist, becomes used for non-trade purposes, or if the person's trade is permanently discontinued.

In addition, a person who ceases to have 'the qualifying interest' in a fixture (or who is treated as ceasing to own it) will be treated as disposing of it. 'The qualifying interest' is, generally, the interest of the person treated as the person to whom it belongs, i.e. the lessee, tenant, etc.

Where, under these rules, a person is treated as ceasing to own a fixture, somebody else may be treated as acquiring the fixture at that time.

Legislation: CAA 2001, s. 188, 196(5)

Tax Reporter: ¶243-100

No disposal in certain circumstances

No deemed disposal arises if:

- the qualifying interest is merged with another interest acquired by the same person;
- on the expiry of a lease, a new lease is granted to the lessee;
- an agreement to acquire an interest results in the acquisition of that interest;
- on the expiry of a licence to occupy, a new licence is granted to the licensee; or
- on the expiry of a lease, the lessee remains in occupation with the consent of the lessor.

In each such case the qualifying interest is thereafter to take into account the change in circumstance.

Legislation: CAA 2001, s. 188–189

114-680 Disposal values of fixtures

The disposal value that has to be brought into account in respect of a fixture will depend on the nature of the event giving rise to the disposal. The legislation contains a table listing the different types of disposal event and, in each case, describing how the disposal value is calculated.

A higher disposal value will need to be brought into account where a disposal event 'is part of, or occurs as a result of, a scheme or arrangement the main purpose or one of the main purposes of which is the obtaining by the taxpayer of a tax advantage' under the plant and machinery rules.

The anti-avoidance rules will apply where the disposal value to be brought into account would otherwise be less than what is termed the notional written-down value. In this case, the person concerned must bring into account the notional written-down value of the asset in question.

Legislation: CAA 2001, s. 196–197

Tax Reporter: ¶243-250

114-700 Buying and selling property

Introduction

It is in the area of buying and selling property that capital allowances become most complex and most valuable. The amounts of tax at stake can be great and there are still many transactions where simple tax planning opportunities are missed.

Common misconceptions

One of the areas that can create surprises for businesses and their tax advisers concerns the tax effect of wording in a contract for the purchase and sale of a property. It is often thought that as long as the vendor and purchaser write agreed figures into a sales contract, this will be effective for tax purposes. In fact, the HMRC officer has a statutory obligation to impose a 'just and reasonable apportionment' where different types of property are sold together, even where separate prices are agreed for separate parts of the overall transaction. Signing a joint election can, however, override this power.

A second misconception is that the allocation of the proceeds/purchase price can be sorted out at the time the relevant tax computations are prepared. In fact, it may be very advantageous for either purchaser or vendor to consider the position before the transaction is completed, not least because the tax effect may well have a legitimate bearing on the value of the property sold and acquired. This is considered in more depth below.

Finally, it is often thought that the interaction of the capital allowances and capital gains tax rules will mean that what is lost on the one side can be gained on the other. This is rarely the case, for the reasons discussed at 114-850.

Legislation: CAA 2001, s. 198, 562

Tax Reporter: ¶243-700

114-750 Just and reasonable apportionments

The need for apportionment

Plant or machinery will often be sold in a single transaction which also involves other assets, such as land or buildings. Where the transaction is at arm's length, HMRC will not be entitled to question the total sale value. However, they do have power (and indeed a statutory obligation) to question the apportionment between plant or machinery on the one hand and other assets on the other.

The HMRC officer may insist on 'a just and reasonable apportionment' but, if he increases or reduces the amount allocated to the plant or machinery, he will need to adjust the figures for other assets accordingly and indeed must justify the value he attributes to those other assets.

In practice, the amount to be apportioned between different assets often features in the negotiations for the sale of a business, etc. In most cases, what suits the vendor does not suit the purchaser, as the latter will often wish to attribute as much as possible to plant and machinery which will produce a balancing charge for the vendor. Each case is different, however, and it may be relevant to take account of many different factors including, for example, the availability of trading losses or the different tax rates of purchaser and vendor. The valuation of plant is not an exact science and so there is usually some scope for obtaining a result that is favourable from the tax point of view if both parties can agree. However, it should be borne in mind that unless a joint election is signed in respect of fixtures (see 114-800) the HMRC officer can impose his own figures 'even though separate prices are, or purport to be, agreed for separate items'.

If no election is made, the question therefore arises of what is 'just and reasonable'. Each case will depend on its own facts, but the following may be considered as a guideline for the approximate percentage of the *overall acquisition price* qualifying as fixed plant when purchasing an existing building:

	Integral features (%)	**Other fixtures (%)**	**Total (%)**
Basic office	10	5–10	15–20
Prestigious office	15	5–15	20–30
Hospitals and nursing homes	15	5–20	20–35
Hotels	15	5–20	20–35
Shopping centres	10	5–20	15–30
Industrial units	4	1–11	5–15
Sports centres	10	5–15	15–25

The apportionment rules apply not only to an ordinary sale but also to any consideration for the exchange or surrender of an asset.

The introduction, from April 2008, of the rules relating to integral features significantly increased the percentages of total expenditure on a building that qualifies for plant and machinery allowances. Nearly every building has cold water and electrical systems (including general lighting), adding to the list of items on which plant and machinery allowances may now be claimed.

Legislation: CAA 2001, s. 562, 572

Tax Reporter: ¶244-300

Method of apportionment

Where necessary, HMRC will involve the Valuation Office for the purposes of reaching a proper apportionment between plant and other items. The Valuation Office Agency manuals are of interest in this respect (see www.voa.gov.uk/instructions/Index.htm). The relevant parts of the manuals are in the 'Capital gains tax, income tax and corporation tax' manual, section 3 of which deals specifically with capital allowances. Within this, part three is entitled 'Approach to apportionments'.

The manuals make it clear that, when apportioning a purchase price between plant and other non-qualifying elements, the approach taken will 'usually' be to use the formula whereby the value of plant and machinery is calculated as:

$$\text{Purchase price} \times \frac{A}{A + B + C}$$

where:

A is the replacement cost of qualifying items of plant;

B is the replacement cost of the rest of the building, (i.e. excluding plant); and

C is the value of the bare land.

Example

Those manuals go on to give an example involving the purchase of a 20 year old building for £5m. They suggest that if the total replacement cost of the building were £6m, including £1.5m representing the replacement cost of qualifying plant, and if the land value were £2m, then the apportionment would be as follows:

$$\text{Value of plant} = £5m \times \frac{£1.5m}{£8m} = £937{,}500$$

The resulting value is likely to lie somewhere between the original cost of the plant and its replacement value, depending on the average age of the plant. Interestingly, the formula has the effect of depreciating the values of all elements of the purchase price, including the land. The manuals go on to explain that 'although land does not of course depreciate in value with age, the bare site in this case is encumbered by an ageing building'. The point is that whatever the actual bare site value, it will not be possible to realise this value as long as there is a building on the site that is not ready for demolition.

A further HMRC example demonstrates that the apportioned value of the plant and machinery may exceed the replacement cost of those assets. This is explained as being because the element of the developer's profit will be apportioned on a pro rata basis and part of it will therefore increase the value of the plant and machinery.

Example

The example illustrating this involves a new property costing £10m. If the replacement cost of the building excluding plant and machinery is £4.5m with £1.5m allocated as the replacement cost of the plant and £2m as the bare site value, then the apportioned value of the plant and machinery will be calculated as follows:

$$\text{Purchase price} \times \frac{A}{A + B + C}$$

$$£10m \times \frac{£1.5m}{£1.5m + £3.5m + £2m} = £1.875m$$

Where agreement cannot be reached, there is legislation enabling a determination to be made by the tax tribunal. Where the tribunal considers an apportionment for capital allowances purposes, HMRC officers are instructed to accept that decision as it will be a question of fact rather than of law.

Legislation: CAA 2001, s. 563

Other Material: HMRC *Capital Allowances Manual* CA12500

114-800 Elections to fix apportionments re fixtures

An important aspect of the fixtures election is the opportunity, in certain circumstances, to choose how the overall value of a purchase and sale should be allocated between different elements. The legislation provides for a possible apportionment of the sale price when the qualifying interest is sold and in certain other circumstances.

An apportionment made by an election under these sections takes precedence over any apportionment that would otherwise be made. Elections made under these rules are irrevocable; but if, as a result of circumstances arising after the making of an election, the maximum amount which could be fixed by the election proves to be less than the amount that has been specified, the election is treated as if it had specified the maximum allowable amount.

The statutory rules relating to elections were not amended when the concept of integral features was introduced from April 2008. However, the election is strictly to be made on an asset by asset basis (as CAA 2001, s. 198 refers to 'a fixture' and 'the fixture' in the singular). Although HMRC do in practice allow assets to be amalgamated, this is only permitted where such amalgamation does not distort the tax computation. HMRC guidance now specifically states that any election must distinguish between fixtures that are integral features (and that therefore qualify for allowances only at the lower 'special rate') and other fixtures that qualify for unrestricted WDAs in the main plant and machinery pool. Specifically, the HMRC guidance states that elections are likely to be unacceptable if they do not include a split between the two categories. Where there is more than one property, HMRC have always insisted that each property must be subject to its own fixtures election.

Legislation: CAA 2001, s. 198ff.

Other Material: HMRC *Capital Allowances Manual* CA26850

Tax Reporter: ¶243-325

Election to apportion sale price on sale of qualifying interest

An opportunity to elect for a particular apportionment of the transaction value arises where the disposal value of a fixture has to be brought into account in accordance with item 1 of the table in CAA 2001, s. 196 (sale of qualifying interest at not less than market value, etc.). The seller and the purchaser may jointly elect to fix the amount (being part of the overall proceeds of the transaction) that is to be treated as the expenditure incurred by the purchaser on the provision of the fixture. The amount fixed by the election must not exceed either the overall sale price or the amount of the vendor's capital expenditure on the provision of the fixture.

Example

A property containing fixtures is sold for £1m. The cost of those fixtures had historically amounted to £160,000 and their current value is £20,000. The vendor company has large trading losses brought forward.

The vendor and purchaser may agree to allocate £160,000 to the fixtures. The vendor will incur balancing charges but these may be covered by the trading losses brought forward. The purchaser can claim capital allowances on the £160,000.

The requirement to bring in a disposal value should not be overlooked. No election is possible, for example, if the vendor is a property developer for whom the property represents trading stock – the vendor will not have claimed any capital allowances on the building and does not therefore bring a disposal value into account. Another effect of the requirement is that no election may be made for any asset on which no capital allowances claim has been made. In practice, many vendors have claimed allowances on certain fixtures but not others and it follows that an election that purports to cover all fixtures, including those on which no claim has been made, is flawed and potentially invalid.

If such an election is made then the remaining amount (if any) of the sale price is allocated to other property which is not the fixture but which formed part of the overall transaction.

Restrictions may apply if industrial buildings allowances or research and development allowances have previously been claimed.

Legislation: CAA 2001, s. 198ff.

Election to apportion capital sum given by lessee on grant of lease

An election may also be made if the disposal value of a fixture has to be brought into account on the grant of a lease.

The lessor and lessee may jointly elect to fix the amount to be treated as expenditure incurred by the lessee on the provision of the fixture. The amount fixed by the election must not exceed either the actual capital sum or the amount of the lessor's capital expenditure on the provision of the fixture.

As before, if such an election is made then the remaining amount (if any) of the sale price is allocated to other property which is not the fixture but which formed part of the overall transaction.

Once more, restrictions may apply if industrial buildings allowances or research and development allowances have previously been claimed.

Legislation: CAA 2001, s. 183

Procedures

Any election under these sections must be made within two years from the date on which the purchaser acquires the qualifying interest or (as the case may be) on which the lessee is granted the lease.

The notice must include:

- the amount fixed by the election;
- the name of each of the persons making the election;
- information sufficient to identify both the plant or machinery and the relevant land;

- particulars of the interest acquired by the purchaser or (as appropriate) of the lease granted to the lessee; and
- the tax district references of both parties making the election (see below).

Once a person has made such an election, he must include a copy of the notice containing the election when submitting his tax return for the first period for which the election has an effect for tax purposes in his case.

Legislation: CAA 2001, s. 198ff.

Overseas buyers

The requirement to provide details of tax district references has in the past been used by HMRC as justification for denying the right to make an election where the purchaser is not resident in the UK, as in the following quotation formerly at CA 26850:

> 'Do not accept an election if the buyer is non resident and outside the UK tax net. The election must give the tax district and reference of each person making the election. If the buyer is outside the UK tax net the buyer will not have a tax district and reference. This means that an election cannot be made because the tax district and reference of the buyer cannot be given.'

That wording was removed from the guidance around October 2007, though the motivation for that change is unclear. This raises an interesting technical issue as to whether or not an election can be entered into by someone who is not a taxpayer. It is clear from the wording of CAA 2001, s. 198(1) that the vendor must be paying tax, but there are possible arguments to the effect that the purchaser does not need to do so.

Other Material: HMRC *Capital Allowances Manual* CA26850

114-850 Fixtures and capital gains tax

Basic principle

Where a property is sold, and the property contains plant and machinery that is sold as part of a single transaction, an issue may arise as to how any capital allowances will affect either the base cost or the disposal proceeds of the property for capital gains tax purposes.

The normal rule is that capital allowances are simply ignored when working out the capital gains tax position. The full consideration still needs to be brought into account in the capital gains computation even where it partly represents disposal proceeds for capital allowances purposes. Similarly, allowable expenditure for the purposes of the capital gains computation does not have to be restricted by reference to any capital allowances claimed. This is subject to special rules where the capital gains tax computation produces a loss.

The following examples illustrate the above principles.

Example

In the ordinary way, where no capital allowances are involved, a small property may be bought for £200,000 and sold for £250,000. This will produce a capital gain of £50,000.

Suppose that when the property is bought for £200,000, a claim is made in respect of £20,000 of that £200,000 as representing fixtures that qualify as plant. Suppose that the property is still sold for £250,000 but at that stage no value is allocated to plant or machinery. In this case, the capital gain is still calculated as £50,000 since the legislation 'shall not require the exclusion from the sums allowable as a deduction in the computation of the gain of any expenditure as being expenditure in respect of which a capital allowance or renewals allowance is made'. The net result is therefore that there is still a capital gain of £50,000 but allowances totalling £20,000 will be available (made up of any combination of first-year, annual investment, writing-down and balancing allowances).

Suppose that, instead, the property is bought for £200,000 and sold for £250,000 and that at the time of both the purchase and the sale an amount of £20,000 is allocated to plant. (The amount allocated as proceeds of plant cannot for capital allowance purposes exceed the cost.) In this case, there will still be a gain of £50,000. However, in these circumstances no allowances will have been given overall since any first-year, annual investment or writing-down allowances will have been recaptured through a balancing charge (or, possibly, a reduced pool value carried down) at the time of the sale.

The above examples make it clear first that there is every benefit in claiming capital allowances even where the property containing the fixtures will be sold, and second that a crucial part of a sales process is to consider how much should be allocated to plant and machinery.

In the above examples, the trader has gained tax relief on £20,000 more in the earlier example than in the latter one; it is not unreasonable to state that the expenditure is relieved twice for tax purposes.

It is worth considering the accounting treatment. The fact that capital allowances are claimed on the £200,000 does not affect the accounting treatment; the full £200,000 will be shown in the accounts as 'additions to freehold property' or whatever. It is likely that there will be another entry in the accounts for plant and machinery (i.e. moveable items) so the capital allowances claim will include the whole of the latter and part of the freehold cost.

Legislation: TCGA 1992, s. 37(2), 41

Tax Reporter: ¶244-350

Modification of normal rule where disposal produces CGT loss

The above rules are modified where under the capital gains tax rules a loss is made. In this case, TCGA 1992, s. 41(1) requires that 'the amount of any losses accruing on the disposal of an asset shall be restricted by reference to capital allowances and renewal allowances'. The effect of this legislation is that the allowable expenditure must be reduced by the amount of allowances actually given. For these purposes, it is necessary to establish the amount of allowances net of any balancing charge.

Example

Suppose, for example, that a property was bought for £170,000 and sold for £140,000. Suppose that £20,000 was allocated to plant at the time of purchase, but nothing was allocated to plant at the time of sale. Without any special rules, there would simply be a capital loss of £30,000. However, the £170,000 needs to be adjusted for the net allowances given of £20,000, thereby reducing the deemed cost of the property to £150,000. As such, the loss arising will be £10,000. Thus the £30,000 'real' loss is relieved as to £20,000 through the capital allowances system and as to £10,000 through the capital gains tax system.

Suppose, instead, that of the sale proceeds of £140,000, £6,000 was allocated to plant. In this case, the capital gains computation would show disposal proceeds of £140,000 and an allowable cost of £156,000 (£170,000 less net allowances given of £14,000). In this case, the real loss of £30,000 is relieved as to £14,000 through the capital allowances system and as to £16,000 through the capital gains tax rules.

Legislation: TCGA 1992, s. 41

Further modification where asset acquired at written-down value

In certain circumstances, the adjustment of the loss (as discussed above) will need to take account of capital allowances enjoyed not only by the vendor but also by previous owners of the asset. This will apply when the vendor had acquired the asset at its tax written-down value where either:

- an election was made under CAA 2001, s. 569 (sales without change of control or between connected persons); or
- the transfer was one to which CAA 2001, s. 268 applied (succession to trade on death).

In these circumstances, it will be necessary to look at capital allowances given both to the actual vendor and to previous owners who had then transferred the asset to the current vendor at the written-down value for capital allowance purposes.

Legislation: TCGA 1992, s. 41(3)

114-900 Basic tax planning

It is important to gain a full understanding of the tax position of the vendor when buying a property. The following simple example illustrates some of the issues.

> **Example**
>
> Macbeth buys a property in 2000 for £2m and sells the property to Macduff in 2010 for £7m. It is agreed, based on the nature of the property, that a fair value of the fixtures would be 25% of the overall property value, so £500,000 in 2000 and £1,750,000 in 2010.
>
> If Macbeth made a claim for allowances on £500,000, then its disposal proceeds will be capped at that figure. This will in turn cap Macduff's expenditure at the same level. However, if Macbeth did not make a claim, Macduff's fixtures claim can be of £1,750,000. However, where the transaction occurs after 5 April 2012 the changes made by FA 2012 referred to in 114-650 above will restrict the allowances available compared to the previous position.

This simple example shows why it is so important to establish the capital allowances history of the property in question and this is particularly important following the FA 2012 changes. It is now necessary to make detailed enquiries relating to the previous owner's claims to ensure that the pooling, fixed value or disposal value requirement is met in relation to the past owner within the meaning of CAA 2001, s. 187A. Otherwise, the new owner will not be able to obtain allowances on the fixtures. The broad effect of these changes is to prevent buyers going back over the history of a building to seek expenditure on fixtures not claimed by a previous owner.

Property refurbishments

A property refurbishment may consist entirely of repairs and be allowable in computing profits of the trade, etc. Typically, however, it will involve capital expenditure. In this case, it will be essential to determine the level of plant and machinery allowances that can be claimed in respect of fixtures.

The extent of allowances claimed will clearly depend on the nature of the project. If the work involves demolition and reconstruction of external walls then the value of the fixtures will be a lower percentage of the total. If, at the other extreme, the shell of the building is retained and the fittings are replaced, a very high percentage of the overall expenditure may qualify for allowances. It is certainly possible that three quarters or more of such expenditure could qualify for relief as plant or machinery.

This is an area where detailed work in analysing expenditure can pay for itself many times over.

Tax Reporter: ¶244-050

114-920 Resolution of disputes

If a dispute arises as to whether an item of machinery has become, in law, a fixture, and that question is material to the tax liability of two or more persons, then the question is settled by the tax tribunal in the same manner as if it were an ordinary appeal. The only difference is that persons other than the parties to the dispute are entitled to appear and be heard, or to make representations in writing.

Legislation: CAA 2001, s. 204

Case: *JC Ducaux (UK) Ltd v Francis (HMIT)* (1996) Sp C 84

Integral features

115-000 Overview

Expenditure on so-called 'integral features' is treated separately from other capital expenditure for the purposes of claiming plant and machinery allowances. Expenditure on these integral features is excluded from the main capital allowances pool and allocated instead to the 'special rate' pool, where writing-down allowances are given at a rate of 8% (rather than the standard 18% rate) on the reducing balance of the pool. (Prior to April 2012, these figures were 10% and 20% respectively.)

Key features of the treatment of integral features are as follows.

- Integral features are unaffected by the restrictions in CAA 2001, s. 21 and 22 (buildings, structures, etc.).
- Certain items (e.g. asset ceasing to belong to him As a result, such assets now unambiguously qualify for plant and machinery allowances but only do so at the lower rate of tax relief.
- Expenditure on integral features is classified (together with certain other expenditure) as 'special rate expenditure', which is allocated to its own 'special rate pool' and which attracts allowances at a rate of 10% on a reducing balance basis.

- Integral features may, however, qualify for 100% relief by way of the annual investment allowance (see, generally, 111-875ff.), subject to the rules applying for the purposes of that allowance.

The mechanics of the legislation are that capital allowances are given *as if* expenditure on integral features were capital expenditure on plant and machinery, incurred for the purposes of the qualifying activity. The person incurring the expenditure is then treated as owning the item in question.

Legislation: CAA 2001, s. 23(2), 33A, 104Aff.

Tax Reporter: ¶243-400

115-030 Definition of 'integral features'

The following assets are integral features for the purposes of applying those rules.

(1) An electrical system (including a lighting system).

(2) A cold water system.

(3) A space or water heating system, a powered system of ventilation, air cooling or air purification, and any floor or ceiling comprised in such a system.

(4) A lift, an escalator or a moving walkway.

(5) External solar shading.

Legislation: CAA 2001, s. 33A

Tax Reporter: ¶243-420

Exclusions

An asset does not qualify as an integral feature if it is one 'whose principal purpose is to insulate or enclose the interior of a building or to provide an interior wall, floor or ceiling which (in each case) is intended to remain permanently in place'. This would apply, for example, to deny allowances on the cost of a wall that happens to form the fourth side of a ventilation pipe.

Legislation: CAA 2001, s. 33A

115-060 Allowances for special rate expenditure

Allowances and charges are not given for integral features in isolation: rather, there are rules for 'special rate expenditure', covering not only integral features but also certain long-life asset expenditure and expenditure on thermal insulation.

Annual investment allowance

There is nothing to stop a person claiming the annual investment allowance for special rate expenditure incurred on integral features, long-life assets, etc. The most basic form of tax planning will therefore be to ensure, each year, that the annual investment allowance is allocated first to absorb any expenditure that would otherwise qualify only for a lower rate of tax relief.

Writing-down allowances

Writing-down allowances are given at a lower rate for expenditure on integral features and other special rate expenditure. The mechanics of achieving this are to exclude such expenditure from the main capital allowances pool and to allocate it instead to a 'special rate' pool. Expenditure on integral features is pooled with other 'special rate' expenditure . Where only part of the expenditure is to be categorised as on such assets (for example, part of the expenditure is on integral features and part on ordinary plant and machinery) then the two parts of the expenditure are treated separately and an apportionment is made to determine how much should be allocated to each pool.

Allowances are given in accordance with normal principles, but with an 8% rate rather than the standard 18% rate that otherwise applies. Allowances are increased or decreased proportionately where the chargeable period is greater or shorter than one year and the normal restrictions apply where the qualifying activity was carried on for only part of the chargeable period. Once the value of the pool has fallen below £1,000, the small pool provisions apply to it as they do to the main pool (see 112-030).

Legislation: CAA 2001, s. 104Aff.

Tax Reporter: ¶243-440

Exclusions from the special rate pool

Expenditure is only allocated to the special rate pool if it is incurred wholly and exclusively for the purposes of the qualifying activity. This is slightly more complex than it may first seem. The interaction of the special rate expenditure rules and those relating to the single asset pool may be summarised as follows:

- expenditure on integral features or other special rate assets is invariably 'special rate expenditure';
- as a general principle, such expenditure is allocated to the 'special rate pool';

- it is instead allocated to a single asset pool if it is incurred partly for other purposes;
- nevertheless, allowances are given at the restricted rate of 8% for such expenditure (and are then subject to further reduction as appropriate. For example where there is private use of the asset).

The same principles apply to any other expenditure on integral features that is required to be allocated to a single asset pool. This would be the case, for example, where a person receives a partial depreciation subsidy.

Legislation: CAA 2001, s. 104C, 104D(2), 211

Disposal value: anti-avoidance rules

Anti-avoidance rules take effect if a disposal event 'is part of, or occurs as a result of, a scheme or arrangement the main purpose or one of the main purposes of which is the obtaining by the taxpayer of a tax advantage' under the plant and machinery legislation.

Legislation: CAA 2001, s. 104E

115-080 Replacement of integral features

When the whole or the majority of an 'integral feature' is replaced, that replacement expenditure is also treated as capital expenditure on the integral feature, rather than attracting a revenue deduction in the accounts.

If the expenditure on the feature in question is a one-off cost then the rule applies if the amount spent on the feature is more than half of the cost that would be incurred if, at that time, the integral feature were to be replaced.

A further rule applies, however, if the amount incurred is initially less than half the replacement cost but if further expenditure is incurred on the same integral feature in the period of 12 months beginning with that initial expenditure. If the aggregate of the initial expenditure and any further expenditure amounts to more than half of the cost of replacing the asset then both the initial and the later expenditure are treated as capital expenditure on the integral feature. Note that the term 'initial expenditure' refers not to the original cost of the asset but to the first amount of additional expenditure incurred on that asset. The test is determined by reference to the replacement cost of the asset at the time that initial expenditure is incurred.

The effect of this is that it may be necessary to re-open accounts and computations that have already been submitted. The legislation specifically allows for the making of all such assessments (and adjustments to assessments) as may be necessary to give effect to the rule.

Example

A company incurs expenditure of £40,000 on a central heating system in June 2014. In drawing up its accounts to 31 December 2015, it claims capital allowances.

A major flaw is discovered with the type of pipes that have been used and the business that installed the system goes bust. The company that paid for the heating system therefore has to bear the costs of replacing many of the pipes. Costs of £17,000 are incurred in October and November 2017. It is calculated at this point that to replace the entire system would now cost £43,000, so the £17,000 is less than half of the replacement cost. These costs are therefore treated as repairs and are written off in the accounts to 31 December 2017, submitted in June 2018.

Further problems arise when some other pipes start to leak in July, and additional costs of £5,000 are incurred in August 2018. The company is advised that the overall costs of this type of system have now increased further and that the whole system would now cost £50,000.

The total costs incurred in the 12-month period are £22,000. This figure has to be compared not with the £50,000 but with the £43,000 ('the cost of replacing the integral feature at the time the initial expenditure was incurred'). As the £22,000 is more than half of that cost, the special rules relating to replacement of integral features are applied. The £5,000 has to be treated as expenditure on integral features. Furthermore, it is now necessary to go back and re-open the accounts to 31 December 2017, adding back the repairs of £17,000 and instead claiming capital allowances on the cost.

Legislation: CAA 2001, s. 33B

Tax Reporter: ¶243-450

115-090 Mains services, lighting, heating, etc.

Mains services to buildings (e.g. electrical wiring, cold water piping and gas piping) are regarded as part of the cost of the building and did not, until April 2008, qualify for capital allowances. However, electrical transformers, ancillary equipment and switchboards have been held to be plant (see *Cole Bros Ltd v Phillips*). Relief is also given for the cost of baths, wash basins, etc.

Since April 2008, the cost of cold water and electrical (including lighting) systems is allowed under the rules relating to integral features. Relief is also given, under the general rules relating to plant and machinery, for the cost of sanitaryware (baths, wash basins, etc.).

Case: *Cole Bros Ltd v Phillips* [1982] BTC 208

Other Material: HMRC *Capital Allowances Manual* CA21170

Tax Reporter: ¶245-820

115-100 Sales between connected persons

Background

The rules relating to integral features sometimes offer a tax advantage but in other circumstances represent a tax cost. The first is illustrated by expenditure on cold water systems (now qualifying for relief at 8% but previously qualifying for no allowances at all in many cases). The opposite effect can be illustrated by reference to an air conditioning system, which previously qualified for full allowances but where the expenditure would now qualify only at the lower 8% rate.

The need for anti-avoidance provisions

Without special anti-avoidance legislation, the rules could be manipulated by selling an asset that did not previously qualify for relief to a related party. For example, Company A might have incurred expenditure on a cold water system in the year 2007, claiming no tax relief on that expenditure. By selling the building in August 2008 to related Company B, the latter company would be able to claim tax relief, under the integral feature provisions, on the element relating to the cold water system.

This opportunity is blocked in certain circumstances. HMRC have summarised the effect of the rules as follows (in the *Explanatory Notes* to Finance Bill 2008):

> 'These rules ensure that in a connected party transaction the buyer is not denied relief for any asset where plant and machinery allowances were available prior to 1 or 6 April 2008 in respect of the integral feature but ensure that historic non qualifying expenditure is not relieved after the changes made by this legislation.'

Legislation: FA 2008, Sch. 26, para. 15

Tax Reporter: ¶243-480

Methods of acquisition and disposal

115-200 Overview

There are numerous different ways in which a person can acquire and dispose of assets.

To obtain allowances for plant and machinery, the taxpayer must have incurred expenditure on 'the provision of the asset for the purposes of a qualifying activity' in consequence of which it 'belongs' to him. A balancing adjustment may arise without a disposal of an asset as such – an occasion must arise for which a disposal value is to be brought into account, i.e. the asset ceasing to belong to him, he permanently loses or abandons it, it ceases to exist, it begins to be used not for the purposes of the qualifying activity or the qualifying activity is permanently discontinued.

Such provision above would clearly encompass an outright purchase (irrespective of whether the price was payable in instalments – although this might affect when it is incurred). It would not include a leasing arrangement or other rental agreement (allowances may be available to the lessor).

Special provisions apply so as to permit allowances in particular cases where the requirements above are not met (gifts where no expenditure is incurred; assets previously used for purposes other than the qualifying activity where expenditure is not incurred on the provision for the qualifying activity; hire-purchase and lease-purchase where the asset does not belong to the taxpayer until he exercises the option to acquire it at the end of the contract and the expenditure is not incurred until each instalment is met). Allowances may also be given in respect of a person's contribution to expenditure in respect of which another person satisfies the requirements.

There are special rules for successions, transactions between connected persons, leasebacks and tax-structured transactions.

115-250 Gifts of plant or machinery

Where a person brings into use plant or machinery which he has been given, that person is treated as though he had purchased the plant or machinery from the donor at its open market value on the date on which it was brought into use and allowances will be calculated accordingly.

In relation to transfers at an undervalue, the general rule is that the actual price will not be disturbed for either the transferor or the transferee, unless the transferee does not bring the amount into account in a capital allowances computation or in a calculation of benefits from his employment; in other cases market value may apply for the transferor.

However, market value may be applied for both the transferor and transferee in the case of certain transfers between 'connected persons' or involving a transfer of trade. They may elect that, where a trade is transferred between them, that plant or machinery be treated as passed from predecessor to successor at a consideration which gives rise to no balancing adjustment. In other words, where there is a transfer between connected persons (including an incorporation) the parties may effectively choose between market value or tax written down value; they do not have the option to use a purely nominal value (e.g. £1) or any other figure nominated by the parties.

Allowances for the transferee may be restricted by reference to the disposal value to be brought into account by the transferor where the parties are connected as above or in the case of a leaseback, etc. or where it is a tax-structured transaction.

No first-year allowances or annual investment allowances are available in these circumstances.

Legislation: CAA 2001, s. 14, 38B, 46(2)

Tax Reporter: ¶236-260

115-300 Appropriation of property for qualifying activity use

Writing-down allowances are normally available to a person who brings plant or machinery already owned by him into qualifying activity use. That person is treated as though he had incurred capital expenditure equal to the market value of the asset on the date it is brought into use (if this is less than the actual expenditure incurred), for the qualifying activity and allowances are calculated accordingly.

No first-year allowances or annual investment allowances are available in these circumstances.

Legislation: CAA 2001, s. 13, 38B, 46(2)

Tax Reporter: ¶236-245

115-350 Hire-purchase

Under hire-purchase agreements, the purchaser is not legally the owner of the property until the final instalment has been paid. However, for capital allowance purposes, the item of plant or machinery is treated as belonging to the purchaser (and nobody else) when he becomes entitled to the benefit of the contract.

Payments under a hire-purchase contract can be divided into capital and interest payments. The interest element is deductible as a trade expense whilst capital allowances are available for the balance.

Instalments of capital paid before the asset is brought into use will have been incurred and allowances due accordingly. Capital payments outstanding at the date the asset is first brought into use, are treated as incurred at that time and capital allowances are given accordingly, except in the case of fixtures. This is unaffected by the specific rules applying to the deemed date of incurring expenditure where the payment date is more than four months after the obligation to pay becomes unconditional.

Example 1

Timmit Ltd, which makes up its accounts to 31 December each year, buys a van for business use under a hire-purchase contract. The cost is as follows:

	£
Cash price	10,000
Deposit	(1,000)
	9,000
Interest	2,160
	11,160

The £11,160 is payable in 36 instalments of £310, made up of £60 interest and £250 capital. Timmit enters into the contract on 1 December 2017, when it pays the £1,000 deposit. The first instalment is due on 1 January 2018 and the van is brought into use on 1 February 2018.

Timmit is entitled to allowances on the deposit of £1,000 in the period to 31 December 2017. The instalment of capital actually incurred on 1 January 2018 together with the outstanding capital instalments at 1 February 2018 (aggregate £9,000) are added to the pool in the year to 31 December 2018.

Where a hire-purchase contract is not completed, allowances which have already been given for capital payments no longer payable are dealt with by bringing into account a disposal value equal to any compensation received and future capital payments not incurred.

If a chattel (i.e. a tangible asset which is not fixed to land) is subject to a hire purchase agreement and it subsequently becomes a fixture, then the previous owner is treated as having made a disposal of it if a different person becomes treated as the owner of the asset.

If someone buys a *fixture* on hire-purchase, they cannot recognise unpaid instalments in their capital allowances computations if they fall due more than four months after the contract becomes unconditional.

Example 2

Pyotr and Pavel both buy assets on hire-purchase. They enter into the agreements on 31 December 2016 and the first instalment is due on 1 November 2017.

They both use the assets immediately for their business, for which they prepare accounts to 31 December each year. The only difference is that Pyotr's asset is a fixture, whereas Pavel's is a chattel.

Pyotr will not be able to recognise the expenditure until it is incurred.

Pavel, however, will be able to bring in all the expenditure in the computations for the year ending 31 December 2016.

Legislation: CAA 2001, s. 5(5), 67

Tax Reporter: ¶240-080

115-400 Contributions to the cost of plant and machinery

Contributions by others

A contribution by somebody other than a public authority towards capital expenditure generally reduces the amount of expenditure on which the recipient can claim capital allowances. Thus where A makes a contribution towards capital expenditure by B, B's allowable expenditure is reduced by the amount of the contribution.

The contributor may obtain capital allowances on his contribution (known as contribution allowances) if made for the purposes of his own (or his tenant's) trade, profession or vocation. Where the contributor is not entitled to claim capital allowances, the person who otherwise incurs the expenditure is entitled to allowances on the amount of his expenditure *including* the contribution, unless the contributor is the Crown, or a government, or public or local authority. However, if a grant or contribution is subsequently repaid by the original recipient then, by concession, the amount repaid will be treated as expenditure on which capital allowances may be given. Where the original contributor is other than the Crown or a public body and had claimed allowances on the contribution the repayment of the contribution will only generate an entitlement to additional capital allowances for the person making the refund if the repayment will be dealt with as a balancing adjustment or trading receipt in the hands of the original contributor.

Where the contributor is not entitled to capital allowances on his contribution (i.e. contribution allowances), but is entitled to deduct the contribution in computing the profits of his business, the recipient is denied allowances on expenditure represented by the contribution. The same applies in cases where the contributor is not taxable, but his contributions would qualify for allowances if he were.

Legislation: CAA 2001, s. 532ff.

Case: *Cyril Lord Carpets Ltd v Schofield* (1966) 42 TC 637

Other Material: ESC B49

Allowances for contributors to expenditure

Where the contributor is entitled to contribution allowances on contributing to the cost of an asset falling to be plant or machinery, his contributions for that asset are separately pooled (i.e. a single asset pool); if there is only one contribution for an asset then the contribution stands alone and contribution allowances are computed in respect of that contribution alone. But balancing adjustments will be made as with the relevant main pool of expenditure when his trade is transferred or discontinued.

If a person carries on more than one qualifying activity, capital expenditure relating to the different activities must not be allocated to the same pool. Writing-down allowances for chargeable periods ending after the date of the transfer are to be made to the transferee instead of to the transferor.

In the case of the transfer of part of a trade, if the contribution relates to the provision of a plant or machinery asset for the purposes of the part of the trade transferred then a balancing adjustment (i.e. a balancing allowance where the contributor has not received anything) will be made in respect of the contribution or single asset pool concerned (where more than one contribution in respect of the same asset is pooled); there would not be a balancing adjustment in the relevant main pool (i.e. because not all of the trade has permanently discontinued).

Legislation: CAA 2001, s. 53, 65, 538

Industrial buildings allowances

116-000 Overview

Industrial buildings allowances (IBAs) were for many decades available for qualifying expenditure incurred on the construction of an industrial building. The allowances for qualifying expenditure on an industrial building were made to the person with the relevant interest in the industrial building to which the qualifying expenditure relates.

In the March 2007 Budget, the Chancellor announced that IBAs (and agricultural buildings allowances) were to be phased out over a four-year period.

For the rates of allowances, see *Hardman's Tax Rates and Tables* at 11-700.

Legislation: CAA 2001, s. 271, 309, 352ff.

Tax Reporter: ¶246-750

116-100 Phasing out of IBAs

Introduction and overview

The Chancellor announced in the Budget of March 2007 that IBAs (and agricultural buildings allowances) were to be phased out over a four-year period.

The phasing-out is put into effect as follows:

- FA 2007 provided that no IBA balancing adjustment was to be made for balancing events occurring (broadly) from 21 March 2007.
- FA 2008 confirms that the annual IBA writing-down allowance is reduced to 3% from April 2008 and by a further 1% per year thereafter, until the allowances are finally withdrawn from 1 April 2011. Where IBA writing-down allowances are given at different rates (e.g. following a sale of the property), then these rates too are reduced year by year from April 2008.
- No IBAs at all are due for expenditure incurred from 6 April 2011.

Different rules apply to qualifying enterprise zone expenditure (see 118-400).

Tax Reporter: ¶246-750ff.

Balancing allowances and charges

118-100 Introduction

As already noted, the Chancellor announced in the Budget of March 2007 that IBAs (and agricultural buildings allowances) were to be phased out. Subject to an exception for enterprise zones, no IBA balancing adjustment is now to be made for a 'a post-commencement balancing event', as defined below. In other words, the vendor of an industrial building will not normally be subject to a balancing charge at the time of disposal (and will not be able to obtain a balancing allowance if selling at a loss).

Legislation: CAA 2001, s. 314

Tax Reporter: ¶249-900

Enterprise zones

118-400 Introduction to enterprise zones

Tax advantages apply to designated areas, known as enterprise zones, to encourage industrial and commercial activity. The last date on which a zone was designated was 21 October 1996 and as a general rule expenditure only qualifies for relief if incurred within ten years of the designation date. Nevertheless, there are some circumstances in which the rules can still be relevant.

The benefits include the availability of initial allowances, calculated as 100% of the qualifying enterprise zone expenditure. Broadly, this means capital expenditure that has been incurred on the construction of a building on a site in an enterprise zone, designated as such by statutory instrument, where:

- the expenditure was incurred within ten years after the site was first included in the enterprise zone; or
- the expenditure was incurred under a contract entered within ten years after the date that the site was first included in the enterprise zone and the expenditure was incurred within 20 years after that date.

In general terms, the initial allowance applies to expenditure on the following:

- construction of a 'commercial building or structure' (see below);
- construction of an 'industrial building or structure';
- construction of a 'qualifying hotel',

providing that expenditure on all or any of the above was generally incurred within ten years of the date when the site was declared an enterprise zone, or under a contract which was entered into during the same ten-year period and actually incurred within the 20 years after that date.

Plant or machinery which is part of the building also qualifies for the 100% allowance.

Legislation: CAA 2001, s. 294ff.

Other Material: HMRC *Capital Allowances Manual* CA37050

Tax Reporter: ¶250-950

End of enterprise zone period

Enterprise zones have a life of ten years, and the position when this period expires was spelt out by the Under Secretary of State for the Environment in a House of Commons Written Answer (*Hansard*, 15 January 1988, col. 430). At the expiry of the ten-year period, the financial benefits are withdrawn immediately; there is no transitional period. As enterprise zones approach their ten-year anniversaries, therefore, the date when capital expenditure is incurred can become crucial. However, someone purchasing a second-hand enterprise zone building after the end of the ten-year enterprise zone period but before the end of the building's 25-year tax life, is entitled to enterprise zone allowances.

118-410 Overview of tax rules

The enterprise zone rules form part of the overall IBA legislation. Unless otherwise specified, therefore, qualifying expenditure on an enterprise zone building will be treated for IBA purposes in the same way as any other qualifying expenditure discussed elsewhere in this Chapter.

Nevertheless, there are some key differences, including in particular, the following.

- The abolition of most balancing adjustments for events occurring from 21 March 2007 does not apply for enterprise zone expenditure.
- IBAs will nevertheless be withdrawn even for enterprise zone expenditure from April 2011.
- At the time of abolition of IBAs, there will be a seven-year run-off period during which taxpayers may still face balancing charges (see below).
- A wider range of buildings, specifically to include commercial buildings, can qualify under the enterprise zone rules than under the general IBA rules.
- A 100% initial allowance is available for enterprise zone expenditure.
- If a full initial allowance has not been taken, expenditure qualifies for writing-down allowances at a much faster rate.
- The tax treatment differs from the main IBA rules where buildings are bought that have already been used.
- In view of the attractive tax benefits, the enterprise zone rules are subject to their own anti-avoidance legislation.

118-415 Phasing-out of IBAs: effect on enterprise zones

IBAs will be completely abolished from April 2011. As a general principle, this will apply for qualifying enterprise zone expenditure as it does for all other allowances under the IBA code.

For enterprise zone expenditure only, balancing adjustments have still been made since April 2007 (without relying on transitional provisions). Furthermore, it will still be possible for a person to incur a balancing *charge* up to 5 April 2018 in relation to such expenditure. More specifically, the balancing charge will (from April 2011) arise if:

- an initial allowance or writing-down allowance has been made under the enterprise zone rules;
- an event occurs which would have given rise to a balancing charge under those rules; and
- the balancing event occurs within seven years of the date on which the building was first used.

Similarly, an initial allowance for qualifying enterprise zone expenditure will be withdrawn if:

- an event occurs which would have caused the allowance to be withdrawn if (from April 2011), CAA 2001, s. 307 had not been withdrawn; and
- the balancing event occurs within seven years of the end of the chargeable period for which the allowance was made.

For chargeable periods that start before 1 or 6 April 2011 (the 'relevant date' for corporation tax and income tax respectively), but end after that date, any writing-down allowances will only be given for the part of the period falling before that date. This is achieved by calculating the allowance for that period according to the following formula:

$(DCPB/DCP) \times WDA$

where:

DCPB	is the number of days in the chargeable period which fall before the relevant date;
DCP	is the number of days in the chargeable period; and
WDA	is the writing-down allowance to which the person would otherwise be entitled for the chargeable period.

Legislation: FA 2008, s. 86 and Sch. 27, para. 31

Other Material: HMRC *Capital Allowances Manual* CA37050

Tax Reporter: ¶250-950

Business premises renovation allowances

120-000 Overview

Business premises renovation allowances (BPRAs) apply to expenditure incurred from 11 April 2007. The scheme was originally due to last until 10 April 2012, but it was announced in the March 2011 Budget that it will be extended for a further five years. *Finance Act* 2016 provides that the scheme will no longer apply for expenditure incurred after 5 April 2017.

The allowances offer 100% up-front tax relief for the costs of renovating or converting certain unused business property in any of the 2,000 or so areas of the UK that are designated as disadvantaged. Allowances can be claimed by an individual or company incurring capital expenditure on bringing qualifying business premises back into business use. The allowances are available both to landlords and to businesses occupying their own properties.

Allowances are due only to the person incurring the expenditure. They can be clawed back if there is a sale or other 'balancing event' within seven years from the date on which the premises are first brought back into use (or on which they are first made suitable and available for letting). A subsequent purchaser of the property has no entitlement to allowances.

Entitlement to BPRAs depends on three conditions:

- a person must incur qualifying expenditure (see 120-100);
- that expenditure must be on a qualifying building (see 120-150); and
- the person must have the relevant interest in that building (see 120-250).

Legislation: CAA 2001, s. 360A

Tax Reporter: ¶252-500

120-050 Giving effect to allowances and charges

Allowances are generally treated as an expense of the trade, profession or vocation and any balancing charge is treated as a trading, etc. receipt.

This rule is varied if a person's interest in the building is subject to a lease or a licence at any time in the chargeable period in question. If the building is an asset of a property business carried on by him, then any allowance will be treated as an expense of that business and any charge as a receipt. In any other case, which will be exceptional, the person is treated as if he were carrying on a property business, and allowances are given as if they were an expense of that business, and charges as if they were a receipt of the business.

Legislation: CAA 2001, s. 360Z

Tax Reporter: ¶252-525

120-100 Qualifying expenditure

Qualifying expenditure must be capital expenditure that is incurred before the fifth anniversary of the scheme coming into effect (though this date may be extended by Treasury regulations).

The expenditure must be incurred in connection with one of the following:

- the conversion of a qualifying building (see below) into qualifying business premises (see below);
- the renovation of a qualifying building that is (or will become) qualifying business premises; or
- repairs to a qualifying building (or to the building of which the qualifying building forms part) to the extent that the repairs are incidental to the above-mentioned conversion or renovation work.

For these purposes, repairs are treated as capital expenditure to the extent that they are not tax deductible in calculating the profits of a trade, etc., or of a property business.

The following expenditure, however, will *not* qualify:

- the acquisition of land or of rights in or over land;
- the demolition of existing buildings;
- the extension of a qualifying building (except as required to provide access to the qualifying business premises);
- the development of land adjoining or adjacent to a qualifying building; or
- the provision of plant and machinery, except for fixtures.

Expenditure will not qualify to the extent it is subject to a claim for a relevant grant or relevant payment meaning a grant or payment which is State Aid or is declared to be equivalent to State Aid by Treasury order.

Legislation: CAA 2001, s. 360B, 360L

120-150 Qualifying building

A qualifying building can be a building or structure, or part of either. It must meet all of the following conditions:

- on the date on which the conversion or renovation work begins, it must be situated in a designated disadvantaged area (see below);
- it must have been unused for at least the 12 months leading to the date on which the renovation, etc. work began;
- it must last have been used either for the purposes of a trade, vocation or profession or as an office or offices (for whatever purposes); and
- it must not last have been used as (or as part of) a dwelling.

A further rule applies in the case of a part of a building or structure. The part must not, on the date on which the renovation, etc. work began, have last been occupied and used in common with any other part of the building or structure. However, this rule can be ignored if the other part was last used as a dwelling or if the other part was unused for at least the 12 months leading to the date on which the renovation, etc. work began.

HMRC have illustrated the rules relating to part of a building as follows:

> 'Jim owns and runs the Morrison hotel. He decides to move to Paris and lets the hotel become disused. He lets all the floors above the ground floor to Leonard, who wants to run it as a hostel. After the ground floor has been unused for two years, Alice says that she is looking for restaurant premises. Jim leases the ground floor to Alice who converts it into a restaurant. Alice's conversion expenditure qualifies for BPRA.'

Legislation: CAA 2001, s. 360C

Other Material: HMRC *Capital Allowances Manual* CA45300

Designated area

The following areas are designated for these purposes:

- The whole of Northern Ireland.
- Any other area of the UK that is specified as a development area by the *Assisted Areas Order* 2007 (SI 2007/107).

The government website, www.opsi.gov.uk/si/em2007/uksiem_20070945_en.pdf gives the following guidance:

> 'Assisted Areas are those areas where regional investment aid can be granted in accordance with European Union (EU) legislation. Regional aid is used to promote the economic development of certain disadvantaged areas within the EU.'

A building may lie on the border of a designated area. In this case, a just and reasonable apportionment has to be made to determine how much of the overall expenditure is attributable to the part located in the disadvantaged area.

Legislation: CAA 2001, s. 360C; SI 2007/945

120-200 Qualifying business premises

The conditions for qualifying business premises overlap with the requirements listed above in relation to a qualifying building. Specifically, premises must:

- constitute a building or structure (or part of a building or structure);
- be a qualifying building;
- be used (or available and suitable for letting for use) either for the purposes of a trade, vocation or profession or as an office or offices (for whatever purposes);
- not be used (or available for use) as a dwelling or as part of a dwelling; and
- not be used, or (broadly) owned, for the purposes of a disqualified trade sector (see below).

Premises do not cease to be qualifying business premises if they are temporarily unsuitable for use or letting, as long as they were qualifying business premises immediately beforehand.

Legislation: CAA 2001, s. 360D

Disqualified trade sectors

A building will not be qualifying business premises if either of the following applies:

- the person with the relevant interest (see 120-250) in the premises is carrying on a relevant trade; or
- the premises are wholly or partly used for the purposes of such a trade.

The term 'relevant trade' covers the following trades (according to the *Explanatory Notes* issued with SI 2007/945):

- fisheries and aquaculture;
- shipbuilding;
- the coal industry;
- the steel industry;

- synthetic fibres;
- the primary production of certain agricultural products;
- the manufacture and marketing of products which imitate or substitute for milk and milk products.

A trade is for these purposes defined to include a part of a trade.

Legislation: SI 2007/945

120-250 Relevant interest

Significance

Allowances are given under the BPRA scheme only to the person who:

- incurred the expenditure (and not, therefore, to any subsequent owner); and
- holds the relevant interest in the qualifying building.

Legislation: CAA 2001, s. 360A(2)

Definition

The rules for determining the relevant interest are very similar to those for flat conversion allowances, which in turn mirror the IBA rules. Generally, the relevant interest is the interest in the qualifying building held by the person when the expenditure was incurred. This will normally be a freehold or leasehold interest in the property.

An interest does not cease to be the relevant interest just because of the creation of a new interest to which it is subject. So, for example, a freeholder who has the relevant interest will not lose that interest just because he grants a lease. No writing-down allowance is given, though, if the person has granted a long lease for a capital sum.

A person who does not have the relevant interest at the time he incurs the conversion or renovation expenditure may claim the allowances provided he is entitled to an interest in the qualifying building as a result of the conversion.

The purchaser of the relevant interest in a qualifying building is not entitled to claim BPRAs, even if the vendor is required to bring in a disposal value. The system of giving BPRAs is in this way like the code for flat conversion allowances but differs from other parts of the capital allowances code in this respect.

The issue of when a lease terminates can have bearing on the definition of 'relevant interest'. The rules exactly mirror those applying for the purposes of flat conversion allowances (see 122-050).

Legislation: CAA 2001, s. 360E–360I, 360Z3

120-300 Initial allowances

The person incurring the qualifying expenditure is entitled to an initial allowance equal to 100% of the expenditure for the chargeable period in which the expenditure is incurred. The person may choose to claim a lesser amount, in which case the balance of relief is given by means of writing-down allowances in subsequent periods.

No initial allowance is given to the extent that the expenditure is taken into account for the purposes of a relevant grant or a relevant payment towards the expenditure.

Legislation: CAA 2001, s. 360G(3), 360L

120-350 Writing-down allowances

The amount of the writing-down allowance is 25% per year on a straight line basis but:

- a lesser amount may be claimed;
- the 25% figure is increased or decreased proportionately for chargeable periods that are longer or shorter than one year;
- no writing-down allowance is available to the extent that the expenditure is taken into account for the purposes of a relevant grant or a relevant payment towards the expenditure; and
- the amount of a writing-down allowance is capped at the residue of qualifying expenditure, the amount of which is to be calculated 'immediately before writing off the writing-down allowance at the end of the chargeable period'. The residue of expenditure is the qualifying expenditure not yet written off.

Writing-down allowances may only be claimed where, at the end of the chargeable period, the claimant has a relevant interest in a qualifying building and has not granted a long lease on the building, i.e. one that exceeds 50 years.

If a relevant payment or grant is made after an initial or writing-down allowance has been made then the allowance is to be withdrawn to that extent; assessments are to be made or adjusted as necessary (but within three years of the end of the chargeable period) to implement this.

For the avoidance of doubt, the 25% figure did *not* reduce to 20% from April 2008 (at which time such a reduction was made for plant and machinery allowances).

Legislation: CAA 2001, s. 360I, 360J, 360L

120-400 Balancing allowances and charges

Principles

If a balancing event takes place within seven years of the date on which the premises were first used, or were first suitable for letting for the purposes of a trade, etc. or as an office, then a balancing adjustment will be made. A balancing charge will recover excess allowances that have been given and a balancing allowance will give further tax relief.

If more than one balancing event occurs, it is only the first that gives rise to a balancing allowance or charge.

No balancing allowance is available, or charge made, if the balancing event occurs more than seven years after the time the premises were first used, or were first suitable for letting for the purposes of a trade, etc. or as an office.

A statutory table in lists the possible balancing events and the proceeds – received or receivable by the person who incurred the expenditure which are deemed to arise from each event.

Legislation: CAA 2001, s. 360M, 360O

Calculation of balancing adjustments

Balancing adjustments are calculated by comparing the 'residue of qualifying expenditure' and the proceeds (per the table referred to above) from the balancing event. The residue is defined broadly as the amount of qualifying expenditure that has not yet been written off (but see below).

If the proceeds exceed the residue, then there is a balancing charge equal to the difference. However, the balancing charge may not exceed the total allowances (initial or writing-down) made to the person in respect of the qualifying expenditure.

If the residue exceeds the proceeds, then there is a balancing allowance equal to the difference.

There is a special rule where the balancing event is the end of a lease. The table shows proceeds equal to the market value of the relevant interest. However, this only applies if there is a person with a superior interest to the relevant interest and who is connected to the person with the relevant interest. Although the legislation does not explicitly provide for this, it is assumed that in other cases the lease ending will give rise to nil proceeds.

Legislation: CAA 2001, s. 360Off.

Residue of qualifying expenditure

The residue can be expressed as:

An initial allowance reduces the residue at the time that the qualifying business premises are first used, or first suitable for letting, for the purposes of a trade, etc. or as an office. A writing-down allowance reduces the residue at the end of the chargeable period for which it is made.

If:

- a balancing event occurs at the end of a chargeable period; and
- a writing-down allowance is made for that chargeable period in respect of the qualifying expenditure,

then the residue should be calculated after deducting the writing-down allowance.

Legislation: CAA 2001, s. 360P, 360R

120-450 Demolition of the qualifying building

A special rule applies if the qualifying building is demolished. In practice, this will only be relevant if the qualifying building is demolished during the first seven years (and, by being demolished, ceases to be a qualifying building). This is because writing-down allowances are only available for chargeable periods at the end of which the property is a qualifying building.

If the person who incurred the qualifying expenditure incurs the cost of demolition, then the net cost of demolition is added to the residue. The result of this is that the net cost of demolition will be relieved as a balancing allowance or will reduce the impact of a balancing charge.

The net cost of demolition is defined as the cost of demolition, less the cost of any proceeds for the sale of the remains of the qualifying building.

Legislation: CAA 2001, s. 360S

120-500 Other issues

Anti-avoidance

Anti-avoidance rules provide for market value if sales are between connected persons or are transactions to obtain a tax advantage. There are also rules to prevent businesses from entering into artificial transactions that depress the market value of an asset prior to a sale to a connected person.

Legislation: CAA 2001, s. 567ff.

Apportionments

Sale receipts (or other types of receipt) which relate partly to buildings subject to business premises renovation allowances and partly to other assets are to be apportioned on a just and reasonable basis.

Legislation: CAA 2001, s. 360Z2

Additional VAT liabilities and rebates

Additional VAT liabilities and rebates may be taken into account for the purposes of giving allowances or making balancing charges.

Legislation: CAA 2001, s. 360T

Flat conversion allowances

122-000 Introduction and overview

As part of the tax simplification programme this relief will not apply to expenditure after 5 April 2013, although the legislation will remain relevant until April 2020 which is the latest date that a balancing allowance or charge may arise.

Capital allowances until then are available in respect of capital expenditure incurred on:

- the conversion of part of a 'qualifying building' into a 'qualifying flat';
- the renovation of a flat in a qualifying building if the flat is, or will be, a qualifying flat; or
- repairs to a qualifying building, to the extent that the repairs are incidental to expenditure on such a renovation or conversion.

The rules are similar to those for industrial buildings allowances, but are considerably simpler. In particular:

- 100% initial allowances will generally be available;
- to the extent that initial allowances are not claimed, or a reduced amount is claimed, writing-down allowances are available at the rate of 25% of the qualifying expenditure;
- there are no balancing charges for events more than seven years after the completion of the flat; and
- entitlement to allowances is not transferable.

Legislation: CAA 2001, s. 393B; FA 2012, Sch. 39, para. 36

Tax Reporter: ¶254-000

122-050 Definitions

Qualifying building

A building is a qualifying building if:

- all or most of the ground floor of the building is authorised for business use;
- it must appear that, when the building was constructed, the storeys above the ground floor were for use primarily as one or more dwellings (in other words, only the ground floor (and basement) were meant for business use);
- the building must not have more than four storeys above the ground floor (excluding the attic unless it is or has been in use as a dwelling or part of a dwelling; and
- the construction of the building must have been completed before 1 January 1980 – later extensions do not fall foul of this rule provided that they were completed before 1 January 2001.

'Authorised for business use' applies the definitions in rating legislation. The actual definition depends on the location of the building and reference should be made to the HMRC manual.

Legislation: CAA 2001, s. 393C

Other Material: HMRC *Capital Allowances Manual* CA43200

Qualifying flat

A flat is a qualifying flat if it is:

- in a qualifying building;
- suitable for letting as a dwelling;
- held for the purpose of short-term letting (no more than five years);
- accessible without using the part of the ground floor of the building that is authorised for business use (as defined);
- has four or fewer rooms – a room does not include a kitchen or bathroom, nor does a room include any closet, hallway or cloakroom not exceeding five square metres in area;
- not a 'high-value flat' (as defined);
- not created or renovated as part of a scheme involving the creation or renovation of a high-value flat; and
- not let to a person connected with the person who incurred the expenditure on the conversion or renovation – 'connected' has the meaning given in CAA 2001, s. 575.

If a flat is a qualifying flat immediately before a period during which it is temporarily unsuitable for letting as a dwelling, then it is to be treated as a qualifying flat during that period.

Legislation: CAA 2001, s. 393D

Flat

A 'flat' is a dwelling which forms a separate set of premises forming part of a building with some form of horizontal division from another part of the building. The definition ensures that duplexes would qualify (as the flat need not be on one level). The horizontal division ensures that converting a property into semi-detached or terraced 'houses' would not qualify. It would seem that maisonettes (with separate entrances) would not necessarily qualify if the entrances are on the same level. However, a separate basement entrance might not fall foul of the horizontal division rule.

Legislation: CAA 2001, s. 393A(3)

High-value flat

A high-value flat is one for which the notional rent exceeds the relevant limit set out in the table in CAA 2001, s. 393E(5), as set out below.

The relevant limits in the table may be amended by Treasury Order.

Number of rooms	In Greater London	Elsewhere
1 or 2	£350 per week	£150 per week
3	£425 per week	£225 per week
4	£480 per week	£300 per week

The notional rent is the rent that could be reasonably expected for the flat when the conversion or renovation expenditure is first incurred on the following assumptions.

- The conversion or renovation is complete.
- The flat is let furnished.
- No premiums are payable to the landlord or any person connected with the landlord.
- The tenant is not connected with the person incurring the expenditure on the conversion or renovation.
- For a flat in England or Wales, it is let on an assured shorthold tenancy.
- For a flat in Scotland, it is let on a short assured tenancy.

Legislation: CAA 2001, s. 393E

Relevant interest

Only the person incurring the expenditure can qualify for flat conversion allowances and only if that person has the 'relevant interest' in the flat. Broadly, the relevant interest in relation to any expenditure is the interest to which the person who incurred the expenditure was entitled when he incurred it.

Legislation: CAA 2001, s. 393A(2), 393F–393G

Qualifying expenditure

Qualifying expenditure is capital expenditure, incurred on or in connection with one of the following two categories:

- the conversion of a qualifying building into a qualifying flat;
- the renovation of a flat in a qualifying building if the flat will be a qualifying flat;
- the renovation of a qualifying flat in a qualifying building; or
- repairs to a qualifying building to the extent that they are incidental to the conversion or renovation listed above.

Conversion or renovation expenditure only qualifies, however, if the building was either unused (or used only for storage) for at least a year before the conversion or renovation work began.

Certain expenditure cannot be qualifying expenditure, namely expenditure incurred on or in connection with:

- the acquisition of land;
- the acquisition of rights over land;
- the development of land adjoining or adjacent to a qualifying building (unless, presumably, it is itself a qualifying building);
- the extension of a qualifying building, except to the extent required for the purpose of providing a means of access to a qualifying flat; and
- the provision of chattels (e.g. furniture) or furnishings.

'Capital expenditure' is any expenditure that would not be allowable as a revenue deduction in calculating the taxable profits of a UK property business.

Legislation: CAA 2001, s. 393B

122-100 Initial allowances

A person who incurs qualifying expenditure on a flat may be entitled to an initial allowance.

Initial allowances are given at 100% of the qualifying expenditure. However, a person can claim a reduced initial allowance. The initial allowance is made for the chargeable period in which the qualifying expenditure is incurred.

However, an initial allowance is not available if it is not a qualifying flat when the flat is first suitable for residential letting.

Any initial allowance made (when the expenditure was incurred) but no longer available must be withdrawn and assessments amended as a result. This will be necessary if when the flat is first suitable for residential letting:

- it is not a qualifying flat; or
- it has been sold by the person to whom the initial allowance was made.

Legislation: CAA 2001, s. 393H, 393I

122-150 Writing-down allowances

Entitlement

Writing-down allowances are available for a chargeable period to the person who incurred qualifying expenditure on the flat, if at the end of the chargeable period:

- the person is entitled to the relevant interest in the flat;
- the flat is a qualifying flat; and
- the person has not granted a lease in excess of 50 years in respect of the flat (but the rules in CTA 2009, s. 243 (corporation tax) and ITTOIA 2005, s. 303ff. apply in certain circumstances to treat a shorter lease be as a longer one).

Legislation: CAA 2001, s. 393J

Amount of allowances

For expenditure for which the 100% initial allowance is not claimed, writing-down allowances are available. They are calculated as the lower of:

- 25% of the qualifying expenditure; and
- the residue of qualifying expenditure (as defined) immediately before writing-down allowances are calculated).

The 25% writing-down rate is increased or decreased proportionately for chargeable periods that are longer or shorter than one year.

Further, a person may claim a reduced writing-down allowance if desired.

Legislation: CAA 2001, s. 393J–393L

122-200 Balancing adjustments

Overview

Unrelieved expenditure can be relieved if a 'balancing event' occurs. This will be in the form of a balancing allowance made on the person who incurred the qualifying expenditure.

However, no balancing allowance is available if the balancing event occurs more than seven years after the flat was first suitable for letting. It is therefore important to ensure that sufficient writing-down allowances are taken before the balancing event, in order to avoid expenditure being stranded.

Conversely, there will be no balancing charge for balancing events occurring after the seven-year cut-off. However, if there is a balancing event during the seven-year period then any surplus allowances are reclaimed in the form of a balancing charge and. The balancing charge will be made on the person who incurred the qualifying expenditure.

If more than one balancing event occurs, it is only the first that gives rise to a balancing allowance or charge.

Legislation: CAA 2001, s. 393M

Balancing events

The following are balancing events:

- the sale of the relevant interest in the flat;
- the grant of a long-lease for the payment of a capital sum;
- if the relevant interest is a lease, the end of that lease – however, this does not constitute a balancing event, if the person with the lease acquires the immediately superior interest in the flat when the lease ends;
- the death of the person who incurred the qualifying expenditure – there does not seem to be an equivalent provision for the winding up of companies or trusts;
- the destruction or demolition of the flat; or
- the flat ceasing to be a qualifying flat without being demolished or destroyed.

Legislation: CAA 2001, s. 393N

Calculation of balancing adjustments

Broadly, a balancing adjustment is based on the difference between the 'residue of qualifying expenditure' and the proceeds from the balancing event. If the proceeds exceed the residue, then there is a balancing charge equal to the difference, but the balancing charge may not exceed the total allowances (initial or writing-down) made to the person in respect of the qualifying expenditure.

If the residue exceeds the proceeds, or if there are no proceeds, then there is a balancing allowance equal to the excess.

There is a statutory table identifying the proceeds to be taken into account.

Where the balancing event is the lease coming to an end and the person, with the relevant interest, is connected with a person with any superior interest, then the proceeds from the event are equal to the market value of the relevant interest. It is assumed that, in other cases where the lease ends, the proceeds will be nil if no proceeds are actually received by the lessee.

Legislation: CAA 2001, s. 393O, 393P

122-250 Residue of expenditure

The residue of qualifying expenditure needs to be ascertained to ensure that the total of initial and writing-down allowances given do not exceed the qualifying expenditure. Similarly, it is needed to determine the type and amount of any balancing adjustment on a balancing event occurring within the first seven years of the flat first being available for letting.

The residue can be expressed as:

An initial allowance reduces the residue at the time that the flat is first suitable for letting as a dwelling. A writing-down allowance reduces the residue at the end of the chargeable period to which it relates.

If:

- a balancing event occurs at the end of a chargeable period; and
- a writing-down allowance is made for that chargeable period in respect of the qualifying expenditure,

then the residue should be calculated after deducting the writing-down allowance.

Legislation: CAA 2001, s. 393K, 393M, 393R

122-300 Giving effect to allowances and charges

Effect is given to allowances and charges by treating them as expenses or receipts of the UK property business.

Legislation: CAA 2001, s. 393T

122-350 Other matters

Demolition costs

A special rule applies if the flat is demolished. In practice, this will only be relevant if the flat is demolished during the first seven years after which it is first suitable for letting as a dwelling (and by being demolished ceases to be a qualifying flat). This is because writing-down allowances are only available for chargeable periods at the end of which the flat is a qualifying flat.

If the person who incurred the qualifying expenditure incurs the cost of demolition, then the net cost of demolition is added to the residue. The result of this is that the net cost of demolition will be relieved as a balancing allowance or will reduce the impact of a balancing charge.

The net cost of demolition is defined as the cost of demolition, less the cost of any proceeds for the sale of the remains of the flat.

The demolition costs may not be used both to increase the residue and to make up qualifying expenditure (under any Part of the Capital Allowances Act) in respect of any replacement property.

Legislation: CAA 2001, s. 393R, 393S

Apportionments

Sale receipts which relate partly to flats subject to flat conversion allowances and partly to other assets should be apportioned on a just and reasonable basis. This applies also to other proceeds arising from balancing events. However, this is subject to the other rules providing for apportionments.

Legislation: CAA 2001, s. 393U

Termination of leases

If a person remains in possession of a flat after the termination of a lease without a new lease being granted to that person, then the old lease is treated as continuing while the lessee remains in possession of the flat.

If a person is granted a new lease as a result of exercising an option available to that person under the old lease, then the new lease is treated as a continuation of the old.

Where a lessor pays a sum to the lessee on termination of the lease, the lease is then treated as coming to an end by surrender – with the payment treated as the consideration for the surrender.

Where:

- on the termination of the lease, another lease is granted to a third party; and
- in connection with the transaction, the new lessee pays a sum to the original lessee,

the two leases are treated as the same lease assigned by the original lessee to the new lessee in consideration for the payment.

A 'lease' includes a tenancy and any agreement for a lease once the lease term has begun; however, a lease does not include a mortgage.

Legislation: CAA 2001, s. 393V, 393W

Research and development allowances

123-000 Overview

Research and development allowances (RDAs) are available for certain capital expenditure on research and development. Separate relief, not under the capital allowances code, is available for qualifying revenue expenditure (ITTOIA 2005, s. 87; CTA 2009, s. 87).

Both the capital allowance relief and the revenue relief are generous compared to reliefs for other types of expenditure.

This division is concerned solely with the allowances available for capital expenditure. These are given where a person incurs 'qualifying expenditure' (see 123-150) on 'research and development' (see 123-100).

Research and development allowances are given at 100% and balancing charges can arise where an asset is sold, demolished or destroyed. Ceasing to use an asset for research and development purposes does not trigger a balancing charge. RDAs are only available for traders, not for those carrying on a profession.

Tax Reporter: ¶256-000

123-050 Giving effect to allowances and charges

An allowance in respect of qualifying expenditure is treated as a trading expense. A balancing charge in respect of such expenditure is treated as a trading receipt.

Research and development allowances are given for the chargeable period in which the expenditure is incurred, but if incurred before the trade was set up, then in the chargeable period beginning with the commencement.

Legislation: CAA 2001, s. 441(2), 447(3), 450

123-100 Meaning of 'research and development'

The capital allowance legislation used to state that the term 'research and development' was to be defined by reference to ICTA 1988, s. 837A, but 'includes oil and gas exploration and appraisal'.

However, CAA 2001, Sch. 1, Pt. 2 (which contains 'defined expressions' for capital allowance purposes) has since 6 April 2007 pointed to CAA 2001, s. 437.

Broadly, the concept is based on generally accepted accounting practice, but subject to certain statutory provisions that can override such practice.

Expenditure on research and development includes both expenditure for carrying out research and development as such, and also the cost of providing facilities for carrying out such work. Examples of capital expenditure which may qualify for allowances include expenditure on the provision of laboratories, pilot plant and other research equipment. There is no requirement that the plant should be fixed so the provision of a car for an employee involved in research work may qualify for allowances.

However, the term excludes expenditure incurred on acquiring rights in, or rights arising out of, research and development. Thus the cost of acquiring patent rights, for example, is excluded.

No allowance is given in respect of expenditure on land, except such proportion as is attributable to existing buildings or structures already on that land, or plant or machinery which has become a fixture. Nor is an allowance given in respect of expenditure on a dwelling; where, however, less than one-quarter of the capital expenditure on a building is attributable to a part-use as a dwelling, the whole building may qualify (CAA 2001, s. 438(3)–(6)).

In applying this 25% test, any additional VAT liability or rebate is to be ignored.

Legislation: CAA 2001, s. 438ff.

Other Material: HMRC *Capital Allowances Manual* CA60300; HMRC *Corporate Intangibles Research and Development Manual* CIRD81900

Tax Reporter: ¶256-200

123-150 Qualifying expenditure

The following conditions must be met if expenditure is to be qualifying expenditure:

- a person must incur capital expenditure on research and development;
- the expenditure must be undertaken directly by the person incurring the expenditure, or undertaken on his behalf (see *Gaspet Ltd (formerly Saga Petroleum (UK) Ltd) v Elliss (HMIT)*);

Example 1

Researcher Ltd pays £1 million for a laboratory (excluding the part allocated to land).

Although very profitable, it benefits from group relief and is therefore able to restrict its claim to £800,000, i.e. leaving £200,000 unclaimed. The laboratory is sold (again, excluding the land value) for £900,000 three years later.

The balancing charge is £700,000, calculated as the excess of proceeds (£900,000) over unclaimed allowances (£200,000).

If, instead, the sale price at the later date was £1.2m, the balancing charge would initially be calculated as £1m, but this would be capped at £800,000, being the amount of allowances claimed in relation to the expenditure in question.

Legislation: CAA 2001, s. 442–443

Disposal events and values

A disposal value has to be brought into account if the person ceases to own the asset in question or if it is demolished or destroyed. The disposal value to be brought into account is as follows:

- If the disposal is a sale for an amount which represents at least full market value, the disposal value is the figure of net sale proceeds.
- If the asset is demolished or destroyed, the disposal value is the amount of any compensation or insurance moneys received, together with any amount received for the remains of the asset.
- In any other case, the disposal value is the open market value of the asset (except that the disposal value of an oil licence may in certain circumstances be treated as nil.

If the person incurs demolition costs, the disposal value is to be reduced accordingly.

Legislation: CAA 2001, s. 443, 553(2)

123-300 Other issues

Sales between connected persons and persons under common control

Where the seller and buyer are connected persons or are under common control, a sale of research and development expenditure is taken at market value for the purposes of any balancing adjustment, even if the sale is at an undervalue or overvalue.

To the extent that capital expenditure on research and development is not already covered by 100% allowances, where there is no significant element of gaining a tax advantage, the transferor and transferee may generally elect by notice in writing to the inspector to treat the sale as taking place at the tax written-down value, if that is lower than market value. The election also has the effect of treating the buyer and the seller as one continuous owner as regards any balancing charge for events after the date of the sale, i.e. in determining allowances to be clawed back, etc.

Where it appears with respect to a sale (or with respect to transactions of which the sale is one) that the sole or main benefit which might have been expected to accrue to any of the parties was the obtaining of certain tax advantages, the provisions which apply for industrial buildings allowances purposes apply equally for the purposes of research and development expenditure.

Legislation: CAA 2001, s. 567–569

Interaction with capital goods scheme

A person may incur allowable research and development expenditure and incur an additional VAT liability while he still owns the asset representing such expenditure. That liability is capital expenditure incurred on the research and development.

Any VAT rebate, which arises while the person still owns the asset, is taxed as a trading receipt for the period in which the rebate is made, unless it is brought into account in making an allowance or charge. If the person no longer carries on the trade, the rebate accrues for tax purposes immediately before the trade ceased.

Any VAT rebate, which arises while the person still owns the asset and which is taxed as a trading receipt under CAA 2001, s. 448, reduces the amount of the expenditure and allowance for the purposes of calculating balancing charges.

Legislation: CAA 2001, s. 443(6), 447ff.

Other allowances

Mineral extraction allowances

125-000 Overview

Mineral extraction allowances (MEAs) are available in respect of capital expenditure incurred in connection with mineral extraction.

To qualify for relief, a person must be carrying on a mineral extraction trade and must incur qualifying expenditure. Relief is not available to lessors of land containing minerals.

The relief applies to mineral extraction activities carried on worldwide, including sand and gravel extraction, hard rock mining, the oil sector and geothermal energy.

Expenditure qualifying for MEAs includes expenditure on exploration, access to a source, acquisition of the source, construction of certain works in connection with the source, the working of the source itself, and restoration of the site after work has ceased. Expenditure attributable to the value of land, rather than to the value of the mineral deposits, is excluded. Other items which do not generally qualify include processing plants, buildings for employees' accommodation or welfare, and offices.

The normal rate of allowance is 25% per annum on a reducing balance basis. In respect of the acquisition of a 'mineral asset', i.e. the mineral deposits or rights over them, the rate is 10% per annum on a reducing balance basis. First-year allowances are available only for expenditure incurred by a company for the purposes of a ring-fence trade.

Each asset is written down individually: there is no 'pooling' as for plant and machinery (but in practice HMRC do not object to the grouping together of assets for computational convenience provided that individual sources are dealt with separately and expenditure that is written down at the 10% rate is distinguished from other expenditure).

Where an asset is sold to a person who in turn carries on a trade of mineral extraction, the purchaser may claim allowances for his acquisition costs to the extent that they do not exceed the residue of expenditure which qualified for allowances in the hands of the seller.

Allowances are available in respect of a part of, or a share in, an asset of any description as they are for the asset itself, so long as the asset is used for the purposes of a trade.

Expenditure which is incurred by a person before commencement of a trade is treated as incurred on the first day of trading. However, the availability of allowances is restricted where pre-trading expenditure is incurred on mineral exploration and access.

Legislation: CAA 2001, s. 394, 401–402, 435

Other Material: HMRC *Capital Allowances Manual* CA50110, CA50410

Tax Reporter: ¶255-500

125-050 Giving effect to allowances and charges

A person carrying on a mineral extraction trade gives effect to allowances in calculating the profits of that trade. So:

- any allowance is treated as an expense of the trade; and
- any balancing charge is treated as a trading receipt.

Legislation: CAA 2001, s. 432

125-100 Qualifying expenditure

Mineral extraction allowances are available in respect of expenditure on :

- mineral exploration and access;
- acquisition of a mineral asset (in the case of acquisition of a Petroleum Act license, or an interest therein, limited to expenditure of the original licensee;
- construction of works which, when the source is worked out, are likely to be of little or no remaining value to the person working it at that time;
- construction of works in connection with a foreign concession, which are likely to become valueless to the person working the source immediately before the concession comes to an end; and
- the cost of obtaining planning permission.

The above general rules are subject to exceptions and qualification.

Legislation: CAA 2001, s. 395

Restriction of qualifying expenditure

Restrictions are applied to the amount of allowable qualifying expenditure where a mineral asset was previously acquired or brought into existence by a 'previous trader' carrying on a trade of mineral extraction whose expenditure was either allowed as qualifying expenditure for capital allowance purposes or allowed as a deduction in computing trading profits.

Legislation: CAA 2001, s. 407–409

Demolition costs

If demolition costs exceed any consideration received for the remains of an asset representing qualifying expenditure, the excess is added to qualifying expenditure in calculating any balancing allowance or balancing charge.

125-150 Land

Expenditure on mineral assets may be qualifying expenditure. While the definition of mineral asset includes land comprising mineral deposits, or any interest in or right over such land, it is not intended that allowances should be available in respect of land. They are only available in respect of mineral deposits contained therein. Various restrictions apply to achieve this effect.

Legislation: CAA 2001, s. 399

Unsuccessful planning applications

Where expenditure is incurred on an unsuccessful planning application, that expenditure is regarded as expenditure on mineral exploration and access, and qualifies for allowances. The cost of pursuing an appeal against a refusal of planning permission is also included in these costs.

Legislation: CAA 2001, s. 396

Land restoration

The rules allow the expense of restoring a site of mineral extraction if incurred within three years of the last day of trading. It must not have previously been deducted for income or corporation tax purposes, and it must be such that it would be qualifying expenditure if the trade was still being carried on. If it qualifies, it is deemed to have been incurred on the last trading day.

Legislation: CAA 2001, s. 416

125-175 Buildings

Expenditure on buildings and 'works' may be qualifying expenditure but only if they are likely to be of little or no value to the person working the source when it is worked out or when a foreign concession ends. The following buildings, however, are specifically excluded.

- Works constructed wholly or mainly for subjecting the new product to any process, other than for preparing the raw product for use as such.
- Buildings for occupation by or welfare of workers (which may qualify for industrial buildings allowance.
- Buildings constructed wholly for use as offices.
- Buildings constructed partly for use as offices, unless 10% or less of the capital expenditure is attributable to office use.

The term 'works' is not defined, but (per HMRC) 'can include railway lines, roads and jetties at the site of mineral extraction'.

There is also a possibility that certain buildings will qualify for allowances under other codes of allowance (especially industrial buildings allowances).

Legislation: CAA 2001, s. 399

Other Material: HMRC *Capital Allowances Manual* CA50230

125-200 Writing-down allowances

Writing-down allowances are given for the accounting period in which expenditure is incurred or the tax year which relates to the 'basis period' in which it was incurred. The allowance is on a reducing balance on the excess of expenditure over 'disposal receipts' for the chargeable period or earlier chargeable periods.

Legislation: CAA 2001, s. 417

Rate of allowance

For expenditure on the acquisition of a 'mineral asset', the rate is 10% and for other qualifying expenditure the rate is 25%. The rate of relief is proportionately reduced or increased where the chargeable period is less or more than a year. Also, the rate of relief is proportionately reduced if the trade has been carried on for only part of a year.

Legislation: CAA 2001, s. 418

Disposal receipts

A person who has incurred 'qualifying expenditure' on assets must bring into account as a disposal receipt the 'disposal value' in respect of any assets disposed of or which otherwise permanently cease to be used for the trade of mineral extraction. Use for certain new development constitutes such permanent cessation. Disposal value is generally determined as in relation to plant and machinery. Any capital sum received which is attributable to the expenditure must also be brought into account.

Where part of a disposal receipt is from land, that part is disregarded for the purpose of calculating subsequent allowances. The excess of disposal value (not land value) as exceeds the 'undeveloped market value' of the interest in land is what is taken into account.

Legislation: CAA 2001, s. 420–424

125-225 Balancing allowances

A balancing allowance arises in the following circumstances.

- Pre-trading exploration expenditure (CAA 2001, s. 426).
- Abortive exploration expenditure (CAA 2001, s. 427).
- Work on mineral deposit ceasing (CAA 2001, s. 428).
- Public works ceasing to be used for mineral extraction (CAA 2001, s. 429).
- Disposal of an asset (CAA 2001, s. 430(1)).
- Loss or destruction of an asset (CAA 2001, s. 430(2)).
- Permanent discontinuance of the trade (CAA 2001, s. 431).

125-250 Balancing charges

Where 'disposal receipts' in a chargeable period exceed the tax written-down value of the asset at the beginning of the period in respect of a particular item of qualifying expenditure, a balancing charge arises. The balancing charge cannot exceed total allowances given on the asset.

Legislation: CAA 2001, s. 417(3), 418(4)

Know-how allowances

125-500 Overview

The term 'know-how' is defined for capital allowance purposes to mean certain industrial information and techniques.

Know-how allowances are not given for expenditure incurred by companies from 1 April 2002. Such expenditure is instead dealt with under the *Finance Act* 2002 rules relating to intellectual property.

For income tax purposes, capital allowances are available where a person incurs qualifying capital expenditure on the acquisition of know-how. The allowances are only available to traders.

Know-how is specifically stated to be property for capital allowance purposes. As such, references in the *Capital Allowances Act* 2001 to the purchase and sale of property include the acquisition and disposal of know-how.

No first-year allowances are given for know-how expenditure. Annual writing-down allowances are available, generally at 25%, on a reducing-balance basis.

As with expenditure on plant or machinery, expenditure on know-how forms a pool, and allowances are given each year on the excess of the written-down value over disposals brought into account. Any sales of know-how on which allowances have been given must be brought into account. Writing-down allowances are not given in the period of permanent discontinuance.

Pre-trading expenditure is treated as incurred on the commencement of trade.

Legislation: CAA 2001, s. 453ff.

Other Material: HMRC *Capital Allowances Manual* CA70001ff.

Tax Reporter: ¶257-000

125-550 Giving effect to allowances and charges

A trader gives effect to allowances in calculating the profits of the trade. So:

- any allowance under the know-how code is treated as an expense of the trade; and
- any balancing charge is treated as a trading receipt.

Legislation: CAA 2001, s. 463

125-600 Meaning of know-how

'Know-how' means any industrial information and techniques likely to assist in the manufacture or processing of goods or materials, or in the working of a mine, oil well or other source of mineral deposits (including the searching for, discovery, or testing of deposits or the winning of access to such deposits), or in the carrying out of any agricultural, forestry or fishing operations.

HMRC have stated that in their view, capital allowances are not available on the acquisition of *commercial* know-how (including, for example, a customer list) and that know-how which does not assist directly in the manufacturing and processing operations is commercial know-how, and is not within the statutory definition.

Examples of commercial know-how which would not qualify for capital allowances would be information about marketing, packaging or distributing a manufactured product, as such information is concerned with selling rather than the manufacture of the product.

Legislation: CAA 2001, s. 452(2)

Other Material: HMRC *Capital Allowances Manual* CA70030

125-650 Writing-down allowances

All qualifying expenditure must be put into a single pool, but with a separate pool for each trade. The plant and machinery concepts of short and long-life assets do not apply for know-how expenditure.

Writing-down allowances are given based on a pool of qualifying expenditure. The method of calculating allowances may be summarised as follows.

- Allowances are normally given each year at 25% of the value of the pool, on a reducing balance basis.
- A balancing charge will arise if a disposal value to be brought into account exceeds the expenditure left in the pool.
- A balancing allowance arises only on permanent discontinuance of the trade.
- Unlike the system for plant and machinery allowances, the disposal value is not restricted to original cost.

A proportionately reduced allowance is available if the chargeable period is less than a year, or if the trade has been carried on for less than the whole year. Conversely, a proportionately increased percentage is available if the chargeable period is more than a year.

Legislation: CAA 2001, s. 456, 458

125-700 Balancing adjustments

When a trader disposes of know-how in respect of which allowances have been given, a balancing charge will arise if the disposal value exceeds the written-down value of the pool. The charge is made on the amount of the difference.

If an allowance falls to be made for the chargeable period related to the discontinuance of the trade, a balancing allowance is made equal to the excess of the written-down value of the pool less the disposal value to be brought into account.

Legislation: CAA 2001, s. 458

Patent allowances

126-000 Overview

Summary of statutory provisions

The rules relating to patents are scattered through various parts of the tax legislation. A summary of how the legislation works is as follows.

- A deduction for the cost of obtaining (i.e. establishing) a patent (ITTOIA 2005, s. 89).
- Capital allowances are given for the cost of buying patent rights (CAA 2001, s. 464ff., though for companies, these rules are broadly superseded by the FA 2002 legislation relating to intangible assets).
- Various taxation issues arise when patent rights are sold (ITTOIA 2005, s. 587ff.).
- Tax relief is granted for certain expenses by offsetting them against income from patents (ITTOIA 2005, s. 600ff.).

Capital allowances

Capital allowances are available when a person incurs qualifying expenditure on the purchase of 'patent rights'.

The system of giving patent allowances is in essence similar to that for plant and machinery, in that:

- expenditure is normally pooled; and
- allowances are given at an annual rate of 25% on a reducing balancing basis.

Allowances are only made to a person if he is carrying on a trade or if any income from the rights would be otherwise liable to income tax or corporation tax. Expenditure incurred for trade purposes by a person 'about to' carry it on is treated as if incurred on the first day of trading unless, before that time, he has sold the patent rights.

Patent allowances are not given for expenditure incurred by *companies* from 1 April 2002. Such expenditure is instead dealt with under the *Finance Act* 2002 rules relating to intellectual property.

Legislation: CAA 2001, s. 464ff.

Tax Reporter: ¶257-500

126-050 Meaning of patent rights

'Patent rights' means the right to do or authorise the doing of anything which would, but for that right, be an infringement of a patent. Expenditure on patent rights includes expenditure on a licence in respect of a patent and on obtaining a right to acquire patent rights in the future in respect of an invention for which a patent has not yet been granted.

Legislation: CAA 2001, s. 464–466

126-100 Writing-down allowances

Writing-down allowances are given at an annual rate of 25% on a reducing-balance basis. A proportionately reduced percentage is available if the chargeable period is less than a year, or (for income tax) if the trade has been carried on for less than the whole year. Conversely, a proportionately increased percentage is available for income tax purposes if the chargeable period is more than a year.

Allowances are thus given on a basis similar to that applying for expenditure on plant or machinery. Expenditure on patent rights forms a pool, and allowances are given each year on the excess of the written-down value over disposals brought into account. Any sales of patent rights on which allowances have been given must be brought into account, but the total disposal value of one or more sales cannot exceed the claimant's capital expenditure.

Writing-down allowances are not given in the period of permanent discontinuance, although a balancing adjustment may be made.

Legislation: CAA 2001, s. 464, 472ff.

126-150 Balancing adjustments

Where in a chargeable period a person's disposals out of the patent rights pool exceed the written-down value of the pool, a balancing charge will arise; the amount of the charge equals the excess.

If an allowance falls to be made in a period when either:

- the trade is permanently discontinued; or
- the last of the patent rights on which allowances have been given come to an end without being revived and without having been disposed of,

a balancing allowance will be given equal to the excess of the written-down value of the pool over any disposal value to be taken into account.

As with writing-down allowances, this closely mirrors the balancing adjustments applicable to plant or machinery.

Legislation: CAA 2001, s. 471–472

126-200 Anti-avoidance rules

Two special provisions apply where a claimant has purchased patent rights from a connected person.

First, the restriction of balancing charges to the total capital expenditure incurred is to be read as if it referred to the capital expenditure incurred by whichever party to the transaction incurred the greatest expenditure. This removes any advantage from sales between connected persons designed to minimise balancing charges or maximise balancing allowances.

Secondly, the amount on which the purchaser is entitled to allowances is restricted to the disposal value brought into account by the seller.

The second rule described immediately above also applies, where the parties are not connected, if it appears that the sole or main benefit expected of the sale (or of transactions including the sale) is the obtaining of an allowance.

Where no value is brought into account by the vendor, if the vendor receives a capital sum chargeable to tax as income, the purchaser's allowable expenditure is restricted to that sum. In any other case, the purchaser's allowable expenditure is restricted to the smallest of:

- the open market value;
- the capital expenditure incurred by the vendor on acquiring the rights;
- the capital expenditure incurred by any person connected with the vendor on acquiring the rights.

Legislation: CAA 2001, s. 477, 481

Dredging allowances

126-500 Initial and writing-down allowances

An annual writing-down allowance of 4% (2% if expenditure was incurred before 6 November 1962) of expenditure is available where all of the following criteria are complied with:

(1) a person is carrying on a 'qualifying trade';

(2) that person incurs capital expenditure;

(3) that capital expenditure is incurred on dredging; and

(4) either:

   (a) the trade consists of the maintenance or improvement of the navigation of a harbour, estuary or waterway; or

   (b) the dredging is for the benefit of vessels coming to, leaving, or using any dock or other premises occupied by the taxpayer for the purposes of the trade.

Dredging carried on by a harbour authority for the purposes of keeping their channels clear for navigation is generally considered to be revenue expenditure (see *Whelan v Dover Harbour Board*).

Legislation: CAA 2001, s. 484

Case: *Whelan v Dover Harbour Board* (1934) 18 TC 555

Other Material: HMRC *Capital Allowances Manual* CA80100

Tax Reporter: ¶258-000

126-550 Dredging defined

'Dredging' does not include anything done other than in the interests of navigation. Subject to this qualification, dredging includes the removal of anything forming part of or projecting from the bed of the sea or of any inland water. The term also applies to the widening of inland waterways in the interests of navigation.

Legislation: CAA 2001, s. 484(3), (4)

126-600 Qualifying trade

A 'qualifying trade' is a trade or undertaking which, or part of which, consists of:

- the maintenance or improvement of the navigation of a harbour, estuary or waterway; or
- a qualifying trade for the purposes of industrial buildings allowances.

Where part of a trade qualifies, or where expenditure is incurred partly for the purposes of a qualifying trade and partly for other purposes, the expenditure is apportioned between the qualifying and non-qualifying parts. Allowances are given for expenditure relating to the qualifying part only.

Legislation: CAA 2001, s. 484(2), 485(2), (3)

126-650 Pre-trading expenditure

Capital expenditure incurred for the purposes of a trade not yet carried on by the taxpayer (but with a view to carrying it on) or incurred in connection with a dock or other premises not yet occupied by the taxpayer for the purposes of a qualifying trade (but with a view to so occupying the premises), nevertheless qualifies for an allowance in the first chargeable period when he both carries on the trade and occupies the dock, etc.

Legislation: CAA 2001, s. 486

126-700 Permanent discontinuance

On a permanent discontinuance of a 'qualifying trade', a balancing allowance is made equal to expenditure less allowances previously given. The term 'permanent discontinuance' does not include a deemed discontinuance (partnership change treated as a discontinuance or company ceasing to carry on a trade), but does include situations where a trade is sold other than to a connected person.

Legislation: CAA 2001, s. 488

126-750 Subsidies and contributions

A person who contributes a capital sum to another person's expenditure on dredging is treated as having incurred the expenditure and is, therefore, entitled to the allowances if he is carrying on a qualifying trade.

A person is not treated as having incurred expenditure for the purposes of any trade in so far as it is met directly or indirectly by the Crown, or by any government or public or local authority in or outside the UK, or by any other person where the sums contributed are not for the purposes of that trade.

Legislation: CAA 2001, s. 532ff.

Employment income

Key principles

130-000 Employment income

Tax is levied by the *Income Tax (Earnings and Pensions) Act* 2003 (ITEPA 2003) on employment income, pension income and social security income.

'Employment income' includes earnings, any amount treated as earnings and any amount which counts as employment income.

The term 'earnings' is in its turn defined to include:

- any salary, wages or fee;
- any gratuity or other profit or incidental benefit of any kind obtained by the employee if it is money or money's worth; or
- anything else that constitutes an emolument of the employment.

Round-sum allowances are generally taxable (subject to claims for necessary expenses: see 140-000ff.).

Although the term 'emoluments' has now largely disappeared from the legislation, its inclusion above ensures that everything treated as an emolument under old Sch. E principles remains within the charge to tax as earnings.

Prior to 6 April 2016, benefits in kind for employees earning less than £8,500 were only taxed *as earnings* if they were capable of being turned into money ('money's worth' as in the second category of earnings listed above) (*Tennant v Smith*). However, for employees paid over £8,500 p.a. ('higher paid employees'), benefits were taxable even if they are not able to be converted into money. This is because they are taxed as 'amounts treated as earnings' (see 132-020). With effect from 6 April 2016, the distinction between 'higher' and 'lower' paid employees was withdrawn.

Legislation: ITEPA 2003, s. 1, 7, 62(2)

Case: *Tennant v Smith* (1892) 3 TC 158

Expenses payments

The *Income Tax (Earnings and Pensions) Act* 2003 imposes a tax charge where:

> 'a sum is paid to an employee in a tax year if the sum is paid to the employee in respect of expenses, and is so paid by reason of the employment.'

In other words, if an employer reimburses an employee for an employment-related expense then the starting position is that that reimbursement is taxed in the same way as any payment of salary or wages. However, where the expenses in question meet certain strictly defined conditions, relief may be available to the employee (see 140-000ff).

Legislation: ITEPA 2003, s. 70, 218

Tax Reporter: ¶400-000

130-025 HMRC guidance for employee tax enquiries: telephone number

HMRC have published a single phone number for employees who need help with their tax enquiries: 0300 200 3300.

According to HMRC, 'employers can use this number too, for example if you need to confirm an employee's tax code. But you should continue to call the Employer Helpline for enquiries relating to running your payroll'.

130-050 Offices and employments

The provisions of the employment income parts of the *Income Tax (Earnings and Pensions) Act* 2003 that apply to employments apply equally to offices. 'Employee' means the office-holder and 'employer' means the person under whom the office-holder holds office. 'Office' includes in particular any position which has an existence independent of the person who holds it and may be filled by successive holders.

Legislation: ITEPA 2003, s. 5

Offices

The definition of an 'office' has been constructed on the basis of case law (notably *Great Western Railway Company v Bater (HMIT)* and *Edwards (HMIT) v Clinch*).

The statutory definition is not exhaustive, and so decided cases on the term 'office' in previous legislation still provide guidance. One important example of the holder of an office, as defined, is a company director: see 130-100.

A barrister's senior clerk who provides services under separate contracts with each member of the chambers has been held not to be the holder of an office (*McMenamin (HMIT) v Diggles*).

However, it is possible for a single contract to provide for both employment and independent services (*McManus v Griffiths (HMIT)*).

Legislation: ITEPA 2003, s. 5

Cases: *Great Western Railway Company v Bater (HMIT)* (1922) 8 TC 231; *Edwards (HMIT) v Clinch* [1982] BTC 109; *McMenamin (HMIT) v Diggles* [1991] BTC 218; *McManus v Griffiths (HMIT)* [1997] BTC 412

Doctors, dentists, solicitors, accountants

When doctors, dentists, solicitors or accountants are in private practice the profits of that practice will be chargeable to tax as profits of a profession or vocation under ITTOIA 2005, s. 5. However, it is quite common for such individuals to hold an office at the same time.

Thus, an accountant in private practice, who is also an auditor of a limited company, would be properly chargeable to tax under the employment income rules on the receipts from the office of auditor (*Walker v Carnaby, Harrower, Barham & Pykett*; *Ellis v Lucas*). Similarly, a solicitor or accountant in private practice who acts as a secretary/registrar to a company is also holding an office and the receipts from that office would also be properly chargeable to tax under the employment income rules (*IR Commrs v Brander and Cruickshank*).

In practice, when the person carries on a profession as well as holding an office, HMRC will often, as a matter of convenience, treat the receipts of the office as profits of the profession and charge them to tax under ITTOIA 2005, s. 5. Guidelines on this matter are given in ESC A37. The *Employment Income Manual* confirms that the treatment continues to apply since the enactment of ITEPA 2003.

Terminal payments in respect of an office (see 142-000ff.) are always dealt with under the strictly correct basis, using the employment income rules.

Cases: *Ellis v Lucas* (1966) 43 TC 276; *Walker v Carnaby, Harrower, Barham & Pykett* (1969) 46 TC 561; *IR Commrs v Brander and Cruickshank* (1970) 46 TC 574.

Other Material: HMRC *Employment Income Manual* EIM02500

Tax Reporter: ¶400-010

130-100 Directors

If a company director does not have a contract of employment with the company, but receives fees in his capacity as director, the director's fees will be derived from his office and will thus be within the charge to tax on employment income.

The term 'director' is defined in different places within the *Income Tax (Earnings and Pensions) Act* 2003, including:

- in ITEPA 2003, s. 67(1) for the purposes of the benefits code; and
- in ITEPA 2003, s. 548(1) in relation to certain priority share allocations.

A difficulty can arise in relation to shadow directors. There is no explicit tax definition of what a shadow director means, though the definition of 'director' at ITEPA 2003, s. 67(1) states that the term 'includes any person in accordance with whose directions or instructions the directors of the company ... are accustomed to act'.

The criminal case of *R v Dimsey and Allen* – and the related tax case – made it clear that the benefits in kind legislation applies equally to shadow directors.

Legislation: ITEPA 2003, s. 67(3)

Cases: *R v Dimsey and Allen* [2000] 1 Crim App R(S) 497; *R v Dimsey and Allen* [2001] BTC 421

Tax Reporter: ¶400-020

130-125 Companies which appoint directors of other companies

Companies sometimes appoint directors to the board of other companies by right or by an informal arrangement. Where companies have a formal right to appoint and the director is required to pass on to the appointing company any fees or other payments which he receives and does pass them on, then the appointed director will not be charged to tax on those fees provided that the appointing company agrees that the fees and payments which have been passed on to it are liable to corporation tax. Where the appointing company is chargeable to income tax rather than corporation tax (e.g. a non-resident company which is not trading through a branch or agency in the UK) and agrees to accept liability, the fees and other payments will be chargeable at basic rate.

Where the appointing company has no formal right to appoint a director but does so and he is required to pass on fees and other payments and does so, then the appointed director will not be charged to tax on those fees or payments provided that the appointing company agrees to accept

HMRC make a distinction between a 'waiver of remuneration' on the one hand and a 'salary sacrifice' on the other. These are not statutory terms, but the distinction is a useful one in practice. HMRC define a waiver of remuneration as what happens 'when an employee gives up right to remuneration and gets nothing in return'; this concept is considered here and in the paragraphs that follow. By contrast, HMRC define salary sacrifice as covering the case 'where the employee gets a non-cash benefit in return'. Commentary on salary sacrifice may be found at 132-080.

A waiver of remuneration may relate to salary, fees, bonus or any other form of cash remuneration.

Other Material: HMRC *Employment Income Manual* EIM42705

Timing of waiver

The key aspect of any waiver of remuneration is its timing. See 130-200 for commentary on when remuneration is treated as received for tax purposes, including the stricter rules applying to directors.

Remuneration waived before receipt

If remuneration is waived before the income is treated as having been received for tax purposes, then the amount waived will not be taxable as earnings from the employment.

Remuneration waived or returned after receipt

By contrast, remuneration waived after it is already treated for tax purposes as having been received nearly always remains taxable, even if the employee returns it to the employer or never actually receives it.

Once remuneration is treated as received for income tax purposes, the employer has an obligation to operate PAYE and the remuneration constitutes taxable earnings for the employee. A subsequent waiver of remuneration is seen simply as a decision by the employee to apply his or her earnings in a particular way by giving the money back to the employer. Such a decision has no impact on the PAYE obligations of the employer or on the tax liability of the employee.

Cases: *Parker v Chapman (HMIT)* (1928) 13 TC 677; *Reade v Brearley (HMIT)* (1933) 17 TC 687

Other Material: HMRC *Employment Income Manual* EIM42715

Tax Reporter: ¶405-500

130-250 Supply of services through a limited company or partnership (IR35)

Rules exist to prevent the use of intermediaries such as personal service companies or partnerships to avoid tax and National Insurance. The proposals are widely known as IR35 after the number of the Budget press release in which they were first unveiled.

The rules apply where the worker would be an employee if he or she worked for the client directly rather than through a company or partnership and the company or partnership meets certain conditions. In deciding whether the worker would have been an employee had he or she provided services direct to the client, normal rules apply for determining whether someone is employed or self-employed, 'as set out at 131-250. It is necessary to consider status on a contract-by-contract basis as some contracts may fall within the rules whilst others do not. Beginning with 2013–14, it is made clear that office-holders of the client are also potentially within these provisions.

In determining whether the worker supplies services as an employed or self-employed person but for the existence of the intermediary, the number of clients to whom services are supplied may be relevant. Where services are supplied to many different clients, this may indicate self-employment, although it is still necessary to consider the actual details of each individual contract.

In May 2012, HMRC published guidance to try and give further clarity as to whether these rules apply. Business entity tests are given to help determine the risk category based on a scoring system but it is up to each taxpayer to come to their own decision on their particular facts. Six case study examples are also given.

For the rules to apply, the company or partnership must meet various conditions. In the case of a company, the rules are in point if:

- the worker (or his/her family, including an unmarried partner) controls more than 5% of the ordinary share capital of the company;
- the worker (or his/her family) is entitled to receive more than 5% of any dividends from the company; or
- the worker receives or could receive payments or benefits from the company which are not salary but could reasonably be taken to represent payment for services provided to the client.

In the case of a partnership, for the worker to fall within the scope of IR35:

- he or his family (including an unmarried partner) must be entitled to 60% or more of the profits of the partnership;

- all or most of the partnership's income must come from providing services to a single client; or
- the profit sharing arrangements in the partnership are designed to ensure that the worker receives an amount based on the payments received for the worker's services to clients.

It should be noted that IR35 will only apply if the company or partnership falls within the above *and* the worker would be treated as an employee if he or she supplied his or her services direct to the client.

Corresponding provisions apply for National Insurance purposes.

Legislation: ITEPA 2003, s. 48ff.

Tax Reporter: ¶407-600

Impact of the rules

Where a contract falls within the scope of IR35 (other than those above providing services to public sector bodies (see 130-270)), the company or partnership should operate PAYE in the normal way on any salary payments made to the worker during the course of the year. However, at the end of the year, it is also necessary to determine whether or not tax and National Insurance is payable in respect of a 'deemed payment'. The purpose of the deemed payment, which is treated as paid on 5 April, is to ensure that the correct amount of tax and National Insurance contributions are paid. To determine whether such a payment is deemed to be made and tax and National Insurance contributions are due, the following procedure should be followed at the end of the tax year.

Step 1

Add up all the payments that the company or partnership has received for the worker's services during the tax year under the contracts to which the rules apply.

Step 2

Deduct 5% from this total to allow for the costs involved in running the company or partnership.

Step 3

Add any other payments or benefits in kind that have been received directly from the client if they are not already taxable.

Step 4

Deduct any allowable expenses met by the company or partnership.

Step 5

Deduct any earnings that have been received from the company or partnership on which PAYE has been operated and NICs paid, and benefits in kind which have been provided by the company and on which tax and NICs are due.

Step 6

Deduct the employer's NIC that the company or partnership has paid on the earnings and any Class 1A contributions due on benefits in kind. National Insurance contributions should be calculated on an annual basis whether or not the worker is a director.

Step 7

The balance represents the amount of the deemed payment plus the associated employer's National Insurance. To find the deemed payment, multiply by 100/(100 + the rate of employer's NIC). If the deemed payment is greater than zero, tax and NICs will be payable as if a payment of this amount had been made on 5 April.

Example

Richard provides his services to clients through a limited company. During the tax year 2017–18, services are provided under a contract that falls within the scope of IR35. The contract is Richard's only work that year. The client pays £50,000 to Richard's limited company.

Richard pays himself a salary of £30,000. The company also pays £3,000 into an approved pension scheme. Richard has a company car provided by the company, the cash equivalent value of which is £4,000.

The deemed payment is calculated as follows.

	£	£
Sum received from client under contract		50,000
Less:		
5% deduction for running costs	2,500	
Earnings paid subject to tax (salary)	30,000	
Benefits subject to tax (car)	4,000	
Contributions to pension scheme	3,000	
Employer's Class 1 NIC		
(£30,000 – 8,060) × 13.8%)	3,028	
Employer's Class 1A NIC		
(£4,000 × 13.8%)	552	
		(43,080)

Balance	6,920
Deemed payment	
$£6{,}920 \times \dfrac{100}{(100 + 13.8)}$	6,081

The deemed payment can be paid to the worker as salary or as dividends or it can be retained within the company. The tax and National Insurance is payable on the deemed payment irrespective of whether it is actually made to the worker.

The deemed payment is deductible in computing the company's profits chargeable to corporation tax.

Expenses

When computing the deemed payment, certain expenses are deductible in addition to the 5% deduction for running costs. These include any expenses met by the company or partnership that the worker would have been able to claim as a deduction for income tax purposes had he or she incurred the expenditure personally (e.g. professional subscriptions, professional indemnity premiums, etc. and certain travelling expenses). Also deductible are any pension contributions paid by the company to an approved pension scheme for the benefit of the worker.

The statutory car mileage rates discussed at 140-550 may be paid by a personal service company.

Legislation: ITEPA 2003, s. 54

IR35 and nannies

Rules introduced in 2003 counteracted the practice of paying nannies and other such domestic staff through the medium of a limited company – these companies are now caught by the IR35 rules and as such now have to pay tax and NIC on a deemed payment.

Legislation: ITEPA 2003, s. 49

Additional information

Further information on the impact of IR35 is available on the HMRC website, including a list of frequently asked questions. The address is www.hmrc.gov.uk/ir35.

HMRC also produce a booklet, *Supply Services through a limited company or partnership* (IR175). It is available from tax offices and enquiry centres and to download from the HMRC website.

130-270 PAYE obligations on public sector organisations engaging intermediaries

Finance Act 2017 introduced a significant change to the IR35 provisions where the end user is a public sector body. These provisions apply for income earned after 5 April 2017.

The definition of a public sector body or 'public authority' is widely drawn and is defined in the *Freedom of Information Act* 2000. It is not limited to simply government institutions but extends to such bodies as healthcare providers, police authorities, Ministry of Defence, etc.

In such cases, the onus of responsibility to establish the status of the contractor moves from the intermediary to the end user. Where it is found that the intermediary would fall within the IR35 provisions, then it is the end user that must operate PAYE on payments to the intermediary. In effect, the intermediary is treated as if they were an employee of the public sector body. There is no 5% 'expenses allowance' in these circumstances.

Where these provisions apply, then the receipt does not form part of the taxable profits of the intermediary.

Legislation: ITEPA 2003, s. 61K–61X; ITTOIA 2005, s. 164B; CTA 2009, s. 141A

HMRC guidance: www.gov.uk/government/publications/off-payroll-working-in-the-public-sector-changes-to-the-intermediaries-legislation/off-payroll-working-in-the-public-sector-changes-to-the-intermediaries-legislation

130-275 Managed service companies

Background

A variant of the standard service company is the 'managed service company' which aims to remove from the worker the administrative burden of running a company. Typically, the third party offering the service will set up the company and deal with the company and tax law issues arising. The worker will be both employee and shareholder and will therefore receive a combination of salary and dividend, as well as expenses payments. HMRC have estimated that as many as 240,000 workers were employed in such companies during the year to 5 April 2006.

The IR35 rules need to be considered in relation to these managed service companies as to any other service company. Nevertheless, various schemes were used to get round the rules and rules introduced in FA 2007 seek to ensure that workers in managed service companies are 'subject to employed levels of tax and NICs'. Companies are now obliged to operate PAYE accordingly in certain defined circumstances. The rules giving tax relief for travel expenses have been brought into line with those applying for other employed workers, thus restricting relief in many cases. The legislation also allows tax debts to be recovered from 'appropriate third parties'.

Legislation: ITEPA 2003, s. 61Aff.

Tax Reporter: ¶408-550

Meaning of 'managed service company'

A company (defined for these purposes to include any body corporate or partnership, including a limited liability partnership) will be treated as a 'managed service company' if it meets all of the conditions set out under the following four headings (ITEPA 2003, s. 61B).

Nature of business

The business of the company must consist wholly or mainly of providing the services of an individual to other persons (whether this is done directly or indirectly). HMRC warned in December 2008 that they disagreed with the interpretation of certain companies claiming not to be MSCs. The particular issue raised concerned companies that:

> 'claim that they are not MSCs, ... by virtue of the fact that the provider of the intermediary is an officer or partner of the intermediary and that consequently as there is no separate MSC Provider, the MSC legislation does not apply. HMRC have now taken Counsel's advice on the matter and have concluded that being an officer or partner in a service company does not preclude that person from being an MSC Provider. Furthermore, HMRC have declared their specific intention of investigating, challenging and litigating cases that rely on this defence to escape the MSC provisions. If the company is unable to pay any resulting liability, HMRC have declared their intention of invoking the transfer of debt provisions (see 130-280).'

Payments to individual

Payments made to the individual providing his services must be equal to the majority, or all of the amount the company is paid for the provision of that individual's services. This seems to be interpreted literally to mean that more than half of the payments received by the company must be paid to the individual. The condition is met whether such payments are made directly or indirectly and whether they are paid to the individual or to an associate of the individual (see below).

According to HMRC guidance (see below), 'the intention of the legislation is to compare on a cumulative basis rather than any particular timeframe.'

Tax saving

The manner of making the payments to the individual, or to the individual's associates, must be such as to result in a tax saving. More specifically, the amount received by the individual (or associates), after deduction of any tax and NIC, must be more than the net amount the individual would have received if the whole amount paid for the services had been treated as his or her employment income.

Involvement of MSC provider

The fourth condition is that an 'MSC provider', or an associate of the MSC provider, must be 'involved with the company'.

An MSC provider is defined as 'a person who carries on a business of promoting or facilitating the use of companies to provide the services of individuals'. No definition is given of the term 'promoting or facilitating', which must therefore be given its ordinary meaning.

Where a person's profession is that of providing independent, legal or accountancy services, then that person is not caught as an MSC provider (ITEPA 2003, s. 61B(3)). Standard employment agencies or businesses are also generally outside the definition and there are tests to define that concept. The HMRC guidance notes, however, confuse this issue, not least by introducing a non-statutory distinction between qualified and non-qualified accountants, and by statements such as the following:

> 'Simply because a person is a lawyer or accountant does not automatically exempt them from being an MSC Provider—the ultimate test is whether a person is carrying on a business (or a discernable part of their business) of promoting or facilitating the use of companies to provide the services of individuals.'

Elsewhere in the guidance, HMRC state that a 'Back Office Service Provider' who 'provides accounting/bookkeeping services exclusively to clients in the service company sector' would be within the rules because 'they are carrying on a business of facilitating the use of companies to provide the services of individuals'.

The Treasury is empowered to make an order providing that certain persons will fall outside the definition of 'MSC provider'.

An MSC provider is said to be involved with the company if, broadly, the provider, or its associate, benefits financially on an ongoing basis from the provision of the services of the individual or has a certain level of influence or control over the provision of the individual's services, over the way in which the individual is paid or over the company's finances or any of its activities. It will also be caught if it provides an undertaking to make good any tax loss. What is envisaged here is that the business of the MSC provider 'is not simply that of promoting or facilitating companies, but specifically promoting or facilitating companies to provide the services of individuals' (from the *Explanatory Notes* to the 2007 Finance Bill).

Legislation: ITEPA 2003, s. 61B

Tax Reporter: ¶408-600

HMRC guidance notes

In July 2007, HMRC issued some guidance notes which provide useful insight into how HMRC intend to interpret and apply the managed service company rules. The notes run to 48 pages, plus additional related material, and may be found in full at www.hmrc.gov.uk/employment-status/msc-guidance.htm. (Unfortunately, they are extremely badly written with garbled sentences, ridiculous punctuation and mistakes of both spelling and grammar. It sometimes seems to be the case that these presentational problems reflect an underlying problem with the guidance itself.)

Deemed employment payment

The managed service company (MSC) rules apply when the following conditions are all met:

- the MSC directly or indirectly provides the services of an individual worker;
- the worker (or his associate) receives from any person a payment or benefit (as defined) that can reasonably be taken to be in respect of the services; and
- the payment or benefit is not taxable as earnings within ITEPA 2003, Pt. 3, Ch. 1 (i.e. as salary or wages subject to PAYE and NIC).

Where these conditions are met, the MSC is treated as making a 'deemed employment payment' to the worker at the time the payment or benefit is received (and the worker is treated as receiving such a payment). The MSC has an obligation to operate PAYE, deducting tax and NIC as appropriate, at that date. It does not matter if the payment is made by someone other than the MSC. In the case of a payment or cash benefit, the payment is treated as made when payment is made or, or on account of, the payment or benefit. In other cases, the rules of ITEPA 2003, Pt. 2, Ch. 4 and 5 are applied.

Legislation: ITEPA 2003, s. 61D

Tax Reporter: ¶408-650

Calculation of deemed employment payment

The legislation provides three steps for calculating the deemed employment payment under the managed service company (MSC) rules. Where payments or benefits are related partly to the provision of relevant services and partly to other matters, then an apportionment is to be made on a just and reasonable basis.

Step 1: amount of benefit

The first step for the MSC is to take the amount of the payment received by the worker (whether or not it was paid by the managed service company).

Step 2: deduction of allowable expenses

The MSC then deducts from that payment any expenses that would be tax-deductible if the worker had been employed by the client to provide personal services, and had paid the expenses from his taxable earnings.

This wording is intended to ensure that travel costs to the client's premises, and associated accommodation and subsistence costs, will *not* be tax-deductible (as all engagements are treated as being part of a single employment with the MSC). Mileage allowance relief is, however, deductible in relation to a company car (or other vehicle) provided by the MSC for the worker if it would have been deductible if the worker had been employed by the client to provide personal services and if the vehicle had not been a company vehicle.

In the case of a partnership, the deduction may also be made if the worker is a member of the partnership and the vehicle is provided by the worker for the purposes of the partnership business. More generally, the HMRC guidance states that 'the expenses met by the worker includes, where the MSC is a partnership and the worker is a member of the partnership, expenses met by the worker for and on behalf of the partnership'.

If the resulting figure is zero or negative, then there is no deemed employment payment.

Step 3: adjustment for employer NIC

The figure resulting from the application of Step 2 is now treated as a figure that represents the deemed employment payment and employer NIC thereon. The MSC must therefore calculate the amount of the net payment to which the employer NIC is added to reach the figure resulting from Step 2. The net payment, known as the 'deemed employment payment' must then be subject to PAYE and employee NIC.

> **Example**
>
> Suppose that the result after Step 2 is £4,000 and that the rate of employer NIC is 13.8%. The net figure is then calculated as £4,000 × 100/113.8 = £3,515 (as this is the figure which, if the employer NIC is added to it, takes the calculation back up to £4,000).

Legislation: ITEPA 2003, s. 61E

Tax Reporter: ¶408-700

130-280 Debts of managed service companies

Rules were introduced in 2007 to ensure that managed service companies (MSCs) cannot avoid tax and NIC liabilities. The rules work by allowing the PAYE liability to be transferred to a fairly widely defined group of persons.

Debts may be transferred to:

- any director or other office holder of the MSC;
- any associate of the MSC;
- an MSC provider;
- a director or other office holder of an MSC provider;
- an associate of an MSC provider;
- a person who (directly or indirectly) has encouraged or been actively involved in the provision by the MSC of the services of the individual (though this category is subject to certain limited exceptions); or
- a director, other office holder or associate of any person in the last bullet point above.

A statutory instrument deals with the mechanics of identifying the debt to be transferred, of how and when such transfer may be made, of how and when the transferred debt must be paid, and of how a person to whom the debt is transferred may appeal.

Legislation: ITEPA 2003, s. 688A; SI 2003/2682, reg. 97A

130-290 Employment income provided through third parties

There had been a proliferation of Employee Benefit Trusts (EBTs) and Employer-Financed Retirement Benefit Schemes (EFRBSs) that caused considerable concern to HMRC. They are already challenging EBTs but this can take an enormous amount of time with considerable uncertainty. To rectify this for the future, FA 2011 introduced a new ITEPA 2003, Pt. 7A.

Although intended to combat EBTs and EFRBs, the provisions are very wide indeed and could in appropriate circumstances be stretched so as to be of concern to other transactions. Exactly how HMRC will interpret these provisions and police them generally is uncertain. They cannot be ignored particularly where there is a third party involved in a transaction, however innocent.

There are gateway tests that must be met to fall within these provisions as follows:

- there must be an employee, which could include a former or prospective employee, of another person;
- there must be an arrangement to which the employee is a party or which otherwise, wholly or partly, covers or relates to that person;
- it must be reasonable to suppose that in essence the arrangement is wholly or partly a means of providing the employee with rewards or recognition or loans in connection with the employment;
- a relevant step is taken by a relevant third person (these expressions are defined); and
- it is reasonable to suppose that in essence the relevant step is taken wholly or partly in pursuance of the arrangement or there is some other connection between that step and the arrangement.

A relevant step is defined and can include payment of money, transfer of asset or making available money or an asset for use as security for a loan. This means that the payment of a sum of money or transfer of an asset can include a loan or hire and the charge to tax will be based on the asset value, ignoring the fact that there has been no outright transfer of ownership. A relevant third person is virtually anyone other than the employee or employer acting as a trustee.

A relevant step can also include the earmarking of a sum of money or an asset without, therefore, any actual transfer to the employee in question. This could include, for example, a sub trust arrangement but is much wider than that in its potential application.

Any attempt to argue that the arrangement is not caught will be difficult as this is widely defined so that all the details of the steps need not be known and it does not matter that the person taking the relevant step is unaware of the arrangement. There is a provision that states that all relevant circumstances are to be taken into account in order to get to the essence of the matter.

The legislation works by excluding certain types of transaction from these provisions given that they are so wide and so the approach has to be to first consider whether the gateway tests are met and then to try and find a specific exclusion, many of which relate to approved share incentive schemes and registered pension schemes.

If a charge arises it will be subject to PAYE as employment income 2, using the best estimate which can be reasonably made where relevant. The deemed payment is treated as having been made by the employer and so the liability will fall on that employer even though the money or asset is transferred from a trust. This will no doubt provide a source of problems in practice, particularly if shares in the company are sold, no doubt complicating matters on due diligence and warranties and indemnities in sale and purchase agreements.

Broadly, the provisions came into effect for payments or transfers after 8 December 2010 with relatively minor transitional provisions. Loans made to individuals before 9 December 2010 are not caught but, for example, the repayment of that loan and then making a further loan will bring these provisions into play.

This explanation can only scratch at the surface of the very detailed provisions that run to many pages. In a given situation reference must be made to the legislation in an attempt to find an answer to a given set of circumstances.

Similar provisions have also been introduced for national insurance contribution purposes albeit with a different starting date.

130-300 Income paid 'free of tax'

The discharge of a director's or employee's pecuniary obligations by the employer is treated as 'money's worth' and therefore as earnings from the employment. This includes the situation where the employer tries to provide a tax-free salary by paying the employee's income tax: the amount of income tax so paid is earnings in itself.

It is prohibited to pay a director remuneration 'free of income tax' or otherwise calculated by reference to, or varying with the amount of, his income tax, or to or with any rate of income tax. Any provision purporting to provide such tax-free remuneration takes effect as if the 'tax-free' amount were grossed up (i.e. multiplied by 100/80 where basic rate income tax is 20%).

Payments in respect of PAYE made by employers on behalf of directors in cases where no deduction in respect of the PAYE tax has been made from the directors' remuneration are specifically charged to tax. Directors who do not have a 'material interest' in the employing company are not regarded as directors for this purpose. Where the employment has ceased before the payment is made, the payment is treated as remuneration for the year in which the employment ceased, unless the payment is made after the death of the director, in which case it is disregarded.

Legislation: *Companies Act* 1985, s. 311; ITEPA 2003, s. 223

Tax Reporter: ¶494-310

Notional payments

Where an employer has paid to HMRC an amount of PAYE on 'notional payments' but has been unable to deduct this from actual payments to the employee, the employee is obliged to pay to the employer the amount which the employer had paid to HMRC within 90 days from the date on which the employer was treated as making the notional payment. If he does not do so, the tax paid by the employer on the notional payment is added to the employee's PAYE income arising on the last day of the 90-day period.

A company and its directors argued unsuccessfully that the application of the legislation should be restricted to cases involving tax avoidance (*Chilcott v R & C Commrs*). The legislation was clear and unambiguous in its terms. Some of its terms dealt with anti-avoidance and others dealt with the practicalities of tax collection. The purpose of the rules was to encourage an employee to make prompt repayment to its employer.

Legislation: ITEPA 2003, s. 222

Case: *Chilcott v R & C Commrs* [2011] BTC 1

Tax Reporter: ¶494-310

130-350 Reward for services

Not all payments to employees are taxable even if they are convertible into money. To be taxable, a payment must be made to reward the employee for services rendered or to be rendered, or be made by reason of those services.

It is insufficient reason to justify taxing an employee for HMRC to say that no payment would have been received by an employee or office holder had he not been in a particular job *Beak v Robson*. The payment must be made as remuneration for services. Viscount Simonds in *Hochstrasser v Mayes* cited Upjohn J's test in the High Court:

> 'The payment must be made in reference to the services the employee renders by virtue of his office and it must be something in the nature of a reward for services, past, present or future.'

However, Viscount Simonds was unsure whether past services should be included.

It is not the case, though, that the payment must be made primarily as a reward for services. Rather, it is sufficient that the payment arose out of or came from the employment. To put it another way, if the source of the payments was the employee's employment then the payment will be earnings of that employment.

Example

A part-time employee earning £10,000 p.a. is paid £200 for passing his examinations. This would not be taxable because it is paid to reward the personal qualities of the employee rather than his business services. Had the employee not been employed he would not have received the payment and to that extent his being an employee is a cause of the payment. But the payment arose from the employee's personal qualities and not his employment (*Ball v Johnson*).

However, if the payment was conditional upon the employee working for a period of time after the exam it may well be taxable (see *Clayton v Gothorp*).

Where an employee's contract provides for the right of the employee to receive a payment or benefit then such payment or benefit will be taxable, because it is paid by reason of his employment.

The case of *Teward v IR Commrs* is helpful in bringing out some distinctions here. The taxpayer was initially employed by G Ltd as operations manager of a chemical plant that G Ltd wished to sell. The proposed purchaser had no experience of operating such a plant and wished to employ the appellant to supervise. During negotiations, it became clear that the taxpayer would lose the benefit of the share options package he had with G Ltd. The taxpayer calculated the gross amount that would be required to compensate him for the loss. The purchaser agreed to pay this amount in consideration of his entering into the new contract of employment, and conditional on his doing so. The taxpayer contended that this payment was compensation for loss of benefits from his employment with G Ltd and not connected with his new employment.

On the authorities, a payment was assessable if it has been paid to an employee for acting, being or becoming an employee. The status of the payment and the context in which it was made were relevant considerations. The nature or character of a payment made in lieu of a sum which might, subject to a contingency, have been payable would be affected by the nature of the sum which might otherwise have been paid. However, it was ultimately a matter of applying the statutory language to each situation. In the present case, the payment was part and parcel of the arrangement that induced the taxpayer to accept employment with the purchaser. As such, it was an emolument of his new employment.

A payment made and received as an incentive to work willingly will be an emolument from the employment, even if it is also paid and received as compensation for a loss of pension or other rights. In *Kuehne & Nagel Drinks Logistics*, certain payments made to the employees did not come from the cessation of their employment, even though there would have been no payment without the cessation. The cessation was the trigger for the payments, but they were made because of a loss of pension rights and to ensure that the employees concerned would continue to work willingly, and without threatening strike action. The threat of that strike action was not merely the means by which the payment was secured but was a substantial cause of the payment and on that basis the payment was taxable. The decision was upheld in the upper tribunal. The earlier judge could not be criticised for focusing on why the payments totalling £5,000 had been made. He was entitled to take the view that the causes and reasons for the payments were key to determining whether they were 'from' employment. Where, as in the present case, a judge decided that it was impossible to separate or rank causes, there could be no basis for deciding that a payment was to be attributed to a non-taxable one as opposed to a taxable one.

By contrast, HMRC failed, in *Thresh*, to convince the tax tribunal that any profit gained by a director arose from his office or employment. The case concerned contractual arrangements to build three properties on a parcel of land and HMRC did not take adequate account of the fact that the director had (from his own private resources) contributed more than £100,000. Any profit was received by the director not by reason of his office or employment but by reason of his funding arrangement with the company. The tribunal was influenced in reaching this decision by the fact that the arrangement was such as might have been agreed by the company with an arm's length joint venturer.

The discharge by an employer of his employee's indebtedness to a third party (e.g. in respect of private school fees, or council tax) is taxable earnings if made to reward the employee.

Cases: *Beak v Robson* (1942) 25 TC 33; *Hochstrasser v Mayes* (1959) 38 TC 673; *Ball v Johnson* (1971) 47 TC 155; *Clayton v Gothorp* (1971) 47 TC 168; *Teward v IR Commrs* (2001) Sp C 270; *Kuehne & Nagel Drinks Logistics* [2010] TC 00314; *Thresh* [2010] TC 00343; *Kuehne & Nagel Drinks Logistics v R & C Commrs* [2011] BTC 1,562

Tax Reporter: ¶412-350

130-400 Payments not to reward services

The employment will not be the source of the payment or benefit in the following circumstances:

(1) where the payment or benefit is made under a contractual right outside the scope of the employment (see below);

(2) where it is a purely personal gift; or

(3) in some cases where it is a terminal payment made after the services have ended.

However, it is incorrect to assume that all payments which fall into the above three categories are tax-free. Provisions exist to tax certain payments in all three categories in particular circumstances.

Restrictive covenants

Payments made to an employee in consideration of his entering into a contract which restricts his conduct or activities (for example an agreement that he will not compete with his former employer within a certain radius) are taxed. Such payments are deductible by the employer as revenue expenses.

The scope of the rules was considered in the case of *Kent Foods Ltd v R & C Commrs*, in which it was found that there was plainly a connection between the holding of the individual's employment (past, present and future) and the giving of the undertakings contained in the non-compete agreement. The fact that the giving of the undertaking was also connected with something else was of no moment.

Legislation: ITEPA 2003, s. 225

Case: *Kent Foods Ltd v R & C Commrs* (2007) Sp C 643

Tax Reporter: ¶423-500

Golden handshakes

Payments made as terminal payments after the services have ended are often called 'golden handshakes' and are in principle taxed under their own special rules. Only amounts in excess of £30,000 are taxable, but there are many pitfalls in this area (see 142-000).

Legislation: ITEPA 2003, Pt. 6, Ch. 3

130-500 Commission receipts, cashbacks and discounts

HMRC issued a detailed statement of practice covering the taxation of commission receipts, cashbacks and discounts on the sales of insurance policies, life annuity contracts, capital redemption policies, personal pension schemes and other financial services products. Paragraphs 23 to 34 deal with the employment income aspects. Key provisions include the following.

- Employees who receive, or are entitled to receive, commission (as earnings) from their employment in respect of goods, investments or services sold to third parties are taxed on the full amount of that commission.
- Even where an employee agrees that commission which is due from his or her employment should be paid to the customer, the employee is still taxable in principle on that commission (but subject to possible deductions).
- Employees who receive commission in respect of their own purchase of goods, investments or services from the employer are liable to tax on the full amount of that commission.
- Where an employee receives a cashback from his or her employer or a third party on the same basis as is available to members of the general public, no amount is normally chargeable to tax as employment income (but this is subject to the necessary conditions being met).

Other Material: SP 4/97

Tax Reporter: ¶129-100

130-550 Tax-free lump sums

Certain lump sum payments from pension policies are specifically declared to be tax-free. This topic is covered in depth in the section on investment income.

For the treatment of termination payments, see 142-000ff.

130-650 Gifts to employees

As a general principle, where any employee receives an asset from his employer then he will be taxable on the market value of that asset. This rule can catch a broad range of possible gifts, from land or a property at one end of the scale to Christmas hampers (see 143-050) or other more modest seasonal gifts at the other.

Finance Act 2016 introduces a statutory exemption for certain trivial benefits (see 133-335). Provided the qualifying criteria are met, then the receipt of these benefits will not attract an income tax (or National Insurance) charge on the employee.

A question may arise of whether a gift is given in a personal capacity rather than because of the employer-employee relationship. Any benefit from the employer is deemed to be provided by reason of the employment unless the employer is an individual and it can be shown that the benefit was provided in the normal course of a domestic, family or personal relationship. If, for example, an employer has ten employees and gives them all a Christmas present, then, subject to the exemption for trivial benefits, the value of the presents will be a taxable benefit. The employment relationship is the reason for the making of the gifts.

Legislation: ITEPA 2003, s. 201(3), 323A

Other Material: HMRC *Employment Income Manual* EIM01040

Tax Reporter: ¶412-450

Personal gift or reward for services

Where there is doubt as to whether a payment is a personal gift or paid to reward services, two points in particular are of relevance. They are:

- the regularity of the payments;
- the expectation of the employee to receive it.

If the payments are regular it is more likely that the court will hold that they are remuneration for services. If the employee expected a payment to be made to him, that is an indication that the payment was part of his earnings and not a spontaneous gift.

Regularity must be in relation to a particular employee and not in relation to a business policy only. In *IR Commrs v Morris*, a £1,000 payment was made by an Electricity Board to a former Atomic Energy Authority worker who came to work for them two years earlier. The Electricity Board had given gifts to other Atomic Energy Authority workers who had come to work for them in the past. Nevertheless, the payment was said to be unexpected by Mr Morris.

The same point was taken up by Lord Evershed in *Moorhouse v Dooland* when he said that the character of the payment is to be ascertained and judged in relation to the recipient rather than the giver.

Cases: *Moorhouse v Dooland* (1954) 36 TC 1; *IR Commrs v Morris* (1967) 44 TC 685

Cash gifts

Payments in money from an employer to an employee will always be taxable if they were made to reward the employee for his services. Strong evidence will be required to rebut an HMRC contention that payments from an employer to an employee are a reward for services.

Non-cash gifts from third parties

An exemption is available for non-cash gifts made by third parties to employees costing less than £250 (including VAT) per tax year.

130-675 Tips

Tips are taxable, and where these are shared among the various employees it is the employer's responsibility to account for PAYE unless the tips are dealt with through a 'troncmaster' (see *Figael Ltd v Fox (HMIT)*).

Troncs

A 'tronc' arrangement is one in which tips to hotel, restaurant or other staff are pooled and then distributed by a person (known as a 'troncmaster') other than the employer. Special tax rules apply to such arrangements.

An employer is required to notify HMRC when a new troncmaster is appointed. HMRC will then set up a PAYE scheme in the troncmaster's name, run entirely separately from the main employer PAYE scheme, specifically to deal with the troncs. The troncmaster is responsible for operating PAYE, though HMRC have confirmed that this role may in practice be carried out by the employer acting effectively as payroll agent.

If the troncmaster fails in any respect to comply with the regulations, he or she may be held personally liable for tax that has not been deducted. HMRC may then require the principal employer to operate PAYE on the tips and, to the extent that they are not so dealt with, HMRC may adjust the employee's coding and require him to deliver a personal return.

The statutory provisions apply where there is 'an organised arrangement' for the sharing of tips among employees by a 'person ... who is not the principal employer'. HMRC's interpretation of this is that the tronc rules do not apply if the troncmaster is a 'business partner or official of the company (for example, a director)'. As such, a company director when acting on behalf of the company cannot be counted a troncmaster and so divert from the company responsibility to operate PAYE.

Legislation: SI 2003/2682, reg. 100

Case: *Figael Ltd v Fox (HMIT)* [1990] BTC 421

Other Material: HMRC *PAYE Online Manual* PAYE72080; booklet E24(2010), entitled 'Tips, Gratuities, Service Charges and Troncs' (see www.hmrc.gov.uk/helpsheets/e24.pdf)

Tax Reporter: ¶412-500

Tips paid out by the employer

If the employer collects the tips and pays them out to the employee then PAYE must be operated on them just as it is operated on ordinary payments of salary or wages. This is the case even if the term 'tronc' is used and even if a troncmaster determines the allocation of the tips to the staff before the employer actually pays them over.

Tips given direct by customers

A tip given directly from a customer to an employee, without any intervention by the employer or by a troncmaster, is still liable to tax but is not subject to PAYE. The employee has an obligation to notify HMRC of the liability and, in an ongoing role, the employee's PAYE code will normally be adjusted to collect any tax due.

National minimum wage

Employers are not allowed to take account of tips, etc. for the purposes of calculating the national minimum wage (NMW) to be paid to employees. Specifically, employers must discount tips, gratuities, service charges and cover charges paid by customers for NMW purposes. The position was more complex before 1 October 2009 but it appeared to be the case that employers who simply took control of distributing tips and operating PAYE on them could until that date count those tips towards the national minimum wage.

130-750 Testimonial matches

Finance Act 2016 introduces a statutory framework for the taxation of receipts arising under 'testimonial' or 'benefit' arrangement. It had become customary for professional sportsmen to be granted a testimonial match at which the player concerned receives the gate takings less expenses.

Attempts by HMRC to convince the courts that such receipts are part of the player's earnings have failed. In *Reed v Seymour*, Viscount Cave in the House of Lords pointed out that the professional cricketer concerned had no contractual right to the benefit. If, on the other hand, the player's contract provided that a public collection is tied to the performance of the player's duties and is made if he attains a certain level of skill, then such a collection, if given to him, will be taxable. In *Moorhouse v Dooland*, the Court of Appeal was persuaded to find the collection taxable because:

- Mr Dooland qualified for the collection by the performance of his duties;
- although the performances were outstanding, they were not exceptional in the sense that they might not be repeated; and
- the employment contract gave him the right to receive the collection if he qualified.

Usually sportsmen are given benefit matches on the *Reed v Seymour* principle, i.e. a 'one-off' collection and/or gate takings from a 'one-off' testimonial game. The player does not expect it and the right to receive it is not part of his contract. There is a line of opinion, however, which suggests that, as such testimonials become customary, then a degree of expectancy on the part of the player must arise and with it a greater likelihood that the payment will be treated as part of his wages.

As noted above, the position was put beyond doubt by the introduction of ITEPA 2003, s. 226E. It remains the case that where a payment is received that is taxable under basic principles, i.e. there is a contractual arrangement with the employer or there is a customary expectation, then such payments will continue to be subject to PAYE as normal income. Where such provisions do not apply then, with effect from 6 April 2017, an individual may receive up to £100,000 without incurring an income tax liability provided certain detailed conditions are met.

Legislation: ITEPA 2003, s. 226E, 306B

Cases: *Reed v Seymour* (1927) 11 TC 625; *Moorhouse v Dooland* (1954) 36 TC 1

Tax Reporter: ¶488-865

130-800 ITEPA 2003 and ITTOIA 2005: priorities of charge

Trading income or income taxed under ITEPA 2003

If a receipt potentially falls within both ITTOIA 2005, Pt. 2 (trading income) and ITEPA 2003, Pt. 2, 9 or 10 (respectively employment income, pension income or social security income), then the provisions of ITEPA 2003 take priority.

Legislation: ITTOIA 2005, s. 4(2)

Savings and investment income or charge under ITEPA 2003

If a receipt potentially falls within both ITTOIA 2005, Pt. 4 (savings and investment income) and ITEPA 2003, Pt. 2, 9 or 10 (respectively employment income, pension income or social security income) then the provisions of ITEPA 2003 take priority.

However, the decision of the Court of Appeal in *PA Holdings Ltd v R & C Commrs* should be taken into account. In the context of an avoidance scheme it was held that, on the facts, a dividend was in reality employment income so there was no need to consider the priority rules in the first place. The appeal to the Supreme Court was withdrawn so the decision of the Court of Appeal is final.

Legislation: ITTOIA 2005, s. 366(3)

Case: *PA Holdings Ltd & Anor v R & C Commrs* [2010] BTC 1626

Other miscellaneous income or charge under ITEPA 2003

If a receipt potentially falls within both ITTOIA 2005, Pt. 5 (miscellaneous income) and ITEPA 2003, Pt. 2, 9 or 10 (respectively employment income, pension income or social security income) then the provisions of ITEPA 2003 take priority.

Legislation: ITTOIA 2005, s. 575(4)

Employed or self-employed

Relevance

131-250 Income tax and NIC

The question of whether an individual is acting on the one hand as an employee (or director) or on the other in a self-employed capacity is critical to the way his or her income is to be taxed.

Employees

The employee is normally taxed at source under the PAYE system. Tax is calculated principally by reference to 'earnings', though other amounts are added to reach the totality of 'employment income'.

An employer has an obligation to deduct a certain level of tax and to hand it over to HMRC at specified intervals, together with appropriate amounts of employer and employee ('Class 1') National Insurance. Benefits in kind enjoyed by employees are subject to their own sophisticated system of taxation (and to Class 1A National Insurance, payable by employers only). Tax relief is tightly controlled for expenses incurred. Many employees need little or no knowledge of the tax system, being free to spend the net-of-tax income they receive on a monthly or other basis.

The self-employed

For the self-employed individual, the tax regime looks very different. Tax is calculated by reference to profits rather than earnings. Instead of deduction of tax at source, such individuals normally pay their tax in two instalments, reaching HMRC by 31 January and 31 July each year; a system of payments on account operates. National Insurance is paid by way of a fixed weekly or monthly amount (Class 2) and a further amount linked to profits (Class 4). The overall level of National Insurance payable by a self-employed individual is far less than that payable in respect of an equivalent employee (though the latter's overall burden is shared with the employer).

If a self-employed individual (or a partnership) chooses to incorporate then the individual (or partners) will start to be employed by the new company. This may simplify their own personal tax affairs (after a period of transition) but will create an array of new tax and administrative obligations as the company operates as employer, especially if the business did not previously have any employees.

No contract

Occasionally, it will be the case that the individual is neither an employee nor a self-employed contractor. In *Convery*, an individual wished to claim industrial injuries disablement benefit, for which he needed to show that he had been employed by a particular construction company. On the facts, it was held that he had no contract with the company at all, in either an employed or a self-employed capacity.

Case: *Convery* [2010] TC 00401

Tax Reporter: ¶400-050

131-275 Employer obligations

The first tax-related obligation for a person providing work is to decide whether the relationship with the performer of that work is one of employment or self-employment. The onus is on the provider to decide the status of the relationship. If the provider incorrectly decides that the relationship is one of self-employment, and he therefore fails to apply

PAYE to deduct tax at source, the provider will be liable to account for the tax. This can be very expensive, because:

- HMRC may treat as a net amount the figure that was intended to be paid gross;
- National Insurance will considerably increase the liability;
- there may be other individuals who have been treated in the same way;
- HMRC will almost certainly review earlier years, typically calculating liabilities for the current year plus a further six years; and
- interest and penalties may well be charged.

Having concluded (or conceded) that an individual is indeed an employee, the employer must then accept the full burden of complying with the PAYE regime.

If an individual has been treated as self-employed but is then re-categorised as an employee, the employer may have a substantial liability, quite possibly going back over a number of years. If the individual has properly declared all income on a personal tax return, i.e. as trading profits, the question arises of how any tax suffered may be offset against the employer's new liabilities. In the past, HMRC would always offset any payments made against any liabilities arising, but the *Demibourne* case affirmed the right of HMRC to deny the offset of tax. The case, and subsequent legislation on the issue, is considered at 131-280.

Case: *Demibourne Ltd v HMRC* (2005) Sp C 486

Tax Reporter: ¶400-050

131-280 The Demibourne principle

Background

It happens fairly frequently that an individual has been treated as self employed but is subsequently found to be an employee. If that individual has paid tax as a self-employed person, there is a difficulty over the extent to which the tax already paid may be offset against the employer's PAYE liabilities for earlier years. In the past, HMRC would generally offset any payments made against any liabilities arising, but the *Demibourne* case affirmed the right of HMRC to deny the offset of tax. Secondary legislation was introduced with effect from 6 April 2008 to allow an offset of tax in some circumstances.

HMRC may issue a 'direction' permitting employers to offset tax paid by the individual in certain specified circumstances. The employer will then be relieved of a PAYE liability that would otherwise be due to the extent of any amount(s) of tax specified in the direction for the tax year.

HMRC can issue a 'direction' where various conditions are met:

- the employee has received relevant payments (which can include notional payments) in relation to which the employer should have applied PAYE;
- the employer has deducted or accounted for less tax under PAYE than is required;
- HMRC are satisfied that a liability to tax has been self-assessed on the income in question by, or on or behalf of, the employee (or has been included in a self-assessment payment on account or as a sub-contractor deduction); and
- one of various specified 'trigger events' has occurred (typically, the issue to the employer of a notice of determination which includes tax on the relevant payment).

HMRC have indicated that 'where the conditions for making a direction are satisfied HMRC will usually exercise its power to make a direction'. There may, however, be exceptional circumstances in which HMRC would not wish to do so, particularly if they suspect an employer of deliberate avoidance of PAYE responsibilities. Employers have no right of appeal against any refusal to make a direction. Employees, by contrast, may appeal – on certain specified grounds – against the making of such a direction.

An employer remains potentially liable to penalties on the full amount of tax which should have been deducted, or accounted for, in accordance with the PAYE Regulations.

Legislation: SI 2003/2682, reg. 72E–72G

Case: *Demibourne Ltd v HMRC* (2005) Sp C 486

Tax Reporter: ¶400-065

131-300 Employment law

The status of the individual – whether employee or a self-employed independent contractor – is also, of course, highly significant in determining the rights enjoyed by the individual. Notice periods, the national minimum wage, maternity and paternity rights, redundancy payments, protection against unfair dismissal, statutory sickness and holiday pay are all features of employment legislation but rarely appear in a self-employed

'Provided that the information you input into the ESI is an accurate account of the work carried out for a particular engagement, you can rely on the ESI outcome as HMRC's view of the status for that particular engagement.'

The guidance goes on to state that employers should retain:

- the printed version of the ESI result;
- the printout of the Enquiry Details Screen showing the engagement details and the replies to the questions asked;
- the engagement contract (where applicable); and
- any other documentation or information that were relied on when completing the ESI.

Tax Reporter: ¶400-100

Factors determining employment status

131-450 Overview

In most cases, it is clear whether a relationship is one of employment or of self-employment. There are, though, significant numbers of cases where this is not true. Given that the issue has such far-reaching consequences, both for tax purposes and otherwise, it would be helpful to have a system or checklist that could determine the issue in any given circumstances. In reality, though, this is an area where judgment, experience and legal precedents all have a part to play, and where there are no easy short cuts.

Subject to the rules for special occupations (see below), the HMRC view expressed in leaflet ES/FS1 is that an individual is likely to be treated as employed if he or she answers 'yes' to *most of* the following questions:

- 'Do you have to do the work yourself?
- Can someone tell you where to work, when to work, how to work or what to do?
- Can someone move you from task to task?
- Do you have to work a set number of hours?
- Are you paid a regular wage or salary?
- Can you get overtime pay or bonus payments?
- Are you responsible for managing anyone else engaged by the person or company that you are working for?'

Again subject to the rules for special occupations (see below), the HMRC view expressed in ES/FS1 is that an individual is likely to be treated as self-employed if he or she answers 'yes' to *one or more* of the following questions:

- '• Can you hire someone to do the work, or take on helpers at your own expense?
- Can you decide where to provide the services of the job, when to work, how to work and what to do?
- Can you make a loss as well as a profit?
- Do you agree to do a job for a fixed price regardless of how long the job may take?'

The HMRC guidance goes on to say that even if a person has to give a negative answer to all of the above, he or she is still likely to be self-employed if the answer 'yes' can be given to *most of* the following questions (i.e. on a literal interpretation, at least three of the four questions):

- '• Do you risk your own money?
- Do you provide the main items of equipment (not the tools that many employees provide for themselves) needed to do the job?
- Do you regularly work for a number of different people and require business set up in order to do so?
- Do you have to correct unsatisfactory work in your own time and at your own expense?'

In reality, certain factors invariably carry great weight (see, in particular, the issues of mutuality of obligation, of financial risk and opportunity, and of substitution and delegation). Other factors gain more or less importance from the part they play in the overall relationship between the person providing the work and the one performing it.

A case which considered many of the factors determining employment status was that of *Datagate Services Ltd*, in which a software developer won his appeal against a finding of notional employment status under the IR35 rules. There was no ultimate right of control. The engager could have continued with the engagement had it chosen to, or chosen not to renew the engagement. There was nothing in the documents requiring personal service. The documentation allowed for a substitute to be provided. The payment was on a fee basis which was entirely consistent with self-employment. There was no employee-type benefit such as sick pay or pensions provisions. There was no requirement that the individual should work exclusively for the company concerned and he was not 'integrated' as an employee. The engagement could be terminated but that was not equivalent to being able to give notice under a contract of employment. The parties did not intend the individual to have employment status.

A similar conclusion was reached in the *First Word Software* case.

Cases: *First Word Software Ltd v R & C Commrs* (2007) Sp C 652; *Datagate Services Ltd v R & C Commrs* (2007) Sp C 656

Tax Reporter: ¶400-200

Special occupations

Leaflet ES/FS1 warns that special rules apply to 'certain occupations and jobs', which it lists as follows:

- individuals working through an agency;
- company directors;
- club secretaries;
- other office holders;
- office cleaners;
- ministers of religion;
- examiners, moderators and invigilators of examining boards;
- school teachers, lecturers and instructors;
- entertainers;
- deep sea divers;
- individuals working for someone in their family.

The special rules may relate to tax only, NIC only, or both tax and NIC.

131-475 Mutuality of obligation

A fundamental condition of employment is that employer and employee must have an obligation to one another. The employer must have an obligation to provide work (or possibly to pay the employee whether work is provided or not) and the employee must have an obligation to perform the work personally. This test is crucial. If it can be shown that there is no mutuality of obligation then there can be no employment. In the Court of Appeal case of *Nethermere (St Neots) Ltd v Taverna and Gardiner*, it was held that 'there must be an irreducible minimum of obligation on each side to create a contract of service'.

Revenue guidance used to play down the importance of this factor, but HMRC now acknowledge that:

> 'There must be an irreducible minimum of mutual obligation for there to be a contract of service. That irreducible minimum is
>
> - that the engager must be obliged to pay a wage or other remuneration, and
> - that the worker must be obliged to provide his or her own work or skill.'

The concept of the 'irreducible minimum' was explored in the case of *Lewis (t/a MAL Scaffolding) v R & C Commrs*, in which HMRC argued unsuccessfully that a number of scaffolders should be treated as employees. The commissioner noted the absence of any obligation on MAL Scaffolding to offer the workers any work; Mr Lewis usually did provide work – that was a service he offered the workers – but there was no mutual obligation on a continuing or future basis. And if extreme weather (for example) meant that the scaffolders could not work, then they did not get paid.

The issue of mutual obligation was explored once more in the case of *Dunne v R & C Commrs*, concerning a transfer of pension benefits. The individual argued that he had been an employee of a company, Holme Ltd, but the special commissioner emphatically rejected that contention. The irreducible minimum of mutual obligation necessary to create a contract of service was a contractual obligation on the employer to provide work and on the worker to do it when offered. The evidence was compelling as it described a situation where the taxpayer was not expected to do any work for Holme Ltd and given no instructions on how to carry out his employment duties. So-called employees were entitled to choose where and when they worked and their contracts of employment contained no provisions about notice to terminate, holiday and sickness pay, and disciplinary procedures. The relationship with Holme Ltd bore no hallmarks of an employment relationship and there was no evidence of the irreducible minimum of mutual obligation between Holme Ltd and the taxpayer that was necessary to create a contract of service. Accordingly, in all the circumstances, the 'employment' relationship between the taxpayer and Holme Ltd was a sham, operating as a cover to enable the taxpayer to draw out pension benefits in advance of his retirement.

By contrast, the case of *Dragonfly Consultancy v R & C Commrs* was under the 'IR35' rules and was thus concerned with a notional contract. The mutuality condition was satisfied by an obligation to work in return for an obligation to remunerate, and that condition was satisfied by the notional contracts. A requirement to make work available (or to pay when it was not) was a significant pointer towards employment.

Some doubt was cast, in the case of *Castle Construction (Chesterfield) Ltd v R & C Commrs*, on the weight to be given to the concept of mutual obligation. The authority of the commissioner to question that weight is doubtful, even though it was supported by reference to a High Court decision (that of *Usetech Ltd v Young* [2005] BTC 48) and to another special commissioner case. The judge in *Usetech* did comment that:

> 'It is an over-simplification to say that the obligation of the putative employer to remunerate the worker for services actually performed in itself always provides the kind of mutuality which is a touchstone of an employment relationship. Mutuality of some kind exists in every situation where someone provides a personal service for payment, but that cannot by itself automatically mean that the relationship is a contract of employment: it could perfectly well be a contract for freelance services.'

In *Novasoft Ltd*, the *Usetech* reasoning was affirmed and applied, with a finding that the hypothetical contract in question 'would have established mutuality of obligations during the term of the contract but, for the reason put forward by Park J in *Usetech*, we consider that that is appropriate to a self-employment contract as well as one of employment'.

Cases: *O'Kelly v Trusthouse Forte plc* [1983] 3 All ER 456; *Nethermere (St Neots) Ltd v Taverna and Gardiner* [1984] ICR 612; *Lewis (t/a MAL Scaffolding) v R & C Commrs* (2006) Sp C 527; *Dunne v R & C Commrs* (2007) Sp C 654; *Dragonfly Consultancy Ltd v R & C Commrs* [2008] BTC 639; *Castle Construction (Chesterfield) Ltd v R & C Commrs* (2008) Sp C 723; *Novasoft Ltd* [2010] TC 00456

Other Material: HMRC *Employment Status Manual* ESM0543

Tax Reporter: ¶400-300

Duration of obligation

The HMRC guidance does go on to state that 'if the ongoing mutual obligation could not be demonstrated, then, from the tax and NICs point of view, we would still look at the separate engagements and determine status based on the factors present in each'.

This moves the argument into more difficult territory. In *Wickens v Champion Employment*, reference was made to 'the necessary elements of continuity and care' that characterised mutuality in an employment contract; the reference to continuity would seem to imply the need for an enduring relationship. On the other hand, the *Montgomery* case noted that the concept of 'mutuality' needed to be considered in the context of the specific assignment. See also *McMeehan v Secretary of State for Employment*. HMRC do accept, however, that 'it is often difficult to establish the necessary ongoing mutuality of obligation to change a series of short-term contracts into a single 'umbrella' contract' (HMRC *Employment Status Manual* ESM7110).

A leading case on this point is that of *O'Kelly v Trusthouse Forte plc*, which concerned casual hotel staff engaged on a function-by-function basis. Many of the individuals worked only for the one organisation. It was held in the Court of Appeal, overturning the decision of the industrial tribunal, that the individual in question was self-employed. It was established that there was neither an 'umbrella contract' nor a succession of single contracts of employment. The hotel had no obligation to provide work and the individual waiters had no obligation to accept it.

In *Parade Park Hotel v R & C Commrs*, HMRC contended that even where there was no ongoing commitment to provide work, there could still be mutuality of obligation in separate engagements, producing a series of contracts of employment. The commissioner accepted the principle (established in *Prater v Cornwall County Council*) that there could be a mutual obligation in relation to a single engagement, but said that it was then necessary to consider whether in fact such mutuality existed within the single engagements. This is an important distinction. In *Parade Park Hotel*, there was no evidence of any greater obligation in respect of each separate day for which the individual actually worked than there was over the whole period of the working relationship. The commissioner therefore found that there was no mutuality of obligation in respect of any shorter period within the time covered by these appeals.

The question of the duration of the obligation was also considered in *Littlewood t/a Window & Door Services v R & C Commrs*. In particular, the commissioner in that case found that a distinction could be made between the mutuality that is necessary in a single assignment and the mutuality of obligation required in a series of assignments. The commissioner gave the example of a shopkeeper who needs help on a single Saturday morning and who engages the services of his nephew, on what is clearly a one-off basis. The commissioner commented that 'whether the bargain amounts to a contract of employment (albeit for a very short term) does not depend on the mutual obligations which the parties have entered into; those obligations already exist, and the contract will either be performed or not. The only way of establishing whether the arrangement amounts to a contract of employment is to look at the other factors'. The commissioner concluded that 'the threshold for mutuality in individual assignments is modest'.

The same commissioner heard the case of *Sherburn Aero Club v R & C Commrs*. He commented in that decision that 'in a case where there is not necessarily a continuing relationship, it is open to question how relevant the normal questions relating to mutuality can be'. He went on to refer back to the *Littlewood* case:

> 'I concluded in Littlewood that in employment status cases, an ongoing relationship is not required. To put this another way, the question is confined to what the relationship is when the worker is actually working for the engager, so that the ability on either side to bring the relationship to an end, or the readiness or otherwise of either party to engage in similar relationships in future, are not relevant questions.'

Cases: *O'Kelly v Trusthouse Forte plc* [1983] 3 All ER 456; *Wickens v Champion Employment* [1984] ICR 365; *McMeehan v Secretary of State for Employment* [1997] IRLR 353; *Prater v Cornwall County Council* [2006] 2 All ER 1013; *Parade Park Hotel v R & C Commrs* (2007) Sp C 599; *Littlewood t/a Window & Door Services v R & C Commrs* (2009) Sp C 733; *Sherburn Aero Club v R & C Commrs* [2009] TC 00006

Other Material: HMRC *Employment Status Manual* ESM0543

Tax Reporter: ¶400-300

Demonstrating that there is mutuality of obligation

The practical question then arises of how to determine whether or not there is in fact a mutual obligation between the provider of the work and the individual performing it. The HMRC perspective is that there are four factors to look for:

(1) how work is offered and accepted;

(2) whether the pay records suggest work is in fact done continuously;

(3) how often work has been refused; and

(4) if work is refused, whether the engager will offer work in the future.

The manner in which work is offered and accepted may offer good evidence that there is no contract of employment. If it is clear that there is a genuine negotiation before each task is performed, then this is a clear pointer that there is no ongoing mutual obligation. For example, is there evidence of negotiating the price for the job, or the timeframe within which it is to be performed?

Pay records showing that the individual is working pretty much full time for the engager over a sustained period may strongly imply an expectation both of providing and of performing the work. The case is less clear cut with work that is regular but on a part-time basis.

Care is needed with the third and fourth factors listed above. Most of those working on their own account are hungry for work, and will rarely turn it down, especially if it is offered by an organisation that provides work on a frequent basis. If work has in fact been turned down, then this is an almost conclusive indicator that there is no mutuality of obligation, but failure to refuse a particular job is only a weak pointer to such mutual obligation. Furthermore, it should be borne in mind that the obligation has to be on both sides – if the worker never turns work down, but is offered it only on an irregular basis, then this suggests that there is no obligation on the engager to provide the work; based on HMRC's own wording at ESM0543 (quoted above), this is enough to demonstrate that the employment test fails.

Common sense requires some consideration of the length of the relationship. If, in fact, the same engager has provided work for the same individual over a sustained period, this may provide some indication of at least an understanding that work will be provided and performed.

Other Material: HMRC *Employment Status Manual* ESM0558

No written contract

The mere fact that there is no written contract does not demonstrate that there is no mutuality of obligation. In *R & C Commrs v Wright*, the facts pointed fairly strongly towards an employment relationship and the commissioners' finding that the individuals were not employees was challenged in the High Court (though that court did not overturn it as such, preferring to remit the matter to the commissioners for further consideration).

The commissioners had concluded that the workers were self-employed on the grounds that the terms of engagement were oral; that there was no formal contract to protect the workers; and that there was no minimum requirement to pay the worker irrespective of demand. The judge remitted the case for further consideration by the commissioners on the grounds that the reasons they had given for their decision were wholly inadequate and did not bear upon the question whether the workers were employed by the taxpayer.

Case: *R & C Commrs v Wright* [2007] BTC 596

131-500 In business on own account

At one level, the most important question in determining employment status is that of whether an individual is performing a task as a person in business on his or her own account. Nevertheless, the test is not always a helpful one. For a start, the argument can be circular, as broadly the same issues are raised by the question 'is he in business on his own account?' as by the question 'is he employed or self-employed?'.

It is important to note that the test is not whether the person is in business on his own account; rather, the question is whether the particular task is performed in that capacity. An engineering consultant may be self-employed for three days of the week, acting for a variety of clients, but have a regular employment for the remainder of the week. Indeed, it is possible that the same engineer will work for the same organisation in both capacities, with a regular salary for an ongoing project and by negotiation for one-off tasks as they arise.

No business structure

The fact that a person is not in business on his own account does not mean that he must therefore be an employee. In *Wickens v Champion Employment*, the judge said that the test of whether an individual is employed or self-employed:

> '… does not include as a necessary element the question of whether the individual carries on a separate business. If it did, then it would follow that a casual worker must always be employed under a contract of service unless he has his own business and that, plainly, cannot be the law.'

The absence of a formal business structure is not a relevant factor if no such structure is required for the nature of the activities in question. As it was put in *Hall v Lorimer*:

> 'A self-employed author working from home or an actor or a singer may earn his living without any of the normal trappings of a business.'

The result of this is that this is something of a one-way bet for those wishing to demonstrate that there is no employment:

- if the task is performed in the capacity of an individual acting in business on his own account, then the relationship is not one of employer and employee; but
- it is quite possible to have a casual engagement of an individual who does not have a business structure, but who is nevertheless not an employee.

Case: *Wickens v Champion Employment* [1984] ICR 365

Tax Reporter: ¶400-400

131-520 Financial risk and opportunity

HMRC attach great significance to this issue, making the following points:

- the financial risk accepted by a worker can be 'a strong indication of self-employment';
- (generally) the greater the financial risk the stronger the pointer towards self-employment;
- a worker who buys significant assets and bears the running costs, or pays for materials or overheads, is likely to be self-employed;
- where a worker is required to put right mistakes or poor workmanship in his own time, then this is another pointer towards self-employment; and
- the pointer to self-employment will be increased where the worker must also supply replacement materials, etc. (e.g. a bricklayer who has to rebuild a wall and who must supply or pay for the cost of the mortar/bricks, etc.).

It is true that the earning of an irregular income, with the chance to do either better or worse than an employee, goes to the heart of what it means to be self-employed. Almost invariably, a self-employed individual can take on additional work (whether for the same or for another provider) and thereby earn more if he or she works better or faster than rivals. An employee, on the other hand, is likely to do this only within a very well-defined framework that specifies the exact terms on which additional income can be earned.

The fact that financial risk is a strong indicator that may clearly separate the employed from the self-employed was confirmed in the (unreported) liability case of *Todd v Adams*, which concerned share fishermen who died when a trawler capsized and sank in 1997. In the Court of Appeal, Lord Justice Mance referred to four factors which outweighed any inference of a contract of service and these related primarily to the question of financial risk.

Case: *Todd v Adams* (unreported)

Other Material: HMRC *Employment Status Manual* ESM0541

Tax Reporter: ¶400-500

131-540 Substitution, delegation and the hiring of staff

The issue of substitution has featured in many cases where the courts have had to determine whether an individual is employed or self-employed. If A asks B to carry out a task, is B obliged to do the work himself, or can he in turn engage C to do the work on his behalf? If B does have this freedom, and will be paying C out of his own pocket, then this is a very strong indicator that B is not acting as A's employee.

A genuine right of substitution, whether 'sideways' to someone of similar seniority or by way of delegation to a junior, is one of the strongest factors favouring self-employment. As Lord Fraser stated in the case of *Australian Mutual Provident Society v Chaplin*:

> 'power of unlimited delegation is almost conclusive against the contract being a contract of service.'

Similarly, in *Express and Echo Publications Ltd v Tanton*, concerning a newspaper delivery driver, it was stated that:

> '[where] a person who works for another is not required to perform his services personally, then as a matter of law the relationship between the worker and the person for whom he works is not that of employee and employer.'

In the same case, the point was also made in the following terms:

> 'it is necessary for a contract of employment to contain an obligation on the part of the employee to provide his services personally. Without such an irreducible minimum of obligation, it cannot be said that the contract is one of service.'

Indeed, this was a critical argument in *Express and Echo*, which otherwise had many features of employment (control, provision of equipment, method of calculating payment).

The principle used to be clearly accepted by HMRC, who stated (*Employment Status Manual* ESM1052 as formerly worded) that:

> 'where a worker does not have to perform the work personally, and can hire a substitute to carry out the work, that is inconsistent with employment and the worker will be self-employed regardless of other factors such as control, etc.'

Important changes have been made to the wording of that guidance, however. The first change was made early in 2006, after which the revised wording was as follows:

> '[The *Tanton* case] shows that, where a worker does not have to perform the work personally but is under an obligation to provide and pay for a substitute to carry out the work, such a provision may be inconsistent with employment. This may well be the case where the emphasis is on the job and not on the individual's skills.'

The wording had changed still further by the autumn of 2008, however, and now reads as follows (ESM3350):

> 'It should be noted that, where a hypothetical contract is considered to contain a right of substitution, that right is likely to be only an indicator of self-employment to be weighed with all the other factors. ... Where you only have the personal service company/agency contract, which contains a substitution clause, you would certainly want to seek evidence about substitution from the end-user. The courts would consider that evidence to be very important. Would the end-user permit the worker to send a substitute or would they only accept a substitute from the agency? Would the worker pay the substitute? And did it happen in practice? In the personal service company situation, the worker and the service company are effectively one and the same. That is not the case in the composite service company situation where the worker is an employee and only one of several shareholders. In those circumstances, you will have a worker/service company contract and it is even more essential that you seek the views of the end user where it is suggested that the worker has a right of substitution.'

There is also a statement at ESM0538, however, that 'a right of substitution is normally a pointer towards self-employment'. In *Talentcore Ltd*, the tribunal noted the 'temporary and ad hoc nature of the Appellant's bookings' and the fact that there were separate contracts for each shift the individual worked. The appeal (against the application of the IR35 rules) was allowed 'on the basis that there is no obligation to render (or provide) personal service(s)'.

The fact that a substitute cannot be used is a much weaker indicator of employment status. As HMRC acknowledge (now at ESM0534):

> 'This factor does not necessarily work the other way. Where a worker has to undertake the work personally that does not mean the worker must be an employee. There are many examples (for example, in the professional field) where self-employed individuals have to undertake the work they have agreed themselves. The lack of a right to provide a substitute may be a pointer to employment but it is certainly not conclusive on its own.'

In *Novasoft Ltd*, it was found that the IR35 rules did not apply even though the notional contract would not have permitted substitution.

Cases: *Australian Mutual Provident Society v Chaplin* [1978] 18 ALR 385; *Express and Echo Publications Ltd v Tanton* [1999] IRLR 367; *Talentcore Ltd* [2010] TC 00454; *Novasoft Ltd* [2010] TC 00456

Other Material: HMRC *Employment Status Manual* ESM0531

Tax Reporter: ¶400-600

Difficulties

Given the strength of the judicial comments referred to above, and their apparent acceptance by HMRC, the right of substitution may be perceived as something of a panacea for anyone seeking to avoid an employment relationship. In fact, there are several hurdles to be overcome.

First, the right of substitution implies that responsibility remains with the person who was originally engaged. If a company engages a sole trader accountant to draw up accounts, the individual may delegate that work to an employee. As far as the company is concerned, the first accountant remains responsible (and legally liable) for the quality of the work.

If a right of substitution is written into a contract, but the courts do not accept that it is genuine, or that the right is unfettered, then it may be ignored. A leading case is that of *Macfarlane and Skivington v Glasgow City Council*, in which two individuals had some right of substitution but were nevertheless held to be employees. In *Synaptek Ltd v Young*, the court commented on the right of substitution and held that 'the commissioners were entitled ... to regard it as simply one fact among others, and, in assessing the weight to be given to it, to take into account the extent to which the provision was utilised in practice'.

Yet another reminder was given in 2008 of the need to show that the right to provide a substitute was genuine. In *Alternative Book Co Ltd v R & C Commrs*, the commissioner found that the substitution clause 'was window dressing and had no practical effect on how the contract would operate'.

In the *MKM Computing* case, the commissioner held that a limited or occasional power of delegation or right to substitute another person might be consistent with an employment. In particular, a contract containing a right to substitute if and only if the employer consented was, until consent was given, a contract which plainly satisfied the personal service condition, although the presence of that right might be an indication of self-employment.

Cases: *Macfarlane and Skivington v Glasgow City Council* [2000] EAT/1277; *Synaptek Ltd v Young (HM Inspector of Taxes)* [2003] BTC 8,044; *MKM Computing Ltd v R & C Commrs* (2007) Sp C 653; *Alternative Book Co Ltd v R & C Commrs* (2008) Sp C 685

Financial arrangements

Where there is a genuine right to substitution, the financial arrangements of the person to whom the work is delegated will not normally be the concern of the person who originally provides the work. This may be contrasted with the treatment of employees.

Suppose that an employer asks an employee (E) to do some work. E is busy and asks a fellow employee (F) to do it in his place. F is also busy but does the work and claims overtime accordingly. That overtime will be paid by the employer. E has no interest in the financial arrangements. If E were in business on his own account, on the other hand, then the payment would have to go through him and it is likely that F would then act as his employee. It is then up to E how he pays F, and E may make a profit or a loss on the transaction.

In *Andrews v King*, a distinction was made between selecting others to do the work and personally engaging them.

The financial arrangements also had importance in *Weight Watchers (UK) Ltd*, where a superficial power to delegate was not sufficient to dislodge a finding that the workers were employees. HMRC contended that 'a proper construction of the clause in its context did not, as it was suggested for the Appellants it did, give an unlimited power to delegate. What happened was different.' In finding that the individual 'Leaders' were employees of Weight Watchers, the tribunal explained its reasoning in relation to substitution as follows:

> 'The true position about replacement Leaders and this clause, the tribunal finds, is that there is no contract for the meeting between WW and the usual Leader. Nor was the tribunal given any evidence of contracts between the usual Leader and the replacement Leader. There was no pattern of offer, acceptance, and consideration in either case. There are contracts directly between WW and the replacement Leaders. If not before, then the acceptance of the contract by WW comes at the latest when WW ratifies the deduction

> by the replacement Leader of her fees from the proceeds of the meeting and thereby confirms the cash consideration received directly by the replacement Leader at the time of the meeting. The tribunal finds that it is clearly understood by all concerned that the replacement Leader is entitled to retain those fees as Leader in the same way that the usual Leader would have been entitled had she taken the meeting. The replacement Leader receives from WW the full fee payable for the meeting and the usual Leader receives nothing.'

Cases: *Andrews v King* [1991] BTC 338; *Weight Watchers (UK) Ltd* [2010] TC 00367

Tax Reporter: ¶400-600

131-560 Control

The issue here is the extent to which the provider of the work can control the manner in which that work is carried out; in principle, or so it is argued, the greater the right of control the more likely it is that the relationship will be one of employer and employee.

The importance to be attached to this factor is debatable; in places, HMRC still attach great importance to the concept but arguably its significance can be overstated. HMRC acknowledge that the attitude of the courts has moved on (i.e. presumably in the light of more modern working practices) so that 'the control test is now considered to be less significant in determining status' and that, whilst still 'a significant factor' is no longer 'conclusive on its own'. Specifically, HMRC accept that:

> 'Where there is evidence of little control this does not mean conclusively that there is self-employment. However, where the engager has no right of control over the worker, there will not be a contract of service.'

Some weight was given to the issue of control in *Dragonfly Consultancy Ltd v R & C Commrs* [2008] BTC 639. The individual in that case was explicitly subject to the client's 'direct supervision and control' – one of a number of difficulties in the contractual terms, and an expression that was never going to be a helpful clause in an IR35 dispute. It was held in the High Court that the special commissioner had been fully entitled to conclude that the individual's work was subject to a degree of supervision and quality control that went beyond mere direction as to where and when he should work.

Other Material: HMRC *Employment Status Manual* ESM0516

Tax Reporter: ¶400-700

131-580 Where work is performed

Employment status may be influenced by the issue of where work is performed. The HMRC view of this matter may be summarised as follows.

- Where a worker is required to work on the engager's premises it is also more likely that there will be a right of control over other aspects, especially where the work is integrated into the daily routine of an office or factory.
- Where a worker can carry out work wherever he wishes, the contract is more likely to be a contract for services.
- But where the nature of the work dictates where it should be carried out, the factor is not likely to be of any significance in determining status.
- A worker will not be accepted as self-employed just because he or she does not work at the engager's premises.

Other Material: HMRC *Employment Status Manual* ESM0522

131-600 Provision of equipment

The question of who provides equipment is another factor that can weigh heavily in favour of self-employment but is less likely to indicate decisively an employment relationship. This factor links to that of financial risk and opportunity (see 131-520).

The provision of *small* items of equipment is of almost no significance at all. Many in the building trade will provide their own small tools, whether they are employed or self-employed, though the treatment of tools in the building trade was given a particular slant in the *Castle Construction* case, where relevance was attached to the fact that the bricklayers who were intended to be self-employed provided their own hand tools. Indeed, the observation was made that if these individuals had been blindfolded they would all have been able to identify their own hand tools by feel, a point that supported the concept of them each having pride in his own ongoing trade, whoever he happened to be working for at any given time. As such, this was a small factor in favour of self-employment.

For those working in an office, the question of who provides a calculator or a pen or a block of paper is similarly irrelevant, more probably determined by personal preference than by employment status. Where more expensive equipment is provided by an individual, however, this is a strong indicator of self-employment.

Case: *Castle Construction (Chesterfield) Ltd v R & C Commrs* (2008) Sp C 723

Tax Reporter: ¶400-800

131-620 Integration into engager's business

The test was formulated by Denning LJ who made the following comment in the Court of Appeal decision in *Bank voor Handel en Scheepvaart NV v the Administrator of Hungarian Property*:

> 'The test of being a servant does not rest nowadays on submission to orders. It depends on whether the person is part and parcel of the organisation.'

Nevertheless, the factor is not in practice given much weight. The HMRC view is that 'little reliance' should be placed on the issue and there is case law authority for this.

There are numerous examples of individuals who may be perceived as integrated into an organisation but who are accepted as self-employed. The waiters in the *Trusthouse Forte* case (see 131-475) must have seemed to those dining at the restaurants to be part of the organisation, yet were held to be self-employed. In *Massey v Crown Life Insurance Company*, the individual was a manager and a former employee but was nevertheless held to be self-employed. Similarly, in *Express and Echo Publications Ltd v Tanton*, a newspaper delivery driver was held to be self-employed even though (for example) he drove a company van and was required to wear a uniform.

But what of cases where the individual is clearly *not* integrated into the organisation? It then seems reasonable to give this factor more weight (i.e. in favour of self-employment) if it clearly distinguishes that individual from others who are employees. Some specific differences of treatment between the worker and the company employees helped the tribunal to reject a notional employment in the IR35 *Novasoft Ltd* case.

Cases: *Bank voor Handel en Scheepvaart NV v the Administrator of Hungarian Property* (1952) 35 TC 311; *Massey v Crown Life Insurance Company* [1978] 1 WLR 676; *O'Kelly v Trusthouse Forte plc* [1983] 3 All ER 456; *Express and Echo Publications Ltd v Tanton* [1999] IRLR 367; *Novasoft Ltd* [2010] TC 00456

Other Material: HMRC *Employment Status Manual* ESM0516

Tax Reporter: ¶400-900

131-640 Number and length of engagements

A classic feature of self-employment is that the individual typically works for many different customers or clients. By contrast, the majority of employees spend all their working time reporting to a single employer, often over a period of many years.

As one factor of many, the number of different engagements is clearly a relevant consideration. However, the matter is more complex than it first appears. As HMRC state, the considerations determining employment status:

> 'apply to casual, temporary, part-time or short-term workers as well as to those working on a full-time basis. The result could be employment, self-employment or a combination of both.'

The mere fact that an individual works for more than one organisation is therefore not enough to determine the nature of each relationship. Nevertheless, it is probably fair to say that the more people an individual works for, the greater the likelihood that his work is carried out in a self-employed relationship.

Case: *Hall v Lorimer* [1993] BTC 473

Other Material: HMRC *Employment Status Manual* ESM0519

Tax Reporter: ¶401-000

131-660 Intention of the parties

HMRC instructions to HMRC officers are that 'if you consider that the case is borderline, you should then, and only then, look at the intention of the parties'. The instructions contrast 'the intention of both parties' with 'the real relationship between the parties' and suggest that the intention will be decisive 'if the relationship is ambiguous and other factors are neutral'. It is debatable, however, whether this relegation to 'casting vote' or 'tie-breaker' status can be justified, and whether it is appropriate to set up the intention of the parties in opposition to the reality.

Certainly, it is useful to turn to the intention of the parties if all other considerations lead to no firm conclusion. Indeed, the point was made in *Massey v Crown Life Insurance Co*:

> 'It seems to me on the authorities that, when it is a situation which is in doubt or which is ambiguous, so that it can be brought under one relationship or the other, it is open to the parties by agreement to stipulate what the legal situation between them shall be.'

So the intention cannot determine the matter if the facts clearly show that a different relationship in fact existed. Similarly, where the contract is a sham, the Courts will not shrink from ignoring it. In *Withers v Flackwell Heath Football Supporters' Club*, the Employment Appeals Tribunal made the following comment:

> 'That both parties put the label 'self-employed' on their relationship is far from conclusive and is to be disregarded when the reality is that the label, and

> the fiscal consequences that flow from its use, are adopted simply for fiscal reasons.'

But where the intention of the parties is not in actual conflict with the reality, is that intention not an important factor in its own right, one to be given its due weight in seeing how the balance lies? In *Global Plant Ltd v Secretary of State for Health & Social Security*, Lord Widgery commented that:

> 'although the parties cannot by intention make a transaction into something which it is not, yet it is recognised that such intention is a factor for consideration in these cases.'

The point was more strongly made in *Carmichael v National Power*, in which case it was stated that 'when both parties are agreed about what they understood their mutual obligations (or lack of them) to be, it is a strong thing to exclude their evidence from consideration'.

An Australian case takes this a step further. In *Australian Mutual Provident Society v Chaplin*, Lord Fraser stated a principle that:

> 'subject to one exception, where there is a written contract between the parties whose relationship is in issue, a court is confined, in determining the nature of that relationship, to a consideration of the terms, express or implied, of that contract in the light of the circumstances surrounding the making of it: and it is not entitled to consider also the manner in which the parties subsequently acted in pursuance of that contract. The one exception to the rule is that, where the subsequent conduct of the parties can be shown to have amounted to an agreed addition to, or modification of, the original written contract, such conduct may be considered and taken into account by the court.'

So if it is accepted that 'the terms … of that contract' can be considered to represent the intention of the parties then this gives greater weight to this particular factor.

HMRC seek to water down the effect of Lord Fraser's comments, making the following points:

- regard is to be had only to the express or implied terms of a written contract;
- the terms of many contracts are not in writing and, even if they are, they are not comprehensive. The agreed oral terms can only be discovered by speaking to the parties (a point confirmed in *Carmichael*);
- where the terms are not express (written or oral), then the courts will look to see whether any terms can be implied by the conduct of the parties, by custom and practice, etc.;
- terms may well have been varied by agreement, either orally or in writing, at a later date; and

- one of the exceptions would be where one or more clauses is ineffective or a sham.

Nevertheless, the statement is an important one. The precedent value of an Australian case is, for the avoidance of doubt, acknowledged by HMRC:

> 'Judgments of the Judicial Committee in Commonwealth cases have no value to UK law where the points at issue only concern interpretation of statute of the Commonwealth country. However, they are of relevance where general law principles are considered.'

On balance, it does seem reasonable to challenge the HMRC view that the intention of the parties should be considered *only* in borderline cases; there is clear case law authority to treat the intention as an important factor in its own right. It seems that it is only inappropriate to do so if the declared intention is a tax-related sham or if it is clear that the intention is not borne out in reality. In practice, it will be relevant to consider the overall terms and conditions of the relationship, as discussed below.

It is essential for the parties to the relationship to be clear about what they are intending to achieve. That intention should be recorded in all documentation, including any contracts, correspondence, etc. It should be clearly stated whether or not the individual is to be treated as an employee.

An important aspect of this will be the various terms and conditions of the relationship, including method and calculation of payment, any benefits in kind provided, treatment of holidays and sickness periods, termination and dismissal clauses.

In *Yetis*, the First-tier Tribunal accepted the individual's argument that, notwithstanding his agreement on joining that he was self-employed, he was in reality an employee. This removed the assessment HMRC had made on him as a self-employed person.

In *Tomlinson,* the fact that both parties intended and believed that the individual was self-employed over a period of 25 years was decisive.

Cases: *Global Plant Ltd v Secretary of State for Health & Social Security* [1971] 3 All ER 385; *Massey v Crown Life Insurance Co* [1978] ICR 590; *Australian Mutual Provident Society v Chaplin* [1978] 18 ALR 385; *Withers v Flackwell Heath Football Supporters' Club* [1981] IRLR 307; *Carmichael v National Power* [1999] 4 All ER 897; *Yetis* [2012] TC 02410; *Tomlinson* [2017] TC 05943

Other Material: HMRC *Employment Status Manual* ESM0521, ESM7090

Tax Reporter: ¶401-100

Occupation	**ESM paragraph**
Careworkers: payments under Court of Protection Order or trust fund	4016
Cleaners	4018
Computer staff supplied by agencies	4020
Demonstrators and merchandisers	4025
Dentists	4030
Directors	4040 and 4240
Divers and diving supervisors	4050
Doctors	4060
Election agents	4080
Electoral Registration Officers	4085
Entertainment industry workers	4100
Examiners	4150
Family employment – by spouse	4155
Family employment – other than by spouse	4156
Fellowships	4160
Guardians *Ad Litem* and Reporting Officers	4170
Journalists	4180
Local Veterinary Inspectors	4200
Lorry drivers	4210
Market research interviewers	4220
Milk roundsmen	4230
Nominee directors	4240
Nursing staff	4250
Parish and Community Council Clerks	4260
Pharmacists (locums)	4270
Recorders, Circuit Judges, Deputy High Court Judges and Deputy Circuit Judges	4280
Returning Officers, etc.	4290
School inspectors	4300
Subcontractors	4320
Sub-postmasters/sub-postmistresses	4400
Teachers, lecturers and tutors	4500
Trustees under a will, settlement, etc.	4520
Voluntary organisation workers	4530

131-810 CCH guidance

The *Tax Reporter* at ¶485-000ff. contains detailed guidance on numerous employment occupations, including employment status issues. See 143-990 for a complete list of such occupations.

131-820 Agency workers

The rules applying to workers supplied by agencies were updated from 6 April 2014. The broad principles are similar to the previous law but have been tightened with the practical effect that more workers are likely to be within these provisions than previously.

If the taxpayer is within these provisions, the relevant individual is treated for income tax purposes as holding an employment with the agency with the effect that PAYE (and National Insurance) must be applied by the agency as a general rule.

This treatment will apply where:

- an individual personally provides services to another person;
- there is a contract between that person (or connected person) and a person other than that person or the individual (the agency effectively); and
- under, or in consequence of that contract the services are provided, or the person to whom these services are provided (or a connected person) pays or otherwise provides consideration for the services.

There are exceptions where the services are:

- as an actor, singer, musician or other entertainer or as a fashion, photographic or artist's model; or
- provided wholly in the worker's own home or at other premises which are neither controlled or managed by the client nor prescribed by the nature of the services.

Apart from these excluded services, the main let out is where it can be shown that the manner in which the individual provides the services is not subject to (or to the right of) supervision, direction or control by any person. Thus, the burden of proving this is clearly placed now on the agency, for practical purposes, as there must be some evidence that this exception does apply on the facts. All the relevant factors must be considered but the main one is whether there is supervision, direction or control over how the work is done. HMRC indicate that where there are procedures, methods and instructions which must be followed, then it would be difficult to fall outside the provisions. However, merely having to comply with statutory requirements such as health & safety procedures would not in itself be determinative.

As part of the fact finding, the agency is likely to ask the person for whom these services are required to give details of the work carried out. If that person provides the agency with a fraudulent document intending to demonstrate the absence of supervision, etc., then after the time when that document is provided, the PAYE, etc. obligation passes to the end user of the services.

There is now a targeted anti-avoidance provision that negates arrangements which have the main purpose(s) of securing that these agency rules do not apply. 'Arrangements' is very widely defined to include any scheme, transaction or series of transactions, agreement or understanding, whether or not legally enforceable, and any associated operations.

Attempts to hide behind the incorporation of companies (including limited liability partnerships) is blocked by a provision that applies from 6 April 2014 to the effect that the directors of the company can be made personally liable for PAYE debts not paid by the company. HMRC have the power to serve a notice on any person who was, on the relevant date, a director requiring that person to pay the amounts as specified within 30 days. They can serve a notice on more than one director and the directors on whom a notice is served become jointly and severally liable for the amount (together with interest thereon). There is an appeal procedure but this is very limited to factual points on the amount of the PAYE debt and whether the person was in fact a director on the relevant date. Unfairness or hardship is not a ground for appeal. An individual cannot escape liability by, for example, appointing a man of straw as a director as the statutory provisions apply the definition in ITEPA 2003, s. 67 of including any person in accordance with whose directions or instructions the directors of the company are accustomed to act.

Generally, the PAYE rules have been updated as well so as to ensure that a liability for PAYE cannot be avoided by the interposition of other persons where there is an offshore entity involved. This could cover arrangements where the individual is engaged by an agency or employer based outside the UK and then placed with a UK end-user via one or more UK agencies. In that case, the UK agency has the obligation to apply PAYE. In a simpler case of an agency based outside the UK without an inserted chain, the PAYE obligation falls upon the end user of the services. It can be seen, therefore, that a business engaging agency workers where there is an overseas element must take great care otherwise they could have the obligation to apply PAYE as far as HMRC are concerned; having to rely on contractual obligations against an overseas person, with all the practical difficulties that could involve.

Finally, simply because an individual has a personal service company does not mean that the agency rules do not have to be considered. The order in which the relevant legislation should be considered is first the agency rules, then the managed service company rules and finally the personal service company (IR35) rules.

Example

HMRC in their employer services manual give examples of certain types of situations where the question of supervision or direction or control must be considered (see ESM2056 onwards). The following is a summary of a scenario involving a joiner and a carpenter. The construction industry is in particular one where the changes will be of concern.

A joiner is engaged to work for a company and is supervised by a foreman. That foreman shows the individual how flooring must be laid and checks on progress from time to time, including ensuring that the fitting has been as instructed. Guidance is given if appropriate. Various jobs are allocated over the period of engagement in addition to this first task and it is made clear that the individual could be moved from job to job as required. Thus, the joiner never has any freedom to choose the actual work he does or where he does that work but more importantly he could not decide how he does the work. This was all carried out as required by the foreman and the fact that he did not need to apply any supervision in certain cases because of the experience of the joiner would not alter the analysis as the foreman always had the right to supervise, etc. the manner in which these services were provided.

On the other hand, if the joiner had simply been engaged to carry out a particular task such as hanging a door in place and he has control as to exactly when he did this and without interruption, then he is likely not to be an agency worker; more particularly because he simply carries out the work without being told how he should go about this.

These scenarios illustrate the difficulties in practice in applying the supervision, etc. rules. They all depend upon the particular facts. It could be said that the more skilled an individual is in providing services the less the need for supervision. As mentioned, it is not up to HMRC to determine that there is supervision, etc. as the presumption is that there is such supervision unless the contrary can be demonstrated and simply having the right to exercise it is sufficient whether or not enforced in practice.

Legislation: ITEPA 2003, s. 44–47, 689, 716B, 972A–F

Benefits and expenses

General principles

132-000 Overview

'Employment income' is defined to include not only 'earnings' but 'any amount treated as earnings'. The latter includes any amount treated as earnings under the benefits code, which is to be found in ITEPA 2003, Pt. 3, Ch. 2–11.

The benefits code in ITEPA 2003, Pt. 3 has the following structure:

- Chapter 2 gives the introduction.
- Chapters 3 to 9 deal with specific types of benefit, viz:
  - expenses payments (Ch. 3);
  - vouchers and credit-tokens (Ch. 4);
  - living accommodation (Ch. 5);
  - cars, vans and related benefits (Ch. 6);
  - loans (Ch. 7);
  - notional loans in respect of acquisition of shares (Ch. 8);
  - disposals of shares for more than market value (Ch. 9).
- Chapter 10 is a general 'sweep-up' provision, catching anything not specifically addressed in the previous Chapters.
- Chapter 11 excludes lower-paid employment from parts of the benefits code.

Legislation: ITEPA 2003, s. 7

Tax Reporter: ¶412-800ff.

132-010 P11D employees

Prior to 6 April 2016, the legislation imposed a general benefits code on employees earning less than £8,500 a year and a raft of special provisions on employees whose earnings were above that threshold. With effect from 6 April 2016, the distinction between 'higher' and 'lower' paid employees was removed completely.

An employer is required to make a return of all payments, benefits and facilities within the benefits code provided to or for employees in a particular tax year on form P11D. The return must reach HMRC no later than 6 July following the tax year to which it relates.

Employees who are obliged to file tax returns are required to include the details from their forms P11D , income tax on their benefits is normally collected by adjusting their tax codes.

Tax Reporter: ¶412-850

132-030 'By reason of the employment'

The benefits, expenses and other payments to be taxed are those provided 'by reason of the employment' of the director or employee concerned.

Benefits, etc. provided *by the employer* to the employee, his 'family or household' are deemed to be provided by reason of the employment. The only exception is where:

- the employer is an individual; and
- the benefit is provided in the normal course of his domestic, family or personal relationships.

Where the expenses payment or benefit is provided by a third party, it will still be assessable if it was provided by reason of the employment.

Family or household includes the spouse or civil partner of the director or employee, his sons and daughters and their spouses or civil partners, his parents (but not step-parents, remoter ancestors or issue), his dependants, his domestic staff and his guests. The First-tier Tribunal case of *Baylis* found that care home fees paid for by a company were a benefit in kind taxable on the spouse of the resident of the care home rather than the daughter. It was found that, where two employees are potentially liable for a benefit in kind charge, it is not open to the employer to decide but it is rather defined within ITEPA 2003, s. 721 which sets out a hierarchy of individuals potentially taxable.

Legislation: ITEPA 2003, s. 71, 192(3), 198(4), 201(3), 721(4), (5)

Case: *Baylis* [2016] TC 05454

Tax Reporter: ¶412-000ff.

132-040 Cash equivalent

The taxable amount of a benefit is known as the 'cash equivalent' and is normally the amount of any expense incurred in providing the benefit, or in connection with it, less any amount made good by the employee. However, specific provisions apply to determine the cash equivalent value of certain benefits, including company cars (see 132-200), vans (see 132-600), employment-related loans (see 132-800) and living accommodation (see 133-100).

For details of the cash equivalent value of other types of benefit, see 133-500.

Legislation: ITEPA 2003, s. 203(2)

Tax Reporter: ¶412-850

132-050 Employees 'making good'

In order to avoid the tax consequences of the provision of a benefit in kind, it is open to an employee to reimburse their employer the full cost of the benefit. F(No. 2)A 2017 put on a statutory footing the requirement for any such reimbursement to be made on or before 6 July in the year following the year of the benefit.

Legislation: ITEPA 2003, s. 87

132-065 Restriction of lower paid employees' exemption to certain ministers of religion post 6 April 2016

With effect from 6 April 2016, the concept of 'lower paid employees' (essentially those earning less than £8,500 per annum including benefits in kind) is only applicable in the context of lower paid ministers of religion. This means that, with the exception of this very restricted group, all employees will be governed by the same benefits in kind provisions regardless of their income.

Legislation: ITEPA 2003, s. 290C; FA 2015, s. 13

Tax Reporter: ¶412-800

132-080 Salary sacrifice (prior to 6 April 2017)

Prior to significant changes introduced from 5 April 2017 (see 132-090), the underlying principle of salary sacrifice is simple. An employee gives up salary and takes instead a benefit in kind, often one that is tax-free. A straightforward example would be as follows:

Example

Beth pays higher rate tax. She agrees to a reduction in salary of £500 in return for which her employer allows her to use a mobile phone for which the employer pays, under contract, an amount of £40 per month. The provision of the phone is potentially tax-free. The cash cost to Beth of lost salary is just £290 (after tax at 40% and 2% National Insurance) and she saves mobile costs of £480, so she gains by £190. Her employer saves £20 (being the salary saved less the cost of the phone) plus National Insurance (at 13.8%) of £69 on the salary not taken.

The issue of flexible benefits is often driven more from a human resources perspective than from one based on tax issues. The provision of a choice from a range of benefits can be an attractive part of a remuneration package, thus helping to attract or retain key employees.

HMRC attitude

It might be thought that with the increasing focus on anti-avoidance legislation, a salary sacrifice scheme will be perceived as provocative and liable to HMRC attack. On the whole, though, that this is not the case. The HMRC website contains a copy of a letter to the Chartered Institute of Taxation, undated but published after 1 August 2004. This includes the general comment that 'we remain committed to ensuring that everyday tax advice does not trigger a disclosure obligation'. It goes on to state more specifically that:

> 'We can confirm again that we do not intend promoters or employers to have to disclose everyday advice and arrangements. In the context of employment products this would include:
>
> - the provision of flexible benefits, such as where employees forgo salary in return for a car or are provided with childcare vouchers
> - salary sacrifice arrangements for cars, computers, childcare vouchers or pension funds [as defined] ...'

Furthermore, the HMRC manuals contain extensive coverage of the topic of salary sacrifice and make it clear that it is both effective and acceptable, as long as the necessary formalities are observed. In relation to childcare, for example, the HMRC manual states that 'a salary sacrifice for childcare vouchers or the provision of an employer provided nursery place can reduce your relevant pay for tax credit purposes as the value of these benefits are not included as income. This may have the effect of increasing your Working Tax Credit award'.

A salary sacrifice arrangement in relation to travelling expenses was held to be ineffective by the Upper Tribunal in the *Reed Employment plc* case. This decision illustrates the need to do things properly, including ensuring that employees are clear as to the arrangement.

The *Employment Income Manual* (see also www.hmrc.gov.uk/specialist/salary_sacrifice.pdf) contains a seven-page document addressing some of the tax, National Insurance, and social security benefit implications of salary sacrifice schemes.

Having said all of the above, some evidence of a hardening attitude did start to emerge around the end of 2009. The hardening is in relation to specific benefits and is considered at the following paragraphs:

- cycle to work schemes: 141-250;
- workplace meals: 141-300.

FA 2015 introduced provisions, effective from 6 April 2016, to limit tax relief where payments are linked to certain salary sacrifice arrangements (140-405).

The changes introduced in *Finance Act* 2017 radically restricted the tax benefits associated with salary sacrifice (see 132-090).

Legislation: ITEPA 2003, s. 289A–289E

Case: *Reed Employment plc* [2014] BTC 511

Other Material: HMRC *Employment Income Manual* EIM42774

Making it work

It is important to ensure that the employee has contractually given up part of his or her gross pay before any amount is treated as received for tax purposes. Legal advice on achieving this may be advisable if tax problems are to be avoided. As long as this reduction in contractual pay has been achieved, the employer will only need to apply PAYE to the reduced salary figure. Any benefits in kind will be taxed under their own rules or, where the appropriate rules allow, may be provided tax free.

The scheme will fail if the employee has a right at any time to give up the benefit and to revert to the higher salary. It will also fail if, on a true construction of the varied contractual terms, the employee is merely asking the employer to apply part of the ordinary remuneration towards the cost of providing a benefit in kind.

HMRC have also indicated on the website that 'it is open to employers, when a salary sacrifice has been put in place, to ask their local HMRC office to confirm the correct tax treatment of the arrangement. This gives the employer reassurance that the arrangement has been implemented properly and they are acting correctly when not declaring benefits for tax purposes, operating PAYE and paying NICs'.

Case: *Heaton v Bell* (1969) 46 TC 211

Other Material: www.hmrc.gov.uk/specialist/sal-sac-question-and-answers.htm

Tax Reporter: ¶412-900

132-090 Salary sacrifice post 5 April 2017, 'optional remuneration arrangements'

The ability to remunerate an employee's tax efficiently by way of a salary sacrifice arrangement was severely restricted with effect from 6 April 2017, subject to certain limited transitional arrangements.

The legislation refers to 'optional remuneration arrangements'. In essence, where an employee is able to choose between receiving a benefit in kind and cash remuneration then, with the exemption of the benefits listed below, the employee will be taxed on the higher of the value of the benefit and the salary foregone. This applies even if the benefit would otherwise be tax-free, such as the provision of a mobile phone.

Certain limited benefits are specifically excluded from the new provisions and these are listed in ITEPA 2003, s. 228A. The principal ones are:

- employer pension contributions;
- qualifying childcare vouchers and employer provided care;
- cycle to work scheme.

Optional remuneration arrangements are not limited purely to traditional salary sacrifice arrangements. They will arise wherever an employee is provided with the option of additional remuneration or a benefit in kind. It will therefore be necessary to review historic employment contracts which may include explicit salary/benefit options, e.g. the provision of a company car or payment of a car allowance.

Timing and transitional arrangement

For the majority of benefits, these provisions will apply from 6 April 2017 for arrangement entered into from that date. Where the arrangement is already in place at 6 April 2017, then the provisions will be effective from 6 April 2018. This date is extended to 6 April 2021 for certain benefits such as accommodation, beneficial loans and company cars but only where there are no substantive changes or renewal of the arrangements before that date.

Legislation: ITEPA 2003, s. 69A

132-100 HMRC compliance checklist

In April 2014, HMRC republished an 'Expenses and Benefits from Employment Toolkit'. Although it is subtitled '2013–14 Employers' end of year forms and 2014–15 record keeping', the document contains some (mainly fairly basic) material that is of enduring interest. In particular, there is a compliance checklist, posing 23 questions under six headings, to help employers to meet their obligations in relation to benefits and expenses. The questions and headings are as follows:

Review of benefits and expenses

(1) Have all reportable benefits and expenses payments been identified and reported?

(2) Have all vouchers, credit/debit cards or other cards given to directors or employees been reported appropriately?

(3) If any directors or employees have employment related loans, has beneficial loan interest been reported appropriately?

(4) Have any loans waived or written off during the period been taxed or reported as necessary?

Tax Reporter: ¶412-830

Vehicles

(1) Have all company vehicles available for private use been identified?

(2) Has the correct list price been used to calculate the car benefit charge?

(3) Have all van benefit charges been reported?

(4) Have any company vehicles made available to a member of the directors' or employees' family or household been reported appropriately?

(5) If a car or van is regarded as pooled have all the necessary conditions been met?

(6) If fuel is provided for company vehicles has the correct fuel benefit charge been reported?

(7) Where a director or employee uses their own vehicle for business journeys, have all mileage payments which exceed the approved amount been reported?

(8) If an Employee Car Ownership Scheme (ECOS) arrangement has been used, have all of the necessary conditions been met?

Tax Reporter: ¶412-832

Travel, subsistence and entertainment

(1) Have payments for travel and subsistence been reviewed and reported appropriately?

(2) If travel and subsistence payments have been made for travel to a temporary workplace, have all the conditions been met?

(3) Has the cost of entertaining been reported appropriately?

(4) Have all staff functions been reviewed to ensure that they qualify as exempt from tax?

Tax Reporter: ¶412-834

Personal bills

(1) Have all directors' or employees' personal bills been identified and treated appropriately?

(2) Have all payments made for household expenses been reported?

Tax Reporter: ¶412-836

Use or transfer of assets

(1) If the employer provides living accommodation has the benefit been reported appropriately?

(2) Has the annual value of the use of land and buildings (other than living accommodation) placed at the directors' or employees' disposal been reported?

(3) Has the annual value of the use of any assets (other than land and buildings) placed at the directors' or employees' disposal been reported?

(4) If an asset has been transferred to a director or employee has the correct value been used?

(5) Has the residual cost of any in-house benefits, for example goods or services provided by the employer been reported?

Tax Reporter: ¶412-838

Company cars

132-200 Cars: introduction

The charge to tax

A company car tax charge will arise if three conditions are all met:

(1) a car is made available (without transfer of ownership) to an employee or a member of the employee's family or household;

(2) it is made available by reason of the employment; and

(3) it is available for the employee's or member's private use.

If these conditions are met, the cash equivalent of the benefit of the car is treated as earnings.

In *Cooper*, the taxpayer was a director of a company. A separate partnership was formed to provide administrative services to the company. The partnership provided cars to the director and family members, the cost of which was covered through the fees charged to the company. The First-tier Tribunal held that the cars had been made available by reason of the employment and dismissed the taxpayers' argument that retaining sums in the partnership constituted a contribution that should be offset against the benefit arising. The arrangement entered into was likely to give rise to an element of double taxation but the taxpayers had made a voluntary decision to arrange their affairs in the way they had chosen.

No benefit arises where a car is provided to an employee in lower-paid employment.

For the treatment of mileage allowance payments and reliefs, see 140-500ff.

Legislation: ITEPA 2003, s. 114(1), 120–148

Case: *Cooper* [2012] TC 02120

Choice of cash or car

If an employee is given the choice between a car and a cash alternative, the employee is taxed on whichever is chosen.

A special commissioner held that the purchase by an employee of a part interest (5%) in a car, with the employer retaining the remaining interest, took the vehicle out of the scope of the normal company car rules but this was overturned in the High Court (*Christensen (HMIT) v Vasili*).

Legislation: ITEPA 2003, s. 114(1), 119

Case: *Christensen (HMIT) v Vasili* [2004] BTC 318

Tax Reporter: ¶415-000

Car leased from employer

The effect of an apparently arm's length lease between employer and employee was considered in the case of *Whitby*. Although there was a slight complication on the nature of the lease, the appeal was argued on the basis that the lessor was the employer or a company associated with the employer, and that there was nothing exceptional about the lease. The directors and employees in question entered into car leasing contracts with the employer. The lessor bore the costs of servicing, insurance and road fund licence and the employees made substantial rental payments (typically of around £5,400 per year). Nevertheless, the individuals were found to be taxable on the company car benefit, on the basis that they were driving cars made available to them by their employer.

The company contended that the cars were not made available (without any transfer of property) in the sense required by the legislation. The argument was rejected. The cars fell within the relevant legislation simply because they were made available to the employees in question within the meaning of ITEPA 2003, s. 114(1)(a). The *Vasili* case had shown that an interest might be conferred upon an employee without preventing the car from being 'made available' in the sense required. If that had been the case for part-ownership, then the same must apply for a relationship between lessor and lessee. However, in *Apollo Fuels Ltd*, the Court of Appeal accepted that a car leasing scheme whereby the company leased cars to employees at a market rate and paid a mileage rate identical to that paid to other employees using their own cars meant that no benefit had been transferred to the employees and did not give rise to a car benefit charge. The result of the *Apollo Fuels* case is effectively overturned by Finance (No. 2) Bill 2016, cl. 7. This states that where certain benefits, including cars, are provided to employees, then a benefit in kind charge will arise even where the arrangement with the employee is on an arm's length basis.

Legislation: ITEPA 2003, s. 114(1A)

Cases: *Whitby* [2009] TC 00255; *R & C Commrs v Apollo Fuels Ltd* [2016] BTC 12

Tax Reporter: ¶415-180

Use of director loan accounts

If a company leases a car, the company car tax charge cannot be avoided simply by debiting the monthly leasing costs to the directors' loan accounts. In *Stanford Management Services Ltd*, the lease contracts were in the name of the company but the full cost of the lease payments was charged to their loan accounts. The company argued that there was no company car benefit as there was a nominee agreement. Alternatively, the substance of the transaction was that the directors had leased the cars and paid for them and were in reality the registered keepers. The tribunal found that there was no evidence for the existence of any agency or nominee agreement, and in any case the legislation was not concerned with agency. The contract was in the name of the taxpayer company. The company provided the cars to the directors. The legislation was satisfied and so a benefit arose.

Case: *Stanford Management Services Ltd* [2010] TC 00409

Tax Reporter: ¶415-180

132-210 Meaning of 'car' and associated terms

'Car'

For employment income tax purposes, a car is a mechanically propelled road vehicle which is not:

- a goods vehicle;
- a motor cycle;
- an invalid carriage; or
- a vehicle of a type not commonly used as a private vehicle and unsuitable to be so used.

The last of these exclusions will clearly take some vehicles straight out of the definition of 'car' for these purposes. Inevitably, however, there will be borderline cases. Note that it is necessary to satisfy two separate tests if the vehicle is to fall outside the definition of 'car' for tax purposes:

- it must be of a type not commonly used as a private vehicle; and
- it must be unsuitable to be so used.

In considering the issue of the 'type' of vehicle, HMRC rely on two capital allowances tax cases and conclude that 'a vehicle which has been modified in some way can be a different type from one that has not been modified'.

The mere painting of a vehicle (e.g. as an advertisement) is not sufficient to establish a different type of vehicle. However, any of the following may succeed in doing so:

- adding fixed flashing blue lights (*Gurney v Richards*);
- fitting dual controls, for example on a driving school vehicle (*Bourne v Auto School of Motoring (Norwich) Ltd*); or
- fitting a loudspeaker or a roof-top sign (e.g. for a taxi or driving school) on top of a car.

The mere fact that a car is usually kept loaded with goods or equipment will not take it outside the definition if simple unloading would make it suitable for private use.

Legislation: ITEPA 2003, s. 114

Cases: *Bourne v Auto School of Motoring (Norwich) Ltd* (1964) 42 TC 217; *Gurney v Richards* [1989] BTC 326

Other Material: HMRC *Employment Income Manual* EIM23125

Tax Reporter: ¶415-050

'Motor cycle' and 'invalid carriage'

In this context, the terms 'motor cycle' and 'invalid carriage' have the meanings given by *Road Traffic Act* 1988, s. 185(1).

Legislation: ITEPA 2003, s. 115(2)

'Goods vehicle'

For the purposes of defining 'car' and 'van', 'goods vehicle' is defined as 'a vehicle of a construction primarily suited for the conveyance of goods or burden of any description'.

This definition will exclude from the definition of 'car' any vans, pick-up trucks and heavy goods vehicles. In practice, it is not always easy to draw the line between a car and a van. The HMRC view is that estate cars do not normally come within the exemption:

> 'Most estate cars (or indeed cars with some sort of boot) are suited to the dual purpose of carrying passengers and some cargo or luggage. But it is clear that what they are primarily suited for is the conveyance of passengers.'

Legislation: ITEPA 2003, s. 115(2)

Other Material: HMRC *Employment Income Manual* EIM23100

'Van'

'Van' is defined as a mechanically propelled road vehicle which:

- is a goods vehicle;
- has a design weight not exceeding 3,500kg; and
- is not a motor cycle (as defined above).

Legislation: ITEPA 2003, s. 115(1)

132-220 Available for private use

Where a car is made available at all to an employee, it is automatically deemed to be available for private use unless:

- there is a specific prohibition on such use; and
- no such private use is made of the car during the tax year.

As such, a tax charge arises where a car is made available for private use even if there is in fact no such use at all in the year. There is evidence that HMRC will indeed pursue a tax charge in these cases.

It follows that, if an employee makes use of a car but never intends to use it for private purposes, there should be a written note from employer to employee prohibiting any private use. This should be in place before the start of the relevant tax year or before the car is first made available to the employee for any use (whether private or business).

'Private use' means any use other than for the employee's business travel.

Legislation: ITEPA 2003, s. 118

Tax Reporter: ¶415-200

132-230 Method of calculating the cash equivalent of the benefit of a car

The legislation sets out eight (formerly seven) steps for calculating the cash equivalent.

Step (1) Find the price of the car in accordance with ITEPA 2003, s. 122–124. See 132-240.

Step (2) If necessary, adjust the price to take account of any accessories in accordance with ITEPA 2003, s. 125–131. See 132-250.

Step (3) Make any deduction under ITEPA 2003, s. 132 for capital contributions made by the employee. See 132-280. The resulting figure is known as the 'interim sum'.

Step (4) This step ceased to apply from 6 April 2011. If the total given by Step (3) exceeded £80,000, the 'interim sum' was formerly capped at £80,000.

Step (5) Find the 'appropriate percentage for the car for the year' in accordance with ITEPA 2003, s. 133–142. See 132-330ff.

Step (6) Apply the percentage from Step (5) to the interim sum from Step (4).

Step (7) Compute the 'provisional sum' by adjusting the result of Step (6) under ITEPA 2003, s. 143 to take account of periods during which the car was unavailable for private use. See 132-290.

Step (8) Deduct from the provisional sum any amounts paid by the employee under ITEPA 2003, s. 144 for private use of the car. See 132-310.

This procedure covers all the statutory eventualities (except for three, noted below). In practice, however, many of the Steps will often not apply. In the simplest case of all, the price of the car (Step (1)) multiplied by the appropriate percentage (Step (5)) will give the cash equivalent of the car, i.e. the amount on which the employee will pay tax.

Special rules apply to cars that run on road fuel gas and classic cars. A reduction may be available if the car is shared.

Tax Reporter: ¶415-250

132-240 Price of a car: list price

The first stage in calculating the cash equivalent is to find what the legislation refers to as the 'price of the car'. This is defined as:

(1) the car's list price, if it has one; or

(2) its notional price, if it does not.

The 'list price' is the price published by the car's manufacturer, importer or distributor (as the case may be) as the 'inclusive price' appropriate for a car of that kind if sold:

- in the UK;
- singly;
- in a retail sale;
- in the open market; and
- on the day immediately before the date of the car's first registration.

It follows from this last point that, whatever the age of the car, and whether it was bought new or second-hand, the relevant list price is that published for the car on the day preceding its first registration.

The 'inclusive price' is the price inclusive of any charge for delivery by the manufacturer, importer or distributor to the seller's place of business and any relevant taxes. 'Relevant taxes' are defined to include VAT, any customs or excise duty, and 'any tax chargeable as if it were a customs duty'. It follows from the definition of 'inclusive price' that the 'inclusive price' does not include any delivery charge made by the local garage to the employer, or indeed to the employer direct from the manufacturer, importer or distributor.

The date of first registration in relation to a car or van is the date on which the vehicle was first registered under the *Vehicle Excise and Registration Act* 1994 or any corresponding foreign legislation. If a second-hand car is imported into the UK, it will be necessary to find out the price for a single UK retail sale on the date when the car was first registered abroad.

HMRC do not accept that a car dealer can be regarded as a 'distributor' for these purposes. As such, no account can be taken of local discounts.

A notional price is (to summarise) what the list price would have been had one been published.

Legislation: ITEPA 2003, s. 122ff., 171

Other Material: HMRC *Employment Income Manual* EIM24110ff.

Tax Reporter: ¶415-300

Reduction for road fuel gas cars

The extra cost of adapting or manufacturing a car to run on road fuel gases (compressed natural gas or liquid petroleum gas) is not included when calculating the company car benefit income tax charge. Thus employees will not be faced with a tax penalty where their cars are made capable of running on cleaner and greener road fuel gases.

Equipment by means of which a car is capable of running on 'road fuel gas' is not regarded as an accessory for these purposes. The price of a car which is manufactured so as to be able to run on road gas fuel is treated as the price given by step one, reduced by so much of the price as it is reasonable to attribute to the car being manufactured in that way, rather than in such a way as to be capable of running only on petrol. Both these provisions prevent an uplift of the company car benefit income tax charge in the circumstances described.

Legislation: ITEPA 2003, s. 125(2)(b), 146(2)

Reduction for certain cars for disabled drivers

If, because of a disability, a driver has to drive an automatic car, the list price of the equivalent manual vehicle will be used if it is lower than the list price of the automatic car; see 132-335.

132-250 Accessories: definitions

Accessories are in principle to be included in calculating the cash equivalent of the car benefit. However, the rules for applying this principle in practice are complicated. The Tax Law Rewrite highlighted, but did not remove, the inherent complexity.

The amounts to be taken into account are the price of any 'initial extra accessory' (in the case of a car with a list price) and the price of any 'later accessory' (in all cases). To apply these rules in practice, it is necessary to define the following terms:

- accessory;
- qualifying accessory;
- standard accessory;
- non-standard accessory;
- initial extra accessory; and
- later accessory.

Accessory

Subject to certain exceptions, an accessory includes any kind of equipment. It follows that an accessory must be a tangible item; it does not include such additional services as extended warranties purchased at the same time as the car. A fitted roof rack or perhaps internal blinds would need to be included. There are five exclusions from this definition:

(1) equipment that is 'necessarily provided' for use in the performance of the duties of the employment, such as a tow bar fitted because part of the employee's job is to tow a trailer carrying the equipment needed to carry out his duties;

(2) equipment used to enable the car to run on road fuel gas;

(3) equipment provided to enable a disabled person to use the car is not an accessory;

(4) a mobile telephone; and

(5) for 2011–12 and subsequent years, a relevant security feature (including armour and bullet resistant glass) and consequential modifications.

Legislation: ITEPA 2003, s. 121(1), 125(2)

Tax Reporter: ¶415-350

Qualifying accessory

A qualifying accessory is one that is made available by reason of the employment, and without transfer of ownership of the item in question. It must be attached to the car, though not necessarily permanently.

Legislation: ITEPA 2003, s. 125

Standard and non-standard accessory

A standard accessory is defined as one that is 'equivalent to an accessory assumed to be available with cars of the same kind as the car in question in arriving at the list price'. In other words, if an accessory is already included in the list price then there is a mechanism to ensure that there is no double charge to tax. The definition is also intended to take into account minor changes that manufacturers may make to particular models of car which do not result in changes in the published price lists.

A non-standard accessory is any other accessory.

Legislation: ITEPA 2003, s. 125

Initial extra accessory

An initial extra accessory is a non-standard accessory that is available with the car at the time the car is first made available to the employee.

Legislation: ITEPA 2003, s. 126(2)

Later accessory

A 'later accessory' is an accessory that meets the following conditions:

- it is available to the employee in the year in question;
- it was not made available when the car was first made available to the employee;
- it was not made available with the car before 1 August 1993;
- it has a list price (or, if appropriate, a notional price) of at least £100.

This raises a point of practice distinguishing the treatment of standard and later accessories. Optional accessories, attached when the car is first purchased, are already included in the list price of the car. As such, the removal of such an accessory will not reduce the tax charge. Accessories added later, on the other hand, are considered on a year-by-year basis and would no longer be taken into account for years following that in which the accessory was removed.

The term 'list price' is defined in relation to a later accessory as the published price of the manufacturer, importer or distributor of the accessory.

Legislation: ITEPA 2003, s. 126(3), 127(2)

Replacement accessories

Special rules apply to deal with replacement accessories. These are intended both (on the one hand) to prevent a double tax charge, and (on the other) to prevent possible tax avoidance where one accessory is replaced with another. The special rules apply where:

- in the tax year in question, a later accessory is available with the car;
- that accessory replaced another qualifying accessory, whether in that year or in a previous year – in which case, the replacement accessory is referred to as the new accessory; and
- the new accessory is of the same kind as the old one.

To determine the tax treatment, it is necessary to establish whether the new accessory is superior to the old one. It is treated as superior if the 'price' (as defined) of the new accessory is higher than both:

- the 'price' of the old accessory; and
- the 'price', immediately before the new accessory is first made available with the car, of an accessory equivalent to the old accessory.

If the new accessory is not superior, the change is ignored. The cash equivalent of the car continues to be calculated as if no replacement had been made, i.e. using the price of the original accessory.

If the new accessory is superior to the old one, the old accessory is normally ignored and the new one is instead taken into account for the tax year in which the change takes place and for all subsequent years.

Legislation: ITEPA 2003, s. 131

A typical case

A typical invoice from a car dealer will include the basic price, certain accessories, road fund licence, number plates, a first registration fee and, often, a 'road pack'. The basic price and accessories will clearly need to be taken into account in reaching the list price. The cost of number plates should also be included and it would seem appropriate also to include the road pack cost, being part of the capital cost of the car. The road fund licence cost should not be included, being a revenue rather than capital expense. Also, HMRC have confirmed that the first registration fee should be excluded.

Other Material: HMRC *Employment Income Manual* EIM24105, EIM24290

132-260 Price of a car: classic cars

There are special rules to increase the tax charge in respect of valuable older cars, which would otherwise be taxed only on the basis of a very low historic list price. The special rules apply where all three of the following conditions are met:

- the car is at least 15 years old at the end of the tax year;
- the market value of the car is £15,000 or more on the last day of the tax year (or if earlier, the last day on which the car is made available to the employee); and
- the market value of the car is greater than the price of the car on ordinary principles, after including in that price any accessories but after deducting any allowable capital contribution.

Where these conditions are met, the market value of the car on the relevant day is substituted for the price that would otherwise be carried forward from Step (3) (see 132-230) so as to produce a higher tax charge. The relevant day is the last day of the tax year or, if earlier, the last day in the year in which the car is available to the employee).

Capital contributions of up to £5,000 may be made so as to reduce the market value for tax purposes. The treatment of such capital contributions follows that of capital contributions towards cars that are not classic cars – see 132-280 for details.

Legislation: ITEPA 2003, s. 147

Tax Reporter: ¶415-400

132-280 Capital contributions by employees

Where a director or employee makes a contribution towards the cost of providing a car, this may be done in one of two ways with quite different tax results.

First, the employee may make a 'capital contribution' towards the cost of acquiring the car or any qualifying accessories. Alternatively, the employee may contribute on a year-by-year basis. This second type of contribution is examined in 132-310 below.

Where a capital contribution is made, it is deducted from the price of the car for the tax year in which the payment is made and for all subsequent years. The contribution towards the cost of one car cannot be carried forward to count against the price of another car. Similarly, a contribution made by one employee is lost if the car is transferred to a fellow employee.

There is a ceiling of £5,000 on the amount of any capital contribution which may be taken into account for these purposes. There is also a trap to avoid if a capital contribution is made towards the cost of an expensive car: see 132-270.

It is tax-effective to have an agreement that a capital contribution by the employee will be partially reimbursed when the car is sold. If the contribution is to be repaid in full then the HMRC view is that the employee would not be regarded as having made a capital contribution. However, if the agreement is that the employee will be repaid the same proportion of the sale proceeds as he has contributed to the purchase cost then he can have the full benefit of the whole capital contribution even though the net cost to him is ultimately less.

Legislation: ITEPA 2003, s. 132

Other Material: HMRC *Employment Income Manual* EIM24365

Tax Reporter: ¶415-500

132-290 Reduction for periods when car unavailable

If the car is not available for part of the year then the tax charge is reduced. However, the concept of not being available is tightly interpreted.

First, the car is treated as being available to an employee at any given time if it is available either to the individual concerned or to any other members of his family or household. If, for example, the employee himself is stationed overseas for a period but the car is still parked at his home then it may well be possible for HMRC to argue that the car is available to members of his household.

Furthermore, the car may still be treated as available to an individual even though he is in no state to drive it. If, for example, the employee breaks his leg and is clearly unable to drive for an extended period, this does not render the car unavailable for that period. The same principle applies if the employee is banned from driving. In such a circumstance, it is suggested that the car should, if possible, be left at the employer's premises and the keys should be handed in. Ideally, there would be a written note from the employer to the employee concerned confirming that, until further notice, the employee is not entitled to drive the vehicle.

The tax charge is reduced proportionately if the car is unavailable throughout a period of 30 days or more. The taxable benefit is also reduced proportionately if the car is only made available for part of the tax year, either because it is first made available after the start of the tax year or because it stops being made available before the end of the year (or both).

Where a reduction is to be made it is calculated on a daily basis, using the formula:

Legislation: ITEPA 2003, s. 143

Tax Reporter: ¶415-550

Car temporarily replaced

The general rules set out above are modified when a car is temporarily replaced.

A driver will on occasions make use of a courtesy car or other replacement car, typically following an accident or during a major car service. If the original car is out of action for – say – 20 days, relief will not be given under the rules relating to periods when a car is unavailable, because those rules only apply if it us unavailable for a period of at least 30 days.

On first principles, the replacement car would need to be treated as a second company car and taxed accordingly, leading to a double tax charge. The legislation therefore introduces rules to avoid this possible unfairness. Generally, a double tax charge will only be made if the employer is deliberately using the replacement as an excuse to provide a better car to the employee for a period (for example, to let the employee go on holiday).

Legislation: ITEPA 2003, s. 143, 145

132-300 Pooled cars

A car is treated as being unavailable for the private use of any of the employees concerned if all of the following conditions apply in a given tax year, i.e. if the vehicle is a 'pooled car':

- the vehicle was made available to more than one employee by reason of his employment;
- it was not ordinarily used by one employee to the exclusion of the others;
- any private use in the year by any of the employees concerned was 'merely incidental' to his business use in the year; and
- the car was not normally kept overnight near the home of an employee (unless an employee happens to live near to the premises of the person making the car available and the vehicle is parked overnight on those premises).

Given that these rules provide a total exemption from any tax charge, it is not surprising that HMRC apply them very strictly. A literal interpretation of the third condition above leads to the conclusion that it is not possible for a vehicle to be a pooled car for only part of any given tax year. If there is any private use (other than that which is 'merely incidental' to the same user's business use) in the year then the third condition is not satisfied.

The term 'pool car' is also widely used, but the legislation opts for 'pooled car'. The terms are synonymous.

Legislation: ITEPA 2003, s. 167

Other Material: HMRC *Employment Income Manual* EIM23475

Tax Reporter: ¶415-600

Meaning of 'merely incidental to'

HMRC issued a statement of practice entitled 'Pooled cars: incidental private use' but more up to date guidance on the concept of 'merely incidental' can be found in the *Employment Income Manual*.

HMRC make the basic distinction between private use of a car which is 'independent of the employee's business use of the car' on the one hand, and private use which 'follows from the business use' on the other. Again, HMRC talk of 'a qualitative rather than a quantitative test [which] does not refer to the extent of private mileage but rather to the private element viewed in the context of a journey as a whole'. The distinction derives from the case of *Robson v Dixon*.

Examples given by HMRC of cases where private use might be accepted as 'merely incidental' to business use include the case of an employee staying away from home overnight because of a business trip. The employee may use the car to go out for a meal in the evening: even though this journey is not 'necessary' in the tax sense, it may still be regarded as 'merely incidental' to the main business journey and to the overnight stay. By contrast, the use of a car for an annual holiday would not be accepted as 'merely incidental' to business use in the year, even if the amount of private mileage is very small in relation to business miles travelled during the rest of the year.

Case: *Robson v Dixon* (1972) 48 TC 527

Other Material: HMRC *Employment Income Manual* EIM23455; SP 2/96

Meaning of 'not normally kept overnight'

HMRC will normally accept that a car is not normally kept overnight at employees' homes within the meaning of the legislation if the nights on which it is taken home for any reason are less than 60% of the nights in the period under review.

HMRC will not accept an argument that a car taken home overnight only because of a risk of vandalism, or because of inadequate parking facilities at work, should be regarded as a pooled car.

The case of *Yum Yum Ltd* serves as a reminder that the rules will be strictly applied even if the resulting taxable benefit is out of all proportion to the value of the car in question. There was no evidence that anyone other than the individual in question had used the vehicle, and the condition about where the car was kept overnight was also not met. In respect of the latter point, it was argued that the employer company occupied the premises in which the director lived but there was no factual evidence to support that assertion.

Cases: *Yum Yum Ltd* [2010] TC 00616; *Jubb* [2015] TC 04760

Other Material: HMRC *Employment Income Manual* EIM23465

Burden of proof

The HMRC booklet 480 states that 'employers need to be able to demonstrate that the conditions for the car or van to be a pooled vehicle have been met, for instance, by keeping mileage records to show when the car was used, by whom and for what journeys'. However, the position is in reality more complex. In *Industrial Doors (Scotland) Ltd*, the tribunal noted that HMRC wording in booklet 480 but also noted that it was not a statutory requirement. In the absence of any proper evidence from

HMRC the tribunal chose to accept the facts as presented on behalf of the company and the appeal was allowed, confirming the status of the vehicles as pooled cars and eliminating the NIC liability. That case may be contrasted, though, with the case of *Ryan-Munden*, where there was an absence of any proper contemporary records as to usage of the car. The tribunal found that the evidence given by one of the company directors, Mr Munden, lacked credibility and was at times evasive. In the circumstances, the tribunal found that the car in question was generally made available to Mrs Ryan-Munden alone, and that she used it for private purposes that were not merely incidental to her other use of the car. She had failed to provide satisfactory evidence to show that all the conditions were met and the car therefore failed to qualify as a pooled car.

Cases: *Industrial Doors (Scotland) Ltd* [2010] TC 00571; *Ryan-Munden* [2011] TC 00889

Tax Reporter: ¶415-600

132-310 Reduction for payments for use of car

The tax charge may be reduced where, in any given year, an employee makes a contribution towards his private use of the car. Any such reduction is made as the last of the eight steps specified for calculating the taxable benefit (see 132-230). As always, there are pitfalls for the unwary.

The deduction is available if:

- as a condition of the car being available for the employee's private use, the employee is required in the tax year to pay an amount of money for that use, whether by way of deduction from his earnings or otherwise; and
- the employee does in fact make such a payment.

It is not sufficient that the employee merely does make the payment. There must be a requirement for him to do so. Nothing in the legislation allows HMRC to insist that the requirement should be in writing. Nevertheless, it would make sense both for tax reasons and commercially to have any such requirement evidenced in writing.

The payment must be made 'as a condition of the car being available' for the employee's private use (or for use by members of the employee's family or household). It would be as well to incorporate this wording into any agreement between employer and employee.

The payment must be made 'for that use', i.e. for the private use by the employee or members of his family or household. This provision is interpreted very tightly. The HMRC view is that where an employee is allowed the use of a more expensive car if he pays a monthly sum representing, for example, the excess leasing cost, then the payments by the employee would not reduce the benefit charge as they do not qualify as payments 'for the private use of the car'. In the HMRC view, they are 'merely for the availability of a more expensive car'. Not everybody would agree with this interpretation but HMRC are likely to defend it if challenged, particularly following the case of *Brown v Ware (HMIT)*.

In *Marshall*, the First-tier Tribunal held that the payment representing the contribution does not have to be in the same tax year but FA 2014, s. 25 put beyond doubt that the contribution from the employee must be made in the tax year for which a deduction is sought.

Legislation: ITEPA 2003, s. 144

Cases: *Brown v Ware (HMIT)* (1995) Sp C 29; *Marshall v HMRC* [2013] TC 02466

Tax Reporter: ¶415-650

132-320 Shared cars and cars provided for family members

Where a car is shared, the benefit for each employee should be calculated separately and a reduction should then be made on a just and reasonable basis. This reduction could, for example, take account of the fact that one employee has made a contribution to use of the car but another has not. No reduction will be made in respect of use by an individual who is not a P11D employee (or by members of his family or household).

Where two or more members of the same family work for the same employer and each is provided with a company car, each is only taxable in respect of the car made available to him or her. This general position may be challenged by HMRC where the provision of a car to a family member is not commensurate with the employee's position and results in a significant tax saving.

Suppose, for example, that the director of a company is a man and that his wife also works for the business, but on a part-time basis and not as a director. He is provided with a company car and so is she. Assume that the wife is a non-taxpayer or basic rate taxpayer and the husband is subject to tax at the additional rate. In this case, the husband may be taxed on the benefit of both cars unless the wife has the benefit of the car in her own right and other conditions are also met. HMRC take a hard line on this and were supported in that stance in the case of *S Barnard Ltd*.

Legislation: ITEPA 2003, s. 148(2), 169

Case: *S Barnard Ltd* [2010] TC 00491

Tax Reporter: ¶415-710

132-330 The appropriate percentage: overview

Introduction

Under Step (5) of the method for calculating the cash equivalent of the benefit of a car, it is necessary to find the 'appropriate percentage'. This is calculated primarily by reference to CO_2 emission levels (though different rules, based on engine size, apply for any remaining company cars first registered before 1 January 1998).

Most company cars registered from the start of 1998 have the taxable benefit calculated by reference to the car's CO_2 emissions figure. Such cars, referred to in this commentary as 'CO_2 certificate cars', will have an official certificate showing their CO_2 emissions figure.

Almost all cars have the CO_2 figure shown on their vehicle registration document (V5). In cases of difficulty, however, see the database of the Society of Motor Manufacturers and Traders (SMMT) at www.smmt.co.uk.

Tax Reporter: ¶415-720

132-335 Cars for disabled drivers

Adjustment to appropriate percentage

A rule is introduced to avoid penalising a disabled driver of an automatic car who, by reason of the disability, does not have the option of driving a manual car. In such a case, if the CO_2 figure for the automatic transmission car is higher than it would have been for an equivalent manual car, then the CO_2 figure for the equivalent manual car is used instead.

The adjustment is available if the employee holds a disabled person's badge at any time in the year when the car is made available for his private use and on the condition that the car is provided at least partly for the employee himself rather than for a member of his family or household.

Legislation: ITEPA 2003, s. 138

Adjustment to list price

Since April 2009, the legislation has also recognised that an automatic car may have a higher list price and that this may unintentionally penalise disabled employees who do not have the option of driving a manual vehicle. Where this is the case, and where a disabled employee who has to drive an automatic vehicle would otherwise face a higher tax charge as a result, the benefit is instead calculated by reference to the lower list price of the equivalent manual car.

To qualify for this special treatment, the employee must hold a disabled person's badge.

Legislation: ITEPA 2003, s. 124A

Tax Reporter: ¶415-800

132-340 The appropriate percentage: CO_2certificate cars

Basic principle

In practice, the great majority of company cars have their taxable values calculated by reference to their CO_2 emission figures. A higher level of emissions produces a higher appropriate percentage figure and therefore a higher taxable benefit.

For the tax year 2017–18, the appropriate percentage will fall between 9% (for a highly fuel-efficient car) and 37% (for a large, high-pollution car). In simple terms, therefore, a driver of a very low CO_2 emission petrol company car with a list price of £15,000 will pay tax for the year on £1,350 (i.e. 9% of £10,000), typically giving an additional tax bill of either £270 (basic rate) or £540 (higher rate). On the other hand, the driver of a company car with high levels of CO_2 emissions, and with a list price of £30,000, will pay tax on £11,100 (i.e. 37% of £30,000), giving a tax bill of (for example, for a 40% taxpayer) £4,440. These figures ignore other adjustments that may be made, for example in respect of any employee contributions for private use or for periods when the car is unavailable.

Legislation: ITEPA 2003, s. 139

Tax Reporter: ¶415-810

How is the appropriate percentage calculated?

The legislation provides a table showing the 'lower threshold' in grams per kilometre.

The need for a table (and the significance of the term 'appropriate percentage for the year') arises because the threshold tend to be decreased each year to encourage ever lower emissions. See *Hardman's Tax Rates and Tables* at 3-380 for details of the lower threshold applying for each year, or see 3-390 for a table of the actual appropriate percentage applying year by year for specified levels of CO_2 emissions.

With the exception of the two very lowest bands, the percentage increases by 1% for each additional five grams per kilometre of CO_2, rounding down any amounts not divisible by five.

Cars meeting this definition have a 'special percentage' of zero for the tax years 2010–11 to 2014–15 inclusive (ITEPA 2003, s. 140(3A)). Thereafter, the special percentage has risen from zero to 9% for 2017–18.

Example

A director drives an electric company car with a list price of £25,000. The car produces no CO_2 emissions while it is being driven.

For periods from 6 April 2010 to 5 April 2015, there is no taxable benefit from the provision of the company car (and no Class 1A NIC charge for the employer). Thereafter the taxable benefit rises to £2,250 (£25,000 at 9%) for 2017–18.

Tax Reporter: ¶415-760

132-350 Other cars

Various discounts applied, for periods to 5 April 2011, to the following types of car:

- road fuel gas cars;
- hybrid (electric and petrol) cars;
- bi-fuel cars.

These discounts have now all been withdrawn.

Legislation: SI 2001/1123, reg. 3–6

Automatic cars made available to disabled drivers

A rule exists to avoid penalising a disabled driver of an automatic car who, by reason of the disability, does not have the option of driving a manual car. See 132-335.

Legislation: ITEPA 2003, s. 138

132-360 Cars in the motor industry

Employees in the motor trade are taxed in the same way as any other employees where a car is made available to them for private use. However, as such drivers typically use large numbers of different cars in quick succession, it can be impractical to follow the letter of the law when calculating the taxable benefit. For many years, local offices of HMRC operated informal arrangements to address the issues arising, but formal guidelines have applied since 6 April 2009.

Other Material: HMRC *Employment Income Manual* EIM23765

Tax Reporter: ¶415-825

Test and experimental cars

Engineers in the motor and components industries are often required, as part of their jobs, to test cars under various driving conditions. HMRC recognise that for certain types of test such as cold starting, the only practical way of conducting them is for the engineers concerned to use the cars for private journeys and to report on their performance.

The strict legal position is clearly that a tax charge arises in these circumstances. However, HMRC have indicated that they will not seek tax under the company car provisions 'where the primary use of the car is for testing and any private use is clearly subsidiary to that testing'.

Other Material: HMRC *Employment Income Manual* EIM23805

Tax Reporter: ¶415-825

Demonstration and courtesy cars

Where, as part of the normal duties, a director, car salesperson or demonstrator takes a car home for the express purpose of calling on a prospective customer, or servicing staff take a car home overnight as part of a collection and delivery arrangement with a customer, the car will not on that account alone be treated as available for private use. In essence, the whole journey is for a genuine business purpose.

If, however, the car is otherwise available for the employee's private use (e.g. journeys home when no such call is scheduled, at weekends or for holidays), the normal car benefit will be chargeable in full. Furthermore, the fact that an employee might occasionally take home a car under such arrangements will not reduce the taxable car benefit.

Other Material: HMRC *Employment Income Manual* EIM23810

Tax Reporter: ¶415-825

Frequent car changes

As explained above, particular issues can arise in relation to company cars for employees in the motor industry. In October 2008, HMRC issued new guidelines addressing some of the practicalities. The guidelines are fairly complex in relation to employees who drive many different cars in the same tax year, and where it would strictly be necessary for the employer to complete separate P11D entries in relation to every vehicle.

Since April 2009, employers in the car industry with employees who frequently drive different cars have been able to choose to report benefits in kind on a non-statutory basis according to principles now laid out centrally by HMRC. The HMRC guidance runs to 18 pages and is contained in the *Employment Income Manual* EIM23825ff. The process involves seven steps that may be summarised as follows:

(1) identify the cars that need to be averaged;

(2) separate the cars into groups;

(3) calculate the average price of the notional car in each group;.

(4) calculate the average CO_2 emissions and appropriate percentage of the notional car in each group;

(5) determine the benefit charge for the notional car in each group;

(6) identify employees within these arrangements;

(7) allocate those employees to groups.

Full details of these steps (including a further amendment announced in March 2009) are given in the *Tax Reporter* (as below).

HMRC do *not* accept that any reduction in the taxable benefit is appropriate just because the employees may be driving older cars or just because they may not know which car will be made available to them from day to day.

Other Material: HMRC *Employment Income Manual* EIM23830ff.

Tax Reporter: ¶415-830

Employee car ownership schemes

132-365 Introduction and overview

One of the many documents published at the time of the 2006 Budget was the 'Report on the Evaluation of the Company Car Tax Reform: Stage 2'. The *Report* advised that company car changes have led to overall revenue losses for the Exchequer and that these losses arise partly because 'some employers and drivers have stopped having company cars'.

In a press release dated 8 May 2006, it was then announced that the Report was being used as the starting point for HMRC's *Review of Employee Car Ownership Schemes* (ECOS). The ECOS is not (yet) a statutory tax concept but the Report states that these schemes:

> 'enable employees to acquire a car often within a specified finance framework. The common feature of the schemes is that the employer is involved in facilitating the arrangement in some way.'

HMRC are conducting the review of such schemes 'to consider the argument for and against taxing (and subjecting to NIC) the advantage that an employee or employer derives from ECOS'.

In October 2007, HMRC reported that they had received a large number of responses to their cars review (which included the ECOS idea), and that the Government would be making 'an announcement on future policy in this area in Budget 2008'. In reality, however, the position remains unresolved even around the middle of 2013. Nevertheless, those making decisions between private and company cars ought to bear in mind at least the possibility that some further tax charge may apply.

Finance Act 2016 makes it clear that whenever a car is provided by an employer to an employee without transferring full title, then the statutory benefit in kind charge will arise regardless of whether the arrangements between the parties are on an arm's length basis and the employee pays a full open market lease charge for the use of the vehicle. The only exception will be where the employer's normal business is the hire of cars to the public.

Legislation: ITEPA 2003, s. 114(1A)

Tax Reporter: ¶415-860

132-368 Tax issues arising in an ECOS

HMRC particularly identify the following tax considerations that may arise in relation to an ECOS arrangement:

- the price at which the vehicle is sold to the employee;
- the amount at which the employee can re-sell the car to the employer or provider (often referred to as the 'guaranteed future value');
- provision of any benefits in kind, such as vehicle excise duty, insurance, repairs and servicing;
- where any payment is made in connection with the vehicle.

Other Material: HMRC *Employment Income Manual* EIM31510ff.

Tax Reporter: ¶415-875

Car fuel

132-380 Overview

A tax charge arises where fuel is provided for the driver of a company car. This charge, which is on top of the taxable benefit of the company car itself, arises irrespective of the method of payment for the fuel and specifically including the use of vouchers, credit tokens, etc.

No fuel charge arises where electrical energy is provided for an electrically propelled vehicle.

No fuel charge arises where fuel is made available only for business travel.

There is no question of applying the fuel scale charge where the vehicle is privately owned (despite an apparent attempt by HMRC to impose such a charge in one case reported in *Taxation* magazine of 12 October 2006 at p. 48).

Again, no fuel tax charge arises where, in the year concerned, the employer initially pays for all fuel but:

- there is a requirement that the employee must make good the *whole* of the cost of fuel provided for private uses; and
- the employee does in fact make good all of that cost.

HMRC interpret these conditions strictly:

> 'Where **any** fuel is provided for a car that attracts a car benefit charge, the car fuel benefit charge will automatically apply (see EIM25510) unless the employee shows that either condition A or condition B in ITEPA 2003, s. 151 is met (see EIM25555).'

HMRC publish advisory fuel rates (see *Hardman's Tax Rates and Tables* at 3-460) for reimbursement of fuel. These rates can be used whether the employee initially pays for fuel and is reimbursed for the cost of business journeys or where the employer pays and then seeks reimbursement from the employee for private journey costs.

Legislation: ITEPA 2003, s. 149ff.

Other Material: HMRC *Employment Income Manual* EIM25650

Tax Reporter: ¶416-000

132-390 Calculating the car fuel benefit charge

The calculation of the charge is relatively simple: an 'appropriate percentage' is applied to a fixed figure of £22,600 (for 2017–18). For earlier years see *Hardman's Tax Rates and Tables* at 3-440. The 'appropriate percentage' is the same as is used to calculate the benefit of the company car itself: see 132-330ff.

This is subject to possible reductions for periods where the car is unavailable or is shared. A reduction may also be made where the benefit of free fuel is stopped part way through the tax year.

If the company car is unavailable then the car fuel charge is reduced proportionately. The car is only treated as unavailable, however, in the circumstances outlined at 132-290 (periods at the start or end of the tax year, or periods exceeding 30 days).

Given that the tax cost of being provided with free fuel is now very high, many employers may consider stopping the benefit part way through the tax year. An employee who stops receiving free fuel part way through the tax year receives a proportionate reduction in the fuel benefit.

Legislation: ITEPA 2003, s. 150ff.

Tax Reporter: ¶416-030

132-395 Car fuel benefit: making good

HMRC publish advisory rates that may be used for reimbursement of mileage driven by company car drivers. The rates, including amendments issued since the concept was introduced, are given in *Hardman's Tax Rates and Tables* at 3-460. The same rates may be used whether:

- the employer initially pays for all fuel and the employee then reimburses the cost of private mileage; or
- the employee initially pays for all fuel and the employer then reimburses the cost of business mileage.

Employer paying for all fuel and then seeking reimbursement from employee

An employer may initially pay for all fuel and then obtain repayment of the private element from the employee driver. As long as all private mileage has been properly identified, and employees reimburse all such mileage at the published rates or at any higher figures, HMRC nearly always accept that no tax or Class 1A NIC liability will arise in respect of a fuel charge. The only exception is for cars with an engine size greater than three litres, where HMRC may argue for a higher repayment figure to apply.

Any requirement that the employee will reimburse the cost of private fuel should be in place before the fuel is first provided. Such reimbursement by the employee would ideally also be made within the tax year, given that the legislation clearly states that this should be done 'in the tax year in question'. F(No. 2)A 2017 introduced legislation requiring any reimbursement to be made on or before 6 July in the year following the provision of the benefit (see 132-050).

Legislation: ITEPA 2003, s. 151(2)

Other Material: HMRC *Employment Income Manual* EIM25660

Tax Reporter: ¶416-040

Employee paying for all fuel and then seeking reimbursement from employer

HMRC will also use the advisory figures to determine the level of payment that can be made by an employer to reimburse an employee for business mileage, without causing the employee to incur a tax liability. This is generally the better way of arranging matters. As long as the rate paid per mile by the employer does not exceed the appropriate figure from the table, HMRC accept that there is no taxable profit and no Class 1 NIC liability. Furthermore, HMRC are open to persuasion in exceptional cases that the true cost per mile is higher than that shown in the table. They might, for example, accept a higher payment per mile by an employer where an employee – in the course of the duties of his or her employment – drives a 4 × 4 car over rough terrain, or perhaps where the employee undertakes numerous short business journeys, such that the fuel consumption is higher than would normally be the case.

Employers may, of course, choose to pay a lower rate per mile. In principle, it is then open to the employee to claim tax relief on the shortfall.

132-400 Car fuel benefit: practical issues

Given the potential tax and NIC cost of the fuel benefit, it is particularly important for employers to satisfy themselves that they are not inadvertently paying for some private fuel. If an employee makes a claim for a particular journey, for example, and the employer reimburses the cost of fuel for the journey, then this could bring into force the whole fuel charge if it was not in fact bona fide business mileage. This is a serious practical problem.

By contrast, HMRC accept that no car fuel scale charge arises merely because the mileage allowance paid in respect of genuine business journeys exceeds the cost of fuel for those journeys. In these cases,

HMRC accept that the excess is not necessarily a payment for private fuel. The difference between the cost of fuel used for the business journey and the allowance received would be assessable to tax in place of the scale charge itself.

Other Material: HMRC *Employment Income Manual* EIM25660

Tax Reporter: ¶416-060

Company vans and van fuel

132-600 Company vans – overview

In principle, a tax charge arises where a van is made available to an employee, or to a member of his family or household. An additional charge may arise if the employer pays for fuel for the van.

Pooled vans are treated in the same way as pooled cars (see 132-300), that is to say, they are exempt where the stringent conditions are met.

'Vans' are defined as mechanically propelled road vehicles of a design weight not exceeding 3,500 kilograms and of a construction primarily suited to the conveyance of goods or burden of any description. Other definitions include:

- 'design weight': the laden weight which the vehicle is designed not to exceed;
- 'age of van': age between first registration and any given time;
- 'first registration': date of first registration under the *Vehicle Excise and Registration Act* 1994 or any corresponding foreign legislation;
- 'business travel': travel which a person is necessarily obliged to do in the performance of the duties of the employment;
- 'private use': any use other than business use.

Vans are deemed to be available for private use unless the terms on which they are provided prohibit such use and no such use is made of them. Any van provided for an employee or his family or household is deemed to be by reason of his employment unless (very exceptionally) the employer is an individual and the van was made available by reason of domestic, personal or family relationships.

There are some important exemptions from the tax charge on drivers of company vans: see 132-610.

Legislation: ITEPA 2003, s. 117ff., 154ff.

Tax Reporter: ¶416-200

132-610 Company vans – exemptions

There are three ways in which the provision of a company van may be exempt.

- Insignificant private use; see 132-612.
- Restricted private use (for commuting); see 132-614.
- Zero emissions when driving; see 132-616.

Tax Reporter: ¶416-260

132-612 Company van exemption: insignificant private use

No tax charge arises from the provision of a company van 'if the private use of the van during the tax year by the employee or member of the employee's family or household is insignificant'. HMRC have provided guidance on how they intend to interpret the word 'insignificant' in this context. At EIM22745, for example, they comment that:

> 'The word "insignificant" is not defined, so it takes its normal English meaning. For example, the New Oxford English Dictionary defines it as, "too small or unimportant to be worth consideration".'

The guidance goes on to say that private use is considered insignificant if is:

> '• insignificant in quantity in the tax year as a whole (i.e. a few days at most);
> • insignificant in quality (e.g. a week's exclusive private use is clearly **not** insignificant);
> • intermittent and irregular;
> • very much the exception in terms of the pattern of use of that van by that employee (or their family or household) in that tax year;
> • insignificant in absolute terms, not merely as a proportion of other use.'

HMRC go on to give the following examples of insignificant use.

> 'An employee who
> • takes an old mattress or other rubbish to the tip once or twice a year
> • regularly makes a slight detour to stop at a newsagent on the way to work
> • calls at the dentist on his way home.'

By contrast, the following would not qualify as insignificant.

> 'An employee who
> • uses the van to do the supermarket shopping each week
> • takes the van away on a week's holiday
> • uses the van outside of work for social activities.'

Legislation: ITEPA 2003, s. 114(3A)

Tax Reporter: ¶416-260

132-614 Company van exemption: restricted private use

No tax charge arises from the provision of a company van where the 'restricted private use condition' is met. This concept in turn introduces a second expression, the 'commuter use requirement'. This latter requirement will be satisfied at any time if two conditions are met:

- the terms on which the van is made available to the employee prohibit private use of the van otherwise than for ordinary commuting (or travel that is 'substantially ordinary commuting'); and
- neither the employee nor any member of his family or household actually makes private use of the van other than for such commuting purposes.

The 'restricted private use condition' is then said to be met for any given tax year if:

- the commuter use requirement is satisfied throughout the whole year or throughout the part of the year during which the van is made available to the employee; and
- the van is at that time made available to the employee mainly for the purposes of business travel.

The rules contain a slight relaxation of the commuter use requirement. The conditions can still be treated as met if the extent to which that requirement is not satisfied during the period is 'insignificant'. This word is interpreted here as for the first van exemption, see 132-612.

Where these conditions are met, no tax is charged in relation to the van – i.e. the cash equivalent is nil.

Legislation: ITEPA 2003, s. 155(2)

Tax Reporter: ¶416-260

132-616 Company van exemption: zero emissions

A further exemption from the van scale charge is available for the tax years 2010–11 to 2014–15 inclusive.

The tax charge is nil in each of these years if the van cannot in any circumstances emit CO_2 by being driven. Typically, this will cover electric vans, but the wording allows for alternative technologies to be developed for vans that have different forms of power. At Budget 2014, the Government announced the van benefit charge (VBC) support for electric vans will be extended to 5 April 2020 on a tapered basis, this was further amended in *Finance Act* 2016. In 2015–16, the VBC rate paid by electric vans was 20% of the rate paid by conventionally fuelled vans, followed by 20% in 2016–17 and in 2017–18, 40% in 2018–19 and 60% in 2019–20, 80% in 2020–21, 90% in 2021–22, with the rates equalised in 2022–23.

Legislation: ITEPA 2003, s. 155(2)

Tax Reporter: ¶416-260

132-620 Company vans – computation of benefit

The taxable benefit for a company van is £3,230 for 2017–18 unless one of the exemptions applies (see 132-610), in which case the benefit in kind is zero.

Example 1

Pete is employed as an electrician in Luton. His employer provides him with a van which he uses every day for work. Pete is allowed to use the van for private journeys within Bedfordshire, though he has to ask for permission if he wants to take the van outside the county. The van is replaced every three years. Pete must pay tax on an annual benefit of £3,230. (He may also incur a fuel scale charge; see 132-630.)

Example 2

Steve works as a plumber. He is provided with a van which is kept full of tools and plumbing accessories. His work involves visits to private houses. His routine varies and on some mornings he goes direct to his first job but on others he has to go first to the employer's depot to pick up supplies. Steve is allowed to take the van home at the end of each day but is strictly forbidden to make any other private use. The insurance of the van reflects these conditions. Steve meets the restricted private use condition as the only permitted private use is for ordinary commuting. His taxable benefit is therefore nil, and he will not incur a fuel scale charge, even if his employer pays for all fuel for the van (see 132-630).

Example 3

Jack is director of a company that imports fruit and vegetables. He works almost entirely from the warehouse. Jack has a luxury car at home but on advice from his accountant he uses an (expensive) van for commuting to and from work, a round trip of 40 miles. The company pays for all expenses, including fuel. Nobody else drives the van. Jack tells his accountant that he almost never uses the van for purposes other than commuting to and from

> work. Jack must pay tax on an annual benefit of £3,230. A fuel scale charge also applies (see 132-630).
>
> The fact that Jack may make occasional private use of the van for other purposes is not the main problem – other private use is not fatal as long as it is insignificant. However, it is clear on these facts that the van is not being made available mainly for the purposes of business travel. It therefore fails the second leg of the restricted private use condition. It also appears on these facts that there may be no formal restriction in place to prevent other private use.

Tax Reporter: ¶416-240

132-625 Shared vans

The rules for shared vans apply where a van is made available by the same employer to more than one employee, and where both employees may use the van for private purposes. The taxable benefit is first calculated in accordance with normal principles. A reduction is then given for any periods during which the van is unavailable. To recognise that the benefit of the van is shared between more than one employee, a further reduction is then made 'on a just and reasonable basis'. Discretion as to what is just and reasonable will presumably be left to employers unless HMRC suspect deliberate manipulation of the rules.

Tax Reporter: ¶416-280

132-630 Van fuel

There will be no fuel benefit where the benefit of the van itself is exempt (see 132-610). In other cases, the taxable cash equivalent of free fuel for a company van in 2017–18 is £610 per year. Many of the principles are similar to those governing fuel for a company car (see 132-380). There is no taxable fuel benefit if fuel is made available only for business travel. Subject to that, the benefit arises unless the employee makes good the whole of the expense incurred by the employer in connection with the provision of fuel for private use.

As with car fuel, it is possible for an employee to give up the benefit of free van fuel part way through the tax year. Where this applies, there is a proportionate reduction in the fuel scale charge. A reduction is also made to the fuel scale charge for any period during which the van is treated as unavailable. Similarly, a 'corresponding reduction' is made where the van is shared and the taxable benefit is reduced accordingly.

Tax Reporter: ¶416-380

Other vehicles

132-640 Heavier commercial vehicles

There is no chargeable benefit in connection with an employee's use of a commercial vehicle exceeding 3,500kg, provided the employee's use is not 'wholly or mainly' private use.

Also excluded from a charge are the payment by the employer of expenses or the provision by him of a non-cash voucher or credit token which is used for obtaining goods or services in connection with the heavier commercial vehicle, which would otherwise be chargeable under the charge on general earnings provisions.

Legislation: ITEPA 2003, s. 238

132-650 Emergency vehicles

There is no tax charge where there is an operational requirement for certain employees to take their emergency vehicles home.

The rules apply to emergency vehicles that are fitted out as such and that are not available for general private use. An emergency vehicle is one which is used to respond to emergencies. It must normally have a fixed lamp that is designed to emit a flashing light for use in emergencies. This rule is relaxed, however, if the use of such a fixed lamp could produce a special threat to the personal physical security of those using the vehicle 'by reason of it being apparent that they were employed in an emergency service'.

For the exemption to apply, private use must be prohibited except where the person is either on call or 'engaged in on-call commuting'.

Legislation: ITEPA 2003, s. 248A

Tax Reporter: ¶416-650

Drivers and chauffeurs

132-660 Volunteer drivers

Where volunteers drive for hospital car services, etc., HMRC accept that they may be reimbursed using authorised mileage rates (see 140-550) even though they are not strictly employees.

Other Material: www.hmrc.gov.uk/cars/volunteer-drivers.htm

132-670 Chauffeurs

Where an employer provides not only a car, but also a chauffeur, the benefit of the use of the chauffeur is charged separately to tax.

Legislation: ITEPA 2003, Pt. 3, Ch. 10

Tax Reporter: ¶416-750

Employment-related loans

132-800 Introduction

Where a loan is made to a director or employee by reason of their employment, and the loan is either interest-free or at a preferential rate interest, there will normally be a charge to tax on the cash equivalent of the benefit obtained.

There may also be a charge if such a loan is made to a 'relative' of the employee, unless the employee derived no benefit from the loan. 'Relative' means the employee's:

(1) spouse or civil partner;

(2) parent or remoter forebear, child or remoter issue, brother, sister, in each case of either the employee or of the employee's spouse or civil partner; or

(3) spouse or civil partner of a person falling within (2).

A loan to a nephew, for example, would not be directly caught, but care should be taken. Whilst there may be no charge under these provisions the loan could give rise to a liability under other provisions if the employer is a limited company and the employee or his relative holds shares in the company.

A loan will be regarded as made by reason of a person's employment if it is made by his employer, unless the employer is an individual and the loan was made in the normal course of domestic, family or personal relationships. The concept of 'making a loan' is given an artificially wide meaning for these purposes and includes the arranging, guaranteeing or facilitating of a loan (or of the continuation of an existing loan). It also includes circumstances where a person assumes the rights and liabilities of the original lender.

A loan will also be regarded as made by reason of a person's employment if it is made by a company in the same group. Since the employer need not be a company, this would include, for instance, a company owned by the individual or partnership by which the person was controlled.

Further, a loan by a person with a 'material interest' in a close company to a person whose employer either had control over, or was controlled by that close company, is within the scope of the legislation. So that, for instance, a loan by a shareholder in a company which was controlled by a person's employer could give rise to a chargeable benefit.

For the purpose of these provisions an employer includes a prospective employer so that a charge cannot be avoided by making a loan before an employment commences.

'Company' is for these purposes defined as including a partnership, except in the reference to a close company.

Legislation: ITEPA 2003, s. 173ff.

Other Material: HMRC *Employment Income Manual* EIM26100ff.

Tax Reporter: ¶417-000

Directors' loan accounts

Where directors withdraw money from the company, it will be necessary to consider whether these withdrawals should be treated as remuneration (or on account of remuneration) or whether they are loans. If the former, then PAYE should be applied at the time of withdrawal. If not, then an employment-related loan is likely to be created by the withdrawal. If expenditure is charged to the loan account, it is important to ensure that this is done at the correct time, and not just at the year end. HMRC made this point in a *Directors' Loan Accounts Toolkit* issued towards the end of 2010, as follows:

> 'If transactions are not posted at the time they occur, for example if they are only posted at the year end, an overdrawn balance during the year may be overlooked. Overdrawn loan accounts may constitute a beneficial loan which should be returned on form P11D.'

HMRC instructions to their own tax officers then reinforce this as follows:

> 'Transactions should normally be recorded as they occur and a detailed transaction history maintained, so that it is possible to identify the director's loan account balance on any given date. Where a contemporaneous record has not been kept consider whether the loan account should be reproduced to identify if it has been overdrawn at any point during the year. Where a director's loan account is overdrawn at any point during the year consider whether there is a beneficial loan and ensure the benefit is returned on form P11D.'

132-805 Alternative finance arrangements

For the purposes of the rules relating to employment-related loans, a reference to a loan is taken to include a reference to an alternative finance arrangement to which FA 2005, s. 47 or 47A applies. These sections are concerned respectively with 'alternative finance return' and 'diminishing shared ownership'. Also included in the definition of 'loan' for the purposes of the benefit in kind rules is any arrangement to which those sections would apply if one of the parties were a financial institution.

Any reference in the employment-related loan rules to 'interest' includes a reference to 'alternative finance return'.

Tax Reporter: ¶417-275

132-810 Calculating the taxable benefit

The cash equivalent of the benefit is the interest which would have been payable at the 'official rate' less any interest actually paid. The amount to be taken into account is the interest actually paid in the income tax year rather than the amount of interest payable. However, where an amount which was payable in a particular year is in fact paid later, a claim can then be made to take the amount into account for the year in which it was payable.

The official rate of interest is published by HMRC and is in practice set in advance for the following year. It was 4% from 6 April 2010 falling to 3.25% from 6 April 2014 and 3% from 6 April 2015. The rate from 5 April 2017 was further reduced to 2.5%. For details of the official rates for all recent periods, see *Hardman's Tax Rates and Tables* at 3-550.

Averaging method

The normal method of calculation is the averaging method. Here, the average rate of interest for the income tax year is applied to the sum of the opening and closing balances divided by two.

Example 1

	£
At the start of the tax year 2017–18, George owes his employer	24,000
At the end of the tax year, he owes	18,000

The official rate of interest for the year is taken to be 2.5%. George pays interest of £400.

Using the averaging method, the cash equivalent of the benefit is as follows:

	£
$\frac{£24,000 + £18,000}{2} \times 2.5\% =$	525
Less: Interest paid by George	(400)
Taxable amount	125

Where the loan was taken out or repaid during the year a proportional adjustment is necessary. The charge is calculated by reference to the number of whole months (calculated from the 6th of each month) for which the loan was outstanding.

Example 2

At 6/4/17, Bill owes his employer £18,000.

This is repaid on 05/11/17.

Bill pays no interest on the loan.

Assuming an official rate throughout the period of 2.5%, the benefit is calculated as follows:

$$\frac{£18,000 + £18,000}{2} \times 2.5\% \times \frac{7}{12} = £262.50$$

Alternative method

There is an alternative form of calculation which is more accurate and which is used either if the employee wishes or if an officer of Revenue and Customs serves notice that he requires it to be used. This alternative basis requires interest to be calculated on a daily basis for each period for which the rate of interest remains the same. The time limit for either party to give the notice is the usual one applying under self assessment, namely the first anniversary of the normal filing date.

Example

	£
At the start of the tax year, Andrew owed his employer	20,000
By the following 5 February, he had repaid	12,000
By 5 April, he still owed	8,000

The official rate of interest for the year is taken to be 2.5% throughout.

Using the alternative method, the cash equivalent of the benefit is as follows:

	£
$£20{,}000 \times \frac{10}{12} \times 2.5\% =$	416.67
$£8{,}000 \times \frac{2}{12} \times 2.5\% =$	33.33
	450.00

Tax Reporter: ¶417-100

132-815 Capitalised interest

In particular circumstances, a lender may roll up (or 'capitalise') interest owing on a loan. The question then arises of whether such an amount of interest can be treated as having been 'paid' for the purposes of calculating any taxable benefit on an employer loan. HMRC take the view that the interest that has been capitalised in this way should not be treated as having been 'paid'. HMRC have case law support for this view, including in particular the case of *Paton (as Fenton's Trustee) v IR Commrs* in which the judge commented that 'it is only by a legal fiction that the interest in such cases ... can be said to have been paid'. This meant that for tax purposes, it could not be said that the interest had been paid: what the tax legislation requires 'is that the sum due as interest shall have been actually discharged, not merely constructively paid'.

Case: *Paton (as Fenton's Trustee) v IR Commrs* (1938) 21 TC 626

Other Material: HMRC *Employment Income Manual* EIM26251

Tax Reporter: ¶417-050

132-820 'Official rate' on foreign currency loans

The Treasury can set a different 'official rate' of interest in respect of foreign currency loans, where the borrower normally lives in the country or territory in question, and has lived there at some time in the past six years, and obtains the benefit of the loan by reason of his employment. The provision enables the cash equivalent of such loans to reflect actual rates of interest prevailing in that country, though an HMRC press release suggests that the measure will only be used to set lower official rates where interest rates in the country concerned are lower than in the UK.

There is no statutory definition of 'normally lives' so HMRC state that the term has its 'natural common sense meaning'. It is not necessary to maintain a residence in the overseas country in the case, for example, of an employee who has come to work for a few years in the UK. On the other hand, the term 'living' is said to imply 'more than returning for a short holiday'.

Alternative rates may be used for employer-provided loans made in Japanese Yen and Swiss Francs (*Taxes (Interest Rate) Regulations* 1989 (SI 1989/1297), reg. 5). See *Hardman's Tax Rates and Tables* at 3-550 for rates.

Legislation: ITEPA 2003, s. 173(2), 181

Other Material: HMRC *Employment Income Manual* EIM26106

Tax Reporter: ¶418-100

132-830 Replacement loans

A replacement loan is not automatically a taxable loan: the same tests apply to determine whether it is an employment-related loan as apply for other non-replacement loans. An employer who wishes to stop providing cheap or interest-free loans to employees is therefore able to transfer the loans to the subsidiary of a commercial lender set up for the purpose without the replacement loans automatically being taxable. The loans will not be exempt as commercial loans (see 132-880) if the subsidiary company does not lend to the general public.

Anti-avoidance: replacement after employment ceases

Anti-avoidance measures deal with the situation where the employment-related loan is replaced after the employment ceases and prevent abuse of the 'averaging' calculation used to determine the taxable value of an employment-related loan. A replacement loan is treated as an employment-related loan obtained by reason of the employee's former employment if it replaces a loan, the benefit of which was obtained by reason of the employee's former employment, and had the employment not terminated or ceased to be an employment, the replacement loan would have been a loan obtained by reason of that employment. This ensures that where the replacement loan is waived by the former employer, a tax charge arises in the same way as a charge would have arisen had the original loan been waived.

> **Example**
>
> Matthew has a loan of £7,000 from his employer, Minefield Ltd. In April he leaves Minefield Ltd. In August, Minefield Ltd transfers all its loans to the subsidiary of a commercial lender set up for the purpose. In December, Minefield Ltd agrees to write off the loan. The amount written off, i.e. £7,000, is taxable as earnings derived from Matthew's employment with Minefield Ltd.

Legislation: ITEPA 2003, s. 188(3)

Anti-avoidance: averaging calculation

To prevent abuse of the averaging calculation (see 132-810) for determining the benefit derived from the loan, the replacement loan is treated as the original loan in two circumstances:

(1) where the original loan is replaced by another loan from the same employment (an 'employment-related loan'); and

(2) where the original loan is replaced by a loan not from the employment (a 'non-employment-related loan'), and that loan is in turn replaced by a loan from the employment, either within the tax year or within 40 days from the end of the tax year.

The purpose of these provisions is to prevent exploitation of the calculation which ignores part months at the beginning and the end of a loan. Where one loan is replaced by another loan, the calculation is performed as if the original loan had continued.

> **Example**
>
> At 6 April 2017, Rory has £20,000 outstanding on an interest-free loan from his employer. The original loan is replaced by a new interest-free loan on 18 May 2017.
>
> At 5 April 2018, the outstanding balance was £13,000. The average official rate of interest for the year 2017–18 was 2.5%.
>
> The value of the benefit is calculated as if the original loan had continued for the whole of the tax year. The benefit derived from the loan is thus:
>
> $$\frac{£20{,}000 + £13{,}000}{2} \times 2.50\% = \underline{\underline{£425}}$$

Legislation: ITEPA 2003, s. 186

132-835 Aggregation of loans

In the past, all loans between an employer and a given employee normally had to be aggregated for the purposes of calculating the tax charge. There are now no cases where this is obligatory. Therefore employers can ignore the rules regarding aggregation of loans if they wish.

Nevertheless, aggregation remains an option in certain limited circumstances concerning loans to *directors* (only). Where aggregation applies, all loans between the same employer and director are to be treated as a single loan for the purposes of the rules relating to taxable cheap loans.

The option exists where:

- the lender is a close company;
- the borrower is a director of that company;
- the loan is obtained by reason of the director's employment;
- none of the loans in question is a 'qualifying loan' eligible for tax relief;
- the loans are all in the same currency;
- the interest payable on the loans is below the 'official rate' throughout the year; and
- the lender makes an election by giving notice to an officer of Revenue and Customs by 6 July following the tax year in question.

Legislation: ITEPA 2003, s. 187

Tax Reporter: ¶417-700

132-840 Exceptions to the charge

There are some situations in which an employment-related loan will not give rise to any charge. These are discussed at 132-850ff.

Tax Reporter: ¶417-750

132-850 Loans qualifying for tax relief

A loan is not treated as a taxable cheap loan if all interest payable on it (or all interest that would be payable if interest were charged):

- is eligible for relief under ITA 2007, s. 383 (general provision for interest relief);

- is deductible as an expense in computing the profits of a trade, etc. carried on wholly or partly in the UK by the person to whom the loan is made; or
- is deductible in computing the taxable profits of a UK property business carried on by that person.

Legislation: ITEPA 2003, s. 178

Tax Reporter: ¶418-000

132-870 Exemption for small loans

The benefit is exempt if:

- the amount outstanding on all cheap or interest-free loans provided by the employer does not exceed £10,000 (£5,000 prior to 2014–15) at any time in the year; or
- alternatively, the amount outstanding on all such loans which are non-qualifying loans (i.e. ineligible for tax relief) does not exceed £10,000 in the year.

Thus, an employee can have a qualifying loan which is not eligible for the de minimis exemption (e.g. to buy shares in a close company), and a non-qualifying loan which is so eligible (e.g. a season ticket loan). In that case, the non-qualifying loan will be exempt so long as there is no more than £10,000 outstanding on it at any time in the year.

An important point to watch is that this is an all or nothing exemption. If, however briefly, the loan balance rises above this limit at any time in the tax year, then the exemption will not be available and the benefit in kind will be taxed in full. This exemption is, however, looked at on a year-by-year basis.

Legislation: ITEPA 2003, s. 180

Tax Reporter: ¶417-800

132-880 Exemption for commercial loans

The background to this legislation was that employees of banks and similar institutions found themselves penalised when obtaining loans from their employers, even though such loans were available commercially to members of the general public at large. This is because any loan between employer and employee is, in almost all cases, treated as made by reason of the employment. Logically, the availability of commercial loans at a lower interest rate would have suggested that the official rate of interest was too high. The method chosen to eliminate this unfairness, however, was not to reduce the official rate of interest but rather to introduce a specific exemption for loans made on the same terms to employees as to members of the public at large.

A 'loan on ordinary commercial terms' is defined for these purposes as a loan made by a person ('the lender') in the ordinary course of a business carried on by him, which includes that lending of money or the supplying of goods and services on credit, and in respect of which certain conditions are satisfied:

- at the time the loan was made, comparable loans were available to all those who might be expected to avail themselves of the services provided by the lender in the course of his business;
- a substantial proportion of the relevant loans (see below) were made to members of the public;
- the loan in question and comparable loans (see below) generally made by the lender at or about the relevant time to members of the public were held on the same terms; and
- if those terms differed from those applicable immediately after the relevant time, they were imposed in the ordinary course of the lender's business.

For these purposes, a loan is regarded as comparable to another loan if it is made for the same or similar purposes and on the same terms and conditions. Further, 'relevant loans', for the purposes of the second bullet above, are the loan in question and comparable loans made by the lender at or about the relevant time.

A 'member of the public' is a member of the public at large, with whom the lender deals at arm's length.

Where a loan is varied, several requirements must be satisfied if the loan is to qualify for the exemption for ordinary commercial loans.

Legislation: ITEPA 2003, s. 176

132-890 Joint loans

To ensure that a joint loan to more than one employee only gives rise to a single tax charge, special rules apply where two or more employees are chargeable to tax in respect of the same loan:

(1) the cash equivalent value of the benefit should be apportioned between them in a 'just and reasonable' manner; and

(2) as far as each employee is concerned, the cash equivalent value of the benefit he or she receives is the portion allocated to him or her.

No indication is given as to what is regarded as a 'just and reasonable' method of apportionment.

Legislation: ITEPA 2003, s. 185

132-900 Other exemptions

Personal loans

An exemption is available where an employer who is an individual makes a loan in the normal course of domestic, family or personal relationships.

Legislation: ITEPA 2003, s. 174(5)

Advances of expenses

There is no charge to tax on advances to meet necessary expenses (or incidental overnight expenses) where:

- the maximum advanced at any one time does not exceed £1,000 (or such higher amount as is agreed by an officer of Revenue and Customs);
- the advances are spent within six months; and
- the employee accounts to his employer at regular intervals for the expenditure of the sum advanced.

There is no need to include such advances on form P11D but, where appropriate, the expenses themselves must obviously be returned.

Legislation: ITEPA 2003, s. 179

Other Material: HMRC *Employment Income Manual* EIM26155

132-910 Loan waiver

Where all or part of an employment-related loan is released or written off, the employee is to be treated as taxable on a benefit equal to that amount. Where the loan was made to a relative the employee will not be taxed under these provisions if he has derived no benefit from the loan waiver.

Where a loan waiver is taxable under other provisions, such as ITTOIA 2005, s. 416, it is not also taxed as a benefit. However, the benefit charging provisions take precedence over any charge under the golden handshake provisions in ITEPA 2003, s. 401 (see 142-000ff.) so the £30,000 exemption is not available.

The cessation of an employment will not prevent a charge on a benefit, which will be assessable in exactly the same way as though the employment had continued. It may sometimes be possible to make a termination payment within the £30,000 exemption and for the employee to use some or all of that payment to repay the loan.

Legislation: ITEPA 2003, s. 174

Tax Reporter: ¶418-200

Forms P11D: loans written off

A tax charge arises where a loan is written off, the benefit being equal to the amount written off. HMRC have provided the following advice on the mechanics of deducting tax and reporting the benefit:

- report on form P11D – section M;
- deduct and pay Class 1 NICs (but not PAYE tax) on the value of the benefit using your usual payroll procedures.

Other Material: www.hmrc.gov.uk/paye/exb/a-z/l/loans.htm#2

Living accommodation

133-100 Living accommodation: introduction

A tax charge potentially arises where living accommodation is provided for an employee by reason of his employment. There can also be a charge if the accommodation is provided for a member of the employee's family or household. This legislation generally takes priority over any other possible tax charge in respect of living accommodation. The tax treatment of living accommodation is one of the more complex benefits.

Legislation: ITEPA 2003, s. 97, 109

Tax Reporter: ¶414-500

133-110 Meaning of 'living accommodation'

The legislation imposes a tax charge on 'living accommodation' but is silent on the definition of that term. According to HMRC, 'examples of what is clearly living accommodation are houses, flats, houseboats, holiday villas and apartments. The term does not cover accommodation in a hotel room, other forms of board and lodging and non-residential accommodation such as a workshop, garage or office'.

In most cases, there will be no doubt as to whether living accommodation is provided. Typically, the accommodation will, for a period at least, be the main residence of the employee concerned. The HMRC view would certainly be that the charge applies to accommodation overseas as much as to UK properties, though this view is not universally accepted.

The prevailing view is that short-term accommodation used, for example, for holiday purposes would still come within the definition of 'living accommodation' for these purposes. Once more, however, there are some grounds for resisting such a view. This argument would be based on the charging provision of ITEPA 2003, s. 105, which in turn leads to s. 110. This latter section refers to a relationship between landlord and tenant which would appear to be inappropriate in these circumstances.

It should be emphasised, however, that any such arguments are likely to meet stiff resistance from HMRC. Furthermore, it should be borne in mind that P11D employees who escape the charge under the normal rules taxing the benefit of living accommodation may well be caught under the general rules governing the taxation of benefits in kind. ITEPA 2003, s. 201 specifically catches 'a benefit or facility of any kind'.

Other Material: HMRC *Employment Income Manual* EIM11321

Tax Reporter: ¶414-525

Living accommodation or board and lodging?

The rules described here do not apply to board and lodging. The HMRC view of the distinction is that: 'Broadly speaking, 'board and lodging' means the provision of the employee's meals, and somewhere to sleep. If the employee is provided with a self-contained living space with most of the facilities necessary for independent habitation, what is provided then is 'living accommodation'.' Elsewhere, HMRC state that living accommodation 'is something which gives the occupant the necessary facilities to live domestic life independently without reliance on others to supply basic needs. In practice we would be looking for an individual to at least have the use of a refrigerator and full cooking facilities, even if such facilities are shared'.

P11D employees in receipt of board and lodgings will be taxed under the catch-all section for general benefits. Board and lodging will also be taxable if the employee is entitled to a fixed income but an amount is then deducted for the cost of the board and lodging (see *Cordy v Gordon*).

Case: *Cordy v Gordon* (1925) 9 TC 304

Other Material: HMRC *Employment Income Manual* EIM01020, EIM11321

Tax Reporter: ¶414-525

133-115 Homes owned abroad through a company

In principle, the living accommodation charge applies in respect of overseas property as it does for property in the UK. A particular issue arises, however, where property is held through a company for legal reasons connected with the country in which the property is owned.

Individuals buying a home abroad through a company, typically for holiday use, will not face a benefit in kind charge in certain specified circumstances. Subject to certain anti-avoidance rules, the exemption disapplies the living accommodation provisions where all of the following conditions are met:

- living accommodation outside the UK is provided by a company for a director or other officer of the company (referred to as 'D'), or a member of D's family or household;
- the company is wholly owned by D (alone or together with other individuals, but not as partnership property); and
- the company has been the 'holding company of the property' at all times since the 'relevant time'.

Legislation: ITEPA 2003, s. 100A–100B; FA 2008, s. 45(2), (3)

Tax Reporter: ¶414-530

Holding company of the property

The main rule is that a company is the holding company of the property if its main or only asset is a relevant interest in the property and the only activities undertaken by it are ones that are incidental to its ownership of that interest.

However, a company is also the holding company of the property if:

(1) a wholly owned subsidiary of the company meets the above conditions;

(2) the parent company's main or only asset is its interest in the subsidiary; and

(3) the only activities undertaken by it are ones that are incidental to its ownership of that interest.

Tax Reporter: ¶414-530

Relevant time

The relevant time is normally the time the company first owned a relevant interest in the property. However, this rule is modified if none of D's interest in the company was acquired directly or indirectly from any connected person with D, and the company owned a relevant interest in the property at the time D first acquired an interest in the company. In this case, the relevant time is the time D first acquired such an interest.

Tax Reporter: ¶414-530

Anti-avoidance

Not surprisingly, the exemption is hedged about by various anti-avoidance provisions. In particular, these will cause the exemption to fail if there is any tax avoidance motive, including especially the case where a property has been acquired at less than its true value from a connected party.

Legislation: ITEPA 2003, s. 100B

Tax Reporter: ¶414-530

133-120 When living accommodation is 'provided'

Meaning of 'provided'

It is normally obvious if living accommodation is being 'provided' but there can be circumstances where the issue is difficult to determine. The HMRC manuals distinguish between 'available for use' and 'actually used' and argue that both can be correct interpretations of the word 'provided' – depending on the circumstances.

The HMRC view is that if living accommodation has been bought as holiday accommodation for a director and his family then 'provided is likely to mean available for use'. The HMRC examples shown in the *Employment Income Manual* bring out some difficult distinctions and make it clear that the tax result could (on HMRC's interpretation) be very different depending on which side of the line any particular facts fall.

Other Material: HMRC *Employment Income Manual* EIM11406, EIM11421ff.

Tax Reporter: ¶414-550

Provided 'by reason of the employment'

For a tax charge to arise, the living accommodation must be provided to a person 'by reason of the employment'.

Where the living accommodation is provided by the employer, it is automatically deemed to be provided by reason of the employment unless the employer is an individual and the accommodation is provided 'in the normal course of the employer's domestic, family or personal relationships'.

If the accommodation is provided by someone other than the employer it will be necessary to determine whether the employment is one factor in its provision. In *Wicks v Firth*, Lord Denning said that 'the fact of employment must be one of the causes of the benefit being provided, but it need not be the sole cause, or even the dominant cause. It is sufficient if the employment was an operative cause – in the sense that it was a condition of the benefit being granted'.

Shadow directors are caught by the tax rules.

Legislation: ITEPA 2003, s. 97(1)

Cases: *Wicks v Firth* [1982] BTC 402; *R v Dimsey* [2001] BTC 421

Other Material: HMRC *Employment Income Manual* EIM20503

Tax Reporter: ¶414-550

133-130 Exemptions

Living accommodation is excluded from the charge, though subject to the caveat discussed below with regard to directors, if it is within any of the following categories:

(1) it is necessary for the proper performance of the duties of the employment that the employee, etc. should reside in the accommodation (sometimes known as 'representative occupation': e.g. lighthouse keepers' accommodation);

(2) the accommodation is provided for the better performance of the employee's duties and it is one of the kinds of employment in which it is customary to provide living accommodation (e.g. hostel wardens' accommodation);

(3) where there is a special threat to the security of the employee or office holder, special security arrangements are in force, and he lives in the accommodation as part of those arrangements (e.g. certain senior politicians);

(4) the employer is an individual and the accommodation is provided in the normal course of his domestic, family or personal relationships (e.g. to a domestic servant);

(5) the accommodation is provided by a local authority on terms no more favourable than those on other accommodation it provides (e.g. a council house for a council employee).

However, where the taxpayer is a director of the company which provides the accommodation, or of an associated company, the first two exceptions listed above are only applicable if the director owns less than 5% of the shares in the company and is either a full-time working director of the company, or the company is non-profit making.

In practice, it is the first two of these five tests that present the greatest difficulty, so these are considered further below.

Tax Reporter: ¶414-600

Proper performance of the duties – the 'necessary' rule

Employees obtaining an exemption by virtue of this rule will typically include certain hotel staff, caretakers, staff on night duty in a boarding school house and others in similar types of occupation.

The 'necessity' to reside in the accommodation concerned must arise from 'the relationship between the proper performance of the duties and the dwelling house' and not from the 'personal exigencies of the taxpayer' (*Vertigan v Brady*). In other words, it is not sufficient that the employer insists that the employee should live in the house in question – the need to live there must be objectively imposed by the nature of the duties. HMRC acknowledge that the following categories of employee 'may be accepted as being within the exemption':

- agricultural workers who live on farms or agricultural estates;
- lock-gate and level crossing gatekeepers;
- caretakers living on the premises (but this does not extend to a shop employee (for example) who is required to live in a flat above the shop so as to discourage burglaries);
- stewards and greenkeepers (living on the premises);
- managers of public houses; and
- wardens of sheltered housing schemes (living on the premises).

See below for circumstances where the exemption does not apply.

Legislation: ITEPA 2003, s. 99(1)

Cases: *Langley & Ors v Appleby* (1976) 53 TC 1; *Vertigan v Brady* [1988] BTC 99

Other Material: HMRC *Employment Income Manual* EIM11342

Better performance of the duties – the 'customary' rule

This next exemption applies where both:

- the accommodation is provided for the better performance of the duties of the employment; and
- the employee's employment is one where it is customary for employers to provide living accommodation for their employees.

Each of these tests can pose its own problems.

As with the exemption discussed immediately above, the 'better performance' test is an objective one imposed by the duties of the employment. In particular, the fact that the accommodation is near to the employee's work will not carry any weight: the test is not satisfied merely because accommodation is provided close to the place of employment so that the employee can get to work more easily.

The courts have interpreted the 'customary' requirement rather strictly. Statistical evidence will be required demonstrating that the practice of providing accommodation for this kind of employee is a common one, that that practice has continued for some length of time, and that the practice has achieved general acceptance 'by the relevant employers'.

The HMRC view is that 'a practice is customary if it is recognisable as the norm and if failure to observe it is exceptional'. The custom must relate specifically to living accommodation and not, for example, to board and lodging.

HMRC will accept that the 'better performance' test is met where the employee is on call outside normal hours, where he is in fact called out 'frequently' (not defined), and where 'the accommodation is provided so that the employee may have quick access to the place of employment or other place to which the employee is called'. HMRC accept that the following types of employee may qualify under this heading:

- police officers;
- Ministry of Defence police;
- prison governors, officers and chaplains;
- clergymen and ministers of religion (unless engaged on purely administrative duties);

- members of HM Forces;
- members of the Diplomatic Service;
- managers of newsagent shops which have paper rounds (but not those which do not);
- managers of traditional off-licence shops, that is those with opening hours broadly equivalent to those of a public house (but not those only open from 0900 to 1700 or similar basis);
- in boarding schools (including schools where some pupils are boarders) where staff are provided with accommodation on or near the school premises:
  - head teacher;
  - other teachers with pastoral or other irregular contractual responsibilities outside normal school hours (for example, house masters);
  - bursar;
  - matron, nurse and doctor;
- stable staff of racehorse trainers who live on the premises and certain key workers who live close to the stables.

ITEPA 2003, Pt. 4, Ch. 8 details exemption from the charge on the provision of accommodation to certain specialist groups of employees. These include ministers of religion, Members of Parliament and, with effect from 6 April 2016, home care workers.

Legislation: ITEPA 2003, s. 99(2) and Pt. 4, Ch. 8

Case: *Vertigan v Brady* [1988] BTC 99

Other Material: HMRC *Employment Income Manual* EIM11347ff.

133-140 Living accommodation as an alternative to hotel accommodation

If an employee is working away from home, an employer may calculate that it is cheaper to buy or rent a property rather than placing the employee in hotel accommodation. If the use of the property is provided in this way for genuine commercial reasons, then it may well be possible to claim relief on ordinary principles.

Subsistence payments, including hotel accommodation, can only be provided tax-free if associated with qualifying business travel. Take, for example, an employer with an exceptional short-term workload who asks an employee to work very late and then to begin work very early the following day. The employer may offer to put the employee up in a hotel adjacent to the workplace for the one night. The employee's daily journey to and from work would be ordinary commuting and so there is no business travel involved. As such, the overnight hotel accommodation (and associated meals, etc.) will be a taxable benefit and the employer will probably wish to meet the liability through the mechanism of a PAYE Settlement Agreement.

No deduction was given for a 'rent' claimed by an employee sales executive for a property in which he had a 40% interest (*Peter Gamble*). The rental figure had been calculated as a proportion of the mortgage interest payments, council tax and utility bills for the property. The employee argued that the property could have been rented to a third party but it was more cost-effective for him to use it for work purposes when in London. The tribunal accepted that he had to spend time in London for work purposes and that he only used the property for such purposes. However, as he had an interest in the property, he was effectively paying the 'rent' to himself. As such, no expense had in fact been incurred and there was no entitlement to any deduction. Furthermore, the tribunal did not accept that the notional cost was incurred in the performance of the duties of the employment (per ITEPA 2003, s. 336); rather, it merely put the employee in a position to perform those duties.

Case: *Peter Gamble* [2011] TC 00815

Other Material: HMRC *Tax Bulletin* TB12/00–3

Tax Reporter: ¶414-650

133-150 Cash equivalent: cost of accommodation not over £75,000

Where there is a charge, the taxable amount is the value to the employee or director of the accommodation less any payment made by him towards the cost. Where the accommodation is rented by the employer, the value will normally be the rent paid by the employer, but where the accommodation is owned by the employer, tax is calculated by reference to the 'rental value' of the accommodation, which is based on the gross rateable value. The use of gross rateable values is anomalous given that domestic rates are no longer payable in parts of the UK and that the rateable values have not been adjusted for many years. Nevertheless, where such a figure exists then it may continue to be used.

Example

Michael occupies a flat owned by his employer. The flat cost £60,000 two years before the start of the tax year. The employer paid £5,000 on improvements. The gross rateable value is £800. None of the special exemptions applies to Michael. He pays £50 per month as a nominal rent for the property but provides his own furniture and pays for all utilities himself.

	£
Rateable value	800
Deduct Michael's contributions	600
Taxable benefit	200

If the employee is not exempted under one of the categories listed at 133-130, but the property is nevertheless used partly for business purposes, then a claim may be made to reduce the taxable benefit accordingly.

Ministers of religion are not taxable on the value of accommodation provided for them unless they are higher-paid employees (see 143-900).

Legislation: ITEPA 2003, s. 110, 290

Tax Reporter: ¶414-675

Deduction of sums made good

The amount taxable under the general benefit charge is after deduction of 'any sum made good by the employee to the person at whose cost the accommodation is provided that is properly attributable to its provision'. It is understood that HMRC accept that the deduction is available in respect of 'sums made good' *subsequent* to the accommodation's provision (e.g. following an HMRC investigation, which may enable penalties and interest to be avoided).

Legislation: ITEPA 2003, s. 105(2)

Shared accommodation

Where a property is provided as living accommodation to more than one employee or director in the same period, the total taxable benefit cannot be greater than it would have been if the property had been provided to a single employee.

To achieve this, the benefit is apportioned between employees. The method of apportionment has been left open, the legislation requiring only that each employee should be taxed on a basis that is 'just and reasonable'. If husband and wife (for example) are both employed by the same employer, but the living accommodation is, as an established fact, provided by reason of the husband's employment only, then only the husband will be taxed; the benefit would not in this case be split. There could be a tax effect if husband and wife have different tax or National Insurance rates.

Legislation: ITEPA 2003, s. 108

Other Material: HMRC *Employment Income Manual* EIM11410

Lease premiums

The HMRC manuals have, for some time, referred to an anti-avoidance scheme involving the payment of a premium on a lease, followed by a small rent. It is argued that only the small rent can be taken into account when calculating any living accommodation benefit. Legislation was introduced in 2009 to ensure that this does not work as a tax saving measure; the legislation introduces a rule whereby the lease premium is taken into account when working out the benefit in kind charge.

The lease premium rules apply only where the term of the lease does not exceed ten years and where the premises are used mainly for the provision of living accommodation provided as a taxable benefit. In such cases, a part of the premium is 'attributed to the relevant period': in other words, part of the premium is treated each year as additional rent paid by the employer (or other provider of accommodation). The amount so attributed is the proportion of the total premium that is calculated as A over B, where A is the length of the relevant period and B is the term of the lease. Both figures are calculated in days.

Legislation: ITEPA 2003, s. 105A; ITEPA 2003, s. 105(4), (4A)

Other Material: HMRC *Employment Income Manual* EIM11415

Tax Reporter: ¶414-675

133-160 Cash equivalent: cost of accommodation exceeding £75,000

A further charge applies where accommodation is provided by reason of the employment and the cost of providing it exceeds £75,000. The further charge is calculated by multiplying the official rate of interest on the first day of the tax year (so 2.5% for 2017–18) to the excess of the 'cost' of the property over £75,000.

'Cost' means the initial cost of acquiring the property, together with the amount of any expenditure incurred on improvements. The costs which must be taken into account are not only those incurred by the person providing the property, but those of any 'relevant person', less any amount reimbursed by the employee.

A 'relevant person' for this purpose is:

- the person who provides the property;
- the employer (if not the person providing the accommodation);
- any person, other than the employee, 'connected with' the employer or with the person providing the accommodation.

As with other benefit legislation, it is unnecessary for the provision to be made by the employer, provided that it is made 'by reason of the employment'. Where the provision is made by the employer, there is a presumption that it is for that reason.

Where the actual cost of the property (including improvements) was less than £75,000 when originally acquired by the employer, it is not within the scope of the charge, even if the market value exceeds £75,000 when it is first occupied.

Example

A company buys a house for £250,000 and spends £20,000 on improvements. Kim, a director of the company, is allowed to live in it, reimbursing 50% of the cost of the improvements and paying rent of £5,000 per year. The gross rateable value is £3,000. The amount on which Kim will be taxed in 2017–18 will be:

		£
Purchase price		250,000
Expenditure on improvements		20,000
		270,000
Less:	£	
(1) Kim's contribution to purchase price	Nil	
(2) Reimbursement by Kim for improvements	10,000	
(3) Premium paid by Kim for tenancy	Nil	
		£
		(10,000)
		260,000
		(75,000)
Taxable value		185,000

	£
Taxable value 185,000 × 2.5%	4,625
Excess rent over gross rateable value (5,000 – 3,000)	(2,000)
Taxable amount	2,625

Legislation: ITEPA 2003, s. 106

Tax Reporter: ¶414-700

133-170 Associated costs

Overview

The tax charge described in the preceding pages relates only to the provision of the accommodation itself. In many cases, a separate tax charge will arise where associated benefits are provided, such as heat and light, repairs and the use of furniture.

Council tax, rates and water charges

Where an employer meets the council tax, or pays water or sewerage charges, on behalf of an employee, this will normally be taxable under normal principles as the employer is meeting the pecuniary liability of the employee. Similarly, a National Insurance charge will arise in these circumstances. However, no charge will arise to either tax or National Insurance if the employer meets the council tax charge of the employee where any of following exemptions applies (as described in detail at 133-130):

- proper performance of the duties – the ‘necessary’ rule;
- better performance of the duties – the ‘customary’ rule;
- special security threat.

This exemption extends to rates, water and sewerage charges and council tax. Water charges are exempt even if on a metered supply.

Legislation: ITEPA 2003, s. 314

Other Material: HMRC *Employment Income Manual* EIM11332

Tax Reporter: ¶414-800

Repairs and improvements

No benefit arises if the alterations or additions are structural in nature. Similarly, no tax benefit arises if the repairs are such as would legally be the obligation of the lessor. This legislation therefore removes a tax charge in respect of repairs for which the landlord would be responsible.

Although expenditure to improve the property is not taxed as a separate benefit, it will affect the cost of the property for the purposes of the additional charge on 'expensive' accommodation.

Legislation: ITEPA 2003, s. 313

Furniture

Where furniture is provided with the accommodation then a tax charge will be made, calculated by reference to the 'annual value' of the furniture. Broadly, the benefit is calculated as 20% of the market value of the furniture at the time it is first provided as a benefit.

No charge will arise if the furniture is on premises owned by the employer and is only used by the employee in the performance of his duties. If furniture is provided on other premises, stricter conditions must be met if a tax charge is to be avoided.

This exemption is most likely to apply to an employee who works mostly from home and for whom the employer provides office furniture. See below for a possible cap on the tax liability arising from the provision of furniture.

Legislation: ITEPA 2003, s. 316

Other expenses

Other relevant expenses met by the employer might include cleaning, gardening, the provision of utility services, the payment of insurance and a host of other possible items.

Insurance of the property is deemed to be a liability of the owner and no tax charge will therefore arise. For other ancillary benefits, the judgment of Lord Denning in *Butter v Bennett* provides a useful distinction. He balanced the cost of making the property habitable on the one hand with the cost of inhabiting it on the other. Any expenses falling within the former category would not be taxable because they are part of the cost of providing accommodation in the first place. Expenses in the latter category, such as cleaning or gardening, or the payment of fuel bills, will generally create an additional tax charge.

Case: *Butter v Bennett* (1962) 40 TC 402

Restriction of the taxable benefit of associated costs

Where the accommodation falls within one of the following categories (see 133-130):

- proper performance of the duties – the 'necessary' rule;
- better performance of the duties – the 'customary' rule; or
- special security threat,

the maximum assessable amount is limited to 10% of the net earnings of the period for which the accommodation is provided. Net earnings include earnings from any employment by an associated company, but are after deduction of capital allowances, mileage allowance relief, deductions under ITEPA 2003, Pt. 5, and certain approved pension payments.

Legislation: ITEPA 2003, s. 315(5)

Tax Reporter: ¶414-800

133-180 Living accommodation used partly for business purposes

If premises consist, for example, of a shop with a flat over it, only the flat will be treated as living accommodation. The same principle will apply to any other premises where the construction of the building clearly divides the premises into a business part and a part that is used as living accommodation.

In such a case, it will be necessary to apportion on a reasonable basis the cost or rent of the premises, unless separate figures are available. The gross rateable value may also need to be split, but in practice separate rating valuations are often made. If an apportionment of any of these figures is needed then floor area may provide a good starting point. However, a more favourable apportionment will often be possible. As HMRC acknowledge, it will sometimes be the case that 'the non-living accommodation part of the premises commands a proportionately higher part of the cost or rent. This may happen where the other part of the premises is business premises'.

A different position arises if the whole building is designed as living accommodation but, in reality, a part is used exclusively for business purposes. In this case, 'the living accommodation would consist of the whole house but there may be a deduction, equivalent to a Section 336 ITEPA 2003 deduction, from the provided living accommodation benefit'. HMRC illustrate this issue with a simple example of a house with ten rooms of which one is used by an employee exclusively for the duties of his employment. In such a case, a deduction of 10% would be given (but only if the employee is 'necessarily' required to provide the accommodation).

Other Material: HMRC *Employment Income Manual* EIM11501ff.

Tax Reporter: ¶414-900

Credit tokens and vouchers

133-300 Overview

With the exception of certain 'trivial' benefits detailed in 133-335, where an employee or director is provided, by reason of their employment, with a credit token (e.g. a credit card) or voucher which can be used to obtain goods, services or money, the employee is taxable on a benefit equal to the cost of providing the token or voucher. The general principle is that an employee is taxable on the cost to the employer of providing the goods or services, less any amount which the employee makes good to the employer. He or she can still benefit from a claim for deductible expenses.

The topic of vouchers is a complex one. The legislation therefore makes a distinction at the outset between three types of voucher:

- cash vouchers;
- non-cash vouchers; and
- credit tokens.

The tax and National Insurance consequences follow according to the type of voucher being considered.

Legislation: ITEPA 2003, s. 73ff.

Tax Reporter: ¶414-000

133-310 Cash vouchers

A 'cash voucher' is defined as a voucher, stamp or similar document which is capable of being exchanged for a sum of money that is not substantially less than the cost of providing it. Cash vouchers are treated as pay, and PAYE must be operated when they are provided. The taxable amount is the amount of money for which they can be exchanged. National savings certificates on which the interest is exempt are not regarded as cash vouchers, but premium bonds are probably caught under these rules. Documents are not taxed as cash vouchers if they only enable an employee to obtain a sum of money that would not be taxable if paid directly to him.

A cash voucher is taxed as earnings for the year in which the employee receives the voucher. If the voucher is somehow appropriated to the employee (for example, by attaching it to a card held on his or her behalf) then it is treated as received by the employee when it is so appropriated.

According to HMRC, 'the cash voucher legislation was introduced to counter specific holiday pay stamp schemes. It is unlikely to have wide application elsewhere'.

Legislation: ITEPA 2003, s. 73, 81

Other Material: HMRC *Employment Income Manual* EIM16110

Tax Reporter: ¶414-000

133-320 Non-cash vouchers

The main definition of this term is that it includes any voucher, stamp or similar document or token which is capable of being exchanged for goods or services. The definition is extended to include childcare vouchers, transport vouchers and cheque vouchers. Common examples would be ordinary retail vouchers (such as from M&S), season tickets and book tokens.

A non-cash voucher is taxed as earnings of the employment for the year in which the voucher is received by the employee. Certain childcare vouchers are in practice exempt from tax (see 133-400ff). See also 133-335 for the exemption for 'trivial benefits'.

Since 19 July 2006, the Treasury have had the power to exempt from tax the provision of any non-cash vouchers or credit tokens where the underlying benefit is itself exempt from tax (ITEPA 2003, s. 96A). In the *Explanatory Note* to the *Finance Act* 2006, the following statement was made in relation to the power introduced in that Act:

> 'Normally we would want the tax position to be the same for every employment-related benefit, however there may be circumstances where we do not want this treatment to follow automatically. This clause has been introduced to exempt certain such vouchers or credit-tokens as may be specified in the regulations.'

Tax Reporter: ¶414-050

Travel cards

A travel card (such as an Oyster card) is a 'transport voucher' and is therefore taxed as a non-cash voucher. HMRC have provided the following guidance on how they intend to apply the voucher rules where such a card is available for both private and business use.

Tax Reporter: ¶414-060

Card provided mainly for private use

If the card is provided mainly for private journeys (e.g. for commuting to and from work) then the taxable cash equivalent will be the cost of providing the travel card (less any part of that cost made good by the employee to the employer).

Legislation: ITEPA 2003, s. 87(2)

Card provided only for business travel

If the travel card is provided to the employee only for business travel, this is still technically a benefit in kind but there will be no resulting tax charge as the employee is entitled to a matching deduction under ITEPA 2003, s. 337 or 338. This would apply, for example, if the employer purchases a rail ticket for a one-off journey for an employee who is visiting a customer or client.

Legislation: ITEPA 2003, s. 362

Card provided for business travel but available for private journeys

The tax position is more complex if the card is provided for genuine work purposes but is also available for private travel (such as a monthly season ticket that may also be used at the weekend). In this case, the employer is providing a benefit in kind but there may or may not be a tax charge. HMRC have advised on their view of the tax treatment as follows:

> 'If the cost of the travel card provided by the employer is matched or exceeded by the individual cost of business travel by the employee, which gives rise to a matching deduction under s. 362, any additional use for private purposes does not result in any additional cost to the employer. Consequently there is no chargeable benefit for the employee.'

This scenario is then illustrated as follows:

> 'An employer provides an employee with a weekly travel card because the employer knows that this employee has to make frequent business journeys. The weekly travel card costs the employer £25. Previously the employee's expenses claims typically included train journeys costing £30 – £50 per week, so the employer considers it cost effective to provide the employee with a travel card instead of paying, or reimbursing the employee, for individual journeys. The travel card can be used during the week by the employee for private purposes as well.

During the week the employee keeps a record of his business journeys and at the end of the week he calculates the cost of those journeys at £30 in total, if paid singly.

The provision of a travel card represents a benefit to the employee but this benefit only results in a charge to tax and NICs if the private use of the card results in an additional cost to the employer in excess of the costs that relate to its use for business journeys. The employer incurs a cost of £25 to provide the travel card but if the employee had not been provided with a travel card, the cost to the employer for the employee's business journeys would have been £30.

Consequently the cost to the employer in providing the travel card is less than the costs that would have been incurred on behalf of the employee for business travel if the employer had not provided a travel card. By choosing to provide a travel card the employer has saved £5.

The employee is provided with a benefit which cost £25, but he is entitled under s. 362 to a deduction for £25 (the deduction under s. 362 is capped at a maximum amount equal to the amount of the benefit, so the employee is entitled to a deduction for only £25, not £30). Any private travel using the travel card does not result in any further cost to the employer.

Consequently there is no chargeable benefit to the employee.'

By contrast, a tax charge may arise if the employee does not make sufficient business journeys to justify the cost of the ticket. As HMRC put it:

'If the employee makes some use of the travel card for business travel for which he or she is entitled to a deduction under s. 362, but the cost of these journeys does not match the cost of the benefit, a chargeable benefit arises on the difference between the two amounts.

The cost of business journeys in these circumstances is 'notional' to the extent that no costs are incurred on individual journeys because the cost is covered by the travel card, but each journey has a real and identifiable cost which should be the basis for the deduction. An employee can seek a deduction for an amount that is equal to the lesser of

- the total cost of the individual business journeys undertaken with the travel card (if paid singly), and
- the cost of the travel card.

Consequently if the cost of individual journeys (if paid singly) exceeds the cost of the travel card, only the cost of the travel card can be allowed as a deduction.'

Once more, the point is illustrated:

'An employer provides an employee with a weekly travel card which costs £25. This employee spends most of his working time at his permanent workplace

– he rarely travels on business journeys. The provision of the travel card represents a benefit to the employee who uses the card for private purposes, including ordinary commuting. During the week the employee visits one client, a business journey which is covered by his travel card, so he incurs no costs. If he had paid for a ticket for this journey the cost was £10. The employee is entitled to a deduction for £10 under s. 362 against the cost of the benefit of the travel card provided to him.'

The HMRC approach has some merit at first glance, and seems fair enough in the above example where the employee 'rarely travels on business journeys', but at least two practical issues arise. The first is the administration – part of the reason for buying a season ticket is to cut down on paperwork and this advantage is clearly lost if it is necessary to establish and record the notional cost of various business journeys. Secondly, the employer may genuinely buy a monthly season ticket to save time and money, without any intention to give a gratuitous benefit to the employee. But supposing that the employee is on holiday abroad for a period, or is sick; does this mean that the otherwise non-taxable private use of the ticket becomes taxable? It is not entirely clear from the legislation and case law precedents that this is how the courts would interpret the rules in practice, if it was accepted that the purpose of buying the card was to save the employer money and administrative time and if it was only by chance circumstances that the cost of the business journeys fell below the cost of the season ticket in a given month.

Other Material: HMRC *Employment Income Manual* EIM16066ff.

133-330 Credit tokens

A 'credit-token' excludes a cash voucher or a non-cash voucher but means a card, token, document, or other thing given by a person to another person who undertakes:

- that on the production of it (whether or not some action is also required) he will supply money, goods and services (or any of them) on credit; or
- that where on the production of it to a third party (whether or not some action is also required), the third party supplies money, goods and services (or any of them), he will pay the third party for them (whether or not taking any discount or commission).

Use of an object to operate a machine provided by the person giving the object, or by a third party, will be treated as production of the object to that person or, as the case may be, third party.

The employee is treated as receiving a benefit on the date on which the employer incurs the expense, unless the employee does not receive the token until a later date, in which case he is treated as receiving the benefit at that later date.

Legislation: ITEPA 2003, s. 92, 96

Tax Reporter: ¶414-100

133-335 Trivial benefits exemption 6 April 2016

With effect from 6 April 2016, certain non-cash benefits provided by an employer will not result in a taxable benefit on the employee. The benefit must not:

- be cash or a cash voucher;
- cost the employer more than £50;
- be connected to any salary sacrifice arrangement;
- be given in recognition of any particular service performed by the employee as part of their employment.

In addition, where the employer is a close company, the total cumulative value of the benefits provided to an individual employee or their family must not exceed £300 per annum.

Legislation: ITEPA 2003, s. 323A

Childcare

133-400 Overview of relief

With effect from April 2017, the Government is introducing a new form of Tax Free Childcare to replace the existing Childcare Voucher scheme. Those parents who join the voucher scheme before 5 April 2018 will have the option of remaining in that scheme or moving to the new Tax Free scheme. The details of the existing voucher scheme are outlined in 133-405 to 133-437 below whilst the replacement Tax Free Childcare provisions are summarised in 133-450.

133-405 Childcare Voucher Scheme

The provision of childcare, by employers, offers significant potential tax savings. Employers wishing to use the tax relief may well wish to implement a salary sacrifice scheme, i.e. offering the benefit of childcare in return for a reduction in the current salary level (or possibly in return for forgoing a pay increase). The implementation of a salary sacrifice scheme need not be unduly onerous but it is important to ensure that care is taken with the paperwork so as to achieve the right end result. Salary sacrifice schemes generally are considered at 132-080.

There are two different forms of exemption for childcare costs. These are referred to (here, as in the legislation) as 'employer-provided care' and as 'other care'.

The relief for the costs of 'other care' is of much wider application than the employer-provided care. The key features of this broader relief may be summarised as follows:

- the scheme must be open to all staff;
- the child must be below a certain age;
- the care must be registered or approved;
- up to £55 per week per employee may be paid by the employer free of tax and all NIC, either directly to a childcare provider or by way of voucher;
- no tax relief is due if the employer pays a cash allowance to the employee or settles the employee's personal liability for childcare costs;
- if an employer pays more than £55 per week, the excess will be taxable but the first £55 will still qualify for relief if the necessary conditions are met;
- no relief is due for the costs of school fees or for unapproved childcare; and
- various restrictions apply, especially where care is provided by somebody connected with the child.

Restrictions applying from April 2011 limit the amount of tax relief for those newly joining such a scheme from that time. The changes are discussed at 133-435.

If an employer simply gives the employee additional salary to pay for childcare, this is still taxable in full.

HMRC guidance

The HMRC booklet 480 confirms that 'spare places in a qualifying nursery or play scheme can be given to people who are not the employer's employees without affecting the employees' tax position'. See also www.hmrc.gov.uk/childcare/childcarefactsheet.htm for a useful starting point when seeking to navigate the extensive HMRC guidance on this topic. That page leads to a number of other pages, including www.hmrc.gov.uk/

childcare/index.htm, which in turn contains links to pages addressing all of the following.

- Development of childcare tax and NICs policy.
- External links.
- Employer helpbook E15 – Pay and time off for parents.
- Flowchart showing the different types of childcare and when they apply.
- Guidance for employees.
- Guidance for employers.
- Guidance for childcarers.
- How to help your employees with childcare – E18 Helpbook.
- Interaction of childcare vouchers and tax credits.
- Maternity leave and salary sacrifice.
- Salary Sacrifice guidance.
- Tax and NICs manuals.
- Tax Credits.
- Childcare Indicator.
- HMRC Research Report 23 – Monitoring of the Reform of the Income Tax and National Insurance Rules for Employer-Supported Childcare: A study of Provision and Experiences of Employers.

In March 2014, the Government announced their intention to radically change the provision of childcare support. It is anticipated that these changes will be much more widely applicable and will no longer be dependent on provision by a participating employer. In essence, the Government will offer 20% support on up to £10,000 of childcare cost for each child. It is intended that these changes will be implemented from the autumn of 2015.

Other Material: www.gov.uk/government/news/millions-of-parents-to-get-help-with-childcare-costs

Tax Reporter: ¶434-500ff.

133-410 Definitions

Definition of 'care'

Certain key definitions apply to both types of relief. The term 'care' is defined as 'any form of care or supervised activity that is not provided in the course of the child's compulsory education'. Guidance on the HMRC website confirms that any of the following may qualify.

- Registered childminders, nurseries and play schemes.
- Out-of-hours clubs on school premises run by a school or local authority.
- Childcare schemes run by school governing bodies under the 'extended schools scheme'.
- Childcare schemes run by approved providers, such as one approved under a Ministry of Defence accreditation scheme.
- In England only, childcare given in the child's own home by a person approved to care for the child or by a domiciliary worker or nurse from a registered agency (but subject to the rule preventing relief for payments to relatives).
- In Scotland only, childcare given in the child's own home by (or introduced through) registered childcare agencies, including sitter services and nanny agencies (but again subject to the rule preventing relief for payments to relatives).
- Approved foster carers (but once more subject to the rule preventing relief for payments to relatives).

Legislation: ITEPA 2003, s. 318B(1)

Definition of 'child'

A person is for these purposes treated as a child 'until the last day of the week in which falls the 1 September following the child's fifteenth birthday'.

Example

Andrea was born on 1 August 1999. Her 15th birthday falls on 1 August 2014. 1 September 2014 is a Thursday and so Andrea will cease to be treated as a child for these purposes from the end of that week.

This is extended by one year (i.e. substituting 'sixteenth birthday' in the above definition) if the child is disabled.

Legislation: ITEPA 2003, s. 318B(2)

Definition of 'parental responsibility'

Both forms of relief make reference to the concept of parental responsibility. The term is defined to mean 'all the rights, duties, powers, responsibilities and authority which by law a parent of a child has in relation to the child and the child's property'.

Legislation: ITEPA 2003, s. 318B(5)

133-420 Employer-provided care

If the stricter conditions under this heading are met then there is a complete exemption for childcare costs, whatever the level of expense incurred by the employer. However, these conditions are onerous and this type of relief for childcare costs is unsuitable for most smaller employers. See, instead, 133-430.

Four conditions (labelled A to D in the legislation) must be met if this total exemption is to be obtained.

- Condition A, concerning the child.
- Condition B, concerning the premises.
- Condition C, concerning the employer.
- Condition D, requiring the care to be made generally available.

Legislation: ITEPA 2003, s. 318

Tax Reporter: ¶434-600

Condition A – the child

A child (as defined at 133-410) qualifies if he or she:

- is a child or stepchild of the employee and is maintained wholly or partly at the employee's expense;
- is resident with the employee; or
- is a child for whom the employee has parental responsibility, defined as 'all the rights, duties, powers, responsibilities and authority which by law a parent of a child has in relation to the child and the child's property'.

Legislation: ITEPA 2003, s. 318(3)

Condition B – premises

The exemption is not available if the premises are used wholly or mainly as a private dwelling. This would mean, for example, that no relief would be due under this heading (but see 'other care' at 133-430) for the costs of a nanny at the employee's home. The rule would also exclude a case where a child-minder operates from her (or his) own home.

Typically, an employer will either use part of ordinary work premises or will purchase or hire premises for the specific purpose of providing childcare. Any such premises will qualify. A further condition is that any applicable registration requirement is met. Various statutes are listed under which the registration may be made.

Legislation: ITEPA 2003, s. 318(4)

Condition C – employer involvement

Relief may be available if the care is provided on premises made available by the employer alone. If this condition is not met, then relief for employer-provided care is due only if the 'partnership requirements' are met. These requirements are met if care is provided under arrangements which are made by people including the employer and on premises made available by one or more of the people providing the care. In this case, the employer in question must be at least partly responsible for financing the care and also for managing the provision of the care.

It is these requirements (financing and managing) that have in practice made the relief unsuitable for many employers in the past. The HMRC view has been that financing 'requires significantly more than merely buying-in places from a commercial nursery'. HMRC have looked for the provision of capital by the employer or 'some real and substantial commitment to funding the facility'. This may involve 'an agreement to meet a set proportion of the overall cost of providing the care'. Alternatively, the condition will be met if the employer gives 'a guarantee to indemnify against losses a primary care provider who would otherwise be at real risk of losses'.

The 'managing' condition presents similar difficulties. In the HMRC view, management responsibility

> 'does not necessarily mean day-to-day management or direct responsibility for the care of the children. But it does mean much more than being occasionally consulted about the broad policies which should apply to the provision of the care or having a right to a place on a committee which has no particular brief and little or no power to influence the way in which the care is provided.'

Legislation: ITEPA 2003, s. 318(6)

Other Material: HMRC *Employment Income Manual* EIM21930

Condition D – general availability

Relief is available only if the childcare is provided under a scheme that is open to all employees of the particular employer, or to all such employees working at a particular location. HMRC have confirmed, however, that this condition:

> '... does not mean that every employee who wants a childcare place in a scheme must receive a place. Employers may need to prioritise places if more employees apply than the number of places available. How childcare places are prioritised is up to the employer but the scheme should not exclude members of your staff from applying for a place on the basis of
>
> - grade or position
> - level of salary
> - length of service
> - gender.'

Booklet E18 adds the further point that an individual must not be excluded on the basis of absence due to maternity leave.

Legislation: ITEPA 2003, s. 318(8)

Other Material: HMRC booklet 480

133-430 Other care

Employers may contribute up to £55 per week for registered childcare. The definitions of 'child' and 'care' are the same as for employer-provided care (see 133-410), though there are some subtle differences between the two types of relief.

Legislation: ITEPA 2003, s. 318A

Tax Reporter: ¶434-800

Restrictions to relief from April 2011

See 133-435 for details of restrictions that now apply in certain circumstances.

The child

For the £55 per week relief, the child (as defined at 133-410) qualifies if he or she:

- is a child or stepchild of the employee and is maintained wholly or partly at the employee's expense; or
- is resident with the employee, and is a person for whom the employee has parental responsibility (as defined at 133-410).

At first glance, this is identical to the provision outlined under 'Condition A' at 133-420. In fact, there is a difference, in that the child must in this case be both resident with the employee and also a person for whom the employee has parental responsibility. For the (otherwise) stricter relief, these are alternatives.

Legislation: ITEPA 2003, s. 318A(3)

Qualifying care

For this type of relief (only), the care must be qualifying childcare, defined as registered or approved care. Different (and detailed) conditions are listed as to the nature of the registration or approval in England, Wales, Scotland and Northern Ireland. Care provided outside the UK can also qualify if it is with a provider 'approved by an accredited organisation within the meaning of regulation 4 of the Tax Credit (New Category of Child Care Provider) Regulations 2002'.

Legislation: ITEPA 2003, s. 318A(4)

General availability

One condition for the relief is that the care must be provided under a scheme that is open to the scheme employer's employees generally, or at least to all of the scheme employer's employees who work at a particular location. HMRC booklet 480 states that:

> '... the condition does not mean that every employee who wants a childcare place in a scheme must receive a place. Employers may need to prioritise places if more employees apply than the number of places available. How childcare places are prioritised is up to the employer but the scheme should not exclude members of your staff from applying for a place on the basis of
>
> - grade or position
> - level of salary
> - length of service
> - gender.'

Booklet E18 adds the further point that an individual must not be excluded on the basis of absence due to maternity leave.

It is advisable for the employer to keep a record of any material used to promote the scheme to employees (i.e. so as to demonstrate that it was open to all). This might include, for example, staff handbooks, letters to staff, company website material or workplace posters.

Salary sacrifice and the national minimum wage

A particular issue may arise if certain employees are earning no more than (or only slightly over) the national minimum wage. If such an employee were to enter into a salary sacrifice arrangement, with the intention of joining a childcare scheme paid for by the employer, this could cause the core salary to fall below the national minimum wage, which would be illegal. The problem has been resolved by legislation to be introduced in *Finance Act* 2011, but backdated to the tax year 2005–06. The effect of the change is that the 'open to all' condition will not be treated as failing merely because the scheme is not open to 'relevant low-paid employees'. For the relaxation of the rule to apply, the scheme under which the care is provided must involve 'relevant salary sacrifice arrangements' or 'relevant flexible remuneration arrangements', as defined.

Legislation: ITEPA 2003, s. 318A(5)

Tax Reporter: ¶435-250

Exclusions

There are some important exclusions (i.e. anti-avoidance measures) to prevent these rules being used simply as a way of reallocating taxable income between close relations. Relief will be denied if the care is:

- provided by the employee's partner; or
- provided by a relative of the child, wholly or mainly in the child's home or (if different) in the home of a person having 'parental responsibility' (as defined at 133-410) for the child.

For these purposes, the term 'partner' is defined to mean 'one of a couple' (within the meaning of SSCBA 1992, s. 137(1)). A 'relative' is a parent, grandparent, aunt, uncle, brother or sister 'whether by blood, half blood or marriage or civil partnership'. The restriction for care provided by relatives is normally limited to cases where it is in the child's home, however. It follows that there is no general block on having a child looked after by a sibling, for example, as long as the other conditions are met, notably the requirement for the care to be 'registered or approved'.

Legislation: ITEPA 2003, s. 318C(7)

Amount of relief

The scheme limits relief to £55 for each week for which care is provided for a child and the relevant conditions are met, though there is also no tax charge on associated voucher administration costs incurred by the employer. A week begins on whichever day starts the tax year. As 6 April 2011 falls on a Wednesday, for example, weeks for 2011–12 will each begin on a Wednesday. There will always be 53 such weeks in any tax year, the final week being either one or two days. No tax-free payment may be made, however, if no care is provided in the week in question – for example, during a family holiday when the child is with the parent.

The relief is limited to £55 per week per employer per employee. In other words, if a mother has two children, her employer can only contribute up to £55 per week, not up to £110. However, if the father also works then his employer can also contribute up to £55 per week if he is also operating such a scheme. Indeed, even if there is only one child, each parent's employer may contribute up to £55.

See 133-435 for details of changes to the tax rules that apply from April 2011, restricting the amount of relief in some circumstances.

Legislation: ITEPA 2003, s. 270A(6)

Vouchers

The £55 per week scheme is extended to ensure that care may be provided by means of non-cash vouchers. Under the general benefit in kind rules, a non-cash voucher includes a cheque and any other document capable of being exchanged for goods or services. Under the childcare rules, the voucher must be capable of being exchanged only for qualifying childcare.

The same £55 limit applies per employee, and any amount paid by way of voucher is taken into account to restrict tax relief for any other form of payment. It will be possible, however, to pay by voucher one week and by other means the next (but not to have a mixed payment for the same week). In practice, most smaller businesses will not wish to use vouchers as these attract an administrative cost (typically between about two and 10%). There is nothing to stop an employer entering into a direct contract with the childcare provider, or to produce their own in-house childcare vouchers, and HMRC have provided some useful guidance material on these topics. Many employers may also wish to consider a salary sacrifice arrangement (see 132-080).

HMRC have specifically confirmed that employees do not have to use the vouchers in the week or month in which they are provided but may save them up, for example to meet higher childcare costs during the school holidays (booklet E18, at page seven).

Other Material: www.hmrc.gov.uk/childcare/smechildcareguide.pdf

133-435 Childcare: restrictions for higher earners

Tax relief has been restricted to basic rate only for all *new* recipients of childcare vouchers from April 2011. The changes do not affect employer-provided care (workplace nurseries). According to HMRC guidance:

> 'These changes will mean that anyone who joins an employer supported childcare scheme from 6th April 2011 will receive the same level of income tax exemption, which is approximately £11 per week.'

The changes only affect individuals *joining a scheme* from 6 April 2011. HMRC have given the following guidance in this respect:

> 'In order to fall within the former arrangements, an employee must have submitted an application to his or her employer on or before 5th April 2011 and be entitled to receive the tax/NICs exemptions on that date. The employee does not have to have received his or her first childcare voucher on or before 5th April 2011 but must be entitled to receive them as at that date.
>
> In the event that the employee is not entitled to the exemptions on that date (e.g. if there is no qualifying child) then the employee will be subject to the new arrangements as and when they do become eligible.'

The fact that an employee may have an agreement that is renewed annually with the same employer does not mean that the individual is treated as joining a new scheme each year.

HMRC have also stated that 'an employee can alter the amount of the childcare voucher they require without affecting the rate of exemption to which he or she is entitled'.

As long as the break does not exceed one year, it is also acceptable for there to be a temporary cessation of vouchers, e.g., if the employee only requires them during school holidays, or if the employee is on maternity or long term sick leave, or is simply having a career break. The 12-month limit applies in all cases.

Basic earnings assessment

The amount of relief that an employer can provide, by way of voucher or direct payment of childcare costs, will be restricted for those who have joined a childcare scheme after 5 April 2011 and who are paying tax above the basic rate. The weekly cap will be £55 for an employee paying tax at no more than the basic rate, £28 for one paying at the higher (40%) rate, and £20 for an individual paying at the additional (45%) rate.

To achieve this restriction, employers will be required to carry out a 'basic earnings assessment' when an employee first joins an employer's scheme and then annually at the start of each tax year. Employers must keep records to justify their assessment, but it remains valid even if circumstances change during the year. HMRC guidance includes the following detailed questions and answers:

> '**Can an employee self assess their own tax position at the start of the year rather than the employer?**
>
> No – childcare vouchers are an employer provided benefit and the employer is responsible for carrying out the basic earnings assessment for those employees who join a childcare voucher scheme from April 2011.
>
> **Can the basic earnings assessment be discarded and replaced by declaration of the benefit received on form P11D?**
>
> No – the purpose of the basic earnings assessment is to ensure wherever possible that the appropriate level of exemption is received in the course of the current tax year.
>
> **Can the earnings figure from the previous year's P60 be used for the basic earnings assessment?**
>
> No – the basic earnings assessment should reflect the expected earnings for the current year rather than the previous year. They should be based only on employment with you, and should not include details of any other employments.
>
> **Personal Allowance to be included in the basic earning assessment**
>
> The personal allowance for the purpose of establishing the appropriate amount of exempt income an employee may receive in the form of childcare vouchers (or directly contracted childcare) will be the personal allowance as shown on the employee's tax code. Some employees will have no or a restricted entitlement to personal allowances.
>
> For example, if your employee is in receipt of the standard personal allowances for the year, the level of income that can be earned before a restriction to tax relief on childcare vouchers applies will be the full level of personal allowances plus the basic rate taxable band for the year. And if your employee is not entitled to personal allowances, the level of income that can be earned before a restriction to tax relief on childcare vouchers applies will be just the basic rate taxable band for the year.
>
> More information will be available by 6 April on how you decide what personal allowance figure you use. It is acceptable to use the tax code as at 6th April of the relevant tax year.
>
> **Earnings and benefits to be included in the basic earnings assessment**
>
> The basic earnings assessment should include the following information:
>
> - Basic pay as stated in the employee's contract of employment.
> - Contractual or guaranteed bonuses.
> - London weighting or other regional allowances.

- Taxable benefits.
- Shift allowances.

Earnings and benefits to be excluded from the basic earnings assessment

- Performance related or discretional bonuses.
- Overtime payments.
- Earnings and benefits that are exempt from tax such as pension contributions, employee share schemes and payroll charitable donations.

Changes in pay after the basic earnings assessment has been done

You should assess the employee's pay at the beginning of the tax year or when the employee first applies to join the scheme. This will fix what level of exempt income the employee is entitled to receive for that tax year. The basic earnings assessment applies for a full tax year based on the level of employment earnings applicable at the time the assessment was carried out.

If your employee's pay changes during the course of the year this may mean that the amount of exempt income your employee will be entitled to receive in relation to employer-supported childcare will change from the start of the following tax year. You will need to carry out a basic earnings assessment at the beginning of every tax year.

Do I need to take account of my employee's previous earnings?

You should carry out a basic earnings assessment for any new employee who applies to joint your scheme on or after 6th April 2011. You do not need to take into consideration any previous earnings from other employment that your employee has received during that tax year. Calculate the estimated earnings from the point at which the employee joins your company and pro-rata them up to establish the notional annual figure.

For example, if your employee joins your scheme on 6th October and will earn £26,000 between then and 5th April in the following year, divide by six to get the monthly earnings and multiply by twelve to establish the notional annual figure – in this case, the level of notional earnings will be £52,000 for the tax year and the employee will be treated as a higher rate taxpayer and restrictions to the value of tax exempt childcare vouchers will apply.

What if my employee is just returning after absence on maternity or paternity leave part-way through the year and their previous earnings would have been statutory amounts or zero?

Where an employee who originally became a member of your scheme on or after 6th April 2011 rejoins your scheme from maternity or paternity leave, the basic earnings calculation is based from the point at which the employee rejoins active employment. Pro-rata this upwards to estimate the notional annual earnings as above.

What happens if the employer gets the basic earnings assessment wrong?

If the employer has based the assessment on the best available information at the time the assessment is carried out, then it will be valid for a full twelve month period until the next assessment is carried out. Any exempt figure used as a result of this assessment will be treated by HMRC as correct for P11D purposes.

If the employer gets the initial assessment incorrect due to a failure to use relevant available information and the employee has received a level of relief they were not entitled to, HMRC can assess for any additional tax that is payable. An employer can also report the additional benefit paid by submitting a form P11D.

Will HMRC provide any online or CD ROM calculators for employers to use when carrying out the basic earnings assessment?

There are no plans to do so at present.

Change of employment

Where an individual joins a childcare voucher scheme of a new employer on or after 6th April 2011 he or she will be treated as a new joiner and the employer will be required to carry out a basic earnings assessment. There are no exclusions for people working in particular types of employment or sectors where change of employer takes place on a frequent basis.'

Other Material: www.hmrc.gov.uk/thelibrary/employer-qa.pdf (guidance for employers) and www.hmrc.gov.uk/thelibrary/employee-qa.pdf (guidance for employees and parents).

Restricting membership of the scheme

Some employers may decide that they wish to close the childcare scheme to new members to avoid the complications arising under the proposals. However, HMRC have warned that

> 'Where an employer closes a scheme to new members after 6th April 2011 the scheme would no longer be considered to be 'generally open' to all employees. The scheme would not therefore meet the requirements for the tax and NICs exemptions to apply.'

133-437 Employment income amount

The legislation refers to 'the appropriate amount', being respectively £20, £28 or £55. The level of that amount in turn depends on the measure of the 'employment income amount'. The legislation and associated guidance notes confirm that the earnings to be taken into account will be based on the taxable employment income for the employment in question only, ignoring any other sources of income. Discretionary income will be ignored. A complicating factor is that a deduction will be made for personal allowances to the extent that they are reflected in the tax code determined for the employment in question. If the employee has two employments, therefore, it may make a difference if personal allowances are given against one employment rather than the other.

If the employee joins the particular employment part way through the tax year, the employee's income (before deduction of the personal allowances) is grossed up by 365/RD where RD is the number of days from the start of the employment to the following end of the tax year.

The assessment of the employee's income is to be made 'at the required time' which is defined to mean that start of the tax year or, if later, the date on which the employee joins the scheme under which the care is provided.

133-450 Tax-free childcare for working families

With effect from April 2017, a replacement for the Childcare Voucher Scheme will be introduced although parents will have the option to join the Voucher Scheme until 5 April 2018 and, once part of that scheme, they may elect to remain within it.

Otherwise the following provisions will replace the above employer provided childcare vouchers. The new scheme will be open to families where both parents work at least 16 hours per week and neither parent earns more than £100,000 per annum. Parents participating in the scheme must not also claim Childcare Vouchers, tax credits or universal credits. Unlike the Childcare Voucher scheme, this is not designed specifically to be administered by employers although employers may offer to deduct contributions from net pay and pass this into the scheme.

Parents will open an online account into which they will pay money and the Government will automatically make top-up payments of 20p for every 80p paid in by the parent up to a maximum top up of £2,000 per child each year. There is no restriction on the number of participating children. All funds held within these accounts must be used to pay for qualifying childcare.

The scheme will be available for all children up to the age of 12 and this is extended to age 17 for disabled children.

Legislation: *Childcare Payments Regulations* 2015 (SI 2015/522); *Childcare Payments (Eligibility) Regulations* 2015 (SI 2015/448)

Tax Reporter: ¶435-300

Other benefits

133-500 Introduction and general principle

Employees pay tax on most benefits in kind provided by employers, the taxable amount being known as the cash equivalent. Many benefits are subject to their own special rules, and some are exempted from tax either completely or within defined limits.

For benefits that are not subject to any special rules, the general charging provision taxes the amount of any expense incurred in providing the benefit, or in connection with it, less any amount made good by the employee.

Legislation: ITEPA 2003, s. 203ff.

Tax Reporter: ¶419-000

133-510 Assets used by employees

Where an asset is made available to an employee for their private use but the employer retains the ownership of it, the employee is assessed for each year for which he has the use of the asset, on an amount equal to 20% of the market value of the asset at the time it was provided, together with any further costs incurred in providing the asset. It follows that if an employer provides an employee with the use of an asset with a life of less than five years, the total assessable benefit should be less than the cost of provision of the asset.

Where the person who provides an asset to an employee does not own it, but it is rented or hired, the value of the benefit is the rent or hire charge.

Finance Act 2017, s. 8 made clear that the calculation of the benefit will be based on availability for the full year reduced proportionately for days in the year prior to the asset being provided and for days when the asset is unavailable. An asset is unavailable on any day where, for a period of more than 12 hours, it is not in a fit condition to be used, could not lawfully be used or is in the possession of a third party unconnected to the employer.

Legislation: ITEPA 2003, s. 205

Tax Reporter: ¶419-050

133-520 Assets transferred to employees

Where ownership of an asset passes from employer to employee, and the asset has been used since it was acquired by the person providing it, the assessable benefit is normally the market value of the asset at the time it was transferred, rather than the original cost of acquisition. However, where an asset has been used by an employee and ownership then passes from the employer to the same or another employee, the receiving employee is assessed on the full cost to the employer of acquiring the asset, less any amount already assessed on him or on the employee in respect of the use of the asset.

Example

Colin, who earns £20,000 p.a., has been provided with the use of a suit.

The original cost was £300 and it was made available to him for two years. It was sold to him in year three at its market value of £20.

The charge for the use would be:

		£
Year 1	20% × £300	60
Year 2		60
		120

In year 3, the charge would be on £300 – £120 – £20 = £160.

(The original cost of the suit, less the amount already assessed for the use of it, less the amount paid.)

It would probably have been more sensible to give the suit to charity and start again.

The rules just described do not apply where a car or a bicycle is transferred to an employee at a time after it has been provided as a benefit in kind; instead any taxable benefit is calculated by reference to its market value at the date of transfer. This special rule applies to bicycles that have met the conditions of ITEPA 2003, s. 244: see 141-250.

Legislation: ITEPA 2003, s. 204

Tax Reporter: ¶419-050

133-540 Benefits for disabled employees

A benefit provided for a disabled employee is not taxable if the following conditions are satisfied:

(1) the main purpose of providing the benefit is to enable the employee to perform the duties of his employment;

(2) the benefit consists of the provision of a hearing aid or other equipment, services or facilities (apart from representative occupation accommodation, which is already exempt under ITEPA 2003, s. 316);

(3) the benefit is provided under the *Disability Discrimination Act* 1995, the Access to Work programme, or any other statutory provision or arrangements; and

(4) the benefit is available to employees generally on similar terms.

A charge to tax may arise, however, if there is significant private use of the facilities, etc.

Legislation: *Income Tax (Benefits in Kind) (Exemption Costs resulting from Disability) Regulations* 2002 (SI 2002/1596)

Tax Reporter: ¶419-100

133-550 Eye tests and special corrective appliances

A statutory exemption is available for certain eye tests and glasses. This exemption applies even if the eye test is provided by means of a voucher or credit token, so that there will be no tax charge however the employer decides to pay.

Specifically, there will be no taxable benefit if an employer provides the following where two conditions are met:

(1) an eye and eyesight test; or

(2) special corrective appliances shown by such a test to be necessary.

The first condition for such exemption is that the provision of the test or appliances is required by regulations made under the *Health and Safety at Work, etc. Act* 1974. Employers are required by law to provide, or meet the cost of, eyecare tests and/or corrective glasses for employees using computers or other visual display equipment in certain circumstances.

The second condition for exemption is that the employer does indeed provide such tests and appliances for all employees for whom the legal requirement applies.

Legislation: ITEPA 2003, s. 320A

Tax Reporter: ¶437-920

133-560 Medical treatment and private medical insurance

Overseas treatment

Where an employer provides medical insurance for an employee, the taxable amount, following normal rules, is the cost to the employer. However, a benefit is exempt if it consists of:

- providing the employee with medical treatment outside the UK (including providing for him to be an in-patient) in a case where the need for the treatment arises while the employee is outside the UK for the purpose of performing the duties of his employment; or
- providing insurance for the employee against the cost of such treatment in such a case.

Medical treatment here includes all forms of treatment for, and all procedures for diagnosing, any physical or mental ailment, infirmity, or defect.

Legislation: ITEPA 2003, s. 325

Other Material: HMRC *Employment Income Manual* EIM21765

Tax Reporter: ¶437-900

Medical check-ups and health screenings

A statutory exemption applies for one medical check or health assessment per employee per tax year. The exemption applies only to employees (and not, for example, to family members unless they are also employees in their own right). There is no requirement that an employer must provide medical checks for all members of staff, so an employer could choose to pay for such services just for its more senior staff members or (for example) for those over a certain age.

An employer may provide, for a given employee in a given tax year, both one health screening assessment and one medical check-up. The former concept is defined as 'an assessment to identify employees who might be at particular risk of ill-health' whereas a medical check-up is defined to mean 'a physical examination of the employee by a health professional for (and only for) determining the employee's state of health'.

If an employee has more than one employer at the same time, the tax exemption only applies to one health-screening assessment and one medical check-up provided by any of them.

The exemption applies whether the employer pays for the services direct or whether the payment is by way of a non-cash voucher or credit token.

Legislation: ITEPA 2003, s. 266(3), 267(2), 320B

Other Material: HMRC statement of 12 October 2007

Tax Reporter: ¶437-900

Recommended medical treatment

With effect from 1 January 2015, no liability to income tax arises in respect of the provision to an employee of recommended medical treatment, or the payment or reimbursement, to or in respect of an employee, of the cost of such treatment, provided the provision is not pursuant to relevant salary sacrifice arrangements or relevant flexible remuneration arrangements. Provided the value of the exemption does not exceed £500 per employee per annum.

Medical treatment is 'recommended' if it:

(a) is made to the employee as part of occupational health services provided to the employee by a service provided:
   (i) under *Employment and Training Act* 1973, s. 2 (arrangements for the purpose of assisting persons to retain employment etc.); or
   (ii) by, or in accordance with arrangements made by, the employer;
(b) is made for the purpose of assisting the employee to return to work after a period of absence due to injury or ill health; and
(c) meets any other requirements specified in regulations made by the Treasury.

Legislation: ITEPA 2003, s. 320C; *Income Tax (Recommended Medical Treatment) Regulations* 2014 (SI 2014/3227)

133-580 Scholarships and school fees

General

There is a fairly complex web of legislation to deal with this issue. ITTOIA 2005, s. 776 specifically exempts from tax certain scholarship income. Unfortunately, however, ITEPA 2003, s. 215 then makes it clear that the exemption is only to apply to the actual holder of the scholarship.

Any scholarship provided for a member of an employee's family or household is normally deemed to be provided by reason of the employment, and taxed accordingly. Scholarships will be caught if provided by reason of the employment or if provided under arrangements entered into by the employer or by a connected person, whether or not the employer or connected person contributes directly to the cost. However, the usual relaxation applies where the employer is an individual (not, for example, a company) and where 'the arrangements are made in the normal course of the employer's domestic, family or personal relationships'.

For these purposes, a scholarship is defined to include an exhibition, bursary 'or other similar educational endowment'.

Legislation: ITEPA 2003, s. 211ff.

Tax Reporter: ¶419-150ff.

'Sandwich' and similar courses

An employee in full-time employment may leave that employment for a period to attend an educational establishment and yet still receive payments from his employer. This might occur, for example, where the employee is on a so-called 'sandwich' course. Such payments will be treated as exempt from income tax, provided the conditions set out in SP 4/86 (8 August 1986) are satisfied. Various conditions apply with regard to the nature and length of the course and the payments made by the employer must not exceed £15,480 for the academic year. (This figure was increased from £15,000 with effect from 1 September 2007.)

Tax Reporter: ¶419-200

Other Material: HMRC *Employment Income Manual* EIM06245

Trust funds and schemes

No charge will arise by virtue of s. 212 if:

- the scholarship is provided from a trust fund or scheme;
- it is held by somebody in full-time education at a university, college, school or other educational establishment;
- during the tax year in question, not more than a quarter of the relevant payments made from the fund are allocated to individuals (whether or not they are P11D employees) who obtain the scholarship by reason of a person's employment (whether or not the employment is in the UK); and
- the scholarship is provided in such circumstances that it would not, on an ordinary interpretation of the expression, be treated as provided by

reason of the employment; for this purpose only, ignore the provision whereby all benefits provided by an employer are automatically deemed to be so provided.

Such exempt awards are described by HMRC as being made 'fortuitously' rather than by virtue of the employment. In *Kutcha*, this exception did not apply and the benefit of scholarship payments was held to be correctly assessed on the employee and not his children.

Legislation: ITEPA 2003, s. 213

Case: *Kutcha* [2013] TC02769

Other Material: HMRC *Employment Income Manual* EIM30005

School fees

The payment by an employer of the school fees of an employee's child is a taxable benefit in kind. The tax exemption for childcare does not extend to school fees. Where an independent school, or other fee-charging establishment, provides a subsidised or free place for the children of employees (or for other members of the employee's family or household) see 133-600 (in-house benefits).

Legislation: ITEPA 2003, s. 318(8)(b)

133-600 In-house benefits

Many employers will provide their own products or services either free or at a discount to their employees. For example, a bus company may allow its employees to travel free on its buses or an independent school may allow its teachers to send their children at a discount to the school in question.

Where a benefit comprises services or facilities shared between the person to whom the benefit is supplied and others, difficulties arise in determining the taxable amount of the benefit. The House of Lords held in *Pepper (HMIT) v Hart* that the cost (and therefore the taxable value) of 'in-house' benefits in kind is only the marginal or additional cost to the employer. In the case of a school, for example, it will be clear that the average cost of educating each pupil will be much higher than the additional marginal cost of having one extra pupil.

The *Pepper (HMIT) v Hart* case concerned a concessionary fee scheme, operated by Malvern College, which allowed sons of staff members to attend the school for 20% of the normal fees. Concessionary pupils had to satisfy the same educational requirements as all other boys and there was no question of any boy admitted under the scheme taking the place

the cost of two suits which he used for work on the grounds that he was required by his employer to wear them and that they were used only for work. His claim failed because the High Court held that the suits were worn to provide 'cover and comfort' and their cost was not therefore incurred wholly and exclusively in connection with his employment; rather, there was a dual purpose. (For allowances for the cost of special clothing or tools, see 143-100.)

This general problem of 'duality' has caused difficulty in a number of cases. However, it is not necessary that the whole of an item of expenditure meets the requirements of the expense rule if there is a severable part that does. In the ordinary way this means that a claim to apportion expenditure can only succeed if the expenditure is variable and the total cost has been increased by the requirements of the office or employment.

In *Nolder v Walters*, claims were made for travelling expenses and for board and lodging whilst the employee was away from home. The claims were opposed by HMRC on the ground that the expenditure was not wholly and exclusively incurred in the performance of the duties of his employment. However, it was held that:

> 'when you get a travelling office, so that travelling expenses are allowed, those travelling expenses do include the extra expense of living which is put upon a man by having to stay at hotels and inns, and such places, rather than staying at home. Of course his board and lodging in a sense, eating and sleeping, are the necessities of a human being, whether he has an office, or whether he has not, and therefore, of course, the cost of his food and lodging is not wholly and exclusively laid out in the performance of his duties, but the extra part of it is.'

In practice, HMRC accept that the home saving will be very small and admit the claim in full. See further 141-300; *Lucas v Cattell (HMIT)*.

Cases: *Nolder v Walters* (1930) 15 TC 380; *Lucas v Cattell (HMIT)* (1972) 48 TC 353; *Hillyer v Leeke* (1976) 51 TC 90

Tax Reporter: ¶453-200

140-150 'Necessarily'

Two cases relating to club subscriptions both turned on the question of 'necessity' (see 140-050). In *Elwood v Utitz*, Mr Utitz, who lived in Northern Ireland, claimed the cost of his subscription to two London clubs on the ground that he needed first-class accommodation and facilities when he visited London for his company. He argued that his sole reason for joining the clubs was to obtain suitable accommodation at the least cost. HMRC argued that the subscriptions entitled Mr Utitz in his personal capacity to a whole range of facilities and that therefore the expenditure was not wholly, exclusively and necessarily incurred in the performance of his duties. The Northern Ireland Court of Appeal found for the taxpayer.

However, in *Brown v Bullock* a Midland Bank manager, who was required to join a local club as a condition of his employment, was denied the cost of his club subscription as an allowable expense.

The mere fact that an employer requires something of an employee will not of itself make the expense a necessary one.

> 'The test is not whether the employer imposes the expense but whether the duties do, in the sense that, irrespective of what the employer may prescribe, the duties cannot be performed without incurring the particular outlay (*Brown v Bullock* above, per Donovan LJ).'

The word 'cannot' in this particular judgment is not in practice taken too literally, but the test remains a harsh one.

The subject of choice was considered by the courts in *Marsden v IR Commrs*. The case concerned an HMRC employee who used his own car to travel from home to various tax offices and the premises of employers. He was not required by HMRC to use his own car and could have used public transport. However, HMRC did pay his car expenses by reference to their car scale. The taxpayer claimed the excess of his actual expenditure over the amount paid by HMRC. His claim was rejected but the general issue of choice was considered. Pennycuick J said:

> 'This question must be an everyday occurrence, for example as between car and train, self-drive or chauffeur-driven car, aeroplane or ship, first or second class, and the like. Mr Phillips [representing the Revenue] submits that this must be a question of fact and degree depending on the circumstances of any particular case, including not only the price of the transport, but such considerations as speed, convenience, the purpose of the journey, the status of the officer, and so forth. I agree with that contention.'

HMRC officers have been known to argue that an expense cannot be necessary if the employer does not agree to bear it. This is of course a fallacious argument since it must be a matter for agreement between the employer and the employee whether the employer pays a high salary out of which the employee then pays his own expenses or a lower salary plus expenses. However, difficulty must be anticipated if the employer bears some, but not all, of the expenses which are held to be necessary.

Cases: *Brown v Bullock* (1961) 40 TC 1; *Marsden v IR Commrs* (1965) 42 TC 326; *Elwood v Utitz* (1965) 42 TC 482

Tax Reporter: ¶453-200

140-200 'In the performance of the duties'

Some expenses will be incurred wholly, exclusively and necessarily in respect of the employment, but will nevertheless fall to be disallowed because they have not been incurred *in the performance of* the duties of the office or employment (see 140-050). These words are interpreted rigidly and many claims are rejected on the ground that they are incurred in order to put the individual in a position to perform the duties of the employment, rather than in the performance of them.

The difficulties in distinguishing between those activities which are carried out in the performance of an employee's duties and those which are not is shown by the two contrasting cases concerning journalists' reading expenses which were heard together by the House of Lords.

The facts in *Fitzpatrick v IR Commrs (No. 2)* and *Smith (HMIT) v Abbott*, were essentially identical. However in *Fitzpatrick* the Court of Session held that expenses incurred by Scottish journalists in purchasing newspapers and periodicals to keep themselves informed for their jobs was not a deductible expense, whereas in *Abbott*, the Court of Appeal held that such expenses of English journalists were incurred 'in the performance of the duties' of their employment and so were deductible. The House of Lords, by a majority, resolved the conflicting decisions in the two cases by finding in favour of HMRC and disallowing the expenses in both cases.

The distinction was between expenses incurred 'in the performance of the duties' and expenses which were not deductible because they were incurred in order to enable the duties to be performed. Lord Templeman said that, applying this distinction, a journalist does not read in the performance of his duties but in order to enable his duties to be performed.

Nevertheless, some preparatory work may be in the performance of an employee's duties so that expenses incurred in relation to it would be allowable. An example given by Warner J in *Abbott*, at first instance, was of an employed solicitor reading a client's papers together with the relevant legislation and cases prior to giving advice to the client.

The dividing line is clearly a fine one and to some extent will turn on factors such as the terms of the employee's contract; whether the particular activities in question are performed in office hours rather than during the employee's own time at home; and how directly the relevant expense is connected with the employee's work.

Case: *Fitzpatrick v IR Commrs (No. 2); Smith (HMIT) v Abbott* [1994] BTC 66

Tax Reporter: ¶454-120

140-230 Abolition of PAYE dispensations from 6 April 2016

With effect from 6 April 2016, all dispensations agreed with HMRC will cease to be effective. From that date qualifying paid and reimbursed expenses will be exempt from tax and NIC. Qualifying payments will be those payments where the employee would be entitled to a full matching tax deduction. HMRC have indicated that they will publish examples of qualifying payments.

140-300 PAYE settlement agreements

Where benefits are not covered by the statutory exemption for trivial benefits outlined in 133-335, the employer may agree to pay a lump sum in respect of minor, or irregular benefits provided to employees, such as reimbursement of telephone expenses or late night taxis. Such a 'PAYE settlement agreement' may also be appropriate where the employer provides a benefit which is shared by a number of employees and where apportionment is impractical. Where a settlement agreement is reached, the employer need not include the items in the end of year returns, and the employee need not include them in tax returns.

HMRC have published a statement of practice detailing the operation and scope of PAYE settlement agreements.

Legislation: ITEPA 2003, s. 703ff.; *Income Tax (Pay As You Earn) Regulations* 2003 (SI 2003/2682), reg. 105ff.

Other Material: SP 5/96

Tax Reporter: ¶495-000

140-350 Claiming relief for expenses

Employees who need to complete a personal tax return will normally claim relief for any qualifying expenses as part of that return. Those who do not do so may instead use form P87 which can be downloaded from the HMRC site, at www.hmrc.gov.uk/forms/p87.pdf (but if the expenses to be claimed exceed £2,500 then HMRC will insist that the employee should instead complete a personal tax return). If an employee has more than one employment then a separate copy of the form should be completed for each employment.

Fixed sum deductions

140-400 Flat rate allowances

Overview

Some employees are required (at their own expense) to provide tools or protective clothing, or to incur other minor expenses for which a tax deduction would be due. To cut down on administrative time to be spent negotiating numerous small deductions, appropriate fixed allowances have in many cases been agreed by HMRC, typically in discussion with trade unions. These are referred to as 'flat rate' allowances (or expenses allowances).

Legislation: ITEPA 2003, s. 366

Tax Reporter: ¶457-500

Amount of deduction

According to the HMRC manuals, 'the flat rate amounts are intended to represent the average annual expense incurred by that class of employees on the repair and replacement of work equipment. This means the repair, maintenance and replacement of loose tools and special clothing'. A table of the agreed figures is given in *Hardman's Tax Rates and Tables* at 3-700.

To the extent that the employer reimburses the expenses, or would do if requested, the deduction is denied. A deduction is thus only available where the employee *necessarily* provides the items himself and does not have the benefit of any reimbursement from the employer. Since the passing of the *Health and Safety at Work, etc. Act* 1974, there has been a tendency for employers to provide what is necessary for their employees to do their job.

Tax Reporter: ¶457-500

Other Material: HMRC *Employment Income Manual* EIM32705

Local agreements

HMRC officers are allowed to agree local figures for flat rate deductions 'where processing individual expense deductions would otherwise involve considerable unproductive work'. These may be appropriate either where 'the employer does not fall within one of the industry groups for which an allowance has been negotiated nationally' or if 'there are special local circumstances that cause workers to incur a level of deductible expenditure substantially different from that in the apparently relevant industry'.

Although HMRC do not normally scale back a current year figure to cover earlier years, the guidance states that:

> 'the 'no retrospection' rule may be relaxed in cases where a flat rate expenses allowance is agreed for the first time for a particular group of employees. Tax offices may then have to deal with requests for expenses for earlier years by employees in that group who have previously had no relief at all. Receipts will rarely be available, though it is clear that some expenses must have been incurred – otherwise, it would not have been possible to agree an FRE deduction for the future. In such a case, it makes administrative sense to use the newly agreed FRE as a starting point in negotiating the relief due for earlier years.'

If flat rate amounts are agreed of up to £165 per year, the intention will be to increase the figure annually as part of the annual coding process. Higher amounts will not be increased automatically in this way.

Other Material: HMRC *Employment Income Manual* EIM32725, EIM32726

Claiming actual costs incurred

Employees incurring higher costs than the flat rate figures are free to claim actual expenses incurred if they so wish. HMRC make the following comments in respect of this point:

> 'If an employee deducts his or her actual expense in one year they are not prevented from deducting the flat rate expense in other years ... .
>
> In practice the most important advantage of a flat rate expense deduction to an employee is that he or she does not need to retain evidence to demonstrate the amount of expenditure they have incurred. Also, the amount of the deduction is calculated to be appropriate for the average employee taking one year with another. So high expenditure in one year may be balanced by low expenditure in another. For this reason many employees do not retain evidence of expenditure and do not request a deduction for their actual expenditure in those years for which it exceeds the flat rate amount.'

Legislation: ITEPA 2003, s. 330(2)

Other Material: HMRC *Employment Income Manual* EIM32715

Round sum allowances

Flat rate expense deductions under this rule should not be confused with the treatment of round sum allowances. HMRC summarise the distinction as follows:

'The payment of a round sum expenses allowance to an employee by his or her employer is taxable as earnings within Section 62 ITEPA 2003 (see EIM 00520 onwards). PAYE applies to such payments.

A round sum expenses allowance is an allowance which is paid to an employee irrespective of whether he or she spends it or not in a particular way. It is to be contrasted with a reimbursement of expenditure actually incurred by an employee and with a scale rate payment intended to reimburse such expenditure (see EIM 05200).

Fergusson v Noble (1919) 7 TC 176 supports our view that a round sum expense allowance is taxable as part of the employee's earnings. In that case, a detective received a cash allowance for buying civilian clothing whether it was spent or not. It was held to be taxable because it was part of the consideration that the detective was entitled to receive in return for his services. It did not matter that he was expected to spend the money in a particular way.'

Case: *Fergusson v Noble* (1919) 7 TC 176

Other Material: HMRC *Employment Income Manual* EIM05100

140-410 Scale rate payments

Terminology

The concept of a 'scale rate payment' is different from that of a round sum allowance and different again from a flat rate allowance.

A *round sum allowance* is paid to an employee whether or not the money is actually spent in a particular way. For example, an employee may receive an additional £200 per month in salary as an entertaining allowance and it is up to the employee whether or not to spend that money on such entertaining. Such a payment by an employer is taxable in full as ordinary earnings.

A *flat rate allowance* is an amount, negotiated on a broad scale between employers or trade unions and HMRC, which may be paid tax-free to cover particular costs incurred by employees, typically on specialist clothing or laundry costs. See 140-400.

Use of scale rate payments acceptable to HMRC

In contrast to the above, a *scale rate payment* is an amount 'calculated to do no more than reimburse the expenditure incurred by employees on allowable expenses'. Such scale rate payments are in principle still taxable, though subject to an appropriate expenses claim by the employee. However, HMRC accept that a dispensation may be given to cover the use of such scale rate payments, subject to the following guidance:

> 'In general, scale rates are only appropriate for expenses which are widely incurred, in broadly similar amounts, but for which it is often difficult to get receipts. For example subsistence, or the expenses of cleaning uniforms or protective clothing (see EIM 32465). Scale rates should be set at a fairly modest level which, taking one day with another, will be enough to cover the relevant expenses. They should not be pitched at a level to cover the highest amount that an employee might spend.'

The guidance goes on to warn that 'scale rate expenses payments should only be paid on days when the employee has incurred an allowable expense.'

Other Material: HMRC *Employment Income Manual* EIM05200

Travel and subsistence

140-500 Travelling expenses – overview

Employees can get tax relief for the full cost incurred in travelling in the performance of their duties, or in travelling to get to or from a temporary workplace. It is unnecessary for employees to offset any savings they make through not undertaking their normal commuting journey.

'Qualifying travelling expenses' are:

(1) amounts necessarily expended on travelling in the performance of the duties of the employment (see 140-850), etc.; or

(2) other expenses of travelling (see 140-900) which:

   (a) are attributable to the employee's, etc. necessary attendance in performing the duties of the employment, etc.; and

   (b) are not expenses of 'ordinary commuting' or 'private travel'.

For the avoidance of doubt, these are two separate tests. If travel meets the first test ('in the performance of the duties of the employment'), then it is not necessary to consider, for example, whether the journey constitutes 'ordinary commuting'.

Separate rules apply to cars used for business travel (see 132-400).

Legislation: ITEPA 2003, s. 337, 338

Tax Reporter: ¶454-000

140-550 Mileage allowances: overview

No tax charge arises in respect of approved mileage allowance payments made by an employer as payment for the business use of a privately owned qualifying vehicle. Separate mileage rates apply for cars, vans, motor cycles and cycles, as shown in *Hardman's Tax Rates and Tables* at 3-475. The rates for cars and vans were increased, for the first time, from April 2011.

In addition, employers may pay a tax-free passenger rate of five pence per mile for each fellow passenger carried by the employee and making the same business trip (see 140-600).

Tax relief is available to the extent that the employer either pays no mileage rate or pays a mileage rate that is less than the statutory rate. However, there is no tax relief in respect of passengers if the employer fails to pay at the passenger rate.

Payments made in accordance with these rules are tax-free. They should neither be reported on form P11D nor shown in the tax returns of the employees concerned. A dispensation is not needed and should not be sought for such payments.

This is the only form of tax relief available to employees who use their cars for business purposes. Calculating the actual cost of a business journey, perhaps by apportioning the overall cost of running the car on the basis of comparing business and private mileage, is not permitted.

Legislation: ITEPA 2003, s. 229ff.

Tax Reporter: ¶432-100

Company vehicles

The principles of statutory mileage allowance and associated mileage allowance relief (see 140-625) do not apply where the vehicle in question is a company vehicle (but see 140-600). For these purposes, a vehicle is a 'company vehicle' in a tax year, if in that year:

- the vehicle is made available to the employee by reason of his or her employment and is not available for his or her private use;
- the vehicle is available for private use, but the employee is taxed on it under the benefit in kind rules;
- the vehicle is pool car or van and as such no charge arises under ITEPA 2003, s. 167 and 168; or

- the vehicle is a cycle that would have been chargeable to tax under but for the exemption for employer-provided cycles in ITEPA 2003, s. 244(1).

Legislation: ITEPA 2003, s. 236(2), (3)

140-575 Mileage allowances: definitions

Mileage allowance payments are amounts other than 'passenger payments' (see below) that are paid to an employee in respect of expenses in connection with the use by him for business travel of a qualifying vehicle (ITEPA 2003, s. 229(2)).

'Business travel' is any travel, the expenses of which if incurred and defrayed by the employee, would otherwise be deductible for tax purposes (ITEPA 2003, s. 236(1)).

A 'qualifying vehicle' is a car, van, motor cycle or cycle (ITEPA 2003, s. 235(1)).

A 'car' is a mechanically propelled vehicle other than a goods vehicle, a motor cycle, or a vehicle of a type not commonly used as a private vehicle and unsuitable to be so used (ITEPA 2003, s. 235(2)).

A 'van' is a 'goods vehicle' that has a 'design weight' not exceeding 3,500 kilograms and is not a motor cycle (ITEPA 2003, s. 235(3)). The 'design weight' is the weight that a vehicle is designed or adapted not to exceed when in normal use and travelling on a road laden and a 'goods vehicle' is a vehicle of a construction primarily suited for the conveyance of goods or burden of any description (ITEPA 2003, s. 236(2), (3)).

A 'motor cycle' is defined as a mechanically propelled vehicle, not being an invalid carriage, with less than four wheels and the weight of which unladen does not exceed 410 kilograms (ITEPA 2003, s. 235(4); *Road Traffic Act* 1988, s. 185(1)).

A 'cycle' is defined as a bicycle, a tricycle, or a cycle having four or more wheels, not being in any case a motor vehicle (ITEPA 2003, s. 235(5); *Road Traffic Act* 1988, s. 192(1)).

The exemption applies only to 'approved' mileage allowance payments. Mileage allowance payments are approved only if, or to the extent that, the total of all the mileage allowance payments made to the employee for the kind of vehicle in question does not exceed the mileage allowance payments applying to the vehicle in question (ITEPA 2003, s. 229(3)).

The approved amount for mileage allowance payments is determined by the formula:

$$M \times R$$

where:

M is the number of miles of business travel by the employee (other than as a passenger), using that kind of vehicle, in the tax year in question; and

R is the rate applicable for that kind of vehicle.

In applying the rates, the reference to the first 10,000 miles is to the total number of miles of business travel in relation to the employment or any associated employment, by car or van, in the tax year in question. For these purposes, employments are associated if:

- the employer is the same;
- the employers are partnerships or bodies and an individual or another partnership or body has control over both of them; or
- the employers are associated companies.

Example

Matthew uses his own car for work. In the tax year, he undertakes 15,000 business miles. His employer pays him a mileage allowance of 35p per mile for the first 5,000 miles and 25p per mile for mileage in excess of 5,000 miles. As the rates do not exceed the approved amounts applying to cars for the year, no tax charge arises in respect of the payments. Matthew can claim tax relief on the shortfall.

Tax Reporter: ¶432-100

140-600 Passenger payments

Overview

No tax charge arises in respect of an approved passenger payment made to an employee for a car or a van, irrespective of whether the car or van is the employee's own vehicle or a company vehicle. Tax-free passenger rates only apply to passengers in cars or vans. Any rates paid in respect of motor cycle passengers, for example, would be taxable. The relief for passenger payments applies only in relation to passengers who are fellow employees and would not apply, for example, to the employee of a sole proprietor who took that sole proprietor as a passenger on a business journey.

Legislation: ITEPA 2003, s. 233

Meaning of 'approved passenger payments'

Passenger payments are defined for the purposes of the exemption as 'amounts paid to an employee because, while using a car or van for business travel, he carries one or more qualifying passengers in it'. A 'qualifying passenger' is a passenger who is a fellow employee also undertaking business travel.

As with mileage payments (see above), passenger payments are only approved if, or to the extent, that the total amount of all passenger payments made to the employee does not exceed the approved amount for passenger payments.

The approved amount for passenger payments is found by applying the formula:

$$M \times R$$

where:

M is the number of miles of business travel by the employee, by car or van, for which the employee carries a qualifying passenger in the tax year in question and in respect of which passenger payments are made; and

R is 5p per mile.

In the event that the employee carries more than one qualifying passenger for all or part of the tax year, the approved amount for passenger payments is the aggregate of the rates calculated separately for each qualifying passenger.

Example

James uses his own car for work. During the course of the year, he drives various colleagues to business meetings. He receives passenger payments in respect of his passengers (all of whom satisfy the definition of qualifying passenger) as follows:

Passenger	*Business miles*	*Actual passenger payment*	*M × 5p*
John	2,000	£80.00	£100.00
Claire	375	£15.00	£18.75
Paul	680	£27.20	£34.00

As the actual passenger payments received by James do not exceed the approved passenger payments, no liability arises in respect of the payments.

Legislation: ITEPA 2003, s. 233

Tax Reporter: ¶432-100

140-625 Mileage allowance relief

Employees are entitled to tax relief in the event that they use their own vehicle (car, van, motor cycle or bicycle) for business travel and either the employer pays no mileage allowance or pays a mileage allowance that is less than the approved amount of mileage allowance payments applicable to the employee's vehicle (see *Hardman's Tax Rates and Tables* at 3-475). If no mileage allowance is paid, the relief is the approved amount for mileage allowance payments applicable to the kind of vehicle in question. Where a mileage allowance is paid, but at a lower rate that the statutory rate, tax relief is given on the shortfall.

There is no corresponding relief if the employer either fails to pay as passenger rate or pays a passenger rate that is less than the statutory rate.

Example

Polly occasionally uses her bicycle for work. During the tax year, she cycles 120 miles on business travel. Her employer pays no mileage allowance. Polly can claim tax relief on £24, being 120 miles at the statutory mileage rate for bicycles (for the year in question) of 20 pence per mile.

Example

Simon uses his own car for work, and in the tax year 2015–16 he undertakes 15,000 business miles. He receives a mileage allowance from his employer of 20 pence per mile. As this is less than the approved mileage rate, Simon is entitled to claim tax relief as follows:

	£	£
Approved mileage payments:		
10,000 miles @ 45p	4,500	
5,000 miles @ 25p	1,250	
		5,750
15,000 × 20p		(3,000)
Tax relief on		2,750

In each case, the amount of tax relief is an amount on which the employee may claim tax relief at his or her marginal tax rate. Polly can therefore claim tax relief on £24 at her marginal tax rate. Simon can do likewise on the amount of £2,750.

Legislation: ITEPA 2003, s. 231

Tax Reporter: ¶432-100

Remittance basis

Where earnings are chargeable on the remittance basis, there may be deducted from those earnings the amount of any mileage allowance relief for that tax year and for any earlier tax year in which the employee was resident in the UK. A deduction cannot be made twice in respect of the same mileage allowance relief.

Legislation: ITEPA 2003, s. 232

140-700 Car parking

The provision of car parking facilities at or near the individual's place of work is not treated as a taxable benefit. It is also specifically stated that no tax charge can arise as ordinary earnings in relation to workplace parking. Likewise, any expenditure incurred or reimbursing expenses in connection with the provision for, or use by, an employee of a car parking space at or near the employee's place of work is not taxed.

The exemption for car parking extends to the provision of a non-cash voucher or credit token to obtain parking.

Legislation: ITEPA 2003, s. 237, 266ff.

Tax Reporter: ¶432-500

140-750 Parking for cycles and motor cycles

A statutory exemption ensures that there is no charge to tax in respect of the provision of parking spaces for motor cycles and cycles. The exemption extends to the use of non-cash vouchers or credit tokens to obtain parking. As in the case of car parking, any expenditure incurred or reimbursing expenses in connection with the provision for, or use by, an employee of a parking space for a motor cycle or cycle at or near the employee's place of work is not treated as earnings of the employment.

Legislation: ITEPA 2003, s. 237, 266ff.

Tax Reporter: ¶432-500

140-800 Overnight allowances: lorry drivers

HMRC have agreed with the Road Haulage Association an overnight allowance which is tax-free without the need for supporting bills and vouchers but subject to production of documentary evidence that the driver was absent from home overnight and based at a particular depot.

The agreed allowance for recent years, accepted by HMRC as representing no more than reasonable reimbursement of accommodation and subsistence incurred as a result of the business journey within the UK, is as follows:

		£
Year ended	31 December 2013 onwards	34.90
	31 December 2012	33.85
	31 December 2011	32.20
	31 December 2010	30.75
	31 December 2009	30.75
	31 December 2008	29.85
	31 December 2007	28.62
	31 December 2006	27.55
	31 December 2005	26.90

The allowance is reduced by 25%, if a sleeper cab is in operation. Various other allowances are available for lorry drivers. The principles are the same as for any other employees, but particular arrangements have been negotiated with representative bodies.

Other Material: HMRC *Employment Income Manual* EIM66110

Tax Reporter: ¶454-350

140-850 Travel in the performance of the duties

If an employee (in that capacity) is obliged to incur travel expenses, relief is available for amounts necessarily expended on travelling in the performance of the duties of the employment. Few people can claim tax relief under this first heading. A distinction has to be drawn between someone who is travelling as an integral part of the duties of the employment and someone else who is merely travelling to the place where those duties will be performed. Employees qualifying under this leg of the travel expenses rule will include travelling salesmen and domestic service engineers who travel routinely from one location to another, visiting a number of different sites each day on an irregular basis.

A number of tax cases have explored the distinction between private journeys and travel expenses incurred in performing employment duties. Although the structure of the legislation was changed in 1998, these cases can still provide guidance as to what constitutes travel in the performance of the duties.

In *Pook v Owen*, a doctor who carried on a self-employed practice was also employed by a local hospital. HMRC sought to disallow his travelling expenses from home to hospital on the ground that they were not incurred in the performance of his duties. By a majority decision the House of Lords held the expenditure to be allowable on the ground that Dr Owen's duties commenced when he answered the telephone at his home, since at that stage he discussed the symptoms and made various arrangements as to what was to be done whilst he was travelling from home to his office.

However, in the much earlier case of *Ricketts v Colquhoun*, a London barrister who was also Recorder of Portsmouth was denied a claim for travelling expenses from London to Portsmouth on the bases that (1) he had not been obliged to incur the travelling expenses (he could have lived in Portsmouth), and in any case (2), while travelling from London he was not performing the duties of the office.

The case of *Elderkin (HMIT) v Hindmarsh* has added to the difficulty in deciding where a person is employed. In that case the taxpayer spent up to two months at a time working away from his normal base and was paid a subsistence allowance by his firm. He sought to claim a deduction for his subsistence allowances but not his travelling expenses. The court agreed that the expenses were necessary, but denied the claim on the ground that the site at which he was temporarily working was his place of employment. The view taken was that in not claiming travelling expenses the taxpayer had effectively conceded that the site at which he was temporarily working was his place of employment.

It was held in *Miners v Atkinson (HMIT)* that a taxpayer who ran a 'one-man company' from his home could not deduct the cost of travelling to his only client's premises from his income as a director of his company. The High Court held that he ran the company from his home for his own convenience. It was not necessary to fulfil what the judge called his 'directorial duties' from his home address. Consequently, the travelling expenses were not 'necessarily' incurred in the performance of his duties as a director.

The important issue as shown by all these cases is the place of employment. As far as home-workers are concerned, tax relief will only be due under this heading (but see 140-900) if HMRC accept that home is a place of work. HMRC apply a strict test and will only allow such a claim where the conditions are met that allow employees to claim relief for home-working costs not reimbursed by their employers: see under 'Claims for relief where employer does not reimburse expenses' at 143-250.

Legislation: ITEPA 2003, s. 337

Cases: *Ricketts v Colquhoun* (1925) 10 TC 118; *Pook v Owen* (1969) 45 TC 571; *Elderkin (HMIT) v Hindmarsh* [1988] BTC 129; *Miners v Atkinson (HMIT)* [1997] BTC 32

Tax Reporter: ¶454-050

140-900 Other travelling expenses

Travel that is not itself in the performance of the duties will still qualify for tax relief if the employee (in his capacity as such) is obliged to incur and pay the cost of travel and if:

(a) the travel is attributable to the employee's, etc. necessary attendance in performing the duties of the employment, etc.; and

(b) the expense is not one of 'ordinary commuting' or 'private travel'.

It is usually clear whether an employee is attending a particular place in the performance of the duties of his employment. The difficulties therefore arise mainly in defining 'ordinary commuting' and 'private travel'.

Legislation: ITEPA 2003, s. 338

Tax Reporter: ¶454-100

Ordinary commuting and private travel

'Ordinary commuting' means travel between a place which is a 'permanent workplace' in relation to the employment and:

(1) the employee's home; or

(2) a place that is not a 'workplace' in relation to the employment.

This definition is construed strictly.

In the case of *Kirkwood v Evans*, the employee lived in Kings Lynn. His work was relocated to Leeds and he chose to commute between Kings Lynn and Leeds rather than relocate to Leeds at his employer's expense. The court held that journeys between his home in Kings Lynn and his office in Leeds were ordinary commuting. A similar decision, on similar facts, was reached in *Lewis v R & C Commrs*.

'Private travel' means travel between:

(1) the employee's home and a place that is not a workplace in relation to the employment; or

(2) between two places neither of which is a workplace in relation to the employment.

The term 'workplace' is in turn defined to mean a place at which the employee's attendance is necessary in performing the duties of the employment.

Travel between any two places which is, for practical purposes, substantially ordinary commuting or private travel is treated as ordinary commuting or private travel.

In the *Reed Employment* case, the First-tier Tribunal decided that, even if wrong on the salary sacrifice point, each separate engagement of temporary employees was under a separate contract of employment so that the travel was ordinary commuting.

Legislation: ITEPA 2003, s. 338

Cases: *Kirkwood v Evans* [2002] BTC 50; *Lewis v R & C Commrs* (2008) Sp C 690; *Reed Employment plc* [2012] TC 01727

Permanent and temporary workplaces

A 'permanent workplace' means a place which the employee regularly attends in performing the duties of the employment, and which is not a 'temporary workplace'. A 'temporary workplace' means a place which the employee attends in performing the duties of the employment for the purpose of performing a task of limited duration or for some other temporary purpose.

In *Warner v Prior (HMIT)*, the deduction of cost of home to work travel was examined. The taxpayer was a supply teacher at various schools. Lack of facilities at school meant that the taxpayer had to prepare lessons and mark work at home. The taxpayer claimed a deduction in calculating tax liability for cost of travelling to schools in her own car but the tax inspector refused her claim. The taxpayer appealed to the special commissioners, arguing that she had two places of work at home and school, that home work was objectively necessary to perform her duties and expenses of travel were allowable. The commissioner held that the taxpayer's secondary place of work was dependent on where she worked not on requirements of work, and so the costs of travelling to work were not deductible. The appeal was dismissed accordingly.

Legislation: ITEPA 2003, s. 339

Case: *Warner v Prior (HMIT)* (2003) Sp C 353

The 24-month rule and fixed term appointments

A place is not regarded as a temporary workplace if the employee's attendance is:

(1) in the course of a period of continuous work at that place lasting more than 24 months, or comprising all or almost all of the period for which the employee is likely to hold the employment; or

(2) at a time when it is reasonable to assume that it will be in the course of such a period.

A 'period of continuous work' at a place is a period over which, looking at the whole period and considering all the employment duties, the employment duties fall to be performed to a significant extent at that place.

HMRC guidance to tax officers is that they 'should treat duties as performed to a significant extent at any workplace if the employee spends 40% or more of his or her working time at that place'. In principle, therefore, a person who works a standard five day week will normally be caught by this rule if working – on average – for at least two days per week at a given site for at least two years.

If a person is sent on secondment for, say, 18 months then the place of secondment may be treated as a temporary workplace even if the person works there full time for that 18 month period. This will mean that all the travel costs to and from that place of secondment will in principle qualify for relief. Subsistence costs will also be allowed.

However, regular attendance at the same place (for example, every Friday at a particular office) will normally cause that place to be treated as a permanent workplace. HMRC give the example of a person who 'works five days each week but spends each day in a different shop in a different town. He works in the same shop on the same day each week.' Such a person would be denied relief for all travel costs as each shop will be treated as a permanent workplace.

A place attended for less than 24 months may still fail to qualify as a temporary workplace if the employee is on a relatively short-term appointment such that all or nearly all of the period of his employment is spent at the location in question. In *Reiter*, an individual was engaged as a locum consultant at a hospital with the engagement made through a recruitment agency. It was found as a fact that his employment was with the hospital rather than the agency and it followed that his attendance at the hospital was for a succession of periods that together comprised all of the period for which he held the employment. As such, the hospital was a permanent workplace and no relief was due for the taxpayer's travel or accommodation costs.

Legislation: ITEPA 2003, s. 339

Case: *Reiter* [2010] TC 00587

Other Material: HMRC *Employment Income Manual* EIM32080, EIM32141

Tax Reporter: ¶454-100

Workers providing services through intermediaries

Anti-avoidance provisions were introduced with effect from 6 April 2016 to ensure that individuals providing their services through an employment intermediary could not exploit the temporary workplace provisions. Where such an individual operates under the supervision, direction or control of another party (typically the end user) then, for the purposes of s. 338 and 339, any number of separate engagements provided through the intermediary would be treated as a single engagement.

Legislation: ITEPA 2003, s. 339A

Depots and bases

A place which the employee *regularly* attends in performing employment duties is treated as a permanent workplace if it is either:

(1) the base from which the employment duties are performed; or

(2) the place at which the tasks to be carried out in performing the employment duties.

This would catch, for example, a bus driver who travels from home to the bus depot each morning. Even though he spends little time at the depot itself, it is still treated as a permanent workplace.

In *Wilkinson*, a doctor was denied tax relief for travel expenses. The tribunal found, on the facts, that the hospital in Portsmouth where the doctor was working was a place which he regularly attended in the performance of the duties of his employment, and that the Portsmouth hospital was a place at which his tasks were allocated. It followed that the hospital was a permanent workplace for the doctor. (The doctor also failed in a claim under the work relocation expenses rule of ITEPA 2003, s. 271: see 141-700.)

Legislation: ITEPA 2003, s. 339(4)

Case: *Wilkinson* [2010] TC 00572

Tax Reporter: ¶455-060

140-950 Incidental overnight expenses

To reduce the burden on employers of identifying and reporting to HMRC what would otherwise be taxable expenses, certain minor personal expenditure, incurred on business trips involving overnight accommodation and reimbursed or borne by the taxpayer's employer, are not taxed. The exemption also applies where the employee is away from home on a training course.

The exemption applies only to amounts reimbursed by an employer. No relief is available for such costs incurred by employees but not reimbursed.

The payments must be made wholly and exclusively for the purpose of defraying, or enabling the employee to defray, expenses which are incidental to being away from the employee's, etc. usual place of abode during a 'qualifying absence from home' (see below), and which cannot otherwise be deducted. Official guidance notes give examples of newspapers, laundry and telephone calls home. Where an allowance is paid specifically to meet incidental expenses, it qualifies for the exemption whether or not the employee spends it on qualifying items; employees are not required to produce receipts to justify the tax exemption.

It is immaterial how the employer deals with the expense: thus non-cash vouchers, credit-tokens (e.g. a credit card in the employer's name), expenses payments and benefits in kind (e.g. where the employer arranges directly with a hotel to pay the bill) are all covered.

Legislation: ITEPA 2003, s. 240, 241, 268

Other Material: HMRC *Employment Income Manual* EIM02710; *National Insurance Manual* NIM06020, NIM06030

Tax Reporter: ¶432-900

Limit on relief

The exemption applies to amounts of personal expenditure up to £5 per night in the UK and £10 for each night overseas. If this limit is exceeded, the whole amount is taxable. Thus, in most cases, it is still necessary to analyse the receipts submitted with employees' expenses claims.

If the employee's incidental expenses are met in a variety of ways, they must be taken together in applying the maximum figure. The authorised maximum does *not* apply separately to expenses met by non-cash voucher, by credit token, by reimbursement, or directly by the employer. The limits include VAT.

If the absence is for more than one night then the costs must be aggregated and relief (or denial of relief) operates accordingly.

> **Example**
>
> An employee claims personal incidental expenses of £20 for a four-night stay away from home in the UK on the basis of £5, £5, £6 and £4 for the four nights involved. The exemption applies to all repayments because the total does not exceed £20 (four nights at £5 exemption per night).

Where, say, a number of employees' hotel bills are aggregated and paid directly by the employer and individual expenditure cannot readily be identified, a reasonable apportionment will be accepted.

Employers should guard against double payment of personal incidental expenses (for example, by paying the standard allowance for personal incidental expenses *and* reimbursing in full a hotel bill already including such charges: e.g. telephone calls home).

Qualifying absence from home

A 'qualifying absence from home' must be a *continuous* period throughout which the person is obliged to stay away from his usual place of abode (ITEPA 2003, s. 240). During that continuous period, there must be at least one overnight stay. The cost of travelling to the place of stay must be of a kind that is allowable, or would be allowable if incurred out of earnings.

141-000 Foreign travel

Travel to or from foreign employment

A deduction from earnings is given for the costs of travel at the start or end of an overseas employment, if three conditions are met:

(1) the duties of the employment are performed *wholly* outside the UK;

(2) the employee is 'resident' in the UK; and

(3) if the employer is a 'foreign employer', the employee is 'domiciled' in the UK.

The deductible expenses are, specifically, 'starting travel expenses' (defined as expenses incurred by the employee in travelling from a place in the UK to take up the employment) and 'finishing travel expenses' (defined as expenses incurred by the employee in travelling to a place in the UK on the termination of the employment). The employee may incur expenses partly in order to travel to or from the employment and partly for other purposes, such as a foreign holiday; in such a case, the deduction is only given for the part of the expenses which is properly attributable to the taking up or termination of the employment.

By contrast, no such apportionment is made if the duties of the employment are performed partly within and partly outside the UK: the duties must be performed wholly outside the UK if the deduction is to be obtained. However, if the employee performs duties of the employment in the UK, and these duties are merely incidental to the performance of duties outside the UK, then they are treated as performed outside the UK.

Legislation: ITEPA 2003, s. 341

Tax Reporter: ¶454-550

Travel between employments where duties performed abroad

A deduction from earnings is given for travel expenses incurred by the employee if all of the following six conditions are met:

(1) the travel is for the purpose of performing duties of the employment at the destination;

(2) the employee has performed duties of another employment at the place of departure;

(3) the place of departure or the destination or both are outside the UK;

(4) the duties of one or both of the employments are performed wholly or partly outside the UK;

(5) the employee is resident and ordinarily resident in the UK; and

(6) in a case where the employer is a foreign employer, the employee is domiciled in the UK.

If the travel has a dual purpose, the deduction is only allowed for the expenses properly attributable to the purpose of performing duties of the employment at the destination.

Legislation: ITEPA 2003, s. 342

Tax Reporter: ¶454-550

Board and lodging

Expenses incurred in providing board and lodging to enable an employee to perform the duties of his overseas employment are allowed as deductions from his earnings provided that the following requirements are met:

- the earnings are assessed under the charge on employment income provisions in the UK;
- the employer either meets the cost directly or reimburses the employee.

Where the board and lodging is provided partly for the performance of the duties of the employment and partly for another purpose, only the expenses attributable to the employment are allowable as a deduction.

> **Example**
>
> David is sent to Nice by his employers on business which takes one week to conclude. He decides to take a further fortnight's holiday in Nice. The hotel expenses of the three weeks are paid for by the company. Only the hotel expenses relating to the first week are allowable as a deduction.

Legislation: ITEPA 2003, s. 376(1)

141-025 Overseas accommodation and subsistence: scale rate payments

HMRC currently accept that employers may use the benchmark scale rates published by the Foreign and Commonwealth Office when paying accommodation and subsistence expenses to employees whose duties require them to travel abroad, without the need for the employees to produce expenses receipts. Links to the rates (as changed from time to time) may be found in *Hardman's Tax Rates and Tables* at 3-580.

Accommodation and subsistence payments at or below the published rates are treated as exempt from tax and NIC for employees who travel abroad either in the performance of their duties or to a temporary workplace. Such payments by employers, which can be on top of any payments for incidental overnight expenses, do not need to be returned on form P11D. Employees who are not reimbursed by their employers may not, however, use the scale rates when seeking a deduction: actual receipts will be required.

Other Material: *Employment Income Manual* EIM05250; www.gov.uk/government/uploads/system/uploads/attachment_data/file/359797/2014_Worldwide_subsistence_rates.pdf

Tax Reporter: ¶457-570

141-040 Subsistence costs associated with UK travel

From April 2016

From 6 April 2016, the regulations stipulating where an employer may make a tax free subsistence payment to an employee have been simplified. Provided the travel and subsistence rules at ITEPA 2003, s. 337 are met, then the employer may make the following tax free allowance payments dependent on the employee's period of absence from their normal place of work:

Minimum period	Maximum meal allowance
5 hours	£5
10 hours	£10
15 hours	£25

Where a meal allowance of £5 or £10 is paid and the qualifying journey last beyond 8 p.m., then a supplementary rate of £10 may be paid. The employee must incur some costs on a meal during the period.

Employers may pay a lesser rate if they wish, but if a higher rate is to be paid, then this must be agreed with HMRC who will require the employer to undertake a random sampling exercise to demonstrate that the proposed higher rate is justified.

Legislation: ITEPA 2003, s. 289B; *Income Tax (Approved Expenses) Regulations* 2015 (SI 2015/1948); ITEPA 2003, s. 289B

April 2009 to April 2016

In April 2009, HMRC issued formal guidance on the tax treatment of day subsistence expenses (Revenue & Customs Brief 24/09). The guidance is described at the start of the document as 'an advisory system of benchmark scale rates which employers can use to make subsistence payments to employees who incur allowable business travel expenses'. It has applied since 6 April 2009.

HMRC accept that business travel expenses include 'the cost of any necessary subsistence costs incurred in the course of the journey [and] the cost of meals necessarily purchased whilst an employee is at a temporary workplace' (EIM31815). In each case, it seems clear that the concept of 'necessary' is being given a much wider interpretation than its statutory meaning in the context of employee expenditure.

As long as employees are incurring subsistence costs, employers may reimburse them using the scale rates. The April 2009 guidance does not remove the need for employers to apply for a dispensation, but employers may now seek a dispensation on the basis that employees will be reimbursed using the benchmark rates.

Scale subsistence rates

The document published in April 2009 is helpful in two particular ways: it identifies the circumstances in which HMRC will accept that an employer may make a tax-free day subsistence payment to an employee, and it quantifies the amount of such payments that may be made in various circumstances. Four such circumstances are specified.

(1) First, a 'breakfast rate' may be paid to 'irregular early starters'. Specifically, 'a rate of up to £5.00 may be paid where a worker leaves home earlier than usual and before 6.00 a.m. and incurs a cost on breakfast taken away from his home'.

(2) Next comes a 'one meal rate' of £5, which may be paid where a worker 'has been away from his home/normal place of work for a period of at least five hours and has incurred a cost on a meal'.

(3) The one meal rate is doubled to £10 where the period of absence is at least ten hours and the worker has incurred a cost on 'one or more meals'. Although referred to as the 'two meal rate', it therefore appears that the employee is not in fact obliged to buy two meals.

(4) Finally, a 'late evening meal rate' of up to £15 may be paid to 'irregular late finishers'. This is available where 'the employee has to work later than usual, finishes work after 8.00 pm having worked his normal day and has to buy a meal which he would usually have at home'. Where the conditions are met, this allowance may be paid in addition to the one meal or two meal rate.

HMRC emphasise that 'the early starter and late finisher rates are for use in exceptional circumstances only and not intended for employees with regular early or late work patterns'. However, such employees may still be entitled to claim at the five or ten hour rates.

The new approach, introduced from April 2009, was therefore that the above scale rate figures may now be used by employers wishing to reimburse their employees for day subsistence costs; as long as the conditions are met, employers will be able to use these advisory rates without demonstrating to HMRC that they correlate to actual expenditure incurred by the employees of the given organisation.

Conditions

Three such conditions are listed when applying for a dispensation using these rates.

- The travel with which the subsistence is linked must meet the statutory rules for a tax deduction. This should present little practical difficulty as employers already need to determine which travel qualifies for tax relief.
- The employee must be absent from the normal place of work for a continuous period 'in excess of' five or ten hours (or 'at least' that long in other parts of the guidance). Employers can probably gain reasonable assurance in most circumstances that this condition is met, but there will certainly be cases where it will be difficult for an employer to prove the point to an HMRC officer.
- The third condition is that the employee must have incurred a cost on a meal after starting the journey. The word 'meal' is specifically (and repeatedly) defined in the guidance as 'food and drink' so the employee on a long drive who stops for a coffee will not qualify, it seems, unless he or she also orders something to eat (which is surely a pointless condition).

The last condition may well prove difficult for employers in practice. In simple terms, how is the employer to know? The obvious answer is for the employee to provide a receipt, but if the total cost is (say) £4 or £6, and if it is still necessary for the employee to obtain a receipt and pass it to the employer, then there seems little logic in encouraging the employer to reimburse a scale rate figure of £5. If a receipt is to be provided in all cases then the employer may as well apply for a dispensation to cover the actual cost rather than using a scale rate. If no receipt is required, then a difficult HMRC officer may well argue that the employer does not have 'adequate management processes in place to ensure that payments are only made where all the qualifying conditions are met'.

Day rates only

These rates apply only for day subsistence payments. Employers wishing to pay subsistence costs to employees staying away overnight can either reimburse actual costs incurred or agree a separate scale rate (covering meals and other expenses) in a dispensation.

Not obligatory

The use of the standard scale rates is not obligatory. Dispensations already in place at 6 April 2009 will in any case continue to be valid until they are next reviewed, typically over a five year cycle. Employers may still apply to use a rate tailored to their own circumstances, though HMRC officers are then likely to insist that employers carry out a 'statistically valid sampling exercise'.

Family and friends

Some employers have in the past agreed tax-free scale rates for payments to employees staying with family or friends. Any dispensations for such payments are to be withdrawn as and when they come up for review. HMRC have advised that 'all agreed tax and NICs free scale rates in existing dispensations covering such an allowance will be withdrawn when the dispensation comes up for review'.

Expenditure not reimbursed

It seems clear that this new non-statutory guidance is meant to apply only where employers reimburse employees, and only under the umbrella of a formal dispensation. It does not appear, therefore, to open the way for claims by employees who meet the travel conditions but who are not reimbursed by their employers.

141-050 Travel expenses of spouses

Business trips

Where a spouse accompanies an employee on a business trip, the expenses of the spouse's travel are only deductible if the normal statutory conditions are met – notably, that the expenses are necessarily incurred. HMRC guidance states that:

> 'Whether or not a deduction is due will depend on the facts. It is vital that these are established, preferably by a meeting with the couple, before a decision is reached.'

However, travelling expenses of a husband or wife accompanying his or her employee/director spouse on a business journey abroad, which are borne by the employer, are not charged to tax on the husband if his health is such that he cannot undertake the travel unaccompanied.

It is assumed that the expenses of a civil partner would now be viewed in the same way.

Legislation: ITEPA 2003, s. 336

Other Material: HMRC *Employment Income Manual* EIM31980ff.; ESC A4(d)

Tax Reporter: ¶454-600

141-100 Armed forces leave travel facilities

Travel vouchers, warrants, allowances and other payments in respect of travel facilities provided for members of the armed forces going on, or returning from, leave are exempt from tax. See 143-920 for further details of various tax exemptions applying to members of the armed forces.

Legislation: ITEPA 2003, s. 296

Tax Reporter: ¶485-300

141-150 Works transport services

No taxable benefit arises where an employer provides a works bus service for employees, provided that certain conditions are met. For these purposes, a 'works bus service' is 'a service provided by means of a bus or a minibus for conveying employees of one or more employers on qualifying journeys'.

For the vehicle to qualify as a 'bus', it must have a minimum seating capacity of 12; the seating capacity determined in accordance with *Vehicle Registration Act* 1994, Sch. 1, Pt. III, irrespective of whether the vehicle meets the definition of a 'bus' in that Act. A minibus has a seating capacity of 9–11 seats.

For the exemption to apply, the bus must be used for qualifying journeys. A 'qualifying journey' is a journey that an employee makes either between his home and his workplace or between one workplace and another in connection with the performance of the duties of the employment. For these purposes, a 'workplace' is a place at which the employee's attendance is necessary in the performance of his or her duties of employment. Further, the service must be generally available to the employees of the employer (or employers) concerned and the main use of the service must be for qualifying journeys. The exemption is also subject to 'substantial' compliance with the condition that it must be used only by employees for whom it is provided and their children (including stepchildren) under the age of 18.

Where an employee is given a voucher to use a works bus service meeting the conditions for exemption, no tax charge arises in respect of the provision of such a non-cash voucher.

Legislation: ITEPA 2003, s. 242, 249

Tax Reporter: ¶432-600

141-200 Subsidised bus services

No taxable benefit arises (as general earnings or under the benefits legislation) where an employer provides financial or other support for a public transport road service used by employees of one or more employers for qualifying journeys. The legislation defines a 'public transport road service' as 'a public passenger transport service provided by means of a road vehicle'. A 'qualifying journey' is defined as for the exemption for works buses, that is to say a journey that an employee makes between his home and workplace or between one workplace and another in connection with the performance of the duties of the employment. A 'workplace' is for these purposes defined as a place at which the employee's attendance is necessary in the performance of the duties.

For the exemption to apply, certain conditions must be satisfied. These are that:

- the terms on which the service is available to employees are not more favourable than those available to other passengers; and
- the service must be generally available to employees of the employer (or employers) concerned.

Legislation: ITEPA 2003, s. 243, 249

Tax Reporter: ¶432-650

141-250 Cycles and cyclists' safety equipment

No taxable benefit arises (as general earnings or under the benefits legislation) where an employee is provided with a cycle or cycling safety equipment, provided that there is no transfer of ownership to him of either the cycle or the safety equipment. For these purposes, a 'cycle' takes the meaning given to it by the *Road Traffic Act* 1988, s. 192(1), i.e. 'a bicycle, tricycle or a cycle having four or more wheels, not in any case being a motor vehicle', with 'cyclist' taking the corresponding meaning.

For the exemption to apply, the following conditions must be satisfied:

- the benefit or facility must be available generally to the employees of the employer concerned (see below); and
- the employee must use the cycle or safety equipment mainly for qualifying journeys.

For these purposes, the meaning of a 'qualifying journey' and of a 'workplace' matches that for the purposes of the exemptions for works buses (see 141-150) and subsidised bus services.

Where an employee is provided with a non-cash voucher providing entitlement to use a cycle or cycling safety equipment to which the exemption applies, no tax charge will arise in respect of the non-cash voucher.

Legislation: ITEPA 2003, s. 244, 266

Tax Reporter: ¶432-550

Available to all employees

A particular issue was identified by HMRC as a problem area towards the end of 2009. If employers offer cycle equipment under a salary sacrifice arrangement then it is possible that certain employees would be unable to participate. According to HMRC:

> '... this may happen because of other statutory considerations, such as ensuring that pay is not reduced below the level of the National Minimum Wage or because of legal barriers to under 18 year olds signing up to the type of agreement typically included in a cycle to work salary sacrifice arrangement.'

HMRC take a hard line on this matter. If even one employee is excluded from the salary sacrifice arrangement, and is thus unable to take up the offer of an employer-provided bicycle, that means that the exemption will fail for all employees. HMRC have provided guidelines on how employers may wish to resolve this situation.

Other Material: HMRC *Employment Income Manual* EIM21664

Tax Reporter: ¶432-550

Pooled cycles

HMRC provided still further guidance in relation to cycles and salary sacrifice schemes around the end of 2010, including the following:

> 'Although cycles must be offered to all employees, there is no requirement for them to be offered on exactly the same terms and conditions. This means that the availability condition can still be satisfied if employees who enter into salary sacrifice arrangements are offered the use of more expensive cycles than those offered to employees outside salary sacrifice arrangements. In addition, there is no requirement that all employees should have access to a cycle that is solely for their personal use. So a pool of cycles for loan to other employees can be taken into account. But if cycles are provided by way of a pool, they need to be provided in sufficient numbers to ensure that there is genuine availability for those employees who wish to make use of the pool of cycles, in other words the employees must be able to access the cycles with a reasonable degree of frequency. However, this does not mean that there needs to be one pooled cycle available for each employee who does not have ongoing use of a cycle.'

Other Material: HMRC *Employment Income Manual* EIM21664

Transfer to employee of used cycles

Special rules apply when assets that have been provided as a benefit in kind are subsequently transferred to employees (see 133-520). However, these rules are disapplied in the case of certain assets, including cycles that have met the conditions of s. 244 (as above). For such cycles, the taxable value is the market value at the date of transfer of ownership.

Establishing the market value can in practice be difficult in respect of certain assets but HMRC have issued guidance and accept that for a cycle that is at least a year old, the 'acceptable disposal value percentage' will not exceed 18% of cost for a cycle originally costing up to £500, or 25% for a cycle originally costing more than that. HMRC have provided a table with percentages that reduce as the cycle ages and HMRC accept that the bike may be treated as having a negligible value after five or six years respectively for cycles costing up to or over £500. A full table of acceptable percentages is given in *Hardman's Tax Rates and Tables* at 3-530. The tax charge will be based on such percentages, or the employee may pay the relevant percentage to the employer to avoid any tax charge. HMRC will ask for evidence if employers seek to use lower figures, normally including a photograph of the cycle, broad details of the extent of its usage and contemporaneous evidence of the amount it could have realised 'in a private sale and in a sale to a cycle retailer'.

Where a cycle is transferred to an employee at a point between the ages shown in the table, a common sense view should be adopted.

Equipment

HMRC have stated that, when calculating the original price of the cycle, it is necessary to include safety equipment fitted to the cycle (such as lights and bells) but to exclude safety equipment worn by the cyclist (such as helmets or reflective clothing).

VAT

HMRC have given the following advice in relation to VAT and the valuation of used cycles:

> 'It is acceptable to use the VAT exclusive amount in calculating the original price of the cycle. However, where the valuation percentage is applied to a VAT exclusive amount, VAT will need to be added to the result in order to arrive at the acceptable market value. This must be done regardless of whether or not the employer is VAT-registered. For example, if the original price net of VAT was £400, then whilst the VAT rate is 17.5%, the acceptable` market value at 2 years old will be £61. ((£400 × 13%) + (VAT at 17.5% × £52) = £52 + £9 = £61).'

The above is for the purposes of reaching a valuation only. It has no bearing on any actual VAT liability. The figures would now need adjustment to use a VAT figure of 20 rather than 17.5%.

Exclusions

The simplified scheme may not be used for cycles that have special value, e.g. because they are antique or collectable or have been ridden by a famous person.

Other Material: HMRC *Employment Income Manual* EIM21667a

Tax Reporter: ¶419-090

141-275 Miscellaneous travel-related exemptions

Introduction

Certain, specified, types of travelling expenses which do not meet the requirements of ITEPA 2003, s. 337–338 (see 140-500) are allowed by concession or statutory exemption. These are detailed below.

Employees travelling between group companies

A director or employee of two or more companies within a group is regarded as having one place at which he is normally employed. The expenses of travelling from that place to others on the business of the group are then treated as allowable expenses. The legislation also applies to employees of one group company who are directors of another company within the same group.

Legislation: ITEPA 2003, s. 340

Other Material: ESC A4(a)

Tax Reporter: ¶455-100

Unpaid directors of clubs, etc

A director who gives his services without pay to a company (such as a club) which is not managed with a view to dividends is not treated as assessable on any travelling expenses paid to him.

Other Material: ESC A4(b)

Directorships held as part of professional practices

Where a directorship is held as part of a professional practice, travelling expenses incurred by the director in carrying out his duties are allowed as a deduction from the profits of the professional practice. Reasonable expenses paid to such a director are accordingly not assessed under the charge on employment income provisions, provided no claim is made to a deduction in calculating business tax profits.

Other Material: ESC A4(c)

Disruption of public transport

No liability to income tax arises where certain travelling and subsistence allowances are paid when public transport is disrupted.

These are:

- provision of overnight accommodation at or near the employee's permanent workplace;
- expenses incurred by the employee in connection with such accommodation;
- provision of transport for the purpose of ordinary commuting or travel between any two places that is for practical purposes substantially ordinary commuting; and
- expenses payments made to the employee in respect of expenditure incurred on such transport.

Legislation: ITEPA 2003, s. 245

Late-night travel

An exemption is given if employers reimburse the cost of late-night travel where employees are required (on an irregular basis) to work after 9.00pm, provided that they are not required to do so on more than 60 days per year. If in these circumstances the employer provides private transport from work to home the cost will not be treated as an assessable benefit, if either:

- there is no public transport; or
- it would be unreasonable to expect the employee to use such public transport as is available.

Circumstances in which it might be considered unreasonable for the employee to be required to use public transport would include those where the journey would be very lengthy or where there was a possibility of danger to the person.

Legislation: ITEPA 2003, s. 248

Tax Reporter: ¶432-800

Severely disabled employees

An exemption is available for the provision of transport for disabled employees or for the reimbursement of any expenditure incurred by a disabled employee in connection with transport for ordinary commuting purposes.

Legislation: ITEPA 2003, s. 246–247

Travel expenses of employees and directors not domiciled in the UK

Travelling expenses to and from the UK of a person not domiciled in the UK, for the purpose of carrying out employment duties, are excluded from taxable earnings if either the individual concerned was not resident in the UK in the two previous tax years, or was not in the UK for any purpose within two years prior to arrival in the UK to carry out the duties. This applies also to a spouse or child accompanying the employee if the period of employment in the UK is for a continuous period of 60 days or more, but in the case of a spouse or child is limited to two return journeys in any tax year.

Legislation: ITEPA 2003, s. 373, 374

Tax Reporter: ¶455-600

Air miles, car fuel coupons, etc

It is understood that in practice HMRC do not charge to tax air miles derived from business travel but redeemed for personal use. No cost is incurred by the employer in the provision of the air miles since the air fare is the same regardless of whether air miles are given or not. The same view prevails as regards car fuel coupons given to employees purchasing fuel for business travel and to points given for the use of a company credit card.

Government ministers and others exempted

The holder of any office in Her Majesty's Government and certain other office-holders (e.g. Leader of the Opposition and the Speaker of the House) are not charged to tax under the charge on employment income provisions in respect of travel and subsistence provided or reimbursed to the office-holder or their family or household. See 143-910.

Legislation: ITEPA 2003, s. 295

EU travel expenses of MPs and other representatives

MPs and members of the Scottish Parliament or of the regional assemblies of Wales and Northern Ireland are exempt from income tax on certain European travel expenses. See 143-910.

Legislation: ITEPA 2003, s. 294

141-300 Provision of subsidised meals

On first principles, the provision by an employer of food and drink for an employee is a taxable benefit. The cost of providing the meals, including any labour costs incurred in preparing or serving them, should be apportioned between employees and declared as a taxable benefit accordingly. Alternatively, a PAYE settlement agreement (see 140-300) should be reached with HMRC. Dietary supplements are not tax deductible, even where the need for extra nutrition arises from the nature of the duties performed (*Ansell v Brown*, *Emms v R & C Commrs*).

There are, however, numerous exceptions to these strict rules. Tax relief may be available for any of the following, considered in more depth below:

- meals provided in a staff canteen;
- other meals provided to all staff;
- certain low-value meal vouchers;
- meals when away from the normal workplace;
- meals enjoyed by staff when entertaining actual or potential customers or clients;
- meals in connection with business meetings; and
- breakfasts for cyclists (see 142-150).

As regards the treatment of staff parties, see 143-050. For the treatment of subsistence costs related to business travel, see 141-040.

Cases: *Ansell v Brown* [2001] BTC 381; *Emms v R & C Commrs* (2008) Sp C 668

Tax Reporter: ¶437-600

Canteen meals

Subject to a complication where salary sacrifice arrangements are in place (see below), there is total exemption from tax where an employer provides free or subsidised meals or light refreshments and where both of the following conditions are met:

- meals are provided in a canteen; and
- are provided in that canteen for all of the employer's employees or for all of those working at a particular location.

The HMRC view is that the term canteen 'has its ordinary meaning' and that it does not include a 'restaurant, cafe, public house or similar establishment which serves meals to the public at large'. The canteen does not have to be on the employer's premises (though it can be) and does not have to be restricted to use only by the employees. HMRC give the example of a canteen, on an industrial estate, serving the employees of several employers.

Where the exemption is available to employees, it also applies to 'other persons who work on the premises of the employer in question ... notwithstanding that the conditions set out in section 317 ... may not be satisfied in respect of those persons'. This therefore ensures that visiting employees of other employers may enjoy the same benefits without tax consequences. An example might be an auditor staying on site for the period of the audit.

Legislation: ITEPA 2003, s. 317; *Income Tax (Exemption of Minor Benefits) Regulations* 2002 (SI 2002/205) (as amended)

Tax Reporter: ¶437-600

Other meals for all employees

There is a further exemption, with stricter conditions, where meals or light refreshments are provided for all employees but not in a staff canteen as such. The conditions are as follows (and see below for a further condition applying to staff working in hotels, etc.):

- the meals must be provided on the employer's premises;
- they must be provided 'on a reasonable scale', though the HMRC manuals indicate that this is not to be interpreted narrowly: a glass of wine with a meal is accepted but not 'the provision of an elaborate menu, fine wines and cigars'; and
- all of the employees working at that location must be entitled to either a free or a subsidised meal, or to a voucher or other document that entitles the person to obtain a meal that is either free or subsidised.

Once the conditions are met, all reasonable meals provided on the employer's premises will be exempt. HMRC illustrate this with an example involving working lunches: 'If all employees may get a free or subsidised meal on the employer's premises or in a canteen, or meal vouchers, then working lunches on a reasonable scale, provided on the employer's premises, will also be exempt even if not all of the employees get the working lunches.'

There is a further complication where the meals are provided 'in a restaurant or dining room of a hotel or a catering or similar business at a time when meals are being served to the public'. In this case, the exemption will only be available if the meal is taken in a part of the room that is designated for use by employees only.

Legislation: ITEPA 2003, s. 317

Other Material: HMRC *Employment Income Manual* EIM21671ff.

Tax Reporter: ¶437-600

Meals when away from normal workplace

When business travel involves an overnight stay, it is clear that an employer can meet the associated costs of subsistence without triggering a tax liability. Any dispensation related to the travel itself should be extended to cover the subsistence costs.

HMRC also accept (by way of very specific examples, rather than as a general statement of principle) that an employer may pay a reasonable day subsistence allowance free of tax in certain circumstances. This was previously more explicitly stated as applying where employees 'are working away from their normal place of employment, have to eat away from their normal eating places and are away during the whole of the meal break, and incur extra expense over their normal meal costs' (old *Employer Compliance Manual* at paragraph 13103).

Tax Reporter: ¶437-600

Business entertaining

The cost of business entertaining is not tax deductible. Where an employee is involved in entertaining for business purposes, however, the disallowance will normally fall on the employer. As such, the employer can reimburse the employee either under protection of a dispensation, or through the PAYE system. In the latter case, the employee can claim tax relief (see 143-200).

Tax Reporter: ¶437-600

Other business meetings

A common practice in certain types of business is to encourage staff to give up their lunch hours for training or similar sessions by providing sandwiches, etc. for those staff. Unless facilities are provided for all employees, then this produces a potential tax liability for the individuals enjoying the free lunch.

This is a genuinely difficult area in practice. Clearly, there can be no tax relief every time work colleagues go out for a drink or a meal together. Nevertheless, there are occasions on which the food is genuinely in second place to the work in hand. HMRC do accept that free or subsidised meals may occasionally qualify for relief as a business expense. The HMRC starting point is that any meal taken with colleagues 'is almost always likely to be predominantly related to social and personal considerations. The expense is unlikely to have been incurred wholly, exclusively and necessarily in the performance of the employee's duties. The discussion of matters related to the work of the individuals concerned in the course of entertainment does not make the cost of that entertainment admissible.' Nevertheless, HMRC go on to give the following examples of circumstances where no tax liability would arise:

- entertainment in the course of negotiating the renewal or alteration of a service contract; or
- entertainment on the occasion of a 'briefing visit' when local staff are detained beyond normal hours to fit in with the visit of a headquarters controller or 'director general'.

Extending that principle, therefore, there seems every reason to try to claim a deduction for lunches provided by employers where the business element clearly outweighs the social side. If staff are expected to attend a lunchtime meeting, and there is a genuine technical or other business-related training session in progress, then it may be difficult for HMRC to argue that the occasion has any social aspect at all.

Finally, there is a possible argument that sandwiches or other light refreshments provided with an informal training course could be exempt from tax under the work-related training rules (see 143-800). Relief under those rules is extended to include costs that are incidental to the training.

Other Material: HMRC *Employment Income Manual* EIM32620

Tax Reporter: ¶437-600

Removal expenses paid

141-600 Introduction

Eligible removal expenses and benefits are exempt up to a limit of £8,000 for each job-related move that an employee makes. Removal expenses or benefits reasonably incurred or provided in connection with an employee's change of residence will be exempt if the following conditions are satisfied:

- the change of residence must result from taking up employment, or from an alteration in the employee's duties or place of work;
- the change of residence must be made wholly or mainly to allow the employee to have his residence within a reasonable daily travelling distance of the place where he normally performs or is to perform his duties; and
- the employee's former residence must not be within a reasonable daily travelling distance of the place where the employee performs his duties.

Legislation: ITEPA 2003, s. 273

Tax Reporter: ¶433-900ff.

141-700 Eligible expenses and benefits

The following qualifying categories of eligible removal expenses and benefits are defined in some detail:

- expenses and benefits in respect of disposal of the employee's former residence, including legal and estate agents or auctioneer's fees; advertising; penalties for loan redemption; public utility disconnection charges; cost of maintenance, insurance, security and rent while the residence is unoccupied during disposal (ITEPA 2003, s. 279 (disposal benefits and expenses));
- expenses and benefits in respect of the acquisition by the employee of an interest in his new residence, including legal expenses of acquisition or for obtaining a loan to acquire the residence; procurement fees for such a loan; the costs of mortgage protection insurance; survey and inspection fees; registry fees and stamp duties; connection charges to public utilities (ITEPA 2003, s. 277 (acquisition benefits and expenses));
- expenses and benefits in respect of abortive acquisition, being expenses incurred on acquiring a qualifying new residence which was not acquired either due to circumstances beyond the employee's control or because he reasonably decides not to proceed (ITEPA 2003, s. 278 (abortive acquisition benefits and expenses));
- expenses of and benefits in respect of transporting 'domestic belongings' of the employee and members of his family or household from the former to the new residence including insurance cover; packing and unpacking; temporary storage; detaching, attaching and adapting of domestic fittings (ITEPA 2003, s. 280 (transporting belongings));
- travelling and subsistence expenses and benefits including, broadly, the costs of the employee and his family making temporary visits

to the new area; travel between the former residence and the new place of work; travel between the former residence and temporary accommodation; travel by the employee and his family from their former residence to their new residence; subsistence of a child under 19 years in the tax year (a 'relevant child') in living accommodation in either the old area or the new area in order to secure continuity of education; travel by a relevant child from its accommodation to either the employee's former or new residence, as appropriate (ITEPA 2003, s. 281 (travelling and subsistence));

- bridging loan expenses, consisting only of interest on a loan raised by the employee to cover the period between the time when acquisition expenditure is incurred in respect of the new residence and when the disposal proceeds are available from the employee's former residence; if the amount of the loan exceeds the value of the former residence, interest on the excess will not be an eligible expense; similarly, interest on any part of the loan which is not applied in either acquiring the new residence or redeeming a loan on the former residence will not be an eligible expense (ITEPA 2003, s. 284 (bridging loan expenses));
- duplicate expenses and benefits in respect of the cost of purchasing domestic goods intended to replace items used in the employee's former residence but which are unsuitable for use in the new residence (ITEPA 2003, s. 285 (replacement of domestic goods)).

The Treasury has the power to make regulations so as to add to the list of eligible expenses and benefits, including any necessary supplementary, incidental or consequential provisions. Such regulations would affect employees whose new residence results from a job-change occurring after a day specified under the regulations (limit on exemption)).

Legislation: ITEPA 2003, s. 272, 286

In *Wilkinson*, a doctor was denied tax relief for travel expenses under these rules (and under the ordinary rules for travel expenses). In order for benefits to qualify as removal benefits or expenses, they had to fall within one of a list of specified provisions. The only provision that was potentially applicable was s. 281. For this to apply, the benefit had to be for travel between the employee's 'former residence' (defined as 'the employee's residence before the change') and the place where the employee's new duties were normally performed. On the facts, this condition was not met.

Case: *Wilkinson* [2010] TC 00572

Tax Reporter: ¶434-100

141-720 Cars provided for relocation purposes

An employer may provide a company car (or van) for the sole purpose of helping an employee with a house removal. It is possible that the benefit of the private use of that vehicle may fall within the removals exemption described at 141-700.

To come within the exemption, the vehicle must be provided only for the purposes of one of the following:

- eligible travel for the employee;
- eligible travel for members of his family or household; or
- continuity of education for a relevant child.

The rules are strictly interpreted and any use of the vehicle for other purposes will mean that the removals exemption is ignored in calculating the taxable benefit of the car. There can be no partial exemption under this rule.

Legislation: ITEPA 2003, s. 271, 283

141-750 The qualifying limit

The aggregate amount of qualifying expenses and qualifying benefits (see 141-700) (as ascertained by the rules for the cash equivalent of benefits) are compared with the qualifying limit of £8,000. Any excess amount over the qualifying limit will constitute a taxable benefit.

Legislation: ITEPA 2003, s. 287

Tax Reporter: ¶433-900ff.

Compensation payments

142-000 Introduction

The term 'compensation' payments may be used as a generic term to encompass redundancy payments, 'golden handshakes', payments in lieu of notice, and a range of other similar payments. Depending on the nature of the payment, it may be tax-free or may fall to be taxed under ITEPA 2003, s. 62 (as earnings) or s. 403 (as a payment treated as employment income). Restrictive covenants are taxed under their own legislation (s. 225) as are non-approved retirement benefits scheme payments (s. 394). Section 309 deals with statutory redundancy payments.

The goal for employers is normally to make a payment that is tax-deductible for the employer, that is tax-free (in whole or in part – typically up to £30,000) for the employee and that leaves the employer in a position where he is not vulnerable to any employment law challenge for wrongful dismissal or otherwise.

The legislation dealing with the taxation of compensation payments as such is found in ITEPA 2003, Pt. 6, Ch. 3 headed 'Payments and Benefits on Termination of Employment, etc.'. Section 401(1) states that the Chapter applies to:

> 'payments and other benefits which are received directly or indirectly in consideration or in consequence of, or otherwise in connection with:
>
> (a) the termination of a person's employment;
>
> (b) a change in the duties of a person's employment, or
>
> (c) a change in the earnings from a person's employment,
>
> by the person, or the person's spouse, blood relative, dependant or personal representatives.'

Where tax arises under that Chapter, it is treated as employment income only 'if and to the extent that it exceeds the £30,000 threshold'. However, s. 401(3) then states that the Chapter: 'does not apply to any payment or other benefit chargeable to income tax apart from this Chapter'.

To obtain the benefit of the £30,000 exemption, it is therefore necessary to show that the payment is not caught elsewhere. In particular, the exemption will be denied if the payment could be taxed as general earnings or as an 'amount treated as earnings'. For example, if HMRC can show that a payment is taxable as salary, as 'money's worth' or as a benefit in kind then the £30,000 exemption will not be available. The general test applies of whether the payment is made to the individual in return for acting as or being an employee. These tests have been brought out in many cases, including that of *Redundant employee v McNally*, a case which also brought out the dangers of badly worded employer documents. In *Allum & Anor v Marsh*, payments of £30,000 to two retired directors were held to be taxable in full. They were voluntary payments made in recognition of services rendered. In *Wood*, by contrast, the tribunal held that the payment made to a taxpayer by his former employer, under the terms of a compromise agreement, did not constitute earnings within s. 62, even though the payment had been made net of basic rate tax and NIC: the employee undertook no duties in return for that payment and did not receive it for acting as an employee.

Cases: *Redundant employee v McNally* (2004) Sp C 440; *Allum v Marsh* (2004) Sp C 446; *Wood* [2010] TC 00577

Tax Reporter: ¶422-000

In connection with

The question of whether the payment was made 'in connection with' the termination of the employment was considered in some detail in the case of *Crompton v R & C Commrs*. The facts of the case, concerning an army employee who was eventually made redundant, were complex. It was found, however, that the payment of compensation was made because the individual had not been selected for posts for which he had applied, and this had a detrimental effect on his earning power. Although his employment was terminated, there was no connection between the payment of the compensation and the termination of the employment; the payment was for his unfair treatment during the selection process for various particular roles, but that unfair treatment did not lead to the termination of his employment. The fact that the individual left the army may have triggered his decision to make a claim, but it had nothing to do with the merits of the claim. As such, the special commissioner held that he should not be taxed on the substantial compensation payment.

A lump sum payment received by a taxpayer in connection with a change to his contractual rights to redundancy pay was initially held not to be a payment in respect of the termination of his employment (*Colquhoun*). This view was reversed, however, by the Upper Tribunal decision released in December 2010 (*Colquhoun v R & C Commrs*). Allowing HMRC's appeal, the tribunal found that the statutory language had deliberately been widely drawn. It was not necessary to read the phrase 'the termination' as meaning a termination which must have occurred at or about the time the payment in question was made. An individual's employment would always terminate eventually either by dismissal, death or retirement (on account of age or some other reason). A payment connected with the termination of employment was treated as income received on the date of the termination in respect of which the payment was made. Thus, the possibility was envisaged that payment and actual termination might not occur contemporaneously. If that was so, then payment and termination need not be within the same tax years. There was nothing in the legislation which limited the period between payment and actual termination. The payment took its character from a redundancy payment which might have been payable, and such a payment fell within the scope of the charge to tax. The earlier tribunal had erred by considering that termination meant an actual termination, and consequently that there had to be contemporaneity between the payment and the termination.

Cases: *Crompton v R & C Commrs* [2009] TC 00012; *Mairs v Haughey* [2011] BTC 1,511

Tax Reporter: ¶422-200

142-050 Redundancy payments

The term 'redundancy' is often used loosely. For tax purposes it is necessary to be clear whether the reason for an employee leaving his employment can genuinely be classed as redundancy. In reality, it may be that the employee has left for some other reason – typically because he has been dismissed (with or without the notice period to which he is entitled) for incompetence, dishonesty, etc., or because he has retired or has resigned.

Tax law provides no definition of 'redundancy' but instead picks up the definition in the *Employment Rights Act* 1996, s. 139 of which contains the following:

> 'an employee who is dismissed shall be taken to be dismissed by reason of redundancy if the dismissal is wholly or mainly attributable to–
>
> (a) the fact that his employer has ceased or intends to cease–
>
> (i) to carry on the business for the purposes of which the employee was employed by him, or
>
> (ii) to carry on that business in the place where the employee was so employed, or
>
> (b) the fact that the requirements of that business–
>
> (i) for employees to carry out work of a particular kind, or
>
> (ii) for employees to carry out work of a particular kind in the place where the employee was employed by the employer,'
>
> have ceased or diminished or are expected to cease or diminish.'

In view of the relatively favourable tax treatment of redundancy payments, HMRC may well scrutinise any claim that such a payment has been made. As such, HMRC will wish to be clear that a payment made to a departing employee is not (for example) one of the following:

- a long service award;
- a contractual payment that is merely triggered by the fact that the employee is leaving;
- a restrictive covenant payment;
- a payment in lieu of notice;
- a payment of 'garden leave';
- a non-approved pension payment; or
- a payment to acquire shares from a departing director or employee.

The HMRC manuals summarise the position as follows:

> 'The statutory definition of redundancy ... means that redundancy involves a reduction in need for employees in the business. A dismissal is by reason of redundancy only when it is caused by such a reduced need.'

A genuine redundancy payment is one of the few payments from employer to employee that can escape tax despite being contractual. The legislation goes through a complex route but the end result is that statutory redundancy payments are tax-free up to £30,000 assuming that that exemption has not already been used to cover other payments. The amount of a statutory redundancy payment is determined under *Employment Rights Act* 1996, s. 162.

Other Material: HMRC *Employment Income Manual* EIM13802

Tax Reporter: ¶422-300

Non-statutory redundancy payments

In practice, non-statutory payments that are genuinely on account of redundancy can also be exempt (though still subject to the overall cap of £30,000 for all termination payments).

Other Material: HMRC *Employment Income Manual* EIM13775

Case: *Mairs v Haughey* [1993] BTC 339

Tax Reporter: ¶422-350

Pitfalls

Even where it is established that there is a genuine redundancy, it will still be a question of fact whether a payment is actually a redundancy payment for tax purposes. HMRC will be looking out for circumstances where the employee has a general right (whether under contract or otherwise) for a payment on termination of the employment for whatever reason, i.e. some sort of 'terminal bonus'. If the redundancy merely triggers this right then the payment will be taxable in full as ordinary earnings. This is to be contrasted with the case where an employee would not normally receive a termination payment but does receive such a payment precisely because he was made redundant (as opposed, for example, to reaching normal retirement age or to leaving voluntarily).

In practice, it is quite common for a payment to include both a genuine redundancy element and, for example, a payment in lieu of notice. It is well established case law that in such circumstances an apportionment must be made. For example:

> 'where a lump sum payment is made in respect of two different matters, one of which would lead to an assessment for tax and the other would not, the Commissioners have to apportion the sum.'

Other Material: HMRC *Employment Income Manual* EIM12856, EIM13765

Case: *Carter v Wadman* (1946) 28 TC 41

Tax Reporter: ¶422-400

Clearance applications

HMRC operate a formal clearance procedure for checking whether a redundancy payment will qualify for the £30,000 exemption. Statement of Practice 1/94 states that:

> 'An employer or any other person operating a redundancy scheme, who wishes to be satisfied that lump sum payments under a scheme will be accepted as liable to tax only under Section 148 ICTA 1988 [ITEPA 2003, s. 401] should submit the full facts to the Inspector for consideration. Applications for clearance should be made in writing and should be accompanied by the scheme document together with the text of any intended letter to employees which explains its terms.'

The clearance will be binding on HMRC as long as the employer has made a full disclosure of all relevant facts.

Other Material: HMRC *Employment Income Manual* EIM13790

Tax Reporter: ¶422-450

142-100 Payments in lieu of notice and post-employment notice pay

The concept of a payment in lieu of notice (PILON) arises where an individual is instructed to leave an employment and the decision is taken that he or she should not work out a notice period. In such circumstances, a payment may be made instead of the salary that the individual would have drawn over that period. Care should be taken to ensure that the payment is not actually of garden leave (see below).

Prior to 5 April 2018, the question of whether a PILON was subject to PAYE or benefited from the tax reliefs of a termination payment was largely dependent upon whether the payment was contractual or non-contractual. F(No. 2)A 2017, s. 5 set aside any such distinction and introduced the concept of 'post-employment notice pay' (PENP).

Where the PENP is greater than or equal to the termination payment, then the whole sum is subject to PAYE. If the PENP is less than the termination payment, then the PENP element will be taxed as general earnings but the excess will potentially benefit from the termination payment reliefs.

PENP is calculated by applying the formula outlined in ITEPA 2003, s. 402D. In effect, this is achieved by multiplying the individual's basic pay by a fraction equal to the number of days' notice the employee is entitled to over the 365.

Basic pay is defined as all pay but excluding overtime, bonuses, benefits in kind and commissions.

The PENP is defined as the period between the actual date of termination and the date on which the employee would have ceased had they completed their notice period.

Example

Philip earns a basic salary of £90,000 and his contract included a notice period of three months. He is given notice of the termination of his employment on 1 July 2018 but is asked to work only one month of his termination period. On 1 August 2018, he receives a total termination payment of £60,000 made up of compensation for loss of office of £40,000 and a non-contractual PILON of £20,000.

Total termination payment	£60,000

The PENP taxed as general earning is:

£90,000 × 2/12 =	£15,000
Balance potentially subject to relief	£45,000

The numerator in the PENP calculation is made up of three months less the one month actually worked.

Legislation: ITEPA 2003, s. 402A

Tax Reporter: ¶423-000

National Insurance

Regardless of the quantum prior to 5 April 2018, payments in relation to an employee's termination that were not taxed as general earning would be completely exempt from employer's and employee's NIC. The exemption from employer's contributions is removed for payments made after 5 April 2018. Relief will only apply to the extent the payment falls within the statutory £30,000 exemption.

Tax Reporter: ¶423-000

142-150 Restrictive covenants

A payment that is not taxable to income as general earnings will be caught under special legislation if:

- a restrictive undertaking is given in connection with a current, future or past employment;
- that undertaking restricts the individual's conduct or activities;
- payment is made (whether to the employee or to somebody else) in respect of the giving of the undertaking or its partial or total fulfilment; and
- one of the following conditions is met:
  (a) s. 15 (earnings for year when employee UK resident) applies to any general earnings from the employment and would apply even if the individual made a remittance basis claim for the year under ITA 2007, s. 809B; or
  (b) s. 27 (UK-based earnings of employee not resident in UK) applies to any general earnings from the employment.

The legislation applies whether the undertaking is absolute or qualified and whether or not it is legally binding. The effect of the rules is that the payment is treated as earnings from the employment for the tax year in which the payment is made. A restrictive covenant is still caught if paid after the employment has ceased. A payment made after the death of the individual giving the undertaking is treated as having been made immediately before the death.

The legislation is extended to cover valuable consideration other than cash that is given for such restrictive undertakings. Assuming an obligation to make over or provide valuable property, rights or advantages is not treated for these purposes as the giving of valuable consideration. However, it will be so treated as soon as that obligation is in fact discharged, whether wholly or in part.

Legislation: ITEPA 2003, s. 225

Case: *RCI (Europe) Ltd v Woods (HMIT)* [2004] BTC 285

Tax Reporter: ¶423-500

142-200 Employer-financed retirement benefits schemes

Introduction

A payment may be taxable under an employer-financed retirement benefits scheme (formerly, as an non-approved pension payment) even if it is labelled as (for example) being on account of redundancy; the tax treatment will depend on a correct interpretation of the underlying facts. The definition of such a scheme encompasses 'benefits consisting of or including relevant benefits'. As such, the benefits provided will potentially be taxable under these rules if they come within the definition of 'relevant benefits' given in ITEPA 2003, s. 393B. This concept is widely defined to include 'any lump sum, gratuity or other benefit' made:

'(a) on or in anticipation of the retirement of an employee or former employee,
(b) on the death of an employee or former employee
(c) after the retirement or death of an employee or former employee in connection with past service,
(d) on or in anticipation of, or in connection with, any change in the nature of service of an employee, or
(e) to any person by virtue of a pension sharing order or provision relating to an employee or former employee.'

One important difference in the rules applying now compared with those applying before 6 April 2006 is that the current definition specifically includes a non-cash benefit (such as a car).

There are also various 'excluded benefits' that are outside the scope of the rules:

'(a) benefits in respect of ill-health or disablement of an employee during service,
(b) benefits in respect of the death by accident of an employee during service,
(c) benefits under a relevant life policy, and
(d) benefits of any description prescribed by regulations made by the Board of Inland Revenue.'

HMRC gave their interpretation of how this legislation should be applied in a statement of practice. Where a payment is not in fact a genuine redundancy payment, the EFRBS treatment will take priority over any possible treatment as a compensation payment. As a result, no £30,000 exemption will be available. On the other hand, a genuine redundancy or dismissal payment does not become taxable under the pension rules merely because the employee becomes entitled at the same time to immediate pension benefits from the employer's scheme.

The effect of this is that the classic 'golden handshake' made on retirement in recognition of services rendered will often be taxable in full without the benefit of the £30,000 exemption. The employer will be bound to apply PAYE and NIC as if it were ordinary remuneration. There can be difficulties in defining the term 'retirement', especially where the word is used, perhaps as a euphemism, in connection with the premature termination of an employment. An 'early retirement' may not be a retirement at all but may, in fact, be a genuine redundancy or a dismissal on the grounds that the individual is not performing adequately. In either of these cases, the £30,000 will potentially be available. If the individual goes on to further paid employment (or self-employment) then this provides a reasonable starting point for an argument that he has not retired. In *Thomas*, it was held that a payment to the taxpayer was a relevant benefit as there was no evidence of it being in relation to the termination of employment.

The question of whether a payment was made 'in connection with past service' was considered in the case of *R & C Commrs v Barclays Bank plc*, concerning payments made to pensioners to compensate them for the withdrawal of a concessionary benefit previously made available to them (the provision of a free tax advice service). It was held that such payments were given 'in connection with past service' within the meaning of the legislation, in the same way as the concessionary benefit had been. For a payment to be given in connection with past service it was not necessary that it should be effectively a deferred reward for past service. Where, as here, the free tax service was provided to retired employees and their spouses, because they had been employees or were married to retired employees, it was clear that the service was provided in connection with past service. Likewise, where a lump sum was paid in substitution for the free tax service and by way of compensation for its termination, it was paid in connection with the past service to which the free tax service was connected.

The decision was upheld in the Court of Appeal. The class of recipients was limited to those who had been employees or who had connections through an employee by being the surviving spouse or personal representatives. No one else could come within the class. The criterion for selection of the recipients was a strong factor to which substantial weight should be given.

Cases: *R & C Commrs v Barclays Bank plc* [2007] BTC 338; *Thomas* [2013] TC 02463

Other Material: HMRC *Employment Income Manual* EIM15024

Tax Reporter: ¶423-900

142-250 Compensation for loss of office

A payment for dismissal ('loss of office') can be distinguished from any of the preceding categories. In practice, there is often confusion between redundancy and dismissal (though both can enjoy favourable tax treatment). An employer may dismiss an employee for a number of reasons but in many circumstances it will be necessary for the employer to make a payment to the employee as compensation for breach of the employment contract.

As the tax treatment of a genuine compensation payment is generally favourable, HMRC will usually seek to probe the true nature of the payment. Nevertheless, a genuine payment for breach of an employee's rights, where the payment does not come within any of the other categories discussed earlier in this chapter, will normally be taxable only with the benefit of the £30,000 exemption. Compensation for unfair or wrongful dismissal paid under the *Employment Rights Act* 1996 will come within this category. In *Moorthy*, the taxpayer was unsuccessful in his claim that a payment made to settle a discrimination claim was not taxable. The First-tier Tribunal ruled that it fell within ITEPA 2003, s. 401 and only up to the first £30,000 was exempt.

In *Walker v Adams (HMIT)*, HMRC withdrew its claim to tax on the part of a compensation award that was in respect of injury to feelings. Similarly, in *A v R & C Commrs* , a small part of an overall settlement (albeit very much less than was claimed) was allocated to injury to feelings and escaped taxation.

Legislation: ITEPA 2003, s. 403

Cases: *Walker v Adams (HMIT)* (2003) Sp C 344; *A v R & C Commrs* (2009) Sp C 734; *Moorthy* [2014] TC 03952

Tax Reporter: ¶424-020

142-300 Garden leave

Sometimes an employee will continue to be employed until the end of the notice period on full pay but will not in fact be required to perform any services and so can stay at home or use the time to seek other employment. The term 'garden leave' (or 'gardening leave') is applied to such an arrangement.

Payments for such a period are taxable as normal earnings; the employee continues to be employed and to receive a salary. The £30,000 exemption will not be available. (Similarly, a payment for garden leave will normally be earnings for National Insurance purposes, and liable to Class 1 NIC in the same way as any salary payment.)

142-550 The £30,000 exemption

Once it has been established that a liability arises under the rules relating to termination payments, the amount of the payment or benefit counts as employment income 'if and to the extent that it exceeds the £30,000 threshold'.

A number of rules apply in practice to determine how the £30,000 threshold is used, as follows:

- set the £30,000 against any cash benefits as they are received;
- if there is any balance of the £30,000 not used then, at the end of the tax year, set it against the total of any non-cash benefits received in that year; and
- where appropriate, set the £30,000 against payments and benefits received in earlier years before those of later years.

A non-cash benefit is received when it is used or enjoyed. A cash benefit is received when any of the following takes place:

- when it is paid;
- when a payment is made on account of it; or
- when the recipient becomes entitled to require payment of, or on account of, it.

Legislation: ITEPA 2003, s. 403ff.

Tax Reporter: ¶424-450

142-600 Foreign service

The legislation recognises the possibility that an individual will receive a compensation payment that relates partly or wholly to a period of working abroad. The salary, etc. for such a period may have been outside the scope of UK tax and an injustice may therefore be created if the compensation payment is taxed in full.

As such, the compensation payment will in some circumstances be wholly exempt from tax and will in other cases be subject to a reduced tax charge, subject in each case to the making of a valid claim. In determining any reduction of the tax charge, account will be taken of service up to the date of termination or change that is triggering the payment. The reduction must be claimed within five years from 31 January following the tax year in question.

No tax will be charged at all under s. 403 if any of the following three conditions applies:

- if at least 75% of the whole period of service ending on the date of termination or change was foreign service;
- if there was a period of foreign service covering the whole of the last ten years to that date; or
- if the period of service ending on that date is more than 20 years, and at least half of that period was foreign service, including at least half of the last 20 years.

Where there is not a total exemption, there may nevertheless be a reduction to recognise the period of foreign service. Any such reduction will be applied *after* application of the £30,000 threshold. In this case, the proportion to which the reduction applies will be determined by the fraction:

$$\frac{\text{length of foreign service}}{\text{total length of service in the employment to the change date}}$$

Example

Alex has worked for his employer for eight years. His time spent abroad is such that exactly five years count as foreign service. He receives a compensation payment of £70,000. The tax position will be as follows:

	£
Payment	70,000
Exemption (s. 403)	(30,000)
	40,000
Exemption (s. 414) – 5 years out of 8	(25,000)
Taxable	15,000

Where this limited reduction applies then there may be a restriction if the individual has income tax which he is entitled to charge against somebody else or which he can deduct, retain or satisfy out of any payment that he is liable to make.

Legislation: ITEPA 2003, s. 413ff.

Tax Reporter: ¶424-500

142-650 Counselling services for employees

Employees are not taxed on the cost of certain counselling services provided by the employer in connection with a termination of any office or employment.

The following types of expenses may be met by the employer without triggering a charge for the employee:

(1) providing services to a person in connection with the cessation of that person's employment;

(2) paying or reimbursing fees for the provision to the employee of such services; or

(3) paying or reimbursing any allowable travelling expenses incurred in connection with the provision of those services.

The provider, etc. need not be the employer.

The only or main purpose must be to enable the employee to adjust to the cessation of his employment, or to enable him to find other gainful employment or self-employment. The services must consist wholly of giving advice and guidance, of imparting or improving skills, or of providing or making available the use of office equipment or similar facilities.

A further condition is that the employee must have been employed by the employer throughout the period of two years ending with the date on which the employment comes to an end or, if earlier, the date on which the services are first provided. An earlier requirement that the employee needed to have been employed full-time was removed with effect from 6 April 2005.

The opportunity to receive the services on similar terms as to payment or reimbursement of any expenses must be made available either generally to employees or past employees, or to a particular class of such persons.

Legislation: ITEPA 2003, s. 310

Tax Reporter: ¶437-050

142-660 Legal costs

There are rules to ensure that a tax charge is avoided where the employer meets certain legal costs in connection with the termination of an employee's employment. No charge is made under ITEPA 2003, s. 403 if certain conditions are satisfied, as follows:

(1) First, the payment is to meet the whole or part of legal costs ('fees payable for the services and disbursements of a lawyer') incurred by the employee exclusively in connection with the termination of the employee's employment.

(2) Second, either:

(a) the payment is made pursuant to an order of a court or tribunal; or

(b) the termination of the employee's employment results in a compromise agreement, providing for the payment to be made by the employer, between the employer and the employee, in which case the payment must be made directly to the employee's lawyer.

Legislation: ITEPA 2003, s. 413A

Tax Reporter: ¶424-090

Employment losses

142-680 Losses in employment

Tax relief for losses suffered in an employment is rare but an employee could sustain a 'loss' in his employment where, for example, his pay substantially consists of commissions, of which a long incapacitation deprives him, yet he continues to incur allowable deductions. Relief may therefore be given, albeit rarely, for a loss from an employment.

A person who sustains a loss in any employment or office may, by notice in writing given by the second 31 January following the tax year, make a claim for relief from income tax on an amount of his income equal to the amount of the loss.

The loss may be set either against income for the tax year of the loss or against income for the preceding tax year. Relief cannot be claimed for the loss (or the same part of the loss) in both tax years. If a person makes a claim for losses of two successive years to be set against the income of one year, relief is given for a current year loss in priority to a loss carried back from the following year.

If such a claim is made, but part of the loss has not been relieved, the balance may be offset against capital gains.

No relief for employment losses may be made 'if and to the extent that [the loss] is made as a result of anything done in pursuance of arrangements the main purpose, or one of the main purposes, of which is the avoidance of tax'.

Legislation: ITEPA 2003, s. 11(3); ITA 2007, s. 128ff.

Tax Reporter: ¶458-500

Other expenses and exemptions

143-000 Accommodation, supplies or services used in the performance of the duties

Subject to conditions, no taxable benefit arises where an employee is provided with accommodation, supplies or services used by an employee in performing the duties of his employment. The detail of the exemption varies according to whether the accommodation, services or supplies are provided on premises occupied by the employer or other person providing the benefit.

The exemption ensures that in most cases no tax charge will arise from the provision by the employer of ordinary office furniture, stationery and similar supplies. Now that the specific exemption for the provision of computer equipment is being withdrawn (see 143-150), this more general exemption may in practice be needed to ensure that no tax charge arises from occasional private use of computers. Certain assets are excluded from relief under these provisions — see below.

Tax Reporter: ¶437-500

Benefit provided on employer premises

Where the provision is on such premises then it will be exempt as long as any private use by the employee, or members of his family or household, is not significant. In this context, use for 'private purposes' means any use that is not use in performing the duties of the employee's employment. Where, concurrently, the use is both for private purposes and for the purposes of performing the employee's duties of employment, such use is for these purposes regarded as private use. See below for a discussion of what constitutes 'significant' private use.

Legislation: ITEPA 2003, s. 316

Benefit provided elsewhere

A stricter rule applies where the benefit (whether accommodation, services or supplies) is provided other than on premises occupied by the employer or other person providing the benefit. In this case, the exemption will only apply if the following three conditions are satisfied:

(1) the sole purpose of providing the benefit is to enable the employee to perform the duties of his employment;

(2) any private use of the benefit is not significant; and

(3) the benefit is not an excluded benefit.

Use for 'private purposes' is as defined above; concurrent private and work use being treated as private use. See below for a discussion of what constitutes 'significant' private use.

Legislation: ITEPA 2003, s. 316

Meaning of 'significant'

No indication is given in the legislation as to what constitutes 'significant' private use. HMRC policy is to accept that the use is insignificant where all the following conditions are met:

- the employer's policy about private use is clearly stated to the employees and sets out the circumstances in which occasional private use may be made;
- any decision of the employer not to recover the costs of private use is a commercial decision because the administrative costs of doing so would exceed the amounts involved, rather than a desire to reward the employee; and
- there are reasonable checks to ensure that the employer's policy is followed in practice.

These are not a statutory test. If, for example, there are no reasonable checks but it is clear that, as a question of fact, the private use is insignificant then the exemption will still be due.

Other Material: HMRC *Employment Income Manual* EIM21611

Excluded assets

The exemption does not apply to private use of certain high-value assets, referred as 'excluded benefits'. The Treasury is given the power to make regulations to specify what is an excluded benefit for these purposes. Any such regulations may prescribe conditions as to the terms on which, and persons to whom, the benefit is provided if it is to be an 'excluded benefit'.

Subject to any such regulations, the following are 'excluded benefits':

- motor vehicles;
- boats;
- aircraft; and
- a benefit involving the extension, conversion or alteration of any living accommodation, or of a building or other structure on land adjacent to and enjoyed with such accommodation.

These are all excluded benefits irrespective of the terms on which they are provided and the person to whom they are provided.

Where an asset in an excluded asset, normal rules apply to tax the benefit arising from private use.

Example 1

Julia is employed as a landscape gardener. She is provided with a lawnmower for use in the performance of her duties. On one occasion during the tax year, she uses the lawnmower for private purposes, when her own personal lawnmower breaks down. As the lawnmower is provided to enable her to perform the duties of her employment, it is not an excluded asset, and as the private use is not significant, the conditions for exemption are satisfied. No taxable benefit arises.

Example 2

Jordon's employer meets the cost of converting his loft to an office, to enable him to work at home. As the benefit comprises the 'extension, conversion or alteration of any living accommodation', it is an excluded asset and, as such, the exemption does not apply. Consequently, any taxable benefit arising is determined in accordance with normal rules.

Legislation: ITEPA 2003, s. 316

143-050 Christmas parties and other annual events

An exemption from tax is available for annual staff parties. Previously given by concession, the exemption is now on a statutory footing.

Typically associated with the Christmas season, the exemption can in fact apply to one or more events during the year. The maximum cost per individual attending the party is £150 (including VAT and all incidental costs). To qualify for tax exemption, the event must be open to all staff, or to all of those working at a particular location.

If the exemption is not available, most employers will wish to meet any tax liability that arises. This will normally be done through a PAYE settlement agreement, whereby the tax and National Insurance cost is grossed up and paid directly by the employer to the HMRC.

Legislation: ITEPA 2003, s. 264

Several functions

Where there are several annual events, the employer can designate which ones should be taken into account to make best use of the exemption.

If, for example, the cost per head of event A is £100, event B is £70 and event C is £75, the employer can nominate events B and C as covered by the exemption, assuming all conditions are met. This allows for the best overall tax result.

Other Material: HMRC *Employment Income Manual* EIM21690

Tax Reporter: ¶433-750

Hampers, etc.

A difficult issue arises if the hamper or gift is supplied in the context of the Christmas party. The exemption applies to an annual party or similar annual function and, where the cost is within the limit, no liability arises 'in respect of its provision'. The question is therefore whether the giving of the hamper or gift can be properly described as part of the cost of providing the party. With effect from 6 April 2016, the matter is much less likely to be of concern with the introduction of the trivial benefits exemption outlined in 133-335. Subject to the issue of very minor benefits mentioned below, the HMRC manuals offer no guidance on the point and, in the absence of any relevant case law, the best approach is probably to take a reasonable line.

Legislation: ITEPA 2003, s. 323A

Other Material: HMRC *Employment Income Manual* EIM21863

143-100 Clothing and tools

The cost of clothing is seldom allowable as a deduction from earnings as it is rarely incurred wholly, exclusively and necessarily in the performance of an employee's duties (*Hillyer v Leeke*, the business tax case of *Mallalieu v Drummond*, and *Williams*). In the last of these, a deduction for the cost of buying and cleaning clothes was denied to a BBC newsreader: on the evidence, the clothing she wore was not of a special character dictated by the occupation as a matter of physical necessity but was rather ordinary clothing of a standard required for her occupation. The fact that the clothing was not worn off duty was irrelevant; it was sufficient that it was the type of clothing that *could* be worn off duty. Even if it had been established as a fact that the newsreader was obliged to vary her clothing, not wearing the same outfit more than two or three times per month, this would not establish a material distinction between the facts of the case and those of *Hillyer v Leeke*.

Uniforms provided by employers and worn as part of the employee's duties of employment are not, however, taxable as a benefit in kind. The difficulty can be to define what is meant by a uniform for these purposes.

HMRC accept that no tax liability arises from the provision of 'a set of clothing of a specialised nature that is recognisable as a uniform and is intended to identify its wearer as having a particular occupation'. Examples given are of police or nursing uniform. By contrast, HMRC do not accept that the exemption would apply merely because 'employees in the same employment wear clothing of a similar design or colour'. To illustrate this, HMRC give the example of a bank that wishes to 'reinforce its corporate image by requiring all counter staff to wear a shirt or blouse in the corporate colours of blue and green'. The HMRC view in such a case is that 'that clothing is not a uniform for this purpose and no deduction can be permitted for the cost of acquiring such clothing'.

The cost of protective clothing is tax deductible (or may therefore be provided by an employer without triggering a tax liability). As it was put in the then Sch. D case of *Caillebotte v Quinn*, 'the cost of protective clothing worn in the course of carrying on a trade will be deductible, because warmth and decency are incidental to the protection necessary to the carrying on of the trade'.

Where employees are required to provide tools and protective clothing because of the nature of their employment, appropriate fixed allowances have been agreed in many cases by HMRC with trade unions. The employees may claim a deduction of this amount without needing to establish their actual level of expenditure. The employee may claim his actual expenditure if he can establish that it is greater. If the employer pays to the employee the appropriate fixed allowance, a deduction will eliminate the charge to tax normally arising in such circumstances.

Legislation: ITEPA 2003, s. 367

Cases: *Caillebotte v Quinn* (1975) 50 TC 222; *Hillyer v Leeke* (1976) 51 TC 90; *Mallalieu v Drummond* [1983] BTC 380; *Williams* [2010] TC 00397

Other Material: HMRC *Employment Income Manual* EIM32465

Tax Reporter: ¶457-500

143-150 Computer equipment

Changing rules

For a number of years there was a tax exemption for computer equipment provided by an employer for use by directors and employees, but this was withdrawn from April 2006 (subject to transitional provisions). Consideration should now instead be given to the question of whether the more general tax exemption can be used that applies to certain accommodation, supplies and services (see 143-000). In June 2006,

HMRC issued a statement suggestion that the exemption can indeed normally be expected to apply:

> 'Section 316 of the Income Tax (Earnings & Pensions) Act 2003 provides that no income tax will arise on accommodation, supplies and services used in employment duties. This includes computer equipment provided for business purposes where any private use made is not significant. Consequently where employers provide computer equipment to employees solely for them to carry out the duties of the employment at home, HM Revenue and Customs accept it is unlikely that private use of the computer will be significant, when compared with the primary business purpose of providing the computer equipment.'

Personal digital assistants

With the rapid advance of technology, it can now be difficult to distinguish between a mobile phone (see 143-750) on the one hand and a computer on the other. This is particularly the case with 'Personal digital assistants' (or 'PDAs', sometimes better known by the brand name BlackBerry).

HMRC have stated that 'technology has developed to such an extent that PDAs and BlackBerrys now have additional functions more typically associated with a computer and so can no longer be considered primarily as a mobile phone'. The same is likely to apply to the Apple iPhone which, according to the company's own publicity, 'combines three products – a revolutionary mobile phone, a widescreen iPod with touch controls, and a breakthrough internet communications device with desktop-class e-mail, web browsing, maps and searching'. In their HMRC Brief 02/12, HMRC state that they now accept smartphones such as iPhones and BlackBerrys qualify as mobile phones.

The statutory tax test is not one of usage but of design. If the item is designed to be used mainly for spoken messages then it can be exempt under the mobile phone exemption; if it is designed primarily for other functions (accessing e-mail messages, texting, storing data and so on) then for tax purposes it is not a mobile phone but a computer.

HMRC guidance (at EIM21701) states that 'the provision by an employer to an employee of a PDA represents a benefit, unless the exemption in section 316 applies': this seems to imply pretty clearly that HMRC acceptance of a complete tax exemption for PDAs will be the exception rather than the rule.

Other Material: HMRC *Employment Income Manual* EIM21611, EIM21701

143-175 Employees of the employee

A characteristic of employment (as opposed to self-employment) is that the individual normally has to perform the duties himself, rather than having the option to delegate them to a third party. Claims for the costs of employing an assistant will therefore be rare. Even if the employment terms allow for such assistance, it will still be necessary to demonstrate that the costs of employing someone else are incurred wholly, exclusively and necessarily in the performance of the duties of the first employee.

The cost of secretarial assistance was, exceptionally, permitted in the 2010 *Evans* case (though the quantum of the claim was successfully challenged by HMRC).

Case: *Evans* [2010] TC 00446

143-200 Entertaining

As a general rule, expenditure on entertainment or a gift in connection with the employer's trade, business, profession or vocation is not allowed as a deduction from earnings. 'Entertainment' includes hospitality of any kind. Where an employee is involved in entertaining for business purposes, however, the disallowance will normally fall on the employer. As such, the employer can reimburse the employee either under protection of a dispensation, or through the PAYE system. In the latter case, the employee can claim tax relief under ITEPA 2003, s. 336 (the general rule for deduction of employee expenses: see 140-050).

It may seem surprising that the employee can obtain relief at all, since the rules regarding employee expenses are notoriously tight. It is difficult, on ordinary principles, to argue that the cost of the employee's meal is incurred wholly, exclusively and necessarily in the performance of the duties of the employment. In practice, however, HMRC do not take the point. The manuals specifically state that

> 'if an employee is required for genuine business reasons to entertain customers, suppliers or other business connections in the course of his or her duties, the expense of doing so can be regarded as satisfying the statutory test in ITPA 2003, s. 336. This is the case whether the purpose of the occasion was to discuss a particular business project or to maintain existing or new business contacts, even though no specific business was done.'

Furthermore, the paragraph goes on to confirm that 'where the entertainment expenses incurred on a particular occasion are admissible no restriction should be made for the cost of the employee's own food and drinks'.

Care is needed, however. Suppose, for example, that an employee personally meets the cost of client entertaining, paying for it out of taxed salary. Typically, this may happen if the employee is to some extent paid by results and therefore has an incentive to incur expenditure in the hope of a greater financial return. In these circumstances, no disallowance can be made in the employer's computations; indeed, the employer will not know how much of his salary the employee has spent on client entertaining. Therefore, the full salary will be allowable in computing the employer's profits. This time, however, the expenditure incurred by the employee is caught by the prohibition on entertaining expenditure. Even though he pays tax on his salary, and even though it is genuine business expenditure, he cannot claim any tax deduction for the costs incurred.

Legislation: ITEPA 2003, s. 356

Other Material: HMRC *Employment Income Manual* EIM32615

Tax Reporter: ¶455-200

143-250 Homeworker expenses

Employers are increasingly requiring or allowing their employees to set up an office at home and this has led to disputes with HMRC over the tax treatment of contributions made by the employer to the employees' additional utility costs. A distinction is made between the treatment of employer contributions towards homeworking expenses and the possibility of a claim for tax relief by employees working from home. The HMRC stance is not generous.

Employer contributions

Employers may make tax-free contributions to the incidental household costs incurred by employees who work at home. The exemption applies where there are 'arrangements between the employee and the employer under which the employee regularly performs some or all of the duties of the employment at home'. To minimise the need for record-keeping, employers may pay up to £4 per week (£208 per year) (up from £3 per week (£156 per year) with effect from 6 April 2012) without supporting evidence of the costs that the employee has incurred. If an employer pays more than that amount, the exemption will still be available but the employer must provide supporting evidence that the payment is wholly in respect of additional household expenses incurred by the employee in carrying out his duties at home.

There is no requirement that part of the employee's home should be used exclusively for the purposes of the employment. Indeed, such an arrangement is best avoided as exclusive use of one or more rooms may jeopardise the full private residence exemption when the home is sold.

Legislation: ITEPA 2003, s. 316A

Tax Reporter: ¶437-550

Claims for relief where employer does not reimburse expenses

A stricter approach is taken for employees who are not reimbursed by their employers but who wish to claim a portion of household expenses.

According to the guidance issued in October 2005:

> 'HMRC will accept that employees who work at home are entitled to a deduction under Section 336 ITEPA 2003 for their additional household expenses where all the following circumstances apply:
>
> - the duties that the employee performs at home are substantive duties of the employment. 'Substantive duties' are duties that an employee has to carry out and that represent all or part of the central duties of the employment (this condition is unchanged),
> - those duties cannot be performed without the use of appropriate facilities,
> - no such appropriate facilities are available to the employee on the employer's premises (or the nature of the job requires the employee to live so far from the employer's premises that it is unreasonable to expect him or her to travel to those premises on a daily basis),
> - at no time either before or after the contract is drawn up is the employee able to choose between working at the employer's premises or elsewhere.
>
> If one or more of those conditions are not satisfied HMRC officers will contend that the employee is not entitled to relief for the expenses of working at home. That contention is of course without prejudice to the employee's right to appeal to the Commissioners in any case where they believe that, notwithstanding what is said in this article, they satisfy the statutory conditions in Section 336.'

In practice, HMRC will accept that all four conditions are met only in rare circumstances. Even where they do accept this, HMRC will grant a deduction only for:

- the additional unit costs of gas and electricity consumed while a room is being used for work;
- the metered cost of water used in the performance of the duties (if any); and
- the unit costs of business telephone calls (including 'dial-up' internet access).

HMRC do not accept that any deduction may be made for rent, council tax, water rates, mortgage costs of any variety or household insurance premiums. The justification for denying all relief for these costs is that, 'in each case the expense is a single indivisible sum (or a series of indivisible sums) no part of which is incurred 'wholly and exclusively' in the performance of the employee's duties'.

To avoid the need to keep records and to make unnecessary calculations, HMRC have in the past announced that they will allow a deduction of £2 per week, mirroring the rules that apply when employers *do* reimburse employees, as referred to above. The amount that employers may reimburse in this way was increased from £2 to £3 per week from 6 April 2008 and it is therefore assumed that the same increased figure now applies to deductions claimed by employees who are not reimbursed. It is open to employees to claim instead the actual additional costs of working from home, by keeping proper records. In either case, the deduction is only available to employees who meet the conditions for relief to be due at all (see above).

Other Material: HMRC *Employment Income Manual* EIM32810

143-300 Employee liability and indemnity insurance

Employees may deduct the following three types of expenditure paid out of earnings:

(1) the cost of discharging a qualifying liability of the office holder or employee;

(2) costs arising out of or connected with a claim that the office holder or employee is subject to a qualifying liability;

(3) so much of any premium paid under a qualifying contract of insurance as relates to covering the office holder or employee for the above costs.

Legislation: ITEPA 2003, s. 558

Tax Reporter: ¶457-000ff.

Guarantees given by directors

The above form of tax relief may be contrasted with the position that arises if a director gives a personal guarantee on behalf of a company. In *Guarantor v R & C Commrs*, tax relief was disallowed for a payment made under a guarantee relating to a debt factoring arrangement. The expense (as opposed to the contingent liability) was not incurred in the course of the employment but only after it had come to an end. Furthermore, it was evident that the director gained some short-lived personal benefit from the fact that the company was able (briefly) to continue to trade.

Case: *Guarantor v R & C Commrs* (2008) Sp C 703

143-350 Long-service awards

Certain awards may be made tax-free by an employer to an employee after 20 or more years of service. The award is not taxable provided that it is either a tangible asset or shares in the employing company and does not represent more than £50 of value for each year of service. An award cannot be made if the employee has had any other award within the previous ten years from the same or from a related employer, even if the earlier award was of only token value. Whilst the exemption is commonly used in relation to retirement gifts, there is no requirement that the employee should retire.

Legislation: ITEPA 2003, s. 323

Tax Reporter: ¶437-800

143-370 Provision of pension advice

With effect from 2017–18, the first £500 of cost incurred in the provision of relevant pension advice is tax free. Relevant advice in this context will include advice in relation to the individual's pension arrangements or the use of their pension funds.

The service must be made available to all of the employer's employees or at least those in a particular location. The employees must be within five years of their anticipated pension age.

Legislation: ITEPA 2003, s. 308C

143-400 Minor benefits

Statutory exemptions

Prior to 6 April 2016, there was no de minimis figure below which benefits generally were exempt from tax. Nevertheless, the Treasury has the power to make regulations exempting minor benefits from the general charging provisions for benefits in kind. Such an exemption is conditional on the benefit being made available to the employer's employees generally, on similar terms. Exemptions have been granted under this power for the following (subject to particular rules in each case):

- welfare counselling (SI 2000/2080: see 143-850);
- cyclists' breakfasts (SI 2002/205, reg. 3: see 141-150);
- lunchtime use of works bus (SI 2002/205, reg. 4: see 141-150);
- certain minor benefits for disabled employees (SI 2002/1596: see 133-540);
- the provision of recreational facilities and subsidised meals to third parties (SI 2002/205, reg. 6); and
- the provision of certain health screening and medical check-ups (SI 2002/205, reg. 7).

With the introduction of the trivial benefits exemption with effect from 6 April 2016 (133-335), most small non-cash benefit will be exempt from tax and National Insurance.

Legislation: ITEPA 2003, s. 210, 323A

Tax Reporter: ¶419-100

143-430 Monitoring schemes for employees working with vulnerable people

An exemption will apply where an employer pays certain costs (whether directly or by way of reimbursement to the employee) in connection with the *Protection of Vulnerable Groups (Scotland) Act* 2007. Without the exemption, the employer would be meeting a pecuniary liability of the employee and a tax charge would arise.

More specifically, the exemption covers an employee's fees in respect of an application to join the scheme administered under s. 44 of that Act. The purposes of the scheme is to collate and disclose information about individuals working with vulnerable persons. The legislation contains a power to extend the exemption, by Treasury Order, so as to cover fees for equivalent schemes for England, Wales and Northern Ireland.

Legislation: ITEPA 2003, s. 326A

Tax Reporter: ¶437-980

143-450 Payroll giving

Introduction

Payroll giving allows employees to give to any UK charity by way of payment out of gross salary. In this way, immediate tax relief is given at source at the employee's marginal tax rate. There is no limit on the amount of the permissible deduction but the deductions must be made under the terms of a scheme which, at the time the sums are withheld from the employee, is approved (or is of a kind approved) by an officer of HMRC. In practice, employers may wish to insist on a minimum monthly payment level (say £5 per employee) so that the administration is proportionate to the amounts involved.

Example

A higher rate employee wishes to donate £50 per month to Sightsavers International. The employer agrees to run a payroll giving scheme and deducts the payment from gross pay. As such, the after-tax cost to the employee is only £30. The employer passes the full £50 to an approved agency. The agency deducts its costs of say £2 (see below) and passes the remaining £48 to Sightsavers.

Alternatively, the employer agrees to pay the agency costs and therefore pays over an additional £2 – under arrangements agreed with the agency – so that Sightsavers receives its full £50. The employer obtains tax relief for the £2 cost.

Some employers choose to increase or even match employee donations, either indefinitely or for a specified period. If the employer in this example chooses to match the £50 then full tax relief is available for that employer deduction.

Various terms are used to describe schemes of this nature, including also Give As You Earn.

Legislation: ITEPA 2003, s. 713ff.; *Income Tax (Pay As You Earn) Regulations* 2003 (SI 2003/2682), reg. 3(1)(b)

Websites: www.hmrc.gov.uk/payrollgiving/index.htm; www.payrollgiving centre.org.uk

Tax Reporter: ¶457-700

Mechanics

The scheme under which the sums are deducted must provide for the employer to pay them to an agent approved by HMRC, which will then pass them on to the charity or charities nominated. The sums must constitute gifts by the employee to charity. Clearly, each payment must fulfil whatever conditions are laid down in the scheme under which it is made. It is possible for the agent to be itself a specified charity, in which case it will obviously retain any sum due to itself.

Legislation: ITEPA 2003, s. 714

Tax effects

If the above conditions are satisfied, then the sums so withheld by the employer will be deductible expenses in computing the income tax liability of the employee for the tax year in which they are withheld, and will be deducted from his pay before computing PAYE income tax.

As the scheme applies only for tax purposes, no national insurance relief is due. As such, employers must take care, when completing form P11, to deduct the amount of any donations from gross pay for tax purposes but not for NIC purposes.

Legislation: ITEPA 2003, s. 713ff.; *Income Tax (Pay As You Earn) Regulations* 2003 (SI 2003/2682), reg. 3(1)(b)

Costs

Agencies charge a fee for their work in administering these schemes and will deduct such costs before handing the money over to the specified charities. Such costs can vary but a figure of 4% of the donation is fairly typical, often with a minimum figure in the region of 25p. Schemes should not normally prove unduly onerous for employers once they are up and running.

Tainted donations

From April 2011, restrictions to tax relief apply where donors enter into arrangements to obtain an advantage from a charity in return for the donation. Broadly, the restrictions apply where a donor or connected person seeks tax relief for a charitable donation but where there are certain 'arrangements' in place. One of the main purposes of the arrangements must include the obtaining of a financial advantage for the donor or connected person.

Legislation: ITA 2007, s. 809ZH and following sections

143-500 Security assets and services

A tax exemption is given for certain expenditure incurred or reimbursed by an employer on the provision of security assets and security services which improve personal security. The security asset or service must be provided for the employee to meet a special threat to his personal physical security which arises wholly or mainly by virtue of the particular employment concerned; this test is interpreted tightly. Examples of qualifying expenditure might include alarm systems, bullet-resistant windows in houses, floodlighting and security guards.

The special commissioners allowed an appeal by a taxpayer in respect of security costs, having concluded that the security services were provided for the taxpayer to meet a special threat to his personal physical security within the meaning of the legislation. The threat arose wholly or mainly by virtue of the particular employment and the employer company had the meeting of that threat as its sole object in bearing the cost.

Legislation: ITEPA 2003, s. 377

Case: *Lord Hanson v Mansworth (HMIT)* (2004) Sp C 410

Tax Reporter: ¶456-000

143-550 Sick pay and benefits

Where a person holding an employment is absent from work for any period by reason of sickness or disability, any sums which:

- are paid to, or to the order or for the benefit of, that person (or a member of his family or household) in respect of any such absence from work; and
- are, by reason of his employment, paid as a result of any arrangements entered into by his employer,

will be chargeable to income tax under ITEPA 2003, s. 221 as earnings of the employment for that period if, apart from this provision, they would not be so chargeable.

Where the funds for making payments under any arrangements are attributable partly to contributions made by the employer and partly to contributions made by the persons employed by him, the above provision will apply only to such part of the sums paid as a result of the arrangements as it is just and reasonable to regard as attributable to the employer's contributions. The provision was introduced to tax benefits paid under schemes established by employers by way of trust or through an insurance company.

The benefit in kind provisions do not apply to any benefit consisting of the right to receive, or the prospect of receiving, any sums which would be chargeable to tax in accordance with the above.

Legislation: ITEPA 2003, s. 201–202, 221

Tax Reporter: ¶420-050

Group sickness, etc. policies

Where employees contribute to a fund for the provision of sick pay, the contributions do not attract tax relief and should be made from income after the deduction of tax and NIC. Payments made to employees when they are sick out of a fund consisting entirely of employee contributions are not taxable as employment income. The benefits covered include those paid under some kinds of long-term care insurance.

Where an employer has taken out a group policy to meet the cost of sick pay for his employees, benefits received under the policy and passed on to an employee are also exempt if and to the extent that the employee has contributed to the premiums. This is extended to cases where the employee retires as a consequence of, say, an illness and benefits continue to be paid to him under a new separate policy derived from the employer's policy.

Legislation: ITTOIA 2005, s. 735ff.

143-600 Sporting and recreational facilities

Employees are not liable to tax on the benefit of in-house sport and recreational facilities provided by employers for use by their staff generally. The facility must be wholly or mainly used by persons deriving their right to use it from employment (not necessarily with the same employer).

The exemption applies to benefits provided by employers to employees and members of their families or households consisting of any sporting or other recreational facilities provided so as to be generally available to employees of the employer in question, or of non-cash vouchers which can be exchanged only for such benefits. The exemption is extended to cover others who, though not employees, are working on the same premises but the facilities must not be open to the public generally.

The following items are not within the exemption:

(1) mechanically propelled 'vehicles' (which includes ships, boats or other vessels, aircraft and hovercraft);

(2) interest in or use of holiday or other overnight accommodation or of ancillary facilities;

(3) a facility provided on domestic premises (private dwellings and land or premises belonging to, or enjoyed therewith); and

(4) a right or opportunity to use any facility falling within (1)–(3) above.

The Treasury may make regulations to prescribe benefits which would then not be exempt under this section, or prescribe benefits which will be within the section only if certain conditions are fulfilled.

Legislation: ITEPA 2003, s. 261ff; *Income Tax (Exemption of Minor Benefits) Regulations* 2002 (SI 2002/205) (as amended)

Tax Reporter: ¶437-700

143-650 Subscriptions paid

Relief is provided for fees and subscriptions paid by employees and directors to professional bodies, etc. provided that the bodies are either listed in the legislation or approved by HMRC for the purpose of the legislation. If the employer bears the cost of such fees, etc., the relief will eliminate the tax charge normally arising in such circumstances.

For such relief to be available:

- the person concerned must be required to retain membership of a professional body as a condition of his employment and must pay the subscription in order to do so; or
- the subscription must be paid to a body whose activities are relevant to that employment.

The fees listed in the legislation are those paid by members of the following professional categories to keep their names on a professional register:

- health professionals;
- animal health professionals;
- legal professionals;
- architects;
- teachers;
- patent agents and trade mark agents;
- occupations in the transport sector; and
- occupations in the private security industry.

The bodies that have been approved by the Board are listed in a publication ('List 3') available for viewing at www.hmrc.gov.uk/list3.

The general requirements are that the body must be national in character and must exist solely or mainly to advance or spread knowledge, maintain or improve the standards of the members of the profession or to indemnify or protect members against claims for liabilities incurred in the exercise of their profession. The body must not be run for profit.

Relief is only due under this heading if the employee has employment income (and not, for example, only pension income) against which to set the subscription (*Singh v Williams (HMIT)*).

Legislation: ITEPA 2003, s. 343

Case: *Singh v Williams (HMIT)* 2000 Sp C 250

Tax Reporter: ¶455-000

143-700 Suggestion scheme awards

Staff suggestion schemes are operated by some employers in both the public and private sectors to encourage employees to suggest ways, outside the usual scope of their work, in which efficiency and productivity, etc. can be improved. Successful suggestions are often recognised by a cash award from the employer.

Without special legislation, such cash awards would be taxable in the same way as any salary payment. However, a tax exemption is given provided certain conditions are satisfied:

- the employer establishes a scheme which is open on the same terms to employees generally, or a particular description of them;
- the suggestion relates to the activities carried on by the employer;
- the suggestion is made by an employee who could not reasonably be expected to make it in the normal course of his duties, having regard to his experience; and
- the suggestion is not made at a meeting held for the purpose of proposing suggestions.

Provided these conditions are satisfied, no liability to income tax arises if the amount of an award does not exceed:

- 50% of the expected net financial benefit during the first year of implementation; or
- 10% of the expected net financial benefit over a period of up to five years,

subject to an overriding maximum of £5,000. Where an award exceeds £5,000 the excess is not covered by this concession.

Where a suggestion is put forward by more than one employee the award is divided between them on a reasonable basis.

An 'encouragement award' may also be made provided it does not exceed £25. An encouragement award is one which is made in respect of a suggestion which though it will not be implemented, has some intrinsic merit and/or reflects meritorious effort on the part of the employee in making the suggestion.

This concession does not apply to any liability to income tax or capital gains tax on income or gains arising from the exploitation or disposal of rights in an invention devised by the employee, e.g. patent rights, know-how, etc.

Legislation: ITEPA 2003, s. 321, 322

Tax Reporter: ¶437-750

143-750 Telephones

Mobile phones

There is no tax charge on the provision by an employer of a single mobile phone for an employee, irrespective of the level of private use. A taxable benefit will still arise if the employer meets the employee's private bill for a mobile phone or if top-up vouchers are provided which can be used on any phone. Vouchers or credit tokens specifically provided for an employer-supplied mobile phone are, however, exempt.

The exemption does not extend to second phones or to those provided for other members of the employee's family or household.

For a discussion of the distinction between a mobile phone and a computer, see 143-150.

Legislation: ITEPA 2003, s. 319

Tax Reporter: ¶437-700

Car phones and related equipment

A car telephone is within the meaning of 'mobile telephone' and is also excluded from the definition of accessories for calculating the price of a car for any given year.

HMRC have given the following guidance in relation to hands-free mobile phone kits:

- if the kit is fitted to a company car, there are no tax implications (unless, exceptionally, ownership of the kit passes to the employee);
- as long as the employer retains ownership of the kit, there will be no tax charge if the employer pays for a kit to be fitted in a privately owned car;
- if the employer does not retain ownership, then a tax benefit may well arise; and

- if the employee buys a kit and retains ownership, but the employer reimburses the cost, that reimbursement will be treated as earnings, whether the kit is fitted to a company or a privately owned car.

Legislation: ITEPA 2003, s. 125(2)(d)

Other Material: HMRC *Employment Income Manual* EIM21781

Home phones

For details of the rules applying where an employer provides a phone at home for an employee who works from there, see 143-000. Subject to that, an employee will be liable to tax if the employer pays the employee's personal telephone bill.

143-800 Training courses

Training paid for by employer or third party

An exemption applies where an employer incurs expenditure on work-related training for one of his employees. The income is exempt from tax in respect of the expenditure by the employee and the benefit of the work-related training.

The exemption is widely drafted and covers the full-range of training delivery methods. The qualification is that the training must be 'work-related'. This is essentially training which is designed to impart skills or knowledge which would be useful to the employee in performing the duties of any 'relevant employment'. The term 'relevant employment' covers the employee's current job, or one which he is to hold with his employer or a person connected with his employer. This brings training for a job which the employee has a reasonable chance of being promoted into, for example, within the scope of the exemption.

The expenditure covered by the exemption is limited to the cost of providing the training and related costs. Related costs are incidental costs arising wholly and exclusively as a result of the employee undertaking the training, expenses incurred in connection with an assessment of what the employee has learned during the training and those costs of obtaining any qualification, reward, etc. to which the employee is entitled as a result. *Additional* childcare costs arising from the employee attending evening lectures, for example, would be covered, whereas *routine* childcare costs would not. Travel and subsistence expenses are allowed to the same extent as if they had been incurred on business travel.

There are a number of exclusions which aim to ensure the exemption is limited to genuine work-related training. These include training provided for recreation or enjoyment or as an inducement or reward and the provision of assets under the guise of work-related training.

In the case of *Silva v Charnock*, an individual undertook an MBA course. Her prospective employer agreed that she should complete the course before commencing her employment and that it would pay her a 'signing bonus' equal to the course fees. The special commissioner held that this did not amount to an inducement, and that the exemption applied even though the employment had not commenced until after the completion of the course. The HMRC view, though, is that the facts in that case were unusual and 'the decision will not necessarily apply in other cases where the facts are different'.

Work-related training which is funded by a third party rather than the employee's employer is exempt to the same extent as if the employer has incurred the expenditure.

Incidental overnight expenditure paid to employees on training courses may be paid tax-free in the same way and to the same degree as incidental overnight expenses paid to employees who are away on business.

Legislation: ITEPA 2003, s. 250ff.

Case: *Silva v Charnock* (2002) Sp C 332

Tax Reporter: ¶432-500

Training paid for by employee

An employee may, of course, pay for his or her own training. The generous rules regarding employer-funded training are in stark contrast to those that apply where an employee provides training at his or her own cost.

The expenses associated with obtaining a qualification are normally non-deductible on the basis that the expense is incurred to put the employee in a position to work rather than in the performance of the duties of employment.

Blackwell v Mills concerned the costs of travel and textbooks, *Lupton v Potts* concerned examination fees and *Humbles v Brooks* concerned the conference fees of a headmaster. All three cases failed on the ground that the expenditure was not incurred in the performance of the duties of the employment. Expenditure incurred to employ a child minder to enable an employee to work was held non-deductible in *Halstead v Condon*.

An even clearer signal was given in *Consultant Psychiatrist v R & C Commrs*, in which the commissioner considered the contract of a psychiatrist who was claiming a deduction for training expenses. Although the costs were very properly incurred, the commissioner decided that 'when she was undergoing the personal psychotherapy sessions and other training, she was not performing any duties under her contract of employment'. For the avoidance of doubt, he went on to state that 'this applies just as much to the expenditure required to meet the minimum CPD requirement as to the rest of the expenditure'.

The point was made yet again in the Chancery Division decision in *HMRC v Decadt*, concerning a qualified surgeon who sought to deduct certain examination fees and associated costs. The Commissioners had allowed the appeal, noting that the healthcare authority that employed him had made the passing of the examination an obligatory part of the contract of employment. However, the HMRC appeal to the High Court was successful – the fact that the training contract required that the taxpayer take the relevant exams was not in itself sufficient to render the expenses in question deductible; costs and expenses involved in training to qualify the taxpayer better to carry out his duties were not deductible from his earnings.

In *Perrin v R & C Commrs*, tax relief was denied for training costs incurred by a trainee accountant: even though attendance on the courses was required by his employment contract, and enabled him to do his job better, it was not the nature of his employment that required the expenditure. As such, the cost of attendance was not incurred in the performance of the duties of the employment. Even if it had been so incurred, it would have been difficult to conclude that it was exclusively so incurred as the expenditure must have been at least partly for the purposes of obtaining the qualification.

After this succession of decisions, all disallowing training costs, it was surprising that a very similar case went the other way early in 2009. In *Banerjee*, the General Commissioners held that training costs incurred by a consultant dermatologist had been incurred wholly, exclusively and necessarily in the performance of the duties of her employment. When that view was confirmed in the High Court, the judge gave some fairly clear indications that the case law had perhaps erred too far against the taxpayer in this area. The decision was upheld in the Court of Appeal, where all three judges agreed that the expenses were 'necessarily incurred' in the performance of the duties, and a majority (two to one) agreed that they were exclusively so incurred: there was no dual purpose even though there was a secondary, or incidental, benefit to the taxpayer in terms of advancing her professional career.

Cases: *Blackwell v Mills* (1945) 26 TC 468; *Humbles v Brooks* (1962) 40 TC 500; *Lupton v Potts* (1969) 45 TC 643; *Halstead v Condon* (1970) 46 TC 289; *Consultant Psychiatrist v R & C Commrs* (2006) Sp C 557; *HMRC v Decadt* [2007] BTC 586; *Perrin v R & C Commrs* (2008) Sp C 671; *R & C Commrs v Banerjee* [2010] BTC 662

143-825 Employee retraining

The treatment of training generally is covered at 143-800 above. An additional form of relief is given for certain training given to individuals who cease to be employed by a particular employer. The relief is therefore typically aimed at retraining those who have been made redundant. An employee will not be taxed on the benefit of the following expenses where the course conditions and the employment conditions are met:

- fees for attendance at a training course;
- fees for examinations taken during or at the end of the course;
- cost of books which are essential for any person attending the course; and
- travelling expenses which would be deductible expenditure (expenses incurred in employment) on the assumptions that attendance at the course is a duty of the employment and, where the employee has ceased to be employed, that he is still employed by the employer.

Course conditions

The training course must provide training that is 'designed to impart or improve skills or knowledge relevant to, and intended to be used in the course of, gainful employment (including self-employment) of any description'. The course, which must last no more than two years, must be 'entirely devoted to the teaching or practical application (or both) of the skills or knowledge'.

Employment conditions

The employee must be employed by the employer or must begin the course within the period of one year after he ceases to be employed and he must cease to be employed by the employer within two years from the end of the qualifying course of training. The course will not be a course of retraining if the employee resumes employment with the same employer within two years of ceasing to be employed. The employee must have been employed by the employer for a period of at least two years ending when the course begins or, if earlier, when the employment ceases.

The opportunity to undertake the course must be available, on similar terms as to payment by the employer, to the employee's fellow employees (or former fellow employees) generally or to a particular class or classes of them.

Legislation: ITEPA 2003, s. 311

Tax Reporter: ¶437-050

143-840 Vouchers and credit-tokens

Overview

Without special rules, certain benefits in kind that are exempt from tax would nevertheless be caught if provided by way of a voucher or credit token. To avoid this outcome, the legislation contains rules to remove the potential tax liability in relation to a range of specified benefits. The structure of the legislation is as follows:

- ITEPA 2003, s. 266: general exemption for non-cash vouchers used for exempt benefits;
- ITEPA 2003, s. 267: general exemption for credit tokens used for exempt benefits; and
- ITEPA 2003, s. 268ff.: exemptions for particular non-cash vouchers and credit tokens.

Legislation: ITEPA 2003, Pt. 4, Ch. 6

Tax Reporter: ¶433-800

Exemption of non-cash vouchers for exempt benefits

Various exemptions from the rules of ITEPA 2003, Pt. 3, Ch. 4 (taxable benefits: vouchers and credit tokens) are provided as follows. The distinctions between the various lists depend on the exact nature of what can be obtained by the voucher (for example, whether the person with the voucher can *obtain* something or whether the voucher merely shows that the holder is *entitled to use* something).

No liability under the vouchers rules arises if, or to the extent that, a non-cash voucher is used to obtain anything, the direct provision of which would be exempt under any of the following provisions:

- parking provision;
- transport between home and work for disabled employees;
- provision of cars for disabled employees;
- late night transport and failure of car-sharing arrangements; and
- third party entertainment.

No liability under the vouchers rules arises if, or to the extent that, a non-cash voucher 'evidences the employee's entitlement to use' anything the direct provision of which would be exempt under any of the following provisions:

- works transport services;
- support for public bus services;
- cyclists and related safety equipment; and
- mobile phones.

No liability under the vouchers rules arises if, or to the extent that, a non-cash voucher can only be used to obtain anything, the direct provision of which would be exempt under any of the following provisions:

- travel and subsistence during public transport strikes;
- recreational benefits;
- annual parties and functions;
- armed forces' leave travel facilities;
- subsidised meals; and
- eye tests and corrective appliances.

No liability under the vouchers rules arises if or to the extent that a non-cash voucher 'evidences the employee's entitlement' to any benefit which is exempt from tax under the residual liability rules because of regulations made under ITEPA 2003, s. 210.

Legislation: ITEPA 2003, s. 266

Tax Reporter: ¶433-805

Exemption of credit-tokens used for exempt benefits

No liability under the vouchers rules arises if or to the extent that a credit-token is used to obtain anything the direct provision of which would be exempt under any of the following provisions:

- parking provision;
- travel and subsistence during public transport strikes;
- transport between home and work for disabled employees;
- provision of cars for disabled employees;
- late night transport and failure of car-sharing arrangements;
- third party entertainment;
- mobile phones; and
- eye tests and corrective appliances.

Legislation: ITEPA 2003, s. 267

Tax Reporter: ¶433-810

Specific exemptions for non-cash vouchers and credit-tokens

Exemptions are also extended to include the use of non-cash vouchers and credit-tokens in relation to the following categories of expenditure:

- incidental overnight expenses;
- cars, vans, HGVs;
- third party gifts; and
- childcare.

Tax Reporter: ¶433-820

143-850 Welfare counselling

No taxable benefit arises in respect of the provision of welfare counselling provided that certain conditions are met. For the exemption to be available, the welfare counselling must be made available generally to an employer's employees on similar terms.

'Welfare counselling' covers counselling of any kind, other than:

- medical treatment of any kind;
- advice on finance (other than on debt problems);
- advice on tax;
- advice on leisure or recreation; and
- legal advice (see below).

HMRC warn that 'the exemption is tightly drawn and there is no intention that all conceivable types of welfare counselling should be exempted from tax'. That is a rather odd statement as the exemption is specifically worded to cover 'counselling of any kind' other than the types listed above. The HMRC guidance goes on, however, to list the following types of counselling that *do* fall within the exemption:

- stress;
- problems at work;
- debt problems;
- alcohol and other drug dependency;
- career concerns;
- bereavement;
- equal opportunities;
- ill-health;

- sexual abuse;
- harassment and bullying;
- conduct and discipline; and
- personal relationship difficulties.

Legislation: ITEPA 2003, s. 210; *Income Tax (Benefits in Kind) (Exemption for Welfare Counselling) Regulations* 2000 (SI 2000/2080)

Other Material: HMRC *Employment Income Manual* EIM21845

Tax Reporter: ¶419-100

Counselling covering different areas

Counselling may include some elements that fall within the exemption and others that do not. The HMRC view in this case is that 'strictly the exemption does not apply to any of the services provided because the exemption does not include any basis for an apportionment of the benefit'. Once more, it is questionable whether that is in fact a correct interpretation of what the legislation really achieves. Nevertheless, the HMRC guidance is sound when it suggests that counselling would ideally be separated into two separate schemes (qualifying and not qualifying). HMRC guidelines go on to state that:

> 'if it is not possible to separate the services in this way, common sense should be applied where the welfare counselling provided by an employer consists substantially of facilities that satisfy the terms of the exemption but also to a not significant proportion of the services provided which do not satisfy the exemption. This applies particularly on occasions where it is difficult to determine where to draw the line between counselling which falls within the exemption and counselling which is outside of the exemption.'

Other Material: www.hmrc.gov.uk/specialist/welfare-counselling.pdf

143-875 Employee-ownership trusts

Finance Act 2014 encourages the disposal of a controlling interest in a trading company to trusts solely for the benefit of employees. As well as capital gains tax and inheritance tax advantages, there is also a limited exemption for bonus payments to employees. The maximum amount that can be exempt is £3,600 in each tax year, applying to payments received after 30 September 2014.

There are many conditions that must be met, including:

- the payment must not be regular salary or wages;
- neither can it be part of a salary exchange arrangement;

- the company must be a trading company or part of a trading group, such that the activities of the company or group do not include non-trading activities to a substantial extent;
- the company must not be a service company, as defined, but there is an exception where the services are provided to a company in the same group;
- the directors or other office holders of the company (and connected persons) must not exceed in number 40% of the total employees and office holders of the company;
- if the payment is made to a former employee, this must be within 12 months of cessation;
- all employees must be eligible to benefit and on the same terms but factors such as remuneration, length of service and hours worked can be taken into account. The scheme must not have features that are likely to confer benefits wholly or mainly on directors and highest paid employees.

It can be seen, however, that this exemption can only apply to employees of companies and not, therefore, to partnerships or sole traders.

Legislation: ITEPA 2003, s. 312A–312I

Rules relating to specific types of employee

143-900 Houses of ministers of religion

An exemption is given for a person in full-time employment as a minister of a religious denomination. No liability to income tax arises on:

- the payment or reimbursement of a 'statutory amount' payable in connection with qualifying premises;
- the reimbursement of a 'statutory deduction' made in connection with qualifying premises; or
- the payment or reimbursement of expenses incurred in connection with providing living accommodation in 'qualifying premises' if the minister is a P9D employee.

The exemption in the first two bullet points does not apply to the extent that the amount or deduction is properly attributable to a part of the premises for which the minister receives rent.

In this context, premises are 'qualifying premises' if:

- an interest in them belongs to a charity or an ecclesiastical corporation; and
- because of that interest and by reason of holding the employment, the minister has a residence in them from which to perform the duties of the employment.

Legislation: ITEPA 2003, s. 290

Tax Reporter: ¶488-100

Accommodation outgoings of ministers of religion

A statutory exemption (formerly given by concession ESC A61) is given from April 2010 for certain ministers of religion in lower-paid employment who are reimbursed expenses of heating, lighting and gardening in connection with living accommodation provided with the employment. A similar exemption is given in respect of allowances paid to ministers and used by them for the purpose of meeting such expenses. However, such expenses must still be taken into account when deciding whether or not the individual is in fact lower paid, so the exemption will now apply rarely in practice.

Legislation: ITEPA 2003, s. 290A

Tax Reporter: ¶488-130

143-910 Members of Parliament, members of regional assemblies, and government ministers

Accommodation expenses of MPs

MPs' accommodation expenses allowances are exempt from income tax. The term 'accommodation expenses' is defined to cover expenses necessarily incurred on overnight accommodation that is required for the performance of the member's parliamentary duties in or about:

- the Palace of Westminster; or
- the MP's own constituency.

Since 7 May 2010, such expenses must be paid under the scheme administered by the Independent Parliamentary Standards Authority (IPSA).

There is also an allowance for necessary overnight expenses for members of the regional assemblies of Scotland, Wales and Northern Ireland.

From 1 November 2010, the exemption is extended to apply to payments made by IPSA, on the authorisation of the MP, to a third party (such as a landlord).

Legislation: ITEPA 2003, s. 292, 293

Tax Reporter: ¶488-000

UK travel and subsistence

Since May 2010, there has been a statutory exemption for travel expenses paid or reimbursed to MPs by IPSA, where the expenses are necessarily incurred in the performance of the parliamentary functions of the MPs. Travel by MPs' spouses or partners, made between the member's London area residence and the member's constituency residence, is also allowable where the spouse or partner shares 'caring responsibilities' as defined in the *Parliamentary Standards Act* 2009.

An exemption is also given for 'relevant subsistence costs' for MPs, where the MP is required to be at the House of Commons because the House is sitting beyond 7.30 p.m. Relevant subsistence costs are expenses necessarily incurred on an evening meal, but excluding alcoholic drinks.

Legislation: ITEPA 2003, s. 293A

European travel expenses of MPs and other representatives

MPs and members of the regional assemblies of Scotland, Wales and Northern Ireland are exempt from income tax on reimbursed European travel expenses, defined as the cost of, and any additional expenses incurred in, travelling between the UK and a 'relevant European location'. This last term covers:

- an EU institution or agency; or
- the national Parliament of:
  - another member state;
  - a candidate or applicant country; or
  - any other country that is a member of the Council of Europe.

Legislation: ITEPA 2003, s. 294

Tax Reporter: ¶488-005

Transport and subsistence for government ministers, etc

An exemption is given to holders of ministerial offices (as defined). Provision of transport or subsistence, and payments or reimbursements of transport or subsistence expenses, by or on behalf of the Crown to such people does not give rise to a liability to income tax.

Legislation: ITEPA 2003, s. 295

Tax Reporter: ¶488-010

Termination payments

No income tax liability as general earnings arises on certain grants or payments (but this does not prevent a liability arising under the rules of ITEPA 2003, Pt. 6, Ch. 3: see 142-000ff.). The exemption applies to grants or payments made:

(1) in accordance with a resolution of the House of Commons to a person ceasing to be a Member of that House on a dissolution of Parliament;

(2) under *Ministerial and other Pensions and Salaries Act* 1991, s. 4 (grants to persons ceasing to hold certain Ministerial and other offices);

(3) made under *European Parliament (Pay and Pensions) Act* 1979, s. 3 (resettlement grants for persons ceasing to be Representatives);

(4) made under *Scotland Act* 1998, s. 81(3) to a person ceasing to be a member of the Scottish Parliament on its dissolution, or ceasing to hold an office corresponding to a relevant office;

(5) made under *Government of Wales Act* 1998, s. 18(1) to a person ceasing to be a member of the National Assembly for Wales on the expiry of the member's term of office;

(6) made under *Northern Ireland Act* 1998, s. 48(1) to a person ceasing to be a member of the Northern Ireland Assembly on its dissolution, or ceasing to hold an office corresponding to a relevant office; or

(7) (for payments made on or after 6 April 2008) under *Greater London Authority Act* 1999, s. 26A (payments on ceasing to hold office as Mayor of London or as a member of the Greater London Assembly).

A 'relevant office' is defined in accordance with *Ministerial and other Pensions and Salaries Act* 1991, s. 4.

Legislation: ITEPA 2003, s. 291

Tax Reporter: ¶488-015

143-920 Members of the armed forces

Leave travel facilities

No liability to income tax arises in respect of travel facilities provided for members of the naval, military or air forces of the Crown going on, or returning from, leave. The exemption applies not only to travel vouchers and warrants for particular journeys but also to allowances and other payments for and in respect of leave travel, whether or not a warrant was available.

Legislation: ITEPA 2003, s. 296

Tax Reporter: ¶485-300

Food, drink and mess allowances

No tax liability arises on allowances paid out of the public revenue to members of the armed forces if the Treasury certifies that the allowances are payable in lieu of food or drink that would normally be supplied to members of the forces. A similar exemption applies to payments towards mess expenses.

Legislation: ITEPA 2003, s. 297

Tax Reporter: ¶485-300

Operational allowance

No income tax charge arises on payments to members of the armed forces of the Crown of the Operational Allowance, where designated as such by the Secretary of State. Although this provision was only introduced by the *Finance Act* 2007, it applies to such payments whenever they were made.

Legislation: ITEPA 2003, s. 297A

Tax Reporter: ¶485-300

Council Tax Relief

An income tax exemption applies for payments of Council Tax Relief (designated as such by the Secretary of State) made from 1 April 2008 to members of the armed forces of the Crown.

Legislation: ITEPA 2003, s. 297B

Tax Reporter: ¶485-300

Lump sum payments on early departure

Lump sums paid under the Armed Forces Early Departure Payments Schemes 2005 and 2014 are free of income tax.

Legislation: ITEPA 2003, s. 640A

143-930 Workers on offshore gas or oil installations

No liability to income tax arises, for offshore oil and gas workers, in respect of:

- the provision of transfer transport, related accommodation and subsistence, or local transport; or
- the payment or reimbursement of reasonable expenses incurred on such transport or accommodation and subsistence.

'Transfer transport' is broadly defined as transport by sea or air between the mainland of Great Britain or Northern Ireland and the offshore installation in question.

Legislation: ITEPA 2003, s. 305

Tax Reporter: ¶488-250

143-940 Miners' free coal

Colliery workers (as defined) are exempt from income tax on coal or smokeless fuel (or an allowance paid in lieu) as long as the coal or fuel does not substantially exceed the amount reasonably required for personal use.

Legislation: ITEPA 2003, s. 306

Tax Reporter: ¶488-050

143-990 Other occupations

The *Tax Reporter* has commentary on an extensive range of employment occupations, in addition to those covered in the preceding paragraphs. The complete list of occupations covered there is as follows:

- accountants: ¶485-050;
- agricultural workers (including racehorse trainers and stable lads): ¶485-100;
- airline pilots: ¶485-200;

- armed forces: ¶485-300;
- bank employees: ¶485-500;
- building industry and civil engineering employees: ¶485-520;
- careworkers: ¶485-550;
- census officers: ¶485-680;.
- cleaners: ¶485-700;
- club secretaries: ¶485-720;
- collegiate bodies: ¶485-750;
- computer staff: ¶485-780;
- construction industry workers: ¶485-800;
- crown servants: ¶486-000;
- deep sea divers: ¶486-020;
- dentists and associated roles: ¶486-200;
- demonstrators and merchandisers: ¶486-050;
- directorships: ¶486-250;
- educational workers: ¶486-300;
- electoral workers: ¶486-600;
- emergency service workers: ¶486-700;
- engineering employees: ¶486-760;
- entertainers: ¶486-800;
- fishermen: ¶486-950;
- government and local government workers: ¶487-000;
- guardians ad litem: ¶487-300;
- gurkhas: ¶487-400;
- insurance agents: ¶487-450;
- journalists: ¶487-550;
- legal professionals: ¶487-580;
- lifeboat crews: ¶487-620;
- lorry drivers: ¶487-650;
- market researchers: ¶487-680;
- medical professionals: ¶487-700;

- Members of Parliament: ¶488-000.
- milkmen: ¶488-025;
- mineworkers: ¶488-050;
- ministers of religion: ¶488-120;
- offshore workers: ¶488-250;
- post office employees: ¶488-300;
- prison officers: ¶488-370;
- public house managers: ¶488-400;
- seafarers: ¶488-500;
- sportsmen and women (footballers, rugby players, cricketers): ¶488-850;
- steel industry workers: ¶488-920;
- tree fellers: ¶488-950;
- trustees and executors: ¶488-960;
- veterinary inspectors: ¶488-975;
- voluntary workers: ¶489-000.

PAYE

Key principles

145-000 Introduction

Primary authority for the PAYE system is found in ITEPA 2003, s. 684, which is headed 'PAYE regulations' and which requires the Commissioners to make regulations for the assessment, charge, collection and recovery of income tax in respect of all PAYE income. The main regulations so made are entitled the *Income Tax (Pay As You Earn) Regulations* 2003 (SI 2003/2682), which were rewritten under the Tax Law Re-write Project and which consolidated earlier regulations. These 2003 regulations are referred to in this commentary as 'the PAYE regulations' and are designated as 'SI 2003/2682'. They came into force from 6 April 2004.

The scope of PAYE is also extended to 'notional payments' to employees, which include payments of PAYE income via intermediaries, such as offshore trusts, or in the form of benefits in kind. Since tax cannot be deducted other than from payments of money to taxpayers, special provision is made for deducting the tax in respect of benefits in kind from other payments. The *Income Tax (Earnings and Pensions) Act* 2003, s. 710 prescribes rules for employers to account for PAYE on notional payments (see 145-060).

Legislation: ITEPA 2003, s. 684(2)(1)(a)

Tax Reporter: ¶493-000

145-005 Real Time Information

General

Real Time Information (RTI) became operative for most employers on 6 April 2013. There had been a prior pilot run for volunteer employers.

RTI is mandatory and it is essential for employers to have the proper software. HMRC have published a list of recognised PAYE software, which it has tested. There is clearly a cost to this although for employers with nine or fewer employees HMRC's basic payroll tool could be used.

The only exceptions to the mandatory compliance with RTI are:

- individuals who are practising members of a religious society or order whose beliefs are incompatible with the use of electronic communications. This would include partnerships and companies if all the partners or directors and company secretaries, as the case may be, are also practising members;
- a care and support employer, being an individual who employs others to provide services to him (or members of his family), that employer or family member having a disability or infirmity. It must be the employer who delivers the return and not someone else on their behalf.

Essential features

Clearly, RTI will bring PAYE fully into the electronic world but a clear motivation for this is the introduction of universal credit. It is vitally important to know the income of individuals and so this needs to be available as soon as possible. Thus, the basic requirement of RTI is that on or before making a payment within the PAYE system an employer must deliver to HMRC detailed information about the payment, which will clearly include the gross payment and the tax deducted. There is also a requirement to indicate the hours worked within specified bands, being linked again to the universal credit regime. Information about the employer and employee must also be given if not already provided and so it is essential that employers have full information about their employees to include date of birth and National Insurance number. Detailed information about employees should be obtained on commencement of an employment, including the employee's address and passport number, if known, and on cessation of employment the date of cessation must be given.

This will all be dealt with online and so there is no longer an obligation to complete a P35 at the end of the tax year, as all the information will be held by HMRC. There is a considerable amount of work in taking on an employee, including checking that the total tax paid to date on the form P45 is correct (and if not use the correct figures when setting up the new employees' payroll record).

Other points

There is a laid down procedure where an employer discovers that an error in the return has been made under RTI. This can be corrected relatively simply if before 20 April following the end of the tax year in question. However, if the information is corrected later than that then a more detailed return must be made in accordance with regulation 67E.

If no relevant payments are made during a tax period an employer may send notification of this to HMRC, which has the practical effect of avoiding reminders from HMRC and dealing with penalty notices when these are introduced.

Where payments are only made once a year, HMRC can be asked to set up an annual scheme, which avoids any need to make nil payment submissions.

There has been recognition by HMRC of the practical difficulties in the international context where employees are assigned from overseas to the UK. There are modified payroll procedures known as either appendix 6 or appendix 7 schemes. Employers need to enter into agreements with HMRC to adopt these and in particular to enter into new agreements from 6 April 2013. The RTI rules are adapted to fit in with these agreements and in some instances are not within RTI at all.

Payments to sub-contractors under the construction industry scheme are not within RTI as such but there is an interaction for an employer in making payments of PAYE, etc. to HMRC.

Penalties

FA 2013 brings in a penalty regime, though, for RTI for failure to make returns that are due from 6 April 2014 onwards. The amendments made to FA 2009, Sch. 55 will be supplemented by regulations to be made by HMRC, including the calculation of the penalty for failure and an exemption during the first tax month and initial period (but these exemptions can be disapplied by the regulations as specified). There are also provisions to impose a 5% penalty for an extended failure, which is one where a failure continues after the end of three months from the filing date.

These penalties are quite distinct from the penalties for failure to make payments on time, which continue to apply, albeit that they have been modified for 2014–15 onwards.

Legislation: *Income Tax (PAYE) Regulations* 2003 (SI 2003/2682), reg. 67B–67F

145-010 Marginal items of pay

There can be practical difficulties in including certain items of pay in the correct earnings period for the purposes of calculating PAYE and NIC. HMRC have issued guidance, updated in June 2010, relaxing the strict rules in relation to so-called 'marginal items of pay'. The guidance includes the following key paragraphs.

> '**When a marginal item of pay can be included in an earnings period later than the one in which it was paid or treated as paid**
>
> Occasionally, your payroll section does not get to know about certain marginal items of pay, for example, expenses, until after they have been paid or treated as paid. So they include the item in a later earnings period because it is time-consuming to have to revisit the correct earnings period and recalculate the Class 1 NICs due. HM Revenue & Customs (HMRC) will allow employers to use a later earnings period when calculating the NICs due, even on the rare occasions when such payments are notified late and the most convenient earnings period falls within the next tax year. But the marginal item of pay must be included in gross pay for the purposes of calculating NICs without any undue delay.
>
> **When a marginal item of pay must be included in the earnings period in which it was paid or treated as paid**
>
> You must allocate the payment to the correct earnings period and recalculate the NICs where the deferred calculation may have a material effect on an individual's benefit entitlement, for example, where an employee earns around the lower earnings limit.
>
> HMRC will also ask you to include the item of pay in the correct earnings period and recalculate the NICs due where it appears that you are deferring the calculation to avoid or reduce NICs.'

HMRC do not accept that 'securities' can be treated as marginal items of pay.

Tax Reporter: ¶493-170

145-020 Definitions

The general principle is that PAYE is to be applied when payments are made 'of, or on account of, PAYE income'. It follows that it is critical to understand what is meant by PAYE income and what is understood by making a payment of such income. It is also necessary to understand who is treated as an employer for these purposes.

Tax Reporter: ¶493-150

Legislation: ITEPA 2003, s. 684(2)(1)(a)

PAYE income: statutory background

The concept of 'PAYE income' is defined through a fairly complex sequence of statutory provisions. Initially, the term includes three elements (ITEPA 2003, s. 683(1)):

(a) any PAYE employment income for the year;

(b) any PAYE pension income for the year; and

(c) any PAYE social security income for the year.

The first of these three elements is then defined in its turn (ITEPA 2003, s. 683(2) to mean income that consists of 'taxable earnings' and 'taxable specific income' from an employment. This then leads to ITEPA 2003, s. 10(2) and (3)). The concept of 'taxable earnings' is thereby defined to mean amounts determined under ITEPA 2003, Pt. 2, Ch. 4 and 5 (covering respectively employees who are and are not resident, ordinarily resident and domiciled in the UK). The term 'taxable specific income' means amounts which count as employment income by virtue of any of a number of provisions, including (inter alia) termination payments and various forms of income relating to securities.

PAYE income: practice

The following non-exhaustive list of payments is based on HMRC practice and guidelines as to what items should be entered in the 'pay in week or month' column of the deductions working sheet:

- salaries, wages, fees, overtime, bonus, pensions, commission, honoraria, perks;
- payments in the form of pensions;
- cash payments such as Christmas boxes;
- amounts voted to a director and credited to an account with the company that a director can draw on;

- payments used for subscribing for shares in a company;
- payments used to reduce a debt that an employee owes the employer unless tax has already been paid on the money when it was advanced to the employee;
- payments made in advance, on account or after an employee has left, including drawings in advance or on account of a director's remuneration;
- pay in respect of sickness or other absence from work;
- statutory sick pay;
- statutory maternity pay, statutory paternity pay and statutory adoption pay;
- holiday pay;
- tool and clothing allowance for employees in the building trade;
- vouchers that can be exchanged for cash including premium bonds;
- certain payments under the Employment Protection Acts, e.g. maternity pay or arrears of pay;
- payments for travelling between the employee's home and normal place of work. In the case of agency workers this is the cost of travelling from home to the client's office;
- round sum allowances;
- payments for time spent travelling;
- cash payments for meals at the normal place of work;
- payments in lieu of benefits in kind;
- certain lump sum payments made when an employee stops work;
- most lump sum payments made when an employee is taken on (including payments made to the employee before he/she has left the old job);
- tips or service charges paid to the employee in addition to the normal wage or salary (but if tips are shared out by a troncmaster, PAYE should be operated separately on these payments by the troncmaster);
- jobseeker's allowance is treated as taxable pay if paid by the employer under an arrangement with the Department for Work and Pensions; and
- payments in the form of readily convertible assets or vouchers or credit tokens which are used to acquire such assets.

In relation to the operation of PAYE where there is no actual payment, the gross amount of earnings should be entered on the deductions working sheet and action taken to ensure that only the net amount is credited or subsequently paid. Where in the same month a director has a bonus credited to him and is paid salary by cheque, to apportion the tax between these two 'payments', the tax is worked out as if only the salary were being paid and that tax is deducted from that salary, the remainder being netted off against the bonus (HMRC press release, 28 July 1989).

Where an employer makes 'notional payments' tax must be deducted from actual payments made to the employee at such time as the PAYE regulations prescribe (see 145-160).

Legislation: ITEPA 2003, s. 710

Payment: general rule

For the purposes of PAYE regulations, a payment of, or on account of, PAYE income is treated as paid when the *earlier* of the following events occur (and see below for the special rules for directors):

- the time when the payment is made; or
- the time when the person becomes entitled to the payment.

Thus, when an employee is entitled to be paid towards the end of a tax year but does not receive payment until the start of the next tax year, PAYE should be operated by reference to the earlier date. Similarly, if an employee is entitled to receive pay on a particular date but decides not to draw it immediately, PAYE should be operated as if the payment was made on the date the employee became entitled to it.

Legislation: ITEPA 2003, s. 686

Payment: special rules for directors

If at any time in the tax year the person is a director of a company and the income is income from employment with the company (whether or not as director), then payment will be treated as made on whichever is the earliest of the following, if this produces an earlier payment date than under the general rule described above:

(1) the time when sums on account of the income are credited in the company's accounts or records (whether or not there is any restriction on the right to draw the sums);

(2) if the amount of the income for a period is determined before the period ends, the time when the period ends; or

(3) if the amount of the income for a period is not determined until after the period has ended, the time when the amount is determined.

Legislation: ITEPA 2003, s. 686

Tax Reporter: ¶493-150

'Employer'

Under ITEPA 2003, s. 4, an 'employment' includes any employment under a contract of service or of apprenticeship and any employment in the service of the Crown. The term 'employer' is to be interpreted accordingly. In *Booth v Mirror Group Newspapers plc*, the High Court held that a company, which had made inducement payments to a person for him to enter into a contract of employment with a third party, was right to have deducted tax from the payment under the PAYE scheme. The payment was an emolument of the relevant employment and the company was therefore within the definition of 'employer' as the payer of emoluments.

Legislation: ITEPA 2003, s. 4

Case: *Booth v Mirror Group Newspapers plc* [1992] BTC 455

145-030 Student loans

Employers have an obligation to deduct student loan repayments in certain circumstances and to account for such payments in like manner as income tax payable under the (*Taxes Acts Education (Student Loans) (Repayment) Regulations* 2000 (SI 2000/944), reg. 14).

HMRC have responsibility for collecting repayment of student loans through the PAYE system. Full guidance on such loans is given in HMRC's *Collection of Student Loans Manual* beginning at CSLM004. See also leaflet CSL2, *The Collection of Student Loans: A guide for employers and employees to help answer common Student Loan queries*, available on the HMRC website at www.hmrc.gov.uk/leaflets/csl2.pdf.

Employers do not have a duty to identify borrowers who are liable to make repayments. However, the role of the employer is summarised as follows at CSLM2030:

> 'It is the employers' role to
>
> - Start and cease deduction of Student Loan repayments following the receipt of Start Notices and Stop Notices from HMRC, when a form P45 is received with a 'Y' in the SL box or when the employee ticks box D (Student Loans) on a P46
> - Calculate the weekly or monthly amount of Student Loan repayments

- Deduct the Student Loan repayments from the borrower's pay
- Account for the Student Loan amounts deducted to Banking Operations along with tax and NIC
- Include the amount of Student Loan deductions on forms P11, P14, P35 and P60
- Ensure that in leaver cases, form P45 is marked with a 'Y' in the SL box when a Start Notice (SL1) has been received (or box D of a P46 has been ticked), but no Stop Notice (SL2), regardless of whether or not any Student Loan repayments have been deducted, (for example, because of the level of the borrower's earnings).'

Student loan deductions are deducted from gross pay alongside tax and NIC. Deductions are rounded down to the nearest pound. Deductions are non-cumulative and employers can therefore ignore the question of amounts already deducted. HMRC provide tables and their 'Basic PAYE Tools' service (available at www.businesslink.gov.uk/basicpayetools) can be used to calculate the deduction which (because of rounding) may not be exactly 1/52 of the annual amount.

If an employee has two jobs, the employer does not need to be concerned with the employee's other income, but should calculate the deduction based only on amounts paid by him. However, if the employee has two employments with the same employer then these should be aggregated for student loan purposes if they are aggregated for NIC purposes.

Tax Reporter: ¶494-380

Deduction and payment of tax

145-040 PAYE as a means of tax collection

The principal method of collecting tax where earnings are charged under the provisions of the *Income Tax (Earnings and Pensions) Act* 2003 (ITEPA 2003) is by means of the Pay As You Earn (PAYE) system. This imposes upon employers the duty to deduct tax when relevant payments are made to employees, to account for the tax deducted and to pay it over to HMRC.

Employers are able to make repayments to new employees when making the first wage or salary payment (if they have been overtaxed under PAYE) without prior reference to the tax authorities. The repayment must be made with the first wage or salary payment. Employers are also able to collect underpayments of tax for a prior year where that underpayment has been included in the calculation of the PAYE tax code, the maximum underpayment that may be coded out in this way, with effect from 6 April 2015, is a graduated sum between £3,000 and £17,000 dependent on the individual's income. With effect from 1 November 2014, regulations were introduced to limit the maximum amount of tax that may be deducted in any period to not more than 50% of the income payable in that period.

Failure to deduct tax may make an employer liable to pay the tax and he may be subject to penalties. The collector may estimate the amount payable if he is not satisfied with the employer's account. The PAYE mechanism aims to match the total tax deducted from relevant payments with the final correct liability.

Employers are required to comply with the rules which are designed to ensure that employees will have the necessary information to complete their self-assessment tax returns on time.

Legislation: *Income Tax (Pay As You Earn) Regulations* 2003 (SI 2008/2682)

Provision of services through an intermediary

Where services are provided by a worker on behalf of an intermediary (a partnership or a service company) for a client, an anti-avoidance regime (popularly known as 'IR35' after the Budget press release that introduced it) may deem the intermediary's receipts from the worker's engagement to be earnings fully liable to income tax (and subject to PAYE) and employer's National Insurance contributions (see 130-250).

Legislation: ITEPA 2003, Pt. 2, Ch. 8

Territorial limitation

In *Clark v Oceanic Contractors Incorporated*, the House of Lords held that a non-resident overseas company with a 'tax presence' in the UK must operate the PAYE system. Their Lordships admitted there was some territorial limitation but declined to determine its extent.

There are special rules where an employee is seconded to the UK but continues to be paid by a non-resident employer. These impose a duty to account for PAYE on the person for whom the employee carries out duties.

Where a non-resident person works partly in the UK and partly abroad, so that only a proportion of total income is chargeable to UK income tax, then an officer of Revenue and Customs may give a direction as to how much of any payment is subject to PAYE.

Legislation: ITEPA 2003, s. 689–690

Case: *Clark v Oceanic Contractors Incorporated* [1982] BTC 417

145-060 Cumulative tables

The PAYE system operates to take account of a proportion of the employee's entitlement to reliefs and allowances when tax is deducted. It operates on a cumulative basis. Each time a payment is made, the running total of tax paid is compared to the tax due on the total earnings to the date of payment. The difference between the tax due and the tax paid is the tax which is deducted from the payment. If the tax paid exceeds the tax due, a repayment is made via the PAYE system.

This is achieved by providing the employer with a series of tables and by notifying him of the relevant code number applying to a particular employee. The tables set out the cumulative allowances and the cumulative tax applying to the employee. A simplified example is given below.

Example

Frank is an employee earning £15,000 p.a. He also has benefits totalling £485 p.a. He is entitled to personal reliefs of £5,225. Frank is paid monthly. In the first month (i.e. month beginning 6 April) Frank is entitled to 1/12 of his allowances (from which the assessable benefit of £485 has been deducted), i.e. £395, and this will be reflected in his PAYE coding. His taxable earnings for that month are therefore £1,250 (1/12 × £15,000) *less* £395 = £855. By the 12th month, Frank will have used up his full personal reliefs and have no further tax to pay.

Tax Reporter: ¶493-510

145-080 PAYE codes

The system of PAYE coding is designed to allow to be taken into account the great variety of possible allowances and reliefs to which an employee might be entitled without actually informing the employer of the employee's reliefs entitlement. Notice of the code determined by the officer is given to the employer by a code authorisation (Form P6 or P9 or, for Budget changes, P7X) and, if it differs from the code notified in the preceding year, the employee is also notified (Form P2). The employee may appeal against such notice of coding.

The exact code depends on the employee's personal circumstances. The following alternative codes reflect an individual's circumstances as indicated:

L – for a code with the basic personal allowance.

P – for a code containing the single age allowance (aged 65–74).

T – used where HMRC are reviewing other items in tax code. Also used where HMRC asked not to use other codes.

Y – for a code with full personal allowance for those aged 75 or over.

D0 – tax is to be deducted wholly at the higher (40%) rate, i.e. normally for a secondary source of income.

D1 (from April 2011) – tax is to be deducted wholly at the additional (50%) rate, i.e. again for a secondary source of income.

K – the excess of taxable benefits, or of a state pension, over allowances is being taxed under PAYE (see below).

BR – tax is to be deducted at the basic rate.

NT– no tax is to be deducted at all.

0T (from April 2011) – no personal allowances are given but tax is deducted at the basic rate, higher rate and additional rate (see below).

Benefits-in-kind are treated as earnings and may therefore be taken into account in determining the appropriate code.

Where an employee's circumstances alter, HMRC should be informed so that the PAYE code can be altered accordingly.

The coding system can, of course, only approximate the tax position of each individual. Adjustments may be made at the year end and if there has been an overpayment of tax, this is repaid. An underpayment of tax may often be taken into account in the following year's coding, i.e. it is 'coded out'.

The Court of Appeal, in the case of *Blackburn (HMIT) v Keeling*, held that a Lloyd's name was not entitled to claim relief from income tax in respect of trading losses before the tax year in which the losses were declared. If the inspector and the commissioners were given a free hand to make provisional allowances for prospective losses then it would add a further layer of complication and uncertainty to the already complex task of preparing PAYE codes.

Finance Act 2012 gives HMRC the power to make regulations to collect income tax arising from the high income child benefit charge through a notice of coding subject to the individual agreeing to this in prescribed circumstances.

An underpayment of up to £17,000 can be collected through an adjustment to an individual's notice of coding. The maximum sum that may be collected through the notice of coding is a graduated figure dependent on the income level of the taxpayer.

Case: *Blackburn (HMIT) v Keeling* [2003] BTC 327

Tax Reporter: ¶493-300

K codes

The 'K' code system provides a mechanism for income tax on benefits to be collected through the PAYE system rather than having to be assessed on the employee at the end of the tax year where the total benefits exceed the employee's personal allowances for the year. The 'K' code instructs the employer to increase taxable pay by an amount (subject to a limit of 50% of pay) to reflect the excess of benefits over personal allowances, tax then being deducted from the resulting total.

0T codes

HMRC have indicated that the 0T (zero T) code is to be used, from April 2011, if:

- a new employee does not complete a form P46;
- an employee receives an occupational pension while continuing to work for the same employer (in which case the 0T code is used for the pension income); and
- if an employee receives payment from the employer after the employment has ceased, and the payment has not been included on the individual's P45. (Before April 2011, the employer was required to deduct basic rate tax in these circumstances.)

Non-cumulative codes

There are circumstances where tax deducted is ascertained on a non-cumulative basis. Tax is calculated as though the payment were the first of the tax year and is generally referred to as 'week 1 or month 1 basis'. The non-cumulative basis is applied whenever an HMRC officer so directs, or there is a payment in week 53 of the tax year, or an employer begins to pay a pension and has not received a cumulative code authorisation.

Legislation: *Income Tax (Pay As You Earn) Regulations* 2003 (SI 2003/2682), reg. 26

Emergency codes

An 'emergency code', equal to one-twelfth or one fifty-second of the single person's allowance, must be used whenever payments are made to an employee for whom no code has been issued and who is paid above a certain rate.

An employee taking up employment for the first time after a period of full-time education will be subject initially to the same code as a new employee, but on a cumulative basis. The figure of 'total payments to date' and of 'total tax to date' before the first payment will be treated as nil. Other new employees are subject to PAYE on a cumulative basis, applying a basic rate code. When a new employee presents the new employer with P45, in most cases the employer will operate PAYE in accordance with that.

Legislation: *Income Tax (Pay As You Earn) Regulations* 2003 (SI 2003/2682), reg. 9, 47–50

145-100 Deductions working sheets

An employer must keep a 'deductions working sheet' (i.e. 'any form of record in which are to be kept the matters required by these regulations in connection with an employee's relevant payments and tax') for each employee to whom he makes relevant payments within the scope of the regulations.

The deductions working sheet must show at least the employee's name, National Insurance number (if known), code and tax year covered.

In respect of every relevant payment made by the employer to the employee, the following must be shown:

- the date of the payment;
- the amount paid; and
- the amount of tax, if any, deducted or repaid on making the payment (or to be deducted or accounted for in respect of notional payments).

If the employee code is used on a cumulative basis, then the employer must either record the following items on the deductions working sheet or keep such records as enable their production:

- the total payments made to the date of payment;
- the total free pay to date (or, where appropriate, the total additional pay to date);
- the total taxable payments made to the date of payment;

- the corresponding total tax to date;
- (in the case of an employee with a K code): the tax due to be deducted at that date, the overriding limit at that date, and the amount of tax not deducted because of the overriding limit; and
- any amount of tax that cannot be repaid because of the rules relating to trade disputes.

If the employee code is *not* used on a cumulative basis, then the employer must either record the following items on the deductions working sheet or keep such records as enable their production:

- the free pay (or, where appropriate, the additional pay) for the employee's code;
- the taxable payments made;
- the corresponding total tax to date; and
- (in the case of an employee with a K code): the tax due to be deducted and the overriding limit.

Although HMRC supply pre-printed deductions sheets (P11) an employer is not obliged to use them. He may keep the records in whatever form is convenient. He may use computer software, for example. What matters is that the statutory information is recorded as required by the regulations.

Legislation: *Income Tax (Pay As You Earn) Regulations* 2003 (SI 2003/2682), reg. 2(1), 66

Tax Reporter: ¶493-200

145-120 Payment of PAYE

Sums deducted under PAYE are a liability of the employer, who must account to the collector within 14 days of each tax month (or 17 days 'where payment is made by an approved method of electronic communication'), receiving a receipt if desired.

If the HMRC officer is not satisfied that the correct amount has been paid he may notify the employer of his best estimate of the liability and request a return in respect thereof, to be made within 14 days. In certain circumstances the tax so estimated will be treated as the amount of the true liability. Alternatively HMRC may issue a formal determination based on the officer's estimate of the unpaid liability.

To combat the failure of a minority of employers who fail to account for PAYE deductions, HMRC have, with effect from 6 April 2012, the power to require a designated person to provide adequate security (usually a cash deposit) for the amounts due from time to time. The designated person will usually be the employer but could also include a director or company secretary or, in the case of an LLP, a member. If more than one person is required to give security the liability is joint and several. HMRC must serve a notice on the person specifying the relevant details. An appeal against such a notice can be made within 30 days to the tribunal. At any time an application can be made to HMRC to reduce the value of the security where there are grounds, such as in cases of hardship and where there has been a significant reduction in the number of employees, with a right of appeal. Failure to provide security when required can result in prosecution, the sanction being a fine. The indications are that HMRC will only use these powers against deliberate evaders; not those with genuine financial difficulties, who should contact HMRC for advice.

HMRC may sometimes revert to the employee. There are two main circumstances in which this may happen. The first is where the employer can show the collector that reasonable care was taken to comply with the PAYE regulations, and that an error had been made in good faith. The second is where the employee has received payments knowing that the employer has wilfully failed to make the proper deduction of tax. This happened in *R v IR Commrs, ex parte Sims*, in which it was admitted that a company employer wilfully failed to deduct tax; the High Court held that as the director in point drew round sums from the employer and had been concerned with PAYE, he knew that the deductions had not been made and tax could be recovered from him directly.

The same applied in *R v IR Commrs, ex parte Cook and Keys*, where the High Court dismissed directors' claims that they were excused because they had delegated the keeping of the records to their accountants who did not carry out their instructions. In *R v IR Commrs, ex parte McVeigh*, a director's loan account was credited with 'net' sums, which were calculated to clear previous gross drawings on the account. The employer did not make the related payment to HMRC, nor did Mr McVeigh include the sums on his personal return. In these somewhat unusual circumstances, where there had been no actual movement of money, no deduction in the normal sense had been made, and HMRC's decision to seek the tax from the employee was upheld. The position would have been different if the employer had been found to have made a deduction and simply failed to make payment to HMRC.

Regulations provide that HMRC may issue a notice absolving an employer from under-deducting PAYE tax from an employee, and consequently restricting the employee's credit for tax deducted. The regulations also provide an appeal procedure for the employee.

For a payment which is less than an employer's full PAYE and NIC liability, the collector is instructed to agree a basis of apportionment (HC Written Answer, *Hansard*, 22 February 1984, vol. 54, col. 543).

Legislation: *Income Tax (Pay As You Earn) Regulations* 2003 (SI 2003/2682), reg. 69ff.

Cases: *R v IR Commrs, ex parte Sims* [1987] BTC 170; *R v IR Commrs, ex parte Cook and Keys* [1987] BTC 339; *R v IR Commrs, ex parte McVeigh* [1996] BTC 35

Tax Reporter: ¶494-510

HMRC Guidance: www.gov.uk/government/uploads/system/uploads/attachment_data/file/356762/140922_CWG2__2014__09_14_revised_helpbook.pdf

Quarterly payments

An option exists for payment to the collector to be made within 14 (or 17) days of each income tax quarter where the employer has reasonable grounds for believing that average monthly amounts will be less than £1,500.

The employer may choose to make quarterly payments at any time and may continue even if the £1,500 limit is exceeded provided there were reasonable grounds for believing the limit would not be exceeded.

Tax Reporter: ¶494-520

145-130 Simplified deduction scheme

A simplified deduction scheme, using simplified tax tables prepared by HMRC for the purpose, may be permitted by HMRC in relation to certain 'personal employees'.

A 'personal employee' is defined as a person who is employed either at the employer's home to provide domestic or personal services for the employer or the employer's family, or to assist the employer with any business, profession or course of study which, solely because of any physical or mental disability, the employer would not be able to carry on without the assistance of the personal employee.

Legislation: SI 2003/2682, reg. 34

HMRC guidance

HMRC provide a 'Simplified PAYE Deduction Scheme Employer Pack', containing the following documents, all of which are available for downloading:

- 'Notes about Simplified PAYE deduction schemes', containing basic guidance on how to operate the scheme;
- 'Simplified Deduction Scheme', advising how to fill in the simplified deduction card;
- 'Employer's report when taking on a new employee';
- 'National Insurance Contribution Tables'; and
- 'What to do if your employee is sick'.

Other Material: www.hmrc.gov.uk/simple_deduction/index.htm

Notional payments

145-160 Overview

In defined circumstances, an employer is treated as making a payment of PAYE income to an employee, even though no money is actually being passed over. The employer is then required to operate PAYE. As the employer is not in reality making a cash payment to the employee there is no amount out of which to deduct the tax due. Nevertheless, the employer still has an obligation to calculate and account for the tax and to pay it over to the collector. Generally, this is done by deducting the tax from other payments made to the employee, but sometimes the employer has an obligation to pay tax over to the collector even though there are no actual cash payments from which to deduct tax, or such cash payments are insufficient for the purpose. The rules were introduced as a measure to counter the avoidance of tax and national insurance.

The rules regarding notional payments apply, in particular, to the following:

- readily convertible assets;
- vouchers and credit tokens;
- certain events, etc. connected with employment-related securities, and with gains from securities options;
- certain payments by intermediaries;
- certain payments to employees of non-UK employers;
- certain circumstances in which the value of an asset is enhanced where the employee (or certain connected individuals) has an interest in that asset, and

the provisions are not intended to extend PAYE to all payments in kind. Rather, the intention is to use the legislation only in cases where payments in the form of assets are being used to avoid PAYE.

Legislation: ITEPA 2003, s. 710

Tax Reporter: ¶494-300

PAYE

In respect of 'notional payments' subject to PAYE, an employer is required to deduct income tax when making actual payments of or on account of PAYE income to the employee within the same income tax period as the notional payment. The term 'employer' here includes a person to whom an employee has been seconded and who pays the employee's remuneration.

If the actual payments of chargeable income to the employee are insufficient to cover the PAYE due on the notional payments, the employer must account for tax within 14 days of the end of the income tax period in which the notional payment was made. This rule is adapted where the notional payment is treated by virtue of any legislative Act as made before the date on which the Act is passed.

Where an employer has paid to HMRC an amount of PAYE on 'notional payments' and has been unable to deduct this from actual payments to the employee, the employee must reimburse the employer within 90 days from the 'relevant date'. The relevant date is normally the date when the employer is treated as making the notional payment but is the date the relevant Act is passed if the employer is treated under that Act as making a notional payment. If the employee does not reimburse the employer within this time, the tax paid by the employer on the notional payment is added to the employee's income for income tax purposes arising on the last day of the 90-day period.

The consequences of breaching this 90-day rule were regarded as penal by the Court of Appeal in *Chilcott v HMRC* but nevertheless enforceable. However, the importance of understanding the scheme rules where an employee exercised share options is clearly demonstrated by the First-tier Tribunal's decision in *Benedict Manning*. In that case, the exercise could not be made validly until the tax was reimbursed and so this had to be within 90 days of the tax crystallisation point.

Legislation: ITEPA 2003, s. 222, 710

Cases: *Chilcott v HMRC* [2010] EWCA Civ 1538; *Benedict Manning* [2013] TC 02666

145-180 Readily convertible assets

PAYE must be operated where taxable income is provided in the form of assets that can readily be turned into cash.

The term 'readily convertible asset' covers items such as gold bars and coffee beans, but also embraces assignments of debts, assets held in bonded warehouses, assets that can give rise to the right to obtain amounts of money without any action being required by the employee (such as reversionary interests), and assets for which trading arrangements are likely to exist in the future as well as those for which such arrangements are already in place. The New York Stock Exchange is also included as a 'recognised investment exchange' for the purpose of determining whether an asset is readily convertible.

The amount on which PAYE is to be operated is the best estimate that can reasonably be made of the amount of taxable income inherent in the provision of the asset. The obligation to deduct or account for PAYE will arise no matter how the money is actually obtained; whether by mortgaging the asset, or using rights comprised in it to obtain other assets for which there are trading arrangements. The definition of trading arrangements is also extended to include arrangements by which a person, or a member of his family or household, can obtain an amount greater than, or not substantially less than, the cost of providing the asset.

A 'security' which is not otherwise treated as a readily convertible asset is treated as such unless the securities are shares that are not otherwise treated as a readily convertible asset and are corporation tax deductible.

Legislation: ITEPA 2003, s. 696, 702

Tax Reporter: ¶497-050

145-200 Notional payments: vouchers and credit tokens

Cash vouchers

Where an employer provides an employee with a cash voucher (see 133-310), the employer is liable for PAYE on the sum of money for which the voucher is capable of being exchanged. However, where the voucher is used to defray expenses or is exchanged for a sum of money which is used to defray expenses, its provision is not within the scope of PAYE provided that had the expense been paid directly by the employer it would not have been chargeable to income tax.

Legislation: ITEPA 2003, s. 693

Tax Reporter: ¶497-000ff.

Non-cash vouchers

Non-cash vouchers (see 133-320) are subject to PAYE provided that one of the following conditions is fulfilled:

(1) the voucher is capable of being exchanged for goods which at the time when the voucher is provided are capable of being sold or otherwise marketed or, at the time when the voucher is provided, would constitute a readily convertible asset;

(2) the voucher would itself constitute a readily convertible asset.

Different rules apply to a marine pilots' benefit fund (ITEPA 2003, s. 587(2)).

Legislation: ITEPA 2003, s. 694

Credit tokens

A credit token (see 133-330) provided by an employer to an employee is within the scope of PAYE where the employee uses it to obtain money or any readily convertible asset. The use of the credit token to defray expenses is excluded from this general rule, provided that had the expense been paid directly by an employer, it would not have been chargeable to income tax.

Legislation: ITEPA 2003, s. 695

Timings

Where a non-cash voucher is exchangeable for goods or services which fit the description of readily convertible asset (see above), or itself fits that description, PAYE is operated at the time it is appropriated to the employee. Similarly, where a credit-token is used to obtain goods, etc. which are readily convertible assets, PAYE must be levied on an amount equal to the cost of providing the goods, etc. at the time the credit-token is used. PAYE on the provision of cash vouchers is operated at the time the cash voucher is appropriated to the employee.

145-220 Employment-related securities and options

Where an event occurs under any of the following provisions in relation to employment-related securities, any taxable amount arising will count as employment income of the employee concerned:

- chargeable events in relation to restricted securities and restricted interests in securities (ITEPA 2003, s. 426);

- chargeable events in relation to convertible securities and interests in convertible securities (ITEPA 2003, s. 438);
- charge on acquisition where market value of securities or interest artificially depressed) (ITEPA 2003, s. 446B);
- charge where market value of securities artificially enhanced (ITEPA 2003, s. 446L);
- securities or interest acquired for less than market value: charge on discharge of notional loan (ITEPA 2003, s. 446U);
- charge where securities or interest disposed of for more than market value (ITEPA 2003, s. 446Y); and
- chargeable benefit from securities or interest (ITEPA 2003, s. 447).

Where a chargeable event occurs under any of these sections, the PAYE provisions apply with the effect that:

- an employee is treated as being provided with PAYE income (in the form of employment-related securities) by the employer at the relevant date; and
- the amount of income likely to be PAYE income is the amount likely to count as employment income.

PAYE is also applied where the employment-related securities are not readily convertible assets but the consideration received is cash or another asset. The legislation specifies the 'relevant date' for PAYE purposes in relation to each case.

Legislation: ITEPA 2003, s. 698(1)

Tax Reporter: ¶497-070

PAYE: gains from securities options

Gains made by the acquisition of securities pursuant to an employment related securities option are (where those securities are readily convertible assets) treated as PAYE income. Other events to which PAYE applies include the receipt of a benefit in relation to the option as well as assigning or releasing the option where consideration is received. PAYE applies to consideration or benefits received in cash or assets, whether or not the underlying securities are readily convertible assets. The 'relevant date' for these purposes is the date on which the chargeable event in question occurs.

Legislation: ITEPA 2003, s. 700

Tax Reporter: ¶497-090

Own-company shares

Companies have to apply PAYE to payments to employees in the form of shares. The arrangements are similar to those applying to payments in the form of assets such as gold bars or coffee beans. However, the requirement does not apply to payments under approved share schemes.

Legislation: ITEPA 2003, s. 701(2), (3)

145-230 Payment through employers' intermediaries

Where an 'intermediary of the employer' makes a payment of or on account of assessable income of an employee, the employer is obliged to operate PAYE on the payment, unless the intermediary himself deducts and accounts for tax under the PAYE regulations. If the payment to the employee by the intermediary is a net payment after deduction of any income tax, the PAYE liability is calculated on the gross amount of the payment. A payment is made by an 'intermediary of the employer' if it is made:

- by a person acting on behalf of the employer and at the expense of the employer or of a person 'connected with' him; or
- by trustees holding property for any person or class of persons which includes the employee.

The provision is intended to counter the avoidance of PAYE by means of payments of wages and salaries through intermediaries like offshore trusts.

Legislation: ITEPA 2003, s. 687

Tax Reporter: ¶496-400

145-240 Enhancing the value of assets

PAYE must be operated where an asset which an employee (or a member of the employee's family or household) already has an interest is enhanced and the asset, in its enhanced state, would be a 'readily convertible asset' (see 145-180).

Enhancement to an asset (or any right or interest over an asset) includes:

- providing services which improve it or otherwise make it more valuable;
- adding any property to the asset etc. which improves it or otherwise makes it more valuable; and
- improving or securing an increase in its value by applying money or property effecting any other enhancement.

Legislation: ITEPA 2003, s. 697

Tax Reporter: ¶497-060

Joiners and leavers

145-280 Form P45 for employee leaving employer/joining new employer

When an employee ceases employment, the employer must prepare a statement on a prescribed form. HMRC have prescribed the familiar P45 for this purpose. Under RTI this is no longer sent to HMRC. Instead the relevant information should be included in the first full payment submission.

Tax Reporter: ¶494-000

145-300 Procedure for new employee without form P45

If a new employee does not have a P45 or fails to provide the starter information under RTI he is taxed on a week 1 or month 1 basis according to the current emergency code.

For employers within RTI, form P46 should no longer be used. Instead, starter information should be obtained from a new employee, including questions similar to those on the old P45 form. The relevant details will then be included in the first full payment submission in relation to the new employee.

145-320 Casual employees

Casual employees are generally treated in the same manner as other employees although they may be paid gross in certain circumstances. Gross payments to 'casual' employees are, however, a common source of dispute in PAYE audit inspections.

If the pay of a casual employee whose PAYE code is not known is below the level of the ordinary personal allowance and the NIC lower limit, no tax is deducted if the employee appropriately certifies his status.

In the case of 'daily casual' harvest workers (those employed for a period not exceeding a day, whose employment ends with that day *with no agreement for further employment*, and who are paid off in cash at the end of that day), no PAYE is deductible; it is no longer necessary (as it used to be) for the employer to take into account the fact that he expects to offer further employment to the individuals concerned, provided there is no contract, verbal or written, for such employment.

HMRC may operate simplified tax arrangements to cover special circumstances, such as in the case of overseas students coming to the UK to work under Home Office-approved Seasonal Agricultural

Workers Schemes, who are exempt from PAYE stoppages (but not NIC) on completion of form P38(S). From 6 April 2013, form P38(S) will be withdrawn. Students will then be treated in the same way as all employees.

In the case of casual employees, the HMRC officer may make an estimated assessment on the employee or else he may issue a deductions working sheet to the employee who then deducts tax from his earnings (and pays it to HMRC) as if he were his own employer.

Legislation: *Income Tax (Pay As You Earn) Regulations* 2003 (SI 2003/2682), reg. 46, 142

Tax Reporter: ¶485-160

Employer returns

145-340 End-of-year returns (P14 and P35), etc. for years prior to 2013–14

For RTI employers form P35 will no longer be relevant for 2013–14 onwards. The following will, therefore, only be relevant to non-RTI employers for the future.

Individual employee's end-of-year summary (Form P14)

By 20 May after the tax year end, an employer must make a return to HMRC on form P14 in respect of each employee, showing the required information.

Legislation: *Income Tax (Pay As You Earn) Regulations* 2003 (SI 2003/2682), reg. 73

Tax Reporter: ¶494-700

Employer's annual return (Form P35) and Form P60

Forms P14 (see above) must be accompanied by a P35, the employer's annual statement of deductions and refunds for all employees. Form P35 contains a declaration and certificate as to the correctness of the end-of-year returns which must be signed by the employer or, where the employer is a body corporate, by the company secretary or a director. Deductions working sheets should not be sent.

The P14 for an employee who has started work during the year must include total pay and tax deducted by previous employers.

A P14 is required in respect of any employee who has left during the year. Total pay (including payments made after issue of P45) and date of leaving should be entered on the return.

The employer must also give to each employee in his employment at the end of the tax year a certificate (form P60) giving details of pay, tax deducted, and the code used. The form must be given to the employee not later than 56 days from the end of the tax year, i.e. by the end of May. As long as this deadline is met, the employer can deliver the P60 to the employee in any manner, e.g. with payslips, separately by post, etc.

Legislation: *Income Tax (Pay As You Earn) Regulations* 2003 (SI 2003/2682), reg. 73

Nil returns

Employers and agents can now notify HMRC online if they have no need to make annual returns (P35 and P14s). Links to do this may be found at www.hmrc.gov.uk/paye/payroll/year-end/annual-return.htm#4.

Electronic P60s

Employers are now able to provide employees with form P60 in electronic format. HMRC have advised that employers should:

> 'take into account the employees ability to easily access that information
>
> provide secure facilities to view and print their P60. If this is not possible the P60 can be issued to an email address that has been agreed with the employee.'

In connection with the matter of electronic P60s, HMRC have revised their guidelines about amended and duplicated P60s.

Tax Reporter: ¶494-370

145-360 Returns (P11D) of benefits and expenses at end of year

Before 7 July following the end of the tax year, the employer must submit to HMRC a return showing, in respect of each director or employee, particulars of 'other earnings'.

The HMRC booklet, *Employer's Further Guide to PAYE and NICs*, contains lists of returnable and non-returnable benefits. No return is necessary in respect of employees who have not received any of the payments listed.

If there are employees or directors, who are not in receipt of any of the above, employers are asked simply to confirm that all necessary forms

P11D have been completed and returned, individual 'nil' returns not being required.

As regards form 42 re certain share transactions, see 147-200.

Legislation: *Income Tax (Pay As You Earn) Regulations* 2003 (SI 2003/2682), reg. 85ff.

Tax Reporter: ¶495-000

Motor mileage allowances

Mileage payments made within the agreed rates (see 140-550) do not need to be returned on form P11D as they are exempt from tax (which is, technically, different from saying that a corresponding deduction can be claimed). Any excess over and above the approved figures should, however, be returned. Dispensations are not required (and should not be sought) for mileage allowance payments.

145-380 Termination payments and other benefits

Before 7 July, an employer (or former employer) must give HMRC details of certain 'termination awards'. Broadly, the term covers payments and/or other benefits that exceed £30,000 and that were awarded in connection with the termination of the employee's employment or with any change in the duties of or earnings from the employment. There is no requirement to file a return if the payment is satisfied purely as cash. Further regulations apply if the amount of the award changes or if awards are provided by more than one employer.

Similar information must be provided before the same 7 July deadline to the employees concerned.

Legislation: *Income Tax (Pay As You Earn) Regulations* 2003 (SI 2003/2682), reg. 91

Tax Reporter: ¶495-050

145-400 Form P46(Car)

Within 28 days from the end of each income tax quarter, employers are required to return (on form P46(Car)), details of changes in the cars made available for private use to employees and directors. The return must contain:

- the employee's name and (if known) National Insurance number;
- details of the car which has become available or which ceases to be available;
- the 'interim sum' (see 132-240);
- any capital sum contributed by the employee towards the cost of providing the car or any qualifying accessory which is included in the cost of the car;
- any amount paid by the employee in the year as a condition of the car being made available for private use; and
- details of any fuel provided for private use.

Details must be provided whenever an employee enjoys the benefit of a company car for the first time, has an additional car, ceases to have a company car (unless it is replaced with another one), or becomes a higher paid employee whilst enjoying the benefit of a company car. However, employers should not complete a form P46(Car) where one car is simply replaced by another (SI 2003/2682, reg. 90(1A)). As a result, the first HMRC will know of a change of car is after the end of the tax year during which the change took place by the submission of a form P11D. The employee may have had a different car for up to 16 months before HMRC become aware of it. HMRC have recognised this problem, however, and the provision of or a change in a vehicle may be notified online (www.gov.uk/government/publications/paye-car-provided-to-employee-for-private-use-p46car).

Legislation: *Income Tax (Pay As You Earn) Regulations* 2003 (SI 2003/2682), reg. 90

Tax Reporter: ¶495-040

145-410 Benefits, etc. provided by third parties

Where expenses payments and benefits in kind are provided by a third party under arrangements with the employer, the employer must include on form P11D the same information as would be required had he provided the expenses payments or benefits directly. This applies where the provision of benefits by the third party has been 'arranged, guaranteed or in any way facilitated' by the employer. Where the expenses payments and benefits are not provided under such an arrangement with the employer, the person providing them must give that information to the employee before 7 July following the year end, but will not generally be obliged to inform HMRC.

Legislation: *Income Tax (Pay As You Earn) Regulations* 2003 (SI 2003/2682), reg. 86(4), 95

Tax Reporter: ¶495-010

145-420 Special return of pay and benefits

HMRC have wide powers to require returns of employees' earnings, etc. Although these powers are supplemented by the more specific requirements of the PAYE regulations, their authority remains available to HMRC as a means of enforcing full disclosure of such earnings.

Every employer must, if so required by written notice by an HMRC officer, deliver a return, within the time limit specified, relating to his employees or former employees. HMRC may require information on 'relevant payments', defined to include:

- payments to the employee in respect of expenses;
- payments made on behalf of the employee and not repaid; and
- payments to the employee for services in connection with a trade or business, whether in the course of employment or not.

Legislation: TMA 1970, s. 15

Tax Reporter: ¶494-750

145-425 Inspection powers

HMRC have a general inspection power under which an employer must produce 'all PAYE records, or such PAYE records as may be specified by the officer'. The concept of 'PAYE records' is widely drawn and includes wages sheets, deductions working sheets, other PAYE documents and all supporting documentation for completion of forms P11D. PAYE records must be kept for three years after the end of the tax year to which they relate, but in practice it is sensible to keep records for a full six years after the tax year to which they relate.

Finance Act 2012 extended the matters for which PAYE regulations can be made to include the obtaining of information from third parties who provide a payroll type service so as to secure that the provision of information will not be a breach of confidence.

Legislation: SI 2003/2682, reg. 97; ITEPA 2003, s. 684ZA

HMRC Guidance

The following 'factsheets' are produced to help employers (and contractors) to understand the compliance processes exercised by HMRC:

EC/FS1: Employers and contractors – reviewing your records

This factsheet, available at www.hmrc.gov.uk/leaflets/ecfs1.pdf has the following headings:

- Compliance checks;
- About your check;
- Arranging visits;
- Asking someone to help you;
- Preparing for our visit; and
- At the visit.

EC/FS2: Large employers and contractors – reviewing your records

This factsheet, available at www.hmrc.gov.uk/leaflets/ecfs2.pdf has the following headings:

- Compliance checks;
- Risk reviews;
- The Customer Relationship Manager and the Customer Manager;
- About your check;
- Arranging visits (with sub-heading: Asking someone to help you);
- Preparing for our visit; and
- At the visit.

EC/FS3: Compliance checks – what happens during and at the end of a check

This factsheet, available at www.hmrc.gov.uk/leaflets/ecfs3.pdf has the following headings:

- When we find something wrong;
- Overpayments;
- Underpayments;
- What happens next, and
- Formal action.

EC/FS4: Compliance checks – types of penalty

This factsheet, available at www.hmrc.gov.uk/leaflets/ecfs4.pdf has the following headings:

- Fixed penalties;
- Maximum penalty of a set amount;
- Tariff based penalties;
- Initial and daily penalties; and
- Maximum penalty of the difference.

EC/FS5: Employers and contractors compliance checks – your obligations

This factsheet, available at www.hmrc.gov.uk/leaflets/ecfs5.pdf has the following headings:

- Regulations;
- Keeping records;
- Producing records;
- Where records must be produced;
- What records must be produced; and
- What happens if you don't meet your obligations.

Reviews and appeals

A further factsheet addresses the arrangements, applying since 1 April 2009, for appeals, reviews and tribunals. The factsheet, entitled 'HM Revenue & Customs decisions – what to do if you disagree', is available at www.hmrc.gov.uk/factsheets/hmrc1.pdf. It has the following headings:

- Disagreeing with an HMRC decision;
- Tell us now if you disagree;
- What to do if we cannot reach agreement;
- How a review works;
- Appealing to the tribunal; and
- Payment of tax during reviews and appeals.

Other Material

HMRC have published an 'e-learning package' (available at www.hmrc.gov.uk/e-learning/compliance-checks/Externalmodule/HTML/Externalmodule_menu.html) to help taxpayers understand the framework for compliance checks introduced from 1 April 2009. The package covers both PAYE and other tax issues.

Interest and penalties

145-500 Penalties for late returns: main employer returns

Penalties for failure to make returns on time may be imposed as follows:

- for employers with 50 employees or less – £100 for each month (but to a maximum of 12 months) for which the failure continues plus a maximum equal to any amount that remains unpaid at 19 April following the tax year in point;
- for employers with more than 50 employees – £100 for each 50 employees (or part) for each month (but to a maximum of 12 months) for which the failure continues plus a maximum equal to any amount that remains unpaid at 19 April following the tax year in point.

The penalties for late end of year PAYE returns are determined automatically in accordance with the legislation without recourse to the tax tribunal.

In practice, automatic penalties will not be charged if returns are received on or before the last business day on or before 26 May.

The maximum penalty for fraudulently or negligently submitting a return is the amount of tax lost.

Legislation: TMA 1970, s. 98A, 100

Other Material: ESC B46

Tax Reporter: ¶499-200

Reasonable excuse

An employer may be saved from any penalty if there was a reasonable excuse for the failure and if the matter was rectified without unreasonable delay after the excuse had ceased. In *Clover Chemicals Ltd*, the tribunal held that the company did not have a reasonable excuse for failing to file a return online. It was not the duty of HMRC to remind companies of the correct method for filing returns. Similarly, in *Brookes* it was held that there was no reasonable excuse for the late filing of the form P35. The business relied on the accountant who was admitted to hospital with cancer. Nevertheless, the tribunal felt that the accountant should have found a locum to cover his absence and did not consider that the illness amounted to a reasonable excuse. Certainly, it was not the case that the reasonable excuse continued for the whole four-month period of delay. In *Currier*, the employer failed to establish a reasonable excuse for the late submission of year end returns, even though he argued that

HMRC had contributed to the delay. The employer also failed to establish a reasonable excuse in *Maddalo* as the tribunal was not able to take into account the difficulties encountered by being a small business.

The First-tier Tribunal in *Hok Ltd* decided that the taxpayer had a reasonable excuse as it took HMRC four months to generate a penalty notice. HMRC had neither acted fairly nor in good conscience. The penalty was reduced to £100 for the initial period of delay. This decision was reversed by the Upper Tribunal as HMRC had acted within the statutory provisions. By discharging the penalties on the ground of being unfair, the First-tier Tribunal had acted in excess of its jurisdiction, as such a tribunal does not have a judicial review function.

Legislation: TMA 1970, s. 118(2)

Cases: *Clover Chemicals Ltd* [2009] TC 00229; *Brookes* [2010] TC 00423; *Currier* [2010] TC 00609; *R & C Commrs v Hok Ltd* [2012] BTC 1,711; *Maddalo* [2012] TC 02117

145-510 Penalties for late returns: P11Ds

Late P11Ds are subject to an initial penalty of £300 and to further penalties of up to £60 a day for each day that the failure to make the return continues after imposition of the initial penalty. An incorrect P11D, submitted fraudulently or negligently, carries a penalty of up to £3,000.

Failure to submit form P11D(b) by the due date attracts a penalty under the *Social Security (Contributions) Regulations* 2001 (SI 2001/1004). Penalties may be imposed as follows:

- for the first 12 months, a penalty of the relevant monthly amount for each month (or part-month) that the failure continues, unless a penalty has already been imposed; and
- for failures continuing beyond 12 months, a penalty not exceeding so much as is due and remaining unpaid at the end of 19 July following the end of that year.

The 'relevant monthly amount' is £100 where the number of earners for whom particulars are included in the return is 50 or less. Where the number is greater than 50, the number is £100 for each 50 earners and an additional £100 where the number of earners is not a multiple of 50. Thus, the relevant monthly amount for a return that includes particulars for 327 earners would be £700 ((6 × £100) + £100). However, the total penalty payable is subject to a maximum limit of the total amount of Class 1A contributions payable in respect of the year in respect of which the return relates.

Legislation: TMA 1970, s. 98; *Social Security (Contributions) Regulations* 2001 (SI 2001/1004), reg. 81(2)

Tax Reporter: ¶499-200

145-520 Interest and surcharges on late PAYE payments

Interest

Where an employer has not paid the net tax deductible by him to the collector within 14 days after the end of the tax year, then unless a direction is made under SI 2003/2682, reg. 72, the unpaid tax carries interest at the 'prescribed rate' from the 'reckonable date' until the date of payment. The 'reckonable date' is the fourteenth day after the end of the relevant year (but the seventeenth day if payment is made electronically) and the 'prescribed rate' is that applicable for the purposes of TMA 1970, s. 86.

Sums recovered from an employee under reg. 72 and 81 likewise carry interest from the reckonable date until either the date of payment, or the date immediately before that on which the sum begins to carry interest under TMA 1970, s. 86, whichever is the earlier.

Interest as such is not charged on late monthly or quarterly payments made during the year, but see 145-530 for details of penalties now charged for late payments.

Legislation: *Income Tax (Pay As You Earn) Regulations* 2003 (SI 2003/2682), reg. 82

Tax Reporter: ¶494-900

145-530 PAYE penalties for late payment: principles

All employers who fail to make their PAYE payments on time have faced penalties since May 2010. As the HMRC guidance puts it, 'from May 2010 you may have to pay a penalty if you do not pay the PAYE due each month, on time and in full'. Extensive HMRC guidance is given at www.hmrc.gov.uk/employers/paye-penalties-faqs.htm.

The scheme of penalties introduced from May 2010 brought to an end a fairly benign attitude that applied before that date for late in-year payments. No changes were made to the dates on which PAYE liabilities fall due, and there is no intention to introduce a system of monthly or quarterly reminders. Employers should therefore ensure that they are clear about these dates.

Legislation: FA 2009, s. 107 and Sch. 56

Tax Reporter: ¶499-100ff.

Employers affected

The penalty regime from 2010–11 applies to all employers and contractors who are obliged to make payments of PAYE to HMRC. HMRC have specifically confirmed that the rules apply even to domestic employers with a single employee (e.g. a nanny). CIS contractors who are not employers will also be subject to the same regime.

Larger employers continue to have an obligation to pay electronically.

Types of payment affected

All of the following are subject to the penalty regime from 2010–11:

- income tax under PAYE;
- primary Class 1 NIC;
- secondary Class 1 NIC;
- Class 1A NIC on benefits;
- Class 1B NIC on PAYE settlement agreements;
- construction industry scheme deductions; and
- student loan deductions.

Employers making payments quarterly are subject to the same rules as those paying monthly.

Tax Reporter: ¶499-130

145-532 PAYE penalties for late payment: calculation

Penalties for late payment of PAYE liabilities work differently for in-year payments of income tax and PAYE on the one hand, and for after-year payments (Class 1A and 1B) on the other.

In-year payments: general rule

The terminology in the legislation is fairly complex as it distinguishes between 'failures' and 'defaults' and states that the first failure does not count as a default. It is really easier, though, to ignore that terminology and to refer simply to the number of occasions in the year on which a PAYE payment is made late. Subject to further penalties if a payment is made six months late, the position may be summarised as follows.

- If there is just one failure in the year to pay on time, no penalty is charged.
- If there are two, three or four such failures, the penalty is 1%.

- This doubles to 2% if there are five to seven failures to pay on time.
- Eight to ten failures will trigger a penalty at 3%.
- 11 or more failures will lead to a penalty of 4%.

In each case, the percentage penalty is applied to the total amount that is late in the tax year, but ignoring the first late payment in the year. Employers are specifically warned that the rules will be applied strictly and that an employer who chooses to 'pay roughly the right amount every month and then make end of year adjustments' will be liable for penalties in relation to any monthly payment that falls short of the amount due.

Example

Suppose, for example, that an employer has a regular monthly liability of £5,000 but pays that amount one week late on five occasions in the year. As there are five failures in the year, the penalty percentage is 2% of the total amount of the late payments, excluding the first. Therefore, the total penalty will be calculated as 2% of £20,000 (rather than of £25,000), so £400.

For 2014–15 and later years the late payment penalty system has been revised, so that it is only the tax owed at each failure stage that attracts the increased percentage.

In-year payments: payment delays exceeding six months

There are additional penalties of 5% of any liability that remains unpaid after six months, with a further 5% after 12 months. The amnesty for the first failure in the year does not apply to these 5% penalties. HMRC are also likely to take separate enforcement action where such lengthy delays occur.

After-year payments

A different regime applies for payments of Class 1A and Class 1B liabilities, as these fall due after the year end rather than on a monthly or quarterly basis.

The penalty for these payments is 5% of the amount that is late if it remains unpaid 30 days from the due date. A further 5% penalty is imposed if the delay exceeds six months, and yet another 5% penalty after 12 months.

Legislation: FA 2009, Sch. 56, para. 6ff.

Tax Reporter: ¶499-140

145-534 PAYE penalties: exceptions to the charge

The regime for penalties is strictly applied. A delay of a single day is enough to count as a failure to pay on time and it is not possible to claim that the underpayment was a simple error. There are, however, certain circumstances in which a penalty will not be imposed.

One error in year

If there is just one failure in the year to pay on time, no penalty will be imposed unless the delay exceeds six months.

Reasonable excuse

No penalty will be imposed where there is a reasonable excuse for the delay in payment.

The HMRC view is that a reasonable excuse will depend on the person's particular circumstances but is likely to be something 'unusual' that could not reasonably have been predicted and that the person was powerless to prevent.

HMRC will not impose a late payment penalty if they accept that the employer had a reasonable excuse. Employers may appeal against a refusal to accept such an excuse. Many cases have been heard by First-tier Tribunals but, despite having sympathy for the taxpayers, HMRC's view has been upheld in the vast majority, given the practical difficulty in establishing a reasonable excuse. Many cases have now been heard by First-tier Tribunals but despite having sympathy for the taxpayers, HMRC's view has been upheld in the vast majority given the practical difficulty of establishing a reasonable excuse.

Business Payment Support Service

In certain circumstances, HMRC may allow employers extra time to meet their tax liabilities. See, generally, 63-550 for details of the scope of that service.

If HMRC have agreed a 'Time to Pay' arrangement under the BPSS then no penalties will be applied from the date the employer approaches HMRC, as long as the employer keeps to the arranged schedule of payments. Penalties will still be charged for earlier times, though those penalties may be included within the agreement.

HMRC will not charge further late payment penalties if they agree to a change in the arrangement.

Double jeopardy

A person is not liable to a penalty under these rules if that person has already been convicted of an offence in respect of the same failure.

Special circumstances

HMRC may reduce a penalty if they deem it appropriate to do so in 'special circumstances'.

Legislation: FA 2009, Sch. 56, para. 9 and 16ff.

Tax Reporter: ¶499-150

145-540 In-year interest and repayment interest

With effect from 2014–15, overpayments and underpayments of PAYE will receive a repayment supplement or will be subject to an interest charge calculated from the normal monthly due date.

Legislation: *Income Tax (Pay As You Earn) Regulations* 2003 (SI 2003/2682), reg. 82

Tax Reporter: ¶494-910

145-542 Remittance to collector

Sums deducted under PAYE are a liability of the employer, who must account to the collector within 14 days of each tax month (or 17 days 'where payment is made by an approved method of electronic communication'), receiving a receipt if desired.

Legislation: *Income Tax (Pay As You Earn) Regulations* 2003 (SI 2003/2682), reg. 69

Tax Reporter: ¶494-510

Failure to pay rebates to employees

If an employer has failed to pay tax rebates due to employees, the employer is liable to pay to HMRC the full amount of tax deducted from other payments, without netting off the rebates.

Legislation: *Income Tax (Pay As You Earn) Regulations* 2003 (SI 2003/2682), reg. 73

Tax Reporter: ¶494-700

145-545 Recovery from employer

Where an employer fails to make a monthly or quarterly remittance, or the Revenue consider that the full liability has not been met, the Revenue may require the employer to make a return of his or her liability for the tax period in question.

HMRC need not require a return. They may give notice to the employer of their estimate of the amount of tax payable under reg. 78. The estimate must reflect the employer's previous payments and be to HMRC's best judgment.

Legislation: *Income Tax (Pay As You Earn) Regulations* 2003 (SI 2003/2682), reg. 77, 84

Tax Reporter: ¶494-820

145-550 Recovery from the employee

An employer is liable for sums due under PAYE whether or not the employer operates it correctly. But, if it appears to the collector that the employer took reasonable care and any errors were made in good faith, then the collector may seek any under-deductions from the employee. In *Equinox Gifted Thoughts Ltd*, it was accepted by HMRC that an error had been made in good faith, but the tribunal confirmed the HMRC view that the employer had failed to take reasonable care to comply with the regulations. The employee had trouble operating a K code and used the same code but without the K prefix, resulting in an underpayment of several hundred pounds.

If it appears to HMRC that the employer did not take proper care and an employee knowingly acquiesces to under-deduction of PAYE, then here too the Revenue may seek recovery from the employee. The employer must have wilfully failed to deduct tax, that is consciously neglected the regulations, and the employee must have had actual knowledge of this.

If it is found as a fact that the employer had not remitted to HMRC any tax in respect of deductions from an individual's earnings, the onus is on the employee to show that (on the balance of probabilities) the tax had in fact been deducted. In *Moran v R & C Commrs*, where the employee failed to show that tax had been deducted, he was assessed to tax to recover the amounts due and the assessments were upheld.

SI 2003/2682, reg. 185 and 188 require there, in particular cases, to be an adjustment to give the taxpayer credit for tax the employer should have but failed to deduct. Where the employer fails to operate PAYE correctly, HMRC can only look to the employer for the under-payment but it is for the taxpayer to show that the assessment levied on him should be amended to include the relevant credit. Accordingly, the taxpayer has to establish that the company did not operate PAYE correctly. In *Burton*, the employee failed to demonstrate that the company had not operated PAYE correctly.

Legislation: *Income Tax (Pay As You Earn) Regulations* 2003 (SI 2003/2682), reg. 72, 84

Cases: *Moran v R & C Commrs* (2008) Sp C 681; *Equinox Gifted Thoughts Ltd* [2010] TC 00478; *Burton* [2010] TC 00263

Tax Reporter: ¶494-530

145-560 HMRC determination

A power is available to HMRC to deal with employers who fail to operate PAYE. It is most often used when HMRC become aware of a private company where a director/shareholder has drawn remuneration gross.

HMRC may determine tax due from an employer if it appears to them that tax has not been remitted to them in circumstances where PAYE should have been operated. The determination must be to the best of their judgment and notice of it must be given to the employer.

The determination may be disputed by the employer by way of an appeal to the tax tribunal, which will hear the appeals and in the same way as appeals against assessments.

Legislation: *Income Tax (Pay As You Earn) Regulations* 2003 (SI 2003/2682), reg. 80

Tax Reporter: ¶494-840

145-570 Senior accounting officers

Background and overview

In the 2009 Budget, the Chancellor made a surprise announcement that senior accounting officers of large companies would be held personally responsible for the adequacy of their company's tax accounting arrangements.

Thus, a senior accounting officer of a qualifying company is obliged to ensure that the company establishes and maintains appropriate tax accounting arrangements, and to provide a certificate to HMRC indicating whether or not this was done for each financial year. Qualifying companies are obliged to provide details of their senior accounting officer to HMRC.

Failure to comply with these requirements will make the senior accounting officer and/or the company liable to a penalty.

PAYE

The main duty of a senior accounting officer is to 'take reasonable steps to ensure that the company establishes and maintains appropriate tax accounting arrangements'. The term 'appropriate tax accounting arrangements' is defined as meaning: 'accounting arrangements that enable the company's relevant liabilities to be calculated accurately in all material respects'. The term 'relevant liabilities' is in turn defined to include 'amounts for which the company is accountable under PAYE regulations'. The scope of this may be narrower than would first be thought. HMRC have issued extensive guidelines on the regulations and, in respect of this item, have commented as follows:

> 'PAYE in the context of the SAO legislation refers to the Income Tax (Pay As You Earn) Regulations 2003/2682. These regulations are given effect in primary legislation by section 684 Income Tax (Earnings and Pensions) Act 2003. "PAYE" does not cover other employer responsibilities administered by HMRC such as student loans, national minimum wage and National Insurance Contributions. These will therefore be excluded.'

Legislation: FA 2009, Sch. 46

Tax Reporter: ¶493-090

Residence issues

146-000 Employees resident in the UK

General principle

Most people who are taxed in the UK on their employment income are not only resident but also domiciled in the UK. Until April 2008 such employees formed a discrete group for tax purposes. From that date, however, the tax legislation carves up the rules on a different basis. As such, ITEPA 2003, Pt. 2, Ch. 4 is now entitled 'Taxable earnings: UK resident employees'.

Employees resident in the UK are in principle taxed on the receipts basis: the full amount of any general earnings which are received in a tax year is an amount of taxable earnings from employment in that year. The operative term is 'received', not 'received in the UK'; it follows that if the employee is resident in the UK, general earnings are taxable whether or not they arise in the UK and regardless of whether they are received in the UK.

The term 'taxable earnings' is used to describe the full amount of 'general earnings' received by the employee in the tax year from the employment in question, whether or not the employment is still held when the earnings are received.

Crucially, however, the above is subject to the remittance basis rules where such rules take precedence: see below.

Legislation: ITEPA 2003, s. 14ff.

Tax Reporter: ¶406-000

Remittance basis

The legislation at ITEPA 2003, s. 14–19 does not explicitly state that the rules are subject to any remittance basis issues. However, this effect is achieved elsewhere. Specifically, s. 22(7) and 26(6) both make it clear that general earnings to which their respective sections relate are only taxed under s. 15(1) to the extent that they do not fall within (respectively) s. 22(1) or 26(1).

Earnings can only fall within those other sections if the individual is 'not domiciled' in the UK, and if certain other conditions are met. See 146-150.

Legislation: ITEPA 2003, s. 15ff.

Tax Reporter: ¶406-200ff.

146-050 The territorial extent of the UK

For tax purposes generally the UK includes territorial waters, the breadth of which is 12 nautical miles. However, for certain tax purposes the UK includes designated areas of the continental shelf. Earnings from exploration or exploitation activities in connection with the oil industry, which are carried on in these designated areas, are treated as though the activities were carried on in the UK. Non-UK resident companies operating in such areas may be required to operate UK PAYE.

Legislation: *Territorial Sea Act* 1987, s. 1; ITEPA 2003, s. 41; ITA 2007, s. 1013; CTA 2010, s. 1170

Tax Reporter: ¶406-500

146-100 Employee resident but not domiciled in the UK

Since 6 April 2008, an individual who is resident in the UK has paid tax on earnings on the basis described at 146-000 unless he or she is not domiciled in the UK *and* the remittance basis rules apply (see, generally,

146-150). This is the effect of applying ITEPA 2003, s. 15, 22(7) and 26(6). Broadly, s. 15 applies the general rule but s. 22(7) and 26(6) say that the general rule only applies to earnings that are not taxed under different provisions.

Legislation: ITEPA 2003, s. 25, 28

Tax Reporter: ¶406-000ff.

146-130 Incidental duties

Where the employment is one which in substance falls to be performed outside the UK, duties performed inside the UK which are incidental to duties performed abroad are treated as if they were themselves performed abroad. Whether duties performed in the UK are incidental duties is a question of fact. It is the nature of the duties which is the most significant factor, but the time spent on such duties is also a factor to be taken into account.

HMRC have provided extensive guidance on residence tax issues in leaflet HMRC6: Residence, Domicile and the Remittance Basis. Paragraph 10.6 contains the following guidance in relation to incidental duties:

> 'Whether or not duties performed in the UK are incidental to an overseas employment will always depend on the circumstances of each particular case. Any decision has to be based on the work carried out in the UK – not the amount of time spent on it. But if you spend more than 91 days working in the UK in a tax year the work **will not** be incidental as it is reasonable to say that someone who spends such an extended period working in the UK is actually working here rather than undertaking duties which are incidental to an overseas employment.
>
> If the work you perform in the UK is the same or is of similar importance to the work that you do abroad, it will **not be** incidental. You will have to show that there is a purpose to the work you did in the UK which enabled you to do your normal work abroad and which you could only do in the UK.'

The guidance goes on to give the following examples:

'***Incidental work***

- time spent in the UK by an overseas representative of a UK company to make reports or receive fresh instructions.
- time spent training in the UK by an overseas employee which does not exceed 91 days in the tax year and provided no productive work is carried out in the UK by the trainee during that time.

Non incidental work

- time spent in the UK as part of the duties of a member of the crew of a ship or aircraft.

- attendance at director's meetings in the UK by a director of the company who normally works abroad.'

Legislation: ITEPA 2003, s. 39

Tax Reporter: ¶406-160

146-150 Foreign earnings: remittance basis

Overview

Major changes were made from April 2008 to the rules taxing overseas income. Individuals aged 18 or over, who are not domiciled in the UK, may in certain circumstances claim to be taxed on a remittance basis, normally in return for an annual payment of £30,000. Subject to de minimis provisions, the individual needs to make a formal claim for the remittance basis to apply. See, generally, 172-050ff.

Employee not domiciled in the UK

For an employee who is not domiciled in the UK, 'chargeable overseas earnings' are taxable on the remittance basis.

Chargeable overseas earnings are calculated by identifying the full amount of overseas earnings, subtracting the deductions listed in ITEPA 2003, s. 23(3), and applying any limit imposed by ITEPA 2003, s. 24.

The label 'overseas earnings' is used to describe earnings where the following conditions are met:

- ITA 2007, s. 809B, 809D or 809E (remittance basis) applies to the employee for that year;
- the earnings are for a year in which the employee is resident but not domiciled, in the UK and who does not fall within overseas workday relief;
- they are from an employment with a 'foreign employer' (see below); and
- the duties are all performed outside the UK.

Legislation: ITEPA 2003, s. 22, 23

Tax Reporter: ¶406-220

Foreign employer

A foreign employer is defined as an individual, partnership or body of persons resident outside, and not resident in, the UK.

Legislation: ITEPA 2003, s. 721

146-200 Employees not resident in the UK

General earnings for a tax year in which the employee is not resident in the UK are charged on the receipts basis if they are:

- general earnings in respect of duties performed in the UK; or
- general earnings from overseas Crown employment subject to UK tax, as defined (see 146-250).

This applies whether the earnings are for that year or for some other tax year, and whether or not the employment is held at the time when the earnings are received.

By implication, an employee who is not resident in the UK in a tax year is not subject to income tax on foreign earnings, i.e. general earnings which do not fall into either of the categories listed above. This holds true whether the employee is domiciled in the UK or not.

As regards the treatment of employees resident in the UK for just part of the tax year, HMRC generally (but conditionally) operate a concession whereby liability to UK tax is computed only by reference to the period of residence in the UK during the year in question. See 170-600ff.

For commentary on the double taxation aspects of salaries and wages, see 174-550.

Legislation: ITEPA 2003, s. 27–28

Other Material: ESC A11

Tax Reporter: ¶406-400

146-210 Overseas workday relief

Requirement of three year period of non-residence

Prior to 2013–14 an individual who was resident but not ordinarily UK resident could apply the remittance basis in respect of overseas earnings from an employment, being earnings for duties performed outside the UK. With the abolition of the concept of ordinary residence, changes have been made to the law to continue this relief and which is now described as 'overseas workday relief'. As before, general earnings from overseas Crown employments subject to UK tax are excluded from this relief.

To be eligible, there is a requirement for the employee to meet one of the following requirements:

- be non-UK resident for the previous three tax years;
- be UK resident for the previous tax year but non-UK resident for the three tax years before that;
- be UK resident for the previous two tax years but non-UK resident for the three years before that;
- be non-UK resident for the previous tax year, UK resident for the tax year before that and non-UK resident for the three tax years before that.

The broad effect of this is that an individual coming to the UK to work will have three years to benefit from this basis, which can include a split year.

There are transitional provisions that can apply where an individual is not UK resident for the tax year 2009–10 but is resident there for 2012–13 and is not ordinarily resident on 5 April 2013. In that instance, the relief will continue as if the changes had not been made for years up to 2015–16 at the latest, continuing to apply the concept of ordinary residence.

Having decided that by virtue of the above the remittance basis can apply to a given year, it is necessary to consider the quantum of the duties performed outside the UK and then apply the remittance basis to those earnings. Previously, this was dealt with by Statement of Practice (SP) 1/09 but legislation has now been enacted in FA 2013.

A new ITEPA 2013, s. 41ZA provides that the extent to which general earnings are in respect of duties performed in the UK is to be determined on a just and reasonable basis. Subject to this overriding requirement, in most cases it could be expected that HMRC would accept time apportionment, based on the number of days worked abroad and in the UK.

As far as the remittance basis is concerned there are now some complex provisions in ITA 2007, s. 809RA–809RD added by FA 2013, which apply to 2013–14 and subsequent tax years. These contain a relaxation of the normal remittance basis rule where it is necessary to look at each particular transfer out of an overseas account. Provided certain conditions are met, transfers to the UK and overseas are deemed to be made at the end of the tax year, treating the UK transfers as having been made first in time. Applying the usual mixed fund rules, employment income, other than relevant foreign earnings, is deemed to have been remitted first to the UK and then the foreign earnings to which the remittance basis applies. In effect, this means that if only the UK element of the earnings is remitted to the UK that is fully taxable under normal rules but there is no remittance of any part of the non-UK duties. Any excess that is brought to the UK will be treated as a remittance, each transfer from the account being treated as containing the proportion which the offshore transfers bears to the total of the UK and offshore transfers. HMRC have indicated that an individual using SP 1/09 before 6 April 2013 can continue to do so.

For this treatment to apply, the taxpayer must give notice to HMRC to nominate an overseas account to be a qualifying account. A qualifying date must be specified, being the first date on which earnings of more than £10 are paid into that account. The notice must be given by 31 January following the tax year in which the qualifying date falls although HMRC have the discretion to allow a later date. A nomination can be withdrawn within the same timescale.

The account must be an ordinary bank account held by and for the benefit of the individual, whether alone or jointly with others and cannot have a credit balance of more than £10 before the qualifying date. There are then further requirements as to the type of sums that can be deposited in the account so that broadly only general earnings of the individual and specific employment income falling within ITEPA 2003, Pt. 6, 7 or 7A, such as involving non-approved pension schemes, termination payments, securities employment income and income provided through third parties. The interest on the account can also be included as can the proceeds from the sale of securities following the exercise of an option where the disposal is at the same time or as soon as reasonably practicable thereafter. The earnings and other amounts must be derived from the employment that is eligible for overseas workday relief. No other earnings etc can be paid into the account, otherwise the special mixed fund rules will not apply. If a prohibited amount is paid into the account this can be remedied provided this is within 30 days from the day on which the individual became or ought reasonably to have become aware of the breach. No more than two breach reversals are allowed in any 12-month period.

Legislation: ITEPA 2003, s. 26, 26A; ITA 2007, s. 809RA

146-250 Crown servants

Crown servants whose duties are of a public nature and whose earnings are paid out of the public revenue of the UK or Northern Ireland are regarded as carrying out their employment in the UK regardless of where the duties are actually performed.

Allowances given to Crown servants representing compensation for the extra cost of living abroad in order to perform their duties are not regarded as income and are therefore not taxable. To qualify for exemption such allowances must be certified by the Treasury as representing such compensation.

Legislation: ITEPA 2003, s. 28, 299

Tax Reporter: ¶486-000

146-300 Commonwealth agents – general and foreign consular staff, etc.

An exemption from income tax applies to Commonwealth agents-general who are resident in the UK, as well as to members of their personal staff employed in the UK; also exempt are official agents for countries included in the *British Nationality Act* 1981, Sch. 3, the Republic of Ireland, or any self-governing colony.

Consuls and official agents for any foreign state are exempt from tax on their income from employment. Consular officers and employees are generally not liable to tax on employment income if they are nationals of the foreign state.

Tax is not charged on certain education allowances payable to officers in the public service of certain overseas territories where, as part of an agreement under the Overseas Service Aid Scheme, the UK Government has undertaken to exempt such allowances from UK tax.

Legislation: ITEPA 2003, s. 300ff.; ITA 2007, s. 841

146-350 Visiting forces

The forces of any country designated by an Order in Council are exempt from income tax on earnings paid to them by the Government of their country; a member of such forces, in the UK in that capacity, retains his normal residence and domicile.

Legislation: ITEPA 2003, s. 303

146-400 Seafarers

Seafarers are eligible for a 100% deduction from their employment earnings provided they attain the required qualifying period of 365 days, subject to days spent in the UK (i.e. not more than 183 consecutive days and not more than one half of the overall period). Up to 5 April 2011, the special tax deduction for seafarers applies only if the claimant is ordinarily resident in the UK. After that date, the Seafarers' Earnings Deduction will be extended to EU and EEA resident seafarers to the extent that their seafarer earnings are liable to UK income tax. This is to ensure that the legislation is compatible with EU treaty rules.

Those employed on offshore installations for oil or gas exploration or extraction do not qualify for the relief. Employment 'as a seafarer' now means an employment consisting of performing duties on a ship (or of such duties and others incidental to them).

The distinction between a ship and an offshore installation was again considered in the case of *Langley v R & C Commrs*. A vessel that was intended to operate under its own power could not rank as a ship until it was capable of doing so. In this case, that meant that it was not a ship until its thrusters had been installed.

To count as an offshore installation, a structure must be standing or stationed in waters (or on the foreshore or certain other land). The special commissioner in *Torr v R & C Commrs* determined that it would be absurd to suggest that a ship could only be stationed if it was either secured by anchors or hawsers. A ship could clearly be stationed in deep water. While the context in which the word 'stationed' was used was as an alternative to 'standing', the word clearly envisaged the ship being substantially stationery. When 'dynamically positioned', the vessel in question was stationed. As such, it was an offshore installation, and therefore not a ship for the purposes of these rules, and tax relief was denied.

The position was further complicated by the decision in *Spowage v R & C Commrs*. Taxpayers working on offshore semi-submersible units were entitled to a foreign earnings deduction as the vessels were excepted from being offshore installations when they ceased to operate as 'flotels' and instead began to operate as support vessels for maintenance and construction work. Following that decision, HMRC have accepted that 'it is no longer possible to class a vessel as either an offshore installation or as a ship, based solely on the vessel type or description'. Further HMRC comment on the *Spowage* decision may be found at EIM33112.

Employees who enter an amount of earnings that attract seafarers' earnings deduction in the employment pages of their personal tax return must also enter the names of the ships on which they have performed employment duties (HMRC Brief 33/07).

Legislation: ITEPA 2003, s. 378, 384; ITA 2007, s. 1001; CTA 2010, s. 1132

Cases: *Clark (HMIT) v Perks; Macleod (HMIT) v Perks; Guild (HMIT) v Newrick* [2001] BTC 336; *Palmer v R & C Commrs* [2007] BTC 126; *Langley v R & C Commrs* (2007) Sp C 642; *Torr v R & C Commrs* (2008) Sp C 679; *Spowage v R & C Commrs* [2009] TC 00110

Other Material: *Employment Income Manual* at EIM33112

Tax Reporter: ¶488-500

Employee share schemes

147-000 Introduction to share incentives

There are a variety of employee share schemes, some involving an immediate acquisition of shares, others involving the grant of options to acquire shares at a later date.

Employee share ownership is generally encouraged, with tax and National Insurance advantages available where shares or share options are issued or granted within the terms of a HMRC-approved scheme.

If shares are issued at less than market value, or otherwise on favourable terms, to a director or employee, the benefit may be taxed under the general charge on earnings provisions as a non-cash emolument. The charge may not arise in the case of allocations of shares to employees:

- in priority to the public (see 147-150); or
- in accordance with an approved scheme (see 148-050).

The layout of ITEPA 2003, Pt. 7, entitled 'Employment Income: Income and Exemptions Relating to Securities', is as follows:

(1) Chapter 1 provides an introduction, definitions and reporting requirements (147-050);

(2) Chapters 2–5 contain details of the income tax charges arising on unapproved securities options under the following headings:
- Restricted securities (147-250);
- Convertible securities (147-350);
- Securities with artificially depressed market value (147-450);
- Securities with artificially enhanced market value (147-600);
- Securities acquired for less than market value (147-700);
- Securities disposed of for more than market value (147-800);
- Post-acquisition benefits from securities (147-850);
- Shares in research institution spin-out companies (147-900); and
- Securities options (147-950).

(3) Chapters 6–9 deal with the plans and schemes under which employees and directors may be offered shares or share options on tax-advantageous terms; and

(4) Chapter 10 deals with exemptions from income tax where employees or directors benefit from an allocation of shares as part of a genuine offer to the public, and Ch. 11 contains various supplementary provisions.

The legislation sets out and clarifies a number of ground rules to be used in calculating any charge to income tax arising. Broadly, the rules apply to any person who has acquired either securities or an interest in securities by reason of an employment of any person. This includes situations where the securities are acquired before the employment starts or after it finishes. A security (or interest) is deemed to be made available by a person's employer where it is made available by reason of employment unless the employer is an individual and is providing the security (or interest) for purely domestic, personal or family reasons.

No charge to tax arises where:

- securities (or interests) are disposed of to someone who is not an 'associated person' within ITEPA 2003, s. 421C;
- the employee dies; or
- seven years have elapsed since the employee ceased employment with the employer who made the right or opportunity available, the company which issued the securities, or any person associated with the employer or the issuer.

Anti-avoidance

The broad intention of the legislation is that all of the value received by way of remuneration in the form of shares or other securities is subject to income tax and NICs at an appropriate time. The rules provide some flexibility in respect of the timing of the charges. For example, the employer and employee can jointly elect to pay tax and National Insurance on a higher proportion when the shares are acquired, leaving future commercial growth in value of the shares in the capital gains tax regime (see 147-950). Various anti-avoidance provisions apply, however. *Finance Act* 2006 sought to strengthen the anti-avoidance provisions concerning employment-related securities further by making it clear that *all* options are within the definition of securities.

Legislation: ITEPA 2003, s. 421B

Other Material: HMRC *Employment Related Securities Manual* ERSM10000

Tax Reporter: ¶464-000

147-010 Employee shareholder shares (pre-23 November 2016)

Between 1 September 2013 and its withdrawal for shares issued after 23 November 2016, it was possible to issue shares under the employer shareholder provisions. This allowed a company to issue tax favoured shares to an employee in return for the surrender of certain employment rights. For shares issued prior to 16 March 2016, then any capital gain on the subsequent sale of the shares would be completely tax free to the extent the market value of the shares at the date of issue was below £50,000. For shares issued subsequent to that date, the maximum tax free capital gain was limited to £100,000.

However, for income tax purposes, there was no general exemption except that an employee would be treated as having 'paid' £2,000 for the shares in lieu of the surrender of employment rights. Thus, if an employee received shares worth £2,000, there was no employment income tax charge. However, if the shares were worth £10,000, then the employee would be subject to income tax on the benefit as earnings from the employment of £8,000.

The deemed payment of £2,000 was not available where the employee had a material interest in the employee company or a relevant parent undertaking or if the employee was connected with an individual who has such an interest. This exclusion also applied if such interests had been held in the period of one year ending with the date of acquisition of the shares. The definition of material for this purpose was, broadly, holding voting rights of at least 25%, which included the rights of connected persons. An entitlement to acquire rights that would give the acquirer a material interest, or arrangements to obtain a material interest were also taken into account for this purpose.

If shares are purchased back by the company from an individual who has acquired shares in this manner there is no income tax charge on a distribution if at the time of the disposal the individual is not an employee or office holder in relation to the employer company or associated company.

Legislation: ITEPA 2003, s. 226A–226D; ITTOIA 2005, s. 385A (This provision, introduced by FA 2013, is effective from 1 September 2013. Withdrawn with effect from 23 November 2016 (FA 2017, s. 12).)

147-020 HMRC guidance

HMRC guidance

Extensive HMRC guidance is available in relation to share schemes and appropriate references are made throughout this chapter. See, in particular, the current *Employment Related Securities Manual* and the (older) *Share Scheme Manual*. It is understood that material from the latter is gradually being updated and transferred to the former.

A list of annual return forms, with downloadable versions and explanatory notes as appropriate, may be found at www.hmrc.gov.uk/shareschemes/ann-app-schemes.htm.

For a lengthy (131 page) HMRC research report evaluating tax-advantaged all-employee share schemes, see www.hmrc.gov.uk/research/report59-main.pdf.

HMRC also publish extensive online guidance in relation to the various share schemes, including the following:

- *Approved Company Share Option Plans: Guidance for employers*; www.hmrc.gov.uk/shareschemes/csop_general.htm;
- *Approved Company Share Option: Plans Guidance for employees*: www.hmrc.gov.uk/shareschemes/csop_general_ees.htm;
- *Share Incentive Plans — A Guide for employees*: www.hmrc.gov.uk/shareschemes/sip-info-employees.rtf; and
- *Share Incentive Plans Guidance for Employers and Advisers*: www.hmrc.gov.uk/shareschemes/share_incentive/sip-guide-employers-advisors.pdf.

147-050 Definitions

Meaning of 'securities'

The legislation in ITEPA 2003, Pt. 7 covers both shares and all securities. 'Securities' includes:

- shares in any body corporate (wherever incorporated) or in any unincorporated body constituted under the law of a country or territory outside the UK;
- debentures, debenture stock, loan stock, bonds, certificates of deposit and other instruments creating or acknowledging indebtedness;
- warrants and other instruments entitling their holders to subscribe for securities (whether or not in existence or identifiable);
- certificates and other instruments conferring rights in respect of securities held by persons other than the persons on whom the rights are conferred and the transfer of which may be effected without the consent of those persons;
- units in a collective investment scheme;
- options and futures; and
- rights under contracts for differences or contracts similar to contracts for differences.

A significant difference introduced by the *Finance Act* 2003 is that government loan stocks, or gilts and now included under these provisions.

The following are not 'securities' for the purposes of ITEPA 2003, Pt. 7:

- cheques and other bills of exchange, bankers' drafts and letters of credit (other than bills of exchange accepted by a banker);
- money and statements showing balances on a current, deposit or savings account;
- leases and other dispositions of property and heritable securities;
- rights under contracts of insurance (within the meaning of the *Financial Services and Markets Act 2000 (Regulated Activities) Order* 2001); and
- securities options.

The Treasury has the power to amend and add to the definition given for 'securities'.

Numerous definitions are given in the legislation in relation to items that do, or do not, qualify as securities.

Legislation: ITEPA 2003, s. 420, 421A–421L

Tax Reporter: ¶555-000

147-100 Replacement and additional securities and changes in interests

Specific provisions deal with company reorganisations, rights issues and bonus securities, maintaining the link with the original employment-related securities. The provisions apply when either:

- the employment-related securities are replaced with other securities (as in a company reorganisation); or
- the additional securities are acquired by reason of the holding of employment-related securities (as with bonus shares or a rights issue).

Any replacement or additional securities are treated as though they were acquired by reason of the same right or opportunity as the original securities. As a result they are subject to the same tax treatment (i.e. Ch. 5 – securities options; see 147-950) as would have been the case if they had been acquired directly by reason of an employment.

Legislation: ITEPA 2003, s. 421D

Tax Reporter: ¶472-280

147-150 Exclusions

The legislation provides for the following exclusions.

Residence

For periods up to 5 April 2015, some of the rules relating to securities do not apply if at the time the securities were acquired, earnings from the employment would not have been general earnings for a year for which the employee was resident and ordinarily resident in the UK.

Legislation: ITEPA 2003, s. 421E

Tax Reporter: ¶480-540

Internationally mobile employees post 5 April 2015

The basis of taxation of internationally mobile employees from 5 April 2015 is greatly simplified and put on a statutory footing. These rules apply to all chargeable events relating to employment related securities arising after 5 April 2015, irrespective of the date of issue or grant. In effect, subject to the override of any specific double tax agreement, any UK tax liability will be calculated by reference to an individual's UK residence and workdays during the period over which the award was earned. If a simple time apportionment gives an unreasonable result, then it should be substituted by an apportionment on a 'just and reasonable' basis.

Where an individual is taxed on a remittance basis and remits foreign securities income, then a proportion of that income may be taxable in the UK regardless of whether he or she is still employed by the issuing company at the time of the remittance. The taxable proportion will be apportioned on a just and reasonable basis between duties performed in the UK and duties performed outside of the UK.

Legislation: ITEPA 2003, Pt. 2, Ch. 5B

Public offers

Public offers, where shareholders are receiving similar benefits are excluded from the scope of some of the provisions. The term 'public offer' includes priority share allocations for employees. Benefits from priority allocation for employees are disregarded.

Legislation: ITEPA 2003, s. 421F

Tax Reporter: ¶472-360

147-200 Duty to provide information

HMRC have the power to require a return from employers and others of employee benefits associated with securities. Broadly, the legislation specifies that a 'responsible person' is required to give details of 'reportable events' to HMRC in writing, using form 42, before the 7 July of the tax year following that in which the reportable event occurred. A 'responsible person' is the employer, host employer (employee of non-UK employer (ITEPA 2003, s. 689)), person from whom the securities were obtained, or the issuer of securities.

HMRC may serve a notice on any person to provide details of reportable events or to state that no such event has taken place. The person receiving such a notice must be given not less than 30 days in which to respond.

'Reportable events' are as follows:

- acquisition of securities or securities option;
- chargeable events affecting restricted securities;
- chargeable events affecting convertible securities;
- events where artificial enhancement of value of securities;
- discharge of notional loan in relation to securities (partly-paid securities);
- disposal of securities for more than market value (stop loss);
- receipt of benefit arising from a security;
- assignment or release of securities option; and
- compensation or other benefit on securities option.

Legislation: ITEPA 2003, s. 421K

Tax Reporter: ¶472-380

147-250 Restricted securities

Overview

Where employees acquire securities (or an interest in securities) by reason of their employment, their value (less anything paid for them) will generally be taxable as employment income. If the securities have restrictions or conditions attached to them, including risk of forfeiture, then those restrictions will affect the value and, generally, the securities will be worth less than they would be without those restrictions (this depression in value is often referred to as a discount). Broadly, the employee is charged to income tax and NIC when additional value in a security is accessed as a result of lifting a restriction. Each restriction placed on securities will have a proportionate effect on its market value. Each time a restriction is lifted or varied, there will be a charge based on the market value of the discount relating to that restriction which represents the proportion of the securities' value that was not taxed on acquisition.

The charge is calculated using a formula. In the simplest case (where there is only one restriction) the charge is equal to the restriction's effect on the market value of the securities at the time it is lifted. The result is that the employee is taxed on the whole share in two stages – an amount at acquisition relating to the unrestricted proportion of the securities and the balance when the restriction is lifted. By focusing on proportions of the securities' market value at each event, the legislation ensures that capital growth on previously taxed proportions is not included in the computation of the income gain.

Numerous restrictions and exceptions apply.

Legislation: ITEPA 2003, s. 422ff.

Tax Reporter: ¶474-500

Elections

Where the charge on acquisition of the securities is deferred there may be a higher charge on the future chargeable event. An employee may, therefore, prefer to pay some tax on acquisition to limit the later charge. The employee and employer may elect jointly (and irrevocably) that the exemption in ITEPA 2003, s. 425(2) is disapplied. Such an election must be in a form approved by HMRC and be made within 14 days of the acquisition.

Legislation: ITEPA 2003, s. 425(3)

Tax Reporter: ¶474-900

Election for outstanding restrictions to be ignored

A joint election may be made for outstanding restrictions to be ignored in computing the charge on the employee, and PAYE and NIC payable by employer. Once such an election has been made the whole of any future growth in the value of the securities will be outside the scope of the charges on restricted securities. The election must be made in a form approved by HMRC. The time limit for making an election is within 14 days of the chargeable event.

The employee and employer may also elect jointly and irrevocably that when restricted securities are acquired one or more of the restrictions should be disregarded in computing the charge. The employee and employer may disregard one or more specified conditions. The market value on acquisition will then not be reduced by those restrictions and there will be a corresponding reduction in the future charge. The election is implemented by agreement between the employer and the employee and is irrevocable. It is not necessary to notify HMRC at the time the election is made, and no formal approval is required. The election must be in a form approved by HMRC and the time limit for making it is within 14 days of the chargeable event.

Legislation: ITEPA 2003, s. 430, 431

Tax Reporter: ¶474-960

147-300 Charge on chargeable event (restricted securities)

Where a chargeable event occurs, the taxable amount arising is treated as employment income of the employee for the 'relevant tax year' (i.e. the tax year in which the chargeable event occurs). A chargeable event occurs in the following circumstances:

- on the lifting of all restrictions from the securities, before they have been disposed of to an unconnected person;
- on variation (including the removal) of any of the restrictions, before they have been disposed of to an unconnected person; and
- on the disposal of the securities to an unconnected person, before all the restrictions have been lifted.

Complex formulae are provided to calculate the amount of the tax charge.

Legislation: ITEPA 2003, s. 427

Tax Reporter: ¶476-240

147-350 Convertible securities

Overview

Prior to 1 September 2003, the legislation provided for convertible shares acquired by reason of employment (on the market value of the convertible share at that time) to be charged to tax. This did not reflect the reality of the employee acquiring a security plus a right to convert that security into another security. As a result the legislation did not tax the right amount of value at the right time. Revised legislation came into force from 1 September 2003 which is designed to rectify this. It does so by treating the convertible security as if it were two assets – the security itself, ignoring the right to convert, and a right to acquire another security (similar to a securities option). On the acquisition of convertible securities tax is charged on what would be the market value if they were not convertible. Later, on conversion, the employee is taxed as if an employment-related securities option had been exercised with the market value of the convertible securities given up being treated as consideration given for the new securities acquired. The rules for computing this charge are similar to those relating to employment-related securities options in Ch. 5 ('Securities Options': see 147-950).

To fall within the convertible securities legislation, the securities have to be capable of conversion either because the right to convert is automatically built into the share (as it would be, for example, if the articles of association of the issuing company specified that the shares carried such a right), or is provided for specifically in the event that certain circumstances arise, or do not arise (for example, where the employer specifies that the shares can only be converted after three years).

Companies can set up schemes under which an employee receives shares of a class with a low value which can later be converted into higher-value shares. The charge does not apply if most of the shares of the class converting are held by persons who are not employees or directors (e.g. on a conversion resulting from a company reconstruction).

Legislation: ITEPA 2003, s. 436

Tax Reporter: ¶475-500ff.

147-400 Charge on chargeable event (convertible securities)

The rules apply to employment-related securities and taxable amounts arising are treated as employment income of the employee for the relevant tax year (i.e. the tax year in which the chargeable event occurs).

Legislation: ITEPA 2003, s. 438

Tax Reporter: ¶475-560

Chargeable events

There are four circumstances that are chargeable events in relation to employment-related securities, or interest in them. These are:

(1) the conversion of the securities, provided that an 'associated person' (see 147-050) has a beneficial interest in those securities before the conversion occurs and in the securities into which they are converted;

(2) the disposal for consideration of the securities by an associated person to anyone who is not an associated person, at a time when the securities carry a conversion right;

(3) the release for consideration of the conversion right where an associated person has a beneficial interest in the securities; and

(4) the receipt by an associated person of a benefit in money or money's worth in respect of the entitlement. This could be, for example, compensation for the loss of the entitlement.

Statutory formulae are provided to calculate the amount of the tax charge.

Legislation: ITEPA 2003, s. 439(3)

Tax Reporter: ¶475-560

Amount of consideration given for entitlement to convert

The legislation is designed to ensure that relief is given on the conversion of shares for any amount of consideration paid for the conversion right that was not relieved against a gain charged on acquisition. For example, an employee pays £20 for a convertible share, which is worth £10 if the value of the conversion is excluded. Subsequently the shares are converted into shares worth £100. The charge on acquisition is nil (£10–£20). On conversion, the employee is charged on £90 (£100, less the £10 unrelieved on acquisition).

Legislation: ITEPA 2003, s. 442, 443

Tax Reporter: ¶475-560

147-450 Securities with artificially depressed market value

Overview

If the value of employment-related securities is depressed by means of one or more non-commercial transactions, then that reduction in value is taxed on the employee accordingly. The rules work in three ways.

(1) There is a charge at the time of acquisition on the effect of artificial reductions in value. This charge is on the proportion of the employment-related securities being taxed at that time.

(2) The market values to be used in the various formulae relating to restricted and convertible securities (see 147-250 and 147-400) are adjusted to reverse the effect on actual market values of such transactions when chargeable events occur. This would include the sale of such employment-related securities while restrictions still apply or the retention of such securities for more than five years without the restrictions being lifted or varied.

(3) If there would not otherwise be a charge in respect of restricted securities, a charge will arise at 5 April following the date of acquisition, as if there had been a lifting of restrictions.

Legislation: *Finance Act 2003, Sch. 22, Para. 3(1) (Appointed Day) Order* 2003 (SI 2003/1997)

Tax Reporter: ¶476-200

147-500 Charge on acquisition

The provisions apply where the market value of employment-related securities at the time of acquisition has been reduced by at least 10% as a result of things done otherwise than for genuine commercial purposes within a period of seven years ending with the date of acquisition. Any subsequent gain arising will be treated as employment income of the employee for the tax year in which the acquisition occurs.

Legislation: ITEPA 2003, s. 425(2), 446B(1)

Tax Reporter: ¶476-220

Amount of charge

The formula for computing the charge arising is as follows:

$$FMV - MV$$

where:

FMV (full market value) is the market value disregarding the effect of anything done within the terms of s. 44B(1) above which reduced that value; and

MV is the actual market value of securities at the time they were acquired. If any consideration is given for the securities and the consideration is greater than market value, that figure is used in the formula instead.

Restricted and convertible securities

Certain post-acquisition charges are imposed where restricted or convertible securities are involved. If the securities are restricted securities, FMV in the formula above will be based on the unrestricted value. There is no subsequent charge under ITEPA 2003, s. 426 or 431 on the securities. The effect on the value of any conversion right in relation to convertible securities is to be disregarded when applying the formula under ITEPA 2003, s. 446C above.

Legislation: ITEPA 2003, s. 446D(1), 446D(2)

Tax Reporter: ¶476-240

Charge on restricted securities

A post-acquisition adjustment of a charge on restricted securities is applied by increasing the market value by the amount of any depreciatory transactions. The provision applies where the value of restricted securities is reduced at the time of a chargeable event or at 5 April. The value of securities is reduced where there have been things done other than for genuine commercial purposes that have reduced the value by at least 10%. Where the charge on restricted securities arises, the values used in the formula in s. 428 will be the values that the securities would have had if the non-commercial things had not been done.

Legislation: ITEPA 2003, s. 446E

Tax Reporter: ¶476-240

147-550 Adjustments

Various adjustments may need to be made. For example, special rules apply where there has been a reduction in the value of the securities and there is a charge on conditional securities under ITEPA 2003, s. 427. In certain circumstances, the relief for an excess of consideration given for acquiring convertible securities over the value of the security (ignoring the right of conversion) may be adjusted. And a conversion charge applies where the market value of securities into which employment-related securities convert is artificially low on conversion.

Legislation: ITEPA 2003, s. 446G

Tax Reporter: ¶476-260ff.

147-600 Securities with artificially enhanced market value

Overview

If the value of employment-related securities is enhanced by means of non-commercial transaction(s) during any tax year, then that appreciation in value is taxed on the employee at the earlier time of the disposal of the employment-related securities or 5 April.

If the market value of employment-related securities is increased by things done otherwise than for genuine commercial reason a tax charge will arise in accordance with a statutory formula. This includes:

- anything done as part of a scheme or arrangement the main purpose, or one of the main purposes, of which is the avoidance of tax or NICs; and
- any transaction between companies which are members of the same group on terms which are not such as might be expected to be agreed between persons acting at arm's length (other than a payment for group relief).

Legislation: ITEPA 2003, s. 446Kff.

Tax Reporter: ¶476-000

147-650 Charge on non-commercial increase

A charge arises in respect of employment-related securities where, on the valuation date, the increase in market value is at least 10% greater than market value. The taxable amount will be calculated as:

$$IMV - MV$$

where:

IMV is the market value of the securities on the valuation date; and

MV is the amount that would be the market value of the securities on the valuation date if any non-commercial increases during the relevant period were disregarded.

Tax Reporter: ¶476-020

147-700 Securities acquired for less than market value

Overview

Special rules apply relating to shares acquired for less than market value by creating a notional loan on the amount of that undervalue. The rules apply principally to partly-paid shares and options exercised by non-resident or not ordinarily resident employees.

The main circumstances in which this legislation are where the person acquiring the employment-related securities pays less than the market value of the employment-related securities. Market value is defined in ITEPA2003, s. 421(1). Any amounts the person acquiring the employment-related securities may be obliged to pay at a later date is ignored in determining the market value of the employment-related securities. If the securities are not fully paid up then the market value is determined as if that were not the case. In other words, it is to be based on what the market value would be if those securities were fully paid up.

These rules do not apply where the securities are of a class and the company is either employee-controlled, or where the majority of the shares of that class are held by outside shareholders. More specifically, they do not apply where:

(1) the securities are shares in a company;

(2) all the shares in the same class as the shares being considered are acquired on payment of an amount less than the market value; and

(3) one of two following conditions are met:

   (a) the shares being considered are shares that control the company, and the majority of those shares are held by employees; or

   (b) the majority of the shares of the class concerned are not held by employees (or persons related to employees).

Legislation: ITEPA 2003, s. 446Q, 446R(1)

Tax Reporter: ¶476-600

147-800 Securities disposed of for more than market value

A charge to tax arises on an employee when an 'associated person' (see 147-050) disposes of the beneficial interest in employment-related securities for more than its market value at the time of that disposal. The scope of the legislation was considered in *Grays Timber Products Ltd v R & C Commrs.*

Legislation: ITEPA 2003, s. 446X, 446Y

Case: *Grays Timber Products Ltd v R & C Commrs* [2010] BTC 112

Tax Reporter: ¶476-800

147-850 Post acquisition benefits from securities

Overview

A charge arises on the employee if a chargeable benefit is received by the person who owns the employment-related securities or by another associated person. The chargeable benefit is treated as employment income for the tax year in which the benefit is received. The provisions do not apply if the benefit is otherwise chargeable to income tax or if the event falls into one of the categories listed in ITEPA 2003, s. 449, which are as follows:

(1) the employment-related securities are shares or interest in shares in a company of a class;

(2) a similar benefit is received by the owners of all the company's shares of the class; and

(3) the following conditions are satisfied:

   (a) immediately before the receipt of the benefit, the company is employee-controlled by virtue of holdings of shares of the class; and

   (b) immediately before the receipt of the benefit, the majority of the company's shares of the class are not held by or for the benefit of any of the following:

      (i) employees of the company;

      (ii) persons who are related to an employee of the company;

      (iii) associated companies of the company;

      (iv) employees of any associated company of the company; or

      (v) persons who are related to an employee of any such associated company.

The taxable amount is the amount or the market value of the benefit.

Legislation: ITEPA 2003, s. 447, 448

Tax Reporter: ¶477-500

147-900 Shares in research institution spin-out companies

Background

Measures were introduced in FA 2005 to help employees of various institutions involved in research. The types of institutions likely to be involved are universities, public-sector research establishments and entities such as NHS Trusts and The Ministry of Defence. According to the relevant HMRC press release, such institutions,

> 'have unique IP sharing policies (sometimes called 'employee incentive or compensation schemes') that allow researchers, who have helped create the IP, to benefit when it is subsequently exploited.'

Typically, the intellectual property created by the employees is transferred by the institution into a spin-out company in which the employees have shares. In practice, though, the way of rewarding employees may vary, as explained further in the press release:

'The form and timing of this reward varies. It may be cash representing a share of royalties received by the institution from licensing or selling the IP. Alternatively, it could be a transfer of value to researchers via their ownership of shares in a spinout company set up to further develop the IP to the point where it can be exploited commercially.'

'Whatever form the reward takes it is subject to PAYE and National Insurance Contributions (NICs) at the time it flows to the employee. Where shares are concerned, this point can be very early on in the life of a spinout, and it can be difficult to value the extent of the reward, leading to difficulties in payment of tax and NICs.'

Effect of legislation

The primary effect of the legislation is that, in calculating the market value of the shares at the time of acquisition, the intellectual property agreement is to be disregarded, as is any transfer of intellectual property pursuant to it. If the shares are acquired before the agreement is made, or before the transfer of intellectual property, a tax charge may potentially arise under s. 447 (post-acquisition benefits from securities) – see 147-850. In such a case, the taxable amount determined under s. 448 is nil.

Legislation: ITEPA 2003, s. 451(1), 452(1), 453(2), 454(1), 454(5); FA 2005, s. 20(5)

Other Material: HMRC *Employment-Related Securities Manual* ERSM100010

Tax Reporter: ¶471-000ff.

147-950 Securities options

Overview

Gains accruing when securities are acquired pursuant to a right or opportunity available by reason of an employment (employment-related securities options) now come within the meaning of the chargeable events. ITEPA 2003, Pt. 7, Ch. 5 therefore now applies to securities acquired under 'long-term incentive plans' as well as to the extended meaning of securities and associated persons. Payments (or money's worth) received by an associated person in connection with an employment-related securities option, where the option has not been assigned, released or employment-related securities acquired, are also within the scope of charge under Ch. 5. This applies also to compensation payments for the unilateral cancellation of an employment-related securities option.

Finance Act 2006 contained measures designed to strengthen parts of the income tax legislation relating to employment related securities to counter avoidance schemes, which use options over shares and securities to deliver employment reward.

Legislation: ITEPA 2003, s. 420

Tax Reporter: ¶472-500

Cases where Chapter 5 does not apply

The rules of Ch. 5 apply only to an employee who was resident and ordinarily resident in the UK during the year in which the right or opportunity was made available. They do not apply in the case of a former employment if the Chapter would not have applied had the option been made available in the last tax year of employment. In addition they do not apply in the case of a prospective employment if the Chapter would not have applied had the option been made available in the first tax year in which the new employment was held. Where an 'old' option is rolled over into a 'new' option the exemption in ITEPA 2003, s. 474(1) for a person not resident or not ordinarily resident in the UK is maintained for the new option.

148-000 PAYE and unapproved schemes

Where a chargeable event occurs under any of the following provisions in relation to employment-related securities, any taxable amount arising will count as employment income of the employee concerned:

- chargeable events in relation to restricted securities and restricted interests in securities;
- chargeable events in relation to convertible securities and interests in convertible securities;
- charge on acquisition where market value of securities or interest artificially depressed;
- charge where market value of securities artificially enhanced;
- securities or interest acquired for less than market value: charge on discharge of notional loan;
- charge where securities or interest disposed of for more than market value; and
- chargeable benefit from securities or interest.

Where a chargeable event occurs under any of these sections, the PAYE provisions apply with the effect that:

- the employee is treated as being provided with PAYE income (in the form of employment-related securities) by the employer at the relevant date; and
- the amount of income likely to be PAYE income provided for in ITEPA 2003, s. 696(2), is the amount likely to count as employment income.

PAYE is also applied where the employment-related securities are not readily convertible assets but the consideration received is cash or another asset. The proportion of the consideration or benefit as a whole that takes the form of an asset and falls to be treated as employment income will also be treated as the amount of income likely to be PAYE income.

The 'relevant date' for PAYE purposes for each category of security is as follows:

(1) restricted securities and convertible securities – the date on which the chargeable event in question occurs;

(2) securities with artificially depressed market value – the date of the acquisition of the securities or interest in securities in question;

(3) securities with artificially enhanced market value – the valuation date in question;

(4) securities acquired for less than market value – the date on which the notional loan in question is treated as discharged;

(5) securities disposed of for more than market value – the date of the disposal of the securities or interest in securities in question; and

(6) post-acquisition benefits from securities – the date on which the benefit in question is received.

Legislation: ITEPA 2003, s. 698, 700

Tax Reporter: ¶472-000ff

PAYE: gains from securities options

Where securities are acquired pursuant to an employment-related securities option under ITEPA 2003, s. 476 (Charge on post-acquisition chargeable events), PAYE is operated in accordance with ITEPA 2003, s. 700. Gains made by the acquisition of securities pursuant to an employment-related securities option (where those securities are readily convertible assets) are treated as PAYE income. Other events to which PAYE applies include the receipt of a benefit in relation to the option as well as assigning or releasing the option where consideration is received. PAYE applies to consideration or benefits received in cash or assets, whether or not the underlying securities are readily convertible assets. The 'relevant date' for the purposes of gains chargeable under ITEPA 2003, s. 700 is the date on which the chargeable event in question occurs.

There are provisions which specify which shares and additional connected or replacement shares are corporation tax deductible.

Legislation: ITEPA 2003, s. 702; FA 2003, Sch. 22, para. 15(2); *Finance Act 2003, Schedule 22, Paragraph 3(1) (Appointed Day) Order* 2003 (SI 2003/1997)

148-025 Approved share option schemes

No charge to income tax will arise under general principles on the grant or exercise, etc. of an option where shares are acquired under an approved share option scheme. If the shares are later disposed of for a gain, that gain will be chargeable to capital gains tax. There is no question of an income tax growth charge. The gain is the difference between the full cost of acquiring shares under option arrangements and the proceeds of disposal.

Where the market value of the shares when the option was received is greater than the aggregate of the amount or value of consideration paid to obtain the right and the price at which the shares are acquired by exercising that right, there may be a charge to income tax. Relief is given in respect of capital gains tax for amounts charged as income tax under these provisions.

To obtain approval as a 'Company Share Option Plan', the scheme must fulfil certain conditions. Some of the main issues are considered below.

The value of shares for which a person may hold options under any approved scheme established by his employer or any associated company is limited to £30,000.

The share price must be specified at the time the option is granted and must not be manifestly less than their market value at that time.

The employee must not exercise his option less than three years or more than ten years after the date on which it was granted. Approved options may only be exercised once every three years. There are special provisions on exercise in relation to individuals who die (see eligible participants, below).

The procedure for obtaining approval is substantially the same as that for approved savings-related share option schemes (see 148-000). A reduction in the time limit at which options acquired under an approved option scheme became exercisable was a fundamental alteration which

HMRC was justified in refusing to approve, the High Court has held (*IR Commrs v Eurocopy plc*). Alterations removing a provision that existing options would lapse unless they were exercised within six months of the company which employed an option holder ceasing to be a member of the group were not such that HMRC could justifiably refuse consent (*IR Commrs v Reed International plc*).

A plan must be notified electronically to HMRC on or before the 5 July in the year following the first awards under the scheme. If this deadline is missed, then the scheme will only be treated as an approved scheme with effect from the beginning of the tax year in which the notification is made.

The rules do not affect share options which were granted before 6 April 1984.

It is possible within limits to subject shares within an approved scheme to restrictions where the restriction is either attached to all shares of the same class or requires that the directors and employees sell all the shares upon cessation of employment and that shares be sold when acquired, if the acquisition of the shares occurs after cessation of employment. Restrictions which are not permissible include those attaching to shares which limit the holder's freedom to dispose of the shares, or their proceeds of sale, or to exercise any right conferred by the shares. They do not include restrictions imposed by the Stock Exchange Model Rules for Securities Transactions by Directors, nor to any terms of a loan relating to repayment or security. This provision regarding restrictions does not apply from the date of Royal Assent to FA 2013. Instead, details of any restrictions must be stated at the time of grant.

Legislation: ITEPA 2003, Pt. 7, Ch. 7, 8 and Sch. 4; FA 2014, Sch. 8

Cases: *IR Commrs v Eurocopy plc* [1991] BTC 459; *IR Commrs v Reed International plc* [1995] BTC 373

Tax Reporter: ¶465-500

Eligible participants

Only full-time directors and employees may participate in a scheme approved before 1 May 1995. The 'full-time' requirement is removed in respect of schemes approved on or after that date.

However, a company may include provisions in a scheme which permit options to be exercised by participators who, by the time of the exercise, may no longer be full-time employees. A provision may also be included allowing options to be exercised by the personal representatives of a deceased participator. In such cases, the exercise must take place within one year of the employee's death but subject to the ten-year limit.

Participators whose employment ends as a result of injury, disability, redundancy or retirement and who exercise the option with six months of cessation of employment receive the option tax free even if exercised within the first three years.

Any person having 'a material interest' in a close company is ineligible to participate in an approved share scheme involving that company. Broadly, a person has a 'material interest' for this purpose if he, alone or with any 'associate(s)', beneficially owns or is able to control more than 25% of the ordinary share capital of the company or on the company's liquidation would be entitled to more than 25% of its assets. Excluded from consideration are the personal shareholdings of fellow beneficiaries, although trust shares remain to be aggregated. A 'close company' for present purposes is, in brief, one which is controlled by five or fewer 'participators' or over half the assets of which could be distributed on its liquidation between five or fewer participators or director participators.

Companies of which a jointly-owned company (JOC) has control can join in approved share schemes run by either of the JOC's parent companies. Consent will only be given where an undertaking has been given by the grantor of the relevant share scheme to notify HMRC of changes in the ownership or control of any of the appropriate parties.

Legislation: ITEPA 2003, Sch. 4

Tax Reporter: ¶466-300

148-050 Approved savings-related share options

Exemptions for savings-related share option schemes have the effect that no charge is made on the grant of the option or on the exercise of it or on the increased value of the shares. Conditions for approval include the following:

- the shares must be bought through a certified contractual savings scheme and any loans must not be payable before a date approved by the Board except where the employee dies or leaves his job before that date;
- the price paid for the shares must not be less than 80% of their market value when purchased;
- all employees or directors must be able to participate in the scheme;
- all those who have worked for a qualifying period must be permitted to participate in the scheme. The qualifying period must not exceed five years; and

- the shares must be fully paid ordinary shares which are non-redeemable and they must be either quoted on a stock exchange or be shares in a subsidiary company.

A plan must be notified electronically to HMRC on or before the 5 July in the year following the first awards under the scheme. If this deadline is missed, then the scheme will only be treated as an approved scheme with effect from the beginning of the tax year in which the notification is made.

An approved scheme must not permit the aggregate of a person's contributions under certified contractual savings schemes linked to approved schemes to exceed £250 a month (£500 with effect from 6 April 2014) or impose a minimum contribution on the amount of a person's contributions which exceeds £10 a month.

Provisions on jointly owned companies apply in the same way as for share option schemes.

As with approved share option schemes it is possible to subject shares within savings-related share option schemes to restrictions connected with the termination of employment.

On a takeover of a company, scheme participants may exchange their rights of option in shares of the company taken over for equivalent rights in the acquiring company or another company. Scheme rules may be changed so that an exchange of rights is permissible and such a transaction will not give rise to a capital gains tax charge.

Legislation: ITEPA 2003, Sch. 3, Pt. 2; ITTOIA 2005, s. 703

Other Material: *Approved Save As You Earn Share Option Schemes – Guidance for employees* (www.hmrc.gov.uk/shareschemes/employee-guidance.pdf); *Approved Save As You Earn Share Option Schemes – Guidance for employers and advisers* (www.hmrc.gov.uk/shareschemes/employer-guidance.pdf)

Tax Reporter: ¶470-360

148-100 Share incentive plans

Broadly, the key features of the scheme are as follows:

- employers can give employees up to £3,600 (£3,000 prior to 6 April 2014) of shares each year, free of tax and National Insurance;
- some or all of these shares can be awarded to employees for reaching performance targets;

- employees will be able to buy partnership shares out of their pre-tax salary, free of tax and National Insurance up to a maximum of £1,800 per annum (£1,500 prior to 6 April 2014); and
- employees can match partnership shares by giving employees up to two free shares for each partnership share that they buy.

For the purposes of the legislation, an 'employee share ownership plan' is a plan established by a company that provides (ITEPA 2003, s. 488(4) and Sch. 2, para. 2):

- for shares to be appropriated to employees without payment (known as 'free shares'); and
- for shares to be acquired on behalf of employees from sums deducted from their salaries (known as 'partnership shares').

In addition, provision may be made to provide employees with further free shares (known as 'matching shares') in proportion to the purchase of their partnership shares. Where a plan contains provision for more than of type of share, the company has the discretion as to when the provisions relating to each type of share take effect.

Each occasion on which matching or free shares are appropriated to an employee, or on which partnership shares are acquired on behalf of employees, constitutes an 'award of shares'; an individual (known as a 'participant'), participating in such an award (an 'individual award') when he or she receives free or matching shares, or when partnership shares are acquired on his or her behalf.

Legislation: ITEPA 2003, Sch. 2

Tax Reporter: ¶468-000ff.

Approval

Companies wishing to set up SIPs need to have the plans approved by HMRC. HMRC will approve plans if they are happy that they meet the conditions of the legislation. To assist companies, HMRC have a dedicated helpline (0300 123 1079) and also make available model rules and trust deeds on their website.

A plan must be notified electronically to HMRC on or before the 5 July in the year following the first awards under the scheme. If this deadline is missed, then the scheme will only be treated as an approved scheme with effect from the beginning of the tax year in which the notification is made.

Legislation: ITEPA 2003, Sch. 2, para. 81 and 81A–81K

Website: www.hmrc.gov.uk/shareschemes

Tax Reporter: ¶468-820

General requirements

The plan must comply a number of general requirements. Broadly, these cover:

- the purpose of the plan;
- all-employee nature;
- participation on the same terms; and
- no preferential treatment for directors.

Legislation: ITEPA 2003, Sch. 2, para. 6

Tax Reporter: ¶468-000ff.

All-employee nature

Employee share ownership plans are all-employee plans. This means that the plan must provide that all employees meeting the 'eligibility of individuals' requirements that are chargeable to tax under the charge on employment income provisions are eligible to participate in an award and are invited to do so. Eligibility may also be extended to those outside the charge to tax.

To participate, individuals must satisfy various conditions:

- the employment requirement;
- the 'no material interest' requirement; and
- the 'non-participation in other relevant share schemes' requirement.

The material interest requirement does not apply to determine eligibility from Royal Assent to FA 2013.

A further important requirement is that every employee who is invited to participate in an award is invited to participate on the same terms, and that those who do participate, do so on the same terms. Shares may, however, be awarded by reference to:

- remuneration;
- length of service; or
- hours worked.

Legislation: ITEPA 2003, Sch. 2, para. 8, 9

Tax Reporter: ¶468-060

Award of shares

Where the plan provides for the award of free shares, the initial market value of shares awarded to a participant in a tax year cannot exceed £3,000.

The plan may provide that the award of free shares is conditional on performance targets (known as 'performance allowances') being met. However, where performance allowances are incorporated shares must be allocated in accordance with one of two methods set out in the legislation.

If the plan provides for the award of partnership shares, qualifying employees must enter into a partnership share agreement with the company. The employee agrees to a deduction from salary for the purpose of purchasing partnership shares and the company agrees to award the shares in accordance with the plan. The sums are subject to agreement between the employee and the company. There is a limit of 10% of the employee's annual salary or £1,500 per tax year. Hence, companies are therefore able to operate a scheme solely for the month in which an annual bonus is paid and the employee will be able to invest up to £1,500 in that month.

The plan may or may not provide for an accumulation period. Where there is an accumulation period, this may last up to 12 months.

The third type of shares that may be awarded under the plan are matching shares. These are free shares that are awarded to employees in proportion to the partnership shares acquired by them. The purpose is to act as an incentive to purchase partnership shares. Matching shares must meet the requirement in ITEPA 2003, Sch. 2, para. 59.

Cash dividends may be reinvested an applied in the acquisition of further shares. Such shares are known as dividend shares.

Legislation: ITEPA 2003, Sch. 2, para. 35, 44, 50, 51, 59

Tax Reporter: ¶468-180

Eligible shares

For shares to be eligible to be awarded under the plan (known as 'eligible shares'), they must satisfy several requirements. Broadly, the requirements are that:

- the shares must be ordinary share capital;
- they must satisfy the listing requirements;

- they must be fully paid up and not redeemable; and
- they must not be in prohibited companies.

Legislation: ITEPA 2003, Sch. 2, para. 25

Tax Reporter: ¶468-280

Income tax relief

No tax charge arises on the award for free, matching or partnership shares under the plan or in respect of the acquisition of dividend shares on the participant's behalf. Similarly, incidental expenses incurred by the trustees do not give rise to taxable fringe benefits.

Legislation: ITEPA 2003, s. 490, 499

Tax Reporter: ¶468-500ff

Capital receipts

The exemption does not extend to capital receipts. Where a participant receives a capital receipt less than five years after the award of free, matching or partnership shares to which the receipt, the amount of value of the receipt is taxable under the charge on employment income provisions. Likewise, a capital receipt received in respect of the dividend shares, less than three years after the acquisition of those shares on the participant's behalf, is also taxable under the charge on employment income provisions.

Legislation: ITEPA 2003, s. 501(1)–(5)

Tax Reporter: ¶468-520

Withdrawal of shares from the plan

Free or matching shares

When free or matching shares cease to be subject to the plan, an income tax charge may arise. This will depend on the period that has elapsed between the date on which the participant was awarded the shares and the date on which they cease to be subject to the plan. If that period is less than three years, the participant is taxed on the market value of the shares on the date on which they ceased to be subject to the plan. If, however, the period is more than three years but less than five years, the participant is taxed on the lower of:

- the market value on the date on which the shares were awarded; and
- the market value of the shares on the date on which they ceased to be subject to the plan.

Where any tax charge arising is based on the market value on the date of the award, the tax payable is reduced by any tax paid on capital receipt received in respect of those shares.

However, no tax charge arises where free or matching shares cease to be subject to the plan as a result of forfeiture.

Where shares are withdrawn from the plan at least five years after they were awarded, no tax charge arises on their withdrawal.

Legislation: ITEPA 2003, s. 497(1), 505

Tax Reporter: ¶468-520

Partnership shares

An income tax charge may also arise when partnership shares leave the plan. As for free and matching shares, this depends on the period that has elapsed between the acquisition date in respect of ITEPA 2003, s. 506(2). If the period that has elapsed is less than three years, the charge is based on the market value of the shares on the date on which they cease to be subject to the plan. Tax relief is given on partnership share money (see below) and thus the full market value is taxed on withdrawal.

In the event that the shares are withdrawn more than three years but less than five years after the acquisition date, the employee is taxed on the lower of:

- the amount of partnership share money used to acquire the shares; and
- the market value when they cease to be subject to the plan.

Where the tax charge is based on the partnership share money, the tax due is reduced by an tax paid on capital receipts received in relation to the shares.

There is no charge if the shares are withdrawn at least five years after the acquisition date.

Legislation: FA 2000, Sch. 8, para. 86(2); ITEPA 2003, s. 497(2), 506(3), (4)

Tax Reporter: ¶468-580

Dividend shares

In the event that dividend shares cease to be subject to the plan before the end of the holding period, the participant is charged to tax on the amount of the relevant dividend. The charge arises for the tax year in which the shares ceased to be subject to the plan.

No tax charge arises where dividend shares are withdrawn at least three years after the date on which they were acquired on the participant's behalf.

Legislation: ITEPA 2003, s. 497(3) and Sch. 2, para. 80(5)

Tax Reporter: ¶468-620

Exceptions

However, no tax charge arises where shares (irrespective of type) cease to be subject to the plan because the employee's relevant employment ceases as a result of:

- injury or disability;
- dismissal or redundancy;
- a transfer to which the *Transfer of Undertakings (Protection of Employment) Regulations* 1981 apply;
- a change of control or other circumstances ending the associated company status of the company, which employs him;
- retirement on or after retirement age; or
- the employee's death.

Legislation: ITEPA 2003, s. 498 and Sch. 2, para. 32, 98, 99

Tax Reporter: ¶468-620

Withdrawal of approval

Where HMRC withdraw approval of the plan, they may also claw back any deductions given in respect of the award of free or matching shares or in respect of any additional expense of partnership shares. If such a notice is given, the aggregate amount of the deductions is treated as a trading receipt of the company for the period in which HMRC notice of withdrawal of approval.

HMRC may withdraw the plan's approval in the event that a disqualifying event occurs. Approval is withdrawn by giving notice to the company that the approval is withdrawn from the date of the disqualifying event or such later time as specified by HMRC. Withdrawing approval has no impact on the operation of the plan prior to the date of the withdrawal.

The following are disqualifying events:

(1) a contravention in relation to the operation of the plan of any of the requirements of the legislation, the plan itself or the plan trust;

(2) an alteration being made in a key feature of the plan, or in the terms of the plan trust, without the approval of HMRC;

(3) if the plan provides for performance allowances in accordance with Method 2, the setting of performance targets in respect of an award of shares which are not consistent targets;

(4) an alteration being made in the share capital of a company any of whose shares are subject to the plan trust, or in the rights attaching to any shares of such a company, that materially affects the value of shares that are subject to the plan trust;

(5) shares of a class of which shares are subject to the plan trust receiving different treatment in any respect from the other shares of that class;

(6) the trustees, the company, or (in the case of a group plan) a company which is or has been a constituent company failing to furnish any information which they are or it is required to furnish under the relevant provisions.

For these purposes, a 'key feature' of the plan is one that is necessary to meet the legislative requirements. In this instance, HMRC approval would only be withheld if it appears to them that in its altered form the plan would be unlikely to gain approval.

A right of appeal exists against a decision of HMRC to withdraw approval.

Legislation: ITEPA 2003, Sch. 2, para. 83

Tax Reporter: ¶468-840

Withdrawal of shares

Shares are withdrawn from the plan when:

- they are transferred either to the participant or to another person at his request;
- the participant assigns, charges or otherwise disposes of his beneficial interest in the shares; or
- the trustees dispose of them at the participant's request and account to the participant for the proceeds.

Where the participant has died, his place is taken by his personal representative.

Legislation: ITEPA 2003, Sch. 2, para. 96

Tax Reporter: ¶468-880

PAYE: shares ceasing to be subject to the plan

An income tax charge may arise when shares leave the plan, depending on the amount of time that the shares were held within the plan.

Where a tax charge arises as a result of shares ceasing to be subject to the plan, PAYE will apply. The readily convertible asset provisions in ITEPA 2003, s. 696(2) have effect as if the amount of income likely to be chargeable is the income brought into charge as a result of the shares being withdrawn from the plan. However, the amount that is brought into charge will depend on the type of shares and the period of time that has elapsed before the shares cease to be subject to the plan.

In the case of free or matching shares, if they have been held in the plan for less than three years, the participant is taxed on the market value of the shares on the date on which they ceased to be subject to the plan. If, however, the period is more than three years but less than five years, the participant is taxed on the lower of:

- the market value on the date on which the shares were awarded; and
- the market value of the shares on the date on which they ceased to be subject to the plan.

In the case of partnership shares, if the period that has elapsed is less than three years, the charge is based on the market value of the shares on the date on which they cease to be subject to the plan. However, if the shares are withdrawn more than three years but less than five years after the acquisition date, the employee is taxed on the lower of (ITEPA 2003, s. 506(3)):

- the amount of partnership share money used to acquire the shares; and
- the market value when they cease to be subject to the plan.

Where PAYE is in point, the obligation to operate PAYE falls on the employer company. The 'employer company' is defined as the company that employs the participant in relevant employment at the time when the shares cease to be subject to the plan (or if the participant is not employed in the relevant employment at that time, the company that last employed him in relevant employment before that time), provided the company is one to which the PAYE regulations apply.

Legislation: ITEPA 2003, s. 505ff.

Tax Reporter: ¶468-600

PAYE: capital receipts

Where a participant receives a capital receipt less than five years after the award of free, matching or partnership shares to which the receipt relates, the amount of value of the receipt is taxable. Likewise, a capital receipt received in respect of the dividend shares, less than three years after the acquisition of those shares, on the participant's behalf, is also taxable. The employer company is required to deduct PAYE when paying the capital receipt over to the participant.

The definition of the employer company makes it clear that the employer company is the company that employs the participant in relevant employment at the time when the shares cease to be subject to the plan (or if the participant is not employed in the relevant employment at that time, the company that last employed him in relevant employment before that time), provided that the company is one to which the PAYE regulations apply.

Legislation: ITEPA 2003, s. 501, 513

Tax Reporter: ¶468-520

Jointly-owned companies

A 'jointly-owned company' is a company that is owned equally by two other companies, with neither having control. A jointly-owned company may participate in a plan run by either of the owning companies, but not in both. The legislation makes it clear that subsidiaries of jointly-owned companies may not be a participating company in more than one group plan. Furthermore, if the jointly-owned company or any other company controlled by it is a participating company in a group plan, a subsidiary of a jointly-owned company cannot be a participating company in a different group plan. This removes any unintended flexibility and aligns the treatment of jointly-owned companies for share incentive plan purposes with their treatment in other share incentive schemes.

Legislation: ITEPA 2003, Sch. 2, para. 91

148-125 Enterprise management incentives

Enterprise management incentives (EMIs) were introduced to help small, potentially high-growth companies to recruit and retain high calibre individuals. The measures aim to reward those who take a risk in investing their time and skills in helping small companies to achieve their potential.

Broadly, under enterprise management incentives:

- independent trading companies whose assets do not exceed £30 million are able to award their employees with tax advantaged share options;
- qualifying companies must have fewer than 250 full-time (or equivalent) employees at the date of the grant of the options;
- the total value of shares that an employee may be entitled to have in respect of his or her unexercised qualifying options must not exceed £250,000 (£120,000 before 16 June 2012);
- the total value of shares in respect of all unexercised qualifying options must not exceed £3 million;
- normally, there will be no tax or National Insurance for the employee to pay when the options are exercised, or any National Insurance charge for the employer;
- when the shares are sold, capital gains tax taper relief will usually apply from the date the options were granted; and
- a simple notification process will apply in place of an approvals system.

If a company wishes to use enterprise management incentives to reward employees, there are various requirements that must be satisfied. In brief:

- options granted must be qualifying options;
- the company granting the options must be a qualifying company; and
- the employees to whom the options are granted must be qualifying employees.

Where the requirements are satisfied, income tax and capital gains tax advantages ensue.

There is no approvals process for enterprise management incentives; however, companies using them are obliged to comply with the relevant notification procedure.

Legislation: FA 2000, s. 62 and Sch. 14; ITEPA 2003, Pt. 7, Ch. 9 and Sch. 5

Tax Reporter: ¶466-000ff.

Qualifying options

Options granted as enterprise management incentives must be qualifying options. This means that, at the time the option is granted, various requirements must be met. The requirements are:

- general requirements covering the purposes for which the option is granted, an employee's maximum entitlement and the maximum number of employees who can hold qualifying options;
- specific requirements governing the terms of the option;
- that the company whose shares are the subject of the option (the 'relevant company') must be a qualifying company;
- that the employee must be an eligible employee; and
- that the option must be granted to the employee by reason of his employment with that company, or, if that company is a parent company, with another group company. This company is known as the 'employer company'.

Legislation: ITEPA 2003, Sch. 5, para. 1, 2

Tax Reporter: ¶466-100

Value of options granted

For an option to benefit from EMI reliefs, it must be a qualifying option and satisfy conditions as to the purpose for which the option is granted and the maximum entitlement of an employee. A limit of £3 million is placed on the value of the company's shares in respect of which unexercised options can exist. Should an option be granted at a time when this limit is already exceeded, it will not be a qualifying option. Similarly, if the grant of an option causes the limit to be exceeded, the excess is not a qualifying option.

Legislation: ITEPA 2003, Sch. 5, para. 3, 7

Tax Reporter: ¶466-380

Example 1

A company has unexercised qualifying options over shares worth £2.97 million. Options are granted to a new employee over shares valued at £100,000. The grant of the new option takes the value of shares over which unexercised options exist to £3.07 million. As the limit of £3 million is exceeded by £70,000, options over shares to the value of £70,000 (the excess) are not qualifying options. Thus of the options granted to the new employee, only those over shares to the value of £30,000 are qualifying EMI options.

A further employee is granted options over shares worth £75,000. As the £3 million limit has already been reached, the option is not a qualifying EMI option.

Example 2

In the event that two or more options granted at the same time cause the limit to be exceeded, in determining whether the options are qualifying options, the excess over the limit is split pro rata among the options according to the value of the shares in respect of which the option is granted. For these purposes, the value of shares is the market value at the time of grant of shares of the same class as those that may be acquired by the exercise of the options.

Example 3

Unexercised qualifying options are held over shares in a company to a value of £2.95 million. Options are granted to two further employees, one of whom is granted options over shares to the value of shares to the value of £100,000 and the other over shares to the value of £25,000. The granting of these options takes the value of shares over which unexercised options exist to 3.075 million. The limit is exceeded by £75,000 and this is allocated in the ratio in the ratio 4:1 between the two employees (i.e. £60,000:£15,000). Thus the employee receiving options over shares to the value of £100,000 receives qualifying options over shares worth £40,000 and non-qualifying options over the remaining £60,000 worth of shares. Likewise, the employee granted options over shares to the value of £25,000 receives qualifying options to the tune of £10,000 and non-qualifying options to the value of £15,000.

Qualifying companies

For a company to be a qualifying company, it must satisfy requirements as to:

- independence;
- having only qualifying subsidiaries;
- the nature of any property managing subsidiaries;
- gross assets and trading activities;
- the number of employees, which must be restricted to less than 250 full-time or equivalent; and
- (from December 2010) having a permanent establishment in the UK.

The following are excluded activities (which would therefore prevent a company from qualifying):

- dealing in land commodities, futures or in shares, securities or other financial instruments;
- dealing in goods, except in the course of an ordinary trade of wholesale or retail distribution;
- banking, insurance, money-lending, debt-factoring, hire purchase financing and other financial activities;

- leasing (including letting ships on charter or other assets on hire) or receiving royalties or licence fees;
- providing legal or accountancy services;
- property development;
- farming or market gardening; holding, managing or occupying woodlands, any other forestry activities or timber production;
- shipbuilding and the production of coal or steel;
- operating or managing hotels or comparable establishments, or managing property used as a hotel or comparable establishment; and
- operating or managing nursing homes or residential care homes, or managing property used as a nursing home or residential care home.

Legislation: ITEPA 2003, Sch. 5, para. 8, 16

Tax Reporter: ¶466-100

Eligible employees

For an individual to be an eligible employee, he or she must satisfy requirements in relation to:

- employment;
- commitment of working time; and
- no material interest.

Legislation: ITEPA 2003, Sch. 5, para. 24

Tax Reporter: ¶466-300

Income tax

Income tax relief is available in respect of the grant or exercise of a qualifying option.

Tax is not chargeable on the grant of a qualifying option.

Relief in respect of the exercise of a qualifying option is only available within ten years from the grant of the option or, if it is a replacement option, the grant of the original option. Where there has been more than one replacement option, the original option is the first one that was replaced.

Legislation: ITEPA 2003, s. 528, 529(1)

Tax Reporter: ¶466-640

Exercise to acquire shares at market value

No amount is chargeable under ITEPA 2003, Pt. 7 ('Employment income: income and exemptions relating to securities') if the option is to acquire shares at not less than their market value at the time the option was granted or, if the option is a replacement option, at the time that the original option was granted.

Where a disqualifying event (see below) occurs, a tax charge may arise under ITEPA 2003, Pt. 7. Where such an event occurs before the option is exercised and the option is not exercised within 90 days of that disqualifying event, the amount of the gain realised on exercise (for the purposes of ITEPA 2003, Pt. 7) is the amount (if any) by which the market value of the shares when the option is exercised exceeds their market value immediately before the disqualifying event (40 days for events occurring before Royal Assent to FA 2013). However, this only applies if the amount so chargeable is more than the amount that would otherwise be chargeable under ITEPA 2003, Pt. 7 on the exercise of the option.

Legislation: ITEPA 2003, s. 532(6)

Exercise to acquire shares at less than market value

Where the option is to acquire shares at less than the market value at the time that the option was granted, or if the option is a replacement option, at the time that the original option was granted, the amount of the gain realised by the exercise for the purpose of ITEPA 2003, Pt. 7 is the lower of:

- the amount of the discount; or
- the amount by which the market value of the shares at the time that the option is exercised exceeds the amount for which they are acquired.

For these purposes, the discount is the amount by which the market value of the shares at the time the option was granted, or if the option is a replacement option, the time the original option was granted, exceeds the amount for which they are acquired.

However, there is no tax charged under ITEPA 2003, Pt. 7 if the market value at the time of exercise does not exceed the amount for which they were acquired.

Where a disqualifying event (see below) occurs before the option is exercised and the option is not exercised within 40 days of that disqualifying event, the amount of the gain realised on exercise (for the purposes of ITEPA 2003, Pt. 7), as computed above, is increased by the amount (if any) by which the market value of the shares when the option is exercised exceeds their market value immediately before the disqualifying event. However, this only applies if the amount so chargeable is more than the amount that would otherwise be chargeable under ITEPA 2003, Pt. 7 on the exercise of the option.

When the option is exercised, the gain charged to income tax for the purpose of ITEPA 2003, Pt. 7 is the amount by which the chargeable market value exceeds the aggregate of the amount or value of the consideration given for the grant of the option and the amount for which the shares are acquired. For these purposes, the 'chargeable market value' is the lower of:

- the market value of the shares at the time that the option was granted or, in the case of a replacement option, at the time that the original option was granted; and
- the market value at the time that the option was exercised.

In the event that the chargeable market value does not exceed the aggregate of the amount of value of the consideration given for the option and the amount for which the shares are acquired, no charge to income tax arises on exercise under ITEPA 2003, Pt. 7.

The changes to the method of calculation ensure that any price paid on the grant of the option is taken into account.

Legislation: ITEPA 2003, s. 531(1), (2), (4), 532

Exercise to acquire shares at nil cost

Exercise to acquire shares at nil cost – in the case where the option is to acquire shares at nil cost, the amount of the gain realised by the exercise for the purposes of ITEPA 2003, Pt. 7 is the lower of:

- the market value of the shares at the time the option was granted or, if the option is a replacement option, at the time that the original option was granted; and
- the market value at the time of exercise.

Where a disqualifying event (see below) occurs before the option is exercised and the option is not exercised within 40 days of that disqualifying event, the amount of the gain realised on exercise (for the purposes of ITEPA 2003, Pt. 7), as computed above, is increased by the amount (if any) by which the market value of the shares when the option is exercised exceeds their market value immediately before the disqualifying event. However, this only applies if the amount so chargeable is more than the amount that would otherwise be chargeable under ITEPA 2003, Pt. 7 on the exercise of the option.

The gain charged to income tax for the purpose of ITEPA 2003, Pt. 7 in respect of an option to acquire shares at nil cost is the amount by which the chargeable market value exceed the amount or value of the consideration given for the grant of the option.

Legislation: ITEPA 2003, s. 531, 532(6)

Disqualifying event

The main disqualifying events in relation to a qualifying share option are:

- the relevant company becomes a 51% subsidiary of another company of another company (or of another company and persons connected with that company) without becoming a 51% subsidiary;
- the relevant company ceases to meet the trading activities requirement (see above);
- the employee ceases to be an eligible employee by failing to meet the commitment of working time requirement (see above) or the employment requirement (see above);
- any variation of the terms of the option that has the effect of increasing the market value of the shares that are the subject of the option;
- any variation of the option such that the necessary requirements are no longer satisfied;
- any alteration of the share capital (as described below) that is made without prior HMRC approval;
- a conversion of any of the shares into shares of a different class (except as described below); and
- the grant of a relevant CSOP option (i.e. an option to acquire shares under a approved non-saving related share option scheme (approved under ITEPA 2003, Sch. 4) if immediately after its grant, the employee holds unexercised employee options in respect of shares with a total value of more than £250,000.

A disqualifying event also occurs if the relevant company was a qualifying company only by reason of preparing to carry on a qualifying trade and either the preparation cease, or within two years of the grant of the qualifying option neither the company, not its parent if it is a group company, has started to carry on that qualifying trade.

If in the tax year, the employee's relevant working time amounts to less than 25 hours a week or, if less, 75% of his working time, a disqualifying event is treated as having occurred.

The above list of disqualifying events is subject to consideration relating to:

- a company reorganisation;
- alterations of share capital;
- conversion of shares;
- grant of a CSOP option; and
- actual relevant working time.

Legislation: ITEPA 2003, s. 533–536

Tax Reporter: ¶466-660

Income tax charge arising on a disqualifying event

Where a disqualifying event occurs, an income tax charge arises. Changes are made to the calculation of the charge to ensure that any option price paid on grant is taken into account in calculating the tax arising on the exercise of an option after a disqualifying event.

The amount of the gain realised on exercise where the option is to acquire shares at market value is the post-event gain (if any) less the amount or value of the consideration given for the grant of the option.

If the option is to acquire shares at less than the market value, the gain realised on exercise is:

	£	£
Chargeable market value		X
Add: post-event gain		X
		X
Less: amount or value of consideration given for option	X	
amount for which shares acquired	X	
		(X)
Gain realised on exercise		X

Where the option is to acquire shares at nil cost, the gain realised on exercise is:

	£
Chargeable market value	X
Add: post-event gain	X
	X
Less: amount or value of consideration given for grant option	(X)
Gain realised on exercise	X

For these purposes, the 'post-event gain' is the amount by which, if any, the market value of the shares when the option is exercised exceeds their market value immediately before the disqualifying event.

Legislation: ITEPA 2003, s. 532(2)–(5)

Tax Reporter: ¶466-680

Notifying HMRC

To minimise the administrative burdens surrounding enterprise management incentives, there is no approvals process. Instead, a notification procedure exists.

For an option to be a qualifying option, HMRC must be given notice electronically of the option within 92 days of its grant using the employment related securities online service.

Legislation: ITEPA 2003, Sch. 5, para. 44

Tax Reporter: ¶466-680

148-150 Priority share allocations

Where a company offers its shares for sale, its directors and employees are often given priority rights so that if the offer is over-subscribed the employees etc. will receive either their full allocation or, where there is a scaling-down, more shares than a member of the public who applies for the same number. A taxable benefit could arise where the shares, at the date they are allocated to the employees etc., are worth more than the public offer price. This benefit is not liable to income tax.

The tax exemption covers share allocations as part of an offer to the public consisting of a package of shares in two or more companies where employees etc. are entitled to shares in one or more but not all of them.

Where employees etc. acquire their shares for a price less than the fixed price or the lowest price successfully tendered, that benefit remains taxable. The benefit arises where the price payable is not the same as, or as near as practicable, to the 'appropriate notional price' for the shares, defined as the price that might reasonably have been expected to be the fixed price for the shares, had the shares of all the companies been subject to separate offers to the public at the time at which the public offer was actually made. Note that, if the sum of the appropriate notional prices differs from the actual fixed price or lowest successfully tendered price, the appropriate notional prices are scaled up or down, using the fraction:

sum of actual fixed prices or lowest successfully tendered prices/sum of appropriate notional prices

However, any 'registrant discount' is ignored for these purposes after 15 January 1991: such a discount is one which is available to employees etc. subscribing for shares as well as (in some form) to individual members of the public who are allocated at least 40% of the rest of the shares.

Legislation: ITEPA 2003, Pt. 7, Ch. 10

Conditions

For the exemption to have effect, certain conditions must be observed. There must be an offer to the public at a fixed price or by tender and a director or employee is entitled, by reason of his office or employment, to an allocation of the shares, in priority to members of the public.

To ensure that the exemption is confined to cases genuinely involving what is primarily an offer to the public, of which the priority allocation to employees etc. forms only a part, the priority allocation must not exceed 10% of the total number of shares (including the priority issue) subject to the offer. The 10% limit applies overall. However, where shares of the same class are the subject of more than one offer (for example, offers at more than one fixed price or offers containing both tender and fixed-price elements) then up to 40% of the shares of a particular element of the offer may be allocated in priority to employees.

All persons entitled to the priority issue must be entitled on similar terms, and, specifically, the persons who are entitled may not be restricted mainly to directors or higher paid employees. However, different provisions may be made based on the levels of remuneration, length of service and similar factors (which are not further defined, but could presumably include seniority marked otherwise than by remuneration or length of service) without infringing the rule as to similar entitlement. Further, the fact that share allocations in one company (the first company) to which directors or employees of another company are entitled are smaller than those to which directors or employees of the first company are entitled does not offend, in relation to offers made after 25 July 1990, the 'similar terms' requirement if:

- each such employee, etc. is also entitled to a priority allocation of shares in another company or companies which are offered to the public (at a fixed price or by tender) at the same time as the shares in the first company; and
- the value of their total entitlement (based on the fixed price or lowest tender price) is the same, or as nearly the same as is reasonably practicable, as that received by directors or employees of the first company.

Relief is also given in relation to such priority allocations for capital gains tax. If the exemption from income tax applies, the individual will not be deemed to have acquired his shares at market value but at the value of his payment for those shares (TCGA 1992, s. 149C). Market value would otherwise apply, because the individual acquires the shares in recognition of his services or past services in an office or employment.

The exemptions extend to individuals who are to be or have ceased to be directors or employees. In practice, this is only likely to include joiners and leavers close to the date of the offer.

Legislation: ITEPA 2003, s. 542, 544, 546, 548

Tax Reporter: ¶472-360

148-175 ESC to maintain reservists' participation in employee share schemes

By concession, employers of Armed Forces reservists may protect the reservist's participation in an approved employer share scheme while the reservist is away on active service. The concession is needed because civilian employment usually ends when a reservist is called up for service under the *Reserve Forces Act* 1996 and, strictly, the reservist can no longer participate in the scheme.

Other Material: ESC A103

Income in trusts and estates

Income in trusts and settlements: background and definitions

150-000 Trusts and settlements – introduction

This chapter deals with the taxation of trust and settlement income, both in the hands of the trustees and in those of the beneficiaries. It also deals with the taxation of the income of estates in administration (see 156-000ff.).

Basic definitions and concepts

A trust exists where a person or persons hold property ('trust property', or 'settled property') for the benefit of another or others.

The person holding the property (the 'trustee') owes a duty (often referred to as 'fiduciary' in nature) to deal with it in the manner prescribed by the terms of the trust. This will involve consulting the interests of the 'beneficiary' or 'beneficiaries' (those for whose benefit the trust exists) and acting in accordance with the stated objects of the trust. A 'breach of trust' will arise when a trustee uses property subject to the trust for his own benefit, for the benefit of someone who is not a beneficiary, or otherwise in a way not authorised by the trust.

A company may be appointed to act as a trustee, so long as its memorandum of association permits it. Trustees may be appointed by name or may be identified by their status, e.g. the senior partner of a firm of solicitors.

A trust is generally created by a person (a 'settlor') transferring funds or other property to trustees with the stipulation that they hold it in the manner set out in a trust deed or other written instrument (such as a will, when the trust will take effect from the death of the testator). This may be for the benefit of a named person or persons, who may be given an 'immediate' or 'contingent' interest in the income of the trust fund or other property, or the right to use it (e.g. a beneficiary may be given the right to live in a dwelling-house) for a defined period, or for life. This will generally create an 'interest in possession', or 'life interest', and the beneficiary will often be referred to loosely as the 'life tenant'. On termination of the life interest, by the death of the life tenant or by the life tenant relinquishing his interest, other interests (usually absolute interests) will succeed: these are known as 'interests in remainder', or 'reversionary interests'.

Alternatively, trust property may be set aside for trustees to apply, according to their discretion, for any one or more of a number of stated purposes for a class of beneficiaries, who may be members of a family, employees of a particular employer, or some other group specified in the trust instrument. No such beneficiaries will have an indefeasible right to the trust property; their entitlement will depend entirely on the exercise by the trustees of the discretion afforded them by the trust instrument. Such trusts are often referred to as 'discretionary trusts', and the exercise by the trustees of their discretion in favour of any one or more of the objects of the trust is known as an 'appointment'.

The law relating to the formation and administration of trusts is both extensive and complex. The interpretation of trust deeds and the dealing with the administrative law relating to trusts is generally regarded as a legal speciality. One unfortunate feature of trust law is an inconsistency in the naming of things, as with interests in remainder and reversionary interests, mentioned above. One consequence of the variable identification within the law relating to trusts is that the different professions involved in trust work often describe the same thing using different wording. An example of this is that tax professionals will usually use the phrase 'interest in possession' (since it is used in tax legislation), whereas professional trustees and solicitors will often use the term 'life interest' (since it is used in administrative trust law) to describe the same thing.

What is known as the Hastings Bass principle has been considerably restricted by the Court of Appeal decision in *Pitt v HMRC* and *Futter v HMRC*. Previously this principle has been adopted to cure erroneous tax advice by applying to the court to set aside the exercise of a trustee's discretion but for the future that will be considerably restricted. The Supreme Court upheld this decision but in the *Pitt* case allowed the appeal, holding that the voluntary disposition to the trust could be set aside on the grounds of mistake. Had there been a tax avoidance motive it seems that the court would not have exercised its inherent equitable discretion.

New trust deeds

HMRC in general no longer ask for a copy of every new trust document, but instead they rely on information shown by trustees on form 41G(Trust) and in their annual tax returns.

HMRC will seek further information only where necessary, and only exceptionally will they ask to see the relevant documents. When a new trust is created, trustees will be sent a form requesting basic information about the identities of the trustees and the nature of the trust in question. However, these arrangements only affect ordinary family trusts – they do not affect special types of trust or the examination of deeds for inheritance tax purposes.

Vested interests, contingent interests

A beneficiary has a *vested* interest in trust property if his entitlement is indefeasible, that is to say the interest cannot be put aside or made void. For instance, he may be entitled to the income of the trust as it arises, or the terms of the trust may provide for him to become entitled at some future date, for example on attaining a certain age. If, however, his entitlement is dependent upon an event which may or may not occur, such as his surviving another beneficiary, it is *contingent*.

There is sometimes a thin dividing line between a vested interest that does not fall into possession until some future date, and a contingent interest; the distinction is basically between becoming entitled *when* something occurs (future vesting) or becoming entitled *if* something occurs (contingent).

Trusts with vulnerable beneficiaries

There is a special tax regime for certain trusts with 'vulnerable beneficiaries', which is intended to ensure that qualifying trusts pay no more tax on the income that accrues for the benefit of vulnerable beneficiaries than the beneficiaries would themselves have paid if the income had arisen directly in their own hands (see 150-800 for details).

Other trusts

A *bare trust* occurs generally when the beneficiary is absolutely entitled to trust property as against the trustee (often called a nominee): see 150-350 for the income tax treatment of such trusts.

A *protective trust* is one under which an interest in possession may terminate on the bankruptcy of the life tenant, or on his attempting to assign his interest. The interest in possession will then be superseded by discretionary trusts of which the former life tenant may be a discretionary object.

Settlement

Where property is set aside on trust for beneficiaries, whether with vested interests or entitlements which depend upon the exercise of a discretion by the trustees, the property may be referred to as *settled*, and the term *settlement* used interchangeably with *trust*. Partly as a result of recent reforms of trust taxation, the term *settlement* seems to be supplanting the term *trust*, at least in relation to tax matters. In the Taxes Acts, the term *settlement* can vary in its precise meaning according to the context; as part of the reform process some terminology relating to the concept of *settlement* has been refined, with common definitions applying for both income and capital gains tax purposes (see 150-220). The term *settlement* can potentially cover any situation in which a person arranges for money or property to be held by or for the benefit of another, otherwise than for full and valuable consideration. The meaning of *settlement* for some anti-avoidance purposes is further considered at 151-000ff. (see 151-200 for specific comment).

Sub-fund elections

It may be convenient for trustees to divide property within a single trust into two or more distinct sub-funds, perhaps to reflect the position of various beneficiaries. Such administrative measures, generally, have no effect on how the trust is taxed. If it is a single trust it is taxed as such. However, in order to enable the taxation of trusts with more than one fund to reflect the manner in which the trust deals with its property it is possible to elect for sub-funds to be treated, generally, as separate trusts.

The trustees of any settlement, described as the 'principal settlement', are able to elect that a fund or other specified portion of the settled property should be treated for most capital gains tax purposes as if it comprised a separate settlement (the 'sub-fund'). The separate settlement created by the election is known as the 'sub-fund settlement'.

Where trustees have made a sub-fund election, the sub-fund settlement is to be treated as a separate settlement for income tax purposes as well. This notional settlement is treated as made at the time the sub-fund election took effect; from that time any trustees of the sub-fund settlement will be treated as trustees of that notional settlement and not the principal settlement, unless they also happen to be trustees of the principal settlement (which will frequently be the case). Similarly, the trustees of the principal settlement will be treated as trustees of that settlement and not of the sub-fund settlement, unless they also happen to be trustees of the sub-fund settlement.

Legislation: *Trustee Act* 1925; FA 2005, s. 23; ITA 2007, s. 466–473

Cases: *Pitt v Holt; Futter v Futter* [2011] BTC 322; *Futter v R & C Commrs; Pitt v R & C Commrs* [2013] BTC 126

Other Material: HMRC *Trusts, Settlements and Estates Manual* TSEM1005

Tax Reporter: ¶350-000

150-100 Powers of trustees

The administrative responsibilities and abilities of the trustees to deal with (e.g. to sell, purchase, mortgage, use, etc.) trust property are generally laid down in the trust deed, but some are created by statute, and these may in turn be excluded, modified or amplified by the trust deed. The common powers of maintenance and advancement should particularly be noted.

Maintenance

By statute trustees may, during the minority of a beneficiary (whether that beneficiary's interest is vested or contingent), at their sole discretion, pay to the parent or guardian of the minor, or otherwise apply for or towards the minor's maintenance, education or benefit, the whole of the income from the trust fund, or such part of it as may be reasonable. This is the case whether or not there is any other fund available for the purpose or any person bound by law to provide for the beneficiary's maintenance or education.

If a beneficiary has reached majority without attaining a vested interest (e.g. because he is still only entitled contingently upon some other event, such as surviving some other person or attaining a specified age) the trustees must usually pay the trust income to him (unless the trust deed expresses some contrary intention) until he either attains a vested interest, or dies, or his interest fails. Income not applied for the maintenance, etc. of a beneficiary during his minority must be accumulated; the beneficiary will then become entitled to the accumulations if he reaches his majority (and if he does not, the accumulations are added to the trust capital). These statutory powers of maintenance exist subject to any prior interests or charges affecting the trust property, and are often supplemented by specified powers in the trust deed.

Advancement

If powers of maintenance relate to the income of the trust, the trustees also enjoy powers of advancement over the capital. They may apply capital for the advancement or benefit, in their discretion, of any person entitled to the capital of trust property, or to a share in it, whether that person's entitlement is absolute or contingent upon his or her attaining a specified age or upon some other event. The money so applied must not exceed one-half of the beneficiary's vested or presumptive share in trust capital; when the beneficiary becomes absolutely entitled to his or her share, the money already advanced to him or her must be brought into account, and no advancement may be made which would prejudice any person entitled to a prior interest, unless that person is in existence, of full age and consents in writing to the advancement. Again, the trust deed may include its own power of advancement which may be wider than that provided for by statute.

Legislation: *Trustee Act* 1925, s. 31, 32

Tax Reporter: ¶350-000

150-150 Non-express trusts

In addition to express trusts created by deed or will or by some deliberate act of the settlor, there are also various non-express trusts. Of particular importance for tax purposes is the 'resulting trust' which arises, for instance, where the initial objects of the trust fail, and the property reverts to the settlor in the absence of any other defined objects.

> **Example**
>
> Alan settles property on trust for such of Bob, Colin and David as should survive him. There is no *gift-over* to any beneficiary entitled in default. Bob, Colin and David all predecease Alan: the trust property reverts to Alan. This is known as a *resulting trust*.

HMRC are often alert to spot a hidden resulting trust in the terms of an express trust because of the principle that if there is any chance that the settlor (or the spouse or civil partner of the settlor) may benefit from the property, the income of the trust will be treated, under special, wide ranging anti-avoidance rules, as that of the settlor for income tax purposes (see 151-000ff.).

Legislation: ITTOIA 2005, s. 619

Tax Reporter: ¶350-000

Other Material: HMRC *Trusts, Settlements and Estates Manual* TSEM4005ff.

Trustees

150-200 Introduction

Trustees are liable to income tax (by self assessment or by deduction at source, as appropriate) in respect of the income of the trust. The income is assessed under the rules appropriate to the particular source. Trusts, being subject to income tax, are within the scope of the Income Tax Acts. So, for example, income from a trade carried on by a trust (a relatively rare occurrence) is assessed as trading income under normal rules and the trustees are entitled to claim any relief applying to that source of income.

Trustees are not treated as individuals for tax purposes. Instead they are treated as if they were a single person, distinct from the actual persons who are (from time to time) the trustees of the settlement. They cannot claim personal reliefs in respect of trust income, and they are not liable to higher rate tax in respect of that income. However, in certain cases where it might otherwise be possible for settlors to avoid higher rate tax by putting their income into a settlement, the settlement income is deemed to be that of the settlor for tax purposes. Also, some trust income is charged at special rates that equate to the higher rates of personal tax.

The rate of tax depends on the source of the income and the type of trust.

Discretionary trusts and accumulation trusts

Most of the income of discretionary trusts and trusts that require income to be accumulated is subject to tax at special rates ('the trust rate' and the 'dividend trust rate').

For 2017–18, the trust rate is 45% and the dividend trust rate is 38.1%.

See 150-250 for further detail.

Interest in possession trusts

The income of an interest in possession (IIP) trust is taxable at the rate appropriate to the source and type of income, except that an IIP trust is not liable at the higher rate or the starting rate for income tax. So for 2017–18, the rates are:

- 7.5% for dividend income (the dividend ordinary rate); and
- 20% (the basic rate) on all other income.

The special rates for trusts can apply to IIP trusts in some cases where capital receipts are deemed to be income (see 150-250).

For commentary on IIP trusts generally, see 150-230.

Bare trusts and nominees

Income arising to a bare trustee or nominee, where property is held on behalf of beneficiaries who are absolutely entitled as against the bare trustee or nominee, is treated for tax purposes as the beneficiaries' own income, so the bare trustee or nominee is generally ignored for tax purposes and any income will be taxed at the rates appropriate to the beneficiary (using the personal allowances and rate bands) (see 150-350).

Service charges and landlords

Most landlords are required to hold any amounts received for service charges and sinking funds, paid by tenants and leaseholders in respect of residential property, in trust for the tenants, etc. Registered social landlords and local authorities are not legally required to hold such service charge payments in trust but in practice they often do.

A 'service charge' is an amount payable by a tenant of a dwelling as part of or in addition to rent directly or indirectly, for services, repairs, maintenance or insurance or the landlord's costs of management. A 'sinking fund' usually involves the long-term setting aside of funds for major repairs and renewals. Over a period such a fund may grow to a significant size and generate substantial investment income. Such income is excluded from the scope of accumulated or discretionary income for tax purposes (so that the special trust rates do not apply). This applies for all landlords (whether social or private), provided the funds relate to dwellings in the UK.

Trustees' administrative and management expenses

Expenses that are deductible in computing profits are allowable (e.g. maintenance and repair expenses in relation to let property), but the general administrative and management expenses of the trustees in running the trust are subject to special rules. See 150-260.

Legislation: *Landlord and Tenant Act* 1985, s. 18; ITTOIA 2005, s. 619; ITA 2007, Pt. 9, Ch. 1–8

Other Material: HMRC *Trusts, Settlements and Estates Manual*

Tax Reporter: ¶350-100ff.

150-220 Common definitions: 'settlor' and 'settled property'

The terms below are applicable except where the context requires otherwise or other provisions apply. (See, for example, 151-200 for definitions of 'settlement' and 'settlor' that are specific to the anti-avoidance rules relating to settlor-interested trusts.)

Settled property

'Settled property' is any property held in trust, but is *not* property held:

- by one person as nominee for another; or
- by one person as trustee for another person who is either absolutely entitled to the property as against the trustee; or who would be

absolutely entitled to the property as against the trustee but for being an infant or otherwise lacking legal capacity.

Any references to property comprised in a settlement are treated as references to settled property.

A person who is absolutely entitled to property as against the trustee means a person with exclusive right to direct how the property should be dealt with. The fact that the trustee has the right to use the property to pay outgoings, taxes etc. does not prevent another person from being absolutely entitled to the property as against the trustee. It is possible for two or more persons to be jointly absolutely entitled as against the trustee.

Settlor

A 'settlor' in relation to a settlement is generally the person who has made (or is treated as having made) the settlement. A settlor can be more than one person.

A person is treated as having made a settlement if:

- he has made or entered into it, directly or indirectly; or
- the settlement arose on the person's death and any of the settled property is, or is derived from, property of which that person was competent to dispose immediately before their death (i.e. property that could have been disposed of by the person's will, including any property subject to joint tenancy).

In this context, a person is treated as having made a settlement if he has provided, or has undertaken to provide, property directly or indirectly for the purposes of the settlement.

Property is derived from other property if it comes, directly or indirectly, wholly or partly, from that other property or from any income from that other property.

Reciprocal arrangements

Where there are reciprocal arrangements in force so that one person ('A') makes a settlement as a result of an arrangement with another person ('B'), B rather than A will be regarded as the settlor.

Ceasing to be treated as settlor

It is possible for a person to cease to be regarded as a settlor, in relation to a particular settlement, if the following three conditions are met:

- the settlement no longer contains or comprises any property of which the person was the settlor;
- the person has not undertaken to provide (directly or indirectly) any further property; and
- the person has not entered into any reciprocal arrangements with another person to provide property for the settlement in the future.

Transfers between settlements

Where the trustees of one settlement ('settlement 1') transfer any property to another settlement ('settlement 2') and the transfer meets the following conditions, the person who provided the transferred property to settlement 1 will be treated as a settlor in respect of settlement 2 and its newly acquired property. The conditions are that the transfer:

(1) is not for full consideration;

(2) is not by way of a bargain at arm's length; and

(3) does not occur:

  (i) only because of a beneficiary transferring rights under settlement 1 to the trustees of settlement 2;

  (ii) only because of the exercise of a general power of appointment; or

  (iii) on the variation of a will.

Variation of a will

Where the disposition of property following a person's death is varied within two years of the death there are special rules to identify who will be regarded as a settlor of any of the property.

Where any property becomes settled property in consequence of a variation and it would not otherwise have become settled property then one of the following will be treated as having made the settlement and as having provided the property for the purposes of the settlement:

- the person who, immediately before the variation, was entitled to the property (or to property from which it derives) absolutely as legatee;
- the persons who would have become entitled to the property (or to property from which it derives) absolutely as legatee but for the variation; or
- any persons who would have fallen into either of these two categories were they not infants or other persons lacking legal capacity.

'Legatee' includes anyone who takes property under a testamentary disposition or under the intestacy rules, whether as beneficiary or trustee.

A person who takes property under a *donatio mortis causa* (gift in consideration of death) is treated as a legatee who acquires the property at the time of the donor's death.

There are also rules that apply where the variation results in property of which the deceased person was settlor in one settlement being comprised in another settlement. The deceased person is deemed to be the settlor of the other settlement.

Legislation: ITA 2007, s. 465–473

Tax Reporter: ¶350-000ff.

150-230 Interest in possession (IIP) trusts

The income of an IIP trust is taxable at the rate appropriate to the income, but the higher rate and the starting rate do not apply.

Some deemed income of an IIP trust is chargeable at the special trust rates; see 150-250.

Administrative and management expenses of the trustees (see 150-260) reduce the beneficiary's income paid out of the trust.

Example

The Smith No. 1 Trust under which Alice has a life interest with the remainder to her grandchildren, receives in 2017–18:

- UK dividends of £3,000;
- building society interest of £2,000;
- bank interest of £2,500;
- rental income of £2,500.

There are trust administrative expenses of £270, and £600 is spent on repairing and insuring the rented property.

The trust's tax liability for 2017–18 is calculated as follows:

Source	*Gross*
	£
Dividends	3,000
Savings income (building society and bank interest)	4,500
	7,500
Rental income (£2,500 less £600)	1,900
Trust's taxable income	9,400

Trust's tax liability		£
Dividend income at 7.5% × £3,000	=	225
Savings income at 20% × £4,500	=	900
Other income at 20% × £1,900	=	380
Assessable		1,505

Tax at the basic rate (20%) and the dividend ordinary rate (7.5%) is directly assessable on the trustees.

There is no relief at any of these rates for the trust's administrative expenses of £270. The expenses will reduce Anne's income from the trust.

Legislation: ITA 2007, s. 11, 12, 14, 479 and 481

Tax Reporter: ¶350–100

150-250 Special rates of tax for trustees

Certain income is charged at 'the trust rate' (45% for 2017–18) and the 'dividend trust rate' (38.1% for 2017–18). These special rates apply to income which:

- is to be accumulated; or
- is payable at the discretion of the trustees or any other person.

The special rates also apply to certain kinds of deemed income in all trusts (see below).

However, the special rates do *not* apply where:

- the trust income (before being distributed) is the income of any person other than the trustees;
- the trust income arises under a charitable trust (see 154-000ff.);
- the income is from property held for the purposes of certain superannuation schemes; or
- the income arises from service charges held on trust by landlords (see 150-200).

The special rates apply only to income which exceeds income used in defraying the expenses of trustees in the tax year which are properly chargeable to income. See 150-260 for commentary on trustees' expenses.

Where untaxed income arises to the trustees by reason of their being non-UK resident, the management expenses must be apportioned between taxable and non-taxable income.

Special trust rates not to apply to first slice of income

The special trust rates do not apply to the first slice of income that would otherwise be charged at those rates. The first £1,000 of such income is chargeable at the basic rate (20%) or dividend ordinary rate (7.5%), depending on the type of income falling into that first slice (generally referred to as the 'standard rate band', although this is not the statutory term).

The standard rate band rates are applied to the income in the following order:

(1) first against income that would, but for the special trust rules, be chargeable at the basic rate;

(2) then, against income that would, but for the special trust rules, be chargeable at the dividend ordinary rate.

The standard rate band applies to income that is net of allowable trust management expenses.

Where a settlor has made more than one settlement, the £1,000 is divided between each of the settlements equally, subject to a de minimis standard rate band of £200 that any qualifying settlement is entitled to. So if an individual has made four settlements, each will have a standard rate band of £250, being £1,000/4. But if he has made six settlements, each will have a standard rate band of £200.

The tax pool

Tax charged on the income of the trust is included in the tax pool (see 150-600). Where UK resident trustees make discretionary distributions of income to beneficiaries the income is treated as an amount from which tax payable at the trust rate has been deducted. Trustees must ensure that they have paid sufficient income tax to cover the amount of that deemed deduction, which is available as a tax credit to the beneficiary, and is disclosed as such on the form R185 (Trust Income). Income tax paid by the trustees at the trust rate or dividend trust rate (prior to 6 April 2016, this excluded the 10% non-payable tax credit on dividend income) goes into the tax pool. This tax pool can be used to cover the amount of the deemed deduction, with the trustees paying any additional tax to cover a shortfall. Any tax charged at the basic rate and, with effect from 6 April 2016, the dividend ordinary rate, as part of the first slice rate band, can be added to the tax pool and can be used to cover the amount of the deemed deduction.

Calculation of tax at the special rates for trustees

The exact method of calculation to be used to ascertain a trust's tax liability at the trust rate or the dividend trust rate is not set out in statute. The method used by HMRC is set out in the self-assessment guide – SA950 *Trust and Estate Tax Return Guide*.

Example

The Abacus discretionary trust has the following assessable income and trust management expenses for the tax year 2017–18:

- profit from property rental business: £2,000;
- UK company dividends: £1,700;
- bank interest: £1,000;
- trust management expenses: £1,480.

Taxable income for 2017–18

	Gross income
	£
Rental income	2,000
Dividend	1,700
Interest	1,000
	4,700

The trust management expenses are treated as paid out of the dividend income in priority to other types of income (see order of priority above). To the extent that the management expenses are paid out of a particular type of income (in this case, dividend income) the income so used is taxed not at the special trust rates but at the appropriate basic, savings or dividend ordinary rate. The amount of income therefore needed to pay the management expenses is the amount of gross income that would be needed, prior to the tax charged at the appropriate rate.

	Non-savings (basic rate)	**Savings (savings rate)**	**Dividend (dividend rate)**	**Tax**
	£	**£**	**£**	**£**
Taxable income	2,000	1,000	1,700	
Non-savings income				
(Rental income)				
First £1,000 at basic rate(1)	(1,000)			
• £1,000 × 20% =				200.00

	Non-savings (basic rate)	Savings (savings rate)	Dividend (dividend rate)	Tax
	£	£	£	£
Next £1,000 at the trust rate	(1,000)			
• £1,000 × 45% =				450.00
Savings income				
(Bank interest)				
£1,000 at the trust rate		(1,000)		
• £1,000 × 45% =				450.00
Dividend income				
First:				
Income allocated to pay trust management expenses expense of £1,480 grossed up at the dividend ordinary rate of 7.5%			(1,600)	
Taxed at the dividend ordinary rate:				
• £1,600 × 7.5% =				120.00
Next:				
Remaining dividend income taxed at the dividend trust rate:				
(£1,700 – £1,600)			(100)	
• £260 × 38.1% =				38.10
Total trust tax liability				1,058.10

(1) The first £1,000 slice of trust income is not subject to the special rates for trusts but to the appropriate basic or dividend ordinary rate.

For commentary on trustees' expenses, see 150-260.

Capital receipts treated as income to which the special rates for trusts apply

Various types of capital receipt (including gains on a chargeable event) are assessable to income tax, at the special trust rates, in trustees' hands (provided the trust is not a unit trust) on receipt or when the trustees become entitled to payment.

The types of capital receipt/chargeable event include:

- any payments made by a company on redemption, repayment or purchase of its own shares, or on the purchase of rights to acquire its own shares;

- gains on contracts for life assurance, etc.;
- deemed income under the accrued income scheme;
- profits on disposal of deeply discounted securities;
- profits of property businesses in relation to lease premiums and similar amounts;
- the profit on the disposal of a future or option;
- profits on the disposal of deposit rights;
- proceeds of sale of a foreign dividend coupon;
- chargeable events in relation to employee share ownership trusts;
- offshore income gains; and
- gains on disposals of land.

Legislation: ITTOIA 2005, s. 619; ITA 2007 s. 479–484, 486 and 491–496

Cases: *IR Commrs v Berrill* (1981) 55 TC 429; *Carver v Duncan; Bosanquet v Allen* [1985] BTC 248

Other Material: HMRC *Trusts, Settlements and Estates Manual* TSEM3010 and TSEM3505

Tax Reporter: ¶351-100ff.

150-260 Trustees' expenses

Expenses that are deductible in calculating profits (e.g. repair and maintenance expenses in a property business) are allowable as a deduction against the specific income source under the normal rules for tax deduction. But trustees' general administrative expenses (often called trust management expenses or TMEs) are subject to special rules.

Interest in possession trusts

TMEs incurred by the trustees reduce the beneficiary's entitlement to income rather than being used to reduce the trustees' tax liability. As the beneficiary is taxed at different rates on different kinds of income, it is necessary to know which trust income has been used to pay the TMEs. The order for the offset is:

(1) company dividends, including non-qualifying distributions, foreign dividends equivalent to UK dividends, scrip dividends, and close company loans released to the trustees; then

(2) other savings income; and

(3) non-savings income.

Discretionary and accumulation trusts

Income which is used to pay administrative expenses is not liable at the trust rate or the dividend trust rate but at the dividend ordinary rate, being 7.5% if paid out of dividend income or 20% if paid out of other income. The expenses must be grossed up at the appropriate rate (7.5% or 20% after 6 April 2016) – before they are deducted. The order of priority for allocating the expenses to particular income is the same as in (1)–(3) above.

The expenses taken into account are those that have been incurred rather than those that have been paid.

Where a non-resident beneficiary is entitled to untaxed income because of his or her non-resident status, the management expenses must be apportioned between the untaxed and taxed income.

Nature of expenses

Expenses are allowable TMEs if they are income (not capital) expenses. The distinction is based on trust law.

HMRC publish guidance on the kinds of expenses that should be treated as allowable TMEs. The guidance is available at www.hmrc.gov.uk/trusts/tmes-paper.pdf. Examples given by HMRC include:

- the cost of preparing the trust's tax return: as far as the costs relate to income they are allowable TMEs, but as far as they relate to capital gains, they are not TMEs; and
- the cost of obtaining tax advice for capital gains tax or inheritance tax: this cannot be said to relate to income and so is not an allowable TME.

Legislation: ITA 2007, s. 484, 486, 500 and 503

Other Material: HMRC *Trusts, Settlements and Estates Manual* TSEM3505 and TSEM8425

Tax Reporter: ¶350-600

150-270 Income of discretionary trusts paid to beneficiaries

Income received by a discretionary trust is liable to tax at the special trust rates. This income is assessed on the trustees for the year in which it arises. The income might not be distributed until some years later, when the rates of tax may have changed. Where:

- UK resident trustees in the exercise of a discretion (exercisable by them or by any other person) make a payment to any person;

- the sum paid becomes for tax purposes the income of the recipient, or the income of the settlor if paid for the benefit of a minor child of the settlor who is unmarried and not a civil partner; and
- the sum would not be income of the recipient apart from the payment,

such a payment is treated as a net payment corresponding to a gross amount from which tax has been deducted at the trust rate in force for the year in which the payment is made.

Example

The Benificent Trust, a discretionary settlement, makes a distribution of £3,250 to a beneficiary in 2017–18. The payment of £3,250 is treated as a net payment after tax at 45% has been deducted from the gross amount. The net payment is grossed up in the hands of the beneficiary to £5,909.

The beneficiary receives (for tax purposes) gross income of £5,909 with a tax credit of £2,659. These amounts will be included on the form 'R185 (Trust Income)' (certificate of deduction of income tax prepared by the trustees and given to the beneficiary). See also 150-600.

Set-off provisions

The tax regarded as deducted is treated as income tax paid by the person to whom the payment is made, and is repayable if the beneficiary's tax liability is lower than the tax deducted. The trustees are required to account for the tax deducted to HMRC, except to the extent that it is covered by income tax already charged on the trustees. The trustees therefore maintain a 'tax pool', and if the tax pool is insufficient to 'frank' the payment to the beneficiary, the balance is recovered through the self assessment (see also 150-600).

The tax pool is made up as follows.

(1) The amount of the tax pool brought forward at the start of the year (after the deduction of the tax due as a result of discretionary payments in the previous year and, where the settlement is an employee benefit settlement, after deduction, any repayments made for that previous tax year in respect of payments treated as employment income of the recipients (see 150-300).

(2) Tax charged in the tax year at the trust rate or the dividend trust rate (including tax charged on deemed income under ITA 2007, s. 482: see 150-250), except where (4) or (5) below applies.

(3) Tax charged at the basic rate (but, prior to 6 April 2016, not the dividend ordinary rate) on the first slice (£1,000) of trust income (see 150-250).

(4) Prior to 6 April 2016, tax charged at the difference between the dividend trust rate and the dividend ordinary rate on:

   (a) dividends, etc. from UK companies;

   (b) stock dividends from UK companies;

   (c) loans from close companies written off; and

   (d) deemed income in respect of payments made by a company on the redemption, repayment or purchase of the company's shares.

(5) Tax charged at the difference between the trust rate and the basic rate on chargeable event gains on life insurance policies.

(6) The income tax liability of the trustees determined following a claim for relief in respect of a vulnerable beneficiary.

Where (4) above applies, then, prior to 6 April 2016, the amount of tax added to the tax pool was the difference between the tax charged at the dividend trust rate and the dividend ordinary rate. This had the effect of excluding the notional tax credit on UK dividends, etc. from the tax pool, thereby preventing any beneficiary who receives income from being able to recover tax credits on dividends.

Example, pre-2016–17

The Delta Trust (a discretionary trust) received UK dividends of £2,700 in 2015–16. There was no tax pool brought forward from previous years. The trustees' tax liability and net income are as follows:

Trustees' tax liabilities	**£**	**£**
Dividends received	2,700	
Add: non-payable tax credit	300	
Total income of trust	3,000	
IT liability of trust:		
• First £1,000 at 10%		100
(Standard Rate Band)		
• Balance at dividend trust rate		
(37.5% × £2,000)		750
Total IT liability of trust		850
Less: Tax credit on dividends		(300)
Tax payable by trustees		550

Net income of trust

Actual amounts received	2,700
Less: tax paid to HMRC	(550)
Net income of trust/cash retained	2,150

The tax pool, for any payments made to a beneficiary in 2014–15, will be as follows:

Tax Pool	**£**
Amount brought forward	Nil
Tax suffered/paid	850
Less: non-payable tax credit	(300)
Tax pool: available to 'frank' tax credit (at 45%) on amounts paid to beneficiary	550

If the whole of the cash retained (£2,150) were to be paid out to a beneficiary there would have been insufficient funds available to the trustees to settle the tax deducted at source from the gross payment, because a net payment £2,150 equals a gross payment of £3,909 with a tax credit (at 45%) of £1,759 from which the tax pool of only £550 is available. A balance of £1,209 would have been needed (but unavailable) to frank the tax credit (£1,759 *less* £550). With a net income of £2,150 and a tax pool of £550, the maximum amount that could have been paid to a beneficiary was as follows:

Maximum amount payable	**£**	**£**
Net income of trust/cash retained	2,150	
Add: tax in tax pool	550	
Amount available to cover:	2,700	
(i) payment to beneficiary; and		
(ii) beneficiary's tax credit at 45%		
Tax credit at 45% of £2,700	1,215	
Less: amount in the tax pool	(550)	
Further tax payable by trustees	665	
Net payment to beneficiary		
Net income of trust/cash retained	2,150	
Less: further tax payable by trustees	(665)	
Net payment to beneficiary	1,485	
Total amount available	or	2,700
Less: tax credit at 45% of £2,700		(1,215)
Net payment to beneficiary		1,485

Effectively the maximum amount that could have been paid out (in the absence of a balance on the tax pool brought forward from earlier years) where only dividend income is received, was 45% of the net dividends received (i.e. £2,700 × 45% = £1,215). The result of this was unfavourable compared to an interest in possession trust where a beneficiary is not wholly in a tax repayment position.

The requirement to have sufficient tax credit in the 'tax pool' continues post-6 April 2016, but there is no longer a requirement to adjust for the notional tax credit on dividend income. This is illustrated below.

Example, post-2016–17

The Delta Trust (as illustrated in the example above) received UK dividends of £2,700 in 2017–18. There was no tax pool brought forward from previous years. The trustees' tax liability and net income are as follows:

Trustees' tax liabilities	**£**	**£**
Dividends received	2,700	
IT liability of trust:		
• First £1,000 at 7.5% (Standard Rate Band)		75
• Balance at dividend trust rate (38.1% × £1,700)		648
Total IT liability of trust		723
Net income of trust		
Actual amounts received		2,700
Less: tax paid to HMRC		(723)
Net income of trust/cash retained		1,977

The tax pool, for any payments made to a beneficiary in 2017–18, will be as follows:

Tax pool	**£**
Amount brought forward	Nil
Tax suffered/paid: available to 'frank' tax credit (at 45%) on amounts paid to beneficiary	723

If the whole of the cash retained (£1,977) were to be paid out to a beneficiary, there would have been insufficient funds available to the trustees to settle the tax deducted at source from the gross payment, because a net payment £1,977 equals a gross payment of £3,595 with a tax credit (at 45%) of £1,618 from which the tax pool of only £723 is available. A balance of £895 would have been needed (but unavailable) to frank the tax credit (£1,618 *less* £723). With a net income of £1,977 and a tax pool of £723, the maximum amount that could have been paid to a beneficiary was as follows:

Maximum amount payable	**£**	**£**
Net income of trust/cash retained	1,977	
Add: tax in tax pool	723	
Amount available to cover:	2,700	
(i) payment to beneficiary; and		
(i) beneficiary's tax credit at 45%		
Tax credit at 45% of £2,700	1,215	
Less: amount in the tax pool	(723)	
Further tax payable by trustees	492	
Net payment to beneficiary		
Net income of trust/cash retained	1,977	
Less: further tax payable by trustees	(492)	
Net payment to beneficiary	1,485	
Total amount available		2,700
Less: tax credit at 45% of £2,700		(1,215)
Net payment to beneficiary		1,485

Effectively, the maximum amount that can be paid out (in the absence of a balance on the tax pool brought forward from earlier years) is 45% of the dividends received (i.e. £2,700 × 45% = £1,215). This is no different from the position prior to 6 April 2016 but, with the removal of the notional tax credits on dividends, the mechanism for arriving at the tax pąyable is different.

Distribution must be income in the hands of the beneficiary

It is essential to establish clearly whether a payment made by a discretionary trust to a beneficiary is income or capital in the hands of the beneficiary, since this will establish whether the trustees have an income tax liability.

Whether a payment by a trust will be regarded as income or capital in the hands of the beneficiary depends on the facts. It is the character of the payment in the hands of the beneficiary which is important and not the character of the funds out of which it is paid.

Legislation: ITA 2007, s. 493–495

Case: *Carver v Duncan; Bosanquet v Allen* [1985] BTC 248

Tax Reporter: ¶354-300

150-300 Discretionary payments to beneficiaries of employee benefit settlements

Payments to employees of the settlor may be treated as arising from the employment and hence taxable as employment income. Payments from an employee trust where the employment has ceased are taxable. Payment of assessable income to an employee by an intermediary of the employer is subject to the obligation to deduct tax and NIC under PAYE. An 'intermediary of the employer' includes trustees holding property for any person or class of persons which includes the employee. Thus, payments by trustees of an employee trust are within the PAYE net. Discretionary payments to beneficiaries in general would fall to be treated as income received after deduction of tax at the special trust rates (see 150-250). This does not, however, apply where the payment is employment income in the hands of the beneficiary. As a result, because the employee receives no credit for the tax borne by the trustees, there is the potential for double taxation on the same income; once on the trustees and again on the employee under PAYE.

This double taxation is avoided because the trustees of an 'employee benefit settlement' may claim a repayment of income tax equal to the lower of:

- tax at the trust rate for the year on the total of the discretionary payments made in the year which are treated as employment income of the recipients; and
- the amount in the trustees' tax pool for the year reduced by the total amount of income tax treated as having been paid as a result of the discretionary payments made in the year.

An 'employee benefit settlement' for these purposes is one where the settled property can only be applied for the benefit of persons within a relevant class, or jointly for those persons and for charitable purposes. A relevant class is one comprising of individuals employed in a particular trade or profession or employed by a body carrying on a trade, etc. or the spouses, civil partners and dependants of those individuals.

Repayment supplement/interest will be payable if the repayment is made later than 31 January following the tax year concerned.

Legislation: ITEPA 2003, s. 17(1)–(3) and 686; ITA 2007, s. 493(2), 496A and 496B

Case: *Brumby v Milner* 51 TC 583

Tax Reporter: ¶351-550

150-350 Bare trustees and nominees

A bare trust arises where the beneficiary has an indefeasible interest in the whole of the trust property, the trustee's powers are purely administrative, and the beneficiary, if of full age and capacity (sui juris), has the right to have the property vested in him absolutely subject only to a proper deduction for trustees' expenses. A similar situation arises where there is a nominee instead of a trustee: this generally arises from a contractual arrangement between the person beneficially entitled and his nominee, and usually the nominee has no administrative powers.

A bare trustee or nominee for a person sui juris is ignored for income tax purposes; the income arising is assessed on the beneficial owner as though it were his income. In practice, the beneficial owner will be assessed, not the trustee or nominee.

Where the beneficiary is not sui juris (e.g. is a minor or incapacitated person) the trustee instead of the beneficiary may be assessed, but the tax due is still calculated on the basis that the income belongs to the beneficiary. Consequently, the trustee may claim any personal allowances or reliefs due on behalf of the beneficiary, but must pay any tax to which the beneficiary may be liable and which is not covered by deduction of tax at source. The trustee has a statutory right to retain, out of funds coming into his hands on behalf of the beneficiary, sufficient to pay any tax due.

Legislation: TMA 1970, s. 72

Tax Reporter: ¶351-000

150-400 Trustees' remuneration

Some trust instruments specify a fixed remuneration to which trustees are entitled. If the trustee is not a professional person, then this remuneration is normally regarded as an 'annual payment' from which tax is deducted and which is taxed under ITTOIA 2005, Pt. 5, Ch. 7 ('Annual payment not otherwise charged'). However, for a professional trustee (e.g. a solicitor or accountant) who is entitled to charge for his services, the income forms part of his professional receipts taxable as the profits of a trade or profession, and is paid without deduction of tax.

For planning purposes, if the settlor is also a trustee, and provides for remuneration for himself in the trust deed, HMRC may argue that the income of the trust should be taxed as income of the settlor on the ground that the settlor has not absolutely divested himself of the trust property. It is understood that HMRC might not wish to take this point if the remuneration paid to the settlor/trustee is reasonable, but since the question of reasonableness is a value judgment, the wiser course may be not to provide remuneration for the settlor/trustee in such circumstances.

Legislation: ITTOIA 2005, s. 686; ITA 2007, s. 494

Cases: *Baxendale v Murphy* (1924) 9 TC 76; *Dale v IR Commrs* (1953) 34 TC 468

Tax Reporter: ¶350-150

150-450 Residence of trustees

The residence status of trustees is relevant in determining their UK income tax liability, and is particularly important in discretionary trusts. Where the beneficiary is absolutely entitled to trust income, it is the residence of the beneficiary that is important, as the trust is looked through to establish the underlying source of the income.

As a single body, trustees have a single joint residence which is determined by looking to the residence position of the individual trustees. The following rules apply.

When either Condition A or Condition B below is met, the trustees (as a deemed single person) are both UK resident and ordinarily UK resident.

When neither of Conditions A or B below is met, the trustees (as a deemed single person) are non-UK resident and not ordinarily UK resident.

Condition A is that all the persons who are trustees are UK resident.

Condition B is that:

- at least one of the persons who are trustees is UK resident;
- at least one such person is non-UK resident; *and*
- a settlor of the trust, at the time the trust was made (or immediately before the settlor's death if the trust arose on death) was UK resident, ordinarily UK resident, *or* domiciled in the UK.

See also 170-000ff.

Legislation: ICTA 1988, s. 685E; FA 1989, s. 110

Tax Reporter: ¶350-800

Beneficiaries

150-500 General treatment of beneficiaries

The distinction between vested interests and contingent interests in income must be borne in mind when dealing with the taxation of beneficiaries. This is explained in outline at 150-000. Where a beneficiary has a vested interest in income, that income forms part of his total income as it arises, even if it is not paid out by the trustees. Where the interest is a contingent interest, the income is that of the trustees and the beneficiary will only be taxed on amounts actually received from the trustees. In general, if a beneficiary has a vested interest, even income which is accumulated by trustees forms part of the beneficiary's total income.

Accumulations for minor beneficiaries

It is sometimes the case that a minor beneficiary has an absolute right to income but, because he cannot give a good receipt for it, the trustees continue to accumulate it until he attains his majority. In such cases, the income is the beneficiary's income as it arises (unless it is treated as the income of the settlor). However, where there is a minor beneficiary, any direction in the trust instrument to accumulate income until, for example, a specified age, will generally prevent the income being that of the beneficiary during the required period of accumulation. Of particular importance is the statutory trust for accumulation, coupled with the power of maintenance (see 150-100). This rule applies unless it is expressly excluded by the terms of the settlement. Any income not applied for the minor beneficiary's maintenance, education or benefit is accumulated until his majority, when the trustees are obliged to pay him the accumulations. If the minor beneficiary does not reach his majority, the accumulations are held as an accretion to the capital. It was held in *Stanley v IR Commrs* that this entailed the beneficiary having only a contingent interest in the trust income during his minority; accordingly the accumulations were taxable as the trustees' income and were not to be treated as the beneficiary's income.

Discretionary payments

Income applied at the trustees' discretion for the maintenance, education or benefit of a beneficiary is treated as the income of the beneficiary in the year of receipt and is grossed up at the trust rate for the year in which the income is paid. It is not treated as savings or dividend income in the beneficiary's hands, regardless of the underlying source of the income.

> **Example**
>
> Ann is an infant beneficiary. In 2017–18, the trustees of a discretionary trust set up by Ann's great uncle pay £550 to Ann's father, for her maintenance. Ann has no other income. Ann is treated as having received £1,000 (£550 grossed up at 45%, i.e. the trust rate) and, as her liability to tax is nil, she is entitled to reclaim the £450 tax treated as paid.

Legislation: *Trustee Act* 1925, s. 31

Case: *Stanley v IR Commrs* (1944) 26 TC 12

Tax Reporter: ¶353-000ff.

150-550 Trust income in hands of beneficiary

Where a beneficiary has a vested interest in the trust income, he will be liable to income tax on the grossed up amount of that income. The individual income sources will usually be grossed up at the 'applicable rate' which will depend on the type of income (see 150-200).

> **Example 1**
>
> Michael, a beneficiary of an interest in possession (IIP) trust, receives £800 of trust income (derived from a property business) in 2017–18. The income has borne 20% basic rate tax. He is treated as having received £1,000 (£800 grossed up at 20%). In making his self-assessment, Michael will be entitled to a tax credit of £200 (£1,000 – £800).
>
> If the income had borne tax at the trust rate (because the trust was a discretionary trust), it would be grossed up at 45% in Michael's hands and he would be treated as having received income of £1,455 (£800 grossed up at 45%). If Michael were only a basic rate taxpayer he would be entitled to a tax repayment of £364 (£1,455 × (45 – 20)%).

The rights of a beneficiary under a UK resident trust subject to Scots law are deemed to include the same right to income as that under English law.

The taxable income of the trustees will often not equate with the beneficiary's income for tax purposes because although trustees are not allowed to deduct their expenses when computing trust income, these expenses are deducted from the beneficiary's income (see 150-260). A consequence of this rule is that the tax credit to which the beneficiary is entitled will be less than the actual tax paid by the trustees.

The beneficiary may reclaim tax if the amount of tax borne on his trust income exceeds the amount due from him in respect of his total income, taking into account personal allowances, except that the tax credit on

UK dividends is not repayable. In other cases, the beneficiary is, where applicable, liable to tax at the higher rates.

Example 2

Trust income (of an IIP trust, with a single beneficiary) for 2017–18 is as follows:

	Gross
	£
Dividends	2,000
Bank interest	4,000
Rent	3,000
	9,000

Income tax of £600 will be due on rental income (£3,000 × 20%), £800 on the bank interest (£4,000 × 20%) and £150 on the dividend income (£2,000 × 7.5%). Trust administration expenses of £800 have been incurred.

	Rent	*Savings*	*Dividends*
	£	£	£
Total net income	2,400	3,200	1,850
Less: administration costs			(800)
	2,400	3,200	1,050

The maximum that the trust can distribute is £6,650 (£2,400 + £3,200 + £1,050). This is treated as the beneficiary's net income (it is an IIP trust), with the net amounts received with appropriate tax credits.

	Net	*Tax credit*	*Gross*
	£	£	£
Dividends	1,050	85	1,135
Bank interest	3,200	800	4,000
Rent	2,400	600	3,000
	6,600	1,511	8,135

The details shown above of the beneficiary's overall net income and tax credit would be notified to the beneficiary by the trustees on a certificate. The administration expenses are allocated to specific types of income (first dividends, then savings, then other income; see 150-260). To the extent the individual beneficiary has unused allowances or dividend nil rate tax bands, then they may be entitled to a repayment of tax paid by the trust on the respective income sources.

Legislation: ITA 2007, s. 11, 12, 14, 464, 500 and 503

Case: *MacFarlane v IR Commrs* (1929) 14 TC 532

Tax Reporter: ¶353-200

150-600 Discretionary trusts: the tax pool

Where trustees make a payment at their discretion (or at the discretion of any other person) which is income in the hands of a beneficiary of a trust, they are liable for the payment of income tax in respect of that income. The income paid to the beneficiary is treated as a sum net of tax at the trust rate for the tax year in which the payment is made.

The liability is satisfied by the trustees primarily out of income tax paid in respect of the tax year in which the payment is made, with any balance being satisfied out of the 'tax pool' that has accumulated. Where the total of the pool and the tax actually suffered in the tax year is insufficient to 'frank' the payment, the trustees are assessable for the shortfall, i.e. any excess of the tax credits attaching to payments to beneficiaries, over and above the available tax credits on the trust income and any tax payments made, are added to the tax bill for the year. Any excess in the tax pool is carried forward to the tax pool for the next tax year.

The tax pool

The composition of the tax pool is set out at 150-270.

The tax pool is reduced by the tax credit given on each 'franked' payment made by the trustees and certified on form R185 (Trust Income).

The pool relates to the entire trust and not to an individual beneficiary. So it is possible for a trust to have, say, two beneficiaries, one of whom ceases to qualify for discretionary payments without having received any such payments. The other beneficiary can then receive franked income payments out of the trust to the extent of the entire tax pool, not just half of it.

The tax pool when tax rates increase

The tax pool is carried forward at its accumulated value irrespective of any change in tax rates. The tax in the tax pool is then applied to 'frank' payments at the rate in force in the year in which payments are made, irrespective of the rate applicable when the tax was credited to the pool.

Where tax rates are lowered, tax credits at the higher rates previously in force will remain in the pool.

150-650 Payments made to beneficiary out of capital

Whether a payment to a beneficiary is taxed as income or is capital in his hands depends on the character of the payment in the hands of the beneficiary, regardless of the character of the funds out of which it is paid (see 150-270). It does not follow that money paid to a beneficiary out of trust capital is necessarily treated as capital in his hands. An annuity payment will, for instance, always be treated as income in the hands of the beneficiary, even if it is clear that it has been paid out of trust capital. In *Brodie's Will Trusts v IR Commrs*, a testator directed his trustees to pay to his widow a fixed annual sum out of the income of the trust fund and, where the income was not sufficient, to raise and pay the balance out of capital. The payments, even when made out of capital, were taxed as income in the hands of the widow. Similarly, in *Baron Inchyra v Jennings*, payments to a beneficiary of a foreign trust were income in her hands, even though they were capital in the hands of the trustees under the foreign jurisdiction.

However, in *Stevenson (HMIT) v Wishart* a series of payments made by trustees of a discretionary trust were held to be capital in the hands of the beneficiary. In that case payments had been made over a three-year period in exercise of a power to appoint capital to maintain an aged beneficiary in a nursing home. The Court of Appeal found that although the payments were used for day-to-day maintenance expenses they were exceptionally large amounts which would normally have been met out of capital and could not be regarded as ordinary income expenses. If the trustees had made a single appointment instead of a series of appointments there would have been no basis for saying that the sum would have been other than capital in the beneficiary's hands. The trustees were disposing of capital in exercise of a power to appoint capital and what they appointed remained capital. Payments made under the exercise of a discretionary power, for the maintenance, education or benefit of a minor normally form part of his income.

Cases: *Brodie's Will Trusts v IR Commrs* (1928–1933) 17 TC 432; *Baron Inchyra v Jennings* (1965) 42 TC 388; *Morant Settlement Trustees v IR Commrs* 30 TC 147; *Stevenson (HMIT) v Wishart* [1987] BTC 283

Tax Reporter: ¶352–850; ¶353–200

150-700 Payments made by the Thalidomide Children's Trust

Payments from the Thalidomide Children's Trust ('The Trust') to victims of thalidomide are within the scope of the tax exemption for personal injury damages paid as periodical payments. Such payments are thus exempt from tax, both for the purposes of calculating the victims' income tax liabilities and also their entitlement to tax credits.

Payments from The Trust prior to this were usually treated for tax purposes as any other payments to the beneficiaries of a discretionary trust (i.e. assessed on the beneficiaries, with a tax credit representing the rate of tax applicable to trusts). To comply with the new statutory requirements the Trust has changed the way it makes payments so that they can be classed as 'periodical' and capable of falling within the scope of the post 5 August 2004 rules.

Legislation: ITTOIA 2005, s. 731 and 732; *Thalidomide Children's Trust (Application of Section 329AA of the Income and Corporation Taxes Act 1988) Order* 2004 (SI 2004/1819)

Trusts with vulnerable beneficiaries

150-800 Introduction and overview

There are special rules for trusts with 'vulnerable beneficiaries' ('qualifying trusts').

Overview of the scheme

The overall aim of the rules is to enable the trustees of qualifying trusts to make a claim so that the trust pays no more income tax for a tax year than would have been paid by any beneficiary who is a 'vulnerable person' if the relevant income had accrued directly to the beneficiary.

Qualifying trusts income

The trustees may claim a deduction from the amount of income tax that they would otherwise pay, apart from the modified regime. The amount of tax actually payable by them is based on the tax situation of the 'vulnerable person'. The trustees:

- calculate what the trust's tax liability on the qualifying trusts income would be, without the special treatment;
- calculate what the vulnerable person's tax liability would have been had the qualifying trust's income arisen directly to the vulnerable beneficiary; and
- claim the difference (if any) between these two amounts as a deduction from the trust's own tax liability.

Settlor-interested trusts

The special income tax treatment is not available if the qualifying trust's income derives (or is treated as derived) from property in which the settlor (or spouse/civil partner) can be regarded as having an interest under the anti-avoidance rules for settlor-interested trusts (see 151-100ff. and 151-700ff.).

Legislation: FA 2005, s. 23–45 and Sch. 1

Tax Reporter: ¶352-000

150-820 Meaning of a 'vulnerable person'

A 'vulnerable person' is defined as someone who is either a 'disabled person' or a 'relevant minor' (or both).

'Disabled person'

A person is a 'disabled person' for these purposes if any one of three requirements is satisfied:

(1) the person is incapable of managing their affairs or administering their property by reason of mental disorder (as defined by the *Mental Health Act* 1983);

(2) the person is in receipt of attendance allowance under the *Social Security Contributions and Benefits Act* 1992, s. 64;

(3) the person is in receipt of a disability living allowance, under the *Social Security Contributions and Benefits Act* 1992, s. 71, by virtue of an entitlement to the care component at the middle or highest rate;

(4) the person is in receipt of a personal independence payment by virtue of entitlement to the daily living component;

(5) the person is in receipt of constant attendance allowance; or

(6) the person is in receipt of armed forces independence payment.

A person who is not in actual receipt of an allowance or payment as in (2) to (4) above, may still be treated as a 'disabled person' for these purposes, if the lack of entitlement is solely due to their failure to meet the allowances' prescribed conditions of residence in the UK. To meet the residence condition the claimant of the allowance should be ordinarily resident in the UK and be physically present in the UK when making the claim and have lived in the UK for an aggregate of 26 weeks out of the 52 weeks immediately prior to the claim. Where these residence conditions are *not* met, attendance or disability living allowance cannot be claimed. But if all the other conditions for receipt of these allowances are met, the failure of the residency conditions will not prevent a person from being treated as a vulnerable person by reason of disability.

Although the number of individuals who will be affected by this rule is likely to be small, it must be of some concern that officers of HMRC (and advisers to trustees and beneficiaries) will have to make decisions about the likelihood of a person's possible entitlement to attendance or disability living allowance, apart from their failure to meet the UK residence condition. It is not obvious that HMRC have particular expertise in this area of entitlement to benefit provision.

It may also be possible to be treated as a 'disabled person' if the lack of entitlement to the allowances is due to the person:

- being provided with treatment for renal failure (whether in hospital or in non-hospital accommodation); or
- being provided with non-hospital accommodation under the *National Assistance Act* 1948, Pt. III or the *National Health Service Act* 1977, Sch. 2, para. 8.

'Relevant minor'

A person is a 'relevant minor', for the purposes of these rules, if:

- the person is under 18 years of age; *and*
- at least one parent has died.

Legislation: FA 2005, s. 23, 38, 39 and Sch. 1A, 9 (as enacted for 2014–15 onwards)

Tax Reporter: ¶356-050

150-840 Qualifying trusts

It may be that a trust will hold only some of its settled property for particular beneficiaries on terms ('trusts') that meet the 'qualifying trusts' and 'vulnerable person' criteria. In such cases the special income and capital gains tax treatment may apply only in relation to that particular property to the extent that it is held in a separate fund or in some other way as a defined part of the overall settled property within the trust. There may also be cases where only a part of an asset is held on qualifying trusts for the benefit of a vulnerable person who is entitled to any income arising from that part of the asset. If it is possible to identify the relevant part of the asset and the portion of the income arising from that part then, for the purposes of determining whether the trusts on which the part of the asset is held are qualifying trusts, that part of the asset is to be treated as if it were a separate asset. When making the 'vulnerable person election' (see 150-860), if the trustees hold an asset (or assets) only parts of which are held on the relevant trusts, the election must include a statement listing each asset concerned, with each part of the asset concerned identified together with details of the allocation of any income arising from it.

There are two 'classes' of vulnerable person (disabled persons and relevant minors; see above) and there are two corresponding types of qualifying trust.

Qualifying trusts: disabled persons

Where property is held on trusts for a disabled person, those trusts will be 'qualifying trusts' if, during the disabled person's lifetime, or until the trusts' termination (if that is before the disabled person's death):

(1) the trusts' property is to be applied only for the benefit of the disabled person; and

(2) either:

    (a) the disabled person is entitled to all (if any) of the income arising from the property; or

    (b) none of any income arising from the property can be applied for the benefit of anyone, other than the disabled person. For 2013–14 onwards this condition is not breached if the trustees have power to make payments to others not exceeding the annual limit. That limit is the lower of £3,000 and 3% of the maximum value of the settled property during the year in question.

A trust is not to be treated as failing to satisfy these conditions solely because the trustees have:

- power under the *Trustee Act* 1925, s. 32 or the *Trustee Act (Northern Ireland)* 1958, s. 33 to advance no more than one-half of the capital to a person entitled to the trust capital provided it does not prejudice existing life interests; or
- a power under those Acts but free from or subject to a less restrictive limitation than the limit imposed by those Acts.

It must be noted that this exception is only available in cases where the statutory provision applies automatically and without variation. If, for example, the *Trustee Act* 1925, s. 32 does not apply or is superseded, e.g. because the statutory provisions are modified or extended by the settlement deed, then the facility to overlook powers of appointment such as those in s. 32 is ineffective.

Qualifying trusts: relevant minors

Where property is held on trusts for a relevant minor, those trusts will be 'qualifying trusts' if either:

(1) the parent of the minor dies without making a will and the statutory intestacy rules provide for the property in question to be held on trusts for the benefit of the child, under the *Administration of Estates Act* 1925, s. 46 and 47(1); or

(2) the parent of the minor dies and establishes a will trust meeting certain conditions, or a trust (meeting certain conditions) is established by the Criminal Injuries Compensation Scheme or the Victims of Overseas Terrorism Compensation Scheme. The minor must become absolutely entitled on attaining the age of 18. There are also restrictions on the application of monies similar to those for disabled persons.

Separate funds within a single trust

The special tax treatment is only available where property is held for the benefit of a vulnerable beneficiary on qualifying trusts. It may be that a single trust may hold property for the benefit of a number of beneficiaries on a variety of terms. With such mixed trusts the special tax treatment can only be applied in relation to property which is held on appropriate terms (qualifying trusts) for the benefit of vulnerable beneficiaries in separate funds or in other defined parts of the settled property.

Where part of, or a partial interest in, an asset is held on trusts for the benefit of a vulnerable person (and the other part is not) and that person is entitled to the income arising from that part of the asset it may be possible to treat that part interest and the income as if it were a separate asset for the purposes of determining whether the trusts on which the part of the asset is held are qualifying trusts. This will only be possible if it is possible to identify clearly the specific part of the asset concerned and the income arising from that specific part. Where it is not possible to identify clearly a partial interest in an asset and its income as being subject to qualifying trusts, claims to the special tax treatment cannot be made.

It may therefore prove difficult for trustees who hold an asset on trust, on terms that would otherwise be qualifying trusts for a number of beneficiaries, only some of whom may be vulnerable, to distinguish which parts of the asset (and its income) actually belong to the vulnerable beneficiaries. Claims may not be possible in such cases.

Legislation: FA 2005, s. 34, 35

Tax Reporter: ¶356-100

150-860 The vulnerable person election

Before the special tax treatment can be claimed for a tax year by the trustees of a qualifying trust, a 'vulnerable person election' must be effective for the whole, or part, of the relevant tax year.

A vulnerable person election must be made *jointly* by:

- the trustees holding property on 'qualifying trusts' (see 150-840); and
- the beneficiary of such trusts, who must be a 'vulnerable person' (see 150-820).

In circumstances where the beneficiary is unable to make a legally valid election, (e.g. because of infirmity, lack of legal or mental capacity, etc.) the election should be made on the beneficiary's behalf by someone legally entitled to do so (e.g. a parent, guardian or a person having the relevant powers of attorney).

The election must be made to HMRC using the specified form(s), providing information and making such declarations as may be required. HMRC may require any information relating to the trusts, the trustees, the vulnerable person and their entitlement under the trusts, and any one else connected with the trusts to be provided as part of the election. They may also require any 'reasonable' declarations to be made as part of the election. There are two specified declarations that must be completed.

(1) A declaration, by the vulnerable person *and* the trustees, that all the information in the election is correct, to the best of their knowledge and belief.

(2) A declaration, by the vulnerable person, that the trustees are thereby authorised to make any claims for special tax treatment for any tax year as they consider appropriate.

The election must specify the date from which it is to be effective (the 'effective date') and must contain a statement that the trusts covered by the election are, in fact, qualifying trusts.

It should be noted that, once validly made, the election is irrevocable and is of continuing validity from the effective date until any one of the following three events occurs.

(1) The vulnerable person covered by the election ceases to be a vulnerable person.

(2) The trusts cease to be qualifying trusts.

(3) The trusts are terminated.

If the trustees become aware that any of the above events has occurred, resulting in the nullification of a vulnerable person election, they are required to inform HMRC of this, by way of a notice containing details of the event that terminated the election, within 90 days of becoming aware of the event. The vulnerable person covered by the election is under no obligation to inform HMRC of any changes that might affect its continuing validity. Any failures to provide timely notices or the provision of negligent or fraudulent information, declarations, etc. are subject to the penalty regime at TMA 1970, s. 98.

Time-limit for 'vulnerable person' election

The election must be made to HMRC no later than 12 months after the 31 January next following the tax year in which the 'effective date' falls. A late election may be made where HMRC have exercised their discretion to issue a notice in writing, extending the time-limit.

The first year for which the special tax treatment is available is 2004–05.

More than one beneficiary

Where there is more than one vulnerable beneficiary entitled to income from qualifying trusts within a single trust a separate joint election is needed for each one.

Legislation: FA 2005, s. 24, 37

Tax Reporter: ¶356-300

150-880 Special income tax treatment

Claiming special tax treatment

Once a valid vulnerable person election has been made (see 150-860), the trustees can submit claims for the special income treatment within the time-limits generally provided for making claims. So the trustees can make a claim for special tax treatment for any tax year, if a valid election is in force for the whole or part of that year, at any time up to four years after the end of that tax year. Assuming that a vulnerable person election has been submitted within the normal time limit for an effective date within 2013–14 (i.e. by 31 January 2016), the trustees have until 5 April 2018 to submit a claim for the special income and/or capital gains tax treatment (as appropriate) to apply for that year.

Effect of an income tax claim

The overall aim of the special income tax treatment is to ensure that the trustees pay no more income tax on the income arising in respect of property held under qualifying trusts than would have been payable by the vulnerable person had such income been receivable directly by the vulnerable person.

Accordingly it is necessary to calculate the vulnerable person's income tax liabilities both:

- *without* any special tax treatment; *and*
- on the basis that the special treatment *does* apply.

The difference between these two amounts is the additional tax that would be paid by the vulnerable person if the qualifying trusts' income arose directly to the vulnerable person. When calculating the income tax liabilities on either basis some special rules and assumptions are to be applied.

(1) If the vulnerable person is 'non-UK resident' (see below) during the tax year under consideration, the individual's income tax liabilities are to be calculated as if the individual was resident (and domiciled) in the UK throughout the year.

(2) Any income that is actually distributed to the vulnerable person by the trustees in the tax year under consideration (irrespective of when it arose) is to be ignored when calculating income tax liabilities.

(3) Any relief given by way of an income tax reduction is to be ignored when calculating income tax liabilities.

One effect of (1) and (2) above is to ensure that the residence status of the vulnerable beneficiary does not prejudice a claim for the special income tax treatment to be applied.

The term 'non-UK resident', when applied to a vulnerable person, has a specific meaning for the purposes of this relief. A vulnerable person is 'non-UK resident' for a tax year if the individual is:

- not resident in the UK throughout the tax year; *and*
- not ordinarily resident in the UK for that tax year.

Once the vulnerable person's tax liabilities with and without the qualifying trusts income included have been determined, using the special rules and assumptions, the amount of extra tax that would be payable by the vulnerable person if the qualifying trusts income in fact belonged to that individual can be determined.

The amount of income tax to which the trustees would be liable, ignoring these special rules, in respect of income arising (or treated as arising) from property subject to qualifying trusts must be calculated.

When a valid claim to the special income tax treatment is made, the trustees' liability to income tax is reduced by an amount equal to the income tax that the trustees would be liable to without any claim in respect of income arising, *minus* the extra tax that would payable by the vulnerable person if the qualifying trusts income in fact belonged to them.

So the trustees' income tax liability, in respect of qualifying trusts income, is reduced by the amount of extra tax to which the vulnerable person would be liable if the qualifying trusts income in fact belonged to the vulnerable person.

In many cases a vulnerable person may have no taxable income of their own. If this is so the vulnerable person's actual tax liability will be nil. The vulnerable person's income tax liabilities on the basis that qualifying trusts income is treated as theirs will then amount to the extra tax that would be due from the vulnerable person. This figure is then the amount that may be deducted from the trustees' tax liability in respect of the qualifying trusts income.

Example 1

Amelie, aged 12, qualifies as a 'vulnerable person' since she is a 'relevant minor'. She is the sole beneficiary of the 'Amelie discretionary trust', which is a 'qualifying trust'. The trustees submitted a vulnerable person election (Amelie's guardian signing it on her behalf). The election has been in force since 2004–05. She has no income of her own. The trusts' income for the tax year 2017–18 is as follows:

- rental profits: £10,000;
- bank interest received: £7,500; and
- UK dividends: £8,000.

The trustees will be liable at the trust rate on non-savings and savings income (i.e. 45%) and at the dividend trust rate on dividend income (i.e. 38.1%).

The trustees make a claim for 2017–18 for the special income tax treatment to be applied to the qualifying trusts income (in this Example, the whole of the trust's income so qualifies).

Trustees' taxable income

	£
Rent	10,000
Interest	7,500
Dividends	8,000

The trustees' tax liability, before making a claim for special income tax treatment, will be:

	Non-savings	Savings	Dividend	Tax
	£	£	£	£
Income	10,000	7,500	8,000	
Non-savings income				
First £1,000 at basic rate[1]	(1,000)			
• £1,000 × 20%				200
Next £9,000 at the trust rate	(9,000)			
• £9,000 × 45%				4,050
Savings income				
£7,500 at the trust rate		(7,500)		
• £7,500 × 45%				3,375
Dividend income				
£8,000 at the dividend trust rate			(8,000)	
• £8,000 × 38.1%				3,048
Tax chargeable				10,673

Note:

[1] The trust rate and the dividend trust rate do not apply to the first slice of income, which would otherwise be subject to such rates.

The amount of extra or additional tax that Amelie would pay if the income from the qualifying trusts arose directly in her hands must now be calculated. In this example, Amelie has no personal income, so the actual tax liability is 'nil'.

The total personal tax liability of Amelie, assuming that all of the income from the qualifying trusts was her income would be as follows:

	Dividends	Savings	Non-savings	Total
	£	£	£	£
Deemed income	8,000	7,500	10,000	25,500
Less: personal allowance		(1,500)	(10,000)	(11,500)
Taxable income less personal allowance	8,000	6,000	0	14,000
Non-savings income: £0 × 20%			0	0
Savings income: First £5,000 at 0%		5,000		0

	Dividends	Savings	Non-savings	Total
	£	£	£	£
Savings allowance				
£1,000 at 0%		1,000		0
£0 at 20%		0		0
Dividend income				
£5,000 at 0%	5,000			0
£3,000 at 7.5%	3,000			225
Income tax payable				225
Less: tax due on beneficiaries actual income; in this case				nil
Additional tax due by beneficiary if the trust income arose directly to the beneficiary				225

The amount by which the trustees' income tax liability is reduced is £10,448 (i.e. (£10,673 less £325). In effect, the trustees' liability is reduced to the additional tax which would have been paid by the beneficiary.

Example 2

The facts are as shown in Example 1 above; Amelie has the following personal income and gains for 2017–18:

- a distribution of £2,500 from the trustees;
- bank interest received: £3,000;
- UK dividends: £2,800;
- rental income: £7,530.

The trustees' tax liability prior to any claim for 2017–18 will be as shown in Example 1 above. Amelie's pre-claim liability for that year will be as follows:

	Non-Savings	Savings	Dividends	Tax
	£	£	£	£
Rental income				
	7,530			
Interest				
		3,000		

	Non-Savings	Savings	Dividends	Tax
	£	£	£	£
Dividend				
			2,800	
Less:				
Basic personal allowance (£11,500 for 2017–18)	(7,530)	(3,000)	(970)	
Taxable	–	0	1,830	
Savings income				
£0 × 0%		(0)		
Dividends				
dividend nil rate				
£1,830 × 0%			0	
Tax due				0

Note:

The distribution received from the trustees is ignored for the purposes of calculating the beneficiary's tax liability as are the tax credits, etc. that would otherwise reduce the tax liability.

The next amount to calculate is Amelie's liability on the assumption that all of the qualifying trust's income is hers.

	Dividends	Savings	Non-savings	Total
	£	£	£	£
Actual income	2,800	3,000	7,530	13,330
Deemed income	8,000	7,500	10,000	25,500
Less: personal allowance			(11,500)	(11,500)
Taxable income less personal allowance	10,800	10,500	6,030	27,330
Non-savings income £6,030 × 20%			6,030	1,206
Savings allowance				

	Dividends	Savings	Non-savings	Total
	£	£	£	£
£1,000 at 0%		1,000		0
£9,500 at 20%		9,500		1,900
Dividend income				
£5,000 at 0%	5,000			0
£5,800 at 7.5%	5,800			435
Income tax payable				3,541
Less: tax due on beneficiaries actual income; in this case				nil
Additional tax due by beneficiary if the trust income arose directly to the beneficiary				3,541

The amount by which the trustees' income tax liability is reduced is £7,132 (i.e. £10,673 less £3,541), so that the reduced liability becomes £3,541. In effect, the trustees' liability is reduced to the additional tax which would have been payable by the beneficiary.

Claims for part years

A vulnerable person election may be made, within the time-limits, as soon as the qualifications are met. Entitlement to the special income tax treatment may, therefore, start part way through a tax year, from the time that the election has effect.

Where the election is in force for only part of a tax year (the 'elected part of the year'), only the qualifying trusts income arising in the elected part of the year will qualify for special income tax treatment. As might be expected, if there are expenses of management and/or income on non-qualifying trusts, the expenses and non-qualifying income must be apportioned to the elected part of the year and the part of the year not within the special tax treatment. Thus multiple apportionments may be needed; for the allocation of trust management expenses between qualifying and non-qualifying income and then for parts of the year subject to the vulnerable person election.

The same principles of apportionment apply where entitlement to make a vulnerable person election begins during a tax year; and where a vulnerable person election ceases to be effective during a year (e.g. where a minor reaches 18 years of age or a vulnerable person dies, etc.).

Tax pool

In Example 2, the trustees made a discretionary distribution to the beneficiary of £2,500. This amount was disregarded only for the purposes of computing the vulnerable beneficiary's tax liability under the rules relating to the relief. The amount will need to be included in the beneficiary's actual personal tax computation, along with the other income received. Therefore, it will still be necessary to consider whether the trustees have paid sufficient tax to cover the deemed deduction of tax from the payment. The payment is to be treated as if it were made after the deduction of tax at the trust rate (45%) and so the £2,500 payment in the example would be treated as £4,545 in the hands of the beneficiary for the purposes of computing their actual income tax liability. A tax credit of £2,045 would be available to the beneficiary and this amount of tax credit can be covered by the trustees' tax pool. The tax pool is the amount of income tax charged on the trustees at the trust rate and the dividend trust rate. Any trust income falling within the standard rate band and liable at the basic and lower rates can also qualify to be included in the tax pool.

In Example 2, assuming that the tax pool brought forward from previous years is nil, the tax pool will be £10,673. This is adequate to cover the tax deemed to have been deducted from the distribution (£2,045) and the balance of £8,628 will be carried forward to next year's tax pool.

For further commentary on the tax pool, see 150-600.

Trusts that qualify in part

A trust may have more than one beneficiary. If some of the beneficiaries are not 'vulnerable persons' an election and claim may still be possible if particular property that produces specific income can be shown to comprise the entitlement of the 'vulnerable person(s)'. In such a case, the property and income that is held for the benefit of such vulnerable beneficiaries is held on qualifying trusts and the election and claim can be made in respect of that element of the trusts property/income and the particular tax position of the vulnerable beneficiary. In order for a claim to be made, the property will need to be held in a separate fund or some other defined part of the settled property will need to be allocated to the 'vulnerable person'.

The legislation gives limited guidance on this matter. It merely specifies that for the purposes of the special income and CGT treatments any reference to property being held on trusts (i.e. qualifying trusts) also includes reference to 'a part of an asset being held on trusts'. It is to be presumed that common-sense apportionments and divisions that are just and reasonable will be accepted by HMRC, provided that the arrangement does not run counter to trust law.

Management expenses

If trustees properly incur any trust management expenses in respect of a trust's income, and that income is only partly qualifying trusts income, the amount claimed against the qualifying trusts income in respect of such management expenses must be apportioned into allowable and non-allowable elements. The proportion of the total management expenses to be excluded from the calculation of the qualifying trusts income is an amount that bears the same proportion to the whole of the management expenses amount as non-qualifying income bears to the trust's total income (i.e. both non-qualifying and qualifying income).

Legislation: FA 2005, s. 24, 27–30, 36, 42(5)

Tax Reporter: ¶356-400

150-900 Enquiries, appeals and adjustments

At any time following the submission of a vulnerable person election HMRC may make enquiries into any aspects of the election, e.g. the status of the vulnerable person, the qualifying status of the trust, etc.

An enquiry is opened by HMRC issuing a written notice to the trustees and/or the vulnerable person, requiring them to furnish HMRC with 'such particulars as [HMRC] may reasonably require'. The notice must specify a time-limit within which the required information must be provided but this cannot be less than 60 days. Penalties may be imposed for any failures to respond to a notice. The negligent or fraudulent provision of particulars, etc. may be subject to a penalty of up to £3,000. A failure to provide information in a timely manner (e.g. the time-limit on the notice) may render the person(s) served with the notice liable to an initial penalty of up to £300 and a continuing daily penalty of up to £60 for each day that such a failure continues. Information to be given jointly by trustees and a vulnerable person is treated, for the purposes of penalties, as given by the trustees only.

If HMRC decide that the election's requirements relating to the status of the 'qualifying trusts' and/or the 'vulnerable person' are not met, or that some event has occurred since the 'effective date' that causes the election to lapse, they may issue a notice to the trustees and the erstwhile 'vulnerable person' determining either:

- that the election never had effect; or
- that the election ceased to have effect from a date that must be specified in the notice.

There is a right of appeal against any such determination, to be exercised within 30 days if it being given. Any notice appeal is to be made to HMRC and it is to be directed to the general commissioners (i.e. there is no right to choose to direct an appeal to the special commissioners).

In order to give effect to a determination HMRC may make any adjustments that are necessary, including repayment and discharge of tax as well as making any assessments to tax, without regard to any time-limits that might otherwise apply.

Legislation: TMA 1970, s. 98; FA 2005, s. 36, 40 and 43

Tax Reporter: ¶356-550

Settlements: the anti-avoidance code

151-000 Outline

There are many uses to which settlements can be put – for instance, facilitating the management and preservation of trust property, stabilising an inheritance, the education and maintenance of children and adolescents – of which tax planning is one of the more common. At one time, the settlement was a favoured means of allowing income to accumulate at tax rates more favourable than those applying to the settlor, and the purpose of the legislation which is now contained in ITTOIA 2005, Pt. 5, Ch. 5 is to ensure that unless settlements are of a 'genuine' nature and fulfil very stringent conditions, their income remains taxable at the settlor's rate.

There are three main charging provisions, affecting:

- settlements in which the settlor retains an interest (151-050ff.);
- payments out of a settlement to a settlor's minor child who is not married or in a civil partnership (151-700ff.); and
- capital sums paid to the settlor (153-250).

Broadly, where during the life of the settlor any property subject to a settlement, or any derived property, can become payable to or applicable for the benefit of the settlor or spouse or civil partner of the settlor in any circumstances whatsoever, the income of the settlement is treated as the settlor's income for all tax purposes. Even where that is not the case, any payments out of the settlement during the settlor's lifetime to or for the benefit of a minor child of the settlor (if the child is neither married nor in a civil partnership) are taxed as the settlor's income to the extent that they match undistributed income in the settlement.

The tax charge in respect of the settlement anti-avoidance code is a 'free-standing' charge under ITTOIA 2005, s. 619(1) and (2). This charges the settlor as if the income treated as arising to the settlor is assessable to income tax in the settlor's hands at the rates that would have applied had the income arisen directly to him. So income from a trade will be charged in the settlor's hands as income under ITTOIA 2005, Pt. 2, bank and building society interest will be assessable under ITTOIA 2005, Pt. 4, Ch. 2, income from property will be assessable under ITTOIA 2005, Pt. 3 and so on, at the rates of tax for individuals that are appropriate to the various sources. There are provisions enabling the settlor to claim reimbursement of tax paid from the trustees.

Beneficiaries' position if settlor charged to tax

Although the income of a settlor-interested settlement is deemed to be that of the settlor for income tax purposes, an income distribution at the trustee's discretion is still treated in the first instance as income of the beneficiary (except where the beneficiary is also the settlor). However, to avoid double taxation the recipient is treated as having paid income tax at the higher rate but no part is treated as repayable. This amount is treated as the highest part of the recipients total income as a general rule. Otherwise, it could be deemed to be taxed at the basic rate only with no right to a repayment because of ITTOIA 2005, s. 685A(4), leaving own income chargeable at the higher rate. This anomaly was corrected by FA 2008 and with retrospective effect to the year 2006–07.

It should also be borne in mind that even though the income is treated as that of the settlor, the trustees must nevertheless account for income tax in the normal way under the discretionary trust regime. In practice, HMRC give credit for the tax paid by the trustees although the actual mechanics and strict legal justification for this are far from clear.

Legislation: ICTA 1988, s. 1; ITTOIA 2005, s. 619–648 and 685A

Tax Reporter: ¶357-000ff.

Retention of interest by settlor

151-050 When settlor retains an interest

Settlement income is to be treated as income of the settlor for all tax purposes unless it arises from property in which the settlor (or the settlor's spouse or civil partner) has no interest or, for income arising after 20 March 2012, where the property originates from a settlor who is not an individual. Effectively, any retention of an interest by the settlor in the settled property will trigger a charge under the anti-avoidance rules unless any of the specific exclusions apply.

There has been some uncertainty over the precise scope of these rules, mainly focused around a series of HMRC articles and pronouncements and the so-called '*Arctic Systems*' case (*Jones v Garnett (HMIT)*; see 151-150).

A settlor has an interest in settled property if there is any possibility of the property or any 'derived property' being paid to the settlor, or to the settlor's spouse or civil partner, or applied for their benefit in any circumstances whatsoever. The question of whether such individuals have a 'power to enjoy' the current or future income or capital of the settlement was tested in the case of *IR Commrs v Botnar*, in this case, although the settlor and his spouse were expressly excluded from benefiting from the settlement, the trustees did have the power to appoint funds to other settlements. It was found that as the settlor could potentially be a beneficiary of those settlements, then he had failed to divest himself completely from the power to enjoy the assets of the settlement.

The term 'derived property' means any of the following:

- income from the settled property;
- other property 'directly or indirectly representing the proceeds of' the settled property;
- other property 'directly or indirectly representing the proceeds of' the income of the settled property;
- income from such proceeds.

Where the settled property or derived property cannot be paid to the settlor or the settlor's spouse or civil partner while someone else is alive unless that person becomes bankrupt or assigns or charges his or her interest, the settlor will not be regarded as having an interest while that person is under the age of 25. Furthermore, there are four circumstances in which property may become payable to the settlor, the settlor's spouse or civil partner *without* triggering a charge on the settlor.

- the bankruptcy of a potential beneficiary;
- a potential beneficiary assigning or charging his or her beneficial interest;
- in the case of a marriage settlement or civil partnership settlement, the death of both parties to the marriage or partnership and all or any of the children of the marriage or partnership;
- the death of a child of the settlor who had become beneficially entitled to the property or any derived property on or before attaining the age of 25.

Decided cases

In general, the courts have not been slow to find that a settlor has an interest in settlement property or income, and even remote possibilities that a settlor might benefit have brought the settlement within the anti-avoidance provisions. Relevant cases include *Glyn v IR Commrs* concerning powers of appointment; *Barr's Trustees v IR Commrs* concerning possible reversion of the funds to the to settlor; and *Hannay's Executors v IR Commrs* concerning an incomplete disposition. The 2003 special commissioners' decision in *Unmarried Settlor v IR Commrs* emphasises that even a very remote possibility of a settlor (or a settlor's future spouse) benefiting from a settlement can bring the arrangements within the scope of the anti-avoidance rules. In that case even though the settlor was a single, elderly, homosexual man who was highly unlikely to marry, the remote possibility of a marriage could not be ignored and so any future wife of the settlor could have benefited under the trust, because such benefit was not explicitly excluded. Since December 2005 the Civil Partnership Act means that had this case been decided in the light of those rules the special commissioner might have decided that the contracting of a civil partnership was more than a remote possibility.

A power to direct investments which is a purely fiduciary power is outside the ambit of the retention of interest provisions.

Legislation: ITTOIA 2005, s. 624–627

Cases: *Barr's Trustees v IR Commrs* (1943) 25 TC 72; *Glyn v IR Commrs* (1948) 30 TC 321; *Vestey's Executors v IR Commrs* (1949) 31 TC 1; *Hannay's Executors v IR Commrs* (1956) 37 TC 217; *IR Commrs v Botnar* [1999] BTC 267; *Unmarried Settlor v IR Commrs* (2003) Sp C 345; *Jones v Garnett (HMIT)* [2007] BTC 476

Tax Reporter: ¶355-550

151-100 Exclusions from the retention of interest provisions

The following categories of income are excluded from the ambit of the provisions.

- Income from settlements made by one party to a marriage or civil partnership to provide for the other party following a divorce or annulment, or a separation pursuant to a court order, a separation agreement, or in such circumstances that the separation is likely to be permanent.
- Annual payments made by an individual for *bona fide* commercial reasons in connection with his trade, profession or vocation (this would normally include an annuity payable by continuing partners to a retiring partner or to the widow or dependants of a deceased partner).

- Donations to charity under the Gift Aid scheme.
- Benefits under approved pension arrangements.

An outright gift between spouses or civil partners does not constitute a 'settlement' for the purposes of the retention of interest provisions.

The outright gift exclusion does not apply to the following.

- A gift which does not carry a right to the whole of the income from the gifted property.
- A gift which consists wholly or substantially of a right to income.
- A gift which is subject to conditions.
- A gift the subject matter of which, or any 'derived property' from which, will or may become payable to or applicable for the benefit of the donor in any circumstances whatsoever.

A totally voluntary return of previously gifted property to the donor would not be regarded as 'circumstances' leading to the denial of relief.

The extent of these exclusions was considered in the *Arctic Systems* case (*Jones v Garnett (HMIT)*; see 151-150).

Legislation: ITTOIA 2005, s. 626 and 627

Case: *Jones v Garnett (HMIT)* [2007] BTC 476

Tax Reporter: ¶355-550

151-150 Uncertainty over the scope of the anti-avoidance rules for settlements

In HMRC Tax Bulletin, Issue 64, April 2003, HMRC set out their interpretation of terms such as 'settlement' and 'settlor', indicating that the scope of the settlement anti-avoidance rules went far beyond trust scenarios and intruded into what had until then been regarded as straightforward, common and unexceptional family tax-planning (see 151-200 for commentary on 'settlement' and 'settlor'). There then followed a series of published exchanges between HMRC and a 'consortium' of tax, accounting and business organisations.

In November 2004, HMRC published '*A Guide to the Settlements Legislation for Small Business Advisers*', a 49-page guidance note that summarised and consolidated much of the arguments that it had used through the articles, etc. referred to above. The note also included comment on what is generally referred to as the *Artic Systems* case (see below).

This case was heard in June 2004 by the Special Commissioners and dealt with the issues raised by HMRC's stance towards the settlements legislation.

HMRC succeeded before the Special Commissioners, but lost in the Court of Appeal and the House of Lords.

The 'Arctic Systems' case

The facts of the case were straightforward. The company was owned equally by Mr Jones and his wife. Mr Jones was the sole director and his wife was company secretary. The company's only business was the supply of computer consultancy services which were performed only by the husband; Mrs Jones performed company secretarial and administrative services only. In some years the company paid modest salaries to both husband and wife and in some years more substantial dividends were paid equally to husband and wife. The principal issue was whether the dividends paid to Mrs Jones consisted of income arising under a settlement of which Mr Jones was the settlor so that they should be treated as his income under the provisions for settlor-interested trusts. Arctic Systems Limited had been originally incorporated on 5 August 1992 by company formation agents as an 'off the shelf' company, and only two £1 shares were issued. On 11 August 1992, Mr and Mrs Jones acquired the company. Mr and Mrs Jones each paid £1 for their share. There were no subsequent changes in the issued share capital, shareholdings or officers of the company.

The House of Lords' decision, delivered on 25 July 2007, found that whilst the arrangement *did* fall within the settlements legislation, the statutory let-out for outright gifts between spouses applied to protect the taxpayer.

This decision does not sit happily with HMRC's Tax Bulletin 64 article and later pronouncements. It is therefore perhaps not surprising that, just one day after the Lords' decision, on 26 July 2007, it was announced, in a written ministerial statement, that the Government would be making changes to the tax legislation to ensure that their view (that 'individuals involved in these arrangements should pay tax on what is, in substance, their own income') would be put on a clear statutory footing. The proposed changes to the legislation would be consulted upon (according to the statement, in order to help ensure that commercial arrangements will not be caught by it). A consultation paper was issued by HMRC, but after adverse comments on the proposals, a March 2008 Budget announcement stated that any changes would be deferred until 6 April 2009. The promised legislation failed to materialise either then or subsequently and the suggestion is that this matter has been placed on the 'too difficult ' pile.

Legislation: ITTOIA 2005, s. 626, 627

Case: *Jones v Garnett (HMIT)* [2007] BTC 476

Other Material: HMRC Tax Bulletin, Issue 64, April 2003

Tax Reporter: ¶357-050ff.

151-200 Settlor-interested trusts: 'settlement' and 'settlor'

Beyond the generic definitions of terms such as 'settled property' and 'settlor' (see 150-220) there are specific meanings attributed to several terms when considering the anti-avoidance provisions relating to settlor-interested trusts.

'Settlement' is defined as 'any disposition, trust, covenant, agreement, arrangement, or transfer of assets'.

In general, the term 'settlement' represents a much wider concept than what is commonly thought of as a 'trust'.

A will is not a 'settlement' for the purposes of the anti-avoidance code (*IR Commrs v Buchanan*), nor broadly speaking is a bona fide commercial transaction (*IR Commrs v Levy*).

A transaction will only amount to a 'settlement' if it involves an element of bounty (*IR Commrs v Plummer*), an important element of the *Artic Systems* case.

Many of the decided cases have focused on the meaning and extent of the term 'arrangement' in the definition of 'settlement' (see, for instance, *IR Commrs v Pay*; *Crossland v Hawkins*; *Butler (HMIT) v Wildin*; *Young (HMIT) v Scrutton; Young (HMIT) v Pearce (HMIT)*; *Chamberlain v IR Commrs*; and of course the *Arctic Systems* case (see 151-150). It seems to be generally held that whilst the term 'arrangement' is a very wide one, any arrangements that are to be included must be clear or at least exist as a reasonable possibility at the time that the settlement is created for tax purposes. Thus in a situation where there are no plans, ideas or agreements about how a future 'arrangement' might be set up it is not possible to use hindsight to catch subsequent plans, etc. as if they had existed at some earlier time (when a settlement of some sort was being considered).

'Settlor'

'Settlor', in relation to a settlement, means any person by whom the settlement was made. This includes any person who has indirectly made or entered into the settlement, for instance by providing or undertaking to provide funds, whether directly or indirectly, for the purposes of the settlement, or has made a reciprocal arrangement for another person to make or enter into the settlement. One common application of this principle applies where a beneficiary under a will enters into a deed of variation; the beneficiary is treated as the settlor for income tax purposes, even though the disposition is treated for inheritance tax purposes as if it had been made by the deceased.

Legislation: ITTOIA 2005, s. 620

Cases: *Chamberlain v IR Commrs* (1943) 25 TC 317; *IR Commrs v Pay* (1955) 36 TC 109; *IR Commrs v Buchanan* (1957) 37 TC 365; *Crossland v Hawkins* 39 TC 493; *IR Commrs v Plummer* (1979) 54 TC 1; *IR Commrs v Levy* [1982] BTC 235; *Butler (HMIT) v Wildin* [1988] BTC 475; *Young (HMIT) v Scrutton; Young (HMIT) v Pearce (HMIT)* [1996] BTC 322; *Jones v Garnett (HMIT)* [2007] BTC 476

Tax Reporter: ¶357-050ff.

151-250 Meaning of 'income arising under a settlement'

The expression 'income arising under a settlement' includes income chargeable to income tax by deduction or otherwise, or income which would have been chargeable if received in the UK by a person domiciled, resident and ordinarily resident there. If the settlor is not domiciled or not resident in the UK in a tax year, then any income arising under the settlement which would otherwise have been treated as his under the anti-avoidance provisions will only be taxable on him if it would have been had it actually been his income. This includes the application of the remittance basis where the settlement income is actually remitted to the UK.

Accrued income on fixed interest securities is specifically included as income. An offshore income gain accruing to the bare trustee of a minor is deemed to be the minor's income but an offshore income gain apportioned to an individual who is a participator in a non-resident company or a beneficiary of a non-resident settlement cannot be reallocated under the settlement anti-avoidance code.

Legislation: ITTOIA 2005, s. 632 and 648

Tax Reporter: ¶357-250

151-300 Multiple settlors

Where there is more than one settlor, it is provided for the settlement anti-avoidance code to apply separately to each settlor as if he were the only settlor in relation to the property or income originating from him. Payments of income to minor children of the settlor who are unmarried and not in a civil partnership are only to be taken into account, in relation to each settlor, to the extent that they emanate from income originating from that settlor, and other such payments to the extent that they represent retained or accumulated income which has originated from that settlor. 'Property originating from a settlor' is defined as property which that settlor has provided for the settlement, and property representing it or accumulated income from it, including an apportioned part of any property which represents both it and other property. The expression 'income originating from a settlor' includes both income from property which originates from the settlor, and income which the settlor has provided. A settlor is treated as providing property or income which has been provided by another person under reciprocal arrangements with the settlor, but not property which the settlor has provided under reciprocal arrangements with another person. This means that where there is a reciprocal arrangement such that A provides assets ('A's assets') for the children of B in return for B providing assets ('B's assets') for the children of A, income arising from A's assets, if caught, will be taxed as income of B (the parent). Similarly, income arising from B's assets will be taxed as income of A.

Legislation: ITTOIA 2005, s. 644 and 645

Tax Reporter: ¶357-100

151-400 Information powers

HMRC have wide powers to obtain information from any party to a settlement. It is for the officer of the Board to form an opinion as to what information is necessary for the purpose of the provisions, in exercise of a proper legal discretion, and the onus is on the taxpayer to show by direct evidence, or proper inference from the circumstances, that the officer does not in fact think such information or particulars necessary for those purposes (*Wilover Nominees Ltd v IR Commrs*). Any notice requiring such information must give the recipient at least 28 days in which to respond, and penalties are chargeable in respect of any failure to furnish information.

Legislation: TMA 1970, s. 98; ITTOIA 2005, s. 647

Case: *Wilover Nominees Ltd v IR Commrs* (1973) 49 TC 559

Tax Reporter: ¶357-550

151-450 Adjustment between settlor and trustees

If a settlor is required to pay tax on settlement income on the footing that it is to be treated as the settlor's for tax purposes, he or she is entitled to recover the tax paid from the trustees or from any person to whom the income is payable under the settlement, and as conclusive evidence of payment of tax may require HMRC to certify the amount of income charged to tax, and the amount of tax paid.

Conversely, if a person receives a repayment of tax which, because of the operation of the anti-avoidance rules, is in excess of what would otherwise have been due to him or her, the person must repay the excess to the trustee or the appropriate beneficiary. Any question as to the amount of such a payment, or as to any apportionment where more than one beneficiary is entitled, is to be decided by the tax tribunal, whose decision is final.

Legislation: ITTOIA 2005, s. 646

Tax Reporter: ¶357-350

151-500 Power to pay inheritance tax

HMRC do not treat settlement income as that of the settlor simply because the trustees have power to pay, or do in fact pay, inheritance tax on assets put into the settlement (SP 1/82). However, if a settlor pays inheritance tax, and is then reimbursed by the trustees, that amount may be deemed to be his income.

Legislation: ITTOIA 2005, s. 633 and 634

Tax Reporter: ¶357-150

151-550 Gift Aid

Qualifying gift aid donations are specifically excluded from the scope of the anti-avoidance legislation which deems settlement income to be the income of the settlor for income tax purpose.

Legislation: ITTOIA 2005, s. 627

Tax Reporter: ¶357-500

Payments to children

151-700 Payments to minor children of settlor who are not married and not in a civil partnership

If a settlement is not already caught by the retention of interest provisions (see 151-050ff.), any settlement income which is paid during the settlor's lifetime to or for the benefit of his or her minor child who is neither married nor in a civil partnership (a 'relevant child') is treated for all tax purposes as the settlor's income for the tax year in which it is so paid or applied.

A 'minor' is defined as a person under 18 years of age, and a 'child' includes a stepchild, even where the natural parent is still alive (*IR Commrs v AB Russell*), and an illegitimate child. References to 'payments' include payments in money or money's worth.

Where there is accumulated income in the settlement, any payment to or for a relevant child of the settlor is treated as a payment of income to the extent that it matches available retained or accumulated income.

The rules also apply to income arising from property held on bare trusts for a relevant child of the settlor, even if the income is accumulated and not paid to or for the child, provided the property was settled on or after 9 March 1999. The rules do not apply where the property was settled before 9 March 1999. This loophole used to allow interest to be accumulated within bank and building society accounts for minors, effectively free of tax.

'Available retained or accumulated income' is all the income that has arisen in the settlement since it began, excluding:

- income treated as income of the settlor;
- income paid to or for the benefit of, or treated as the income of, a beneficiary other than a relevant child of the settlor, whether as income or as capital;
- income treated as the income of a relevant child of the settlor in 1995–96 to 1997–98, but only to the extent that it was taxed and not covered by allowances or deductions; or
- income applied in defraying the expenses of the trustees which were properly chargeable to income, notwithstanding any express provision of the trust.

Where an offshore income gain accrues to a bare trustee or nominee for a beneficiary who is a relevant child of the settlor, the gain is treated as the settlor's income for tax purposes.

If no more than £100 is paid to a relevant child of the settlor in any tax year, the income is not treated as that of the settlor under these provisions.

Legislation: ITTOIA 2005, s. 629 and 631

Case: *IR Commrs v AB Russell* (1955) 36 TC 83

Tax Reporter: ¶357-300

Capital sums paid to settlor

153-000 General

Under special anti-avoidance rules capital sums (including loans and repayment of loans) paid to the settlor (or the settlor's spouse or civil partner) where the settlement has undistributed income are treated as the income of the settlor.

There are also rules designed to prevent a settlor transferring to trustees shares in a company controlled by him or her and borrowing money from the trustees who use the dividends to make the loans. The repayment of loans made to the settlor by trustees and loans made by the settlor to the trustees may also be caught.

Capital sums paid to the settlor by a company connected with the settlement are also potentially taxable.

Legislation: ITTOIA 2005, s. 633–644

Tax Reporter: ¶358-000

153-050 Capital sums paid to settlor

The rules apply where capital sums are paid directly or indirectly in any tax year by the trustees of a settlement to:

- the settlor;
- the settlor's spouse or civil partner; or
- the settlor (or the settlor's spouse or civil partner) jointly with another person.

In these circumstances the capital sums are:

- treated for all income tax purposes as the income of the settlor for that year to the extent that the payment falls within the amount of income available up to the end of that year; and
- for each of the following ten years (i.e. eleven years in total) any excess is treated for all income tax purposes as the income of the settlor for each subsequent year to the extent that the payment is within the amount of income available.

> **Example**
>
> Simon, the settlor, receives in May 2017 a capital payment of £100,000. The undistributed income of the settlement is as follows:
>
> | | |
> |---|---|
> | 2017–18 | £30,000 |
> | 2018–19 | £10,000 |
> | 2019–20 | £20,000 |
>
> Assume that undistributed income for the 20 subsequent years is £1,000 per year.
>
> The sums of £30,000, £10,000 and £20,000 are treated as Simon's income in 2017–18, 2018–19 and 2019–20, respectively. £1,000 for each of the following eight years (i.e. 20120–21 to 2027–28) is also treated as Simon's income. Thus, in total, £68,000 of the capital sum will be treated as Simon's income.

Trustees of settlements for the maintenance of historic buildings, etc. may elect not to treat capital sums as income of the settlor (see 155-050).

Legislation: ITTOIA 2005, s. 620 and 634

Tax Reporter: ¶358-050

153-100 Settlement income available

The amount of settlement income available up to the end of a tax year, in relation to any capital payment, is the aggregate amount of income arising under the settlement in that year and any previous tax year which has not been distributed. It includes:

(1) the amount of income already taken into account in this and previous years as the settlor's income by reason of the capital payment in question;

(2) income taken into account in relation to any other capital sum paid to the settlor (or the settlor's spouse or civil partner) in any previous year before the capital payment in question was made;

(3) any income arising under the settlement in the year in question or any previous year which has been treated as income of the settlor under the provisions on retention of interest by settlor or payments to or for the benefit of a minor children of the settlor who are unmarried and not in a civil partnership;

(4) any income arising or sums paid which have been treated as the settlor's income in a previous year under earlier anti-avoidance legislation; and

(5) an amount equal to tax at the trust rate on the aggregate amount of undistributed income in the year in question and any previous year, less the aggregate amount of the income/sums referred to in (4).

Legislation: ITTOIA 2005, s. 635

Tax Reporter: ¶358-250

153-150 Loans

If the capital sum paid to the settlor (or the settlor's spouse or civil partner) is a loan only, then the sum ceases to be treated as the settlor's income for any tax year *after* that in which the loan is wholly repaid.

Example 1

Trustees of a settlement make a capital payment of £30,000 in May 2013 to Ann (the wife of Stephen, the settlor) as a loan. Settlement income available for distribution is as follows:

2015–16	£9,000
2016–17	£8,000
2017–18	£7,000

The loan is repaid in 2016–17. Only the £9,000 in 2015–16 and the £8,000 in 2016–17 are treated as the settlor's income.

If after the first loan is wholly repaid a further sum is lent to the settlor (or the settlor's spouse or civil partner), the amount which may be treated as the settlor's income takes into account earlier charges. The amount of the second loan is effectively reduced by any amounts already taxed as the settlor's income due to the first loan.

Example 2

The facts are the same as in Example 1. In 2017–18, the trustees make a further loan of £20,000 to Stephen's wife. This sum is treated as a capital payment of £3,000 (i.e. £20,000 – (£9,000 + £8,000)) and as the income of the settlor to that extent in 2017–18.

In some cases, a settlor might have made a loan to trustees of the settlement. If the loan is *completely* repaid, then if the settlor re-advances an amount not less than the original loan, no part of the repayment is treated as the settlor's income for any tax year after that in which the further loan is made.

> **Example 3**
>
> Richard, the settlor, makes a loan to trustees of £100,000 in 2012–13. The loan is completely repaid in 2017–18. In that year, the settlement has £40,000 of undistributed income to cover the repayments. The repayment is treated as Richard's income in 2017–18 to the extent of £40,000. In the same year, Richard makes a subsequent loan of £100,000 to the trustees. The remaining £60,000 of the trustees' repayment in 2017–18 is not treated as Richard's income when future income arises in the settlement.

Legislation: ITTOIA 2005, s. 634 and 638

Tax Reporter: ¶358-150

153-200 Charge to tax on settlor

Any sum treated as the income of the settlor is treated as income grossed up at the trust rate (see 150-250) applicable to the year of payment. The trust rate for 2017–18 is 45%.

> **Example**
>
> Anthony receives £5,500 from the trustees of his settlement in 2017–18. Assuming that available income in that year is sufficient to cover the receipt, Anthony is treated for income tax purposes as receiving gross income of £10,000.

The settlor is entitled to set off against the tax charged the lesser of:

- the trust rate for that year on the amount treated as his income; or
- the tax actually charged.

So if in the above example Anthony had only been liable to tax at the basic rate his tax liability would have been discharged, but he would not be entitled to a repayment.

The settlor is entitled to the same deductions and reliefs as would have been allowed if the amount treated as his income had been received by him as income.

Legislation: ITTOIA 2005, s. 623 and 640

Tax Reporter: ¶358-050

153-250 Capital sum

A capital sum is:

- any loan or repayment of a loan; and
- any other sum not paid as income and which is not paid for full consideration in money or money's worth.

However, this definition of 'capital sum' does not include any sum which could not have become payable to the settlor except in one of the following events:

- a beneficiary becoming bankrupt or assigning or charging his or her interest;
- the death of both parties to a marriage settlement or civil partnership settlement and of all or any of their children;
- the death of a child of the settlor who had become beneficially entitled before attaining 25;
- the death under 25 of any object of a protective trust.

It can be seen that 'capital sum' includes any loan or *repayment of a loan*. The reason for this is illustrated by the example below.

> **Example**
>
> Charles creates a settlement by lending trustees £10,000. The trustees buy shares in Sigma Ltd and Charles withdraws the dividend income in the form of the repayment of his loan. The result is the same as if Charles had transferred the shares in Sigma Ltd into the settlement and had later withdrawn the dividends in the form of loans.

Certain sums are deemed to be capital sums paid to the settlor by the trustees of a settlement. These are sums which:

- are paid by the trustees to a third party at the settlor's direction or because of the assignment by the settlor of his or her right to receive it; or
- are otherwise paid or applied by them for the benefit of the settlor.

Legislation: ITTOIA 2005, s. 634

Tax Reporter: ¶358-100

153-300 Capital sums paid by a company connected with settlement

A capital sum is treated as having been paid to the settlor by the trustees of the settlement if:

- a capital sum is paid to the settlor by any body corporate connected with the settlement in the tax year of payment; and
- an 'associated payment' has been made directly or indirectly to that company by the trustees of the settlement.

A company is connected with a settlement if it is a close company (or would be a close company if it were resident in the UK) whose participators include the trustees of the settlement or it is a company controlled by such a close company.

An associated payment is:

- any capital sum paid to the company by the trustees of the settlement; and
- any other sum paid, or asset transferred, to the company by the trustees which is not so done for full consideration in money or money's worth,

and the sum is one which is paid or transferred in the five years ending or beginning with the date on which the capital sum is paid to the settlor.

Example

Daytime Systems Ltd, a company connected with the settlement, pays a capital sum of £10,000 to Robert, the settlor, on 1 May 2017. The trustees, on 30 April 2011, made a loan to Daytime Systems Ltd of £10,000. The £10,000 is treated as having been paid to Robert by the trustees of his settlement.

'Capital sum' has the same meaning as in 153-250.

A capital sum paid to the settlor is only taken into account in the year of payment to the extent of the total of associated payments made by the trustees to the company up to the end of that year. If the whole sum is not taken into account, the unmatched part is treated as having been paid to the settlor in the following year (so long as it falls within the total of associated payments to the end of that year) and so on for each subsequent year.

The provisions do not apply to any sum paid to the settlor as a loan or repayment of a loan if:

- the whole of the loan is repaid within 12 months; and

- the period for which loans are made to the settlor by any company connected with the settlement, or by the settlor to such a company, does not exceed 12 months in any period of five years.

Legislation: ITTOIA 2005, s. 637 and 641

Tax Reporter: ¶358-200

153-350 Interpretative and administrative provisions

Certain interpretative and administrative provisions applicable to the rest of the settlement anti-avoidance code are also applicable to the provisions on capital sums payable to the settlor. These deal with the meanings of 'settlement', 'settlor', and 'income arising under a settlement', the question of multiple settlors, and HMRC information powers (see 151-050ff.).

153-400 Meaning of 'undistributed income'

Income is undistributed income to the extent that it exceeds the aggregate of:

(1) sums paid to any persons by the trustees of the settlement as the income of the recipient (including sums which would be so treated if the recipient were domiciled, resident and ordinarily resident in the UK), except:

  (a) payments of interest;

  (b) sums paid to a body corporate 'connected with' the settlement (see below);

  (c) sums paid to the trustees of another settlement made by the settlor or the trustees of the settlement;

  (d) sums paid to the settlor otherwise than as income;

(2) trustees' expenses chargeable to income, in so far as they are not included in the sums mentioned in (1). Interest paid by trustees is excluded in so far as the income is paid to the settlor or the settlor's spouse and where income is also paid to others a corresponding proportion of such interest is excluded. This does not apply to interest paid to the settlor or the settlor's spouse or civil partner if living with the settlor, or where the interest attracts tax relief; and

(3) where trustees are charitable trustees, the excess of tax-exempt income over the aggregate of (1) and (2) above.

Legislation: ITTOIA 2005, s. 636 and 637

Tax Reporter: ¶358-250

Charitable trusts

154-000 Charitable trusts – overview

Charities are entitled to various tax exemptions and other privileges. The exemptions extend to the formation, funding and income of the charity and certain conditions must be met if they are to apply.

Prior to 6 April 2010, HMRC's policy, based upon case law, was that the term charity could only apply to bodies established in the UK and thus within the jurisdiction of the UK Courts. As a result of pressure from the European Commission, which regarded this policy as incompatible with EU Law, a statutory definition was introduced by *Finance Act* 2010, applicable to all main taxes, which extended charitable treatment to bodies established in the EU and other specified territories.

To qualify as a charity, a body must:

- be established for charitable purposes only (as defined by the *Charities Act* 2006);
- be subject to the jurisdiction of the UK Courts or the Courts of a Member State of the EU or a territory specified by Treasury Order (Iceland and Norway), in relation to charity law;
- comply with any requirement to be registered imposed on it by the laws of England and Wales or of any other country; and
- have 'fit and proper' persons as the managers exercising general control and management of its administration.

A charity may be a trust, a limited company, an unincorporated association or a Royal Charter body. This chapter deals with charities which are constituted as trusts ('charitable trusts').

The *Small Charitable Donations Act* 2012 gives relief to certain charities equivalent to gift aid for donations in cash of no more than £20. There are many conditions to be met including a requirement to have made a successful gift aid claim in at least two of the previous four tax years.

Legislation: *Charities Act* 2006, s. 2; FA 2010, Sch. 6, para. 1(1), (2); *Small Charitable Donations Act* 2012

Tax Reporter: ¶138-500ff.

Application of trust law

A charitable trust may be valid even if it may last beyond the normal period permitted by the perpetuity rules. Also, where it can be shown that the settlor clearly intended to transfer funds to a charitable trust the trust will not fail for uncertainty of objects; instead, what is known as the cy pres doctrine applies to make the objects more certain. This doctrine enables a court to determine, in some situations, that a trust, which would otherwise fail the charitable purposes test, because of some impracticability or impossibility within the trust deed, is to be treated as if it succeeded in meeting the requirements for charitable status.

Tax special trust rates

Charitable trusts are specifically excluded from the application of the trust rate and the dividend trust rate (see 150-250).

Legislation: ITA 2007, s. 479(1)

154-050 Charitable purposes

The definition of 'charitable purpose', applicable from 6 April 2010, is imported from the *Charities Act* 2006 and that definition is to apply regardless of where the body is established.

Under that definition a charitable purpose is one which is 'for the public benefit' (see below) and which also falls within one of the following categories:

- the prevention or relief of poverty;
- the advancement of education;
- the advancement of religion, including religions which involve belief in more than one god or even no god at all;
- the advancement of health or the saving of lives, including the prevention or relief of sickness, disease or human suffering;
- the advancement of citizenship or community development, including rural or urban regeneration and the promotion of civic responsibility, volunteering, the voluntary sector or the effectiveness or efficiency of charities;
- the advancement of the arts, culture, heritage or science;
- the advancement of amateur sports or games which promote health by involving physical or mental skill or exertion;
- the advancement of human rights, conflict resolution or reconciliation or the promotion of religious or racial harmony or equality and diversity;
- the advancement of environmental protection or improvement;
- the relief of those in need by reason of youth, age, ill-health, disability financial hardship or other disadvantage including the provision of accommodation or care to those persons;

- the advancement of animal welfare;
- the promotion of the efficiency of the armed forces of the Crown or of the efficiency of the police, fire and rescue services or ambulance services;
- any other purposes reasonably analogous to the above;
- any purposes not falling within the above categories but recognised as charitable purposes under either the charity law existing immediately prior to the date the *Charities Act* came into force (1 April 2008) or by virtue of *Recreational Charities Act* 1958, s. 1, together with any other reasonably analogous purposes.

Legislation: *Charities Act* 2006, s. 2; FA 2010, Sch. 6, para. 1(4)

Public benefit test

The *Charities Act* 2006 contains nothing to assist in the interpretation of the term 'for the public benefit' other than to say that 'reference to the public benefit is a reference to the public benefit as that term is understood for the purposes of the law relating to charities in England and Wales'.

However, the Act places a statutory obligation on the Charities Commission to issue guidance as to the operation of the public benefit objective. This can be found on the Commission's website.

Website: www.charity-commission.gov.uk/Library/guidance/publicbenefittext.pdf

Tax Reporter: ¶138-600

154-100 'Charitable purposes only'

A trust which is established for charitable and non-charitable purposes will generally fail as a charitable trust, although it may be a valid private trust. If, however, the non-charitable purposes are merely incidental or ancillary to the main purposes, then the trust will often be capable of being considered charitable.

Similarly, trustees of a trust to encourage the holding of a company's shares by its employees, and which when wound up was to be distributed in part in repayment of a loan to the company, with the balance being paid to a named charity, failed in their application for charitable status on the grounds that the obligation to repay the loan was dispositive, not administrative, in character, and hence the trust funds were not applicable for charitable purposes only.

154-150 Income tax exemptions

To be able to claim these exemptions a charity must now register with the Charity Commission where required to do so. There is also a requirement that the trust's managers are fit and proper persons.

Investment income

Charitable trusts established in the UK are exempt from income tax on the following:

- gifts from donors that qualify for gift aid relief and equivalent gifts from companies, and UK-source payments received from other charities;
- the profits of charitable trades (that is, trades carried out in the course of carrying out the trust's primary purpose, or where the work in connection with the trade is mainly carried out by beneficiaries of the trust);
- with some exceptions, miscellaneous income and deemed income to which ITA 2007, s. 1016 applies (e.g. deemed income under the accrued income scheme);
- profits from fund-raising events;
- profits from lotteries;
- property business profits, including dividends from real estate investment trusts (REITs);
- certain savings and investment income (dividends, interest, income from authorised unit trusts, profits on deeply discounted securities, and annuity payments under purchased life annuities);
- public revenue dividends;
- gains from the disposal of certain deposit rights;
- offshore income gains;
- miscellaneous income such as royalties and other income from intellectual property rights that are not trading receipt and certain annual payments;
- income from estates in administration.

In order to qualify for any of these exemptions, the income must be applied for charitable purposes only.

From 22 April 2013, charities and Community Amateur Sports Clubs have been able to sign up with HMRC to make repayment claims electronically using Charities Online.

Restriction of exemptions

The exemptions from income tax are restricted in a year if a charitable trust incurs non-charitable expenditure. Non-charitable expenditure for this purpose includes certain transactions with substantial donors.

The non-exempt amount is the lesser of:

- the charitable trust's non-charitable expenditure for the year; and
- its (otherwise) exempt income and gains for the year.

Legislation: ITA 2007, s. 521–536 and 539–557; FA 2010, Sch. 6; *Small Charitable Donations Act* 2012

Tax Reporter: ¶139-900ff.

Heritage maintenance settlements

155-000 Introduction

There is a special tax treatment for certain settlements which provide funds for the maintenance of heritage property. Broadly, they are excluded from the anti-avoidance rules that deal with settlor-interested trusts.

The trusts that qualify for this treatment are 'heritage maintenance settlements'. A heritage maintenance settlement is a trust that comprises property which is the subject of a direction under IHTA 1984, Sch. 4 ('heritage maintenance property'). Heritage maintenance property is settled property that is used within six years of being settled for:

- the maintenance, repair, preservation of, or the provision of public access to, certain land and buildings designated by the Treasury (a 'property maintenance purpose'); or
- for the benefit of various bodies ('heritage bodies') as defined in the inheritance tax legislation, including, e.g. the National Gallery, national museums, the National Trust, universities, local authorities and Government departments.

The trustees must be approved by the Treasury.

If the settlement includes both heritage maintenance property and other property, the two types of property are treated as being comprised in two separate settlements.

Legislation: IHTA 1984, Sch. 3, 4, para. 1, 2 and 3; ITA 2007, Pt. 9, Ch. 10

Tax Reporter: ¶354-500

155-050 Income tax treatment

Trustees of heritage maintenance settlements may elect that in relation to a tax year:

(1) any income arising in that year from heritage maintenance property which would be treated by the settlement anti-avoidance provisions (see 151-000) as the income of the settlor is not to be so treated; and

(2) sums applied in that year out of the heritage maintenance property for a property maintenance purpose are not treated as the income of the settlor if they otherwise would have been so treated by virtue of the anti-avoidance rules on capital sums payable to the settlor (see 153-000ff.) or because the settlor has an interest in the property or occupies it (see 151-050).

The election must be made in writing on or before the first anniversary of the normal self-assessment filling date for the year to which it relates.

If no election is made, (2) above applies in relation to any sums used in that year for a property maintenance purpose which exceed the settlement's income from heritage maintenance property.

If the election is made, the trustees become liable to tax on the income and this will be charged at the trust rate.

If a direction under IHTA 1984, Sch. 4 is in force for at least part of the tax year and if the income is treated as the settlor's income for at least part of the tax year, but one of those two conditions is not met (or neither is met) for another part of the tax year, then the year will be split into two and each part treated as a separate tax year, and the trustees may make the election in respect of one of those deemed tax years.

Legislation: ITA 2007, s. 508 and 509

Tax Reporter: ¶354-600

155-150 Reimbursement of settlor

Income arising from heritage maintenance property could be treated as the settlor's income if it is applied in reimbursing the settlor for expenditure incurred by the settlor for a property maintenance purpose. If the settlor is carrying on a trade or a property letting business which includes the property then the reimbursement would ordinarily prevent the settlor from deducting the expenditure in calculating the profits of the trade or business.

To prevent double taxation, where reimbursed amounts are treated as the settlor's income, the settlor may deduct the expenditure in calculating the profits of the trade or business.

Legislation: ITA 2007, s. 511

Tax Reporter: ¶354-600

Asbestos compensation settlements

155-200 Income tax exemption

The trustees of an asbestos compensation settlement are to be exempt from income tax on income arising from the settled property with effect from 2006–07 onwards.

Such settlements are those made before 24 March 2010 under an arrangement made under the Insolvency or Companies Acts (or similar laws overseas) which have a sole or main purpose of making compensation payments in respect of those who have, or have had, an asbestos related condition.

Legislation: ITA 2007, s. 838A

Income of estates in administration

156-000 Introduction

When a person dies the person's property passes to his or her personal representatives, i.e. either executors appointed by his or her will or administrators of his or her estate appointed by the court. Personal representatives are liable for any tax liability of the deceased to the extent that there are sufficient assets of the deceased coming into their hands to meet the debt. A personal representative who neglects or refuses to pay may be proceeded against as any other defaulter; but the personal representative may deduct any payments of tax made out of the assets of the deceased.

A personal representative may also be assessed to tax in respect of income (and chargeable gains) accruing to the deceased but not assessed on him or her. Such an assessment cannot be made later than three years after 31 January next following the tax year in which the deceased died.

The income of the deceased's estate is regarded as the income of the personal representatives and is liable to tax at the dividend ordinary rate, the savings rate or the basic rate, as appropriate (but not at the trust rate) in their hands. The income is computed in the usual way appropriate to the source of income and the appropriate reliefs and deductions are taken into account. Personal representatives cannot, however, utilise personal reliefs against estate income, nor are administration expenses deductible in computing tax payable.

Tax is assessable on the personal representatives to whom the income of the estate arises, and any personal representatives subsequently appointed (the 'relevant personal representatives'). Any one or more of the relevant personal representatives may be assessed. The chief aim of this rule is to permit a UK resident personal representative to be assessed in cases where some of the personal representatives are non-resident.

The estate income is treated as part of the income of the beneficiary in computing his total income. The extent of the income taken into account will depend on whether the beneficiary has a limited or absolute interest in the residue. The following paragraphs deal briefly with these rules and also with the position of legatees and annuitants.

When the administration of the estate is complete, the personal representatives hold the property as trustees until such time as the property vests in the beneficiaries or in other trustees. Even if the personal representatives continue to hold the property as trustees, the beneficiaries will generally be absolutely entitled as against their trustees and the income tax position will therefore be identical to that applicable to bare trusts (see 150-350). These provisions only apply during the administration period, i.e. from the date of the deceased's death to the completion of administration.

Tax legislation gives no definition of when the administration of an estate is considered complete, except in relation to Scotland where the administration is completed when debts, specific legacies and liabilities of the estate have been discharged or provided for and the residuary estate can be ascertained. This also seems to be the general position in England and Wales.

Administrative procedures for personal representatives' returns

Personal representatives may make an informal payment of the total liability for the whole period of administering the deceased's estate if certain conditions are met. The main condition is that the total tax liability (income tax plus capital gains tax) for the entire administration period is less than £10,000. The other conditions are that:

- the probate/confirmation value of the estate is less than £2.5m;
- the proceeds of assets sold in any one tax year are less than £250,000; and
- the estate is not regarded as complex, so it can be dealt with without the personal representatives having to complete an SA return.

The office that handled the deceased's tax affairs should normally accept informal payments.

An informal payment may not be accepted where any part of the payment relates to:

- tax deducted from annual payments;
- a recovery of tax overpaid; or
- the recovery of excessive tax credits.

Informal payments may not be accepted where a self assessment return has been issued to the personal representatives. In such circumstances, the personal representatives are under an obligation to complete and send back the return.

CGT liability can be accounted for informally where the proceeds of any disposals from the estate are less than £250,000 in any one tax year.

The informal procedures are in place because the tax affairs of most estates are not complicated, and most estates only last for a short time. In the great majority of cases, it is easier for both the personal representatives and HMRC to resolve the estate's tax position without setting the estate up within self assessment. It is envisaged that agreeing the tax liability will be fairly straightforward with only minor adjustments needed to tax computations.

The exceptions are where agreement is unlikely without entering into protracted correspondence. There might be a dispute over the basis of assessment, for example, or a difference of opinion about HMRC's interpretation of legislation or practice. In these situations the informal procedures are not appropriate and formal self assessment returns will be required. A formal enquiry into the return(s) will then be opened to raise queries on and ask for explanations for the entries in the return.

To help personal representatives settle the tax affairs of the administration period quickly HMRC will, on request, issue a tax return before the end of the tax year in which cessation occurred.

Whether the tax return is issued before or after the end of that tax year, HMRC will, on request, give early written confirmation if they do not intend to enquire into that return. This confirmation does not preclude, in exceptional circumstances, HMRC enquiring into the tax return at a later date if they discover that the return was incomplete or incorrect. But in the vast majority of cases, receipt of this written confirmation will signify the end of HMRC's interest in the income and capital gains tax affairs of the administration period and, where that is the only open matter, will enable the personal representatives to finalise tax liabilities and distribute the estate. This practice is not statutory, but was included in the Budget announcement for *Finance Act* 2007.

Other Material: HMRC *Trusts, Settlements & Estates Manual* TSEM7410

Tax Reporter: ¶363-300

Intestacy

Where a person dies intestate (i.e. without leaving a valid will), their estate will be distributed or held on trust according to detailed rules laid down by statute (*Administration of Estates Act* 1925, as amended). The operation of the intestacy rules will inevitably have tax implications.

Particular attention should be given to the matrimonial home. If the spouses own the matrimonial home as joint tenants, the property automatically passes to the surviving spouse, so that the intestacy rules will only apply to the remainder of the estate. Where the matrimonial home is, however, owned by the husband and wife as tenants in common, on the death of one spouse the deceased's share forms part of his or her estate and the intestacy rules will apply (this will also be the case where the matrimonial home was owned solely by the deceased spouse).

The rules for the distribution of an estate under intestacy where significantly changed with effect from 1 October 2014. While a detailed examination of the intestacy rules is outside the scope of this work, there follows a general description of the main aspects of their application pre and post these changes:

Deceased survived by:	Pre-1 October 2014	Post-1 October 2014
Spouse/civil partner and children	Spouse/civil partner receives:	Spouse/civil partner receives:
	Personal chattels	Personal chattels
	Cash legacy of £250,000	Legacy of £250,000 (now index linked)
	Half of residue on life interest trust	Half of residue outright
	Children inherit balance absolutely at 18	Children inherit balance absolutely at 18

Spouse/civil partner, no children	Spouse/civil partner receives: Personal chattels Cash legacy of £450,000 Half of residue outright Balance passes to other relatives	Spouse/civil partner receives: Whole estate
No spouse/civil partner	Whole estate to children outright at 18 If none, estate passes to other relatives If no relatives, to the Crown	No change

Legislation: *Administration of Estates Act* 1925, s. 36(2); TMA 1970, s. 40, 74; FA 1989, s. 151; ITTOIA 2005, s. 649–682

Tax Reporter: ¶362-000ff.

Income of the deceased

156-100 General

As explained at 156-000, a personal representative may be assessed to income tax on the unassessed income of the deceased within three years and ten months after the tax year in which the deceased died. Outstanding income tax owed by the deceased is dealt with by the personal representative in the same way as other debts of the estate. This generally means that outstanding tax cannot be paid until after a grant of representation is obtained to the estate, as in practical terms a personal representative cannot collect the assets of the estate until he or she can prove his or her title. HMRC are generally lenient where the ensuing delay renders the personal representative liable to an interest charge. HMRC policy is also to be co-operative about issuing tax returns before the end of the tax year in order to facilitate the early settlement of the deceased's tax affairs, and under self-assessment they are prepared to give early confirmation that they do not intend to enquire into the return.

Certain complications can arise where income credited after the death of the deceased accrues partly during the deceased's lifetime and partly after his or her death, necessitating an apportionment.

Legislation: TMA 1970, s. 40

Other Material: HMRC Press Release, 4 April 1996

Tax Reporter: ¶362-500ff.

156-150 Apportionment of income straddling date of death

The *Apportionment Act* 1870 requires that certain income received after the deceased's death is nevertheless treated as capital of the estate when establishing the beneficiaries' entitlements. So, for example, dividends received by personal representatives after the deceased's death but relating also to a prior period are to be apportioned on a time basis. However, for the purposes of income tax the Apportionment Act does not apply. For income tax purposes, the deceased is treated as having no right to the dividends until they are declared, and income received after death will be the income of the personal representatives (*IR Commrs v Henderson's Exors*). In practice, many wills bar apportionments to avoid these complications.

Case: *IR Commrs v Henderson's Exors* (1931) 16 TC 282

Tax Reporter: ¶362-500ff.

156-200 Inheritance tax on accrued income

Income accrued before the death of the deceased may form part of the residuary income of the estate and yet also be taken into consideration as capital and so be chargeable to inheritance tax. This applies, for example, to dividends paid for periods prior to death which are reflected in the price of the underlying shares, or added to the price where the shares are valued 'ex div'. Relief is provided from higher-rate tax in such a situation for any person who has an absolute interest in the residue of that or any other estate (or part of it). The residuary income is treated for higher-rate purposes as reduced by an amount equal to the grossed-up amount of inheritance tax on that income. The inheritance tax must be grossed up at the rate of tax applying to the underlying income, i.e. the dividend ordinary rate of 7.5% on dividends, and the basic rate of 20% on other income.

Legislation: ITTOIA 2005, s. 669

Tax Reporter: ¶362-500ff.

156-250 Death of taxpayer: interest and penalties on late tax

A taxpayer may die before the date on which the payment of tax charged on him or her is due. In such circumstances, the personal representatives may not be able to settle the liability until probate or letters of administration have been obtained.

The date from which interest may be charged on unpaid tax may in this situation be extended according to the date on which probate or letters of administration are granted. The 'relevant date' for interest charged is to be either determined by the statutory provisions or treated as 30 days after the day on which probate or letters of administration are granted, whichever is the later.

Penalties

Ordinarily, a failure to deal properly with an individual's tax obligations will give rise to a penalty, except in the case of innocent adjustments. However, where an individual has died, HMRC's practice is not to seek to impose a penalty on the personal representatives for tax offences committed by the deceased prior to the date of death. The basis for this is that to impose a penalty in such circumstances is not compatible with the Human Rights Act. However, under declarations of tax by the personal representatives, relating to matters after death can be the subject of a penalty, as in that instance they are the culpable party.

Legislation: TMA 1970, s. 86 and 100–103

Other Material: ESC A17

Tax Reporter: ¶362-750

Income of the estate

156-500 Limited interests in residue

A person is deemed to have a limited interest if he or she does not have an absolute interest and the income of the residue (or part of it) would be properly payable to him or her, or directly or indirectly paid for his or her benefit, if the residue had been ascertained at the commencement of the administration period.

Any sum paid during the administration period in respect of a limited interest is deemed to have been paid as income in the tax year in which the sum was paid. Where the sum is paid in respect of a limited interest which has ceased during the administration, the sum is deemed to have been paid in the last tax year in which the interest subsisted. Where on completion of the administration there is still an amount due to the beneficiary in respect of his or her limited interest, it is treated as income of the beneficiary for the tax year of completion. In the case of a UK estate the personal representatives will have paid tax at the dividend ordinary rate of 10% on dividends or 20% on other income ('the applicable rate') and any sum paid to a beneficiary is treated as a net amount after tax at the applicable rate for the year of payment has been deducted.

Example

John has a life interest in the residuary estate of Betty, which is invested entirely in building society accounts. During the administration period, the executors pay the following sums to John:

2015–16	£200
2016–17	£220
2017–18	£230

John is treated as having received £250, £275 and £287.50 respectively (being the amounts paid grossed up at the savings rate relating to the year of payment). John is entitled to tax credits of £50, £55 and £57.50 respectively.

Where the estate has more than one beneficiary, payments of income bearing tax at different rates are apportioned between them on a just and reasonable basis according to their different interests. Otherwise, it is assumed that payments are made out first of income bearing tax at the basic rate, secondly out of income bearing tax at the savings rate and finally out of income bearing tax at the dividend ordinary rate.

Legislation: ITTOIA 2005, s. 650, 653, 663 and 679

Tax Reporter: ¶364-600ff.

156-550 Absolute interests in residue

A person is deemed to have an absolute interest if and so long as the capital of the residue (or of the relevant part) would, if the residue had been ascertained, be properly payable to him or her, directly or indirectly, payable for his or her benefit.

Where a beneficiary has an absolute interest in residue, he or she is entitled to both the capital and the income of the estate. Payments made to the beneficiary may be paid out of income or capital and there are provisions designed to distinguish between these two elements in order to arrive at the correct income tax position. This is done by first calculating the 'residuary income' during that part of the administration period in which the beneficiary had an absolute interest.

The residuary income is ascertained by deducting from the aggregate income of the estate (see below) for that year:

- annual interest and annual payments for that year which are properly payable out of the residue, except for any interest, etc. which has already been allowed in computing the aggregate income of the estate (see below);

- management expenses (unless already allowed in computing the aggregate income of the estate) which, in the absence of any express provision in the will, are properly chargeable to income;
- the aggregate income of the estate (see below) to which any person is specifically entitled as a devisee or legatee.

The basic rule is that sums paid to a beneficiary during the administration period are treated as income of the beneficiary for the tax year in which they are paid. If, however, the payment exceeds the beneficiary's entitlement to residuary income in respect of each year up to and including the date of payment less any amounts previously treated as income, the excess is treated as capital. The sum he or she receives is, in the case of a UK estate, net of income tax at the applicable rate (see the discussion below). If on completion of the administration the beneficiary has not yet received his or her full entitlement to income accrued during the period of administration, the balance is treated as paid to him or her immediately before the end of the administration period. 'Payments' include assets transferred to the beneficiary.

Where there has been a change in the rate of tax between the year in which the income arose to the personal representatives and the year in which it was distributed to the beneficiaries, the applicable rate to be used for grossing up the net amount is the rate actually suffered by that income when it arose. Thus, income which arose in 2007–08, but not distributed until 2010–11, should be grossed up at 22% (the rate prevailing in 2007–08).

If inheritance tax is chargeable in relation to income accrued before the death, and that income is also taken into account in arriving at the residuary income of the estate for any year of assessment, then in ascertaining the liability of a person with an absolute interest in the residue a deduction is allowed of the grossed-up equivalent of the inheritance tax attributable to the income, net of liabilities, taken into account.

Aggregate income of the estate

'Aggregate income of the estate' means income from all sources for that year which is chargeable to UK tax (by deduction or otherwise) and any income which would have been so chargeable if it had arisen in the UK to a person resident and ordinarily resident in the UK. Income from property devolving on the personal representatives other than as assets for the payment of the deceased's debts is excluded.

Applicable rate

The 'applicable rate', when referring to the rate at which tax is deducted, or treated as deducted, from a gross amount which a beneficiary is deemed to receive or be entitled to, is the dividend ordinary rate, or the basic rate of income tax, depending upon the rate at which the underlying residuary income is taxed. To determine how much of any payment should be treated as made out of income which bears tax at one rate rather than another, apportionments of amounts bearing tax at different rates are made between different beneficiaries on a just and reasonable basis, and payments to beneficiaries are treated as made first out of income bearing basic rate tax, and then out of income bearing tax at the dividend ordinary rate.

Residuary income of non-residents

Under Extra-statutory Concession A14 if income is paid to a non-resident residuary beneficiary, the beneficiary may claim that his or her tax liability should be calculated as if the income had arisen directly from the underlying sources.

Excess deductions

If in a tax year deductions allowable against residuary income exceed the gross income, the excess is an allowable deduction in calculating the net residuary income for the following year.

Example

Eleanor died in year 1 and the period of administration extends to year 4. The personal representatives are required to pass the income arising from the residue to Julia after paying a prior charge of £3,000 per annum to Elissa.

Income arising from the residue before the prior charge is:

	£
Year 1	6,000
Year 2	2,000
Year 3	5,000
Year 4	4,000

Income assessable on Julia is calculated as follows:

	Total income	*Prior charge*	*Reallocation*	*Assessable income*
	£	£	£	£
Year 1	6,000	(3,000)		3,000
Year 2	2,000	(3,000)	1,000	Nil
Year 3	5,000	(3,000)	(1,000)	1,000
Year 4	4,000	(3,000)		1,000

Absolute interest for part of administration period

An absolute interest in the residuary estate may come to an end during an administration period. This could be the case, for instance, where the person absolutely entitled dies during the administration period (in which case his personal representatives are deemed to have an interest in the residuary estate or the relevant part of it). In such a case, the residuary income is ascertained for each whole tax year, and for each part of a tax year, during which that person had an interest.

Legislation: ITTOIA 2005, s. 650 and 659ff.

Other Material: ESC A14

Tax Reporter: ¶364-800ff.

156-600 Successive interests in residue

Where there are successive interests in residue, the earlier or earliest of them is a limited interest and each interest is brought about by cessation of the preceding interest otherwise than by death (i.e. by disclaimer, assignment, etc.), the following rules apply for the purpose of calculating the residuary income of a beneficiary during the administration period:

(1) all the successive interests are treated as one and the same interest;

(2) that one interest is treated as belonging to the person who has whichever limited interest is subsisting at the time the payment is made;

(3) where one of the later interests is an absolute interest, any residuary income treated as paid to previous beneficiaries is treated as having been paid as income to the holder of the absolute interest.

Example

Gaius is entitled to a life interest in the estate of Marcus, who died in May 2012. In 2007, Gaius assigns his life interest to his cousin Sextus. In June 2015, Sextus receives a payment of £10,000 from the estate. Up to and including 2015–16, the estate has residuary income of £12,500. In July 2016, Sextus disclaims his life interest, whereupon Calpurnia becomes absolutely entitled to the residue. A further £1,500 residuary income is available on the completion of the administration in August 2017, and Calpurnia receives a payment of £5,000 from the estate.

As the payment to Sextus is fully covered by residuary income, he is treated as receiving the sum of £10,000 as his income in 2015–16, notwithstanding Gaius's earlier limited interest. Calpurnia is treated as receiving income of £4,000 (£12,500 + £1,500 – £10,000) in 2017–18.

Similarly, successive absolute interests in residue are treated as if they were the same interest. The aim is that each beneficiary is taxed on the income he actually receives.

Legislation: ITTOIA 2005, s. 659 and 672–675

Tax Reporter: ¶365-050

156-650 UK and foreign estates

A foreign estate is 'an estate which is not a UK estate in relation to that year'. A UK estate is an estate the income of which comprises only income which either:

- has borne UK income tax by deduction; or
- in respect of which the personal representatives are directly assessable to UK income tax.

Dividends (including stock dividends), close company loans written off and chargeable gains on life policies are ignored in determining whether an estate is a UK estate or a foreign estate, except that if the estate receives no other income it is treated as a UK estate.

To be a UK estate the personal representatives must not be entitled to claim exemption from UK income tax (in respect of any part of the income of the estate) by reason of their residence or ordinary residence outside the UK.

In the case of a foreign estate, an amount deemed to have been paid to a person as income is not normally grossed up and is charged to tax as if it were income arising from securities outside the UK. Relief is available for any UK tax already borne on such income.

Where the personal representatives of a deceased person include at least one person who is UK resident and at least one who is non-resident, the non-resident personal representative(s) are also treated for all income tax purposes as UK resident if the deceased person was at his death:

- UK resident; or
- domiciled in the UK.

Otherwise, the UK resident personal representative(s) are treated as non-resident.

Legislation: ITTOIA 2005, s. 651, 677 and 678; ITA 2007, s. 834

Tax Reporter: ¶365-500

156-700 Discretionary payments to beneficiaries

If the will provides for all or part of the estate to be held on discretionary trusts, then any income paid to the trustees is liable to tax at the trust rate or the dividend trust rate as appropriate. Commonly the trustees will be the same persons as the personal representatives, but the income will not accrue to the trustees until the personal representatives make a decision to pay over the income, or the period of administration comes to an end.

If the payment is made to the trustees at such a time that the income falls to be the income of a beneficiary under the terms of the trust, then the payment is treated as the beneficiary's income, not the trustees' income.

> **Example**
>
> The residue of an estate is held for a beneficiary, Ben, contingent on his attaining the age of 25. If a payment is made to the trustees whilst he is under the age of 18 the income can be accumulated (assuming the *Trustee Act* 1925, s. 31 applies), and will be liable to tax at the trust rate or the dividend trust rate as appropriate. If a payment is made to the trustees once Ben has attained the age of 18 the trustees must pay the income to Ben, and the payment by the personal representatives will be treated as if it had been made direct to Ben.

Legislation: ITTOIA 2005, s. 655 and 662

Tax Reporter: ¶365-150

156-750 Information

The personal representatives of a deceased person are obliged to supply to a beneficiary, if he so requests, a statement of amounts deemed paid to him as income and the tax deemed to have been deducted, with amounts bearing tax at the basic rate shown separately.

Legislation: ICTA 1988, s. 700(5) and (6)

Tax Reporter: ¶365-100

156-800 Legatees and annuitants

The previous paragraphs have dealt with interests in residue. This paragraph deals with non-residuary interests only.

In the case of a specific legacy, the legatee is entitled to the income (subject to a contrary provision in the will) from the relevant property from the date of the testator's death. The income from the property, therefore, forms part of the legatee's total income as it arises.

In the case of a general legacy, the legatee is entitled to interest which is generally payable only after the end of the executor's year (i.e. the year allowed to the personal representatives to wind up the affairs of the deceased before they are obliged to pay any legacies). Such interest is paid gross (out of the executors' taxed income) and is charged to tax as part of the legatee's total income. However, a legatee may refuse to accept payment of the interest and in such instances the interest on the legacy is not generally treated as the legatee's income.

In general an annuitant is not entitled to the capital value of his or her annuity, although he or she is entitled to have a fund set aside to secure the annuity. The first instalment of the annuity is payable only at the end of the executor's year but (subject to a contrary intention) the annuity runs from the testator's death and forms part of the annuitant's total income from that date.

In some cases, and in particular where the estate is insufficient to provide an annuity fund and also to pay the pecuniary legacies in full, the annuitant is entitled to the actuarial value of his annuity (duly abated, if necessary). This is regarded as a capital payment and is not included in the annuitant's total income (*IR Commrs v Lady Castlemaine*).

Legislation: *Administration of Estates Act* 1925, s. 44

Case: *IR Commrs v Lady Castlemaine* (1943) 25 TC 408

Tax Reporter: ¶365-200ff.

156-900 Relief on loan to pay inheritance tax

Where the personal representatives of a deceased person borrow money:

- to pay inheritance tax on personal property before the grant of representation; or
- to pay off an earlier loan taken out to pay such tax,

then any interest on the loan is available for relief provided it is paid in respect of a period ending within one year from the making of the loan.

Relief is given by setting off against or deducting from income of the estate the amount of the interest for that tax year. However, if the interest paid is above a reasonable commercial rate, then relief will only be given on that part which is reasonable.

Where there is not enough income in a particular tax year against which to set the relief, the relief may be given against income of the preceding year, and so on, or otherwise against the income of the following year, and so on.

Legislation: ITA 2007, s. 403–405

Tax Reporter: ¶115-550

156-950 Deed of variation

Where a deed of variation is entered into within two years of the death and it contains a statement made by all of the parties to the deed that it is intended to be effective for inheritance tax (IHT) and capital gains tax (CGT) purposes, any liabilities to CGT and IHT can be computed as if the variation took place at the time of death.

There is no equivalent statutory provision in respect of income tax. Consequently income arising from the date of death to the date of the deed of variation is taxable by reference to the interest that the beneficiaries receive under the will, *without* any regard being taken of the subsequent deed of variation (*Schnieder v Mills*). The effect of the rules regarding limited interests and absolute interests (see 156-500 and 156-550 respectively), is therefore that the allocation, for tax purposes, of income received during the period of administration is by reference to each separate period during which each beneficiary's interest subsisted. From the date of the deed of variation, income arising during the period of administration is taxed by reference to the beneficiary's interest under that deed.

A deed of variation is regarded as a settlement by the individuals joining in the deed. Thus, when a parent enters into a deed of variation so that an asset passes not to him but to his child, income arising from that asset is assessable on the parent, so long as the child is a minor and unmarried. By contrast, HMRC appear to take the view that a disclaimer is not a settlement. See 150-220 for details of how a 'settlor' is defined and identified in such circumstances.

The HMRC view on the income tax effects of variations/disclaimers relies on the dictum of Rowlatt J in *Waddington v O'Callaghan (HMIT)* that 'no deed can alter the past'. In that case, a deed of partnership was entered into on 11 May 1929 but expressed to have been operative since 1 January 1929. However, the commissioners had found in fact that the parties to the deed had not been acting in partnership in the intervening period and so the deed could not relate back to 1 January. The application of the principle of this case to a deed of variation has been criticised on the grounds that a beneficiary does not have a right to income arising during a period of administration until either the end of that period or, if earlier, when the income is made available to the beneficiary. It is generally accepted that an individual who disclaims income *before* it arises is not taxable on that income. A deed of variation, if made during the period of administration and before income is made available to the beneficiary, can be seen as such a disclaimer. The effect is then that income is taxable on the beneficiaries who receive it and not necessarily those who have an entitlement under the will. HMRC do not appear to accept this argument.

Legislation: IHTA 1984, s. 142; ITTOIA 2005, s. 629–632, 653(1) and 659(1)

Cases: *Waddington v O'Callaghan (HMIT)* (1931) 16 TC 187; *Schnieder v Mills* [1993] All ER 377

Tax Reporter: ¶366-000

Residence and international aspects

Residence

General

170-000 Why is residence relevant?

An individual's residence status determines the extent of his or her liability to UK tax. In general, an individual who is 'resident' in the UK is liable to tax on his or her worldwide income and gains. On the other hand, an individual who is not resident in the UK is only liable to tax in respect of income which arises in the UK. Tax treaties can affect these basic principles (see 174-050).

The exception to this principle applies to those who are resident but who are not 'domiciled' here (see 172-050).

170-025 Introduction to statutory residence test

A new statutory residence test (SRT) applies for all tax years commencing with 2013–14. The legislation is contained in FA 2013, Sch. 45 and is self-contained.

Before then, the question of an individual's residence for tax purposes was based largely on case law that had developed over many years, there being very little statutory material on the subject. HMRC produced their booklet IR20 in the 1970s which set out their practice in determining residence. However, there remained uncertainty which culminated in various decisions of the courts over the past few years, and in particular in the *Gaines-Cooper* case that reached the Supreme Court.

The statutory provisions in Sch. 45 are very detailed and although in most cases it should be relatively straightforward by careful application of the rules to the facts to determine an individual's residence there will no doubt be disputes in border line cases, particularly in applying the sufficient ties test. Sufficient records should be kept to establish, and demonstrate, if required, key facts such as where and when working, including the hours involved, and whether accommodation qualifies as a home.

These rules only apply in determining the residence of individuals. There are separate provisions for trusts but even there it is necessary to determine the residence of individual trustees and so to that extent these new rules will be relevant to trusts. The definition of residence for National Insurance contribution purposes has not changed and is not affected by Sch. 45.

The concept of ordinary residence has been abolished at the same time and where necessary consequential amendments in FA 2013, Sch. 46 have been made to the legislation although the broad effect of this abolition should be quite limited. Ordinary residence is now only relevant for specified aspects of the foreign service rules for termination payments, transfer of assets abroad legislation and overseas workday relief, but only where the individual is not ordinarily resident at the end of 2012–13.

Finally, in considering the tax impact of being resident in the UK the effect of double taxation treaties must be considered as it is possible for an individual to be resident in more than one country. Most treaties contain a tie breaker provision to determine residence for the purposes of the treaty (and only for those purposes). It should also be borne in mind that aspects of the anti-avoidance rules referred to below can override double taxation treaties.

170-050 Basic principles of SRT

Each tax year is considered on its own according to these rules although in some cases, in particular in applying the sufficient ties test, it is necessary to consider whether an individual has been UK resident in previous tax years. Years prior to 2013–14 must be determined according to the previous law. However, it is often relevant to determine whether or not an individual was UK resident for preceding years and when the years in question are any of 2013–14 to 2017–18 the individual can elect to determine residence for this purpose (and only for this purpose) on the basis of the SRT rules. Such an election, which is irrevocable, must be made no later than the first anniversary of the end of the year in question. There are other transitional rules where it is necessary to consider the residence status of an individual in a year prior to 2013–14, including split years.

The structure of the legislation is on the following lines:

- first, determine if one or more of the automatic overseas tests applies;
- if not, look at the automatic UK residence test rules for the year;
- if these tests do not determine residence, consider whether the sufficient ties test is met for the year.

There are special rules for split years, being the years of arrival and departure, on which the legislation is very detailed and for the year in which an individual dies so as to avoid anomalies that would otherwise arise in applying the SRT rules.

There are also rules under the heading of anti-avoidance, to require individuals to be resident for periods of longer than one tax year (usually five years) so as not to avoid the tax charge otherwise arising.

170-100 The automatic overseas tests

If, as mentioned above, any of these tests is met for a tax year then the individual will not be UK resident for that year. The first three tests apply if the individual does not die in the year and the other two apply if death does occur. The tests to be automatically non-resident are:

(1) The individual has been UK resident for one or more of the three preceding tax years and spends fewer than 16 days in the UK in the tax year.

(2) The individual has not been UK resident for any of the three preceding years and the number of days spent in the UK in the tax year is fewer than 46.

(3) An overseas work test that requires the following to be met:
- sufficient hours worked overseas for the year;
- no significant breaks from overseas work in that year, which means that at least 31 days go by and not one of those is a day on which more than three hours' work is carried out overseas or would have been but for annual, sick or parenting leave;
- the number of days in the year on which the individual does more than three hours' work in the UK is fewer than 31;
- the number of days spent in the UK by the individual is fewer than 91 (being any days by reference to the individual being in the UK at midnight on a day).

Particular complication comes in determining the sufficient hours overseas test. The legislation requires the completion of five steps involving the following:
- First identify the days on which the individual has worked for more than three hours in the UK whether or not overseas work is carried out on the same day. These are referred to as disregarded days.
- For the employments held and trades carried on by the individual total up the total number of hours that the individual works overseas in the year but ignoring the hours spent overseas on the disregarded days referred to in the previous bullet point. This produces the net overseas hours figure.
- It is then necessary to work out the reference period which is broadly the number of days in a year (being 366 if a leap year) excluding the disregarded days in step one (where more

than three hours' work is carried on in the UK on a day) and other days that are allowed to be disregarded such as annual leave, sick leave and certain non-working days, which is dealt with in more detail below.

- The number of days resulting from the previous step is to be divided by seven and the answer if not a whole number should be rounded down to the nearest whole number (unless the answer is less than one in which case it is rounded up to one).
- The net overseas hours resulting from the second step above must then be divided by the number determined in the previous step and if the answer is at least 35, the individual is considered to have worked sufficient hours overseas.

This is very convoluted and is best illustrated with an example.

Example

Peter has always been UK resident but takes up a job abroad on 1 March 2017. In the year to 5 April 2018, he is in the UK for his annual three weeks' holiday and on 24 days he is working in the UK for at least 5 hours each day. His work when abroad totals 1,600 hours of which 10 hours are on the same days he is in the UK. Thus, his net overseas hours are 1,590.

Peter's reference period is 365 less UK disregarded days of 24 and annual leave of 21 (including weekends assuming this is 'embedded' time), i.e. 320 days under the fourth step. Divide this 320 day figure by 7, producing 45.7 which is rounded down to 45.

Then divide the net overseas hours of 1,590 by 45, which produces 35.33. As this is at least 35, Peter is treated as working sufficient hours overseas. Given also that in the year there are no significant breaks from work, he works in the UK on fewer than 31 days and is in the UK for fewer than 91 days he will pass the third automatic overseas test and be regarded as not resident for 2017–18.

This test does not apply, however, if the individual has what is called a relevant job on board a vehicle, aircraft or ship at any time in the year and at least six of the trips that the individual makes in that year as part of that job are cross border trips that involve the UK. A relevant job is defined as one where the duties or trade of the individual, as the case may be, consist of carrying out duties or activities on board such a vehicle, etc. while it is travelling and substantially all of the trips made in performing those duties or activities are ones that involve crossing an international boundary, whether at sea, in the air or on land. Moreover, it is expressly stated that duties for activities of a purely incidental nature are to be ignored. Generally, this rule will prevent, as an example, lorry drivers who go backwards and forwards to the continent to use the working abroad day test to become non-resident.

(1) If the individual dies in the year and was not UK resident for either of the two preceding tax years and the days spent in the UK are fewer than 46 then the automatic overseas test is met. For this purpose, if the first of the two years preceding the relevant tax year was a split year by virtue of falling in case 1, 2 or 3 (see below) that is also treated effectively as a year of non-residence.

(2) If the individual dies in the year but has not been UK resident for either of the two preceding years by virtue of the automatic working overseas test mentioned above (including where the first of the two years is a split year falling within case 1) then there are modifications in determining the overseas test for that year of death. Those modifications include reducing the number of days from 365 or 366 as the case may be to the number of days from the start of the tax year up to and including the day before death and otherwise only considering the period up to the date of death where relevant.

Legislation: FA 2013, Sch. 45, para. 11–16, 29

170-200 Automatic UK tests

There are four such tests. If any are met, and assuming none of the automatic overseas tests apply, the individual is UK resident for that year. Those tests are:

(1) Spending at least 183 days in the UK in the tax year. If this applies it is impossible to meet any of the automatic overseas tests so for practical purposes this test is overriding.

(2) Having a home in the UK for any part of the tax year in which the individual spends a sufficient amount of time in that year, being at least 30 days in the year, a day counting when the individual is present for at least some of that day and no matter how short that time. There should also be at least one period of 91 consecutive days in respect of which the individual has that home in the UK where at least 30 days fall within the tax year and throughout that 91-day period either the individual has no home overseas or has such a home(s) and there are fewer than 30 days in the tax year when the individual is present at any time on a day in the year in that home. Where the individual has more than one home then each of those homes has to be looked at separately to see if this test is met. It is important to understand the difference between a home and accommodation, which is explained in more detail below.

(3) The third is a test that determines the hours spent in the UK working, which involves a similar procedure to that for the automatic overseas work test set out above by looking at a period of 365 days, part of which falls within the relevant tax year, so as to determine whether sufficient hours are worked in the UK in that period. There must also

be no significant breaks from UK work, which is defined on the same lines as that for the overseas work test so that there must be at least 31 days that go by and not one of those days is a day on which at least three hours' work is carried out in the UK or would be but for annual leave etc. Three quarters of the total number of days in that period on which the individual does more than three hours' work must be days in the UK, at least one of those days being in both that period and the relevant tax year. This test is also not applicable, in the same way as the overseas working test, where the individual has a relevant job on a vehicle, aircraft or ship in that year where at least six of those trips are cross border ones including the UK.

Again, this is also best illustrated by an example which, as indicated, corresponds with that for the automatic overseas test.

Example

Rachel has lived and worked wholly abroad until taking on a new employment on 1 November 2016 that involves her working both in the UK and abroad. She rents a flat in the UK retaining her home abroad in which she spends at least 50 days a year. Thus, she would not meet the second automatic UK test, as she has a home overseas in which she spends a sufficient amount of time.

In the period of 365 days from 1 November 2016, she works her standard eight-hour day on 220 days of which 190 are in the UK. Her annual leave that can be deducted in the third step totals 20 days.

Thus, more than 75% of the total number of relevant work days are in the UK (190 out of 220 equals 86.4%) and at least one day is spent in both 2016–17 and 2017–18.

The determining question is then whether she works sufficient hours in the UK. Her reference period is 365 less 50 days work overseas and annual leave of 20 days, i.e. 295. Divided by 7 produces 42.14, rounded down to 42. Then divide the UK hours worked of 1,520 (190 days at 8 hours per day) by 42 and as the resulting figure (36.19) is at least 35 she will meet the sufficient hours in the UK and be UK resident for the year (but split year treatment will apply for 2016–17).

(4) The last test applies when the individual dies in the year and for each of the previous three tax years is UK resident by virtue of meeting the automatic residence test, provided the preceding year had not been a split year if the individual were assumed not to be a UK resident for the relevant tax year, and at the time of death the individual had a home in the UK. If the individual had a home overseas this test will not be met if a sufficient amount of time is spent there in the tax year of death. Sufficient time is spent there if either the individual was present there as a home on at least 30 days (no matter how short a time) in that year or on each day of the year up to and including the

day on which the individual died. If more than one home overseas was owned this test must be met for each of them.

Legislation: FA 2013, Sch. 45, para. 6–10, 29

170-300 Position if none of the automatic tests applies

If having considered first whether the individual is automatically non-resident and, secondly, whether automatically UK resident, there is no clear answer applying the SRT rules it is necessary to consider if the individual has sufficient ties for the relevant tax year.

General

The broad principle behind this is that if an individual wishes to spend more days in the UK then to achieve non-UK residence there must be fewer ties with the UK than would be if a reduced number of days were spent in the UK. The number of ties also depends on whether or not the individual has been UK resident for any one of the three previous tax years, as follows.

Where UK resident in any of the three preceding tax years

Days spent in the UK	Number of ties that are sufficient to become UK resident
16 – 45 days	At least four
46 – 90 days	At least three
91 – 120 days	At least two
121 – 182 days	At least one

Not UK resident for any of the three preceding years

Days spent in the UK	Number of ties that are sufficient to become UK resident
46 – 90 days	All four ties
91 – 120 days	At least three ties
121 – 182 days	At least two ties

There are special rules that apply where an individual dies in the year so that in the first table above the days spent in the UK should read up to 45 rather than 16–45 days. Moreover, if death occurs before 1 March then the days spent in the UK are time apportioned on a monthly basis by reducing the days, taking only whole months in the year after the month in which the individual dies. The resulting number of days is rounded up or down on conventional principles. Thus, if an individual dies on 22 January in a year the number of days in the 46–90 days bracket becomes 38–75 days, applying the fraction 10/12ths. A whole month is determined according to calendar months but, at the start of a tax year, April is counted as a whole month.

There are five types of tie, which are explained in more detail below, being:

- a family tie;
- an accommodation tie;
- a work tie;
- a 90-day tie; and
- a country tie (which only applies if the individual was UK resident for any of the three preceding tax years).

The ties in more detail

Some of these are quite involved and the following is a summary of the five ties referred to above.

Family tie

Broadly, this is relevant if at any time in the tax year the individual is not separated from an individual with whom they have a spouse or civil partner relationship or living together as if in one of those relationships. Separated has the same meaning as for income tax purposes. The tie applies if the other person in that relationship is UK resident for the year in question.

The family tie is also met if there is a child of the individual under the age of 18 who is UK resident unless the individual sees that child in the UK on fewer than 61 days in the tax year, but ignoring days after the child turns 18. This child family tie can also be disregarded if the child is in full-time education in the UK at any time in the year and would not be UK resident if the time spent in full-time education in the UK were disregarded.

Clearly, in determining whether or not the person with whom the individual has a relationship is UK resident there is a potential for going round in a circle. To avoid this, it is expressly provided that in determining the partner's residence the relationship with the individual in question is to be disregarded in determining that family member's residence.

Accommodation tie

There is an accommodation tie if the individual has a place to live in the UK which is available for a continuous period of at least 91 days and the individual spends at least one night at that place in the relevant tax year. A gap of fewer than 16 days between periods in a particular place that is available is treated as if available to the individual during that gap period.

Whether or not an individual has a place to live in the UK is widely defined so as to include a holiday home or temporary retreat, or is otherwise available, where the individual can live when in the UK, irrespective of whether the individual owns a freehold or leasehold interest in the property. However, if the accommodation is the home of a close relative of the individual then for that accommodation to count at least 16 nights in the year must be spent in that home. A close relative includes ancestors, siblings, children and grandchildren aged 18 or over, including relationships of the half blood or of marital/civil partnership.

Work tie

This tie is met if the individual works in the UK for at least 40 days in the relevant year, whether continuously or not, but the day only counts if the individual does more than three hours' work in the UK on that day.

There are special rules where the individual has a relevant job on board a vehicle, aircraft or ship so that broadly it is assumed that if the trip begins or ends in the UK the individual will carry out more than three hours' work in the UK on the day on which it begins or ends.

90-day tie

The individual has a 90-day tie by spending more than 90 days in the UK in either or both of the two tax years preceding the relevant tax year.

Country tie

This tie only applies if the individual has been UK resident in any of the three preceding years and is met if the country in which the individual meets the midnight test for the greatest number of days in the year is the UK. If there is a tie between the UK and another country for the greatest number of days, this test will also be met.

Example

Alice has been UK resident for four years but on 1 April 2017 she decides to move abroad to live. She sells her house in the UK and buys a house abroad for her use. She does, however, spend some time in the UK living with her sister. She spends 40 midnight days living with her sister and in addition she attends concerts on seven days in the UK, flying in in the morning and leaving the UK by 11 p.m. in the evening.

The part days can be ignored because they do not exceed 30 and so the deeming rule does not apply. Given that the days spent in the UK do not exceed 45 days she will not be UK resident unless she has at least three UK ties. So looking at these:

- she is single without any minor children so would not meet the family tie;
- she should not meet the accommodation tie unless the accommodation with her sister is available for a continuous period of at least 91 days, assuming also that she has to make arrangements each time to stay with her sister;
- the work tie is not met as she is not working abroad;
- the 90-day tie is met because she has spent more than 90 days in the UK in 2016–17;
- the country tie is not met as she will spend the greatest number of days in the country in which she has her new home.

Thus, she meets one tie definitely, and possibly the accommodation tie, but does not reach the three UK ties that would make her UK resident. Thus, she is not resident for UK tax purposes for the year 2017–18. The same procedure should then be applied for succeeding years unless one of the automatic overseas tests is met.

Legislation: FA 2013, Sch. 45, para. 17–20, 31–38, 145

170-400 Split year treatment

The basic rule under Sch. 45, para. 2(3) is that an individual is either resident or not resident in the UK for the entire tax year. This was also the strict principle behind the previous residence rules but in practice HMRC did allow a year to be split between periods of residence and non-residence where the facts so permitted.

The SRT rules bring in a statutory basis for split year treatment but only in the circumstances specified, which are set out in Cases 1 to 8. The legislation then goes on to specify how the charging rules are varied for specific types of income where an individual falls within one of those cases.

If a type of income does not fall within those statutory rules then notwithstanding that the individual falls within one of the cases for split year treatment, this does not affect income not specifically covered by that treatment. For example, an individual moving abroad to work is likely to be eligible for split year treatment in the year of departure but any UK dividend income will be taxed in full without the benefit of the limitation of liability to income tax for non-UK residents.

The eight cases can be divided into two broad categories. Cases 1 to 3 are concerned with departure from the UK such that from the date of departure the individual will be treated as non-UK resident and be available for split year treatment for the earnings in the period when overseas. Cases 4 to 8 are involved in instances where an individual arrives in the UK having been non-UK resident previously. These cases are dealt with in more detail below.

Cases 1 and 2

In very broad terms, Case 1 is concerned with instances where an individual goes to work abroad so as to follow the previous practice of treating an individual as non-UK resident from the date of departure. Case 2 is linked to this as it deals with an individual's partner who goes with his or her working partner.

The following conditions must be met for the working individual to have split year treatment where, as indicated above, the individual was resident in the UK for the previous tax year.

(1) There must be a period of one or more days in the relevant tax year that begins with the day on which the individual does more than three hours' work overseas and satisfies the overseas work criteria, which is dealt with in more detail below.

(2) The individual must not be UK resident for the next tax year by virtue of meeting the automatic overseas working test.

The overseas work criteria test follows the broad principles in determining the automatic overseas working test, those criteria being met if:

- the individual works sufficient hours overseas assessed over the period from the first day of the overseas working period to the following 5 April;
- during that period there must be no significant breaks from overseas work, which is where at least 31 days go by and not one of those days is a day on which the individual does more than three hours' work overseas (which may include annual leave, sick leave or parenting leave);
- the number of days in that period on which the individual does more than three hours' work in the UK does not exceed the permitted limit; and
- the number of days spent by the taxpayer in the UK (being midnight days) does not exceed the permitted limit.

Whether the individual satisfies the sufficient hours overseas test is based on the same principles as the automatic overseas test but looking only at the period under consideration and using the permitted limit number of days instead of 30 where there is a gap between different periods of employment. The permitted limit, where more than three hours' work is spent in the UK, is found by apportioning 30 days on a time basis for the period from departure (but including a part month as a whole month) so the number of relevant working days in the UK should not exceed that resulting figure. The permitted limit for the number of days spent in the UK (whether working or not) is calculated on a similar basis but by applying the same fraction to 90.

Where the split year treatment in Case 1 applies to an individual for the same year or the previous year, and that individual's partner moves overseas so that they can continue to live together, then that other partner can also have split year treatment provided that partner meets the following tests:

- not resident in the UK for the next tax year;
- have no home in the UK or, where there are homes both in the UK and overseas, spend the greater part of that time living in the overseas home; and
- the number of days spent in the UK must not exceed the permitted limit, which follows the same calculation as for Case 1.

The deemed departure date for this individual is the date they move overseas to join their partner or, if later, the first day of that partner's split year period.

Example

John started a new job on 5 August 2017 with a view to being posted overseas to work full-time. He has an induction period in the UK spending two full days (8 and 9 August 2017) for an initial overseas briefing meeting. He then starts work overseas on 1 October 2017. Assume that he continues the overseas job for the next tax year spending hardly any time in the UK so he is clearly non-UK resident for the year 2018–19 (applying the overseas working automatic test). From 1 October 2017 to 5 April 2018, he is in the UK on four days (counting midnights) and works a total of 30 hours. The time spent working overseas in that period amounts to 950 hours. Also in that time he spends part of his annual leave in the UK on 10 consecutive working days commencing on the Monday of one week and ending on Friday the next week. He does not work at weekends.

The split year test requires looking first at the period from 8 August (the first overseas working day) to 5 April 2018 to see if the split year test can be met for that period. He will fail that test, however, because of the number of days spent in the UK. The maximum number of days is 60 (being the maximum allowed for the year of 90 days less the fraction of whole months up to 8 August being 4/12ths, hence the net figure allowed of 60 days). He has clearly spent at least that period of days between 8 or 9 August and 5 April, allowing also for the time spent in the UK on annual leave.

It is then necessary to look at the period from 1 October 2017 (the next relevant day on which there is overseas work) and apply the tests for the period from 1 October 2017 to 5 April 2018.

He would meet that test so that that period would be the overseas part of the year and therefore not resident for that part because:

- there are no significant breaks from overseas work as there is no period of at least 31 days on which he does not do more than three hours' work overseas;
- the number of days in the UK does not exceed the permitted limit, which is 45 days (being 6/12ths of 90);
- the number of days on which he does more than three hours' work in the UK does not exceed the permitted limit of 15 (being 30 × 6/12) as he is only working in the UK on four days;
- he works sufficient hours overseas applying the test in paragraph 14(3) in that period from 1 October 2017 to 5 April 2018 (170 days). The disregarded days are 4 days in the UK and the paragraph 28 days (being 12 days annual leave including one embedded weekend and, say, three bank holidays). That resulting reference period of 170 days is divided by 7 which produces 27 (rounded down). Then divide 950 hours worked overseas by 27, i.e. 35.18, and given that this is at least 35 means that he does work sufficient hours overseas.

Case 3

This case effectively deals with an individual who goes to live abroad as the requirements for this are:

- having held one or more homes in the UK, there must be a day in the tax year of departure when that individual ceased to have any home in the UK and continues not to have a home in the UK for the remainder of that year;
- from the day when the individual ceases to have a home in the UK, they have spent fewer than 16 days in the UK in that split year;
- must not be UK resident in the next tax year; and
- at the end of the period of six months from the date of ceasing to have a UK home there must be a sufficient link with an overseas country, which requires being a resident only of that country in accordance with its domestic laws; or being personally present in that country at the end of each day of that six month period; or the only home or all homes, if relevant, are in that country.

Case 4

This is effectively the reverse of Case 3 where an individual comes to live in the UK, not having been UK resident for the previous tax year. It is necessary to look at the part of the year from 6 April to the day on which they cease to have any homes outside the UK. That prior period is then treated as the overseas part under the split year treatment, provided the individual did not have sufficient UK ties in that part.

In determining those sufficient UK ties the same principles apply as for the SRT generally except the number of UK days will be time apportioned by reference to the number of whole months in that overseas part and generally looking at the circumstances in that part only (except where it is necessary to look at the residence status of family members).

Case 5

This covers an individual who was not UK resident in the previous tax year but then comes to carry out work in the UK where the following conditions are met for a period of at least 365 days (taking the date of arrival as the start of the longest period if more than one):

- that period begins with a day in the year of arrival on which at least three hours' work in the UK is carried out;
- in the part of the year before arrival the individual does not have sufficient UK ties, which is arrived at applying the same principles as in Case 4 above;
- sufficient hours in the UK are worked as assessed over that period, applying the same principles as for the automatic UK working test; and
- at least 75% of the total number of days in the period in which the individual does more than three hours' work are days when working in the UK.

If those conditions are met then the period to the date of arrival will be the overseas part and the remainder of the tax year will be the UK part.

Case 6

This case will apply where an individual has not been UK resident for the previous tax year by virtue of meeting the automatic overseas working test, but was UK resident for one or more of the four preceding years, and is UK resident for the following year. The split year treatment will then apply for the year of arrival back in the UK, the overseas part beginning with 6 April of the year of return and ending on the last day on which more than three hours' work is carried out overseas, provided the overseas work criteria are satisfied.

The overseas work criteria apply the same principles as for Case 1 above, dealing with the period after leaving the UK as opposed to the period prior to arriving.

Case 7

This deals with the treatment of an individual where an individual's partner falls within Case 6 for the year in question or the previous tax year and follows the same principles as in Case 2 above. The UK part runs from the day of moving to the UK or, if later, the working partner's arrival date.

Case 8

This is similar in many ways to Case 4, involving circumstances where the individual is not UK resident for the previous tax year and did not have a home in the UK at the start of the year of arrival.

Split year treatment will then apply if the individual for the first time in that year has a home in the UK and continues to have such a home for the remainder of that tax year and the whole of the next year (and resident in the UK for that next tax year provided that is not a split year).

The period from 6 April to the date of having that first home will be treated as the overseas part to which split year treatment will apply, provided the individual did not have sufficient UK ties in that part, which follows the same principles as in Cases 4 and 5.

Priority rules

It is possible that an individual's circumstances could fall within one or more cases. Between Cases 1 to 3 priority is given in that order in determining the overseas part. For Cases 4 to 8 the rules are:

- if both Cases 5 and 6 apply, the overseas part is effectively treated as the shorter of the two resulting periods;
- if Case 7 (but not Case 6) and Case 5 also then again the overseas part is the shorter of the new period;
- if any two or more of Cases 4, 5 and 8 apply (but neither Case 6 nor 7) the overseas part is the shortest of these three periods.

Legislation: FA 2013, Sch. 45, para. 39–56

170-475 Variation of taxation rules for overseas part where split year treatment applies

The following types of income, and only these, are affected when there is split year treatment for a tax year.

Employment income

General earnings related to the overseas part of the split year are not subject to UK tax provided they are neither in respect of duties performed in the UK nor from overseas employment subject to UK tax. Where necessary any apportionment should be on a just and reasonable basis.

There are also consequential amendments to achieve the same broad overall effect where the remittance basis applies whether under ITEPA 2003, s. 22 where there are duties under employment of a foreign employer performed wholly outside of the UK, or under ITEPA 2003, s. 26 where the new overseas workday relief applies.

The complex employment related security provisions only apply generally if the employee is UK resident. In the case of a split year, those provisions as set out in ITEPA 2003, Pt. 7, Ch. 2, 3 do not apply where the acquisition of the security is in the overseas part of a split year. Neither do those chapters apply if the acquisition occurs in the UK part of the split year but the earnings are not general earnings falling within s. 15, 22 or 26.

The rules in Ch. 3A–3D dealing with securities with artificially or enhanced or depressed market value which are acquired or disposed at other than market value do apply where the acquisition takes place in the overseas part of the split year where Case 1, 2 or 3 applies (i.e. where there is a departure from the UK). The provisions dealing with share options, etc. in Ch. 5 do not apply to the split year where the option is granted in the overseas part (or in the UK part and the earnings from the employment are not general earnings falling within s. 15, 22 or 26).

Foreign pensions

Where an individual receives a foreign pension falling within ITEPA 2003, s. 573, then in a split year it is only the pension arising in the UK part that is subject to income tax (subject to the special rules applying for temporary non-residence).

Trading income

There are consequential amendments to ensure that the deemed cessation and commencement of trade where split year treatment applies will be linked to when the UK or overseas part, as the case may be, starts.

Overseas property business

The apportioned part of the profits from overseas property letting is only subject to tax to the extent of the UK part of the split year. Where there are capital allowances, the profits before capital allowances are apportioned first on a just and reasonable basis and then capital allowances applied for the UK part of the year.

Savings and investment income

Income arising to an individual in the overseas part of a split year is treated as if it arose to a non-UK resident under ITTOA 2005, s. 368 purposes, which has the broad effect that any income from a source outside the UK of a savings and investment income nature in that overseas part will not be subject to UK tax.

Detailed changes are made to the taxation of gains on life assurance policies to deal with split year treatment, given the apportionment required where for part of the period in which the policy is owned the individual is not UK resident.

Other matters

Where foreign income is charged on the remittance basis, that will only apply to such income remitted in the UK part of a split year.

The *Income Tax (Trading and Other Income) Act* 2005, Pt. 5 deals with miscellaneous income, which includes income from estates in administration and income not otherwise charged. As with the savings and investment income tax charge, where such income has a foreign source and arises in the overseas part of the split year it will not be subject to UK income tax.

For trusts, to be non-UK resident a trust must not have a UK resident trustee. The residence of a trust will not be prejudiced simply because an individual becomes UK resident in a year, provided the individual is not a trustee in the UK part of the year.

Legislation: FA 2013, Sch. 45, para. 57–91

170-500 Important definitions

Certain key concepts are defined in detail in Sch. 43, Pt. 2 and the above commentary should be read in conjunction with the following summaries of those concepts.

Days spent in the UK

The basic rule, as indicated above, is that an individual is present in the UK if there at the end of the day. The corollary to this is that if an individual is not in the UK at the end of the day then it is not counted as being a day in the UK. There are exceptions to this:

- The first is where the individual is a passenger who arrives in the UK on one day and leaves the UK the next day provided between arrival and departure that individual does not engage in activities which are to a substantial extent unrelated to passage through the UK.
- The second is where the individual would not be in the UK at the end of the day but for exceptional circumstances beyond their control and the individual leaves the UK as soon as those circumstances permit. There is no definition as such of exceptional circumstances but examples given are national or local emergencies such as war, civil unrest or natural disasters and sudden or life threatening illness or injury. HMRC's view on what is exceptional is fairly restricted so as not to include foreseeable or predictable circumstances or travel problems. The maximum number of days on which such days can be disregarded is limited to 60 and so, counting forward from the start of the tax year, once the number of exceptional circumstances days reaches that figure the remaining days will count as days in the UK.
- The third exception is to prevent perceived abuse of the midnight rule. Taking that rule on its own, it would conceivably be possible for an individual to leave the UK at the end of one day and return as soon as possible the next day so as to limit the midnights here. To deal with this para. 23(4) contains a deeming rule. This applies where the individual:
  - has at least three UK ties for a tax year;
  - the number of days in the tax year when present in the UK at some point, but not at the end of the day, is more than 30;
  - the individual was resident in the UK for at least one of the three preceding tax years.

  In that case, once the number of part days reaches 30 each subsequent day is treated as spent in the UK. This does not apply, however, in determining whether the individual has a 90-day tie.

Home

This is widely defined to include not only a building or part of a building but also a vehicle, vessel or structure of any kind. All the circumstances must be considered to determine whether there is a sufficient degree of permanence or stability about the arrangements so as to count as an individual's home. As with the accommodation tie, there is no requirement to hold a freehold or leasehold interest in a property.

There are two specific exceptions so that a place does not count as a home where:

- the individual uses the place periodically as nothing more than a holiday home or temporary retreat; and
- where the individual has moved out of a place that was a home, that place does not count as a home merely because the individual continues to hold the legal right to it, such as where in the process of selling or letting it.

Work and location of work

It may be necessary to determine whether a person is working and this is treated as including carrying out something in the course of the duties of an employment or in the course of a trade carried on by the individual, whether alone or in partnership.

Time spent travelling counts as working if the cost of the journey would be an allowable expense for employment tax purposes or to the extent that the individual does something else during the journey that would itself count as work.

Time spent undertaking training counts as time spent working if in the case of employment it is provided or paid for by the employer with a view to helping an individual perform their duties, and, in the case of a trade, where the cost is allowable in arriving at the profits of the trade for tax purposes.

It may be that the employment or trade is carried on outside the UK and, therefore, not within the charge to UK tax. In that case where relevant it should be assumed that the activity is within the charge to UK tax in applying these provisions.

Where work is carried out in the course of travelling to and from the UK by air or sea or via a tunnel under the sea it is assumed to be done overseas even during the part of the journey in or over the UK. Travelling to and from the UK is assumed to begin when the individual boards the aircraft, ship or train and ends when disembarking. There are special rules for individuals with relevant jobs on board vehicles, aircraft or ships as mentioned above. When travelling over land, work is treated as carried out according to the country in which the work is actually performed.

Finally, a voluntary post for which the individual has no contract of service does not count as employment.

Calculating the days in the reference period for the sufficient hours in the UK or overseas tests

In arriving at the days in the reference period in the third step of the automatic working test (whether overseas or in the UK) a deduction can be made for disregarded days (i.e. days on which the individual works in the UK for more than three hours) and also the following days:

- reasonable amounts of annual or parenting leave;
- absences on account of sickness where the individual cannot reasonably be expected to work as a result of the illness or injury in question;
- non-working days embedded within a block of leave falling within the above.

A non-working day is one where the individual is not expected to work based on their contract or usual pattern of work and does not in fact work and is embedded within a block of leave only if there are at least three consecutive days of leave before the non-working day or series of non-working days and at least three consecutive days of leave taken after such day or days.

Where there is a gap between two employments and the individual does not work at all in that gap period a deduction can also be made for the number of days within that period, subject to a maximum of 15 days per change of employment and 30 days overall.

Legislation: FA 2013, Sch. 45, para. 21–30

170-600 Anti-avoidance – overview

Part 4 of Sch. 45 is headed 'anti-avoidance'. Its basic aim is to ensure that by becoming non-resident for a relatively short period an individual cannot avoid significant amounts of tax. There are already provisions in place for capital gains tax purposes requiring five tax years of non-residence in many instances and the broad thrust of that rule has now been introduced for specified types of income.

Without this it would be possible, as an example, for an individual who has been UK resident and has built up a company with significant value to go abroad and spend fewer than 16 days in the UK in a tax year. In that tax year he would then arrange for his company to pay a significant dividend and without the anti-avoidance provisions there would effectively be no tax payable on that dividend.

These anti-avoidance rules only apply where an individual becomes 'temporarily non-resident', the meaning of which is set out below. Moreover, they only apply if the year of departure is 2013–14 or a subsequent year. For departures in an earlier year, the previous provisions will apply (and are more limited in scope).

170-650 Meaning of temporarily non-resident

This definition is met if the individual:

- has sole UK residence for a residence period and for this purpose a residence period can include the UK part of a split year;
- immediately following that period there are one or more residence periods for which the individual does not have sole UK residence;
- in at least four out of the seven tax years immediately preceding the year of departure the individual had sole UK residence or a split year in which he was so resident; and
- the temporary period of non-residence is five years or less.

The reference to sole UK residence means that the individual is resident in the UK for an entire year or the UK part of the split year, as the case may be, and there is no time in that year or part when the individual is non-resident for the purposes of a double taxation treaty.

For capital gains tax purposes, the previous rule was that the five year period of non-residence related to tax years. However, the way in which the period of non-residence is defined means that it is the actual period of non-residence is relevant, being when the overseas part of a split year commences to the date of return (i.e. when the UK residence part of a split year starts). If an individual wishes to push this to the limit of five years and one day great care would have to be taken in applying the split year treatment.

Once it has been determined that an individual is temporarily non-resident, the income of that individual must then be considered to determine whether or not it is caught by the anti-avoidance rules.

170-700 Types of income affected by this rule

Income from close companies

In practice, dividends and other distributions are likely to be the most common matters caught by this rule.

The definition of close company has its normal meaning for corporation tax purposes and other definitions, such as having a material interest, follow the corporation tax definitions so that material interest means having, in broad terms, a shareholding of more than 5%, taking into account the rights of associates. The strict position regarding dividends from UK companies received by a non-UK resident is that the income is liable to income tax but ITA 2007, s. 811 imposes a limit on that liability. The practical effect is that such income is exempt from UK tax even though technically taxable.

A new ITA 2007, s. 812A has been added by Sch. 45 so that if s. 811 applies and the individual receives dividends or other distributions from a close company in which he has a material interest and that is within a tax year within the temporary period of non-residence then that income is brought into charge in the year of return. The dividend then becomes taxable in that year. Stock dividends issued by a close company are also caught (ITTOIA 2005, s. 413A).

However, this rule does not apply to a cash dividend or stock dividend to the extent that these are in respect of post-departure trade profits. These are effectively the trading profits that arise after the date of departure and the amount is to be determined on a just and reasonable basis.

A new ITTOIA 2005, s. 401C has similar effect if a distribution of a close company is made in a year when the individual is UK resident (which could be a split year as an example) but double taxation relief is available which has the effect of reducing the income tax charge. Effectively, the double taxation arrangements are disregarded.

If a close company releases a debt owed by a participator or associate then in the year of release or writing off that amount is treated as the income of the individual in a similar way to a dividend. If a release or write off occurs during the period of temporary non-residence then a charge to tax arises as if that had occurred in the period of return.

Dividends from certain non-resident companies

A non-resident receiving foreign source income is not subject to income tax in the first place but it would be again relatively easy to avoid income tax by arranging for a short period of non-residence. Similar to the dividend rule for close companies above, ITTOIA 2005, s. 408A has been added. This applies to dividends paid by a company that would be a close company if UK resident and where the individual or associate has a material interest in the company. Any dividends paid in the period of temporary non-residence are deemed to be paid in the year of return in the same way as UK dividends and there is a similar exception for post-departure trade profits.

Other types of income

The anti-avoidance rule also includes:

- pensions from non-UK flexible drawdown plans. There is already provision to cover this and amendments have been made to interact with the new SRT provisions;
- also simply varying existing law to be consistent with SRT, remittances of a non-domiciled person while temporarily non-resident are treated as remitted in the year of return;
- inevitable amendments to the complex provisions in the ITEPA 2003, Pt. 7A dealing with employment income provided through third parties to make sure there can be no avoidance by using the SRT rules;
- chargeable event gains on contracts of life insurance can give rise to a charge in the year of return when a gain arises in the temporary period of non-residence unless the policy was issued after the period of non-residence began. There is also no charge if death is the event giving rise to the gain or there is a deemed gain on a personal portfolio bond. If such a gain is brought back into charge then some allowance should be made for the period of non-residence in the normal way;
- there is a somewhat obscure provision that adds ITTOIA 2005, s. 689A to the residual charge for income tax (the old Schedule D Case VI) where a distribution of a company that is a close company, or would be if UK resident, is made to an individual with a material interest or an associate of such a person and the amount would not be liable to tax. This is perhaps aimed at income type distributions of non-resident companies to ensure that in the year of return the amount is brought into charge. Distributions from UK resident companies would ordinarily be treated as income in any event and taxed in the same way as a dividend.

Legislation: FA 2013, Sch. 45, para. 109–138 and 153

Bodies of persons

170-800 Trustees

For income tax purposes trustees have a single joint residence which is determined by looking to the residence position of the individual trustees and consequently:

- where each individual trustee is not resident in the UK, the trustees as a body are treated as not UK resident;
- where each individual trustee is resident in the UK, the trustees as a body are treated as UK resident; and

- where the trustees include at least one person who is UK resident and at least one who is not, the body of trustees will be UK resident for income tax purposes if, when the settlor provided funds to the settlement, he or she was either resident or ordinarily resident or domiciled in the UK. (Where the settlement is created by a will or intestacy, the test is applied with respect to the residence, ordinary residence and domicile of the deceased at the date of his or her death.)

Trustees who become or cease to be non-resident are treated as resident throughout the tax year in which the change of residence status occurs. The split year treatment (see 170-400) does not apply to trustees.

The residence of individual trustees is determined by their personal situations as individuals.

The residence of trustees is relevant when dealing with discretionary trusts where no beneficiary is indefeasibly entitled to the trust income as it arises. Where the beneficiary is absolutely entitled to the income of the trust it is the beneficiary's residence, and not that of the trustees, that is relevant for income tax purposes.

Legislation: ITA 2007, s. 474, 475, 476

Tax Reporter: ¶350-800

170-850 Partnerships

A partnership is not regarded for tax purposes as being a separate and distinct entity from the partners themselves and each partner is taxed on his appropriate share of the partnership profits. There is thus no single residence status for the partnership as a body; each individual partner's residence status will be determined independently from that of the other partners.

Legislation: ITTOIA 2005, s. 848

170-900 Personal representatives

The residence of personal representatives is determined as a body on the following basis:

- where all the personal representatives are UK resident, they are treated as a body as resident, irrespective of the residence of the deceased;

- where none of the personal representatives are UK resident, they are treated as a body as not resident, irrespective of the residence of the deceased; and
- where at least one personal representative is UK resident and at least one is not, they are treated as a body as UK resident if the deceased was either resident or ordinarily resident or domiciled in the UK at the date of his or her death. Otherwise they will be treated as not resident.

Legislation: ITA 2007, s. 834

Tax Reporter: ¶350-700

Domicile

171-000 Why domicile is relevant

Liability to UK income tax and CGT are founded upon residence. However the *domicile* of an individual may also be of importance in determining his liability particularly in respect of 'relevant foreign income' and the taxation of overseas earnings.

Legislation: ITTOIA 2005, s. 831

171-025 Deemed domicile status from 6 April 2017

The Government has for many years believed that the tax benefits associated with being non-domiciled but UK resident are open to abuse. Major change in 2008 and the introduction of the Remittance Charge significantly reduced the benefits for all but the wealthiest non-domiciled individuals. The July 2015 Budget proposed further radical changes to the taxation of UK resident non-domiciled individuals. The following points were introduced in F(No. 2)A 2017 and are effective from 6 April 2017.

Abolition of non-domicile status for long-term residents

Where an individual has been resident in the UK for more than 15 of the previous 20 tax years, they will be deemed to be domiciled in the UK for tax purposes.

This provision will not apply where the individual is not resident in the UK and there is no tax year after 5 April 2017 and preceding the relevant tax year in which the individual is resident in the UK.

Non-domicile status for UK born individuals

In addition, those who had a domicile in the UK at the date of their birth will revert to having a UK domicile for tax purposes whenever they are resident in the UK, even if under general law they have acquired a domicile in another country.

A technical briefing has been published outlining the above two proposals, with a technical consultation to be published later in the year.

Legislation: ITA 2007, s. 835BA

171-050 What is meant by domicile

The concept of domicile is one of general law and has been described as the jurisdiction which covers the location of an individual's permanent home, though not perhaps in the sense of where the individual permanently resides, but more where he or she 'belongs'. As a result, whilst an individual may be a resident of more than one country, he or she can never have more than one domicile at any one time.

Domicile is related to legal jurisdictions and, as a result, an individual is not domiciled in the UK as such but rather in one of the areas of jurisdiction that together constitute the UK, viz. England and Wales, Scotland, and Northern Ireland.

There are three kinds of domicile:

(1) domicile of origin (171-100);

(2) domicile of choice (171-150); and

(3) domicile of dependency (171-200).

Certain key principles need to be constantly borne in mind:

- every individual must have a domicile and no person may be without one;
- there is a presumption in favour of the existing domicile continuing; and
- the burden of proving a change lies upon those who allege a change has occurred.

171-100 Domicile of origin

Each individual, at his or her birth, acquires a domicile of origin. In the case of a legitimate child this will be the father's domicile,, otherwise that of the child's mother. There need be no connection between an individual's place of birth and his or her domicile of origin, e.g. a legitimate child born in England to a father of Scottish domicile would acquire a Scottish domicile of origin.

No individual may have more than one domicile at any point in time. The domicile of origin subsists until it is displaced by a new domicile of either choice (see 171-150) or dependency (see 171-200).

Domicile of origin is characterised by two factors, its tenacity and the heavy burden of proof required to displace it. In a case where the taxpayer had a domicile of origin in Nova Scotia, Canada but had lived in England for over 40 years, he was held not to have acquired a domicile of choice in England.

He always had the stated intention of returning to Canada. However, his wife, who was English, wished to remain living here. All his assets were in Canada and he appointed a Canadian trust company as the executor of his will, which contained a declaration that his domicile was in Nova Scotia, Canada, and that he intended to return to that country upon his wife's death. He maintained close contact with Canada and never voted in UK elections. The Court of Appeal held that for the taxpayer to have acquired a domicile of choice in England he must have intended to make his home there until the end of his days unless and until something happened which was not indefinite or vague. The possibility that the taxpayer would survive his wife was not unreal. He had not formed the intention necessary to acquire a domicile of choice in England and over 40 years of residence in the UK was insufficient to displace his domicile of origin.

The domicile of origin can never be completely lost. Since a person cannot be without a domicile, English law, in the absence of any other form of domicile, will assume a domicile of origin. Thus, if an individual abandons a domicile of choice (see 171-050) without acquiring a new domicile of choice, the individual will revert to his or her domicile of origin.

Case: *IR Commrs v Bullock* (1976) 51 TC 522

Other Material: HMRC6: *Residence, domicile and the remittance basis*, 4

Tax Reporter: ¶199-525

171-150 Domicile of choice

An individual of legal capacity, who is not dependent for his or her domicile upon another person, may acquire a domicile of choice by taking up residence in another country with the intention of permanently residing there. Generally, children under 16 years of age cannot exercise a domicile of choice.

A domicile of choice is difficult to acquire but is less retentive, and therefore more easily abandoned, than a domicile of origin. Where a domicile of choice is abandoned, the domicile of origin will revive unless and until it is replaced by a new domicile of choice.

In order to establish a domicile of choice an individual must demonstrate both residence and intention.

It is necessary to sever ties with the domicile of origin and establish permanent ties with the domicile of choice. This will involve considering accommodation, employment and business arrangements, the amount of time spent in each country and where a person's social life is centred.

It is not possible to retain a residence in the domicile of origin and establish a new domicile of choice unless a new 'chief' residence is established there. In the case of *Plummer v IR Commrs*, the taxpayer's family moved to Guernsey, and it was her intention also to settle there. However, she remained in the UK to continue her education at school and, later, university. Her claim to have established a Guernsey domicile of choice failed, since Guernsey had not become her chief place of residence. The taxpayer continued to reside in London during the week and, during the time she was studying, only visited the family's Guernsey residence at weekends.

To acquire a domicile of choice in a particular country, there must be the intention to reside permanently or for an unlimited time in that country. In *Furse v IR Commrs* an individual had a domicile of origin in Rhode Island, USA. In 1923, he and his family came to England, and purchased a farm in Sussex where he resided until his death in 1963. He had indicated that he would not return to the USA until such time as he was rendered incapable of leading an active life on his farm in England. In view of the individual's stated intention, it was clear that he had no intention of leaving England, save on a vague and indefinite contingency. It followed that at the time of his death he had acquired a domicile of choice in England.

Cases: *Furse v IR Commrs* [1980] 3 All ER 838; *Plummer v IR Commrs* [1987] BTC 543

Tax Reporter: ¶199-530–¶199-540

Domicile for tax purposes of overseas electors

In order to determine either a person's domicile for income tax purposes any 'relevant action' taken by that person in connection with electoral rights is ignored unless the person wishes these actions to be taken into consideration.

A 'relevant action' in connection with electoral rights occurs where a person takes any action in order to become registered as an overseas elector or votes in any election which that person is entitled to vote in by virtue of being registered as an overseas elector.

A person is registered as an overseas elector if the person is a registered voter under the *Representation of the People Act* 1983.

In effect, therefore, a former UK domiciliary claiming to have acquired a domicile of choice outside the UK will not prejudice his or her case if he or she exercises his or her UK voting rights as an overseas voter.

Legislation: FA 1996, s. 200(4)

Tax Reporter: ¶199-555

171-200 Domicile of dependency

The domicile of a dependent person is the same as the domicile of the person on whom he or she is dependent. Therefore, any change to the latter will change the domicile of the dependent person. A dependent person cannot unilaterally change domicile. There are two categories of dependent persons: children and the mentally incapacitated.

Children

At birth, a child acquires a domicile of origin which will normally be the father's domicile. Where a child is illegitimate or born after the father's death, the child's domicile will follow that of the mother. The only way a child's domicile can be changed from that domicile of origin is if the parent acquires a new domicile of choice; the child will then also acquire that new domicile.

Once a child is 16 years old (or on marriage at a younger age) he or she becomes capable of acquiring an independent domicile of choice). Until such an independent domicile is acquired, the domicile of dependency is retained as a domicile of choice.

In Scotland, a minor with legal capacity (i.e. girl of 12 or over, or a boy of 14 or over) is capable of acquiring an independent domicile.

Legislation: *Domicile and Matrimonial Proceedings Act* 1973, s. 3

Mentally incapacitated persons

A mentally incapacitated person cannot acquire an independent domicile of choice by his or her own act as he or she is incapable of forming the requisite intention. Therefore, if the person became mentally ill before the age at which he or she could acquire an independent domicile, the person's domicile will change with that of the person's appropriate parent until he or she reaches the prescribed age. From then onwards the person will retain the domicile held at that age. Conversely, if he or she becomes mentally ill after being able to acquire an independent domicile, he or she will retain the domicile held at the date of the onset of the illness.

171-250 Married women where marriage occurred prior to 1 January 1974

Before 1974, a woman acquired her husband's domicile on marriage. If he acquired a new domicile of choice then she acquired it too. She retained this domicile not only as long as her husband was alive and she was legally married to him but also during widowhood or following divorce unless and until it was changed by the acquisition of another domicile. This rule was abolished from 1 January 1974 and the domicile of a woman marrying after that date is determined independently from that of her husband.

A woman who was married prior to 1974, retains her husband's domicile until it is changed by the acquisition of a new domicile of choice or revival of the domicile of origin.

American wives of UK-domiciled taxpayers

A special provision in the US-UK Double Tax Treaty applies to US wives of UK residents where the marriage took place before 1 January 1974. This treats a pre-1974 marriage as having taken place on 1 January 1974 for the purposes of determining her domicile for UK tax purposes. As a consequence, the wife's domicile is to be determined independently from that of her husband.

Legislation: *Domicile and Matrimonial Proceedings Act* 1973, s. 1

Other Material: UK-US Double Tax Convention of Convention of 24 July 2001 (SI 2002/2848)

Tax Reporter: ¶199-550

Foreign income of UK residents

The arising basis

172-000 Tax on worldwide income

A UK resident or ordinarily resident individual who is also domiciled in the UK is liable to tax on income regardless of where that income arises. The amount chargeable is the actual income arising to the person whether that income is enjoyed in this country or not.

Legislation: ITEPA 2003, s. 15(1) (earnings); ITTOIA 2005, s. 6(1) (trade profits); ITTOIA 2005, s. 269(2) (property income); ITTOIA 2005, s. 368(1) (savings and investment income); ITTOIA 2005, s. 577(1) (miscellaneous income)

172-025 Unremittable foreign income

Where the arising basis applies, income falls chargeable to UK tax whenever it arises, irrespective of whether it is actually received in the UK or not. This may result in hardship if the taxpayer is unable to remit his or her overseas income to the UK.

Taxpayers who find themselves in such a position may claim relief where they have:

- been prevented from remitting the income to the UK, either because of the laws or other actions of the Government of the country in which the income arose or because of the impossibility of obtaining foreign currency in that country; and
- not remitted the income to a third country and converted it into sterling or some other currency which can be transferred to the UK.

No claim for relief can be made if a payment in respect of that income is received from the Export Credits Guarantee Department (ECGD).

A person seeking relief must give notice in writing by the first anniversary of the 31 January following the tax year in which the income arises. Appeal lies to the special commissioners and not to the general commissioners.

Where the conditions for relief are satisfied, the unremitted income is omitted from the taxable income for the year it arises. Once the income ceases to be unremittable or a payment from the ECGD is subsequently received, it becomes part of the taxable income for the tax year in which that event occurs. The relief is therefore a postponement of the tax liability on the income, not an exemption.

Where previously unremittable income becomes taxable, it is valued at the time of that event.

Where, by the time the income becomes taxable, the individual is dead, the tax is payable by the person's personal representative and is a debt due from his or her estate.

If no claim to relief is made, but the income nevertheless qualifies as unremittable, it will still be taxable for the year in which it arose. The value of that income to be taken as the generally recognised market value in the UK of the currency in which the income is denominated or, if there is no such value, calculated by reference to the official rate of exchange of the territory where the income arises.

Legislation: ITTOIA 2005, s. 841–845

The remittance basis

172-050 Remittance basis for non-domiciled taxpayers or those (prior to 6 April 2013) not ordinarily resident

Finance Act 2008 has made far reaching changes to the taxation of foreign domiciliaries. The new legislation is the result of the residence and domicile review that began in 2002 and has effect from 6 April 2008.

The legislation provides that the remittance basis will only automatically apply for individuals who are either not domiciled or, prior to 6 April 2013, not ordinarily resident in the UK in respect of a tax year in which:

- the individual's aggregate unremitted foreign income and gains are less than £2,000;
- the individual either has no UK income or gains, or has no UK income and gains other than taxed investment income not exceeding £100 and does not remit any foreign income or foreign gains and either has not been UK resident for more than six out of the previous nine years or are under the age of 18 throughout the year.

Individuals within these categories will remain entitled to the personal allowance and the annual exempt amount for capital gains.

Finance Act 2009 provides that an individual with unremitted foreign income and gains of less than £2,000 in a tax year does not need to file a self-assessment tax return in order to use the remittance basis. Similarly an individual who has no UK income and gains other than taxed investment income of less than £100 in a tax year does not need to file a self-assessment tax return in order to use the remittance basis. This extension comes into effect from 6 April 2008.

In all other circumstances, from 6 April 2008, foreign domiciliaries will be taxed on the arising basis unless they make a claim for the remittance basis to apply.

To make a claim, the individual must not be domiciled in the UK in that tax year or not ordinarily resident in that year. The claim will be made in the self-assessment return and will result in the individual losing entitlement to personal allowances and the capital gains tax annual exemption.

Finance Act 2008 also overturns the 'source doctrine', i.e. that no tax liability can apply if the source of the income benefiting from the remittance basis no longer exists in the year of remittance. This means that if an individual arranged for a bank account to be closed at the end of one tax year and remitted the interest in the next year, there was likely to be no tax liability. Legislation in *Finance Act* 2008 means that a charge can now be imposed where the foreign income that has benefited from the remittance basis is remitted, whether or not the source exists in the year of remittance.

Finance Act 2009 also removes the obligation to file a return with effect from 6 April 2008 where individuals employed in the UK also receive overseas employment income of less than £10,000 and overseas bank interest of less than £100, all of which is subject to a foreign tax. Such individuals will typically be migrant workers employed in seasonal work in the agricultural or service sectors in the UK, and in other countries, in the same tax year, and whose overseas income is subject to tax where it is earned.

Legislation: ITA 2007, s. 809B, 809D and 809E; FA 2009, s. 51 and Sch. 27

172-075 Remittance basis charge

Where a foreign domiciliary is aged 18 or over, has been resident in the UK for at least seven out of the preceding nine tax years and wishes to make a claim for the remittance basis to apply for a tax year, the person will be required to pay an additional tax charge, the remittance basis charge (RBC) set at £30,000. The individual must 'nominate' foreign income or chargeable gains with respect to which the RBC will be calculated. The RBC will be the higher of:

- the additional tax payable as a result of the nominated foreign income or foreign gains being taxed on the arising basis; and
- £30,000.

The period of residence may be broken or unbroken.

The charge of £30,000 is increased to £50,000 for 2012–13 to 2014–15 and £60,000 for later years where the individual has been UK resident in at least 12 of the 14 years immediately preceding the relevant year. With effect from 5 April 2015, individuals resident in the UK for more than 17 out of the last 20 years will pay a charge of £90,000 to claim the remittance basis.

> **Example**
>
> A is resident in the UK in 2015–16, but is not domiciled and not ordinary resident. A has been continuously resident in the UK since 6 April 1991 except for 2007–08 and 2008–09. The RBC of £90,000 will be payable.

The RBC has been expressed in such a way as to provide a possibility for it to qualify for double tax relief in other countries. However, where other countries have lower rates of tax than the UK, full credit for the RBC may not be obtained.

Legislation: ITA 2007, s. 809C, 809H

172-100 What is meant by 'remittances'

From 6 April 2008, there is a single wider definition of remittance which covers non cash remittances and payments offshore with respect to UK linked services and debts. The new rules mean that goods purchased out of relevant foreign income after 11 March 2008 and imported to the UK after 5 April 2008 will be deemed remittances. The amount remitted will be equal to the foreign income or gains which were used to acquire the asset.

Four conditions are specified to determine whether income or chargeable gains are remitted to the UK. Conditions A and B are required to be satisfied as one, whereas Conditions C and D are freestanding.

Conditions A and B

Condition A is that the individual or other relevant person (for definition see below) has either brought money or property into the UK or has received it here or it has been used here for the person's benefit. The condition is also satisfied if a service is provided in the UK for the person's benefit. (This presumably includes the completion and submission of the person's UK tax return.)

If that condition is satisfied, then Condition B must also be satisfied. This requires that either:

- the property or service referred to in Condition A or the consideration given for that service must either be, in whole or in part, income or chargeable gains of the individual, or be derived from such income and gains; or
- property (including income and chargeable gains) of the individual, or anything deriving from them, are used outside the UK in respect of a debt which relates to the property or service referred to in Condition A. (This is aimed at preventing the individual from borrowing funds abroad to remit to the UK and then using foreign income to repay those borrowings.)

Legislation: ITA 2007, s. 809L(2), (3)

Condition C

Condition C is that property of a donee (termed in the legislation a 'gift recipient'), which derives from a gift by the individual, is used in the ways mentioned in Condition A or used in respect of a debt which relates to that property. The gift must be of money or property which itself derives from the individual's income or chargeable gains.

Legislation: ITA 2007, s. 809L(4), 809N

Condition D

Condition D is that property of any other person is used in the ways mentioned in Condition A or in respect of a debt which relates to that property. This must be as a consequence of a connected operation whereby the individual or other relevant person has made a corresponding transfer to that person of money or property which derives from the individual's income or chargeable gains.

Legislation: ITA 2007, s. 809L(5), 809O; FA 2009, Sch. 28, para. 6

Relevant person

A relevant person is:

(a) the individual;

(b) the individual's husband or wife;

(c) the individual's civil partner;

(d) a child or grandchild under 18 of any of the above;

(e) a close company in which any of the above is a participator or a company, which is a 51% subsidiary of such a close company;

(f) a company, which, if it was UK resident, would be a close company and any other relevant person would be regarded as a participator, or a 51% subsidiary of such a company;

(g) the trustees of a settlement in which any of the above is a beneficiary; or

(h) a body connected with such a settlement.

For this purpose co-habitees are to be treated as husband and wife or civil partners as appropriate.

Legislation: ITA 2007, s. 809M; FA 2009, Sch. 28, para. 7

Tax Reporter: ¶199-730–199-755

172-175 Exempt property

Property will not be treated as remitted where funds are brought to the UK to settle the RBC. Specific categories of exempt property are:

- property that meets the public access rule (a work of art, collectors' item or antique that is available for public access at an approved establishment);
- clothes, footwear, jewellery and watches that meet the personal use rule; or
- property if:
  - the property is in the UK for repair or restoration;
  - the property is only in the UK temporarily (275 days or less in total); or
  - it cost less than £1,000.

There will be a tax charge where exempt property is sold in the UK or ceases to be exempt property. There is a relaxation from 6 April 2013 for property that would cease to be exempt because it is lost, stolen or destroyed. There is a further relaxation where compensation monies are taken offshore within 45 days or a qualifying investment is made.

Legislation: ITA 2007, s. 809X, 809Y, 809YF, 809Z, 809(Z1)–(Z4); FA 2009, Sch. 28, para. 10

172-176 Non-domiciled individuals – relaxation for remittance of monies to make business type investment

Following consultation, *Finance Act* 2012 includes provisions to allow, in certain cases, a UK resident individual who is not domiciled in the UK to make tax free remittances here provided the monies are used for a qualifying investment. The rules are very detailed but can be summarised as follows.

(1) The qualifying investment can be either shares in a company or a loan whether secured or unsecured.

(2) The target company must be either a trading company within the definition, which broadly requires a commercial trade with a view to making profits, or a holding company of a trading group. The qualifying trades must be all (or substantially all) of what the company or the group, as the case may be, does.

The definition of trade also includes a business carried on for generating income from land but as with an investment in a trade, the activity must be carried on by a private limited company and not held directly by the individual.

An eligible stakeholder company can also qualify, which is broadly a company which exists wholly for the purpose of making investments in eligible trading companies. In all cases, only private limited companies fall within the relief, i.e. any company whose shares are not listed on a recognised stock exchange. Limited liability partnerships are specifically excluded.

(3) Generally, the investment must be made within 45 days of the day on which the money or other property is brought to or received in the UK. There must be no expectation of receiving a benefit linked to the investment other than in the ordinary course of business or not on arm's length terms.

(4) The sale of the investment can give rise to what is called a potentially chargeable event. Such an event can also include a company ceasing to be eligible as a trading company and breaching the extraction of value rule.

(5) In the case of a disposal, if this is of the entire holding and the whole of the disposal proceeds have been taken offshore or reinvested in other qualifying investments, the period to avoid a chargeable event is 45 days. This is limited, though, to the amount originally invested less any amount dealt with under para. 6 below to meet a capital gains tax liability. In arriving at disposal proceeds, it is possible to make allowance for fees and other selling costs of the disposal.

(6) An individual may have a liability for capital gains tax on the disposal. In that case, an individual can retain funds to meet those liabilities but only where the subject supplies a certificate of tax deposit with a letter confirming that the relevant provision is intended to apply to the deposit.

(7) To obtain the benefit of this relaxation, a claim for relief must be made before the first anniversary of 31 January following the tax year of remittance.

(8) This relief does not apply if the investment is concerned with tax avoidance to a material extent.

Legislation: ITA 2007, s. 809VA–809Z10

UK income of non-residents

Computation of UK tax

173-000 Personal allowances

Normally only UK resident individuals are entitled to personal allowances. However, the following categories of non-residents are also entitled to claim:

- nationals of a European Economic Area state (i.e. the member states of the European Union plus Iceland, Liechtenstein and Norway);
- residents of the Isle of Man or Channel Islands;
- persons who are or have been Crown servants;
- widows, widowers or surviving civil partners of Crown servants;
- missionaries;
- persons in the service of a British protectorate; and
- persons who have been resident in the UK but are now resident abroad for the sake of their health or the health of a member of their family who is resident with them.

In addition, the UK's double taxation treaties normally allow residents of the other country to claim personal allowances against their UK income.

In the year in which a non-resident arrives in the UK to take up permanent residence, full allowances and reliefs are given.

An individual who departs the UK to take up permanent residence abroad is entitled to full allowances and reliefs for the year of departure. He or she may cease to be regarded as being resident and ordinarily resident in the UK from the date of departure.

Claims for personal allowances may made on the 'Non-residence, etc.' supplementary pages to the self-assessment return by ticking box 9.7. Claims for repayment of UK tax deducted can be made on Form R43.

Finance Act 2009 withdrew the entitlement for non-resident individuals who qualified for UK personal allowances and reliefs from income tax solely by virtue of being a Commonwealth citizen, from 6 April 2010. This is because HMRC have been advised that this is not compliant with the Human Rights Act. The vast majority of individuals affected will still benefit through Double Taxation Treaties.

Legislation: ITA 2007, s. 56; FA 2009, Sch. 1

Other Material: HMRC Booklet R43 Notes (2005), Chapter 3

173-050 Limitation of UK liability

The income tax payable by a non-resident in any tax year is not to exceed the sum of:

(1) tax deducted at source, or treated as deducted from income received under deduction of tax; and

(2) tax on the non-resident's total UK income, but ignoring what is termed 'excluded income' and any personal allowances which may be due.

Where that sum is less than the total liability which would normally arise, taking into account any personal allowances which may be due, the effect is that no further tax will arise on such income as has already borne basic rate tax by deduction at source and only trade profits (derived from a trade carried on in the UK via a permanent establishment) and UK property income could be liable to unlimited liability.

As a rule of thumb the limitation will apply where the higher rate tax saving on excluded income is greater than the increased tax on trading or property income due to the loss of any personal allowances which might otherwise be due.

'Excluded income' for these purposes includes:

- interest from banks and building societies;
- dividends from UK companies;
- unit trust distributions;
- purchased life annuities (except annuities under personal pension schemes;
- profits on deeply discounted securities;
- profits on transactions in deposits;
- royalties from intellectual property;
- certain non-trading receipts from telecommunications rights;

- annual payments;
- taxable social security pensions and benefits (except income support and jobseeker's allowance);
- annuities paid under a retirement annuity contract or a specified superannuation scheme; and
- any other income which may be designated for this purpose by Treasury regulations (no such regulations have yet been issued).

Example

Pedro is a 54-year-old non-resident Commonwealth citizen who has the following income arising in the UK for 2017–18:

	£
Trading profits from a restaurant in the UK	50,000
Dividends from a UK company	6,000
Bank interest	4,500

His normal UK liability for the year would be:

	Total income	Trade profits	Savings income	Dividend income
	£	£	£	£
Trade profits	50,000	50,000		
Savings income	4,500		4,500	
Dividends	6,000			6,000
	60,500	50,000	4,500	6,000
Less: personal allowance	(11,500)	(11,500)		
Taxable income	49,000	38,500	4,500	6,000
Tax rates applicable:				
Basic rate on	33,500	33,500		
Savings income allowance 0% on	500		500	
40% on	9,000	5,000	4,000	
Dividend nil rate 0% on	5,000			5,000
32.5% on	1,000			1,000
	49,000	38,500	4,500	6,000

	Total income	Trade profits	Savings income	Dividend income
	£	£	£	£
Tax due:	£	£	£	£
At basic rates	6,700	6,700		
At 40%	3,600	2,000	1,600	
At 32.5%	325			325
Tax liability	10,625	8,700	1,600	325
The maximum UK liability is limited to:				
			£	£
Tax deducted from interest				0
Tax on trade profits ignoring personal allowance:				
£33,500 at basic rate			6,700	
£16,500 at 40%			6,600	13,300
Tax liability				13,300
As this sum is more than the total liability which would normally arise, taking into account any personal allowances, tax payable is £10,625.				

Legislation: ITA 2007, s. 810–814

Other Material: HMRC Help Sheet IR300

173-100 Partnership profits

Where a non-resident individual is a member of a partnership carrying on a trade in the UK, income tax is charged by treating the individual's share of the partnership profits as arising from a deemed trade carried on in the UK by him or her alone.

In situations where the partnership carries on a trade partly in the UK and partly outside, the effect of this provision is to limit the charge on the non-resident to his or her share of the profits from that part of the trade carried on in the UK.

Legislation: ITTOIA 2005, s. 849(3)

Tax Reporter: ¶288-500

Collection of UK tax

173-500 Property income

Income from property in the UK arising to non-residents is taxed by way of deduction at source under the 'Non-resident Landlords Scheme'. The scheme provides for letting agents, or, where there is no letting agent, the tenants of a non-resident landlord, to:

- deduct tax at the basic rate from the landlord's UK rental income;
- pay the tax quarterly to HMRC; and
- submit annual information returns of details relating to income, expenses and tax deducted for each non-resident landlord.

There are different implications for letting agents, tenants and landlords, each of which is considered in turn below.

Letting agents

A 'letting agent' is defined as a person who acts on behalf of the non-resident in connection with the management or administration of a UK property business.

HMRC regard this definition as potentially very wide. However, they regard the requirement to operate the scheme to apply only to those who handle or control UK rental income of a non-resident landlord. The letting agent must produce a separate quarterly tax calculation for each of the non-resident landlords for whom he or she acts. This calculation will apply basic rate tax to:

- property income received in the quarter; *plus*
- other property income paid away by the tenant in the quarter at the letting agent's direction; *less*
- expenses paid in the quarter by the letting agent (or paid at the agent's direction) which the letting agent can reasonably be satisfied are allowable expenses of the non-resident landlord's property business.

Where, for a particular landlord, the calculation for a quarter results in a loss, that loss can be carried back to earlier quarters within the tax year where tax has been paid, thus producing a repayable amount. This amount may be set off against tax which the letting agent is due to pay in respect of other landlords for the quarter in which the excess arose. Failing this, it is repaid to the agent. Any excess of expenditure that cannot be carried back in this way is carried forward and set against the future income of the landlord concerned. Excess expenditure may be carried forward beyond the year-end. The total tax due for all non-resident landlords must then be submitted with the quarterly return within 30 days of the end of the quarter.

HMRC's Centre for Non Residents (CNR) publish guidelines on allowable deductions. Provided these guidelines are followed, there will be no penalty imposed for deducting an item that turns out not to be deductible. Where there is doubt about the deductibility of an item, it should not be deducted.

Tenants

Tenants have a similar quarterly obligation where there is no letting agent. In this case, the calculation of tax due is based on:

- property income paid in the quarter to the non-resident landlord; *plus*
- property income paid to a third party in the quarter, unless the tenant can be reasonably satisfied that this represents an allowable expense of the business (see above with regard to HMRC guidelines).

Since there is no requirement to deduct expenses, there is no need for provisions dealing with excess expenditure. There is an important de minimis exception for tenants paying rent of £100 per week or less. This is subject to HMRC issuing a notice requiring the scheme to be operated.

Landlords

Non-resident landlords may apply to CNR for approval for rents to be paid gross. Where approval is not given, or earlier approval is withdrawn, appeal lies to the First-tier Tribunal. Approval may be given where:

- the non-resident landlord's UK tax affairs are up to date;
- the non-resident landlord has never had any UK tax obligations; or
- the non-resident landlord does not expect to be liable to UK income tax for the year in which the application is made.

Undertakings must also be given that:

- where the basis of the application is that no UK tax liability is expected to arise, CNR will be notified if any liability does in fact arise;
- all UK obligations will be complied with fully; and
- the Board will be notified if the applicant's normal place of abode ceases to be outside the UK.

Where approval is given, CNR will write to the relevant letting agents or tenants informing them of the date from which payments may be made gross. Gross payment is conditional on the receipt of this notice, and should not be made before receipt. The non-resident landlord should receive a certificate from letting agents/tenants showing the amount of tax deducted for the year ended 31 March. This should be available by 5 July following that year. The amount of tax deducted can then be set off against the tax liability arising in the self-assessment for the year ended 5 April.

Legislation: ITA 2007, s. 271 and 272; *Taxation of Income from Land (Non-residents) Regulations* 1995 (SI 1995/2902)

Other Material: HMRC Booklet *The Non-resident Landlords Scheme: Guidance notes for letting agents and tenants*

Website: www.hmrc.gov.uk/cnr/nrl_guide_notes.pdf

Tax Reporter: ¶303-200

173-550 Entertainers and sportspersons

A withholding tax is applied to certain earnings of non-resident visiting entertainers and sportsmen and women, termed in the legislation 'visiting performers'. Broadly speaking, any person making a payment in relation to an appearance or performance in the UK by a visiting performer is required to withhold from that payment an amount equivalent to basic rate income tax upon it, no matter to whom the payment is made. An arrangement can be made with HMRC for a nil or lower rate of deduction, to recognise a deduction for expenses, but in the absence of such an arrangement, the full basic rate of tax should be deducted at source.

The legislation is in two parts. First, it treats the activities of the visiting performer in respect of which a payment is made as forming part of a trade, profession or vocation being carried on in the UK. This is necessary to bring the receipt of the payment within the UK tax net. Secondly, it permits regulations to be made to impose an obligation on the payer to deduct basic rate income tax from the payment.

The Non-resident Entertainers Unit has been established especially to administer the scheme and has issued a guide for those who will be responsible for complying with the requirements to deduct tax at source.

Legislation: ITTOIA 2005, s. 13; *Income Tax (Entertainers and Sportsmen) Regulations* 1987 (SI 1987/530)

Other Material: HMRC Booklet FEU 50: *Payer's Guide – Foreign Entertainers*

Tax Reporter: ¶281-000

Treatment as trade, profession or vocation

Where a payment is made which is subject to the obligation to withhold tax, the relevant activity which gave rise to that obligation is treated for income tax purposes as performed in the course of a trade, profession or vocation exercised in the UK by the visiting performer. In other words, any profits and gains arising from the relevant activity would be assessable to UK tax as trading income.

This deeming provision will not apply (because it is unnecessary) where the performer:

- is already exercising a trade, etc. in the UK and the relevant activity is part of that trade; or
- carries out the relevant activity as part of the duties of an office or employment. In such a case the performer would be assessable anyway in his or her capacity as employee.

The obligation to deduct tax

The regulations contain, inter alia, the essential definitions of:

- entertainers and sportsmen;
- the activities falling within the scope of the rules; and
- the types and extent of income subject to (or excluded from) the withholding system,

as well as provision for rates of tax, deductions of expenses and losses and for the administration of the withholding arrangements.

Although it is the making of a payment connected with an appearance in the UK that actually triggers the operation of the withholding arrangements, they will only apply where a number of requirements are satisfied:

- the performer must be not resident in the UK for the tax year in which the relevant activity takes place;
- the performer must fall within the description of entertainer or sportsman, namely an individual (whether alone or with others) who gives performances in his or her character as an entertainer or sportsman in any kind of entertainment or sport. This means performing any activity of a physical kind, which is or may be made available to the public (or any section of the public), whether or not for payment;
- the relevant activity must be performed in the UK by the performer in his or her character as such or on or in connection with a 'commercial occasion or event' as specifically defined in the regulations; and

- the payments involved must have a connection 'of a prescribed kind' with the relevant activity. In essence they must be in respect of, or derive directly or indirectly from, the performance of the activity.

It has been established by the House of Lords that the obligation to deduct tax applies to payments made by non-resident companies to other non-resident companies in connection with activities performed in the UK.

Payments of less than the personal allowance (£1,000 per year prior to 1 June 2012) to any performer are excluded from the scheme.

Case: *Agassi v Robinson* [2006] BTC 372

173-600 Deduction of tax at source

The following payments made to non-resident recipients are to be made under deduction of income tax:

- annual interest paid by any person, other than a bank. Generally this is interest paid by a company or, in exceptional circumstances, an individual who, due to an insufficiency of income, is not paying the interest out of profits or gains brought into charge to income tax;
- annual payments or annuities;
- royalties or other sums in respect of the user of a UK patent; and
- interest paid by banks on 'relevant deposits', except where a declaration has been given to the bank that the person beneficially entitled to the interest is not ordinarily resident in the UK.

Legislation: ITA 2007, s. 874, 889, 900 and 903

Tax Reporter ¶117-000ff.

173-650 Assessment of UK representative

Where the non-resident carries on a trade, profession or vocation in the UK via a branch or agency, that branch/agent becomes the non-resident's 'UK representative' in respect of the trading income arising directly or indirectly from the branch, including any income arising from property or rights held by the branch.

As a result, the branch/agent is made responsible for filing appropriate self-assessment returns, paying the tax due and complying with all the other obligations in connection with the assessment, collection or recovery of tax or the interest on the tax.

Not all agents can be treated as UK representatives. Specifically exempted is any agent who transacts business at arm's length for the non-resident. In the main, this means that independent agents such as Lloyds' members' agents, brokers and investment managers are not to be regarded as UK representatives for this purpose.

Legislation: ITA 2007, Pt. 14, Ch. 2C; TCGA 1992, Pt. 7A

Tax Reporter: ¶293-400; ¶293-450

Double taxation

Causes and remedies

174-000 How double taxation arises

In simple terms, double taxation arises when an amount of income, profit or capital gain is charged to tax in two different tax jurisdictions, either on the same person or on different persons.

In general, the UK, in common with most other countries, levies tax on a person's income where either:

- the source of that income is within its fiscal jurisdiction (the 'source basis'); or
- the person resides within its fiscal jurisdiction (the 'residence basis').

The fiscal jurisdiction of the UK extends to England, Wales, Scotland and Northern Ireland and the territorial sea of the UK.

Thus a person resident in the UK is, in normal circumstances, charged to tax not only upon his or her income arising within the UK, but also upon any income arising elsewhere in the world. It follows that as other countries adopt a tax charging regime similar to that of the UK, certain items of income will fall to be taxed in more than one country.

Double taxation also occurs where two or more countries each regard the same person as being resident in their country, under their respective domestic law, and seek to tax that person on his or her worldwide income.

Legislation: *Interpretation Act* 1978, Sch. 1; TCGA 1992, s. 276; ITA 2007, s. 1013

Tax Reporter: ¶170-000

174-050 The methods of relieving double taxation

In order to alleviate double taxation, a country may enter into an agreement with another country to either:

- grant an exemption in one country, so that the other has exclusive taxing rights for that particular source of income; or
- provide for one country to have primary taxing rights and for the other to reduce its tax charge by giving credit for the tax charged by the first country.

The agreements may be either comprehensive, covering all sources of income, or limited to certain operations such as shipping or air transport.

Primary taxing rights are determined by the residence position of the taxpayer and agreements contain provisions, colloquially termed 'tie-breakers', for determining the residence where the person would otherwise be resident in both countries under their domestic legislation.

Although double taxation agreements are ostensibly intended to give relief, they also contain provisions relating to the exchange of information to assist each jurisdiction to counter tax avoidance and evasion (see 146-450).

Tax Reporter: ¶170-050; ¶170-550

174-100 Resolving dual residence situations

The benefits of a double taxation agreement are only available to persons who are residents of one of the countries concerned. The vast majority of the UK's current double taxation agreements define a resident of one of the countries as any person who is liable to tax in that country by virtue of some connection with it in the form of either residence, domicile, place of business or similar test. It is not sufficient that a person's income may arise in that country.

Therefore, a person's residence is to be determined initially under the domestic laws of each country. In many cases that will result in the person being regarded as being resident in only one of the countries. However, it is possible for both countries to regard the person as resident for the whole or part of a chargeable period and specific rules are needed to determine that person's residence for the purposes of the agreement. By this means, one of the countries will be given taxing rights on total income on the basis of residence and the other country will be limited to taxing only that income which derives from a source within its jurisdiction.

In order to cope with the situation, where an individual is regarded as resident under each country's domestic law, those treaties usually contain four 'tie-breaker' tests to be applied in order to determine the tax residence for the purposes of the agreement. The tests are to be applied in the following order until one of the countries can be clearly identified.

(1) In which country is the individual's permanent home located? This test need only be applied to the period when the individual's residence position affects tax liability and this period may be less than an entire tax year where, for example, during that year, the individual either acquires a second home in the other country or emigrates to the other country.

(2) If the individual has a permanent home in both countries (but not otherwise), where is his or her 'centre of vital interests'? This is the country with which the individual's personal and economic relations are the closest. Regard should be had to the individual's family and social relations, occupation and place of business, political and cultural activities and the place from where the individual administers his or her property. It is clear, by definition, that an individual cannot have more than one centre of vital interests.

(3) If the individual does not have a permanent home in either country, or if the location of the person's centre of vital interests cannot be determined, where is his or her 'habitual abode'? This term means the country in which the individual stays more frequently. Regard must be had to periods spent by the individual at *any* place in either country, not just a permanent home. The comparison must be over a sufficiently long period to be able to determine whether the residence in any country is habitual.

(4) If the individual has his or her habitual abode in both countries or in neither of them, of which country is the individual a 'national'? This will be a question of fact.

Where the answer to the 'nationality' test is that the individual is a national of both countries or of neither of them, they are to settle the matter by mutual agreement.

Tax Reporter: ¶170-550

Double taxation agreements

174-300 Relationship with domestic law

In the UK, the Crown is empowered to make Orders in Council setting out the detail of arrangements with other countries with a view to giving relief from double taxation in relation to income tax, capital gains tax, corporation tax and 'any taxes of a similar character' imposed by the laws of the other country. Therefore, double taxation agreements override UK domestic law.

Where there is no double taxation agreement in existence with a particular country, or a treaty does not provide for relief on that particular source, the UK will grant relief unilaterally in respect of any foreign tax paid (see 175-250).

HMRC may make regulations for carrying out the provisions of double taxation agreements. These powers include the ability to make regulations:

- to ensure that the benefits of UK double taxation agreements only accrue to persons entitled to them; and
- where earlier payments have been made under the mistaken belief that relief under an agreement eliminated or reduced the tax otherwise deductible, to recover that tax either by assessment or by deduction from subsequent payments.

The regulations made under these powers are concerned with payments (e.g. interest or royalties) where the UK domestic law may require the deduction at source of income tax at the basic rate, but where this withholding requirement is reduced or eliminated by a double taxation agreement. (They do not, however, apply to dividends or other distributions.)

Legislation: ICTA 1988, s. 788, 790, 791; TIOPA 2010, s. 2–7; *Double Taxation Relief (Taxes on Income) (General) Regulations* 1970 (SI 1970/488)

Tax Reporter: ¶170-000

174-400 Property income

The term used in double taxation agreements is 'income from immoveable property' and the term itself is to be determined by reference to the domestic law of the country in which the property is situated. However, in general, certain items such as livestock and equipment used for the purposes of agriculture and forestry and payments for the working of mineral deposits and other natural resources are specifically within the definition, whilst ships, boats and aircraft are specifically excluded.

This article applies irrespective of the means by which the property is used to generate income, whether by direct use, letting or any other form. It also applies to income of this nature generated by an enterprise.

Generally, a right to tax such income is given to the country in which the property is located (the 'state of source') but the country of residence of the taxpayer is not prohibited from taxing that same income.

In the case of an unincorporated business, the taxing rights of the state of source would have priority over those of the state of residence where the income arises to a business which does not have a permanent establishment in the state of source.

174-450 Business profits

A UK resident individual trader is taxed wherever the trade is exercised and non-residents are taxed on the profits derived from trading in the UK.

The UK's double taxation agreements normally provide that the profits of any business carried on by a resident of one country are taxable only in the country of residence unless the business is carried on in the other country through a 'permanent establishment' in that other country.

Where such a permanent establishment exists in the other country, the profits of the business are taxed in that country but only to the extent that those profits are attributable to the permanent establishment.

Legislation: ITTOIA 2005, Pt. 2, s. 6

174-500 Interest, dividends and royalties

Interest is generally defined as income from 'debt-claims', government securities, bonds or debentures. Tax will be levied by the country of residence, whilst the tax levied by the source country is usually limited to a withholding tax at a maximum of 10%.

Dividends are generally taxable only in the country of residence (of the recipient) or are taxed in both countries but at a reduced rate in the source country. They are usually defined in double taxation agreements as:

- income from shares and other rights which participate in profits and are not debt claims; and
- other income which is taxed under the same rules as dividends by the state in which the distributing company is resident.

Royalties in respect of patents, copyrights, etc. are generally exempt from tax in the source country and are taxed only in the country of residence. Where the beneficial owner of the copyright, etc. carries on business in the source country through a permanent establishment and this rule does not apply, the source country may also tax the royalties where they are effectively connected to that permanent establishment.

Tax Reporter: ¶171-200; ¶171-250; ¶171-300

174-550 Salaries and wages

Normally salaries, wages and similar remuneration are only taxed in the country where the individual is resident. However, if the duties of the employment are carried out in the other country (the 'host state'), that country may also tax the remuneration to the extent that it is derived from those duties.

Special provision is usually made for:

- company directors (see 174-600);
- artistes and sportspersons (see 174-650);
- pensioners (see 174-700); and
- those engaged on government service (see 174-750).

For other individuals, an exemption from 'host state' taxation is usually available where the following three conditions are satisfied.

(1) The individual is present in the host state for less than 183 days in any 12-month period which begins or ends in the fiscal year concerned.

(2) The remuneration is paid by, or on behalf of, a non-resident employer.

(3) The cost of that remuneration is not borne by a permanent establishment of the employer located in the host state.

The object is to exempt the remuneration of employees temporarily working in the host state for non-resident employers. It is not intended to apply where the employment services are rendered by its employees to an enterprise which is liable to tax in the host state, either on the grounds of residence or because of a business carried on via a permanent establishment there. Put in basic terms, the host state is saying 'if we allow a deduction in computing the profits of the enterprise for the cost of the remuneration of its employees, we want to balance that loss of tax by taxing that remuneration'.

Short-stay employees: HMRC practice

The third condition for the short-stay exemption is that the cost of the visiting employees' remuneration is not borne by an employer in the host state. HMRC policy is to identify the true 'economic employer' of a visiting employee.

Often, the formal contract of employment is with the overseas employer, but the employee works in the business of the UK company, which benefits from the work undertaken by the employee. The overseas employer often recharges the cost of the employee to the UK company, which is effectively the 'economic employer'. HMRC policy is that the exemption will not be applied in cases where the economic employer is UK resident.

However, HMRC will not consider that a short-term business visitor was sufficiently integrated into the business of a UK company for it to be regarded as the employer where:

- the employee concerned is in the UK for less than 60 days in a tax year; and
- that period does not form part of a more substantial period when the taxpayer is present in the UK.

This has become known as 'the 60-day rule'.

Other Material: HMRC *Tax Bulletin* TB06/95–3, TB10/96–9 and TB12/03–3

Tax Reporter: ¶171-410

174-600 Company directors

Directors' fees and other similar payments are taxable by the country in which the individual is resident and also by the country of residence of the company concerned, regardless of where the duties of that office are performed. This is in contrast to the normal rule for wages and salaries, where the host state may only tax remuneration attributable to duties performed there. (However, under certain double taxation agreements such as the 2003 agreement with Australia, such fees will be treated in the same way as wages and salaries.)

The scope of the article is limited to fees and similar payments, including benefits in kind, received in a person's capacity as a director. Other remuneration received in respect of other functions, such as an executive or consultant, falls to be treated in the same way as wages and salaries.

Tax Reporter: ¶171-420

174-650 Artists and sportspersons

In the case of entertainers and sportspersons, the rules applicable to business profits and wages and salaries are usually overridden by special rules. The income from the exercise of their personal activities as such may be taxed in the country in which those activities are exercised (the 'host state') regardless of the length of the individual's presence there. The right of the host state to tax the income is also given where the income accrues to a person other than the entertainer/sportsperson. Most UK agreements in recent years contain such special rules.

The country of residence of the individual will, of course, also tax the earnings.

See 173-550 for commentary on the deduction of UK tax at source on amounts paid in respect of visiting artistes and sportspersons.

Tax Reporter: ¶171-430

174-700 Pensions

The general rule is that pensions and other similar remuneration paid in respect of past employment are taxed only in the state of residence of the recipient.

In practice, the UK agreements often make a distinction between occupational pensions and social security pensions paid by a contracting state. The treatment of occupational pensions usually gives exclusive taxing rights to the country of residence, although where the pensioner was previously resident in the country of source, that country might also be given taxing rights. Social security pensions on the other hand are often to be taxed only in the country of source, on the basis that as the government of that country pays the pension, it should have the exclusive right to tax it.

Finance Act 2011 introduces an anti-avoidance provision which will apply where amounts are transferred out of a pension scheme into another scheme out of which pension type income is paid with a view to taking advantage of a double tax treaty. Where the transfer is part of a tax avoidance scheme the pension type income paid will remain subject to UK income tax notwithstanding the terms of the treaty.

Legislation: TIOPA 2011, s. 130A

Tax Reporter: ¶171-440

174-750 Government service

The general rule is that tax on salaries, wages and other remuneration (but not pensions) paid in respect of services rendered to a government or local authority of a country is only to be levied by that country.

However, the country of residence of the individual may have exclusive taxing rights, but only if the services were rendered in, and the individual is a national of, that country. An additional requirement is that the individual did not become a resident of that country solely for the purpose of rendering those services. In this context, government service does not include services rendered in connection with a business carried on by a contracting state or a local authority. Remuneration in respect of such services falls to be treated as wages and salaries, directors' fees or pensions, as appropriate.

Pensions paid in respect of government service are to be taxed only in the country of source. However, they may be taxed exclusively by the country of residence if the individual is a national of that country.

Tax Reporter: ¶171-450

174-800 Students and apprentices

A student, or business apprentice, who is normally resident in one country but is present in a second country (the 'host state') for purposes of education, training, etc. is normally exempt from tax in that host state in respect of any sums received in respect of his maintenance, education or training, provided the source of those payments is outside that host state.

However, there are variations in the UK's double taxation agreements and it will be essential to check the relevant treaty in any specific case.

HMRC may assist in particular cases by modifying the provisions of the PAYE system. An instance is the case of overseas farm students working in the UK on a Home Office approved Seasonal Agricultural Workers Scheme. Such students are not normally liable to UK tax and are therefore given form P38(S) enabling employers to pay them without deducting tax.

Tax Reporter: ¶171-460

174-850 Teachers and professors

The UK's double taxation treaties generally provide that a teacher who is normally resident in one country, but who visits the other (the 'host state') for purposes of teaching, is not to be taxed in that host state on remuneration accruing in respect of that teaching, provided the period of the visit does not exceed a period of, generally, two years.

Where the teacher visits the UK on a number of separate occasions, the two-year 'clock' starts running from the date of his or her first arrival in the UK and the exemption only applies to remuneration earned from visits in that two-year period.

Case: *IR Commrs v Vas* [1990] BTC 52

Tax Reporter: ¶171-470

174-900 Other income

To cater for situations where a type of income or gain does not fall within a particular article, most UK double taxation agreements provide a 'residual' article to cover income not expressly mentioned elsewhere in the agreement.

This gives exclusive taxing rights to the country of residence unless the income is 'effectively connected' with a permanent establishment in the country of source through which the recipient carries on a business. In that case, the provisions of the business profits article will apply and the state of source may also tax the income.

Earlier UK agreements may lack an 'other income' article, in which case where income does not fall within a specific article, it is to be taxed under the domestic law of both countries. Where this results in double taxation, UK residents will be entitled to unilateral relief (see 175-200ff.).

Tax Reporter: ¶171-480

174-950 Income from discretionary trusts and estates in the course of administration

In the absence of an article in the UK's agreements containing any specific article dealing with the income arising from discretionary trusts and the estates of deceased persons in the course of administration, this income falls to be dealt with under the 'other income' article.

HMRC's policy in such cases is to treat the source of the income as the trust or estate itself and, where the article granted exclusive taxing rights to the state of residence of the beneficiary, to repay the tax suffered by the trustees.

Where the relevant agreement does not contain an 'other income' article, or where there is no agreement in force, a 'look-through' policy will be applied, i.e. it would look through the trust or estate to the underlying source of income and apply the article appropriate to that source.

Other Material: SP 3/86

Tax Reporter: ¶171-485

Relief in the absence of an agreement

175-500 Unilateral relief: introduction

Relief for foreign tax may still be given against the UK tax on the same income, even though there is no double taxation agreement with that country or the agreement does not include a particular tax or source of income. This is known as 'unilateral relief'.

If relief is available under a double taxation agreement but has not been claimed, unilateral relief cannot be claimed instead. If the foreign tax was eligible for a relief in that country, which was not claimed, that tax is also not available for unilateral relief.

An agreement may explicitly preclude double tax relief in specified circumstances. In such cases, unilateral relief is not available either.

Essentially, unilateral relief is calculated in the same way as credit relief by treaty, and the same restrictions apply.

Legislation: TIOPA 2010, s. 8–17

Tax Reporter: ¶171-500

175-600 Entitlement to unilateral relief

The normal rule is that credit given for tax paid under the laws of another country and which is computed by reference to income or gains arising in that country, is allowed as a credit against the UK tax on that same income or gain.

However, relief is also specifically available in respect of:

- tax levied by the Isle of Man or the Channel Islands on income without limitation to where it arises;
- tax levied by the Isle of Man or the Channel Islands on a person resident there who is not also resident in the UK (normally only UK residents are entitled to double taxation relief); and
- tax levied by a foreign country on a resident there in respect income from an office or employment in that country which is also charged to UK tax on employment income.

Legislation: TIOPA 2010, s. 18

Tax Reporter: ¶171-550

175-700 Foreign tax eligible for unilateral relief

The foreign tax eligible for unilateral relief is that calculated by reference to the income or gain arising in the foreign country. It is to be allowed as a credit against the UK tax charged on that same income, etc. In this connection, remuneration from personal or professional services performed in the foreign territory is deemed to be income arising in that territory.

The foreign tax concerned must also be 'computed by reference to income'. Thus the foreign tax must correspond to income tax, capital gains tax or corporation tax. In a case where Venezuelan tax was charged on 90% of the total contract value, the question before the court was whether this was a tax on income or a turnover tax. It was held that the tax was similar to and served the same function as an income tax. The 10% deduction from turnover was intended to arrive at a statutory profit figure on which tax was levied (although this was a gross over-estimate of the actual profit the company derived from the contract).

As a result of this judgment, a statement of practice was issued explaining that HMRC will examine a foreign tax in its legislative context to decide whether it fulfils the same function as income tax and corporation tax served in the UK. Turnover taxes, as such, will therefore not be admissible for relief.

Unilateral relief extends to taxes imposed under the laws of a province, state or other territory, or taxes levied by a local authority or similar body provided such taxes correspond to income, corporation or capital gains tax.

A number of foreign taxes have been admitted by HMRC as being allowable for purposes of unilateral relief. The list of admissible taxes is shown in the *Tax Reporter* and also the HMRC *Double Taxation Relief Manual*, under the country concerned.

Legislation: TIOPA 2010, s. 8 and 9

Case: *Yates (HMIT) v GCA International Ltd (formerly Gaffney Cline & Associates Ltd)* [1991] BTC 107

Other Material: SP 7/91; HMRC *Double Taxation Relief Manual* DTRM2150ff.

Tax Reporter: ¶171-600

176-000 Relief by deduction: entitlement

A person may elect not to take relief by credit for foreign tax paid. If the person so elects, or if relief by credit (either under an agreement or unilaterally) is otherwise unavailable, he or she is entitled to a deduction from his or her foreign income of any tax paid.

It is not possible to claim both tax credit relief and a deduction in respect of the same item of income. However, HMRC accept that, where there are a number of different items of income, it is possible to claim credit relief for some and a deduction for others.

Example 1

Terence has foreign income of £5,000 on which he pays foreign tax of £1,000. If he elects for relief by deduction he will be taxed in the UK on income of £4,000 (i.e. £5,000 – £1,000).

Assuming the rate of UK tax is 40% he will pay £1,600 in UK tax. Had Terence claimed relief by credit his UK tax liability would be as follows:

Income	*UK tax*
£5,000	$£5{,}000 \times \frac{40}{100} = £2{,}000$

The tax credit for foreign tax paid (£1,000) is set off against UK tax liability, leaving a liability to UK tax of £1,000. Terence would therefore claim relief by credit.

Relief by deduction cannot be claimed where the foreign income is taxed on the remittance basis (see 172-050). Also relief does reduce total income for the purposes of calculating personal allowances for non-residents (see 173-000).

Legislation: TIOPA 2010, s. 2

Tax Reporter: ¶171-750

176-100 Relief by deduction: time limits

Where foreign tax is relieved as a deduction from taxable income, instead of by means of a credit against the income tax itself, an assessment or claim may be made within extended time limits where the foreign tax is subsequently increased or reduced. Where foreign tax deducted becomes excessive or inadequate as a result of an adjustment in the UK or the foreign territory, the time limit for:

- making an assessment or a claim, becomes six years after the date of the adjustment; and
- the taxpayer notifying HMRC of an adjustment to the foreign tax which renders a deduction excessive becomes one year after the date of the adjustment (subject to a penalty up to the amount of tax payable as a result of the excessive adjustment).

The requirement to notify an adjustment which renders a deduction excessive (and consequent penalty for failure to do so) does not apply to Lloyd's members in respect of their membership liabilities.

HMRC's interpretation of what is meant by an adjustment, and when it should be considered to have been made was contained in Tax Bulletin and although issued specifically in connection with adjustments to foreign tax relieved under an agreement will also apply to tax relieved by deduction, since both provisions are couched in similar language.

Legislation: TIOPA 2010, s. 114 and 115

Other Material: HMRC Interpretation, IRInt. 198 (Tax Bulletin, June 1999)

Tax Reporter: ¶171-750

Claiming relief

176-500 Calculation of credit relief

The amount of the foreign tax credit which is set against the UK tax payable is limited to the difference between:

- the UK tax chargeable on his total income for the year (any foreign income being 'grossed up' at the appropriate rate of the foreign tax); and
- the tax chargeable on his income but excluding the foreign income.

In other words the credit is limited to the UK tax on the foreign income, taking it as the top slice of the taxpayer's income. It follows, of course, that should the foreign rate of tax be higher than the UK rate, no UK tax is payable. The corollary, however, is that any excess of foreign tax cannot be reclaimed or carried forward.

Where there is more than one foreign source of income in a tax year, the calculation needs to be repeated in respect of each source but in such a way that foreign income already taken into account in the first calculation is excluded from total income for purposes of the second calculation. The order in which foreign sources are considered is a matter for the taxpayer and may produce a different overall result.

Example 1

Bill is aged 30, single and UK resident. In 2017–18, his taxable income is as follows:

	Income	Foreign tax
	£	£
UK salary	32,000	
Rental income (Ruritania) – gross before tax deduction at 50%	6,000	3,000
Rental income (Eldorado) – gross before tax deduction at 20%	3,000	600
	41,000	

	Income	Foreign tax
Less: personal allowance	(11,500)	
Taxable income	29,500	

Bill has decided to calculate the maximum relief on his Ruritanian income first. The maximum credit for Ruritanian tax is calculated as follows:

	Income	Foreign tax
Step 1	£	£
UK tax payable on taxable income of £29,500:		
£29,500 at 20%		5,900
Step 2		
UK tax payable on taxable income *less* Ruritanian income (£29,500 – £6,000 = £23,500):		
On £23,500 at 20%	4,700	
Maximum credit for Ruritanian tax		1,200

Thus £1,800 of Ruritanian tax would be unrelieved.

The calculation is then repeated in respect of the Eldoradian income.

	Income	Foreign tax
Step 1	£	£
UK tax payable on taxable income *less* Ruritanian income (as previously calculated at Step 2 of the Ruritanian calculation)		4,700
Step 2		
UK tax payable on taxable income *less* Ruritanian and Eldoradian income (£29,500 – [£6,000 + £3,000] = £20,500)		
On £20,500 at 20%	4,100	
Maximum credit for Eldoradian tax		600

Thus the full amount of the Eldoradian tax, £600, is available for credit, bringing the total credit for foreign tax to £1,800, with £1,800 Ruritanian tax being unrelieved.

It is important to give priority to the source which has suffered the highest rate of foreign tax.

Legislation: TIOPA 2010, s. 36

Tax Reporter: ¶152-000

176-550 Basis periods

It may be that the basis period on which foreign tax is calculated differs from the basis period applying in the UK. The tax year for which credit is given for an amount of foreign tax strictly depends upon whether the relevant double tax agreement provides for credit to be given on a 'root income basis' or a 'statutory income basis'. With the exception of the agreement with St. Kitts-Nevis, all current UK double tax agreements now prescribe the root income basis.

Under this basis, the foreign tax charged on a particular amount of foreign income is credited against the UK tax charged on that same amount of income, regardless of the year for which the other country assesses the tax. This applies where the double taxation agreement contains words to the effect that the foreign tax paid in respect of a source of income is to be allowed as a credit against the UK tax computed by reference to the same income.

Example

Kevin is UK-resident and operates a nightclub in Benidorm. He prepares accounts for the club annually to 31 December. Spanish tax is levied on a calendar year basis. The Spanish tax due for the year to 31 December 2017 will be credited against the UK tax due for the year 2017–18.

Other Material: HMRC *International Manual* INTM161170

Tax Reporter: ¶152-040

176-600 Overlap profits of foreign trades

In the opening years of a trade some part of the profits may be taxed twice, e.g. once in the opening year and again in the second year. Credit for overseas tax on foreign trade profits is allowed against the UK tax for any tax year during which that income forms the basis of assessment for UK purposes.

Example 1

Brian is resident, ordinarily resident and domiciled in the UK. He carries on a business there. On 1 January 2017, he opens a branch of his business in Ruritania. He makes up his accounts to 31 December each year. In the year ending 31 December 2017, the profits of his Ruritanian branch are £40,000. Ruritania charges tax on such profits at a rate of 20%.

The Ruritanian profits are assessed to UK tax in the following manner:

UK tax year	*Profits forming basis of assessment*
2016–17	£10,000 ($^3/_{12}$ × first 12 months profit of £40,000)
2017–18	£40,000 (first 12 months profit of £40,000)

On profits of £40,000 Ruritania charges tax in the sum of £8,000 (£40,000 × 20%). Brian therefore has a credit of £8,000 in respect of foreign tax paid. This credit may be set off against his UK tax for 2016–17 and 2017–18.

The amount of credit to be allowed, however, is subject to a prescribed maximum, as is the credit available in respect of any particular tax year. The amount of credit allowed in respect of any income for any tax year may not exceed the difference between:

- the total credit allowable against income tax for all the tax years for which credit is allowable; and
- the amount of credit in fact allowed for earlier years.

The total credit allowable is the amount of the overseas tax, suitably adjusted where the number of UK periods of assessment exceeds the number of foreign periods of assessment.

Example 2

In Example 1 (above) the number of UK periods of assessment is 1 $^1/_4$ and the number of foreign periods of assessment 1. Thus the maximum total credit allowable for all tax years is £8,000 × 1 $^1/_4$, i.e. £10,000.

Therefore, the maximum credit available to Brian in respect of Ruritanian tax paid is as follows:

UK tax year	*Credit*
	£
2016–17 ($^3/_{12}$ × £8,000)	2,000
2017–18 (first 12 months)	8,000
	10,000

The total credit allowed is £10,000, as compared to the actual foreign tax paid of £8,000. The foreign tax has, therefore, been 'expanded' to recognise the fact that some part of the foreign profits have been taxed twice.

The time limit for making claims for this expanded relief is five years from 31 January next following the tax year in which relief is claimed or, if more than one, the later year.

Legislation: TIOPA 2010, s. 22

Clawback of relief where overlap profits reverse

On a change of accounting date giving rise to a long basis period or on cessation, an amount of profits representing a period of more than 12 months may become taxable. In such a case the overlap profits created in the opening years may be deducted from the profits otherwise taxable.

HMRC will clawback the excess credit, where the overlap profits, which have previously attracted the 'expanded' foreign tax credit described above, are deducted from subsequent profits.

A comparison is made between:

(1) the total of:

  (a) the double tax credit given against the original overlap profit which has subsequently been credited; plus

  (b) the amount of credit which without 'expanding' the foreign tax would have been allowed against the overlap profit subsequently credited; and

(2) the amount of double tax credit which would have been given, on income from the same source, in the year when the overlap profits are credited, had no overlap credits been given.

If 1 exceeds 2, the taxpayer will be taxed on such an amount as, at basic rate, will give tax equal to the excess. If 1 is less than 2, then the taxpayer can have a tax credit equal to the shortfall.

If overlap profits are relieved in stages, a proportionate amount of clawback operates on each occasion.

Legislation: TIOPA 2010, s. 22 and 24

Tax Reporter: ¶152-060

176-650 Claiming relief under a double taxation treaty

Claims for relief by virtue of any double taxation agreement are to be made before the later of:

- the fourth anniversary of the end of the year of assessment; or
- the 31 January next following the year of assessment in which the foreign tax is paid.

There are two main exceptions to the time limits above:

- where there is any later adjustment made in the amount of foreign tax payable (see 176-700); and

- where the special rules applicable to overlap profits apply (see 176-600).

Legislation: TIOPA 2010, s. 19

Tax Reporter: ¶175-900

176-700 Subsequent adjustments to foreign tax already relieved

Additional claims or assessments may be made where relief for foreign tax has become inadequate or excessive respectively, as a result of an adjustment to the amount of foreign tax. Taxpayers who have claimed relief must notify HMRC if there is an adjustment and the relief claimed has become excessive. This latter requirement does not apply to Lloyd's underwriters.

Where double tax credit relief has been rendered inadequate because of an adjustment to the tax payable either in the UK or under the laws of the foreign country, a claim for additional relief may be made within six years of the time when the adjustment was made.

Similarly, where relief or a deduction has been rendered excessive because of such an adjustment, then an assessment, adjustment or determination to correct relief already given may be made within the same extended time limit.

Taxpayers who have claimed tax credit relief must notify HMRC if there is an adjustment to the amount of foreign tax and the relief claimed has become excessive as a consequence. A similar notification must be made for adjustments where foreign tax claimed as a deduction becomes excessive (see 176-100).

Notification must be made in writing within one year of the time the adjustment was made. A penalty up to the amount of the excessive relief (or tax payable as a result of the excessive adjustment where tax is claimed as a deduction) may be applied where there is a failure to notify.

HMRC's views on what is meant by an adjustment, and when it should be considered to have been made for these purposes is contained in Tax Bulletin.

Legislation: TIOPA 2010, s. 134

Other Material: HMRC Interpretation, IRInt. 198 (Tax Bulletin, June 1999)

176-750 Self-assessment returns

Claims for foreign tax credit relief can be made on the 'Foreign' supplementary pages to the self-assessment return. These pages enable foreign income to be declared together with the country of source and the amount of foreign tax paid or deducted.

The accompanying 'Notes on Foreign' contain worksheets to assist in the calculation of the maximum tax credit relief (see 176-500) and a separate Help Sheet IR260 contains a worksheet to deal with overlap profits (see 176-600).

Relief for special withholding tax

177-000 Background

The EC directive on the taxation of savings income was responsible for the introduction of a 'special withholding tax' on payments of savings income by institutions in member states and their dependent or associated territories to individuals resident in the EU. Provisions introduced into UK domestic legislation allow credit for the tax and provide for certification to enable UK-resident beneficial owners to claim exemption from the tax.

A particular feature of the special withholding tax is that it is to be shared 25% by the state where the source of income is located and 75% by the state of residence of the individual beneficial owner of that income.

The UK-resident individual can, by making a claim, be entitled to credit for the full amount of the tax against his or her UK liability on the savings income. Where the special withholding tax exceeds the UK liability, the excess is repayable. This is unique; only 75% of the special withholding tax is due to the UK authorities, but HMRC are obliged to repay 100% if there is no UK liability. Normally, for double tax relief purposes, HMRC will only give credit for the foreign tax up to the amount of the UK liability; any excess of foreign tax is lost.

Legislation: Directive 2003/48

177-050 Credit for income tax purposes

A UK-resident individual in receipt of savings income which has been subject to special withholding tax may make a claim to treat that tax as if it were UK income tax suffered by deduction at source. From this, the normal consequences flow; that deemed UK tax will be set against the individual's total UK liability. Where the deemed UK tax exceeds the individual's income tax liability, the excess is to be set against his or her capital gains liability (if any) and any remaining excess repaid.

A claim cannot be made, however, if relief for the special withholding tax has already been obtained in another jurisdiction because the individual is resident there or is treated as resident there under a double taxation agreement.

The provisions do not set a time limit for a claim, nor do they prescribe a particular form of claim. The normal time limit of four years from the end of the year of assessment will therefore apply.

Legislation: TIOPA 2010, s. 137

177-100 Interaction with other foreign tax

Although, by making a claim, special withholding tax is to be deemed to be UK tax, it is nevertheless tax deducted by the country in which the source of the income is situated. If a claim is not made, the special withholding tax is simply foreign tax and eligible for double tax relief just as any other overseas withholding tax on that source of income.

However, the credit given by HMRC will be limited to the amount of UK tax due on that income and any excess will be unrelieved. By contrast, a claim to treat the special withholding tax as UK tax will ensure full relief for that tax, as any excess over the UK liability will be repaid. Where the individual has suffered special withholding tax, which is treated as UK tax, and any other foreign tax, that other foreign tax is to be set off against the UK liability in priority to the special withholding tax. By this means, the maximum possible foreign tax will be relieved and any unrelieved special withholding tax will be repaid by HMRC.

Legislation: TIOPA 2010, s. 138 and 141

177-150 Computation of income

Special rules apply for the calculation of the amount of the income where the amounts involved have suffered only special withholding tax or both special withholding tax and foreign tax. In essence, the rules are the same in both cases; it is merely the applicable legislation which differs.

In this particular context, 'special withholding tax' means that in respect of which a claim has been made to treat it as UK tax.

The following rules apply:

- where the income tax is assessed on the income arising in the year, the income will be calculated without any deduction for the special withholding tax (or foreign tax if applicable) deducted; and
- where the individual is non-domiciled and the income tax liability is based on the remittance basis (see 172-050), the gross income for UK tax purposes will be the total of the net income received plus the amount of the special withholding tax (or foreign tax, if applicable) relevant to that amount.

Legislation: TIOPA 2010, s. 143

177-200 Exemption certificates

Provision is made for the issue of certificates to individuals to enable them to claim exemption from special withholding tax in the country where the source of income is located. An application for a certificate has to be made in writing and provide:

- the name and address of the applicant;
- the applicant's National Insurance number or the date, town and country of his or her birth;
- the account number or some other means of identifying the investment from which the income arises;
- the name and address of the payer of the income;
- the period for which the certificate is to be valid, not exceeding three years; and
- such documents as HMRC require to verify that information.

If HMRC are satisfied that they have been provided with all the information required, they are obliged to issue a certificate within two months from when the required information and documents are provided by the applicant. The certificate must set out the required information and its period of validity.

Where HMRC refuse to issue a certificate, they must issue a written notice to that effect setting out the reasons for the refusal. Any appeal must be made within 30 days of the refusal notice and lies to the special commissioners, who may either confirm the refusal notice or quash it and require HMRC to issue an exemption certificate.

Legislation: TIOPA 2010, s. 144

Tax credits

Introduction to tax credits

190-000 Introduction

Working tax credit (WTC) and child tax credit (CTC) began to be paid from April 2003. Their immediate predecessors, working families' tax credit (WFTC) and disabled person's tax credit (DPTC), introduced in October 1999, were the first attempt for some three decades to integrate parts of the social security system with the tax system. In this case, administration and responsibility for payment of two welfare benefits (family credit and disability working allowance) was transferred from the Department of Social Security to the then Inland Revenue.

The policy objectives behind WTC and CTC (the 'new' tax credits to distinguish them from their predecessors) were twofold: to make work pay better than staying on benefits, and to reduce child poverty. To that end, WTC is paid to low-income working families and individuals, whether or not they have children; while CTC is paid to those with children, whether or not they are in work. The costs of childcare, often cited as a disincentive to work particularly for lone parents, are supported through the childcare element of WTC.

It was intended that the CTC should, along with child benefits, become the principal means of child support within the welfare system. To this end, the child premiums in income support (IS) and income-based jobseeker's allowance (IBJSA) were abolished for new claims from April 2004 and recipients paid CTC instead. Some people, mainly those who claimed prior to April 2004, still receive the child premiums in IS and IBJSA. The effective date for migration of these remaining families to CTC has been continually postponed since the originally scheduled date of 6 April 2005 and is now unlikely to happen due to the introduction of universal credit (UC).

Both WTC and CTC are gradually being replaced by UC. This new benefit will be administered by DWP and will bring together several separate benefits into one benefit with several elements.

It is clear that the new benefit will be very different to tax credits both in terms of qualification rules and income measure and whilst some people will be better off under UC there will be others who will lose out financially. The next few years will be challenging for both HMRC and DWP as preparations start for the migration of tax credits claimants to UC (see 190-500).

The main piece of primary legislation governing WTC and CTC is the *Tax Credits Act* 2002 (TCA). The main legislative provisions in tax credits are regulations, made under enabling provisions in the TCA 2002. These are referred to where appropriate in footnotes to each paragraph in this commentary, and a full list can be found in Key Data. The *Welfare Reform Act* 2012 also contains some provisions that are relevant to tax credits. These are primarily related to tax credits fraud.

Her Majesty's Revenue and Customs (HMRC) is the Government department responsible for the payment and management of tax credits. This contrasts with other welfare payments which fall mainly within the responsibility of the Department for Work and Pensions (DWP) or, in the case of housing benefit and local council tax support schemes, local authorities. When tax credits are replaced by Universal Credit, responsibility will once more pass back to DWP in Great Britain (Department for Communities in Northern Ireland). HMRC however will still play an important role through the development of their Real Time Information (RTI) system which will be used to pass earnings information to DWP on a regular basis so that UC claims can be amended by DWP in 'real time'. HMRC will also retain responsibility for child benefit and the new Tax-Free Childcare scheme.

Claims

A claim to tax credits must be made; if there is no claim there is no entitlement. A single claimant must make a single claim; couples must make a joint claim. See further 190-300.

Age limit

There is no upper age limit for claiming tax credits, but no claim may be made by a person under 16, and in the case of a joint claim both partners must be at least 16.

Meaning of 'in the UK'

For both WTC and CTC, a claimant must be 'in the UK'. A person is treated as not 'in the UK' if he or she is not ordinarily resident in the UK: 'ordinarily resident' here takes its social security meaning of 'normally residing in the UK (apart from temporary or occasional absences) and their residence here has been adopted voluntarily as part of the regular order of their life for the time being'.

EU workers exercising their right to work or reside in the UK are treated as ordinarily resident in the UK.

As well as being ordinarily resident, a person must also be physically present in the UK. However, this physical presence requirement is somewhat relaxed where a claimant (or a partner in a claiming couple) is 'temporarily absent' from the UK. In such cases the person's entitlement continues for the first eight weeks of his or her absence, or 12 weeks where the person's absence is related to medical treatment for or death of the claimant or claimant's partner, or of a child or relative of either. After the first eight (or 12) weeks, the person making the claim is no longer 'in the UK' and his or her entitlement ceases. However, if that person is part of a couple, the person's partner – if still 'in the UK' in his or her own right – can make a new claim as a single person for the remainder of the period of absence.

A person is temporarily absent if at the beginning of the period of absence the person is not expected to be away for more than 52 weeks.

From 1 July 2014, certain EEA nationals need to be living in the UK for at least three months before they will be treated as 'being in the UK' for CTC purposes. These rules will generally not apply to workers who are exercising their EU rights.

Crown servants posted overseas, together with their partners, are treated as 'in the UK' and therefore entitled to claim, if they were ordinarily resident in the UK before their posting, or were 'in the UK' in connection with that posting. While overseas, they may be temporarily absent from their overseas post on the same basis as if they had been in the UK.

There is an additional requirement for CTC (not WTC). A person is also treated as not 'in the UK' if the person makes a claim for CTC on or after 1 May 2004 and does not have a right to reside. This is in addition to the requirement that the person is present and ordinarily resident. From 8 November 2012, a small group of claimants will not be treated as in the UK even if they do have a right to reside. In summary, this rule applies where the claimant's right to reside only exists because they are the primary carer of a person who has their own right to reside and that person could not live in the UK without their primary carer.

There is no statutory definition of right to reside. Whether a person has a right to reside will depend on many factors including nationality, nationality of spouse, work status and immigration status. Right to reside can also be established under various EU law provisions as well as UK provisions. There are some changes to Right to reside for certain EU nationals. From July 2014 onwards, closer scrutiny applies to the question of whether an EEA national can be defined as a worker or self-employed person for the purpose of establishing their right to reside. Both HMRC and DWP introduced a minimum earnings threshold which is linked to the Primary Earnings Threshold set for National Insurance purposes. This approach supposes that in order that the work or self-employment is genuine and effective (as required under EU law), the individual must earn minimum amount from the work. In cases where the person does not meet that income threshold, HMRC will consider their full circumstances including whether their right to reside may be established under other criteria (as in the above list).

The HMRC *Tax Credits Technical Manual* (TCTM) contains further detailed information about establishing a right to reside.

Immigration

Except in certain circumstances set out in regulations, a person subject to immigration control cannot claim tax credits. However, asylum seekers, though not entitled to tax credits on arrival in the UK, can have their claims backdated to the date of their arrival on receiving confirmation from the Home Office that they have been granted refugee status. This is subject to the provision that the tax credit claim is made within one month of receiving notification of refugee status. Prior to 6 April 2012, this time limit was three months. It is therefore important that people in this situation contact HMRC immediately after receiving notification of their status to allow time for a form to be issued, completed, sent back and received by HMRC within the one-month time limit.

One further notable exception is that if one member of a couple is subject to immigration control and the other member is not (or falls within another exception), the joint claim will be determined as if that person were not subject to immigration control. Note, however, that unless either or both of the claimants are responsible for a child, the second adult element will not be included in the claim where one person is subject to immigration control.

Legislation: TCA 2002, s. 1, 2 and 3; CPA 2004, Sch. 24, para. 144; *Tax Credits (Immigration) Regulations* 2003 (SI 2003/653); *Tax Credits (Residence) Regulations* 2003 (SI 2003/654)

Case: *Shah v Barnet London BC* [1983] 1 All ER 226

Other Material: HMRC *Tax Credits Technical Manual* TCTM02001; TCTM02100

Tax Reporter: ¶160-000

190-050 Practical aspects of tax credits for tax advisers

While the current tax credits system incorporates many of the social security antecedents which they supplanted, the way in which they interact with the tax system means that they cannot safely be ignored by tax practitioners advising individuals, whether in their personal or business affairs. Some examples of where the tax credit system interacts with the mainstream tax system follow.

- Tax credits can be claimed by relatively high-earning couples where both parties work and pay maximum childcare costs (although changes to tax credits in the last couple of years have somewhat reduced the number of people who qualify at higher incomes). In such cases, depending upon the numbers of children in the household, the cost of any childcare and whether there are any disability elements included, the couple can earn in excess of £60,000 or £70,000 per annum between them and still receive tax credits. See further 190-280.
- Clients who seem at first sight too wealthy to be entitled to tax credits should nevertheless consider making a 'protective claim' to preserve their entitlement for the whole tax year if their income should take a sudden drop (e.g. through redundancy or an unexpected bad debt). See further 190-340.
- Computation of income taken into account in assessing tax credits entitlement follows quite closely the income tax model, but there are subtle differences which can give rise to serious financial consequences if the variations are not taken into account (see, e.g. computation of trading loss relief – 190-260). It should be noted that calculation of income for a final tax credits award on transition to universal credit is calculated differently (see 190-500).
- If a self-assessment enquiry gives rise to a tax credits enquiry, the one cannot be settled without considering the impact of its outcome on the other; and HMRC usually work the two together.

In reality, therefore, the stark choice now open to advisers is to include tax credits in the service they offer clients, or to state very clearly in letters of engagement that they do not.

Agents' phone line

HMRC have set up a priority telephone line for agents who have an ongoing relationship with their clients and for whom a form 64-8 is lodged as authorisation. The agents' phone number is 0345 300 3943. All agent calls are routed to one contact centre site, where the adviser will have the necessary guidance for verifying and dealing with agents. The phone line is not for use by members of the public.

Working tax credit

190-150 Introduction

The working tax credit (WTC) consists of a number of different 'elements', listed below. To qualify for WTC, a person must at least fulfil the conditions of the basic element. The remaining elements are paid according to the circumstances of the claimant.

Legislation: TCA 2002, s. 10–13; *Working Tax Credit (Entitlement and Maximum Rate) Regulations* 2002 (SI 2002/2005)

Tax Reporter: ¶164-000

190-160 The basic element of WTC

To be entitled to the basic element, the claimant (or one or both of them if a couple) must be in 'qualifying remunerative work'. This means that the claimant must be working at the date of claim or expecting to start a job within seven days.

Lone parents and claimants who qualify for the disability element are eligible for WTC provided they work at least 16 hours a week and are aged 16 or over. From April 2011, claimants aged 60 or over also qualify by working at least 16 hours a week. The 50 plus element was abolished from 6 April 2012 which means people who met that criteria prior to that date can no longer qualify by working at least 16 hours.

The rules for couples responsible for a child changed from 6 April 2012. From that date, couples responsible for at least one child are required to work at least 24 hours a week between them with one person working at least 16 hours a week. Prior to this rule change, they qualified as long as one person worked at least 16 hours.

There are a number of exceptions to this rule. If one person works at least 16 hours and the other partner is incapacitated (the same definition as for the childcare element), in prison, in hospital or entitled to carer's allowance they will be entitled to WTC with no requirement to meet the 24-hour rule.

Other workers are eligible provided they work at least 30 hours a week and are aged 25 or over.

Not all work counts for tax credit purposes. The work must be expected to continue for at least four weeks and must be done for payment (or in expectation of payment). A social security benefit is not payment for the purposes of satisfying this condition. Gaps between jobs of up to seven days are ignored. The claimants must also be employed or self-employed (this requirement was added from 6 April 2015).

The definition of 'self-employed' has also been changed from 6 April 2015. To qualify as self-employed, a person must be engaged in carrying on a trade, profession or vocation on a commercial basis and with a view to the realisation of profits, either on their own account or as a member of a business partnership. The trade, profession or vocation must also be organised and regular.

Determining number of hours worked

Employees, apprentices and office-holders are usually treated as working the number of hours they normally perform under their contracts of employment, apprenticeship or the office in which they are employed. This may not necessarily be the same as their contractual hours.

Self-employed people are treated as working the hours they 'normally perform for payment or in expectation of payment'. This includes not only work done and billed to the customer, but also time spent in 'activities necessary to the employment'.

Other points to note, in brief, are:

- any period of 'customary or paid holiday' is disregarded in computing hours worked;
- time allowed for meals and refreshments is treated as time spent working if it is paid;
- similarly, time spent in hospital or clinic visits are treated as time spent working if it is paid;
- people who have a 'recognised cycle of work' of less than a year such as seasonal workers must claim on the basis of their normal working hours each week to determine whether they work on average 16 or 30 hours a week;
- people who have a 'recognised cycle of work' over a period of one year such as term-time workers in schools, educational establishments or other places of work must average their hours over the whole year (but ignoring vacations);
- those who receive statutory maternity, paternity, shared parental or adoption pay or maternity allowance are treated as in qualifying remunerative work during such periods. Similarly those who are absent from work during ordinary maternity, paternity, shared parental or adoption leave are treated as continuing in work for these periods; and they can also be paid WTC during the first 13 weeks of any

additional maternity, shared parental or adoption leave under the *Employment Rights Act* 1996, s. 73 or 75B;

- parents of babies due on or after 3 April 2011 but before 6 April 2015 had the right to take additional paternity leave. During this period, they were treated as continuing in work during any period of additional statutory paternity pay providing the *Additional Statutory Paternity Pay (General) Regulations* 2010, Pt. 2 or 3 have been satisfied;
- those on statutory sick pay, employment support allowance, or those in the first 28 weeks of receiving IS, or national insurance credits on the grounds of incapacity for work or limited capacity for work are, similarly, treated as working so long as they were working up to the point when their sickness period began – claimants are only treated as working for the first 28 weeks of claiming the benefits listed;
- self-employed people taking time off for maternity, paternity, adoption, shared parental leave or sick leave are treated as working for the statutory leave periods that would apply to them if they were employees;
- recipients of pay in lieu of notice are not treated as working during the period for which they receive the pay;
- periods of strike action are treated as periods of work provided they do not exceed ten days;
- periods of suspension from work while complaints or allegations against the worker are investigated are treated as periods of work; and
- an agency worker is deemed to work 'the number of hours for which remuneration is normally paid to him by an employment agency with whom he has a contract of employment'. In practice, this is often unhelpful, as agency workers may not have a 'normal' weekly pattern of work if their working hours fluctuate from week to week.

From 6 April 2007, a four-week run-on was introduced which meant that claimants who ceased to be entitled to WTC on reducing their working hours below 16, or on stopping work altogether, normally continued to receive WTC for four weeks afterwards. However, this run-on did not apply to those who only qualified for tax credits by working at least 30 hours per week and who started to work for less than 30, but remained at 16 or above. To address this problem, the four week run-on was clarified and extended from 31 July 2009 so that it applied to this group of claimants as well.

As a result of changes to the qualifying rules for couples with children from April 2012, the four-week run-on will also apply where a couple's combined working hours cease or reduce so that they no longer meet the requirement that one member of a couple works at least 16 hours a week and between them they work at least 24 hours a week.

The run-on will apply to all elements which are lost as a result of the fall in hours, including the childcare element where the other conditions for entitlement to that element are met.

A person who does work while in custody on remand, whether inside or outside a prison, cannot after 6 April 2007 claim WTC in respect of that work. This does not affect prisoners who have been released into the community to be supervised by probation staff or electronic tag, post-custody.

The normal income test applies during the four-week run-on even if someone is claiming means-tested benefits during that period (under normal rules this would automatically entitle them to maximum tax credits).

Tax Reporter: ¶164-040

190-170 Other elements of WTC

Provided they are eligible for the basic element of WTC, claimants to WTC may be entitled to various other elements, based on their circumstances.

- *A second adult element.* This is automatic where a joint claim to WTC is made, unless one of the claimants is serving a custodial sentence of more than 12 months or one of the claimants is subject to immigration control under the *Immigration and Asylum Act* 1999, s. 115(9). These two exclusions do not apply if one or both of the joint claimants are responsible for a child or qualifying young person.
- *A lone parent element*, where a single claim is made and the claimant is responsible for a child or children.
- *A 30-hour element.* This is designed to encourage those with a disability, or families with children, to move to full-time work. This element is included where a single claimant, or in a joint claim at least one of the claimants, works at least 30 hours. Couples with children are entitled to this element if one of the couple works at least 30 hours a week, or if they jointly work 30 hours a week, provided that one of them works at least 16 hours.
- *A disability element.* Joint claimants may each claim this if they both meet the qualifying criteria (which includes requiring the person with the disability to be working at least 16 hours a week).
- *A severe disability element.* Joint claimants may each claim this if they both qualify (unlike the disability element, to qualify for this element the person with the disability does not need to be working at least 16 hours a week).

- *A 50 plus element.* This element was available to those aged 50 or over who were returning to work after 6 April 2003 following a period of at least six months out of work. It was divided into two rates – one for those working at least 16 hours, and one for those working at least 30 hours. Joint claimants were each able to claim the 50 plus element if they both met the qualifying criteria. It was generally payable for up to 12 months. This element was abolished on 6 April 2012 for everyone (including claimants who had not received it for a full 12 months).

The childcare element

Families are eligible for the childcare element where a lone parent or both partners in a couple work at least 16 hours a week and one (or both) of them is responsible for a child or children in respect of whom they incur qualifying childcare costs.

There are exceptions to this rule in respect of couples. Where only one member of a couple works at least 16 hours a week, the couple will still be eligible for the childcare element if the other member is incapacitated, an in-patient in hospital, in prison or or entitled to carer's allowance (from 6 April 2012).

Although an element of WTC, it is paid directly to the main carer with any CTC, either weekly or four-weekly at the claimant's request. It is worth up to 70% of qualifying childcare costs (70% for tax years up to and including 2005–06 and 80% up to and including 2010–11), although a maximum limit to those costs is set. That is £175 a week for one child and £300 a week for two or more.

Claimants can therefore claim up to 70% of those maximum figures, currently £122.50 for one child and £210 for two or more children. Childcare costs are calculated on the basis of the average weekly cost, either using the four weeks immediately prior to the claim if the costs are fixed or by aggregating the charges for the previous 52 weeks and dividing the total by 52 where costs are variable. In the case of fixed monthly payments, multiplying by 12 and dividing by 52 or if the monthly payments are variable by aggregating the charges for the previous 12 months and dividing the total by 52. If childcare has been used for less than 52 weeks/12 months, then the averaging should be done using an estimate of costs going forward for 52 weeks/12 months. From 6 April 2010, where claimants have childcare only for short fixed periods, they can choose to average the costs only over the fixed period rather than 52 weeks. This method does not apply if they have childcare for most of the year.

Qualifying childcare means care provided by a registered or approved provider. A relative of the child, even if registered or approved cannot provide qualifying childcare where the care is provided in the child's own home. A relative who is registered may qualify if the childcare is outside of the child's own home. In some parts of the UK, there is also a requirement for those who are approved childcare providers to also look after other, non-related children.

A 'relevant' change in childcare costs occurs where:

- there is an increase or decrease in average weekly childcare costs of £10 a week or more; or
- childcare costs cease.

For the purpose of determining whether there has been increase of £10 per week of more, those with fixed weekly costs must look at the previous four weeks and those with fixed monthly costs must multiply that monthly cost by 12 and divide by 52. Those with variable costs must take an average of their anticipated costs over the following 52 weeks (if paid weekly) or following 12 months (if paid monthly).

Decreases (not increases) in childcare costs of £10 a week or more are ascertained in the same way, and must be reported to HMRC within one month of the later of the date of the change, or the date the claimant first became aware of the change. Before 6 April 2007, the time limit for reporting was three months from the date of the change.

When a relevant change occurs, the child care element of WTC must be recalculated. It is important to note that where childcare costs decrease, and therefore less WTC is due, the recalculation will be made from the first day of the week following the four consecutive weeks in which the change occurs. Where, from 6 April 2010, claimants have a short fixed period of childcare costs, and choose to average over this period only (rather than 52 weeks), the recalculation of WTC will take place on the first day of the week immediately following the end of the fixed period where costs decrease.

Where costs increase, so that more WTC is due, the recalculation is made from the later of:

- the first day of the week in which the change occurred; and
- the first day of the week in which falls the date one month prior to the change being notified to HMRC.

Hence, there is the possibility of obtaining the increase from the first day of the four-week period (any decrease begins from the end of the four-week period) – but any delay in notification of more than one month will mean a loss of credit.

Tax Reporter: ¶164-130; ¶164-280

Child tax credit

190-200 Introduction

Child tax credit (CTC) brings together support for children from the diverse provisions of the former WFTC, DPTC and the children's tax credit, and has replaced the child premiums in income support and income-based jobseeker's allowance for new claimants. Claimants do not have to be in work. Child tax credit is paid to some six million families and can be paid to those on fairly high incomes. It is paid by HMRC directly to the main carer.

Children are eligible up to their 16th birthday. After that date, the child becomes a qualifying young person up until 31st August following his or her 16th birthday. There is no requirement to satisfy the full-time education or approved training conditions during the period, but other conditions relating to being a qualifying young person must be met. After that date, the credit remains payable only to those who continue in full-time, non-advanced, education or training up to the age of 20, provided the course of education or training started before the young person became 19.

The usual test to be applied is that the child is 'normally living with' the claimant(s). Where there are competing claims, the test is who has the 'main responsibility' for the child. This is subject to a joint election as to who has the main responsibility, but in the absence of such an election HMRC will decide on the information available.

Child tax credit remains payable for up to eight weeks following the death of a child.

Significant changes have been made to CTC from 6 April 2017 with the introduction of the two-child limit policy.

Legislation: TCA 2002, s. 8 and 9; *Child Tax Credit Regulations* 2002 (SI 2002/2007)

Tax Reporter: ¶165-000

190-220 Elements of CTC

Prior to 6 April 2017, CTC was made up of the following elements:

- A *family element*. This was the basic element, paid to all families eligible for CTC and taking the place of the former children's tax credit. A higher family element was also available during the first year following the birth of a child, however this was abolished from 6 April 2011.
- A *child element* for each child in the family – the child element was payable at one of three rates. The standard rate was paid unless the

child qualified for the disabled child rate or the severely disabled child rate:

- the *disabled child rate* was payable where disability living allowance, personal independence payment or armed forces independence payment was payable (or has ceased to be payable solely because the child is an in-patient) or the child was certified as severely sight impaired or blind by a consultant ophthalmologist (or ceased to be certified in the last 28 weeks); or
- the *severely disabled child rate* was payable for families caring for a child with severe disability, where the highest rate of the care component of disability living allowance or the enhanced daily living component of the personal independence payment was payable (or would be payable but for a suspension of the benefit or abatement as a consequence of hospitalisation).

In the Summer Budget 2015, the Government announced major changes to the child element of CTC so that support would be limited to two children for those born on or after 6 April 2017 unless certain exceptions apply. Prior to 6 April 2017, the child element was paid for each child or qualifying young person that the claimant was responsible for.

From 6 April 2017, CTC is made up of three elements:

- A *family element.* This is the basic element; from 6 April 2017, it is only paid to families who have responsibility for a child or qualifying young person born before 6 April 2017.
- A *child element.* The claimant will receive a child element for all children or young people born before 6 April 2017 that they are responsible for. Where the claimant is responsible for a child or qualifying young person born on or after 6 April 2017, they will not receive the child element for them unless:
  - there is no more than one child already on the claim;
  - an exception applies.
- A *disability element.* From 6 April 2017, this is an element in its own right and is no longer part of the child element. The two-child restriction does not apply to the disability element and so it will be paid for as many children or young people that qualify. The disability element is payable at two rates – disabled child rate and severely disabled child rate. The conditions for each are the same as the previous disabled child rate/severely disabled child rate of the child element.

Even if a claimant is not entitled to a child element for the child, they should still report the birth of a child or an older child joining their household to ensure any disability element or the childcare element of WTC (which is not affected by the two-child restriction) is paid.

There are five exceptions to the two-child limit for children born on or after 6 April 2017. In summary, these are:

- *Multiple births* – This exception is needed where the claimant already has at least one child on the claim before the multiple birth or there are no children on the claim already but the multiple birth results in triplets (or greater). The first child in a multiple birth will only get the child element if they are the first or second child on that claim; if they are not, then they will not receive the child element.
- *Adoption* – If a child has been placed for adoption with the claimant (or their partner) or adopted by them under certain legislation, this exception may apply. There are some exceptions, for example, if the claimant or their partner were the step-parent of the child immediately before the adoption.
- *Non-parental care arrangements* – This exception will apply where the claimant or their partner is a friend or family carer of the child. This has a specific meaning and requires the person to be a carer in formal situations under certain legislation. It can also apply in informal care situations where care has been undertaken where it is likely that the child would otherwise be looked after by the local authority. There are some exclusions from the general rule.
- *Child of the claimant has a child of their own* – Where the claimant is responsible for a child or young person that they receive a child element for and that child/young person has a child of their own, the CTC rules allow the claimant to claim for both their own child and their child's child.
- *Non-consensual conception* – Where the claimant is the child's parent and HMRC determine that the child is likely to have been conceived as a result of sexual intercourse to which they did not agree by choice, or did not have the freedom or capacity to agree by choice, this exception may be applied. There is also a requirement that the claimant is not living at the same address as the other party to that intercourse.

HMRC will normally ask for supporting documents in relation to the exceptions. Full details can be found on the GOV.UK website (link below). In the case of the non-consensual conception exception, there is a statutory requirement for a form to be signed by an approved third-party professional.

Other Material: www.gov.uk/guidance/child-tax-credit-exceptions-to-the-2-child-limit

Tax Reporter: ¶165-020

Calculations

190-250 Introduction

An award of tax credit normally lasts for a tax year, and this may have to be divided into 'relevant periods'. A relevant period is a part of the period of award (i.e. the tax year) where there is no change to the elements of WTC or CTC which the claimant is entitled to, and no relevant change in child care costs or arrangements. Thus, a fluctuation in income does not trigger a new relevant period, but changes in circumstances (such as a material change in working hours) do. It follows that if there is no change in circumstances during the tax year, then the relevant period is the whole tax year.

The general method of calculation is to compute the maximum that can be claimed, and then to reduce this figure if income exceeds the threshold. But that rule does not apply during any period in which the claimant is entitled to income support, income-based jobseeker's allowance, income-related employment and support allowance or pension credit – for the whole of any such period, the claimant is automatically entitled to maximum tax credits. Note that from 6 April 2010 people who are in receipt of these benefits only during the four week run-on period are not automatically entitled to maximum tax credits and instead remain subject to the income test.

Legislation: TCA 2002, s. 7, 8 and 13; *Tax Credits (Income Thresholds and Determination of Rates) Regulations* 2002 (SI 2002/2008)

Tax Reporter: ¶165-500

190-260 Income for tax credit purposes

'Income' is the gross income (i.e. before tax and NIC) of the claimant or, in the case of a joint claim, of the couple for a tax year. There are anti-avoidance provisions to ensure that income is not artificially reduced so as to increase credit entitlement.

Income for tax credit purposes is arrived at in a series of steps, as follows.

Step one

Add together (in joint claims, add together income from both claimants):

- pension income;
- investment income;
- property income;

- foreign income; and
- notional income.

Each of these items is subject to complex definition in regulations but they largely mirror the tax treatment. HMRC have produced Worksheet TC825 which contains specific guidance on self-employed losses.

If the sum of these items is £300 or less, it is treated as nil. If it is more than £300, only the excess is carried forward to the next stages in the computation.

For property income, from 6 April 2017, there are changes to the tax rules for residential landlords. Under the new tax rules, the amount of tax relief that a landlord can get on finance costs (including mortgage interest) will be restricted to the basic rate of tax. The changes are being phased in over four years. Once fully implemented, finance costs won't be taken into account when calculating taxable property profit. Instead, the person's income tax liability will be reduced by a basic rate tax deduction which for most landlords will be the basic rate value of the finance costs. Most basic rate taxpayers will not pay any more tax but their taxable income for tax credit purposes would be higher.

In order to mitigate this, HMRC amended the income legislation for tax credits from 6 April 2017. The impact of the latest legislation is that the new treatment of finance costs for tax purposes is ignored for tax credit purposes and tax credit claimants can continue to deduct finance costs as an expense when calculating their property income for tax credit purposes.

Step two

Add together:

- employment income;
- social security income (mainly, taxable state benefits, but not including income-based job seeker's allowance);
- student income (certain grants); and
- miscellaneous income.

Once again, these items are subject to detailed regulations, but there is some HMRC guidance available in the notes accompanying claim and renewal forms.

Employment income, like other categories in this list, broadly follows tax principles, so that most employees are able to use the entries on their forms P60 or P45. Some taxable benefits are included in the definition – these are broadly the cash equivalent of company cars and fuel, taxable expenses payments and mileage allowances, cash and non-cash vouchers and credit tokens, and money's worth. Share-related income is also included. Some taxable benefits in kind are excluded as income for tax credits so advisers should check the position carefully.

Various deductions can also be made from employment income such as work expenses that have not been paid back by an employer, fees to professional bodies, agency fees. If statutory maternity, paternity, adoption or shared parental leave payments were received, a £100 for each week it was paid can be deducted from the earnings figure. For example, if statutory maternity pay was received for 30 weeks, £3,000 can be deducted from the earnings figure. A helpful working sheet is included in the TC600 claim form notes as well as the TC603R reply required renewals notes.

Step three

Add together the results of steps one and two.

Step four

Calculate taxable trading income or allowable loss. This is broadly the same profit figure as for tax, but the loss computation proceeds differently although there are some exceptions such as averaging for farmers which is not allowed for tax credits. Add the income or deduct the loss from the result of step three. The notes accompanying worksheet TC 825 provide useful guidance on trading losses.

There are the following important differences between the computation of loss relief for income tax and tax credits.

- In the case of a joint claim, the partner whose business it is must set off any trading loss in a tax year against the joint income of both himself or herself and his or her partner.
- Losses may not be carried back to prior years for tax credits.
- Any surplus after setting off against current year income of the trader and the trader's partner may be set off against future profits of the same trade.

Deductions

In calculating income for tax credit purposes the following may be deducted:

- any banking charge or commission for conversion of income into sterling;

- gross gift aid, payroll giving or give as you earn donations made in the current year; and
- gross contributions to an approved retirement benefits scheme, an approved retirement annuity contract, or an approved personal pension scheme.

Note that the information in this section applies to normal tax credit claims and not the finalisation of claims in-year when a claimant is moving to universal credit.

Legislation: *Tax Credits (Definition and Calculation of Income) (Amendment) Regulations* 2017 (SI 2017/396)

190-270 Calculating WTC

The first step is to calculate the maximum daily rate for each of the elements of WTC to which the claimant is entitled, other than the child care element (see below). This is done by dividing the annual maximum figures by the number of days in the tax year and rounding up to the nearest penny.

Having calculated the daily entitlement, the maximum rate for the relevant period is obtained by multiplying the daily rate by the number of days in the relevant period.

Example 1

Roger, who has no children, is registered blind and works full-time. From 1 September 2017, he chooses to work part-time, working 20 hours a week. His maximum rate of WTC is found as follows:

Relevant period 6/4/2017–31/8/2017 (148 days)

		£
Basic element:	$\frac{£1,960}{365}$ = £5.37 × 148 =	794.76
30 hour element:	$\frac{£810}{365}$ = £2.22 × 148 =	328.56
Disability element:	$\frac{£3,000}{365}$ = £8.22 × 148 =	1,216.56
Maximum rate for relevant period		2,339.88

Relevant period 1/9/2017–5/4/2018 (217 days)

Basic element: £5.37 × 217 =	1,165.29
Disability element: £8.22 × 217 =	1,783.74
Maximum rate for relevant period	2,949.03

The maximum rate for the relevant period is then reduced by 41% (39% for 2010–11, 2009–10, 2008–09 and 37% 2007–08 and earlier years) (rounding down to the nearest penny) of any income falling above a designated threshold. The annual threshold and income figures are apportioned between relevant periods (rounding income down to the nearest penny and the threshold up to the nearest penny).

Example 2

Assume that Roger earned £12,000 in 2016–17 (and in 2017–18). His rate of WTC is as follows:

Relevant period 6/4/2017–31/8/2017 (148 days)

		£		£
Maximum rate:				2,339.88
Income:	$\frac{£12,000}{365} \times 148 =$	4,865.75		
Threshold:	$\frac{£6,420}{365} \times 148 =$	(2,603.18)		
		2,262.57	× 41% =	(927.65)
Rate of WTC for relevant period				1,412.23

Relevant period 1/9/2017–5/4/2018 (217 days)

		£		£
Maximum rate:				2,949.03
Income:	$\frac{£12,000}{365} \times 217 =$	7,134.25		
Threshold:	$\frac{£6,420}{365} \times 217 =$	(3,816.83)		
		3,317.42	× 41% =	(1,360.14)
Rate of WTC for relevant period				1,588.89

The child care element

The calculation for the child care element for the relevant period is slightly different, since child care costs are reckoned on a weekly basis. The costs for the relevant period are found by obtaining an annual figure (multiply weekly cost by 52) and apportioning this using the number of days in the tax year and the number of days in the relevant period.

This must then be compared with the maximum that may be paid (for 2005–06 onwards: £175 per week for one child and £300 if more than one child). Once again, the figure for the relevant period must be computed. The relevant maximum figure is divided by seven, rounded up to the nearest penny, and multiplied by the number of days in the relevant period.

The lower of the two figures (the actual child care costs of the relevant period and the maximum allowable for the relevant period) is then multiplied by 70% (rounding up to the nearest penny). The result is the maximum rate of child care element for the relevant period.

Example 3

Tom and Barbara start the tax year 2017–18 paying £350 per week in child care costs. On 1 September, one of their two children starts school, but they still pay for out of school hours child care. Nonetheless, the overall cost decreases to £290 per week. The maximum rate for the child care element of WTC is as follows:

Maximum rate for relevant period 6/4/2017–31/8/2017 (148 days)

	£
Actual cost:	
$£350 \times \frac{52}{365} \times 148 =$	7,379.73
Maximum:	
$\frac{£300}{7} = £42.86 \times 148 =$	6,343.28
Maximum rate is therefore: £6,343.28 × 70%	4,440.30

Maximum rate for relevant period 1/9/2017–5/4/2018 (217 days)

Actual cost:	
$£290 \times \frac{52}{365} \times 217 =$	8,965.37
Maximum:	
£42.86 × 217	9,300.62
Maximum rate is therefore: £8,965.37 × 70%	6,275.76

If income is high enough to result in a reduction of credit greater than the other elements of WTC, the excess is set against the child care element.

Example 4

If, in the preceding example, Tom worked full-time and Barbara part-time, producing a joint income of £30,000 for 2017–18, the calculation of their final WTC entitlement is as follows (note that their initial entitlement would in fact be based on their joint income for 2016–17):

Rate of WTC for relevant period 6/4/2017–31/8/2017

		£	£
Basic element:	£1,960 / 365 = £5.37 × 148 =		794.76
Second adult element:	£2,010 / 365 = £5.51 × 148 =		815.48
30 hour element:	£810 / 365 = £2.22 × 148 =		328.56
Maximum rate:			1,938.80
Reduction in credit			
Income:	£30,000 / 365 × 148 =	12,164.38	
Threshold:	£6,420 / 365 × 148 =	(2,603.18)	
		9,561.20 × 41% =	(3,920.09)
Excess reduction carried forward			(1,981.29)
Child care element (see previous example)			4,440.30
Rate of WTC for relevant period			2,459.01

Rate of WTC for relevant period 1/9/2017–5/4/2018

		£	£
Basic element:	£5.37 × 217		1,165.29
Second adult element:	£5.51 × 217		1,195.67
30 hour element:	£2.22 × 217		481.74
Maximum rate:			2,842.70
Reduction in credit			
Income:	£30,000 / 365 × 217 =	17,835.61	
Threshold:	£6,420 / 365 × 217 =	(3,816.83)	
		14,018.78 × 41% =	(5,747.70)
Excess reduction carried forward			(2,905.00)
Child care element (see previous example)			6,275.76
Rate of WTC for relevant period			3,370.76

190-280 Calculating CTC

An award of CTC is also for a tax year, and may have to be divided into relevant periods. A relevant period for CTC purposes is any part of the period of award where the maximum rate of CTC to which the claimant is entitled stays the same. Since the maximum rate is calculated before any reduction on account of income, changes in income will not trigger the end of a relevant period. However, changes in circumstances which affect the gross amount of CTC due (such as the birth of another child) will.

If WTC is being claimed at the same time as CTC, the definition of a relevant period is different. In addition to the requirement that the maximum rate of CTC stay the same, the two requirements for WTC relevant periods must also be met (i.e. no change in the elements of WTC the claimant is entitled to, and no relevant change in child care costs or arrangements).

The first step in calculating the rate of CTC for a relevant period is to compute the maximum daily rate. Divide the annual maximum amounts by the number of days in the tax year, rounding up to the nearest penny. This figure is then multiplied by the number of days in the relevant period.

Example 5

Continuing the example of Tom and Barbara from 190-270, since they have two children their maximum rate of CTC entitlement for the two relevant periods is as follows:

Maximum rate of CTC for relevant period 6/4/2017–31/8/2017 (148 days)

			£
Child element:	$\frac{£2,780 \times 2}{365}$	= £15.24 × 148 =	2,255.52
Family element:	$\frac{£545}{365}$	= £1.50 × 148 =	222.00
Maximum rate of CTC for relevant period			2,477.52

Maximum rate of CTC for relevant period 1/9/2017–5/4/2018 (217 days)

Child element:	$\frac{£2,780 \times 2}{365}$	= £15.24 × 217 =	3,307.08
Family element:	$\frac{£545}{365}$	= £1.50 × 217 =	325.50
Maximum rate of CTC for relevant period			3,632.58

A reduction of 41% (rounding down to the nearest penny) of any income falling above a designated threshold is then applied to the maximum rate for all elements.

Where only CTC is being claimed, the threshold figure is straightforward (the annual figure is £16,105 for 2017–18). However, where both WTC and CTC are claimed the threshold figure is the greater of:

- the annual figure (£6,420 for 2015–16, 2014–15, 2013–14, 2012–13, 2011–12, 2010–11, 2009–10 and 2008–09, £5,220 for 2007–08 and earlier years); or
- the amount of income needed to absorb all entitlement to WTC.

This produces some very fiddly computations, but fortunately the practical effect is simply to carry forward to CTC any amount of reduction left over from the WTC calculation. In practice it is easier to carry out WTC and CTC calculations using the £6,420 threshold as the result is the same. For the 2017–18, 2016–17, 2015–16, 2014–15, 2013–14 and 2012–13 tax years this carried forward figure of reduction may be set against all elements of CTC. Prior to 6 April 2012, the carried forward figure was set against all elements of CTC apart from the family element, which was subject to a different rate of reduction (see below). If the income level has not led to a reduction of all of the WTC elements (including childcare) then there will be no reduction of the CTC elements.

The annual threshold and income figures are apportioned between relevant periods (rounding income down to the nearest penny and the threshold up to the nearest penny) where necessary.

Example 6

If Barbara's and Tom's tax credits income was £47,000 for 2017–18, the final position would be as follows:

Annual rate of WTC & CTC for relevant period 6/4/2017–31/8/2017

		£	£
Maximum rate of WTC (other than child care)			1,938.80
Reduction:			
Income:	$\frac{£47,000}{365} \times 148 =$	19,057.53	
Threshold:	$\frac{£6,420}{365} \times 148 =$	$\frac{(2,603.18)}{16,454.35} \times 41\% =$	(6,746.28)
Reduction carried forward			(4,807.48)
Childcare element of WTC			4,440.30
Reduction carried forward			367.18
CTC (including family element)			2,477.52
Actual rate of CTC for relevant period (2,477.52 – 367.18)			2,110.34
Total tax credit for relevant period			2,110.34

Actual rate of CTC for relevant period 1/9/2017–5/4/2018

				£	£
Maximum rate of WTC (other than child care)					2,842.70
Reduction:					
Income:	£47,000 / 365	× 217 =	27,942.46		
Threshold:	£6,420 / 365	× 217 =	(3,816.83)		
			24,125.63	× 41% =	(9,891.51)
Reduction carried forward					(7,048.81)
Child care element of WTC					6,275.76
Reduction carried forward					773.05
CTC (including family element)					3,632.58
Actual rate of CTC for relevant period (3,632.58 – 773.05)					2,859.53
Total tax credit for relevant period					2,859.53

Family element of CTC

Until 6 April 2012, the family element was treated differently to the other elements of CTC. This meant that any carried forward figure in the above calculations was only set against any CTC other than the family element. This is because the family element was protected until income reached at least £40,000 (£50,000 in 2010–11 and earlier years). The point at which the family element was tapered away was called the second income threshold. Above that point, the family element was reduced by 41% only when income was the greater of:

- £40,000; and
- the income needed to absorb all other elements of WTC and CTC.

Prior to 6 April 2011, the family element was tapered away more slowly at a rate of 6.67%. If income was below £40,000 (£50,000 in 2010–11 and earlier years), the family element was not reduced and was paid in full. This protection for the family element was removed from 6 April 2012. This makes the calculation much less complex and means that the family element is added to other CTC elements and the total of those CTC elements is reduced by any carried forward amount. This change has meant many families who were receiving only £545 per year now receive Nil.

Example 7 shows how the family element was calculated in 2011–12 for a family whose second income threshold was higher than £40,000. The same scenario is repeated in Example 8 for 2017–18 to show how the calculation is done under the new rules from 6 April 2012.

Example 7

Terry is a self-employed engineering consultant. His profit for 2010–11 was £60,000. He is married to June, who works part-time as a teacher, earning £15,000 in 2010–11 (initial claims for 2011–12 are based on 2010–11 income). They have five children, and incur child care costs of £290 per week.

Their initial entitlement to WTC and CTC for 2011–12 is:

	£		£
WTC entitlement (other than child care)			
Basic element			1,920.00
Second adult element			1,950.00
30 hour element			790.00
			4,660.00
Reduction			
Income:	75,000		
Threshold:	(6,420)		
	68,580	× 41% =	(28,117.80)
Reduction carried forward			(23,457.80)
Child care element of WTC (maximum child care £290 p/w × 52 × 70%) =			10,556.00
Reduction carried forward			(12,901.80)
CTC other than family element: £2,555 × 5			12,775.00
Reduction carried forward			(126.80)
Family element of CTC			545.00
less reduction carried forward			(126.80)
CTC award			418.20

Example 8

Terry is a self-employed engineering consultant. His profit for 2016–17 was £60,000. He is married to June, who works part-time as a teacher, earning £15,000 in 2016–17 (initial claims for 2017–18 are based on 2016–17 income). They have five children, and incur child care costs of £290 per week.

Their initial entitlement to WTC and CTC for 2017–18 is:

	£		£
WTC entitlement (other than child care)			
Basic element			1,960.00
Second adult element			2,010.00
30 hour element			810.00
			4,780.00
Reduction			
Income:	75,000		
Threshold:	(6,420)		
	68,580	× 41% =	(28,117.80)
Reduction carried forward			(23,337.80)
Child care element of WTC (maximum child care £290 p/w × 52 × 70%) =			10,556.00
Reduction carried forward			(12,781.80)
CTC (including than family element) (£2,780 × 5 + 545)			14,445.00
Note – We assume that all children are born before 6 April 2017 and are not affected by the two-child limit			
CTC award (£14,445.00 – £12,781.80)			1,663.20

Claims, adjustments and renewals

190-300 Claims

A claim to tax credits must be made: if no claim is made, there is no entitlement. A single claim may be made by a single person, or a joint claim by a couple (or polygamous unit).

Couple

A 'couple' is defined as:

- a married couple or civil partners who are neither separated under a court order nor separated in circumstances in which the separation is likely to be permanent; or
- two people living together as if they were husband and wife or civil partners.

Same-sex couples were not recognised for tax credits purposes until the *Civil Partnership Act* 2004 entered into force on 5 December 2005 – before then each partner in a same-sex couple had to make a single claim.

Two people of the same sex are regarded as living together as if they were civil partners only if they would be regarded as living together as husband and wife if instead they were two people of the opposite sex.

Single claims and joint claims

When a single person enters into a relationship, the person's entitlement under his or her single claim comes to an end automatically but the person can, if appropriate, make a joint claim with his or her new partner. Similarly, when a couple separate, or one of them dies, their entitlement under their joint claim automatically comes to an end, but the remaining member(s) of the couple can, if they are entitled as single person(s), (each) make a single claim. It is vital that claimants in this situation notify HMRC promptly of their change of status to prevent an overpayment on their old claim (see 190-380).

Making and adjusting claims

Initial claims to WTC and CTC are based on current circumstances and the previous tax year's income. On the basis of this information HMRC will make an initial decision as to the award of tax credit. HMRC are empowered to require what further information or evidence they need for this decision from the claimant(s) or from an employer or – where the child care element of WTC is claimed – from the child care provider.

If claimants think that their income for the current tax year will be lower than the previous year, they can request that HMRC recalculate their award to be based on an estimated current year income (subject to the £2,500 income disregard for falls in income from 6 April 2012 – see 190-340). However, if the estimate turns out to be too low, the claimants will most likely have an overpayment.

Claims may generally be backdated for up to 31 days. Prior to 6 April 2012, this was 93 days. HMRC backdate some claims automatically. However, some claimants will need to ask for the backdating to be applied. Claimants who only qualify for tax credits due to the disability element of WTC or existing claimants (including children on a claim) who later qualify for the disability elements of WTC or CTC can get longer backdating if their qualifying disability benefit has also been backdated and they meet various reporting requirements. Asylum seekers who are awarded refugee status may also be entitled to longer backdating providing they claim within one month of being notified of their refugee status.

The Tax-Free Childcare (TFC) scheme was rolled-out from 21 April 2017 providing a new childcare support scheme run by HMRC. The general rule is that you cannot claim tax credits (both WTC and CTC) and TFC at the same time. Tax credit regulations were amended to stop backdating of a tax credit claim to a period where someone held a TFC account and was in a live TFC entitlement period (normally three months long). In such cases, the tax credit award will start from the date of the tax credit claim.

However, where HMRC make a TFC account restriction order, the childcare account is closed or the child ceases to be a qualifying child for TFC, the claim for tax credits can be treated having been made on the latest of either:

- the day following that event; or
- 31 days before the actual date of the tax credit claim.

An appeal may be brought against HMRC's initial decision on the award of tax credit.

Legislation: TCA 2002, s. 3; *Tax Credits (Claims and Notifications) Regulations* 2002 (SI 2002/2014), reg. 26, 26A, 30 and 31; *Tax Credits (Claims and Notifications) (Amendment) Regulations* 2017 (SI 2017/597)

Tax Reporter: ¶162-000

190-340 Adjustments to claims during the period of award

Claims to WTC and CTC will run for the remainder of the tax year unless there is a change in circumstances or income. The system provides for adjustments to be made during the year. Tax credit awards can be affected by:

- changes in the adults heading a household;
- changes in the circumstances giving entitlement to tax credits or the various elements of those tax credits; or
- changes in income.

Changes in circumstances

There are a number of changes of circumstance of which it is compulsory to inform HMRC on pain of incurring a penalty of £300:

- changes in the adults heading a household. This is because an award of tax credit is made to a household based on the income of those adults. Any change signifies the end of that particular claim;
- average weekly childcare costs go down by £10 or more or ceases altogether; and

- the claimant (or in a joint claim one partner in the couple) goes abroad for more than 8 weeks, or 12 weeks if the reason for the absence is a death in the family (see further 190-300) or loses their right to reside.

From 1 November 2006, it has also been compulsory to report to HMRC the following changes of circumstances:

- ceasing to work for at least 16 hours a week, thereby losing entitlement to WTC, or to one of the following elements of WTC – disabled worker, 30 hours or childcare;
- ceasing to work for at least 30 hours a week and thereby losing entitlement to WTC, or to the 30 hour or second adult element of WTC;
- where one or both members of a couple with children (who are subject to the requirement to work at least 24 hours between them with one person working at least 16 hours in order to qualify for WTC) cease to meet that condition;
- where a couple, who between them have been working 30 hours a week or more, begin to work fewer hours and thereby lose the 30 hour element;
- ceasing to be responsible for a child or a qualifying young person, so losing entitlement to CTC in respect of the child or young person, or to WTC (including the childcare element);
- a child or young person dropping out of full-time education or training, or not meeting the conditions to continue to be a 'qualifying young person', where a claim to CTC has previously been made or extended on the basis that the child or young person will continue to be a 'qualifying young person';
- a young person ceases to be a 'qualifying young person', other than by virtue of attaining the age of 20;
- the death of a child or qualifying young person.

Changes should be notified to HMRC within one month of the change or, if later, the date the claimant first became aware of the change (other than a young person ceasing to be a qualifying young person for tax credit purposes). Before 6 April 2007, the time limit for reporting was three months from the date of the change.

Apart from these mandatory notifications, it is up to the claimant whether to tell HMRC about changes in their circumstances. A change that increases entitlement – e.g. the birth of a child – should be reported to HMRC promptly, and in any event, within one month as it is generally not possible to backdate a claim to tax credit, or to more tax credit, by more than that.

Changes in income

Increases in income are subject to a £2,500 disregard. That is to say, the first £2,500 of any increase in income in a tax year, as compared to previous year income, is ignored in assessing tax credits entitlement for that tax year. In the tax years from 2003–04 to 2005–06, the disregard was £2,500 and in 2006–07 to 2010–11 inclusive it was £25,000. It reduced to £10,000 for 2011–12 and 2012–13 and then to £5,000 for 2013–14, 2014–15 and 2015–16. The disregard only applies when comparing current year income to previous year income.

The reason for the size of the increase in the disregard from £2,500 in 2005–06 to £25,000 in 2006–07 was to reduce the volume of overpayments in the system, which in 2003–04 and 2004–05 had been running at approximately £1.9 billion and £1.7 billion respectively. The Government decided that this level was unsustainable, and had been facing sustained criticism on account of the hardship faced by low-income families forced to pay back large sums of overpaid credit. Along with other changes announced in the Pre-Budget Report 2005, the disregard has contributed to a fall in overpayments from £1.7 billion in 2005–06 to £1.0 billion in 2006–07 and 2007–08.

Despite the success of the increased disregard in reducing the number of awards overpaid, the Government announced a reduction in the disregard to £10,000 from 6 April 2011. This was reduced further to £5,000 from 6 April 2013 and then back to £2,500 from 6 April 2016 which could lead to an increase number of income-related overpayments.

Three points about the increased disregard are worthy of note.

(1) Because the disregard only operates in the tax year of the increase in income ('the current year'), the following tax year's award will be based initially on the actual income for the current year. Therefore, even if the increase does not affect the current year's entitlement, it is advisable to report it to HMRC by January or February of that year so that the provisional award for the following tax year starting in April can be determined accurately. Otherwise the provisional award for that later year (the run-on from the previous year's payments – see below) will be based on the last income figure known to HMRC, and if that does not take into account the increase, a large overpayment could have accrued by the time the renewal papers are received in May or June and the right amount of credit computed.

(2) Some commentators have suggested that tax credit entitlement can be kept artificially high by manipulating income from year to year, although there is little benefit to doing so now due to the lower disregard for income rises coupled with the newer disregard for income falls. This, it is suggested, can be achieved by, e.g. making

some pension contributions in alternate years. It is considered, however, that this device would be made ineffective by the notional income rules (see above) under which HMRC can treat claimants as still having income of which they have deprived themselves if their motive for doing so was to secure a tax credit entitlement, or a higher tax credit entitlement.

(3) The disregard is measured by reference to previous year's income as finalised for tax credits. Therefore, if a claimant's income falls below that level in the current year, then starts to rise again, the subsequent rise is not covered by the disregard. Consequently, any extra tax credits paid on the basis of the lowest level of current year income are liable to be clawed back as an overpayment. While claimants are fully entitled to ask for more tax credit if their income falls (subject to the £2,500 disregard for falls in income below), and may not be able to do without the extra credit, if they over estimate the fall in their income for the tax year *as a whole* then they risk having to repay an overpayment at the end of it. Because of this risk, HMRC now restrict the extra credits they pay initially so that if someone estimates an income lower than previous year income, any underpayment that has accrued is held back to offset against any overpayment that may accrue if the estimate is wrong. Any underpayment remaining at the end of the tax year will be paid to the claimant as a lump sum if income has remained at a low level.

In April 2012, HMRC introduced a disregard for falls in income. Although this power has always existed in the *Tax Credits Act* 2002, HMRC have never implemented it. The £2,500 disregard means that if a claimant has a fall in income, the first £2,500 of that fall will be disregarded.

Example

Georgina is a lone parent who earns £15,000 a year. She loses her job in July 2017. She contacts HMRC to tell them about this fall in income and that her estimated income for 2017–18 is now £8,000. The revised award will be calculated using estimated income of £10,500, because the first £2,500 of the fall from 2016–17 income is disregarded. Providing her actual income for 2017–18 is £8,000 as estimated, the 2017–18 award will be finalised using £10,500 and the award for 2018–19 will be calculated using the £8,000 previous year income (i.e. the actual income rather than the deemed income figure of £10,500). This means the effect of the new disregard only lasts until the end of the tax year.

Had this situation occurred in 2011–12 or earlier years, Georgina would have had her tax credits for 2017–18 calculated on her actual estimate of £8,000.

'Protective' claims

Because tax credits are computed on an annual basis, the fact that a person's income is too high at the start of the tax year to make a claim does not mean that the person might not suffer a decrease in income sufficient to bring him or her within the scope of tax credits later in the year. For example, a high earning executive might be made redundant, or a successful businessperson might encounter a bad debt that will wipe out his or her profits for that year.

In such cases, the person might wish to claim tax credits. But if he or she waits until misfortune strikes, the person will find that his or her claim can only be backdated by one month. If, on the other hand, the person had made a claim at the start of the year, and been given a nil award, the person's position would be protected for the entire year in the event of him or her experiencing a downturn in income or profits later on.

Claims on this basis resulting in nil awards are known as 'protective claims', and should be considered by everyone who is potentially eligible for tax credits, particularly if they are responsible for children. While there may be drawbacks in entering the tax credit 'club' in terms of the paperwork it entails, and the burden of reporting changes in personal circumstances to HMRC, it is understood to be HMRC's practice not to charge a penalty where a claimant with a nil award fails to notify a change of circumstances which has no effect on their entitlement.

An appeal may be brought against HMRC's decision to adjust an award of tax credit.

Legislation: TCA 2002, s. 3–7; *Tax Credits (Claims and Notifications) Regulations* 2002 (SI 2002/2014)

Tax Reporter: ¶166-060

190-360 Finalising and renewing claims

After the end of the tax year renewal papers are issued by HMRC. Some claimants receive both forms TC603R (the annual review) and TC603D (the annual declaration) others may only receive one form (the annual review). The annual review is a statement of the claimant's last known income and circumstances on which the person's award is based. The purpose of the renewal process is to finalise the claim for the year just ended, and act as a claim for the new tax year (unless the claim ended at some earlier point).

If the claimant receives the full family element (£545), has been in receipt of income support, income-based JSA, income related ESA or pension credit for the whole year or falls into one of the groups for which HMRC have enough employment or pension income information from the Real Time Information (RTI) system, the claimant will receive the TC603R only, and is not required to respond if his or her circumstances remain the same and his or her income is as stated on the notice so that there is no change in entitlement. These are known as 'auto-renewal' cases.

Other claimants ('reply required' cases) are required to complete form TC603D with details of their income for the current year (i.e. the tax year just gone) and to return it, whereupon their entitlement for the current year will be finalised as follows.

- If current year income is greater than previous year income by no more than £2,500, final entitlement is based on previous year income.
- If current year income is greater than previous year income by more than £2,500, final entitlement is based on current year income less the disregard (£2,500).
- If previous year income exceeds current year income by no more than £2,500, final entitlement is based on previous year income.
- If previous year income exceeds current year income by more than £2,500, final entitlement is based on current year income plus £2,500.

If they have made more than one claim during the year, e.g. because they started the year as part of a couple and ended it as a single claimant, they must complete a set of forms for each claim, even if they show the same information.

The actual amount of current year income returned on form TC603D also forms the basis of the initial award for the coming tax year.

While HMRC are awaiting the return of the completed renewal form the existing level of tax credit payments continues, although HMRC are likely to base them on the RTI data they hold for the year just ended which may not reflect the claimant's declarable income for that year. These run-on payments are known as 'provisional payments' and they can be a significant cause of overpayments if the information on which they are based is out of date.

From 6 April 2014, HMRC have been using RTI data provided by employers and pension providers to finalise tax credit claims. This exercise means that many claimants who were previously required to fill in a declaration form or phone the helpline with their income will now only need to contact HMRC if the information replayed on their renewal form is incorrect (auto-renewal). It should be noted that the RTI figure may not be the correct figure for tax credit purposes as there are a number of deductions that may be made – for example, deductions relating to statutory maternity, paternity or adoption pay, certain pension contributions, mileage allowance and other allowable deductions. If a claimant or their partner has more than one job, they may find it difficult to check the figure as it is not broken down by individual employers. Where it appears there is a discrepancy, claimants or their advisers should contact the tax credits helpline in the first instance but if they refuse to amend the award then an appeal will need to be lodged once the award notice is received.

Claimants must normally return their renewal papers by 31 July following the tax year end (unless the notice states otherwise). Claimants can complete the process by using the online service, sending back the paper forms (if required) or by phoning the tax credits helpline. In 2003–04 to 2005–06, the date was 30 September; it was brought forward in 2006–07 to 31 August as part of that year's package to reduce the volume of overpayments in the system, and forward again in 2007–08. If income details for the previous tax year are not available by that date, claimants must return estimated figures by 31 July and confirm their estimates, or submit the final figures, by 31 January following the tax year end.

If the renewal papers are not returned by the deadline, HMRC will terminate provisional payments and issue a statement of account. Everything paid between April and the date payments are terminated becomes overpaid and HMRC will seek recovery of this amount. This is because the renewal forms act as a claim for the new tax year, and without the form there is no valid claim. In addition, any overpayments from previous years being recovered by deductions from ongoing payments will be demanded immediately via direct recovery.

Providing a claimant contacts HMRC within 30 days of the statement of account issue date, and gives HMRC the renewals information they need, payments can be reinstated and the claimant's claim treated as made from the previous 6 April. Outside of this 30-day period, a claim can still be reinstated up to the following 31 January providing there was 'good cause' for missing the deadline – however, if the claimant lives in an area where full service UC has been rolled-out, they may not be able to have their claim reinstated for good cause under the legislation, although HMRC may be willing to reinstate the tax credit claim. Advice should be taken before making a claim for UC in this situation.

If both of these deadlines have passed, the claim cannot be reinstated and a new claim will have to be made. In some postcode areas, new claims for tax credits are not possible by certain people and so the claim would need to be for UC. Any new claim for tax credits can be backdated up to 31 days.

Thus, the tax year end sees HMRC having to make adjustments to the amount of credit paid out during the year. If credit has been underpaid, HMRC will make a single payment of the amount they owe. If credit has been overpaid, HMRC will recover the excess, normally by adjusting the credit due in the following year (see 190-380).

HMRC's 'finalising' decision on a claim may be appealed.

From 6 April 2010, HMRC will allow one member of a continuing couple to make the declaration rather than both. HMRC also introduced the ability to withdraw from the system by finalising the year just ended without making a claim for the new tax year. However, withdrawal must be notified to HMRC by 31 July if the claimant wishes the claim to stop for the current tax year. Any payments made after 6 April may need to be repaid. If the claimant requests withdrawal at any other time, the claim will carry on to the end of the current tax year. Once a person has left tax credits, they will need to make a completely new claim if they change their mind.

The renewals process described in this section will change for people who are moving from tax credits to universal credit. The new process is called 'in-year finalisation'. This means that HMRC will seek to finalise the tax credits claim at the point the person leaves for universal credit rather than after the end of the tax year. This means HMRC will use a slightly different method of calculating income for such cases. It may mean that some people end up with an overpayment or underpayment that they would not have had if the current finalisation process was used (see 190-500).

Legislation: TCA 2002, s. 17 and 18; *Tax Credits (Claims and Notifications) Regulations* 2002 (SI 2002/2014)

Guidance: www.revenuebenefits.org.uk – detailed information on the transition from tax credits to universal credit

Tax Reporter: ¶162-000

190-370 Payment of credits

Both CTC and the child care element of WTC are paid by HMRC directly to the main carer. Working tax credit apart from the child care element is paid directly to the person or persons in work. The default position is for four-weekly payments, although the claimant may opt for weekly payments. Normally payments are made in arrears, although those on four-weekly payments may receive part of their payment in advance and part in arrears depending on where in the cycle of payment they fall.

In 2005–06 and previous tax years, WTC minus the childcare element was paid to those in employment mainly via their employer, who added it to the payroll in accordance with instructions given by HMRC. Between November 2005 and February 2006 payment via employer (or PVE) was phased out, and after March 2006 WTC minus childcare was paid directly to all employees.

In April 2010, HMRC introduced rules requiring claimants to provide bank account details or risk suspension of their payments. This was in order to reduce HMRC's costs in paying claimants via cashcheque (previously called giro payments). From April 2012, claimants who do not provide account details on their initial claim form will receive a written notice from HMRC giving them four weeks to provide the relevant details (eight weeks prior to 6 April 2012). If no response is received, HMRC have powers to postpone payments.

Tax Reporter: ¶166-500

190-380 Overpayments and underpayments

An overpayment in the strict sense arises when the end-of-year renewal process has identified that too much tax credit has been paid during the year, based on the claimant's income and circumstances as reported on the renewal papers. These are known as 'cross-year overpayments'. But HMRC are also empowered to adjust an award during the year if, in their opinion, an overpayment is likely to occur by the year end. These are known as 'in-year overpayments' and may happen following a change of circumstances, or if provisional payments were set too high earlier in the year.

Other causes of overpayments include claimant error or delay, HMRC error or delay (whether human or computer), or adjustment of an award following an investigation.

HMRC have complete discretion whether or not they recover an overpayment. Usually they will decide to recover it, and there is no independent right of appeal against their decision to recover an overpayment. However, it is possible to dispute the overpayment and ask HMRC not to collect it back. Their practice on recovery is set out in Code of Practice COP26.

The current test is based on a series of responsibilities for both HMRC and the claimants. If the claimant has met their responsibilities, and HMRC have failed to meet theirs, the overpayment will be written off. Conversely, if HMRC have met their responsibilities and the claimant has failed to meet theirs, the overpayment will be recovered. Where both sides fail to meet responsibilities, a partial remission will be carried out. The full list of responsibilities can be found in the current COP26.

COP26 has a provision which states that HMRC may decide to write off an overpayment in exceptional circumstances where recovery would cause the claimant undue hardship. This appears to be rarely used by HMRC.

Prior to 15 July 2013, when a dispute was received by HMRC they would suspend recovery of the overpayment. However, this suspension was removed from 15 July 2013 therefore recovery will continue whilst the dispute is considered. It is important that claimants in the direct recovery process (where the overpayment cannot be collected from an ongoing award) engage with Debt Management to arrangement repayment during the dispute process otherwise recovery action may be taken.

One other notable change to the dispute is the introduction of a three month time limit from 6 April 2013. Claimants have three months from:

- date of the final award notice;
- date of the final decision if an auto-renewal case (normally 31 July); or
- date of the letter giving an appeal decision (if an appeal is lost or partially lost at tribunal).

This means that for 2016–17 finalised awards, only overpayments that occurred in 2016–17 can be disputed within three months. Any earlier overpayments shown can no longer be disputed unless the claimant can show exceptional circumstances were present.

If the dispute cannot be resolved between HMRC and claimant, once the internal complaints procedure with HMRC has been exhausted there may be recourse to the Adjudicator or Parliamentary Ombudsman (see 18-400). It is currently not HMRC policy to suspend recovery of an overpayment whilst progressing through the complaints process. The right to apply to the High Court for judicial review of HMRC's decision may exist in certain limited circumstances, but is unlikely to be of any practical use to the vast majority of tax credit claimants whom it may affect.

HMRC generally recover a cross-year overpayment by reducing payments of an ongoing award by a maximum of:

- 10% if the claimant is on maximum tax credits, or on income support or income-based jobseeker's allowance, income-related ESA or pension credit;
- 25% if the claimant receives less than maximum tax credits but more than the family element of CTC; or
- 50% if the claimant receives less than maximum tax credits and annual income exceeds £20,000. This 50% recovery rate applies from 6 April 2016.

For the new 50% recovery rate, annual income is defined as the income that HMRC are, for the time being, treating as income for that tax year. This may be different to the income figure used to calculate the tax credit award. For example, if a claimant has income in 2016–17 of £15,000, their 2017–18 award will be based on £15,000 initially. If the claimant contacts HMRC and estimates that their 2017–18 income will be £21,000, HMRC will recalculate their tax credits to be based on 18,500 (due to the £2,500 disregard); however, the 50% recovery rate will apply because the estimated income for 2017–18 is over £20,000.

For those on the family element of CTC only, their award may be reduced without limit or stopped in order to collect the overpayment.

Adjustments of awards in-year to reduce or eliminate an overpayment (in-year overpayment) have, since January 2007, been subject to the same percentage restriction as recovery of cross-year overpayments. From 6 April 2015, HMRC will stop tax credits in year if they believe the claimant has already received their full entitlement, previously they would continue paying in order to avoid causing hardship to the claimant.

COP26 states that HMRC can consider reducing the amount being recovered from ongoing payments where the claimant is suffering hardship and cannot meet his or her essential living expenses. In exceptional circumstances, HMRC can stop recovery from an ongoing award.

Prior to October 2014, where an award ended and the claimant was no longer entitled to tax credits, overpayments were generally recovered from the claimant directly. Similarly, where there had been a change of household – for example, a couple split up, or a single claimant moved in with a new partner – an overpayment that accrued on the previous household could not be set against a tax credit award made to the new household and had to be collected directly.

From October 2014, HMRC upgraded their IT to allow them to implement cross claim recovery in certain situations. Cross claim recovery can apply in these situations:

- a joint ongoing claim can be reduced to recover debts from old single claims of one or both members of the couple;
- a single ongoing claim can be reduced to recover debts from an old single claim of the same person;
- a joint ongoing claim can be reduced to recovery debts from an old joint claim if the same two people are involved in each claim.

While direct repayment is generally demanded within 30 days, HMRC should accept repayment without question over 12 months or if circumstances dictate enter into arrangements for time to pay over a much longer period (currently up to 10 years). HMRC may also recover overpayments by adjusting a claimant's tax code; however, HMRC stopped using this method in April 2016 ahead of the move of claimants across to UC.

Under legislation in the *Welfare Reform Act* 2012 and subsequent regulations, DWP has the power to recover tax credit overpayment debts from UC payments. Once the UC award ends, the debt remains with DWP and negotiation for time to pay and hardship will be dealt with by DWP.

Any time to pay arrangement with HMRC will be cancelled at the point the claimant moves to UC.

From April 2018, DWP will start to collect tax credit debts on behalf of HMRC even if the person has not yet moved to UC or will never transfer to UC. This is because DWP has a wider range of powers than HMRC – for example, they can use Direct Earnings Attachment orders.

HMRC state, in COP26, that overpayments can be written off in cases of financial hardship. Suspension of recovery can also be requested in cases where a person is in receipt of certain means-tested benefits, with an eventual request for remission if the situation is unlikely to improve (for example if the person has ill-health.

In cases where couples separate, HMRC policy is to ask each person to pay 50%, and providing the engaging partner repays his or her 50%, HMRC will not go back to the person for the remaining amount should the person's ex-partner refuse to pay or if the partner cannot be traced.

HMRC have a 'notional offsetting' policy which means that, where an overpayment is caused by a delay in reporting a change of household, the overpayment can be reduced by the amount that would have been due had the new claim been made at the correct time. The policy applies to overpayments outstanding as of 18 January 2010. Prior to Autumn 2016, HMRC's policy was to refuse notional offsetting in cases of 'deliberate error'; however, HMRC have relaxed the policy so that it should be available in all cases involving late reporting of a change of household.

Underpayments

Where tax credit is underpaid, HMRC generally make good the underpayment by immediate payment of the whole amount.

Legislation: TCA 2002, s. 28 and 29

Other Material: COP26, www.revenuebenefits.org.uk

Tax Reporter: ¶166-840; ¶166-860

Investigations, penalties and appeals

190-400 Investigations

HMRC may enquire into the entitlement of the claimant(s) to tax credit and to the amount of tax credit before an award is made, during an award or after the end of the tax year of the award. In order to pursue their enquiries they may require information from the claimant(s) or an employer or a child care provider.

Examinations

Investigations undertaken before an award is made or during the tax year of an award are known as 'examinations', and are usually triggered by a computer-generated risk assessment. They may range from simple checks focusing on known discrepancies, e.g. between information on the claim form and information held about the claimant elsewhere on HMRC's computer systems, or they may be more intrusive questions about a claimant's income or circumstances (e.g. the validity of a claim for childcare).

Such examinations will usually take place once an award is in payment, but they can also be generated before the award is paid and can delay payment in some cases. HMRC are currently carrying out a large number of pre-award and post award examinations in order to reduce overpayments. By statute the purpose of an examination is 'to provide any information or evidence which [the Board] consider they may need for making their decision' on an award, which precludes random investigations. There are penalties for failure to comply with an information notice, but there is no right of appeal against its issue, although the claimant may appeal against any decision on an award that results from the examination and against any penalty. In addition, HMRC have the power to suspend payments where claimants have not complied with a formal request for information under TCA 2002, s. 16(3). It should be noted that for decisions under TCA 2002, s. 16 the burden of proof is on HMRC to show that they have reasonable grounds for believing the award is wrong. The burden is reversed in s. 14 examinations (pre-claim).

Enquiries

Investigations undertaken after the end of the tax year and after the previous year's award has been finalised are known as 'enquiries'. Where a claimant is also a self-assessment taxpayer and an income tax enquiry has been opened, HMRC will generally work the two together. Practitioners will generally find it in the client's interests to conclude both together in order to gain finality. Like income tax enquiries, tax credit enquiries may be conducted at random, but there are more safeguards in place for the claimant than there are for examinations.

As for income tax, HMRC must comply with the enquiry time limits, give notice that they are opening an enquiry, and also give notice when their enquiry is finished. Also, the claimant may ask the First-tier Tribunal to direct HMRC to close their enquiry.

Once the enquiry window has passed, HMRC have discovery powers under s. 20 which allow them to change an award in two situations. The first is where a person's income tax liability is revised and as a consequence HMRC have reason to believe that the tax credits decision is not correct. The second is where HMRC have reasonable grounds for believing that a final tax credits decision is wrong by virtue of fraud or neglect. There are certain limitations on when this can be used and strict time limits.

Legislation: TCA 2002, s. 14(2), 15(2), 16(2), 19 and 20

Tax Reporter: ¶166-700

Penalties

There is a penalty of up to £3,000 for fraudulently or negligently making an incorrect statement or declaration in connection with a claim for tax credit, or for supplying incorrect information or evidence in response to a notice requiring information. This applies also to any person acting for another in connection with the claim or notice. The penalty is imposed by an HMRC determination. An appeal may be lodged with the First-tier Tribunal.

Failure to comply with a request for information or evidence, or with the requirements of a renewal notice, may result in an initial penalty of up to £300, after proceedings in front of the First-tier Tribunal, whose decision may be appealed to the Upper Tribunal. Their decision may be appealed to the Court of Appeal. Continued failure results in a penalty of up to £60 per day, to be imposed by HMRC (an appeal against the determination may be lodged with the appeal tribunal).

Where notification of a change in circumstances is mandatory (see above), failure to do so may result in a fine of up to £300. This is imposed by HMRC determination, and appeal is to the First-tier Tribunal.

Legislation: TCA 2002, s. 31, 32 and Sch. 2

Tax Reporter: ¶166-880

Fraud

There is an offence of being 'knowingly concerned' in any fraudulent activity undertaken with a view to obtaining payments of a tax credit. It is triable summarily or on indictment. On summary conviction they will be liable to imprisonment for a term up to six months, a fine not exceeding the statutory maximum or both. On conviction by indictment they can be imprisoned for a term not exceeding seven years, given a fine or both. Section 35 will be substantially amended by *Welfare Reform Act* 2012, s. 124. However, at the time of writing, this section has not come into force.

Welfare Reform Act 2012, s. 120 has also introduced four new sections into the TCA 2002 that relate to fraud. The new provisions allow the loss of working tax credit for a period of time when certain offences are committed. Section 120 was brought into force in 2013.

Legislation: TCA 2002, s. 35, 36, 36A–36D; *Welfare Reform Act* 2012, s. 120, 124

Tax Reporter: ¶166-940

Interest

Where an overpayment occurs because of fraud or neglect, HMRC may decide that all, or any part of, the overpayment is to carry interest. Interest runs from 30 days following the 'appropriate date', which is:

- in a case where the overpayment arises because the claimant was never entitled to the credit, the date of HMRC's decision to terminate the award; and
- in any other case, the date given in the end-of-year renewal notice.

HMRC must issue a notice stating their decision regarding interest, and the notice must refer to the right of appeal against the decision.

Penalties carry interest from the date on which they become due and payable. However, HMRC may reduce the amount of interest due, including down to nil, if they think it appropriate.

Legislation: TCA 2002, s. 37

Tax Reporter: ¶166-960

190-420 Appeals

Appeals lie against nearly all decisions on entitlement by HMRC or a penalty, except a decision to recover an overpayment and the issue of an information notice.

Initial appeal lies to the Social Entitlement Chamber of the First-tier Tribunal. This First-tier Tribunal is administered by Her Majesty's Courts and Tribunals service, an agency of the Ministry of Justice, and began operating in November 2008. Onward appeals can be made to the Upper Tribunal only with permission and on a point of law, or on the amount of a penalty. The Upper Tribunal replaced the Social Security and Child Support Commissioners under the old structure. From the Upper Tribunal, final appeal routes lie to the Court of Appeal, or the Court of Session in Scotland or the Court of Appeal of Northern Ireland.

The answer is that it very much depends on what postcode a claimant lives in. Broadly speaking, if they live in a full (digital) service area, any person who resides in that postcode is eligible to make a claim for UC. Those who are over state pension credit age cannot claim UC (unless, for now, they have a partner who is under state pension credit age).

There is one temporary exception to this broad rule. Until 31 January 2019 (changed from 31 October 2018 following Autumn Budget 2017), claimants who are responsible for three or more children will not be able to make a claim for UC unless they:

- have claimed UC in the previous six months and are able to make a reclaim for UC; or
- are a single person and were claiming UC with someone else as part of a couple and that claim ended in the last month.

In full (digital) service areas, claims for WTC and CTC are no longer possible by the majority of claimants. There are of course some exceptions to this rule including for anyone who has reached the qualifying age for state pension credit and those with three or more children who are unable to claim UC (until 31 January 2019). If someone in one of these postcode areas applies for tax credits, HMRC should check if an exception applies and if it doesn't they will send letter TC601U stating that they do not qualify for tax credits and that they should claim UC instead. This decision does carry normal tax credit appeal rights.

If the claimant lives in a live service area, then they are only eligible to claim UC if they meet very strict gateway conditions. The three-child rule mentioned above also applies in live service. Following the Autumn Budget 2017, it was confirmed that DWP intend to close down the live service for new claims from 31 December 2017. Tax credits remain open for everyone in live service postcode areas.

Existing tax credit claimants

Existing tax credit claimants are currently unaffected by the roll-out of UC. Their awards of tax credit will continue at present until DWP introduces rules to migrate those people across to UC. Existing claimants will only be affected if:

- they choose to move to UC;
- they need to make a new claim for another benefit that UC has replaced, such as housing benefit;
- their tax credit claim ends due to a change of circumstance, e.g. a couple separating.

UC and tax credits cannot be claimed at the same time. Some people will be better off under the UC system but many people will be worse off; therefore, it is imperative that existing tax credit claimants seek advice before choosing to move to UC.

New tax credit processes

Many tax credit rules have been changed in order to facilitate the introduction of UC. The biggest change will be seen in the finalisation process. When a claimant moves from tax credits to UC, instead of finalising their claim after the end of the tax year as is currently the process, HMRC will seek to finalise their claim at the point they move to UC. To do this, the calculation of income will be different to the normal tax credits system which will create winners and losers.

In-year finalisation (IYF) applies where:

- a claim for UC is made or is treated as being made;
- the claimant is, or was at any time during the tax year in which the UC claim is made, entitled to tax credits; and
- DWP is satisfied that the UC claimant meets the basic conditions for UC (other than those the claimant is not required to meet and those in relation to a claimant commitment).

There is a general power allowing HMRC to opt-out of using IYF where they deem it is not reasonably practicable to do so. In such cases, the normal end of year finalisation will operate.

IYF involves a two-step process. The first step requires calculation of part tax year income (as defined in regulations). The second step involves using that part year income to calculate a 'notional current year income'. This notional income is then compared to previous year income, applying the relevant disregards. This will give the relevant income figure to be used in the calculation of tax credits.

'Notional current year income' is defined specifically as income for the part tax year to which the claim relates, divided by the number of days in that part tax year, multiplied by the number of days in the tax year in which the part tax year is included and rounded down to the next whole number of pence. For couples, it is joint income that is used.

For the self-employed, the legislation states that the claimant's trading income is the amount of 'actual or estimated taxable profits attributable to that part tax year'. Actual or estimated taxable profits attributable to the part tax year are called the 'relevant trading income' and are to be calculated by reference to the basis period ending during the tax year in which the claimant made, or was treated as making, a claim for UC.

To calculate the relevant trading income:

- take the figure for the actual or estimated taxable income earned in the basis period;

- divide that figure by the number of days in the basis period to give a daily figure;
- multiply that daily figure by the number of days in the part tax year in which the self-employment was carried out.

The legislation does not give any guidance on how claimants are to estimate their taxable trading profits, nor does it give any information about what happens if the estimate is wrong. It is therefore not clear how HMRC will deal with claimants who provide estimates that turn out to be very different to the actual figures declared for tax purposes by the following 31 January.

IYF has the potential, for both the employed and self-employed, to create winners and losers. Overpayments and underpayments are possible even if the claimant has done everything with their award correctly. These overpayments will be recoverable.

Legislation: *Welfare Reform Act* 2012; *Universal Credit (Transitional Provisions) Regulations* 2014 (SI 2014/1230)

Guidance: www.revenuebenefits.org.uk – detailed information on the transition from tax credits to universal credit and the in-year finalisation process (http://revenuebenefits.org.uk/universal-credit/guidance/stopping-tax-credits/finalising-tax-credit-claims)

Case table

(1) Short Bros., Ltd. v IR Commrs.; (2) The Sunderland Shipbuilding Co., Ltd. v IR Commrs.; Short Bros., Ltd. v IR Commrs VOL 12 TC 955 97-140

Legislation finding list

Index to concessions and statements

Index